D1568446

THE MEDICI
Rise of a Parvenu Dynasty
1360-1537

ALSO BY DANNY CHAPLIN

Strenuitas. The Life and Times of Robert Guiscard and Bohemond of Taranto: Norman Power from the Mezzogiorno to Antioch 1016 – 1111 A.D.

The Medici

Rise of a Parvenu Dynasty
1360-1537

DANNY CHAPLIN

On the front cover: Medici family members and their political associates incorporated into *The Procession of the Magi* by Benozzo Gozzoli, painted between 1459-1461 (Magi Chapel, Eastern Wall, Palazzo Medici, Florence).

In memory of Michael 'Mihangel' Cusato
(1960–2016)
A true Renaissance man

CONTENTS

Map of Italy in the 15th and 16th century   i
A Note on Noble Titles and Usage   iii
Medici Leaders and Rulers of Florence   v
Preface   vii
Introduction: The Ultimate Parvenu Family   xi

PART ONE ↩ THE RISE OF THE MEDICI

Chapter 1: The Emergence of Florence   1
Chapter 2: Giovanni di Bicci and the Pirate Pope   31
Chapter 3: Florence's War with the *Lucchesi*   57
Chapter 4: Cosimo in the *Alberghettino*   81

PART TWO ↩ CONSOLIDATION OF MEDICI RULE

Chapter 5: Humanists and Ecclesiastics   109
Chapter 6: The Pivot towards Milan   133
Chapter 7: Cosimo Triumphant   157
Chapter 8: The Crisis of 1466   189

PART THREE ↩ THE GOLDEN AGE OF THE MEDICI

Chapter 9: *Magnifico* Rising   215
Chapter 10: The Pazzi Conspiracy   239
Chapter 11: Naples and into the Lion's Den   263
Chapter 12: The Settling of Scores   289

PART FOUR ↩ THE MEDICI WILDERNESS YEARS

Chapter 13: Charles VIII's Invasion of Italy   323
Chapter 14: The Medici in Exile   353
Chapter 15: Italy Aflame   383

PART FIVE ↩ THE MEDICI RESURGENT

Chapter 16: The Lion Pope   425
Chapter 17: The Battle of Pavia   459
Chapter 18: The Sack of Rome   501
Chapter 19: The Humbling of a Medici Pope   525
Chapter 20: Florence's Black Prince   555

Afterword: The Grand Dukes of Tuscany   597
Select Bibliography   605

Bergamo

Milan   Padua   *Venice*

Turin   *Pavia*

Asti   *Parma*   *Ferrara*

Genoa   *Modena*
          Bologna   *Ravenna*
          Forlì/Imola   *Rimini*

Pisa   *Florence*

          Arezzo   *Ancona*
Siena

Rome

Naples

N
W   E
S

*Italy in the
15th & 16th century*

i

A NOTE ON NOBLE TITLES
AND USAGE

There seems to be as many different styles of imposing grammatical capitalisation on aristocratic titles as there are history books. Some go with one methodology, others go with another. I accept historians' different preferences in regard to this and the key thing is consistency. As I'm something of a stickler for these things I find it necessary to explain the style I have chosen for the writing of this text. Aristocratic titles will be capitalised (or not) in my narrative as per the following rules:

The duke/duchess of Milan. *
The duchy of Milan. †
The Duke/Duchess. ‡
Duke Francesco Sforza of Milan. §
Francesco Sforza, Duke of Milan. **
Francesco Sforza, the duke of Milan. ††

The marquis/marquess of Mantua. *
The marquisate of Mantua. †
The Marquis/Marquess. ‡
Marquis Ludovico Gonzaga of Mantua. §
Ludovico Gonzaga, Marquis of Mantua. **
Ludovico Gonzaga, the marquis of Mantua. ††

The king of France/queen of France. *
The kingdom of France. †
The King/Queen. ‡
King François of France. §
François, King of France. **
François, the king of France. ††

The pope of Rome. *
The papacy. †
The Pope. ‡
Pope Leo X. §
Giovanni de' Medici, Pope Leo X. **
Giovanni de' Medici, the pope of Rome. ††

Rules used.
*   Title uncapitalised when it doesn't replace anyone's name.
†   Singular proper noun (e.g. duchy) uncapitalised in generic use.
‡   Title capitalised when used in place of person's name.
§   Title capitalised when used with person's name.
**   Title capitalised when used as an appositive.
†† Title uncapitalised when used purely descriptively.

Additionally, I have also made certain stylistic decisions to use Anglophile titles with some individuals whilst retaining local-sounding titles for their compatriots. Thus: Charles, Duke of Bourbon (not Charles, Duc de Bourbon) or John Stewart, Duke of Albany (not John Stewart, Duc d'Albany) might sit alongside Louis d'Armagnac, Duc de Nemours; or Gilbert de Bourbon, Comte de Montpensier. Likewise, instead of the more usual King Francis I of France, I have used the more gallic-sounding King François I. These are purely stylistic preferences on my part for which I make no apology.

Likewise, many names may be spelled or styled in different ways: Gonzalo Fernández de Córdoba instead of Gonsalvo Fernández de Cordova; or Georg von Frundsburg instead of Georg von Frundsberg. Again, one has to make a decision either way but the key thing is consistency. Fortunately the Borja clan residing in Rome have made things easier for us historians by subsequently electing to be known as Borgia by the time that Cardinal Rodrigo Lanzol y de Borja (Pope Alexander VI) came to precedence – this was mainly due, it is true, to the tendency of the Italians to soften the more guttural Spanish consonants.

MEDICI LEADERS AND RULERS
OF FLORENCE

- ❖ Giovanni di Bicci (1360-1429)

- ❖ Cosimo di Giovanni de' Medici, 'Pater Patriae' (1389-1464)

- ❖ Piero di Cosimo de' Medici, 'the Gouty' (1416-1469)

- ❖ Lorenzo di Piero de' Medici, 'the Magnificent' (1449-1492)

- ❖ Piero di Lorenzo de' Medici, 'the Unfortunate' (1471-1503)

- ❖ Cardinal Giovanni di Lorenzo de' Medici, Pope Leo X (1475-1521)

- ❖ Cardinal Giulio di Giuliano de' Medici, Pope Clement VII (1478-1534)

- ❖ Giuliano di Lorenzo de' Medici, Duke of Nemours (1479-1516)

- ❖ Lorenzo di Piero de' Medici, Duke of Urbino (1492-1519)

- ❖ Cardinal Ippolito di Giuliano de' Medici (1511-1535)

- ❖ Alessandro di Lorenzo de' Medici, Duke of Penne and Duke of Florence (1511/12-1537)

- ❖ Cosimo di Giovanni de' Medici, Grand Duke of Tuscany (1519-1574)

The main focus of this volume is anchored firmly in the late Middle Ages and early to late Renaissance periods, culminating in the Medici family fortunes as they reached their zenith during the early Baroque era. My interest lies in establishing the answers to three principal questions: firstly, how did a parvenu family like the Medici first gain political power in Florence? Secondly, how did the Medici maintain that power in the face of numerous determined revolts in 1433, 1458, 1466, 1478, 1494 and 1527? Thirdly, to what extent did their alternating strengths and weaknesses of ruling style affect Florence and the lives of Florentine citizens?

I have approached these three basic questions within the framework of a conventional narrative history of the Medici family between the years 1360 to 1537. What I have written is intended for the general reader, or rather the 'educated layman', as shown by the conscious decision to eschew detailed footnotes which are rarely of interest to general interest readers outside of academia. The decision to end the narrative around 1537 with the advent of the grand duke Cosimo I is also a very conscious one. The present work makes no attempt to tell the later story of Cosimo I's rule, or indeed the subsequent grand dukes of Tuscany, although it does of necessity cover the early life of Grand Duke Cosimo and such important Medici personages as Catherine de' Medici, the renowned and somewhat infamous queen of France. With the advent of Grand Duke Cosimo and Queen Catherine there would, within just a few generations, be a Medici bloodline descendant sitting on practically every major throne of Europe. Not only would all the remaining Valois kings have Medici blood flowing through their veins but other royals too would be direct descendants of the Medici; King Charles I of England's wife, Queen Henrietta Maria, for example, was the daughter of Marie de' Medici – the daughter of Francesco I de' Medici, Grand Duke of Tuscany (and the son of Grand Duke Cosimo I.) Their admittedly fascinating stories belong more to the Baroque Counter Reformation era and well beyond into the seventeenth and eighteenth-centuries. My main concern here, however, is with the Medici family as it rose to initial prominence in Florence from the late medieval era onwards and laid the solid groundwork for the family's subsequent ennoblement and 'royal apotheosis'.

In examining the rule of the Medici during this period, I have tended to focus on the threefold approach of exploring: (1) Florence's cultural milieu and the cut-and-thrust of domestic politics, (2) Florence's foreign policy as well as the wider military and strategic background, including (in later chapters) the competing claims of France, the Swiss cantons, Spain and the Holy Roman Empire, and (3) the personal lives of the individual Medici family members themselves. I have also taken time to cover Florence's ever-fluctuating relationship with Rome and the post-Avignon papacy, giving some essential background on the evolution of this key religious institution during the period in question, as well as also devoting attention to Florence's relations with its most powerful northern neighbour, the duchy of Milan. One chapter deals almost exclusively with the Ecclesiastical Councils of Ferrara and Florence along with the flowering of humanist learning in Florence. I hope the reader won't be switched off too much by the pedantry of such topics, but I nevertheless felt it important to provide some background on late medieval/early Renaissance theology and humanism since an awareness of these subjects can only serve to broaden our understanding of the actual social, cultural and political events taking place in this period.

Additionally, there are occasional winding detours in the narrative to explore the lives of certain key non-Medici personalities such as, for example, Francesco Sforza and his son Gian Galeazzo, the antipope John XXIII, Pope Sixtus IV, Caterina Sforza and her husband Girolamo Riario, Charles the duke of Bourbon, Niccolò Machiavelli, Cesare Borgia, Francesco Guicciardini, Baldassare Castiglione, Michelangelo, Leonardo da Vinci, Charles V and certain others who are nevertheless central to the Medici story. If this has served to significantly lengthen what might otherwise have been an economical whistle-stop narrative on the key events in Medici family history, I can only offer the reader my apologies whilst at the same time hoping that these 'excursions' will nevertheless deepen your feel for the period and broaden your knowledge of some of the most illustrious and fascinating personalities of the age.

In the course of recording the lives of the Medici I have of course touched upon many of the great Renaissance artists, those painters, sculptors and architects who benefited from generous Medici patronage and thereby established a new artistic awakening first in Renaissance Florence and later throughout Italy. Characters such as Brunelleschi, Michelangelo, da Vinci, Cellini and Vasari naturally figure quite prominently. However, although I do inevitably touch upon questions of Medici artistic patronage, especially as it pertains to the political and propagandistic value of the arts, this book makes no claim to cover in any systematic or comprehensive sense the history of art during the Florentine Renaissance. There are an abundance of fine works that cover this expansive subject far better and more eruditely than could ever be achieved in these pages. Instead, what I have attempted to do is to show how the lives of some of these key Renaissance artists, poets and humanist scholars meshed with the everyday social, political and cultural life of the Florentine state and give some insights into their on-going interactions with individual members of the Medici family, relationships which were usually of the client-patron variety but which occasionally (as in the case of Michelangelo's relationship with Lorenzo de' Medici or Cellini's relationship with Pope Clement VII) touchingly veer into warm personal friendships.

Cosimo de' Medici's personal motto, which his family subsequently adopted as their own, was 'Make haste slowly' (Latin: *Festina lente*). It was a saying, derived from the Greek maxim σπεῦδε βραδέως, which Cosimo had borrowed from the writings of Suetonius, who in turn attributed the expression to the Emperor Augustus, a cautious man who detested rash action above all else. Kindred spirits if you will. Anyway, this delightfully oxymoronic adage from imperial Rome is perhaps good advice as you progress through the pages of *The Medici: Rise of a Parvenu Dynasty, 1360 – 1537* for this is both a lengthy and a complex story involving an intertwined cast of hundreds. I have tried my best to tell the whole story with a complete list of the most important dramatis personae. Therefore, in the early chapters of the book we learn about the main political families of Florence, houses which the Medici would eventually emerge from obscurity to challenge. As we progress through the middle part of the book we encounter those characters such as Francesco Sforza, Pope Sixtus IV, Girolamo Riario or Cesare Borgia – fellow Italians who would be important in the unfolding Medici saga on the national stage. The final section of the book inevitably widens the story out even further to encompass the many personalities of those rapacious international powers who sought to dominate Italy from the late fifteenth to the mid sixteenth-century. By this time, we find the stories of France, Spain and the Holy Roman Empire themselves very much overlapping with the story of the Medici, especially at the point when the family evolve, under the twin Medici pontificates of Pope Leo X and Pope Clement VII, from being national rulers to their role as leaders of Christendom. The story of the Medici becomes, in fact, the story of Italy herself, at least until 1534 when Clement ingested his fateful meal of *Amanita phalloides* mushrooms, fell sick and died.

In my past reading about the Medici I was deeply dissatisfied with the quality of *recent* books that were available on the market for the slightly more sophisticated general reader. This volume therefore has its genesis in my entirely selfish motivation to create the sort of narrative that I would have liked to have had available on the subject when I first began my own research. Such a narrative would necessarily be exhaustive, detailed, and comprehensive (as well as entertaining) and would encompass digressions into the individual stories of many of the era's central historical players. Inevitably this has made for an unusually long book for which I again apologise to those who prefer brevity. On the other hand, I make *no* apology for any minutiae or trivia which the reader might consider unnecessary or irrelevant. For me, the study of history will always be a process of uncovering connections that lead to other connections. For these characters, sometimes even relatively minor ones, to live in the historical imagination, most importantly *my* narrative imagination, it is necessary to know as much about them as possible. As I have already confessed, this book was written from a personal need to fill a vacuum that I felt existed out there in the wide world of Medici literature.

I hope that by the time you reach the Afterword you will have gained a unique, in-depth and, one hopes, thought-provoking perspective on the House of Medici as it evolved in the early years, as well as–in equal measure–the gritty and yet alluringly glamorous Renaissance stage on which its members strutted, fretted and acted out their individual dramatic roles for the later edification of scholars and historians. Above all, I hope that you will find the journey an interesting and rewarding one and absolve me from my gleeful tendency to often gallop off and explore the highways and byways of my subject matter.

Danny Chaplin
Singapore, 2016

The Ultimate Parvenu Family

La gente nuova e i sùbiti guadagni
orgoglio e dismisura han generata,
Fiorenza, in te, sì che tu già ten piagni!

An upstart multitude and sudden gains have in thee
Engender'd arrogance and intemperance
O Florence, so that now, in tears thou mourn'st!

Inferno, Canto XVI, Dante Alighieri

Italy in the Quattrocento was a society obsessed with hierarchy and social standing. As a culture that was still only just emerging from the dim feudalism of the Middle Ages, it was anchored to traditional concepts of inherited title and nobility. But as the intellectual re-awakening that later came to be known as the Renaissance dawned and as artists and scholars, rediscovering the wisdom of the ancient Greeks and Romans, freed themselves from the shackles of outmoded ways of thinking and looking at the world, these medieval concepts of title and nobility were being increasingly called into question.

In the Tuscan humanist Poggio Bracciolini's work *De nobilitate* (1440), which explored the nature and foundations of 'nobility', the character Niccolò snobbishly asserts: 'I certainly cannot see what kind of nobility can be acquired by trade, for trade is judged by wise men to be vile and base, and nothing that can be regarded as contemptible can be related to nobility in any way'. The essential point being made was that although wealth was admitted as one of the key criteria of true nobility, it only applied to wealth which had been inherited from one's noble, presumably titled, predecessors. By contrast, if a parvenu tradesman, merchant or moneylender accumulated great wealth through his own enterprise and ingenuity the endeavour, no matter how fabulously wealthy he may subsequently become, was nevertheless regarded as somehow 'base' or 'ignoble'. Bracciolini (who was a close friend of the banker and statesman Cosimo di Giovanni de' Medici) was certainly *not* vindicating or endorsing these Old World ideas on nobility; on the contrary, this self-made man from the obscure Tuscan village of Terranuova who had achieved the position of *Apostolicus Secretarius* or papal secretary under Pope Martin V, defended the concept of *true* nobility as being based on 'virtue' rather than on mere attributes of birth and background.

This 'meritocratic' elucidation of nobility, which was favoured by the rich 'bourgeoisie' of Florence, lay right at the heart of Quattrocento Italy's evolving social, political and cultural milieu and was widely debated in intelligent circles at the time. Neither was Bracciolini the only Florentine civic humanist scrutinising this issue, for Buonaccorso de Montemagna's work *Controversia de nobilitate* (1420) also raised much the same kinds of questions two decades earlier. In an era of newly established fortunes based on trade and commerce built by clever *arriviste* families, Italian society at-large required a reformulation of its previous hierarchical principles that was altogether more flexible and all-inclusive. And yet, as early as 1320, we find Dante Alighieri already lamenting in *La Divina Commedia* the 'arrogance and intemperance' (*orgoglio e dismisura*) of the newly-wealthy and their alarming tendency towards political factionalism.

The feudal Old World Order in Italy was a society founded very much upon the family and extended networks of kinship, clan allegiances and patronage. In this respect Italy was no different from late medieval northern Europe, which was even more deeply entrenched in the feudal system of the Middle Ages. That system had given a veneer of respectability and 'nobility' to rapacious tenth-century and eleventh-century dynasties which, when all is said and done, had been little more than well-armed and well-organised families of gangsters. Within Italy there were, aside from the various titled nobility, the three states that had the more exalted 'sovereign' or royal status of monarchies: these were the kingdom of Naples (*Il Regno di Napoli*), the elective theocratic monarchy of Rome and the papacy, and Venice which, although ostensibly a maritime republic, was in reality far closer to an elective quasi-monarchy which was governed by an elected Doge who ruled for life. Apart from these three 'sovereign' powers all other Italian societies–regardless of whether they were urban or rural–were usually always based on old, established landholding families who were given the respectability and legitimacy of intergenerational inherited titles.

These titles were dispensed either by the Holy Roman Emperor, by the pope of Rome, or by the king of Naples. Late medieval Italy had been no different in this respect from the rest of Western Christendom and the older Italian families–not only the great landowners themselves but also sometimes the extremely wealthy urban élite–sought, wherever possible, to preserve their social standing and political sovereignty and keep newcomers *out* of their ranks. They intermarried only amongst other noble families and condescended towards the lower social classes and the lumpen peasantry struggling to eke out a living in the widening base of the social pyramid that stretched out beneath them. Amongst such élite families there was an insatiable craving for honours, titles and emoluments which frequently manifested as an obsession with complex and esoteric heraldic one-upmanship. And as always with this class of lords there was the tireless obsession with acquiring more lands, estates, castles and fortresses in the *contado*, which is to say, the surrounding rural countryside that lay outside every walled Italian city-state.

But by the thirteenth and fourteenth-century the complacent world of this landed, feudal nobility was drawing to a close. In a social sense, city-states like Florence had become extremely fluid and dynamic due to a whole range of factors. Frequent epidemics of plague for example regularly depopulated the commune, in the aftermath of which fresh *contadini* (rural dwellers) always migrated to the urban areas to replenish the depleted manpower. Many set about diligently making their fortunes and some, like the Medici family, proved extremely successful in their chosen speciality. The urban city-states had spawned a rising class of merchants, bankers and businessmen whose increasing wealth gave them the practical means with which to challenge the landed, feudal élite who went by the designation of *magnati*. The Medici, who ruled the city-state of Florence (with several notable intermissions or 'interregnums') from the year 1434 until the death in 1737 of the impotent seventh and final Medicean grand duke of Tuscany, Gian Gastone, belonged to this rising class of urban nouveau riche. They came from a clan of rural moneylenders from the Mugello region of Tuscany and, since lesser rural folk were just as obsessed with heraldic snobbery as their social betters, they too had their own idiosyncratic heraldic device. The Medici arms comprised several red or gold *palle* or balls arranged in a pattern against a shield. Other humble families desirous of portraying themselves in a noble light could pay a visit to Luca della Robbia's workshop in Florence and purchase a family coat-of-arms in an attractive glazed terracotta roundel. The Medici family was indeed emblematic of this growing new class of Italian families that had migrated to the city and established their fortune. These two rival groups, old money and new money, were meanwhile also divided by their loyalty to either the Holy Roman Emperors or the popes of Rome, a holdover from the partisan politics of the Middle Ages.

In the city of Florence there were numerous such exemplars of old and new money. Certain distinguished houses like the Calvalcanti or the Pazzi, whose engaging coat of arms comprised two golden dolphins and whose properties at one time extended along either side of the Borgo degli' Albizzi, could trace their family origins back centuries, in the case of the Pazzi all the way back to the eleventh-century. Their family stories were intertwined with the very history of Florence itself. These urban families, along with others that had grown to prominence between the eleventh and fourteenth-century, held sway within the commune of Florence. With the enacting of the Ordinances of Justice in 1293 these urban families achieved their final victory over the feudal *magnati* of the *contado*, depriving them of their former political power and marginalising them within the political life of the commune. In the fourteenth-century Florence then flirted briefly with a period of experimentation with despotic rule before ultimately introducing its unique guild-based system of republican government.

But although it introduced a more democratic electoral process to the city the guild system itself remained little more than a caste system in miniature. Those 'major guilds' dealing with prestigious white collar professions like law and banking tended to look down on and take precedence over the trade-based 'minor guilds' which were more concerned with the so-called 'mechanical arts'. It honestly seemed that, however the Florentines came to organise their precious republic, matters always ultimately came back down to that old chestnut of social class. In the place of the *magnati* a new social élite came into being. This social élite were the *ottimati*, the descriptor for which is derived from the Latin *optimates*. The *ottimati* were, in the specific political and social context of Florence, those who held the lion's share of political positions and indeed most of the economic power in the city. Such families ruled the roost, as it were, often using the services of lesser though still well-to-do families as their political placemen. In popular parlance such families were referred to as 'having the state' (*avere lo stato*).

As members of one of the major guilds, that of banking and moneylending, the House of Medici was able to quietly bide its time and concentrate on building up its financial capital largely by avoiding the errors of their older, more flamboyant rivals in the banking arena. Giovanni di Bicci de Medici's decision to become the banker to a future pope (later an antipope) was the watershed in the family's fortunes. From this point on the Medici family's reputation was established on the wider Italian stage thanks to a timely interlude as bankers to the papal court of Rome – a privileged position which the Rothschilds hold in the present day for instance. At the same time the family also entered into dynastic marriages with the daughters of old aristocratic (though often impecunious) Florentine families such as the Bueri, the Bardi and the Cavalcanti. Certain earlier members of the family had, it was true, served in Florence's government, so the family were not entirely nonentities; but it is also true to say that the Medici's early participation in public life had been lacklustre. Several early Medici had been embroiled in either civil rebellions or else military misadventures and all ultimately paid the price for their personal or political shortcomings.

All this seemingly changed when a young Giovanni di Bicci arrived in Florence from the Mugello to join his relative's moneylending business as a young trainee banker. His older kinsman promptly sent his young protégé to Rome to learn the family business and sometime after his return he bought over the business and thereby founded the Medici Bank. Within just two generations, Giovanni's particular branch of the family had gone from banking nonentities to being in effect the single wealthiest family in Florence according to tax assessments of the time. With growing wealth came upward social mobility, increased participation in government affairs, and the extraordinarily generous patronage of the arts for which the Medici are of course most well-known. Success also brought with it a backlash from Florence's older, more established élites. That a family-run counting house should rise to such social and financial prominence in Florence was nothing exceptional in itself; however, by late 1434 we find the Medici also predominating in Florence's system of government too.

The political pre-eminence of the Medici in Florence after the year 1434 was due to a conjunction of factors, not all of them of the Medici's own making. The paranoia and persecution of one of their chief political adversaries, Rinaldo degli Albizzi, had led Giovanni's son Cosimo de' Medici to consolidate his extended family network and reach out to form political alliances with several *ottimati* families. Through the political ineptitude of his enemy, Cosimo was able to transcend the opposition ranged against him and thereafter establish control over the republic's supposedly democratic election processes. It is not so much that this had been the Medici plan all along, more that the Medici were forced to take political control of Florence simply in order to ensure their own personal survival. Cosimo and his son Piero's astute stewardship of the family fortunes managed to transcend two subsequent political crises in 1458 and 1466 and after Cosimo's grandson Lorenzo de' Medici succeeded his father Piero in 1469 the Medici were by now the undisputed first family of Florence. As the principal *ottimati* family, they naturally also harboured ill-concealed aristocratic pretensions, as revealed for example in their marital habits. The Medici began to look outside of Florence in order to find their social equals. Though already socially established in Florence, they were therefore forced to endure the snobbery of the Romans when Lorenzo de' Medici and his son Piero sought wives in Rome, or the French, when Giuliano di Lorenzo, Lorenzo di Piero and Catherine de' Medici sought marriage partners in France and Savoy.

It was not until Giuliano di Lorenzo became duke of Nemours in 1515 that the family finally entered the official ranks of the nobility. Up until then the

Medici had ruled Florence not as lords but only as first citizens. Italy had more than its fair share of counts, dukes and princes however. In the south there was the kingdom of Naples, *Il Regno*, which had previously been under Angevin rule, but would be reconquered in June 1443 by the Aragonese ruler Alfonso V, who would once more reunite the divided thrones of Naples and Sicily (what used to be known as the kingdom of Sicily). In Florence's neighbouring imperial duchy of Milan a republic, newly arisen from the ashes of a brutal Visconti hereditary dukedom, would be overthrown by a *condottiere* from simple peasant stock, Francesco Sforza, who proceeded to impose his own ducal dynasty on the long-suffering *Milanesi*. Other northern Italian city-states such as Genoa, Bologna, Mantua and Ferrara were similarly ruled by families who had either purchased or else assumed the mantle of titled nobility, even though some of them came from humble *condottiere* origins just like the Sforza. Venice meanwhile was very much a hybrid 'sovereign oligarchy', one perhaps arguably more obsessed by money than with titled nobility. In Rome too, a lifelong elected pope assumed both spiritual and temporal power over the city and its associated Papal States, that confusing patchwork of territories and fiefdoms where an assemblage of petty lords and tyrants ruled ostensibly as 'vicars' of the Supreme Pontiff.

In Florence the situation was somewhat different. Whereas a city like Rome might look proudly to the glories of the Roman Empire to justify its system of autocratic rule, Florence's commune was exceedingly attached to its republican heritage, which it too quarried from essentially classical sources, and which gave the city-state its collective identity and informed its unique local culture. The tolling of the *vacca* to call the citizens to a public meeting in the Piazza della Signoria, a *parlamento*, was part of the collective memory of all Florentine citizens. Such traditions could not be so easily dispensed with as in other more tyrannical city-states. When, in 1422, Pope Martin V had honoured Giovanni di Bicci with the noble title of count of Monteverde he refused to assume the title knowing that aggrandising himself in this way would anger and alienate his fellow Florentines. Besides, anger and alienation were bad for business. His feel for the republican mentality of his city is also shown in the counsel he gave to his sons and grandsons, namely to present a modest appearance to the Florentines at all times and to refrain from putting on airs and graces.

Therefore, when these initial generations of Medici bankers ruled Florence they largely accomplished this through the established institutions of government, taking care not to innovate too much unless circumstances demanded it. Fortunately for them, Florence's seigniorial, guild-based government had been fashioned by the *ottimati* into a system that lent itself especially well to manipulation, favour-buying and the packing of the official seats of government with Medicean adherents. The Medici essentially inherited an off-the-shelf plutocratic system of rule. A plutocracy (Gk: *ploutokratia*) differs from a common-or-garden oligarchy (Gk: *oligarkhia*) by virtue of the fact that the former is 'rule by the wealthy' whereas the latter is 'rule by the few'. The two often collide and a plutocracy can also therefore be an oligarchy – rule by 'a few wealthy individuals/families'. Florence's republicanism was *always* plutocratic, in that the wealthy usually always wielded greater political influence, but whether it was always oligarchic is up for debate since the (wealthy) ruling families sometimes numbered in the several hundred and sometimes, especially towards the end, were very few indeed. But relatively speaking, since the guild system ensured that only a tiny percentage of the wealthier guildsmen ever had genuine access to political power, as contrasted with the disenfranchised unguilded masses, it's perhaps fair in Florence's case to use 'plutocracy' and 'oligarchy' fairly interchangeably.

As additional political weapons the Medici also became adept at wielding the twin expedients of banishment and selective tax assessment. In 1434, 1458 and 1466 many of Florence's aristocratic *ottimati* families were exiled in order to protect Medici hegemony. The enactment of such sentences was no doubt helped by a certain *schadenfreude* on the part of those less well-off Florentines who witnessed with satisfaction the downcast exodus of their social superiors. Cosimo de' Medici was the *maestro* at these political arts but his grandson Lorenzo the Magnificent also inherited his immense political acumen, to which was added a certain additional glamour and charisma which has led many historians to regard the period of Laurentian rule from 1469 to 1492 as being the so-called 'golden age of Medicean Florence'. But, even as Lorenzo was spending vast sums of Medici largesse on beautifying his city and commissioning some of the greatest artworks of the Renaissance, there were many in Florence who still regarded the Medici as parvenu imposters. Most notable amongst these were the Pazzi whose infamous assassination plot against Lorenzo and Giuliano de' Medici in 1478 effectively resulted in that family's social and political annihilation.

The Medici during this period were also great statesmen who managed to stabilise and bring peace to Italy through a delicate balance of power, of which they were the chief architects. Cosimo de' Medici guided the republic through a long period of rivalry with the neighbouring city-state of Milan and forged an intergenerational alliance with its new duke, the *condottiere* Francesco Sforza. In conjunction with Pope Nicholas V, Cosimo also brought the various city-states together in the ground-breaking Peace of Lodi and Most Holy League that bound Florence, Milan, Venice, Naples and the Papal States, along with their various client city-states, to an unprecedented twenty-five year epoch of truce. Both Cosimo and Lorenzo, and to a lesser extent Lorenzo's father Piero the Gouty, also successfully fended off the growing power of France, Spain and the Holy Roman Empire. These formidable rival powers had not only begun to take a renewed interest in individual possessions like Naples and Milan, but they increasingly viewed Italy as little more than a proxy battlefield for their own ever-intensifying conflicts, what were in effect the teething pains of the emergence of the great Western European nations.

Following Lorenzo the Magnificent's death in 1492, however, Medici family fortunes took a marked turn for the worse as Lorenzo's son Piero 'the Unfortunate' squandered all the social and political capital that the Medici plutocracy had painstakingly accumulated up until that point. The backlash that chased him and his two brothers into exile from Florence in 1494 demonstrated, if nothing else had, that the Florentines might have tolerated Medici rule, and indeed prospered under it, but they still resented the tight grip that the Medici *reggimento* or 'dominant ruling regime' held on Florentine politics. The loss of Medici power was in part due, not only to Piero's personal cowardice and incompetence, but also to his social pretensions. By this time the Medici had shed the sound advice of Giovanni di Bicci and now regarded themselves as great and important lords.

It is also probably true to say that after Lorenzo the Magnificent's death in 1492 the overall calibre of the Medici's male descendants tended to degenerate. Piero de' Medici was vain, lazy, venal and irresponsible; his brother Cardinal Giovanni was corpulent and pleasure-loving; his younger brother Giuliano was genial, bluff and well-intentioned but politically naïve, the classic affable underachiever. Their cousin Giulio de' Medici was the illegitimate son of the assassinated Giuliano de' Medici, who had spilled his seed into a woman of low birth some time prior to his murder. The child had been taken under the Medici roof (like Cosimo's own illegitimate, half-caste offspring Carlo) and been given a privileged Medici upbringing. Piero the Unfortunate's own son, Lorenzo, Duke of Urbino, was–beneath his fine silken trappings–yet another venal and syphilitic Medici wastrel who fortunately met his end before he could do further harm to the dynasty's already heavily dented reputation.

It was, ironically enough, during the reign of these arguably incompetent and self-serving Medici scions that the family made its real appearance on the world political stage, as the renowned family of the Medici popes Leo X and Clement VII. But this was only due to the wise and far-sighted Laurentian policy of 'Romanisation' – which was inaugurated when Giovanni de' Medici became the first member of the family to wear a cardinal's red bonnet. It was under Pope Leo X that the first Medici family members became ennobled: his younger brother Giuliano became the duke of Nemours; Lorenzo illegally seized the dukedom of Urbino for himself, at immense cost to the papacy, and several Medici cousins and kinsmen were also destined to become cardinal princes of the Holy Roman Church. Prior to becoming pope, Cardinal Giovanni de' Medici was able to finesse imperial-papal politics to obtain a Spanish army which he then used to intimidate Florence into submission by brutally sacking her neighbour Prato on 29 August 1512. The Florentine republic buckled and gave way just as quickly as they had ejected the Medici and the long interregnum lasting from 1494 to 1512 ended with the ever fickle Florentines rushing to acclaim their new Medici pope upon his elevation in March 1513.

Cardinal Giovanni de' Medici's eight-and-a-half year long papacy became, quite literally, one long extravagant party. But who was counting the cost? If it was Pope Leo X's profligacy that gave rise to the Protestant reformer Martin Luther (through Leo's cynical efforts to raise money from the spiritually fraudulent sale of indulgences), it was Pope Clement VII who finally lost the German Lutheran congregations altogether by electing to wage war on the Emperor Charles V, the one man who was his natural ally against the heretics. By this time, as popes, the House of Medici was operating on a truly international world stage, although with mixed results, and accordingly the stakes were exceedingly high. A superb papal adviser and cardinal-legate, Giulio di Giuliano de' Medici was a complete and unmitigated disaster once he shed his cardinal's hat for the triple tiara. His indecisive foreign policy, which gyrated wildly between support for France one minute and the Empire the next, resulted in the disastrous Sack of Rome in May 1527 that ended the period of the High Renaissance in that city-state when all the most talented artists and architects of the day were either maimed, murdered, traumatised or dispelled to other, safer, corners of Italy. After the sacking, as Pope Clement sat impotently in exile at his ramshackle makeshift papal court in Orvieto, his continued ineptitude at handling the king of England's 'Great Matter' also ultimately cost the Roman Catholic Church its English congregations too. It was under these two Medici popes, one short-sighted the other inclement, that the See of Rome was stripped of much of its northern faithful through the upheaval of the Protestant Reformation.

Both popes meanwhile ruled Medici Florence almost as an afterthought and the city chaffed under the proxy rule of 'foreigners' like the cardinals Silvio

Passerini and Innocenzo Cybò, and their privileged charges the two unruly Medici scions Alessandro and Ippolito de' Medici. In the immediate aftermath of Rome's 1527 sacking, the Medici were ejected from Florence for the last time and Pope Clement was forced to make terms with the Emperor Charles V, crowning him in Bologna in return for the loan of an imperial army with which he reconquered Florence within the course of a single year. The death of Pope Clement VII was followed by the rule of the young Alessandro de' Medici, Duke Lorenzo of Urbino's mulatto bastard, but who many rumoured was in fact the late pope's progeny. Known as 'the Black Prince' due to his swarthy mixed-race appearance, Duke Alessandro's reign marked the Medici family's final ignominious descent into depravity, madness and ultimately murder.

Although they were by now entrenched titled nobility (Alessandro, already the duke of Penne, was created duke of Florence in 1533), the downward moral and spiritual trajectory of the Medici since the death of Lorenzo the Magnificent was, with Alessandro's scandalous murder, only arrested by the accession of Cosimo de' Medici as the grand duke of Tuscany. Cosimo I united within himself the two main branches of the Medici family which had split off from Cosimo de' Medici and his brother Lorenzo the Elder. The grand duke's father had been Giovanni della Bande Nere, the renowned *condottiere* who was the son of Caterina Sforza and Giovanni *il Popolano* (a descendant of Lorenzo the Elder). His mother had been Lorenzo the Magnificent's granddaughter Maria Salviati. It was somehow fitting that the Medici should assume their role as grand dukes through a candidate who, aside from being a passably competent and responsible ruler, boasted such an impeccable Medici lineage.

As we shall see, individual members of the House of Medici either rose spectacularly to the occasion (Cosimo de' Medici, Lorenzo the Magnificent, Giovanni della Bande Nere) or else they were tragically miscast in roles for which they were monumentally unsuited (Piero the Unfortunate, Pope Clement VII, Alessandro de' Medici). Others like Piero the Gouty, Pope Leo X, Giuliano the duke of Nemours, or Lorenzo di Piero the duke of Urbino merely coasted complacently along on the success and vast wealth of the family holdings. The difference in Medici sons puts one in mind of the Emperor Tiberius, who in Robert Graves's *I Claudius* is made to observe: 'They say the tree of the Claudians produces two kinds of apples, the *sweet* and the *sour*'. This was also somewhat true of the Medici, except that when the Medici produced the third category mentioned above, the *indifferent*, they usually had the good grace to die relatively young. Despite their later failings, the Medici were by this time able to sustain themselves in power through their entry to the international world of the papacy and thus international power politics. But by the time of Duke Alessandro the family had done about as much damage as it could possibly have done and, in a sense, his assassin Lorenzino de' Medici provided a service in cleansing the family of this last remaining degenerate element which then cleared the way for the advent of the grand duke Cosimo I. What follows is their story.

Festina lente ('Make haste slowly').
The motto of Cosimo de' Medici.

'I love my native city more than my own soul'.
Niccoló Machiavelli.

PART ONE

THE RISE OF THE MEDICI

CHAPTER 1

The Emergence of Florence

Nihil est incertius vulgo, nihil obscurius voluntate hominum, nihil fallacius
ratione tota comitiorum.

Nothing is more unpredictable than the common mob, nothing more
obscure than public opinion, nothing more deceptive than the whole
electoral process.

Marcus Tullius Cicero

In *The Civilisation of the Renaissance in Italy*, the historian Jakob Burckhardt
wrote of Italy during the fifteenth-century: 'No trace is here visible of that
half religious loyalty by which the legitimate princes of the West were
supported; personal popularity is the nearest approach we can find to it. Talent
and calculation were the only means of advancement.' To the attributes 'talent
and calculation' we might perhaps add the additional quality of 'wealth and
plenty of it' if we are to describe the political milieu of Quattrocentro Florence.
The Medici family, or at least those four crucial generations which spanned the
lifetimes of the two founding patriarchs Giovanni di Bicci and Cosimo de'
Medici, as well as their immediate descendants Piero de' Medici and his son
Lorenzo de' Medici, also known as *il Magnifico*, boasted abundant amounts of
intelligence, talent, calculation and of course *wealth*. Indeed, to extrapolate that
such qualities were and indeed are often interdependent, Cosimo de' Medici
rose eventually to become the single wealthiest man in Florence. Because of
these underlying attributes, as well as their family's on-going popularity and
association with the *popolo minuto* (the so-called 'little people' or commoners of
Florence), the Medici were signally well qualified to assume the mantle of quasi
'princely' government within the context of a democratic republic which
supposedly frowned upon such despotic pretensions.

But by what strange alchemy does a parvenu family from the Mugello
countryside transform itself from small time financiers and wool factors into
princes (in all but name) in a city-state where setting oneself up over and above
one's peers was a treasonable offence punishable by the harshest of means?
Well, for a start, it certainly helped to have a strong, cohesive and single-
minded family to begin with. In an era when allegiance to family was the pre-
eminent imperative of life this was, of course, nothing remarkable in and of
itself. Nevertheless, it also helped for the aforementioned family to inhabit a city
in which republicanism was vaingloriously trumpeted but where a narrow
plutocracy still ruled the roost. In this respect at least, the city of Florence was
being true to its own history.

The Florence of Cosimo and Lorenzo de' Medici owed its existence to that towering and ubiquitous demagogue of antiquity, Julius Caesar. In 59 B.C., the great Roman general and dictator established a colony to settle some recently retired legionary veterans on the marshy banks of the River Arno. Nearby Fiesole had itself been settled since pre-Roman times, having formerly been a centre of Etruscan power, and it is from the word *Etruscan* that the name of the region of *Tuscany* is derived. During the early days of the republic it had long been the practice to settle hoary veterans of the legions on recently conquered or hostile territory. However by the time the encampment on the Arno was initiated the Italian peninsula was by now irrevocably Roman. The settlement of agricultural legionary veterans soon thrived, first under Caesar's rule and then, following his assassination in 44 B.C., under the Triumvirs, and later the Roman Empire of the Augustii.

The town or, to give it its correct Latin name *colonia*, was laid out along standard Roman lines in rectangular fashion. From north to south ran the main street, the *cardo maximus*, *cardo* meaning 'hinge' and so the *cardo maximus* was the 'main hinge' of the town (the ecclesiastical title cardinal is also derived from the same Latin word for hinge, hence the cardinals are literally 'the hinges on which the door of the Church swings'). This main street was filled with shops and vendors of all kinds and constituted the principal economic hub of the settlement. From east to west ran another street, the *decumanus maximus*, whose name derived from the path that, in military terminology, separated the ninth cohort from the tenth (*decima*) cohort in a Roman legionary encampment. Where these two main streets intersected was called the *groma*, and was usually the location for the *forum urbis*, that is to say the main civic centre of the *colonia*. In Roman times the forum was situated where the modern day Piazza della Repubblica (which replaced the older Mercato Vecchio, the 'Old Market') is still located to this day. The *cardo* meanwhile became the Via Roma and Via Calimala, and the *decumanus* became the Via degli Strozzi, Via degli Speziali and Via del Corso. In Roman times, the Arno was navigable all the way upstream to Florence itself and the town had its own little thriving river port. The settlement was also favourably situated for land communications and trade routes and grew prosperous on commerce. *Florentissimo* in Italian means 'flourishing' and so this bustling town of legionary veterans, soon to be the leading town in northern Etruria, became known as *Colonia Florentina* or the 'flourishing colony'.

At the site of the Arno River crossing the battle-hardened legionaries had erected a temple to Mars the Roman god of war. The town was first exposed to Christianity during the second-century with the advent of Christian cults associated with the Deacon Lorenzo and the Palestinian Saint Felicita. These cults were the basis for two of Florence's earliest churches, San Lorenzo, consecrated in 393 C.E., and Santa Felicita, which has its origins slightly later in the fifth-century. When Christianity supplanted paganism the citizens of *Florentina* reconsecrated the Temple of Mars to that obstreperous though least martial of figures John the Baptist, who henceforth became the city's patron saint. The temple/church itself was to endure until as late as 1333 when in that year it was washed away by a particularly devastating flooding of the River Arno.

Like the temple to Mars, for the next thousand years, until the advent of the early Middle Ages, Florence weathered the coming storms. These storms included the decline and fall of the Roman Empire in the West to Rome's own

2

barbarian mercenaries; the devastating Gothic Wars of Belisarius and Totila; a peninsula-wide invasion by the barbaric northern race known as the Lombards; and the coming of Charlemagne's even more savage Germanic Franks. It was during the Frankish intermission in the eighth and ninth-centuries that Florence and Fiesole were combined into a single county under Charlemagne's Holy Roman Empire, both now coming under the proximate jurisdiction of the March of Tuscany, an entity in the *Regnum Italiae* whose capital was situated at nearby Lucca. But Florence's fortunes waxed anew when Hugo the Margrave of Tuscany switched his capital from Lucca to Florence around 1,000 C.E. and initiated a period of building that heralded the city's arrival as both an economic and a cultural power to be reckoned with.

It was around the turn of the millennium too that the phenomenon of individual city-states began to come into its own across Europe. This was especially the case in Italy, where the absenteeism of the Holy Roman Emperors, the ostensible feudal suzerains of imperial northern Italy, left key cities such as Venice, Genoa, Pisa, Milan, Bologna, Ferrara, Lucca and Florence free to appropriate an ever-increasing degree of civic autonomy. By the twelfth-century, and in the continued absence of their Emperor, these northern Italian city-states had comfortably assumed control over law and order and the judicial process, taxation, the levying of duties on commercial imports, and the minting of coinage. As their political and economic independence grew the Empire, which could hardly have been expected to complacently sit back and dispassionately observe this trend, decided to take action. So it was that Frederick Barbarossa embarked upon a re-conquest and pacification of the *Regnum Italiae* designed to bring the increasingly autonomous city-states firmly back within the imperial fold. Barbarossa's attempt, however, was ultimately crushed at the Battle of Legnano in May 1176, when the city-states of the Lombard League banded together to defy their unwelcome suzerain from the frosty north. The defeat of the Emperor left five main city-states to dominate the Italian peninsula during the centuries that followed.

In the heart of the Lombard plain sat the great city of Milan, surrounded by her symmetrical walls of red brick and home to 90,000 people in the thirteenth-century, a number that would double by the turn of the fourteenth-century and reach a quarter of a million by the mid-fifteenth-century. As a result of the Battle of Legnano and the subsequent Peace of Constance in 1183, Milan had become a duchy. This new duchy of Milan would, after the year 1277, come to be dominated by the House of Visconti when the city's archbishop Ottone Visconti defeated the rival della Torre faction at the Battle of Desio. With its solid economic foundation of prosperous manufacturers, merchants and farmers, the Visconti rulers of Milan would embark upon a fiercely expansionist policy with regard to the independent neighbouring Lombard communities of Verona, Brescia, Bergamo, Piacenza, Pavia, Lodi and Alessandria, all of which would eventually fall under *Milanese* rule between the thirteenth and fifteenth-century.

To the east, squatting on oak and larch wood piles driven deep into the mud of her coastal lagoons lay *La Serenissima*, the Most Serene Republic of Venice. Ruled by her elected lifetime monarch the Doge, Venice had largely eschewed expansionism on the Italian mainland for a shrewd alternative policy of maritime development instead. This policy led to a giant international Venetian trading empire that extended as far afield as Acre, Alexandria, Cherson,

Constantinople, Sardinia, Sicily and Tunis. Venice's citizens were descended from refugees who had fled the ancient Roman towns of Padua, Aquileia, Treviso, Altino and Concordia in the wake of successive waves of invasions by the Visigoths, the Huns and the Lombards during the tumultuous fifth and sixth-centuries. In their coastal lagoons, where their enemies had lacked both the means and the inclination to pursue them, the Venetians felt safe and in the centuries that followed they had taken naturally to the sea where their abilities as a traditionally coastal people served them well. Numbering fewer more than 100,000 in the year 1300, their intelligence, their canny aptitude for survival and their unsurpassed ability to build fast, light, sea-going galleys led to their reputation as the acknowledged masters of the sea lanes. By the early fifteenth-century Venice's huge trade income, combined with her tough and uncompromising inhabitants, stood her in good stead to face down the growing expansionist threat from Milan, with whom she shared a common frontier.

To the south lay the Kingdom of Sicily, a realm that amalgamated in a single dominion the island of Sicily and the Mezzogiorno, namely those regions of the southern Italian mainland such as Apulia, Calabria and Basilicata. Known simply as the *Regno*, the kingdom had been created in 1130 following a gruelling and systematic Norman conquest which had lasted throughout the entire eleventh-century and one quarter of the way into the twelfth. Sicily itself had briefly flourished under the enlightened Norman King Roger II but those southern mainland regions centred on Naples were torn by endless feudal squabbling which had largely reduced the agricultural Mezzogiorno to an archaic economic and commercial backwater as compared to the more progressive and industrious city-states to the north. The inhabitants of the *Regno*, an exotic racial blend of Greek, Lombard, Roman, Norman, Saracen, Angevin and Aragonese, spoke a dialect which was almost as incomprehensible to the northern Italians as the Germanic languages spoken by those Europeans to the cold north. Successively ruled over by élite foreign dynasties like the Normans, the imperial Germans, the French Angevins and the Spanish Aragonese, the *Regno* had never been allowed to develop a unified cultural identity of its own and a wide gulf always existed between the rulers and those whom they lorded it over.

In Rome and the Papal States, meanwhile, the pope reigned as both spiritual and temporal ruler. From the eleventh-century onwards the institution of the papacy was deeply preoccupied with efforts to establish greater independence from the Western Emperors. These efforts came to a head under the influential reformist Pope Gregory VII, better known as Hildebrand of Sovana. When Pope Gregory antagonised the Emperor Henry IV during the so-called Investiture Controversy, the latter swept down on Rome with his army in 1081 to chastise the pontiff and, when Hildebrand's Norman protector Robert Guiscard came to his rescue, a large portion of the city was razed to the ground in the process. Later, with the signing of the Peace of Venice in 1177, Frederick Barbarossa and Pope Alexander III were reconciled. The Emperor acknowledged the pope's sovereignty over the Papal States in return for Alexander's acknowledgement of Frederick's overlordship of the imperial Church. But by 1309, following decades of civil war between the rival baronial factions of the Annibaldi, Caetani, Colonna, Orsini and Conti, as well as on-going friction with the French King Philip the Fair, the papacy was relocated from Rome to Avignon. During this interlude the city, which had once boasted a population of one million inhabitants during the reign of the Emperor Augustus, shrunk to around 15,000 people by the year 1350.

Despite a well-meaning attempt by Cola di Renzo to resurrect the former greatness of the ancient Roman republic, Rome degenerated into a neglected, dilapidated and sparsely-populated slum where the once magnificent temples, forums, baths and triumphal boulevards became filthy, disease-ridden havens for brigands and cut-throats. In the absence of the pope the most dominant force in Rome consisted in the all-powerful feudal barons. With their vast country estates and private armies, these immensely powerful families operated in Rome from the safety of their urban palaces-cum-fortresses. In the north, the landed barons would ultimately be expunged by the growing power of the mercantile city-states with their emergent upper middle class, but in Rome they continued to shape the social and cultural life of the city. In 1377 the last French pope, Gregory XI, decided to return the papacy from Avignon to Rome, which in turn only gave rise to the so-called Western Schism of 1377 to 1418 during which competing popes vied for power. Although the city of Rome would begin to see its gradual reconstruction and revitalisation from this point forward, especially under the later Pope Nicholas V who oversaw the commencement of Rome's civic and architectural renovation, all popes were obliged to deal with the authority of the Roman barons, and especially the two most important families of all, the Orsini and the Colonna.

Nestled amidst the vineyards and olive groves of Tuscany and inhabited by an industrious, intellectually-disposed and freedom-loving people, the city of Florence had benefited considerably from its association with *la Gran Contessa*, Matilda of Tuscany. When the Emperor Henry IV had descended upon Italy to reprimand Pope Gregory VII he had been forced to traverse Tuscan lands but the Pope's ally Matilda had defied the Emperor's demand to be allowed free passage through her territory. As a result, Matilda had been charged by Henry with *lèse-majesté* and was formerly deposed from her lands and dignities. Every town and city in Tuscany had abandoned her and sided with the Emperor, all except for loyal Florence that is. Once the crisis had blown over and Henry had been chased back across the Alps, as a gesture of thanks to the only city which had stood by her side she had contributed to the rebuilding and strengthening of Florence's walls and graciously acquiesced to its citizens' increasing predisposition towards civic independence and self-government. Upon Matilda's death in 1115, Florence reorganised itself into a commune and in 1138 the other cities and communes of Tuscany came together in a defensive league. By the year 1250 Florence's population numbered around 110,000. It was during this period that Florence saw a dramatic rise in foreign trade with a corresponding increase in the city's mercantile classes.

In the breathing space which the victory at Legnano had created now came the relatively new concept of the 'consular city state', one in which northern Italy's cities began to assume a form of government comprising representative bodies. In Florence's case the civic life of the city was guided by eight consuls who worked in cohort with jurists named *causidici*. These officials were in turn supplemented by a deliberative and consultative council of one hundred members, beneath which lay a popular assembly known as the *arengo*. The reality, however, as indeed in much later periods of Florence's history, was that the consuls and assemblymen were carefully cherry-picked by the city's social élite. These mainly comprised the *magnati*, the old, feudal nobility working in cahoots with the city's wealthiest merchants. At the same time, with the new concepts of government came a growth in collective civic pride and a corresponding increase in the importance of civic symbolism. In Florentine heraldry the two most important symbols became the red cross on a white background, which was the cross of the people and represented all Florentine citizens, and the red iris flower (*il giglio*) against a white background, which was the symbol of Florence itself.

Although the city and the countryside's most privileged citizens colluded in the governmental process to monopolise Florence's political life and dominate policy-making this did not mean that they still did not compete with each other. The debilitating Italian penchant for factionalism and vendetta was graphically displayed by the many fortified towers which rose high above the roofline of Florence throughout the course of the thirteenth-century. Indeed the situation grew so bad that in 1250 civic ordinances were passed that restricted the height of all private towers to just ninety-five feet. A still-extant example of one of these old fortified family towers is the Torre dei Mannelli, which perches sentinel-like on the south-east corner of the Ponte Vecchio. No aristocratic faction worth its salt could be taken seriously if it did not own a stout, intimidating private tower such as this. At street level, meanwhile, the soldiers and armed retainers, the so-called *bravi et capitani*, of the various 'Tower Societies' fought spur-of-the-moment skirmishes for control of different sections of the city, making Florentine street life quite often a brutal, hazardous and deadly affair. The city's attempted solution to its increasingly unruly civic life was the creation of a new official with wide-ranging powers called the *podestà*, who combined within his person the offices of magistrate, chief justice and chief of police. Usually a lawyer by training, it later became necessary to stipulate that the *podestà* always be a non-Florentine. In this way his neutrality could be better assured when he was called upon to adjudicate disputes between Florence's various influential families. For this reason too, the *Liber de regimine civitatum* ('Book of City Management') enjoined that the *podestà* was to limit his day-to-day social contact with Florentine citizens and even discouraged him from dining out with locals lest he be suborned to look with anything less than full impartiality upon any law suit that came before him.

Europe in the thirteenth-century was experiencing a fresh spurt of commercial growth and development, a wave which Florence was able to ride to the full. The Venetian Marco Polo had discovered and explored a whole new world to the East which led to the opening of profitable new trade markets in exotic silks and spices. Maritime states such as Venice, Pisa and Genoa were particularly well-placed to exploit these new frontiers of trade. Their swift, streamlined galleys plied as far even as the Caspian Sea and the seacoast of West Africa. Meanwhile, the egregious sacking of Constantinople by the Fourth Crusade in 1204 had resulted in a staggering infusion of gold bullion and precious gemstones into the markets, banks and counting houses of Italy and especially Lombardy; this was primarily thanks to the machinations of Venice whose blind Doge Enrico Dandolo had perfidiously orchestrated the city's conquest and subsequent sacking.

Meanwhile, from the go-downs and warehouses of Italy's seaports, a profusion of Oriental luxury goods snaked north across the Alps to Europe, a hazardous journey of hundreds of miles under difficult conditions, but one that could bring rich rewards for a forward-thinking thirteenth-century entrepreneur. Florence meanwhile received trade goods through the nearby port of Pisa which, to the undying chagrin of the passionately independent *Pisani*, was eventually conquered and assimilated by the landlocked Florentines as late as 1406. Florence and Genoa also shared a virtual monopoly of trade with the troubled kingdom of Sicily when it came under the sway of the Angevin ruler Charles in 1266.

Whilst the factions fought and litigated and the merchants increased their capital holdings, the Florentines–both grand and humble alike–devoutly prayed in an ever-increasing number of churches. By the beginning of the thirteenth-century the city had as many as forty-eight churches, comprising twelve priories and thirty-six parishes. Meanwhile, at the turn of the thirteenth-century, construction work was commenced on the new cathedral of Santa Maria del Fiore. Around this time, Florence also became host to many of the new religious orders such as the Franciscans, Dominicans, Augustinians, Servites and Carmelites. The Dominicans established themselves in 1221 in the church of Santa Maria delle Vigne whilst the Franciscans' basilica of Santa Croce ('Holy Cross') dates to the fourth quarter of the thirteenth-century. Most of these orders rebuilt and expanded their original churches over time, evolving into fully-fledged monasteries which played an active role in the spiritual, cultural and even the political life of the community. However all of this economic and cultural life growth needed defending.

Matilda's improved city walls of 1078 had, over the years, been further expanded to encompass Florence's rapidly growing suburbs. In 1172 the commune decided to enlarge the city walls to incorporate the newest districts and the new walls, which were finished in 1175, enclosed an area three times as great as before. A portion of the Arno was also enclosed by this new structure whereupon the river served the multiple functions of infrastructure, communications route, a source of hydrodynamic energy as well as a water supply for Florence's ever-expanding textile industries. But as the population continued to expand new city walls were eventually required. In 1282, construction on a belt 8,500 meters long was begun which enclosed an area of 435 hectares, five times larger than before. These sixth and final city walls took over fifty years to complete and represented the single greatest financial expenditure ever undertaken by the commune. Access to Florence was gained through one of twelve gates. The Porta San Gallo (begun in 1285) was the northern gate whilst–self-explanatorily–the Porta Romana (completed in 1326) was the gate that led southward to Rome. Erected in 1324, the Porta San Niccolò was the tower gate from which the southern part of the city walls began and today it remains the best preserved of all the city gates, retaining its original height of about one hundred feet.

Also important to the city's infrastructure were the various bridges which had over time been built across the River Arno. A new bridge directly opposite the populous southern bank of the Oltrarno district (*Oltrarno* meaning literally 'beyond the Arno') was completed in 1237, whilst another bridge constructed across the widest point of the Arno called the Ponte alle Grazie was named after the small church which was built on one of its piers in the middle of the fourteenth-century. Meanwhile, the area around the stone bridge known as the Ponte Vecchio was one of the main centres of town life. The older structure, which had stood since the twelfth-century, was destroyed in the great floods of 1333 but was rebuilt again in 1345. The reconstituted bridge had little shops and houses built upon it, much like our image of medieval London Bridge, and the bridge's thoroughfare was lined first with tanners and purse makers who later gave way to rows of butcher's shops. This then was where the people of Florence came for their choice cuts of meat; if indeed their social and economic station permitted them this luxury. Following the usual urban uptrend of gentrification, the butchers in their turn would eventually give way to goldsmiths and jewellers shops by the end of the sixteenth-century.

Like Genoa and Venice, where land was at a premium, the central precincts of Florence consisted of houses built to four or five stories in height. The ground floor would often comprise a shop or an artisan's workshop or *bottega* with private dwelling space above for the building's owners. Different crafts were commonly concentrated along single streets or neighbourhoods and the practice of living above the *bottega* itself meant that work and leisure life were usually localised in a familiar and village-like community. Many private apartments and tenements in the city would have been rented by tenants rather than owned outright. The narrow city streets were often devastated by fire, however, as in the years 1293, 1301 and 1304 and fresh constructions grew up to replace those structures which had been gutted and subsequently levelled by the municipal authorities.

Before the second half of the fourteenth-century there was little emphasis on the extravagant urban *palazzi* of Florence's later generations of wealthy citizens. Building façades were relatively unadorned and ground floors customarily took on the uniform nature of an open loggia fronting the busy street, which provided little in the way of privacy. Influential families like the Rucellai or the Peruzzi, who were clustered around the church of Santa Croce, showed little inclination to adorn their urban dwellings until around the year 1400 when private *palazzi* began increasingly to make their appearance. Even so, the decorative element of such structures was largely confined to stone rustication or the painted plaster known as *intonaco*. Foreign visitors to the city, especially northern Europeans, often praised the city's pavements, which, in the words of the Florentine silk merchant and diarist Goro Dati, were paved 'with flat stones of equal size so that they were always clean and neat, no more so than in any other place'. The streets, unlike many cities of the period, were kept largely clean and free of effluent by an effective, well-planned system of drains which fed directly into the River Arno. Having said that, like all medieval cities of the era there was however still a certain degree of everyday filth to have to contend with.

Throughout much of thirteenth and fourteenth-century Europe power still resided in the hands of feudal lords of the countryside who operated from impregnable private castles and who commanded small personal armies comprised of obligated serfs and feudal retainers. In Italy the societal situation was by contrast far removed from much of the rest of Europe due to the predominance of prosperous city-states which, like Florence, had developed from earlier towns previously established by the ancient Romans. This factor tended to limit the power of the landed feudal lords based in the *contado*, the so-called *magnati*. Embryonic tensions between the *magnati* based in the countryside and the urban middle classes were exacerbated by the notorious thirteenth and fourteenth-century conflict between Guelph and Ghibelline. This lengthy and frequently bloody dispute was precipitated by the Holy Roman Emperor Frederick II's renewed struggle with the independent-minded Italian city-states and by his rivalry with the Bavarian house of Welf (which became transposed to 'Guelf' or 'Guelph' in Italian). The intricacies of this conflict need not concern us here suffice it to say that Italy's city-states aligned themselves either with the Emperor or with the pope of Rome. The former were referred to as 'Ghibellines', a name that was derived from the supporters of the House of Hohenstaufen, who were known as Waiblinger, which became *Ghibellini* when transposed into Italian. The supporters of the pope meanwhile became known as the 'Guelphs'.

More often than not these allegiances ran along longstanding political fault lines. Pisa and Siena's enduring enmity with Florence for example saw these two city-states aligning themselves with the Ghibelline faction and favouring a more aristocratic semi-feudal sort of society whilst Florence, which differed in being based on a form of merchant plutocracy, adhered to the papal Guelph faction. Other Tuscan communes such as Prato and Lucca also remained in the Guelph camp. Socially speaking, the old feudal nobility of the surrounding *contado* tended to side with their suzerain the Emperor and so were traditionally aligned with the Ghibellines whilst in the towns and cities the urban middle classes, which were struggling to free themselves from outdated feudal systems of vassalage, tended to gravitate towards the side of the pope and the Guelphs.

During the thirteenth and fourteenth-century the Ghibelline armies had adopted as their own the war banner of the Holy Roman Empire, which consisted of a white cross against a red field. Guelph armies usually bore the same colours only in reverse, a red cross on a white field. Since these two heraldic schemes often predominate in the civic heraldry of northern Italian towns and cities they offer a revealing glimpse into their past factional affiliations. Traditionally Ghibelline towns like Pavia, Novara, Como, Treviso and Asti continue to sport the Ghibelline white cross. The Guelph red cross meanwhile can be found on the civic arms of traditionally Guelph towns like Milan, Vercelli, Padua, Reggio, Bologna, Florence and Alessandria, which had been founded by *Milanese* refugees who fled after Frederick Barbarossa burned Milan to the ground in 1162. These damaging schisms were, furthermore, played out within the city precincts of Florence itself and distinct Guelph and Ghibelline parties had emerged within the commune each with their own headquarters. The building which for example housed the powerful Guelph faction, the Palazzo di Parte Guelfa, still exists today two blocks west of the Piazza della Signoria.

In 1250, Florence's Guelph faction defeated the Ghibellines, who under Frederick of Antioch had ruled Florence since 1244, and a new Florentine Republic was established the same year under the enlightened government of the so-called *primo popolo*. This new administration extirpated its rivals the Ghibellines, who were subsequently sent into exile. However, a decade later, one of these exiles by the name of Farinata degli Uberti, who was the scion of an ancient and distinguished Florentine family, rode out against Florence at the head of a *Sienese* army and at the Battle of Montaperti in September 1260 left the field of battle littered with 10,000 Florentine Guelph dead. Florence's rival Siena had wanted to raze a vanquished Florence to the ground, just as Rome had done to her bitter enemy Carthage, but it had been Farinata degli Uberti who had averted this disaster by declaring himself 'a Florentine first and a Ghibelline second' and vowing to defend his native town with his life if necessary. With the subsequent resurgence of Guelph fortunes in 1266, the Uberti family's properties were demolished and ordered never to be rebuilt, thereby creating the civic open space later known as the Piazza della Signoria.

9

But, for his role in preventing Florence's destruction, Farinata degli Uberti would be honoured much later with a niche statue in the Uffizi colonnade, the only Ghibelline citizen of Florence to be so recognised.

With the final victory of the urban mercantile Guelphs over the landed Ghibelline *magnati* at the Battle of Campaldino in 1289, the latter were forced from their feudal estates in the *contado* and compelled to live in the city where a close watch could be kept on their activities. In 1293 the Ordinances of Justice were enacted, a kind of new constitution which severely circumscribed the political privileges of the *magnati* and left them few outlets for government participation beyond the token post of ambassador. Out of this triumph of the middling mercantile and artisan classes now arose a new system of seigniorial Florentine government which was structured closely around the guild system. However, even with the final defeat of the Ghibellines, factionalism continued to plague Florentine life and the victorious *Parte Guelfa* now ruptured into its own antagonistic sub-factions: the *neri* ('blacks') who were more extreme papal supporters and the more moderate *bianchi* ('whites'). The *neri* commanded the support of Pope Boniface VIII and eventually managed to run the *bianchi* out of the city; the poet Dante Alighieri was perhaps the most well-known personality amongst the 'whites' to be exiled in the year 1302.

As was usual in Florentine politics, this feud also corresponded with existing vendettas between old aristocratic families; the *neri* had been backed by the Donati and Spini families on the one hand and the *bianchi* by their rivals the Cerchi on the other. Unhappily, rising good fortunes in the economic and financial arena had never entirely eclipsed the city's predilection for factional violence and wealthy houses feuded with other wealthy houses, often for no other reason than a perceived insult or slight to this or that family member's pride. It is no accident that we favour the Italian word for seeking reprisal in a feud, *vendetta* ('vengeance'), as this violent pastime seems to have been a part of the very fabric of Italian life since time immemorial.

Florence's early prosperity had been built on the wool and cloth industries. Her street names even reflect this early debt; one block to the north-west of the Piazza della Signoria lay two parallel streets, one of which was named the Via Calimala ('Wool Street') and the other which was called the Via Pellicceria ('Fur Street'). From England and the Low Countries Florence imported vast quantities of wool and cloth to be dyed and finished in the city's many workshops, known as *botteghe,* before being re-exported to the markets of Italy and Northern Europe. Florence's wool and cloth workshops are believed to have employed as many as 30,000 people at their height before the Black Death denuded the city's population between 1346 and 1353. From 95,000 inhabitants in 1338, Florence's population had dwindled to just 40,000 in 1427, yet despite this devastating blow to its labour force, wool and cloth-finishing still continued to be the stricken city's commercial lifeblood.

The businessmen who set up the wool and cloth workshops were, like many other professionals and tradesmen in Florence, affiliated with a number of *arti*, or trade guilds. These *arti* were, in effect, an early form of corporation and their importance to the commercial and civic life of medieval Florence cannot under any circumstances be underestimated. There were twenty-one guilds in total, chief amongst which were the seven influential *arti maggiori* or 'major guilds'. Florence's economic life rested on the first four of these guilds which comprised the judges, lawyers and notaries (*arte dei giudici e notai*), the wool manufacturers and merchants (*arte della lana*), the merchants, finishers and dyers of cloth (*arte di calimala*), and finally the bankers and money-changers (*arte del cambio*). The remaining three *arti maggiori* were somewhat less influential and these were the silk weavers and merchants (*arte della seta*), the physicians and pharmacists (*arte dei medici e speziali*), and the furriers and skinners (*arte dei vaiai e pellicciai*).

Beneath these preeminent *arti* were a further fourteen lesser guilds which themselves were sub-divided into five *arti mediane* ('middle guilds') and nine *arti minori* ('minor guilds'). The *arti mediane* comprised butchers and graziers, blacksmiths, shoemakers, master stonemasons and wood-carvers, and linen manufacturers, retail cloth dealers and tailors. The *arti minori* comprised vintners, innkeepers, curriers and tanners, olive oil-merchants and provision-dealers, saddlers and harness-makers, locksmiths, toolmakers and braziers, armourers and sword smiths, carpenters, and bakers and millers. The *arti mediane* and *arti minori* are often subsumed into a single 'minor guilds' category in any general discussion of Florence's guild system, but the distinction should be made that there was very much a three-tier stratification of the Florentine guilds. In this system, the major guild members looked down on the middle guild members, whilst the middle guild members looked down in turn on the minor guild members. Meanwhile, all members of the guild system looked down through their noses on the so-called *popolo minuto*, those semi-skilled or unskilled workers and day labourers who lacked guild membership or a *bottega* to call their own. Such workaday drudges constituted more than two thirds of the entire population of Florence during the city's late medieval heyday. Nevertheless, although the guildsmen considered themselves to be a cut above the disenfranchised mass of the *popolo minuto* they often, as we shall see, condescended to support them when it suited them politically to do so.

Each *arte* had its own elected officials, its own guild hall, coat-of-arms and *gonfalon* (ceremonial banner), together with its own set of ordinances and statutes. What the rise of the Florentine guild system demonstrated was the supreme importance of the mercantile bourgeoisie to the economic life of the commune. This wealthy parvenu élite comprising bankers, wool and cloth finishers, merchants and other skilled tradespeople had formed the backbone of those Guelph forces which had successfully challenged the old feudal order and it was only right that the guild system itself should now come to dominate the republic's political life and dictate the formulation of state policy. Firstly, the guilds were behind the city's re-organisation for the purposes of administration and defence. Florence was partitioned into four *quartiere* or 'quarters' which were further sub-divided into four 'wards' or 'companies' (making sixteen wards in total). The character of each *quartiere* and each ward came to reflect the kinds of trades which were carried out within its jurisdiction. This system had its origins in Florence's early security and defence requirements. In time of conflict each of the sixteen municipal wards would muster a certain quota of armed and able-bodied young men, who would march behind their own *gonfalon* or banner. This civilian militia was a palpable symbol of the will of the citizens, who were ready, able and willing to fight to defend their city.

The prosperity of the guild-based economy led to the first flowering of Florentine art and architecture for which the city is famously renowned. With the considerable profits garnered from the highly lucrative wool and cloth trade, for instance, the three associated wool and cloth guilds had lavished vast expenditure upon the city, sponsoring many of Florence's finest buildings. In

1298 the architect Arnolfo di Cambio commenced work on the design and construction of the new Cathedral of Santa Maria del Fiore, more commonly known as *Il Duomo di Firenze*, which was built on the foundations of Florence's former cathedral of Santa Reparata. The wool merchants who had commissioned di Cambio gave him the following brief: that the cathedral 'should be designed so as to be worthy of a heart expanded to much greatness, corresponding to the noble city's soul, which is composed of all the souls of all its citizens'. When you are spending small mountains of florins for the greater glory of God it is important to let people know *who* is doing the bankrolling. Accordingly, the Duomo bears on its façade numerous stone motifs of the Holy Lamb of God as an indication of the wool guild's financial involvement in the project.

Around the same time di Cambio also began work on a strong new fortified building which would serve as the seat of Florence's government. This would be known as the Palazzo della Signoria, the palace of the *signoria*. It was built offset to one side of the Piazza della Signoria as it had been decreed that no buildings should ever be raised on the former site of the demolished properties of the Ghibelline Uberti family. After di Cambio's death the work on the Duomo was continued under the *capomaestro* Giotto di Bondone, who also built the cathedral's associated bell tower known as the Campanile.

As magnificent as the Duomo or the Campanile or the Palazzo della Signoria undoubtedly were, however, the beating heart of late-medieval Florence lay in her vibrant centres of trade. Foremost amongst these were the bustling Mercato Vecchio, formerly the old Roman forum, and the Orsanmichele which served officially as the public granary but which also doubled up as an alfresco centre for banking and money-changing. Here, amidst the rowdy clamour of the busy marketplace, bankers and money-lenders set up their portable trestle tables covered with green felt and scribbled in their huge ledgers. The trestle table on which the Florentine moneylender conducted his trade was called a *banco*–quite literally 'bench' or 'board'–and from the word *banco* we derive the modern expressions 'bank' and 'banking'. The Florentines being perhaps the most fastidious of Italian city-states when it came to the question of keeping records, the regulatory authorities at the exchangers guild, the *arte del cambio*, insisted that all moneylenders keep thorough accounts of every financial transaction that took place on their *banco*. From this practice is probably derived our modern day expression 'above board'.

To the more staunch Christians of the city the banking trade was still regarded askance as being usurious and hence deeply sinful in the eyes of Almighty God. But long before the Jews became synonymous with banks and banking throughout Europe it was actually the Christian Italians, particularly the Lombards, who perfected the techniques of money-lending. The perceived sin of usury did not however prevent the Florentine exponents of the trade from continually pushing the envelope in financial innovation. The singular breakthrough of double-entry bookkeeping was followed in quick succession by other advances like the bill of exchange, letters of credit and the deposit account. The prohibition on charging interest was cleverly circumvented and the restriction on paying interest out on deposit accounts was likewise finessed in such a way that even cardinals in Rome thought nothing of placing their fortunes, which had been gathered primarily from church tithes, into special 'discretionary' interest-paying accounts.

The ordinary Italian's ambivalence towards banking was best expressed by Boccaccio in The *Decameron*. In one of his stories, Boccaccio tells of a crafty usurer named Ciappelletto who comes to stay with his two Lombard moneylender friends in Florence. While residing in their home Ciappelletto suddenly falls gravely ill and the two Lombards are torn with indecision about what to do with him. If they turn the possibly contagious man out of their house while he is sick the locals will descend on them in righteous anger and use their sinful profession as a pretext for robbing them blind. Ciappelletto offers them a solution to their dilemma, proposing to give a dishonest last rites confession to the local priest so that after he dies he can be buried in consecrated ground without any undue public fuss. However, when the hapless priest takes Ciappelletto's confession, the dying man gives such a glowing account of himself that he is quickly declared a saint and the place where he died, the moneylenders' home, becomes a shrine for public veneration. So much for keeping a low profile! Boccaccio captures perfectly in this story the sagacious desire of the Christian usurer not to draw overly much attention to oneself.

The cornerstone of Florence's reputation in trade and finance was the small gold coin containing fifty-four grains of fine gold which bore on one side the city's Latin name *Florentina* and, on the other, a *fleur-de-lis*. This gold coin, the *fiorino d'oro* or 'florin' for short, was to become a mainstay of trade and business transactions right across the medieval world, supplanting the much heavier silver bars that were then in common usage as the preferred medium of currency and exchange. First introduced in 1252 by the city's new republican government the *primo popolo*, the florin established a critical mass of confidence in Florence as a centre of reliable and trustworthy banking houses. The florin was to change very little from its inception until the mid-sixteenth-century and the lucrative banking industry which it helped create came to be dominated by three influential mercantile families: the Bardi, the Peruzzi and the Acciaiuoli.

The Bardi had arrived in Florence in the eleventh-century; they were lords of the castle of Ruballa near Antella and took their name from Pagano di Bardo, who made a donation of land to the cathedral church of Santa Reparata. By the thirteenth-century they had settled in the Oltrarno district and established a powerful banking business extending from the kingdom of Naples all the way to England on the periphery of Europe. The Peruzzi on the other hand had not been native to Florence or indeed Tuscany. This family hailed originally from Rome and were known as the della Pera until they appropriated their new name from the Piazza Peruzzi in Florence where they held property. The Acciaiuoli meanwhile were originally from the town of Brescia in Lombardy. They arrived in Florence around 1160 and settled down around the Lungarno or 'river-side street' that runs just north-west of the Ponte Vecchio which still bears their name to this day, the Lungarno degli Acciaiuoli. Originally metalworkers, the Acciaiuoli acquired their great wealth initially through the wool trade and then later in banking.

Other prominent Florentine banking families around this time were the Antellesi, who had been the lords of Antella, near where the Bardi were originally from, and also the Castellani, an ancient family which enjoyed exceptional political prominence in the years predating 1434. Florentine banking houses began to predominate, especially after the rival *Sienese* banking clan the Bonsignori collapsed amidst a mountain of bad loans to European royalty, following which the main focus of European banking shifted from Siena to Florence. Formerly the *Sienese* had been the undisputed masters of Italian banking; Orlando Bonsignori's innovation in creating a consortium known as the *Gran Tavola* or 'Great Table' had led to the city, and the Bonsignori family, being catapulted into international prominence as bankers to the Papal States and custodians of the ecclesiastical tithes from the Holy Land. Orlando Bonsignori had also shrewdly gambled his family's fortunes on Charles of Anjou in his struggle with the Hohenstaufen for mastery of the kingdom of Sicily. However, under Orlando's son Fazio Bonsignori the *Sienese* 'Great Table' foundered and went into liquidation.

The Florentine banking houses gladly filled the gaping vacuum left in the wake of the Bonsignori Bank's collapse. Correspondingly, Florence's new leadership position in the international banking industry therefore inevitably led to the pre-eminence of the *arte del cambio* within the commercial life of the commune. This, and the flourishing of many new Florentine family banking houses, tended to cause friction with the traditional artisan guilds, particularly the influential wool and cloth associations which had enjoyed a long period of dominance in Florence's civic and commercial life. These tensions were in turn played out in the guild-based system of government which had been instated by the *primo popolo*.

Compared with the rest of feudal Europe, the Italian city-states bore a remarkable resemblance to the ancient Greek *polis*, that is to say a human community that is brought together by man's innate sociability directed by the intrinsic human principle of justice, a principle by which Aristotle had distinguished humans from other social animals which existed in hives, herds or packs. In the *polis* government was founded and implemented by its own citizens, who Aristotle had described as 'an association of free men'. The *polis* of free and democratic Athens differed therefore from monarchy, in which the king received the sacred mandate of heaven (Zeus) for his rule. It also differed from a tyranny, where the ruler 'owed his power to force or deception'. In the Italian context, as we have noted, examples of monarchy would have been the kingdom of Naples and the papacy, and an example of a tyranny would have been Milan under the iron rule of the House of Visconti. In neither autocratic form of government did the citizens necessarily *consent* to their being ruled. On two distinct occasions Florence would flirt with a form of 'consensual tyranny' in 1325 and 1342 but both these experiments ultimately floundered and failed.

The republican guildsmen of Florence would have agreed with the ancient Athenians that the best form of administration was one in which free born citizens consented to govern their own affairs. A 'citizen' was defined as any male over thirty years of age who was enrolled in one of the guilds and who paid his taxes on time. This only applied, however, to the inhabitants of Florence itself, because residents of subject cities could not qualify as Florentine citizens. Where the Florentines might have argued was over the question of exactly how wide political representation and participation should be and in this respect they conformed to the division in ancient Athens between the supporters of democracy, those who favoured the widest possible participation, and the supporters of oligarchy, those who advocated restricted participation. Fifth-century Athens went the way of democracy. Florence, by contrast, opted for a more oligarchical and plutocratic system which nevertheless incorporated elements of 'democratic' practices such as filling public posts by lot. The unique form of plutocracy/oligarchy which arose in Florence was mainly based on the guild system as it conveniently corresponded with the prevailing hierarchical structure of the commune.

In Florence, the main governing council was known as the *signoria* and it comprised eight 'priors' or *priori* plus a ninth member known as the *gonfaloniere della giustizia* or 'gonfaloniere of justice'. In Florence, only members of the *arti* or trades guilds who were aged above thirty years old were entitled to hold public office. All serving guild members who were eligible to hold public office had their names deposited into a ballot box which in Florence took the form of eight leather electoral purses which were collectively known as the *borse*. Every two months, later extended from two to six months, in an open and public ceremony held at the church of Santa Croce, the eight *priori* and the *gonfaloniere* were drawn randomly by lot from the *borse*. But this system was by no means democratic across the board of all the trades guilds because it effectively ensured that only members of the four principal *arti maggiore* dominated the political life of Florence. This was achieved by having six of the *priori* selected by lot from the *arti maggiori* only, with the remaining two priori being selected randomly from the middle and minor guilds. Naturally the *gonfaloniere* was also drawn from the election purse of the major guilds. In a further pre-screening procedure, the names of those entitled to be placed in the sealed *borse* were first subject to a qualifying *scrutiny*. Debtors were prohibited from inclusion in the ballot, as were those who had recently held office. Also excluded were close relatives of those who had previously been drawn for public office.

The ninth member of the *signoria*, the *gonfaloniere della giustizia*, served as the nominal and ceremonial leader of the *signoria*. His ceremonial role was to bear and maintain the city's banner, which depicted Florence's red iris flower on a white field. In all respects he was the titular head of state for the relatively brief duration of each presiding *signoria*. In addition to his voting rights on the *signoria*, the *gonfaloniere* also controlled the internal security forces of the city and was tasked with maintaining public order. Sumptuously clad in their ermine-trimmed scarlet robes of office, the eight *priori* together with the *gonfaloniere*, separately distinguished by his crimson coat embroidered with golden stars, were required to move into the seat of government, the Palazzo della Signoria, and domicile there for the duration of their two-month electoral term. Here, they were attended by a modest though adequate administrative support staff and a number of stewards and were compensated for their civic duty with a modest stipend. Like the *podestà* they also tended to take their daily meals secluded together in the official *palazzo* of government.

The *signoria* did not rule Florence in isolation, however, but was required to consult with two other elected councils which were collectively known as the *collegi*. Drawn from the guilds and the four quarters of the city, these two councils were the *dodici buonuomini* ('twelve good men') and the *sedici gonfalonieri* ('sixteen *gonfalonieri*'). Other ad hoc *collegi* were summoned to counsel the *signoria* as and when required. The *dieci di balia* ('ten of war') was appointed to handle all military and defence-related matters whilst the *sei di commercio* ('six of trade') looked after trade and commerce. A further council, the *otto di guardia* ('eight of security'), fulfilled the ever-necessary role of secret police and domestic intelligence-gathering agency and worked in tandem with the gonfaloniere. The *signoria* also governed alongside several permanent officials including, of course, the non-Florentine *podestà*.

The republic also incorporated the position of chancellor. Although not drawn by lot like the members of the *signoria*, the chancellor of Florence held the most important executive position in the bureaucracy. His role, which was equivalent to the head of the civil service, encompassed both ceremonial as well as practical functions and holders of the post included some of the most celebrated scholars and humanists of Renaissance Florence. The chancery of the Florentine commune was divided into different departments. One of these was headed by the official notary or *notaio della riformagioni* who was in charge of recording the results of meetings of the legislative assemblies and of drafting the legislation approved by those assemblies. Another department was headed by the chancellor himself. The traditional duty of the chancellor was to compose letters on behalf of the commune and to write the commissions and instructions of Florence's ambassadors. The chancellor, however, was not in charge of all the business and correspondence of the *signoria*. It was frequently the case that orders, warrants or announcements were despatched in the name of the *signoria* itself rather than of the commune as a whole and these were therefore drawn up by the *signoria's* own notary who, as head of a third autonomous section of the chancery, was responsible for the day-to-day deliberations and business of the *signoria*.

This system of government had its well-rehearsed procedures, and this was especially the case in times of trouble. When the city experienced any sort of crisis, whether foreign or domestic, the *signoria* would order the great bell known as *la vacca* to be sounded in the *campanile* of the Palazzo della Signoria. *La vaccha* was named for its deep mooing tone which sounded to everyone like the lowing of a cow. The tolling of this bell would be the signal for all Florentine males above the age of fourteen to assemble in their respective wards and then to proceed behind their *gonfaloniere* to the Piazza della Signoria. Here, the assembled ward members would constitute a *parlamento*. The members of the *signoria* would then emerge from their official palazzo and array themselves behind the *ringhiera*, the raised dais specially created outside the Palazzo della Signoria for official announcements and speechmaking. The *gonfaloniere* would then ask the crowd if they wished to form a *balia*. A *balia* was an extraordinary commission convened to deal with the specific crisis in hand and its powers could, in theory at least, eclipse those of the *signoria* and the *collegi*. The assembled members of the *parlamento* would usually shout '*Sì! Sì!*' and the *balia* would duly be created.

As may be concluded from the above description, Florence's government was henceforth by no means 'democratic', although it flattered those in power to promulgate the idea that the *seigniorial* system was both 'representative' and 'supportive' of the ideals of equality and parity. 'Government by popular acclamation' was, for example, a common enough phrase that was rolled out by the oligarchs to describe the Florentine system of which everyone was so proud. This seemingly democratic form of republican government was an immense source of patriotic pride to the free-born Florentines, who favourably compared their city to more tyrannical systems such as existed in Milan under the cruel Ghibelline Visconti family, or in Venice under its ruling aristocratic plutocracy and Doge. Beneath the veneer, however, it was all a clever sham. In truth, the community which actually ruled supreme in Florence was that small plutocratic group of wealthy mercantile families who belonged almost exclusively to the *arti maggiori*. We might describe these families as the *ottimati* or alternately as the *nobili popolani* who had over time organised themselves into the *Parte Guelfa* or the Guelph faction.

The members of the community who were effectively side-lined from the political process lay on radically different ends of the social divide. On the one hand, the old feudal *magnati* were still restricted from government participation by the Ordinances of Justice. The Parte Guelfa generally saw to it that those amongst the *magnati* who were suspected of Ghibellinism were effectively excluded from the political process. The struggle with the feudal *magnati* had been both protracted and bitter. Now that the Guelphs had triumphed they saw absolutely no reason why they should share power with their old adversaries. With little choice now open to them, some of those old *magnati* families effectively downgraded themselves, becoming actively involved in commerce and joining the various trades guilds merely as a ways and means to participate in the political life of the commune. Other distinguished *magnati* families continued to exist on faded memories of their past glory and so eventually disappeared into political, if not always social, oblivion. The Florentines, who were inveterate snobs, inevitably pandered to and hankered after old money and the prestige of marriage into one of these illustrious *magnati* houses continued, ironically, to offer great caché to parvenu newcomers like the Medici and others.

On the other hand, the non-guild members of the *popolo minuto*, the lumpen mass of the unguilded labouring classes, were also barred from participation and suffered from having very little genuine representation in the political process. These disenfranchised workers, the so-called *sottoposti* or 'subjects', were the employees and labour forces of the city's innumerable cloth and wool workshops and dying factories. These people were frequently referred to as the *ciompi*, which is often explained as an onomatopoeic word for the sound that their cheap wooden clogs made against the flagstones. The word's true etymology lies in the French word *compères*, which means 'companions'.

Despite the homespun pride in Florence's republicanism, the growing tendency towards plutocracy which arose from the ascendancy of the wealthy *ottimati* families portended an increasing cynicism in how the political process was executed. *Parlamento* and *balìa* could both be 'fixed' and stage-managed to a certain extent and ways could always be found to lawfully oust any truculent or uncooperative prior who refused to enact the mandated policies of the few. The *scrutinies* could likewise cynically be used to exclude from the electoral *borse* all those deemed either troublesome to the prevailing regime or disloyal to the commune itself. In this way, although seigniorial elections could preserve the appearance of being drawn impartially by lot, in reality the pool of eligible governmental candidates could be tightly controlled.

Socially, we can break Florentine society down into five main categories during this time. Firstly there were the *magnati*, comprising those old and prestigious feudal families who were legally excluded from holding public office. Secondly there were the *ottimati* or *nobili popolani*, those wealthy major guild members and prestigious merchant families who monopolised Florentine government. Thirdly were the *gente nuova* or 'new men', meaning the *arriviste* major guilds members whose families were only admitted to the *signoria* much later, after the events of the year 1343. Fourthly were the members of the middle and minor guilds. Finally was the vast disenfranchised underclass of the *popolo minuto*. Studies have been conducted which appear to show that as the political influence of the *magnati* contracted, so they became more endogamous in their marital habits preferring, like the aristocrats that they were, to intermarry amongst themselves. Since the *ottimati* families apparently never discriminated against the feudal aristocrats in quite the same way, a *magnati* marriage alliance was always regarded as a social triumph. The *magnati* reserved the lion's share of their distaste, however, for the *gente nuova*, those 'new men' whose fortunes seemed to be rising even as theirs was inexorably falling. Beneath these three upper social classes came the lesser guild members and the largest social class in the commune, the much despised *popolo minuto*, who were regarded in much the same way as the ancient Romans looked down upon the plebeians and derided them as 'the mob'.

In neighbouring Italian states the term 'signoria' referred specifically to a very personal form of government by the patriarch of a single, powerful oligarchic family, known as the *signore*. For the most part Florence managed to sidestep any devolution of its system into personal rule, but on two occasions during the fourteenth-century the city voluntarily gave itself over to the autocratic rule of two non-Florentines. The Ghibelline forces of Castruccio Castracani, allied with the Visconti family of Milan, had routed Florence's Guelph army at the Battle of Altopascio in September 1325. As a result Florence reached out that same year for protection to the Angevin King Robert the Wise of Naples, the titular overlord of the Guelphs on the Italian peninsula. Robert agreed with the Florentines to unify the Guelph military command on Tuscan territory and assigned his son Duke Charles of Calabria as *signore* of Florence for a ten-year period from 1326 to 1336. Charles ruled in absentia but even so did not miss his chance to tax Florence senseless all the same. As a result of this largely unsatisfying experience, the Florentine *ottimati* vowed never again to hand over the government of their commune.

In 1342, however, seeking to restore their military and economic potency following an ill-conceived war with the city of Lucca, the Florentines once again extended an invitation to an outside powerbroker–this time Walter Brienne, Duke of Athens–to become *signore* of their city. On the one hand, the duke of Athens proved popular with the disenfranchised *popolo minuto*, the lowly wool workers, for whom he created a brand new guild called the *arte dell'agnolo*, which had its own unique *gonfalon* depicting–as per the new guild's name–an angel. On the other hand, Walter ruled with scant regard for the wealthy *ottimati* burghers who had invited him to assume power. He introduced the unpopular system of taxation known as the *estimo* and his squeezing of the mercantile classes forced the city to the brink of fiscal ruin. A popular uprising within the commune soon led to his ejection just ten months later and the Florentine oligarchs resolved that no further experiments in personal rule would ever be undertaken.

Florence's two brief flirtations with lordly dictatorship had proven singularly unsatisfactory to the heavily republican leaning commune. During the intervening half-century the city's *ottimati* happily reverted to their previous oligarchic ways and the *popolo minuto* went back to being largely unrepresented in the day-to-day life of the government. The on-going, palpable manipulation by the wealthy families was not, however, entirely without its consequences. In 1378, the resentful *popolo minuto* erupted in a spontaneous and bloody uprising, what was to become known as *il ribellione dei ciompi* or 'the rebellion of the *ciompi*'. Led by an illiterate wool-worker, the *ciompi* rioted through the streets of the city, merrily ransacking and setting fire to the *palazzi* of the wealthy merchants of the ruling upper classes, and installing their own more populist version of seigniorial government.

The destabilising conditions for the *ribellione dei ciompi* had been laid decades in the past and were many. Firstly, there was growing tension within the guild system between the patrician *ottimati* of the major guilds on the one hand and the more humble exponents of the middle and lesser guilds on the other. Patrician politics had by this time polarised around two prominent families of the so-called *popolani grassi* ('fat cats'), the Ghibelline Albizzi and the Guelph Ricci. The Black Death had overwhelmed Florence in the years 1348 and 1363, depleting the population and severely denuding the patrician class itself. The situation had been graphically illustrated by one Florentine observer who wrote of plague victims that 'Many died without being confessed or receiving the last sacraments, and men died of hunger, for when somebody took ill to his bed, the other occupants in panic told him, "I'm going for the doctor", and quietly locked the door from the outside and didn't come back'. Many citizens at this time fled Florence to seek safety in neighbouring city-states. The resulting economic depression had led to numerous bankruptcies and layoffs in the textile industries whilst many new immigrants were drawn to the city from the impoverished Tuscan *contado*. Into this highly fluid situation arrived the *gente nuova*, a class of 'new men', many of whom were recent immigrants who had made their money from trade and commerce but who were as yet excluded from politics. The *gente nuova* now made common cause with the disgruntled members of the *arti minori*, the under-enfranchised poor relations of the guild system. The two alienated groups became natural bedfellows.

On top of all these negative factors, a group of citizens antagonistic towards the Parte Guelfa had embroiled Florence in a war with Pope Gregory XI between 1375 and 1378 over the republican independence of the cities of the Papal States. This was known as the War of the Eight Saints and it had resulted in the Pope placing Florence under an interdict of excommunication. The divisive conflict had dragged on for three years and undermined both the political and spiritual basis of the commune. Florence was only saved when they paid a crippling 130,000 florin bribe to the Pope's English *condottiere*, Sir John Hawkwood (whose name is sometimes Italianised to 'Giovanni Aucut'). This forestalled Hawkwood's main offensive against Florence and when the Florentines also later agreed to pay the *condottiere* a generous regular stipend he came over into Florence's service altogether. But the expense of the three year-long war and the resulting taxation had only added to the hardship of the Florentines. In 1378 the captains of the Parte Guelfa conspired to seize the Palazzo della Signoria and take possession of the State. It so happened that a member of the Medici family, a banker named Salvestro de' Medici, was serving as *gonfaloniere* at this time.

Salvestro set about penalising the Parte Guelfa using the old Ordinances of Justice against them and appealing to the Council of the People. This move so inflamed the city that the discontent now spilled over into the thorny issue of political representation itself. The tidewaters eventually broke in June 1378 with a full-scale riot. The disenfranchised wool-workers labouring under the wealthy and influential *ottimati* merchants of the *arte della lana* armed themselves and took to the streets, attacking first the *palazzi* of the leaders of the Parte Guelfa and then widening their ire indiscriminately to government buildings, monasteries and prisons. During the unrest they had also released inmates from the city prisons which only contributed to the general chaos and lawlessness. The uprising may be seen as being closely connected to a growing tendency on the part of the lower orders to question the accepted social hierarchy. This was not only happening in Florence but was indeed a Europe-wide awakening. Just several years later, in 1381, the participants in the English Peasants' Revolt would pose the simple yet devastatingly subversive question: 'When Adam dalf and Eve span, who was thanne a gentilman?' This had been the question articulated by an itinerant English Lollard preacher named John Ball, 'the mad priest of Kent' as the historian Jean Froissart called him, who was later hanged, drawn and quartered for the treasonous offence of not only uttering such dislocating speculations on the social order but of having the impudence to act upon them.

Having provoked these events in the first place through their wilfully partisan actions the embattled anti-Guelph *signoria* were now caught on the back foot. They sought to contain the unrest by entering into futile negotiations with the *ciompi* which nevertheless still left that group without guild membership and therefore still unrepresented in politics. The procrastination and insincerity of the oligarchy in the face of this popular rising led to a worsening of the situation and, between 20-22 July, the lawless mob captured the palace of the *podestà*, torched many of the wool merchants' *botteghe* and took over the Palazzo della Signoria by force, installing an illiterate wool-comber named Michele di Lando as their populist *gonfaloniere*. It was already widely known that Salvestro de' Medici was comfortable wielding populism as a political tool but his task of containing the working class rebellion had not been helped by the scurrilous rumour that Salvestro himself had foolishly augmented the *ciompi's* numbers by freeing the criminal element from the city prisons. Now, with the city's riff-raff mingling freely with the rioting workers, the crisis had worsened. Salvestro was now displaced by Lando and in the ensuing two years the latter proceeded to establish a far more democratic commune in place of the previous narrow oligarchy. To signify their takeover of the city the *ciompi* had gleefully hoisted aloft their blacksmith's banner atop the Bargello, the inviolable palace of the *podestà*.

Under Lando the *ciompi* established three new *arti minori*, each of which reserved for them a post in the civil government. But the common woolworkers' government that they had created was widely disparaged by the more well-to-do. The sixteenth-century Florentine soldier, diplomat and historian Francesco Guicciardini later sneered: 'The men left in the government were mostly plebs, men of the crowd rather than nobles ... and with popular support they governed three years in which time they did many ugly things'. Lando himself struggled with his newfound power and was check-mated by the *ottimati* who now closed their *botteghe* to the *ciompi* thereby preventing them from earning a living. In a sense this was deeply unfair for the *ciompi* did not have a revolutionary agenda per se; they merely sought political reform and greater political representation for the underclass. They sorely missed the democratising reforms of the duke of Athens and failure to have a say in government meant that they were frequently blindsided by exploitative civic ordinances pertaining to wages and working conditions. As well as the notables, Lando also faced increasing disobedience from the unruly *ciompi* themselves who now suspected him of conspiring with Salvestro de' Medici to return the *ottimati* to power. In his hour of need Lando had turned to Salvestro de' Medici, whose own actions had sparked the rebellion, and he now sought out Salvestro's more experienced counsel. Lando created Salvestro a knight on 21 July 1378 along with sixty-three other citizens and shortly afterwards, as an additional show of favour, also gave him a lucrative tax farm on the revenue of shops along the Ponte Vecchio. Understandably, this pandering to an already wealthy burgher inflamed the impoverished *ciompi* who now howled for redress. But when they decamped once more to the streets to express their collective displeasure at Lando and Salvestro's machinations they were ready for them. Barricading all exits to the Piazza della Signoria, Lando called out the city militia which was mostly manned by tradesmen from the middle and minor guilds who resented the rule of the *ciompi*. Quickly and efficiently these more reactionary forces quelled the woolworkers' uprising.

Tragically, most of the *ciompi* who had taken to the city streets that day were butchered in a bloody massacre. The *ribellione dei ciompi* had been a discordant wake up call to the city's complacent mercantile élite and had shaken up the comfortable status quo hitherto enjoyed by the *ottimati*. Nevertheless, the wealthy *popolani grassi* families, most notably the Albizzi, the Capponi and the Uzzano, quickly reasserted control once more. The three new guilds established by the *ciompi* were dismantled in 1382 and the labouring classes of Florentines, who in fact constituted the majority of the population, grumblingly returned to their former disenfranchised and exploited condition. The poet Franco Sacchetti hailed the new anti-*ciompi* government in a *canzone* proclaiming that Prudence, Justice, Fortitude and Temperance had once more been reinstated in Florence. Although most of Sacchetti's kin had been banished by the earlier pro-*ciompi* signoria he himself had been exempted by the *ciompi* for being '*per esser tanto uomo buono*' or 'a really good man'.

The oligarchy now reverted to its previous tightly-controlled and largely self-regulating system. The *arti maggiori* reassumed control of government and promptly seized three-quarters of the government posts for themselves. Further genuine reform from within under the existing conditions was impracticable; not only was the *signoria's* two-month term of office too little in which to effect any real change or self-reform but, on a purely personal basis, any placemen who failed to do the ruling families' bidding soon found themselves discarded. In grudging recognition of their role in suppressing the *ciompi* Lando and Salvestro had meanwhile escaped a grisly execution. Instead they were both exiled from Florence, Lando himself being placed under bounds at Chioggia in the Veneto with twenty-five others before eventually returning to Florence where he died in 1401.

The Medici family name had, on reflection, gained little from the whole sordid affair. Indeed, the political track record of the Medici up to this point was arguably quite dismal. In 1343, some years prior to the whole *ciompi* débâcle, Salvestro's cousin Giovanni de' Medici had belligerently taken the Florentines to war against the city of Lucca with high hopes of establishing his standing in the republic through skill-at-arms. In the event, the incompetent war commissioner Giovanni had failed miserably and had been executed for his hubris and misplaced ambition. But this was a common enough problem in Florence, as indeed in ancient Athens. Antisthenes had advised the Athenians to pass a vote that asses were horses and, when they thought that irrational, he had replied, 'Why, those whom you make generals have never learnt to be really generals, they have only been voted such'. But nevertheless, in the wake of both of these high-profile fiascos, the Medici family now sensibly kept their heads down during the ensuing years and waited.

When Salvestro's successor, Vieri di Cambio de' Medici, took over the family business upon the former's death in 1388, the new patriarch demonstrated by contrast a marked diffidence towards politics, preferring instead to quietly concentrate on building up the family's banking interests. When, in 1393, yet another popular rebellion was ignited amongst Florence's *popolo magro* or 'skinny people', the commune's poor and unskilled sub-underclass, Vieri was approached to be their leader and to provide them with more enlightened and educated political direction. His response was to lead the agitators *en masse* to the Piazza della Signoria where, much to the astonishment of the rebels, he abased himself before the *priori*. Unctuously confessing that he himself had played no part in the rebellion, Vieri humbly pleaded for clemency for the misguided *popolo magro* and, thanks to his conciliatory actions, the crisis was averted and the malcontents dispersed back to their hovels. But the harrowing experience of being singled out as a potential rebel leader had taken its toll on the mild mannered moneylender's nerves and Vieri died later the same year, thus extinguishing the senior Medici line.

One of the *ottimati* families to re-emerge pre-eminent in Florence in the immediate aftermath of the *ribellione dei ciompi* was the House of Albizzi. Its members were not originally Florentines at all but instead hailed from Arezzo and the family name first appears in official Florentine records in 1251. In 1282 Ser Compagno became the first of ninety-eight Albizzi priors of Florence. The recent fortunes of the Albizzi had been highly chequered however. The former *capo* or 'head' of the family, Piero degli Albizzi, had sided with the tyrannical captains of the Guelph party and been beheaded by the *ciompi* regime. The new *capo* was Maso di Luca degli Albizzi, who was Piero's nephew and had been raised beneath Piero's roof. Maso was a capable man who had, amongst other things, carried out a diplomatic commission for Florence to the city of Milan in 1368. Although Ghibelline in their sympathies, Piero and Maso had aligned their family with Guelph interests and in 1372 had formed an alliance with their notional Guelph rivals the Ricci, who were led by Uguccione de' Ricci; this had alarmed the rising class of *gente nuova* who feared that these two *popolani grassi* families were planning to stage an outright coup d'état. The *signoria* had decreed as a precautionary measure that all political sects be dissolved and, in the confused street disturbances which followed, a member of the Ricci clan had allegedly bludgeoned an artisan to death with a stone ashlar. In January 1373 both the Ricci and the Albizzi were as a consequence banned from communal office for a period of ten years. Unable to participate in Florentine politics, the disgraced thirty-year-old Maso degli Albizzi went into voluntary exile to the north where, in the freezing wastes of the Baltic, he fought under the banner of the Teutonic Order against the grand duchy of Lithuania.

When the *ribellione dei ciompi* broke in 1378, Maso was still away from Florence and could do nothing to prevent the Albizzi *palazzi* and several other properties from being torched by the disgruntled wool carders. However, when news reached the erstwhile Teutonic Crusader of the death sentence for conspiracy which had been passed on his uncle Piero by the ciompi, who had been working in cahoots with the influential Alberti family, he swore vengeance. Following the collapse of the *ciompi*-led government in 1381, Maso returned from self-exile and rapidly recovered his family's former position of dominance. One of his most earnest actions was the retributive annihilation of the House of Alberti in the year 1393. On the pretext of an alleged Alberti conspiracy, Maso orchestrated the convening of an emergency *balia* of eighty-one members and had the rival family proscribed and sent into exile. Benedetto degli Alberti, one

22

of the leading figures in the Alberti's championing of the *ciompi* cause was banished from Florence and ended his life miserably on the island of Rhodes. For the next thirty-five years, until their banishment was revoked in 1428, the Alberti had effectively been obliterated as a political force in Florence.

Maso degli Albizzi had the foresight to pacify the still truculent disenfranchised *popolo minuto* and *popolo magro* through a sensible policy of fostering economic prosperity, something which most social classes, even the politically disenfranchised ones, could readily participate in. Outside threats also served to galvanise and entrench the ruling élite during the later years of the fourteenth-century, especially the continuing threat posed by Duke Gian Galeazzo Visconti of Milan. A fierce rival in the silk trade, Milan was Florence's traditional enemy and her ambitious and expansionist duke made her an exceedingly dangerous adversary. Gian Galeazzo was the eldest son of Galeazzo II Visconti who had established himself as co-ruler of Milan together with his brothers Bernabò and Matteo. Galeazzo II is famously known for instituting the *Quaresima*, a diabolically protracted 41-day series of tortures, alternating with 'days of rest', which was reserved for traitors to the state which has been preserved in the record of his court notary Petro Azario, who detailed for posterity such lurid agonies as whippings, flaying of skin, removal of limbs and eyes, mutilation of the face and genitals and finally breaking upon the wheel. Following Galeazzo II's death in 1378, Gian Galeazzo had wrestled sole control of Milan from his surviving uncle Bernabò and ruled the duchy as *signore* in addition to Pavia which the Visconti family also held. In 1395 he purchased the duchy of Milan from King Wenceslaus IV of the Romans for 100,000 gold florins and became duke. Following his assumption of ducal power in Milan, Gian Galeazzo then went on to conquer the cities of Verona, Vicenza, and Padua, his cherished hope being to unite all of northern Italy into one revived Lombard empire ruled over by the House of Visconti from the duchy of Milan. Eventually, he aspired to be crowned in Florence itself. For their part the Florentines endearingly referred to him as *il Grande Serpente*.

But Maso degli Albizzi, the former Teutonic Knight with liquid steel in his veins, was more than equal to the challenge posed by Gian Galeazzo Visconti. In dogged opposition to *Milanese* ambitions in Lombardy stood the independent cities of Bologna, ruled since 1401 by the pro-Guelph Giovanni I Bentivoglio, and the Florentine republic itself. In 1396, Maso concluded a league with the lords of Bologna, Ferrara and Padua which now defied the up-till-now unchecked expansionism of the Visconti. Gian Galeazzo unleashed his armies on both city states in 1402 and, supported by his allies the Malatesta of Rimini and the Gonzaga of Mantua, scored a rapid victory over the *Bolognesi* and their Florentine allies at the Battle of Casalecchio on 26 June. Giovanni Bentivoglio was killed in the battle and the House of Bentivoglio was temporarily deposed as the rulers of Bologna. In 1402, the Emperor Robert confirmed an alliance with Florence and appointed Maso degli Albizzi as Count Palatine. However the withdrawal soon afterwards of Robert from Tuscany led to a resurgence of Visconti aggression. Fortunately for Florence, by September that same year Gian Galeazzo Visconti was dead and, under his thirteen-year-old heir Gian Maria Visconti, the duchy disintegrated amidst bitter family feuding and in-fighting. The immediate threat from Milan was for the time being suspended.

With the subsequent break-up of the duchy of Milan between Gian Galeazzo Visconti's squabbling heirs, Maso redirected Florence's foreign policy towards the conquest and absorption of the maritime city-state of Pisa and also took a hand in promoting the foundation of Florence's university, the *Studio Fiorentino*. By 1414 the oligarchy was at the top of its game. 'One may rightly say', lauded Francesco Guicciardini, 'that it was the wisest, the most glorious, the happiest government that our city ever had'. The Florentine bookseller and biographer Vespasiano da Bisticci echoed these sentiments readily: 'In that time, from 1422 to 1433, the city of Florence was in a most blissful state, abounding with excellent men in every faculty, and it was full of admirable citizens'. Florence's chancellor Coluccio Salutati also extolled his city's virtues, asserting, somewhat disingenuously it must be said, that 'the foundation of our government is the parity and equality of all the citizens'. The position of the Albizzeschi (as the extended Albizzi clan was called) seemed so entrenched and unassailable within the ruling oligarchy at this time that few could have imagined that a parvenu family, the Medici, would shortly dust off its past indiscretions and enter the political arena to challenge them.

Being merely the most prominent figure in Florence's oligarchy, Maso degli Albizzi nevertheless shared power to a certain extent with half a dozen other wealthy and experienced *grassi* including men like Niccolò da Uzzano, Gino Capponi, Lorenzo Ridolfi, Agnolo Pandolfini, Palla Strozzi and Matteo Castellani. Such notables conducted Florence's foreign embassies and were habitually to be found presiding over the war council, the *dieci di balìa*. But despite the acknowledged oligarchy, on the surface at least Florence's much vaunted civic humanism appeared to be thriving. Between 1393 and 1420 the number of those eligible to sit on the *signoria* actually increased from 600 to over 2,000. On closer inspection however this growth reflected not so much an increase in outsiders to the oligarchy, such as the upwardly mobile *gente nuova*, as a reallocation of eligibility amongst the dominant oligarchic families themselves. Following the 1390s the number of new entrants to the electoral rolls probably decreased if anything and by the 1420s the *reggimento* revolved around no less than sixty or seventy key plutocratic families.

Another important body which these key families constituted and dominated was known as the *consulte e pratiche*. The *pratiche* were consultative commissions which had arisen during the earlier years of the *signoria*. These commissions comprised only leading members of the Florentine community and were occasionally called to order by the nine amateur politicians of the *signoria* for the purpose of providing them with informal guidance and consultation on important matters of state policy by experts, or at least, by those who were supposedly 'in the know' about such specialised matters. Following the *ribellione dei ciompi* these consultative *pratiche* took on an even greater permanence and ubiquity, effectively assuming the role of, as it were, a shadow government behind the *signoria*. As Florence descended into its hugely destabilizing period of struggle with the Visconti dynasty of Milan, these *pratiche* became an important factor in maintaining continuity of state policy and provided a firm hand on the tiller of public affairs. This was already sorely lacking in the case of the more short-term, rotational *signoria*. But the growth in influence of the *pratiche* was not the only way in which Florence's political institutions had been undermined and denuded of their original integrity by the *ottimati*.

The vaunted institution of the *parlamento* had, by this time, come to be cynically manipulated as a tool of oligarchic rule. The *parlamento* was only meant to be called during serious crises and, when summoned, offered all the benefits of what we today would call a plebiscite, where the entire adult community is consulted and asked to vote on a matter of supreme importance. At the intoning of the *vacca* the citizens would march to the Piazza della Signoria where the *signoria* would make proposals to the assembled crowd who would give their assent 'by popular acclamation'. In later years it was however realised that if the *piazza* was carefully secured in advance by armed guards obedient to the dominant oligarchy then voting could effectively be influenced and controlled. Those in opposition to a given proposal were loath to risk their lives by dissenting publicly in the presence of armed militia, and furthermore the *parlamento* would anyway be packed with the oligarchy's obedient acolytes. Likewise, when the *parlamento* was called upon to appoint a *balia*, that committee of two or three hundred citizens tasked with the reform of the *signoria*, the oligarchy could easily manipulate the *balia's* composition and its political affinities. The reality of such practices was of course an open secret in Florence by the time of the *ribellione dei ciompi* and was unquestionably one of the many grievances of the politically dispossessed classes.

The 'ruling regime', known in local parlance as *il reggimento*, did not as we have seen comprise merely the Albizzeschi but up to seventy other influential *ottimati* families. Indeed, the way that the political mechanism was structured at this time did not lend itself to a system whereby any single family could entirely dominate the political life of the republic and the smooth operation of the Florentine state still very much depended on the mutual cooperation of a diverse network of *ottimati* houses (during the later more autocratic period of Medici rule this self-regulating era in Florentine government would be regarded as a sort of 'golden age', whimsically looked back on through rose-tinted glasses). However, the plutocratic oligarchy at this time still failed to assume the outward appearance of an aristocracy as we might typically understand it. The imperial Ghibellinism of the feudal order, with its preoccupation with noble titles and ennoblements, was still regarded with suspicion by Florentines; it tended not to manifest in the outward show of the social status of these urban mercantile families. These men were not from the great landed estates but instead comprised for the most part white collar professionals like judges, lawyers, bankers, merchants and such like. The manipulation of the city's political life was therefore skewed more towards securing economic benefits for the oligarchy's individual members – the fixing of wages for instance or the creation of new civic or commercial ordinances favourable to the interests of business owners. But all the same, the other families tended to defer to Maso degli Albizzi during this period and, all things considered, his predominance was a beneficial thing for Florence. The republic needed a firm hand on the executive levers of power at this time given the ever-present hostility of Milan and Maso was at least a trained, experienced professional soldier.

With the *Milanese* peril in temporary abeyance, Florence had turned her thoughts towards territorial expansion of her own and cast her greedy eye upon the Ghibelline city of Pisa. Formerly one of the four powerful maritime republics of Italy, Pisa's naval power had been broken forever by her rival Genoa at the Battle of Meloria in 1284. Six years later the *Genovesi* had finished the job by dismantling the *Porto Pisano* and by maliciously sewing the surrounding agricultural land with salt to ruin it for cultivation. Despite her woes Pisa had, however, managed to inflict a crushing defeat on the combined armies of Florence and Naples at the Battle of Montecatini in 1315. But Pisa's last possession of any value, the island of Sardinia, was lost to her in 1324 thus marking the final catastrophic decline in the maritime state's fortunes. By the early fourteenth-century Pisa had also inevitably entered the orbit of Gian Galeazzo Visconti of Milan. When Gian Galeazzo died in late 1402 he left the state to his illegitimate son Gabriele Maria who was accepted as Lord of Pisa. By July of 1405 the *Pisani* had ejected him with enthusiastic cries of '*Viva il popolo, morte al tiranno!*' Peevishly, Gabriele Maria then agreed to sell Pisa to Florence for the sum of 200,000 gold florins.

Florence despatched Gino Capponi to take control of Pisa's main citadel and two other outlying fortresses, which he did, leaving a garrison of mercenaries behind to secure the new possession. However, before Florence could take official tenure of the city, the *Pisani* recaptured the citadel and instead nominated the Raspanti family as their new rulers. The Raspanti were then quickly supplanted by a newly returned *Pisano* exile named Giovanni Gambacorta. Pisa appealed to Florence for the return of its other fortresses but handled the negotiations ineptly; as Gino Capponi recorded in his diary: 'With these and like phrases they talked in such a disgusting manner that every man in Florence determined he would go naked rather than *not* conquer Pisa'. In response to the crisis, a *dieci di balìa* was called, on which Maso degli Albizzi presided together with representatives from the Capponi, Corbinelli, Castellani and Cavalcanti families, and a Florentine mercenary army was placed before the walls of Pisa in March 1406, supplied by sea through Livorno. Maso and Gino Capponi then assumed joint personal command of the army and proceeded to lay siege to Pisa with great cruelty.

Enclosing Pisa in a ring of steel, Maso's strategy was to starve the city into submission. The weeks and months passed. Inside the walls, the inhabitants were soon reduced to consuming cats, dogs, beasts of burden and *in extremis* even vermin. When all the living creatures had been hunted down and devoured the *Pisani* tore up any roots and any vestiges of greenery they could find growing within the city walls. 'The grass in market places had been torn up, dried, and ground into a powdery dust for bread', reported one eye witness inside the city. Smugglers from the nearby city of Lucca risked their lives by attempting to sneak into Pisa with a few handfuls of grain; such were the huge potential profits to be made from supplying the starving inhabitants with food. But, in spite of their enormous suffering, the *Pisani* were determined to hold out.

To save food supplies, they expelled from their city the 'destitute and useless' non-combatants such as beggars and other poor people. Maso warned the *Pisani* that anyone found leaving the city in future would be summarily hanged. Still the *Pisani* ejected those considered inessential to the defence of their city and this time it was the turn of Pisa's womenfolk to tremulously emerge from the city gates and make their way towards the entrenchment lines of their enemy. Not wishing to hang scores of poor women, the Florentines instead tore their dresses open to expose their buttocks and, using red hot pokers, branded their cheeks with the Florentine *giglio*. When even this failed to discourage the constant exodus, the Florentines cut off the women's noses and shoved them rudely back towards the city gates. Any men unwise enough to flee the siege were hanged on the spot, usually within sight of the walls as a grisly example to those watching from the ramparts.

Throughout all of this cruelty Maso degli Albizzi had grimly presided. When it became clear that Pisa would fall of its own accord through starvation the *signoria* issued strict instructions to its mercenaries forbidding the sacking of

26

the city. This was done not out of any compassion for the inhabitants themselves, however, but out of the pragmatic desire not to see Pisa's considerable wealth transferred into the pockets of their hired *condottieri* as they swiftly departed for home. Eventually, the misery of those trapped within the city grew too great to contend with. Gambacorta now entered into negotiations with the Florentines to hand the city over to them in return for a personal amnesty, property in Florence, and a payment of 20,000 ducats. At dawn on 9 October 1406, Gambacorta opened the city gate of San Marco to admit the triumphant Florentine troops. Some of the mercenaries entered Pisa with loaves of bread which they threw to the starving people whom they found cowering pitifully inside. To their horror the *Pisani*, especially the children who were by now completely feral, had reacted like 'ravenous birds of prey'.

The prestige that Florence earned from this 'bloodless' conquest was considerable. The families which had been instrumental in the victory were showered with adulation, especially the Albizzeschi and the Capponi (Gino Capponi was named governor of Pisa following its capitulation). It had been the practical guidance of the *pratiche* which had carried the day but behind this consultative council sat the looming presence of Maso degli Albizzi himself. Florence's church bells rang out *a stormo*; there were bonfires, Masses in all of Florence's churches and holy processions of thanksgiving. Land-locked, mercantile Florence now had a seaport of its very own. Unfortunately, in the aftermath of Pisa's conquest, the city's fortunes plummeted. In 1305 Pisa's population had been one third that of Florence but by 1427 it was down to less than one fifth. Rather than concentrating on Pisa's economic contribution to the Florentine polity by rebuilding the vanquished city's economic base, its new overlords were instead preoccupied with security-related issues. As the native *Pisani* themselves emigrated from their ailing city, creating an economic brain drain, Florentines seeking their fortune migrated to Pisa in growing numbers. As Florence's economic migrants settled and began integrating amongst them, the *Pisani* themselves would remain bitter and resentful. They had no right to Florentine citizenship and they would never truly forget the cruelties which the Florentines had inflicted upon their defenceless womenfolk. Their odium would quietly simmer for another eighty-eight years until a dwarfish king of France would march south and release them from Florence's servitude.

As well as Pisa and Milan, Florence also found herself locked in a life-or-death struggle with King Ladislas of Naples. Ladislas was the last male of the senior ruling Angevin line who was also titular king of Jerusalem and Sicily, count of Provence and king of Hungary and Croatia. The disagreement was triggered by the King's growing propensity for interference in the affairs of central Italy, a tendency which his predecessors Charles and Robert of Anjou had also shared. The Florentines were especially troubled by Ladislas's alliance with nearby Lucca's *signore* Paolo Guinigi who was a traditional enemy of the republic. Additional friction also arose over the existence of three competing popes around this time: Gregory XII, his Avignon-based rival Benedict XIII and Alexander V, whom the Florentines themselves had opted to support. Eventually, the situation erupted into open war by the early 1400s and by 1410, although Florence had captured the town of Cortona in Arezzo, Ladislas had counter-attacked deep into Tuscany. As with Gian Galeazzo Visconti, the dire situation had only been saved by the death of King Ladislas in August 1414.

The following year the Ecumenical Council of Constance deposed all three popes, including Pope Alexander V's successor the antipope John XXIII, and, two years later in 1417 on the feast of St. Martin, it elected the *capo* of the Genazzano branch of the Colonna family, Oddone Colonna, as Pope Martin V. Pope Martin returned the Holy See from Avignon to Rome (described by Petrarch in his *Rerum senilium libri* as 'that most disgusting city') thus ending the Western Schism. Even so, Pope Martin was unable to take up immediate residence in Rome due to an on-going battle for supremacy between the city's warring factions, combined with outside interference from King Ladislas's successor Queen Joanna II of Naples. He therefore relocated to a more peaceful and congenial Florence, making his temporary home at the Dominican church of Santa Maria Novella, and therefore Florence briefly became the epicentre of Western Christendom. Eventually, a treaty with Queen Joanna finally allowed the Pope to move back to Rome in 1420.

Amidst these two major outside threats presented by Naples and Milan, Florence had needed strong leadership and the dynamic Maso degli Albizzi and the wealthy *ottimati* houses of the oligarchy had provided exactly that. But there was, as always, a political price to pay for strength and what was becoming increasingly apparent by the turn of the fifteenth-century was that the oligarchic manipulation of the so-called *popolani grassi*, the 'fat cats', was threatening to evolve into rule by Maso degli Albizzi and his family alone. Florence was, in effect, now threatened with being transformed into a de facto *tirannia*. Jealousy of the upper echelons of the *reggimento* by those at the bottom rungs of the establishment had already riven the government with factionalism by the time of King Ladislas's death in 1414. Gino Capponi had created a party which stood opposed to the final peace treaty with Ladislas, a treaty which had had the backing of Maso and his faction. The affronted Maso, unused to being challenged in this way, had reacted somewhat ungraciously by accusing Gino of plotting to assassinate him. Three years later in 1417, however, Maso degli Albizzi himself was dead and the reins of power devolved not to his son Rinaldo but to the most senior statesman in Florence, Niccolò da Uzzano.

Born sometime around 1359, and thrice *gonfaloniere* of the republic, Niccolò da Uzzano gladly took to his newfound authority. Although Albizzeschi rule remained strong through their nominees and placemen within the *signoria*, Rinaldo was devoid of his father's undisputed wisdom and personal charisma. The inevitable brake on Albizzi power created by the passing of the baton to da Uzzano caused resentment not only with Rinaldo himself but also with other younger scions of the oligarchy. So celebrated had Maso's legacy been that in 1426 an anonymous bill had even been posted on the doors of the Palazzo della Signoria asserting that Maso was worthy of being regarded as king (*re*), a remarkable proclamation for republican Florence. But all that the proposal celebrated was Maso's shrewd aptitude for manipulating Florence's electoral apparatus. Meanwhile, the extremely narrow monopoly on rule was generating fresh discontent amongst the disenfranchised masses. The minor *arti* were restricted by their paltry two *priori* to all but a vestigial share in government. Even certain members of the major *arti* were unable to pass the *scrutinies* and become eligible to hold office. Still others, even amongst those fortunate enough to have passed the *scrutinies*, were unable to wield real executive power in the *signoria* due to their lack of patronage from the ruling *ottimati* families. Ironically, many of these stymied men belonged to Florence's nouveau riche:

28

merchants and artisans who had become as prosperous, if not even more wealthy, than the *ottimati* themselves.

This class of nouveau riche, the *gente nuova*, inevitably found common cause with the old feudal *magnati* as well as with the vast underclass, both of whom complained that they were being heavily and unfairly taxed. But, although there was a strong undercurrent of general dissatisfaction with the political realities of the republic, the opposition had in no wise coalesced into a united front or indeed appointed any real leaders worth their salt who could successfully vocalise their grievances. That is not to say that such men had not come forward in the past. Salvestro de' Medici, for instance, was one such individual, even if his courage had manifested itself at the cost of his family's reputation. Vieri di Cambio de' Medici had, as we have seen in 1393, been offered the leadership of a popular rebellion due to the Medici's growing reputation as 'a family of the people', even if Vieri's instincts for survival had in the event led him to remain wisely aloof. Past precedent for going up against the dominant ruling élite was clear and the consequences were almost always the social and political obliteration of one's entire family. It therefore took a strong stomach to become involved in Florentine politics at the highest level.

The oligarchy further weakened its position by squabbling amongst itself; contemporary *ricordi* and *ricordanze* provide ample evidence for this growing loss of cohesion. The wealthy patrician Bonaccorso Pitti, for example, complained in his own *ricordi* how he had been the victim of an unjust kangaroo court merely because his family were rivals of the Ricasoli family. Worse still, the feuding *ottimati* further undermined their own position by adopting and promoting members of the disenfranchised classes in order to swell their own parties' numbers. Niccolò da Uzzano himself was wise enough to foresee that this foolish and short-sighted policy would eventually result in a critical dilution of their political power. New councils such as the Council of Two Hundred and the Council of One Hundred and Thirty-One had been set up, supposedly to provide a bulwark for the minority's rule, but the extension of power to more and more people, many of whom were now acting independently, was an unnecessary and short-sighted blunder. These councils grew increasingly unruly and sometimes even refused to rubber stamp the decisions of the *signoria*, a snub to the influential *pratiche* which lay behind the visible show of government. Sensing a descent into mob rule, da Uzzano urged the calling of a *parlamento* and the creation of a *balìa*. This could then go to work reviewing the *scrutinies* in such a way that only those partisan to the ruling élite would be admitted and all those suspected of disloyalty could be prohibited from participating in Florence's civic life. Unwisely, in the event, da Uzzano's recommendations were ignored. The fifty-eight-year-old Niccolò da Uzzano had seen it all and by now had a jaundiced view of Florentine politics. 'All these citizens, some through ignorance, some through malice, are ready to sell this republic; and thanks to their good fortune, they have found the purchaser', was his pessimistic remark on the matter. Little known to da Uzzano at this time was that an obscure offshoot of the Medici family were about to stage a political comeback. His remarks might have been tailor-made for their future relationship with Florence.

CHAPTER 2

Giovanni di Bicci and the Pirate Pope

> But in this year of 1415, the fate of the Roman pontiff and of the Church of Rome are inextricably enmeshed with the details–sometimes sordid, sometimes pathetic, always regrettable–of this one man, Baldassare Cossa. As of this May morning, he claimed to be pope for five years. His papal name: John XXIII. Those have been five years of energetic cunning, twisting and turning, confusing some enemies, liquidating others, buying off still others, parleying, temporising, compromising, warring, raiding, massacring, lying, perjuring, betraying.
>
> Malachi Martin,
> The Decline and Fall of the Roman Church

There was an old Medici family legend which was greatly revered and it went something like this. During the time of Charlemagne, there was a brave knight named Averardo who had fought for the great Frankish king as he conquered the Italian lands of the Lombards. This Averardo was passing through the valley of the Mugello, which lies to the north of Florence, when he heard from local peasants a story concerning a cruel and brutal giant who had been pillaging the region. Setting off in search of this marauding giant, the knight soon came face-to-face with his quarry and a battle inevitably ensued. Now, this giant carried a massive cudgel in which were embedded many fearsome-looking iron balls. As Averardo fought the colossus, using all his skill, he fended off the giant's club with his shield. When he had finally triumphed over the creature, Averardo wearily turned his shield over to inspect it and found that the giant's weapon, thanks to its iron balls, had left several circular indents in it. When Charlemagne heard of Averardo's valiant exploits he was so impressed that he granted the knight the privilege of his own coat-of-arms featuring red *palle* (or balls) against a golden backdrop. Ever afterwards, the *palle* would be known as the insignia of the Medici family.

It was an engaging myth to be sure but a more prosaic explanation for the *palle* was that the Medici had previously been apothecaries (as per their family name 'Medici' which derives from the Latin *Medicinae* meaning 'medicine') and that the balls represented the medicinal pills that they dispensed. This story too was just as apocryphal; the fact of the matter was that pills had not come into use so early in medieval history and so could not possibly account for the *palle* symbolism. More likely was the even simpler explanation that the *palle* were a traditional sign put up outside money-changing and pawn broking shops. The Medici themselves had, for as long as anyone could recall, been in the money-changing/lending business and this is perhaps the most likely explanation for their heraldic insignia. Indeed, the coat-of-arms of the *arte del cambio*, the banking guild, was practically identical, consisting as it did of several balls arrayed on a shield.

The mention of the Mugello had at least been correct; the Medici hailed from the village of Cafaggiolo, which was situated in the Mugello's relatively compact Sieve River Valley some eighteen miles north of Florence. Around the turn of the thirteenth-century however the family had left the rural, homespun comforts of Cafaggiolo and migrated to Florence, settling in the locality of San Lorenzo. This bustling neighbourhood, situated close to the animated market places of the city, derived its name from the Basilica di San Lorenzo, the fourth century Romanesque church which had served for several hundred years as the city's cathedral (the Basilica di San Lorenzo would in fact serve as Florence's de facto cathedral until the official seat of the city's bishop was later transferred to the church of Santa Reparata). San Lorenzo and the Medici family were to develop a close and abiding relationship over the coming centuries and the Medici were instrumental in its later remodelling into one of the icons of Florentine Renaissance architecture. San Lorenzo would also lend his name to many of the scions of the Medici, including of course the illustrious Lorenzo de' Medici, who would become known to the Florentines as *il Magnifico*.

The first member of the Medici family who we know from official public records is a man named Chiarissimo de' Medici, who is mentioned in the year 1201 in some legal documents. Then, an interlude of 95 years elapses before we next hear of a Medici being elected to the high office of *gonfaloniere della giustizia*. This man was Ardingo de' Medici. Just three years later, in 1299, Ardingo's brother Guccio was the second member of the Medici family to become *gonfaloniere*. Upon his death, he was distinguished by being laid to rest outside the Baptistery. In 1314, yet another Medici was honoured with the same high appointment; this was Averardo de' Medici who bore the same name as the family's legendary Frankish ancestor. Since it was an open secret that the wealthier families kept a tight rein on political elections, clearly by this time the Medici–though not themselves from the ruling *ottimati*–had proven themselves sufficiently capable of delivering the proxy political decisions required by the oligarchic powers operating behind the scenes. Averardo's grandson, Filigno di Conte de' Medici, rhapsodized about these halcyon days of civic honour and family good fortune in his memoirs.

Following Averardo's indenture there had sadly been no further preferments for the Medici and indeed one of their number, Giovanni de' Medici, had been executed in 1343 by Walter de Brienne. Decades later Salvestro de' Medici was elevated to *gonfaloniere* in 1370 and then again in 1378. But Salvestro's complicity in the *ribellione dei ciompi* had ended his career and tainted the reputations of many of the guiltless members of his family. Salvestro's sympathetic identification with the disenfranchised *popolo minuto* had placed the Medici beyond the pale, rendering them useless as proxies for the oligarchs. For an up-and-coming parvenu family like the Medici the inability to hold political office was a major constraint on their growing status. When they judged and evaluated you, the civic-minded Florentines still elevated political office above all other practical attainments. As has been seen, however, when the Medici could not participate in politics they turned to what they were best at, that is to say, making money. Wisely eschewing involvement in any form of popular rabble rousing, Vieri di Cambio de' Medici instead focused his energies on capitalising on the mistakes of his more established competitors.

Those pre-eminent Florentine banking families the Bardi, the Peruzzi and the Acciaiuoli had repeated the same errors as the by now defunct Bonsignore of Siena. By chasing the prestigious yet hazardous whimsy of royal clientage, in this case King Edward III of England and King Robert of Naples, they had left themselves exposed to staggeringly large debts and royal lines of credit. Edward III had borrowed vast sums from Florentine counting houses before embarking upon what would later come to be known as the Hundred Years War with France, a ruinously expensive undertaking; by some peoples' reckoning the war-loving English king is reputed to have borrowed 900,000 gold florins from the Bardi family and a further 600,000 florins from the Peruzzi. When King Edward found himself in the inconvenient position of being unable to repay the debt he simply reneged and both the Bardi and the Peruzzi bank instantaneously collapsed. These banks had failed to adequately ring-fence the liabilities of their individual branches therefore the bad debts of one branch became the liability of the entire bank. Thanks to such systemic instability the banks owned by the Bardi and Peruzzi, and to a lesser extent also the Acciaiuoli, had become extremely cumbersome to manage; the growing number of partners and investors in both banks caused management to squabble and make exceedingly poor decisions. They now found their places usurped by the rising Alberti bank which, prior to the family's banishment from Florence in 1393, was just large enough to capture the lucrative business of the Roman Catholic Church.

So Vieri di Cambio de' Medici worked modestly though assiduously at his green felt table at the Orsanmichele, his fingers counting florins and silver *piccioli*, or scribing entries in his great ledger. By all accounts his business was thriving; in addition to Florence, Vieri's bank had branches in Venice, Genoa, Rome, Naples and Gaeta. One of Vieri's more prescient actions had been to employ two distant Medici relatives in his growing banking concern. As Leon Battista Alberti wrote in *Della Famiglia*, since the family is the fundamental social unit of any society, anything which is done to benefit or enrich it or enhance its honour is justifiable. Family gives the individual a transcendent meaning beyond simple enrichment as a result of business. This could conveniently be interpreted by those successful banking families as a ready solution to the moral and spiritual dilemma of having achieved great wealth through the 'sinful' practice of usury. Loyalty to family comes above all else and, with the necessary degree of sophistry, justifies almost anything.

These *paisanos* whom Messer Vieri employed, two young members of the extended clan of Medici families which had been spawned over the decades, were Giovanni di Bicci de' Medici and his elder brother Francesco. The brothers were from the ancestral Medici village of Cafaggiolo and were sons of the late Averardo detto Bicci, who owned a smallholding there. Averardo detto Bicci was married to a daughter of the aristocratic Spini family and so could not exactly have been a Tuscan nobody; however, the plague of 1363 carried him off and, following his death, his wife's dowry of 800 gold florins was restored to her and what remained of his legacy afterwards was divided up equally between the widow and her five sons, leaving nobody in the family especially well-off. The brothers had only been toddlers at the time of these unhappy events but, upon attaining adulthood, Giovanni di Bicci and his brother had gravitated to Florence and were almost certainly in the city around the time of the *ribellione dei ciompi* and the subsequent rule of the commune.

Born in 1360, Giovanni would have been in his early twenties when he witnessed his distant relative Salvestro de' Medici's ignominious fall from grace. Perhaps as a result of the spectacle of Salvestro's disgrace and subsequent banishment, Giovanni, like his remote cousin and patron Vieri di Cambio de' Medici, prudently chose to remain out of the limelight. Instead, he applied himself to the business of banking and was despatched to his employer's Rome branch where he soon revealed a natural aptitude for finance. Rome at this time was a far cry from the ancient splendours of the Caesars and had yet to evolve into the luxurious Baroque Rome of the High Renaissance. The city's once grand ruins were now silent, dilapidated and crusted with centuries of accumulated filth. Over most of the seven hills sheep and cattle roamed freely and in the old Roman forum goats and cows grazed amongst the collapsed temples and Corinthian columns leading the Romans to refer to it as *Campo Vaccino* or the 'Cow Field'.

The Pope had his seat in the decrepit Basilica of St. Peter, which was essentially a fourth-century structure which had been haphazardly added to during medieval times. In front of the basilica was an atrium known as the 'paradise' in which a large bronze pinecone and a fountain took centre stage. It was a place of relative peace and tranquillity compared to the rest of the city. The Roman streets across the River Tiber were controlled by the vicious private armies of ancient feudal families, pre-eminent amongst which were the Orsini and the Colonna. Before these two houses had arisen, the Frangipani and Pierleoni families had clashed just as bitterly and before them the Romans had borne witness to the feud between the Crescenti and the Tusculani. Intergenerational feuding and vendetta were in the Romans' blood and had transformed much of Rome into an armed camp; the Frangipani had even converted the timeless Coliseum of Rome into a fortress which controlled the city's western approaches to the Lateran basilica. As in medieval Florence, numerous fortified towers dotted the city, breaking up the Roman skyline. Nevertheless, despite its dilapidation and in spite of the open warfare that occasionally broke out between the warring aristocratic families, Rome was renowned throughout the medieval banking world as a rich source of income. Through the city's unholy environs flowed a golden stream of hundreds of thousands of gold florins in ecclesiastical tithes and indulgences from all across Europe.

Rome was unique in the medieval world in drawing its income not only from its own citizens and the surrounding *campagna* (as well as the Papal States) but in tapping the rich financial vein of Western Christendom itself. The vast wealth which was sent to Rome, or more specifically to the Curia, was extracted from the remotest corners of Europe, often under duress, and occasionally even under direct threat of excommunication. Within this exploitative system, ecclesiastics were extorted just as efficiently and systematically as peasants. Before he could take up his benefice a cardinal was forced to cough up to the papal court his *annates*, equivalent to one-half of his first year's income; meanwhile all newly appointed abbots, bishops and archbishops were forced to pay to the papal court the appointment fee known as the *pallium*. This of course presented the practical problem of how exactly to move such large amounts of coin over huge distances. Due to the perils of travelling with large wealth, Church exactions were seldom carried in gold or silver coin across isolated mountains and through wild forests where thieves and cut-purses lurked. Instead, money was deposited in bank branches in European capitals in exchange for letters of credit which were cashed only upon arrival in Rome. The traveller himself purchased peace of mind whilst the bank earned moderately on commissions and exchange rates. However this system only worked west of the River Rhine and for those visiting Constantinople or the exotic cities of the East there were no such convenient financial services.

This constant stream of ecclesiastical income allowed the worldly red-bonneted cardinals of the Eternal City to splurge lavishly on their *palazzi*, their banquets and other costly entertainments, each cardinal seemingly eager to outdo the other in the extravagance of their soirees. Such free-flowing largesse inevitably spawned a corrupt city overflowing with fawning flatterers, hangers on, adventurers, poets, pornographers, parasites and whores. For the prudent and conservative Florentine banker there was an element of personal risk in doing business in a place like Rome, but there was even greater potential reward. Within just three years, Giovanni di Bicci had, through the diligent pursuit of his craft, leap frogged from junior partner to general manager of the Rome branch. This was soon followed by the opening of a second Rome branch as well as another new branch in Geneva across the Alps. Through steady application he had learned of the best ways to parlay his capital through mixed trades. He had mastered the art of the triangular transaction, whereby a bank becomes as much a commodities trading company as a financier. He had learned the importance of having bank branches in all the major business and political centres of Europe. He had become knowledgeable in when to accept risk and when to decline it. He had schooled himself not to be taken in by royalty or nobility; a royal line of credit might look good on a bank's resume but, as the Bardi and Peruzzi had shown, it could be positively disastrous on that same bank's balance sheet.

Giovanni had learned how to operate a bank in the teeth of Christendom's strictures against earning or paying out interest, known in medieval times as 'usury'. Although usury was officially prohibited by the Church and punishable by eternal damnation, nevertheless in an exquisitely immoral city such as Rome ways and means could always be found to circumvent the consequences of practices which might otherwise imperil one's immortal soul. Wealthy cardinals rolling in the fat incomes from multiple ecclesiastical benefices may have railed against 'interest' in their sermons but, at the end of the day, a large portion of their wealth was deposited into so-called 'discretionary accounts' with the bankers and moneylenders. The bankers discreetly kept their cash deposits safe whilst at the same time paying out annual 'discretionary' gifts to their ecclesiastical depositors. In the absence of either a definite contract promising to pay interest or a guaranteed gain this was conveniently viewed by much of the Curia as side-stepping the inconvenient dogmatic issue of usury.

Such an ambiguous arrangement, though not without its element of risk and involving costly litigation if moneylenders went bust, was nonetheless deemed necessary. Cardinals who put too much of their wealth into visible assets, such as for example property, ran the constant risk of having their possessions seized by an incoming pope eager to be seen as a reformist intent on making a clean sweep of Church corruption. Visible clerical wealth was always a target for Church administrators and the main reason for prohibiting the clergy from marrying had been to keep the assets of the Church *in* the Church rather bled away to the secular world through inheritance. Depositing one's money with a usurer and a sinner was therefore far safer for an ecclesiastic than building up his property portfolio. Furthermore, if Rome itself came under threat a Churchman could transfer most of his wealth to a different Italian city-state, or indeed to any other European capital outside the Holy Father's jurisdiction, while he safely waited out the crisis. With the creation of brand new financial instruments, many of which were developed by the innovative bankers of Florence, this advantage sent most wealthy Churchmen scurrying to find the most trustworthy and reliable bankers who could give them the best security and return on their deposits.

The Rome in which Giovanni di Bicci was learning the ropes of the banking business was at that time under the rule of Pope Urban VI. Bartolomeo Prignano had formerly been the archbishop of Bari and had, up until his election in 1378, led an exemplary life as a bureaucrat in the cloisters of the papal chancery. Upon ascending to the Chair of St. Peter, however, his demeanour had completely changed; he had gone from being an unassuming administrator to an overbearing, threatening bully of a pope who was determined, come what may, to impose his sanctimonious reforms on the Curia. Those indignant French cardinals who, up till now, had been habituated to dictating papal terms from Avignon, where the papacy had been held 'captive' for sixty-nine years from 1309 to 1378, now escaped from Rome to Anagni. Here, they promptly elected an antipope who took the name Clement VII. The Western Roman Church was now effectively in a state of Schism; this mind you was in addition to the Great Schism which already existed between the Roman Catholic and Eastern Orthodox Churches ever since 1054. This present Western Papal Schism would last until 1417 and, unbeknown to him at the time, Giovanni di Bicci himself would play a significant role in the Schism from behind the scenes through his backing the financial dealings of one of the schismatic popes.

In the meantime, Giovanni continued working at building up his skills and knowledge of the multifaceted world of banking. He learned everything that went into the setting up of a bank branch with sufficient capital. He learned how to staff that branch with *paisanos* that he could trust implicitly. As we have already seen, above all he learned the complexities of how to turn a profit whilst seeming not to charge interest on the money paid out as loans. This technique often veered into the mercantile world and involved structuring triangulated deals in which goods and services crossed international borders and were paid for according to complicated rates of exchange which ultimately favoured the banker who put the deal together. There was a certain kind of financial trickery, or 'alchemy', involved in such transactions because they always ensured that the banker turned a profit despite the ever fluctuating exchange rates. As these professional methods were something in the nature of a trade secret it was all the more important to employ only those trusted individuals who could be counted upon to be discreet and not flap their gums too much. As Giovanni slowly rose in prominence within the world of Florentine banking other prominent financier families like the Bardi, the Peruzzi, the Acciaiuoli and the Alberti waned in importance. With fortune smiling on his endeavours the time had now come for Giovanni to make a favourable wedding match.

In 1385, at the age of twenty-five and at the height of his success with the Vieri Bank, the young Giovanni di Bicci made a fortuitous union with a young woman named Piccarda Bueri. This Veronese beauty was the daughter of

Edoardo Bueri, an aristocrat with a long and noble lineage in Florence. Piccarda brought to the marriage an exceedingly handsome dowry of 1,500 florins. To put this amount somewhat in perspective, the sum of thirty-five florins would be sufficient to rent a modest townhouse with a garden for a whole year. We are told that Giovanni wisely reinvested his wife's dowry in his own business schemes, although we remain oblivious of the specific details. It would be the sons and grandsons of Giovanni di Bicci and the beautiful Piccarda Bueri who would be destined to shape the future of their city and indeed, through their involvement with the movement of the Renaissance and the institution of the papacy, of Italy and much of the rest of Europe as well. A son, Cosimo, was born to the couple in 1389 and in 1395 he was followed by a brother named Lorenzo, who would be known to later historians as 'the Elder' to distinguish him from Cosimo's own grandson Lorenzo *il Magnifico*. The descendants of Cosimo and Lorenzo the Elder would form two twin branches of the Medici family which would gain fame as the future rulers of Florence.

In 1393, Vieri di Cambio de' Medici, who was by then approaching seventy, decided to retire and divest himself of his business responsibilities and Giovanni di Bicci, who was by now Vieri's executive partner in the Rome branch, astutely stepped in to buy out his relative's interests. The young man took over Vieri's Rome office, whose business he had carefully grown over the past few years, and assumed Vieri's debts and liabilities as part and parcel of the deal. In this venture, Giovanni took on a talented young business partner named Benedetto di Lippaccio de' Bardi from the former esteemed Bardi banking family. In 1397, Giovanni associated yet again with Benedetto, as well as with another partner from Pisa named Gentile di Baldassare Buoni, when he relocated back home to Florence. With an initial paid-up capital of 10,000 florins (5,500 florins from Giovanni and 2,500/2,000 florins from his two partners respectively), he registered the Florence branch of his new bank with the *arte del cambio*. The date of 1 October 1397 therefore sees the establishment of the great Medici Bank on which the family's later financial and political fortunes would be solidly founded.

Just to place this event in its historical context, in 1397 King Richard II (the son of Edward the Black Prince) had been on the English throne for twenty years and had only just moved against the Lords Appellant who had usurped power from him. In France, Charles VI 'the Mad' had ruled for seventeen years and his wife Isabeau of Bavaria had just given birth to their eighth child Louis, Duke of Guyenne. The last Holy Roman Emperor Charles IV had died in 1378 and his heir apparent Wenceslaus IV of the Romans was having so many problems with his kingdom of Bohemia and with the Reichstag diet of Nuremberg that year that he neglected to seek coronation as Holy Roman Emperor. A replacement Emperor would not be found until the election of Sigismund in 1433. That same Sigismund, at this time king of Hungary and Croatia, would lead a Crusade against the Ottoman Turks the year previous and be defeated at the Battle of Nicopolis on 25 September 1396. In 1397, the Ottomans would capture the Vidin Empire, the last remaining independent Bulgarian state, and its ruler Ivan Sratsimir would be taken into captivity and never seen again. Meanwhile, in Constantinople the *basileus* of the old Eastern Roman Empire was the capable Manuel II Palaiologos. Also in 1397, Richard ('Dick') Whittington was nominated as Lord Mayor of London for the first time and the Florentine painter Paolo Uccello and the future Pope Nicholas V were born.

After several months, Gentile di Baldassare Buoni withdrew from the venture, leaving the two remaining partners to grow rich while he himself ended his life in Florence's notorious debtor's prison known as the Stinche. Giovanni meanwhile increased his capital contribution to 6,000 florins and within the space of two years the new bank had turned a modest profit of 1,200 florins. Wisely and carefully, Giovanni guided his fledgling bank through the vicissitudes of start-up. Prudently, he did not over-extend his initial capital and he adamantly refused to be lured by the siren call of prestigious, but risky, royal clientage. Instead, in 1402, he established a small wool-finishing *bottega* with a modest investment of just 3,000 florins. For business purposes the workshop was put in the name of Giovanni's thirteen-year-old son Cosimo but it was in fact run as a joint venture with an experienced artisan named Michele di Baldo. In 1408, a second *bottega*, this time for the making and finishing of cloth, was set up with 4,000 florins in start-up capital. Once again, the going concern was placed in his other young son Lorenzo's name, but the business was managed by an experienced tradesman partner. Additionally, Giovanni also bought farmland, never a bad investment, around his ancestral family home of Cafaggiolo.

One especially forward-thinking strategic move that he did make, however, was to open a Venetian branch of the Medici Bank in March 1402. The new office, which was managed by one of Giovanni's factors and junior partners, Neri di Cipriano Tornaquinci, would exploit the growing need for business capital focused around the luxury goods trade with the Orient. This was a trade which the maritime giant Venice (together with, to a lesser extent, Genoa) had practically monopolised over the centuries. Additionally, the Rome branch opened two sub-branches in Naples and the nearby port city of Gaeta. During the initial two decades of the Medici Bank's operations there was therefore, a pervasive policy of conservatism and restraint that was uncharacteristic of the high-flyers of fourteenth-century and fifteenth-century banking and finance. Still more prudent purchases of Tuscan farmland soon followed as well as assorted urban properties within the precincts of Florence itself. Giovanni had placed his fledgling business upon a modest yet solid foundation.

But although Giovanni distinguished himself at this time as a careful and cautious operator, building up his business and his capital in slow and steady increments, he was not so successful in some of the early protégés whom he took on board. Hiring the aforementioned Neri Tornaquinci would prove one of his early mistakes, not least because–impressed by Neri's early promise–the *maggiore* or senior partners of the Medici bank had generously overpaid their Venice branch manager. Tornaquinci would repay their kindness with incompetence compounded by outright fraud. Early bad experiences dealing with German clients had led the bank's senior management to declare a moratorium on all further loans to residents of the Holy Roman Empire. Not only did Germans have an irritating tendency to renege on their debts and scamper back to *das Vaterland* at the first available opportunity but Germany's primitive financial laws provided insufficient recourse for the honest banker to recover those debts legally through the court system. Circumventing the approval of his head office in Florence, Tornaquinci had nonetheless lent large sums of cash to some German and Polish merchants who had subsequently absconded from Venice without repaying their debts.

Tornaquinci's further folly of replenishing capital by borrowing at extortionate rates of interest in the hope of making back the shortfall through the daily operations of the Venice branch only made matters worse. Eventually the errant Tornaquinci had been reduced to cooking the bank's books in order to conceal the staggering losses. When the *maggiore* got wind of their general manager's deception, he was promptly fired and sued in the mercantile court known as the *sei della Mercanzia*, which succeeded in recovering his house and some farmland as collateral for the losses. But this was not the end of the story, however, for Tornaquinci himself then decamped across the Alps to Cracow where he somehow succeeded in recouping some of the outstanding arrears from his Polish clients. But, with ducats now clinking in his pocket, he decided to remain in Poland rather than return to Italy and face the music. A few years later, Giovanni learned that Tornaquinci, having by now spent all his money, was living in such abject poverty in Cracow that he benevolently sent his former employee some florins to alleviate his hardship.

The caché of political populism with which the Medici family had always flirted was not initially emulated by Giovanni di Bicci. Humble, self-effacing, lacking all outward manifestations of ostentation, there is little doubt that this banker of growing repute was looked upon as a potential leader who might articulate the dissatisfaction of both the *magnati* and the *popolo minuto*. Indeed, Giovanni di Bicci was already becoming fairly well known in civic life. In 1401, the forty-one-year-old banker had served on a committee of citizens who judged the winner of an international competition to fashion a new set of bronze doors for the octagonal church called San Giovanni Battista, better known as the Baptistery. The new doors were intended as a supplicatory offering to Almighty God to refrain from visiting upon the Florentines such plagues as had devastated the population in the years 1348 and 1363. The judges had selected a talented twenty-three-year-old Florentine sculptor by the name of Lorenzo Ghiberti and this marked the Medici family's first foray into the world of artistic patronage for which they would later become world-renowned.

The first set of Baptistery doors took twenty excruciating years to complete. A second set, which Michelangelo later fulsomely remarked were 'fit to be the gates of paradise', was to take several decades more, making Giovanni de' Medici's commission practically a lifelong affair for Ghiberti (who did rather well for himself and became moderately wealthy through the two contracts). This public duty was followed in 1402 when Giovanni became prior of the *arte del cambio*, the guild of bankers and money-changers, and so accepted nomination to the *signoria*. The following year he served as ambassador to Bologna and in 1407 he was appointed governor of the client city of Pistoia. His membership of the *signoria* was then repeated again in 1408, 1411 and 1421, in which year he was nominated to the top post of *gonfaloniere*. In 1419 he had also sat on the *dieci di balìa* and, as a member of the *pratiche*, he had also demonstrated his trustworthiness and political utility to the ruling oligarchy. In 1424, when he was sixty-four, he served in yet another embassy, this time to Venice. Although evidently still a place-holder politician, and not overly politically ambitious in his own right, Giovanni was nevertheless making powerful business and governmental friendships during this time which would set the Medici on their eventual course for political ascendancy.

The almost fatal kind heartedness which Giovanni had shown in the case of Neri Tornaquinci was to manifest next in Giovanni's most notorious client, who was a man by the name of Baldassare Cossa. It was an association–indeed a close, lifelong friendship–which was astonishing not least because of the vastly divergent personalities of the two individuals. Born on the island of Procida in the Gulf of Naples to an illustrious though impoverished *Napoletano* family, Baldassare Cossa seemed destined to follow his two brothers into the family business of piracy. Before this, he had fought in the Angevin-Neapolitan wars when the junior and senior lines of the House of Anjou fought savagely for possession of the kingdom of Naples. Unhappily, Baldassare Cossa was to see his brothers executed by King Ladislas of Naples for their piratical ways, whereupon he left his lawless former life and instead took up the study of canon law at the University of Bologna. After obtaining his doctorate, in 1392 he entered the service of Pope Boniface IX, one of the two schismatic popes then claiming legitimacy. In 1402, as the next step in his ecclesiastical career, he sought to become a cardinal-deacon and approached his Florentine banker friend Giovanni di Bicci in Rome for the necessary loan of 12,000 florins with which to purchase the sinecure.

Giovanni obliged his *Napoletano* friend and, after 1403, Baldassare Cossa now settled down to his first post as papal legate to the town of Forlì, which was followed some time thereafter by an assignment to the city of Bologna. Evidently, his old piratical ways had not been entirely left behind him because it was rumoured that, wherever he went, Baldassare Cossa maintained links with local robber bands which held up carriages and intimidated Cossa's political and ecclesiastical rivals. Cossa had also by now acquired a reputation as a famous voluptuary. In Bologna he was rumoured to have seduced 'two hundred maids, wives and widows, and many nuns'. His spiritual qualities were admittedly questionable, if not downright non-existent, but what this unscrupulous, scheming and amoral prelate *did* possess was an unquenchable drive and ambition to become the Vicar of Christ and Supreme Pontiff of the Holy Roman Church. With a pope of Rome as his client, Giovanni di Bicci surmised that he could take the Medici Bank all the way to the top of the heap. The banker therefore put aside his usual restraint and hitched his business firmly to the coattails of Baldassare Cossa's ascendant pontifical career and went along for the ride.

After eight years of having to finance Cossa's sensual and indulgent lifestyle the extraordinary and audacious gamble paid off. On 25 May 1410, Baldassare Cossa was consecrated as pope, assuming the name John XXIII. True to form, he had only bothered to be ordained as a priest the day before. Immediately, the loyal Medici Bank now became the official bank to the Curia with all the boosts to its income and profitability that this naturally entailed. Giovanni's business partner, Benedetto's brother, Ilarione di Lippaccio de' Bardi, was instantly elevated to Depositary of the Papal Chamber and assumed responsibility over the papal deposit accounts and collection of Church incomes. This intimate position of trust would later allow Giovanni to put in a good word for this or that candidate for any upcoming episcopal vacancies, a useful insider privilege which gained the Medici a chip in the game of Curial power politics. Since any incoming senior cleric was obliged to forward one-half of his first year's income to the Curia, his *annates*, which the Medici Bank was appointed to collect, Giovanni made a point of recommending to the Pope only those well-heeled candidates who would be in a position to settle up their dues promptly. But there was one significant drawback in all of this; the papacy into which Pope John XXIII now stepped was still currently in the grip of the Western Schism and at this time there were no less than three competing popes. Such a scandalous situation had not existed since the simultaneous reign of Popes Benedict IX, Sylvester III and Gregory VI during the 1040s.

Due to the unreasonable conduct of Pope Urban VI, the French cardinals had, as we have already seen, elected a rival pope named Clement VII. In 1410, the successors to these two popes were the Italian Pope Gregory XII and the Avignon Pope Benedict XIII. Two years earlier, the Sacred Colleges of both pope and antipope had put their respective differences aside and got together at Livorno in 1408, and later at a General Council at Pisa (by now under Florentine control) in 1409, at which they ruled unambiguously that the Schism needed to come to an end. The French and Italian cardinals declared both popes as schismatic and–for good measure–as heretics and formally deposed the pair of them. In their place they had elected a new pope, the cardinal archbishop of Milan, Pietro Philarghi, who took the name of Pope Alexander V. But in deposing two competing popes, the Council had been proceeding on the erroneous assumption that the papacy was subordinate to the Sacred College, something which was entirely unsupported in canon law, and consequently neither Gregory XII nor Benedict XIII agreed to step down, leaving no less than three popes on the throne of Christendom.

When Alexander V died, Baldassare Cossa had subsequently succeeded him and was consecrated as the resident pope in Rome. He was recognised as the rightful pope by England, France, Bohemia, Prussia, Portugal and elements of the Holy Roman Empire and certain city-states of Italy. Benedict XIII, meanwhile, was recognised by the Spanish kingdoms of Castile and Aragon, amongst others, whilst Gregory XII was recognised primarily by King Ladislas of Naples. Unfortunately, Pope John XXIII's sensual and sybaritic reputation had preceded him and he was not held in especially high esteem by many Churchmen. More damagingly still, he was popularly rumoured to have poisoned Pope Alexander V so he could steal the papal tiara from him. King Ladislas of Naples evidently believed along these lines for, not only did he openly back Pope Gregory, but he launched an outright invasion of the Papal States. Although Pope John was allied with Louis II of Anjou, Ladislas proved irresistible and he captured Rome in 1413, causing the Pope to flee to Florence. The conflict was ended only by a demeaning settlement in which the Pope was obliged to pay Ladislas the crippling recompense of 95,000 florins. Although the sum amounted to more than the entire Medici Bank's profits over a twenty year period, Giovanni di Bicci made the judgement call to extend the necessary line of credit to the Holy Father in order to maintain Medici business interests in the Eternal City. By way of collateral, Cossa released into Giovanni's safe-keeping some precious pieces from the papal treasury including one particularly fine jewel-encrusted papal mitre.

During his enforced stay in Florence, Pope John XXIII had encountered Sigismund of Luxemburg, King of the Romans, as well as King of Germany, Hungary, Bohemia and Croatia. Harbouring ambitions to become Holy Roman Emperor, Sigismund hoped to end the papal schism and persuaded Pope John to summon a general council for this express purpose. John did so, in the mistaken belief that chairing such a council would enable him to claw back some of his evaporating prestige as well as help him regain overall control of the Church. Sigismund called for the council to be assembled on German territory and Pope John duly convened the Council at the city of Constance on 30 October 1413.

Seeking to deflect attention from his own widely-publicised shortcomings, Pope John had decided to make a centrepiece of the Council the condemnation of two recent heresies which had lately arisen in Europe, those of the Hussites in Bohemia and the followers of John Wycliffe in England. As patron of the Council he also sought the active involvement of Sigismund. As ruler of Bohemia, Sigismund had good reason to be concerned about the ecclesiastical reform agenda of the Czech priest Jan Hus, who might be regarded as being a precursor to Martin Luther and other reformist Church leaders of the sixteenth-century. With a considerable personal interest in the upcoming proceedings, therefore, Sigismund demanded the prerogative to preside over the Council in person and John XXIII had little alternative but to stand aside and take a mere spectator's role in the proceedings, a fatal decision which would remove the Council of Constance from the Pope's careful control and direction.

With so much at stake, Giovanni di Bicci ordered his son Cosimo to accompany the Pope on his journey north to Sigismund's court at Constance, which was the venue for the coming ecumenical Council. In fact, the Medici Bank operated in Rome as two distinct branches, one to service the needs of the city of Rome itself and the other to serve the needs of the papal court. The latter, as in the case of the ecumenical Council of Constance, might well be travelling on papal business and require general financing and stop-gap loans while they carried out their work away from the city of Rome. For the twenty-five-year-old Cosimo de' Medici the assignment was, of course, a hugely important learning experience. Aside from the obvious responsibility that it entailed, that of acting as the Pope's banker-in-attendance, Cosimo would also have the opportunity to rub shoulders with other famous bankers of the era such as the Fuggers of Augsburg and the valuable international connections made at Constance would last Cosimo for a lifetime.

The Council of Constance, which would ultimately sit until 22 April 1418, had as its first order of business the task of dealing with the unfortunate business of the two heretics John Wycliffe and Jan Hus, surely one of the most shameful episodes in the history of the Roman Catholic Church. Wycliffe was an Oxford don, sometimes described as 'the Morning Star of the Reformation' for championing an early form of justification by faith and for denouncing the illegitimacy of the papacy; suspected of being the founder of the notorious Lollard heresy, Wycliffe, who had also translated the Scriptures into a superb vernacular English Bible, was roundly condemned in the eighth session. Fortunately for him he was not physically present at Constance, having prudently declined to answer the Pope's summons to attend. Jan Hus, on the other hand, had been given a personal assurance of safe passage by King Sigismund himself and had ventured to Constance in good faith to respond to the charges against levelled against him. For this trusting act of naiveté Hus was roundly denounced as a heretic by the council members and promptly turned over to the secular court, which lost no time in condemning him to be executed by burning. On 6 July 1415, the forty-five-year-old Hus was bound with chains to the stake and, refusing to recant, declared instead that 'God is my witness that the things charged against me I never preached. In the same truth of the Gospel which I have written, taught, and preached, drawing upon the sayings and positions of the holy doctors, I am ready to die today.' After his burning Hus's remains were treated like common refuse and thrown into the River Rhine.

Next there followed the adjudication of the claims of the three rival popes. Because John XXIII was not himself presiding over the Council he was now forced to appear as an appellant alongside Gregory XII and Benedict XIII to answer to charges of misconduct. The implications of Cossa's failing to retain full control of his own Church Council, as well as his allowing Sigismund free rein to set the agenda, now returned to haunt him. Not only was he openly accused of poisoning his predecessor but his lewd and outrageous personal life now came under uncomfortably close scrutiny. After due deliberation, Cossa was eventually arraigned on no less than seventy separate charges, although a number of them were subsequently dropped due to their being 'too indecent to repeat in public'. We can nonetheless glimpse what some of those charges may have been from the historian Edward Gibbon who salaciously recounts a litany of offences including: 'piracy, murder, rape, sodomy and incest'. Cringing under these stinging rebukes to his private life, and fearing any further probing into his personal peccadilloes, Pope John XXIII now promised to abdicate as pope so long as his two competitors reciprocated.

Having stepped down, the former pope disguised himself in the garb of a common crossbowman and, on 21 March 1415, fled the city under cover of darkness, evading the clutches of the famous *condottiere* Pippo Spano, Count of Temesvár, whom King Sigismund had charged with the antipope's custody. By boat he travelled down the Rhine to the city of Schaffhausen. John XXIII had been accompanied in his flight by one of his secular supporters, Duke Frederick IV of Austria, commonly known to his subjects as 'Frederick of the Empty Pockets'. Frederick ruled over Tyrol and the scattered Habsburg territories in south-western Germany and Alsace which were collectively referred to as *Vorderösterreich* or 'Further Austria'. Whilst the deposed former Pope and his ducal ally made their way down the River Rhine an enraged Sigismund declared the Duke deposed and his lands forfeit. By the time that Frederick and John had reached the Rhine town of Freiburg im Breisgau, which recognised the Duke as its feudal lord, Sigismund's lieutenant Ludwig III, Elector Palatine, had caught up with them both. He persuaded the Duke, who admittedly had much to lose, to hand the fugitive former pope over into his custody and Baldassare Cossa was flung into gaol at Heidelberg Castle where he languished for several months. In Cossa's absence the Council of Constance carried on its retributive cleansing work. Not only was John XXIII formerly deposed but so too were Gregory XII and Benedict XIII.

On 11 November 1417 the Sacred College finalised its reform of the schismatic papacy by electing a brand new pope, the forty-eight-year-old Oddone Colonna, cardinal-deacon of San Giorgio al Velabro. Cardinal Colonna had accompanied John XXIII to Constance and had even taken part in the pope's flight to Schaffhausen. Now he was elevated as the Vicar of Christ, taking the name of Pope Martin V, his predecessor Baldassare Cossa having retrospectively been declared an antipope. One of Pope Martin's first acts as pope was to hound Cosimo de' Medici for the return of the valuable papal mitre which Cossa had left in the young banker's safekeeping as surety for the loan made in order to pay Naples its reparations. But this was not the only financial demand that the Medici had to contend with over their former papal client. By this time Cossa had been transferred from Heidelberg to Mannheim Castle. King Sigismund was demanding a ransom of 38,500 Rhenish guilders, equivalent to about 35,000 florins, in return for the former pope's release from prison.

To put this ransom amount in its proper perspective, you could build a brand new *palazzo* in Florence at this time for around a thousand florins. To place matters in even starker perspective we must also consider that in 1420 Giovanni's profits over the previous twenty-three years amounted to 152,820 florins, or 6,644 florins annually (before disbursements of 25% to his business partners, leaving him with an actual profit of 114,615). The ransom he was obliged to pay out to purchase his friend's liberty amounted therefore to just over one third of all the profits he had ever made during his lifetime. In Florence, Giovanni di Bicci received this positively ruinous news from Constance with his usual stoical equanimity. For years he had subsidised Cossa's exorbitant lifestyle and occasional ruinous debts and now he was being asked to fork out a vast sum to free a man who had no official title, standing or importance and who, as an asset, was now essentially worthless. It is a testament to Giovanni's character both as a banker and as a friend that he lost no time in paying Sigismund's extortionate ransom demand in full and welcomed the liberated and no doubt hugely relieved Baldassare Cossa back to Florence.

The aging former pope had spent the last three years languishing in a dank German prison cell and cannot have cut the same imposing figure as before upon his return to Florence. Nevertheless, Giovanni still cleverly managed to turn the situation to gold for his friend and erstwhile client. Craftily, Giovanni had negotiated Cossa's ransom and release on the condition that Pope Martin V came to Florence for a public reconciliation with Cossa, the former 'pope'. As Pope Martin himself was obliged to seek sanctuary in Florence while Rome was still being occupied by Queen Joanna of Naples he agreed, regarding Giovanni's proposal as a convenient way to rubber stamp his undisputed papacy by having his predecessor Cossa 'endorse' him. It was, as they say, a win-win arrangement. In a touching display of felicity and reconciliation the two men came together in Florence and publicly embraced and Baldassare Cossa was duly bestowed with the cardinal-bishopric of Tusculum, which he held until his death just a few months later in December 1419. Baldassare Cossa, the pope, antipope and pirate as was, was laid to rest in a magnificent tomb created for him in Florence's Baptistery by the sculptor Donatello and the architect Michelozzo. In one final snub from beyond the grave, however, Pope Martin V was incensed to learn that the inscription on Cossa's tomb had been made to read: *Ioannes Quondam Papa XXIII*, or 'John XXIII, the former pope'. Officially, in the eyes of the Church, John XXIII was not a *former pope* but an *antipope*.

As Giovanni di Bicci's final unstinting disbursement to his dear friend, the tomb had been financed by the Medici Bank and it was a powerful restatement of the way in which Baldassare Cossa had lived. Only three other bishops up until now had ever been buried in the Baptistery and custom dictated that their final resting place be little more than a plain stone sarcophagus. John XXIII's tomb, by comparison, stretched twenty-four feet from floor to ceiling, was resplendent with naked cherubs and bas relief figures depicting Faith, Hope and Charity and was topped with a bronze sarcophagus where Baldassare Cossa's effigy reclined supine, his face turned provocatively towards the congregation, still poignantly confrontational even in death. It was a remarkable statement of aggrandisement for an acknowledged antipope, but more importantly it was a statement about the Medici family's growing wealth and influence. Thumbing their nose at the conservative guilds which were responsible for the city's holy places, the Medici had the clout to purchase

44

radical stylistic changes in Florence's cherished conservative sepulchral traditions.

Giovanni was not–at least for the time being–able to preserve the Medici Bank's exclusive status as bankers to the Court of Rome. For this, Pope Martin had selected Florence's aristocratic Spini family, to whom Giovanni was distantly related through his late mother. Nonetheless the Medici still continued to do business in Rome and indeed to a certain extent with the Curia too, although not to quite the same extent as before. But, notwithstanding this slight drop in the family fortunes, Medici respectability was on the rise. Giovanni had been honoured as one of the four *Cavalieri* who had seen the Pope off from the gates of Florence and so was by now regarded as a highly respected dignitary with considerable political capital. Business cycles seldom last and, in the event, the Medici had only to wait patiently and bide their time. Just a few years later the Spini banking business would collapse and the Medici Bank would avidly step into their shoes, opening deposit accounts and lines of credit not only for Pope Martin V but also for several of his cardinals, not to mention the apostolic treasurer. The Medici Bank was back in business at the lucrative Court of Rome.

Less encouragingly, Giovanni di Bicci had been unable to bring about any great rapprochement with the powerful and dominant political oligarch Niccolò da Uzzano. Although da Uzzano and Giovanni had jointly persuaded Baldassare Cossa to reconcile with Pope Martin V, this was as far as da Uzzano himself was prepared to allow his fraternisation with the Medici banker to go. Niccolò da Uzzano had himself risen to the heights of political success from a relatively small but wealthy banking family which hailed from the Santo Spirito quarter of Florence. The family took its name from the Castle of Uzzano in Greve, situated in Tuscany's Chianti region. Niccolò's father Giovanni had been the first member of the family to hold a position in the *signoria* and, following his death, Niccolò's inheritance had enabled him to marry his daughters off to the wealthy and aristocratic Soderini and Capponi families. Nevertheless the Uzzani were still relative newcomers on the social and political scene and Niccolò's rapid ascent may be understood in the light of his own exceptional personal qualities.

These qualities enabled him as ambassador to represent Florence's interests to many of the important city-states of Italy, and to sit as war councillor on the prestigious *dieci di balìa* no less than five times. As Lapo Mazzei described da Uzzano to Francesco Datini in 1400, 'He is a man of courage, wisdom and integrity; he is powerful and respected'. By this time, da Uzzano and the more conservative *ottimati* oligarchs behind the *signoria* were growing increasingly suspicious of the Medici family's alleged populist leanings. Niccolò da Uzzano tried unsuccessfully to block Giovanni's election as *gonfaloniere* in 1421, fearing that the banker was using his vast wealth to purchase acolytes within the *signoria*, which in all fairness was probably at least partly true by this time. To defuse allegations of seeking to rise above his station, and at the same time preserve his carefully-crafted image as a man of the people, Giovanni rode around town on an old flea-bitten mule accompanied by just one servant, instead of sitting astride an expensive and finely caparisoned horse.

In 1420, Giovanni's business partner in the Florence bank, Benedetto di Lippaccio de' Bardi, had died thereby dissolving all existing partnership agreements between the Medici and the Bardi. Giovanni took full advantage of this interregnum to reorganise the Medici Bank's business structure. Firstly, the bank's partnership interests in Michele di Baldo's by now loss-making wool *bottega* was terminated. Secondly, Giovanni himself withdrew from active involvement in the bank. When the time came to draw up fresh contracts with Benedetto de' Bardi's brother, Ilarione de' Bardi, the agreements were drawn up in favour of Giovanni's two sons Cosimo and Lorenzo. Of the paid up capital of 24,000 florins, the Medici would contribute two thirds and the Bardi one third. A new general manager was also meanwhile hired to run the Florence head office. The principal claim to fame of this man was that his great-grandfather was brother to the poet Dante's legendary muse Beatrice di Folco Portinari. With the bank's affair's now settled, Giovanni largely ignored the mistrust of his political rival da Uzzano retired to his unassuming town house in the shadow of the Duomo.

In retirement, Giovanni focused his energies on philanthropic pursuits, arts patronage and the civic duties of government, when of course permitted this luxury by Niccolò da Uzzano. Notably, he chaired the public committee which appointed Filippo Brunelleschi to design and build the city's new orphanage, the Ospedale degli Innocenti. The building, which was the world's first ever hospital for foundlings, and which was financed by the guild of weavers, the *arte della seta*, was distinguished by its ancient classical design and simplicity. The aspect of the building that was most revolutionary for its time was the loggia which had been created as the centrepiece of the building's cloister, and comprised nine round Romanesque arches behind each of which was a separate domed bay. The building, the like of which nobody had ever seen before in Florence, had been inspired by what the architect had observed during his study-trips amongst the ruins of Rome. Citizens sensitive to the novelty value of the structure gathered in the streets on a daily basis to watch the on-going construction. Often the bystanders were so numerous that the poor builders grumbled as they tried to go about their work.

Brunelleschi was also later hired by Giovanni in 1421 to renovate the church of San Lorenzo, which was by now considered very much the Medici clan's local church and which became strongly identified with the family. Again, the architect made fullest possible use of the techniques he had observed in ancient Roman ruins. Unlike the gothic churches and cathedrals of Europe, San Lorenzo's space did not soar upwards to be diffused in a conflagration of flying buttresses and randomly placed stone gargoyles. Instead, the colonnaded nave was neatly enclosed beneath a flat vaulted roof, whilst the Corinthian capitals of the classical columns were carved identically and not for individual effect. The entire makeover was planned on the basis of symmetrical, geometrical proportion which imparted a sense of harmony to the space. These classical techniques would be repeated by Brunelleschi ten years later in the Pazzi Chapel of Santa Croce, whilst other architects like Leon Battista Alberti would also be heavily influenced by ancient Roman stylisation. With Brunelleschi's death in 1446, San Lorenzo's facade would ultimately remain unfinished until the great Michelangelo was commissioned to explore plans for the completion of the work in 1515.

Giovanni would no doubt have preferred to continue devoting his attention to such edifying and salvific pursuits, *Charity* being one of the cardinal Christian virtues alongside Faith and Hope, but political events were destined to overtake his philanthropic interests. During the 1420s, these events–as they played out–would place even further strain on his already overwrought and mutually suspicious relationship with the ruling oligarchy led by Niccolò da

Uzzano and to a lesser extent Rinaldo degli Albizzi. The origin of the problem lay with the ever-present thorn in Florence's side, the Visconti family of Milan.

Gian Galeazzo Visconti's second son, Filippo Maria Visconti, had come to power in the duchy in 1412 after his brother, Duke Gian Maria Visconti, had been assassinated in a Ghibelline plot. Not long after taking power, Filippo Maria had set his cap to the re-acquisition of Genoa as well as the towns of Bergamo, Brescia and Parma, all of which had been lost to Milan in the immediate aftermath of his brother's murder and the subsequent death of Gian Maria's *condottiere* Facino Cane. The late duke had been a cruel man by nature; one of his favourite diversions was breeding dogs that were trained to tear men apart. Filippo Maria was no less sociopathic and to his sadism was added the additional trait of extreme paranoia. This may have been on account of his appearance, for the Duke was reputed by contemporary commentators to have been exceptionally ugly. He was said to have been grotesquely pallid and obese with weak, malformed legs which could not support him unaided without the assistance of a flunky. The Duke was extremely sensitive about his unattractiveness. He was also neurotically frightened of thunder and lightning and had a soundproofed bedchamber built for himself deep within the bowels of his fortress in Milan. To entertain himself he played crude and boorish practical jokes on his long-suffering courtiers.

In September 1418, Filippo Maria had ordered the beheading of his first wife, Beatrice Lascaris di Tenda, after she had sought a greater share in the running of the state. Beatrice was the widow of his brother's manipulative *condottiere*, Facino Cane, who had grown astonishingly wealthy from playing upon the former Duke's weaknesses. The cash-strapped Filippo Maria had married Beatrice, who was twenty years his senior, to shore up his own fiscal problems; she had not only brought to the union a 400,000 ducat fortune but had returned control over numerous *Milanese* towns and lands that had been in her late husband's possession. She also brought into the Duke's army an influx of many of the late *condottiere's* experienced former troops. The reasons why the couple's marriage soured are potentially many. Not only had Beatrice demanded a greater share in the Duke's political power but Filippo Maria was also possibly jealous about her first husband's illustrious reputation as a respected *condottiere*. His vindictive personality led him to take his insecurities out on the late *condottiere's* widow.

Being an older woman, Beatrice had borne the Duke no children and so instead he lavished his affection on his younger mistress, the *Milanese* noblewoman Agnese del Maino. Agnese bore the Duke two illegitimate daughters named Bianca Maria and Caterina Maria. Ultimately, Filippo Maria had used as his pretext for ridding himself of Beatrice the trumped-up charge that she had committed adultery with a handsome young troubadour named Michele Orombelli. The unhappy Beatrice, her ladies-in-waiting and Orombelli himself were cruelly tortured on the rack to obtain their 'confessions' before having their heads hacked off. But before this, the tragic Beatrice was also given twenty-four lashes just for good measure.

Filippo Maria's ambitions to recover Genoa, currently enjoying independence under her Doge Tommaso Campofregoso, and to take possession of the cities of Bergamo, Brescia and Parma, now provoked a foreign policy emergency back in Florence. Filippo Maria despatched ambassadors to the Florentine *signoria* to notify them of his intentions and gain their acquiescence.

This precipitated the formation within the commune of a war party and a peace party. The war party was galvanised by such oligarchic figures as Gino Capponi and also included the Albizzeschi as well as their de facto leader Niccolò da Uzzano. The war party, which was primarily concerned with containing the growing power of Milan, saw little advantage in standing by and allowing the Visconti duke to wage an expansionist war at Florence's expense.

The peace party comprised for the most part those majority *popolo minuto* who saw little tangible benefit in pursuing a war for the sake of long term commercial or geopolitical advantage. These were people for whom the stark, day-to-day economic realities of life made them preoccupied with keeping food on the table and taxation low, which in turn meant keeping Florence out of needless and expensive foreign entanglements. Such figures as Giovanni di Bicci and Agnolo Pandolfini, a former Florentine ambassador to Bologna and the Angevin court of Naples, tended to back the cause of peace. The peace party won the day and an agreement was reached with Filippo Maria by which Florence agreed to turn a blind eye in return for the duke of Milan's agreement not to advance his troops south of the rivers Magra and Panaro into sovereign Florentine territory.

The appeasement of Florence's peace faction gave Duke Filippo Maria the necessary green light to initiate military action against the lost *Milanese* cities and in due course war broke out. The Duke entrusted his forces to an officer who had formerly served in the late *condottiere* Facino Cane's army. This officer was the remarkable thirty-year-old Francesco Bussone da Carmagnola. From simple Turin peasant stock, Carmagnola had entered the service of Facino Cane at the age of twelve and by adulthood had grown into a dynamic and highly charismatic military commander. In 1421, Carmagnola cut an agreement with the Aragonese which enabled him to move against Genoa, sparking a passionate outcry from the war party within Florence. The peace party had mistakenly assumed that Genoa would be able to look after herself and were shocked when the duke of Milan conquered the city with relative ease. Now that he was in control of Genoa and much of the Ligurian coast Filippo Maria posed a direct threat to Tuscany and to Florence itself. Carmagnola's inspired command of Milan's army had also resulted in a string of rapid victories further north as the strategic Lombard towns of Lodi, Crema, Bergamo, Brescia and Parma all fell domino-like in quick succession. Florence's peace party had assumed that Venice would come to the aid of these towns but once again they were mistaken in their calculations.

In gratitude to Carmagnola, Duke Filippo Maria fêted his talented general by showering him with money, landed estates throughout Lombardy and even a fine new *palazzo* in Milan. In 1417, the Duke had given the *condottiere* the hand in marriage of his cousin Antonia Visconti. However, in late medieval Italy being an unqualified success in the military sphere could, so to speak, prove a double-edged sword. On the one hand there were the obvious tangible benefits to being of service to one's lord – Carmagnola himself was evidence of this. But, on the other hand, it tended to make powerful men rather uncomfortable. The capable Carmagnola would prove a victim of his own success. In a characteristic fit of paranoia, Filippo Maria suddenly refused to assign any further active military commands to his star general. Instead, in October 1422, he made him the governor of the newly pacified *Milanese* possession of Genoa. Although this was arguably a fairly prestigious appointment, nevertheless to the proud Carmagnola it was construed, correctly as things turned out, as a demotion and he brooded darkly on what he now perceived as the downgrading of his once glittering military career.

In the course of achieving his strategic designs Duke Filippo Maria had by now also violated his prior treaty with the Florentines, having captured territory south of the River Magra contrary to his earlier undertaking. On this pretext, Florence's war party now gained the ascendancy and the moral traction which they needed and a *dieci* of war was duly appointed whilst taxes were raised to fund troops. But Milan's incursions across the Magra were not, in themself, sufficient grounds for an open declaration of war on Milan. As Florence readied itself for the coming confrontation with the duke of Milan, the flame which lit the powder keg eventually came not in Lombardy but in the Romagna the following year.

The region of the Romagna had been officially ceded to the Papal States by Rudolf I of Germany in 1278. In practice the region was not governed by the Pope directly but instead by a variety of *signori* and petty tyrants who in theory ruled as papal vassals, despite the fact that many such rulers were essentially Ghibellines and hence implicitly anti-papal in their sympathies. In practice, however, most of these men ruled not as vicars of the Pope but as completely independent warlords. Both Florence and Venice regarded parts of the Romagna as their exclusive property or spheres of influence. Certain towns such as Forlì or Imola, for instance, which lay on the old Roman road known as the Via Emilia, were regarded as being *raccomandati* of Florence or 'coming under the traditional protection' of the Florentine republic.

The town of Forlì at this time had been ruled by Giorgio Ordelaffi since 1411, which was when he had been awarded the vicariate of the town by Pope Gregory XII. Upon Giorgio's death in 1423 he left behind a child heir named Tebaldo. The boy, who was still far too young to rule, was rendered up by his mother Lucrezia degli Alidosi into the guardianship of her father Ludovico Alidosi, lord of the neighbouring town of Imola; this left Lucrezia free to assume the regency of Forlì herself. But the *Forlìvesi* were not happy about coming under the dominion of the Alidosi family of Imola. They rebelled against Lucrezia's rule and called upon Milan for military assistance to dislodge her from the town's fortress. At the same time they demanded that Tebaldo Ordelaffi be 'rescued' from Ludovico Alidosi and placed instead under the guardianship of the duke of Milan. There is no question that Duke Filippo Maria planned to take full advantage of this offer of guardianship to assimilate both Forlì and eventually Imola within Milan's growing possessions. Milan's emissary Guido Torello was despatched to Forlì to seize the town, which he duly accomplished without too much difficulty. As a diversion the *condottiere* Agnolo della Pergola was meanwhile sent against Imola, which he stormed and captured in February 1424. Both Ludovico Alidosi and the young ruler of Imola, Luigi Alidosi, were sent in chains back to Milan. As a result of these victories the lord of neighbouring Faenza, Guidantonio Manfredi, bowed to the greater power and subsequently threw in his lot with the duke of Milan.

Since Forlì was meant to be under at least nominal Florentine protection, the belligerent war party finally got their way and in 1424 the commune moved to openly challenge Milan in the Romagna over the whole Forlì affair. Florence purchased a mercenary contract or *condotta* from Pandolfo III Malatesta, the lord of Fano, who also conveniently happened to be the former lord of Bergamo and Brescia, two towns currently under the occupation of Filippo Maria's forces.

Pandolfo was the second son of the late Galeotto I Malatesta, lord of Rimini which was situated on the Romagna's Adriatic coast. The House of Malatesta was a proud one whose members mostly made their living as *condottieri*. They first came to prominence in 1293, when Malatesta da Verucchio became *podestà* of Rimini, and the family eventually came to rule the towns of Rimini, Pesaro, Fano, Cesena, Fossombrone and Cervia. But they were an especially vicious and sociopathic family, even by the relatively cruel standards of the time. Malatesta II Malatesta had been known disquietingly by his soubriquet *Guastafamiglia*, the 'family destroyer'. For the Malatesta, the fact that the towns of Forlì and Imola had both been captured by Milan was grave cause for concern and they made the not unreasonable assumption that their Romagnol possessions might be next on the list. The family's attempts to seek support from Pope Martin V, by now residing in Rome and casting his own greedy eye on the Malatesta lands, had been politely but firmly rebuffed. It therefore made sense for the Malatesta to find common cause with Florence in this business.

Pandolfo was quickly despatched by Florence to assist the Alidosi at Imola but, finding it already in *Milanese* hands, he diverted his efforts instead against Forlì which was duly invested. Pandolfo then hired Alberico Novello da Barbiano, the lord of Zagonara, to harry the territories surrounding Forlì so as to make it difficult for Agnolo della Pergola to come to the town's relief. At this point, realising that a direct assault on the Florentines presently laying siege to Forlì was unfeasible, Agnolo della Pergola decided to stage a counter-siege against Zagonara and thereby draw the Florentine army away from Forlì to relieve their beleaguered ally Alberico in his home fortress. The plan worked like a dream. On 28 July 1424, Pandolfo Malatesta abandoned the siege of Forlì and advanced with his brother Carlo, the lord of Rimini, together with a Florentine force which included 8,000 cavalry supported by 3,000 infantry. However, having marched for hours through the pouring rain and knee-deep in mud, the Florentines were exhausted by the time they reached the castle of Zagonara and their cavalry assaults soon flagged, leaving Agnolo della Pergola's infantry and horse to take the field. Pandolfo himself fled back to Cesena but his brother Carlo was taken prisoner along with most of the Florentine troops. As an aside, the 'Battle' of Zagonara was typical of the *condottiere* battles of the era in which not that many people were usually injured. Throughout the entirety of the day's skirmishing, so the historian and political theorist Niccolò Machiavelli informs us, the sole casualties had been the *condottiere* Lodovico degli Obizzi who, along with his two companions, fell off their horses and drowned in the mud.

Whilst in captivity, Carlo Malatesta deserted Florence and, like Guidantonio Manfredi of Faenza, now went over to the Visconti. Disenchanted with the performance and loyalties of the Malatesta, Florence replaced them with two new *condottieri*: Oddo da Montone and an especially able commander named Niccolò Piccinino who was the son of a *Perugino* butcher. Unfortunately, whilst on an initial expedition to convert the Manfredi lord of Faenza to Florence's side, both commanders were confronted by forces loyal to Milan and roundly defeated. Oddo da Montone himself was killed and Niccolò Piccinino was taken as a prisoner to Faenza. Here, he succeeded in persuading Guidantonio Manfredi to defect to Florence's side; but this is where he himself parted ways with Florence. Sensing that his services would be far better rewarded by the Visconti duke, the newly liberated Piccinino made his own way to Milan where, duplicitously, he offered his services to Filippo Maria.

The Florentines, so Niccolò Machiavelli would write later, were 'alarmed by this circumstance and reduced to despondency'. Piccinino's loss was keenly felt. For his treachery, he would be made the subject of a notorious *pittura infamante* ('defaming portrait') on the wall of the Palazzo della Signoria which depicted him hanging upside-down in chains. This defamatory genre of painting, which was common in Renaissance Italian city-states, usually depicted *condottieri* who changed sides as hanging by one foot like the hanged man of the Tarot deck. In a society governed by rules of honour, the depiction was intended to degrade the victim and shame his family and was quite literally the social destruction of one's reputation. Since the *condottieri* fought so sparingly and continuously changed sides during conflicts, Piccinino's depiction would soon be joined by the likenesses of numerous other unreliable or untrustworthy professional soldiers. Yet Piccinino was not the only talented mercenary leader that the Duke would acquire, for Filippo Maria had also recently hired another promising young *condottiere* by the name of Francesco Sforza.

As their next move, Florence and Naples sent twenty-four Aragonese galleys north in an attempt to provoke an uprising by the *Genovesi* against Milan's rule. But frustratingly this intervention proved unsuccessful and Florence remained stymied by Milan's superior skill-at-arms and hamstrung by the defection of her key commander. Florence now looked to Venice to be the equaliser in this conflict and appealed to her, as a sister trading republic, to help counter Visconti tyranny and expansionism. Venice at this time had already embarked upon her own expansionist phase on the Italian mainland. In the aftermath of the War of Chioggia, which she had fought with Genoa from 1378 to 1381, Venice neutralised the powerful Carraresi family of Padua by 1405 and had extended her possessions all the way to Lake Garda near Verona. The 1418 war that she fought against the patriarch of Aquileia, meanwhile, had secured for Venice the whole of the region of Friuli including the capital city of Udine. But regardless of her recent territorial successes, Venice was still not prepared to go head to head with Milan and Florence's envoys were politely yet consistently rebuffed. Under the leadership of the cautious eighty-year-old Doge, Tommaso Mocenigo, Venice had kept aloof from the opening movements of the war. Mocenigo reminded his fellow Venetians that a war made little economic sense when the Most Serene Republic was moving goods worth in excess of ten million gold ducats through her ports each year. Maritime business and commerce must always be the first consideration and that meant the preservation of peace with her Lombard neighbour. Besides which, lacking a standing army of her own, it was cripplingly expensive to hire mercenary armies to fight her battles for her on terra firma.

But when Mocenigo died in 1423 his more belligerent rival Francesco Foscari (who is distinguished as being not only the subject of a play by Lord Byron but of an opera by Giuseppe Verdi) took his place as Doge. Foscari, who gained election through widespread vote-buying, and whom Mocenigo had earlier called 'an arrogant windbag', put an immediate end to the more populist leanings of the Venetian system of government. The *arengo*, a general assembly of all adult citizens, was abolished and the law requiring that the Doge's election needed to receive the formal endorsement of the entire populace was removed from the statutes. Soon, Foscari had adopted the royal 'We' and steered the Venetian ship of state towards the 'sovereign oligarchy' which, to be candid, it had already been for some years. Foscari was also instrumental in bringing about Venice's transition from a primarily maritime trading state to an imperial power on the Italian mainland itself. This was an ambition which the Venetians had always studiously avoided; they had known for generations that those 'prestigious' dry land territories and possessions could not, unlike the inaccessible lagoons where they had built their city on pile after oak pile hammered into the murky waters, be so easily defended by a basically seafaring people. Yet even Foscari was unable to compel the Venetian senate to go to war through the considerable force of his personality alone. One exasperated Florentine envoy had exclaimed to Venice's rulers: 'Signors of Venice! When we refused help to Genoa, the *Genovesi* themselves adopted Filippo Maria as their lord; we, if we receive no support from you in this our hour of need, shall make him our *king'*. It was enough of a hint. Venice, like her sister trading republic of Florence, could no longer continue to ignore the growing power of the duke of Milan who ranged freely in her backyard of the Po Valley.

Foscari immediately began putting Venice on a war footing and a pact was finalised between Florence and Venice on 4 December 1425. Venice would take charge of the war in Lombardy, whilst Florence would be responsible for the prosecution of the war in both Tuscany and the Romagna. Siena, Ferrara, Savoy and Mantua also joined this alliance of the two wealthy trading republics and, as a result, the balance was now tipped against Filippo Maria and the *Milanesi* experienced a rapid string of military reversals. The Venetians advanced quickly from the Veneto along the Po Valley, reaching and capturing the town of Brescia from Francesco Sforza after an eight-month siege which ended on 20 November 1426. This, as Machiavelli writes, 'was in those days considered a most brilliant exploit'. The Florentine forces meanwhile recaptured all their possessions in Tuscany and the duke of Milan was ultimately forced to cede Forlì and Imola to the Pope in order to curry papal favour. With no advantage to gain at this stage, the duke of Milan wearily called for mediation and, through the intervention of the papal legate Niccolò degli Albergati, a peace was signed on 30 December 1426 at San Giorgio Maggiore in Venice. Although the status quo was largely reinstated for now, Filippo Maria did regain those lands formerly occupied by Florence in Liguria, a state of affairs that was largely regarded as a diplomatic defeat for Florence.

In fact, as a result of locking horns with powerful Milan, all that Florence really had to show for the misadventure were four years of suffering, grinding poverty, as well as a crippling war debt later estimated by Niccolò Machiavelli as being in excess of 3,500,000 florins. War had proven a devastatingly expensive pursuit for Florence; in 1420 the commune's expenditure on military *condotte* had been less than 100,000 florins, still a considerable peacetime burden. However in 1423, the first year of the *Milanese* war, that amount had ballooned to over 400,000 florins, rising to over 500,000 florins the following year. Indeed, military expenditure amounted to twice the amount of all communal taxes being farmed at this time. The peace party were livid. They argued, not unreasonably, that both Forlì and Imola fell under the jurisdiction of the Papal States and were therefore technically none of Florence's concern. They questioned why the state was being financially crippled to exert Florence's influence in places like the Romagna where she had no business.

A fresh groundswell of public opposition to oligarchic rule stirred ominously. The question of how to pay for this cripplingly expensive war now arose and the focus of public discontent came to bear upon the incendiary issue of taxation.

Traditionally, the Florentine government preferred to tax its population through indirect excise taxes and gabelles which tended to mostly penalise the lower and middle-class citizens. Additionally, in times of emergency–such as during a prolonged state of war–extraordinary revenue was raised through a system known as the *estimo*.

The *estimo* was based both on inheritances (the taxpayer's 'patrimony') as well as an *estimo* or 'assessment' of each individual person's wealth, with a focus on their income as opposed to their physical wealth, such as land or estates. The result was that the landed wealthy and the urban mercantile wealthy who were members of the *ottimati reggimento* were not taxed to their true net worth, whilst those with smaller incomes bore the brunt of the tax farming as it was harder for them to conceal their meagre earnings in the form of landed or fixed assets. In practice too, the way in which the *estimo* was calculated from case to case was woefully arbitrary and tax collectors tended to base their assessments on all-inclusive target quotas for each of the city's quarters or parishes. Perhaps worst of all, the *estimo* was used as the basis for exacting *prestanze* or 'forced loans' from the public which were levied by the *signoria* as and when required. Such loans could sometimes be considered 'voluntary', in which case they received interest payments at Florence's public fund the Monte Commune. In reality, however, these loans were compulsory and payment of interest was both unreliable and spasmodic. During the war with Milan over 114 such *prestanze* were collected. Even the inhabitants of the *contado* and Florence's subject cities like Pisa were not immune from the demands of the *estimo*, which was in time expanded to cover these subject cities as well.

The *estimo* and the *prestanze* were unfair, arbitrary and burdensome and even the threat of punishment (including in some extreme cases the death penalty for those who refused to pay their back taxes) could not wring blood from the proverbial stone. Many skilled Florentine artisans voted with their feet and left the commune altogether, which only served to further weaken Florence's economic base. It soon became clear that a radical overhaul of the tax system was needed; as early as 1424 Niccolò da Uzzano himself had sounded the warning bells on the matter of taxation but, ever the conservative, even he had been reluctant to undertake the daunting task himself. Early experiments at testing new systems proved woefully ineffective. In 1426 an especially punishing new tax called the *ventina*, because it was assessed by a committee of twenty (*venti*) citizens, met with signal disfavour from both wealthy and lower income citizens alike. Instead, it fell to Rinaldo degli Albizzi to propose an entirely new system of progressive taxation known as the *catasto* or 'register'. The spirit of the *catasto* system, and what made it so popular with the common people, was that fixed rules were finally laid down for assessing taxable wealth which could not be arbitrarily skewed by tax collectors to suit the *ottimati* whenever it suited them.

The *catasto* broadened the tax base so that all forms of wealth, including landed property, Monte Commune credits, business investments and mercantile trade income, were factored into individual tax assessments; this now made it difficult for the wealthier classes to evade a proper scrutiny of their entire portfolio of assets. The way the new system worked was as follows. The assessors demanded from every householder an exact accounting of his assets and sources of income and this income was then capitalised at a rate of 7 per cent. Tax was then charged at the rate of ½ per cent on the person's assessed capital (or, to look at it another way, on a 14th part of the person's income). However there were also deductions from the estimated capital for the necessities of life before tax; one's dwelling or place of business was tax deductible, also the necessary furniture, utensils, animals and beasts of burden, tools, plus a two-hundred florin allowance for each member of the household. The result was that for many of the poorer folk, their capital (after these deductions) failed to reach the minimum taxable sum and therefore exempted them from having to pay the *catasto*. Out of these, some were required to pay a small, discretionary tax which was privately and discreetly agreed with the assessors, whilst others instead paid a poll tax of between two to six soldi. The Registers of household wealth were maintained for a three year period after which they were revised to reflect the changed circumstances of individual homes.

The *catasto* was voted into law on 24 May 1427. At a stroke, it removed the main burden of taxation from the disenchanted masses and–with some long awaited semblance of social justice–now caused the wealthy members of the plutocracy themselves to bear the brunt of public taxation. As Rinaldo degli Albizzi stated: 'It is impossible for the citizens to bear these great burdens unless their distribution is equal; which it is not, since some pay fifty soldi in the pound, some only ten'. To give some idea of how the tax landscape changed post-*catasto*, an ordinary person might be assessed as having seven florins of income giving him capital extrapolated at one hundred florins, a ½ per cent of which would be taxed, meaning a tax bill of half a florin before deductions. By contrast, Florence's wealthiest citizen, Palla Strozzi, was assessed as owing 500 florins of *catasto*, whilst Giovanni di Bicci was assessed at 300 florins and Niccolò da Uzzano at 200 florins. Moreover, these payments were not one-off annual payments; often several discrete *catasto* demands would be made in any given year depending on fiscal necessity, and in this respect it was still somewhat similar to the *estimo*.

The *catasto* should by rights have served to assuage public discontent. Magnates like Niccolò da Uzzano and Giovanni di Bicci were, as we have seen, now assessed at hundreds of florins instead of the nominal amounts for which they had previously been liable. But, instead of applauding Rinaldo's reforms, the masses now called for the *catasto* to be enforced retroactively so that the élite would be accountable for taxation on decades' worth of back income. Not only this but, gallingly for Rinaldo, the kudos for introducing the *catasto* fell not to himself but to the new man Giovanni di Bicci who, by all accounts, does not seem to have played a major role in the introduction of the new tax. The *catasto* also alienated those well-to-do merchants who had previously been aligned with, but not expressly part of the inner workings of, the plutocracy; they felt aggrieved at their additional tax burdens and resented having to disclose their ledgers to the nosy and intrusive *catasto* committee.

Malcontents from the wealthier sections of the middle classes thronged to a number of secret societies which sprang up in the wake of the tax reforms. These societies met, under the pretext of being religious sodalities, in the city's numerous churches to privately discuss and criticise the government. Laws were passed for the suppression of these allegedly 'seditious' secret societies but were of little practical use since the citizens continued to meet and continued to grumble safely behind closed doors. At the same time Rinaldo degli Albizzi mooted the possibility of reducing the fourteen minor *arti* to just seven so as to deal with what many in the oligarchy saw as the pernicious influence of the minor guilds. Reducing the number of minor guilds would proportionally reduce their already limited involvement in government.

What seems to have followed next was a war waged by proxy between, on the one hand, Niccolò da Uzzano and the old guard and, on the other, Rinaldo degli Albizzi who had now aligned himself with the enigmatic *gente nuova* Giovanni di Bicci. This was very much a low-intensity conflict waged in the sombre halls and corridors of the Palazzo della Signoria. It was played out through retributive acts of political spite and each faction succeeded in dismissing from office certain key acolytes of the other. In 1427, da Uzzano's man Pagolo Fortini, the chancellor of the *signoria*, was dismissed from office; several months later, a known political agent of the Medici, Martino Martini the *notaio della riformagioni*, was likewise dismissed. Following the fall of Fortini we find Rinaldo degli Albizzi–a man who 'did not know how to dissemble'–writing warmly and effusively to Cosimo's older cousin Averardo di Francesco de' Medici of 'thy Cosimo, to whom all my desire is known'.

Giovanni's motivations in toppling Pagolo Fortini are murky and somewhat hard to discern. It has been suggested that his removal foreshadowed a direct move by Giovanni against Niccolò da Uzzano with the objective of having the latter banished. If so, this would have been a repetition of Maso degli Albizzi's masterful banishing of Benedetto degli Alberti. If this was in fact the case there remains no written evidence that this was his ultimate endgame and yet, concerning the recent costly war against Milan, Giovanni had jumped into the political ferment feet first and, in da Uzzano, had come up against the most able and experienced politician of the day. The experience may have proven disconcerting for Giovanni. An enemy of Niccolò da Uzzano's calibre and intellect would, once roused, prove dangerous to a family of relative *arrivistes* like the Medici. Better to remove the problem root and branch before it had the opportunity to strike back at you. Be that as it may, the political feuding remained for now frustratingly indecisive and tit-for-tat. The Medici would be obliged to bide their time and develop their family influence in other respects and by incremental steps.

By this point, Giovanni di Bicci was not only a growing political force to be reckoned with but also a financial one too. In the *denuncia del catasto* or tax return of 1427, at the age of almost seventy Giovanni di Bicci had declared no less than 81,072 florins, making him the next richest man in Florence second only to Palla Strozzi. The latter boasted gross taxable assets of 162,925 florins, including fifty-four farms, thirty houses, a banking firm with a capital of 45,000 florins, and communal bonds. But unlike Strozzi, who lived well beyond his means and who generally neglected his financial undertakings, Giovanni governed his affairs with the same prudence and caution with which he had managed the Medici Bank in the years when he had been active in its business. The unsurpassed financial strength of the Medici would prove decisive in buying votes and political favours and in shoring up support as and when it was required. A common way in which this manifested was where the Medici would pay off an individual's debts so that he became eligible for public office in the *signoria*, whereat the individual in question would become politically indebted to the Medici. Giovanni also continued to buy valuable goodwill from the Church with his generous and unstinting 'charitable' donations.

This political élite were not shy of self-documentation and self-glorification. In 1427 the painter Masaccio depicted a procession of prominent contemporary

Florentines in a cloister fresco known as the *Sagra* ('Consecration') created for the Brancacci Chapel of Santa Maria del Carmine in Florence. The fresco, which was given an antiquarian look by being painted in a green earth monochrome called *terra verde*, depicted the assembled personages witnessing the church's consecration on 19 April 1422. As three of the key magnates and civic dignitaries of the day, the painted figures in the crowd would presumably have included Giovanni di Bicci, Niccolò da Uzzano and Rinaldo degli Albizzi. It would have been interesting to see Masaccio's rendering of these three prominent figures in our story. Due to his skill in recreating lifelike three-dimensional figures the sixteenth-century artist Giorgio Vasari would later praise Masaccio as the best painter of his generation. Sadly, however, we no longer have their likenesses preserved for posterity because during the eighteenth-century some shoddy Florentine builders, who were engaged in renovating the church, plastered over the priceless painting and it was lost forever. Michelangelo did however leave us a tantalising sketch copy of several of Masaccio's figures, but who exactly these depicted today we have no idea.

CHAPTER 3

Florence's War with the Lucchesi

The war will thus last longer than we wished, and all because we would
not when we could. May God forgive those who are the cause. If some of
the present Signori had not enough sense to be of the Ten of the *balia*,
instead of ten they should be made nine.

Cosimo de' Medici to Averardo de' Medici, 21 October 1430

I f Giovanni di Bicci began his career seeking to evade the vicissitudes of
Florentine public office, he eventually ended up holding many of the most
important posts in the republic. His championing of the cause of peace with
Milan projected him to the very front-and-centre of the politics of the day and
brought him recognition as a man of the *popolo minuto*. But it had also led him
to square off against the most influential and experienced politician in the
oligarchy, Niccolò da Uzzano. How far Giovanni was pressed in the direction of
political involvement and how far it was pressed upon him is still a matter for
scholarly debate. But what is clear is that in fourteenth and fifteenth-century
Florence no wealthy merchant could realise his true potential unless he rose to
some prominence in civic life. Naturally, Giovanni had even bigger plans for his
business and high hopes for his two capable heirs, especially his eldest son
Cosimo, to whom he entrusted the most important portfolios such as the
mission to Constance. It is difficult to imagine that Giovanni would have gone to
such lengths to build his enterprise just in order to bump uncomfortably up
against the glass ceiling of Florentine politics. If the Medici were to evolve, both
as a family and as a business, then they would need to stake their place amidst
the cut and thrust of Florence's political life.

In 1429, the sixty-nine-year-old Giovanni di Bicci – banker, patron of the
arts, politician and champion of the *popolo minuto*, lay dying. Cosimo and
Lorenzo hastened to their father's bedside, where Giovanni offered them the
following sage words of wisdom: 'To those citizens who are rich and powerful, be
inoffensive, whilst at the same time being charitable to those who are poor and
weak ... Be wary of hanging around the Palazzo della Signoria, as if it is just
another ordinary place of business. Only go there when summoned, and–when
called to go there–only accept those offices which are bestowed upon you, and
nothing more. Never make a show before the people should you receive many
votes, but if a show is unavoidable, let it be the least show necessary. Avoid
litigation, keep out of the public eye, and never go against the will of the people–
unless they are advocating some disastrous project...' These prudent words of
advice belied the fact that Giovanni, by now the second richest man in Florence,

had for some time already been able to afford to purchase political supporters and favours and thereby build a notional political following.

But on 20 February 1429 his political service to the republic came to an end with his death. Despite his strictures to his sons about 'not making a public show' his sizable funeral cortege included the members of the *signoria* as well as the city's *gonfaloniere*, numerous dignitaries, foreign ambassadors, fellow bankers and money-changers and many of his depositors. Before he could be placed in his funeral bier and carried through the streets of his beloved Florence, Giovanni was–according to ancient Etruscan tradition–carried out of his house through a hole which had been knocked in the wall. He was buried near the Duomo in the Basilica of San Lorenzo, in a sacristy designed by his friend, Florence's most famous architect Brunelleschi. His resting place was for the time being a simple affair. In later years, Cosimo de' Medici would induce his own artist friend Donatello to spruce the space up, embellishing the four corners of the sacristy with shields bearing the Medici *palle* and thereby transforming the basilica into what became essentially a Medici family church.

In his history of Florence, Niccolò Machiavelli left us a vivid eulogy of sorts to Giovanni di Bicci who, so we are told, was charitable and generous in his alms giving towards the poor and who 'loved everybody', praising the good but pitying the wicked. 'He loved peace, he avoided war. In times of adversity, he gave men support; in times of prosperity, he gave them aid. He was far from plundering the treasury, and to the common good he made additions. In city offices he appeared well: not much of eloquence but of very great wisdom. He presented the appearance of melancholy, but later in conversation he was pleasant and witty. He died very rich in money, and still richer in good reputation and good will. His legacy, both of the goods of Fortune and those of the spirit, Cosimo not merely preserved but increased.' Just four years later Piccarda Bueri would follow her husband Giovanni to the grave.

There is a famous portrait of Giovanni di Bicci hanging now in the Galleria Degli Uffizi and completed in the Mannerist Bronzino School of Agnolo di Cosimo (1503–1572), usually known as il Bronzino. Painted around a century after Giovanni died, it may well have been based on an earlier, non-extant portrait that was painted from life. Giovanni di Bicci's face, though earthy, unrefined and–it must be said-somewhat melancholic, has a certain shrewd and determined cast to it. The eyes gaze out openly yet resolutely, the worry lines across the forehead suggest a man who was always ruminating on how to gain a favourable business angle. The mouth is not that of a voluptuary but rather a person of a much more puritanical mind-set for whom sound business dealings and propriety supersede the frivolity of sensual enjoyment. Like the portrait itself, a certain patina of ambiguity lies over Giovanni's legacy and we are drawn once more to his dying advice to his two sons to hold aloof, if they could, from Florentine politics. For a man who was held in such high esteem by so many of the disenfranchised, he himself possessed a definite political footprint in the city's civic affairs. But, when any attempt is made to pin down or delineate his political motivations in concrete terms, we find only the studied, impenetrable neutrality of an impresario walking Florence's hazardous political tightrope with aplomb.

Venerated by the people, he consistently refused to initiate any governmental reform that might alleviate their situation. Yet, badgered to align himself more closely with the oligarchy, he stoutly resisted their advances. Meanwhile, through his almsgiving and patronage to the Church, Giovanni enhanced his popularity and common appeal amongst the ordinary pious folk. When, in 1422, Pope Martin V bestowed on him the title of count of Monteverde, he refused to assume the honour for fear of antagonising the ruling *ottimati* on the one hand and the *popolo minuto* on the other. That being said, it seems conclusive that quietly, behind the scenes, Giovanni and his loyal adherents, men like Martino Martini, were assembling a powerful faction through financial gifts, favours and the discharging of debts. The faction would enjoy a groundswell of support amongst the ordinary people of Florence. This ability to tap into grassroots support, a Medici trademark, would prove an important political atrribute in the years to come.

Cosimo de' Medici was already thirty-nine years old and in the prime of his life when he assumed leadership as *capo* of the Medici family. As a seventeen-year-old youth he had seen military service at the siege of Pisa, serving under Maso degli Albizzi and Gino Capponi. Still barely only a youth, he had accompanied the antipope John XXIII to the Council of Constance, after which he had travelled alone through France and Germany, before returning to Florence in the year 1416. Upon Giovanni di Bicci's death, Cosimo now became the chief inheritor of the family wealth and, although he was always on good terms with his brother Lorenzo the Elder, the career of the latter would from now on be eclipsed by and subordinated to that of Cosimo and his more senior branch of the family.

As the baton passed from Medici father to eldest son, Florence at this time was still rocked by division and sedition. Within the confines of the secret societies, which had proven difficult if not impossible for the authorities to eradicate, certain disgruntled members of the community had woken up to the fact that Florence's system of taxation had been rigged against them for centuries. They were deeply unhappy and continued to demand that the more progressive and equitable *catasto* be made retroactive. Prior to his death Giovanni di Bicci, who was himself one of the wealthiest citizens of the commune and had much to lose, had counselled the general population against implementing a retroactive tax demand on the rich. 'it is not well to go into things so long past unless to learn something for our present guidance', Machiavelli records Giovanni as arguing, 'and if in former times the taxation has been unjust, we ought to be thankful, that we have now discovered a method of making it equitable, and hope that this will be a means of uniting the citizens, not of dividing them; which would certainly be the case were they to attempt the recovery of taxes for the past, and make them equal to the present.'

Giovanni had in effect threatened to withdraw his personal support for the popular *catasto* system if the citizens insisted on plundering the wealthy for back-taxes. He had, however, couched his position in agreeable and easily digestible rhetoric that was designed to tease and tickle their conscience. Machiavelli has Giovanni conclude that 'He who is content with a moderate victory is always more successful; for those who would more than conquer, commonly lose'. Don't get too greedy in your zeal for reform Giovanni had cautioned the ordinary people. In the meantime, the secret societies still proliferated and the *signoria* vainly attempted to ban them with recourse to a new law called the *Lex contra Scandalosos*. The so-called scandal laws strove to identify and punish those 'who wish to be more powerful than the commune itself'. As usual though, all the new tell-tale law succeeded in doing was to whet the appetite of those who had an axe to grind with their neighbours or rivals.

The result was an avalanche of grudges and even more 'scandal' and confusion than ever before. On top of everything else, as if the domestic situation in Florence was not unstable enough, the war in Lombardy against Milan was about to be reignited. The reopening of the conflict would now push the commune to the brink of political and financial disaster.

The Peace of 30 December 1426 with Filippo Maria Visconti had been a dead letter. Advised by the meddlesome King Sigismund of the Romans not to ratify it, Visconti had re-opened hostilities against both Venice and Florence in May 1427. In this continuing phase of the war Visconti could count for support upon some of the most illustrious *condottieri* of the era, men such as Agnolo della Pergola, Florence's turncoat captain Niccolò Piccinino, Guido Torello and Francesco Sforza. As was common with the wars of the *condottieri* the conflict now see-sawed endlessly back and forth with all the indecisiveness of early twentieth-century trench warfare. As was also common in the changeable world of the *condottieri*, allegiances had by now also shifted. For one thing the renowned commander Francesco Bussone da Carmagnola had been fighting on the side of Venice for a full nine months before the conclusion of the last peace treaty. How this came about deserves a brief detour since it illustrates the tightrope that the *condotteri* often walked in offering their loyalty in return for pay. By the same token, it also demonstrates the liabilities faced by employers who were forced to depend for their military needs on hired mercenary muscle.

Deeply unhappy by his downgrading to peacetime governor of Genoa, the ambitious Carmagnola had grown increasingly paranoid about his employer's seeming ambivalence towards him. This was not without justification though for Filippo Maria Visconti knew from experience the fickleness of the *condottieri*. A strong, capable and celebrated mercenary commander like Carmagnola was quite capable of changing sides at any moment if the enemy bribed him with higher pay. As was common practice amongst noble employers, the Duke had therefore attempted to bind Carmagnola in loyalty to Milan through wealth, marriage and gifts of property. He had also sought to side-line Carmagnola in Genoa in order to reduce his potential threat. Naturally, Carmagnola had grown jealous of the other *condottieri* who had been selected to lead Milan's offensive against Venice and Florence, and this was especially true in the case of the up-and-coming young captain named Francesco Sforza. To make matters worse, Carmagnola's post in Genoa placed him at some distance from Milan's court so his enemies there could intrigue against him with impunity.

Carmagnola's worst fears seem to have been vindicated in the autumn of 1424 when he found himself summarily dismissed from his post as Genoa's governor. Bowing to the whispering campaign against him back in Milan, the Duke had apparently shelved him. This was too much for any proud *condottiere* to bear. He hurried to Milan to remonstrate with Filippo Maria on why he had been cast aside in favour of far less experienced generals? At Milan he was denied an audience with the Duke by his adversaries, the smirking lackeys and flunkies at court. This was all Carmagnola needed to make up his mind. Abandoning his wife and child in Milan he fled in fear of his life to Piedmont to wait out the winter. By February 1425, Carmagnola was in Venice offering his services to Milan's enemy the Doge. Venice had been only too glad to hire such an illustrious soldier but on-going negotiations between Venice and Florence for a formal alliance meant that a year would elapse before Carmagnola would enter active service. By February 1426, however, Venice was in a position to grant Carmagnola a *condotta* of 1,000 gold ducats a month to fight the *Milanesi* and, in a lavish ceremony which took place in the Patriarchal Cathedral Basilica in Venice, Francesco Foscari proudly handed him the banner of St. Mark to carry into battle.

Deeply offended at having been jilted by Carmagnola, yet refusing to acknowledge any responsibility for his commander's desertion, Filippo Maria still held Carmagnola's wife and child captive in Milan. The *condottiere* was therefore under considerable pressure to proceed against Milan with caution, so as to prevent the Duke from taking revenge on his family. Carmagnola's first assignment from the Venetian senate had been to retake the town of Brescia from Francesco Sforza, which he had accomplished after a half-hearted eight month investment of the city during which he was twice absent due to bouts of sickness. As part of the terms of the peace treaty of 30 December 1426, Filippo Maria had not only agreed to cede Brescia and the Bresciano to Venice but also consented to release Carmagnola's wife and child. War broke out again in May 1427 and, with his family now safe, Venice expected their seemingly tepid supreme commander to prosecute the war with less restraint. But Carmagnola was in for a fresh surprise when the duke of Milan's forces attempted to eliminate him and 200 of his guards and retainers in an ambush at the Venetian frontier town of Chiari in Brescia.

Despite the forbearance of the Venetian senate, Carmagnola's performance continued to disappoint. Carmagnola was at Abano taking one of his periodic spa cures when Milan's army advanced and invested Casalmaggiore near Cremona, one of Venice's key trading bases on the River Po. Carmagnola's dilatory response led to Casalmaggiore being captured and, although the Venetians succeeded in burning Filippo Maria's river fleet near Cremona on 21 May 1427, Carmagnola himself was ignominiously defeated at the hamlet of Gottolengo by Niccolò Piccinino just one week later on 29 May. The Tuscan humanist and Florentine chancellor Leonardo Bruni would use the Battle of Gottolengo to eulogize one of the other *condottieri* who had fought and died that day, the anti-republican Florentine political exile Nanni Strozzi. In his *Funeral Oration for Nanni Strozzi* Bruni would use the genre of civic panegyric to praise Florence for its liberty and equality, favourably comparing Florence's *signoria* to the alternatives of monarchy and oligarchy. In Bruni's view, Florence was a meritocracy where virtue and ability were considered the essence of 'true nobility'. It was characteristic of Florentine intellectuals to make propaganda capital out of what was essentially a military defeat and, as Florence's chancellor Bruni waxed lyrical, as always it was left to the common soldier to make good the tactical deficit in the real world.

Carmagnola, by now under a dark cloud for his ponderous manoeuvring, was nevertheless quick to re-establish his reputation by pushing Piccinino back and recapturing Casalmaggiore. When the Venetians followed up by advancing on Cremona they were checked at Casalsecco by a fresh force of *Milanese* reinforcements under the personal command of Duke Filippo Maria himself. On 12 July 1427 the *Milanese condottieri* sought to win favour from their duke by forcing an engagement but the resulting skirmish, fought in clouds of dust kicked up by their horses' hoofs, proved inconclusive at best and, having had his fill of campaigning, the Duke promptly retired to the comforts of Milan. Carmagnola then blotted his copy book once more by himself threatening to retire to winter quarters even though it was still only early September. A flurry of indignant correspondence followed between the Doge and his supreme commander. Action was urged, the very safety and security of the Venetian state hung in the balance. Finally, Carmagnola relented, jolted from his indolence perhaps by the realisation that his employers were nearing the end of their saint-like patience. Advancing into Mantuan territory, Carmagnola's troops seized the city of Cremona after a lightning assault which had seen them using their own dead as a bridge across the city's moat.

Positioning his forces in solid defensive positions amongst the marshy dunes near Maclodio, Carmagnola next set a trap for the *Milanesi* on 11 October 1427. Milan's newly appointed supreme commander Carlo Malatesta was eager to prove his worth to his fellow captains Piccinino, Sforza and Torello. Against their advice he gave the order to attack through a narrow causeway which Carmagnola had deliberately left open. Taking the bait, the *Milanese* troops were assailed on every side by withering projectile and artillery file and could not deploy within the narrow strip. As three of the *condottieri* captains made their escape, Carmagnola's cavalry crushed the remaining resistance by enveloping the *Milanesi* from the rear. As the dust settled over the marshland, the town of Maclodio itself lay in ruins and the lord of Rimini was taken along with 8,000 of his soldiers. Suddenly, all Carmagnola's former wrongdoings were forgiven and the Venetians fell over themselves pell-mell to praise and flatter their gifted *condottiere*. The Doge wrote him a fulsome letter of appreciation; he was lavished with property formerly owned by the Malatesta family; he was even given the town of Chiari as a fief, the same place where Filippo Maria had once attempted to have him murdered.

But the foolish, incorrigible Carmagnola now made the fatal mistake of pushing his employer's patience to the limit. By the following morning he had given orders for the release of all but 400 of the 8,000 captives, including Carlo Malatesta himself. These prisoners of war now returned to Milan and began the process of re-arming all over again. Venice's war commissioner, the *provveditore*, was absolutely livid. Challenging Carmagnola on his actions, the *condottiere* justified himself by claiming that his troops had acted humanely by releasing their adversaries. But the Venetians knew, as did Carmagnola, that making the duke of Milan a gift of his own army could only serve to prolong the war and keep the fees pouring in every month. The Venetians were many things, but they were certainly not stupid where money was concerned. To add further insult to injury, Carmagnola had made it an open secret that he still remained in diplomatic contact with his former employer the duke of Milan; Filippo Maria's envoys had established contact with Carmagnola as early as 1426 and, not wishing to burn any bridges, the *condottiere* had gladly entertained their overtures. Admittedly, he had kept Venice's *signore* fully informed of this fact, but even so there was a creeping suspicion on the Venetians' part that Carmagnola may still be colluding with the Duke.

While the Venetians were entertaining second thoughts about their supreme commander, the duke of Milan had remarried. To the west, Amadeus VIII of Savoy and John Jacob Palaeologus of Montferrat had invaded Lombardy from their respective territories. In order to neutralise the former threat Visconti had made a hasty dynastic marriage with Amadeus's eighteen-year-old daughter Marie. True to form, the superstitious and mentally unbalanced Filippo Maria had treated his hapless new wife with as little consideration as he had done his first. After a dog had yowled during their nuptials, the superstitious Filippo Maria had had the poor girl locked up for the remainder of their wedding night. Despite this dynastic stopgap however the *Milanesi* still could not gain significant ground. Francesco Sforza was defeated by returned *Genovese* exiles and Sigismund had failed to provide the military support he had promised. Needing a breathing space in which to reconstitute his army, Filippo Maria sued for peace again. In Florence, Cosimo de' Medici's cousin Averardo de' Medici was despatched together with Palla Strozzi as joint peace envoys and a treaty was duly signed at Ferrara on 18 April 1428 through the mediation of Pope Martin V, who was represented by the Cardinal di Santa Croce.

Although the news of the Peace of Ferrara reached Florence on 20 April it was only officially proclaimed on 16 May 1428. It had been an exhausted Florence which had in fact called loudest for this latest truce. As was customary, a period of celebration ensued with fireworks and bonfires being lit in the many *piazze* of the city. The *signoria* ordered that the venerated portrait of the Virgin from Impruneta be carried through the streets at the head of a large procession comprising both clerics and laypeople. This was Florence's most sacred icon and acted as an intermediary between the city and the realm of the divine. At the Piazza della Signoria, in the loggia of the *signoria*, the procession paused while the chancellor Leonardo Bruni delivered the proclamation of peace to the *priori* and their entourage, as well as the assembled citizens of Florence. This moment was also chosen for Bruni to hand over the first six books of his officially commissioned history of Florence, the *Historiarum Florentini populi libri XII*. This was a potent piece of civic propagandising and state theatre. In Bruni's view, Florence owed its ancestry not to the Roman Emperors, whose counterpart might be seen in the tyrant Filippo Maria Visconti, but instead to the Roman people themselves, those free-born citizens who had been the driving force behind the Roman republic. The handover ceremony of Florence's, as it were, 'state-endorsed' history was a reminder to all of Florence's power and legitimacy and the superiority of its republican system to that of its despotic adversary Milan.

Another exponent of classical Roman values had ventured to Florence that merciful year of peace. Leon Battista Alberti had been born in Genoa around the year 1404, a member of the Florentine family that had been ruthlessly exiled by Maso degli Albizzi in 1393. He proved to be something of a prodigy, mastering Greek and Latin at a relatively young age and studying law at the University of Bologna. In 1428 the banishment of the Alberti family was revoked and Leon Battista travelled for the first time to Florence where he came into contact with Brunelleschi, Donatello and Ghiberti. His love of classical art and architecture would ultimately lead Leon Battista to become the first theorist of humanist art. In his *Della Pittura* (1435) he would explore the theoretical basis of painting, whilst his monumental ten-volume work *De re aedificatoria* (1452) would examine the principles of architecture, borrowing heavily from the classical ideas of Vitruvius.

By the spring of 1428 the commune was in dire financial straits and incurring regular losses from raids mounted by her neighbour Lucca, a Tuscan city-state which had aligned itself with Milan in the recent wars for, so she claimed, purely defensive purposes. Under the terms of the latest treaty Milan had been obliged to relinquish Bergamo, Brescia (including the surrounding *contado* of Bresciano) and Cremona to Venice, who now luxuriated in the largest ever extent of her possessions on terra firma. Florence meanwhile duly regained a number of her former cities and territories, amongst which was the town of Volterra. Like Pisa, Volterra was seldom content under Florentine hegemony. It was a very old Etruscan town which had been raised to great prominence in ancient times thanks to the minerals extracted from the mines of the nearby Colline Metallifere or 'Metalliferous Hills'. The town itself sits astride an acropolis which surges some eighteen-hundred feet into the sky and dominates the surrounding country on all sides. The acropolis was, in those days, protected by walls and a *rocca* dating back to 1343.

During the Lombard invasion of Italy Volterra had been established as a *gastaldato* dependent upon the protection of the Emperor, however Berengar the king of Italy had sacked the city and reduced it to ruins in the tenth-century, whereupon it had become an episcopate subject to the temporal rule of its resident bishops. From the twelfth to the fourteenth-centuries the commune of Volterra had fought the power of both the bishops as well as the Pannocchieschi family, whose principal member Bishop Ildebrando Pannocchieschi had been bestowed with the title Count Palatine in Tuscany and prince of the Holy Roman Empire by Henry VI. The ensuing years saw an on-going struggle for control of Volterra among the great feudal families of the Panocchieschi, the Ubertini and the Belforti. Florence, allied to the Belforti, gradually strengthened its influence over the city and in 1427 succeeded in establishing control over the commune. But Florentine rule did not sit well with the proudly independent *Volterrani* and any taxation from the *dominante*, the 'dominant city' was deeply resented. Also, Florentine citizenship and enfranchisement only applied to the inhabitants of Florence itself, being customarily denied to the people of any towns or cities which Florence annexed. When the Florentine élite gleefully imposed the *catasto* upon the resentful *Volterrani*, a tax under which they themselves had moreover been groaning, it was the touch paper which ignited a popular rebellion against Florentine overlordship.

The *catasto* assessments were regarded by eighteen citizens of Volterra as an affront to their liberties and they publicly opposed the Florentine assessors. This led to the eighteen dissidents being seized and transported to Florence, whereupon they were imprisoned in the city's notorious debtor's prison known as the Stinche. Located at the junction of the Via dell' Isola delle Stinche and the Via Ghibellina, the Stinche was a featureless, windowless cube with only a single small entranceway through which visitors and inmates had to stoop down low upon entering. Its forty-four feet high walls occluded any natural sunlight and left the cells dark, humid and foetid. The entire forbidding structure was regarded with a deep sense of dread by the Florentines; the bleak words *oportet misereri*, ('we ought to be compassionate') were inscribed above the gaol's entrance. The city of Volterra was outraged by this affront to its citizens' liberty but after some time the debtor-dissidents grew weary of the deprivations of the Stinche and reluctantly they agreed to have their property assessed in return for their freedom. They subsequently returned embittered to their home town where one of them, a common man named Giusto, was chosen to be one of the city's new priors. Once elected, Giusto—who by now hated the Florentines bitterly—roused the people of Volterra to open revolt against Florence. In short order the Florentine captain and magistrates were thrown out of the city by the enraged *Volterrani*.

At the same time, the dissidents called for help from both Paolo Guinigi, the *signore* of Lucca, as well as the *Sienese*. Both states declined to help, Siena because it was currently allied to Florence and Lucca because its *signore* wished to curry favour with the Florentines after having lost their goodwill by supporting Filippo Maria Visconti in the recent Lombard Wars. Volterra being a highly profitable source of alum, a precious resource which could not be given up so lightly, Florence could not stand idly by while the city revolted against its rule. A council of war was duly constituted and Rinaldo degli Albizzi and Palla Strozzi were jointly appointed as commissioners to oversee Volterra's return to the fold. They approached the *condottiere* Niccolò Fortebraccio for assistance in regaining the town. Fortebraccio, who had been employed by the *signoria* during the recent war with Milan, was at this time quartered at the town of Fucecchio west of Florence. He consented to sell his troops and, together with some men-at-arms recruited from Valdarno and Pisa, Florence's commissioners moved them to a siege encampment beneath Volterra's formidable acropolis.

Giusto, however, was given no opportunity to prove himself as a popular leader, either in war or in peace. Soon afterwards, some well-to-do *Voterrani* citizens assassinated him on the pretext that if they handed Volterra back to Florence, not only would their city's ancient privileges be restored, but the grateful Florentines would permit them to become the de facto rulers in the city. But they had miscalculated badly. Upon handing Volterra back to the Florentine commissioners, the latter promptly ordered Niccolò Fortebraccio to occupy the town before any meaningful terms or conditions could be struck. The result was therefore far worse for Volterra since they lost not only the last vestiges of their political liberty, but also their surrounding *contado*, which now instead became a vicariate of Florence.

The presence of Florence's mercenary army on Volterra's soil now begged the question of whether to continue her military conquest against nearby Lucca, whose ruler Paolo Guinigi had not only sided with the hated Visconti but who had also appeared, at least on the surface, sympathetic to Volterra's rebellion. Florence had censured the *Lucchesi* for their close ties to the Visconti of Milan but the rapprochement had not arisen out of naked antagonism towards Florence; rather it was regarded as Lucca's best strategy for maintaining her independence. Florence at this time seemed rapacious, a wealthy and predatory neighbour which would turn Lucca into another Pisa given the opportunity. In fact, Florence's normal instinct once the situation had been settled with Milan and Volterra would have been to retire once more into peaceful trade and commerce. However, in the case of Lucca, there was a certain amount of simmering resentment at the attacks which Lucca's troops had made on Florence's *contado*. Retaliation was felt to be an appropriate response to Lucca's opportunism and, even though Florence did not have access to the most gifted *condottiere* of the era Francesco Bussone da Carmagnola (whose services were currently being monopolised by Venice), she could just as easily find another equally willing to do her bidding in this grim business.

Bad blood had existed between Florence and Lucca for centuries. In the thirteenth-century the formerly Guelph city had been ruled by a captain of the people, after which it had been conquered by the Ghibelline lord of Pisa, Uguccione della Faggiuola. When he was expelled by the *Lucchesi*, his former *condottiere* Castruccio Castracani was elected to rule over the city in his stead. Castruccio, also a staunch Ghibelline, had then prosecuted a long and vigorous war against the republic of Florence. It had been his victory over Florence at the Battle of Altopascio in 1325 which had caused the Florentines to embark upon their brief but unsuccessful flirtation with Angevin despotic rule. In thanks for his long years of imperial service the Emperor Louis the Bavarian had appointed Castracani as duke of Lucca, Pistoia, Volterra and Luni and he had shortly thereafter gone on to conquer Pisa, of which city he was made imperial vicar. Under Castracani's stern hand Lucca had been a power to rival nearby Florence until its duke's death in 1328. In the decades that followed the city was then passed around by a dizzying array of different rulers. Occupied by the troops of Louis the Bavarian, the city was sold to a rich *Genovese*, Gherardino Spinola, and then seized by King John of Bohemia. Pawned by John to the Rossi of Parma, it was next ceded to Mastino II della Scala of Verona and then sold to the Florentines, who surrendered it to the *Pisani*. Next, Lucca had been nominally liberated by the Emperor Charles IV and governed by his vicar. Finally the Guinigi family came to power in Lucca.

Despite a chequered history of being handed round between a series of despots, traditionally the people of Lucca had strong republican sentiments when it came to their government. They were also fiercely independent in their stance towards any aggression from neighbouring states like Florence. The House of Guinigi had long been the wealthiest family in Lucca and the Guinigi and the *Lucchesi* had, over time, settled down into a convenient coalition in which the Guinigi were rewarded with rule in return for keeping the state strong and autonomous. Paolo Guinigi had been the youngest sibling in a clan of elder brothers and had never been expected to rule but their untimely deaths had opened the way for him and on 21 November 1400 Paolo took power in Lucca as *capitano* and defender of the people. Lucca at that time was still slowly recovering from a disastrous plague from which many of the more prominent citizens had fled; certain of her political offices lay vacant whilst outside predators hovered on the fringes. The people of Lucca were again content to relinquish their republican dreams in return for good, robust central government under the effective Guinigi family. For their part, the Guinigi built their state not upon oppression but instead upon ideals of kinship, marriage alliances, clientage, and neighbourhood ties. By not allowing themselves to degenerate into mere *tiranni*, they henceforth governed Lucca with the general consent of the people.

Paolo Guinigi himself was, after the fashion of the times, a regular patron of the arts. Especially notable amongst his commissions was the stately Villa Guinigi as well as the sarcophagus of his second wife Ilaria del Carretto which was sculpted in 1408 by Jacopo della Quercia. Paolo's marital life was perhaps the least satisfactory aspect of his reign. Ilaria had died whilst giving birth to his second daughter in 1406 and prior to that his child bride Maria Caterina Antelminelli had died at the tender age of eleven, virtually as soon as the wedding festivities had been concluded. Maria Caterina had been a distant relative of Duke Castruccio Castracani and their union had been an attempt to unite the old and new ruling houses of Lucca. Paolo had nevertheless married twice more after this and had a capable son named Ladislao by Ilaria.

Guinigi was also an efficient defender of his city. The fall of Pisa to Florence in 1406 left an uncomfortable Florentine presence along Lucca's borders. In response to this, that same year Paolo strengthened Lucca's defences by ordering that all the trees within a mile of the city walls be cut down with the order that nothing else be replanted there. No cover was to be allowed for any besieging army. He had also built a new citadel within the city that became the seat of Lucca's government. The city was protected by particularly strong medieval walls. These were about thirty-five feet high with various semi-circular and square towers and four monumental gates which were flanked by cylindrical towers, according to the Roman custom. The walls which existed in the 1400s were the third cycle of wall-building before Lucca's defences were upgraded for a fourth and final time during the sixteenth-century. These were the so-called 'Renaissance walls' when Lucca's signory decreed the need to keep pace with advances in military technology and guarantee better defences for the city.

The main access point to Lucca was the Porta San Gervasio, the gateway to the ancient Roman and early medieval walls. This gate tower, which was also known as the Annunciation, was completed in 1255. The entrance had a large eight meters high opening and was decorated with an arch. In the inner bezel could be seen the image of the Madonna and Her Child with two saints. The two towers were built out of grey sandstone and ornamented with white limestone. The walls and gate of Lucca, which are relatively well-preserved to this day, presented a considerable barrier to any army that might attempt to lay siege to the town. They were the guardians of her sovereignty and the *Lucchesi* would not suffer historic enemies like Florence to enter so easily.

As had happened before over Milan, Florence's population coalesced again into competing war and peace parties. In 1422, when the commune was desperately seeking a solution to its fiscal and taxation problems, the *reggimento* had stood together united. Here were some of the most illustrious citizens of the republic all calling for reform: Rinaldo degli Albizzi, Niccolò da Uzzano, Lorenzo Ridolfi, Bartolomeo Valori, Salamone and Palla Strozzi, Bartolomeo and Giotto Peruzzi, Francesco Machiavelli and Niccolò del Bellaccio. Now that coalition fractured once more into opposing sides. The doves led by Niccolò da Uzzano, Agnolo Pandolfini and Palla Strozzi urged prudence and caution. Florence, they argued, was still dangerously weak–not to mention fiscally broke–from the first round of wars with Milan. Attacking Lucca would only put neighbouring Siena on her guard and Visconti would meanwhile use the opportunity of Florence's distraction to renew his campaign of conquest in Lombardy and the Romagna. Besides, they reasoned, Paolo Guinigi had recently been petitioning Florence to enter into a defensive league; hence attacking the *Lucchesi* at this point would remove a potential future ally against Milan whilst creating an unnecessary threat. Above all, Niccolò da Uzzano argued, Lucca was a fellow Guelph city and therefore a natural brother to Florence.

The peace faction put Guinigi's actions in previously turning away from Florence to embrace Milan down to Florentine arrogance, which was in large measure a fair assessment. The free citizens of Lucca had only to remember how methodically Florence had subjugated neighbouring Pisa. In 1403 the Florentine *dieci* had, through their agent in Pisa, Bartolomeo Valori, initially sought to purchase Pisa for 100,000 florins. When this deal proved inconclusive the following year the *dieci* despatched a military force to gain entry through a weak and poorly defended section of the *Pisano* curtain wall, but in this too they had proven unsuccessful. When, in March 1404, the Florentines ordered more troops into the region of Lunigiana intending to stir up anti-Visconti feelings in Lucca's *contado* both the *Genovesi* as well as the French had come to the support of the *Pisani*. The lesson for the *Lucchesi* was clear; once Florence had set her cap at a given acquisition she would stop at nothing to achieve it and would try all means, both fair and foul, to secure her ends.

Florence's peace faction was, nonetheless, drowned out by the vociferous war faction who, in a reversal of recent trends, now comprised most of the *popolo minuto*. The introduction of the *catasto* had fallen squarely on the shoulders of the rich and powerful; the seemingly inexhaustible public funds this generated now gave the lower classes the impression that there was infinite funding available for war. Whereas past wars had been a heavy and unwelcome burden on the commoners, those same *popolo minuto* now realised that war need not encumber them personally. Enthusiastically they took to the streets to call for war against the perfidious *Lucchesi* who, they protested, had stood shoulder-to-shoulder with their enemy Milan. It was inevitable that some in the oligarchy would opportunistically tap into the will of the common people and hawks like Rinaldo degli Albizzi and his rival Neri Capponi (the son of Gino Capponi) now emerged as the main advocates for war. Not only did Albizzi and Capponi hope to cover themselves with glory, as indeed their predecessors had done during the conquest of Pisa in 1406, but cynically they used the hue and cry to distract the lower classes from their existing grievances over political disenfranchisement. As every politician knows, war is and always has been a powerful distraction in times of domestic turmoil.

Albizzi and Capponi argued that Florence must acquire Lucca as a buffer state to safeguard Pisa against any future aggression from Milan. The city stood on Florence's Tuscan border with *Genovese* Liguria and also controlled access to certain strategically important Apennine passes which were essential to Florentine trade with the towns and cities of Lombardy and the Po Valley. Lucca had moreover developed into a serious economic rival to Florence in the field of silk manufacturing, which was emerging as a major alternative to the wool trade in Florence. Inconveniently, Lucca also threatened Florence's interests by excelling in banking and the quarrying of high quality marble. Besides, argued Rinaldo, Lucca would be easy to capture, 'since she was in servitude to a citizen and had lost her natural vigour and her ancient zeal for defending her liberty. Hence, either the people drive out the tyrant, or by the tyrant in fear of the people, she would be surrendered.'

Even the relatively neutral Cosimo de' Medici, who was by now beginning to emerge onto the public stage, was reluctantly driven to admit that Lucca's rich and extensive lands were tantalisingly independent of Florentine control and exploitation. Since the *popolo minuto* were in favour of war, the Medici were able to side with popular feeling and support the coming conflict without alienating their groundswell of lower class supporters. Cosimo's cousin Averardo de' Medici and the late Giovanni' di Bicci's agent Martino Martini also gathered in Rinaldo's corner; Martini himself led an opposing faction to the other hawk Neri Capponi in the *signoria*. In fact, so friendly was the feeling between them that Rinaldo counselled his son to treat Martini 'as a father'. Nevertheless, at the same time Averardo was also father-in-law to Alamanno Salviati and must therefore have been exposed to Alamanno's own grumbles about Rinaldo, to whom he was politically opposed.

Niccolò Fortebraccio, the *condottiere* who had previously acted for Florence against the rebel city of Volterra, was now approached by Rinaldo degli Albizzi at his headquarters at Fucecchio. Rinaldo persuaded the commander that if he were to attack Lucca on some feigned pretence he would manage things so that Florence subsequently declared war on Lucca and appointed him as commander-in-chief; with Volterra by now subjugated Fortebraccio was himself currently unemployed. Fortebraccio agreed to this scheme and devised a suitable plan. Claiming to be acting in his own personal interests with no connection to Florentine foreign policy, Fortebraccio proclaimed that Lucca still owed his uncle Braccio da Montone an outstanding 50,000 florins from a previous *condotta*. On this pretext he began mobilising his troops and in November 1429, claiming that he was simply moving to collect the outstanding balance owed to his family, Fortebraccio embarked upon initial operations against Lucca's territory. With only 300 horse and an equal number of infantry, he quickly captured two of Lucca's outlying *castelli* at Ruoti and Compito and descended to the plains despoiling the countryside as he went. The Florentine castellans of the nearby fortresses at Pescia and Vico looked on greedily, expecting these fallen *Lucchesi* strongholds to sue to come under their protection. They sent word back to Florence to alert the *signoria* that the whole of Lucca's *contado* would in this way soon fall 'like a ripe fruit into their hands'.

Back in Florence, Neri Capponi justified the thinly veiled offensive to the Florentines by drawing attention to the republic's need to rebuild its lacklustre military reputation in the wake of the previous conflicts with the Visconti. 'We should not', he asserted, 'give up on the Lucca campaign simply because we are afraid of the duke of Milan, since conquering the city will restore the republic's reputation and give our citizens hope, thereby meaning the Duke will refrain from entering the fray'. The hawks were given additional impetus from an unlikely source, Lucca's own ambassador to Florence, Jacopo Viviani. A political rival of the Guinigi who had formerly been imprisoned by Paolo, Viviani had subsequently been released, appointed to serve as the city-state's envoy to Florence, and given the task of carrying a message of reconciliation to the *signoria*. It was, to say the very least, a strange and foolish choice of emissary. Viviani had not forgotten his personal vendetta against the Guinigi-ruled *signore*, even if Paolo himself apparently had, and no sooner had he arrived in Florence than he secretly began encouraging the Florentines to mount an invasion of his home city so as to topple his political enemy.

After two weeks of debate, Albizzi's war party seized the day by a four-to-one majority and Neri Capponi was elected to the *dieci*, the creation of which was recognised by all as a virtual declaration of war. A citizen of growing power and influence, Cosimo de' Medici was another appointee to the *dieci*. Rinaldo degli Albizzi meanwhile, although not elected to the prestigious *dieci*, was despatched in December 1429 alongside Astorre Gianni as Florence's joint war commissioner to the military camp outside Lucca. The commissioners were those political officials assigned by the *signoria* to accompany a *condottiere* whilst on campaign in the service of the republic. As well as acting as a liaison point between the military and the government, they also served to ensure that the general followed orders and carried out the *dieci*'s implicit instructions.

Astorre Gianni wasted little time however in dishonouring both himself and Florence. Marching with half of the Florentine army into the Guelph lands of Seravezza around Pietra Santa, his troops embarked on a shameful orgy of rape and despoliation. The surviving *Seravezzesi* streamed into Florence carrying word of Astorre's atrocities. They described him, in the later words of Machiavelli, as being 'nothing of man except his appearance, nothing of a Florentine except the name – a death-bringing plague, a cruel wild beast, a repulsive monster, such as never has been described by any writer'. For his cruelty and disregard for the people of Seravezza, Astorre was soon recalled by the *signoria* and stripped of his citizenship. As for Rinaldo degli Albizzi, he fared little better. Astorre Gianni's poor conduct had seemingly rubbed off on Rinaldo who was also now accused in Florence of conducting the war against Lucca purely for his own private profit and advantage. He had been caught stocking his own extensive estates with stolen booty and even speculated to acquire, at a preferential price, the goods taken as plunder by his own troops.

When an incompetent individual is assigned a task far in excess of his abilities it is customary for such a person to spend most of his time justifying and defending his actions rather than focusing his efforts on improving his performance. This was the case with Rinaldo degli Albizzi during the three fruitless months that he spent with the Florentine army beneath the walls of Lucca. As the letters flew home to Florence so the doves under da Uzzano obstructed his and the war council's labours at every turn. Whilst the political conspirators hampered his efforts with infrequent supplies and contradictory instructions, Rinaldo was at the same time barraged with impatient demands for a rapid and glorious Florentine victory. These demands caused Rinaldo to now lock horns with the *condottiere* Niccolò Fortebraccio over questions of military strategy. A shrewd general, Fortebraccio preferred to first reduce Lucca's various *castelli* dotted around the surrounding countryside. Once the threat which they posed had been removed, Florence's forces could move forward and reduce the city of Lucca itself. For Rinaldo, however, under pressure to win a speedy political victory over the enemy, this was too ponderous a methodology. He was already prickly from the imputations against his reputation back home and, swollen with galled pride, was completely unable to command the situation.

When there seemed no solution to the impasse between the two commanders on the ground the *dieci* despatched Neri Capponi and Alamanno Salviati to Lucca as new commissioners to expedite matters. Capponi and Salviati found the Florentine troops encamped in their winter quarters at Capannole, far away from Lucca, and they ordered the army back into its siege posture. Moodily the soldiers refused to budge, citing the inclement weather as the reason for their inactivity. It was not a good sign. What is more, the political rivals Albizzi and Capponi were also bitter personal rivals. Indeed, their animosity towards one another had quite a long pedigree. It had begun in 1424 when Rinaldo had been based in Rome acting as Florence's representative to the Curia. The *signoria* had subsequently despatched Capponi to Rome on his own independent diplomatic mission, something that intruded upon Rinaldo's ambassadorial remit. From its origins as a simple diplomatic turf war the situation had gone rapidly downhill from there.

Capponi had served on the *dieci* several times but Rinaldo had not even served once; furthermore, Capponi had been present at the siege of Pisa but Rinaldo had not. Neri Capponi had even revised a self-glorifying chronicle that his father, Gino Capponi, had written concerning that glorious conquest and the Capponi family's central role in the entire campaign. As part of his duties Capponi also had experience in recruiting foreign mercenaries for service with the republic and was highly respected by these rough-and-tumble fighting men. By contrast, Rinaldo was not held in the same high esteem by the professional soldiers, even though he craved recognition as a leader of men. Simple jealously can therefore be seen to account for a large part of Rinaldo's sour motivations towards Neri Capponi. In hindsight, sending Neri to interfere with Rinaldo's military command could not have been more inflammatory and counterproductive to Florence's war effort. In the stark conditions of the military camp, the simmering resentment between these two uneasy colleagues now flared up into open animosity. Neri Capponi was already an intimate of

Niccolò Fortebraccio and the two men blithely acted together without bothering to first consult with their joint commander, Rinaldo. When they gained a victory, as for example over the *castello* of Collodi, they claimed exclusive credit for it, which further upset the proud and unstable Rinaldo.

Rinaldo responded by initiating a smear campaign against his political rival, strongly inferring that Capponi's influence with the army was such that, should he wish to do so, he could easily initiate an armed coup against the *signoria*. The spectre of an armed takeover by a potential tyrant-in-the-making seemed at last to have the desired effect and the *signoria* now grew alarmed at Rinaldo's allegations. Neri Capponi was recalled to Florence to answer the charges. Meanwhile, his replacement Alamanno Salviati proved no less intractable in matters of command. If anything in fact, he seemed even worse than Neri Capponi. Further miscalculations on the part of the *signoria* shortly followed. Requesting additional troops to enable him to close the noose around Lucca, ineptly the *dieci* sent Rinaldo the *condottiere* Bernardino Ubaldini, a man who was the sworn enemy of Niccolò Fortebraccio. So bad was the feeling between these two ranking commanders in fact that their armies were required to remain physically separate from each other at all times. When the *dieci* refused to confer upon Fortebraccio his long-awaited title of supreme commander for fear of offending his bitter rival Ubaldini, the former grew disinterested in the war, refusing to prosecute it with any sense of vigour or commitment.

Disgusted, Rinaldo engineered his own recall to Florence in March 1430. Rushing back to appear before the *dieci* he querulously justified his own lacklustre efforts: 'I know how difficult it is to serve an undisciplined people and a divided city', he declared, because 'the first accepts every rumour; the second is hard on evil deeds, and does not reward good ones. Hence, if you are victorious, nobody praises you; if you make a mistake, everybody censures you; if you lose, everybody slanders you; the friendly party strives to injure you through envy, the hostile party through hatred.' Rinaldo then pompously went on to remind the *dieci* that, as citizens of the republic serving in the government, they too may come under the censure of the people at any time. It was the haughty and self-serving argument of the fatally incompetent. Maso degli Albizzi had fought with the Teutonic Knights in the frozen north against savage pagans; indeed the Albizzi family's coat of arms consisted of two concentric golden rings beneath the black cross of the Teutonic order; but Maso's ungifted son could boast no such accomplishments. Sent unprepared and inexperienced before the city walls of Lucca, he had unwittingly allowed himself to become a political scapegoat. Unhappily for him he had played that role proficiently by simply whining about his misfortunes. All he could hope to do in future was to deflect his sad failings onto others. This, as we shall see, would have grim repercussions for the Medici.

Cosimo de' Medici, influential but still not yet at the forefront of Florence's political life, nevertheless had his own opinions on current affairs. The course of events having been embarked upon, and most being in favour of the war, Cosimo believed they should do all they could to ensure the venture's success. Writing to his cousin Averardo de' Medici in Pisa, Cosimo remarked: 'I think this enterprise is generally popular, and seeing things have gone so far as to implicate the honour of the Commune, every one ought to favour it as much as possible'. Nevertheless, at the same time he noted how 'There are those who, hoping to see injury and infamy inflicted on others, would inflict injury and infamy on the Commune, and try with all their might to bring this about; which

71

shows an evil nature'. However, like many others in Florence, he increasingly bemoaned the poor performance of the inept Florentine commissioners who seemed to be the source of all their military problems.

Under increasing pressure from the citizenry to win the war with Lucca, a fraught *dieci* now authorised an audacious civil engineering plan which involved the damning of the River Serchio to redirect its waters against the city walls of Lucca. This was a scheme originated by the architect Filippo Brunelleschi who, like many masters of his era, was equally accomplished in both civil and military engineering. The military arena was widely regarded at this time as an acceptable platform on which the brilliant, inquiring, artistic minds of the Italian Renaissance could shine. Before Leonardo da Vinci's prototype tanks and multi-barrelled 'organ guns', the Quattrocento antecedent of the Gatling gun, other artistic minds were avidly applying themselves to military problems. Andrea Pisano and Orcagna had, for example, previously worked on the problem of strengthening Florence's defensive walls, whilst in their scholarly treatises Alberti and Filarete devoted as much time to military as to civil architecture. Brunelleschi himself nurtured a particular fascination for siege engines. Together with his artistic colleagues Michelozzo and the sculptor Donatello, Brunelleschi now decamped to Lucca to personally supervise the engineering works along the River Serchio.

The ingenious plan involved the deflection of the river waters onto the city using a clever system of hydraulics, effectively creating an artificial island out of Lucca. Whether this stratagem was intended to contribute to the invested city's isolation or to simply undermine the walls through inundation is not entirely clear. They perhaps hoped that the torrential floodwaters, once released, would serve to simply wash the defences away. Everything had initially gone to plan and the damned waters soon brimmed ready to do their worst. Unbeknown to the Florentines, however, the *Lucchesi* had secretly dug their own dike along the line of the meadows outside their city. One night they sallied out and silently cut a fresh channel from the River Serchio into the dike that they had created. Cleverly, this released torrents of water into the Florentines' own siege encampment, entirely washing it away and cutting it off from the city! This embarrassing fiasco became widely known in Florence as the 'Lucca Disaster'. Scrutinising Brunelleschi's blueprints some weeks earlier, Neri Capponi had foreseen that the plan would fail but had nevertheless been politely ignored. The diarist Giovanni Morelli later lamented how 'It was child's play, we lost time, money and works, there were forty thousand of us and we didn't conclude anything, but we lingered amidst the shame and damages'.

The public relations ramifications of this disaster were devastating. In Florence, the war went from being popular to being intensely disliked. Those who had initially supported the war now tried to distance themselves from it. As the man on the spot, Alamanno Salviati continued meanwhile to botch the prosecution of the war on every conceivable level. The *dieci* impotently complained that 'Every day the reputation of our office and of this undertaking is declining, and the murmuring and complaining of the citizens increases'. Tax burdens too had risen once more to unprecedented levels. A single collection of forced loans equivalent to thirty-six *catasti* was imposed in one fell swoop in 1431; intended to give the war council a viable military budget to work with, the massive exaction instead created outrage amongst the general public. Although on paper such forced loans were interest-bearing shares on Florence's Monte, and therefore continued in theory at least to be assets of the household, this was only the case for those who could afford to pay the *catasto* in full. For those who could not afford to pay, the *prestanze* became a true tax with no entitlement to any interest. Meanwhile, the ordinary taxpayer could see that the wealthier citizens such as the Strozzi and the Medici were tax exempt on certain expensive assets such as their *palazzi*.

Efforts to mollify popular discontent proved largely ineffective. In 1429, on the eve of war, Lorenzo Ridolfi had organised a great meeting of Florence's citizens during which they all took an oath to keep peace with each other upon the Book of the Gospels. This had been repeated again in 1430 to the same disappointing effect. Rinaldo together with his supporters now tried to salvage his own reputation by shifting the blame onto his former allies the Medici. What, may we conjecture, had been the reason for his change of heart? Cosimo had by now resigned from the *dieci*, having lost confidence in the war altogether. The reason he gave was that he wanted to 'let others have their turn' but his real motivation was to distance himself from a conflict which, he now saw with belated perspicacity, could never be won. Fortunately for the Medici they had not been directly involved in the disastrous prosecution of the war on the ground and, unlike the Albizzeschi, were left largely untainted by it.

Rinaldo degli Albizzi's resentment of his fair weather allies now festered. He was determined to punish them and used as his weapon of choice the pretext of the many secret societies which still flourished around this time, sodalities which the *signoria* regarded with distrust and suspicion. Rinaldo now publicly accused the Medici of having instigated the Lucca war with the intention of stirring up the city's factional squabbles. It was an unqualified accusation that was aggravated by Rinaldo's fondness for rhetoric and his ability to turn an effective metaphor to his favour. He now stood up and denounced the city's rampant factionalism as being a *morbum* ('disease') which 'needed a cure'. The corollary of this metaphor was clear, the Medici were the cancer which needed to be excised from the body politic.

The allegation was of course spurious, or at the very least pedestrian. The Medici created no more factionalism during this period than any other wealthy and influential Florentine family. Likewise, secret societies and confraternities were long acknowledged to be a normal part of Florence's political life. Typically, such societies operated quietly and unobtrusively. When their members were happy and content that they were gaining a fair share of the commune's wealth they participated in lubricating the political machinery of government by advancing favours and political positions. When, however, the *reggimento* was dysfunctional or exploitative, as it was during the period of the 1420s, the secret societies represented an extended network of friendships, ties and alliances that could help offset the imbalances of the day-to-day political system. They functioned essentially as a collegiate self-help network. Nonetheless, when such confraternities were debated in the *signoria* and the *pratiche* they were almost universally denounced as a subversive influence. Francesco Machiavelli had once condemned the societies as fomenting 'dissension, hatred and evil' and Cosimo de' Medici is unlikely to have publicly deviated from this party line.

A new *dieci* was elected in the summer of 1430 which now included the Peace faction members Niccolò da Uzzano, Palla Strozzi and Giovanni Guicciardini, the latter having been appointed as the latest commissioner to the

Florentine army. Few worse developments could have come to pass; da Uzzano now publicly undermined the whole expedition by presenting a divided front and lamenting the fact that Florence had gone to war with Lucca in the first place. Rinaldo meanwhile continued desperately to justify the war, proclaiming that those who had initiated it, meaning he himself, should not be held to blame by those who were currently prosecuting it so ineptly, meaning of course da Uzzano. His argument was not without merit. As for Cosimo, ever the pragmatic realist, he was by this time writing privately to his agents that he lacked any real conviction that the war could be won and would therefore 'rather be out of it altogether'. His risk-averse banker's mentality could only look askance at any venture which, seemingly promising at first had later acquired the taint of 'unprofitability'.

Meanwhile, what was already a fiasco of a war was now threatening to escalate beyond the confines of Lucca. As predicted by da Uzzano and the doves, their traditional enemy Siena had felt threatened by Florence's actions against Lucca and consequently the ten *priori* of that city were now making overtures to Paolo Guinigi. This was only exacerbated by the undiplomatic attitude of the Florentines themself. When the *Sienese* orator Antonio Petrucci was despatched to mediate between Florence and Lucca he was shocked to witness Florentine urchins openly proclaiming in the streets: 'Hail Mary, full of grace, once we conquer Lucca, we'll also conquer Siena!' Appalled at Florence's rampant jingoism he sent word to Siena to support the *Lucchesi* at all costs. The *Sienese* duly nominated a war committee and despatched troops to assist the besieged city. As the *Sienese* began probing Florence's outlying borders and infiltrating Pisa's countryside, so Genoa and Pope Martin V were also increasingly drawn to this growing anti-Florentine coalition. Although the papacy was a traditional ally of Lucca, the Pope had up till this time been too preoccupied with Milan to become involved in the local situation. The fact that Florence had given the Pope sanctuary in the immediate aftermath of his election cut little ice with the pontiff. Politicians like da Uzzano openly predicted that it would only be a matter of time before the Visconti duke of Milan entered the conflict once again.

The *dieci* summoned Cosimo de' Medici's brother Lorenzo to the *signoria* and despatched him with an ambassadorship to Milan in a pre-emptive effort to dissuade Filippo Maria from embroiling himself in Tuscany's affairs. This unfortunately had the same effect as baiting a bull with a red *gonfalon*. The opportunity to embarrass the Florentines was too good for the Duke to pass up and he seized the moment. Besides which, Milan could not afford for Lucca to fall into Florence's hands as the city had already been earmarked as the jumping off point for any future *Milanese* invasion of Tuscany. Filippo Maria was, nonetheless, still bound by the Treaty of Ferrara and could not act openly, therefore he employed subterfuge; first he pretended to discharge from his service the rising star Francesco Sforza. But it was all a masquerade; once the *condottiere* was a free agent the Duke commanded him privately to ride to Lucca with 3,000 horse where he concluded a hasty *condotta* worth 24,000 ducats with Lucca's Paolo Guinigi and Siena's Antonio Petrucci. This officially enabled him to come to Lucca's assistance. Upon arrival outside the walls of Lucca in July 1430, Sforza's forces drove the Florentine troops before them enabling the *condottiere* to enter the city in triumph.

By enlisting Sforza's aid, the unfortunate Guinigi had however reaped the whirlwind. The two men quickly fell out over operational matters and Sforza temporarily removed himself from Lucca and decamped to the vicinity of the Serchio River, where he entered into negotiations with Florence to hand the city over to them. By this time, both Niccolò Fortebraccio and Bernardino Ubaldini had been replaced by the *signoria* with the experienced *condottiere* Guidantonio da Montefeltro, Count of Urbino. Although he felt it beneath his honour to offer Lucca up to Florence on a silver platter, Sforza nevertheless succeeded in wringing a payment of 55,000 florins from Florence, in return for which he would support a popular uprising inside Lucca which would depose Paolo Guinigi and his son Ladislao. This was duly engineered under the auspices of two *Lucchese* dissidents named Pietro Cennami and Giovanni da Chivizano who went to Guinigi's *castelli* with forty armed men and captured him. Paolo's son Ladislao was, meanwhile, already safely quartered with Sforza himself at the Serchio River encampment. Guinigi's palace was looted and a further 60,000 ducats pilfered, following which Sforza withdrew and allowed the Florentine troops to regroup beneath the city walls once more. The former *signore* and his unfortunate son were despatched by Sforza to Milan where they would ultimately perish in the duke of Milan's dungeons. In Lucca, meanwhile, a republic was declared in their place.

The expensive and unnecessary deal with Francesco Sforza led to public outrage back in Florence; as Cosimo de' Medici wryly observed, the plague which was raging in Lucca at that time would surely have achieved the same result for free. Besides, after all was said and done, Lucca still remained in the hands of the republican *Lucchesi* rebels despite the fact that money had changed hands. To the Florentines' disgust, everything which Francesco Sforza had done whilst at Lucca was revealed to be little more than a sop to his own high-falooting sense of honour. As Cosimo complained in a letter to his cousin Averardo on 21 October 1430, 'The affairs of Lucca do not appear to turn out as we expected, which displeases me; and the money spent on Count Francesco [Sforza] was thrown away. Everyone laughs at us because he could not remain on account of the plague, and only consumed the provisions of the people.' Guidantonio da Montefeltro was now ordered to resume the siege which Sforza had prematurely abandoned.

Worse was still to come, however, for the butcher's son Niccolò Piccinino was now sent by Duke Filippo Maria to resume the conflict with Florence on Lucca's side. Once again, this had been done under the cover story that the captain had been dismissed from Visconti's service and was a free and independent agent. Piccinino was given a *condotta* by Genoa which–at Visconti's instigation–had recently signed a defence pact with Lucca. In December 1430, the Florentines under Guidantonio da Montefeltro attempted to halt Piccinino's advance towards Lucca at the banks of the River Serchio but were utterly defeated. The Florentine war commissioner Giovanni Guicciardini managed to escape with a few of his men to Pisa but was immediately held up to stinging scrutiny back in Florence; many now accused him of having accepted bribes not to conclude the war after the paying off of Francesco Sforza. That same month Cosimo lamented to Averardo de' Medici: 'We certainly seem to have shown but little prudence; we will talk of this when we meet. Our people ought to hear what is said of us and how little we are esteemed; if we go on thus we shall be treated like Jews.'

Piccinino meanwhile retired inside Lucca for the winter and looked set to threaten Pisa, the jewel in Florence's Tuscan crown, whilst most of Pisa's possessions in the *contado* were now snapped up by forces loyal to Lucca. As if this was not bad enough Duke Filippo Maria now also drew Lucca, Genoa, Siena and Piombino into his own defensive league against Florence and appointed Piccinino as the alliance's commander-in-chief. Fortunately however for Florence, on 20 February 1431 Pope Martin V died and was replaced by the Venetian Gabriele Condulmer who became Pope Eugenius IV. With a Venetian on the Chair of St. Peter, the Venetian Republic felt confident enough to once more declare war on Milan and so Filippo Maria had little choice but to recall both Piccinino and Sforza (who were both officially 'rehired' by the Duke) in order to meet the imminent threat from Venice. The old battle lines had been redrawn and Florence and Venice found themselves back once more, shoulder to shoulder in alliance against Milan.

Milan won a series of swift, early victories over the revivified League. The count of Carmagnola (who, true to form, had renegotiated a cripplingly expensive new *condotta* with his employer Venice) was defeated by Francesco Sforza at the Battle of Soncino on 17 May 1431. The Venetians had offered Carmagnola ever more enticing emoluments in a bid to retain his loyalty and increase his motivation. In August 1430 the senate had even promised him the dukedom of Milan provided that he capture the duchy and end the war as soon as possible, but still he prevaricated. At Soncino he had allowed himself to be surrounded by the enemy forces; before that at Lodi he had neglected to capture an undefended town when he had shown up on the battlefield too late. The Doge and the senate of Venice were livid. Worse was to follow however. When, in June 1431, the Venetians sent a fleet of eighty-five river galleys under the admiralship of Niccolò Trevisani to support Carmagnola's army at Cremona it was intercepted by a superior *Milanese* fleet and defeated with the loss of twenty-eight of Venice's best vessels.

While Carmagnola was proving himself to be the expensive white elephant that he by now unquestionably was, Milan's *condottiere* Luigi Colonna was defeating the Venetians at Cremona and Piccinino was entrenching himself in Tuscany. On the broader front, to the west, Filippo Maria's father-in-law, Amadeus VIII of Savoy, agreed to align himself with Milan in exchange for *Milanese* help against Amadeus's rival John Jacob Palaeologus of Montferrat, who was at that moment being engaged successfully by Milan's *condottiere* Cristoforo Lavello. Not to be outdone, the Emperor Sigismund meanwhile marched across the Alps with his own army, intending to receive his Imperial Crown in addition to the crown of Italy. The Emperor's presence now only served to bolster Milan's efforts. Venice managed to turn the tide when it defeated a *Genovese* fleet at San Fruttuoso on 27 August 1431; however on land Carmagnola continued to prosecute Venice's offensive with undue caution whilst continuing to entertain envoys from Filippo Maria. It was no particular secret that the latter was promising his former supreme commander treasure and emoluments if only he returned to *Milanese* service.

A deeply flawed and tragic figure, Carmagnola seems to have been under the misapprehension that he could flirt with both sides indefinitely, acting as the power broker or kingmaker of Lombardy's affairs. However he had reckoned without the ruthlessness of the Most Serene Republic. Managing to evade censure for his latest failures at Lodi, Soncino and Cremona, in part at least by making Niccolò Trevisani a scapegoat, Carmagnola was commanded to renew the offensive against both Soncino and Cremona even if he had to campaign all through the winter. In October, in express contravention of Venice's instructions, he was in the process of moving the first units of his army into winter quarters when he entirely missed an opportunity to retake the town of Cremona. This failure was the final straw for the Venetian senate, which now secretly began to plan how they could rid themselves of this inept commander who in the words of one Venetian functionary was no more than a source of 'perpetual anxiety and expense'. Recalled to Venice in March 1432, ostensibly for the purpose of discussing future military strategy, he complied unsuspectingly and was received with all due honour and much festivity. But when the last cup of wine had been drained in his honour, Carmagnola was promptly arrested, arraigned and condemned on charges of treason. The hapless count of Carmagnola ended his career by being beheaded between two stone columns on the Molo, the paved dock in front of the Ducal Palace, on 5 May 1432.

One month after Venice had executed its most gifted though duplicitous general, the Florentines and *Sienese* locked horns at the Battle of San Romano on 1 June 1432. Florence had purchased the services of the *condottiere* Micheletto Attendolo da Cotignola and another capable mercenary leader, Niccolò Mauruzzi da Tolentino, had been found to replace Bernardino Ubaldini who had deserted Florence and gone over to the *Sienese*. Tolentino had advanced alone with his forces to the village of San Romano to observe the enemy and gain intelligence on their numbers but, having done so and despite being clearly outnumbered, he decided to mount an impromptu attack on the *Sienese* troops known as the *ducheschi*. For seven to eight hours Tolentino's men mounted a series of heavy cavalry charges against the *Sienese* and their *Milanese* allies commanded by Bernardino della Ciarda and Niccolò Piccinino's adoptive son, Francesco Piccinino. Tolentino's lack of numbers and the enemy's preponderance of crossbowmen began to tell on the *condottiere's* mounted troops, however, and he was only saved by the timely arrival of Cotignola and his reinforcements. Although the *Sienese* and *Milanesi* took flight the Florentine mercenaries were too exhausted to give chase and deliver the coup de grâce. In the event, both sides therefore claimed victory.

Back home the wealthy Florentine wool magnate and politician Giovanni di Paolo Rucellai publicly proclaimed San Romano as a triumph of Florence's republican ideals. More importantly, Cosimo de' Medici turned what was in effect Florence's sole military success in an otherwise mediocre campaign to his advantage, making capital from the fact that it was only his personal friendship with the *condottiere* Tolentino, the hero of the hour, that had succeeded in getting him involved in the war on Florence's side. But the victory at San Romano proved merely an interlude in Florence's and the League's ailing military fortunes. Later that same year Niccolò Piccinino inflicted yet another crushing defeat on the League in November 1432 at the Battle of Delebio. Now, as had happened twice before, both sides found that they had fought themselves to a standstill and consequently a general peace was reached at Ferrara in May 1433. Palla Strozzi was despatched there to oversee negotiations between Milan, Venice and Florence and later stood signatory to the peace on behalf of Florence.

The treaty restored the status quo and Florence, Milan, Lucca and Siena all returned conquests which had been made at each other's expense. Once again,

Florence had essentially gained nothing new from her misguided adventurism and there were no fresh territorial acquisitions from which to defray the ruinous cost of the war. Rinaldo degli Albizzi had meanwhile been side-lined in Siena as ambassador to treat for peace with the Emperor Sigismund acting as mediator. Cosimo de' Medici had likewise been despatched to Padua. Politically speaking the Florentine republic, though at last thankfully at peace, was by now hopelessly divided against itself. The simmering personal resentments of the various key members of the ruling oligarchy had come into stark contrast over the mishandling of the war against Lucca. But these antipathies, which required public catharsis, had yet to play out in any meaningful or satisfying resolution.

Although the heat had been removed from Florence for now, the republic was left in a pitiful and shambolic condition and lacked all confidence in itself. Predictably, Rinaldo degli Albizzi still upheld the flimsy reasons justifying the war and was supported publicly by Cosimo's cousin Averardo de' Medici. But the *dieci* and the war commissioners were now hopelessly riven by disagreement and bitter mutual recrimination. Unable to evade his accusers any longer, the disgraced war commissioner Giovanni Guicciardini was made to stand trial for misconduct. This was certainly a fillip to the Medici for Messer Giovanni was closely linked with the anti-Medicean elements within Florence at this time, although his brother Piero Guicciardini was also a passionate supporter of the Medici. Rinaldo degli Albizzi's chief opponent, Neri Capponi, had already been ordered by the *signoria* to remain at least twenty miles from Florence for a period of ten years. This had been decreed on 28 March 1432 under the *Lex contra Scandalosos* but, as with all convictions under these cumbersome 'scandal laws', the charges had been frivolous at best and Capponi's banishment was only temporary. The next *signoria* to hold office was friendly to his cause and promptly recalled him to Florence. While the republic was doing her internal governmental housecleaning, the elder statesman Niccolò da Uzzano carped that some dignitaries had been elevated higher than their natural talents warranted and that this was the source of all their woes.

Public finances were in complete disarray. For some time, the wealthiest members of Florentine society had, as we have seen, financed the commune's war effort through high interest loans. A situation eventually arose, however, in which nobody would lend the republic any further funds except for the Medici Bank. It has even been suggested that Cosimo de' Medici diverted the profits from the Medici Bank's branches in Rome, Venice, Geneva and elsewhere so that they could be reinvested in the form of huge loans to the commune. Despite his services to Florence, Cosimo would nevertheless soon become the lens of the oligarchy's misguided wrath over the disastrous prosecution of the Lucca war. Giovanni di Bicci had said 'keep out of the public eye' but for a growing family concern like the Medici this was by now practically impossible. The *catasto* register revealed the extent of the family's wealth: two wool-finishing factories within the city, a silk factory, villas at Careggi, Trebbio and Cafaggiolo, and a good deal of agricultural land in addition to the flourishing Medici Bank. They were by this time too high profile to take a back seat in local politics.

The House of Medici was also at this time forming highly visible alliances with other, much older grandee families. The Medici bank was managed by paid-up partners from both the Bardi and the Portinari families. Such alliances were more than just inter-family business for in effect they constituted a political faction. This was in spite of the fact that founding a political party was at this time defined as treason and punishable by death or banishment. Meanwhile, the Florentines were making puns based on the meaning of the name Medici, meaning doctor or healer. Many now joked that, far from being Florence's 'disease', the Medici were the potential 'healers of Florence's problems'. As far as many observers could tell it was only Medici ducats that were keeping the republic afloat. With such vast wealth as the Medici commanded what problems could not be 'cured' provided the Medici were given a greater share in government decision-making? Rinaldo degli Albizzi looked on with repugnance. Despite his illustrious background and the great reputation of his father, Rinaldo had failed to even gain a seat on the war committee. Florence had not given him his due and his resentment burned bright; how could the Medici *not* be his natural enemies?

CHAPTER 4

Cosimo in the Alberghettino

On September ... 1433 our grandfather Cosimo was imprisoned in the
Palace, and in danger of losing his head. On September 9th he was
banished to Padua, together with his brother Lorenzo, a sentence
confirmed by the Balia of 1433 on the 11th, and on the 16th December
he was permitted to reside anywhere in the Venetian territory, but not
nearer to Florence than Padua.

The *Ricordi* of Lorenzo de' Medici

Born on 27 September 1389, Cosimo di Giovanni de' Medici was educated
together with his younger brother Lorenzo at the monastery school of
Santa Maria degli Angeli. The monastery belonged to the Camaldolese
congregation, a reformed branch of the Benedictine Order which was founded in
1012 by the hermit Saint Romuald at Camaldoli, near Arezzo. A Camaldolese
church was first established in Florence in 1294 and quickly gained favour and
funding from the city's élite, the Albizzi family being their main source of
finance during the fourteenth-century. However the church complex was sacked
in 1378 during the rebellion of the *ciompi*, who regarded Santa Maria degli
Angeli as unacceptably patrician-funded.

During Cosimo's childhood, under such scholars as Ambrogio Traversari,
the monastery had already acquired a reputation for being a centre for the new
learning which sought–after centuries of barbarism and stultifying
scholasticism–to rediscover the cultural and intellectual brilliance of classical
Greece and Rome. Here, alongside the scions of other wealthy Florentine
families, the two Medici brothers learned German, French and Latin as well as a
smattering of Hebrew and Greek. Cosimo–as would become apparent in his later
pursuits–was especially diligent in his studies of the classical world and as an
adult he would have been able to look with pride upon his father's
commissioning of Florence's first neo-classical revivalist building, the Ospedale
degli Innocenti or foundling hospital. Giovanni di Bicci had been a strong
formative influence on the young Cosimo and indeed, professionally speaking,
he was to remain in Giovanni's shadow for much of his adult working life.

Later, Giovanni procured for his two sons an exceptionally gifted tutor who
would further develop the young Cosimo's interests in the mysteries and
wonders of antiquity. This was none other than Roberto de' Rossi, a wealthy
Florentine bachelor who shunned public life and instead retired to his home in
the Oltrarno district of Florence to read and study the ancients. The first local
pupil of Manuel Chrysoloras, who is credited with bringing the study of Greek
from Constantinople to Italy, de' Rossi was the first man in Florence to be able

to read ancient Greek, which had not been studied in Italy for seven hundred years. His translations of Aristotle and other classical Greek writers brought them to the attention of a wide Latin-speaking public. These early experiences under de' Rossi ignited in Cosimo a lifelong interest in classical manuscripts, which he began to avidly collect, spurred on by his admiration for such humanists as Niccolò de' Niccoli, an obsessive Florentine scholar who had spent his entire family fortune on amassing Florence's largest library of over eight hundred classical volumes. It was Cosimo's devotion to humanist study that would later lead Pope Pius II, himself the son of a common soldier, to grudgingly admit that Cosimo was 'more lettered than merchants are wont to be'. When Niccolò de' Niccoli bankrupted himself with his ceaseless purchases of rare books, Cosimo opened an unlimited line of credit for him at his bank on condition that he be permitted to dispose of the scholar's celebrated book collection after his death.

Of Cosimo's enduring love of classical antiquity and the arts we shall learn more in due course. But for now, as the oldest son, he was needed in the family business and was duly inducted into the Medici Bank's Florence branch where his more practical education in high finance now commenced. He would have been just twenty-five when he was packed off by Giovanni to attend on the former pirate and antipope John XXIII at the Council of Constance in 1414. The sixteenth-century historian Scipione Ammirato describes the young Cosimo physically as being 'of middle height, with an olive complexion, and of imposing presence'. The youth had already begun to exhibit the same conservative disposition as his father. Throughout his entire life Cosimo abjured gambling, preferring instead a thoughtful game of chess. The cautious Giovanni would not have entrusted his son with such an important assignment had he not believed him both responsible and equal to the challenge; as we have seen, the papal assignment would in an important sense prove to be Cosimo's professional baptism of fire. Baldassare Cossa had first called upon Cosimo to authorise lines of credit while they were in residence at Constance, something that–given the Pope's expensive and indulgent proclivities–would have required some forbearance on Cosimo's part. Later, abandoned in Germany by the deposed runaway pontiff and in possession of an extremely valuable jewel-encrusted papal mitre, Cosimo had hastened back to Florence leaving it to Giovanni to assuage the anger of Pope Martin V, who was now calling loudly for the papal treasure to be restored.

Cosimo discharged his early political duties in 1415 and 1417 by serving as a member of the *signoria* and would have been in the city to witness the antipope John XXIII's return and eventual death the following year. It is interesting to speculate on the reunion that the two men must have had and one is tempted to imagine Cossa nonchalantly slapping his former Medici protégé heartily on the shoulder with a roguish twinkle in his eye as if to say, 'Well boy, I *almost* escaped that time!' Around this time Cosimo was sent by his father Giovanni on an extended educational and business tour of Europe which took in several far-flung regions of Europe including Germany, Flanders and France where the Medici Bank had representatives. It was around 1416 that Medici Bank sole agents were established in Bruges in Flanders as well as in London and this may have been Cosimo's doing while he was in situ. Bruges at this time was extremely important to the commercial life of Europe being a centre of the wool trade with links to England, southern Europe and the powerful cities of the Hanseatic League which dominated the Baltic Sea trade.

We can be confident too that Cosimo was also using his travels to acquire rare books and manuscripts from antiquarian dealers and monasteries, an enduring hobby that had not left him since his studious days in thrall to the likes of Roberto de' Rossi and the eccentric literary hermit Niccolò de' Niccoli.

Giovanni di Bicci's business partners Benedetto and Ilarione di Lippaccio de' Bardi, had an unattached cousin by the name of Contessina de' Bardi, whose name meant literally 'little countess'. The Bardi family fortunes had suffered dreadfully at the hands of their royal clientele like England's King Edward III and had never really recovered. Worse still, the rival Acciaiuoli family had colluded in many of their business misfortunes and had certainly benefited from the family's business downfall. Under these circumstances it was quite fortunate that the Bardi were able to partner with the Medici Bank albeit as junior shareholders. However in Renaissance Italy, as indeed elsewhere, 'old money' always trumped 'nouveau riches' in the social stakes. The Bardi still held tremendous reserves of social caché in snobbish Florentine circles. It was therefore advantageous for the Medici and the Bardi to seal their relationship through a marriage alliance. The Bardi would benefit in a commercial sense and the Medici would gain social advantage from the ancient Bardi family name.

Sometime around 1415, the exact date has not been recorded for posterity, Cosimo de' Medici and Contessina de' Bardi were joined in matrimony. Cosimo himself was around twenty-six years old at this time and his bride no more than about fifteen or sixteen. It was common in Renaissance Florence for husbands to be at least ten years older than their spouse. Contessina was not an especially educated girl (we cannot yet call her a *woman*), but she was a Florentine aristocrat. What's more, since the collapse of the Bardi Bank in the 1340s the Bardi had eked out a living as landowners and occasionally too as *condottieri*. Their speciality in the arts of war might stand the Medici in good stead in years to come if a show of military muscle was called for to shore up their position in the political arena. Cosimo's relationship with the loyal *condottiere* Niccolò da Tolentino had already proven politically advantageous. The relatively poor Bardi could not bring an especially large dowry to the table so instead Contessina conveyed to the marriage a dilapidated family property, the Palazzo Bardi, where the newly married couple now went to live near the banks of the River Arno. The *palazzo* was situated on the Oltrarno along the Via de' Bardi, a street which the once affluent Bardi family had previously redeveloped and which had formerly been a notorious slum known as the Borgo Pigiglioso ('the Fleapit'). Cosimo busied himself with the renovation of the Palazzo Bardi, which he decorated liberally with the by-now famous Medici *palle*.

Contessina was known throughout her life as being a sensible person who was careful with money and with the management of the household almost to the point of parsimoniousness; she was also a tender and loving mother to their children as well as offering a stable anchoring point for her more intellectual and ethereally-minded husband. Her letters to Cosimo reveal that mixture of comfortable chattiness in which household matters are casually combined with family news and gossip: 'This evening I have a letter from thee and have understood how much we are to pay for the barrels at Careggi; as soon as they arrive I will do as thou sayest', writes Contessina to her husband who is away in Ferrara on business. 'I have a letter from Antonio Martelli saying that he is sending nine bales of our linen cloth, which were at home, by now I think they must have arrived, give orders that they be put in a dry place so that the linen be not spoiled', and she goes on to add that 'Ginevra and Pierfrancesco are in the Val d'Arno and Amerigo Cavalcanti is with them. They are all well.' Finally, Contessina follows up with a little postscript: 'Matteo gave me the little keys, if thou hast need of them tell me. Thy mother who put that Santelena into the bag with the others thou hadst from here is much surprised that thou hast not found it, she remembers to a certainty putting it into the bag the first thing after thy departure.'

Cosimo's brother Lorenzo the Elder would meanwhile also marry into another 'old money' family, the Cavalcanti. One year after his older brother's marriage he would wed Ginevra Cavalcanti who was also able to boast aristocratic Malespini blood on her mother's side of the family. The Venetian Francesco Barbaro presented Lorenzo and Ginevra with a wedding gift, a slightly pompous treatise entitled *De re uxoria* which he had written concerning wifely duties. Completed in just three weeks, the treatise offered the Medici bride helpful advice in a number of different areas. 'Noble women should always try to feed their own offspring so that they will not degenerate from being fed on poorer, foreign milk', advised one of its chapters solicitously. 'But if, as often happens, mothers cannot for compelling reasons suckle their own children, they ought to place them with good nurses, not with slaves, strangers, or drunken and unchaste women. They ought to give their infants to the care of those who are freeborn, well mannered, and especially those endowed with dignified speech.' Both marriages were considered good matches and the union of the three houses served to bring this parvenu family from the Mugello considerable social standing within Florence.

Between 1416 and 1421 Contessina would give birth to two sons – Piero followed a few years later by Giovanni. However, not long after the couple's marriage, Giovanni di Bicci reassigned his son Cosimo to look after the Medici Bank's all-important Rome branch and he left Contessina alone in Florence to raise their family whilst he attended to business there. At this time in Rome the Spini family were still the Pope's preferred bankers and so Cosimo was unable to make capital from the previously lucrative Court of Rome branch of the Medici Bank. Nevertheless Rome was still by far and away the bank's most profitable branch, contributing perhaps more than half of the bank's total revenues. Despite his hard work and long hours at the bank, Cosimo still found time for some 'extra-curricular' activities.

It was in Rome that Cosimo fathered an illegitimate son by a Circassian slave girl named Maddalena. Most female slaves came from Caffa, a frontier slaver town in the Crimea, and in terms of their racial origins were usually Circassian, Tartar, Turkish, Armenian or Georgian, or else Arab, Russian or Greek. From the busy slave markets of Caffa the girls were shipped to either Genoa or Venice, where slaving had existed as a thriving industry since the eighth-century. Here, in Venice, Maddalena had been purchased by one of Cosimo's agents to take care of the banker's Roman household. In addition to their household duties, slaves and servants of either sex often ministered to the 'needs' of the master of the house and this girl, so Cosimo had been assured by the agent, was 'a sound virgin, free from disease and aged about twenty-one'. He named the mixed-race child which she bore him Carlo and he would turn out to be a quiet, bookish man similar to his natural father.

Such illicit relationships, even in the case of married men, were fairly common in Italy at the time and were a frequent topic for long and censorious

Church sermons and moralising harangues from the pulpit. Slaves purchased from abroad were still regarded as chattels, even in Christian regions like Italy. But poor local females often fared little better. Young Italian girls from poorer families who could not afford a dowry were often placed in brothels, consigned to the more lower class nunneries, or else pushed into domestic service where they were frequently exposed to sexual abuse. Few were prepared to champion the case of these poor girls although there was the occasional enlightened exception. Bernardine of Siena (1380-1444) had preached in more concrete terms against the moral turpitude of the age than most of his contemporaries. He instructed mothers to bring their daughters to church so that he could instruct them about the commonplace fact of sexual abuse within marriage. In his sermons he spoke out about allowing girls from impoverished backgrounds to slip through society's cracks, whereupon they became 'the scum and vomit of the world'. Then again, we are speaking of a time when women's rights were bad enough outside of marriage and perhaps even worse within the marital state. It was a chauvinistic era during which the short story writer Franco Sacchetti (1332-1400) could matter-of-factly opine in *Il Trecentonovelle* that 'both good women and bad women alike need to be beaten'.

This notwithstanding, no merchant who fathered a bastard child as Cosimo de' Medici had done would find it an undue impediment and it carried little in the way of social stigma. The nobility were notorious for fathering illegitimate children who often went on to inherit. Indeed, in what must surely seem a refreshingly enlightened practise for such pious times, in many cases legitimate and illegitimate children were raised together beneath the same roof. This was the case with young Carlo himself, who was acknowledged and brought back to Florence at the end of Cosimo's stint in Rome along with his mother, who was put to work in the Palazzo Medici and who, according to Medici household records, was still working in service to the household as late as 1457 at the ripe old age of forty. Carlo de' Medici would eventually enter the Church, rising to become Rector of Prato and Protonotary Apostolic. The single concession which Cosimo made to family propriety was that the illegitimate boy was not given one of the customary generational Medici names, such as 'Lorenzo' or 'Giovanni' or 'Averardo'. Contessina de' Medici's reaction to Carlo's patrimony, or her husband's unapologetic philandering, is left conveniently unrecorded; we can only wonder at her personal feelings towards the new addition to their household.

Around 1420 Giovanni di Bicci had, as we have seen, handed over the running of the family business to his two sons Cosimo and Lorenzo, the former having all-round seniority. Cosimo was already entering his thirties by this time and his father was about to be elected *gonfaloniere* in 1421, the first time that a Medici had been honoured with this position since the ill-fated Salvestro de' Medici had sided with the *ciompi*. The recent collapse of the Spini Bank had meanwhile allowed Cosimo to lobby Pope Martin V for the transferral of the Court of Rome's business back to the Medici. His time in Rome had been well spent and he had cultivated numerous high level contacts in the city that were close to the Curia as well as the Holy Father himself. His tactful overtures now bore fruit. Papal business was duly resumed and the Medici strongboxes groaned appreciatively once more from the inflow of Church florins and ducats. During the 1420s, with business back on an even keel, Cosimo increasingly delegated the day-to-day running of the bank to his younger brother Lorenzo while he started taking a more prominent role in the city's political life; although still relatively low key at this time, Cosimo would be supported in this by his cousin Averardo de' Medici.

By the time that Giovanni di Bicci died in 1429, Cosimo had effectively already been in the driving seat of the family business for nine years. His father had still continued to show his face at the bank's Florence head office and was naturally deferred to on any important decisions, but other than that Cosimo was given latitude to run the bank as he saw fit. According to the *ricordi* of Lorenzo the Magnificent, Giovanni left behind an estate worth close to 180,000 florins. He had refused to write a last will and testament because, due to Church laws at this time, this could well have opened him up to accusations of usury, which would have had damaging legal ramifications for his descendants. Upon his father's death Cosimo was now unquestionably recognised as the *capo della casa Medici* or the 'head of the house of Medici'.

Florence's opportunistic war with Lucca was rapidly turning sour. Francesco Sforza had been bought off at enormous and largely unnecessary expense and had departed from Lucca leaving the Florentines no nearer their goal than before. To fund the war the Florentines were being bled dry by *prestanze* and the heavy taxation was starting to impede Florence's civic growth and development. For example, in 1434 Filippo Brunelleschi was commissioned by Matteo and Andrea Scolari (the heirs of Pippo Spano, the *condottiere* who had let slip John XXIII at the Council of Constance) to design a new church for Cosimo's old school, the monastery of Santa Maria degli Angeli. Brunelleschi's design, probably inspired by ancient Roman temples, consisted of an elegant domed octagon with eight radiating chapels and a sixteen-sided exterior. Sadly, the funds which had been set aside for this innovative project were appropriated by the *signoria* to fund the war with Lucca instead and building work on the chapel had been discontinued. It would not be recommenced until the 1920s when Brunelleschi's original structure was finally completed and named the Rotonda degli Scolari, presumably after the two noblemen who had commissioned it a mere 495 years before.

By the autumn of 1430, Cosimo's reaction to the on-going farce beneath the walls of Lucca was to finally withdraw what little personal support he still had for the war. Resigning from the *dieci* of war on the flimsy grounds of wanting 'to let others have their turn', and also 'partly because, on account of party divisions, I do not think the affairs of our city can prosper', Cosimo physically distanced himself from the on-going political recriminations by visiting the city of Verona. Cosimo was by no means isolated at this time for he drew around him a coterie of men with shared political interests and objectives. These included of course his cunning and ambitious cousin Averardo whose innate cruelty served Cosimo well as the Medici's tip-of-the-spear. There was also Martino Martini, who had been Giovanni di Bicci's trusted confederate, as well as Puccio Pucci, a member of the *arte minori* who had distinguished himself over the years for his craftiness and sagacity. The Pucci in particular were to prove loyal friends of the Medici. They were an illustrious old *ottimati* family which had produced a total of twenty-three *priori* and eight *gonfaloniere*. Others too flocked to the Medici faction including Averardo de' Medici's son-in-law Alamanno Salviati, Agnolo Acciaiuoli, Dietisalvi Neroni and Luca Pitti, all of whom were greatly discouraged by Rinaldo degli Albizzi's growing tendency towards megalomania.

These men were effectively walking a tightrope. On the one hand Florentine humanism deplored all forms of despotism, tyranny and monarchy. Citizens who participated in the political process needed to be careful not to be seen to be elevating themselves above the rest of the commune, as the Albizzeschi had come close to doing. But on the other hand populists such as the Medici still needed to resist the temptation to fall prey to the will of the mob, a phenomenon which was even more hated and despised than despotism itself. As Florence's chancellor Leonardo Bruni put it in his official history of Florence, the commune should avoid well-meaning but ill-advised political reforms which made 'poor guildsmen and men of base condition the rulers of the city'. Above all, the enlightened burghers of a republic should not pander to the 'stupidity of the aroused multitude. For there was no end or order to the unleashed appetites of the poor and the criminals, who, once armed, lusted after the possessions of rich and honourable men, and who thought of nothing except robbing, killing and exiling citizens.' Another commentator, Giovanni di Pagolo Morelli, did not mince his words when he stated in his *ricordi*: 'If a poor man sees that you have grain to sell and that you are holding on to it in order to increase its price, he will damn and curse and rob you and burn your house, if he has the power to do so, and he will make you hated by the entire lower class, which is a most dangerous thing. May God preserve our city from their rule.'

Rinaldo degli Albizzi may have been a tyrant-in-the-making but this hardly altered the fact that just about everyone else in Florence–regardless of whether they were supporters of the Medici or of the oligarchs like the Albizzeschi–was, according to Florentine custom, an inveterate gossipmonger. As the wars dragged on to their unsatisfactory conclusion, bringing low some of the most prominent men of the time, focus now inevitably shifted to the alleged role of Cosimo de' Medici and his faction in all of this. Cosimo had unquestionably started out in favour of the war with Lucca, if only for the reason that war aligned with the desires of the common masses. Averardo de' Medici came under particular scrutiny and it was put about that Averardo had been instrumental in getting Neri Capponi assigned to Lucca. This, it was widely suggested, had been done with the express intention of creating strife between Neri Capponi and Rinaldo degli Albizzi, thus sabotaging the smooth prosecution of the war. Cosimo was not regarded as being the architect of this policy per se but even so people still complained that on a personal level he had apparently done little to reduce the tensions between the two rival war commissioners.

Blaming the Medici for the deep-seated personal rivalries of two of the most influential men in Florence must, from our viewpoint, seem grossly unfair. But it should be understood that rumours and speculation had as much political currency in the fifteenth-century as they do today. Gossip and hearsay, when given enough traction, had the tendency to acquire the brute force of fact. Political discontent requires a safety valve and scapegoats have always been a political fact of life in all societies down through history. Thus, rightly or wrongly, and regardless of the strength of the actual evidence against them, many Florentines now grumbled–without perhaps even understanding the finer arguments behind the allegations–that Cosimo de' Medici and his family were the source of all their ills. Rinaldo degli Albizzi, still anxious to deflect public censure away from his personal shortcomings at Lucca, further inflamed the situation with slanderous talk of his own. Soon, anti-Medici feeling in Florence had worryingly escalated into petitions and calls to action against the family.

Shortly before his death in 1431, a deputation of concerned Florentines from all walks of life called upon Niccolò da Uzzano at his *palazzo* in the Via de' Bardi to seek his opinion on what should be done about Cosimo de' Medici. Niccolò da Uzzano's family was not one of the oldest or most well-established in Florence, although his wealth was admittedly great. Mostly, he drew his political influence from the high esteem in which he was almost universally held. A man of great cultivation and Ciceronian integrity, he was essentially a sensible, conservative politician; an elder statesman of age, rank and wisdom who was able to transcend the petty squabbles of the commune. Niccolò da Uzzano kept his distance from the Medici. He and the rising superstar banker Cosimo de' Medici had somewhat different temperaments which are revealed in one particularly telling anecdote. A minor disagreement had arisen between the two over the practice of young men during carnival time to block the city streets and extort an entry charge from the general public. As the author of the *Pseudo-Burlamacchi* later described the dodge, the lads 'would take a long beam of wood and they used it to stop people, and especially young women and they would not let them pass unless they gave them money, which they then spent on their wanton desire and vain pleasures'. Cosimo had been the stickler who was in favour of eliminating such practices and establishing the stern rule of law. By contrast, da Uzzano had advocated toleration. Such practices, though illegal, allowed the young men to let off some of their pent-up steam. Although Cosimo is seen as upholding the letter of the law in this case, in his more mature awareness of human nature Niccolò da Uzzano is seen to embody the truer wisdom.

When those who expressed unhappiness with the Medici came to visit him at his house da Uzzano, sagacious as always, gave them his ear but remained largely noncommittal. The elder statesman waited until they had finished and then offered them his own opinion. In seeking the proscription of the Medici were they, he asked, willing to trade this for greater empowerment on the part of the Albizzeschi? Removing the counterweight of the Medici would almost certainly unleash an even greater potential tyrant in the form of Rinaldo degli Albizzi. Niccolò da Uzzano had himself been on the receiving end of unremitting Albizzeschi political assaults. Rinaldo had the makings of another Filippo Maria Visconti; the man was a natural autocrat - haughty, strait-laced and eager to dominate others whilst claiming credit for everything. He had already threatened to halve the number of Florence's lesser guilds to safeguard his own ascendancy and it was but a short step from here to positioning himself as Florence's despot.

This had happened in too many Italian communes to mention; a strong man inveigled his way into a position of power and soon afterwards the historical rights of the people had been despoiled. Niccolò da Uzzano posed the question: did the honourable citizens truly desire the arbitrary rule of one man, an unhappy situation which their neighbours the *Milanesi* were forced to endure? Besides, da Uzzano was quick to point out, if it came down to a political dog fight there was no certainty that the Albizzeschi would prevail against the Medici. The latter were, on the one hand, beloved by the *popolo minuto* and, on the other, they were aligned through business and marriage ties with some of Florence's most celebrated and revered families like the Bardi, the Tornabuoni, the Portinari, the Malespini and the Calvalcanti. Many of Cosimo's humanist associates also came from old, established families and would almost certainly rush to lend their weight to their friend in any political crisis. Niccolò da

Uzzano's wise counsel managed to keep the peace for a year or so but soon the elderly leader of Florence's Guelph party lay dead.

In the Bargello today is a polychrome terracotta bust of Niccolò da Uzzano, who is portrayed in the lively and animated guise of a Roman republican senator. Attributed to Donatello and dating to 1432, the year after his death, the bust imbues da Uzzano with the expected civic *dignitas* and *gravitas* of a Florentine statesman, but there is much in the depiction which is nevertheless rather approachable. The artist has moreover presented us with a lifelike and truthful representation of the man as he was in real life, from the close-cropped hair and the wrinkles in the skin to the distinctive wart near his mouth. The statesman's wisdom and innate humanism helped stem some of the worst excesses of Florentine politics during this period and his natural sense of restraint was in harmony with Cosimo's own tendency to shy away from more extremist stances or the overt show of force. Niccolò da Uzzano's departure from the political scene and his removal as a kind of buffer or insulator between the two antagonistic factions could only result in a drastically polarised and divided Florence. Rinaldo degli Albizzi would increasingly regard Cosimo de' Medici as the last remaining barrier between him and the ability to dictate Florence's civic life as he saw fit. He now went into high gear, initiating a malicious whispering campaign against the Medici which soon took on a life of its own.

When they were not persecuting the Medici, Florence's puritanical Albizzi-influenced *signoria* were preoccupied with other weighty matters of state such as the long-awaited overhaul of Florence's sodomy laws. Florence had always enjoyed a reputation as a major breeding ground for sodomy and in certain districts the practise was rife. The Ponte Vecchio, lined on either side by butchers shops and therefore quite literally 'a meat market', was a place where no self-respecting adolescent boy could venture unless he wanted to 'have his cap stolen'. Homosexuality in Florence usually took the form of 'dominant' older men above the age of eighteen or nineteen penetrating teenage boys below these ages and most liaisons tended to be casual encounters. Even as late as the early sixteenth-century, a German dictionary defined *Florenzer* as 'buggerer' and the verb *Florenzen* as 'to bugger'. In 1432 the *gonfaloniere* Doffo di Nepo degli Spini established a special magistracy which examined the issue. Harsher laws were decreed as a result and the penalty for sodomy was fixed at fifty gold florins for a first offence and execution for a fifth offence. Older men who assumed the 'passive' role in the act of sodomy itself were held up for special repugnance, but despite these new measures the conviction rates were low. Two years prior to the passing of these laws, Cosimo de' Medici had commissioned his friend the homosexual artist Donatello to create his famous free-standing statue of *David*, probably the most homo-erotic sculpture of the early Florentine Renaissance. Hardly a conformist, Cosimo de' Medici would always tend to go his own way, even to the extent of swimming against the tide of current opinion on morals.

When Cosimo traded Verona for Ferrara and Rinaldo degli Albizzi went to Rome in 1432, the city of Florence erupted in a maelstrom of malicious gossip, rumour and counter-rumour. For all their scholarship even some of the more prominent humanists found themselves indulging in the low rumour-mongering. Francesco Filelfo, who was not in fact a Florentine but hailed instead from Tolentino, was only too glad to impugn Cosimo's reputation while he was absent. Filelfo, we are told, was a man of inexhaustible intellectual energy but he was also a man of violent passions and unquenchable cravings, hungry for florins and hungry too for fame and recognition. These qualities often set him at odds with his fellow humanists, the friends of Cosimo de' Medici, who could not stand his insufferable vanity and abominable one-upmanship. Filelfo helped damage Cosimo's reputation during his absence by freely putting it about that the Medici *capo* was engaged in secret intrigues with the Visconti duke of Milan. Cosimo's brother Lorenzo's embassy to Milan had resulted not in Milan's neutrality but had had quite the reverse effect, Visconti's military intervention. From this it was inferred that Cosimo had somehow precipitated the duke of Milan's involvement for some vague and treasonous reason known only to the banker. It was clearly slanderous talk and there was never any question of Cosimo's loyalty towards Florence. Nevertheless, Cosimo's cousin Averardo was soon berated by the junior members of their faction to urge Cosimo to address these accusations openly. But thanks to Filelfo and other malicious slanderers the damage to the family reputation had already been done.

Cosimo himself returned, in September 1433, to a Florence that was fragmented and fractious, the rumours being peddled about him as virulent as ever. Rinaldo degli Albizzi, Francesco Filelfo and their cohorts were now putting it about that Cosimo's popularism was just a sham; that he was no more 'a man of the people' than were the old feudal *magnati* and that his plain clothes and studied humility were just a pretence. He gave money freely to the Church it was true but, at the end of the day, he was a usurer and a sinner because Christendom had forbidden usury in all its forms. Why, they asked, were the Medici *palle* to be seen everywhere throughout Florence adorning their many houses and *palazzi* if this was not at root a greedy, expansionist and politically ambitious family? Three months after the Peace of Ferrara, the open wound of the war with Lucca still festered. The Medici were reproached with having stirred up the war so they could indulge in war profiteering. The truth of the matter was that the individual who had profited most from the war with Lucca was Rinaldo himself. Averardo de' Medici was meanwhile censured for conspiring to prevent Neri Capponi and Rinaldo degli Albizzi from achieving military success. Again, this was a contemptible calumny. Rinaldo had been very much the architect of his own failure when it came down to the issue of military leadership. And so the accusations flew in the wind, almost all of them detrimental to the Medici.

In his book *Renaissance Princes* Vespasiano da Bisticci has Cosimo remarking 'that in most gardens there grew a weed which should never be watered but left to dry up. Most men, however, watered it instead of letting it die of drought. This weed was that worst of all weeds, Envy.' Rinaldo degli Albizzi had watered this most dangerous of plants. He was stung by personal affronts, whether real or imagined, that he believed himself to have suffered at Cosimo's hands. Cosimo, for example, had served twice on the *dieci* of war when he, Rinaldo, had not even served once throughout the entire duration of the war. Cosimo had been intimately involved, together with Palla Strozzi, in the peace negotiations which brought the war to a close. Once again, Rinaldo had sat those important proceedings out from the side-lines in Florence and Siena. It had become clear to all that Rinaldo had at some stage transferred his enmity from Neri Capponi to Cosimo de' Medici, who was now regarded as his *bête noir*. To be sure, the Medici name was an easy one for an oligarch to dislike; the long memories of the Florentine major guildsmen stretched back to the military failures of Giovanni de' Medici and the championing of the *ciompi* by Salvestro de' Medici. They had long memories and long grudges to go with them.

With so many damaging rumours and imputations being hurled at him, Cosimo kept his focus on the most important matter of all, Florence's well-being. Following the end of the war with Lucca Florence was bankrupt and being kept fiscally alive only through forced loans from the city's banking houses, who only agreed to lend out to the republic at ruinous rates of interest. Cosimo immediately ordered that the requisite funds be released to the government to settle its more pressing debts; this act gave a welcome fillip to his popularity, especially amongst his loyal supporters the *popolo minuto*, who saw the ship of state being kept afloat solely by the House of Medici. But, despite the efforts of the Medici in keeping Florence financially solvent, the situation within the city was by this time growing increasingly fraught and deteriorating for them day-by-day. The oligarchy was split down the middle, clan feuded with clan, Albizzi quarrelled with Medici, and everybody was unhappy that Florence had been brought to such a low pass by a war which had seemed like such a good idea at the time, but which had turned out to be pure folly. Armed bands roamed the streets by night and the tension between the factions erupted into open violence when a scion of one noble family was 'seized by the hair and struck in the face' by–it was alleged–two knaves 'from the Medici quarter of San Giovanni'. Aristocratic families barricaded themselves in their *palazzi* at twilight and a war of nerves ensued. One night the doors of the Medici residence were smeared with animal blood, an unsettling statement of threatening intent. The gloves were about to come off in this war of words and under these circumstances Cosimo was forced to consider the safety of Contessina and the children. Discretion would be the better part of valour for Cosimo and his family.

In the Sieve Valley of the Mugello stands the castellated Medici Villa del Trebbio. This small medieval fort was originally owned by Giovanni di Bicci and was bequeathed to Cosimo upon the former's death. Thereafter, Cosimo had commissioned Michelozzo di Bartolomeo to rebuild the castle, which he did commencing in 1428. A pre-existing watchtower was reconstituted by Michelozzo into a strong defensive bastion featuring arrow embrasures and stone machicolation which can still be seen today (machicolation was a defensive feature of castles whereby parapets were thrust outward until they overhung, enabling defenders to drop rocks or pour boiling oil onto enemy forces at the foot of the wall; they were a more developed and permanent form of wooden 'hoarding' which served much the same purpose during the middle ages). The entire defensive structure was surrounded by a moat with a sturdy drawbridge. It was to the robust sanctuary of *il Trebbio*, rather than to his usual summer residence at Cafaggiolo, that Cosimo now withdrew with his family and retainers 'in order to escape from the contests and divisions of the city' as, with characteristic understatement, he couched it in his diary. The Villa del Trebbio boasted a delightful walled garden set on two terraces which was the first of its kind to be created for a villa during this time, and Contessina would have had the luxury of allowing her children Piero (seventeen) and Giovanni (twelve), not to mention the illegitimate mulatto infant Carlo (five), to gambol in the grounds free from the perils of the city.

Amidst this rural idyll, Cosimo busied himself with the practicalities of transferring vast amounts of funds out of Florence to the Medici Bank's other

Italian branches in Rome, Venice and Naples. The Medici *libro segreto*, basically the bank's master ledger, reveals that on 30 May 1433 some 2,400 florins worth of gold Venetian ducats were sequestered with the Benedictine monks of the hillside monastery of San Miniato al Monte just outside Florence. The same day, a further 4,700 florins worth of ducats were spirited away to the Dominicans at San Marco. Within days, Cosimo had taken the necessary and prudent precaution of moving most of the Medici Bank's working capital out of Florence and beyond the control of the Albizzeschi and their allies. The movement of such a large amount of wealth was simply unprecedented but, under the circumstances, Cosimo could do little else but prepare to protect his more liquid assets.

As soon as Cosimo had departed for *il Trebbio*, Rinaldo degli Albizzi had manipulated the electoral rolls to ensure a good turnout of Albizzeschi partisans on the *signoria*. In the elections which followed all but two of the nine *priori* turned out to be in the Albizzi camp and the incoming *gonfaloniere* Bernardo Guadagni–the scion of an old eleventh-century Florentine family–was also firmly in Rinaldo's pocket. Guadagni was *a specchio*, behind in his tax payments, and should ordinarily have been disqualified from holding political office; Rinaldo had however discharged the man's debts so he could represent the Albizzi family interests, thus placing him firmly in Rinaldo's debt. Bernardo Guadagni's father had also been Rinaldo's closest friend, and so the latter regarded the new *gonfaloniere* with a sort of reverse benefactorial avuncularity. With clarity, Cosimo's political allies could see the writing on the wall. Alamanno Salviati wrote to Averardo de' Medici that 'the magistrates are behaving as badly as, or worse than, ever' and lamented that 'we shall gain no advantage because of Rinaldo's pride and ambition'.

By the first week of September the incoming *gonfaloniere* Bernardo Guadagni had summoned Cosimo back from the Mugello to assist in 'some important decisions' and the Medici *capo* duly arrived in Florence on 4 September 1433 prepared to confront his persecutors. He went that same afternoon to the Palazzo della Signoria to meet Guadagni, where he disclosed that certain rumours had come to his attention to the effect that the *signoria* was planning some sort of 'revolution' directed against Medici interests. Guadagni flatly denied that this was the case and reassured him, telling Cosimo 'to be of good cheer, for they hoped to leave the city at the end of their office in the same condition as they had found it'. Guadagni told Cosimo to return again on 7 September and participate in a council of eight select citizens which had been summoned to help observe and counsel the *signoria* on the city's current political crisis. After his conference with the *gonfaloniere* had ended, Cosimo writes in his diary that he then went straight to the house of one of the *priori*, 'Giovanni dello Scelto who I thought was my friend, and who was under obligations to me, as were also the others'. The 'friend' dello Scelto proceeded to reiterate Guadagni's reassurances and Cosimo, for the time being satisfied, left for his office at the Via Porta Rosa to settle some outstanding business there.

Three days passed and Cosimo returned once more to the Palazzo della Signoria for the meeting of the government at which he–together with Rinaldo degli Albizzi and six others–was earmarked to serve as an informal adviser. When he arrived at the *palazzo*, however, he was taken aback to find that the *signoria* was already in session. Had he been given the wrong timing by mistake? Furthermore, instead of being ushered into the council chamber where he could hear the discussions already being held, he was rudely bundled up the narrow flight of stairs by the captain of the seigniorial bodyguard to the 300 feet high tower which sits asymmetrically atop of the building. Here, he was flung into a small room-cum-gaol-cell which was wryly known amongst Florentines as the *Alberghettino* or 'the little inn'. Cosimo's astonishment was complete and in his diary he later noted that 'such underhand proceedings were indeed unlike the Rinaldo of old!' But the fact remained that Rinaldo degli Albizzi had successfully blindsided him. He was suddenly the prisoner of a wayward and recalcitrant *signoria* and his life now hung precariously in the balance, with his rival Rinaldo as its arbiter.

It did not take long for word of Cosimo's imprisonment to spread like wildfire through the streets of Florence. Cosimo himself later recollected how 'on hearing this, the entire city rose'. The *popolo minuto*, the lower classes, were the most fearful for his safety. In the San Lorenzo district word spread from door to door and anxious prayers were offered up in the gloom for the deliverance of their patron, the only wealthy man in all of Florence who appeared to understand them and their everyday problems. Rinaldo degli Albizzi's rhetorical warnings to the *signoria* against the perils of Medici *governo di uno solo* ('rule by a single man') tended to cut little ice with the ordinary man in the street. At the Palazzo della Signoria, meanwhile, the government was seemingly in the grip of an attack of panic at the sheer enormity of what they had just done. Admittedly, they had not sleepwalked into this course of action and had obviously planned it all out; however they now seemed unsure what their next steps should be. The whole city was by now murmuring about the treacherous events of the afternoon and it could not be taken for granted that the general population would yield peacefully to these shocking developments.

Inside the *palazzo* all was alarm and urgent activity as armed men rushed hither and thither laden with weapons, making preparations for a possible defence of the seat of government. Downstairs in the *piazza* below, Rinaldo's son Ormanno degli Albizzi was feverishly directing the stationing of seigniorial guards, blocking the entrances to the government quarter and making precautions against any impromptu rescue attempt by Cosimo's dedicated supporters within the city. Inside the *Alberghettino*, Cosimo was said to have fainted when his jailor entered the room and he refused point blank to touch the food offered to him, fearing he might be poisoned before he could even be brought to trial. This was in fact a very real possibility; the presiding Albizzeschi *signoria* wanted Cosimo out of the way and his sudden death while under detention would have obviated many unnecessary legal entanglements.

Efforts to arrest Cosimo's brother Lorenzo in the Mugello, as well as his cousin Averardo who had been at Pisa during this time, had meanwhile failed and both men regrouped in the Medici's Mugello stronghold surrounded and protected by bands of loyal peasants. They were supported by the *condottiere* Niccolò da Tolentino, who brought his troops to the town of Lastra which lay within several miles of Florence. 'Had they taken us all three, we should have been in evil plight', Cosimo noted with relief in his diary. Rather than attempt to enter the city, however, they soon halted for fear that any further advance towards Florence might endanger Cosimo's life. Cosimo himself was to later reproach them in his journal for their hesitancy but the fact remains that an armed offensive against the lawful government would have set an entirely different cast on these events and would have enabled the enemies of the Medici to level the more serious charge of treason against the family. Having made captive the man whom they were now painting as public enemy number one, the *signoria* were still undecided about what actually to do with Cosimo. Could they run the risk of a long, drawn-out trial and have their flimsy arguments rebutted by expensive and clever Medici advocates? No, open trial was considered far too great a risk and there was always the possibility that Cosimo would get off the hook and return later for his revenge; the crisis needed a quick resolution.

The decision was therefore taken to call a *parlamento* and dragoon the subsequent *balìa* into rubber-stamping whatever summary punishment the *signoria* had already privately decreed for their captive, which–at least as far as Rinaldo degli Albizzi was concerned–was preferably execution. The *vacca* was duly sounded on 9 September 'and those who had been the cause of all assembled on the Piazza with much infantry' Cosimo recorded. Those citizens entitled to constitute the *parlamento* began to jostle in murmuring crowds towards the Piazza della Signoria, 'but few of the people were present', Cosimo added, 'because in truth the mass of the citizens were ill-pleased'. When they arrived at the *piazza* they were stopped by cordons of armed guards who prevented access to all those individuals who were confirmed Medici supporters or adherents. As a result only a pitifully small group of individuals was eventually granted access to the *piazza*. From the towering vantage point of his tiny gaol cell Cosimo himself could look down and count no more than about twenty-three citizens, 'verily a small number' as he observed. When the *notaio della riformagioni* then asked this pathetically meagre group if they wished to form a *balìa* for the reform of the city and 'for the good of the people' the sparse crowd enthusiastically shouted their approval as loudly and as convincingly as a couple of dozen men could.

When Cosimo's matter was discussed the crime of which he was charged now emerged. Cosimo, so the *signoria* claimed, had been guilty of raising himself up above the rank of any other ordinary citizen, the insinuation being of course that Cosimo de' Medici was an anti-republican tyrant-in-the-making. As evidence of this allegation that the Medici regarded themselves as standing above other Florentines, the *signoria* pointed to Cosimo's new house, which was currently under construction on the Via Larga. The *capo* of the household had required a suitable *palazzo* expressing his true status and *gravitas*, not a fixer-upper *palazzo* that had come to him in a dowry. Cosimo had therefore commissioned the tempestuous architect Filippo Brunelleschi, who had already received the considerable patronage of his father Giovanni di Bicci, to design a sumptuous *palazzo* on the corner of the Via Larga (now known as the Via Camilo Benso Cavour). For this purpose, a number of adjacent properties were purchased and demolished along this recently constructed road which skirted the eastern boundary of the *gonfalone* del Leon d'Oro, the largest of the sixteen 'companies' or 'wards' into which the city was divided. The Via Larga was a serene, residential road filled with the mansions of the wealthy; the busier commercial life of the *gonfalone* was restricted to a long road running parallel to the Via Larga and which extended from the Borgo San Lorenzo (coming off the Piazza del Duomo) to Florence's northern city gate the Porta San Gallo (which no longer exists but which is marked today by the Piazza della Libertà).

However Brunelleschi's blueprints would, Cosimo shrewdly noted, prove far too grand for his fellow Florentines to swallow. Cosimo had therefore turned to his other architect friend Michelozzo to come up with a simpler alternative design, the foundations and first story of which were already going up around the time of Cosimo's incarceration. Nevertheless, even this second design was considered too ostentatious and Rinaldo degli Albizzi now held this building up as the future *palazzo* from which the putative tyrant Cosimo de' Medici intended to rule over a once proudly republican Florence. It was a persuasive demagogic argument designed to appeal to the jealousy and resentment of the Florentines; indeed a favourite distraction of the lower classes often involved burning down the houses of the more well-to-do. However baseless they may have been, the charges against Cosimo began to stick.

But when it came down to the pronouncement of the defendant's sentence, Rinaldo could not browbeat the *balìa* into accepting the most serious capital penalty of all: execution. For every council member who called for beheading there was another who felt banishment to be more appropriate, and still others who thought that Cosimo should simply be released. Still stinging from the cold shoulder he had received from many of Cosimo's humanist friends, the vain and contentious scholar of Greek, Francesco Filelfo, kept up his enthusiastic call for capital punishment. Cosimo's other humanist friends such as the monk Ambrose of Camaldoli meanwhile interceded with the *signoria* in Cosimo's favour. Florence's neighbours had also by now weighed in on the Medicean side; official envoys quickly arrived from Venice and Ferrara to entreat for his release. Cosimo also received word that Pope Martin V's successor Pope Eugenius IV was also firmly in his corner.

Undaunted, Rinaldo had meanwhile tortured two Medici associates on the rack and one of them, the poet Niccolò Tinucci, had broken down and 'confessed' that Cosimo had conspired with Milan against his own city. This enabled Rinaldo to now widen the allegations into the more severe charge of treason. However, neither the Venetian ambassador nor the Pope–himself a Venetian by birth–would countenance the idea that Cosimo had intrigued against them with their traditional enemies the *Milanesi*. With the diplomatic pressure mounting daily, Rinaldo was forced to face the fact that the most he could hope for was Cosimo's banishment from Florence. Arrangements were meanwhile made to reward the venal *gonfaloniere* Bernardo Guadagni, who received a one thousand florin bribe for doing Rinaldo's bidding in this whole dirty business.

So it was that on 3 October 1433, after almost one month of imprisonment in his lofty gaol cell, Cosimo de' Medici was led down the stone steps from the *Alberghettino* to finally receive judgement from the *signoria*. He was sentenced to be exiled to the city of Padua for a period of ten years. According to his own later recollection he put a brave face on things, stating: 'I declare that I am content to go, and to stay wherever you command, not only in the Trevisian State, but should you send me to live amongst the Arabs, or any other people alien to our customs, I would go most willingly'. Then, looking pale and ill, his guards brought him from the government building and proceeded to lead him across the Piazza della Signoria which thronged with curious onlookers. Feeling suddenly vulnerable and exposed, Cosimo grew fearful that one of Rinaldo's assassins may be lurking in the crowd, ready to strike him down. To the assembled and watching *priori* Cosimo now exhorted them: 'Have a care that those who stand outside in the piazza with arms in their hands anxiously desiring my blood, should not have their way with me'. He cautioned them that should he meet his death at some cut throat's dagger as he was being led to the city gates, his own suffering would be brief but *their* disrepute would be eternal:

'nothing is so brief as death. But you would earn perpetual infamy by having made me a promise which was broken by villainous citizens: infamy is worse than an innocent death.'

Continuing in the same vein, he took pains to impress upon the *signoria* his years of public service and his unstinting contribution to the republic of Florence, remarking tartly: 'With no small pride I affirm that none can say my ill-behaviour ever caused a city to rebel or to be taken from you; on the contrary, our [Medici] money bought several: ask your soldiers how many times they were paid by me for the commune with my own money, to be returned when convenient to the commune'. The *signoria* relented and saw reason; the prisoner would be held until nightfall whereat he would be spirited quietly from Florence via the Porta San Gallo. An armed escort would then take him the forty or so miles to Florence's borders where he would be handed over into the custody and safekeeping of the marquis of Ferrara, who would then take him the remaining distance to Padua.

Cosimo's journey through the lands of Ferrara and Padua was a fitting precursor to his exile. All along the route, instead of receiving peoples' scorn for having been banished from his home state he was instead fêted by the *contadini*, those poor country peasantry who always felt close to the Medici. As he rode through their lands and villages they offered him presents and cheered him on his way. It was a relief for the banker to receive such support and understanding for his predicament from the common people. More adulation followed at Ferrara and finally at Padua, where the rulers of those two cities greeted Cosimo with all honour and their best Lombard hospitality. 'Messer Jacopo Donato went with me [to Padua] and lodged me in his fine house, furnished with linen, beds, and eatables fit for the greatest personage', reflected Cosimo. Two months passed and Cosimo secured permission from Padua, Venice and Florence's new *gonfaloniere* Bartolommeo de' Ridolfi to be permitted 'to live at Padua, Venice, or elsewhere, in the Venetian territory, and the permission was given, but with orders not to approach within 140 miles of Florence'. At Venice he was reunited with his brother Lorenzo, who had meanwhile also been sentenced to five year's exile in the maritime state. He was again accorded all the esteem and status of a Florentine ambassador, leading Cosimo to note in his journal, 'It could hardly be believed that, having been driven from my home, I should find so much honour'. The two brothers were shortly thereafter joined by their cousin Averardo, who had himself been banished to Naples for ten years.

In Venice he took up residence with the monks at the old tenth-century Benedictine monastery of San Giorgio Maggiore which lies on its own little island at the mouth of Venice's Grand Canal. Cosimo had over the years retained close links with the Benedictine Order; not only had he been educated at the reformed Benedictine monastery school of Santa Maria degli Angeli, but he also had 2,400 florins worth of Venetian ducats on secret deposit with the Benedictine monks of San Miniato al Monte just outside of Florence. To express his gratitude to the Benedictines for giving him sanctuary, and to give thanks to the city of Venice itself, Cosimo now commissioned the architect Michelozzo–who, downing tools on the Medici *palazzo* in the Via Larga, had loyally followed him into exile–to design a new library for the Order's monastery. This was an astute move on Cosimo's part since the Venetian Pope Eugenius IV had himself formerly been a monk at San Giorgio Maggiore; garnering papal goodwill with this display of patronage might prove useful in the future. He therefore busied himself with this project, as well as with the oversight of his banking business, which still carried on as usual at his Venice, Rome and Naples branches and elsewhere. Indeed, this almost transnational independence of the Medici Bank was predicated on its vast capital, as well as on equally large reserves of international goodwill; as Cosimo observed in one of his diary entries: 'They thought to ruin us by preventing me from making use of what was mine. But in this they failed, for we lost no credit, and many foreign merchants and gentlemen offered us, and even sent to Venice, large sums of money.'

Meanwhile, Cosimo's supporters who remained behind kept him updated on all the major political developments in Florence so that he was not left entirely in the dark. Astonishingly, despite his having been exiled by the Florentine *signoria*, he still continued to furnish their emissaries with useful intelligence of his own concerning on-going international affairs, for which he was duly and politely thanked for his contribution. Cosimo evidently did not believe in burning his bridges and back in Florence it seemed that his valuable presence was already being missed. In his history of Florence, Niccolò Machiavelli later wrote that the city 'remaining widowed of a citizen so universally loved, everyone was confounded, both the conquered and the conquerors'. Moderates like Agnolo Pandolfini and Palla Strozzi–who himself had taken up the calm, steadying role previously fulfilled by Niccolò da Uzzano–were appalled at what Rinaldo's faction had done and, although the Albizzeschi appeared to be in the ascendant, the truth of the matter was that the government was by now as deeply divided as it had been in the aftermath of the war with Lucca. Cosimo's humanist friend Niccolò de' Niccoli even wrote openly to the exile about how 'so many errors are made every day by this government that a folio of paper would not be sufficient to contain them all'.

In February 1434, Cosimo was informed that Agnolo Acciaiuoli–one of the main critics of Rinaldo degli Albizzi's increasingly autocratic methods–had been seized and banished to Cosenza for a term of ten years. His accusers alleged that he had urged Cosimo to engineer a new foreign war to cause Florence hardship and also to make overtures to Neri Capponi. Capponi–together with the known Medici faction member Alamanno Salviati–was in turn accused of plotting to procure the services of the *condottiere* Niccolò da Tolentino to invade Florence and secure Cosimo's restoration by force. Not long afterwards, Acciaiuoli, Capponi and Salviati were all followed into exile by one of Cosimo's own distant relatives, Mario Bartolommeo de' Medici, who was also accused of disloyalty and sentenced to ten years in exile. Another notable Medici supporter, Puccio Pucci, had already been banished sometime earlier along with his brother Giovanni.

Although these desperate moves by the Albizzi faction had stripped Cosimo of some of his most important potential supporters in Florence he took pains to remain studiously aloof from the allegations and counter-allegations flying around at this time. Sagely, he knew that Rinaldo's clique was deeply unpopular and, given enough time, it would squander its last reserves of bankable Florentine goodwill. He was therefore content for the moment to sit back and give Rinaldo just enough rope with which to hang himself. In this, Rinaldo was apparently happy to oblige. By the summer of 1434, starved of Medici funding, the Albizzeschi-controlled *signoria* had embroiled Florence in yet another military fiasco when their troops were defeated by the *Milanesi* just outside the town of Imola.

It was by now time to elect a fresh *signoria* and it was at this point that Rinaldo degli Albizzi revealed the true extent of his naiveté and political ineptitude. Having previously achieved, in effect, a coup d'état by securing the election of his family friend Bernardo Guadagni as *gonfaloniere* and rigging the subsequent *parlamento* that he had called, Rinaldo now lapsed into complacency and failed to maintain a continuous grip on the levers of government. In doing so Rinaldo betrayed his Achilles heel, which is to say his constitutional scruples. Like most Florentines he was far too heavily invested in the republican tradition and pledged to upholding the commune's ancient constitution to perceive that, for his party to rule through the existing governmental structure, he needed to prevent the *signoria* from exercising even the slightest quasi-independence of action. In the wake of Cosimo's banishment what he should therefore have done was completely purge the electoral *borse* of all remaining Medici sympathisers. Under normal circumstances this would have been achieved through the manipulation of the *accoppiatori*.

The *accoppiatori* was a committee of the most powerful and trusted members of Florence's oligarchy. They were usually called to office in times of emergency by the *balìa* and their purpose was to screen and pre-select *a mano* ('by hand') those citizens deemed eligible to serve on the *signoria*. The names of the candidates who passed muster in this way went into the sealed electoral *borse* and the *signoria* was randomly drawn by lot from the leather purses as usual. In practice, the *accoppiatori* therefore enabled the dominant regime to carefully remove from the running any political opponents whilst still maintaining the subterfuge that Florence's venerable electoral procedures had been observed. Like the *parlamento* and the *balìa*, the *accoppiatori* was originally designed to be used as an emergency measure in times of crisis, but inevitably it came to be used simply to manipulate the outcome of seigniorial elections. Had Rinaldo used the *accoppiatori* in this way to predefine a set of sympathetic electoral candidates he could have ensured that no Medici party followers could in future be admitted to the ranks of the *priori*. Unfortunately for the scrupulous Rinaldo, the presiding *accoppiatori*–which was only valid for a period of one year–was due to expire before the election of the new *signoria* could take place and there was no time to nominate a fresh one before the coming election. Under such circumstances the more pragmatic Cosimo would undoubtedly have railroaded through a new *accoppiatori*. By failing to do so and by introducing into the electoral process an unacceptable element of chance, Rinaldo had unwittingly broadcast to the entire city that the upcoming government was being released from its obligation to toe the Albizzi party line. This wild card was to be his undoing.

When the *signoria* was duly drawn by lot in September 1434, Rinaldo's failure to censor the candidates resulted in a landslide for the Medici party. Even the new *gonfaloniere*, Niccolò di Cocco, was known to be a strong adherent of Cosimo de' Medici. Rinaldo realised his mistake too late. Knowing that the tide of public opinion was turning against his faction he now back peddled desperately; summoning Palla Strozzi he suggested calling a *parlamento* and a *balìa* and empowering them to select a replacement *signoria* to that which had just been elected. Strozzi replied in no uncertain terms that it was far too late for such measures. Fearing that Rinaldo would resort to armed force to prevent the new *signoria* from sitting, Strozzi guaranteed him that the new government would not recall Cosimo de' Medici from exile. Despite his reservations Rinaldo was apparently assuaged and grudgingly left the city, but this was only to recruit several hundred country ploughmen, whom he armed and brought back with him to Florence in late September. 'The whole city was teeming with boorish peasants, who lusted after other people's goods and bayed for their blood', complained the chronicler Giovanni Cavalcanti. Rinaldo's absence at this critical juncture was arguably his second grave mistake. After he had left Florence earlier that month the *signoria* immediately arraigned the previous *gonfaloniere* Bernardo Guadagni on charges of corruption and sent word to Cosimo de' Medici in Venice to return to the city with all haste.

Upon his return to Florence, Rinaldo was distressed to learn that two of his stalwarts, Ridolfo Peruzzi and Niccolò Barbadori, had been ordered to report to the *signoria* but, somewhat ominously, had not been given the reason. Mindful of Cosimo's own fate when he had been given similar orders one year earlier, and informed that the signoria was planning to call a *parlamento* on 29 September, Rinaldo decided to act. Hastening to the Palazzo Albizzi, he set about the business of calling his faction to arms. He still felt reasonably confident that he had the support of such influential figures as Palla Strozzi, Giovanni Guicciardini, Ridolfo Peruzzi and Niccolò Barbadori. If he could get most of the more respected moderates in his corner his actions might be interpreted as having some degree of legitimacy. On 26 September 1434, Rinaldo ordered 600 of his armed supporters to take up positions next to the church of San Pier Scheraggio which formerly stood on the present day site of the Uffizi.

Rinaldo's plan was to surround the palace with his men, bolstered by armed peasants who were marching in from the countryside, occupy the seat of government and overthrow the rightfully elected pro-Medici *signoria*. Rinaldo's ramshackle coalition of wealthy merchants, unemployed soldiers, country bumpkins and idlers hoping for easy plunder duly regrouped just behind the Piazza della Signoria at the spacious Piazza Sant'Apollinare (today known as the Piazza San Firenze) and from there they now advanced on Florence's seat of government. To ensure that the front door of the Palazzo della Signoria would be opened to them when the time came the guard who had been posted there that morning was bribed with a brimming helmet full of ducats.

Meanwhile however, unbeknown to Rinaldo, his erstwhile nemesis Neri Capponi had alerted the *signoria* to his plans for armed rebellion and reinforcements, weapons and food stores had been hurriedly laid in at the Palazzo della Signoria. Word had also been sent to loyal troops waiting outside the city to come as quickly as possible to the government's relief. Despite the bribing of the door guard all the gates and entrances to the *palazzo* were now barred and barricaded in preparation for a siege. As Rinaldo's men began to take up position outside the towering, fortified building they were discouraged to note that, rather than rushing to join their ranks, the masses of the ordinary people and the law-abiding middle classes had timidly shut themselves indoors to await the outcome.

The *signoria* now sought to buy time for their reinforcements to arrive by sending out several neutral representatives to negotiate with the rebels. These envoys pledged not to recall Cosimo de' Medici on condition that Rinaldo's men agreed to stand down; this was sufficient reassurance to win the support of Ridolfo Peruzzi, who left Rinaldo and proceeded inside the Palazzo della Signoria where he was received with great honour and clemency. If Peruzzi's defection was a calamity worse was however to follow. Into the tense *piazza* rode Rinaldo's other key ally Palla Strozzi attended by only two armed bodyguards instead of the 500 men that he had earlier promised. There had been terse words and a fierce altercation arose between Strozzi and Rinaldo and in a fit of pique Strozzi indignantly spurred his horse and rode off. Rinaldo's support, what little he thought he had to begin with, was crumbling piecemeal. If he wasn't to lose the initiative altogether it was time to order his men to try to capture the Palazzo della Signoria.

It was at this point that Pope Eugenius IV now entered the picture by offering his services as a mediator in the crisis. The Supreme Pontiff, who had been staying at Florence's convent of Santa Maria Novella, was currently in exile from Rome. Following the death of Pope Martin V his contentious Colonna kinsmen had challenged Eugenius's election and Eugenius, for his own part, had been rather too vocal in *his* objections to the transferral of the papal treasury to the Colonna family *palazzo*. As a result the Colonna had instigated an insurrection which had brought a secular republic to power in Rome. Joining the new pope in exile was the captain-general of the papal armies, Cardinal Giovanni Vitelleschi, whose parting shot to the rebels had been to raze the old Colonna family base of Palestrina to the ground. It had been Rinaldo degli Albizzi who had been responsible for offering the Supreme Pontiff sanctuary in Florence; Eugenius was aghast that his host had turned rebel against his own city. Pope Eugenius divined that Rinaldo's actions would only serve to weaken and destabilise Florence and that this in turn threatened to undermine the alliance that existed between Rome, Florence and Naples against the duchy of Milan.

The Pope was not about to see his main defensive bulwark crumble without even attempting to intervene. He despatched his envoy, Cardinal Vitelleschi, a fierce *condottiere* by training who was known in Rome as 'the fighting bishop of Recanati', to discuss terms with Rinaldo at the Piazza Sant'Apollinare. All day long, as the two small armies waited in the Piazza della Signoria in a tense standoff, Cardinal Vitelleschi shuffled backwards and forwards between Rinaldo and the *signoria*; eventually Pope Eugenius prevailed upon Rinaldo to come and meet with him in person at Santa Maria Novella. Rinaldo consented to the proposal and so left the government quarter to go and meet the Pope together with his motley crew of *bravi*. This was his third mistake. Upon arrival at the convent his fourth and final mistake was leaving his supporters to their own devices while he went inside to confer with the Pope. When he came into the Holy Father's presence, Eugenius greeted him–so we are told–with 'crocodile tears' at Florence's domestic turmoil. Pulling himself together the Pope then reassured Rinaldo that he would prevail upon the *signoria* for a satisfactory decision concerning Cosimo de' Medici. He also reassured Rinaldo that he would do everything within his power to secure a pardon for his own rebellious actions that day and that no reprisals would be taken against either him or his property. Reassured by these seemingly sincere words from the lips of the Pope himself, Rinaldo saw that the day could not be won by force and consented to stand his men down.

While Rinaldo was enjoying a long audience with the Pope his assorted band of armed retainers and cutthroats had been left kicking their heels outside the convent. Disheartened at the lack of action and in the absence of any fresh news or developments from their leader the group of several hundred men had grown bored and drifted off home. When Rinaldo learned that his army had evaporated, rather than venture through the dark and hostile streets to his family *palazzo*, he instead decided to spend the night with the Pope, together with his son Ormanno and Ridolfo Peruzzi. The rebellion, such as it was, was by now effectively over. Soon loyal detachments of mercenaries from the *contado* had entered the city under cover of darkness and taken up position in defence of the seat of government. The following day the streets resonated with the familiar mooing sound of the *vacca* and those entitled to form a *parlamento* obediently made their way bleary-eyed, for it had been a long and anxious night, to the Piazza della Signoria where the *priori* asked if they wished to form a *balìa*. They loudly affirmed 'Sì! Sì!' and a three-hundred-and-fifty-member *balìa* was duly elected packed with Medici supporters as well as moderates like Palla Strozzi. Their first order of business was to reverse the Medici banishments and recall Cosimo de' Medici, his brother and his cousin from Venice. Also pardoned were Agnolo Acciaiuoli, Puccio Pucci and many others loyal to the Medici.

On 28 September 1434, accompanied by 'a large body of foot-soldiers' and 200 Venetian horsemen as his escort, Cosimo set out for Florence crossing over into Florentine territory to almost universal jubilation. In exile he had remained gracious and honourable, refusing to condemn either Florence or the *signoria* for their actions against him. He even nobly stated that 'He and his family have always defended their country with everything in their power, and now, to regain it, he would rest content not only to stay in Padua but even at the top of the world, even until death itself'. Within a few days Cosimo had reached his own estates at Careggi where he and his entourage enjoyed a hearty homecoming meal amidst familiar surroundings. By now, so many people had begun to throng the streets and thoroughfares of the city to catch a glimpse of Cosimo's return that the *signoria* sent urgent word for him not to enter Florence until after nightfall; as Cosimo later noted in his diary: 'The *signoria* did not wish us to enter by daylight lest we should be the cause of an uproar in the city'. He obediently complied, entering Florence by a postern gate east of the Bargello and proceeding from there directly to the Palazzo della Signoria. Here, one of the sympathetic *priori* put him up for the night in his own personal bedchamber in the government *palazzo*.

The following morning Cosimo called on Pope Eugenius IV to thank him personally for interceding on his behalf. He then went directly home, across the river, to the Palazzo Bardi and was cheered through the streets by the city's population, which had by now learned of his presence in Florence. Despite the assurances of the Pope, the Medici-controlled *signoria* lost little time in pronouncing sentence upon Rinaldo degli Albizzi and his son Ormanno. Together with their adherents such as Ridolfo Peruzzi, Niccolò Barbadori, Giovanni Guicciardini and the disgraced *gonfaloniere* Bernardo Guadagni, they were all promptly banished. Rinaldo was fined 4,000 florins and sent into exile at either Naples or Trani, his son Ormanno to Gaeta for ten years. Barbadori, whose association with Rinaldo dated back to 1408 when he had served as one of the ten supervisors of the recently-conquered Pisa, was sent into exile at Verona for ten years. According to Machiavelli, before being exiled, Rinaldo was sent for by Pope Eugenius who told him that he blamed himself for the consequences that had befallen him since Rinaldo had trusted his word; the Pope exhorted him to have patience and to hope for a change of fortune. In response, Rinaldo had apparently tartly shot back at the Pope: 'I blame myself for believing that you, who were driven out of your own country, could keep me in mine'. Rinaldo was not, however, joined in exile by his brother Luca degli Albizzi. Luca had enjoyed a creditable career as an official envoy of Florence on several occasions and as commissary had been present with Florence's captain-general Niccolò da Tolentino when he fought the battle of San Romano, of which he left us a historically important account in his personal diary. Prior to that Luca had served as the head of Florence's galleys from 1429 to 1430. A loyal lifelong friend to Cosimo de, Medici, Luca degli Albizzi would even later be appointed *gonfaloniere* in 1442.

Aside from Rinaldo degli Albizzi over seventy others went into exile, amongst them the hapless Palla Strozzi who had started out lukewarm towards Rinaldo's plans and had ended by withdrawing his support altogether. But this would cut little ice in Cosimo de' Medici's eyes; a far shrewder political operator than Rinaldo degli Albizzi had ever been, Cosimo had decided that it was advantageous for Medici interests if the hugely wealthy and influential Strozzi were now deftly removed from the political life of the city. A long list of aristocratic Florentine families departed with them into exile; not only the Albizzi and the Strozzi but also the Altoviti, the Branacci, the Castellani, the Gianfigliazzi, the Lamberteschi, the Panciatichi, the da Panzano and the Ricasoli. Their names were a veritable roll call of Florence's most illustrious *ottimati* houses. Emptying Florence of her leading citizens now led some to ask how the political life of the republic could go on as normal. When Cosimo himself was asked about this we are told that he looked up briefly from his papers and remarked laconically that 'it only took seven or eight yards of scarlet cloth to make a new prior'. The world-weary combination of cynicism and pragmatism were entirely characteristic.

One of those who had called loudest of all for Cosimo's execution, the humanist Francesco Filelfo, gave the Florentines no opportunity to pronounce sentence upon him, having already fled Florence of his own accord. Filelfo's strange journey from humanist client of the Medici to their most vociferous and outspoken enemy is worth pausing and reflecting on. Cosimo, who was almost universally esteemed by the Florentine humanists for his generous patronage, not to mention his own humanist credentials, gave Filelfo his initial start in Florence by supporting him financially when he first arrived in the city to lecture at the *Studio Fiorentino* in 1428. Initially his classes on Cicero, Livy, Terence, Thucydides and Xenophon were well-received by such notable students as Carlo Marsuppini and Niccolò Niccoli. However Filelfo's arrogant and overbearing manner had soon alienated many of his former pupils and colleagues, most of whom were associated in some way with Cosimo. He found his tenure at the *Studio* abruptly cancelled in 1431. When a certain Filippo da Casale assaulted him in the street, leaving him badly wounded, Filelfo had jumped to the conclusion that his erstwhile patron Cosimo de' Medici was behind the attack. By 1432 relations between the two men had soured with Filelfo claiming that his former benefactor was now actively working against him. Writing to his friend Niccolò Albergati, Filelfo ungraciously remarked: 'Cosimo, while he behaves as though he were devoted to me, I observe to be the sort of person who pretends to be and pretends not to be all things; he's so taciturn that even his intimate friends and family cannot understand him'. Filelfo's public hostility towards Cosimo throughout the latter's exile made him persona non grata once the Medici were restored to power. He fled to Siena where, for the next four years, he unleashed a deluge of propaganda against Cosimo and encouraged the Florentines to rise against him. Making a fresh set of enemies in Siena, Filelfo was then obliged to relocate to Milan. Filelfo's antagonistic broadsides from his new place of refuge drew an indignant backlash from such Medici loyalists as Poggio Bracciolini, who responded in kind with his tract *Invectivae in Franciscum Philelphum*.

In these days of euphoric return, it would have been perfectly within Cosimo's power to have had his chief adversaries executed had he wished. However unless it was for the most extreme charge of treason against the state execution was generally considered to be somewhat un-Florentine. Such barbarities as beheading, garrotting or tearing limb from limb could be left to tyrannies such as Milan for the merchant Florentines felt proud of their pragmatic leniency when it came to dealing with political rivals. Besides, for any wealthy citizen with considerable business interests or property holdings in Florence, the penalty of proscription and banishment was quite severe enough. To be removed from Florence was to be cut off from the wellspring of one's financial interests as well as from the succour of one's own family, friends and kinship network. To the average upper class Florentine it was akin to being cast into some gloomy Dantesque purgatory. Another alternative to banishment was to re-categorize a family as *magnati*, that is to say one of the feudal families who were restricted by law from participation in government. This effectively served the same purpose of keeping certain blacklisted families out of civic life, although it did not entail physical exile. In the end, a total of eleven of the wealthiest families in Florence were proscribed in perpetuity from taking any part in Florence's government including, not unsurprisingly, the Albizzeschi. Cosimo used the opportunity to make a clean sweep of all those *ottimati* families who had monopolised Florence's government since the creation of the guild-based republican system.

If Rinaldo degli Albizzi had been slow to make use of the *accoppiatori*, Cosimo most certainly was not. Moving forward he employed the *accoppiatori* to keep the *signoria* packed with his own acolytes. He was assisted in this by his able handler Puccio Pucci as well as by the newly returned Agnolo Acciaiuoli. Averardo de' Medici had meanwhile died in exile in Venice. Now truly in the ascendant, the Medici party began to grow exponentially. Cosimo flattered the feelings of the *popolo minuto* by allowing them greater–though still judicious–participation in government. At the same time he continued to keep the old aristocratic families out. Some semblance of political opposition was maintained by permitting Cosimo's friends–so-called 'loyal opponents' or 'internal adversaries'–like Neri Capponi for example, to occasionally give utterance to their misgivings about the extent of Medici power. But by and large this was all just convenient window dressing. The chronicler Giovanni Cavalcanti had once described Neri Capponi as being 'the wisest' whilst describing Cosimo as 'the richest', but Capponi eventually died anyway and his successor was the hugely wealthy member of the Colleges and erstwhile humanist Gianozzo Manetti. Capponi's replacement in this subterfuge, Manetti had at different points in his career held such wide-ranging briefs as sea consul, grain officer, night officer and ambassador.

For those politicians who refused to toe the Medici line there were always methods designed to hit them where it hurt most – in their purse. Puccio Pucci and other Medici-controlled 'tax officers' could, if they so decided, impose a crippling *catasto* assessment designed to ruin an opponent financially. Often this would result in self-exile as the persecuted opponent fled from Florence in order to preserve their fortune from confiscation by the Florentine Monte. Gianozzo Manetti himself was to feel the effect of selective Medici taxation in the early 1450s and was driven into exile in Naples, a departure which Vespasiano da Bisticci was at pains to point out was purely *volontariamente*. In Naples, Manetti continued nevertheless to correspond cordially with Cosimo's son Giovanni about family affairs, expressing thanks for Giovanni's help in arranging marriages for his children. Manetti is often cited as a political adversary who was driven off because of his opposition to Cosimo's foreign policy. On closer examination of the circumstances, however, it seems more likely that he was targeted by another member of the *reggimento*, Luca Pitti, who served as tax commissioner in the crucial year in question – 1452. Manetti and Pitti had crossed swords over their dual, overlapping governance of the subject town of Pistoia and Pitti had wielded the *catasto* as a means of simply ridding himself of his rival. But if taxation was indeed used as a surgical means with which individual members of the élite could persecute their less empowered enemies, there is little doubt that Cosimo himself also wielded taxation as a weapon to break his opponents when the need arose. This would sometimes make him exceedingly unpopular and in 1458 feelings ran so high in Florence as a result of taxation and Medici fiscal policy in general that Cosimo would rent a house in Pavia for himself, Contessina and the children as a precautionary measure.

What few people had realised by this time was that the social dynamics of Florence's political life had by now undergone a sea change. The old *ottimati* families of the oligarchy, including the Albizzi and the Strozzi, were no longer the wealthiest families in the city. They were now replaced by upstart families like the Medici, the Pitti and the Pucci and some of the newly powerful were still only members of the *arte minori*. It was these families, backed by their enormous fortunes, which were able to eventually force themselves to the forefront and edge out the old families by establishing better funded and numerically superior political factions. The new éminence grise was now unquestionably Cosimo de' Medici himself and, as it was observed at the time, 'No important decision was ever reached without reference to the Medici Palace. Foreign ambassadors were frequently to be seen passing through the gateway; Florentine ambassadors invariably called upon Cosimo before taking up their appointments.'

Although surprisingly little is known about Cosimo de' Medici's real personality except that which we can infer from his political actions, nonetheless tantalising glimpses of the man occasionally penetrate the murky gloom of history. Vespasiano da Bisticci describes, for instance, a conversation between Cosimo and a political rival in which the Medici *capo* enunciates his political philosophy:

> 'Now it seems to me only just and honest that I should prefer the good name and honour of my house to you: that I should work for my own interest rather than for yours. So you and I will act like two big dogs that, when they meet, smell one another and then, because they both have teeth, go their ways. Wherefore now you can attend to your affairs and I to mine.'

Hard-nosed though the comment was this was no notional threat of implied machismo, it was merely an expression of the hard political realities of wealthy family politics in fifteenth-century Italy. Cosimo's gladiatorial arena were the closed doors and back channels of Florence's *palazzi* and in most cases he

104

achieved his ends through only implied, not actual, intimidation. Unlike the other princes of Italy he did not use judicial murder against his rivals but instead the less extreme modus vivendi of exile or punitive tax assessments. His was the triumph of the rational and calculating mercantile mentality, which could find no place in the political process for wild and undue passion. Instead, he bound others to him not by naked fear but by generosity and obligation. As Vespasiano da Bisticci put it: 'He rewarded those who brought him back [from exile], lending to one a good sum of money, and making a gift to another to help marry his daughter or buy lands'.

Cosimo may not have employed cutthroat murder but in business he could be ruthlessly decisive when the situation demanded. One year after returning from exile Cosimo had cut all ties with his business associates the Bardi family. Up until then the Bardi had held key executive positions with Ilarione di Lippaccio de' Bardi serving as general manager in Florence and Bartolomeo de' Bardi acting as the Medici Bank's director in Rome. In addition, the bank relied upon independent Bardi banking agents in two key northern cities – Gualterotto de' Bardi in Bruges and Ubertino de' Bardi in London. The problem with this arrangement consisted largely in the fact that, because of the huge imbalance in trade between north and south, with most goods and services flowing north but little returning south to Italy, the independent Medici agents in London and Bruges were hard pressed to send their cash earnings south to Florence and Rome. For example, the wool which the Florentines usually bought from the English for finishing in Florence, the English had now decided that they wanted to finish themselves. The punitive export duties which the English imposed on their wool removed one important source of exchange revenue which previously had happily flowed south. Furthermore, those Florentine galleys conveying silks and luxury goods to northern shores were forced to return empty-handed to Florence's showcase port of Pisa, which was an expensive and wasteful arrangement for both shippers and financiers alike.

Cosimo may justifiably have suspected some measure of under-the-table collusion between the various members of his Bardi in-laws. The Bardi agents in London and Bruges owed the Medici Bank a grand total of 22,000 florins in 1437 and these funds were simply not finding their way back to Florence. In the meantime, the Bardi had access to interest-free Medici capital which they could conveniently re-invest and profit from. This was simply unacceptable and so Cosimo despatched Bernardo Portinari to audit the Medici's northern agents and assess the feasibility of opening two wholly-owned Medici bank branches in both London and Bruges. In doing so Cosimo was at last learning from the practices of the Fuggers who, greedy to retain every scrap of profit for themselves, avoided partnerships and joint ventures like the plague, even though it meant that risk could not be spread across a network of agents, nor larger amounts of capital pooled for particularly choice investment opportunities. Portinari's journey proved fruitful and in 1439 the Medici Bank's new Bruges branch was opened followed by a London branch, both with a paid up capital of only 6,000 florins. At the same time, Portinari managed to secure the repayment of some of the Medici's outstanding debts, sending the equivalent of 9,000 florins to the Medici Bank's Geneva branch hidden in a bale of cloth. When circumstances could not be helped, bankers did occasionally smuggle physical coin across international borders. It was a hazardous business, both for the banker as well for the courier, but with a little inventiveness the florins or ducats could be safely and ingeniously hidden from the many cut-purses lying in wait along the route.

After parting ways with the Bardi, Cosimo then strengthened his ties with the Portinari by taking three Portinari children into his home to be raised alongside his own sons Piero, Giovanni and Carlo. These were the orphaned sons of Folco Portinari, brother to Giovanni Portinari, who was the patriarch and general manager of the bank's Venice branch. The Medici Bank's housecleaning had therefore been accomplished, a changing of the managerial guard was enacted and dynastic alliances had been duly reshuffled. As when Cosimo brought home an illegitimate half-caste son from Rome, the reaction of Cosimo's wife Contessina de' Bardi to seeing the relegation and dismissal of her Bardi relatives is not recorded. She would no doubt have been aggrieved by Cosimo's treatment of her Bardi family members, but he was her husband and under his roof she had little recourse but to dutifully obey him in all things.

Earlier, in 1436, another Medici Bank branch had also been established in Ancona on the Adriatic. Ancona was an important transhipment port for goods being sent east to Constantinople and beyond and Cosimo had set up the branch with a capital of 13,000 florins. Traditional masters of the Adriatic, the seafaring Venetians had by now also established themselves firmly on land as well. On 20 July 1437, the Doge of Venice Francesco Foscari was invested by the Emperor Sigismund as duke of Treviso, Feltre, Belluno, Ceneda, Padua, Brescia, Bergamo, Casalmaggiore, Soncino and San Giovanni in Croce in addition to all fortresses in Lombardy east of the River Adda. If Pope Eugenius IV had wanted to protest the investiture he could do little in reality. Eugenius had himself invested Sigismund in Rome in 1433 and was in no position to contest the appointments.

But the formalisation of Venice's territorial gains in Lombardy and the Po Valley would only serve to foment fresh trouble with the duke of Milan. Inevitably, this also meant that Florence would be drawn into the renewed troubles. Venice would call for a renewal of their previous alliance with Florence and Cosimo de' Medici, as *capo* of the Florentine *reggimento*, would be obliged to reinstate it. But would he? Could Florence really continue to be opposed to her neighbour Milan and, if so, where was the profit in it? Cosimo could not help thinking like a banker even if he was effectively now Florence's acknowledged, though unofficial, head of state. From this point on he had more to ponder than simply the continued expansion of the Medici Bank for he must also decide the future strategy of the Florentine state as well. Fortunately for a man of Cosimo's refined tastes he could always escape into his books and manuscripts when the need arose. Banking was Cosimo's forte, political leadership was his necessary burden, but humanist learning would always remain his first and only love.

PART TWO

CONSOLIDATION OF
MEDICI RULE

CHAPTER 5

Humanists and Ecclesiastics

Athens has not been destroyed by the barbarians
but has migrated to Florence.

Angelo Poliziano

The great Italian scholar and poet Petrarch (1304–1374) is traditionally cited as being the founder of the new Latin scholarship which came to be known as humanism. Humanism, that volcanic renewal of interest in classical antiquity which appeared in Italy from around the mid fourteenth-century, is a historiographical watershed often dated for convenience from the year 1345 when Petrarch had rediscovered a collection of letters by the Roman orator Cicero, the compendium known as *ad Atticum*. Cicero's reasoned, grounded arguments and observations about Roman civic and moral life led Petrarch to a startling epiphany, namely that the millennium which had followed the fall of the Western Roman Empire had been a kind of intellectual 'Dark Ages'. Far from their being dismissed as mere 'pagans', Petrarch realised that the ancients should in fact be lauded as having much to teach us about all aspects of mankind's existence upon the earth and how he moved in civilised society.

Petrarch's father Ser Petracco had been a public notary who had held various important posts in Florence, including that of ambassador to Pisa, before being banished in 1302 in connection with an unnamed criminal charge. His son Francesco Petrarca (Anglicised to simply 'Petrarch') was therefore born in exile in Arezzo in the year in 1304, although he always regarded himself as an accidental *Aretine* on account of his father's unfortunate legal circumstances. Ser Petracco pressured his son to enter the legal profession as he had done, forcing him to devote several years of his life to the study of the law at the University of Montpellier and later also in Bologna. Petrarch, whose true interests lay in writing and Latin scholarship, deeply resented this but his proficiency in Latin had nevertheless benefited considerably from his exposure to the legal discipline. When his parents died he and his brother Gherardo found clerical work in Avignon; this work gave him sufficient spare time to perfect his writing and scholarship. His first full scale work *Africa*, an epic written in Latin on the life of the great Roman general Scipio Africanus, was a late medieval 'best-seller' and established Petrarch as a major European author. In 1341, in recognition of his achievement, he was created poet laureate, the first to hold that honour since antiquity. He then travelled widely throughout Europe, serving as an ambassador, and has with some justification been described as 'history's first tourist'.

Petrarch discovered in writers like Augustine and Cicero his abiding curiosity for Latin literature and moral philosophy and he also perfected his vernacular Italian poetry in such works as the *Canzoniere* ('Songbook') the central theme of which is Petrarch's love for his muse, the immortal literary figure of Laura. Petrarch is principally known however for his Latin writings, including *Secretum* ('My Secret Book'), *De Otio Religiosorum* ('On Religious Leisure'), *De Vita Solitaria* ('On the Solitary Life') and *De Sui Ipsius et Multorum Ignorantia* ('On his Own Ignorance and that of Many Others'). The latter was a pamphlet in which Petrarch responded to critics from Padua who decried Petrarch's ignorance of scholasticism. Petrarch's spirited defence of Ciceronian rhetoric, as applied to the real world of practical politics and diplomacy, embodied the essence of humanism as it was later to be practised in the Florentine republic. As Petrarch eloquently put it in *Remediis Utriusque Fortunae* ('Remedies for Fortune Fair and Foul'), 'Philosophy offers not wisdom but the love of wisdom. Therefore, whoever wants her must win her through love ... True wisdom can be grasped and loved only by pure and pious minds.' This yearning for sanctification and purification in order to be made worthy of true knowledge was a recurring theme in Petrarch's corpus and consequently the poet was always battling the inner demons of the mystical versus the profane (a similar battle would play out nearly two-hundred years later in the theocratic Florence of Fra Savonarola). Petrarch's championing of classical authors and his adoption of their arguments to the cut-and-thrust of medieval politics was eminently 'modern' in spirit and would set the tone for much of the scholarship which would follow in Renaissance Florence.

Petrarch's friend and correspondent, the Florentine Giovanni Boccaccio (1313-1375), was also introduced early on in life to a profession for which he had distinctly little taste (in Boccaccio's case it was banking) and just like Petrarch he realised that his real vocation lay in writing, specifically in verse composition. His early works included *Filostrato and Teseida*, which were the sources for Chaucer's *Troilus and Criseyde* and *The Knight's Tale*. Much of the material for his verse was drawn from Boccaccio's own everyday experiences in Naples, where he had spent several years studying canon law at the *Studium*, and then later on in Florence. The work for which he is most well-known is the *Decameron*, the first important work of literature to be composed in the argot of Tuscan, what would later become modern Italian prose. Returning to Florence, he entered the *arte dei giudici e notai* as a lawyer and served the republic faithfully as an ambassador and administrator. Like Petrarch, he travelled widely and was despatched by the state on official business to cities such as Brandenburg, Milan, and Avignon.

In October 1350, he was delegated to greet Petrarch during the latter's visit to Florence and was asked to put the great humanist up as a guest at his home. With the time and leisure to converse and get to know one another's minds, the two men formed a strong lifelong friendship. Boccaccio would compliment Petrarch by describing him as his 'teacher and magister'. Petrarch also embarked Boccaccio on his initial study of classical Greek and Latin literature, and the following year they met again in Padua where Boccaccio was trying to persuade his mentor to accept a chair at the university in Florence. It was as a direct result of this second fortuitous meeting that Boccaccio was encouraged to write the *Genealogia deorum gentilium* ('On the Genealogy of the Gods of the Gentiles'). Written in elegant Latin prose, the *Genealogia* was a ground-breaking compilation of the genealogies of the classical pantheons of Ancient Greece and

Rome in fifteen books. Boccaccio advocated the principle that the writers of antiquity often enshrined the deepest truths in allegorical formulas.

Though he was not a native of Florence, having been born in the commune of Stignano near Buggiano, Coluccio Salutati (1331–1406) was another loyal administrator of Florence who was appointed chancellor in 1375 and held the post until his death in 1406. As the most important bureaucrat of the Florentine republic, Salutati was privy to the innermost dealings of the *signoria* and his classical education was enshrined in the commands, orders and instructions that he issued to the government servants of Florence. An accomplished Latin grammarian who had learned his skills in Bologna, Salutati was to become one of Renaissance Florence's most important political and cultural leaders. 'I have always believed', Salutati wrote, 'I must imitate antiquity not simply to reproduce it, but in order to produce something new'. Accordingly his ideal was personified in the civic humanism of the Roman republic and his hero would have been the guardian of the republic, Marcus Junius Brutus, rather than the tyrant Julius Caesar. When he was granted citizenship in 1400 his citation read: 'especially for his capacity in rhetoric and the *ars dictaminis*'.

Salutati was one of Florence's earliest bibliophiles, amassing a collection of eight-hundred books (considered the largest library in Florence at the time) at the cost of most of his workaday salary. His valuable work as a manuscript collector and researcher led to the discovery of Cicero's *Epistulae ad Familiares* ('Lost Letters to his Friends') which completely revised the medieval world's notion of the great Roman statesman and orator. Meanwhile, his more politically-inclined research into antiquity established Florence's origins firmly in the era of the Roman republic as opposed to the imperial period. Like Boccaccio he was also an ardent correspondent of Petrarch and he inspired and promoted the careers of many of the younger emerging humanists such as Poggio Bracciolini, Niccolò Niccoli and Leonardo Bruni. In 1397, he was instrumental in bringing the revered Byzantine scholar Manuel Chrysoloras to Florence to teach one of the first ever university courses in Greek since the end of the Roman Empire. By bringing Chrysoloras to Florence, Salutati enabled a small group of scholars to learn to read Aristotle and Plato in the original ancient Greek.

What Petrarch, Boccaccio and Salutati all brought to the study of classical and even contemporary literature was a search for hidden layers of meaning and symbolism in textual material. In doing so they were merely applying the tools which medieval scholasticism had already bestowed on them. Conventional Church wisdom held that Biblical texts for example embodied no less than four different layers of meaning (literal, allegorical, moral and anagogical) and the habit of deconstructing writings in this meticulous way naturally led to the same rigorous analysis of profane literature. The Florentine humanist Cristoforo Landino pointed this out by alluding to the truth that when poetry 'most appears to be narrating something most humble and ignoble or to be singing a little fable to delight idle ears, at that very time it is writing in a rather secret way the most excellent things of all, which are drawn forth from the fountain of the gods'. This was anagoge (ἀναγωγή), a literary device whereby a commonplace and visible motif points upwards to things both invisible and divine.

But at the heart of these literary techniques and discoveries lay the central motivation of humanism itself which was the desperate need to question, re-evaluate and thereby better understand conventional received wisdom. This urge to inquire into all forms of knowledge, both ancient and modern, was inherent in the career of Cosimo de' Medici's humanist friend the Florentine chancellor Leonardo Bruni (1370–1444). An *Aretine* foreigner like Petrarch, Bruni was in the same mould as Coluccio Salutati, who had first encouraged him to pursue Latin and Greek. His subsequent translations of Aristotle broke new ground but provoked the ire of the conservative Church schoolmen who regarded the pre-existing Aristotelian texts with the sanctity of holy writ.

Bruni took Petrarch's concept of the Middle Ages as having been *tenebrae* or 'darkness' and developed the idea into the world's first 'three-period' view of history as being composed of Antiquity, Middle Ages, and Modern. His most important work was the *Historiarum Florentini populi libri XII* ('History of the Florentine People in 12 Books'), often described as being the world's first modern history book and which was widely imitated by humanist historians at the time. Bruni's *Historiarum* betrays an infectious level of pride and enthusiasm for Florence in a non-Florentine resident. In Book XI he describes for instance the novel festivities laid on to celebrate the birth of the French king's son in 1392. The revelries featured: 'an equestrian battle with arms and equipment, representing a real battle in the form of a contest. Parti-coloured vestments gleaming with purple and gold covered their armour. The only thing that distinguished the contest from true battle was that they fought with blunt swords.' Pride of one's adopted state could provoke a reaction in kind in humanist circles and Latin and Greek scholars were not immune from stirring feelings of patriotism. Bruni's *Laudatio Florentinae Urbis* ('In Praise of Florence') incited Pier Paolo Decembrio to compose his own 'panegyric' on Milan which was dedicated to Duke Filippo Maria Visconti.

Another foreigner and an even closer confidant of Cosimo de' Medici's was Marsilio Ficino (1433–99) whose reconciliation of classical with Christian ideals revolutionised not only Renaissance philosophy and literature but also the visual arts, deeply influencing such artists as Michelangelo and Raphael. Born in Figline Valdarno, fifteen miles southeast of Florence, Ficino was to spend his career focusing less on Petrarchan *tenebrae* than on Platonic illumination. Some in the humanist movement like Leonardo Bruni would be less interested in the vague metaphysics of Plato than in the concise political lessons of Cicero or Livy. Ficino, however, had a marked disposition towards the transcendent and the eternal and his talented, eclectic mind flitted and glided in the Platonic realm of Forms with consummate ease. Under Cosimo's indulgent and understanding patronage he translated Plato's entire collection of dialogues from Greek to Latin, adding in the process a neat twist. If the secular humanists saw the study of the humanities as being central to a well-rounded modern education, then Ficino preached that the human soul was the proper centre of nature itself.

With sprite-like mischievousness Ficino always took pleasure in calling himself 'a priest of the Muses' thereby perpetuating the general Renaissance tendency to sanctify the profane and profane the sanctified. Ficino was a great syncretist who was effortlessly able to combine and blend the symbols and tropes of classical antiquity with those of scholastic Christendom. From the farm that he owned in rural Careggi in the Mugello, where he and Cosimo de' Medici enjoyed protracted philosophical conversations, we even get the slightest whiff of heresy in his suggestion that all those ancient high priests of antiquity (Zoroaster, Hermes and Orpheus) were essentially selling the same spiritual truths as the saints and apostles of Christendom. Around Ficino would coalesce the tight-knit group of humanist philosophers which would form Cosimo's grandson Lorenzo *il Magnifico's* inner intellectual circle; amongst others it would include both Angelo Poliziano (also known as Politian) and the headstrong Giovanni Pico della Mirandola, whom Machiavelli would later describe as '*uomo quasiché divino*', meaning that Pico's genius was of an 'almost divine provenance'.

While his translation of Plato's complete writings established the humanist basis of what we would call 'modern philosophy', this versatile scholar, philosopher, doctor, musician and priest was no dry academic but a fun-loving individual who indulged his taste for fine wine and the arts, dabbled in vegetarianism centuries before it even became fashionable and accompanied himself on the lyre whilst intoning plangent Orphic hymns. Ficino's ambivalent attitude towards love and sex, and especially towards homosexuality, have been contemplated and discussed at length. Ficino and indeed most of the humanists were eager to explore the meaning of physical and emotional forms of love, free of the shackles of Church scrutiny and dogma. The Church was always too quick to cast the pronouncement of sin on practically every species of love except for that which concerned the Heavenly Father. Florence's Platonic Academy made a special point of meeting each year on 7 November, the putative date of Plato's birth, in order to read his central text on the subject of love, the *Symposium*. As a result, Ficino had developed a *Commentary* on the work in which he expounded his own views on the subject, writing: 'The man enjoys the physical beauty of the youth with his eyes; the youth enjoys the man's beauty with his mind. The youth, who is beautiful in body only, by this practice becomes beautiful in soul; the man who is beautiful also in soul only, feasts his eyes upon bodily beauty.'

Such sentiments might, it was true, lead to the physical expression of love between men and indeed after Ficino's death scurrilous tongues in Florentine society speculated about the true nature of the relationship he had shared with one of his devotees, Benedetto Varchi, who was openly accused of being a sodomite. Ficino's correspondence with another of his constant followers, the good looking young Giovanni Cavalcanti, also belie a strong romantic interest and are nothing short of love letters. On the one hand, Ficino replies to his own question that physical relations between men was 'a wicked crime' but on the other he also acknowledged that it was possible to have 'too great a love for the body' and comments, 'that is not strange either, since the body is the companion and child of the soul ... the best hope is to remember that God understands how difficult and dangerous is the province which he has given us to live in and govern.' There is no doubt that priests such as the Dominican friar Savonarola were to later use Ficino's freethinking example to preach that, spiritually speaking, Florence was sailing awfully close to the winds of damnation. But regardless of his exact position on an act which was still punishable in Florentine society by the most brutal means, through his work on Platonic dialogues such as the *Symposium* and *Phaedrus* Ficino was the first in history to coin the phrase 'Platonic love'. It was fortunate that academics like Ficino were at least laying the foundation for greater toleration of such practices otherwise great geniuses like Michelangelo and Leonardo da Vinci may have fallen foul of Florence's draconian sodomy laws long before they had had a chance to shine – Leonardo had indeed been accused by the Night Watch of sodomising a known male prostitute named Jacopo Saltarelli in April 1476 but was later acquitted.

What was the true dynamic between the established Church and the emerging humanist movement? Renaissance humanism and the intellectual fever which it engendered, particularly that which arose in the Florence of the Quattrocento with its apparently overwhelmingly rational and secular preoccupations, is often misinterpreted as having been somehow in opposition to the prevailing 'religious' worldview of Christendom and the Church. This is a common though quite misleading way to perceive humanism's relationship with the Churchmen. Indeed, as humanism took root in the fertile intellectual scholarly soil of Italy we find amongst its chief exponents not only sundry members of the Curia like Francesco Nelli, Poggio Bracciolini, Ambrogio Traversari (St. Ambrose Traversari) or Basilios Bessarion but also popes such as Innocent VII (who is widely credited with being the first 'humanist pope'), Nicholas V, Pius II, Sixtus IV, Alexander VI and Leo X. Indeed, by the time of Æneas Silvius Piccolomini (Pope Pius II), we encounter a man who was not only the Supreme Pontiff of Roman Catholic Christendom but also a prolific author who could pen such humanist treatises as *On the Education of Boys* (1450), not to mention works of highbrow smut like *The Tale of Two Lovers*.

These humanist scholars, many of whom were high Churchmen, had no innate desire to contradict the teachings of the Church or collapse its edifice. Instead they sought, through these ancient manuscripts, to further develop their understanding of man's purpose on earth within the existing Christian framework. This is clearly shown by the fact that, when humanism transmuted into the kinds of illicit Hermetic knowledge exemplified by scholars and thinkers like Giordano Bruno, the ecclesiastical establishment could still close ranks and come down hard on what they perceived to be dangerous and heretical ideas; ideas moreover that encroached on their own jealously-guarded spiritual preserve. Indeed, even during the first flourishing of the movement, a 'humanist pope' such as Sixtus IV could still be followed just as easily by a conservative like Innocent VIII who was only too eager to convene an inquisitorial tribunal to investigate the unorthodox and revolutionary declarations being put forth in Giovanni Pico della Mirandola's *900 Theses*. The difference between the edifying rediscovery of ancient knowledge and outright heresy was often marked by an exceedingly fine line. What the humanists sought above all else was a timeless space–instructive and educational in character–where they could increase their awareness of truth and beauty free of the stultifying omnipresent canonical constrictions of Christian dogma. The early Church Fathers had already appropriated Plato and Aristotle and spliced the pagan teachings of these classical philosophers into a Christian theological context; the feeling was therefore that Christianity was already so well-represented in the intellectual life of Europe, through the medieval Scholastic movement, that it should not be able to lay further claim to the enlightening wisdom of the ancients that was newly coming to light around this time. In this sort of territoriality lay the basis for the Renaissance humanists' deprecating remarks about the *scholastici*.

The lawyer and notary Poggio Bracciolini conducted much of his freelance investigative, bibliophilia under the aegis of his on-going work for the Church as well as for popes like Martin V and Eugenius IV. Although he consorted regularly with his lifelong collaborator, the great Florentine manuscript collector

Niccolò de' Niccoli, he could not have overtly followed any lines of study regarded by his employers as being dangerously unorthodox. This notwithstanding, humanism often had its own impetus independent of the Church. When Bracciolini discovered the only surviving manuscript of Lucretius's *De Rerum Natura* ('On the Nature of Things') at a German monastery in January 1417, little would anyone know that this 7,400 line Latin verse poem based on the ideas of the ancient Greek philosophers Epicurus and Democritus would impact the entire subsequent development of the Renaissance, contribute to the subsequent Reformation of the Church and lead to the development of modern secular science as we understand it today. It is from these two ancient Pre-Socratic Greek philosophers that modern science derives its concept of the 'atom', which comes from the ancient Greek word ἄτομος (*átomos*, 'indivisible'), which in turn derives from the root etymology ἀ- (a-, 'not') + τέμνω (*témnō*, 'I cut'), hence 'not-cuttable'. Bracciolini is, therefore, in certain important respects one of the architects of the modern scientific era.

Poggio Bracciolini was indeed typical of the early humanists, walking a fine line between conventional religious orthodoxy on the one hand and, on the other, adulation of their pagan Italian forebears who, despite their unredeemed condition and their habitual tendency to sacrifice to strange gods, yet still evinced all the recognisable moral and civic traits of a fourteenth-century citizen of Florence, Milan, Rome or Bologna. Bracciolini himself was no great paragon of Christian saintly virtue; like the Epicureans of antiquity he loved rich food and the company of pretty young women and, satyr-like, had cheerfully fathered fourteen bastards. At the age of fifty-six he married a coltish eighteen-year-old beauty who bore him six more legitimate offspring. Aside from his more highbrow pursuits and accomplishments, Poggio Bracciolini might also be considered the founder of the modern joke book for, in 1470, he published the *Facetiae*, an anthology of scatological jokes touching on such subjects as farting and defecation.

Born in Arezzo in 1380 to poor parents, Bracciolini had gravitated to Florence with empty pockets but, despite his penury, had somehow managed to enrol in the *Studio Fiorentino*. Here he studied first Latin under Giovanni Malpaghino of Ravenna, the friend and protégé of Petrarch, as well as Greek under Manuel Chrysoloras, then later notarial law, being inducted into the *arte dei giudici e notai* at the age of twenty-one. His unrivalled abilities and dexterity as a manuscript copyist soon brought him to the attention of humanist royalty in Florence, such as Coluccio Salutati and Niccolò de' Niccoli. Gaining entry to the Chancery of Apostolic Briefs in the Roman Curia in 1403, Bracciolini was promoted up to the rank of *scriptor apostolicus* by the antipope John XXIII and accompanied the ill-fated pontiff to the Council of Constance in 1414 where he came into contact with, and subsequently became a close friend of, Baldassare Cossa's private banker Cosimo de' Medici.

Despite a fifty-year career in papal service, where he eventually rose to the top job of *apostolicus secretarius* under Pope Martin V, Bracciolini found time to undertake frequent sabbaticals to France, Germany and Switzerland where he rummaged through the libraries of sundry abbeys and monasteries for rare books and manuscripts. An archivist or librarian's worst nightmare, Bracciolini raised book-theft to a fine art during these expeditions; pocketing, bribing and copying his way across Europe, he spirited most of the works that his detective efforts recovered back to Italy, where the manuscripts wound up in the growing collections of Niccolò de' Niccoli and Cosimo de' Medici. Bracciolini's extraordinary find of Lucretius's *De Rerum Natura* subsequently made its way into Niccoli's possession whereat he initiated a copy in his own italic handwriting. Bracciolini would later grumble that Niccoli had sat on his original copy for fourteen years and indeed the copy that he found subsequently did disappear and, no doubt, eventually found its way, centuries later, into the private collection of some billionaire industrialist.

Bracciolini was resident in Florence from 1434-36 where his employer Pope Eugenius IV had based his papal court whilst in exile from Rome. In 1434, he sold one of his rarer manuscripts, a work by Livy, and with the proceeds he commissioned a tasteful villa in the Valdarno Valley of the Arno which he fastidiously decorated with antique sculptures and busts of classical thinkers and philosophers. Following his return from exile Cosimo de' Medici was a frequent guest during this time and the two enthusiastic humanists indulged their passion for conversation and speculation amidst the congenial, rustic surroundings. A recurring topic of conversation may well have been the justifications of classical writers for money lending. Cosimo himself was always troubled by guilt at having made his fortune through 'unchristian usury'. The Scriptures were quite clear on this subject. Exodus 22:25 stated: 'If you lend money to one of my people among you who is needy, do not treat it like a business deal; charge no interest', and this was further reinforced by Leviticus 25:37, Ezekiel 22:12 and numerous other problematic passages. Cosimo might have been somewhat assuaged by Deuteronomy 23:20, which compromised somewhat in stipulating that 'You may charge a foreigner interest, but not a fellow Israelite, so that the LORD your God may bless you in everything you put your hand to', but this did not alter the fact that Cosimo *did* still lend money at interest to his fellow Florentines. Unfortunately, profane literature provided no more comfort than Scripture. Boccaccio's *Decameron* derides the two usurers who are afraid of the townspeople's' reaction to their shameful trade, while in Circle 7, cantos 12-17 of Dante's *Divina Commedia*, Virgil offers a long explanation as to why usurers are placed at the same level as sodomites, blasphemers, suicides and murderers. Indeed, officially speaking the Christian Church denied the burial of usurers in sanctified ground, stipulating that 'their bodies should be buried in ditches, together with dogs and cattle'.

The learned and widely-read Bracciolini would have been only too glad to salve Cosimo's Christian conscience by stressing that great figures are not subject to the same laws as other men. In a thinly-veiled reference to Cosimo de' Medici himself, a speaker in one of Bracciolini's many humanist tracts proclaims: 'Only the little people and lower orders of a city are controlled by your laws'; Cosimo might therefore have speculated whether this insight extended to divine law as well. When not relaxing in Bracciolini's philosophical garden the two men were off investigating old Roman ruins together at the sea port of Ostia. While they rummaged and dug in the clay they doubtless continued their musings al fresco. Cosimo's friend observed that ancient Roman civic leaders had seen themselves as living and acting (for the common good) above the common run of man – the 'mob' as the Romans had disparagingly referred to the lower orders. And, as in the days of republican Rome and later Augustus, great deeds often sprang from great acts of cruelty too, as when Julius Caesar starved the women and children at the Siege of Alessia, a hair-raising tale which recalled Florence's more recent treatment of the unfortunate women of Pisa. Yes, these were all valid points with impeccable classical credentials but they certainly ran counter to what he had been taught by his father, Giovanni di Bicci, who had impressed upon him the need to treat the *popolo minuto* with kindness and benevolence. There was no getting away from the recurrent theme of cruelty in the ancient world and it was all too easy to use this as a justification for unchristian conduct.

In 1453, Bracciolini was granted the considerable public honour of being nominated chancellor of the Florentine republic upon the death of his intimate friend Carlo Aretino, the previous incumbent. The worldly appointment, which had probably been engineered at the behest of his friend Cosimo de' Medici, sounded prestigious but was, to the inveterate scholar, merely a worldly distraction from his more cloistered and scholarly interests. Public duties interfered with the writing of his *History of Florence* and when he eventually passed away in 1459 this outstanding humanist, researcher, copyist, educator and celebrant of profane humour was commemorated sparingly with a statue by Donatello and a portrait by Antonio del Pollaiuolo. Men like Bracciolini were archetypical of these Florentine humanists; often deeply flawed human beings, these men did not allow their mortal vagaries to prevent them from devoting themselves to studying and teaching the *studia humanitatis*, a phrase first coined by Leonardo Bruni and referring to the study of human endeavours (the five core subjects of which comprised: grammar, rhetoric, poetry, history and ethics). The *studia humanitatis* were henceforth held separate and distinct from the disciplines of theology and metaphysics.

The reproduction of this knowledge salvaged from the ancient world was becoming increasingly standardised in Florence by the turn of the fifteenth-century. Although individual manuscripts might be hand-copied on a case-by-case basis by gifted copyists like Bracciolini, the reproduction of texts was also achieving a certain level of standardisation and commercialisation. *Stationarii* (*stationarius*, or plural, *stationarii*, from which we derive the modern word 'stationer') like Vespasiano da Bisticci were responsible for organising the wholesale bulk copying of books and manuscripts as well as their retail distribution afterwards. Vespasiano himself records how he completed an impressive collection of two-hundred volumes for Cosimo de' Medici in just under two years by employing a workforce of forty-five professional scribes. Such copyist workshops later had to compete with the first printing presses to arrive in Italy. In 1465, the Germans Sweynheym and Pannartz set up Italy's first printing press at the Benedictine monastery at Subiaco near Rome and within five years of commencing operations had produced a prodigious twelve-thousand volumes, a feat which Vespasiano would have required a workforce of one thousand scribes to equal in the same time frame. By the end of the century Italy was already home to around one hundred and fifty similar modern presses.

Florence in the fifteenth-century lent itself to a remarkable cross-fertilisation between the intellectual ideas of the humanists and the wider artistic and cultural community. Researchers, copyists and archivists like Bracciolini and Niccolò de' Niccoli mingled freely with the prominent artists of the day, luminaries like Brunelleschi, Ghiberti, Donatello and Michelozzo. The great artistic patrons of Florence like the Medici provided another important nexus for the interplay of ideas and artistry. Central to the concept of the Renaissance was innovation, and this was often not true innovation but instead *revivalism*. The structure of Brunelleschi's dome for the Duomo was not an original invention of the Quattrocento but a revival of similar, though not identical, techniques which had been used in the Pantheon of Rome.

117

Meanwhile, Florentine writers of comedy tried to emulate Terence and Plautus; tragedians emulated Seneca; purveyors of epics strove to imitate Virgil or Homer. The ideas of antiquity, articulated by the humanists and graphically depicted by the artists, found especially fertile soil in an Italy which had been less deeply affected by the Greek style of the Byzantines or the Gothic style of Germany. The most fecund ground in Italy was likewise found in Florence whose republicanism made the beautification of the city by its wealthy patrons practically a civic duty.

Another significant factor which allowed Florence to become a magnet for the peninsula's greatest intellectual and artistic talent was the fact that the city did not permit its *arti* to railroad these thinkers and craftsmen into becoming guild members. All writers and artists of merit were entitled to venture to Florence and work freely as foreigners alongside the locals. By contrast, Albrecht Dürer complained after his visit to Venice in 1506 that he had been summoned before the magistrate no less than three times and been forced to pay four florins to the arts guild in return for the work he was doing. Dürer had bitterly criticized the intolerance of the Venetian artists towards outside competition. So it was that Florence was uniquely able to provide a fertile, libertarian soil in which the intellectual currents of humanism could co-exist with traditional, conservative forms of Church worship, communion, fellowship and piety.

Florence's brand of 'civic humanism' meanwhile stood diametrically opposed to despotic forms of government, as existed for instance in Milan, the former Roman city of Mediolanum, or other city-states which were ruled over by a *signor* or, even worse, a *tiranno* (tyrant). Florence's humanist intellectuals argued instead for the level-headed execution of power and the upholding of the rule of law. They judged the safety and security of the person and his private property to be sacrosanct and looked to the state to confer honours and career openings fairly and equitably to all deserving and qualified citizens. Above all, Florentine humanism gave a gloss of republican and democratic acceptability to a political system which was, deep in its bones, fundamentally an entrenched oligarchy. For all their talk of the beauty of truth, many practising humanists, like Bracciolini for example, were enamoured of good old fashioned Roman rhetoric and its ability to sway the common masses. It was Ciceronian persuasion, not love of the eternal Platonic Forms, which had the power both to coax and justify unpalatable courses of political action and the practical-minded Cosimo de' Medici knew this as well as most. Cosimo also knew of the importance of making a public show of civic piety too. Humanism was a force to be reckoned with but the traditional power of the Church still demanded to be acknowledged as paramount. Cosimo de' Medici now made a show of putting his state at the disposal of the Holy Roman Church for the resolution of some of its most pressing issues.

In 1439 Florence became host to an Ecumenical Council of the Roman Catholic Church, what was to be the most brilliant convocation of combined Latin and Greek ecclesiastical intellect in several hundred years. The council had begun life as the Seventeenth Ecumenical Council and had been convoked as the Council of Basel by Pope Martin V before his death in February 1431 and in nature was a strongly conciliar Church council. The earlier Council of Constance, which deposed the antipope John XXIII, had already established this 'conciliar' precedent in which Church councils had the authority to impose their will on the pope himself, or if necessary even depose a pope as had happened at Constance. In reality, however, the Council of Constance had done little to heal the breach and its assertion that General Councils of the Church were possessed of an authority derived directly from God (and were by extension superior to the Pope's own authority) was both inflammatory and dangerously inimical to Church discipline. In December 1431 Pope Martin's successor, Pope Eugenius IV, contrived to exert his authority over the conciliarists and reclaim papal supremacy by ordering the Seventeenth Ecumenical Council dissolved and all future Church councils to be held in Italy under close papal scrutiny. It was around this time that he resolved to convene a gathering of the Eastern and Western Churches in order to repair the Great Schism, that crucial set of differences in ecclesiastical doctrine that had arisen between the Latin and Byzantine world and which had prevented their two Churches from being in full communion since the middle of the eleventh-century.

The Great Schism can be regarded as a result of doctrinal differences or it can be regarded as a difference between the two fundamentally divergent management styles of both Churches, with doctrine being held up as the superficial pretext for the divide. To the Latin papacy there was no question of the ultimate supremacy of the See of Rome and of the rule of the Pope–the bishop of Rome–on ecclesiastical and doctrinal issues (although this 'supremacy' had, as we have already seen, been challenged recently by the conciliar movement). The Eastern Church on the other hand took a more collegial approach in which jurisdictional authority was seen to be vested not in the pope alone but in an ecumenical council representing the five patriarchs of both East and West. In this way, Eastern Orthodoxy was seen to reside in the rulings of the first seven ecumenical councils of the Church, decisions concerning deep matters of dogma and doctrinal uniformity which had been passed down from antiquity pure and inviolate. Additionally, in the East the *basileus* or 'Eastern Roman Emperor' retained a certain degree of practical power to bend the Church to the needs of the state when the situation demanded it, although this had of course created many unnecessary problems in the case of issues such as Iconoclasm or the Monophysite heresy where the *basileus* had become heavily embroiled in directing Church policy. In the Latin West, by contrast, the pope had on many occasions during the last half millennium come out in direct opposition to the wishes of the Western Holy Roman Emperor and indeed the jurisdictional disputes between papacy and Empire (most obviously expressed in the struggle between Guelphs and Ghibellines) had coloured much of Western European development since Charlemagne's time.

It was not a foregone conclusion that the council would be held in Italy at Pope Eugenius's pleasure. Despite the Pope's call for its dissolution, the Council of Basel was still sitting and the conciliarists were indeed calling for the great reunification of East and West to be attempted within *their* jurisdiction. Attempts to discuss the Schism at Basel had not gone smoothly however and, on one occasion when the matter had been debated, the arguments were so boisterous that Æneas Silvius Piccolomini, later consecrated as Pope Pius II, was led to complain, 'You would have found drunkards of a tavern better behaved'. Besides, the Greek side were making it a precondition of their attendance that the Roman Pope must be present in person for the deliberations and there was little likelihood of that if the proceedings were held at Basel or Avignon or Savoy where the conciliarists had their three key strongholds. As the *basileus* of Constantinople John VIII Palaiologos regarded these other Italian locations for the new council to be too distant and inconvenient for consideration, Pope Eugenius instead chose Ferrara as the venue. Seven years of diplomatic negotiation ensued and, in February 1438, John VIII Palaiologos arrived in Italy with a seven hundred strong delegation from the East. As an incentive for them to accord the council at Ferrara their full weight the Pope had generously, though somewhat hastily, offered to foot the Byzantines' costs throughout their sojourn in Italy. Meanwhile, the move drew the inevitable backlash in Basel and the conciliarists retaliated by electing Amadeus VIII, Count of Savoy and Bonne of Berry, as an antipope taking the name of Felix V.

On both sides of the great East-West schism there was, after 384 years, a strong desire for union. Broadly speaking, there came into being a body of opinion, reflected in the ideas of the more idealistic clerics of both worlds, which regarded reconciliation between East and West as being the only effective way that Christendom could begin to address its larger problems. In the case of the Latin Church there was an additional unspoken ambition for the papacy, once the rift had been healed, to consolidate and extend its supremacy over the Eastern Orthodox Church. The West's intentions had already been revealed earlier during the Latin conquest of Constantinople in 1204, when the Latin Church had forced the conquered Greeks of Constantinople to convert to the Roman Catholic rite at sword point. This had been the single most damaging episode in recent East-West relations. Not only had the Latin Crusaders rode roughshod over Orthodoxy, but–as if in some cruel parody of the Western European feudal system–the Byzantine domains themselves had been fractured into a number of despotates subject to Latin lords. The people of the Greek Orthodox faith had never fully recovered from this betrayal and arguably still haven't to this very day.

For the Byzantines in particular the gathering had as much a political dimension as it did an ecclesiastical one, however, for the desire for union on the part of successive Greek *basileis* was usually a function of their need for Latin military support against their Eastern aggressors and tended to fluctuate accordingly. But as late as the mid-1400s the need for Western aid had plainly become critical; the former Seljuk Sultanate of Rum, against which the Christian Crusaders had fought to liberate Jerusalem and the Holy Sepulcher from 1095–1291, had by this time been supplanted by a ferocious new Muslim superpower: the Ottoman Turks. Under Sultan Murad II, the Ottomans had been making steady, relentless progress in conquering large tracts of formerly Byzantine Greek territory. Ultimately, in the spring of 1422, Murad had laid siege to Constantinople itself, establishing countless catapults, mangonels and trebuchets all along the length of the famous Theodosian Walls which pounded the defenders within both night and day. The siege, like so many before it, had miscarried thanks both to the strength of the city's ancient defences and the vigour of its co-*basileus* John VIII Palaiologos, who comported himself well as an inspired wartime leader. In the immediate aftermath of the siege, the Pope had despatched Antonio da Massa, Provincial of the Franciscan Order, to discuss a nine-point plan for Church union but as usual the Latins expected their pound of flesh in return. The discussions had foundered on the customary Latin demand for the Orthodox congregation to return to the Roman fold as a precondition of any military relief forces being despatched from the West.

Worse was yet to follow. In 1430 Thessalonica had fallen and been sacked after a gruelling eight-year-long siege and that same year Ioannina, the capital and largest city of Epirus, had reverted to the Turks who now also pressed hard against the borders of Albania, threatening both Transylvania and Hungary. The once proud and mighty Byzantine Empire had by this time been reduced to little more than the city and suburbs of Constantinople and it would only be a matter of time before the Sultan once more set his sights on this final, ultimate (and by now considerably denuded) prize. To the collective psyche of the inhabitants of Western Christendom the Turk was a savage and barbarous enemy. When one thought of the Turk, if one dared to think of him at all, one could not help but remember their habit of impaling their victims through the anus with a pointed stake, the sharpened end of which would emerge from between the victim's collar bone. This form of execution was peculiarly unique to the Turk, until at least the career of Vlad III, Prince of Wallachia (1431–1476) who adopted the Turk's own methods as a grisly form of retaliation. The fact that Christians themselves burned their own heretics alive on bonfires was conveniently overlooked in this tendency to imbue the Turk with all the trappings of an apocalyptic and demonic foe. To make matters worse, the Turkish offensives were spearheaded by the Janissaries, the crack regiments of élite troops who had been abducted from their families as young Christian boys for service in the Sultan's armed forces and raised as Muslims.

There had nonetheless been some elements of cooperation between East and West on military matters. In 1423, the Byzantine despot Andronikos Palaiologos (son of the Byzantine *basileus* Manuel II Palaiologos and brother of the co-*basileus* John VIII Palaiologos) offered a beleaguered Thessalonica to the Republic of Venice, which then assumed the burden of its defence in return for Venice's upholding of Greek Orthodoxy. In September 1423, the new Doge of Venice Francesco Foscari had sailed into the harbour of Thessalonica with six transports full of food and provisions for the city; however the commissioners he left behind had proved largely incompetent, had rapidly alienated their Greek population, and moreover had been obliged to pay the Sultan annual protection money of 60,000 ducats per year to keep his army from storming the city. The final Turkish onslaught, when it came, was every bit as barbarous as the defenders within the walls had anticipated and when the bloodletting had finally subsided no less than 7,000 mostly women and children were carried off into captivity.

The Great Schism between the Eastern and Western Churches had, in the secular domain, been hampering effective military cooperation between the Greek and Latin world for too long. John VIII Palaiologos had done more than most Byzantine leaders to try to heal the rift. In 1424, following the recent Turkish siege of Constantinople, he had travelled to Venice, Milan, Mantua and Hungary for discussions with Western rulers on how they could come to Eastern Christendom's much-needed aid. Negotiations had been disappointingly inconclusive, however, and when he arrived in Hungary the future Emperor Sigismund refused point blank to provide military assistance unless the East-West Schism was first resolved. Furthermore, he was outraged–as only an Emperor could be–that the Byzantines should have entrusted the defence of Thessalonica to the Empire's traditional enemy Venice.

Now the situation was deemed critical enough for the *basileus* himself to make the journey to Ferrara. Here, he hoped to meet with the assembled princes of Europe and create an alliance which could counter the Turks on a more equal footing. John VIII's reign had been depressingly overshadowed by the Turkish threat. As a child he had been removed from the capital to the safe haven of Monembasia while a beleaguered Constantinople endured a siege by the previous Sultan, Bayezid I. In 1422, when Sultan Murad II had advanced into Greek territory and again laid siege to the capital, he had–in addition to the usual siege engines–employed frightful anti-personnel swivel guns called falconets for the very first time. John VIII found himself caught in the middle of the rapacious Turks on the one hand and the growing power of the Italian mercantile city-states and the Western Empire on the other. Meanwhile, his Imperial Court was but a shadow of the heyday of the Byzantine Empire, reduced to the indignity of occupying a few rooms in the once grand imperial palace. Union with the West was therefore imperative. He left his brother Constantine in control of Constantinople and set out for Italy with an impressive entourage.

It is hard, on the face of it at least, to find fault with John VIII's tireless efforts to resolve the doctrinal Schism and, with the West's help, reconstitute the former power and stability of the Byzantine Empire in the East. John was a great *basileus* in this respect, one of the last great ones in fact. But his broad strategic agenda was deeply criticised as folly by his own father. Before his death in June 1425, the *basileus* Manuel II had confided in his old friend the historian George Sphrantzes that:

> 'At other times in our history, my son might have been a great *basileus*; but he is not for the present time, for he sees and thinks on a grand scale, in a manner which would have been appropriate in the prosperous days of our forefathers. But today, with our troubles closing in upon us from every side, our Empire needs not a great *basileus* but a good manager. And I fear that his grandiose schemes and endeavours may bring ruin upon our house.'

The older man could see the writing on the wall and plainly realised that the Ottoman star was now in the ascendant. The Turks would never be beaten militarily, as in the halcyon days of the first three Crusades; and Byzantine military greatness had ended on the field of Manzikert as far back as 1071 with the annihilation of the Eastern Empire's professional standing army the *tagmata* (τάγματα).

Traditionally, when Constantinople could not defeat an enemy on the field of battle with superior numbers, she would play one foe off against another and if that was not possible she would parlay and negotiate a resolution, often by paying either a bribe or a financial tribute. If necessary, and if her military resources were at a particularly low ebb, she would even agree to pay protection money to forestall any immediate threat. Byzantium no longer had the military muscle of earlier centuries, therefore her bargaining position with Murad remained hopelessly weak, but even so negotiation still remained her sole recourse. Now was not the time for grand designs or the recovery of past greatness; now was the time for simple survival. But this was not on John VIII's mind as he set out for Italy thirteen years after his father's death, and the grandiosity of his entourage betrayed his high hopes of finding help in Italy.

Accompanying John VIII, in addition to his brother Demetrius Palaeologus the Despot of Mesembria and Lemnos, was one of the most eminent delegations of clerics to have ever visited the Latin West. Leading the Churchmen was the Patriarch Joseph II of Constantinople who was already in his eighties by this time and seriously ill. Joseph had been born in Bulgaria in the 1360s, the son of Ivan Shishman of Bulgaria and had been Metropolitan of Ephesus before becoming Patriarch of Constantinople in 1416. His was an attractive and likable manner and, combined with his simple spirituality, made Joseph highly popular amongst his fellow Churchmen. Amongst the eighteen Metropolitan bishops and countless theologians whom he led to Ferrara were the patriarchs of Alexandria, Antioch and Jerusalem, as well as Bishop Bessarion of Nicaea and Isidore, abbot of St Demetrius and bishop of Kiev. The lay scholars who made the journey were equally distinguished. They included George Scholarius, George Gemistos Plethon from Mistra and Mark Eugenicus the Metropolitan of Ephesus. In addition to the learned clerics the Byzantines had also brought that essential imperial accessory, a menagerie of wild animals. The Byzantines were eager to put on a good show.

The delegation's arrival in Venice had been truly magnificent. Doge Francesco Foscari rode out to the flagship of the *basileus* in his state barge and made fulsome obeisance after which the entire cortege had made its way up the Grand Canal to the cheers of the Venetian populace. But when they arrived in Ferrara in April, despite the attempts by Niccolò III d'Este and his two sons Leonello and Borso to put on a suitable show by accompanying the *basileus* into the city on 4 March, it was driving with rain and freezing cold and the various parties now busied themselves instead with endless wrangling over the correct protocol for receiving the Byzantine *basileus*. Pope Eugenius had appointed Cardinal Giuliano Cesarini to lead the Latin commission appointed to confer with the visiting Greek delegation; Cesarini was largely encumbered with the series of protocol nightmares which ensued.

The patriarch Joseph had been mortified at being informed that it was necessary for him to kneel and kiss the pontiff's slippered foot. He quickly sent word back to the *basileus* that he would not step ashore unless this outrageous piece of protocol was rescinded. The relative height of Eugenius's and John's throne in Ferrara Cathedral was yet another bone of contention. Still another was John's refusal to dismount from his horse at the door of the cathedral and walk to his throne; in the event it was decided that a hole would be knocked in the cathedral wall and that the *basileus* would be carried through it on a litter. Behind all this wrangling over etiquette lay John VIII's concern to be received not as a supplicant to the Latins but in his full Imperial Majesty. At Venice he had written to the European heads of state and now delayed the Council's proceedings for a full four months to allow time for their representatives to gather at Ferrara.

The Council's magnificent opening public session took place on 9 April 1438. Despite its serious objectives, John VIII nevertheless treated the Council as a recreational trip. Hunting was his overriding passion and such was his appetite for the hunt that he had even left the Greek fleet transporting the delegates at Cenchrea (Kechries in the municipality of Corinth) and travelled by horseback to Navarino (Pylos in Messenia, in the Peloponnese) where he subsequently re-joined the flotilla. The reverse of the commemorative medal commissioned to celebrate the Council by the Italian artist Pisanello (who specialised in the classical Roman medallic art form) had appropriately depicted John VIII on horseback. Upon arrival at Ferrara his passion quickly outlived his welcome with his hosts, the d'Este family. An exasperated Niccolò d'Este was forced to beseech the *basileus* 'to restrain his enthusiasm for the chase owing to the damage he was causing to the property of the country folk and the decimation of the game that the Marquis had imported for his own pleasure'.

Pope Eugenius and the d'Este family were meanwhile faced with the financial and logistical problem of how to play host to seven hundred pampered Greek delegates in a cold and inhospitable city which barely had enough lodgings to house them all. Pope Eugenius's financial problems were at least partly a result of the parallel and competing claims of the Council of Basel, whose dissenting ecclesiastics had diverted their episcopal incomes from Rome's coffers. Another reason for the Pope's impecunious state was Filippo Maria Visconti's on-going raids on the Papal States which denied him the revenues from certain towns and cities there, in addition to the cost of raising and maintaining troops to defend papal territory. He solved the immediate need by borrowing 10,000 florins from the Medici Bank in April 1438 but this barely proved adequate and he was forced to go further into debt in June 1439 just in order to keep the proceedings going. This trend continued with the pledging of half the income of the Camera Apostolica as security against a further loan of 12,000 florins and the selling of indulgences. In addition, Pope Eugenius sold off selected papal cities to raise ready cash; in this way Florence acquired the town of Borgo Santo Sepolcro, which had formerly been under the vicariate of the Malatesta family. Meanwhile, as the *basileus* hunted the rapidly diminishing game of the *Ferrarese* countryside, the other European princes showed little inclination to participate and so the clerics finally got the Council's proceedings underway. The first items on the agenda included such matters as the Procession of the Holy Spirit, the *filioque* clause in the Nicene Creed, Purgatory and Papal Primacy.

The most critical and divisive issue which the ecclesiastics hoped to resolve, and which had effectively separated the two Churches since the eleventh-century, was the so-called *filioque*; this Latin word meaning 'and the son' had been added to the Nicene-Constantinopolitan Creed by the Church of Rome in the eleventh-century and stated that the Holy Spirit proceeded from both the Father 'and the son'. The clause was first used in 1014 when Pope Benedict VIII was pressured by the Emperor Henry II to include the phrase at Mass. Later in 1054, when a variety of personal and doctrinal differences led Cardinal Humbert of Rome and Patriarch Michael Cerularius of Constantinople to excommunicate each other in the Church of the Hagia Sophia, thus sparking the Great Schism, the *filioque* was again cited as a major bone of contention. Although the Greeks accused their Latin brethren of having originated the *filioque* it had in fact first been created in the Syrian Christian tradition of the Persian East. Later, St. Augustine had also taught that the Holy Spirit had also come from the Father as well as the Son. However, by the time of the Third Ecumenical Council of Ephesus in 431, the Eastern Church had forbidden any further alterations to the Nicene-Constantinopolitan Creed. For the most part, the bishops of Rome had capitulated to these wishes until the year 1014. The *filioque* made no difference to the question of the fundamental unity of substance of the Trinity and was, if truth be told, a rather subtle and esoteric distinction when scrutinised more closely. The Greeks saw in the Father a single creative principle and it seemed natural to them that the Holy Spirit should flow exclusively from this dominant 'royal' principle. By contrast, the Latins were more apt to reflect on the three-in-one Trinitarian aspect of the

124

Godhead and so, by extension, the Holy Spirit proceeded from both Father *and* Son.

If the two Churches sought to find common ground over the *filioque* none would have suspected it for in the opening rounds the Metropolitan of Ephesus, Mark Eugenicus, categorically refused to countenance any alteration in the formulation laid down by the Ecumenical Council of Ephesus and the other Church councils. He argued that the individual merit of the *filioque* clause itself was totally irrelevant; it was the fact that it had been added outside of the jurisdiction of conciliar Orthodoxy. It was a patristic line that threatened to remove the rug from beneath the Latins before the debate had even begun. The Greeks were on the whole disinclined to subject questions of Orthodoxy to reasoned, logical debate. George Scholarius had addressed his fellow Orientals thus: 'I know that you, O Greeks, in matters of this sort have no confidence in proofs from reason but consider them suspect and misleading', whilst Bessarion himself wrote, 'The words (of the Fathers) by themselves alone are enough to solve every doubt and to persuade every soul. It was not syllogisms or probabilities or arguments that convinced me, but the bare words (of the Fathers).'

To the Latins the *filioque* clause was a common sense addition which had been included to forestall the Arian heresy, which denied the full divinity of the Son. The *filioque* had therefore first been officially advanced in the West at the Council of Toledo in 589 for this specific purpose (Arianism being especially strong in Spain thanks to the Visigothic invasions). To counter the arguments of Mark Eugenicus the Roman delegates disparagingly played down the importance of the *filioque*, so much as to say 'it's not so important, let's just keep it'. Eugenicus inevitably rebutted why, if it were so trivial, were they so eager to keep the clause? By the same token the *filioque* could be abandoned! The Romans, led by Cardinal Giuliano Cesarini and the Dominican Andrea of Rhodes, advanced a compromise formulation based on the Latin expression *ex filio* but once again Mark denounced the attempt, falling back on the Orthodox position of St. Photius the Great in the ninth-century. Underlying the fierce Orthodox resistance to the *filioque* now, as ever, was a deep-seated fear of the encroaching 'Latinisation' of Orthodoxy, of a fundamental loss of Greek identity as the papacy called the shots concerning Christian doctrine. Again, this inevitably arose from the sense of trauma that the Greeks still felt at having been conquered by the Latins in 1204. Orthodoxy was one area where they could still exert a large degree of control and they were loath to relinquish it at the say so of the papacy.

These deliberations were, however, brought to an abrupt end in the summer of 1438 when the city was stricken by a plague epidemic which laid the Latin hosts low and further alienated them from their troublesome Greek guests. As if plague was not bad enough, the duke of Milan's troops had recently been brought precariously close to Ferrara through the machinations of Æneas Silvius Piccolomini and the Pope could not risk being captured by the Visconti. Pope Eugenius briefly considered relocating the Council to either Padua or Treviso but the cooperation of Venice could not be counted upon. It was at this point, therefore, that Cosimo de' Medici despatched his brother Lorenzo as plenipotentiary to propose bringing the Council to Florence which, plague-free and with its balmier climate, was not only more congenial than Ferrara but was a safe haven from the clutches of Milan.

As an additional incentive the republic of Florence undertook to 'willingly provide houses for them [the Greek delegates] *gratis*, without demanding any rent, and that we shall strive to render the houses suitable for their various degrees of nobility'. As for underwriting the council's costs, Lorenzo was instructed by the *signoria* to offer the Pope a maximum of 1,500–1,700 florins per month for a period not exceeding eight months and stipulated that this be regarded as a loan to be repaid at a later date, 'otherwise it would seem as though we had bought his visit, which would not be at all to the honour of our Commune'. Hampered by dwindling funds, Pope Eugenius avidly consented to the relocation and, by 18 December 1438, an agreement was signed between the *signoria* and the Cardinal Treasurer. Cosimo had played a shrewd hand; bringing the prestigious Ecumenical Council to Florence would not only confer prestige on the republic but would also stimulate trade and commerce. The Greek delegates had, by this time, already been away from Constantinople for many months, most of them were running out of funds and they were growing weary of the endless deliberations, particularly over the troublesome *filioque*.

Cosimo was elected as *gonfaloniere della giustizia* on the 28 December 1438 and was thus able to welcome the papacy as Florence's official head of state. Upon relocating to Florence, the clerics eagerly sought middle ground on the contentious matter of the *filioque*. Differences in both language and normative usage were cited in order to arrive at the conclusion that the Roman formula that the Spirit proceeded from both Father 'and Son' was not substantially different from the Greek formulation that the Spirit proceeded from the Father 'through' the Son. When the ailing Patriarch Joseph finally gave up the ghost on 10 June 1439, the remaining clerics on both sides of the divide hurried to affirm a decree of union between East and West on 6 July 1439, sparking the exclamation: *Laetentur Coeli* ('Let the heavens rejoice'). Mark Eugenicus was, however, alone in refusing to become a signatory to what he regarded as a palpably heretical compromise. Mark's objections notwithstanding, the result was a huge victory for Church unity and, for the first time since 1054, the Eastern and Western Churches returned to full communion with each other.

The victory could not have been other than a huge triumph too for Cosimo de' Medici whose city had played host to the epoch-making reconciliation. The notional victory over the question of the *filioque*, however, was still qualified as the clerics continued to wrangle over the equally thorny issue of pontifical supremacy. While the ecclesiastics agonised over the limits of papal jurisdiction in the midsummer heat, the Florentines indulged their love of carnival with the feast of St. John the Baptist, the eve of which fell on 23 June and heralded a public holiday. This was always an occasion of great pomp and the more prominent citizens of the commune appeared in public wearing crowns and bearing olive branches whilst religious effigies, stilt walkers, relics, banners, crosses and musicians paraded through the festooned city streets. During the feast itself those same wealthy citizens prominently displayed their gold and silver and a myriad lamps and candles illuminated the darkness. Both the feast and the presence of the Ecumenical Council were cause for great celebration and the *basileus* was presented with an official gift from the citizens of Florence.

More pomp was to follow. On 6 July (the day on which *Laetentur Coeli* was announced) Florence celebrated the new Church union in the form of a communion ceremony held at the Duomo and attended by the council members and the entire city of Florence, who were given yet another public holiday. Present was John VIII Palaiologos, described as being 'clad very richly in Greek style in a brocade of damask silk, with a hat in Greek style on the point of which was a beautiful jewel, a handsome man with a beard in Greek style'. Also present was Pope Eugenius IV in his finest vestments who, garbed in his chasuble for Mass, received the kiss of both Western and Eastern bishops and archbishops as a sign of reconciliation between the two communions. The presiding *gonfaloniere* of Florence, the wealthy merchant and friend of the Medici, Filippo di Giovanni, attended the Pope as one of the servers at Mass and after litanies and the blessing of the congregation, cardinals Cesarini and Bessarion both mounted the pulpit near the papal throne and read out the decree of union one after the other. The Pope, Latin prelates and Greek priests each agreed to the decree in turn and finally Pope Eugenius chanted the *Te Deum*. Official union between Eastern and Western Christendom had finally been achieved. The reconciliation had been witnessed by all the citizens of Florence and those who could not gain admittance to the cathedral watched the proceedings as best they could from outside. The reunification, and the fact that it had been orchestrated in Florence, was universally acknowledged as a diplomatic triumph for Cosimo de' Medici.

In other respects too Cosimo was also making considerable capital from the presence of the Council. The attendance at Florence of the Platonic scholar George Gemistos Plethon was to have considerable influence on the humanist intellectual life of the city. Born in Constantinople, Plethon had studied in the nearby city of Adrianopolis which, under the rule of Sultan Murad II, was modelled on the enlightened caliphates of Cairo and Baghdad. From there he had gravitated to Mistra in the despotate of Morea where he studied and taught Platonic philosophy, history and astronomy. Plethon's work *De Differentiis* which evaluated the differences between Plato and Aristotle's conception of deity had opened him up to charges of heresy from his former pupil George Scholarius, who was also present in Florence with the ecumenical delegation. Plethon had nonetheless weathered the storm and later been invited by the *basileus* to consult on the issue of the East-West schism in the Church. This in turn had led to his being invited to the Council of Ferrara by John VIII Palaiologos.

Since he was not actually a cleric Plethon did not need to participate in all the sessions of the council and he spent the balance of his time lecturing to the Florentine humanists on the subject of Plato. When Cosimo de' Medici sat in on several of these lectures he was so impressed that he was inspired to set up the *Accademia Platonica* in Florence. This informal discussion group, whose members saw themselves as the natural successors to Plato's famous Academy of Athens, gathered at the Medici Villa di Careggi. The *Accademia* later came to include such notable scholars as Angelo Poliziano, Marsilio Ficino, Cristoforo Landino, Leonardo Bruni, Carlo Marsuppini, Giovanni Pico della Mirandola and Gentile de' Becchi, who would become tutor to Cosimo's grandson Lorenzo. Plethon did not only promote Plato (above Aristotle) but was also an exponent of polytheism and suggested that Christendom ought to return to the devotion of the pagan pantheon of deities. His influence on the Italian Renaissance as an advocate of such classical ideas was paramount and some academics have even gone so far as to remark that the advent of the Council of Florence with its wealth of Greek scholars marked the real beginning of the Italian Renaissance.

The most distinguished student of Plethon was Bishop Bessarion of Nicaea. He was less interested in the ideas of Plato however than in the very real need to unify the Churches of East and West. Amongst those in the Byzantine delegation he was one of the most willing to seek reconciliation. His readiness to compromise on thorny issues of Christian creed and Church dogma earned him the rebuke of more conservative Orthodox Churchmen. But on the other hand he won the plaudits of Pope Eugenius IV who elevated him to the College of Cardinals in 1439. Bessarion duly converted to Roman Catholicism and, after the Council had been dissolved, he remained behind in Italy. His palazzo in Rome became a centre for Greek scholarship and translation and he sympathetically sponsored and patronised all the Greek émigrés from Constantinople who congregated there. Like the teaching of Plethon, the patronage of Bessarion opened Italy up to an influx of Greek learning which nourished the growing classical humanism of the Renaissance. Much of the growing Diaspora of Greek scholars and academics found its way to Italy. The rare manuscripts that they carried with them exposed Italian humanists to such exotica as the Hermetic teachings of Alexandria as well as Hebrew Qabbala (קַבָּלָה) which was studied and popularised in Italy by Pico della Mirandola. Many of these manuscripts subsequently found their way into Cosimo's own library at the monastery of San Marco.

The Ecumenical Council finally concluded in February 1440 and the *basileus* John VIII Palaiologos returned to Constantinople by way of Venice. What ought to have been a victory of mediation, compromise and reunification (and an important stepping stone to Byzantium receiving the urgent Latin military support that it so desperately needed in the face of the Turk) devolved however into yet more destructive and divisive controversy back home. Those Greek clerics who had sanctioned *Laetentur Coeli* were roundly disparaged for their 'heretical' conciliation whilst Mark Eugenicus was extolled as the very pillar of Orthodoxy. The Sees of Jerusalem, Antioch and Alexandria now rallied behind the Metropolitan of Ephesus and condemned the reunification agreement. All who had supported it became persona non grata in the East and in some cases were even physically accosted; such was their pariah status that a group of them later came together to sign a manifesto formally withdrawing their support for it. More damaging still, the loss of prestige which John VIII himself had suffered from the affair led to an attempted coup by his brother Demetrius, who cynically claimed to be acting in support of Orthodoxy. Although the rebellion had been quashed the affair had opened up damaging rifts within the Byzantine regime which the *basileus* could ill afford in the face of a unified, determined Ottoman front. Those returning clerics and scholars like George Scholarius only made the situation worse by continuing to fuel the whole reopened debate surrounding the *filioque*.

What issues lay beneath the unravelling of the conclusions of the Council of Florence? On first analysis it seems quite counterintuitive for the people of Constantinople, under constant threat as they were from the Ottoman hordes, to disregard any agreement which would surely guarantee them Western military assistance. On deeper analysis, however, the wounds which afflicted the collective Greek psyche since the outrageous and traumatic Fourth Crusade had never truly healed. These wounds tended to manifest in a general antipathy towards Latins in general as well as a divergence in mentality between East and West. Since these two attitudes were also expressed in two completely different languages there was a habit for fundamental differences of temperament to show up as conflicts over the meanings of obscure ecclesiastical phrases and

128

formulas. The problem was only compounded by the fact that in Latin there was no equivalent for certain Greek terms and vice versa. It was this fundamental problem which rendered most attempts of the East and West to come together as an impotent talking shop in which debate circled round and round in ever more pedantic and obscurantist loops. To make matters worse, the Eastern patriarchs themselves were known for their love of doctrinal dispute whereas Western archbishops were rather more inclined to toe the line when it came to the ruling of their acknowledged pope.

With John VIII's unruly and independent ecclesiastics threatening to undo all the constructive work of the Ecumenical Council it was incumbent on the Latin Pope Eugenius IV to proceed on the basis that the Council had been an undisputed success. That meant providing the promised secular military support to the *basileus* in his war to roll back the Turk. Although the Western princes had largely ignored or evaded John's call-to-arms at Ferrara and Florence, the Pope published a Crusading bull on 1 January 1443 and war was duly declared on Sultan Murad. Murad had returned to the offensive during the late 1430s and by 1439 Smederevo had capitulated reducing Serbia to the status of an Ottoman province. The despot of Serbia, George Brankovich, fled to his estates in Hungary. In 1440, Murad's attempt to lay siege to Belgrade had foundered and Hungary's borders had held. Nevertheless it was clear that once Murad had settled matters with his Karaman rebels to the East, he would redouble his efforts to conquer Hungary. By 1441 Turkish forces had already probed Transylvania, which was being vigorously defended by the talented military commander John Hunyadi, who had lately been appointed as Voyevod of Transylvania by Władysław III, King of Poland, Hungary and Croatia. In quick succession in 1441, Hunyadi had defeated the Turkish generals Ishak Pasha and Mezid Bey when they made incursions into Transylvanian territory. However, despite his success the last major Serbian city Novo Brdo fell to the Ottomans that same year.

Pope Eugenius IV's call for a righteous Crusade was received positively by these three capable Christian rulers: King Władysław III, George Brankovich and John Hunyadi. The plan was for their combined armies to advance south-east to the Black Sea where they would rendezvous in the vicinity of the Danube River Delta with the Pope's Crusader fleet comprising a mixture of Venetians and Burgundians commanded by the Pope himself. Cardinal Cesarini, who had proved his reliability throughout the Councils of Ferrara and Florence, was placed in overall charge of coordination and logistics. Cesarini had already been in the Balkans since 1442. He had mediated a dispute between the court of the infant King Ladislaus V of Hungary and King Władysław of Poland, who had been summoned to rule Hungary during the infant's minority in the face of the Turkish threat. His effectiveness as a papal diplomat had led to his becoming Władysław III's confidante and he had also conducted an ambassadorial mission to the court of the Emperor Frederick III.

In the fall of 1443 the combined forces of the Polish, Hungarian, Serbian and Transylvanian Crusaders launched their campaign in the knowledge that Murad's levies were preoccupied with harvesting their crops, an essential task not only for the food which it created but also because this was the main way that they paid the Sultan's taxes. The Crusaders quickly overran the troops of the Pasha of Rumelia outside the city of Nish, who retreated to Sofia in Bulgaria leaving a trail of scorched earth in his wake. Regardless of this, the Crusaders proceeded to pacify Sofia by January 1444 after only token resistance from the city. Murad was thrown onto the defensive; in the East he was still preoccupied with quelling the Karamans; in Albania George Kastriotes–better known to history as Skanderbeg–had embarked upon his own rebellion against Turkish domination. The younger brother of John VIII, Constantine Palaeologus, was meanwhile threatening both Athens and Thebes and advancing across the Gulf of Corinth. Constantine had rebuilt the Hexamilion, the ancient defensive wall constructed across the narrow Isthmus of Corinth which guarded the land route into the Morea, otherwise known as the Peloponnese peninsula. As Władysław and Hunyadi were greeted in Buda as heroes for their rapid string of victories, Murad knew that his only option at this point lay in diplomacy.

In an attempt to forestall Ottoman incursions into Serbia, Brankovich had in 1435 agreed to the concubinage of his daughter Mara to Sultan Murad. This had gone ahead and Mara had duly entered Murad's harem. In June 1444, after some lobbying from Murad's sister as well as his new Serbian concubine, peace negotiations were entered into and envoys from Władysław, Brankovich and Hunyadi were duly received at the Sultan's court in Adrianople, the modern day Turkish city of Erdine. Here, the two sides agreed to institute a ten-year truce and Murad consented to pull back from Wallachia and restore Brankovich's Serbian lands. On 15 August 1444, the Peace of Szeged was sworn into effect by both Murad and Władysław in Hungary. The Sultan, believing the Christians to be sincere in their desire for peace, was able to turn east once more to deal with the ever-troublesome Karamans. For their part, however, the Christians were far from earnest; scarcely had the truce been brokered than the Pope's envoy Cardinal Cesarini pushed belligerently for a resumption of hostilities and now rushed to Szeged to absolve Władysław of his oath to the Ottoman Sultan. Fatally, the Polish king caved in to the pressure from the papal nuncio and mobilised his army. However, Władysław's forces were by now depleted by the abandonment of Brankovich who, safely restored to his Serbian lands, was perfectly content to abide by the general peace.

Władysław and Hunyadi therefore proceeded to gather a diverse army comprising Hungarian, Polish, Bohemian, Wallachian, Czech, Bosnian, Croatian, Lithuanian and Bulgarian troops bolstered by fierce papal and Teutonic knights. The plan, as before, was for them to march across Bulgaria to Varna on the Black Sea where they would link up with a Roman Catholic papal fleet sailing up the Dardanelles. The two forces would combine and advance southwards towards Constantinople, expunging the Ottomans from Thrace and the Balkans as they went. Hopes were high. On 4 July 1444, Władysław wrote to the Senate of Florence: 'If Almighty God gives us a safe passage of the Danube, as we hope, we are quite confident of expelling the impious sect of Maumett to parts across the sea, to the praise and glory of our Omnipotent God. This will come about especially with God's mercy and with the assistance of the fleet which, in order to do such a great good, our most Holy Lord, the Lord Pope Eugenius and our most illustrious and dearest brother, the duke of Burgundy and, in addition, the entire *signoria* of Venice have built and sent to the Straits of Gallipoli.'

On 9 November 1444, the Crusader army was confronted on the plains outside Varna by a huge Ottoman army of 50,000 men led in person by Sultan Murad II himself. In the face of such overwhelming odds Cardinal Cesarini counselled a defensive retreat. This was not viable however as the Crusaders were by now hemmed in by Lake Varna on one side and the Black Sea on the

130

other. Advising instead that the army adopt the Hussite defensive technique called the *Wagenburg*, basically a circle of wagons, the bellicose John Hunyadi scornfully declared: 'To escape is impossible, to surrender is unthinkable. Let us fight with bravery and honour our arms.' His rallying cry was supported by King Władysław and grimly the Crusaders deployed into a two mile-long arc to receive Murad's fearsome host of Kapikulus, Sipathis, Anatolians and Janissaries. The ensuing Battle of Varna which took place on 10 November 1444 would be a crushing defeat for the Christian army. The Crusaders failed to coordinate their forces effectively and, when John Hunyadi left Władysław alone for a brief moment to personally lead a counter-attack against an Ottoman assault, Władysław ignored Hunyadi's entreaties to stay put and instead launched an ill-conceived cavalry charge directly at Sultan Murad himself. Spurring his charger forward, Władysław attempted to break the line of Murad's Janissaries and capture the Sultan alive. Władysław's brave and impulsive gambit even came close to succeeding, but tragically his horse foundered in the mud and the Ottoman mercenary Kodja Hazar slayed the King and decapitated him, sending Władysław's head back to the Sultan as tribute.

Hunyadi, unable to stem the ensuing rout, barely escaped the field with his life. Cardinal Giuliano Cesarini, who had confusingly urged strategic aggression whilst advising tactical caution, was himself slain in the course of the battle. Back in Rome, the Curia was stunned by the news of their representative's death and rumours abounded for a short while that Cesarini had somehow survived the disastrous events of Varna. Cosimo de' Medici too was taken aback by the news. Cesarini had worked closely with Cosimo on the arrangements for transferring the Ecumenical Council from Ferrara to Florence. When the Council delegates had been en route from Ferrara at Faenza they had run out of ducats and urgently needed two hundred horses and mules with which to complete the journey to Florence; Cardinal Cesarini had written to Cosimo begging him 'For the honour of our Latin Church which is in question, and so that we can keep our promises firmly made to the Byzantines, I beseech you to take all possible steps to send the horses and mules'.

The Battle of Varna was a crushing blow to shared Christian hopes that the Ottoman floodtide might somehow be contained. Had the original peace treaty with Murad been observed, there may have been ten years of peace during which the Church could have organised a more durable resistance to the Turk in the East. As it was, the end result was merely a divisive new civil war in Hungary, which lasted until John Hunyadi was elected regent for the infant King Ladislaus in 1446. Another result of the defeat at Varna was that the West was now disinclined to assign further military help to the East, a policy of restraint that would have tragic consequences just seven years later in the watershed events of 1453. Ironically too, it was John VIII Palaiologos who, as his vassal, was obliged to welcome Sultan Murad after his triumphant victory over John's fellow Christians at Varna. The failure of the *basileus* was complete. Despite travelling to Italy and risking the scorn of Constantinople's citizens by seeking to heal the Great Schism with the Latin West, his father had proved prescient about John VIII's overly grand endeavours, all of which had ultimately come to nothing.

CHAPTER 6

The Pivot towards Milan

Let what will happen, as long as none can say that I have been the cause of any troubles. I am not; and I believe I shall be held guiltless by God and by the world. But whoso tries to take from me what is mine will find it far harder and thornier than to demand it, as at present.

Francesco Sforza to Cosimo de' Medici, 28 May 1438

According to the story, Francesco Sforza's father Muzio Attendolo had been working in his family's fields in Cotignola in the Romagna when a band of mercenaries had marched past in search of new recruits. Intrigued by these brightly-attired soldiers of fortune, Muzio had stolen his father's horse and rode after them and this supposedly was how his career as a famous *condottiere* had begun. Another, somewhat less romantic variation records that the young Muzio had simply been abducted by the soldiers. Entering the service of the first and original Italian *condottiere*, Alberico da Barbiano, Muzio and two of his brothers fought in Barbiano's renowned *Compagnia San Giorgio* under the eponymous banner of St. George. In appreciative recognition of the young recruit's steadfast performance on the battlefield his employer Barbiano bestowed upon his protégé Muzio the soubriquet *Sforza*, meaning 'Strength' or 'Force' and the apt name had stuck. As the years passed the nom de guerre 'Sforza' had proven useful to the budding mercenary's efforts to establish a bankable reputation in a crowded market of competing *condottieri*. It became the most useful means by which he was able to promote or, as we might say today, brand his professional services. Sforza henceforth became the family name of all his descendants, of which there were a great many by his numerous wives and mistresses. Sforza's employer Barbiano was, it may be of interest to note, no great lover of Florence; in his *Historiarum Florentini populi libri XII*, Leonardo Bruni has him berating the Florentine ambassador with the words 'How arrogant you are, you Florentines! Nowadays nobody in all of Italy can fart without you sticking your noses in'. For Muzio's son Francesco Sforza, the relationship with Florence was destined to be somewhat more engaged and certainly more complicated than Barbiano's had been.

Muzio Attendolo had married three times in total, but none of his three official wives had been Francesco Sforza's mother. Instead, Muzio had spilled his seed into Lucia Terzani da Marsciano, one of two mistresses that he kept on the side. Lucia had borne Muzio a prodigious litter of no less than eight bastard children, of whom Francesco, born on 23 July 1401, was the eldest. Taking naturally to the military life, just like his father before him, the sixteen-year-old Francesco first joined Muzio Attendolo 'Sforza' on the field of battle in 1417 when Queen Joanna II of Naples commissioned his family's services. However, in 1423, Muzio himself was unexpectedly drowned during the pacification of the city of Aquila whilst attempting to save one of his pages from the fast-flowing Pescara River, a waterway which his army had been trying with difficulty to ford that day. True to the family reputation, the twenty-two-year-old Francesco immediately took command of his late father's rank and file and, despite his youth, had soon proven himself to be a leader of exceptional courage and ability.

From the time of his father's death until the year when we see him in action with his cavalry against Florence at Lucca, Francesco Sforza worked alternately for the Visconti of Milan, the Pope, the Venetians and the *Napoletani*. His fortunes grew with every new *condotta* awarded to him. Indeed, as early as 1412, while still only eleven-years-old, and in gratitude to his father Muzio for defecting to his side in an on-going war with both the papacy and Louis II of Anjou, King Ladislas of Naples had granted Francesco the marquisate of Tricarico, a town in the southern Italian region of Basilicata. Muzio himself had meanwhile been hanged in effigy on the bridges and gates of Rome by a disgruntled Pope John XXIII. Francesco's conquest, meanwhile, of certain lands in the Romagna was particularly galling for a much later pope, Eugenius IV. Ever since the papacy had returned from Avignon the Roman popes had tended to regard these lands as Church property which, ruled by recalcitrant tyrants and warlords, needed to be brought back into the fold.

Allowing himself to be bribed by the Florentines with the sum of 50,000 florins to depart from the city of Lucca in 1431 had been an enviable coup for the young *condottiere* and his legend grew in tandem with the contents of his strongbox. The future Pope Pius II later said of him: 'He appeared the only man of our time whom Fortune loved ... He was rarely ill. There was nothing he greatly desired which he did not obtain.' Despite the rise in Sforza's own personal fortunes, however, his soldiers tended to be poorly paid and so they quickly acquired a reputation for ferocity and plundering and were therefore greatly feared (which was not in itself a bad thing for a *condottiere* company). New mercenary recruits were expected to foot their own initial expenses for weapons and armour, as well as for food, clothing and other incidentals, which they paid for out of a meagre monthly allowance. The only way most of these men could turn a profit was through plundering the countryside or sacking the occasional town or city.

As his fortunes and reputation grew, so too did Sforza's ambition. Francesco soon set his sights on the hand in marriage of Filippo Maria Visconti's sole surviving daughter Bianca Maria, whom the Duke had illegitimately squired by his lover Agnese del Maino. As Bianca was the Duke's only child such an advantageous match would, Francesco knew, give him legal claim to the Visconti duchy after Filippo Maria died. The duke of Milan was both jealous and suspicious of the powerful and successful *condottiere* in his employ, a rising star who he suspected (correctly as it turned out) of coveting his ducal throne. Surmising that the key to controlling Francesco Sforza lay in his acting as gatekeeper to Bianca Maria, the duke of Milan was to drag the engagement out interminably throughout the ensuing decade. When Sforza's efforts pleased him, he renewed the prospect of the betrothal but, whenever he felt that Sforza was growing too powerful, he conveniently kept off the whole subject. In this manner, wielding Bianca Maria as both carrot and stick, Sforza could be kept on a tight leash and, in theory at least, prevented from taking employment with the Duke's enemies. Although the Duke was an old hand at this game of dynastic brinkmanship, Visconti's other actions around this time had the effect however of driving Francesco Sforza into the waiting and appreciative arms of his rivals Cosimo de' Medici and the Florentines.

In 1434, Florence's loyal *capitano generale* Niccolò da Tolentino had been captured by the duke of Milan and flung into a ravine; the severe wounds which he sustained in the fall eventually proved fatal the following year. He was buried in Santa Maria del Fiore in Florence and a celebratory equestrian fresco by Andrea del Castagno was commissioned over his tomb by an appreciative Florentine commune. Tolentino's death had left an appreciable military command vacuum in the League between Florence, Venice and the Papal States. During the first years of his return from exile, Cosimo had dutifully adhered to Florence's traditional foreign policy of maintaining the League in opposition to a still hostile Milan. Venice had shown him every kindness during the year that he had spent there as a stateless émigré and, so far as Rome was concerned, Pope Eugenius IV had interceded personally in Florence's affairs to secure a favourable outcome for the Medici. Although there was no reason to abandon the regional status quo, the League did now require a suitably competent military leader who could replace Tolentino, the heroic victor of San Romano. Cosimo now therefore took a calculated gamble which, based partly on calculation and partly on Cosimo's own impeccable political instincts, was to eventually lead Florence down a drastically alternate path. In the winter of 1435-6 and at the huge risk of alienating both the Pope and his own countrymen–many of whom had fought against Francesco Sforza's troops at Lucca and elsewhere–Cosimo invited the up-and-coming young *condottiere* to pay an official visit to Florence.

To say that the two men bonded at this initial meeting would be putting it rather mildly. The tall, physically powerful and brusque young mercenary general took an immediate liking to the charismatic, middle-aged Florentine banker who knew exactly how to charm him; so much so that we soon find Francesco referring to Cosimo in his correspondence as his 'second father'. Fortunately for Cosimo the Florentines themselves soon warmed to Sforza on account of his Tuscan origins and upbringing. For his part, Francesco Sforza had astutely realised that Florence's support, not to mention the immense wealth of the Medici Bank, would prove indispensable in his proximate ambition to inherit the duchy of Milan. In this meeting of minds and agendas lay the genesis of a whole new balance of power that was later to dominate the geopolitics of the Italian peninsula.

The new alliance was also timely in other respects too. Since their banishment from Florence, Rinaldo degli Albizzi and his supporters had fallen into the orbit of Filippo Maria Visconti. It was a classic case of 'the enemy of my enemy is my friend' and in a manifestly cynical sort of way it suited both sides down to the ground. Now, from the safety and succour of Milan an embittered Rinaldo was urging Filippo Maria to invade Florence with his *Milanese* troops, an action which–he optimistically assured the Duke–would be followed by a spontaneous uprising in favour of the exiled Albizzeschi faction. The duke of Milan fell short of direct intervention against Florence itself but instead despatched Rinaldo's combative son Ormanno in 1437 to occupy Lucca's territory in support of Lucca against Florence. This move was ostensibly in retaliation for the assistance which had earlier been rendered by Florence and

Venice to Genoa which had itself recently revolted against *Milanese* rule. On the second such *Milanese* expedition to Lucca in 1438, Visconti sent his capable *condottiere* Niccolò Piccinino to supplement Ormanno's efforts. Under these circumstances, Cosimo's inspired countermove was to send his new friend and ally Francesco Sforza to rendezvous with Florentine troops commanded by Neri Capponi in the vicinity of Pisa. Together, their combined forces engaged Piccinino beneath the walls of the mountain town of Barga to the north of Lucca and completely routed the *Milanese* army. Piccinino had no choice but to raise his siege of Lucca and withdraw.

Now, however, the Florentines found themselves overreaching. Sforza arrived outside the gates of Lucca and in an optimistic whirlwind of opportunism the *signoria* assigned him to capture Lucca for Florence. According to Machiavelli, Francesco Sforza set about this new assignment with gusto and he now 'laid waste all their corn-fields, burnt their villages, cut up their vines and fruit trees, drove away their cattle, and spared nothing that an enemy can pillage or destroy'. Lucca appealed to Filippo Maria Visconti for help, urging him to send either a fresh *Milanese* army into Tuscany, or else attack the Venetians in Lombardy and thereby force the Florentines to lift the siege and march to their assistance. When the *signoria* got wind of this request they in turn urged the Venetians to open a new front against the duke of Milan so as to confine him to Lombardy. The Venetians consented to this but only on condition that Florence loaned them Francesco Sforza so he could lead their army in person. Venice's argument had been to object to bearing their share of Sforza's stipend when the latter only ever seemed to embark on expeditions which benefited Florence's own territorial adventurism. Given the fact that Florence had earlier shared in the joint military expenses which had secured the capture of Bergamo and Brescia for Venice during the earlier round of the Lombard Wars this was bare-faced hypocrisy on Venice's part. Yet Florence relented with good grace and Sforza marched to Venice's aid, having first erected some breastworks around Lucca to keep its inhabitants hemmed in.

However, Venice had calculated without Francesco Sforza's reluctance to offend the Duke, who was once more cleverly dangling the carrot of his affianced Bianca Maria before his nose. Earlier, Sforza had made a private agreement with his prospective father-in-law to refrain from crossing the River Po into *Milanese* territory. But, fearing a repeat of the situation which had arisen with Carmagnola some years before, Venice sought to test Sforza's loyalties. No sooner than he was in their direct employment than they ordered him to cross the Po with his troops. The *condottiere* objected that his original *condotta* with both Florence and Venice made no mention at all of fighting north of the River Po; a move which he knew would only antagonise Filippo Maria. This resulted in a violent quarrel between Sforza and Venice's commissioner Andrea Mauroceno. With the Venetians refusing to settle payment of his arrears, Francesco Sforza now indicated to Florence's *signoria* that for pecuniary reasons he may need to reassess his entire commission from the Florentines and the Venetians, by which he strongly implied that he might need to come to some alternative arrangement with the duke of Milan. To show his displeasure the *condottiere* now dithered and went through the motions of a deliberately half-hearted and unconvincing campaign.

At this point Cosimo de' Medici decided to trust in the relationship which he–at least earnestly believed–he had built up with the Venetian Republic during his brief exile there. Orchestrating his own appointment as Florence's ambassador to Venice, he hastened to the maritime city-state and was granted an audience with the Doge. He urged Venice to relinquish its claims upon Francesco's Sforza's services and cease and desist from ordering Sforza to cross the Po. Should Sforza choose to defect out of frustration at Venice's treatment, his and the duke of Milan's combined forces would, Cosimo confidently assured the Doge, prove more than sufficient to push Venice right into the sea. The Doge's reply was to inform Cosimo that Venice had no objection to Florence acquiring Lucca; just that Venice should not be expected to bear the cost of its conquest. It was not, replied the Doge, the practice of the republic to pay for mercenaries who fought chiefly for others. He then went on to point out Francesco Sforza's 'insolence' and suggested that the best way to deal with this manner of *condottiere* was to humble his pride rather than indulge him, for this would only encourage Sforza to return with even more outrageous demands at some later date (one suspects that Venice's prior experience with Francesco Bussone da Carmagnola may have had a great deal to do with her intractability). Following this, a confounded Cosimo de' Medici then took a brief detour to Ferrara where, as we have seen, he successfully lobbied Pope Eugenius IV to relocate the Seventeenth Ecumenical Council from chilly and plague-ridden Ferrara to the more congenial environs of Florence. On his return to Venice, however, Cosimo found that his allies had gone from being unhelpful and uncooperative to be being distinctly frosty in their diplomatic reception.

Venice was deeply unhappy that Cosimo seemed to want all the glittering prizes for himself – the conquest of Lucca, exclusive access to Francesco Sforza's services, Florence's hosting of the prestigious Ecumenical Council; they made no bones about telling him as much. In Venice's eyes, in their marriage of convenience against Milan, Florence had always been the poor relation; they were glad for Florence to stabilise the overall balance of power in northern Italy but, at the same time, they were still concerned that Florence's fortunes did not rise too high, too fast. As a direct result of Venice's obstinacy, just as Cosimo had predicted, Francesco Sforza now went over to Filippo Maria Visconti. The stipulation that Sforza must fight on *Milanese* territory proved to be the main deal-breaker. The defection to Milan of one of Sforza's favourite captains, Taliano Furlano, was another. As a condition of Sforza's defection the duke of Milan agreed however not to intervene in either Tuscany or the Romagna. With Sforza's desertion, the Florentines had no option but to abandon the siege of Lucca and so a treaty was concluded with the city in April 1438. Cosimo de' Medici would never truly forgive Venice for her duplicity and short-sightedness in this business. It would be one of the main factors in his decision to later distance Florence from Venice and instead align with Francesco Sforza and the duchy of Milan.

In the interim, Cosimo was–with no small sense of satisfaction–nevertheless able to enjoy watching Venice 'hoist with her own petard'. With Florence now effectively neutralised over Lucca and with Sforza temporarily out of the game, Milan greedily turned her attentions once again towards Venice's Lombard territories, sending the *condottieri* Niccolò Piccinino and Gian Francesco Gonzaga to mount assaults on Brescia (which was defended by an untried civilian militia), Bergamo and Verona. In this time of crisis Venice turned to her other gifted *condottiere*, a man of similar stature and reputation to the late Carmagnola. This was Erasmo da Narni, better known as 'Gattamelata' ('speckled cat'), whose famous equestrian statue by Donatello still graces the

Piazza del Santo in Padua, which he briefly ruled on Venice's behalf. Gattamelata was one of those men for whom the word 'impossible' seemingly did not exist, a visionary general in the classical mould of Caesar, Napoleon or Patton. When Niccolò Piccinino besieged Brescia, a city which was staunchly Venetian in its loyalties, Gattamelata and his engineers achieved the unbelievable task of dragging a whole flotilla of barques and galleys across the snow-covered alpine countryside around Lake Garda in order to ferry relief troops to the beleaguered town from across the lake. This astonishing achievement in military engineering was only check-mated when the *Milanesi* brought their own ships to the lake and blocked the Venetians in Torbole harbour.

Shamelessly, Venice now appealed to Florence for help, despatching as their envoy Jacopo Donato, the man who had been Cosimo de' Medici's host throughout his Venetian sojourn. Donato used all his powers of persuasion on Cosimo, persuading him that, as gratifying it was for Florence to see Venice on her knees, it was not ultimately in Florence's interests to stand by whilst Milan swallowed up vast tracts of territory in Lombardy. Aside from Brescia itself, Piccinino's troops were also threatening Bergamo and Verona and looked set to erode most of Venice's territorial gains in the Po Valley, despite the fact that the republic had hired other reputable *condottieri* to help hold the line. Donato's words penetrated Cosimo's stony reserve and the latter relented. Putting aside his personal enmity for Venice, Cosimo resolved to entice his friend Francesco Sforza back into the League's corner. Despite the two men's friendship Francesco had initially proved skittish; he had no wish to jeopardise his marriage plans to Bianca Maria which (to him) lay tantalisingly close. He was only brought round by a Florentine delegation led by the indefatigable Neri Capponi, who achieved the unthinkable when he successfully convinced Francesco that the duke was only using his daughter to manipulate him and check his freedom of action. The penny finally dropped; realising the Duke's chicanery, Sforza relented and signed a fresh *condotta* with the League, upon news of which there were jubilant scenes of relief in Venice and great public acclaim for Neri Capponi upon his return to Florence.

Marching into the disputed Lombard territories, the vigorous and potent Francesco Sforza carried all before him. In this campaign he was joined by other notable *condottieri* such as Astorre II Manfredi, Pietro Persaliano and Niccolò III of Ferrara, who together quickly reversed Niccolò Piccinino's initial successes. Francesco Sforza had never been especially intimidated by Piccinino. On 28 May 1438, he wrote to Cosimo de' Medici expressing his opinion that 'all these intrigues and demonstrations, and loud talk, wherein Niccolò shows such valour, are rather scarecrows to frighten people; but scarecrows are good for frightening kites and such-like birds of prey, I do not heed them, being the son of a Sforza and not of a kite'. Even so, on 22 August 1438, Francesco was again writing to Cosimo on the subject of the intense pressure that the duke of Milan was exerting on him, complaining that he 'will never give me Madonna Bianca, or anything else I desire from him, unless I am in perfect accord with and make an alliance with Niccolò Piccinino'.

Then, suddenly, disaster struck. Niccolò Piccinino suddenly quit Lombardy, altered direction and changed his route-of-march towards Tuscany itself. The long-feared *Milanese* attack on Florence was finally afoot. With Piccinino's army was Rinaldo degli Albizzi himself as well as many other prominent anti-Medici exiles. Rinaldo had finally persuaded the duke of Milan that a rapid advance on

Florence would restore the anti-Mediceans to power and neutralise Florence's threat to Milan's southern borders. The pertinacious Rinaldo, always injudiciously quick to crow his perceived advantage, now sent word to Cosimo that in his haste to engage the loyalist Florentine forces he 'was not sleeping', to which the unruffled Cosimo drolly replied 'Probably not, since I have deprived you of sleep'.

During the interval that Rinaldo had been in exile, an intellectual war of words had arisen between the *fuoriusciti* ('exiles') and their apologists such as Francesco Filelfo, and the staunchly pro-Medici humanists of Florence. Filelfo was especially eager to elevate his consolatory tracts on the subject of exile to the level of an art form. His imagined dialogues between notable exiles, such as Rinaldo degli Albizzi and others like Palla Strozzi and his dim-witted son Onofri, cast the exiled rebel patriarchs in the flattering light of wise but essentially unlucky men who had fought high-mindedly for the good of their country; noble and upright men who had gambled but lost thanks to the dice-throw of capricious fate. Now, unjustly maligned and hounded by the 'ungrateful' Medicean politicians of Florence, the exiles could only commiserate and console one another, offering pompous disquisitions on the philosophical lessons to be learned from their unhappy predicament.

Filelfo's self-serving dialogues, casting what were essentially traitors in a positive light, were almost certainly a response to similar pamphlets by Cosimo's ardent humanist supporters, foremost amongst which was Poggio Bracciolini. In 1435, Bracciolini had compared Cosimo to a modern day Scipio Africanus who had gone into exile 'lest he stand in the way of liberty in his country'. This led Filelfo to lash out in an ad hominem attack on Bracciolini himself in which he parodied the notorious sensualist, making him complain that the pleasures of the flesh and a full stomach are the world's only real consolations. Rinaldo degli Albizzi and Palla Strozzi and their cohorts, so it was implied, were above such self-indulgent preoccupations. Filelfo has Palla Strozzi declaim: 'Only the wise man is great, only he is powerful, only he is fortunate, only he belongs to himself. He knows that nothing can perturb him... If you will contemplate this, you will not be downcast but rejoice that we are exiles despised by the unjust mob.' For the caustic Filelfo, the exiles were blameless martyrs whilst the Medici were painted as vindictive, pleasure loving, jumped-up despots.

A proxy war waged on parchment was all very well, but a real life war still remained to be fought with boots on the ground. Not all of it was fought in a way which was open and above board. Amidst the latest developments in Tuscany a piece of unwelcome subterfuge had come to light concerning Pope Eugenius IV's 'fighting bishop' Cardinal Vitelleschi. Despatches had been recovered from Vitelleschi to Niccolò Piccinino that were coded in ciphers and which implicated the cardinal in sundry acts of disloyalty towards his master the Pope. Vitelleschi as it turned out had been offended by Cosimo's removal of the Ecumenical Council from Ferarra to Florence and furthermore was jealous of the Florentine banker's close and affectionate relationship with the Supreme Pontiff. For his own part, Niccolò Machiavelli in his *History of Florence* accuses Vitelleschi of being 'bold and cunning; and, having obtained great influence, [he] was appointed to command all the forces of the church, and conduct all the enterprises of the pontiff, whether in Tuscany, Romagna, the kingdom of Naples, or in Rome. Hence he acquired so much power over the pontiff, and the

139

papal troops, that the former was afraid of commanding him, and the latter obeyed no one else.' Despite his mediating role during the Albizzi crisis, the Florentines could never wholeheartedly bring themselves to trust Cardinal Vitelleschi. They despatched Luca Pitti on a mission to Rome to convince the Pope of his captain-general's perfidy. Pope Eugenius was convinced by the evidence presented to him and, as recounted by Machiavelli, Cardinal Vitelleschi was subsequently captured at Rome's Castel Sant'Angelo by its castellan, Antonio Rido of Padua, and discreetly put to death in the dungeons.

Niccolò Piccinino and Rinaldo degli Albizzi meanwhile continued their ominous march on Florence, snaking through the Medici family lands of the Mugello and Fiesole, crossing the River Arno and interposing themselves between Florence and Pisa. Despite the clear and present danger which they posed Cosimo obdurately refused to call Francesco Sforza to his assistance; that would have meant abandoning his erstwhile ally Venice to Visconti's other *condottieri* who were still active in Lombardy. To his credit, Cosimo was anxious to maintain the integrity of the League despite Venice's recent personal slights and diplomatic rebuttals. Once again, Cosimo was staking his political survival upon a huge gamble. If the *Milanese* and Florentine exiles should interdict the roads by which Florence's food supplies were sent from the port of Pisa they could easily create enough hardship within the city to precipitate an anti-Medici uprising. Indeed, Rinaldo degli Albizzi's own proximity to Florence made this a very real possibility, for he was still not entirely without influence in the commune. Despite his downfall Rinaldo still possessed a certain charisma and there was no small sense of panic as word of his approach reached Florence's citizens. For a brief moment the durability of Medici rule would be severely tested.

Fortune however intervened and, in the event, the *Milanesi* ruined their chances of conquering Florence. This came about when Niccolò Piccinino ordered his army to break off and go to the support of one of Rinaldo's supporters in the *contado* the count of Poppi, who was *capo* of the ancient Guido family. The Count had offered to help Rinaldo against Florence on the proviso that the *Milanesi* come to his assistance against his own parochial rivals. From this point on, Piccinino entirely lost his focus; abandoning his overlook position threatening Florence, he trudged off into the Casentino region of Tuscany where he squandered several crucial months in an isolated region of Florence's *contado* where poor terrain made it difficult to move or resupply his troops. After this largely fruitless diversion, Piccinino then decamped with the army to his homeland in Perugia where he wasted several further weeks pursuing the quixotic personal agenda of establishing a lordship for himself there. Piccinino, angrily recalled from these pointless diversions by the duke of Milan to Lombardy to check Francesco Sforza, his pride stroked by an impatient Rinaldo degli Albizzi, the *condottiere* staked the outcome of his directionless Tuscan expedition on a single climactic battle with the Florentine republic. This came to pass on 29 June 1440 at the town of Anghiari in the province of Arezzo on the Florentine border.

Niccolò Piccinino reached the area on the night of 28 June, at which point his already numerically superior forces were further augmented by around 2,000 irregulars from the nearby town of Sansepolcro. Simultaneously the League's army, which had been fully reconstituted during the enemy's interlude in the Casentino, also converged on Anghiari. It comprised 4,000 papal troops under

Cardinal Ludovico Trevisan (the former Paduan metropolitan bishop of Florence, now a papal legate with special powers in the Romagna), as well as a Florentine detachment of similar size, together with a company of 300 men-at-arms sent from Venice under the command of Micheletto Attendolo, one of the heroes of the Battle of San Romano. The League's army was also bolstered by sympathetic men from the town of Anghiari itself. Piccinino was by now acting on the false intelligence that the Florentine military leadership under the war commissioners Neri Capponi and Bernardetto de' Medici was divided and their army disordered. Confident in his superior manpower, Piccinino ordered a surprise attack on the afternoon of the following day.

Micheletto Attendolo and his commanders had, however, been afforded ample warning of the *Milanese* advance by the prodigious amounts of dust that the enemy kicked up on their march along the Sansepolcro-Anghiari road. Accordingly, he drew his men up in good order in effective defensive positions on the sloped far bank of a small stream. When the *Milanese* vanguard appeared, Micheletto's Venetian knights blocked their progress across the only bridge for miles around. The Venetians doggedly held this defensive position until they were eventually pushed back by *Milanese* reinforcements led jointly by Niccolò Piccinino's son Francesco and Astorre II Manfredi. The *Milanesi* advanced until, their right wing flanked having been overwhelmed by Cardinal Trevisan's papal troops, they were obliged to withdraw. The battle continued for a further four hours during which time the League attempted to surround the *Milanesi* who were still abandoned on the League's side of the stream. Ignominiously, Niccolò Piccinino was not only soundly defeated and forced to retire back into Lombardy, but in the process he also left behind a huge number of prisoners.

The victory at Anghiari was commemorated in Florence with a mural on the wall of the Palazzo del Podestà depicting Cosimo de' Medici's rebel adversaries hanging ignominiously by their heels. The mural was painted by the precocious young artist Andrea del Castagno, who had also earlier commemorated Florence's loyal *condottiere* Niccolò da Tolentino. Andrea, so it was said, had been discovered by Cosimo's relative, Bernardetto de' Medici, who had brought him to Florence to practise his art. As usual, the Medici had lost no time in transforming a military triumph into solid public relations mileage through the art of the young maestro. The propagandistic fresco earned the artist the nickname *Andreino degli Impiccati* or 'Little Andrea of the Hanged Men'. As things fell out, this was not to be the last time that rebels against the Medici would be plastered, in various shades of indisposition, all over the walls of Florence's public buildings.

In the aftermath of the Battle of Anghiari, Florence recovered those territories and fortresses that had previously been lost to Piccinino and the duke of Milan. The count of Poppi, who had fought alongside Florence's enemies, was duly punished and his lands assimilated by the republic. This proved a boon for Florence's defences as it secured the strategically important territory of the upper Arno River Valley and created a buffer against the Romagnol. It was rumoured that the count of Poppi had only rebelled out of distemper, because Cosimo de' Medici had declined his offer to marry one of his sons to the Count's daughter. At this time the Medici were still not thinking like princes and the marriages they made were still between other *ottimati* families in Florence and not with the feudal nobility. All this would change in time as the family's fortunes continued to outstrip even their nearest Florentine

141

contemporaries in terms of wealth and power. The lands of Borgo San Sepulcro, which had been ruled by the count of Poppi and which had been contested by the Pope, were duly released to the papacy and then repurchased by Florence at a cost of 25,000 florins. The town commanded a key strategic point in the upper Tiber valley and was an advantageous acquisition for Florence. Cosimo's Medici Bank conveniently advanced the commune the funds for the purchase price. Around the same time another family, the Pietramala of the Montedoglio, also located in the upper Tiber valley, were deprived of their property too, which was subsequently placed under Florentine rule.

The Battle of Anghiari was a watershed for Milan whose duke, now considerably weakened, realised that he could no longer prevaricate over the matter of his daughter's promised wedding to Francesco Sforza. He had tried to keep her just out of reach but this had only alienated the *condottiere*. Finally driven to play his ace, in October 1441 Filippo Maria Visconti consented to the long-awaited marriage. The wedding subsequently took place in Cremona where, one month later, a peace treaty dubbed the Peace of Cavriana was concluded between the various belligerents. The terms of the treaty were mediated by a triumphant Francesco Sforza himself who, newly married and positively aglow, radiated to all and sundry his expectation of eventually being able to inherit the duchy of Milan. In the meantime, the forty-year-old *condottiere* gained, as part of Bianca Maria's dowry, the towns of Cremona and Pontremoli and his lordship there took immediate effect. Pisanello was in this year commissioned by Francesco to cast a commemorative medal of himself; on the reverse side from his portrait was a depiction of a horse, a sword and a book, which was indicative of the *condottiere's* desire to be regarded as a man of letters and of learning as well as a soldier.

In deference to his new family Francesco Sforza adopted the coat of arms of the House of Visconti, which consisted of a large blue serpent surmounted by a golden crown and devouring a naked Saracen. Francesco Sforza and Bianca Maria would later go on to have nine children: seven sons and two daughters. The first child, his heir Galeazzo Maria, was born three years after their marriage. The union would not be entirely without scandal. In *De Europa*, Pope Pius II would record the story of Francesco's affair with one of Bianca Maria's ladies-in-waiting, a certain Perpetua da Varese from Novara. When Perpetua fell pregnant with Francesco's child he arranged for her to be married off to a local *Milanese* of good social standing so as to conceal the indiscretion. During the nuptial celebrations, however, the poor girl was unceremoniously bundled off to Francesco's citadel leaving the groom unable to consummate the marriage. According to the author, when Bianca Maria learned of this, she arranged for Perpetua to be murdered, but not before Perpetua had given birth to Francesco's illegitimate son, Polidoro Sforza.

From this moment onwards it became a cardinal aspect of Cosimo de Medici's foreign policy to maintain the interests of his new friend Francesco Sforza in the face of all those who sought to bring him low. It was a policy not without immense opposition from certain quarters but Cosimo recognised this new policy as being unquestionably the right one for Florence's future interests. Not only had Sforza's mercenaries been pivotal in winning at Anghiari but he was no longer merely a *condottiere*, he was Milan's heir apparent and, as such, how Florence treated him would determine the republic's future relations with her powerful old rival in Lombardy.

During the intervening six years there were, as a direct result of this policy, several none too subtle changes in the alignments of regional power politics. One of the most significant of these was the ineluctable movement of Rome and the papacy away from its previous state of friendship with Florence. The main sticking point was the Medici pact with Francesco Sforza, who still continued to occupy Church lands in the Romagna and also the Marches, what was formerly known in ancient times as the region of Picenum where Pompey the Great had been born. In November 1433, Sforza had demanded access to the Marches in order to reach his fiefs in Apulia. Certain cities in the Marches, including the city of Ancona, were however dissatisfied with the oppressive rule of the papal legate, Cardinal Vitelleschi and they rushed to embrace Sforza as their lord. On 25 March 1434, the Pope had little choice but to declare Francesco Sforza vicar of the March of Ancona and *gonfaloniere* of the Church. These appointments had served to provide Sforza with the firm foundation for his future career; however Pope Eugenius IV was increasingly resentful about having to accede to the *condottiere's* promotion and now set his mind on winning his territories back.

Each time Cosimo de' Medici tried to engineer a truce either between Francesco Sforza and the Pope or Sforza and Niccolò Piccinino, Eugenius proved uncooperative, either ignoring or evading the proffered olive branch. Relations between Florence and Rome were to deteriorate still further thanks to a peculiar occurrence in 1441. The *condottiere* Baldaccio d'Anghiari, who was ostensibly in the republic's service, was murdered and then flung, by person or persons unknown, from the window of the Palazzo della Signoria. Upon landing in a crumpled heap on the stone flags of the *piazza*, the corpse was immediately beheaded by shadowy figures and left on public display. This act of what can only be described as 'judicial murder', Baldaccio's assassination having been committed inside Florence's seat of government no less, had in fact been ordered by the resident *gonfaloniere* Bartolomeo Orlandini. The motives for the murder were complex. Baldaccio d'Anghiari's reputation as a soldier was unrivalled at this time and Niccolò Machiavelli was to later describe him as 'an excellent soldier, for in those times there was not one in Italy surpassed him in vigour either of body or mind'.

On the surface it seemed as though Orlandini had acted simply out of revenge for Baldaccio had publicly accused him sometime earlier of an act of cowardice. It was also said that the Florentines had begun to fear that the strong and capable Baldaccio, who had been awarded Florentine citizenship in 1437, would eventually grow strong enough to make himself duke in Florence. However, what was not commonly known at the time was that Baldaccio d'Anghiari had recently accepted an 80,000 florin *condotta* from Pope Eugenius IV to drive Francesco Sforza from the papal lands of the Marches. Cosimo had got wind of the Pope's secret contract through his intelligence channels and had almost certainly acted decisively to prevent d'Anghiari from joining forces with Niccolò Piccinino and moving against his new friend and ally Francesco Sforza. What is more, d'Anghiari was an intimate of Cosimo's political rival Neri Capponi, who had recently achieved public popularity both through his victories in the Casentino as well as at the Battle of Anghiari. Neutralising Baldaccio in this way also therefore served to weaken Neri's growing influence. It had fallen to the unfortunate humanist Giannozzo Manetti to have to explain the *signoria's* actions in this matter to an outraged Pope Eugenius IV.

This bloody and unfortunate incident had nevertheless proven too much for the Holy Father, who finally quit Florence for the city of Rome; he made his entry to the Eternal City on 28 September 1443 after an exile of almost ten years. By virtue of Pope Eugenius's shift away from the orbit of the League of the two republics he now gravitated towards the kingdom of Naples which was ruled by King Alfonso V of Aragon, the traditional ally of Milan and the Visconti, who had entered Naples on 26 February 1443 as the *Regno's* new King Alfonso I of Naples amidst the full spectacle of classical Roman triumphalism. In aligning himself with Alfonso and recognising him as the rightful king of Naples, the Pope reversed his previous policy of favouring the Angevin succession to the Neapolitan throne. King Alfonso's victory over René of Anjou had succeeded in reuniting the old kingdom of Sicily under the Aragonese House of Trastámara but this would only last for fifteen years. Before his death in 1458, Alfonso would divide the two kingdoms once more, giving the rule of Naples and the mainland to his illegitimate son Ferrante, whilst Sicily and the rest of the Crown of Aragon escheated to Alfonso's brother John II.

The Pope's previous opposition to King Alfonso had nevertheless rebounded back on him and stung him. When popes questioned the legitimacy of kings (and also emperors as in the case of Pope Gregory VII's disagreement with King Henry IV) it was usually on the quasi legal basis of the document known as the *Constitutum Constantini* or 'Donation of Constantine'. This document, said to have been decreed by the Roman Emperor Constantine the Great during the fourth-century, effectively transferred the whole of the Western Roman Empire to the Roman Catholic Church as an act of gratitude for Constantine's having been miraculously cured of leprosy by Pope Sylvester I. Since it supposedly predated Pepin the Short's own 'Donation of Pepin' in 754, which consigned to the Church all the Lombard holdings north of Rome, the *Constitutum Constantini* was seen as being 'all-inclusive' and it was on this authority that Pope Leo III had crowned Charlemagne as Emperor of the Romans on Christmas Day 800 C.E. In order to confront the legal authority of the Pope in feudal matters it was therefore necessary to first dismantle, or at least call into question, the legitimacy of the *Constitutum Constantini*. From 1439 to 1440 this was exactly what one humanist, rhetorician and philologist in service to King Alfonso had attempted to do.

The Roman scholar and educator Lorenzo Valla had used his extensive knowledge of classical Latin style to compile *De falso credita et ementita Constantini Donatione declamatio* in which he demonstrated that the *Constitutum Constantini* could not possibly have been written in the historical era of Constantine I since its vernacular style dated conclusively to a much later era closer to the eighth-century. Valla himself was something of a paradox. On the one hand he was an adventurous and zealous sort who had earlier contemplated a career as a Roman Catholic missionary in China; on the other, he had seized the opportunity of Poggio Bracciolini's rediscovery of *De Rerum Natura* to argue (in his book *De voluptate* or 'On Pleasure') on behalf of the Epicurean benefits of good food, drink and sex. Drawing attention to certain anachronistic words and terms which were not in general use during the fourth-century, Valla argued that popes had been subordinate to the Emperors of the West even *after* the era of Constantine. He asserted, moreover, that the claim that the papacy had transferred the imperial dignity 'from the Greeks to the Germans' during Charlemagne's time was palpably unhistorical. Valla's treatise naturally met with great resistance and criticism from an outraged

Curia. Unfortunately however for Pope Eugenius IV, his rapprochement with King Alfonso of Aragon came too late to stuff the genie back inside the bottle and Valla's devastating thesis was so conclusively argued that its conclusion still holds good to this day, with most modern scholars conceding the illegitimacy of the notorious 'Donation'.

Another direct result of the cooling of relations between Pope Eugenius IV and the Medici, though much closer to home for the Florentine banking house, was that the latter lost the Court of Rome's banking business yet again, even though its general branch in the city continued to enjoy a healthy turnover. Just as potentially damaging to Medici interests, however, was the perceived loss of prestige in being no longer associated in peoples' minds with the institution of the papacy. The Catholic Church of the Quattrocento carried immense prestige and, in the minds of the Florentines, their close association with the papacy served to amplify the Medici's authority in Florence. Now this was unfortunately no longer a reserve of standing on which Cosimo and his family could, for the time being, draw.

The jockeying for power continued. Aside from the Marches, Francesco Sforza also held lands in *Napoletano* territory which had been ceded to him from the French and furthermore his recent acquisitions in the Papal States also served to threaten Naples's borders. When Alfonso of Naples personally invaded Sforza's domains in the Marches at the head of his own army Visconti now switched sides and joined the two republics and Sforza (also newly bolstered by the Bentivoglio family of Bologna) against the Romans and the *Napoletani*. Thwarted by this, King Alfonso fled and the Pope's forces, left to face the northern alliance alone, were crushed. Again, this victory was a direct result of Cosimo's foresight in foreign policy and his investment in Sforza military power. However, although *Napoletano* power may have been curbed for the time being, it had still not been completely bridled.

Since the victory over Milan and the Florentine exiles at Anghiari, much of the wind had by now been removed from the aging duke of Milan's sails. This left Naples under King Alfonso of Aragon as arguably the more potent power on the peninsula. For his part, Alfonso continued to look askance at Florence's traditional championing of the Angevin cause in the *Regno* as well as her alliance with Naples's territorial interloper Francesco Sforza. *Napoletano* troops now moved to lay siege to Piombino on the border with Tuscany and in 1444 Alfonso appointed Sigismondo Pandolfo Malatesta, the son of Venice's former captain-general Pandolfo III Malatesta, to attack the Florentines. Again, however, fortune smiled on Cosimo de' Medici and Florence. Dissatisfied with *Napoletano* employment, possibly over pay-related issues, Sigismondo (who had acquired the nickname of 'the Wolf of Rimini' for his intemperate conduct), eventually went over to the Florentine side and, by 1448, had helped confound his former employer Naples and had raised the siege of Piombino.

Meanwhile, Francesco Sforza had, since his marriage to the duke of Milan's daughter, emerged as another powerful supporter of the Angevin cause in Italy. His increasingly fraught relations with Pope Eugenius IV over his occupation of Church lands had led Sforza to enter into negotiations with Eugenius's rival the antipope Felix V. This he shrewdly turned to his own advantage. Offering Felix his friendship with René of Anjou as leverage over the king of France (who could be persuaded to support Felix over Eugenius), Sforza persuaded the antipope to reciprocate by granting him fresh land concessions in the March of Ancona. He even proposed a broad new strategic alliance comprising René, Pope Felix and Frederick III Habsburg against Alfonso of Naples. His animosity towards Naples made logical sense. Alfonso was still occupying certain lands within the *Regno* which had been granted to Sforza by the Angevins and furthermore the continued presence in the area of the king's son Ferrante was a threat to his newly acquired territory in the March of Ancona. By the end of 1444 Sforza had also entered into active discussions with Cosimo de' Medici and Giovanni Cossa, one of the exiled *Napoletano* barons and an ardent Angevin sympathiser, for the prosecution of René of Anjou's interests in Naples. The humanist Gian Antonio Porcellio de' Pandoni described Francesco Sforza as 'the standard-bearer of Holy Church and the hope and salvation of Florence'. This was not far off the mark and was certainly beneficial to Cosimo's strategy. With Sforza established in the Marches, Naples was thus effectively contained. By the same token, when Sforza eventually took over Visconti's duchy upon his death, a strong barrier would also be placed between Florence and an expansionist Venice. Thus, in a strategic sense, Cosimo's alliance with Francesco Sforza was able to vanquish two birds with one stone.

There were other Italian states too that feared the expansion of Aragonese Naples and actively sided with the Angevins. The *Genovesi* for example were caught in the twin jaws of a vice which consisted, on the one hand, of the *Milanese* Visconti state and, on the other, of a sea which was now rapidly becoming an Aragonese lake (soon after arriving in Italy Alfonso had embarked on an aggressive programme of naval and dockyard construction). In 1436 Genoa had forged an alliance with both Florence and Venice designed to give it added leverage against the Visconti but which in reality also protected the maritime republic from King Alfonso as well. In 1440 this alliance was further extended to include the papacy, although Genoa also later showed her perfidy against her fellow Christians by actively supporting the Ottoman Turks against the papal and Hungarian Crusaders at the Battle of Varna in 1444. Genoa would henceforth remain the lynchpin in any future French attempts to regain her former Angevin possessions in Italy and would provide both the port and the navy necessary for such efforts.

Cosimo de Medici's first faltering steps towards being the architect of an enduring new balance of power on the Italian peninsula were, however, destined to be frustrated by the perpetual fickleness of Duke Filippo Maria. The Duke's changeableness and randomness was not merely a product of cunning brinksmanship on his part, but also stemmed from his intensely superstitious nature. At the *Milanese* court, the Duke actively consulted his astrologers concerning all important political and foreign policy decisions. This was a by-product of his fearful and irrational character, which also led him to be equally superstitious about birdsong, lightning strikes, comets and darkness. In his *Life of Filippo Maria Visconti* the Duke's private secretary Pier Candid Decembrio wrote that his master:

> 'Gave so much credit to astrologers as a *scientia* that he attracted the most experienced practitioners of this discipline, and he almost never took any initiative without first consulting them: among those who were held in the highest esteem were Pietro from Siena and Stefano from Faenza, both very experienced in the art, while towards the end of his time as lord of Milan he drew actively from the advice of Antonio Bernareggi,

146

sometimes Luigi Terzaghi, and often Lanfranco from Parma. Among his physicians he counted also Elia, the Jew, a famous soothsayer.'

Deciding once more that his son-in-law was growing too powerful for his own good, and perhaps having been advised by a court mage that the time was propitious for a change of direction, pendulum-like, Visconti switched his allegiance back to the Pope and King Alfonso of Naples. Together, all three waged war on Francesco Sforza as he tried with difficulty to re-occupy his territories in the Romagna.

When Duke Filippo Maria loaned Pope Eugenius IV his most capable *condottiere* Niccolò Piccinino, to help the Supreme Pontiff drive his son-in-law out of the Marches, the Pope leapt at the opportunity to have the illustrious commander fight under a papal *gonfalon*. Cosimo did his best, under the circumstances, to heal the rift and mend fences. Sending his cousin Bernadetto de' Medici twice to establish peace between Sforza and Piccinino, each treaty was broken in turn thanks to the Pope's secret connivance. To further bolster Sforza, Cosimo turned to his old allies Venice, who at first affected disinterest at Cosimo and Sforza's plight. The Venetians reluctantly consented to join forces with Florence and Sforza, however, after a Venetian embassy to Milan was rudely and foolishly disregarded by the Duke. Inflicting a crushing defeat on the *Milanesi* at the Battle of Casalmaggiore in September 1446, the Venetians relieved the pressure on Sforza's possessions in Cremona and Pontremoli and advanced to within a few miles of Milan itself. But their easy victories only served to increase the Venetians' arrogance towards Sforza who, seemingly dependent on their help, suddenly appeared to them to be the weaker party in the alliance. The war of nerves between these two uneasy allies intensified until Venice staged an assault on Sforza's possession Cremona which, naturally enough, now drove Sforza back into the willing arms of his father-in-law.

This situation divided public opinion and led to an emergency within Florence itself for most Florentines still favoured maintaining the old alliance with Venice rather than siding with Sforza and the Visconti. Always practical, with some justification the mercantile Florentines now perceived Filippo Maria as a spent force in Italy; at the same time, their costly association with the ambitious and seemingly insatiable *condottiere* Francesco Sforza was no longer bringing them any tangible returns on their investment. So far as anyone could make out, Sforza's only real agenda seemed to be the struggle to maintain his own power base and possessions in Lombardy, the Romagna and the Marches. However, they had failed to grasp that this was precisely the cornerstone of Cosimo de' Medici's longer term policy of establishing a bulwark against Naples in the Romagnol and a barrier to Venice in the Po Valley. The *signoria* was also deeply troubled by rumours, which probably had some credence, that the increasingly desperate and imprudent Filippo Maria Visconti had invited the French *Dauphin* to intervene in Italy. The party of those hostile to maintaining amity with Francesco Sforza now coalesced around the person of Neri Capponi.

Cosimo de' Medici, who was finding it increasingly difficult to secure Florentine subsidies for his *condottiere* friend, saw things quite differently. For Cosimo it was suicidal for Florence to permit Venice to conquer Milan and extend her territories right across Lombardy, not to mention down into the Romagna. As Cosimo saw things, Venice was not interested in any kind of balance of power within Italy; like her old rival Naples she was purely interested in outright conquest until the entire peninsula lay under her control and domination. Backed by the vast wealth of her maritime trading empire, and ruled by the bellicose and warlike Doge Francesco Foscari, Venice's imperial aspirations in this regard were not only a distinct possibility but a clear and present danger to the future safety and security of Florence. The latter *needed* a strong, independent and friendly warlord like Francesco Sforza interposed between Florence and Venice.

On 23 February 1447, Pope Eugenius IV died and his successor, the bishop of Bologna, Tommaso Parentucelli, was elected as Pope Nicholas V. Parentucelli was the orphaned son of a doctor from Sarzana, a town on the border between Tuscany and Liguria. During his youth, and to fund his future university studies in Bologna, he had lived in Florence and been employed as tutor to the children of the exiles Rinaldo degli Albizzi and Palla Strozzi. It was here that he had made Cosimo de' Medici's acquaintance and the two had indulged their lifelong appreciation for rare books and manuscripts. A voracious reader known for his wide-ranging humanist knowledge, Parentucelli's interests had been fed by Cosimo's unstinting patronage and generosity. Inspired by Cosimo's own impressive library, the new pope founded the Vatican Library with an initial stock of twelve hundred manuscripts and would base his new library along the same lines as Cosimo de' Medici's own. 'The Pope', it was commented, 'cordially loves Cosimo and I am certain that he will place everything in his disposition, for there is no one in the world in whom he trusts so much as he does in Cosimo'.

But not even the two men's fraternal, bookish rapport could assuage Nicholas V's intractability when it came to the question of relinquishing Church lands in the Marches. Like his predecessor Pope Eugenius IV, Tommaso Parentucelli made this issue an everlasting obstacle to securing any resolution to the impasse. So much so that Cosimo feared that Milan would fall to the Venetians whilst pope and embattled Sforza haggled over a few inconsequential vicariates in the Papal States. In retrospect, Nicholas V cannot entirely be blamed for fighting for what he understood belonged to the Vatican. For decades the institution of the papacy had been undermined by the Northern European champions of imperial primacy, principally manifesting in the form of the divisive conciliarist movement within the Church. Pope Eugenius IV had made great strides at the Councils of Ferrara and Florence in eroding much of the momentum of the conciliarists, effectively taking the wind out of their sails by assuming the lead in reunifying Eastern and Western Christendom, but it was left to his successor Nicholas V to complete this work and entice the remaining influential dissidents back into the papal corner. That he achieved this was due in considerable measure to his personal temperament and flexible, forbearing attitude.

Recognised widely for his scholarly inclinations, Pope Nicholas V was an attractive figure to such prominent conciliarists as the *Sienese* humanist Æneas Silvius Piccolomini, who had lately served as the personal secretary to the antipope Felix V. Drawing Piccolomini into his orbit, Pope Nicholas won him over by creating him bishop of Trieste and Siena. Another leading conciliarist and advocate of imperial supremacy, Nicholas of Cusa, meanwhile received a cardinal's hat in return for his own change of allegiance. Eventually, even the antipope Felix V himself was won over in return for his appointment as a legitimate cardinal (as opposed to an illegitimate pope) and the conciliarist movement simply withered on the vine. Although well-intentioned, reformist conciliarism had ultimately been found to be largely unworkable. Through the ineptitude of the concilarists themselves the movement failed to deliver the reforms that were so desperately needed within the Church. Afterwards, those few dedicated conciliarists still remaining found it easier to work within the context of national Church assemblies overseen by secular princes who were largely immune from threats from a still weakened papacy.

As Cosimo de' Medici occupied himself with guiding the long term strategic alliances of Florence into uncharted new territory, Pope Nicholas V concerned himself with the rehabilitation of both the papacy itself and the city which that institution called home. If Martin V can be said to be the first real Renaissance pope, then Nicholas V was the pope who got the Renaissance truly underway in Rome itself. In so doing he laid the foundations for the future greatness of High Renaissance Rome, the beautified and marble-hewn city of Donato Bramante, Giorgio Vasari, Melozzo da Forlì and Michelangelo. A number of factors, including the Avignon Papacy from 1309 to 1377 and the conciliar movement which followed, had seen the centre of gravity shift away from Rome for a century and a half. Rome itself produced virtually nothing of value; its sole source of income was derived from the presence of the papal court and the revenue generated from ecclesiastical tithes, not to mention the fees and tributes extracted from throngs of pilgrims and other spiritual tourists who passed through her gates each month. As a result of having been starved of its principal sources of revenue, Rome's fortunes had contracted sharply.

By the beginning of the fifteenth-century, the city's population had dwindled to a pitiful 20,000 inhabitants but these were hardly the senators and knights of earlier times. Writing to Giovanni di Cosimo de' Medici in 1443, Alberto Averardo de' Alberti had commented that 'The men of the present day, who call themselves Romans, are very different in bearing and in conduct from the ancient inhabitants. *Breviter loquendo*, they all look like cowherds.' Most of these people subsisted within the Borgo which lay isolated from the main part of the city on the west bank of the River Tiber. The Borgo, which was not considered a part of Rome proper but a separate walled city–the *Civitas Leonina* or Leonine City–complete with its own magistrates and governor, dated from the reign of Pope Leo IV who had built the walls in 852 in response to Saracen raids which had been mounted against Rome and St. Peter's. The pope's traditional seat was at St. John Lateran, the pontiff's official cathedral in his capacity as bishop of Rome; however by the time of Nicholas V's pontificate, the papal court had relocated from the crumbling Lateran basilica, which had originally been commissioned by Constantine the Great, and transferred its permanent residence to the Vatican Palace.

The eternally feuding Colonna and Orsini had made residence in Rome proper a hazardous affair anyway and the relocation also made a virtue out of necessity by offering a much better quality of life. As the late Pope Martin V had grumbled in 1425, 'many inhabitants of Rome have been throwing entrails, viscera, heads, feet, bones, blood and skins, besides rotten meat and fish, refuse, excrement, and other fetid and rotting cadavers into the streets'. Alberto Averardo de' Alberti had observed that Rome had 'many splendid palaces, houses, tombs, and temples, and other edifices in infinite number, but all are in ruins; much porphyry and marble from ancient buildings, and every day these marbles are destroyed by being burnt for lime in scandalous fashion. What is modern is poor stuff, that is to say the buildings; the beauty of Rome lies in what is in ruin.' The Vatican Hill and the Borgo would be where Western Christendom would rebuild in all her Renaissance splendour.

A man who was as fond of *fabbrica* ('building') as he was of books, Pope Nicholas hired Leon Battista Alberti and the Tuscan sculptor and architect Bernardo Rossellino to draw up plans for the rebuilding of the Vatican and the Basilica of St. Peter. Alberti himself harboured even grander dreams of remodelling the entire city, thus stimulating its revitalisation and repopulation, a visionary common purpose that he shared with the Pope. On paper, Alberti prepared a great scheme of reconstruction whilst the Pope's contractors cleared streets, demolished slums and rescued the city's once life-giving aqueducts from centuries of accumulated waste. Meanwhile, Rossellino began the practical work of stabilising the walls of the old Vatican basilica. The restorative interventions and extensions by both masters considerably improved and upgraded the functional aspects of the decaying basilica and Rossellino also contributed a welcome new choir to the building. Overall, Rossellino was concerned to give the Vatican the isolated aspect of a fortress, whilst from the writings of the Florentine politician and diplomat Giannozzo Manetti we know that Alberti planned to make the tomb of the Apostle at St. Peter the epicentre of the revivified city. The proposal of both architects was not only one of the earliest examples of town planning in fifteenth-century Italy but was, indeed, the first organised effort to rebuild the city since the 'fall' of the Western Roman Empire in 476.

On 17 December 1450 a terrible tragedy on the Ponte Sant'Angelo also indicated the dire need for improved human traffic management planning. As the Jubilee of 1449-50 was nearing its close, Pope Nicholas announced that he would display the relic of the *sudarium* of St Veronica at the Vatican. The *sudarium* was what was known as an *acheiropoieton*, that is to say a Christian icon said to have come into existence 'miraculously' and not by human agency. The news that such a revered icon would be on public show caused many hundreds of pilgrims to gather at the spacious *piazza* in front of St. Peter's basilica. However, the Pope was subsequently taken ill therefore it was announced to the tightly packed masses that the relic would not be displayed after all and the crowd began to disperse. As this seething mass of humanity surged back across the little bridge which sat beneath the sombre machicolations of the Castel Sant'Angelo, something spooked the crowd and general panic took hold. During the ensuing stampede and resulting crush two hundred pilgrims were killed, either trodden underfoot or else cast into the Tiber where they drowned. The calamity would have a deep and traumatising impact on the collective psyche of the city.

The Ponte Sant'Angelo stood at the intersection of several streets converging from different parts of Rome on the Rione Ponte, the cone-shaped district nestling within the Tiber's bend directly opposite the Castel. One street, the Canale di Ponte (today known as the Via del Banco di Santo Spirito) received its name because of its propensity to flood whenever the Tiber was at high tide. As a result, Pope Nicholas not only restored the bridge itself, installing in the process two commemorative chapels in honour of the victims, but he also made certain overall improvements to the processional route to and from the Borgo. Ever the journeyman, Bernardo Rossellino was to later replicate and improve upon these town-planning and tourist-management concepts in his later civic improvements for Pope Pius II's birthplace of Pienza.

Despite all the distractions of on-going regional wars and internecine squabbles between competing lords, the first half of the fifteenth-century in Italy was marked by a true rebirth in the arts and civic architecture. The energy and enthusiasm of popes such as Martin V and Nicholas V to rebuild the past glory of their city was being echoed all over the peninsula, and nowhere was this more so than in Florence. A year before Pope Nicholas V's election a genius had died who had done much to beautify Florence and consolidate her standing in the new Italy of the Renaissance. That genius was Filippo Brunelleschi. On 15 April 1446, Brunelleschi had died from a sudden illness and had been laid out on his funeral bier beneath the great pointed cupola of the Duomo which he had built, brick-upon-brick, to the collective wonder of the Florentines. Later, he was interred down in the crypt, a high honour at that time for a mere architect, but a fitting tribute to a craftsman whose sublime talent had created Florence's most recognisable and iconic landmark. Brunelleschi's magnificent dome atop the city's cathedral advertised the fact that Florence's main religious building could outshine anything that Gothic Europe had to offer. Previously, the Gothic cathedrals of Northern Europe had claimed supremacy as the unsurpassed architectural sensations of the world. After Brunelleschi, the focus of attention would shift away from the north and towards Italy and the vibrant rebirth in the arts and architecture which was taking place there.

The artists who made this kind of civic prestige possible increasingly came to be regarded less as artisans and more as minor dignitaries in their own right, as celebrities even. The logical conclusion of this process was the shameless self-promotion of a Cellini or a Vasari, the forerunners of today's cult of 'artistic celebrity'. But the fact is that as early as the turn of the fifteenth-century painters, sculptors and architects were already coming to regard themselves in a new and more exalted light. But the simple fact was of course that the inspired artists and craftsmen of this time and the rising families of new money both needed each other – the craftsmen needed patronage and the wealthy were dependent on their skills to consecrate their political power through the visual arts and architecture. When Vespasiano da Bisticci recorded Cosimo de' Medici as regretting 'that the great mistake of his life was that he did not begin to spend his wealth ten years earlier' he was making it implicit that Cosimo was acutely aware that fine private and public buildings would enduringly advertise his family's identity, status and power like nothing else could. In an age of growing conspicuous consumption, nothing was more conspicuous than architecture, a field in which Brunelleschi was by now the undisputed king. But it is all too easy to forget that Brunelleschi's public career began not with the cupola of the Duomo but with that other iconic artistic landmark of Florence, the Baptistery doors, a project which he ultimately failed to secure and which instead made the name of his great adversary Lorenzo Ghiberti.

Arguably the first great landmark work of art of the Italian Renaissance, the pair of exquisite bronze Baptistery doors commissioned from Lorenzo Ghiberti in 1401 was in the manner of a pagan votive offering to a malevolent Christian God who visited seemingly endless plagues upon a hapless humanity. The competition, in 1401, for a design for the east doors of the Baptistery, coming as it did on the cusp of the fifteenth-century, had been the city's most prestigious public commission to-date, a watershed in Florence's aspiration to position itself as the intellectual and artistic capital of southern Europe. This 'first great artwork of the Renaissance' had also, as we have seen, been connected with the Medici, the first and greatest patrons of Italian Renaissance art. Giovanni di Bicci had sat on the panel of judges; thirty-four native-born citizens of Florence who were tasked by the *arte di calimala* with awarding the Baptistery commission. The judges had decided in favour of Ghiberti, who was barely out of his twenties at the time, and had rejected a competing concept from the goldsmith Filippo Brunelleschi, who had subsequently decamped in disgust to Rome to study the ancient pagan ruins with his friend the homosexual sculptor Donatello. After Ghiberti had won, he had immodestly exclaimed: 'To me was conceded the palm of victory by all the experts and by all my fellow competitors. Universally, they conceded to me the glory, without exception. Everyone felt I had surpassed the others in that time, without a single exception, after great consultation and examination by learned men.' Humility could not be said to be Ghiberti's especially strong suit.

Ghiberti set up a large workshop in which many renowned artists both contributed to the commission and trained, including Donatello, Masolino, Michelozzo, Uccello and Antonio Pollaiuolo. The gilded bronze Baptistery doors which they fashioned comprised a total of twenty-eight panels, twenty of which depicted New Testament scenes from the life of Christ. A further eight panels showed the four evangelists and the Church Fathers Saint Augustine, Saint Ambrose, Saint Jerome and Saint Gregory. Originally installed on the east side, in place of Pisano's pre-existing doors, Ghiberti's replacement doors were later moved to the north side. It took Ghiberti a staggering twenty-one years to complete this first commission. In 1425, Ghiberti won a second commission to design the east doors of the baptistery, which were this time fashioned to depict scenes from the Old Testament. Astonishingly, Ghiberti laboured on the second assignment for a further twenty-seven years. Lorenzo Ghiberti had been twenty-three years old when he began work and was seventy-one years old by the time his two Baptistery commissions were completed, an ancient age by the standards of the time.

Ghiberti's bronze panels embody a crucial element of the Italian Renaissance, the rediscovery of lost classical or early Christian ideas. His depiction of the Noah's Ark story, for instance, incorporates an Ark in the shape of a pyramid, a clear reference to the writings of the Egyptian Church Father Origen who had envisaged the Ark as a truncated pyramid with three decks. This idea was reproduced by other Renaissance artists like Paolo Uccello who also depicted the Ark as an implied pyramid in his work *Flood and Waters Subsiding*. Ghiberti's figures, carved in bas-relief and draped in classical togas, were dramatically fluid and lifelike, almost as though they were paintings upon canvas rather than sculptures in bronze. The classical nature of their surroundings also hearkened back to a different, lost era.

So goes the traditional story at least. In reality, however, the panel of judges could not decide between the two finalists and had therefore commanded them to collaborate on the commission *together*. Predictably, Brunelleschi's volcanic ego could not tolerate such a rank compromise; he was already widely acknowledged amongst Florentines to be a somewhat 'difficult' personality. The writer Marsilio Ficino was to conjoin Aristotle's suggestion that all great men are melancholic with Plato's idea that inspiration was a kind of divine frenzy and argue, as a result, that all creative people (*ingeniosi*) are by nature melancholic and frantic (*furiosi*). This might have been the perfect description of the fiery yet intensely secretive, and often morbid, Brunelleschi. Although his concept for the Baptistery doors had been regarded as the close runner-up, the fact is that his interpretation of the sacrifice of Isaac ushered in an entirely new kind of dramatic realism in the world of the visual arts and was therefore revolutionary in its own right.

When we think of Brunelleschi today it is usually in connection with his engineering feat of the cupola of Florence's Duomo. The story goes that, having been disappointed by the outcome of the Baptistery competition, Brunelleschi chose an entirely new field of endeavour in which he might perfect his art and thereby reign supreme; this may well have been his main motivation in switching his interests from sculpture to architecture and civil engineering. For an ambitious craftsman wishing to make his personal statement through art and craft the cupola could not have been a more inspired choice for it accomplishes much more than merely provide a cathedral with a dome. In effect, what Brunelleschi did was to create a resonant central focal point for the city, an omphalous as it were, which was not only visible and recognisable from any point within the city limits, but which was also discernible from anywhere in the surrounding countryside too, thus providing an artistic and cultural anchoring point. By means of such engineering alchemy, the urban commune and the *contado* therefore became parts of a dynamic whole, a synergy, thus achieving by artistic means a political objective usually only enforceable through wise central government and the occasional, judicious use of military force.

In light of these innovations, which served to draw the parts towards the orbit of the centre to create a whole, it was also fitting that Brunelleschi should have been the one to revolutionise our sense of linear perspective as well. The proportionally receding transversal lines which he innovated not only provided a completely new way of measuring and creating a three-dimensional space on a two-dimensional plane. His new artistic framework for seeing 'in perspective' was entirely appropriate to an awakening age of the intellect in which scholars, bankers and statesmen alike sought to discern more clearly how different elements existed in relation to each other. We see this trend not only in the desire of the humanists to understand the more secular 'human sciences' more clearly, free of the fog of received scholastic wisdom, but also in the banker's operant use of different financial instruments towards a unified end: *profit*. We see it too in the writings of Niccolò Machiavelli, who adduced a whole new 'science' of political cause and effect in the world of princely affairs. It was only natural under such circumstances that everyday people should begin to experience visual representation in a way which was far more representative of the evidence of their own senses. For the first time in centuries people were able to discern what was immediate and important and what was not, and to move away from 'seeing' in the childish idiom of medieval times, where all objects both great and small jostle for equal billing and attention.

If Ghiberti's bronze doors and Brunelleschi's dome and elucidation of the new rules of perspective broke new ground, both technically as well as artistically, then the increasing tendency towards artistic patronage had its origins firmly in devotional life. Wealthy Florentine families like the Bardi, Peruzzi, Alberti, Strozzi and Tournabouni sunk their wealth into a proliferation of private altars, chapels and sacristies in existing churches. This tendency was by no means exclusive to Florence. In Pope Martin V's Rome there had been a papal proclamation to the effect that cardinals and nobles ought to invest in establishing family chapels in Roman churches and that this was to be done for the spiritual hygiene of their souls. This had led to the small boom in ecclesiastical construction which would only continue to gather pace as the fifteenth-century dovetailed into the pious sixteenth-century of Reformation and Counter Reformation. In both Rome and Florence the preference, for those who could afford it, was to assume corporate family sponsorship of the high altar, but if that was not possible then equally prestigious was the sacristy or the chapter room.

The Medici were to contribute wholeheartedly to the trend in ecclesiastical building. In 1418, a prominent group of families residing in the neighbourhood of the church of San Lorenzo agreed to contribute equal funds towards the restoration of their parish church. This group included Giovanni di Bicci, despite the fact that he was at that time currently engaged in negotiations for the release of the antipope John XXIII at positively ruinous cost. The different families would each construct their own family chapel around the transept of the reconstructed church. The Medici agreed to contribute the *Sacrestia Nuova* or 'New Sacristy' of the building and also provide a double chapel at the end of the transept. Their contribution of these two new spaces gave the Medici almost double the space of any other family taking part in the project. Furthermore, in commissioning a renowned architect like Brunelleschi to design the sacristy, the structure acquired a special prominence all of its own.

Although Giovanni di Bicci himself had not lived to see the completion of the Sacristy in 1440, Cosimo had lovingly completed the subsequent adornment and beautification of the space. The decorative details are by Donatello, who designed the tondos in the pendentives, the lunettes, the reliefs above the doors and the doors themselves. Giovanni and his wife Piccarda were both entombed here whilst Cosimo himself later chose the crossing of the church for his own mausoleum. The choice of San Lorenzo itself as the family church and last resting place was also highly symbolic. The church sat on the site of an eleventh-century Romanesque church which itself had replaced an early Christian basilica dedicated by St. Ambrose in 393. As a far older structure than the Duomo itself, San Lorenzo was synonymous with Florence; hence Medici patronage of the sacristy was a powerful political statement of association of the clan with the commune itself. Above these frenetic programmes of public and private works stood the artist or architect; no longer dismissed as a mere craftsman-for-hire, he was a loci for patronage, adoration and emulation by other young up-and-coming talents. When, as in the case of Donatello, the artist was awarded a pension and thus relief from the ordinary exigencies of everyday life, he was henceforth free to exercise his virtuosity and grapple with his own creative and impassioned soul without encumbrance. Humanism's revival of classical literature also fuelled this quasi-Romantic trope; the Greeks in particular saw artistic inspiration as a kind of divine madness, *furor poeticus*, which was sent by the very gods themselves.

Indeed, the artist as virtuoso and tortured genius came to be a fairly recognisable cultural trope from the time of the Quattrocento onwards. He is embodied in the story of the painter Filippo Lippi who first came to Cosimo de' Medici's attention with the 1441 altarpiece that Lippi painted for the church of Sant'Ambrogio. Equally as smitten with the profane as with the sacred, Lippo was for the entire duration of his life deeply enamoured of the low life, dredging the taverns and brothels of Florence and Padua for diversion. When he was working on another altarpiece for the convent of Santa Margherita in Prato he ran off with the nineteen-year-old nun Lucrezia Buti who had been modelling for him. It was only through the intervention of Cosimo de' Medici, who interceded with Æneas Silvius Piccolomini–by now Pope Pius II–that Lippi and Buri were absolved from their vows and allowed to marry and happily procreate. Behind the endless scandals, however, was a prodigal talent and the works that he produced throughout his dissolute life took the techniques he had learned from his mentor Masaccio and broadened them to produce such animated and lifelike figures as to be positively revolutionary for the painting of that time.

The gilded gutter life of Fra Filippo Lippi, and other artists with a similar appetite for life in the raw–the notorious homosexual sculptor Donatello for example–was perhaps one of the reasons why Vespasiano da Bisticci carefully omitted from his biographies of the eminent men of his time any mention of visual artists, even though certain *maestro* like Ghiberti had grown wealthy and socially respectable on the back of their art. If artists themselves, however gifted, were not yet suitable to be counted alongside the names of the wealthy merchants and nobles who patronised them then at least patronage of the arts itself was seen to be a special quality of the more refined type of Quattrocento man. And, if the artists themselves were not worthy of record, then their works most certainly began to be, for as early as the second half of the fifteenth-century we find Francesco Albertini compiling his *Memoriale di molte picture e statue sono nella inclyta cipta di Florentia*, which is widely regarded as the first artistic and cultural guidebook of Florence. Although criticised for his inaccuracy and superficiality, Albertini's tract nevertheless stands as a remarkable monument to the enduring cultural pride of the Florentines.

CHAPTER 7

Cosimo Triumphant

Nothing is denied to Cosimo. He is the arbiter of peace and of war, and
the moderator of the laws. Not so much a private citizen as the lord of
the country. The policy of the Republic is discussed in his house; he it is
who gives commands to the magistrates. Nought of royalty is wanting to
him save the name and the state of a king.

Pope Pius II

In August 1447, at the age of fifty-four, Duke Filippo Maria Visconti finally
gave up the ghost and, with Cosimo de' Medici watching carefully from the
sidelines as always, the struggle for mastery of Milan commenced in earnest.
If Francesco Sforza had been calmly awaiting his father-in-law's impending
death in hopes of a smooth transition from *condottiere* to acknowledged duke he
was to be sadly disappointed. Filippo Maria's demise disgorged a slew of
powerful competing claims from as far afield as Naples, France and even
Germany.

The French claim hinged upon Filippo Maria's older sister, Valentina
Visconti of Orléans. Valentina had been married in 1387 to Louis I of Orléans,
the younger brother of the future Charles VI of France. The bride's marriage
contract contained the clause that, in the absence of any male heirs of Filippo
Maria's, then Valentina herself would inherit the Visconti title and dominions,
which would subsequently be passed down through her male line. As Louis had
died in 1407 and Valentina had followed him to the grave the following year, the
claim had devolved upon their son the fifty-three-year-old Duke Charles of
Orléans, who was Filippo Maria's nephew. Not only was this pernicious clause
to give occasion for Valentina's French son's claim to the duchy of Milan, but it
was also, much later, to provide the pretext for France's protracted and
disastrous involvement in Italian affairs during the reigns of the future French
kings Charles VIII, Louis XII and François I. Indeed, in this ill-conceived
marriage clause were laid the seeds of the devastating Italian Wars which would
extend from 1494 through to 1559, a catastrophic series of conflicts in which
the Medici themselves would play a central role.

For his part, in the absence of any male heirs, the Holy Roman Emperor
Frederick III meanwhile claimed Milan as its feudal suzerain. However the
Emperor was not overly committed to pressing his own claim and only ventured
south in 1452 at the age of thirty-seven to receive his eighteen-year-old bride
Donna Eleanor of Portugal and be crowned by Pope Nicholas V in Rome
(enjoying the considerable improvements which Nicholas had made to the

157

processional route since the time of the Ponte Sant'Angelo tragedy of 1450). A far more enthusiastic claimant was Alfonso V of Aragon, the king of Naples. Eager to sew strife and discord from beyond the grave as well as in life, Filippo Maria had snubbed his son-in-law and in his will had instead mischievously named Alfonso as his sole heir. The fact that Naples and Milan lay at opposite ends of the Italian peninsula seemed to bother neither man. The so-called bracceschi, the Milanese supporters of Alfonso's claim, had been quick to seize Milan's castello on the night of the Duke's death. As if these three competing claims were not enough, Venice–in line with her long-term regional strategy of achieving ascendancy in northern Italy–also still hoped to assimilate both Milan itself in addition to most of western Lombardy.

None of the aforementioned claimants had reckoned, however, on the citizens of Milan. Drawing on the glorious traditions of the old Milanese republic and influenced by the College of Jurisprudence in Pavia, the Milanesi now expelled Aragon's sympathisers the bracceschi and declared that Milan would henceforth be known as the Golden Ambrosian Republic after the fourth-century bishop of Milan, St. Ambrose. They had seen enough of ducal despots, of which the Visconti had been a particularly egregious example. Both Filippo Maria and his brother Giovanni had been a particularly detestable iteration of the Visconti dynasty, determined to maintain power through sheer terror and intimidation rather than making any real effort to seek the support and devotion of the Milanesi. Giovanni Visconti had been an unalloyed sadist who had revelled in the 'sport' of using savage hounds to hunt human beings. His dog handler Squarcia Giramo had trained the Duke's hunting dogs to a high degree of ferocity by feeding them on human flesh. Giovanni's propensity to control knew no bounds and often went to absurd lengths. When, on one occasion, a group of Milanese citizens unhappy with the endless Visconti wars had gathered in a city square calling loudly for peace, Giovanni's response had been to send in the troops. After the crowd was dispersed, the Duke had officially banned any further use of the offending word pace ('peace') in Milan. The obese and paranoid Filippo Maria had been marginally less sociopathic than his loathsome older brother but still ruled Milan as a ruthless overlord at the point of a sword. The Milanesi now looked admiringly towards cities like Florence, which had grown affluent through trade and which had evolved reasonable and for the most part democratic republican political institutions which had stood the test of time. The idealistic and libertarian aspirations of the Milanesi at this point certainly cannot be disparaged and it was tragic that, through no fault of her citizens, Milan was unfortunately surrounded on all sides by four separate ravening powers that were eager to possess her.

One of the first acts of the Golden Ambrosian Republic was to tear down one of Milan's main symbols of oppression, the old fourteenth-century Visconti fortification known as the Porta Giovia which took its name from its proximity to a gate in the city walls. Many of the former Visconti regime's official records were also destroyed in the process of tearing this fortezza down. Despite this promisingly liberating beginning, however, the business of managing a fledgling republic in the golden age of predatory Quattrocento warlords was an extremely delicate business. No sooner was the Golden Ambrosian Republic openly declared than Milan's former client possessions including Pavia, Lodi, and Piacenza also declared their own separate independence from Milan and, as a result, Venice opportunistically moved in, capturing both Lodi and Piacenza and closing her ears to Milan's new government's earnest entreaties for peace on the troubled Lombard Plain. So it was that Milan was compelled with some considerable measure of irony to issue a *condotta* to Francesco Sforza to come to the city's defence, which he did in full awareness that his own objectives were materially the same as Venice's. The unfortunate Ambrosians were fully aware that their champion might well turn out to be their worst enemy but had little choice. Sforza quickly seized the newly independent city of Pavia, ostensibly to block Venice's advance along the Po River and secure its formidable arsenal, but in reality as part of his own grand plan to carve out a personal power base in Lombardy. Therefore, when the *Milanese* captain Bartolomeo Colleoni subsequently captured Tortona, whose inhabitants had previously decreed Sforza as their lord, the *Milanesi* rejoiced. Although he was their *condottiere*, it was good to see Francesco Sforza cut down to size for once. Such was the nature of the relationship between these two mutually-suspicious bedfellows.

Within Florence the Golden Ambrosian Republic had supporters amongst the old, conservative oligarchic faction, such as Neri Capponi and Giannozzo Manetti, who believed that Florence should remain committed to the old confederacy with Venice whilst simultaneously nurturing the promising fledgling *Milanese* republic. Venice, they suggested, could be bought off with some of the choicer cuts from Lombardy excluding Milan herself. But this conservative Florentine faction overlooked the salient fact that expansionist Venice was by now a major rival to Florence in both trade and geopolitical matters. Florence traded avidly with the Ottoman Empire of Asia Minor, whereas Venice's trading relationship with the Levant and the city of Constantinople set her at odds with Florence. Furthermore, Venice's maritime capabilities, still as powerful as ever in the fifteenth-century, were a check on Florence's own growing maritime pretensions centred on the annexed city of Pisa. There may also have been more personal motivations in Cosimo de' Medici's disagreement with Manetti over Florence's foreign policy. A man of considerable erudition, Manetti had acquired his own extensive humanist library and had earned something of a reputation as a vast resource for humanist knowledge. In so doing he had unwittingly challenged Cosimo's primacy in the humanist field and the latter's right to rule as Florence's 'scholar prince'. Cosimo would ultimately destroy Manetti through his favourite weapon, selective taxation.

Revealing himself as a far shrewder practitioner of 'realpolitik' than the old oligarchs, Cosimo objected that Florence needed a strong buffer state between herself and an increasingly predatory and ambitious Venice. He advocated that a powerful Sforza-dominated ducal Milan suited this role far better than a milquetoast republic that was still unsteadily finding its feet. Cosimo's friendship with Francesco Sforza would, meanwhile, serve to neutralise the last remnants of Florentine resistance in exile. In fact, the Battle of Anghiari had sounded the death knell for the hopes of Florence's *fuoriusciti*. It was a battle which, predicated as it was on the unrealistically sanguine hopes and expectations of Rinaldo degli Albizzi himself, should never have been fought. If Rinaldo had convinced Piccinino to fight, then Francesco Filelfo had persuaded Rinaldo to persuade Piccinino to commit to battle. It was an object lesson, if ever one was needed, in how a proxy war waged through polemics should not be permitted to dictate the strategy of a very real war in the field. After the débâcle Milan had understandably washed its hands of the exiles' cause. It was a simple fact of life that exiles were always dependent upon the (often changeable) mercies of the city-states which took them in. The Florentine exiles who had settled in Milan had outlived not only their welcome but also their usefulness. Rinaldo himself, having left the field of Anghiari in disgust, consoled himself by going on a pilgrimage to the Holy Land whilst his sons eventually settled and became citizens in Ancona. By 1442 he had died, removing much of the wind from the exiles' cause.

It must be said that Cosimo de' Medici was not without his vocal public critics at this time, especially in underground literary circles. Giovanni Cavalcanti (1381–1450), a former Guelph party captain who came from an influential old patrician family, had spent years of his life in prison for debt and during this time he penned the *Istorie Fiorentine*, a bitter and scathing commentary on first the *ottimati* oligarchy and then the Medici ascendancy which had followed, his history covering the period from 1420 to 1447. Upon his release from prison he went on to write a further instalment called the *Seconde Storie* which continued this vengeful and moribund narrative. Cavalcanti's lengthy imprisonment had prevented him from taking his proper place in the political life of the commune which he felt to be his due. This was by no means an isolated sentiment in the Florence of this time. One of Cavalcanti's more stinging though well-justified rebukes concerned the fact that political debate and decision-making in Florence did not always take place in the appropriate seat of power, the Palazzo della Signoria, but was more often than not conducted behind the private walls and bolted doors of the city's many wealthy *palazzi*.

Cosimo de' Medici's entire foreign policy from the period 1447 to 1450 consisted in maintaining the financially insatiable Francesco Sforza in funding while he manoeuvred himself into a favourable position to conquer Milan and install himself as duke. But if support for Sforza's long-term objectives was the *sine qua non* of Cosimo's policy, this was to be no easy course for him to steer and he continued to encounter dogged opposition from within. As Sforza's agent in Florence, Nicodemo Tranchedini, reported to his master: 'the more Cosimo urges, the more the others hold back; and one spiteful person is more able to spoil an undertaking than ten favourable to carry it through'. In pursuit of this policy Cosimo was nevertheless resolved, if necessary, to put his life and his reputation on the line. When Venice's ambassadors mounted the *ringhiera* in the Piazza della Signoria to publicly harangue the Florentines for their support of Francesco Sforza and the *Milanesi*, Cosimo himself had in turn mounted the platform to denounce the *Veneziani* themselves as the aggressors. As Venice had allied with Alfonso of Naples and threatened to invade Tuscany, the accusation was at least materially true and Cosimo had some justification for his indignant response. To this it should however be added that Cosimo de' Medici, though himself a scholar of such classical rhetoricians as Cicero and Quintilian, could hardly be described as one of Florence's great orators. Public speaking did not come easily to him and for this reason he largely shunned the limelight if he could. What is more, he would have been addressing many disabled Florentines who would have received their wounds and disfigurements during the long wars against the Visconti and his *condottiere* Francesco Sforza, hardly an amenable audience to receive what was in essence a pro-*Milanese* message.

Nevertheless, despite these difficulties and the opposition which he faced, Cosimo stayed the course. It took three more years of tiresome moves and countermoves on the chessboard of Lombardy for Francesco Sforza to finally checkmate Milan. By this time Lodi, as well as certain other towns, had already followed Tortona's suit and awarded Sforza their town's seignory. Equally worrying for the fledgling Golden Ambrosian Republic was Sforza's alliance with William VIII of Montferrat and, in 1448, with Venice too. Cosimo de' Medici watched cautiously, keeping the critical streams of funding open to his *condottiere* friend. In the meantime he attended to his own family affairs. On 1 January 1449 Cosimo celebrated the birth of his first grandson Lorenzo. His father, Piero di Cosimo, arranged matters so that the infant's baptism coincided with the celebration of the Magi, a theme with which the Medici themselves had increasingly come to be associated, its story of the Three Wise Men reflecting as it conveniently did on the Medici as 'wise' rulers of Florence. Little Lorenzo was baptised in Florence's famous Baptistery and one of his godfathers was the powerful *condottiere* Federigo da Montefeltro, the lord of Urbino. Unlike Cosimo de' Medici this was a child who was truly 'born to rule' and the accompanying baptismal celebrations broadcast this fact to Florence's citizens. The child's father, meanwhile, had not been blessed with an especially good constitution. At the height of his manhood the young Piero de' Medici was already afflicted by the same genetically inherited maladies which plagued Cosimo and, indeed, he had already come to be jokingly known around Florence as Piero *il Gottoso* or Piero 'the Gouty'.

By 1450, Francesco Sforza was by now laying siege to the main prize itself, Milan. In seeking to preserve its independence the commune had been wracked by years of hardship and famine and riots were a regular occurrence in the streets of the city. As with any lengthy siege conditions inside the walls had soon grown unbearable. Once the city's regular provisions had been exhausted the siege had progressed to the inevitable next stage, during which the beleaguered inhabitants were driven to ever more desperate and creative measures to appease their starving bellies. First, all the vermin such as mice and rats mysteriously disappeared from the city streets along with household pets and animals such as cats, dogs and goats (dog stew was considered a particularly handsome meal). When all the living creatures were gone, and the last working horses and livestock had been butchered for their meat, the starving people resorted to boiling the leather from harnesses or the skin from drums in an attempt to create a kind of broth. Anything green and vegetable-like was consumed, including grass and weeds from peoples' gardens. Rudimentary breads were made from the flour of all sorts of things, both organic and inorganic, which could be ground down and made into 'dough' for baking. The more desperate souls avidly sought out and consumed human dung and, when there was absolutely no other alternative, there was always cannibalism, that final horrific taboo which was punishable by the most serious penalties such as burning alive. Long before the final horrific phase, in which parents butchered their dead infants for the cooking pot, a city would usually capitulate and make the best terms it could under the circumstances. So it was with Milan as it lay prostrate before the forces of the fearsome and determined *condottiere* Francesco Sforza.

On 26 February 1450, having forever abandoned their republican dreams, the city's leadership reluctantly called on Francesco Sforza to accept the seignory of Milan and offered him the ducal title. Sforza and his troops entered Milan in triumph through the Porta Nuova bearing gifts of bread and wine for the starving townspeople. On 20 March he repeated his triumphal *ingresso* once again in a grand theatre of ritual accession. Proceeding on horseback from the

Ticinian gate to the city's Duomo attended by his wife Bianca and his sons, guarded by his cavalry whose squadrons glittered in their best armour, he was robed in the traditional white silk vestment of the dukes of Milan and solemnly handed the keys to the city. The *Milanese* signory had wanted Sforza to ride in a chariot which they had prepared for him and which was topped with a canopy of white silk interwoven with gold thread; however Sforza had modestly demurred as he believed this to be a dignity more properly belonging to a monarch than a duke. The exiled humanist Francesco Filelfo was meanwhile inspired to write to his son Senofonte Filelfo of his intention to compose a twenty-four book Latin panegyric to Francesco Sforza's rise to power in the wake of his father-in-law's death and covering the period from 1447 to March 1450. Entitled the *Sphortias*, almost as soon as it appeared in print this ingratiating work of versified propaganda was lambasted for its literary and metrical flaws by Filelfo's contemporary Galeotto Marzio. Sforza's treasurer had refused to settle the bill for Filelfo's work and the desperate humanist had been forced to borrow ducats from the Duke's long-suffering chief minister Cicco Simonetta.

As Cosimo de' Medici had with his acute humanist's eye for the vagaries of human nature so perceptively foreseen, no sooner had Milan capitulated to Francesco Sforza than the Florentines, carried away by Sforza's irresistible glamour, had forgotten all about their former sympathies for Venice. Florence quite literally fell in love with Duke Francesco Sforza. Soon the infectious public excitement took on an official tone when the *signoria* despatched Neri Capponi, Luca Pitti, Dietisalvi Neroni and Cosimo's own thirty-four-year-old son Piero di Cosimo to Milan to offer Francesco Sforza the republic's formal congratulations. Giovanni Cambi recorded in his *Istorie* that the delegation 'proceeded in triumph through the *Milanese* territory ... The number of horsemen was so great when they arrived within five miles of Milan that it seemed like a manoeuvring ground. Then the Duke in person advanced to meet them, and embraced and kissed them. Never was greater honour paid to Florentine ambassadors.'

Cosimo's patience and forbearance had paid off and Florence now had a strong military check in Lombardy to the voracious Republic of Venice to the east and Naples to the south. It was an alliance based on solid friendship, mutual respect and co-dependency. Make no mistake, Francesco Sforza needed Medici money just as badly as Cosimo de' Medici needed *Milanese* arms. As evidence of this close reciprocal relationship one of the new duke's first acts was to set aside a spacious *palazzo* in the centre of Milan to serve as the head office for the Medici Bank's first ever branch in the duchy. Later enlarged and expanded by Cosimo's architect and friend Michelozzo, the Medici Bank's *Milanese* office would, over time, become virtually indistinguishable from the *Milanese* Treasury and would serve much the same function.

Venice's response to these events was predictable; not only were Florentine merchants expelled from the Most Serene Republic but Doge Francesco Foscari turned to the Holy Roman Emperor Frederick III of Austria to apply cool Germanic pressure on the new Florentine-*Milanese* alliance, arguing (somewhat disingenuously given her own territorial ambitions) that this new coalition threatened the whole of Lombardy. As an additional act of spite the Doge also persuaded the Byzantine *basileus* Constantine XI Palaiologos to break off Florence's trade concessions in Constantinople which, given the future events of 1453, may be regarded as an incredible blessing in disguise for the many expatriate Florentine merchants then residing in the Eastern imperial capital. Even so, Venice's retaliation caused great upheaval amongst the Florentine mercantile community and in trade circles Cosimo de' Medici was roundly criticised for disrupting their commercial interests. The banishment of Florentine traders and bankers from Venice fell especially hard on many prominent trading families.

Cosimo's countermove to Venice's troublemaking in 1451 was to despatch his friend, the humanist Agnolo Acciaiuoli, to the court of King Charles VII of France. Chosen for his family's loyalty to the Medici during the turbulent days of the Albizzi ascendancy (Acciaiuoli had himself been banished by Rinaldo degli Albizzi) Acciaiuoli was also selected for his unique Ciceronian gifts as an accomplished orator. An exquisite, cultured, honey-tongued, humanist ambassador, he was the perfect choice to seduce the king of France. By the terms of the Treaty of Montils-les-Tours in April 1452, Charles VII lost no time in reaffirming the Florentine-*Milanese* coalition, recognising Francesco Sforza as the rightful duke of Milan and opening up new trade channels between France and Florence to compensate for those which had been recently lost with Venice. Thenceforth, the white lily of France would stand alongside the red iris of Florence. This strategy of alignment with France already had its antecedent. After Filippo Maria Visconti's defeat by Venice at Casalmaggiore in 1446, he too had flirted with the idea of involving France in Venice's backyard and as an incentive he had offered the *Dauphin* the cities of Asti and Genoa. But Charles VII was seemingly disinterested in such territorial bribes; rather, he was more entranced by Agnolo Acciaiuoli's deeply cultured embassy. Medicean Florence had become the talk of Western Christendom and, to some of the kings and princes of Europe, the Medici were undeniably starting to resemble princes like themselves in all but name. As Pope Pius II later wrote, 'His [Cosimo's] life was full of honour, his glory extended beyond his own city to Italy, nay, to the whole world'.

If King Charles had one caveat in return for his assistance it was that Florence and Milan should stand neutrally aside should René of Anjou decide to renew his claim to the throne of Naples. Allowing French troops to traverse the Tuscan countryside was risky but, on the other hand, Cosimo could also use the threat of French force to make King Alfonso think twice before any future move against Florence. Alfonso had already shown no compunction about sending his troops into Florence's zone of control in the immediate aftermath of Filippo Maria Visconti's death. On that occasion his *Napoletano* army had trudged into Volterra and captured several important *castelli* in the province. Despite the hasty summoning of a *dieci* of war and the appointment of the promising, twenty-five-year-old *condottiere* Federico da Montefeltro, the Florentines could do little to dislodge Alfonso at the time. Cosimo knew that Alfonso took the Angevin threat seriously; it played on his deep-seated insecurities concerning his Neapolitan throne, and Cosimo was therefore determined to use the French as psychological intimidation rather than any real, tangible threat. On the diplomatic front, meanwhile, Agnolo Acciaiuoli was carefully instructed to make no specific promises to the French of any Florentine military help for an Angevin restoration in Naples.

The same year that this accord with France was being forged, Cosimo de' Medici was also able to work his considerable charms on the Holy Roman Emperor Frederick III, thus defusing Venice's meddling on this front too. In

163

January 1452, Frederick had set out for Italy on the dual mission of being crowned Emperor at Rome and also to rendezvous with his new bride, the eighteen-year-old *Infanta* Eleanor, the daughter of King Edward of Portugal. Eleanor had recently landed at Livorno after a gruelling 104-day voyage. On the way to collect her, the Emperor's entourage had already passed through Ferrara, where Frederick had been subjected to an official welcome speech by Francesco Sforza's son Galeazzo Maria which had been 'as long as two chapters of St. John's Gospel'. After that he progressed on to Bologna where he was met by the papal legate Cardinal Bessarion, at which point Cosimo had sent word inviting the Emperor on an 'all expenses paid' state visit to Florence. As the ordinary Florentines griped about the ruinous cost to the city's exchequer of Cosimo's expansive gesture, 1,500 boisterous Austrian and Styrian knights now descended on the city to eat and drink their fill and make merry at the republic's expense, although in reality underwritten by Cosimo's Medici Bank.

The entry of the Emperor to Florence itself had been less than auspicious as a sudden downpour had reduced the fine procession of German notables to a clutch of soaking wet and shivering men and women who quickly sought shelter at the monastery of Santa Maria Novella. The following morning, Frederick III, King Ladislaus of Hungary and numerous other assorted German princes were greeted by the *gonfaloniere* Mariotto Benvenuti and the rest of the *signoria*. Recording the scene, Giovanni Cambi remarked that 'The Emperor seated himself on a most splendid chair under the loggia of the church, and all the gentlemen stood round him while the Ten of the Balia bent the knee before him on either side, representing the Magnificent Signori'. However now it was the Florentines' turn to be crestfallen. A carefully prepared Latin welcoming oration by Florence's chancellor Carlo Marsuppini (a Medici man) was deftly fielded by the Emperor's secretary, the imperial poet laureate Æneas Silvius Piccolomini. Piccolomini's response had required an extempore reply from Marsuppini in Latin but the chancellor's skills had proven sadly unequal to the task. As Marsuppini gaped blankly, desperately trying to frame a worthy reply, the *signoria* now groaned collectively under the unfolding shame of it all. The offering of accomplished humanist orations and repartees had come to play a major role in humanist Florence's diplomatic niceties and was part and parcel of *le usate e anticate cerimonie* (the 'customary ancient ceremonies') and yet here she was being outdone by a group of foreigners. Finally, with the Emperor's secretary pressing for a reply, Giannozzo Manetti (a non-Medici man) came to the rescue with some improvised Latin *bon mots* of his own which were deemed suitably elegant to assuage Florentine pride and move the formalities swiftly along. Indeed, Manetti's impromptu remarks were considered vastly superior to Marsuppini's prepared oration.

Diplomatic and rhetorical one-upmanship aside, however, the Florentines realised that there was little to fear from this rather underwhelming Emperor who, with his modestly-sized retinue, appeared in Florence more like a visiting dignitary than as the feudal suzerain of all Lombardy. He even condescended to entertaining Francesco Sforza's own ambassadors and listened to them openly, albeit non-comitally, the plain fact being that Sforza had seized Milan without his permission. On Frederick III's return from Rome later that same year he passed through Florence once more, but by this time Cosimo had already received word from Agnolo Acciaiuoli concerning the enactment of the French treaty. The Emperor now seemed to pose even less of a threat than he had before and was comfortably discounted as a political or a military force in Italy.

Nevertheless, for all this, Frederick ultimately refused to acknowledge Cosimo's friend and ally Francesco Sforza's ducal title. This was a tit-for-tat response on Frederick's part since he had been unable to obtain the Iron Crown of Lombardy from its *Milanese*-controlled cathedral at Monza and had instead been forced to fall back on being invested with the German crown which he had brought with him to Italy.

The refusal by his imperial suzerain to acknowledge his ducal legitimacy did not seem to concern Francesco Sforza in the slightest. He disdained both Frederick and his equally impecunious father Sigismond for their propensity to pawn imperial preferments for ready cash. This was how Giovanni Francesco da Gonzaga had come by the marquisate of Mantua in 1432, with a payment of 12,000 florins to the Emperor's late father. Likewise, as Frederick travelled through northern Italy in May 1452, Borso d'Este had purchased his dukedom of Modena and Reggio for a much higher price (nineteen years later Borso would also receive the dukedom of Ferrara, a papal vicariate, from Pope Paul II). None of this buying and selling of imperial titles especially impressed the hard-nosed, practical-minded solider Sforza; as de facto ruler of Milan he hardly felt he needed a parchment diploma or an imperial seal to underscore his very tangible, de facto ducal authority. Neither was Frederick the type who was disposed to spend valuable time and money to dislodge Sforza from Milan merely to make a point.

In the event, the Emperor's lack of intervention did not divert Venice from her own strategic goals. On 16 May 1452, disregarding the threat of French intervention, Venice called Cosimo de Medici's bluff and declared war on Milan. The following month Naples followed suit and declared war on Florence. Alfonso's son Ferrante, illegitimately sired by the King's mistress Giraldona Carlino, swept northwards into Tuscany with a *Napoletano* army with the full consent and connivance of neighbouring Siena. But Alfonso's son proved unequal to the task. No sooner had he arrived in enemy territory than Ferrante squandered more than one whole month attempting to reduce the two relatively insignificant Florentine *castelli* of Cortona and Fojano. By winter all he had to show for his efforts were Cortona and the village of Rencine, which gave Florence ample time to reinforce her other more important strategic garrisons.

Nevertheless, the continued presence of the Spaniards and *Napoletani* in Tuscany was worrisome and, by winter time, Ferrante's presence had engendered a real sense of panic. One morning an unnerved merchant burst into Cosimo de' Medici's study at the Palazzo Medici with the news that 'Rencine has fallen!' Cosimo could only glance up and drolly retort 'Rencine? Where is Rencine?' Still, at the news of Rencine's fall to the Spaniards, a large crowd had gathered at the Medici *palazzo* seeking reassurance. Cosimo, bothered now by constant agonising bouts of gout and arthritis, could not spare the energy to speak to the crowd and reassure them personally and merely retired to his bed. Meanwhile, Venice too persisted in her mischief. The maritime republic had actively encouraged the city-states of Savoy and Montferrat to attack Florence's lands from the north-east.

That winter Cosimo de' Medici was also forced to countenance another unwelcome political crisis, this time in Rome. A Roman knight with republican leanings named Stefano Porcari had hoped to restore the mid-fourteenth-century glories of Cola di Rienzo and end the rule of the priesthood in the Eternal City. His rebellious leanings had already come to the attention of Pope

Nicholas V when Porcari had used the death of his predecessor Pope Eugenius IV to publicly call for the Roman people to cast off the papacy's yoke. Following this indiscretion Pope Nicholas had shown merciful tolerance, merely banishing Porcari to Bologna where he was placed under the supervision of Cardinal Bessarion. However, by December 1452 Porcari had returned once again to Rome whereupon he recruited a small army of 300 like-minded conspirators.

Porcari's plan had a child-like simplicity to it: his supporters would first set fire to the Vatican stables and then, in the mayhem, they would kidnap the Pope and his cardinals whilst simultaneously raising the Romans to rebellion. Due to the large numbers of people who were party to the conspiracy the news of their plan had soon leaked out to the authorities. The house in the Piazza della Minerva where Porcari and seventy of his armed accomplices had congregated was quickly surrounded by the papal guard and the conspirators rounded up and brought to book. Porcari himself escaped out the back door but was soon apprehended and executed by hanging on 9 January 1453. Diplomatically, the plot was perceived by the Court of Rome as an international republican intrigue which had been fomented in republican Florence and recently-republican Golden Ambrosian Milan. Adding to this perception was the fact that Stefano Porcari himself had been raised in Florence at the *palazzo* of the Bardi family and from 1427 to 1428 had even served as the commune's *capitano del popolo* or police magistrate. To the Pope and his cardinals, it had been Porcari's exposure to Florentine humanism which had unquestionably fed his idealistic dreams of a classical Roman republic. Florence, meanwhile, was seen to be hovering in the background waiting to pick over the Curia's massive wealth like a vulture scavenging a carcass.

Fortunately for Florence, Pope Nicholas V expended most of his remaining vitality in exacting his revenge on the Roman conspirators, following which–deeply depressed by the whole affair–he slumped into a general malaise of despondency. The more tangible threat from Venice and Naples however still remained. The silver-tongued Agnolo Acciaiuoli was quickly despatched on a second urgent embassy to France. Unlike before, Acciaiuoli was now instructed to encourage Charles VII to actively move against Naples on behalf of René of Anjou. Charles's response was initially lukewarm. He was willing to use France's influence to intervene with Savoy to call them off from attacking Florence but the continued presence of the English on France's territories in Bordeaux still claimed the lion's share of his attention. Nevertheless, by April 1453 the English situation had been sufficiently resolved for Charles to turn his attention to Italy once more. As a precursor to a French invasion of Naples, several thousand mounted knights were initially despatched to ride south to counter both Ferrante and the Venetians.

Quick reversals followed for both of Florence's adversaries. When René reached Brescian lands and joined forces with Francesco Sforza a whole string of towns surrendered to the French without so much as a fight. It would be a chilling foreshadowing of another French invasion forty-three years later; the Italians had been deeply intimidated by the no-nonsense, business-like approach of the French soldiers and they could see that, unlike their own preening *condottiere*, these battle-hardened Gallic veterans were a real force to be reckoned with. Discouraged, Ferrante relinquished what few inconsequential Florentine towns he had captured while his men–now confined for the most part to *Sienese* territory–were ravaged with sickness after spending a miserable winter in camp.

166

René's objective was to force Venice into mediation with Milan and then enlist a grateful Francesco Sforza's aid in conquering Naples. However the French had reckoned without the self-interested pragmatism of the Florentines. France and Anjou's victories had come at so rapid a pace that, their enemy having been chastened, the minds of the Florentines and also the *Milanesi* turned inevitably once more towards the resumption of trade with their former adversaries Venice and Naples. Milan in particular, with its 200,000 inhabitants, had transformed itself into an economic powerhouse with a particular speciality in silk production and the forging of fine suits of armour. Her farmlands in the *contado* were extensive and fertile and, in the intellectual sphere, she would soon also show her worth. Under the rule of Francesco Sforza a printing shop would be established in 1469 by Philip of Lavagna; this was a mere four years after Italy's first printing presses were established at the Benedictine monastery at Subiaco and a full eight years before Bernardo Cennini set up the first ever printing press in Florence.

Sforza had also lost little time in rebuilding the slighted Visconti fortress at Porta Giovia, which he renamed the Castello Sforzesco, and from which he stood sentinel over his newly thriving and revivified city. Its drum towers and heavily rusticated masonry were purposely designed to project an image of strength towards the city which it faced, but it had also been created for gracious living too and the Duke was able to enjoy its walled gardens, courtyards and sumptuously furnished apartments.

The desire for peace on the Lombard Plain was mutual. Venice had by now also been dealt a body blow to her eastern maritime trade interests by the Turkish conquest, in May 1453, of the Byzantine capital of Constantinople which, in an economic sense, had left her reeling. She too was anxious to patch up her differences with Florence and Milan so that she could attend to the threat now posed by the triumphant Ottoman Empire. Her trading posts in Constantinople had been lost but she still held Crete, Euboea, Kythira, Kasos, Karpathos, Mikonos and various other Venetian enclaves up and down the Dalmatian littoral, all of which now lay dangerously exposed to the ever-expanding sphere of influence of the Turk. Indeed, it was widely acknowledged by most of the major city-states of Italy that sooner or later they would all need to come together as one to confront this looming heathen threat.

René of Anjou had realised meanwhile that Florence and Milan had been somewhat insincere in their calling him south to Italy; even now they were proceeding to make their own discrete peace agreements with Venice which left France out in the cold. Not only was René's presence no longer needed to intimidate Venice but neither state wished, as a result of any residual obligation to France, to become embroiled in any protracted Angevin invasion of the *Regno*. Cosimo de' Medici and Francesco Sforza could not have been entirely unaware of the dangerous game they were playing with the French; when all was said and done, Florence's (and by extension Milan's) mercantile fortunes were inextricably bound up with cordial dealings with France. Neither was their policy entirely free of the inevitable fall-out. As a result of their double-dealing the House of Anjou would never quite bring itself to forgive either Florence or indeed the House of Sforza and, as we shall see in due course, the ramifications of this would have adverse effects on future relations between France, Anjou and Orléans on the one side and the unhappy future descendants of Cosimo de' Medici and Francesco Sforza on the other. With the subsequent departure of

René of Anjou, Italy's affairs were left to settle themselves back into some sort of equilibrium.

Constantinople's fall and the wholesale massacre of Orthodox Christians which had followed in its wake had injected a note of sobriety into the Italian peninsula. Italy herself had experienced incidents of sporadic Muslim piracy, slaving and sundry other unspeakable atrocities in centuries past. Italians paused and reflected on who exactly posed the greater, external threat. During the ninth and tenth-century the Saracens had shown just how vulnerable the Italian peninsula could be to a swift and nimble assailant. Not only had North African Muslims conquered the entire island of Sicily from the Byzantines between 827 and 964 but seagoing Muslim pirates and mercenaries had even established their own autonomous emirates on the Italian peninsula itself at Taranto in 840, at Brindisi in 841, and at Bari in 847. In 846, during the pontificate of Sergius II, they had even sailed up the Tiber from Ostia and sacked St. Peter's Basilica, which was not at that time enclosed by the defensive structure later known as the Leonine Walls. The Crusades, though undertaken in a spirit of fanaticism cheered on by the Church Militant, had ultimately failed to stem the infidel tide and the Latin Kingdom of Jerusalem which had been established lasted for a mere 192 years before it was once again re-absorbed. As for the utterly scandalous Fourth Crusade, this venture had merely served to fatally weaken the only effective bulwark against Islam in the East, Constantinople and the Byzantine Empire.

Against this rather uninspiring backdrop, Western Christendom now decided to put its domestic squabbles on pause and unify for another Crusade with which to answer Constantinople's conquest. The Crusade was preached, somewhat unconvincingly, by Pope Nicholas V but his efforts rapidly deteriorated into a mere talking shop. The Pope cannot be entirely blamed for this since in an important respect the moment for concerted action had already passed. When previously approached for help by the Byzantine *basileus* Constantine XI in 1452, Pope Nicholas had issued the bull *Dum Diversas* on 18 June 1452; the bull authorised King Alfonso V of Portugal to 'attack, conquer, and subjugate Saracens, pagans and other enemies of Christ wherever they may be found'. Just one year later, Western Christendom had seemingly lost interest, despite the energetic support of the two Greek cardinals Bessarion and Isidore. Gone, it seemed, were the halcyon days when popes could summon great Crusading armies at will and the militancy issuing from the papal court fell largely on deaf ears.

Cardinal Isidore himself had been physically present at the fall of Constantinople. Sent as papal legate to the doomed city in 1452 with the vestigial token force two hundred soldiers to help in its defence, Isidore had evaded the vengeance of the Ottoman troops and survived the bloody sacking of the city by dressing up a nearby corpse in his ecclesiastical vestments while he himself donned the garb of an ordinary servant and hid. Although subsequently sold into slavery and despatched to Asia Minor Isidore had, somewhat miraculously, escaped Turkish bondage and made his own way back to Italy. Here, he gave his chilling eyewitness account of the terrible events of Constantinople's fall in a letter to Pope Nicholas and was duly compensated for his travails with the bishopric of Sabina. Isidore's tale was a remarkable story of luck and endurance calculated to instil in all Christians the desire for revenge, but even this proved insufficient motivation for Europe's princes to act.

Pope Nicholas V resigned himself miserably to the fact that Eastern Christendom had fallen on his watch. It was the only real blemish on an otherwise spotless pontificate. Nicholas V had ended the conciliarist schism, strengthened the papacy, begun the rebuilding of the city of Rome and, on a personal level, could never be reproached with the sort of self-serving corruption or nepotism which was true of subsequent Renaissance incumbents of St. Peter's throne. He remained to the end a modest man, as he self-deprecatingly described himself to Vespasiano da Bisticci: 'a mere bell-ringing priest'. To his lasting credit the final act of his pontificate was the bringing together of all the belligerent city-states of Italy.

Venice and Milan came together in the Peace of Lodi, an accord that was reached on 9 April 1454, and which ended the hostilities between the two city-states in the wars for the latter's succession. In August 1454, thanks to Medici Florence's diplomatic intercession on behalf of Francesco Sforza, the Peace of Lodi was further upgraded into the Most Holy League (also known as the 'Italic' or 'Italian League'), a twenty-five-year truce between Venice, Milan and Florence. This alliance was later joined in November 1454 by the Papal States and finally, in January 1455, by Naples too. Naples made it a condition of her joining that Genoa be excluded from the League on the pretext that Genoa was friendly towards France. The Most Holy League expressly forbade separate alliances or treaties between the signatories, whilst committing them to maintaining their established territorial boundaries. For the purposes of record, the territorial status quo was codified and a complete list of each city-state's *amici*, *collegati*, *aderenti* and *raccomandati* were set forth in the treaty's supporting documentation. The list of each signatory's territorial spheres of influence was to be maintained and respected by all the other members.

The Most Holy League was designed to achieve two objectives: firstly, to establish a mutual defence agreement against the Turk in the wake of the fall of Constantinople, and secondly to provide a bulwark which would keep the powerful and destabilising influence of France *out* of the Italian peninsula. It was reasoned that the Italian city-states had the best chance of achieving both of these aims provided only that the peninsula was restored to a more lasting and durable peace. The problem of Naples' continued exclusion from this League required deft handling by Cosimo de' Medici. When René of Anjou departed from Italy he had left behind in Florentine pay his son Jean, Duke of Calabria, and Jean's continued provocative presence in Italy was naturally enough resented by King Alfonso. Cosimo, however, was able to finesse both parties sufficiently for Jean to assent to Florence's 'temporary' truce with Naples, and for Alfonso to join the League in January 1455. All was done under the enlightened supervision of Pope Nicholas V, who was to die just two months after Naples formally entered the League.

The creation of The Most Holy League signified the crowning achievement of Cosimo de' Medici's foreign policy. It marked the point at which the Medici had not only made their mark upon the civic life of Florence but, working closely with the Pope, had wrought a significant new political peace on the Italian peninsula itself. The importance of this on so many different levels cannot possibly be understated. Under Cosimo's guidance, Florence had emerged from being a subordinate ally of powerful Venice to exerting a central role as the arbiter of a new regional balance of power. She was no longer willing to be intimidated by either Venice or the kingdom of Naples. To check the aggression and expansionism of wealthy Venice, Cosimo had orchestrated the robust buffer state of Sforzese Milan; to check unruly and capricious Naples he had deftly introduced the invincible French to Italian affairs, whilst drawing them back like an impresario at the critical moment. The cumulative benefit to Florence would be the resumption of a more lasting peace–the first in more than fifty years–which brought with it the inevitable and much longed-for trade prosperity craved by all. War taxation would be reduced and Florence would also now be free to pursue her maritime interests without the interference of the formidable Venetian or Neapolitan navies.

The Medici themselves had also enhanced their standing and esteem within the republic, as well as throughout Italy. It was understood by the leaders of all the other Italian city-states that if they wished something from Florence they would have to go through the good offices of Cosimo de' Medici. Furthermore, Cosimo had achieved this primal, almost 'princely' status whilst not deviating from the communal republican trappings of which the Florentines were so fond. It was a necessary artifice for, in reality of course, Florence was still neither a princely state nor indeed a true republic but a plutocracy run by a coterie of wealthy and powerful families clustered around the Medici. Despite his success in walking this fine line, Cosimo still harboured doubts that his personal achievement would stand the test of time. The Florentine bookseller turned biographer Vespasiano da Bisticci recorded these misgivings when he wrote: 'knowing well the disposition of his fellow citizens, he was sure that, in the lapse of fifty years, no memory would remain of his personality or of his house save the few buildings he might have built'.

These reservations notwithstanding, Cosimo de' Medici's achievement by 1455 was actually both subtle and clever. Like Niccolò Machiavelli, self-taught in the rudiments of how great men thought and the reasons why they acted, Cosimo had stumbled upon a political science of human nature. This way of thinking was admittedly a by-product of the Renaissance, when men constantly questioned and analysed every subject pertaining to the human sciences. However, such analysis had still to reach many of the noble courts of Italy and the despotic, dynastic rulers of the various city-states forever feuded with each other because, deep down at heart, they were fundamentally insecure in themselves. Blinded by their own pride, they acted and reacted on a purely instinctual level. King Alfonso of Naples was of course the supreme example of this tendency, basing his foreign policy on every personal slight which befell him regardless of whether it was real or imagined.

By contrast, Cosimo de' Medici approached geopolitics dispassionately in a more modern and objective way. Like Machiavelli, we get the sense that Cosimo played the game of statesmanship as though it were a game of chess. Free of the personal insecurities of his noble contemporaries, he had the gift of being able to elevate his mind above the petty squabbles of the moment and was able to call into play whatever was needed to adjust a given situation to Florence's advantage. It was this ability which had enabled him to remain faithful to Francesco Sforza when most Florentines resented having to subsidise what they regarded as a pointless and profligate *condottiere*. Cosimo was able to divine the long-term consequences of the courses of action on which he embarked. His foresight worked well for Florence and proved a useful counterweight to a governmental system where executive power was conferred for two-months at a time, a situation hardly conducive to long-term continuity of policy. Just as he found his stride in fine-tuning the Medici *reggimento*, so Cosimo de' Medici now set about fine-tuning the affairs of all Italy; a touch here, a finesse there, an overt threat backed by the required resources when it was called for, this was the Medici way.

On 24 March 1455, Pope Nicholas V, Cosimo's collaborator and fellow architect of The Most Holy League, died after a lengthy period of illness. Italy would need to brace itself for a new pope, but would he prove as wise and as foresighted as the pontiff who had just passed, and would he help to preserve the newfound *pax Italia*? The papal conclave of April 1455 comprised fifteen members of the Sacred College, the remaining five cardinals being absent. Of those fifteen, seven were Italian, two (Cardinals Latino Orsini and Prospero Colonna) were from Rome's old baronial families, another two (Cardinals Bessarion and Isidore) were from the East, and a further four were Spanish and would vote according to how their patron King Alfonso of Naples directed them. The conclave soon polarised into the usual scramble between the Orsini and Colonna candidates, the former commanding Alfonso's Spanish vote, giving him an insufficient total of five votes, just one third of the total. In the horse-trading which followed, the Venetian Cardinal Pietro Barbo (the nephew of Pope Eugenius IV) and Cardinal Capranica emerged as twin favourites but these were not favoured by the Orsini or Colonna cardinals. It was therefore resolved to select instead a neutral candidate as a stop-gap transition pope.

The decision ultimately came down to a two-horse race between two outsiders: the seventy-seven-year-old Aragonese bishop of Valencia, Alfons de Borja, and the former Eastern Orthodox prelate Cardinal Bessarion, who was then only fifty-two years old. The latter was a capable scholar, humanist and Churchman, as indeed he had proven during the Ecumenical Councils of Ferrara and Florence; however, a former Orthodox Christian candidate was not the first choice of clean-shaven, staunchly Roman Catholic cardinals. Aside from their reluctance to elect a churchman only newly emerged from the Schism between East and West, the fourteen cardinals could not find it within themselves to transcend their prejudice towards Eastern-style beards. Beards, which were quintessentially worn by Jews and Turks, tended to signify foreign *otherness* and unhappily for Bessarion his facial hair, as with most Greek males, was particularly luxuriant. The porcine, clean-shaven Alfons de Borja on the other hand was already conveniently advanced in age and therefore his papacy, should it prove unsatisfactory, could not in the nature of things last very long.

On 8 April, the bishop of Valencia was duly elected as the new Supreme Pontiff of the Holy Roman Church and assumed the name Pope Callixtus III. An austere, bone-dry devotee of canon law, Pope Callixtus III's reign would be a brief and largely undistinguished three-and-a-half-year interlude. As a Spaniard and therefore an outsider he lacked any interest in rebuilding Rome, an endeavour to which Nicholas V had previously devoted himself. He kept himself aloof from the partisan baronial politics of the city and Rome's high society gossips, pundits and observers found little that was scandalous or even interesting in his day-to-day affairs. His pontificate would principally be marked by the twin concerns of mounting a great Crusade which would drive the Ottoman Turks from Constantinople and in advancing the careers of his own Aragonese relatives. With regard to the latter, Callixtus immediately brought three of his Valencian nephews to Rome and, in 1456, two of whom were raised to the cardinalate. These were the fifty-four-year-old Luís de Milà y de Borja and his twenty-five-year-old cousin Rodrigo Lanzol y de Borja, later to become notorious as Pope Alexander VI.

Rodrigo was the son of Callixtus III's widowed sister, Isabella, towards whose family he behaved like a father. Following an accelerated sixteen month preparation in the law school at Bologna, Rodrigo was made cardinal-deacon of San Nicola in Carcere Tulliano; having advanced six more non-Borja cardinals to feign impartiality, the Pope then nominated Rodrigo in 1457 as the new vice-chancellor of the Church, the highest and most lucrative position to be had in the Curia. Rodrigo Lanzol y de Borja would eventually become known simply as Rodrigo Borgia, the Italians showing a propensity to soften the harsh guttural consonants of Spanish names. The fortunate young man had definite charisma. Rodrigo's Italian tutor Gaspare da Veroba would later describe how 'beautiful women are attracted to him and are excited by him in an extraordinary manner, more powerfully than iron is attracted by a magnet'.

The Pope's third nephew, Cardinal Rodrigo's twenty-four-year-old younger brother Pedro Luís, was meanwhile named captain-general of the Church and given control over the Castel Sant'Angelo in March 1456. Like Rodrigo, he was also further promoted in 1457, receiving the prestigious accolade of prefect of Rome. Surrounded at all times by his Spanish *bravi*, a swaggering band of adventurers and fortune-seekers, the cruel and arrogant Pedro Luís quickly earned the enmity of the xenophobic Romans. Regardless of whether they hailed from Aragon or Castile, they derided the Borja clan as 'Catalans'; indeed, the poet Dante had already immortalised the Italians' general disdain for Spain when he wrote in the Divine Comedy of 'the greedy poverty of Catalonia'. Pedro Luís and his entourage were only too happy to return the animus of the Romans in kind. To this general dislike of the arrogant Spaniards in their midst was added vendetta when Pedro Luís crossed swords with the powerful Orsini clan. When the Pope despatched his new captain-general to recover certain Orsini fortresses for the papacy the latter declared their undying enmity for the Borja pontiff. Relations with the rival Colonna was somewhat more cordial. A rumour soon circulated to the effect that Don Pedro Luís would be married to a Colonna bride. Although this prospect never actually materialised the new Catalan papal regime would continue to receive succour and support from the Colonna. It was also widely bruited that Pope Callixtus intended to make his swaggering secular nephew the *basileus* of the Byzantine Empire as soon as Constantinople had been recovered from the Ottomans.

To this end, on 15 May 1455, the Pope announced that a new Crusade would depart for the East on 1 March 1456 and he despatched his prelates to the four corners of Europe to drum up support amongst the princes of Christendom. The Dominican archbishop of Florence, Saint Antoninus, declared himself pleased with the decision, nodding his approval of the pontiff's declaration to 'promise and swear, were it to cost me my own blood, to do, so far as my strength allows me with the help of my venerable brothers, all in my power to recover Constantinople which has been seized and destroyed by the enemy of the crucified Saviour, the son of Satan, Mahomet, prince of the Turks'. However, as in the case of Pope Nicholas V before him, Pope Callixtus III's solicitations for troops yielded a disappointing crop. European monarchs were still largely preoccupied with their own affairs; the devastating Hundred Years War in France had only just drawn to a close in 1453, whilst in England the Wars of the Roses were just getting underway from around 1455. The rising European nation states were, moreover, less inclined than they had been in the past to make common cause with each another against the Muslim foe; they would even ally with the Ottoman Turks against fellow Christian powers if it suited their objectives to do so. Word came back from France, England, Spain, Portugal and Germany rebuffing His Holiness's call to arms. Nevertheless, despite these setbacks the Pope was still determined to send a Crusader fleet to the East.

To pursue his proposed naval Crusade, Pope Callixtus embarked on a fanatical drive to generate the necessary funding. He sold papal jewels and art in large quantities, stripped the gold and silver bindings from rare books in the Vatican Library, sold papal castles and landholdings and even ordered his servants to melt down the silver gilt from the salt cellars on his dining table. The Crusade became his overweening and all-encompassing obsession. Unfortunately, in the process Pope Callixtus also halted the rebuilding and civic revitalisation program which had been commenced under Pope Nicholas V and diverted the funds instead to the construction of war galleys in the revivified boatyards of Ripa Grande on the River Tiber. A modest navy comprising twenty-five galleys (supplemented by a further fifteen vessels supplied by the king of Naples) had subsequently been despatched to the Balkans under the Cardinal-Admiral Ludovico Trevisan on 31 May 1456.

Fortunately for Christian Europe, the burden of halting the Ottoman advance did not fall solely on the Catholic kings and the Pope of Western Christendom as in the East there were doughty and capable commanders who also played their part. As it advanced north-west up the Balkans from Constantinople, Sultan Mehmet the Conqueror's army of 70,000 men was stopped dead in its tracks by the heroic efforts of the Transylvanian and Hungarian Voyevod John Hunyadi at the Siege of Belgrade in July 1456. Accompanying Hunyadi were two of the Borja Pope's legates, Fra Capestrano and Cardinal Carvajal. Pope Callixtus had ordered the bells of every European church to be rung every day at noon as a call for believers to pray for the defenders of beleaguered Belgrade. The ringing of the noon bell would subsequently pass down into common practice, even amongst later Protestant congregations, in commemoration of this crucial victory. John Hunyadi did not live long to enjoy his momentous victory, however, and by 11 August 1456 he was dead of a plague which was ravaging his military encampment.

Other Balkan champions now mercifully filled Hunyadi's shoes. Amongst them was the Albanian hero Skanderbeg, the so-called 'athlete of Christ' as Pope Callixtus flatteringly called him, who would soon score another crushing victory over a 70,000-strong Ottoman army at the Battle of Albulena on 2 September 1457. Killing or capturing 30,000 Turks, Skanderbeg's devastating triumph led to a five-year truce with the Sultan which afforded Western Christendom a valuable breathing space in which to regroup. In eastern Mediterranean waters the small papal fleet of Cardinal Trevisan followed up these land victories by defeating an Ottoman attack on Mytilene in August 1457. Capturing many Turkish vessels in the process and winning plaudits for his abilities as a papal admiral, Cardinal Trevisan returned home to Rome to find Pope Callixtus III benignly satisfied that he had contributed, in his own modest way, to the effort to halt the relentless Ottoman advance.

For the next nine years, extending over the reign of three successive popes, Cosimo de' Medici's foreign policy was destined to hold the general peace of Italy together. When conflict did become inevitable, Florence itself always somehow contrived to remain aloof from the actual dirty business of fighting. However, in the immediate aftermath of the Peace of Lodi, Italy was not entirely immune from instability or military infractions, most of which stemmed from issues between the papacy and the *Regno*. Some of these problems were caused by the activities of disgruntled professional *condottieri* whom the recent Peace of Lodi had left sidelined and unemployed. One such *condottiere* was Jacopo Piccinino, the son of the late Niccolò Piccinino who had died in 1444.

Jacopo was a *condottiere* who had served for many years with the duke of Milan but who had lately been employed as captain-general of the Republic of Venice. After the Peace of Lodi, Venice had scaled back its armed forces and was privately quite glad to see the back of Piccinino's unruly mercenary troops. For his own part, Jacopo Piccinino was disappointed not to have been showered with the expected lands, titles and emoluments which had been forthcoming when the renowned Francesco Bussone da Carmagnola had taken the field on Milan's and Venice's behalf. Thwarted in his ambitions for wealth and title, Jacopo had redirected his efforts instead against Siena and the Papal States, forcing Pope Callixtus to counter the unruly warlord with the troops which had so painstakingly been recruited for his upcoming Crusade against the Turk. Soon, Venice, Florence and Milan had all pledged their support to Callixtus in an effort to contain this most troublesome and ungovernable *condottiere*.

King Alfonso of Naples, however, had different ideas and opted to support Piccinino. When a Neapolitan fleet attacked a papal fleet in the port of Civitavecchia and then sacked the *Sienese* port of Orbitello, the Pope was compelled to issue the bull *in Coena Domini* which excommunicated all the anti-papal belligerents. This implicit excommunication of King Alfonso led to a damaging rift between the king of Naples and his former protégé the Spanish Borja pope. Naples' king also caused further internecine problems over Genoa, a city which he had earlier managed to have excluded from the Peace of Lodi. Alfonso's main problem with Genoa lay in its being a potential staging post for any Angevin invasion of the *Regno*. In 1455, an Aragonese fleet had attacked Genoa and, though unsuccessful, it had the cumulative effect of driving the city-state's Doge Pietro Campofregoso into the waiting arms of the French Crown in May 1458. Genoa, the stepping stone to Naples, would thereafter continue to be a principal objective of the Angevin duke of Calabria. Since issuing his bull of excommunication, Pope Callixtus had relented somewhat and attempted to mend relations between himself and Alfonso. When he learned that the King's mistress Lucrezia d'Alagno planned to visit Rome in October 1457 the Pope, at Cardinal Rodrigo Borgia's prompting, had offered to play host to her. Alfonso was very much in love with Lucrezia and had earlier asked the Pope for an annulment to his loveless, childless dynastic marriage to Maria of Castile but Callixtus had denied his request out of hand. At this latest inept attempt to mend fences between them, Alfonso had bridled and rejected the Pope's entreaties and his olive branch.

His pride badly bruised, Callixtus vowed never to recognise Alfonso's illegitimate son Ferrante as his rightful successor. When Alfonso subsequently went to his grave on 27 June 1458, Pope Callixtus followed through on this promise by churlishly refusing to confirm Ferrante as king of Naples, declaring instead that the *Regno* had escheated back to the Holy See. Whilst letting it be known that he would consider the claim of Réne of Anjou to Naples' throne, the Pope meanwhile transferred many Aragonese benefices to members of his own family and close associates, including the bishopric of Valencia which was worth 18,000 ducats and which went to Cardinal Rodrigo. Rumour also abounded that the Pope really intended to make his nephew Pedro Luís king of Naples (preparatory to also making him *basileus* of Constantinople and also king of Cyprus). Undaunted by these rumours, and as a necessary step in securing his succession, Ferrante had gone through the traditional custom of showing himself publicly to the people of Naples on the day of his father's death.

The Pope's ambitious plans to annex the *Regno* and bring Naples and the Papal States under the unified rule of the House of Borja were interrupted by a severe bout of gout in the summer of 1458 which worsened until the Pope lay stricken in his bed. By 6 August Pope Callixtus III was dead and it was now that the Roman cardinals and ecclesiastics acted. With 200 men, the archbishop of Ragusa seized the Vatican and stripped the hated Pedro Luís of his title of captain-general of the Church. Handing over the keys to the Castel Sant'Angelo, the former captain-general fled Rome accompanied by an armed escort of several hundred men together with Cardinal Rodrigo and Cardinal Pietro Barbo. Outside Rome, the two brothers parted company. When the younger brother subsequently reached Ostia, however, the galley he had been promised was nowhere to be seen and, while taking a fishing boat from Ostia to the papal port of Civitavecchia, Pedro Luís 'mysteriously died'.

Unaware of his brother's death, Rodrigo Borgia had returned to Rome where he mournfully witnessed the sacking of his own *palazzo* by the Roman mob. This was situated near the small hill known as the Monte Giordano which lay just across the Tiber from the Ponte Sant'Angelo and which was home to a complex of Orsini palaces and strongholds. Just several months before his uncle the Pope's death, Rodrigo had purchased from him for the sum of 2,000 florins a string of dilapidated buildings here on the former site of the papal mint. Rodrigo had been in the process of renovating it into a *palazzo* at some considerable expense when the mob had descended on his new home like vultures. Naturally, the Orsini were elated at their enemy Callixtus's death, as were the Borja Pope's other adversaries. In the Papal States the ever-irrepressible Jacopo Piccinino used the opportunity to seize Assisi and, together with a jubilant Ferrante of Naples, laid siege to Foligno.

The papal conclave which duly assembled on 16 August comprised eighteen cardinals, eight of whom were Italians who were absolutely dedicated to prohibiting another foreigner from ascending the throne of St. Peter. This notwithstanding, the Frenchman Cardinal d'Estouteville of Rouen soon embarked upon a vigorous campaign of bribery (incommodiously carried out in the latrines) and promised an abundance of 'priesthoods, magistracies and offices and divided his provinces among them'. D'Estouteville had arrogantly proclaimed that he was the most senior cardinal in the Sacred College and that royal blood flowed in his veins. As the only feasible Italian contender, the spotlight now fell on the *Sienese* humanist and former imperial poet laureate, Æneas Silvius Piccolomini. Piccolomini was a relatively new entrant to the Sacred College, having only recently been made a cardinal by Pope Callixtus in December 1456. The wealthy Cardinal d'Estouteville now made an unscrupulous open attack on the fifty-three-year-old Piccolomini's poor health and relative poverty, asking 'shall we put a poet in Peter's place?' In the subsequent voting Piccolomini obtained nine votes with the Frenchman coming a close second with six votes, however it was still insufficient for election and so the conclave instead moved to appoint a new pope by popular acclamation. As silence fell upon the deadlocked conclave it was Cardinal Rodrigo Borgia who stood up and loudly declared 'I accede to the cardinal from Siena!' The chameleon-like Piccolomini–poet, traveller, diplomat, scholar and inveterate gossip–was duly crowned with the papal tiara on 3 September 1458 and took for himself the name of Pope Pius II.

'In our change-loving Italy', Piccolomini had written in his poetic days, 'where nothing stands firm, and where no ancient dynasty exists, a servant can easily become a king'. The lines–which were most certainly applicable to himself–could also have been written for low-born men like Francesco Sforza (who had been one of Piccolomini's main backers along with Ferrante of Naples), not to mention Cosimo de' Medici, the banker's son who rose to command a city-state. The pontificate of Pius II would continue the papacy's convenient alliance with the Colonna; Cardinal Prospero Colonna, having himself been acknowledged as *papabile* (one of the papal frontrunners) and who was closely associated with Piccolomini, had cast the deciding vote in his election. Despite the Orsini backlash in the wake of Pope Callixtus III's death, the Colonna had still not relinquished their power in Rome and all incoming popes would find it necessary to either cooperate with them or else ally themselves with the Orsini.

The accession of Pope Pius II was a generally positive development for the continued peace of Italy. As Niccolò Machiavelli later pointed out in his *History of Florence*, Pius II abandoned his predecessor's vendetta against King Ferrante and refused to countenance the competing Angevin claim to Naples since 'he believed he could more easily secure the tranquillity of Italy by confirming one already in possession, than by favouring the French in making the conquest of that kingdom; or, attempting, as Callixtus had designed, to seize upon it himself'. In his Letters, the fifty-three-year-old former *littérateur* was more candid and less lofty concerning his own election. 'One worthy of the papacy by nobility, conduct, and learning', wrote Piccolomini, 'is more worthy because he held it in contempt'.

Relations between the new humanist pope and humanist Florence would be cordial. Pius II would deal with Cosimo de' Medici as with one who was synonymous with the Florentine state itself. This was not to say, however, that–when it flattered him to do so–Cosimo did not still maintain the artifice of being merely an influential private citizen or *primus inter pares*. As Cosimo was to later pen to Pope Pius: 'you write to me not as a private man who is satisfied with the mediocre dignity of a citizen, but as though I were a reigning prince ... you know well how limited is the power of a private citizen in a free state under popular government'. But this was less genuine modesty and more a desire to excuse himself from having personally to foot the bill for two Florentine war galleys destined for the new Pope's upcoming Crusade. On another occasion Cosimo, just as unhelpfully, had suggested to the Supreme Pontiff that the Venetians and the Ottomans be left to their own devices so as to 'wear each other out'.

The remainder of Cosimo de Medici's rule was not entirely immune from domestic political problems. In 1458, he was beset with a particularly independent-minded *signoria* which proposed a new *catasto* assessment. This threatened to re-assess Cosimo's wealthy faction leaders on the basis of everything they had materially gained since the 1430s and naturally the oligarchs were both threatened and displeased by this proposal. Cosimo himself was caught on the horns of a dilemma; if he approved the *catasto* he ran the risk of offending the wealthy, influential men who constituted his *reggimento*, but if he failed to approve it he would upset the *popolo minuto* who were clamouring for it. Whether he personally paid the *catasto* himself was immaterial for the vast wealth of the Medici Bank could easily absorb any tax demand, however large. The presiding *gonfaloniere* Luca Pitti favoured calling a *parlamento* and allowing the *balià* to scrutinise the incumbent *signoria* and bring them to heel. Cosimo however played coy. He sought to use the crisis to teach his faction leaders the lesson that, influential as they undoubtedly were, they still could not do without his leadership in delicate matters such as this. Reluctant to relinquish power, the *signoria*, councils and *collegi* had meanwhile enacted a ruling that no *balià* could be called without their express and unanimous approval. A political showdown therefore became inevitable.

Into this simmering constitutional controversy now stepped the figure of Girolamo Machiavelli, a professor of law at the University of Florence. A man of known republican sympathies, Machiavelli addressed one of the councils, denouncing the *balià* and the other electoral controls formerly imposed by the Medicean oligarchs as being inimical to the freedom and rights of the citizens and he called for greater democratic representation. Having schooled Luca Pitti and the others in the lesson that they could not altogether dispense with his leadership, Cosimo now sprang into action. A *parlamento* was called and duly assembled in the Piazza della Signoria which had been secured, according to Nicodemo Tranchedi's *ricordi*, 'with three-hundred horse and fifty foot'. A *balià* was appointed and gave Cosimo's security apparatus the mandate to arrest and imprison Machiavelli, together with a gaggle of his associates on the charge of having slanderously described the *signoria* as 'tyrants'. Girolamo Machiavelli himself was tortured for several days and on 18 August sentenced to exile in Avignon for twenty-five years. In a postscript to this episode, the errant lawyer had still clearly not learned his lesson and persisted in conspiring against Florence's government. He was declared a rebel *in absentia* in November 1459 and in the summer of 1460 was recaptured by the authorities and died in the Bargello as a result of either maltreatment or torture.

Girolamo had been the cousin of Bernardo Machiavelli, the father of the future writer and political theorist Niccolò Machiavelli, who would be born eleven years later. As Nicodemo Tranchedi wryly described 1458's brace of political prosecutions: 'They have beaten the kittens in order to frighten the lions'. The Medici had in effect achieved a stunning political victory over the forces of dissension. But Cosimo's usual policy of leniency (Machiavelli had initially merely been banished) was now tinged with a note of *schadenfreude*. The recent crisis was also used as a pretext for extending the scope of the earlier political banishments of 1434. Not only were the former exiles' terms of banishment increased to twenty-five years but it was also retroactively extended to all the male descendants of these *fuoriusciti*, regardless of their age or relative blamelessness. This vindictive ruling fell hard on families like the Strozzi for example. The matriarch Alessandra Macinghi Strozzi was married to Matteo Strozzi who had been exiled in 1434 together with three of their children: Andreuola, Piero, and Simone. Now, she was forced to stand impotently by while her three remaining younger sons Filippo, Lorenzo, and Matteo were sent into exile, even though they had only just been born around the year 1434. After prosecuting the dissidents of 1458 and extending the exile laws, the *balià* next set up a new Council of One Hundred known as the *cento*. Its job was to elect new *accoppiatori* and make fresh *scrutinies* of the electoral rolls; in this way, the *signoria* was chastised, reformed and brought to greater obedience. The fiscal and tax issues which had led to the political crisis were meanwhile addressed by another new body, a magistracy known as the Thirty Reformers of the Monte.

With a robust peace descending upon Italy, and with Florence's domestic politics finally put back into order, Cosimo devoted his remaining years to his sponsorship of the arts as well as to the affairs of the Medici Bank. As always, the lynchpin of the family business remained the city of Rome and especially the resident branch at the papal court. However, as if wishing to demonstrate his concept of 'change-loving Italy', Pope Pius II had immediately transferred the Curia's business from the Medici Bank to one of his own *Sienese* acolytes. This led Cosimo to now invite the pontiff to Florence where he mounted his usual Medici charm offensive. The state visit took place within the context of the Supreme Pontiff's wider tour through other Italian city-states including Siena, Bologna, Ferrara and Mantua, in which city a congress was to be convened for the representatives of Christendom's temporal princes to discuss support for the Pope's impending Crusade. Pope Pius II reached Florence on 25 April 1459 and was greeted by the two young princes Galeazzo Maria Sforza of Milan and Cosimo's nine-year-old grandson Lorenzo de' Medici. The Pope was borne aloft on a litter beneath a golden canopy to the cheers of the crowd. Later, so it was rumoured, the epicurean pope was fêted by Cosimo de' Medici with the most lavish banquets, the most exquisite wines and, more divertingly, the company of Florence's most engaging professional courtesans. Cosimo had not forgotten how to entertain his rascally old humanist friend Piccolomini and the Pope was also kept constantly amused with a series of theatrics, balls, jousts and hunts.

When Cosimo had greeted his old friend his gout was so bad, however, that he was unable to kneel and give the Pope's slipper its customary kiss. He therefore made light of his debility with an impromptu joke about two corpulent Florentines who were unable to embrace each other properly due to the considerable size of their bellies. Both men laughed and all was well. Although the two men had chortled over the amusing quip, no offence having being taken, Cosimo de' Medici was nevertheless unable (despite the variety and lavishness of his papal distractions) to retain the lucrative business of the papal court. This failure was particularly inopportune in the light of the discovery, in 1461 near the small town of Tolfa near Civitavecchia, of large quantities of untapped alum by the Paduan Giovanni de Castro. Since this region lay within the Papal States the Pope lost no time in claiming these deposits for the Apostolic Treasury. By 1463, the mountains near Tolfa were being mined by 8,000 Roman *contadini* and were bringing in huge revenues of 100,000 ducats annually. This in itself was a bloodless victory over the Ottomans who, since the conquest of Constantinople, now controlled most of the known deposits of alum in the East and were extorting more than 300,000 ducats a year from Italian businesses for the essential mineral (whose scientific name is hydrated potassium aluminium sulfate) which was absolutely essential in the process of dyeing, glaziery and armour manufacture. The Medici Bank would need to bide its time, however, before it could obtain a piece of this lucrative new trade in precious papal alum deposits.

The pontificate of Pope Pius II was a largely mild and benign affair, quite different from that of his immediate predecessor. This was due in large part to Pius's improved relations with the *Regno* and, on 17 October 1458, the Pope had agreed to recognise Ferrante as Alfonso's rightful successor as king of Naples. A papal bull was duly proclaimed investing him as such. Towards his vice-chancellor Rodrigo Borgia, who had been the first to acclaim him during the last papal conclave, Pope Pius was all indulgence. He had retained the ambitious but capable young Spanish cardinal in the lucrative, important and highly complex position of vice-chancellor whilst appointing his own nephew Antonio Piccolomini to succeed the dead Pedro Luís as captain-general of the Church. When Cardinal Borgia became embroiled (together with Cardinal d'Estouteville) in a scandal concerning an 'orgy' which allegedly took place whilst on official papal business in Siena, the Pope turned a blind eye. Firing off a terse missive to Rodrigo Borgia he merely offered the question: 'We leave it to you to judge whether you can court women, give them presents of fruit and wine, indulge yourself in every kind of amusement all day long and, finally, send the husbands away so that you can be free to pursue your pleasures– whether you can do all these things without surrendering your position'. Chastened, Borgia assured the Pope that the allegations had been embellished and that his meeting with Siena's gentlewomen had been no debauch.

Never a prude, it had probably been no more than Piccolomini himself had done in his youth. During his former career as a *littérateur* he had been asked by the Emperor Frederick's young ward Sigismund of Tyrol in 1443 to ghost-write an epistle which would help Sigismund seduce a virgin with whom he had recently become romantically enamoured. The humanist poet had replied to the young man: 'Some play must be permitted to them [adolescents]. There must be a little bit of indulgence for their pleasure so that they may obtain heart and soul, know good and evil, know the stratagems of the world and how to avoid them when they have become men', and he had reassured the lovesick youth that 'as the bees sip honey from flowers, so you should learn virtue from the blandishments of Venus'. As a sixty-two year old *roué* who was to fall in love with a much younger married woman in 1493, Cardinal Borgia might well have taken heed of Piccolomini's additional observation to young Sigismund: 'For I know the condition of human life, since whoever does not love in adolescence loves later in old age, in which time he is derided and is a joke to the crowd since that age is inept at love'.

Where Pius II's pontificate converged with that of his two predecessors, popes Callixtus III and Nicholas V, was in his earnest desire for a Crusade to halt the advance of the heathen Turk. For all his humanist scholarship, deep down Piccolomini really saw himself as a Crusading pope in the traditional mould and he devoted most of his six-year-long papacy to gathering a Crusader army which, somewhat implausibly given his age, he planned to lead in person against the savage Ottomans. When Pius II proclaimed his Crusade in a papal bull at Mantua in 1458, Florence dutifully despatched a delegation to Rome and one of their number, Agnolo Acciaiuoli, wrote back to the *gonfaloniere* Otto Niccolini: 'We ought to help in this undertaking against the Turks; it is necessary that we should do our duty, because it would be too greatly to our discredit if all other Christians were to act and we alone were not to join them... It is necessary that you should take counsel with your own self and you should think of what great importance this matter is, when it concerns the defence of our faith for our honour and profit.' It was perhaps easy for Acciaiuoli to write thus, for his ancestors had been great lords in Greece and his family had more to lose than most at the hands of Muslim expansionism.

In March 1461 the court of Rome had received Thomas Palaiologos the despot of Morea and youngest son of the former Byzantine *basileus* Manuel II Palaiologos. Thomas had recently been unseated from his territories by the Sultan and he arrived in Italy in an impecunious state, his first act being to change his religion from Orthodoxy to Roman Catholicism in an obsequious attempt to curry favour with the Pope. When he met the Pope at St. Peter's Basilica, Thomas's first act was to present the Supreme Pontiff with the head of the Apostle Andrew, which had been preserved on the island of Patras. Despite the influx of such high-level eastern refugees as Thomas of Morea, the princes of Europe still remained largely unmotivated at the prospect of another Crusade. The French, Germans and Burgundians were at best noncommittal and, even more counterproductively, the House of Anjou had recently sent its navy against a fleet of galleys which King Ferrante had built and paid for out of the Pope's crusading fund.

Pius, more than most, ought really to have foreseen this kind of lukewarm response to his call. When Constantinople had fallen in 1453 it had been Æneas Silvius Piccolomini who had posed the question 'how might one persuade the numberless Christian rulers to join forces?' and he himself had concluded wearily that France was still too afraid of England to bleed her country of troops, Germany was hopelessly disunited, and Castile was too preoccupied with her own Reconquista against the Moors of Al-Andalus for any of these disunited powers to come together against the eastern Turk. Surprisingly too, even the Eastern European monarchs were unenthusiastic towards the venture; the Holy Roman Emperor Frederick III, King George of Podebrady of Bohemia, King Casimir IV of Poland and the grand duke of Moscow Ivan III all shrugged and made their excuses. Meanwhile, Pius II fulminated in vain: 'Every victory for him will be a stepping-stone to another, until after subjugating all the Christians of the west, he will have destroyed the Gospel of Christ and imposed that of his false prophet over the entire world!'

But not every Christian ruler was as apathetic in the face of the Sultan. In the Balkans, Vlad Țepeș III, Voyevod of Wallachia and effective ruler of Transylvania, had by now incurred a fresh Ottoman offensive through his wanton acts of disobedience. In their youth, both Vlad and his brother Radu had been held as hostages of the Ottomans for the continued loyalty of their father Vlad II. His experience in Turkish captivity had left a deep scar on Vlad's psyche and a festering hatred for the Turk. He eventually succeeded to his father's lordship of Wallachia and had resolved to rule with an iron fist. In a striking presentiment of Machiavelli's *The Prince*, Vlad III would state his personal philosophy thus: 'You have to reflect ... when a prince is powerful and brave, he can make peace as he wishes. If, however, he is powerless, some more powerful than he will conquer him and dictate as he pleases.' He was fundamentally disgusted by the readiness with which his fellow rulers made their peace with the Sultan and was the only Balkan lord to respond to the Pope's call for a new Crusade. Initially, though, he bided him time, paying his dues to the Sultan as an obedient vassal for three years. But when one year the Sultan's representatives arrived in his lands demanding 500 young Wallachian boys for induction into the famous Janissaries, his memory of his own imprisonment stirred within him and his response was fierce. Vlad III's strength and his resolution not to be intimidated by the Ottoman Sultan earned him the praise of such Italian city-states as Venice, Genoa, Milan, Ferrara and especially Pope Pius II in Rome. Not only had Vlad III refused to offer the boys up into

Turkish custody or pay tribute to the Sultan but, when the latter despatched two emissaries named Hamza and Katabolinos to summon the errant Voyevod to the Sublime Porte to explain himself, Vlad had them both put to death.

In the winter of 1461-2, Vlad Ţepeş III proceeded to sack the Turkish fortress of Giurgiu, putting 23,000 Turks and Bulgarians to the sword. Following this atrocity he ravaged the rich Ottoman lands around the Danube basin, which was made easier for him by a particularly cold winter in which the frozen Danube could be forded anywhere at will. Mehmed II raised an army of 150,000 men and invaded Wallachia with the intention of replacing Vlad with his less troublesome brother Radu. When Mehmed entered the town of Târgovişte at the end of June 1462, however, he was–according to an account by the Greek chronicler Laonikos Chalkokondyles–greeted with the following unholy vision:

> 'The sultan's army entered into the area of the impalements, which was seventeen stades long and seven stades wide. There were large stakes there on which, as it was said, about twenty thousand men, women, and children had been spitted, quite a sight for the Turks and the Sultan himself. The Sultan was seized with amazement and said that it was not possible to deprive of his country a man who had done such great deeds, who had such a diabolical understanding of how to govern his realm and its people. And he said that a man who had done such things was worth much. The rest of the Turks were dumbfounded when they saw the multitude of men on the stakes. There were infants too affixed to their mothers on the stakes, and birds had made their nests in their entrails.'

In Rome, Pope Pius II was notified of Vlad's grisly yet effective methods by Nicolas the bishop of Modrussa, the papal envoy to Budapest. Vlad, by this time, was known as *Dracul* which was the Romanian word for 'dragon'. This in turn derived from The Order of the Dragon, a Hungarian chivalric order whose stated intent was the defence of Christianity from its heathen Turkish enemies. In 1464, Nicholas of Modrussa wrote back to the Pope that Vlad III *Dracul*: 'killed some by breaking them under the wheels of carts; others stripped of their clothes were skinned alive up to their entrails; others placed upon stakes or roasted on red-hot coals placed under them; others punctured with stakes piercing their heads, their breasts, their buttocks and the middle of their entrails, with the stake emerging from their mouths; in order that no form of cruelty be missing he stuck stakes in both the mother's breasts and thrust their babies until them. Finally he killed others in various ferocious ways, torturing them with many kinds of instruments such as the atrocious cruelties of the most frightful tyrant could devise.'

Nearly six years elapsed before Pope Pius II was finally able to send a Crusader fleet east to the Balkans to assist in this bloody struggle against the Turk. But by this time, Vlad III *Dracul* himself was in the custody of Matthias Corvinus, who was by now locked in his own personal struggle against Mehmed II in Bosnia, Srebrnica and Zvornik. Together with a promised Venetian fleet, the Pope would have enough transportation for around 5,000 Western Christian Crusaders. From Italy they would sail across the Adriatic and join forces with Matthias Corvinus and Skanderbeg's armies at Ragusa. Both the papal fleet as well as the land forces would assemble at the Adriatic port of Ancona in the Papal States in the spring of 1464. The Pope certainly recognised the Turkish threat and was firmly committed to rolling back the Muslim tide, even going to the unpopular lengths of commanding all able-bodied cardinals to join him on the Crusade. His protégé Rodrigo Borgia was there as well as other considerably less enthusiastic prelates, who were far from happy at being forced to leave the fleshpots of Rome on such a hazardous expedition. But, alas, as badly as the Western troops were needed in the Balkans, none of these plans were destined to come to fruition. The Venetians kept the Crusader army waiting interminably for their fleet of transports and Pope Pius II's moribund delay at the plague-ridden port city of Ancona became a final depressing coda to what had otherwise been a well-intentioned pontificate. By the time the Venetians, horribly late, had sailed into Ancona's harbour, Pius's army, disheartened by the constant postponements, had melted away to practically nothing. Racked by pain, the fifty-eight-year-old pope could do little but observe his impressive papal fleet, *sans armée*, from a high tower window. On 14 August 1464, the crusading humanist Pope Pius II was given the last rites before going to meet his maker.

Pope Pius II was replaced by the Venetian Pietro Barbo who took the name Pope Paul II on 30 August 1464. A pleasure-loving sybarite pope who relocated the entire papal court from the dilapidated and uncomfortable Vatican to the Palazzo Venezia, a vastly more comfortable and salubrious new home across the Tiber, Paul II had much in common with the equally pleasure-seeking Cardinal Borgia. Barbo's election was, however, a generally positive development for Florence and the Medici since the Pope was the nephew of Cosimo's former friend and ally Pope Eugenius IV.

The initial months of Paul II's rule were not without their dangers though. When he made the unpopular move of reversing certain nominations which his predecessor Pope Pius had introduced to the chancellery there was a revolt of ecclesiastics led by Bartolomeo Sacchi de Piadena (also called Platina) which also involved the respected humanist scholar Pomponius Laetus, a professor at Rome's famed university the *Sapienza*. The graduates of the implicated scholar had been accused of plotting to assassinate the Pope as the prelude to re-introducing a republic but Pope Paul II had reacted decisively, rounding up the disaffected academics and crushing the rebellion before it could gain traction. The allegations against the men were serious: conspiracy, heresy and *lèse-majesté* against the Pope, as well as sundry irreverent and incautious remarks concerning priests and the act of sodomy. Platina himself was tortured during the subsequent investigation although eventually, thanks to the timely advocacy of Cardinal Bessarion, most of the accused were quietly released. Meanwhile, the Pope's quick witted response and firmness in handling the crisis earned him greater respect amongst the Romans from this point forward.

As Pope Paul II was growing into his new papacy, the Medici patriarch was meanwhile carefully expanding the Medici Bank and opening new branches in virtually every important mercantile city in Europe. Disliking the more conservative methods of his father's partners the Bardi family he had, as we have already seen, gradually replaced them with the Portinari. To the Portinari were now also added other innovative new partners like Antonio di Messer Francesco Salutati in Rome and Giovanni d'Amerigo Benci in Geneva. Cosimo de' Medici came to like and trust Benci the most; his astute and systematic mind made him an efficient and successful banker and it was under Benci's stewardship from 1435 until 1455 that the Medici Bank achieved its greatest expansion and profitability. Like Cosimo himself, Benci enjoyed his peccadilloes, having sired an illegitimate son by a slave girl belonging to his friend Lorenzo Barducci, in addition to a daughter sired by his own household slave Maria. Happily, these two birds of a feather poured over the Medici Bank's ledger books together, consolidating, making future plans, adjusting the delicate machinery of the family, the bank and the state.

As he entered his late sixties and early seventies, Cosimo's frequent bouts of gout together with other debilitating ailments common to old age caused him increasingly to withdraw from public life. One of his favourite refuges was his cell at the Dominican monastery of San Marco, which had been adorned with a large fresco depicting the Procession of the Magi painted by Fra Angelico's student Benozzo Gozzoli. Here he could meditate undisturbed on his business, on weighty state affairs, and on the events of his own life. But, as always, behind the art lay Medici political propaganda. The supreme expression of a wealthy family broadcasting its reputation through the creative arts was when they included their own illustrious likenesses in the paintings and frescos that they commissioned. The ultimate example of this came in a second painting of the Procession of the Magi, which was completed by Gozzoli between 1459 and 1461 for the Medici Chapel in the Palazzo Medici. Gozzoli had already earned Cosimo's lasting admiration for the devotional fresco at San Marco and the patron had subsequently commissioned the artist to adorn the family's private chapel on the *piano nobile*, the first floor of the palazzo, a convenience which permitted the entire family to worship in private like princes rather than having to celebrate Mass in public with other citizens. Gozzoli painted his fresco over three of the walls, each wall depicting the journey of one of the three Magi to Bethlehem to watch the Nativity. The religious theme was secularised by the inclusion of likenesses of numerous Medici personalities as well as their faction members and international associates. All the individuals are portrayed travelling through rich imaginary Tuscan landscapes.

Members of the Medici family and their entourage are depicted in the fresco which adorns the chapel's east wall. Leading the Magi is the youngest Magus Caspar who is elegantly and luxuriously attired in his *guarnacca ad ali* or 'winged cloak' made of gold brocade, a graphic reminder of the sumptuous, courtly fashions which would soon become increasingly commonplace in High Renaissance Medici Florence. Riding behind him is Piero de' Medici on a white horse whilst, next to Piero, Cosimo de' Medici sits somewhat more modestly astride a humble donkey. Behind them come the *condottiere* and lord of Rimini, Sigismondo Pandolfo Malatesta, riding a chestnut war horse and distinguishable by his bare head and thick bull-like neck. Next to him rides Duke Galeazzo Maria Sforza of Milan on a magnificent white charger. After them comes a procession of eminent Florentines, including the humanists Marsilio Ficino and the Pulci brothers, the members of the art guilds and the fresco painter Benozzo Gozzoli himself. The painter glances out from the fresco directly at the viewer and is identifiable by the scroll which he wears in his red hat, which reads *Opus Benotii*. Little Lorenzo de' Medici is the boy positioned directly below and to his left with the distinctive snub nose, whilst Lorenzo's younger brother Giuliano stands next to him.

Other major political personalities are presented in the fresco on the south wall. The Byzantine *basileus* John VIII Palaiologos is depicted as the bearded

Magus Balthasar riding a white horse. On the west wall, Melchior, the oldest Magus, is a depiction of either Joseph the Patriarch of Constantinople, who died in Florence during the Ecumenical Council, or else the Holy Roman Emperor Sigismund who convoked the Council of Constance in 1414. Like Cosimo, he is shown as a peacemaker riding on a donkey and is preceded by a page dressed all in blue with a leopard on his horse. The fresco is the ultimate self-glorification of the Medici family and presents their mythical apotheosis as travelling in the entourage of the scriptural Three Wise Men. The metaphorical implications are quite clear: the Medici family constitutes the group of all-wise, all-knowing civic leaders in whom complete trust is to be placed by the citizenry of Florence.

When not found in contemplation in his cell at San Marco, or at the private Medici chapel, Cosimo could be found at the Villa di Cafaggiolo, which continued to be his favourite Medici country residence. Like the Villa del Trebbio, Cafaggiolo had also been improved by his architect friend Michelozzo and served the dual role of a fortress, but in his later years Cosimo would doubtless have been more entranced by its ornamental gardens, an impression of which can be gleaned from the lunette of the Villa di Cafaggiolo painted by the Dutch artist Justus Utens in 1599. The property would also later be favoured by his grandson Lorenzo who would use the villa to entertain important and influential humanist friends such as Marsilio Ficino, Giovanni Pico della Mirandola and Angelo Poliziano. In this regard the elderly humanist Cosimo de' Medici would have greatly approved of his grandson's tastes as well as the uses to which he put this delightful Medici country property.

Less favoured it seems was the splendid sprawling urban *palazzo* which he had built for himself, Contessina and the children on the Via Larga. Giovanni di Bicci had always cautioned his heirs to maintain a low profile but Michelozzo's grandiloquent statement, with its imposing rusticated masonry and fortress-like aspect, ran somewhat counterintuitive to his father's homespun advice. Although the style of rustication which Michelozzo incorporated into the lower story of the Palazzo Medici was more or less typical of other Florentine *palazzi* of the fourteenth and early fifteenth-centuries, still the extreme heaviness of the rustication and the double lancet windows of the upper stories tellingly echoed the design of the Palazzo della Signoria, thus linking the Medici architecturally and symbolically with the city's official seat of government. The Palazzo Medici was therefore not so much a home as an unsubtle political statement of power and unspoken political sovereignty.

When Cosimo's obese younger son Giovanni died tragically of a heart attack in 1463 at the age of forty-two, the grieving patriarch had even more reason to bemoan the unnecessary size and expanse of his *palazzo*, lamenting that he was encumbered with 'Too large a house for so small a family!' He had remained emotionally close to his sons Piero, Giovanni and his illegitimate son Carlo even though they themselves were now well into their own middle ages. A celebrated anecdote from Nicodemo Tranchedini tells of how he called on Cosimo at the Palazzo Medici one afternoon only to find *il padrone* supine on his large bed flanked on either side by Piero and Giovanni, all three of them simultaneously stricken with debilitating attacks of the gout. It is a rather vulnerable and touching cameo which again displays Cosimo in a modest, unassuming light – as an old and sick man surrounded by his two equally poorly sons.

In 1452, Giovanni de' Medici had married Maria Ginevra di Niccolò Alessandri, the daughter of one of Cosimo's staunchest supporters during the dark year of 1433. Tragically, their only child Cosimino died in 1459 at the age of six. Although more corpulent and self-indulgent than his abstemious father, Giovanni di Cosimo had taken an active role in Florentine civic and cultural life (he served as a prior in 1454) and had also been an energetic patron of the arts, commissioning works by such Medici-sponsored artists as Donatello and Filippo Lippi. The gentleman's residence that he and Cosimo jointly purchased at Fiesole from Niccolò Baldi was transformed by Michelozzo into the celebrated Villa Medici a Fiesole and signalled the desire to lead an elegant life revolving around the arts and humanities. Built on an orthogonal ground plan and solving the problem of its hillside location by occupying several distinct levels, this delightful villa with its abundant 'hanging gardens' was to have been Giovanni's own private dwelling. Unfortunately, however, by the time it was completed around 1458, Giovanni would have precious little time to truly enjoy it or indeed the splendid library and art collections that it was built to house.

Upon the death of his right-hand-man Giovanni d'Amerigo Benci in 1455, Cosimo had come to increasingly depend upon the more competent of the two legitimate sons, Giovanni, for the smooth running of the Medici Bank. He continued to depend on him even when Giovanni himself persisted in socialising with ribald critics of the Medici such as the notorious Florentine barber and entertainer, Burchiello. A master of *motti* ('witty sayings') and *facezie* ('witty remarks'), Burchiello's tale of the cat which mistook its owner's testicles for a mouse is immortalised in the scatological *Facetiae* of Poggio Bracciolini. As well as Giovanni de' Medici, Burchiello's barbershop was still nevertheless the gathering place of other cultural luminaries such as Leon Battista Alberti. There is something endearing and disarming about Giovanni's readiness to rub shoulders with this versifying, satirising scoundrel who refused on principle to defer to the all-powerful Medici. It seems to suggest that the Medici around this time were still not too big for their boots. They were still willing to mingle with the great unwashed and accept idle street criticism with good grace.

But the death of Giovanni had come as a bitter blow to Cosimo, regardless of the Stoic facade that he strove to project to the outside world. To Nicodemo Tranchedini he had offered words worthy of Marcus Aurelius: 'Give thyself no trouble to console me; for I should be ashamed not to behave myself in this trouble as I have often admonished you and others to do. I tell you that there are two sorts of men who in such circumstances need consolation; the one are those who do not stand well with our Lord God; the others are those who want self-control.' Despite the intense sorrow that he felt at Giovanni's passing his nature prevented him from allowing his grief to overflow into effusive and unseemly demonstrations of public mourning. Giovanni de' Medici's funeral *corteggio* through the streets of Florence was to be kept simple; the austere republican traditions were, at all costs, to be maintained.

Cosimo de Medici's own death followed, barely a year after that of his favourite son Giovanni, on 1 August 1464. True to form, the funeral procession was deliberately understated and nothing fancy. The contemporary chronicler Marco Parenti, a simple bourgeois silk merchant who had married into the upper class Strozzi, vividly recorded the banker's funeral in his *Memoir*: 'Cosimo di Giovanni de' Medici, pre-eminent citizen of Florence whether in wealth or prudence or authority or power, died on the first day of August, 1464, around the twenty-second hour, aged a little less than seventy-six years, in his villa at Careggi. The next day, putting aside the customary pomp of funerals of great citizens, with little display, as he wished, accompanied only by the priests of San Lorenzo and the friars of San Marco and the Abbey of Fiesole, churches he had built, and a few citizens who were relatives and friends walking behind the corpse, he was buried in San Lorenzo in Florence in a low tomb in the ground under the tribune.'

In deference to the sensibilities of middling merchants such as Marco Parenti, men who were arguably the beating economic heart of Florence, Cosimo was as assiduous as ever in keeping his final public promenade, his *corteggio*, within the bounds of republican taste and propriety. The Ciceronian title *Decreto Publico Pater Patriae* ('Father of His Country by Public Decree') which had been granted to him, and which was subsequently inscribed upon the understated marble and porphyry memorial that Verrocchio had designed for him, had only been voted in a full year after Cosimo's death by a Committee of Ten Men which had been called to deliberate how to honour the late first citizen. Cosimo would no doubt have approved of the procedure as much as he may have been embarrassed at the actual honorific itself. This tribute was also underscored in Cosimo's funeral oration, which was delivered by the scholar Donato di Neri Acciaiuoli. Cosimo's death was described by Donato as 'taking away from the citizens the humaneness, wisdom, excellence of that best father in whom all good qualities were found, which are sought by men'. Many of the mourners were monks and priests, which was fitting in light of Cosimo's rebuilding of the monastery of San Marco, and the dead banker had been duly reciprocated with a papal bull absolving his immortal soul of all sin for his lifetime of usury. In the Roman Catholic faith ways and means could always be found to liberate an imperilled soul, provided of course that the right amount of funds found their way into the right collection boxes at the right time.

In the field of the visual arts and architecture, Cosimo de Medici's contribution had been unsurpassed and the father of the state had left his city considerably more beautified at his passing than he had found it. Many young artists had been given their first patronage under the Medici and others, who were already established in their own right, benefited too from the family's generous and wide-ranging artistic commissions. Recipients of early Medici largesse included, for example, the painters Andrea del Castagno and Filippo Lippi. The Medici, as we have already seen, frequently used such artists unashamedly to legitimise and propagandise their regime and its unofficial leadership role through art and the subjects for their paintings and frescoes were more often than not blatantly political as well as devotional. But it was Donatello to whom Cosimo had always felt closest. Donatello, whose love of the classical past resonated so closely with Cosimo's own personal humanist interests. Donatello, who refused to pay attention to his physical appearance and who uncivilly returned the fine robes which Cosimo sent him in an effort to spruce up the artist's dowdy image. Donatello's ground-breaking bronze statue of *David* which stood in the *cortille* of the Palazzo Medici remains the single most important artwork to be identified with the Medici. Sensuous, sexually ambiguous and pushing the envelope of accepted sculptural styles, Donatello's *David* is emblematic of the Medici's championing of cutting edge art and the use of such art to impress and overawe its observer.

Donatello's close friend Paolo Uccello was yet another artist who was especially linked to Cosimo de' Medici. His early paintings of wild animals, commissioned for the Medici family *palazzo*, led to later commissions which remain amongst his most well-known. From 1435 to 1460, Uccello painted his three famous panels depicting The Battle of San Romano. The triptych, only one of which was ever commissioned for the Palazzo Medici (Lorenzo the Magnificent later stole the other two from the Bartolini Salimbeni family and installed all three in the ground floor lobby of his own *palazzo*) depicted the famous 'victory' of Florence's *condottieri* Micheletto Attendolo da Cotignola and Niccolò da Tolentino over the *Sienese* in 1432. Again, boldly propagandistic in tone, the House of Medici was seldom afraid of advertising great political and military accomplishments. In one of the panels, the Medici's *condottiere* Tolentino is famously seen unhorsing the enemy commander Bernardino della Ciarda; if there was one thing better than trouncing an enemy on the field of battle it was immortalising their shame in paint and canvass, and this the Medici were seldom afraid to do.

Uccello was also commissioned in 1436 by the *signoria* to paint the funerary monument to Florence's great *condottiere* Sir John Hawkwood in the Duomo. We should never forget that such grand and imposing monuments were mostly divorced from the actual character of the people they depicted. Although many of the more successful *condottieri* flirted with the pretension of being lofty humanist scholars and patrons of the arts, these were in fact basically callous men whose lives were devoted to mastering the science and technicalities of killing. Hawkwood himself had, for example, presided over the sacking of the town of Cesena in 1377 in which 4,000 civilians are said to have perished, the murderous frenzy of his men deplorably urged on by the Cardinal of Geneva from the safety of the town's citadel. Although Hawkwood himself had died in 1394 the surprising proposal to honour a man who had not only fought against Florence but also extorted huge amounts of florins from the republic during his lifetime, was initially resurrected by the Albizzi-led *signoria* in May 1433 several months before Cosimo's exile. It is likely that Rinaldo degli Albizzi intended the monument to hearken back to a glorious time when Florence's oligarchic *ottimati* had their fingers firmly on the levers of power. In July 1433 an announcement was made tendering for proposals for Hawkwood's thirty-nine-year-late commemorative monument. With the banishing and subsequent return of the Medici in 1434, however, the project was temporarily shelved when the Albizzi were expelled. For political reasons Cosimo de' Medici could not afford to abandon Rinaldo's scheme altogether so instead he appropriated it for his own propagandistic uses; he dismissed Rinaldo's own artisans and called in Uccello to execute the work. Uccello's revised plan for the monument cast Sir John Hawkwood in a 'classical' theme, his relief style of painting giving the quasi-three dimensional appearance of an actual statue. The painting would prefigure actual bronze equestrian statues of other famous *condottieri* like Bartolomeo Colleoni and Gattamelata, not to mention Leonardo da Vinci's abortive equestrian Francesco Sforza.

While Florence's mercenary generals like Hawkwood and Tolentino received the gift of artistic immortality the Medici continued to maintain the modest appearance of merchant leaders. Of course, by now there was not a soul in Florence who was deluded by Cosimo de' Medici's pose of appearing as a simple journeyman banker who was no grander than any other Florentine. This studied pretence belied the fact that during his own lifetime he had ruthlessly crushed his political rivals whilst exalting his allies. Giovanni di Bicci had moved around the streets of Florence and rubbed shoulders with the city's ordinary shopkeepers and artisans. When Cosimo appeared in public or put in an appearance at the Mercato Vecchio or the Orsanmichele everyone knew that sooner or later he would return for the night to his refined *palazzo* on the Via Larga, or else commune in his monastic cell adorned with those magnificent, expensive frescos by Benozzo Gozzoli. The die was now well and truly cast; Florence was in the hands of an élite oligarchic dynasty and *not* an inclusive plutocracy of *ottimati* families, as before. If an old, wealthy *ottimati* family wished to prosper in Cosimo de' Medici's Florence, they had to agree to be *amici* of the Medici and become assimilated into the Medici's extended network of patronage. But how did Cosimo himself ensure that the people of Florence continued to tolerate this level of political power concentrated in the hands of just one family?

Medici power was, for one thing, not founded upon tyranny but upon the semblance of democratic process and on the will of the general population. Cosimo did not habitually sit on the *signoria* or have himself elected as *gonfaloniere* in the executive branch of government where he would have been an obvious potential target. He ruled from behind carefully chosen candidates who whose names were slipped into the electoral purses with a nod and a wink. In thirty years he served as *gonfaloniere* for a total of only six months. By the same token, neither did he always have himself elected to the *dieci* during time of war. He also served as official ambassador only once, that time when he visited Venice in 1438 to plead for Venetian support. In essence, he remained quite inconspicuous in the outward forms of Florence's government. When he got involved in government at all it was with the restricted practical objectives of controlling the election of officials, dictating foreign policy and directing the raising of taxation. Through these three key enablers he was, in effect, able to run the Florentine state from behind the scenes. Meanwhile, the outward show of popular government was preserved in the dignity and ceremonial of the *priori*, officials whom Cosimo had earlier dismissed as being little more than several yards of red silk accompanied by some pomp and ceremonial.

Had the Medici attempted to seize the state by force and rule as dukes the commune in all likelihood simply would not have tolerated it; but by observing the outward manifestations of Florence's ancient guild-based bylaws and republican constitution the Medici astutely secured the acquiescence of the citizens. Vespasiano da Bisticci had observed that more than anyone else Cosimo de' Medici had learned the supreme difficulties of ruling a state against the constant opposition of families and citizens who considered themselves to be the equals of the Medici in former times. It was this understanding of the essential difficulty of his task that led to a marked gloominess on Cosimo's part for in his heart-of-hearts he suspected that his eldest son Piero would be hard-pressed to emulate and continue his and his father Giovanni di Bicci's political success. Following the death of his younger and more capable son Giovanni, Cosimo de' Medici was honest enough not to permit family pride to blind him to the fact that his own flesh and blood may be unequal to the continued task of ruling. Prior to his death, Cosimo's mind had ranged gloomily over the inevitable succession crisis; this would be something, certainly the only thing that he could neither adjudicate nor stage-manage in person.

CHAPTER 8

The Crisis of 1466

I always considered myself beholden to you, but if you examine your
conscience you will see that you have exempted me from any
obligations; nevertheless I am willing to remain your debtor in so far as
it touches me privately, but the public injury I cannot, will not, and may
not pardon. For myself personally I forget everything, forgive all wrongs,
and remain as a son ought to be towards such a father.

Piero de' Medici to Agnolo Acciaiuoli, 22 September 1466

For three decades Cosimo de' Medici had governed Florence firmly as *signore* in all but name, dealing on equal terms with other princes, kings and popes in Rome. His extraordinarily generous patronage–as much as 600,000 Medici florins had been spent during his lifetime on public buildings– had beautified Florence beyond all other cities. He was not only the patron-architect of his city but was also the grand architect of an enduring peace in Italy and his glowing achievements made him politically unassailable during the final years of his life. Throughout this time too he had built up a powerful *reggimento* which ruled from behind the scenes in the council chambers and meeting rooms of the Palazzo della Signoria. The *reggimento* was based very much on that unique form of hierarchical Quattrocento Italian patronage which survives today in such modern iterations as Sicilian Mafioso 'families'. The extended clan comprised not only those clients, employees and dependents of the Medici but also loosely encompassed the people of the neighbourhood in which the Medici had for decades made their home and their business, namely those few city blocks centred on the church of San Lorenzo as well as the north-west wards of the gonfalone del Leon d'Oro, the Golden Lion. Here, amidst the grocers, fishmongers, butchers shops and artisan workshops lay the Medici's real groundswell of support, those petty bourgeoisie and working classes who had always regarded the family as being supporters of the common man since the time of Salvestro de' Medici and the *ribellione dei ciompi*.

Cosimo's successor, the forty-eight-year-old Piero de' Medici, tried to emulate his father's habit of playing effortlessly to this image of the Medici as men of the people. Like his father, in his personal tastes and habits he was by nature a frugal man and his late brother Giovanni always had far more of a reputation for indulgence and ostentation than Piero (in taking account of his father's funeral expenditure, for example, he made careful note of such trifling costs as 43½ lire for the wax candles, or the money spent on mourning clothes for their servants and four female slave girls). The family's well-appointed *palazzo* in the Via Larga remained the actual seat of Florence's government and the loggia which Michelozzo had designed abutting the main thoroughfare thronged each day with messengers and anxious petitioners. On days when his gout was playing up, Piero *il Gottoso* often received ambassadors and other important guests from the relative comfort of his bed, as Cosimo had sometimes done. 'Thus his chambers were almost always crowded with men of every sort on various errands, and often it was difficult to speak with him', recorded Marco Parenti in his *Memoir*.

Piero's wife and helpmeet, Lucrezia Tornabuoni busied herself meanwhile with the management of the Medici household. Together with her mother-in-law Contessina, she did so with maximum efficiency and minimum waste like any practical and self-respecting Florentine matron. Lucrezia's family had previously been called the Tornaquinci and had been one of the old *magnati* families which had been prohibited by the Ordinances of Justice from participating in Florentine government. Like other families of their ilk they had subsequently changed their name to Tornabuoni and entered the mercantile guild system in order to assume a more active role in Florence's political life. They had prospered moderately, owning one of the better *palazzi* of the city, although Lucrezia's dowry was a surprisingly modest 1,000 florins, but this was no matter because her aristocratic connections were worth their weight in gold in snobbish and image-conscious Florence. Lucrezia's father was Francesco di Simone Tornabuoni, an intimate friend of Cosimo de' Medici's. Her brother Giovanni Tornabuoni was the Medici Bank's general manager in Rome, a trusted key position in Cosimo's family business. Lucrezia wrote passably good devotional poetry and dabbled successfully in business, having purchased a mineral baths upcountry which she turned into a well-managed and profitable going concern. Like her gout-ridden husband, Lucrezia was afflicted by poor health for much of her life, being a martyr to both arthritis and eczema.

In addition to their two sons Lorenzo and Giuliano, Lucrezia bore Piero three daughters who were named Maria, Bianca and Lucrezia (who was more commonly known as 'Nannina'). Maria, who was to die relatively young in 1473, married Leonetto de' Rossi and their son Luigi de' Rossi was destined to rise to the position of Protonotary Apostolic and cardinal in the Church. Bianca was to be married off to Guglielmo de' Pazzi, the scion of another ancient and illustrious Florentine family the Pazzi. Guglielmo and his brother-in-law Lorenzo de' Medici were destined to become firm friends. Nannina, a scholarly bluestocking poetess in her own right, saw to it that her brother Lorenzo, on whom she doted, was favoured with a humanist education of the highest possible standard. She was married in 1466 to the thirteen-year-old Bernardo Rucellai amidst considerable pomp and ceremony. Bernardo was the grandson of a Strozzi daughter, the Strozzi having been one of those families which had been heavily proscribed in the aftermath of 1434 and then again in 1458. Bernardo's father Giovanni di Paolo Rucellai had however remained politically neutral; taking no part in public life for almost three decades he eventually became Cosimo de' Medici's firm friend in 1461. Nannina and Bernardo's marriage was therefore noteworthy for marking the social and political rehabilitation of the Rucellai family name in Florence.

One of Piero de Medici's entourage, the Florentine sculptor Mino da Fiesole, has left us a bust of him done in the stiff medieval reliquary style. Piero's facial features have been meticulously described: a penetrating gaze beneath a furrowed brow, the clenched mouth and the long, aquiline nose. It is a surprisingly handsome and determined face, certainly not at this point the face of a person in perpetual misery from gouty and arthritic joints or ground down by the weighty affairs of state. Not shown is the eczema of which Piero was a known sufferer and which he shared in common with his rather ugly son Lorenzo, whose face was as unsightly as Piero's was apparently masculine and attractive. But Piero also had a reputation for a certain coldness of manner, arising no doubt from his methodical banker's temperament. In the animated streets of Florence where every conversation seemingly hinged around how to turn a ducat or two, and where deals were sealed with a spit and a handshake, Piero's more aloof style of doing business and directing government did not count as a mark in his favour. The common touch which the Medici had deliberately cultivated seemed to be evaporating as the family grew in stature, a fact which could not have gone wholly unnoticed amongst the talkative, gossip-loving denizens of Florence. Some openly derided the Medici for their noble pretensions. Had not King Louis XI of France (a man whose paranoia easily equalled that of the late Filippo Maria Visconti) granted the Medici the right to emblazon one of the Medici *palle* with the royal fleur-de-lis of the House of Valois? The implication was all too clear; the Medici regarded themselves as princes-in-waiting. Worse still, many of Piero's contemporaries simply did not perceive any innate talent on Piero's part. The *Stationarii* and biographer Vespasiano da Bisticci devoted an entire chapter to his friend and customer Cosimo de' Medici in his *Lives of the Illustrious Men of the Fifteenth Century* but of Cosimo's son Piero he gave barely even a mention.

In a city enlivened by active political discussion, the central irony of Cosimo de' Medici's rule could not have been lost on those who were steeped in the classical humanist learning of the era. Cosimo had been a wise and benevolent 'father' to Florence and such was his love for the writings of Cicero that he had modelled himself on the archetypal Ciceronian statesman. Yet at the same time, whilst Cicero had lived and flourished during the final years of the Roman republic, Cosimo's ruling style was narrowly oligarchic and–truth be told–had more in common with Plato's philosopher kings or the dictator Julius Caesar than with Rome's most famous republican orator. Cosimo had also, in the process, inadvertently prevented other prominent Florentines from modelling themselves on the Ciceronian ideal of statesmanship. The removal of his formidable restraining influence from Florence's by now intensely frustrated political life could only result in a succession crisis as those more politically active citizens now sought to reassert their traditional rights. With the passing of Cosimo de' Medici there was a sense amongst a great many Florentines that the Old Order had been replaced by an exciting New Order of resurgent republican liberty.

Cosimo must surely have foreseen this scenario. He was nothing if not an astute judge of his fellow countrymen and was well aware of the depth of their attachment to the outward show of their communal traditions. It was this awareness of Florence's enduring love affair with republicanism which guided his public life, his liberal patronage, his restraint and his dislike for showy ostentation. It was one thing to wield real power but rubbing peoples noses in it, especially his closest associates, was quite another. Outside of the *reggimento* the solid mercantile classes represented by the likes of the silk merchant and memoirist Marco Parenti would never have stood for it. Parenti was entirely representative of those who were dismissed as being *un poco di stato* or 'of little political standing', men of small wealth who had been edged out of the political process. Parenti was, at the same time however, also the son-in-law of Alessandra Macinghi Strozzi. Alessandra, an inveterate letter-writer and diarist, was later to become one of the most celebrated chroniclers of Medici Florence. She had been badly affected by the Medici political monopoly and was still fretting over the exile of her three young sons Filippo, Lorenzo, and Matteo. Like many in the city she kept a weather eye on the local political scene in Florence and awaited any indication that the House of Medici was lessening its death grip on civic affairs.

The cracks in the façade of the Medici's *reggimento* came initially from within, from the ungrateful *principali* whom Cosimo himself had elevated to prominence. This situation arose not merely from Cosimo's death but, on the contrary, had been a gradual process dating back well over a decade. Before the Peace of Lodi removed the wider strategic threat to Florence in 1454, Cosimo had been careful to keep the more influential non-Medici members of his regime busily preoccupied with foreign diplomacy. With the advent of peace, however, their thoughts had again turned inevitably to domestic politics. They watched Cosimo growing older and frailer, and noted the lack of distinction in his eldest surviving son Piero. They thirsted for a greater share in government, as in the good old days when a coterie of Florence's most wealthy families ran the city together rather like a cosy ruling gentleman's club. For these moneyed old guard individuals it was a bitter pill that Florence's government should now be exclusively dominated by one single parvenu banking family.

The Medici meanwhile continued to play it low key and, for this reason, Medici family funerals–Giovanni's as well as Cosimo's own–were deliberately kept simple and private. Public envy was to be avoided at all costs. But Piero's less-than-endearing ways, his taking for granted of the succession of political power and his condescending habit of receiving petitioners in his bedchamber had already ruffled powerful feathers. As Marco Parenti put it: 'This difficulty, added to the resentment of his excessive power, stimulated in the minds of many citizens a great hatred, and the greater and more generous of mind they were, the more insupportable they found it. And among the others there were three men of the highest prestige who showed themselves openly to the people as being impatient of bearing this arrogance any longer.'

As mentioned, the cracks in the façade came from within the dominant Medici *reggimento*. Two of its members, Agnolo Acciaiuoli and Dietisalvi Neroni, were friends of the Medici family and indeed senior members of the oligarchy. Following Cosimo's death, both had served on the Committee of Ten Men which had been appointed to determine the state's formal commemorative tribute to its first citizen. Indeed, as a direct result of Agnolo's participation, it had been his own younger cousin Donato di Neri Acciaiuoli who had been given the honour of delivering Cosimo's public funeral oration. Both patriarchs, however, already seem to have become psychologically estranged from the Medici *capo* and his family prior to Cosimo's death. Already in their early sixties by the time that Piero took up the baton, both men had flocked to the Medici colours during the upheavals of the early 1430s. As Cosimo de' Medici's contemporaries they had been inured to his having been honoured as the 'father of the state' and had often referred to him as 'brother' in their correspondence. But this was out of grudging respect for Cosimo's abilities and on account of his considerable political standing.

Piero, on the other hand, was not from Agnolo's or Dietisalvi's generation and could not hope to command the same level of deference as had been given to the father. Neither could Piero be regarded as the 'father of the state' in quite the same way. Donato di Neri Acciaiuoli may have eulogised that 'you, Piero, are not only the legitimate heir of a very generous patrimony but you are also a most careful imitator of his admirable virtues, in the very esteemed tasks which public as well as private affairs bring to you', however the fact of the matter was that these older and more experienced men were loath to bend the knee to a Medici scion who was not only their junior in age but also in political experience. Agnolo Acciaiuoli was a contemporary of Cosimo's and the two boys had acquired a shared passion for learned humanist scholarship from the Camaldolese monk Ambrogio Traversari. The Acciaiuoli themselves came from an old and esteemed family which had migrated to Florence from Brescia in the twelfth-century. They had made their fortune in steel (*acciaio*) hence their family name. They also had the strongest ties to the East of any Florentine family of its time. Their forefathers had parlayed their relationships with the Latin kingdom of Constantinople to become lords of Corinth and Thebes and dukes of Athens. When Agnolo had followed Cosimo into exile in 1434, it had been to his ancestral home in Greece that he had fled. In his *Life of Neri*, Vespasiano da Bisticci declares that 'others may go about begging nobility for their family, the Acciaiuoli have enough and to spare'.

Upon Cosimo's return and subsequent triumph over the Albizzeschi, Agnolo Acciaiuoli had become an important right-hand-man to Cosimo, travelling twice to France to negotiate the French king's intervention in Italy. Through his diplomatic skill Acciaiuoli had effectively saved the republic from the imminent threat from Naples. Acciaiuoli's role in securing France and René d'Anjou's military backing earned him a place within the Medici inner circle and thereafter he came to be described as 'one of the principal citizens and could do what he wished in the city'. With such a career, bathed as it was in the blessed nimbus of Medici favour, Agnolo Acciaiuoli could have secured his family's fortunes were it not for his growing resentment at Medici interference in his own personal affairs. Acciaiuoli had even gone to the lengths of writing to Cosimo's friend and ally Francesco Sforza to complain that both Cosimo and his son were 'cold men (*huomini freddi*), whom illness and old age have reduced to such cowardice that they avoid anything that might cause them worry or trouble'. In yet another letter he went so far as to describe both father and son as 'more cowardly than rabbits that were afraid of everyone'. Acciaiuoli's insinuation, extraordinary as it was in the light of Cosimo and Francesco's close relationship, was that he and his family would make a more robust ally in Florence than the perpetually sick, gouty and indisposed members of the Medici.

The genesis of Agnolo Acciaiuoli's bad feeling towards Cosimo de' Medici lay in two separate incidents in which Cosimo had disrespected the client-patron relationship which existed between the two men. The first disagreement occurred in 1462 and arose in connection with an archiepiscopal appointment. Agnolo had attempted to have his son Lorenzo elected as bishop of Arezzo but Cosimo had used his personal relationship with Pope Pius II to have his own relative Filippo de' Medici appointed to the bishopric instead. Cosimo had nevertheless promised Agnolo that Lorenzo would receive the next available vacant Tuscan seat. Unfortunately, that seat turned out to be the archbishopric of Pisa, politically a far more important and prestigious sinecure that was naturally coveted by the Medici themselves. Cosimo now reneged on his earlier promise to Agnolo and instead offered his son the far less desirable bishopric of

Arezzo, whilst Filippo de' Medici was shuffled around and given the See of Pisa on 14 January 1462.

The second disagreement followed in 1463, the year just prior to Cosimo's death, and was even more inflammatory. Agnolo's other son Raffaello had married the wealthy Alessandra d'Ubertino de' Bardi in 1456 but by 1463 relations between the couple had deteriorated to such an extent that some of Alessandra's kinsmen had appeared in the middle of the night at the Acciaiuoli family *palazzo* to rescue her and bring her home. In her petition to the court of the bishop of Cortona, Alessandra had attested that her father-in-law Agnolo had acted most cruelly towards her, whilst Raffaello himself had misrepresented his marriage suit since he clearly preferred the company of boys to that of his lawful wife. Losing the girl was one thing but handing back to the Bardi family her not inconsiderable dowry of 8,500 florins was quite another matter and so a divorce had been ruled out by the Acciaiuoli. Cosimo however, out of a sense of decency and fair play, had mediated in favour of his erstwhile in-laws the Bardi for the return of the dowry. In the event, the marriage was eventually patched up, the husband reoriented his sexual preferences and the couple went on to produce several children. But the damage had been done and Agnolo Acciaiuoli's resentment at Cosimo's interference in a private family matter precipitated his personal break with the Medici.

It has been suggested that, for his own part, Cosimo had been motivated to intervene not only because his wife was a Bardi (Contessina and Alessandra were in fact cousins) but because his nephew and ward Pierfrancesco de' Medici the Elder had lately married Agnolo's daughter Laudomia Acciaiuoli. Born not in Florence but in Greece, Laudomia was a cousin of the last 'Frankish' duke of Athens, however Cosimo regarded Pierfrancesco's new father-in-law as being 'a bad influence' on his ward. Pierfrancesco's own father, Lorenzo the Elder, had died in 1440 aged forty-five and the ten-year-old boy had been raised together with his brother Francesco under their uncle Cosimo's roof, mostly at his country estates to the north of Florence. During these years Pierfrancesco had grown fat and lazy and frittered his time away in idleness or hunting. But his indolent temperament had not prevented him serving as Florence's ambassador to the Pope in 1458, as well as to Mantua in 1463, and Cosimo's feelings towards him remained both avuncular and protective.

Dietisalvi Neroni, meanwhile, had been one of the chief protagonists of Cosimo's Peace of Lodi in 1454 and, as late as 1464, was still counted as one of Cosimo's closest political advisers. His father, Nerone di Nigi, whose house lay quite literally across the street from Cosimo's own *palazzo* on the Via Larga, had furthermore played a central role in Cosimo's recall from exile in 1434. In the 1420s, the Neroni had been one of the original eight families in the city ward of the Golden Lion who, together with Giovanni di Bicci, had clubbed together to rebuild and beautify the church of San Lorenzo. Dietisalvi's brother, moreover, had been appointed as archbishop of Florence in 1462, a sinecure which spoke volumes about the Neroni family's influence within 'the Medici state'. As an *accoppiatori* during the greater part of Cosimo's rule, Dietisalvi continued to play an important role in the maintenance of Medici power. As a member of the *dieci*, he alone had supported Cosimo's controversial policy of backing Francesco Sforza when the majority in Florence had been anxious to resume the traditional alliance with Venice. Dietisalvi Neroni was widely acknowledged to be a clever and capable statesman.

On the other hand, like Agnolo Acciaiuoli, Dietisalvi Neroni was also a closet political reformer. As early as 1454, during his term as *gonfaloniere*, Neroni had advocated democratic reform and a decade later in 1465 he wrote candidly to Francesco Sforza that 'the citizenry would like greater liberty and a broader government, as is customary in republican cities like ours'. Meanwhile, Nicodemo Tranchedini–a far better judge of character perhaps than Piero de' Medici himself–ominously reported to his master the duke of Milan that 'Cosimo and his men have no greater or more ambitious enemy than Dietisalvi Neroni'. Dietisalvi's animus towards the Medici does not seem to have been personally-motivated in quite the same way as that harboured by Agnolo Acciaiuoli. Instead, it was more a by-product of his deep-seated political convictions. With the succession of Piero de' Medici, both Acciaiuoli and Neroni now converged to form the basis for a notional fledgling anti-Medicean party that was centred on the half-completed *palazzo* of a third collaborator named Luca Pitti. Pitti, a wealthy banker with a distinctly unrepublican taste for self-aggrandisement, had begun making his name during the 1440s and over time had come to regard himself as Cosimo de' Medici's natural heir apparent. In his *chronicle*, Luca Pitti's father Buonaccorso wrote that the Pitti family, being Guelphs, had earlier been expelled from the *castello* of Semifonte by the Ghibellines in 1202, whereupon they divided into three branches. 'We of the third branch', he recorded, 'settled at Castelvecchio in the Val di Pesa, where we bought large and rich estates ... A few years later our ancestors came to live in Florence'.

Like Agnolo Acciaiuoli and Dietisalvi Neroni, Luca Pitti had also prospered under the Medici regime. Unlike his two compatriots, Pitti was himself linked with the Medici through the marriage of his sister, Maddalena di Bonaccorso Pitti, to Rosso di Giovanni de' Medici (from the lesser Foligno di Conte de' Medici line of the Medici family). He had been a prominent figure in the Medici victories of 1434 and 1458 and was, in Marco Parenti's words, 'devoted to Cosimo'. He had been one of the eight *priori* who had recalled Cosimo from exile in 1434, had served as *gonfaloniere* and, like Neroni himself, was an almost permanent fixture on the *accoppiatori*. As Parenti describes the 'reformist' cabal: 'Though superior to M. Luca in prudence, they consented to his having such prestige, and to increase it they too frequented his house. All this they did to block Piero de' Medici to whom previously everyone was accustomed to going to consult on public affairs as well as private, and to take away from him the great arrogance which he had put on–something already obnoxious and insupportable to all.'

As Cosimo had declined in health and increasingly taken to spending more time at his beloved villa in Careggi he had been content to leave much of the day-to-day business of government in the hands of Luca Pitti. This would have suited Cosimo anyway as he always abhorred being in the limelight, but this highly visible relinquishing of power had had an undesirable side effect. Petitioners now began circling around Luca Pitti, instead of the Palazzo Medici and inevitably this gave the conceited Pitti an unjustifiably inflated sense of his own self-worth in the scheme of things. That the narcissistic Pitti was naturally prone to self-importance was another factor. His father Bonaccorso had earlier celebrated in a sonnet the Pitti family's right to incorporate the heraldic arms of Rupert of Bavaria in their own coat of arms and just before Cosimo's death Luca Pitti had had himself knighted by the commune in great pomp. Alessandra Strozzi watched Pitti's meteoric rise with singular distaste, commenting sourly that this latest honour of knighthood would 'truly swell his gut'.

The impressive *palazzo* that Pitti had commissioned the architect Brunelleschi to build for him around the year 1440 was still only half-completed but the growing pile of rusticated stone, quarried from the Boboli Hill, which stood on the far side of the River Arno was more imposing than anything that had been built by any private Florentine citizen up until that time. Local legend has it that Luca Pitti ordered Brunelleschi to make his *palazzo*'s windows as big as the doors of the Medici residence and create an internal courtyard that was large enough to contain Cosimo's entire house on the Via Larga (at this time the Palazzo Medici was far smaller than the present day Medici Ricardi Palace; shorter by seven Medici-sized windows to be precise). The Palazzo Pitti, which completely dominated its hillside setting in the Oltrarno, became the informal meeting place of the reformist cabal. By this token, the anti-Medicean faction became known as the Party of the Hill whilst the Medici faction, centred on the Palazzo Medici along the flat concourse of the Via Larga, was referred to as the Party of the Plain. Likewise, both factions had their preferred sacred buildings which they occasionally used as alternative meeting places. The Party of the Hill favoured La Pietà whilst the Party of the Plain flocked to La Crocetta.

The sheer magnitude of the Palazzo Pitti was telling and spoke of unfulfilled ambition; it was the expression of political power in a compensatory form. Men like Pitti, Acciaiuoli and Neroni had served Cosimo loyally and well and had been members of the Medici inner circle of *amici* for the better part of thirty years. Amongst themselves they were also subject to the famous Florentine trio of social obligations arising from their being each other's *amici, parenti e vicini* ('friends, relatives, and neighbours'), this in spite of the fact that each hailed from a different quarter of the city. Now that Cosimo de' Medici was gone they saw it as their due to succeed to a greater share in real political power. The historian Francesco Guicciardini unkindly remarked of Luca Pitti that 'he had not sufficient brains that Cosimo need fear him' but, as Cosimo had known, proud men such as these would nevertheless begrudge taking orders from his son Piero. Instead of the Medici being able to maintain a monopoly on civil power, as over the past thirty years, their traditional supporters now abjured Medici primacy and a worrying bifurcation now arose in the political life of Florence.

Whether such reformers genuinely strove to dismantle the oligarchic system which had grown up around the restrictive Medici *reggimento* or whether they disingenuously pandered to the popular aspiration for reform in order to further their own independent political careers is difficult to ascertain. Certainly, they were never able to manipulate the system quite as adeptly as Cosimo de' Medici himself. Acciaiuoli and Neroni had flirted once before with popularism back in 1454–5 when they had succeeded in abolishing first the *balia* and then also the *accoppiatori*, probably in the misguided belief that a more open electoral *borse* would favour their own political ambitions. Cosimo had watched and said nothing, knowing that all they were doing was undermining the basis of their own élite power (chiefly by depriving themselves of the means of manipulating the seigniorial elections). When, in 1458, a newly liberated and unfettered *signoria* called for a fresh *catasto* assessment which ate into their own élite wealth, they subsequently took fright and lobbied Cosimo for the speedy return of the *accoppiatori*. Nevertheless, this clique, who began to be known as the *poggeschi*, continued to harbour the desire to see the electoral purses opened to a wider spectrum of political candidates; indeed they hoped to see the return to eligibility of all those prominent citizens who had been purged and exiled during the preceding three decades of Medici rule. Luca Pitti had used the unrest stirred up by Girolamo Machiavelli to deliberately make trouble for Cosimo, causing the latter to issue Pitti a stiff reprimand: 'You strive towards the indefinite, I towards the definite. You plant your ladder in the air, I place mine on the earth so that I may not climb so high as to fall.'

However idealistic the political objectives of the *poggeschi* it is worth remembering that someone like Dietisalvi Neroni was not above cynical dissimulation in the pursuit of these objectives. Not only did Neroni maintain a friendly semblance of clan loyalty to Piero's face, but behind his back he was avidly spreading the seeds of doubt. Most damagingly of all, he used his position as ambassador to the court of Milan in 1465 to conduct a malicious whispering campaign designed to detach Francesco Sforza from the Medici. In this he was assisted by Acciaiuoli who, as we have seen, was already in clandestine communications with Milan's duke. To Sforza, Acciaiuoli would write that whilst 'Piero is as honoured in this city as he was before', nevertheless, 'because of his illness he cannot handle such burdens and cares'. This effort to weaken the Medici-Sforza alliance was especially pernicious since the coalition between these two houses was the pivot upon which the general peace of Italy was based. Cosimo de' Medici's policy of maintaining a balance of power predicated upon Medici-Sforza friendship and military cooperation was a practical and necessary hinge of Florentine foreign policy but, if they could, the *poggeschi* were quite prepared to undermine it in the pursuit of a far narrower political agenda.

Neroni was able to inflict the first blow to the Party of the Plain from a position of concealment and he struck resolutely at the basis of Piero de' Medici's political power, the Medici Bank. When Piero called upon their old family friend for an audit of the bank's books, Neroni responded by grossly exaggerating the bank's liabilities and advising Piero to call in a number of bad debts across their entire network of branches from London, Bruges and Geneva to Venice and Rome. Piero had been badly shaken by this assessment. Since Constantinople's fall to the Turks, the eastern spice and luxury goods trade hitherto dominated by Venice and Genoa had been under considerable pressure. Traders who banked with the Medici were habitually over-stretched, running sizeable overdrafts as they prayed for their ships to evade not only the Ottomans but also Muslim pirates operating securely from bases ranged along the coastline of North Africa. The instruction to call in all debts granted out of the Medici's overseas branches met initially with disappointing results. In 1465, the English King Edward IV had just crowned Elizabeth Woodville as his queen but was still heavily embroiled in the Wars of the Roses; the debts he owed to the Medici Bank–reported the London factors drearily–seemed as little likely to be repaid as Edward III's earlier debt to the Bardi Bank. News from Bruges was equally dismal. More damagingly still, Piero's stoppage of lines of credit to many Florentine merchants resulted in a whole slew of bankruptcies. This only served to intensify the general feeling of resentment towards the Medici amongst those middling merchant classes who, in these lacklustre years, were already being battered by the winds of ill fortune.

With such an undercurrent of bitterness towards the Medici it was perhaps inevitable that a demagogic figure should emerge with the rhetorical skills to manipulate this considerable reservoir of ill-feeling. That man was another erstwhile member of the Medici *reggimento*, Niccolò Soderini. Like the Pitti and the Manetti, the Soderini were one of Florence's old illustrious Oltrarno families. Niccolò Soderini and his brother Tommaso had hailed from an illegitimate branch of the family which was begun when their grandfather, a prominent Soderini, fathered a bastard son by a French woman. At Niccolò da Uzzano's instigation their father had been tried and executed by Florence's authorities for fraudulently counterfeiting credentials proving his legitimacy. In an act of revenge the hot-headed Niccolò Soderini had in 1429 allegedly hired a band of cut throats to murder da Uzzano; however the second-rate assassins he hired proved incompetent and were soon apprehended by the authorities. Quickly implicated by the subsequent police investigation, Niccolò Soderini was arraigned before the *signoria*, who called for the death penalty, and would indeed have met with the same fate as his unhappy father were it not for the personal intervention of Cosimo de' Medici himself. Cosimo had intervened in the imbroglio purely for political reasons since sparing Soderini would naturally embarrass and distress his political rival Niccolò da Uzzano. In the 1430s Niccolò and Tommaso Soderini had been duly inducted into the loyal ranks of the Medici *amici*.

When Cosimo went into exile in 1433, Niccolò Soderini had lobbied so vociferously for the return of his former patron that Rinaldo degli Albizzi had contemplated extending the exile to include Soderini as well. As an interesting coda to the Soderini brothers' story, these two offshoots of an illegitimate cadet branch of the family were able to gloat some years later when the major line of the Soderini fell on hard times and they were able to buy up all the Soderini *palazzi* at rock bottom prices. However, despite this family coup the two brothers were destined to go their separate ways in the years to come. Niccolò Soderini's younger brother Tommaso was destined for a long and venerable career as a wise and loyal Medici statesman. Soon after the death of his first wife Maria Torrigiani in 1440 he married Lucrezia Tornabuoni's sister Dianora Tornabuoni, thus making him both Piero de' Medici's brother-in-law and Lorenzo and Giuliano's uncle-in-law (although his relationship with his headstrong young nephew Lorenzo was often a stormy one). Niccolò Soderini had meanwhile married in quite another political direction; his wife Ginevra was the daughter of Filippo di Niccolò Macinghi and therefore the sister of Alessandra Macinghi Strozzi whose family had been exiled in 1434.

Though older than Tommaso and an extremely gifted orator to boot, Niccolò however was by nature an embittered, combustible and troublesome personality. In Florence he was widely known for his tendency to bring finicky law suits against members of his own extended family. Given the great honour by Cosimo de' Medici of being appointed Florence's ambassador to Genoa, he soon demonstrated his diplomatic ineptitude by embroiling himself in matters which Duke Francesco Sforza saw as his private preserve. Angrily recalled by Cosimo from Genoa in 1453, he was subsequently sidelined by being given relatively low level ambassadorships, first to Rimini and subsequently to Pesaro. Here he could supposedly do little diplomatic damage although, in reality, it was this perceived slight that ultimately set him on a collision course with the Medici. To the twisted logic of Soderini's resentful mind he could simply advance no further with the Medici in power.

It had been the volatile and high-spirited Luca Pitti who had initially urged a more open, forceful expression of opposition against Piero's unsteady new regime. Soderini, by far the more astute operator, knew that open insurrection could never be successful. Instead, he advocated a perfectly legal assault through the existing instruments of government. Soderini's arguments proved more persuasive and the rest of the cabal duly yielded to his more restrained strategy. These shadowy forces now began manoeuvring openly by the middle of 1465 to contain Medici executive power. Since 1434, the Medici had consolidated their rule by means of institutional controls and *amici* like Acciaiuoli, Neroni, Pitti and Soderini had aided and abetted this process; however, the same men who had helped consolidate the institutions of Medici authority would now seek to dismantle it piece-by-piece. They began first with the *otto di guardia*, that eight man committee which oversaw state security. Piero de' Medici had attempted to renew the committee's mandate but was unexpectedly defeated by the cabal. Agnolo Acciaiuoli in particular had led the charge to abolish the secret police apparatus, a move which appreciably hampered the Medici's ability to intimidate political opponents. Neroni had spoken out publicly on 3 September 1465, labelling the Medici-led government as 'corrupt and repressive'. Tommaso Soderini meanwhile tried to lobby for the preservation of the *otto di guardia* but in the end the Party of the Hill carried the day, thereby drawing first blood in the battle for constitutional reform.

The cabal's next victory, several days later, was to abolish the *accoppiatori*, that indispensable committee which had for years been scrutinising and hand-selecting those Florentines who were eligible to be drawn by lot for political office. Leading the attack this time was Manno Temperani, who was himself one of the presiding members of the *accoppiatori*. Temperani told a *pratica* that the people disliked the very word '*balià*' and were dissatisfied with the fact that 'all power had been entrusted to the will of a few and that all things were being governed according to their wishes'. The campaign proved overwhelmingly popular and the electoral *scrutinies* were henceforth abolished. In one fell swoop, all those who had been disqualified in the *scrutinies* of 1458 and 1463-4 were now re-qualified for government office. By opening up the electoral *borse* to the full spectrum of political opinion, the Party of the Hill had at a stroke removed one of the Medici's main mechanisms for maintaining continuity of political control. The inclusion of citizens who had been excluded by the Medici since 1458 would inevitably result in the election of many who were roundly unsympathetic to the Medici.

This major blow threatened to return Florence's political machinery to its traditional pre-1434 situation. It had been Rinaldo degli Albizzi's reluctance to re-nominate a compliant *accoppiatori* which had lost him control of the *signoria* in 1433-4. Piero de' Medici now found himself in the same precarious situation. Commenting cheerily on the victory, Agnolo Acciaiuoli wrote that 'The whole city liked it, except Piero'. Neroni meanwhile crowed in a letter to Francesco Sforza that 'the citizenry would like a more broadly based and freer government, as is appropriate in a *citta popolari* like ours'. To his credit, Neroni seemed to cherish loftier ideals which had far more to do with genuine political reform and greater enfranchisement and less to do with the settling of any personal score with Piero de' Medici, as seemed to be the case with Acciaiuoli.

In November 1465, a new *signoria* was drawn by lot from the considerably expanded electoral *borse* and the reformers were swept into power on a tide of renewed political fervour. Niccolò Soderini himself was elected to the office of *gonfaloniere della giustizia* and was carried aloft to the Palazzo della Signoria wearing a triumphal wreath of olive leaves. 'At the beginning of Soderini's term, Piero di Cosimo feared him and followed along, because never had there been a *gonfaloniere* who took office with such a spirited welcome from the people and with such expectation of good', Marco Parenti had observed hopefully. Knowing how to play to the crowd, Soderini's initial political enactments were calculated to garner as much mass support as possible. His first act as *gonfaloniere* was to reduce taxes on wine and the people loved and blessed him for it. Despite this cheaply-bought early victory, however, things rapidly moved downhill from there. Once in office, Soderini openly associated his own personal affairs with the affairs of the commune, seeking to enact laws and regulations which benefited him personally. When he tried to have himself created a knight a determined coalition of Medici supporters stepped forward and blocked him. When he next tried to engineer nepotistic favour for his illegitimate son he was blocked once again. Soderini's by-now estranged brother Tommaso lamented that 'he went in like a lion and will leave like a lamb' and so indeed it was. When the *gonfaloniere* and his eight *priori* left office at the beginning of January 1466, some wag posted a notice on the vacant *signoria* door which mockingly declared: 'Nine Fools have thus departed'. In his place came a new *gonfaloniere*, the nondescript Francesco Bagnesi, who was nevertheless known to be a solid and reliable Medici man.

In his wake, however, Soderini had left a ticking time bomb. During December 1465 he had called for a new *scrutiny* of the electoral rolls. Soderini the consummate orator, playing to the crowds as usual, had conceived this parting shot as a measure which would be popular amongst the disenfranchised masses. Amongst his own confederates Acciaiuoli, Neroni and Pitti the measure was not a popular one since it threatened to dilute the basis of their own support in the electoral purses. Neither was the Medici *reggimento* overjoyed at this prospect either since manipulating the contents of the *borse* had long been a mainstay of their own power. The move was, in short, a massively destabilising act right across the board. If the electoral purses had remained closed and not subject to fresh attention the political differences between the Medici and their reformist opponents may well have been healed and smoothed over given enough time. The two factions might even have come together in a shared mission to maintain their oligarchic hegemony, even if this had meant the Medici relinquishing some of their authority and Florence reverting to a more balanced plutocracy based on the pre-1434 model. In calling for a radical shakedown of the electoral rolls, however, Soderini inadvertently split Florence right down the middle and caused the usually fluid, shifting state of Florentine political alliances to harden and solidify. From January 1466 onwards an open confrontation between the Party of the Hill and the Party of the Plain became tragically inevitable.

As 1465 gave way to the first wintry months of 1466, both factions garnered support for the armed struggle that they both knew must inevitably come. In addition to their respective militia forces drawn from the immediate countryside around Florence, the Party of the Hill looked for support to Venice as well as Ferrara. Venice consented to provide armed support to Florence's reformers, offering the services of her best general the *Milanese condottiere* Bartolomeo Colleoni. Ferrara's Duke Borso d'Este meanwhile also pledged troops to the Party of the Hill under the command of his brother Ercole. Borso in particular was leery of the *Milanese*-Florentine alliance and saw its dismantling as a necessary prerequisite for Ferrara's own expansionist ambitions. A vain and brutal *condottiere*, Borso had once ordered that a notary's eyes and face be crushed as punishment for attempting merely to move a civil case from *Ferrarese* to Roman jurisdiction. He was also involved in later years in an otiose attempt to build an artificial mountain at Monte Santo, a folly which made him unpopular amongst those of his citizens expected to both pay for it and labour on it. A bumptious and self-important ruler, Pope Pius II later described Duke Borso in his memoirs as 'eloquent and garrulous and listened to himself talking as if he pleased himself more than his hearers'.

The Party of the Plain meanwhile despatched the young Lorenzo de' Medici on an urgent diplomatic mission to Rome and Naples to neutralise any potential support for the reformist party there. On first impression this was a daunting task. Though a nephew of Cosimo de' Medici's former ally Pope Eugenius IV, the incumbent Venetian Pope Paul II had distrusted Florence ever since she, Milan and Naples had signed their mutual defence agreement; he might reasonably therefore be expected to fall into step with the strategic alliances of his home state the Most Serene Republic. The Acciaiuoli family meanwhile handled the banking account of King Ferrante of Naples; another of Agnolo's many sons, Jacopo Acciaiuoli, was known to have the ear of King Ferrante himself. At the beginning of March, Lorenzo arrived in Rome and was greeted by his uncle Giovanni Tornabuoni who was still in charge of the Medici Bank's Rome branch. Amongst Lorenzo's business-like entourage was his old tutor Gentile Becchi, whom Piero had assigned to keep a weather eye on his son, as well as the mercenary *condottiere* Roberto Malatesta (the successor to Sigismondo Pandolfo Malatesta of Rimini) a huge and imposing soldier who was presumably present for added effect and–if needs must–muscle and protection. Drawing on the deep pockets of the Medici Bank, Lorenzo de' Medici mounted an expensive charm campaign comprising lavish banquets and entertainments which impressed the venal and pleasure loving Roman cardinals who, curious about this new Medici prince in their midst, now gravitated to his dazzling orbit.

As for Pope Paul II, he was no cultured poetic humanist like his forerunner Piccolomini, the man who had put Florence's chancellor, Carlo Marsuppini, to shame with his fluency in Latin. For one thing, many gossiped that Pietro Barbo was not in fact Pope Eugenius IV's nephew but his bastard son from an incestuous relationship with his sister. Thanks to his papal connections Barbo had been given his cardinal's hat at the relatively young age of twenty-three and had spent the interval during which Pope Eugenius IV had been in exile at the papal palace of Bologna. Here, it was said, he routinely lavished his income on comely male prostitutes and fine living. As pope, he ran the papal court as well as the Apostolic Treasury from his enormous private residence the Palazzo Venezia, which was nestled just below the silently deserted Capitoline Hill and constructed around an old medieval tower. Incorporating within itself the ancient basilica church of San Marco, the Pope's titular benefice, the *palazzo* arguably made for a rather more salubrious setting for his pleasure-loving pontificate than the aging and drafty St. Peter's basilica.

During 1466, the year of Lorenzo's visit, Pope Paul II hosted a notorious carnival in Rome which famously boasted every conceivable sort of vice and debauchery. For the amusement of the Romans the Pope ordered not only horse racing, of which he was inordinately fond, but forced Rome's Jews to race naked through the streets. This took place on a street known as the Corso which doubled-up as the city's unofficial racecourse; as one later source described the disturbing event: 'Races were run on each of the eight days of the carnival by horses, asses and buffaloes, old men, lads, children, and Jews. Before they were to run, the Jews were richly fed, so as to make the race more difficult for them, and at the same time, more amusing for the spectators. They ran from the Arch of Domitian to the Church of St. Mark at the end of the Corso at full tilt, amid Rome's taunting shrieks of encouragement and peals of laughter, while the Holy Father stood upon a richly ornamented balcony and laughed heartily.'

As an individual, Pope Paul II was a vain man who had allegedly tried to name himself Pope Formosus, which meant 'the Handsome', before being dissuaded by his cardinals in the merciful name of propriety. He enjoyed looking his best, making it his practise occasionally to apply rouge to his sallow cheeks. He was especially notorious for being both spendthrift and cruel. Recognising that the Pope's greed was his Achilles Heel, Lorenzo de' Medici promptly seduced him with the promise of endless Medici ready credit with which his pleasure-loving pontificate could be bankrolled. Pope Paul instantly rose to the bait, taking readily to the charismatic Medici youth who, as with himself, seemed to live and breathe the virtues of ease and enjoyment. As a result, the immensely lucrative contract for the marketing of the recently discovered papal alum deposits was duly transferred to the Medici Bank. Since the Medici had both a ready-made international network, as well as practical experience in wool and cloth finishing, of which Florence was a regional centre, this was a natural fit for the bank's business. Thanks to his innate charm Lorenzo now found that he had this most licentious and venal of popes tamely eating out of his hand like a cooing pigeon.

Sometime after 8 March 1466, news of the most unwelcome kind reached Piero in Florence and Lorenzo in Rome. The *condottiere* friend and ally of Cosimo de' Medici, Duke Francesco Sforza of Milan, had suddenly died. At a stroke the political landscape of the Italian peninsula was turned upside down. In October of the previous year, Francesco Sforza and Ferrante of Naples had managed to strike a dynastic alliance through the marriage of Francesco's daughter Ippolita Maria Sforza to King Ferrante's son Duke Alfonso of Calabria. On a less helpful note for Florence, however, due to Francesco's reluctance to provide military assistance the republic was never able to re-acquire Lucca despite Cosimo's unflagging lobbying of Milan for troops. By 1465-6, the late duke was unwilling to see Tuscany and Liguria destabilised in order for the Medici to emulate the achievements of the Albizzi and the Capponi when they had annexed Pisa. France's own designs on Genoa had scared and upset Sforza and he was still sensitive to the claim laid on Milan by the House of Orléans based on the bloodline of the late Valentina Visconti.

At the time of the Duke's death his heir, the twenty-two-year-old Galeazzo Maria Sforza, was away from the duchy in military service with the king of France. His mother Bianca Maria Visconti sent word for his urgent return and Galeazzo Maria had lost no time hastening south through the Gran Croce Pass. Riding in disguise and under an assumed name through the Alpine territory of hostile Savoy, he had been delayed by an attempt on the part of the duke of Savoy to capture him. Evading the duke's trap, he arrived safely back in Milan on 20 March. Here, he was quickly crowned as the new duke of Milan by his relieved mother, the Dowager Duchess. The death of the late Duke Francesco had sent Piero de' Medici into a paroxysm of dread. Writing to Lorenzo in Rome, he confessed: 'I am in such affliction and sorrow for the sad and untimely death of the illustrious duke of Milan that I know not where I am'. Piero momentarily considered diverting Lorenzo to Milan in order to cement relations with Galeazzo Maria Sforza, the new duke. However, it was decided to adhere to the original plan of having Lorenzo proceed from Rome to parlay with King Ferrante and the young Medici representative duly reached Naples by mid-April.

Meanwhile, the dowager duchess of Milan sent envoys to request the payment of an annual Florentine subsidy of 60,000 florins to tide over Galeazzo Maria's new regime during the immediate succession period. The Party of the Hill strongly opposed the granting of this loan. Medici power in Florence was predicated upon Sforza military muscle therefore, if the loan were granted, Piero's relationship with the new duke would be confirmed and the Medici could continue to count upon Milan's military support. To weaken Piero and besmirch his international reputation it was hence necessary to drive a wedge between him and the House of Sforza. Both Agnolo Acciaiuoli and Dietisalvi Neroni had for two decades provided an unofficial back channel between Florence and Milan and both were convinced that the new duke could be persuaded to work with the reformist party in preference to the House of Medici. All that was needed to accomplish this was a demonstration of their domestic political power. Piero tried vainly to force the loan bill through the *signoria* but was defeated by the reformist coalition who, Niccolò Machiavelli later recorded, objected that 'the alliance was made with Francesco and not Galeazzo; so that Francesco being dead, the obligation had ceased; nor was there any necessity to revive it, because Galeazzo did not possess his father's talents, and consequently they neither could nor ought to expect the same benefits from him; that if they had derived little advantage from Francesco, they would obtain still less from Galeazzo'. With this latest victory the Party of the Hill appeared to be driving Florence away from Milan and back into the waiting arms of Venice.

Fortunately, in Naples Lorenzo de' Medici was able to charm King Ferrante just as he had charmed Pope Paul II a week or so earlier. Together they hunted in the countryside outside the city, closely watched by Naples's small but flourishing community of Florentine expatriates. Gentile Becchi was able to report back to Piero that Ferrante seemed well disposed towards his son, having on one occasion remained closeted in private with Lorenzo for one whole hour. Cosimo de' Medici had, even in death, laid the groundwork for his son's fulsome and diplomatically expedient welcome. Ferrante's father the late King Alfonso had, like Cosimo, been a dedicated humanist whose favourite author happened to have been Livy. Cosimo had on one occasion stroked Alfonso's ego by sending him a rare copy of a valuable manuscript, Livy's sweeping history of Rome, the *Ab Urbe Condita*. Alfonso's physicians had cautioned the King not to read from it, fearing that its pages may have been poisoned by the cunning Florentine, but Alfonso had shrugged off their concerns and was genuinely flattered that Cosimo should regard him as an equal in classical scholarship. The respect and consideration which Cosimo had shown to the father was appreciated by the son; Ferrante's gracious reception of Lorenzo sprang from the 'love which we bear towards his Magnificence, your father, to you, and to your house which merits even greater demonstrations'. Lorenzo de' Medici thus left Naples with Ferrante's tacit agreement to stand behind the Medici in any emerging conflict.

However, in the event of any military offensive against the rebels and their international backers, Ferrante would not be sending Jacopo Piccinino, the bothersome *condottiere* who had previously sewn such havoc and discord in Cosimo de' Medici's Tuscany. After fighting for the King's Angevin rivals, Piccinino had briefly been reconciled with Ferrante and in 1464 had married an illegitimate daughter of Francesco Sforza. The following year he was summoned to Naples to receive the position of viceroy of the Abruzzi and commander of

Ferrante's troops in that province. Upon arrival he was afforded all due honours but shortly afterwards had been treacherously arrested on Ferrante's orders, thrown into prison, and then savagely put to death on 14 July 1465. Lorenzo de' Medici was under no illusions as to the treachery and unreliability of the man he had just come to an accommodation with and on whom he was so dependent. Before departing the Bay of Naples, Lorenzo managed to devote some time to calling on Ippolita Sforza, whom he had befriended during her earlier wedding in Milan. This would prove to be an immensely worthwhile investment of Lorenzo's time, as much later events would attest. On his return through Tuscany, Lorenzo experienced a further welcome triumph when Arezzo, one of Florence's client cities, and one moreover which had formerly maintained close ties with Luca Pitti, pledged their unequivocal support for the Medici cause.

As Piero lobbied behind closed doors throughout the tense summer months of 1466 to further shore up the Medici party's local support, Lorenzo energetically trained up the local militia bands that had been recruited from the numerous Medici estates dotted around the Mugello. This was being done even as some 400 of Florence's most illustrious citizens were drafting a petition in late May 1466 calling for a return to the older, more democratic system of republican government. They were demanding the dismantlement of the *cento*, or Council of One Hundred, which had been created in the wake of the political rupture of 1458. One of the signatories to this damaging public oath had been Piero's own first cousin Pierfrancesco de' Medici, who had seemingly been poisoned by jealousy over the success of the main branch of the Medici family (this was notwithstanding the fact that Pierfrancesco's cadet branch of the family had prospered marvellously under Cosimo's rule). As Cosimo had feared, his former ward Pierfrancesco had come under the disturbing influence of his father-in-law Agnolo Acciaiuoli. It was also around this time that the *signoria* itself took the unprecedented step of issuing a proclamation calling for the antagonists to make peace with each other. That the eight *priori* and the *gonfaloniere* felt themselves sufficiently autonomous and empowered to make such a remarkable declaration suggested that the Florentines were already growing more comfortable with the idea of independent political of action.

The peace proclamation was followed by the notorious public oath which was engineered by the Party of the Hill on 27 May 1466 and which constituted an implicit attack on the Medici's right to control the political processes of the Florentine state. It was signed by 396 prominent citizens who solemnly swore to uphold the traditional republican system of government. Luca Pitti signed first, followed by Agnolo Acciaiuoli, whilst Dietisalvi Neroni signed fourth and Niccolò Soderini signed seventh. It was endorsed by many of the great families of Florence including those which had previously been subject to exile, including the Strozzi and the Brancacci. Pierfrancesco de' Medici also signed the oath under the Svengalian influence of his father-in-law Agnolo Acciaiuoli. The oath was a clever move on the part of the reformers. What it did was to publicly demonstrate that opposition to the Medici-dominated *reggimento* was not, as the latter themselves claimed, merely the actions of a few isolated and alienated citizens but was in fact a substantial mass movement involving many of the most illustrious names in the republic.

The final act of this political *pavana* came in June and July when the *pratiche* debated the abolition of the *cento*, the Medicean Council of One Hundred. In pushing for this latest restructuring, the Party of the Hill seem to have been genuinely advocating republican reform and a return to the pre-1434 status quo, rather than any narrowly-defined élite agenda of their own. Neroni, for instance, freely admitted: 'I like the council of the *cento*, but if it causes trouble it should be abolished'. Acciaiuoli, meanwhile, went further still, stating that 'the *cento* is alright for me, but not for the lower classes, and it can serve as an instrument for despotic government'. Soderini was critical of the *cento* for similar reasons and also because it contained a disproportionate number of lesser guildsmen. The debates over the *cento* became increasingly acrimonious, discordant and divisive, threatening to spill over into armed conflict. Acciaiuoli, for his part, expressed concern for the maintenance of good law and order and averred that the republic itself stood at risk of destruction as a result of the ever-widening political fault lines. In this rancorous climate both parties continued to mobilise armed support. The Party of the Hill continued to solicit help from both Venice and Marquis Borso d'Este of Ferrara. An attempt was also made, through Agnolo Acciaiuoli's son Jacopo at King Ferrante's court, to enlist the support of Naples too but Ferrante maintained his policy of goodwill towards Lorenzo de' Medici and his father.

In a welcome fillip to the ruling faction, word soon arrived from Bianca Maria the dowager duchess of Milan and her chief minister Cicco Simonetta that Duke Galeazzo Maria Sforza would continue to stand by the Medici, as his father had done before him. This was notwithstanding the fact that the Florentine subsidy had not been granted to Milan. The Duke pledged 1,500 *Milanese* knights to the Medici cause and stationed them in the Romagna to be ready for action at a moment's notice. Upon receiving this news, Piero and Lorenzo de' Medici therefore felt confident enough to leave the city for a few days on 27 August. Piero had been stricken by a particularly bad attack of gout and needed to retire to the nearby Medici villa at Careggi so as to recover in the cool recuperative air of the countryside.

The day after they left Florence a new *signoria* was scheduled to be drawn by lot. Meanwhile, whilst resting in the peaceful *contado*, word reached Piero by courier that Borso d'Este's troops had been reconnoitred passing through Bentivoglio territory on their way towards Tuscany. Their objective, so it was reported, was Florence and their orders were to apprehend Piero and Lorenzo de' Medici personally and link up with the Florentine militia belonging to the Party of the Hill. The report itself was deemed to be reliable; the House of Bentivoglio was a Medici asset whose agents kept the family well apprised of any potential troop movements through the Apennine Passes. As if this news wasn't bad enough, however, it also came to Piero's attention around the same time that a Venetian mercenary army was also on the move. Nicodemo Tranchedini wrote to his new lord Galeazzo Maria Sforza that Ferrara's troops were 'already on the move to come here on the invitation of Piero's enemies, together with horse and riders of [the Venetian *condottiere*] Bartolomeo Colleoni'.

From his sick bed the Medici party patriarch Piero de' Medici now swung into action. Firstly, he sent word to the commander of the 1,500 *Milanese* lances posted at Imola in the Romagna to bring his forces without delay towards Florence. Next, he sent a rider to the friendly town of Arezzo asking the burghers to send him as many armed men as they could spare. Simultaneously, the Medici's loyal lieutenants at Careggi were instructed to mobilise the peasant militia which Lorenzo had been so diligently training in the weeks prior to this crisis. Nevertheless, despite these measures, Piero and his son knew they could never hope to confront two separate, professional mercenary armies. Their only tactical hope lay in securing the city from the Party of the Hill and fortifying it until Milan's reinforcements could reach them from Imola. Piero, who was still badly afflicted by gout, was despatched to the city on a litter alongside his attendants, whilst Lorenzo and a small party of riders was sent on ahead of the main party to scout the route back to the city. At the little hamlet of Sant'Ambrogio Lorenzo was waylaid by some men aligned with the Party of the Hill but managed to evade the trap; spurring his horse dramatically through the ranks of his ambushers he galloped back to alert Piero to the danger.

Travelling by a different route so as to evade their pursuers, father and son arrived safely at the Palazzo Medici where the Medici Party mechanism now clicked smoothly into gear. Nicodemo Tranchedini, Milan's ambassador and a long-time friend of the Medici, immediately set about fortifying and defending the Medici *palazzo* on the Via Larga. Lorenzo meanwhile sent their supporters to buy up all the bread, wine and arms that were available in the city. Piero's wealthy cousin Pierfrancesco the Elder was sought out, disentangled somehow from the destructive influence of his father-in-law, and a loan of 10,000 florins was either obtained or extorted from him to cover the costs of both the victualing as well as other emergency purchases. Meanwhile, Medici supporters from across the city arrived and planted themselves in defensive positions around the various Medici residences while other followers of the *reggimento* secured the city gates. In this way, following a plan of action which had probably been worked out weeks in advance and which accounted for every contingency, the Party of the Plain moved to gain the tactical initiative.

Agnolo Acciaiuoli, Dietisalvi Neroni and Luca Pitti were, meanwhile, seemingly caught entirely unawares by events which their own rash actions had precipitated. No concerted plan of action seems to have been formulated by the Party of the Hill beyond the gathering of a ragtag band of armed supporters which now congregated at the construction site of the half-built Palazzo Pitti. Aside from this, none of Florence's city gates had been secured and provisions for a protracted struggle had not been laid in. Furthermore, nobody seemed able to grasp the bull by the horns and each of the conspirators had taken it for granted that his fellows would issue the necessary instructions concerning what to do next; the net result of course was that no preparations had been made whatsoever. Piero and Lorenzo de' Medici's rapid actions had fatally blindsided them and, as Marco Parenti, himself a partisan of the Party of the Hill, wrote disconsolately in his *Memoir*: 'M. Luca, M. Dietisalvi, and M. Agnolo, seeing so great a commotion suddenly fall upon them, stupefied and unprovided, remained almost bewildered'. As the reformers waited at the talking shop of the Palazzo Pitti and blabbed impotently, Niccolò Soderini rode up with his own supporters in tow.

Soderini was the only person at this point who seemed committed to some definite course of action. According to Marco Parenti's account, he insisted that the armed men at the *palazzo* join with his own and together they would call on various friends of his who had hidden themselves away out of feint heartedness. Impressing and cajoling these waverers into service, Soderini planned to 'ride through the city shouting Liberty! and rouse the whole city to arms. And with this support he wished to rise to Piero's house and attack him and with every available means overcome him, capture him, put him to flight, and rout him entirely.' In the event Soderini's plan, which had at least the merit of being reasonably proactive, was cautiously overruled by the others. The more conservative Acciaiuoli, Neroni and Pitti feared that initiating armed conflict, such as Soderini was proposing, would lead to the *popolo minuto* being unleashed in the form of a violent and uncontrollable Florentine mob. Once they had been given a free rein they could not be held in check and would soon be running through the streets, clubs and pitchforks in hand, clamouring for greater power as in the chaotic days of the *ribellione dei ciompi*. Instead of instigating open confrontation both factions instead barricaded themselves into their respective *palazzi* and settled down for the night to await the results of the following morning's seigniorial elections.

The election of 28 August 1466 proved to be the undoing of the reformist Party of the Hill. The outgoing *gonfaloniere* Bernardo Lotti, an official favourable to the reformers, was replaced by Roberto Lioni. Lioni, although a man of the *popolo minuto*, now pledged his loyalty to the Party of the Plain in self-interested hopes of personal advancement from the powerful Medici *reggimento*. Lioni now instigated a four day long period of horse-trading during which both sides were persuaded to ratchet down their respective levels of hostility. As representatives of their respective factions, Luca Pitti and Piero de' Medici were both summoned to the Palazzo della Signoria to give an account of themselves. Luca Pitti dutifully presented himself at Florence's seat of government. Piero de' Medici, on the other hand, sensing his newly resurgent power, feigned illness and instead delegated his two sons Lorenzo and Giuliano to meet with Luca and the *priori* in his place. Attempts by the Party of the Hill, meanwhile, to suborn King Ferrante proved futile as Sforza's troops advanced closer to Florence and, besides, King Ferrante still preferred at this point to hedge his bets and wait for the eventual outcome.

Piero de' Medici now systematically went about dividing the ranks of his adversaries. One of Piero's loyal fixers, Francesco Sassetti, was despatched to detach Luca Pitti from his three co-conspirators. Following his terse cross-examination by the *signoria*, the somewhat unnerved Pitti was privately approached by Sassetti who reassured him of Piero's continued love and goodwill, telling Pitti that he remained deeply appreciative for the part he had played in his father's recall from exile in 1434. Always a conceited man who thrived on praise, the gullible Pitti had been taken in by Sassetti's overtures and offered Piero his terms and conditions for a truce. These were as follows. He wanted, first of all, to be appointed as one of the *accoppiatore*. Secondly, he wanted his brother to serve on the Eight of *Balià*. Thirdly, he insisted on a Medici marriage for his young daughter and dropped none too subtle hints that he wished for the groom to be Lorenzo. Piero consented to all of these terms, whilst at the same time managing to remain vague concerning Pitti's third condition of the dynastic marriage for his daughter, and he sent Francesco Sassetti back to seal the agreement with Pitti. Almost immediately, Luca Pitti's defection became general knowledge; its effect on the Party of the Hill was devastating. On 29 August, Agnolo Acciaiuoli pleaded for peace between the two warring factions, calling on both Piero de' Medici and Luca Pitti to remain at home in their respective *palazzi*, and urging the city authorities to move against any armed foreigners who were found within the city limits. That same day, Piero closeted himself with the archbishops of Florence and Pisa, Giovanni Neroni and Filippo de' Medici, to determine how Pisa might assist in the crisis. The discussion escalated into a shouting match. The Medici prelate from Pisa had pledged 1,500 *Pisano* soldiers to defend Medici interests in Florence.

Florence's own Archbishop Giovanni Neroni, related as he was to the reformer Dietisalvi Neroni, was forced to vacate the city and take refuge in Rome.

From 30 August to 6 September 1466 events moved rapidly towards their inevitable climax. With a sympathetic *gonfaloniere* and body of *priori* in his corner, and with the newly-subverted Luca Pitti now declaring that he would 'live or die with Piero', the Medici faction used their control of the city gates to bring a further 6,000 peasant militia into the city, flouting Agnolo Acciaiuoli's strictures against the presence of foreign mercenaries. 'The city was up in arms' noted the poet and historian Benedetto Dei, who in later life would find himself implausibly in far distant Timbuktu. Piero ordered the tolling of the *vaccha* and a *parlamento* was called to order. The Piazza della Signoria thronged with armed men, all supporters of the Medici, and every point of access to the *piazza* was studded with the usual Medici checkpoints. Wearing full armour and with sword drawn, Lorenzo de' Medici cut a *bella figura* as he cantered up and down the files of men on his favourite white charger. As the city teemed with armed Medici supporters and the lieutenants who urgently directed them, new measures were introduced which tightened the security apparatus of the state. One observer, Carlo Gondi, complained that 'a very large number' had called for the *parlamento* 'against their own will and against the good of the city'. Lorenzo de' Medici, only seventeen at the time, was illegally admitted to the *balià* and would also be nominated to the *cento* by December of the same year. Aside from such shortcuts, everything was done according to the outward show of correct form, although nobody was under any illusion that the machinery of Florence's government was now firmly back beneath the Medici thumb. The full force of that machinery could now be turned against the reformist faction which was by now hopelessly divided, paralysed and starved of any tangible armed support within Florence itself.

The Medici-controlled *signoria* lost little time in portraying the Party of the Hill in the simplest of terms as traitors – men of avarice and cupidity who had gambled on seizing political power for themselves and who had lost. Nonetheless, Medici propagandising aside, the inconvenient truth was that everything that the Party of the Hill had done up until this point, in a reformist sense, had resulted in greater political participation rather than less. The scrapping of the post-1458 electoral purses for one thing, and the abolition of the *cento* for another, had certainly contributed to a more egalitarian climate. Although it was also true that the Party of the Hill sought a return to a more equitable pre-1434 distribution of power, one in which they themselves could cultivate their own independent networks of political patronage, their actions were nevertheless in the best traditions of Florentine republicanism. It is also tempting to dismiss the motivations of someone like Agnolo Acciaiuoli as being merely personal in nature. The Medici had intervened in his private affairs and it was only natural that he should seek the retributive curtailment of Medici power. In light of this it was therefore strange that no desire for personal score-settling seems to have manifested itself in any written evidence. In an era when uncensored personal feelings were commonly shared in personal correspondence with relatives, not a single letter exists between Agnolo and his son Jacopo in which the former alludes to any bitterness at the personal affronts endured at the hands of Cosimo de' Medici. Certainly, if Agnolo did hold a personal vendetta against the House of Medici, he was curiously reticent about it.

Regardless of the personal motivations of each of the reformers, the *signoria* now evaluated the events of the previous weeks and came to their inevitable judgement. Agnolo Acciaiuoli, Dietisalvi Neroni and Niccolò Soderini were all duly sentenced to death, although according to Florentine custom their sentences were commuted instead to exile for a period of not less than twenty years. In fact, by this time they had already vacated a city which was teeming with Medici peasant soldiers hastily imported from the *contado*. Neroni and Soderini set out for Venice where they continued to conspire until Florence lost patience and re-imposed the death sentence on them *in absentia*. Acciaiuoli was banished to Barletta in northern Apulia, something of a social and political backwater, where he vainly persisted in his attempts to win his way back into the regime's good graces and thus engineer for himself a recall to Florence.

Of all the reformers, Luca Pitti remained perhaps the most tragic figure despite having been spared the sentence of exile. Despite his deal with Piero de' Medici he was now hopelessly politically marginalised; having openly conspired against the Medici *reggimento* he could therefore no longer be trusted. No longer regarded as an *amici* of the Medici, as such he was now consigned to a dreary political limbo. Pitti's own supporters from the days of the Party of the Hill, those who had not already been banished, now shunned him in disgust as feckless and unreliable. By now a thoroughly broken man, he ended his days in 1472 as a social and political pariah in Florence. Work on his grand *palazzo* in the Oltrano, that great ill-conceived statement of Pitti family ambition, had already shuddered to an abrupt halt in 1466. As befitting a man who could not see an important project to its conclusion, he was never to see it completed during his lifetime. Much later, the Palazzo Pitti would become the seat of Medici ducal power. The dynastic marriage between Pitti's daughter and Lorenzo de' Medici, which he had so trustingly assumed would be honoured, never materialised. For his eldest son, Piero had set his sights on higher quarry than the mere daughter of a turncoat. Instead, the propitiatory match with the Pitti girl had been made with Piero's brother-in-law Giovanni Tornabuoni, the manager of the Medici Bank's Rome branch. Marco Parenti, who clearly divined the far loftier ambitions of the Medici, wrote that 'Piero wished to reserve Lorenzo for a marriage with nobility since he already felt himself to be more than a mere citizen'.

The immediate political situation in Florence had been solved but the belligerent foreign armies of Venice and Ferrara still remained dangerously at large. Venice's mercenary commander Bartolomeo Colleoni in particular had trained under the late Francesco Sforza and had taken up his mantle as the pre-eminent *condottiere* of his day. Although he fought for Venice and the Florentine exiles against Florence his actual agenda was to seize Milan from the Sforzese. Against him, Florence employed another former Sforza apprentice, the rising star Federico da Montefeltro, the ruler of Urbino. For several years prior to 1450, Federigo had fought for Florence against King Alfonso of Naples. In the year that Francesco Sforza became duke of Milan, Federico had been hired by Sforza at the age of twenty-eight in what was to become a long and profitable association. The following year, Federigo sustained a potentially debilitating injury when he lost his right eye in a freak jousting accident. Shrugging off the wound with the nonchalant comment that he could 'see better with one remaining eye, than with a hundred others' he had the bridge of his nose surgically removed in order to expand his field of vision (the nasal deformity which he had added to his injury may be seen in the iconic portrait of Federigo painted by Piero della Francesca). In 1460, the thirty-eight-year-old Federigo had married his employer's fourteen-year-old niece Battista Sforza and he remained a staunch friend to the duchy of Milan. During the uncertain transition of the Duke's son Galeazzo Maria Sforza in March 1466, Federigo had come to the aid of Bianca Maria Visconti and Cicco Simonetta; the troops that he despatched from Urbino had helped shore up support for the new regime while awaiting the incoming duke's arrival from France. Now would follow the lord of Urbino's greatest test, the defence of Milan against the military prodigy Bartolomeo Colleoni.

The armies of Federigo da Montefeltro and Bartolomeo Colleoni marched and counter-marched in the Romagna, jockeying for a tactical advantage. Soon the forces of Milan under Galeazzo Maria Sforza, those of Naples under his brother-in-law Duke Alfonso of Calabria and those of Bologna under Giovanni II Bentivoglio conjoined with Federigo's own army and engaged Colleoni's 14,000 men on 25 July 1467 at the Battle of Riccardina. The battle, which is immortalised in a fresco in the Castle of Malpaga in the province of Bergamo, was fought on the banks of the Idice River near the villages of Riccardina and Molinella. The resulting carnage was inconclusive at best, but no less shocking for that. On the face of it merely another example of the innumerable *condottieri* battles of the Quattrocento, Riccardina in fact broke new ground as it was the first time that artillery and firearms were used extensively in an Italian battle. The matchlock harquebus was a muzzle-loaded, hand-held weapon which could fire an iron or lead shot of around a half an ounce in weight. It had been developed about seventeen years earlier by German gunsmiths and with a range of between 100-200 yards its effects were devastating. At Riccardina (also known as the Battle of Molinella) the field of battle was strewn with the corpses of over 1,000 horses. But the carnage had effectively stopped the Venetians in their tracks and for the time being saved Milan from being overrun.

Galeazzo Maria's own involvement in the campaign had been moot and it was obvious to the more experienced *condottiere* Federigo that the boy had inherited none of his father's or grandfather's skill-at-arms. Eager to demonstrate his underwhelming martial prowess he felt demoralised and undermined by his doting mother Bianca Maria. His well-meaning mother persisted in constantly checking up on him and–to Galeazzo Maria's intense annoyance–even reminded him to say his prayers before he retired to bed each night. This volatile mother's boy took easy offence. When his former friend and companion Donato 'del Conte' from the noble *Milanese* Bossi family fled Milan in the winter of 1466, the Duke treated him as a traitor, offering a reward for his capture and publicly humiliating Donato by having his likeness 'painted on cards with a harp in the right hand and a shoe in the left, and attached [them] to the columns of the Duomo and the Broletto'. He then took out his spite on Donato's mother, ordering that twenty-six horses be brought into her *palazzo* courtyard where they were led round in a circle, the clattering of their hooves making an unbearable clamour for the poor woman and presumably preventing her from sleeping. Neither was Donato the only disaffected *Milanese* to abscond from the duchy. He was soon joined by Galeazzo Maria's own half-brother Sforza Secondo, the son whom Francesco Sforza had with his French mistress Jeanne d'Acquapendente. Sforza Secondo, who sought refuge in Venetian territory, wrote to Bianca Maria complaining that Galeazzo Maria's behaviour towards him was worse than if he had been 'a rebel or a Turk'.

This, therefore, was the measure of the man whom the level-headed Federico da Montefeltro was forced to fight alongside; understandably, he had soon outstayed his welcome in the command tent. Federico made his unhappiness known to the *signoria* and they contrived to recall Galeazzo Maria to report in person on the war's progress. Hurrying to Florence convinced that his personal report was central to the League's success, he was put up at the official 'state apartment' at the convent of Santa Maria Novella but by the second day, '*e chiamava Piero suo padre*' ('calling Piero his father'), the insecure young duke had elected to foist himself on Piero de' Medici's household at the Via Larga. It was only later that he realised he had been duped by Federico, who had only wanted Galeazzo Maria out of the way so that he could fight the war his own way, *in pace e tranquillità*. The Duke bristled with secret resentment at Florence and Federico, as well as at his own interfering mother. Miserably he complained, with an uncommon glimmer of perceptivity, that his mother treated him 'as if he were a boy of little intelligence'.

Bartolomeo Colleoni's troops had meanwhile emerged from the recent Battle of Riccardina still largely intact; however Venice had by now lost its stomach for the fight. They ordered Colleoni to disengage and permitted Pope Paul II to broker a ceasefire between the various belligerents in 1468. Regional peace had been restored, at least for the time being. Peace had also been established within the Sforza household too. Tired of his mother's continual interference, Galeazzo Maria eventually banished Bianca Maria to her dowry city of Cremona. From here, against the better advice of her counsellors, the aggrieved matron intrigued with Venice. She eventually died of fever at Melegnano on 28 October 1468, while en route from Cremona to Milan to attend her son's wedding to Bona of Savoy. Her death inevitably raised both concerns and gossip. It had been strongly suspected by certain people, including the *condottiere* Bartolomeo Colleoni himself, that Galeazzo Maria had been complicit in ordering her poisoning. There may indeed have been some merit in these allegations. It is certain that during her illness she was attended by men who were not only close to Galeazzo Maria but also complicit in other known cases of poisoning. Besides which, in light of Bianca Maria's threat to hand Cremona over to Venice out of spite towards her estranged son, the Duke certainly had good reason to see the demise of his mother.

As for Piero de' Medici's regime, it was left unquestionably strengthened in the aftermath of the crisis of 1466. The *balià* had, for one thing, empowered the return of elections *a mano* to the *signoria*. The *otto di guardia* was reinstated and went about rounding up enemies of the state; that is to say, the enemies of the Medici. The *cento* too was also re-established. The enterprise of restoring pre-1434 republicanism was never completed; in fact, for the remaining twenty-eight years of the Medici regime, the *signoria* was never more drawn by lot. Many of those who had lent their signatures to the Oath were banished. Such was the depletion of old *ottimati* families on account of this latest exodus that Piero de' Medici was forced to recall some of the exiles of 1434 and 1458, including the Strozzi brothers Filippo and Lorenzo, whose banishment was finally lifted on 20 September 1466 much to the elation of their mother Alessandra Strozzi, who had been tireless in her lobbying and campaigning on their behalf.

Not content with establishing an iron grip on the instruments of government, Piero also sought to add his own historical gloss on the events of

211

1466. According to him, the reformers had been nothing more than conspirators who had plotted his death on the road from Careggi to Florence. They were scoundrels who brazenly plotted to use foreign mercenaries to seize control of the city. As evidence in support of this allegation Piero adduced the confession of Dietisalvi Neroni's brother Francesco, which had nevertheless been obtained under torture and was therefore of questionable validity. More sophisticated contemporary chroniclers like Marco Parenti were under little illusion that the story of a 'conspiracy' was nothing more than a confection dreamed up by Piero himself to justify the presence of so many thousands of Medici peasant militia in the city. The reality was that Francesco's confession spoke only of seeking to 'exile' Piero and not have him murdered. In the marketplaces, meanwhile, the assassination hypothesis gained common currency and was championed by such Medicean diarists as Luca Landucci.

On 13 December 1466, Cosimo de' Medici's friend and client the sculptor Donatello had died. One of his final creations for the Medici had been the bronze statue depicting the assassination of the Assyrian general Holofernes by Judith. Like the *David* before it, Donatello's creation was a powerful symbol against tyranny – a representation of virtue and liberty triumphant over the strong in a just cause. Like the *David*, *Judith and Holofernes* also stood in the Medici *palazzo* where it decorated a water fountain in the courtyard. After 1467 and the final victory over the reformers, all opposition had been so effectively crushed as to set up a one-party state which no longer felt the need to hide or dissemble its supremacy. But, unlike *Judith and Holofernes*, this was no *just* victory of the weak over the strong, but a well-orchestrated crackdown by the Medici on their political enemies. Two years later, on 7 February 1469, Lorenzo de' Medici would marry into the Roman nobility. The House of Medici was now obliged to look outside of Florence in order to find their social equals. If this gave rise to private mutterings about the hubris of the Medici in setting themselves up as princes in the making, in practice there was by now very little anybody could actually do about it.

PART THREE

THE GOLDEN AGE OF
THE MEDICI

CHAPTER 9

Magnifico Rising

Magnificent Lorenzo, to whom heaven has given charge of the city and
the State, first citizen of Florence, doubly crowned with bays lately for
war in S. Croce amid the acclamations of the people and for poetry on
account of the sweetness of your verses, give ear to me who drinking at
Greek sources am striving to set Homer into Latin metre.

Angelo Poliziano to Lorenzo de' Medici

Of Cosimo de' Medici's two sons, only Piero had succeeded in producing
for the late *padrone* any grandchildren that had survived into adulthood.
He had sired a total of three girls and two boys and, of those five
grandchildren, young Lorenzo had always been Cosimo's favourite and
consequently the aging statesman doted on the child. One day, when Cosimo
was in conference with the ambassadors from Volterra, young Lorenzo had
wandered into the room and asked his grandfather to fashion him a flute from a
piece of wood. Without even giving it a second thought, Cosimo had interrupted
the meeting by taking a blade from beneath his robe and spending the next few
minutes whittling the wood into the instrument that the child had requested.
Afterwards, when the affronted ambassadors remonstrated with Cosimo for
giving the boy precedence over them, Cosimo had simply replied with a
rhetorical question: 'don't you all have children and grandchildren?' To Cosimo,
affairs of state were important but family was no less so; and since the House of
Medici was now effectively synonymous with the state itself it was in the
interests of the state to raise prodigious numbers of Medici offspring and devote
adequate time to their nurturing and education. To the elderly *capo* this duty
was every bit as important as the hosting of routine diplomatic conferences.

Young Lorenzo grew up on the Via Larga in the sprawling Palazzo Medici, a
building which was inhabited by no less than three different family generations.
There was his grandfather Cosimo and his grandmother Contessina de' Bardi;
there was his father Piero and his mother Lucrezia Tornabuoni; and finally
there were his siblings, his younger brother Giuliano plus his three sisters
Maria, Bianca and Nannina. The *palazzo* was home to the main family line of
the Medici and was a place where they lived in relative privacy as compared to
the old days when entire extended clans would cluster together in a single
street, though inhabiting separate houses. This had been the case when Cosimo
and Contessina had occupied the Palazzo Bardi in the Oltrarno, where their
palazzo was located in the midst of a number of other Bardi family properties.
Still, it was perfectly normal for such *palazzi* to house at least two generations
of males, along with their wives, children and servants. Where the Medici had

215

innovated was in their decision to demolish a row of pre-existing buildings along the Via Larga and build their new *palazzo* on the ruins from the foundations up. The more common practice was–as for instance in the case of the Palazzo Rucellai–for wealthy families to acquire two or three adjacent houses, knock internal doors in their separating walls and then envelop all of them in a thin facing of stone, thereby presenting a uniform façade to the outside world. The interiors, however, would often inevitably retain the somewhat chaotic layout that you might expect from the amalgamation of several different properties.

It was within the expansive and well-designed confines of the Palazzo Medici that Lorenzo passed his childhood years and here he was groomed for civic duty from an early age. In 1454, when he was barely five years old, the child had been dressed in an exquisite miniature French livery and paraded before Jean, the duke of Calabria, who had been newly-knighted by the *priori* of Florence. In 1459, at the age of ten, he and his younger brother Giuliano were made to recite lines of verse at the first state visit of Francesco Sforza's eldest son Count Galeazzo Maria Sforza of Pavia, who was only several years older than Lorenzo himself. The poetry recital had been followed by a procession in which the 'boy prince' Lorenzo had rode a white horse and had his personal banner proudly displayed – a golden falcon trapped in a net. It was while growing up at the Palazzo Medici that Lorenzo developed an uncommonly close relationship with his doting mother Lucrezia Tornabuoni. An unusually liberated Renaissance matron, Lucrezia had inherited property outside the city limits of Florence over which she had retained complete and independent control free of her husband Piero. She was also an accomplished poetess in her own right and freely gave her opinion on the *volgare* love poetry composed by the teenage Lorenzo and his friends, who referred to themselves collectively as *l'allegra brigata* or 'the Happy Gang'.

The humanist and member of Cosimo's Platonic Academy, Gentile de' Becchi, was selected to be Lorenzo's private tutor. The fact that he was a consecrated priest did not prevent him from inculcating in his charge the full range of classical writers as well as the great Italian poets Dante, Petrarch and Boccaccio. He would remain Lorenzo's friend, ally and occasional chaperone on Lorenzo's future diplomatic missions for Florence and would later be proposed by his former pupil for the bishopric of Arezzo in 1473. Thanks to Becchi's superb and wide-ranging humanist education the precocious Lorenzo was writing letters of patronage to his own coterie of 'clients' by the age of eleven and by the following year he was bombarding his father Piero with a steady stream of requests on their behalf. At the age of fourteen he was permitted leave to go on an educational tour of the Florentine possessions of Pistoia, Lucca and Pisa.

Towards the end of his life it had become evident to Cosimo that Piero possessed neither the health nor the constitution to survive him by many years. The burden of managing the family's fortunes would inevitably fall therefore to his grandson Lorenzo, who was by far and away the more intelligent of Piero's two sons. Everything that the boy did from this moment onwards was shrouded with the glamour of expectation. Neither Cosimo nor his own father Giovanni di Bicci had been born to rule; they had acquired political power gradually and as a necessary, sometimes onerous, corollary of their wealth and social standing. Prior to 1466 the people of the republic were only grudgingly willing to extend inherited power to Cosimo's son Piero, however between 1466 and 1469 there was a sea change in Florentine acceptance of Medici overlordship and towards

Lorenzo himself there was something approaching almost universal acclaim. But on Cosimo's death Lorenzo was still only fifteen years old and still considered unusually young to be groomed for such leadership responsibilities. In Renaissance times the period called *giovinezza* or 'youth' was regarded as a notoriously unstable time of untutored violence and unbridled sexuality. Those who were below the age of maturity were to be excluded from the political life of the state until they had acquired sufficient experience and maturity to be able to make calm, reasoned decisions. In the meantime, a whole host of activities awaited the young prince or scion of a wealthy family. Tournaments, fairs and carnivals, hawking and hunting, carousing with friends, the selection of colourful and elaborate clothing; such diversions occupied the youthful mind, along with that universal rite of passage the discovery of the opposite sex, which was usually facilitated through the sweet embraces of the most exquisite courtesans of the higher class bordellos.

In fifteenth-century Florence the 'carnival song' or *canto carnascialesco* was used to celebrate the city's carnival season, those weeks preceding Lent and the *Calendimaggio* lasting from 1 May to the 24 June. The festivities included song and dance led or performed by masked actors and singers. Lorenzo's own poem *Canzona di Bacco* in his collection *Canti Carnascialeschi* captures the ephemeral spirit of youth:

> *Quant'è bella giovinezza,*
> *Che si fugge tuttavia!*
> *Chi vuol esser lieto, sia:*
> *di doman non c'è certezza*

> How beautiful is youth,
> That quickly flies away!
> He who would be happy, let him:
> Since of tomorrow none can say.

The verse was a poignant ode to Lorenzo's own rapidly fleeting youth. On the one hand he would always hearken back to his days spent idly composing youthful poetry but, on the other hand, his time and his being would increasingly be claimed by the practical demands of politics; although still in his *giovinezza* Lorenzo was the senior Medici scion and therefore next in line to 'rule' albeit unofficially.

Nevertheless, this did not prevent him from living life to the full while he still had the opportunity and Lorenzo enjoyed nothing better than the outdoors life of riding, hunting and falconry with his peers. Galeazzo Maria Sforza had made a gift to Lorenzo of his favourite falcon trainer, Pilato, and after 1473 Lorenzo enjoyed engaging in falconry at his newly acquired villa at Poggio a Caiano. The active, alfresco existence suited him well. He was blessed with considerable physical strength and endurance. A contemporary of his described him thus: he stood 'above the average height, was broad shouldered, robustly built, muscular, remarkably agile, and olive complexioned'. Lorenzo's facial features were, however, somewhat less inviting. His broad, squashed nose looked as though it had been broken and badly re-set and was completely devoid of the sense of smell, a congenital defect also suffered by Lorenzo's mother Lucrezia. The pronounced under bite of his jaw, moreover, made him look coarse and possibly even vulgar to some and he was so 'short-sighted that his eyes could make out very little from a distance'. Yet, once you got beyond the physical impairments, Lorenzo's natural poise as well as his very obvious intelligence and poetic sensibilities made him undeniably appealing to the fairer sex, a man who was truly *molto galante*.

It was around the year 1465, when he would still only have been around sixteen years old, that Lorenzo's name became associated with that of the beautiful Lucrezia Donati. The aristocratic Lucrezia was wife to Niccolò Ardinghelli, a silk merchant who was connected with the exiled Strozzi family. Lorenzo first came into contact with Lucrezia at the marriage of his friend Braccio Martelli to Constanza de' Pazzi. Inflamed by passion, Lorenzo had presented Lucrezia with a clutch of violets, the floral motif used repeatedly throughout his love poems. Watching the mutual attraction unfold between the pair, Martelli had vulgarly hinted to Lorenzo that her husband Ardinghelli was 'hung like the horn of a bull'. Another of Lorenzo's friends Giovanfrancesco Ventura added, rather more helpfully, that Ardinghelli would soon be conveniently overseas on business, adding that 'it would be a pity to leave unploughed such sweet terrain'.

According to the rules of Florentine courtly love it was perfectly permissible for a young blood like Lorenzo to court the 'Platonic love' of even a married woman and the connection between Lucrezia Donati and Lorenzo de' Medici was certainly fairly common knowledge in aristocratic circles at the time. In 1465 we find Alessandra Strozzi gossiping in a letter to her son Filippo in Naples that Lucrezia had ordered an expensive dress adorned with pearls for a ball and how Lorenzo and his companions also wore outfits festooned with pearls in Lucrezia's colours. Lorenzo's biographer Niccolò Valori later wrote that '[Lorenzo] loved Lucrezia Donati, who was a woman of rare beauty, honesty, and nobility ... when he was young; Lorenzo composed beautiful poems and songs in the vernacular in her honour.' As for the unfortunate cuckolded Ardinghelli he must have been either oblivious or else indifferent to their liaison. For all its courtly and poetic trappings, given Lucrezia Donati's obvious charms it is difficult to conceive that the relationship had been exclusively Platonic.

Dalliances such as this were all well and good but Lorenzo's romantic reverie would soon be rudely interrupted for the greater good of the state. For better or worse the hopes of the republic had been placed unequivocally upon his shoulders and, like his contemporary Galeazzo Maria Sforza of Milan, Lorenzo de' Medici was destined to wear the mantle from a young age. Unlike his less talented and increasingly unregenerate contemporary, however, Lorenzo would rise wholeheartedly to the considerable mental and emotional challenge of being publicly paraded as 'the hope of Florence'. As Piero's health seesawed unpredictably, Lorenzo was deliberately rolled out as the official face of the Medici *reggimento*, assuming ever greater responsibility for state ceremonial and even taking point on important diplomatic missions.

Two such missions, to Rome and to Naples in the midst of the political crisis of 1466, tested Lorenzo's credibility in the eyes of Italy's other heads of state and enabled him to perfect his ability to charm and cajole in the service of Florence. He had acquitted himself well, winning the friendship of both the Pope and the king of Naples. The year before, in April 1465, Lorenzo had earned his diplomatic spurs when he had been despatched on a ceremonial mission to Milan. Piero had assigned Lorenzo to represent the Medici and Florence at the proxy wedding of Francesco Sforza's daughter Ippolita to Duke Alfonso of

Calabria. Alfonso was married to Ippolita by proxy, his younger brother Federigo standing in for him, following which Federigo together with an entourage of noblemen brought Ippolita back to Naples. Lorenzo was a tender yet mature sixteen-year-old at the time yet he was called upon to comport himself with the studied gravity of an experienced diplomatist. Lorenzo had travelled to Milan by way of Ferrara, Verona and Venice where he benefited from the opportunity to experience other Italian cities and widen his personal contacts. In Venice he was accorded the honour of being greeted by the Doge himself, Cristoforo Moro. He was joined on the state visit to Milan by his brother-in-law Guglielmo de' Pazzi and by a modest entourage of Medici retainers; Piero would have been careful to ensure that Lorenzo's usual coterie of hellraisers from *l'allegra brigata* remained safely behind in Florence.

The marriage itself cemented a much-needed and long-awaited diplomatic alliance which had deep ramifications for the continued peace of the peninsula. The rift between Milan and Naples prior to the Peace of Lodi and the Most Holy League had been problematic. The wedding brought the former belligerents together in a spirit of healing and dynastic unity which stimulated a newfound hope throughout Italy. In the wake of Cosimo de' Medici's death it was also important for Duke Francesco Sforza to meet Lorenzo de' Medici face-to-face and be afforded the opportunity to evaluate his future Medici ally in Florence. This was especially pressing given the fact that Dietisalvi Neroni was using his ambassadorship to Sforza's ducal court to undermine Medici authority, a situation which Piero was aware of thanks to his own agents in Milan. As things turned out, Piero need not have worried, for the deft application of Lorenzo's unique personal charisma soon assuaged any misgivings the duke might otherwise have had.

Lorenzo de' Medici and the Duke's eldest son Galeazzo Maria Sforza were contemporaries, the Sforza scion being five years Lorenzo's senior. But although both youths were in the first flush of their *giovinezza* even at this age one could see that they were entirely different personalities. Both young men were under incredible pressure to live up to the respective legacies of their fathers or, in Lorenzo's case, his grandfather. At the same time, both were at the cusp of youth and still focused on enjoying their lives as only a wealthy Renaissance male knew how. But whereas Lorenzo was known to be thoughtful, intelligent and mature beyond his years, Galeazzo Maria showed an early tendency towards mental imbalance and even derangement. His early, fruitless attempts to live up to his father's legacy on the battlefield would, once removed from the inhibiting scrutiny of his mother Bianca Maria, soon degenerate into a life of idleness, pretension and casual sadism. Once he had assumed sole power his cruel reign had been softened only by the intervention of his late parents' chief minister Cicco Simonetta. To compensate for his appalling lack of ability and poor judgement in military affairs, Galeazzo Maria turned instead to hunting dumb beasts in his extensive parks and game reserves outside the city of Pavia. As Alfonso of Castile had aptly declared, 'A knight should always engage in anything to do with arms and chivalry and if he cannot do so in war then he should do so in activities that resemble war. And the chase is most similar to war.' All the Sforzese children participated in hunting and the acquisition of military skills, including Galeazzo Maria's capable and intelligent daughter Caterina Sforza, who would later go on to earn her well-deserved reputation as Italy's warlike Virago.

Galeazzo Maria Sforza had first been married in 1466 to Dorotea Gonzaga the daughter of Ludovico III Gonzaga, Marquis of Mantua, and Barbara of Brandenburg. Gonzaga's female offspring were rumoured to suffer from congenital hunched backs so Galeazzo Maria had delayed his marriage to Dorotea until such time as the *Milanese* court was able to ascertain whether her affliction was identical to her unfortunate older sister's. Dorotea died tragically just a year after their marriage and her widower was betrothed again, this time to Bona of Savoy. Bona, who was also the sister-in-law of King Louis XI of France, was originally promised to King Edward IV of England but the revelation of his secret marriage to Elizabeth Woodville had placed Bona back on the international marriage market. The Sforzese had reverted to the strategic Visconti practice of marrying into the Savoy dynasty as a means of securing their north-eastern borders (Filippo Maria Visconti's second wife had been Marie of Savoy, whilst his grandfather Galeazzo II Visconti had been married to Bianca Maria of Savoy). To the obvious strategic benefits of this policy were added the additional advantages of Bona's reputed beauty. Galeazzo Maria had been personally assured by his ambassador to France that the Duke would be 'much pleased with so beautiful a lady' and in an uncharacteristic display of courtly romance Galeazzo Maria had refused to be parted from a portrait of Bona which had been painted by the court painter Bonifacio Bembo. Galeazzo Maria was married to Bona of Savoy by proxy with his half-brother Tristano standing in for him. In Renaissance times, the practise was for the proxy bridegroom to kiss the bride on the cheek and climb briefly into bed with her; there they would symbolically touch each another's bare leg 'according to the custom'. When she arrived at court Bona certainly lived up to all expectations. She was physically attractive and also a good horsewoman, an attribute that was much valued at the hunting-obsessed Sforza court. She was also intelligent and politically savvy and possessed strong willpower.

Galeazzo Maria's married life unfortunately failed to quell the Duke's lurid passion for meanness and lasciviousness. His many inventive acts of cruelty towards his own subjects we can perhaps pass over in judicious silence, but his priapism towards the noblewomen of Milan is well-documented. The well-bred ladies of Milan were regularly abducted and raped by their duke, who went especially out of his way to target the women of the late Visconti dynasty, as well as another prominent *Milanese* family the Olgiati. Galeazzo Maria betrayed no evidence of contrition as he went about his lustful amusements, even going so far as to boast to members of his court that he possessed lasciviousness 'in full perfection, for I have employed it in all the fashions and forms that one can do'. Even the machinery of state finance was geared towards ameliorating the worst excesses of the Duke's carnality and a state fund was set up to discreetly pay off the victims of his lechery. Whilst openly boastful of his own sexual conquests, the Duke was illogically touchy when gossip about his nocturnal pursuits found its way back to him. When the Mantuan ambassador Zaccaria Saggi indiscreetly let it slip that Galeazzo Maria was involved in a homosexual relationship with the son of the Florentine ambassador the Duke was furious. Saggi, who had just recently moved his entire family from Mantua to Milan to take up his new diplomatic post, was immediately forced to leave the city under a cloud.

Soon, it was Lorenzo's turn to experience matrimonial bliss. Although under normal circumstances he could have expected to have enjoyed another ten years of carefree bachelorhood, Piero's poor health meant that Lorenzo was expected to produce heirs as quickly as possible and thus secure the future of the dynasty. Lorenzo's brother Giuliano was four years younger than him and, as was customary for the junior sons of the wealthy or the nobility, Piero may have intended him for a career in the Church. This made it all the more imperative for Lorenzo himself to marry and procreate. In the spring of 1467, while the Florentine mercenaries of Federico da Montefeltro squared off against the Venetian army of Bartolomeo Colleoni, Lucrezia Tornabuoni slipped out of Florence and journeyed to Rome with the express purpose of securing a suitably aristocratic wife for her son. In Rome, she was to scrutinise a daughter of the powerful Orsini family as a potential match for Lorenzo. In between his banking duties her bank manager brother Giovanni had been keeping her abreast of potential candidates from amongst the Roman nobility. He now welcomed his sister to the Eternal City to make the final selection in person.

In the wake of the political crisis of 1466 Florence was now considered too narrow and parochial to find a Florentine bride for Lorenzo. Lucrezia's three daughters had already been married into Florentine high society, Maria to the Rossi, Bianca to the Pazzi, and Nannina to the Ruchellai. But when these marriage contracts had been negotiated the Medici had not been the undisputed first family of the republic. Now, with their pre-eminence assured, a marriage alliance made outside of Florence's pool of élite families would broadcast that the Medici no longer depended upon insular alliances forged amongst the local *principali*. A prestigious Roman match would move the Medici name up a notch and open important new doors in the spiritual heart of Western Christendom. Indeed, in their marriage habits the Medici were beginning to see themselves as princes who, unable to marry into equal rank within their own city-state, were forced to look beyond their own narrow borders in search of marriage partners of equal rank and status. The rumour that the House of Medici was actively seeking a Roman alliance was in fact already known to the Party of the Hill prior to 1466. The imputation was clear to many in Florence; that the Medici now considered themselves too good for even the better sort of Florentine nobility. Machiavelli would later sum up the opposition's feelings in his *History* when he wrote that 'he who does not want citizens as relatives wants them as slaves'.

In many respects the ancient Orsini family fitted all the Medici's requirements for a suitable dynastic match. Firstly, they were one of Rome's oldest surviving feudal families, which appealed to the Medici's innate Florentine snobbery. As a parvenu family of merchant bankers, marriage into the venerable Orsini would give the Medici entry to the world of established old money beyond the narrow confines of Florence. Secondly, the Orsini were an established *condottiere* family with considerable military resources at their disposal, including a private army, as well as castles and fortified strong points located in a strategic arc around Rome. These assets could, if needed, enable Florence to project considerable force beyond the periphery of its own Tuscan territory and even apply direct pressure on the city of Rome. Thirdly, the Orsini had historical ties to the papacy, having fielded no less than two former popes: Celestine III (1191–98) and Nicholas III (1277–80). Admittedly, these were not necessarily what you might describe as 'good' popes. In fact the latter had been such a notorious nepotist, having elevated three close Orsini relatives to the Sacred College and appointed other relatives to high lay positions in the Papal States, that the poet Dante had immortalised him in *The Inferno*. Dante had used the wordplay *orsatti* to denote the three 'bear cubs' that hung from his coat tails, Pope Nicholas himself having admitted that he was guilty of favouring the 'cubs' in his family. The Orsini also boasted the presence of Cardinal Latino Orsini, a sitting member of the Sacred College. This was always a useful asset for a politically ambitious family and moreover the fact that Latino was also in charge of the Camera Apostolica, the Roman Curia's financial department, was a convenient synergy for a family of bankers.

Lucrezia's arrival in Rome hardly went unnoticed. The Florentine exile Agnolo Acciaiuoli–who had relocated to Rome from remote Barletta–sourly remarked: 'She goes around with merchants, visiting each cardinal and is awaiting an audience from the Pope. She behaves like a great lady and tarts herself up like a fifteen-year-old. Here everyone laughs at her, but even more at Piero.' Given his own straightened circumstances Acciaiuoli can be forgiven for expressing more than a soupçon of distaste, but the sour grapes of one Florentine exile was less concerning that the disdain of an entire city. The Roman nobility looked askance at the Medici as nouveau riche and pointed to the sinfulness of wealth that had been established through moneylending. That Medici wealth had funded prodigious clerical entertainments in Rome was conveniently brushed aside. Pope Paul II paid no heed to the snobbery of the Romans and was as enchanted by the gracious and intelligent Medici matriarch as he had been the year before by the glamorous and charismatic son. Not long after her arrival in Rome, the Medici envoy Filippo Martelli was writing fulsomely that Lucrezia 'acquired high favour with the Pope's entire court' and affirming that 'I know that the cardinals have decided that no finer lady has ever visited Rome'. Like or loathe the Medici, the Romans certainly could not ignore them.

The mission to the Orsini had progressed well. Lucrezia set her sights on the sixteen-year-old Clarice Orsini, daughter of Jacopo Orsini the Lord of Bracciano and Monterotondo in the Papal States. Lucrezia approved of the young girl, writing expansively to Piero that: 'She is fairly tall, and fair, and has a nice manner, though she is not as sweet as our girls. She is very modest and will soon learn our customs. Her face is rather round, but it does not displease me.' Continuing in a more candid vein, Clarice went on to report that 'We could not see her bosom as it is the custom here to wear it completely covered up, but it seems promising'. The fact that there was only one year's difference in age between Lorenzo and Clarice was overlooked even though it was customary for Florentine husbands not to marry before the age of thirty and for their brides to be at least ten years their junior. Upon Lucrezia's departure from Rome the on-going marriage negotiations were continued by her brother Giovanni and Filippo de' Medici, the archbishop of Pisa, and were finally concluded to everyone's satisfaction by November 1468.

According to the final deal that was struck between the two families the Orsini would bestow a dowry of 6,000 florins on the girl with the wedding agreed to take place in the summer of 1469. A detached and dispassionate Lorenzo dryly noted in his *ricordi*: 'I, Lorenzo, took to wife Clarice, daughter of the Lord Jacopo Orsini; or rather she was given to me'. This apparent coldness and disinterestedness on Lorenzo's part persisted throughout the long months of their betrothal. He was enjoying himself far too much in Florence to spare much thought for his future arranged bride and when the Orsini invited him to visit them in Rome to meet Clarice and strengthen relations between the two families he politely declined. On those few occasions when he did write to

Clarice she replied back to him with needy and enthusiastic gratitude, but otherwise he evaded any obligation on his part to make the girl feel either welcome or indeed wanted. At the same time a kind of inverse snobbery was at work amongst local observers of the match. Florence's reputation as a centre of intellectual leadership in Italy caused Lorenzo's highbrow coterie of friends to look down on Clarice as a cultural inferior; their judgement was that she would be a pious Roman wife who might, at best, be moulded into a frugal Florentine matron.

Inevitably the announcement of the upcoming marriage was used as an excuse for the Medici to put on a good show. To celebrate his betrothal to Clarice, Lorenzo announced *La Giostra*, a magnificent jousting tournament that would take place in February 1469. The exercise of martial skill-at-arms was always popular with the young bloods of the Renaissance world and a common arena for such exploits was the joust. Such tournaments were often lavish affairs, especially when princes were involved. The Passage of the Tree of Gold, which was held in Bruges in 1468 to mark the wedding of Charles, Duke of Burgundy, to Margaret of York, the sister of Edward IV of England, was arranged around an elaborately detailed allegory designed to honour the bride. According to the fashion of the era it featured knights who often made their appearance in disguise; one of these knights–a particularly strong and robust young man–drew the delighted plaudits of the crowd for making his entrance masquerading as a feeble old man being carried into the tilt-yard on a litter.

Lorenzo's marvellous jousting tournament was destined to be immortalised and live on in the collective memory of the Florentines thanks to Luigi Pulci's poem *Stanze per la giostra di Lorenzo* or 'Stanzas on the Joust of Lorenzo' (in reply, Angelo Poliziano would later compose *La giostra di Giuliano de' Medici* – 'The Joust of Giuliano de' Medici' – for Lorenzo's brother). It was held at the Piazza Santa Croce, which was fitted out for the occasion with public grandstands and special seating areas for the dignitaries. Before even coming to blows in the tilt-yard, the various aristocratic opponents fought with each other to outshine all the rest in the sheer finery of their trappings. Here was a spectacle worthy of majesty, the closest that republican Florence could come to emulating a royal gala all couched in the esoteric code of high medieval chivalry. Clarice herself was not invited and, instead of his prospective bride, Lorenzo jousted as the courtly champion of his muse, the beautiful Lucrezia Donati. Lorenzo rode into the piazza accompanied on either side by Giovanni Ubaldini and Carlo da Forme, the very *non pareil* of courtly Renaissance chivalry. Each companion represented a famous *condottiere*; Ubaldini was Federigo da Montefeltro's man, whilst Forme was employed by another well-known *condottiere* Roberto da Sanseverino. The five horses that Lorenzo rode that day had been contributed by other supporters of the regime: King Ferrante of Naples, Cesare Sforza of Milan and Borso d'Este of Ferrara who, having backed the losers of 1466, was by now anxious to ingratiate himself with the victorious Medici.

The day was an unmitigated success both in terms of sheer spectacle and in view of the accumulated political capital. Long after the tilt-yard had been dismantled and the tipsy revellers had staggered off home, congratulations continued to pour in from across Italy and the rest of Europe complimenting Lorenzo on his martial skill-at-arms and the magnificence of the occasion. On a personal level it was the peak of his young career, the transformation of a mere banker's son into a chivalrous prince and the undisputed future ruler of

Florence. From Rome, Clarice's brother Rinaldo Orsini wrote to Lorenzo: 'God be praised for all and especially that you emerged safe and unhurt; in which I think you were aided by the prayers of your Clarice'. Clarice and Rinaldo were perhaps made fully aware of the fact that Lorenzo had worn the colours of his courtly lover Lucrezia Donati during this astonishing festival, but polite discretion would have caused them to pass over it in silence. In his *ricordi*, Lorenzo matter of factly noted his victory and his having been awarded a silver helmet fashioned with a crest of Mars the god of war.

As in the case of Galeazzo Maria Visconti's marriage to Bona of Savoy, Lorenzo's marriage to Clarice Orsini was performed by proxy with his kinsman the archbishop of Pisa, Filippo de' Medici, standing proxy for him. Filippo later wrote glowingly to Lorenzo of his future bride: 'according to my opinion, a maiden of such physical gifts, appearance, and manners, that she deserves no other bridegroom than him whom, I believe, heaven has destined for her'. In May 1469, a deputation led by Giuliano and which included Lorenzo's cousin Pierfrancesco, his brothers-in-law Bernardo Rucellai and Guglielmo de' Pazzi, and his former tutor Gentile Becchi was despatched to Rome to collect the happy bride. On 4 June, with much lavish pomp and spectacle, Clarice and Lorenzo rode through the teeming streets of Florence, which were gaily bedecked for the occasion with rich hangings and arrases, and which were lined with assorted heralds, pages and trumpeters in Medici livery. It was a glamorous affair which saw the young bride riding through the festooned streets on Falsamico, one of two magnificent horses (the other being a horse named Abruzzese) which had been gifted to Lorenzo by the king of Naples. Lorenzo himself was resplendent in 'a cape of white silk, bordered in scarlet, under a velvet surcoat, and a silk scarf embroidered with roses'. At the Palazzo Medici the couple celebrated their wedding feast.

This ostentatious showcasing of Medici opulence was becoming a recurring motif of official Medici life and was as visible in the family's private as in their public ceremonies. Medici funerals, as well as wedding festivities such as Lorenzo's, were now also becoming more elaborate and more expensive. In the past, flamboyant unseemly displays of wealth and conspicuous consumption had been curtailed not only by the stern sumptuary laws but by a natural Florentine aversion towards undue extravagance. Indeed, had it not been Dante himself who had described the Florentines as 'sobria e pudica' meaning 'temperate and chaste'? With the onset of the Quattrocento these habits, which were firmly rooted in the more conservative mercantile mentality of the medieval era, were fast changing; the leading families of the dominant plutocracy had grasped that the projected image of the family corresponded in large measure to its actual political power. The wealthy merchant élites of the Florentine commune were increasingly permitted the same latitude and freedom of expression as the dynastic princes of Italy and, to all intents and purposes, began to act and resemble princes in all but name. Records of the Medici family's expenditure on such events and ceremonials show both their increasingly elaborate nature as well as their escalating cost.

The wedding feast and celebration had been a palpable demonstration of Medici wealth and power to the rest of the commune but unfortunately this showy ostentation also had its more negative side effects. Some of Piero's regime members and *amici* now began to view themselves, by association with the Medici, as being immune from the normal constraints of the law. Members of other leading families were increasingly waylaid and either robbed or assaulted

224

in the vicinity of San Lorenzo, often in broad daylight. Niccolò Machiavelli later described the conduct of the Medici *amici* in his history of Florence, lamenting that it was 'as though God and fortune had given them the city for a prey'. In the end, matters had gotten so out of hand that Piero was forced to assemble the most pertinacious of these *amici* in his bedchamber. With as stern an aspect as he could summon given the agony inflicted upon him by his gout, the Medici *capo* warned the ringleaders in no uncertain terms that if they did not cease and desist from their bullying he would bring Agnolo Acciaiuoli, Dietisalvi Neroni and Niccolò Soderini back from exile so that they could protect their families in person. Piero's ultimatum had the necessary palliative effect and the muggings promptly ceased. But, on the other hand, the strain of having to deal with this domestic emergency told badly on Piero's already delicate health.

Towards the end of 1469 Piero's health deteriorated further and, like Cosimo de' Medici before him, he was forced to spend more of his time confined to the tranquil environs of the villa at Careggi, leaving Lorenzo and Tommaso Soderini to jointly manage family affairs in his absence. What should have been a relatively smooth transition to power for Lorenzo in the aftermath of his triumphal joust and marriage celebrations was, unfortunately, to prove a thorny period in Florence's foreign relations. Although the Peace of Lodi and the Most Holy League still held firm, Italy was nevertheless still bedevilled by internecine squabbles between the smaller cities and fiefs of the peninsula. One of these tiffs concerned the city of Rimini on the Adriatic coast which theoretically lay within the purview of the Holy Roman Emperor and the Pope but which was to all intents and purposes an independent despotate ruled by its tyrant, Sigismondo Pandolfo Malatesta.

Sigismondo was the *condottiere* who had helped Florence to confront Alfonso of Naples in the mid-1440s and had thereby earned himself a place in Gozzoli's Magi Chapel at the Palazzo Medici. However, he was also one of the more unsavoury figures whom the Medici occasionally found it necessary, for political reasons, to associate with. Indeed, Sigismondo's reputation for cruelty was legendary throughout Italy and throughout his life he was accused of a plethora of heinous crimes. Pope Pius II not only excoriated him as a heretic, burned him in effigy, and excommunicated him, but also afforded Sigismondo the distinction of being the only man aside from Judas Iscariot ever to be gazetted by the Roman Catholic Church as 'officially residing in Hell'. 'Until now, no mortal has been solemnly canonized in Hell. Sigismondo will be the first man worthy of this honour,' Pope Pius had declared with grim metaphysical certainty. Sigismondo had not only burned his bridges with the Pope in Rome. His arrogant, headstrong and sociopathic behaviour had also earned him the enmity of most of the other *condottieri* of Italy and he bore a particular grudge towards Federigo da Montefeltro. Sigismondo had invested considerable time and effort in gaining the trust of Federigo's fifteen-year-old half-brother Oddantonio da Montefeltro, who had earlier been created duke of Urbino by Pope Eugenius IV. This had been done to make Oddantonio utterly dependent on Sigismondo, following which he planned to move in and annex Urbino to Rimini. Federigo, however, had stymied this plan by arranging for Oddantonio's death under mysterious circumstances in July 1444, whereupon he himself assumed the lordship (although not for the time being the dukedom) of Urbino.

Enigmatically for such an ogre, Sigismondo was nevertheless renowned as an enlightened patron of the arts. In 1446 he commissioned Leon Battista Alberti to rebuild the old Church of San Francesco in Rimini as a memorial to himself and his former twelve-year-old lover (later on his wife) Isotta degli Atti, following which the building became more commonly known as the Tempio Malatestiano. No less an artist than Pierro della Francesca had been brought in to paint the interiors. Sigismondo had died in October 1468, not only consigned to the pits of Hell but vilified by his adversary Pope Pius II as 'the worst of all men who have ever lived or ever will live, the shame of Italy, the disgrace of our age'. In Sigismondo's absence, Rimini came to be held by his widow Isotta on behalf of their legitimised son Sallustio. Isotta and Sallustio could both count on the support and backing of Pius's successor Pope Paul II.

Sigismondo, however, had another illegitimate son, Roberto, with whom he was scurrilously rumoured to have had an incestuous homosexual relationship. Roberto Malatesta lost little time in marching on Rimini, which he captured on 20 October. Having deposed Isotta, Roberto had ordered that his two half-brothers Sallustio and Valerio be put to death. Outraged by this infringement of his prerogative in the Papal States, Pope Paul II turned to his home state of Venice for support in the dispute. Fearful of papal ambitions in the Romagna, Milan, Florence and Naples all took Roberto's side and the Most Holy League which Cosimo de' Medici had so painstakingly knitted together rudely collapsed. Roberto Malatesa was already a *condottiere* in the service of the three city-states who supported him; now he was also given the added military support of his late father's rival, Federico da Montefeltro, in addition to Alfonso of Calabria. Together, the three capable generals easily defeated the joint papal and Venetian army that was sent against Rimini in August 1469. This however, was merely the prelude to an unwelcome conundrum for Lorenzo de' Medici.

Having beaten the Pope, Milan and Naples now diverged in their policy objectives and Florence was caught in the middle of both allies. Galeazzo Maria Sforza favoured a quick end to the conflict which would leave him free to address on-going problems of his own pertaining to Savoy. King Ferrante on the other hand wished to prosecute the war further, thus weakening the papacy's position and allowing Naples to pursue her own expansionist goals to the south of Rome and the Papal States. The Medici naturally preferred to align Florence with the objectives of the House of Sforza, whilst dissenters within the *signoria* called for the abandonment of Milan if the latter persisted in appeasing the Pope. Sick and caught in the middle of his allies' conflicting objectives, Piero de' Medici equivocated, much to Galeazzo Maria's intense annoyance. The Duke's envoy Filippo Sacromoro made it abundantly clear that his master's continued friendship towards the Medici was predicated on Florence's compliance with Milan's policy wishes. The chilling insinuation was that the House of Sforza was circumspect in its choice of allies; if the Medici could no longer be depended upon, then Milan would find another wealthy and influential Florentine family who could be. Indeed, the reformers of 1466 had sought to offer the former duke of Milan this very option.

For the good of Sforza-Medici relations Lorenzo had made a second visit to Milan that same summer, standing godfather to Galeazzo Maria's firstborn son, Gian Galeazzo. In a display of Medici munificence–some might have called it a bribe–Lorenzo presented the Duchess Bona with an exquisite gold and diamond necklace worth a staggering 2,000 ducats. Upon his return to Florence, and as his father's health continued to decline, Lorenzo now wrote to Galeazzo Maria in increasingly obsequious tones. In one such letter he gushed: 'I would like to declare myself as the devoted servant of Your Excellency and to recall the ancient devotion of our house and myself in particular toward Your Illustrious Lordship'. A long-time diplomatic ally of the Medici, Filippo Sacromoro in particular rallied to Lorenzo's support, reporting to the Duke in December that Lorenzo had 'so arranged and secured his affairs in the city in regard to the leading citizens that he seems to be squarely in the saddle'. In his private discussions with Lorenzo throughout August 1469 the *Milanese* envoy observed that Lorenzo carried himself 'like an old and knowledgeable man' and noted that Lorenzo intended to rule in the style of his grandfather, 'with as much civility as he could manage'. Beneath this volley of blandishments, endorsements and expensive bribes Galeazzo Maria appears to have relented and Milan once more renewed its partnership with the House of Medici. As a gesture of goodwill, the Duke pledged 1,000 soldiers to Florence's assistance should they be needed.

While Lorenzo de' Medici was finessing the Sforzese, the loyal Tommaso Soderini was meanwhile bolstering support within the Medici *reggimento*. Soderini had, over the past decades, proven his steadfastness towards the Medici cause just as surely as his brother Niccolò had exhibited treachery. Whilst the ambitious and incautious Niccolò had met his political demise at the hands of Piero and Lorenzo in 1466, his brother Tommaso had thrived. Now already well into his sixties and, with three decades of political experience behind him, regarded as one of Florence's elder statesmen, Tommaso had also used his position to shamelessly enrich himself over the years. This was principally achieved through his role as gatekeeper to the Medici leaders and he would accept large bribes from foreign ambassadors as well as locals seeking access to the inner Medici circles of power. Furthermore, in the aftermath of the crisis of 1466, Tommaso had now also become the only politician confident enough to publicly oppose the Medici. On one level this was politically healthy for it at least gave some semblance of opposition and helped appease Florence's more republican sentiments, but on another level it raised questions as to whether Soderini might seek to create his own faction after Piero de' Medici was gone. Indeed, Filippo Sacramoro had speculated aloud to his master the duke of Milan as to Soderini's true loyalty to the regime. Soderini himself seems to have acquired a rather high an opinion of his own role in the greater scheme of things. Increasingly, his conduct betrayed his own view of his position as being entrenched and unassailable, that of both a power broker and a kingmaker. Like the unfortunate *condottiere* Francesco Bussone da Carmagnola who had allowed himself to fall into similar hubris, this conceit that he could manipulate the key players to his own benefit would prove to be Tommaso Soderini's undoing.

On the morning of 2 December 1469, Soderini called a meeting of the Medici *reggimento* at the convent of Sant'Antonio, which was situated near the Porta Piacenza, in order to discuss the transition of power from Piero de' Medici to his son Lorenzo. Filippo Sacramoro recorded that 700 members of the regime attended the meeting but how, just as the meeting was about to get underway, word reached Florence that Piero had already died at Careggi. The regime members nevertheless proceeded with the meeting as planned, whereupon Tommaso Soderini made a statesmanlike speech in favour of a smooth transition of power from Medici father to son. As Niccolò Roberti records, Soderini had remarked: 'Out of regard for their predecessors, and especially

Cosimo and Piero, who had always been friends, protectors and preservers of the commonwealth and benefactors of the State, for which reason they had taken the first rank and borne the whole weight of government wisely and with dignity, always displaying courage and mature judgement, it seemed to him that they should leave to Piero's family and sons, notwithstanding their youth, the honourable position which he himself and Cosimo had enjoyed'.

The following morning, Soderini and a delegation of leading Florentine citizens and politicians descended on the Palazzo Medici where they humbly and respectfully handed over the reins of power to the twenty-year-old Lorenzo de' Medici. The succession had passed without major event and some 1,000 soldiers whom the duke of Milan had prudently placed on standby were, in the event, not needed. Piero de' Medici was laid to rest alongside his beloved son Giovanni at the Church of San Lorenzo, in an arch between the Old Sacristy and the former Chapel of Sacrament, in a tomb created by Andrea del Verrocchio. The native Florentine sculptor had designed Cosimo's funerary monument in 1464 and now made use of the same materials–marble, porphyry, serpentine, bronze and the grey sandstone known as *pietra serena*–in order to emphasize the continuity of the dynasty. A marked step towards a freestanding tomb, Piero and Giovanni's shared sepulchre was impressive for its originality of composition and remains to this day an elegant example of late fifteenth-century funerary art.

On the surface at least, the circumstances in which Lorenzo assumed power in December 1469 were markedly different from those in which Piero had succeeded his own father Cosimo de' Medici. In 1464 there had been a pregnant expectation on the part of many of the *reggimento's principali* that they would be allowed to assume a far greater share in political power as a reward for three decades of loyalty. By contrast the delegation of *principali* that was led by Tommaso Soderini on 3 December 1469 was unequivocal in handing the unofficial mantle of government to the son. This was, as usual, all done under the proper forms and observances of Florentine government and, at least officially, the head of the government was still the *gonfaloniere della giustizia*, who was a man by the name of Piero di Lutozzo. The memoirist Marco Parenti dismissed the deputation as being 'of little weight' but this did little to alter the fact that the delegation at the Palazzo Medici had exhibited the collective subservience of Florence's leading political families.

Or had it? In Florence's sophisticated political milieu Soderini's gesture could also be interpreted quite differently, as a carefully calculated pact. Far from being a subservient and docile act of submission, by making a very public show of handing Lorenzo the mantle of political power, Florence's political élite made it implicit that Medici authority originated with the plutocracy itself and was not simply Lorenzo's by pure right. The underlying assumption was that Lorenzo would rule, not only for the Medici, but also for the benefit of the wider ruling plutocracy which had made a visible show of handing him the reins of government. This 'provisional offer' of power was, by extension, therefore dependent upon the continued good graces of the plutocracy comprised, as it was, of those many influential Medici supporters and *amici*.

Lorenzo's extreme youth combined with Tommaso Soderini's decades of experience in the tough world of Florentine political horse-trading gave these *principali* the impression that it may now be possible for the Medici to be harnessed, subtly and with constitutional finesse, without recourse to open rebellion. Oblivious for the time being of this hidden undercurrent, but nevertheless groomed for power practically from birth, Lorenzo mundanely recorded the transition in his *ricordi*: 'The second day after his death, although I, Lorenzo, was very young, in fact only in my twenty-first year, the leading men of the city and of the ruling party came to our house to express their sorrow for our misfortune, and to persuade me to take upon myself the charge of the government of the city, as my grandfather and father had already done. This proposal being contrary to the instincts of my age, and entailing great labour and danger, I accepted against my will, and only for the sake of protecting my friends, and our own fortunes, for in Florence one can ill live in the possession of wealth without control of the government.' In the very last part of this statement by Lorenzo lay the very nub of Florentine politics. Namely, that in the cut-and-thrust world of Florence's economic life the burgher who lacked political influence was always vulnerable to those business rivals who *did* have access to power. A man could easily be destroyed by spiteful tax assessments or by malicious and impartial court cases brought for political reasons. In the final analysis, the Medici had taken power purely because, as Florence's wealthiest citizens, they had little choice in the matter if they were to protect their wealth from those rivals who reviled them as jumped-up parvenus. Piero's tutor had done his work well and it is clear therefore that Lorenzo comprehended this cardinal rule of Florentine politics from an early age. Tommaso Soderini would find the young Medici 'princeling' a far more difficult political adversary than he had perhaps bargained for.

It would not take long for Tommaso Soderini to lock horns with Lorenzo de' Medici in the sphere of foreign policy. In late December 1469, the *signoria* convened a conference between Milan, Naples and Florence in order to resolve the on-going strategic differences between them concerning the war with the papacy over Rimini. The conference, however, was hamstrung by internal dissent. When the duke of Milan heard rumours to the effect that Naples had entered into clandestine negotiations with Venice he withdrew his envoys. This was followed in the April 1470 by the withdrawal of the *Napoletani* as well. In Florence, opinion was once more polarised into hawks and doves: those who (like the Medici) favoured supporting Milan's desire to end the war, and their opponents who preferred to continue prosecuting the war with vigour alongside Naples. Any official distancing of Florence from the Sforza regime in Milan would serve, as before in 1466, to threaten the military underpinnings of Medicean power. This alliance was still strong and in the aftermath of Piero de' Medici's death, Duke Galeazzo Maria had fulsomely declared his support for Lorenzo, telling the *signoria* that their relationship was like that of two brothers. Tommaso Soderini now sought to leverage Lorenzo's dependence on Milan in an attempt to divert Florence from the Medici's traditional source of power.

Soderini had lately defeated an impeachment attempt by Luigi Guicciardini and Antonio Ridolfi which had targeted his well-known corruption, and was newly resurgent as an independent political force. At this point Soderini now induced his friend Otto Niccolini, the Florentine ambassador to Naples, to craft deceptive intelligence reports that indicated that Naples had already concluded a unilateral defensive treaty with Venice. This artifice now gave Soderini the pretext to publicly call for Florence to join the new Naples-Venice alliance rather than be left out in the cold. Hoodwinked, the mass of the Florentine public fell prey to Soderini's propaganda campaign and began clamouring for a return to the old Venetian coalition. Soderini quickly called a *pratiche* in May, packed it with his own supporters and railroaded through an official communiqué to Niccolini authorising him to 'join' the (in fact, non-existent) Naples-Venice axis. Lorenzo, who had not even been notified of the sitting of the *pratiche* until it was too late, was left embarrassingly uninvolved in the entire episode. In fact, it had been a dismal political debut for the young Medici *prince* and his reputation had sustained a considerable blow. Made determined by this reversal, Lorenzo was resolved not to be caught off guard again by the political sleight of hand of the 'elder statesman' Soderini.

Soon, the Naples-Venice alliance began to move closer to reality, thanks in large measure to the actions of King Ferrante, who now stepped up his campaign pressuring Florence to join with them. Lorenzo played for time, persuading the *signoria* not to decide either way until after Galeazzo Maria had given his official response to the developing diplomatic situation. Meanwhile, Lorenzo worked with the *Milanese* duke and his ambassador Filippo Sacromoro to line the pockets of all those *principali* who had a say in the upcoming vote. At the same time the Medici party apparatus put it about that Tommaso Soderini was in the pay of the king of Naples. When a further *pratiche* was called in June, Lorenzo this time managed to take the initiative, packing the committee with obedient Medici clients and adherents. The *pratiche* now instructed Otto Niccolini to under no circumstances agree to any new treaty with Naples which would serve to leave Milan diplomatically isolated. Thankfully for Lorenzo the news broke soon afterwards that Venice herself had declined to join with Naples under the unfavourable terms which King Ferrante had offered. Lorenzo's victory was complete. Naples's wilful attempt to go her own way had been scuppered and, on pain of being left isolated, the southern kingdom was sheepishly forced to return to the fold. Meanwhile, Soderini's spirited though hubristic attempt to ride the tide of popular Florentine feeling had failed ignominiously and he was compelled once more to bend his will to the Medici.

While the showdown with Soderini over Naples had been afoot, Lorenzo was also grappling with another problem which had developed slightly closer to home in the commune of Prato, one of Florence's dependencies. Encouraged by the internal dissension of the Florentines, the exile Bernardo di Salvestro Nardi, along with a band of followers from Pistoia, stormed Prato with cries of: 'Long live the Marzocco and the Florentine exiles, and down with the *estimo*!' Nardi's men had then marched on the commune's government *palazzo* and captured and imprisoned the town's *podestà*, a man named Cesare Petrucci. Word of this incursion soon reached Florence itself and panic gripped the city as citizens succumbed to the somewhat alarmist vision of Prato's armed artisans and shopkeepers hammering at the gates of their city. The letter writer Alessandra Strozzi commented to her son Filippo that 'For two hours there was complete confusion, with people running about the streets, and particularly around Lorenzo di Piero's house'. Bernardo di Salvestro Nardi had clearly struck a chord in the hearts of the *Pratesi* and, writing some years later, Niccolò Machiavelli would attribute the uprising of the disaffected of Prato to their distaste for the 'pride and avarice' of their Florentine overlords.

The *condottiere* Roberto da Sanseverino, nephew to the late Francesco Sforza, was quickly instructed to marshal his men and march them into Prato to restore order but no sooner had his troops been mustered than the *signoria* received fresh word that the rebellion was over as abruptly as it had begun. Prato's *podestà* Cesare Petrucci had somehow escaped his confinement, rallied the opposition forces within Prato and overwhelmed Nardi's largely undisciplined rebels. Put to the torture, Bernardo Nardi had subsequently implicated the duke of Modena as well as Borso d'Este of Ferrara, two lords who were no particular friends to the Florentines. Nardi and his brother Salvestro had both been exiles of the crisis of 1466; what the Prato affair had vividly demonstrated was that such impenitent *fuoriusciti* as Niccolò Soderini and Dietisalvi Neroni who still remained at-large must be regarded as an ever-present threat. At the same time, the affair had also demonstrated that rustic country officials like Cesare Petrucci could often prove more loyal than select members of the Medici *reggimento*. Men such as these needed to be given a place to match their abilities and, in gratitude for his swift and capable actions, Petrucci was moved to Florence where his political career was placed on the fast-track. This promotion was to prove a remarkably fortunate one for the Medici and, as we shall see, Petrucci would find himself strategically well-placed to assist his new benefactor Lorenzo de' Medici some years later.

On 15 March 1471, having witnessed how adeptly Lorenzo de' Medici had dealt with his first political crises as first citizen of Florence, Duke Galeazzo Maria Sforza, accompanied by his wife Bona of Savoy, made a ten-day state visit to the republic. This was the Duke's second visit, ostensibly in fulfilment of the couple's vows to visit the Church of Santissima Annunziata in Florence, but which would also take in the neighbouring cities of Mantua and Ferrara. Galeazzo Maria had earlier visited Florence as the fifteen-year-old count of Pavia in 1459 in connection with the state visit to Florence of Pope Pius II. On that occasion the young Galeazzo Maria had felt especially honoured as he had been allowed to stay in the private inner sanctum of the Palazzo Medici's women's quarters, which were strictly off-limits to outsiders. In 1471, he was again lodged at the Palazzo Medici while his wife Bona was lodged separately at the *palazzo* belonging to Pierfrancsco de' Medici.

The paranoid and safety-conscious duke was impressed by the fact that Lorenzo did not inhabit a castle protected by moats, walls and embrasures but, like other wealthy Florentines, resided in a normal *palazzo*, albeit a slightly more magnificent one than the rest. However the fact was that the Palazzo Medici was, like most wealthy *palazzi* of the era, based on the strongly fortified design of such official buildings as the Palazzo della Signoria and the Bargello. As in the case of these latter buildings, the private family palaces often had ground floor windows that were smaller than usual and placed high up so as to prevent rioters from gaining entry. Many *palazzi* also boasted their own wells so that a supply of fresh drinking water could be assured in the event that the occupants should be barricaded inside for several days. The visit itself had been a somewhat spur of the moment enterprise as Galeazzo Maria's original plan had been to visit Louis XI of France in order to ingratiate himself with the king and strengthen Milan's French alliance. Characteristically, however, the impulsive duke–who could no longer be bothered to travel all the way to France– had changed his mind at the last moment and opted instead to pay a call on Florence and the Medici, who were conveniently closer to Milan.

It was said of the highly image conscious Galeazzo Maria that he intended to make the court of Milan 'one of the most resplendent in the Universe' and he certainly demonstrated this ambition upon his arrival in Florence. The splendour of his repeat visit amazed even the Florentines. The Duke led a procession of some 2,000 knights through the city's streets on brightly caparisoned mounts. These were followed in turn by 500 foot soldiers and

231

retainers, 'all lords and worthy persons and ... all in courtly style with pomp and without arms'. The members of the entourage were all richly clad in silk and brocade and displayed the red and white ducal livery of the Sforzese. They comprised not only soldiers and retainers but also musicians, grooms, falconers and enough attendants to look after the 500 blood hounds that the Duke had brought with him (it was rumoured that the Duke spent as much as 5,000 ducats a year maintaining his hunting dogs, about the same amount that he spent annually on cathedral-building). The Florentines were also treated to the spectacle of twelve carriages covered in embroidered gold and silver cloth which transported Duchess Bona's ladies-in-waiting. After fulfilling their vows at the Santissima Annunziata, which was the church towards which the Sforzese were traditionally devoted, Galeazzo Maria and Bona proceeded to the Palazzo Medici on the Via Larga where they were given a sumptuous reception and were impressed by the Medici's splendid works of art such as Donatello's bronze statue of *David* in the *cortille*. Amongst the waiting crowd of onlookers that gaped and gawked at the ostentatious spectacle of the duke of Milan's visit was a nineteen-year-old artist from the workshop of the artist Verrocchio who was named Leonardo di ser Piero and who hailed from the small Tuscan town of Vinci.

As the state visit took place during Lent, courtly diversions such as jousts, tournaments and banquets were prohibited. Instead, the Duke and Duchess were treated to no less than three religious performances in the Oltrarno: the Annunciation in San Felice in Piazza, the Ascension in Santa Maria del Carmine, and the Pentecost in Santo Spirito. However, if Duke Galeazzo Maria had intended to dazzle the Florentines with Milan's display of courtly wealth, the native inhabitants of the city were less than impressed with their guests. Some of the more frugally-minded citizens deeply resented the huge expense which Lorenzo had lavished on the duke of Milan's state visit. Not only were the *Milanese* visitors boisterous and haughty but they also indulged heartily in meat dishes despite the Lenten prohibition. Non-observance of the Lenten fast by the rude and impious *Milanesi* was later cited by many Florentines to be the reason why, during the course of the religious performance, a devastating fire broke out in the ancient Augustinian church of Santo Spirito which destroyed all the altars and the numerous works of art. The *Milanesi* in their rich, bejewelled attire also fell afoul of the Florentine sumptuary laws which restricted undue extravagance in dress. As a result of these rather puritanical laws the Florentines themselves tended to garb themselves in drab and simple wool rather than rich silk and in spite of the fact that Florence was a major finishing centre for some of the most luxurious dyed fabrics in all of Europe. But as we have seen, these trends were fast changing in Medici Florence and people had become more inured to luxury items of dress. Niccolò Machiavelli himself later caustically remarked that if Galeazzo Maria Sforza had found Florence to have a marked predilection for 'courtly finery and customs contrary to any well-ordered society, he left it even more so'. It is probably true to say that the ladies of Florence were enviously scandalised by their stylish *Milanese* counterparts.

While he sojourned in Florence, Galeazzo Maria sat for a portrait commissioned from an artist then at the height of his fame in Florence, Piero Pollaiuolo. The maestro created the most famous painting by which the Duke is remembered to this day. In Pollaiuolo's depiction, Galeazzo Maria is shown wearing a green, ermine-trimmed doublet festooned with golden fleur-de-lis. In his gloved right hand he holds his left hand glove; the expression on the face is attentive, directed, even faintly concupiscent. Upon departing, Galeazzo Maria made a gift of the painting to his friend Lorenzo who hung it in pride of place at the *camera grande tenerra*, which is to say in Lorenzo's own personal quarters at the Palazzo Medici. He would cast his eye over it before going to sleep at night and also upon waking. This may seem strange to us but on deeper reflection the gesture shows the enduring bonds between the House of Medici and the House of Sforza and the mutually-dependent relationship that had developed between the two families over the preceding decades.

During his stay at the Palazzo Medici, Duke Galeazzo Maria developed a taste for Medici style artistic patronage and, upon his return to Milan, began commissioning artists and architects to adorn his ducal city. On his state visit to Mantua, Galeazzo Maria had also been mightily impressed by the *Camera Picta* in the Gonzaga castle at Mantua. The four walls of this room displayed the family, friends and political allies of the Gonzaga in a stately procession against a sumptuous Italian landscape which was intended to project the family's influence and power. One trifling detail which had however troubled and irritated him was the absence of his own likeness from the impressive mural. Enthralled by the *Camera Picta*, Galeazzo Maria embarked upon his own cycle of decorative and adulatory art in the Castello Sforzesco and in the spirit of true Sforza one-upmanship he extended his own mural to two rooms instead of one. He then dragooned two of Lombardy's finest artists, Bonifacio Bembo and Vincenzo Foppa, to commence work on the vanity project. The work, however, would never be completed due to the Duke's endless interference, revisions and redactions.

In the summer of 1471 a serious crisis arose between Florence and the people of the semi-independent commune of Volterra. The commune had its origins in ancient Roman times and had always been an important mining town which produced alum, iron, copper and silver. In 1361, Volterra had placed itself under Florentine protection, agreeing to pay large sums of tribute each year and consenting to the placement of a Florentine representative in the town. In 1470, an alum deposit had been found on Volterra's public lands and, as it was not considered an especially important mine, the contract to exploit it had subsequently been awarded by the town government to a consortium led by Lorenzo's client and agent in Volterra, Paolo Inghirami. But in time the mine turned out to be a highly lucrative one and the townspeople grew displeased that the contract for its exploitation had been given to the Medici agent instead of having its profits flow into Volterra's own municipal revenues. An incoming government rode this tide of popular feeling and in June 1471 they reversed the earlier decision, voiding Inghirami's contract and re-allocating it instead to a consortium that was owned by the commune. The act threw down not only an economic but also a political challenge to both Florence and the Medici.

Paolo Inghirami came to Florence to confer with *il padrone* about the dispute. Lorenzo attempted to mediate between Inghirami and the *Volterrani* although, mindful of the alum mine's value to Florence's wool and silk dyeing industry, predictably he adjudicated in favour of his own agent. When, in February 1472, Inghirami and his business associates returned to Volterra accompanied by a party of armed Florentine guards their aggressive efforts to re-appropriate the alum mine provoked the *Volterrani* to anger and a spontaneous riot broke out. In the course of this disturbance both Inghirami and his father-in-law were separated from their Florentine guards and subsequently slaughtered in the family *palazzo*. Florence's own commissioner, Piero Malegonelle, barely escaped Volterra with his life.

On the face of it this seemed, to all intents and purposes, to be purely a rebellion by the *Volterrani* over mining rights. Closer scrutiny revealed, however, that Volterra had been covertly aided and abetted by certain malcontents within Lorenzo's own domestic regime. Furthermore, Dietisalvi Neroni and several relatives of Agnolo Acciaiuoli were also rumoured to be conspiring with the *Volterrani* against Florence. The *Volterrani* had been working in consort with these various dissident elements and their act of disobedience had been timed to coincide with a rebellion of the *signoria*. Surprisingly, one such faction member to come out in opposition to Medici policies was Antonio Ridolfi, who had just recently shown his public support of Lorenzo's friendly policies towards Milan during the previous crisis concerning Naples and Venice. Also waiting in the wings was Tommaso Soderini, who now urged conciliatory measures in response to the Volterra crisis in marked contrast to Lorenzo, who advocated that the rioting be suppressed by force. The government rebellion was, however, easily crushed by Lorenzo who packed the following *signoria* with his own supporters.

A *dieci di balìa* was appointed by April 1472, in which Lorenzo himself took an active role in the military preparations. In response the *Volterrani* sent envoys to Venice, Naples and the Pope in Rome to entice them to enter the coming conflict on their side. The Venetian *condottiere* Bartolomeo Colleoni was also said to be waiting for the right opportunity to link up with the malcontents and his presence and interest in the whole affair was a particular source of concern for Lorenzo. With Galeazzo Maria's envoy Filippo Sacromoro keeping his master carefully abreast of developments, the duke of Milan observed these developments closely. Lorenzo meanwhile succeeded in concluding a 100,000 ducat *condotta* to suppress the *Volterrani* with his godfather Federigo da Montefeltro, lord of Urbino, who would be invested as duke just two years later. By the end of May, Montefeltro had invested the city with an army which, according to Scipione Ammirato in his *Istorie fiorentine*, comprised 5,000 foot and 500 cavalry, including elements contributed by the Pope and the duke of Milan. To defend herself, Volterra mustered a hopelessly inadequate force of 1,500 mercenaries.

Many of those trapped inside the commune regarded it as foolish to defy the Florentines with such meagre resources, even though the city's walls were stout and Volterra itself was well situated atop an escarpment. With no real commitment to the fight, the *Volterrani* therefore soon lost heart and tried desperately to seek a negotiated surrender with Florence. Lorenzo, however, was now determined to teach the recalcitrant commune a stern lesson in obedience. In his belligerent reprisals against Volterra he seems to have forgotten a cardinal precept of Medici rule as practised by his late grandfather: namely, to treat subservient towns and cities well lest they rise up against you. Meanwhile, Montefeltro concluded his own separate agreement with the besieged city on 16 June. Volterra would be surrendered to the lord of Urbino who guaranteed in return that his troops would refrain from sacking the town. But, when a party of Montefeltro's soldiers entered Volterra to take control of the citadel, an altercation arose with some of the townspeople and the rest of the army poured through the gates and mercilessly sacked the city in violation of the truce. In the chaos of rape and pillaging that followed hundreds of *Volterrani* lost their lives as Urbino's troops slaughtered both Medici sympathisers and non-Medici supporters alike. The lord of Urbino himself seems to have made little attempt to avert the sacking and knowingly let it run on for several hours before putting an end to it by rounding up the ringleaders amongst his own men and hanging them in the town square.

In the aftermath, a number of prominent *Volterrani* families were sent into exile. As a symbol of Florentine rule, Lorenzo then also commissioned a massive new fortress on the ruins of the bishop of Volterra's palace. It was built by Francesco di Giovanni, also known as Francione, in consultation with the lord of Urbino. It was revolutionary in conception and boasted an innovative polygonal design, a precursor to the bold new citadel designs of the late fifteenth and sixteenth-century. With Medici rule firmly re-established in Volterra, Lorenzo finally seized complete control over the contested alum mine. But although he had done what he felt needed doing at the time, according to the seriousness of the rebellion, nevertheless on a more personal level Lorenzo was mortified at the tragic and needless loss of life. Soon afterwards he visited Volterra personally and did all in his power to alleviate the suffering of the surviving townspeople. Soon after his visit, the apostolic scribe Inghirami di Volterra wrote to Lorenzo: 'You have seen the afflicted and faithful friends and servants of Your Magnificence naked, despoiled of all their goods, robbed without mercy, for everything was taken during the sack of the city; and I doubt not that Your Magnificence with your kindly nature was moved to great compassion. Your arrival and seeing with your own eyes has been the sole hope of this people and has consoled and comforted them greatly.' Nonetheless, the story of Volterra still remains one of the least edifying chapters in Medici history.

Seeking perhaps to redeem himself in the aftermath of the Volterra massacre, Lorenzo removed himself from Florence to Pisa the following year, where he set himself the task of rejuvenating the Pisan Academy. This two-hundred-year-old institution of learning, which in its heyday had eclipsed even Florence's own university (there were too many 'amusements' for students to seriously apply themselves in Florence), had lately fallen into neglect and disrepute. The decision to do something about this situation was certainly laudable. The Florentines had never been especially kind to Pisa. During the Florentine siege of Pisa in 1406 the war commissioners had shown a singular lack of pity towards the subject city, which had never quite been able to forgive and forget Florence's wrongdoings. To Pisa therefore, Lorenzo rode with four commissioners, this time not of war but of the intellect, whose appointed task it was not to subjugate Pisa but to revivify its deteriorating Academy. These four men were Tommaso de' Ridolfi, the humanist scholar Donato di Neri Acciaiuoli (the humanist who had read Cosimo de' Medici's funeral oration), Andrea de' Puccini and Alamanno de' Rinucci.

Upon arrival the delegation found a great many *Pisano* scholars in residence, many of whom were men of considerable learning. Nevertheless, the long neglect of their institution had led some of them to fall into undisciplined and lackadaisical ways. One such scholar was Mariano Soccini, who had absconded to Venice with some valuable books and property of the Pisan Academy which he had artfully concealed inside some wine casks. Soccini was returned to Florence where a sentence of death had been pronounced upon him. However Lorenzo intervened to commute the sentence, whereat he was later restored to his former position at the Academy and even given a stipend of 1,000 florins a year. Lorenzo, himself a dedicated scholar, had argued that a man of such great learning should not have to suffer an ignominious death no matter how badly he had erred. Lorenzo spent a good while in Pisa sorting out the affairs of the Academy and in his absence he was bombarded by letters from his humanist friend Angelo Poliziano, who missed him and begged him to return to Florence.

The expedition to Pisa had been time well spent. In addition to the 6,000 florins per year budget from Florence, Pisa's Academy also received cash infusions from Lorenzo's personal fortune. Like Volterra, Pisa had once been a prosperous, proud and independent city-state in its own right. Whilst both communes had eventually come under Florence's jurisdiction, Lorenzo was determined to demonstrate to the *Pisani* that, having been a cruel overlord, Florence could also be a benefactor as well. Soon after the Pisan Academy was reinvigorated it received one of its most famous students, Lorenzo's own younger brother Giuliano de' Medici. Arriving at Pisa in May 1474, he wrote gaily to his mother: 'Today we dance, and tomorrow we joust, which, as is the custom of this country, should be very fine'. His friend and tutor Poliziano left us a vivid description of the young Medici princeling: 'He was tall and sturdy, with a large chest. His arms were rounded and muscular, his joints strong and big, his stomach flat, his thighs powerful, his calves rather full. He had bright lively eyes, with excellent vision, and his face was rather dark, with thick, rich black hair worn long and combed straight back from the forehead. He was skilled at riding and at throwing, jumping and wrestling, and prodigiously fond of hunting. Of great courage and steadfastness, he fostered piety and good morals... He was both eloquent and prudent, but not at all showy; he loved wit and was himself witty. He hated liars and men who held grudges. Moderate in his grooming, he was nonetheless amazingly elegant and attractive.' Giuliano, an engaging figure who was also a budding scholar in his own right, was adored by the people of Florence, perhaps even more so than Lorenzo himself. In 1474 Giuliano would have been twenty-one years old and just coming into his majority. After the lacklustre years of Piero the Gouty, Florence it seemed had been blessed by two singularly appealing and accomplished young leaders.

By 1475, Lorenzo already had four surviving children by his Orsini wife Clarice. These were Lucrezia Maria (born 1470), Piero (born 1472), Maria Maddalena (born 1473), and Giovanni (born 1475). Clarice had also given birth to twins in 1471 and a further daughter who was named Contessina Beatrice but unfortunately the three children had died in early infancy. Clarice Orsini herself had by this time settled down into the largely humdrum existence of a Florentine matron. Almost constantly in a state of pregnancy, she tended Lorenzo's various homes together with her mother-in-law Contessina and her grandmother-in-law Lucrezia. When she wrote to her husband it was to express disappointment at not seeing him as often as she liked. When the couple were together under the same roof they would, as wealthy members of society, have enjoyed a considerable degree of privacy in their private lives. Even in their sleeping arrangements it would have been customary for husband and wife to have had separate rooms of their own. 'The husband and wife must have separate bedrooms, not only to ensure that the husband be not disturbed by his wife, when she is about to give birth or is ill, but also to allow them, even in summer, an uninterrupted night's sleep whenever they wish. Each room should have its own door, and in addition a common side door, to enable them to seek

236

each other's company unnoticed.' These had been Leon Battista Alberti's prescriptions for a comfortable married life in his 1452 treatise *On the Art of Building*.

For his own part, Lorenzo much preferred to devote any spare time off from the running of the state to his favourite pastimes of hunting and hawking, not to mention his humanist studies and book collecting. Around this time he welcomed into his patronage a Byzantine Greek named Janus Lascaris who had formerly worked for Cardinal Bessarion until the latter's death in 1472. Lascaris joined the ranks of Lorenzo's agents whose sole task was to scour Europe and the Middle East for rare and valuable manuscripts which would be brought to Florence for copying in the Medici scriptorium. These were still the halcyon days for Lorenzo de' Medici. Despite the unfortunate affair pertaining to Volterra his life was still largely devoid of any major international political worries or upheavals. But this was merely the proverbial calm before the storm. To paraphrase what Lorenzo himself had earlier written, youth is a beautiful time but it flies away so quickly, therefore enjoy both youth and happiness while you can for who can say what will happen tomorrow? In 1471 these words were never truer. A cold wind would soon be blowing from the south, from the faithless and venal city of Rome. The days of youth, and beauty and carefree happiness would soon be interrupted in the most deadly way imaginable.

Around this time, Lorenzo received, evidently from Rome, a playful yet portentous letter from a former artistic member of his household, the sculptor Bertoldo di Giovanni, who had been a former pupil and assistant of Donatello's. The artist was a minor talent notable chiefly for his development of a lesser art form, the bronze commemorative medal. In the letter Bertoldo vows to throw away 'burin, chisel, compasses, square, wax, modelling tools, architecture, perspective' and instead take up the art of cookery since Girolamo Riario's untalented chef Luca Calvanese (who had stolen Bertoldo's treasured cookery book) was 'more esteemed by Count Girolamo than all other talents, sciences, or arts, they having obtained for him knighthood.' At the end of this strange piece of correspondence, in which the medal-caster clearly reveals himself to be on somewhat casual and intimate terms with the exalted ruler of Florence, Bertoldo finally added, 'May God send all that court to the devil. I pray Him that I may see the Pope, the Count, and Messer Luca suffocated in a vat full of pepper, and you, *beware of their treachery.*'

CHAPTER 10

The Pazzi Conspiracy

The state of this city was then that while all the good people were on the
side of the brothers Lorenzo and Giuliano and the rest of the Medici
family, a branch of the Pazzi family and some of the Salviati began, first
in secret and then even openly, to oppose the existing government. They
envied the power of the Medici family in public affairs and its brilliance
in private ones, and they sought to destroy it as much as they could.

della congiura dei Pazzi, Angelo Poliziano

On 26 July 1471, Pope Paul II had died, some gossiped whilst being
sodomised by one of his beloved page boys, others putting it about that
he had unwisely been overindulging in watermelon. His pontificate had
achieved little of any lasting value except perhaps in raising the bar on the free
public entertainment enjoyed by the Roman people. It had been Pius II who had
first introduced the law whereby Jews were forced to identify themselves in the
streets of Rome by displaying a yellow handkerchief. His replacement, in August
1471, was Francesco della Rovere, the son of a well-to-do merchant from
Savona in the republic of Genoa whom Paul II had earlier created a cardinal.
Francesco della Rovere, whom many Romans would later disparage as the
offspring of a poor Ligurian peasant fisherman, assumed the name Sixtus IV.

Della Rovere had entered the Curia from the Franciscans where he had
steadily risen to become minister-general of the Order by the age of fifty. He was
generally regarded as being intelligent, pious and studious, having studied
philosophy and theology at the University of Pavia and having also lectured in
these subjects. However his election as pope served to transform his character
from unassuming scholar into nepotistic megalomaniac. Upon his election,
Sixtus IV happily aggrandised himself by commissioning a brand new chapel on
the derelict remains of the old Cappella Maggiore where Pope Nicholas V had
said daily Mass and which had been decorated with frescos by Ghirlandaio,
Perugino and Botticelli. The new chapel was to be designed by Baccio Pontelli
and was built under the supervision of Giovannino de Dolci between 1473 and
1481. It was named for Pope Sixtus IV as the Sixtine Chapel, which later
became simplified to 'Sistine'. As a concession to such vanity projects as his
new chapel, Pope Sixtus also continued the civic minded improvement and
beautification of Rome that had been begun under his earlier predecessors. He
erected a new bridge over the Tiber which he once again named after himself,
the Ponte Sisto. He also widened streets, improved the sewerage system, cleared
slums and founded a new orphanage for Rome's numerous foundlings. In
addition he initiated the now legendary Vatican Archives.

It is from the Italian word for nephew, *nipote*, that we derive the modern word 'nepotism'. As the Romans were soon to find out, if Pope Sixtus IV possessed one flaw it lay chiefly in his extended family of nephews. These largely impecunious and low born Ligurian relatives of his now descended on Rome in their droves and Sixtus was only too happy to indulge their insatiable appetite for preferments. Sixtus's principal favourite was his nephew Pietro Riaro, the son of his sister Bianca and her shoemaker husband Paolo Riario. Like Pope Sixtus, Pietro Riaro had also risen through the ranks of the Franciscans. Upon ascending to the throne of St. Peter, the new pope nominated him bishop of Treviso as well as cardinal and in 1473 he would also create him archbishop of Florence upon the death of the previous incumbent Giovanni Neroni (who, as we have already noted, was the cleric brother of the Florentine political exile Dietisalvi Neroni). Pietro immediately had a villa built for himself on the Janiculum and also commenced work on a magnificent *palazzo* near the church of Santi Apostoli, embarking on a lavish lifestyle which was considered legendary even for decadent Rome. When the daughter of the king of Naples visited Rome in June 1473, Cardinal Riario constructed in the *piazza* outside his own *palazzo* a magnificent faux palace for her to stay in; amongst other attractions it featured a courtyard, fountains, a theatre and a huge banqueting hall. A six-hour banquet was staged for the princess during which more than forty dishes were served including roasted stag, herons, peacocks and even a full-grown bear. Such was Cardinal Riario's extravagant desire to impress that day that even the loaves of bread had been gilded.

Pietro's older brother Girolamo, whom Niccolò Machiavelli later described as springing from a 'very base and vile condition', had even less to recommend him. When his uncle became pope he had quickly graduated from selling raisins in the streets of his hometown to the position of minor customs official. Arriving in Rome he was promptly ennobled as the count of Bosco and promoted by Sixtus, despite his complete lack of military training, to captain-general and *gonfaloniere* of the papal army. A year later he found himself at the court of Milan where he was betrothed to the eleven-year-old Costanza Fogliani, niece to Duke Galeazzo Maria Sforza. Both Francesco Sforza as well as his son had experienced on-going difficulties in having their dukedoms officially recognised by the Holy Roman Emperor. When Frederick III had come to Italy in 1452 for his coronation he had avoided *Milanese* territory altogether and had consequently been denied the use of the Iron Crown of Lombardy from the cathedral of Monza near Milan. That quarrel had spilled over into Frederick's subsequent relations with Galeazzo Maria, who was rather more sensitive about the lack of imperial acknowledgement for his title than his father had been. Despite repeated overtures from Milan's ambassadors the Emperor steadfastly refused to officially recognise the Sforza duke and eventually, in a fit of desperation, Galeazzo Maria had sought to lay to rest all doubts concerning Sforza legitimacy by instead forging a marriage alliance with the new papal family from Savona.

Pope Sixtus had condescended to offer his dissolute, wastrel nephew Girolamo in order to create this nascent alliance and the twenty-nine-year-old had been despatched to attend the *Milanese* court's Christmas celebration in 1472. It was a gathering of generally disreputable characters – present were such notables as Ludovico Gonzaga of Mantua (Costanza's grandfather through her mother Gabriella, who was Ludovico's illegitimate daughter) and Giovanni Bentivoglio of Bologna. Also present was the notorious fratricide Pino Ordelaffi of Forlì, who had not only stabbed his brother Cecco to death to obtain his lordship but who had also poisoned his first two wives as well as his mother-in-law. The express purpose of Girolamo's attendance was to seal the marriage contract with Costanza Fogliani's family. Much to Gabriella Gonzaga's indignation, however, as soon as the marriage contract had been negotiated the debauched Girolamo had demanded to consummate his marriage without further delay. This was unheard of since consummation, the climactic moment when the husband 'possessed' his wife, was but the third and final stage of a formal three-step process that could take anywhere up to a full year or more of complicated preparation, procedure and anticipation. Naturally, the negotiations had quickly broken down with Costanza's outraged parents refusing this request to copulate with their daughter.

In order to salvage the common purpose of their Papal-*Milanese* alliance, Galeazzo Maria had instead offered the hand of his own illegitimate ten-year-old daughter Caterina, whom he had sired by his lover Lucrezia Landriani. The wedding contract was signed in January 1473 and the subsequent wedding, which took place in the Sforzese castle at Pavia with the Duke himself in attendance, was a low key affair involving only a few necessary officials. None could have anticipated how, in later years, Girolamo's child bride would become one of the most remarkable women of the Italian Renaissance, a Virago and a stateswoman with a shrewd and incisive mind for politics and leadership. As she herself would always boast: 'I am not Duke Galeazzo's daughter for nothing: I have his brains in my head'. As for the concupiscent Girolamo, he was permitted to hastily consummate his marriage with the immature Caterina before departing Milan for Rome without his new bride.

Bianca della Rovere's third child, a daughter named Violante, had a nine-year-old son named Raffaele Sansoni Riario who, like his uncle Pietro, was also destined to enter the clergy and would later rise to prominence under the pontificates of Innocent VIII and Alexander VI. Pope Sixtus's brother Rafaello della Rovere, meanwhile, had four sons: Giuliano, Bartolomeo, Leonardo and Giovanni and all prospered under their uncle's papacy. Whilst Leonardo became Prefect of Rome and duke of Sora, Giuliano della Rovere was made cardinal and assumed the same title formerly held by his uncle, Cardinal of San Pietro in Vincoli. Pope Sixtus and two of his nephews, Giuliano della Rovere and Girolamo Riario, may be seen in the famous painting by Melozzo da Forlì. In real life the two young men could barely tolerate each other and therefore, significantly, while Pope Sixtus reposes in the painting like some powerful Roman Caesar, the two young men face in opposite directions turning away from each other, as indeed they were to do in real life. Melozzo's rendering of Girolamo is somewhat flattering, showing a handsome young man, however contemporary accounts of Girolamo's features habitually speak of him as being pale, overweight and generally peasant-like in his appearance. Giuliano della Rovere meanwhile stands slightly taller than Girolamo and faces directly towards the Pope. He is a massive presence with a determined cast in his eye but for some reason Pope Sixtus never seemed to favour him as highly as the feckless and far less competent Girolamo. It was for this reason perhaps that many in Rome scurrilously speculated that Sixtus may have been a closer relation to both Girolamo and Pietro than merely an 'uncle'.

Another sister of Pope Sixtus, Luchina, had a further three children and two of these also entered the clergy, one becoming an archbishop and the other a cardinal. Lorenzo de' Medici would subsequently support Cardinal Giuliano della Rovere during his steady rise to prominence, and Lorenzo's relative Archbishop Filippo de' Medici of Pisa had reassured him that the news of Pope Sixtus's elevation would prove generally positive for the Medici (which only goes to show how wrong such predictions can be). Unlike his predecessor, Sixtus IV was constrained in his foreign policy by serious fiscal problems that had been bequeathed to him by the late Pope Paul II. Paul had emptied the papal coffers by not only embarking upon the divisive war over Rimini but by dedicating himself to the costly pursuit of expunging the powerful counts of Anguillara from the Papal States. Sixtus's relative poverty, which as financiers the Medici would be able to manipulate, would–so Lorenzo hoped–surely mean a period of peace for central Italy and prosperity for the family Bank.

In September 1471, Lorenzo set out for Rome at the head of a Florentine delegation to congratulate the new pontiff on his recent election. Their initial meeting showed every indication that the good relations that the Medici had enjoyed with the Court of Rome ever since Giovanni di Bicci had first bankrolled the antipope John XXIII would continue under the new regime. Pope Sixtus IV, who unlike the anti-humanist Pope Paul II prided himself on being a classicist and a dedicated humanist, made Lorenzo the splendid gift of two ancient marble busts of Agrippa and Augustus and thanked him personally for the support of Florence and the Medici Bank. The Pope also reconfirmed Lorenzo's uncle Giovanni Tornabuoni as depositor-general of the Apostolic Chamber, in effect returning the Medici Bank to the heyday of its previous good fortune at the Court of Rome. Pope Sixtus also extended the Medici Bank's involvement in the lucrative papal alum business.

In addition to state affairs and bank business Lorenzo de' Medici also took the opportunity to make overtures to the Supreme Pontiff on the matter of installing a native-born Florentine cardinal. Ecclesiastical preferment had always been an area in which the wealthy Florentines had inexplicably lagged behind, even in their own city-state (as evidence of this Sixtus was soon to appoint his own nephew Pietro as archbishop of Florence following the death of Giovanni Neroni in 1473, and even the antipope John XXIII, in debt to the Medici for his entire papacy, had appointed a Paduan as bishop of Florence in 1410). Meanwhile, the archbishop of Pisa, Filippo de' Medici, was never quite able to secure a cardinal's hat for himself and for the family. Having a Florentine elected as cardinal would provide some long-awaited balance and privately Lorenzo had already earmarked his younger brother Giuliano as the pre-eminent candidate for such an honour.

On the surface the worldly and carefree Giuliano seemed an unlikely candidate for the College of Cardinals. Like Lorenzo in his earlier years, Giuliano's time was taken up with pleasant diversions such as hunting, falconry and womanising with his devoted entourage. He was enjoying his years as Florence's golden boy with all his heart and soul. His main diversion seemed to be mooning over the beauty of all Florence, the *Genovese* noblewoman Simonetta Vespucci, who was known as *la bella Simonetta* and whose cousin Ginevra Vespucci also held a particular attraction for his brother Lorenzo. But Giuliano's worldliness would not prove an unnecessary barrier to his advancement within the Church, the reality being of course that the institution of the papacy was a worldly institution dominated by the sons of the most prominent families of Italy. It was usually the practice for a second or third son to enter the Church and those of high birth could, with the right amount of behind-the-scenes family lobbying, expect rapid advancement to the Sacred College. Aside from Archbishop Filippo de' Medici the family had no other major representative in the Church at that level, despite the fact that the Court of Rome was one of the family bank's most lucrative business silos. A well-placed cardinal at the Curia would be invaluable, for instance, in lobbying for new papal contracts or maintaining the Medici Bank's existing business. It was also a continuation of the same 'internationalising' strategy that had led Lucrezia Tornabuoni to select a prestigious Orsini bride for her son Lorenzo. Giuliano for his part had already demonstrated his ability to deputise for Lorenzo when he was away from Florence, and a state visit that his younger brother would later pay to Venice in 1472 would prove an unmitigated success, despite Lorenzo's reservations as to his younger brother's readiness for such a responsibility.

Back in Florence Lorenzo found himself blindsided, however, when in December 1471 the list of new cardinals was published and revealed that the only two elevations to the Sacred College had been Pope Sixtus's own nephews: Pietro and Giuliano della Rovere. It soon became plain to all that the new pontiff intended to pack the Sacred College with his own low-born Ligurian relatives. The strong paternal instincts he showed towards his wayward nephews, especially the two sons of his sister Bianca, could be traced to his days as a struggling friar. Bianca's husband Paolo had supported him financially during this difficult time and had even hired him to tutor his sons Pietro and Girolamo. Sixtus was to write to his brother-in-law: 'I well know that to you, after God, I owe it that I have become what I am; I will show myself grateful; let me have your son Pietro for my son: I will give him the best possible education, and make a notable man of him'. The story of Pietro Riaro's rise and rise is surely an object lesson in Church nepotism and ecclesiastical luxury the likes of which Martin Luther was later to fulminate most earnestly against. Like other Churchmen of the period, Pietro piled benefice upon benefice, few of which he had any intention of ever setting foot in, while his income skyrocketed. Within a couple of years his annual ecclesiastical revenues were said to be in the region of 60,000 ducats, which is how he was able to organise such lavish entertainment for a princess of Naples and barely bat an eyelid at the ruinous cost.

Much to Lorenzo de' Medici's increasing frustration, the Pope seemed therefore to be pursuing a studiously self-interested policy of packing the College of Cardinals almost exclusively with della Roveres and Riarios. In November 1472, Lorenzo was compelled to write to the Pope reminding him of his earlier undertaking to create a Medici cardinal: 'Sanctisimme et Beatissime Pater,— To avoid troubling your Beatitude I have written to Giovanni Tornabuoni and told him to talk with you about the long-standing desire of our house to have a Cardinal. Although I have such entire faith in Your Sanctity that I am sure it is needless again to solicit what was so freely promised.' By April 1473, the news spread that Pope Sixtus intended to create a fresh batch of cardinals in consistory the following month. From Rome, Jacopo Ammanati the cardinal of Pavia wrote reassuringly to Lorenzo: 'It will not be long before the Holy Father will be obliged to make new Cardinals, particularly for those States which have none. You, for instance, are without, which for many reasons is unseemly.' Cardinal Ammanati then went on to add, 'There has been much talk here of your Giuliano, and by fishing at the fountain-head I find he has been mentioned in the proper quarter.' Nevertheless, in the consistory held on 7 May

1473, none of the eight new cardinals created by Sixtus turned out to be a Medici, or even for that matter a Florentine.

On the hapless Girolamo's shoulders Sixtus meanwhile placed the burden of advancing the family's secular ambitions. Sixtus planned to use his pontificate to set Girolamo up as a great feudal baron within the lands of the Papal States in the Romagna. This was done in the hope that, together with his young, noble-born *Milanese* wife Caterina Sforza, Girolamo would found a dynasty which would project their family name far into the future.

Although the title count of Bosco had been a beginning for Girolamo Riario it was hardly grand enough to suit Pope Sixtus's aspirations for his nephew, even if that same nephew had been hawking dried fruits on the grubby streets of Savona only a few years before. The town which the pontiff settled on as the next stage in Girolamo's aggrandisement was Imola, one hundred miles north-east of Florence across the Apennines. Imola and its proud citizens, the *Imolesi*, had previously been under the seigniory of the *condottiere* Guidantonio Manfredi, who had captured it during Florence's war with Milan in 1425-6, and had passed upon his death in 1448 to his son Taddeo Manfredi. Taddeo was afflicted with serial family problems, being in conflict both with his uncle Astorre II Manfredi, lord of nearby Faenza, as well as his son Guidoriccio. Captured and imprisoned briefly by Roberto da Sanseverino, he was freed only to have the *Imolesi* themselves rebel against him in May 1473, following which he agreed to exchange the seigniory with Galeazzo Maria Sforza for the lordship of a less troublesome town.

When the Florentines learned that Milan had acquired Imola it became incumbent upon Lorenzo de' Medici to enter into negotiations with the Duke to purchase the seigniory for the republic of Florence. Although located within the Papal States, Imola was regarded as being within Florence's sphere of influence and moreover straddled the crucial trade route between Florence and Venice; it was therefore only natural that the *signoria* should look to expand the commune's influence by annexing this small but important town of 7,000 souls, just as Florence had annexed other, closer settlements like Pisa and Volterra. Unlike those other territories, however, the *Imolesi* were of an entirely different breed. Living as they did off the sparse, unforgiving land of the Romagna they were tough and resilient and spoke the vulgar Latin of the Roman empire known as Romagnol instead of the various Tuscan romance dialects more common to the Florentines. Galeazzo Maria accepted with alacrity the sale of Imola to Florence and charged a 50,000 ducat 'transfer fee' on top of another 50,000 ducats to defray the 'expenses' which he claimed he had already incurred in the administration of the town. It was a hard bargain from his *Milanese* friend but Lorenzo considered the price a worthwhile sacrifice for the further projection of Florence's mercantile power in central Italy.

Florence and Lorenzo had, however, bargained without Pope Sixtus IV who–like many other rulers of northern Italy–had been outraged by Milan's acquisition of Imola from Manfredi and was furious when he learned of the deal which the duke of Milan had subsequently struck with Florence. He immediately intervened, seeking his own separate contract to purchase Imola and manipulatively threatening the Duke with possible excommunication should he go against his wishes in this matter. To Lorenzo's disgust, he was forced to stand by as Galeazzo Maria caved in to the pontiff's harassment and agreed to transfer the town for a heavily discounted price of 40,000 ducats, which had been negotiated by Cardinal Pietro Riario, who had travelled north to Milan to conclude the transfer. The conclusion of the Imola deal on 23 October 1473 marked the point at which the Medici, after decades of having assiduously cultivated the papacy, experienced a sudden and decisive rift with the Court of Rome. Florence's ambassador to Imola throughout this entire sorry affair was a highly capable professional diplomat by the name of Guido Antonio Vespucci, yet even his tireless efforts were inadequate at this point.

As if to further rub salt in Lorenzo's wounds, Sixtus now asked for a 40,000 ducat loan from the Rome branch of the Medici Bank for the town's purchase (despite already having a 10,000 ducat overdraft with the bank). Lorenzo had to consider this request very carefully; the imbroglio in which Sixtus had placed him through this demand created a dangerous conflict of interest between his family business and the state affairs of Florence. To grant the loan might restore the Medici Bank to the good graces of the Supreme Pontiff, but it could also be construed by the *signoria* as being contrary to Florence's political interests. On the other hand, to refuse Sixtus the loan might assuage the displeasure of the *signoria* but it would inevitably inflame the anger of a powerful enemy, the Pope. It was an impossible lose-lose situation and after deep reflection Lorenzo found that he could not do other than decline the Pope's application and send the politically-correct signal that the Medici were properly in step with Florence's government in this affair. Naturally, given the Pope's unforgiving temperament, Lorenzo's decision sounded the death knell for relations between Sixtus and Lorenzo and the former lost little time in seeking the loan from a rival Florentine bank run by the Pazzi family.

In January 1474, not long after his return from Milan, Sixtus's twenty-eight-year-old nephew Cardinal Pietro Riario suddenly fell sick and died. His two-year stint as one of Rome's most highly paid ecclesiastics had allowed him to indulge his appetites to the very limits of his (and everybody else's) imagination. During his final visit to Milan in 1473, for example, he had been accompanied by a two-hundred strong entourage and had been given a sumptuous welcome by Galeazzo Maria Sforza which had encompassed much pomp, extravagance, hunting parties and seemingly endless banquets, entertainments and amusements. Devastatingly successful with women, Cardinal Pietro had charmed the noble ladies of Milan with his easy charisma and worldly humour and his new sister-in-law Caterina Sforza had been much enamoured of him, reciting verses of welcome in Latin while Pietro flattered her in return. During his private moments he had even taken Galeazzo Maria aside and suggested that the Duke create himself king of Lombardy. Such a move would enable him to sponsor Pietro to advance on Rome with Lombard troops and seize the papal throne for himself. His uncle Pope Sixtus had strongly implied that he would be willing to yield to Cardinal Pietro in the interests of transforming the papacy from an elective monarch into a hereditary dynasty based around the Riario and della Rovere family.

Suddenly, however, Pietro's illustrious cardinalate and the extreme ambition that it foreshadowed came to a premature end. Pietro's elaborate marble sepulchre in the Church of Santi Apostoli continued his short-lived but prodigious flair for indulgence beyond the threshold of death itself. An effigy of the late cardinal is depicted supine on a bier above a decorated sarcophagus. He also appears a second time in the relief above his effigy, being incongruously presented by Saint Peter to the Virgin and Child while his brother Girolamo kneels at the right with Saint Paul. The Supreme Pontiff was devastated at his favourite's death and, whilst his affections were now transferred to the lesser brother Girolamo, who had in the meantime been designated as count of Imola, the blow must have further hardened his heart towards Florence at this sensitive moment. Pietro's brother Girolamo wasted little time in appropriating the dead cardinal's vast wealth, which now legally escheated to him, and together with his new lordship of Imola this unexpected windfall now made him even prouder and more insufferable than ever. This also no doubt gratified Galeazzo Maria Sforza, who now found himself in possession of a considerably more prosperous and important son-in-law at the Court of Rome.

Following their marriage ceremony, Girolamo's child bride Caterina had, as we have noted, not accompanied him back to Rome. While she remained behind in Milan for three years to mature properly, he happily busied himself with his various Roman mistresses, siring a bastard child named Scipione in the interval. Neither did the new count of Imola deign to visit his fiefdom to take formal possession. Instead he loafed in the Eternal City effortlessly adding to his ever-growing list of enemies. The latest to take a dislike to the count of Bosco and Imola were the working class citizens of Trastevere who described him as *malizioso* and *birichino*, a cunning rogue who was not to be trusted an inch. Riario was going to be a difficult and contentious lord for the Florentines to have to tolerate, perched as he was right at the edge of their territory. However Girolamo was by no means the only potential cuckoo in the Florentine nest for his brother Cardinal Giuliano della Rovere had lately arrived outside the walls of Città di Castello at the head of a papal army.

Città di Castello was another of those Romagnol towns like Rimini, Forlì or Imola which lay ostensibly within the jurisdiction of the Papal States but had established a considerable degree of independence during many years of benign papal neglect. Like Imola it was also regarded by the Florentines as coming within their de facto sphere of influence. Città di Castello was contested by two rival clans the Vitelli and the Giustini but Pope Eugenius IV had previously adjudicated in favour of the former, making Vitelozzo Vitelli *signore* of the fiefdom. Following Vitelozzo's death his son Niccolò made the town a virtual protectorate of Florence. The *capo* of the rival clan, Lorenzo Giustini, began a lobbying campaign with his friend and confidante Girolamo Riario and, as a result, Pope Sixtus had ordered Cardinal della Rovere to capture and restore Città di Castello to the bosom of the Papal States and reinstate the Giustini as its 'rightful' papal vicars. Giuliano della Rovere, who always seemed more comfortable on horseback and clad in armour than he did wearing clerical vestments, had already been making progress through the Romagna pacifying such unruly towns as Spoleto and Forlì for the Holy Father in Rome. He now drew up his forces beneath the city walls of Città di Castello on 24 June 1474.

Desperately, Niccolò Vitelli called upon his patrons Florence and the Medici to come to his town's relief and Lorenzo made urgent overtures to his allies Galeazzo Maria in Milan and King Ferrante in Naples. Whilst he found the *Milanese* duke hopelessly vacillating, the response of the Neapolitan king was to deploy his own troops alongside those of Cardinal della Rovere's. Lorenzo's relationship with the fickle King Ferrante had lately been eclipsed by a fresh alliance between Naples and the papacy, which was the result of Sixtus's own recent backroom lobbying with the *Regno*. Lorenzo also found himself constricted by Sixtus's practical *Milanese* connections, facilitated by the recent dynastic marriage between Girolamo Riario and Caterina Sforza. Hopelessly isolated over Città di Castello, Lorenzo now went through the disinterested motions of despatching 6,000 Florentine troops to Borgo San Sepolcro to threaten della Rovere's flank but in reality his gesture carried no teeth and even less conviction. Then, another former Medici ally, Federigo da Montefeltro, also came down and sided with the Pope. When Federigo arrived at Città di Castello with his own private army the town quickly grasped the futility of its situation and capitulated. Combined with the recent problems over Imola, the Città di Castello affair had been another shameful climb-down for Florence and, in light of its inability to shield its clients the Vitelli family, the republic was seen by its other dependencies as being incapable of defending them in the face of a determined aggressor. Considerable diplomatic prestige had been lost.

Lorenzo's defiance now made the Pope fully resolved to twist the knife to the hilt. Having twice wounded the Medici politically, he now had it within his capability to threaten the dynasty financially as well. On 16 July 1474 the inevitable happened and Pope Sixtus IV transferred the Court of Rome's banking business from the Medici Bank to the rival Pazzi Bank. This in itself was devastating enough as the Court of Rome traditionally supplied the lion's share of the Medici Bank's profits, but shortly thereafter Sixtus also took the equally unwelcome measure of auditing the Medici's papal alum accounts, an immeasurably insulting action which deeply offended Lorenzo, prompting him to complain to the pontiff that the Medici Bank had serviced the Court of Rome for over a hundred years without an audit. At this point Girolamo Riario also became involved and he now joined his uncle the Pope in asserting that Sixtus was well within his rights to review the Medici Bank's alum accounts regardless of the vigorous protests of Lorenzo and Giovanni Tornabuoni. Even more exasperating than the Pope's behaviour, however, had been the conduct of the Pazzi family themselves.

The Pazzi were one of Florence's oldest and most noble feudal families. In 1099 during the First Crusade, Pazzo de' Pazzi earned the admiration of the Crusader Godfrey of Bouillon for reputedly being the first to scale the walls of Jerusalem. In thanks and recognition of this achievement the future king of Jerusalem had vouchsafed the knight a flint from the tomb of Christ in the Church of the Holy Sepulchre and, upon his subsequent return to Florence, that same flint was used to light the altar flame in the city's cathedral each year. The chivalry of the Pazzi continued down through the ensuing centuries. In 1260 during the great Battle of Montaperti between Guelph Florence and their rivals Ghibelline Siena, the standard bearer of the Florentine army had been one Jacopo de' Pazzi. When the Florentine Ghibelline traitor Bocca degli Abati sliced off Jacopo's hands with his sword the wounded knight had bravely continued to hold the commune's banner aloft with his bloodied stumps. The Pazzi themselves had always been Guelphs. Jacopo's son Pazzino took over the family fortunes directly after this and, despite achieving victory for the Black Guelphs over the White Guelphs during the urban factionalism of the thirteenth-century, he too met a grisly end when he was lanced in the kidneys by a rival scion of the Calvalcanti family while he was out falconing with a lone manservant. These events were on-going even as parvenu families like the Medici were drifting into Florence from rustic areas like the Mugello to try their hand at making their fortune in moneylending or as artisans in the newly emerging and increasingly influential guild system. Feudal families such as the proud Pazzi would continue to look down on these nouveau riches at least until the rude awakening delivered by the Ordinances of Justice of 1293. Their solution to the Ordinances was to have themselves declared *nobili popolani* and to begin engaging in trade and commerce, at which they had subsequently flourished.

The Pazzi family *capo* had formerly been Andrea de' Pazzi, who had three sons: Antonio, Piero and Jacopo. Since 1464, the head of the family had been Jacopo. Angelo Poliziano would later unkindly describe Jacopo as 'a man both insolent and ambitious for bankruptcy' who as 'great proof of his shiftiness, never kept his mouth, nor his eyes, nor his hands still'. Jacopo's nephew, Francesco (the son of Antonio de' Pazzi) managed the Pazzi Bank's business interests in Rome. Poliziano tells us that he was 'a man of wilful nature from which arose his enormous arrogance and pride'. Pazzi and Medici coexisted amicably to begin with. Jacopo's brother Piero had, according to the biographer Vespasiano da Bisticci, become good friends with the late Piero de' Medici. It was Francesco's brother Guglielmo, meanwhile, who was married to Lorenzo's beloved older sister Bianca de' Medici. Lorenzo was therefore certainly no stranger to the Pazzi and would have mingled with them socially from at least the age of ten, when Bianca and Guglielmo celebrated their wedding in 1459. Thereafter Lorenzo seemed to remain on fairly good terms with his brother-in-law, visiting Milan with him in 1465 and trusting him with accompanying and assisting his mother Lucrezia during her matchmaking visit to Rome. But Guglielmo's relationship through Lorenzo's sister made him a special case. The rest of the family Lorenzo had begun to scorn, confiding in correspondence to Galeazzo Maria Sforza in September 1475 that the Pazzi only owed their continued prominence to Medici political largesse.

There was no question that the Pazzi were, like all wealthy Florentine families of that period, political animals. The Pazzi patriarch Andrea had, from 1439 to 1472, held regular political office along with his three sons and grandsons; Piero and Jacopo had both held the prestigious position of *gonfaloniere della giustizia* in 1462 and 1469 respectively. Following his term as *gonfaloniere* Jacopo had also been knighted by Tommaso Soderini as a sign of his service and personal distinction. Piero in particular was the shining star of the Pazzi family, much as the handsome and elegantly mannered Giuliano de' Medici outshone his brother Lorenzo when it came to public popularity. When Piero had been knighted by King Louis XI while on an embassy to France he had returned to Florence in the spring of 1462 to much acclaim; he was accorded the honour of being greeted outside the city gates by the commune's knights, doctors of law, ambassadors and other high officials and was triumphantly handed the banner of the Guelph party. Around this time, the letter writer and social analyst Alessandra Strozzi was writing perceptively to one of her exiled sons in Bruges that he should nonetheless avoid doing any business with Piero de' Pazzi. The Strozzi boy had confessed to his mother that he had been impressed with Piero after making his acquaintance, but Alessandra soberly counselled that 'those who are with the Medici have always done well, and if with the Pazzi, the opposite, since they are always destroyed. So be advised.' By the time of his father Piero de Medici's death in 1469, Lorenzo too seems to have noticeably cooled to his Pazzi in-laws, going out of his way to mock them in private and quietly hindering their political advancement when and wherever he could.

Lorenzo's intensifying efforts at marginalising the Pazzi were not always successful however since the political machinery of the *reggimento* was, even now, still far from watertight. What's more the Pazzi had real financial clout;

catasto returns of 1457 showed that the Pazzi were already the second-wealthiest family in Florence next to the Medici themselves. Sometime between 1462 and 1470 they had constructed a *palazzo* to equal that of the Medici in their traditional quarter of San Giovanni and Andrea had commissioned Filippo Brunelleschi to create an exquisite family chapel in the Franciscan basilica of Santa Croce. This was a family to be reckoned with. In 1471, Lorenzo had conspired to keep Jacopo de' Pazzi from the *balìa*, offering instead to place his brother-in-law Guglielmo in the council; this attempt had been thwarted and Jacopo and several of his associates had subsequently been voted in. The Medici party machinery soon tightened the *scrutinies* and, in the next selection round that took place towards the end of 1472, the Pazzi were found to have only three names eligible to be deposited into the electoral *borse*. Interestingly, whilst old Medici stalwarts like Tommaso Soderini had openly shown their disobedience to the *reggimento* by backing support for Venice rather than Milan, it was the Pazzi whom Lorenzo singled out for censure and political muzzling. We can only conclude that by 1471-2 Lorenzo distrusted his in-laws sufficiently to want to distance them from the machinery of the *signoria*.

Lorenzo had shown himself to be remarkably prescient about Pazzi ambition as the Imola affair had subsequently confirmed. After instructing Giovanni Tornabuoni to refuse Pope Sixtus the loan from the Medici Bank's Court of Rome branch, not only did the Pazzi Bank put up the money (despite having been expressly instructed not to by Lorenzo as a matter of state policy) but Francesco de' Pazzi had perfidiously leaked Lorenzo's discreet private instructions to deny the loan to Sixtus. This had of course only served to further inflame the Pope's resentment towards the Medici. These acts of disobedience towards Lorenzo himself, not to mention his disloyalty towards Florence, were typical of Francesco de' Pazzi who inclined neither towards the balanced and astute practical wisdom of his father Jacopo, nor the urbane fellowship of his uncle Piero. Francesco was inflated by that characteristic brand of Renaissance pride and ambition which frequently led to hot heads being prematurely parted from their torsos. Puffed up by dreams of ancient Pazzi greatness and interpreting the complex Florentine political scene simplistically from far-off Rome, Francesco was wholeheartedly in favour of challenging the dominance of the Medici. Not content to benevolently look on and condone Lorenzo's unofficial primacy as *maestro di bottega* or 'boss of the shop' (the Florentines' laconic expression for whosoever happened to be the republic's éminence grise of the moment), Francesco considered that the Pazzi was by now the only family whose reputation was sufficiently exalted to compete with the Medici. In this respect he had sadly forgotten the salient political lessons of 1434, 1458 and 1466 when other *principali* had seen their entire families sent into exile for the crime of daring to pose a direct challenge to the Medici *reggimento*.

The die was therefore now cast and the Medici and the Pazzi looked set to collide at some point in the future with the locomotive force being copiously provided by the curdled papacy of Sixtus IV. If Lorenzo had felt addled at the transferral of the Court of Rome's business to his muscle-flexing Pazzi in-laws, far worse was yet to come. In October 1474, without deigning to confer with the *signoria* of Florence, Pope Sixtus appointed his friend and supporter Francesco Salviati as archbishop of Pisa. The archbishopric, which had formerly been held until his death that same month by Lorenzo's own kinsman Filippo de' Medici, was a key political and ecclesiastical appointment within the Florentine republic and the *signoria* felt deeply offended that their blessing for Salviati's candidacy had not been sought beforehand.

Francesco Salviati was himself a Florentine from a noble family, an educated man as well as a humanist, but upon the death of his father he had relocated to Rome where he felt he would have better chances of advancement under his patron Francesco della Rovere. Angelo Poliziano was even less kind in his characterisation of Salviati than he was of Jacopo or Francesco de' Pazzi, calling him 'an ignorant disparager of every law, human and divine' who was 'ruined by an excess of lust and infamous for pandering'. Salviati himself, however, regarded himself as having an impeccable pedigree and entirely deserving of his prestigious new appointment. But the *signoria* was having none of it. Egged on by Lorenzo (who was no doubt also unhappy that the Pope was stonewalling his entreaties for a cardinal's hat for Giuliano), they countered Sixtus by asserting that even if they had no ultimate authority to veto a papal appointment they did still have the right to deny to whomsoever they chose the right to step foot on Florentine territory. As Pisa was unquestionably within Florence's jurisdiction the *signoria* now took the step of denying Francesco Salviati permission to enter their borders, effectively preventing him from taking up his appointment as archbishop in Pisa. A livid Pope Sixtus retaliated with that predictable weapon of any pope's arsenal, the threat of excommunication. Lorenzo, he declared would be excommunicated and the city of Florence would be subjected to a papal interdict.

In theory at least, a papal interdict had the power to bring the spiritual life of the entire commune to a standstill. Not even Lorenzo would be able to pacify angry citizens who had been denied baptisms for their infants, the sacrament of Holy Communion, the rite of confession, the last rites, or Christian burial on sanctified ground. At the same time the anti-Medici malcontents were uniting; as Salviati himself was a distant kinsman to the Pazzi (one of his aunts happened to be Jacopo de' Pazzi's mother) the ambitious and conniving Francesco de' Pazzi now came within his orbit in Rome, seeking not unreasonably to make common cause with the thwarted *arcivescovo*. These two also came into increasingly regular contact with Girolamo Riaro, who was always eager to hasten to his uncle's side in any dispute with the ever-intransigent (and now clearly recalcitrant) Medici. The cabal was emboldened by the knowledge that, aside from Pope Sixtus IV himself, they could also draw on two especially powerful players: King Ferrante of Naples, who was increasingly keen to see Florence's growing power curbed, and Federigo da Montefeltro, Duke of Urbino, who was by now widely regarded as the foremost *condottiere* in all of Italy as well as one of the wealthiest.

Federigo's daughter Giovanna had recently been married to Pope Sixtus's nephew Giovanni della Rovere, effectively making him part of the Pope's extended family. From the magnificent Palazzo Ducale in Urbino which Maso di Bartolomeo had designed for him, Federigo held court like a scholar-prince. Pietro di Spagna has immortalised the Duke in his study wearing full armour, the Aragonian Order of the Ermine about his broad shoulders, his helmet as *gonfaloniere* of the Church set down on the floor beside him. He reads from a book, *The Writings of Pope Gregory the Great*, as casually as though he is merely taking time out from an on-going campaign whilst beside him stands his young son Guidobaldo, dressed in rich clothing and holding a baton. This is not a man anyone would knowingly wish to cross. 'Look at me', di Spagna's portrait seems to say, 'I am both a fierce warrior *and* exceptionally well-read!'

As the crisis over Salviati's appointment dragged on, Lorenzo attempted ways of defusing the impasse, offering Salviati the pick of alternative sees such as Arezzo, Pistoia or Volterra. Churlishly however, Salviati rebutted all of these suggestions, countering that none of them provided a sufficient income for his anticipated needs and hinting that, under the circumstances, nothing short of a cluster of benefices would truly satisfy him at this stage of the dispute. Salviati meanwhile smouldered with resentment that Lorenzo had kept him away from his lucrative *Pisano* benefice. Lorenzo's friends and supporters assured him on the other hand that he was doing the right thing. His friend the humanist Angelo Poliziano described Salviati as 'an ignoramus, contemptuous of both human and divine law, steeped in crime and disgrace of all kinds'. Frustrated, Lorenzo wrote to his ally Galeazzo Maria Sforza, urging him to intervene on Florence's side and complaining: 'I would think that I could bring about [Salviati's] possession of the archbishopric, but I do not think that I should consent to such a public shame for my own sake, for this city does not deserve the like from me'. He added, with more than a tincture of self-pity, 'Over this offence, if it be one, which is being committed by our entire city, he [the Pope] wants to revenge himself on me alone'.

The Duke was no doubt sympathetic to his old ally but his hands were effectively now tied by his daughter Caterina's marriage to Pope Sixtus's boorish nephew Girolamo Riario. Eventually, by October, even Lorenzo recognised that he had no aces in this particular game and was reluctantly forced to concede to Salviati's appointment at Pisa. Salviati took formal possession of his archdiocese on 31 October 1475. Lorenzo swore bitterly to ambassador Sacromoro that if his Pazzi relations 'continued making trouble for him ... thinking that they had got the better of him in this affair, then he would make them regret it ... and if they refused to live in peace, he would see to it that they recognise themselves in their mistakes.' As if in fulfilment of his own prophecy, in June 1476, a division of the Pazzi Bank under the management of Jacopo's brother-in-law Guglielmo and Giovanni de' Pazzi now acquired the former Medici contract for the papal alum monopoly. Lorenzo's response was swift and vindictive. Using his control of the *signoria* he forced through a bill preventing daughters from inheriting any property left by their intestate fathers. This 'this law made for the occasion', as the historian Jacopo Nardi would later describe it, was seemingly conceived and drawn up with the sole purpose of preventing Giovanni de' Pazzi's wife, Beatrice Borromeo, from inheriting a large family fortune from her father, a member of the wealthy Borromeo clan, who had himself died intestate. Instead of passing to his daughter and her Pazzi husband, Giovanni Borromeo's wealth escheated instead to the late man's nephew, Carlo Borromeo, who had contested Beatrice's claim and who also just so happened to be Medici supporters.

Even Lorenzo's own brother Giuliano was appalled by the openly malicious nature of his intervention in this matter. However, as Lorenzo would have seen it, Giuliano was still young and inexperienced in political affairs, blithely fluctuating between an indeterminate future which led either to the clergy or else to a noble dynastic marriage, and his opinion could therefore be safely disregarded. In the game of vendetta there was no room for pity and Lorenzo himself may have been well aware of his grandfather's ungentlemanly intervention in Agnolo Acciaiuoli's personal affairs. Neither a prince nor merely a private citizen but some intangible hybrid of the two, in seeking to maintain his influence over both the *signoria* and the commune Lorenzo appreciated that he walked a fine line. Playing for high stakes, the Medici found it necessary to fire a timely shot across the bow of Pazzi ambition. Unfortunately, however, for Lorenzo he was on the cusp of losing one of his most enduring political allies and would soon find himself, and his party, standing alone and isolated in uncharted waters.

On 26 December 1476, the thirty-two-year-old Duke Galeazzo Maria Sforza of Milan was cut down on the steps of the Basilica di Santo Stefano Maggiore by three young conspirators who left his corpse riddled with fourteen dagger wounds. Two of the conspirators, Carlo Visconti and Giovanni Andrea Lampugnani, held personal grudges against the Duke. Carlo Visconti was motivated by dishonour, the Duke having allegedly deflowered his sister. Lampugnani was angry over a property dispute with the bishop of Como in which the Duke had refused to intercede. Both men were caught *in situ* and summarily executed by the ducal bodyguards, Lampugnani having fled to the women's section of the church where he tripped and became entangled in the ladies' flowing dresses. The third conspirator, Girolamo Olgiati, who managed to escape the scene of the assassination, was driven by somewhat more idealistic motivations.

Olgiati had studied under the *Bolognese* humanist Cola Montano who had previously enjoyed a successful career as a scholar and printer in Milan under the Duke's patronage. After giving offence to certain powerful elements at court, however, Montano had subsequently lost Galeazzo Maria's support and been accused of 'corrupting' the family of an unnamed count. Summoned to the court at Pavia, he was punished by having his bare buttocks whipped in public, a particularly humiliating penalty for the proud academic, following which he was banished from Milan. The deeply embittered Montano had introduced the impressionable young Olgiati to Sallust's book on the Catiline Conspiracy and thereafter Olgiati had developed something of an idealistic fetish for the work, dreaming of emulating those noble deeds by freeing his state from the tyranny and mistreatment of the Sforza family. The three young men had anticipated that their selfless act would be followed by a spontaneous uprising of the *Milanesi* in favour of freedom and liberty. Their hopes, though naïve, were not entirely unfounded.

Under the Golden Abrosian Republic the *Milanesi* had enjoyed a brief, tantalising taste of republican freedom during which the cruelty of the Visconti regime (who could forget the cruelties of the *Quaresima*?) had been temporarily suspended. That experiment had come to an end with the advent of the Sforzese. But whereas Francesco Sforza had proven a sensible, fair and enlightened ruler, his son was the complete opposite. As his reign had progressed the full extent of Galeazzo Maria's madness and depravity had become increasingly apparent to his subjects. Many speculated that the taint of madness carried by the Visconti blood inherited from his mother had been to blame. His raging priapism was by now legendary throughout Italy and he was rumoured to buy and sell the daughters of Milan's nobility at will for his own sexual gratification, discarding the poor girls to his courtiers after he had finished with them. His lust was exceeded only by his cruelty. The Duke had already starved his court astrologer to death for even daring to suggest that his reign would not exceed eleven years (a prediction which, in the event, was

252

proven accurate). When on another occasion a poacher was brought before him, Galeazzo Maria had forced the hapless man to swallow an entire hare, fur included, a meal which had naturally enough proved fatal. Thanks to such lurid stories the Duke was far from loved by his population and was felt to have strayed far from the wise and just rule of his father Francesco.

But whilst the Duke had been feared and hated by the people he had governed it did not necessarily follow that his brutal assassination would lead to their spontaneously rising up in support of the murderers. Rather than stoking feelings of liberty the act instead left people shocked and traumatised. So traumatised were the population in fact that the Duke's corpse was left overnight on the Basilica's cold stone slabs since nobody had the courage to venture out of doors that night and recover the body. The sole remaining killer, Olgiati, was soon apprehended by the authorities and forced to undergo the ordeal of being torn in two from the neck to the groin whilst still alive, the four quarters of his carcass joining those of his co-conspirators above the city gates of Milan. Before the butchers went about their grisly work the twenty-three-year-old *litterato* Girolamo Olgiato declared in Latin to the assembled crowd '*Mora acerba, fama perpetua, stabit vetus memoria facti*' ('Death is bitter, but glory is eternal, the memory of my deed will endure'). While his pupil Olgiato was staking his place alongside the celebrated tyrant-slayers of the Greek and Roman world, Cola Montano meanwhile went on the lam. He was destined to be apprehended six years later in Florentine territory carrying incriminating documents and was put to the rack, whereupon he revealed a wide network of international conspiracy against both Lorenzo de' Medici and Florence. He was subsequently hanged from the walls of the Bargello.

As the decapitated heads of Visconti, Lampugnani and Olgiati glowered sightlessly down from Milan's Broletto belltower, the city was thrown into crisis. What was, on the face of it, clearly the just deserts of an overly-entitled sexual predator sent shock waves across the Italian peninsula. Galeazzo Maria's rightful heir Gian Galeazzo was still but a child. His widow Bona of Savoy assumed the regency but in reality had little time for affairs of state, spending most of her time scandalously closeted with her new 'favourite', a handsome young footman in her household named Antonio Tassino. The more serious business of ruling was left to her chief minister Cicco Simonetta. Cicco, who originally owed his appointment to Francesco Sforza, before transferring his services to the late Duke's son, was an extremely capable administrator and statesman who had taken pains to develop a robust intelligence network throughout Italy and had implemented what was in effect the first diplomatic corps throughout the various courts of Europe. Bona was content to leave the details of rule to Cicco, who quickly established order in the duchy.

However, into the resulting power vacuum stepped the late Francesco Sforza's nephew Roberto da Sanseverino in addition to four of Galeazzo Maria's estranged and exiled brothers, Sforza Maria, Ludovico, Ottaviano and Ascanio, who now returned like hungry wolves to claim their patrimony. Ludovico was often simply known as '*il Moro*', which is often mistakenly thought to be on account of his dark 'Moorish'-looking complexion (on the contrary Ludovico was a fine example of the fair, good-looking Lombard *Milanese* type). In reality, the name derived from his baptismal name 'Maurus' but in adulthood Ludovico would adopt both the Moor's head and the mulberry tree as his personal badge and the artists whom he sponsored were allowed a free rein to creatively interpret both of these devices; a Moorish page would later be depicted for example brushing the robes of Italy in a fresco in Milan's Castello Sforzesco. The colour mulberry would also meanwhile become *à la mode* among the ladies of the Moro's court and was commonly adopted for the livery of Ludovico's servants and pages.

The four Sforza siblings had lately been banished to France on suspicion of fomenting their own plot against the Duke's life and they had quite literally only just arrived in exile when news arrived of Galeazzo Maria's assassination. Their argument was that their father Francesco had never intended for their brother Galeazzo Maria to rule alone and that they were meant to have a share in government. It did not take long for the five men to initiate a fresh conspiracy against both Cicco Simonetta and Bona, who had tried to lure them away from Milan by inducing Milan's allies to offer them various *condotte*. When Cicco had the Sforza *condottiere* Donato del Conte arrested he divulged details of the brothers' plot and they attempted to rouse Milan's population against their duchess. The rebellion failed miserably and three of the brothers were exiled once again (Ottaviano having drowned in the River Adda as he fled). Roberto, whom Bona regarded as a disloyal ingrate, was outlawed as a rebel. While Cicco was busy foiling the Sforza brothers' plots and fending off their increasingly injurious attacks and assassination attempts on his own person he wrote to Lorenzo de' Medici in Florence, sending the gift of four falcons on behalf of his amorously preoccupied mistress. The symbolism was as clear as day. Milan was threatened by four predators: the Pope in Rome, King Ferrante of Naples, the Most Serene Republic of Venice and the duke of Urbino. Milan, specifically the regency of the new infant duke, was unofficially calling on Florence for a continuation of the help and support which the republic had always shown towards the House of Sforza.

The Duke's murder had created a watershed in Italian geopolitics. '*Oggi è morta la pace d'Italia*' ('Today, the peace of Italy lies dead') had been the Pope's grim though disingenuous pronouncement on the assassination. The unfortunate affair of Città di Castello had already given the lie to the integrity of the triple alliance between Florence, Milan and Naples which had survived more or less intact since Cosimo de' Medici's authorship of the Peace of Lodi in 1454. Strategic differences between Milan and Naples over how best to deal with the late Pope Paul II had already frayed the delicate alliance and Florence, always seeking to walk the path of neutrality and please both sides, had usually ended up giving offence to both. The marriage alliance between the Sforza and the Riario/della Rovere clans had knocked the delicate diplomatic gyroscope for six, whilst Pope Sixtus IV had also managed to sweet talk Ferrante of Naples into preferring the papacy over Florence. The small fortune which had been expended by the late Cardinal Pietro Riario over the lavish entertainments and banquets for Ferrante's daughter Leonora's visit to Rome had apparently been money wisely invested. Particularly so since, upon cancelling the Medici Bank's business, Sixtus had effectively reneged on his overdrafts to the Medici's Court of Rome branch. Ferrante had begun to regard Rome less as a northern barrier to his expansionism and more as a partner against his troublesome former allies to the north. Besides which, Ferrante had always resented Florence's and Milan's close ties with the Anjou of France, who still laid claim to his kingdom. What common ground could Naples possibly still have with such contrary-minded city-states?

The Florentine *signoria* treated the crisis with the gravity which it rightly deserved, calling an emergency meeting on 29 December and despatching Tommaso Soderini and Luigi Guicciardini to reaffirm Florence's support and commitment to Milan. Lorenzo also wrote to Bona that he would sustain the Sforzese duchy of Milan 'as long as he had life in his body, and if that failed, to leave instructions in his will for his sons to do the same'. In other respects, however, during the uncertain year that followed Lorenzo continued to do himself no favours in the arena of foreign policy. When the *Perugino* mercenary Carlo Fortebraccio initiated his unilateral war of ancestral conquest against Perugia and Siena he was countered, in Florence's own backyard, by the papal armies of Girolamo Riario and the duke of Urbino. Although the disruptive *condottiere* Fortebraccio was chastened and forced out of his fortress of Montone by September 1477, Lorenzo himself had stood impotently on the sidelines professing no involvement or interest either way. For his impartiality he still incurred the displeasure of Siena whose seignory put it about that Lorenzo had in fact been behind Fortebraccio's acts of aggression. The fact of the matter was that Lorenzo would have had nothing to gain by stirring up additional problems on Tuscany's borders.

Lorenzo, during this surreal interval, seems to move almost as if in a dream. So much had happened and within such a short span of time: the humiliating climb down over Imola and Città di Castello, Florence's acceptance of Archbishop Salviati, now happily ensconced in Pisa, the loss of the Court of Rome's account as well as the papal alum monopoly, the unravelling of the Peace of Lodi of his grandfather Cosimo, the politically devastating loss of Galeazzo Maria Sforza and the geopolitical uncertainty it had engendered, and finally the business surrounding Carlo Fortebraccio. But all of these diplomatic problems paled into insignificance in relation to an event much closer to home. On a personal level both Lorenzo and Giuliano had been most deeply affected it seems by the death of Florence's fabled beauty and muse, Simonetta Vespucci.

Born Simonetta Cattaneo, she was married in Florence to Marco Vespucci, a distant relation of the future explorer and cartographer Amerigo Vespucci. Lorenzo had taken such a liking to Simonetta that he had made the Palazzo Medici and Villa di Careggi available to the couple for a lavish wedding ceremony and reception. Simonetta had quickly been discovered by the genius Botticelli, although her status as his model for some of his most celebrated works such as *the Birth of Venus* remains unsubstantiated and the topic of much artistic speculation even today. The muse almost certainly became the lover of Giuliano de' Medici at some point. Gay, lively and enchanting, Simonetta Vespucci died on 26 April 1476 at the age of twenty-two. Lorenzo had requested daily updates on her condition throughout the term of her illness and he, Giuliano and all of Florence were profoundly saddened at her passing. Later, around the turn of the decade, the Florentine Piero di Cosimo would paint the ethereal Simonetta in the guise of Cleopatra, her pale breasts bared and wearing a necklace around which is entwined an asp. Behind her, thunderclouds gather in the distance signifying the ominous approach of her own untimely death.

While Lorenzo's grief-stricken mind hazily countenanced his recent defeats and reversals, the conspiracy to remove the Medici from power rapidly gathered momentum in Rome. By 1478 we can be confident that Francesco de' Pazzi had convinced himself that the removal of the Medici *reggimento* could only be achieved if Lorenzo and his brother Giuliano were permanently put out of the way. If the Medici were defeated politically in the *signoria* and exiled, assuming even that the Pazzi could pack the government with enough of their supporters to make this a reality, there would always be the risk of Lorenzo returning to Florence to exact his vengeance as Cosimo de' Medici had done in 1434. The only way was to strike the head from the Medici cobra through a necessary act of political violence. Francesco was quite capable of such an act and Poliziano describes him as 'a man of blood who, when he meditated any design, went straight to his goal, being hindered by no regard for morality, religion, reputation, or fair fame'. Francesco's duplicitous strategy was fully endorsed by Count Girolamo Riaro. Should his uncle the Pope die unexpectedly he was at least cunning enough to know that Florence would probably move to unseat him from his possessions in the Romagna.

The precedent for such an act had already been set the year before by the assassination of Galeazzo Maria Sforza although what it had lacked was the political coordination to follow up the initial deed of 'liberation' with a rapid and efficient assumption of the political levers of power. Lampugnani and his cohorts had acted idealistically and in isolation whereas Francesco de' Pazzi and his anti-Medicean confederates Girolamo Riario and Archbishop Salviati would plan their actions methodically and back it up with the full force of the Pazzi factional machinery within Florence itself. They would also put in place the necessary military elements from outside of the republic so that their coup d'état would be ultimately enforceable. The Medici themselves, so Francesco may have justified to himself, had created the necessary conditions for the conspiracy. In refusing to share power equally with any of Florence's other established families they themselves had mandated that political change could only come about through extreme means. The memoirist Marco Parenti had almost certainly reached the same conclusion earlier in 1466-7 and Niccolò Machiavelli would later share much the same sentiments as well. The Medici had effectively left their political opponents with no other choice or course of action but assassination and open rebellion.

With this in mind the three conspirators now approached an *Abruzzese* soldier in Riario's retainer, Giovanni Battista the count of Montesecco. Montesecco was not only a practical and experienced soldier but he also held high rank within the papal forces, being both the commander of the Apostolic Palace Guard as well as commandant of the Castel Sant'Angelo. They met initially on two separate occasions, first in Archbishop Salviati's residence in Rome, followed by a second meeting in Count Riaro's own chambers. According to Montesecco's own recorded account, the professional soldier remained throughout both diffident and sceptical as the three unlikely allies enthused over their plans to 'tear to pieces both Lorenzo and Giuliano, and to have armed men ready to go to Florence'. Montesecco was bothered not so much by the whiff of treachery itself but by their lack of a firm, workable proposal to remove the Medici brothers. He was also concerned by the plotters' seeming lack of grounded realism in executing the enterprise. The old soldier coolly pointed out to his interlocutors that 'Florence is a great undertaking and the Magnificent Lorenzo is well loved, according to all I know'. To this, Count Riario rebutted that in his own opinion Lorenzo did not seem to be loved and Salviati then condescendingly chimed in, telling Montesecco: 'you have never been to Florence; how things really are there and how Lorenzo is regarded *we* know better than *you*'. Still unconvinced by the conspirators' arguments, the soldier asked what Pope Sixtus himself thought of their plans, to which they replied that the pontiff would fall in step with whatever course of action they decided since 'His Holiness is ill disposed towards Lorenzo'.

To soothe his concerns the conspirators agreed to arrange a meeting between Montesecco and Pope Sixtus, which took place several days later, the record of which the cautious solider faithfully recorded for posterity. In the sumptuous grandeur of the pontifical apartments Montesecco knelt, kissed the Pope's ring and asked whether the Holy Father did indeed sanction this plot to assassinate the ruling lords of Florence. On being questioned in this way, the Supreme Pontiff and Vicar of Christ grew evasive. After cataloguing Lorenzo's long list of transgressions against his holy person, Sixtus asserted that he was in favour of a revolution in Florence that would remove the Medici from power. He was adamant, however, that he wished the death of no man. When the perplexed soldier pushed further, insisting that such a feat may not indeed be possible without incurring certain people's deaths, the Pope was once more obdurate in stressing that he wished to see no fatalities. The audience continued in this vein until finally, towards the end, Archbishop Salviati asked the Pope if he would be satisfied with 'how safely they steered the bark' to which His Holiness said that he was content. In this extraordinary account we therefore see the Pope disingenuously denying his *official* blessing for a proposed act of political murder whilst, like the consummate politician he was, still sanctioning it with a nod and a wink. Of course we only have Giovanni Battista's testimony at the end of the day. The actual conversation may have gone any number of ways and the record of it changed later on for political reasons. The unwilling but heavily cajoled soldier may have changed the Pope's comments to protect his reputation afterwards; he was after all the commander of the Apostolic Guard and ultimately loyal to His Holiness the Pope. More likely still is that Lorenzo de' Medici later doctored Giovanni Battista's confession to avoid making a bad situation even worse by publicly driving the Pope into an embarrassing corner. Whatever lay behind the occlusion, the fact remained that throughout 1478 the plot had attained an impetus all of its own.

To be successful, an assassination plot needs to be based on both attention to detail and the right choice of manpower. During this period, further conspirators were drawn into the inner circle whose job it would be to provide both the intelligence and the personnel to make the enterprise a success. For the manpower, the conspirators looked to the count of Montesecco himself as well as the duke of Urbino and Giovanni Francesco da Tolentino who together would field around 1,500 troops for the enterprise. In terms of inside intelligence they sought out Jacopo di Poggio Bracciolini, the son of the great humanist scholar and bibliophile who had been Cosimo de' Medici's close friend, and who had died some while back in 1459. Despite his father's impeccable Medici connections, Jacopo Bracciolini had been accused of being involved in the political rebellion of 1466 and had been duly exiled from Florence. He would return from exile as the private secretary to Cardinal Raffaele Sansoni Riario, Bianca della Rovere's son, who had been given his cardinal's hat on 22 June 1478 at the tender age of seventeen. It had been decided that the assassination would take place on Florentine territory. In fact it could not have been otherwise for these days Lorenzo clung limpet-like to Florence and wisely shunned foreign travel. Girolamo Riario had already tried to entice Lorenzo to Rome for a state visit, during which he intended to carry out the assassination with all the considerable local resources at his disposal. 'I do not in the least doubt that the Holy Father would receive you with joy' Girolamo had gushed. Lorenzo, however, had sensed insincerity and danger lurking behind Riario's honeyed words and had sensibly demurred.

Another cohort whom the conspirators hoped to have on their side when they made their move in Florence was the Pazzi family *capo* Jacopo de' Pazzi. Jacopo would, in theory at least, be able to mobilise the considerable wealth and influence of the Pazzi in the hours and days following the assassination. The reality, however, was that the patriarch–who was by then in his late fifties–had little stomach for the venture. When Montesecco was sent to Florence to meet clandestinely with Jacopo in a private room at the Albergo della Campagna, the old man had avowed that in no way did he wish to be involved 'because those two, who wished to make themselves lords of Florence, would end up breaking their skulls'. Such defeatism was not what Francesco de' Pazzi and his co-conspirators wished to hear. Returning personally to the city some weeks later, Francesco and Montesecco met again with the hesitant head of the family and somehow managed to win him over to the plot. Jacopo had by now realised that his nephew would act with or without his blessing and so decided to throw his support behind the conspiracy as he was already heavily implicated anyway. Jacopo knew from prior experience of the proscriptions of 1434 and 1466 that anti-Medici rebellions hatched by individuals always had wider ramifications for their entire extended family. If Francesco made his move and failed then the Pazzi would effectively be finished in Florence. It was a calculated gamble and when Francesco reassured him that the plan had the full backing of Pope Sixtus IV Jacopo relented and warmed to the enterprise.

During those two visits to Florence, Montesecco also met with Lorenzo on two different occasions. On the surface he came as an envoy of potential concord from the Pope but in reality his likely intention was to glean some helpful intelligence about the man he had pledged to help murder and get his measure. Against his better judgement Montesecco had felt himself irresistibly drawn to Lorenzo during both of these visits. The Medici ruler was evidently warm, charming and personable and showed few airs and graces. Cordially, Lorenzo conducted him on guided tours of the Palazzo Medici and the Villa di Cafaggiolo, where he endearingly boasted about the agricultural improvements which he had made to the estate. To his soldier-visitor Lorenzo also now spoke amiably of Count Riario. The tough, practical-minded soldier could see that here was not some despotic ogre in the mould of Duke Galeazzo Maria Sforza, nor a spoilt and entitled rich man's son like Francesco de' Pazzi. In terms of the scope of his humanist learning, his humility and his vision not only for his own family fortunes but also for the commune of Florence, Lorenzo de' Medici was fully deserving of the title his respectful people had begun to bestow upon him – *il Magnifico*. If Montesecco began to harbour doubts or regrets about his duplicitous mission he nevertheless kept his own counsel and reported back to his chiefs with the helpful intelligence he had obtained. He also continued to recruit hardy and experienced mercenary soldiers from towns in the Romagna like Imola and Città di Castello.

Montesecco's interactions with Lorenzo nonetheless had the desired effect of lulling Lorenzo into a false sense of security, giving him the impression that Pope Sixtus and his nephew Girolamo Riario were reaching out to him with the proverbial olive branch. The opportunity for reconciliation was implied when Lorenzo was shortly afterwards notified of a visit to Florence by the Pope's seventeen-year-old relative Cardinal Raffaele Sansoni Riario, who would be accompanied by Cardinal Francesco Salviati. The conspirators had alighted on the young cardinal as a convenient and innocuous cover story for the assassination. Cardinal Riario would pay a visit to Jacopo de' Pazzi's country villa at Montughi from whence he would issue an invitation to Lorenzo to come visit him there. The killing would be done either here or else at Lorenzo's own villa at Fiesole well away from the scrutiny (and retribution) of the Florentine masses. The appointed day arrived and Lorenzo rode to Montughi together with his young son Piero and his friend, the humanist poet Poliziano. Giuliano however was unwell that day and remained behind in Florence. Learning that the younger Medici brother would not be joining them, the assemblage of conspirators clustered together for a quick confab and deferred their plans until Giuliano and Lorenzo could both be targeted together in one place.

An alternative plan was now formulated. Knowing that Lorenzo was proud of his collections of various valuable art and craft objects, Cardinal Riario asked to view the Medici treasures housed at the Palazzo Medici on Sunday, 26 April 1478. Following this visit he would officiate at a High Mass in the Duomo. Seeing only the long hoped for papal reconciliation, Lorenzo readily agreed to the proposal and began planning a banquet in the cardinal's honour which would take place immediately after Mass. Both the service and the banquet would be attended by most of the notables of Florence including the foreign ambassadors of Milan, Venice, Naples and Ferrara. It would be during this banquet that Lorenzo and his brother would be struck down and, in full view of the emissaries and envoys of all the most powerful city-states of Italy, the Medici would be expunged from Florence's political life. As Poliziano would later record in his account of the plot: 'The fine young men did not suspect a trap. They got their home ready, exhibited their beautiful things, laid out the linens, set out the metal and leather work and jewels in cases, and had a magnificent banquet ready.' But once again fate intervened and the plotters got wind that Giuliano's condition had still not sufficiently improved for him to attend the banquet. An alternative venue would have to be found. As ill as he was, it was considered that Giuliano would be unlikely to miss the High Mass itself–deemed a politically important event–and so the Duomo itself was finally chosen as an alternative setting for the assassination. This decision was made despite the fact that Florence's cathedral was consecrated holy ground.

The responsibilities were now apportioned between the various conspirators. Francesco de' Pazzi and an adventurer named Bernardo Bandini Baroncelli, who was deeply in debt and beholden to the Pazzi family, would strike down an unsuspecting Giuliano. The more important Lorenzo was reserved for the professional attention of the more experienced soldier Montesecco. Montesecco, however, had experienced second thoughts since having his face-to-face meetings with Lorenzo. Beyond all persuasion, he could no longer be induced to participate directly in Lorenzo's murder, especially in a sanctified place 'where God would see him'. The soldier had from the very beginning harboured doubts as to the wisdom of his superiors' devices and this latest revision in the venue was the tipping point for him. He had no wish to imperil his soul by adding the sin of sacrilege to the crime of murder. Relieved of this duty he was therefore permitted instead to take position with his mercenaries, who would converge on the various city gates in the immediate aftermath of the assassination. Montesecco's squeamishness, though understandable, had not prevented other assassins from striking down their victims on sanctified ground. The fact was that there were plenty of precedents for petty tyrants being slain in church.

Francesco Castelli di Vico was killed in 1387 in the Church of S. Sisto at Viterbo, whilst Galeazzo Maria Sforza had been struck down in Milan's Cathedral. In practical terms alone there was much to be said for conducting an assassination inside a church, which was a setting where tyrants tended to relax and let their guard down. Montesecco, however, was adamant that he would not commit murder on sanctified ground.

The unwholesome task of cutting Lorenzo down would fall instead to two hastily recruited priests: Antonio Maffei, a Volterran Apostolic notary who held the Medici a deep grudge for the brutal sacking of his native city, and Stefano da Bagnone, the parish priest of Montemurlo and tutor and chaplain to Jacopo de' Pazzi's illegitimate daughter. Though both of these men were clerics such was their enmity for the Medici that they were strangely untroubled at the prospect of committing murder inside a church and the fact that any actual real-life experience of taking a life with a weapon was a desideratum was disastrously overlooked. The pre-arranged signal for all the assassins to strike would be the tolling of the sanctuary bell at the elevation of the Host during Mass. This was considered ideal as the eyes of the entire congregation would be downcast in reverence just at the moment when the first daggers found their mark in the unsuspecting bodies of the two Medici brothers. While the bloody deed was being done, Archbishop Salviati would meanwhile proceed together with Jacopo di Poggio Bracciolini and an armed band to the Palazzo della Signoria. Here, this second group would pacify the members of the Florentine *signoria* and occupy the official seat of government. While this was happening Montesecco's professional mercenaries would infiltrate the city and provide military security against any response from the Medici faction. Federigo da Montefeltro would meanwhile position himself not far from Florence with his own troops standing by to lend additional support if required.

Sometime before eleven o'clock on 26 April, the young Cardinal Raffaele Sansoni Riario rode into Florence from Montughi with his retinue and called upon Lorenzo de' Medici at the Palazzo Medici as arranged. He was led through the *cortille* of the *palazzo*, past (appropriately enough) Donatello's bronze sculpture of *David* slaying Goliath, to an upstairs chamber where he was given some privacy to change into his ecclesiastical vestments. Lorenzo seems to have been oblivious that the cardinal would call upon him before the service and, when the young cardinal arrived at the *palazzo*, Lorenzo was already waiting at the cathedral and had to hasten back the short distance to his home to greet him. When the cardinal came downstairs Lorenzo had only just arrived and stood breathlessly waiting for him at the foot of the stairs, a wide and affable smile of welcome on his face. Together they made their way south through the crowded Sunday streets towards the Duomo where Cardinal Riario would celebrate Mass that morning. Lorenzo de' Medici could not be happier. It was a lovely day and, through the cardinal's official visit, he was it seemed finally enjoying the breakthrough of re-establishing cordial relations with the Sixtine papacy.

As they strolled arm-in-arm to Florence's cathedral the townspeople parted for the young Medici statesman and the cardinal in his expensive, finely-tailored vestments. Along the way the banker and the cardinal bumped into a somewhat distracted Archbishop Salviati. There may have been an awkward moment or two; Salviati and Lorenzo had after all locked horns not so long ago. In the event, Archbishop Salviati articulated his greetings but politely declined

Lorenzo's offer to accompany them to the cathedral. Mumbling his apologies, he insisted that he needed to pay a visit to his mother who had suddenly fallen sick. The two dignitaries therefore finished the rest of the short walk alone. Upon reaching the Duomo, Lorenzo walked the cardinal to the High Altar and then turned on his heel and strolled back towards the general congregation which, since there were no chairs that day, mingled freely with each other in the ambulatory, talking, gossiping and catching up on the Sunday morning news.

As the conspirators now noted with alarm, however, Giuliano was still nowhere to be seen. Francesco de' Pazzi and Bernardo Baroncelli therefore left the cathedral and quickly walked the few hundred yards to the Palazzo Medici where they were told that the younger Medici brother was still feeling under the weather and had decided to forgo High Mass. Horrified, Francesco begged to see Giuliano. Finding him resting in his *camera*, or bedchamber, he used all his powers of persuasion to induce Giuliano to rise from his sick bed and attend the service. Giuliano, always affable and anxious to please, relented and agreed to accompany them back to the Duomo; the event was after all an important symbol of political reconciliation between the Medici, Riaro and della Rovere families and his presence would be expected. As it was Giuliano's leg which had been bothering him, Francesco and Baroncelli locked their arms in his and offered him their support as he hobbled rather uncomfortably along the busy street towards the cathedral. Francesco observed that Giuliano had neglected to buckle on his sword. This was good. Putting his arm playfully around his waist and remarking on Giuliano's expanding midriff, he now also detected that the younger Medici brother had also neglected to wear his protective cuirass beneath his robes. This was also very good. When the time came, Francesco and Baroncelli would be able to strike home in the vital parts of Giuliano's unprotected torso.

When they reached the Duomo they took their place at the northern side of the choir together with Giuliano. Across the aisle, about twenty yards away, stood Lorenzo on the right hand side of the High Altar together with his friends Poliziano, Filippo Strozzi the Elder, Antonio Ridolfi, Lorenzo Cavalcanti, a childhood friend named Sigismondo della Stufa and Francesco Nori, one of the Medici Bank's branch managers. The two priests Antonio Maffei and Stefano da Bagnone had taken care to position themselves just a few feet behind Lorenzo himself and were partially obscured by the dense crowd. The choir, one of the most accomplished in Europe thanks to generous Medici patronage, now began to intone as the ceremony began. The assassins stiffened and readied themselves for the chiming of the sacristy bell, gripping the pommels of their concealed daggers tightly beneath their Sunday robes.

Then, the bell rang out as the priest began to raise the Host ready for communion. This was the designated signal. At once the assassins began their cruel assault on the Medici brothers and all was suddenly panic and commotion as knives and daggers flashed in the bright morning sun. Bernardo Baroncelli's stiletto found its prey first and the adventurer now plunged the glinting metal deep into Giuliano de Medici's chest with a cry of: 'Here traitor!' Giuliano's body spasmed at the unexpected assault; he tried to cry out but only a gargle of pain and astonishment seemed to emerge from his throat. Before the reeling Giuliano could recover from this onslaught Francesco de' Pazzi joined in the attack, repeatedly stabbing at Giuliano's unprotected chest and stomach so furiously that in his frenzy he accidentally plunged the dagger deep into his own thigh, leaving him with a nasty laceration. When the two assassins had finished their

261

work, Giuliano's lifeless corpse lay bloody and motionless on the stone slabs incised with no less than nineteen stab wounds.

As Giuliano was being butchered just twenty yards away by Baroncelli and Francesco de' Pazzi, the two embittered priests surged forward to stab Lorenzo de' Medici in the back. One of them, however, ineptly placed his hands on Lorenzo's shoulder to steady himself as he drove the blade home. It was an amateurish mistake that the professional soldier Montesecco would never have made; startled by the man's touch, Lorenzo quickly spun round just as the priest's dagger missed its mark and merely grazed his neck. Comprehending that he was under attack, he instinctively wrapped his cloak around his arm to ward off the priest's knife blows. Lorenzo then drew his sword and parried the two assassins' dagger thrusts. Quickly his friends made a protective cordon around him and began bundling him from the ambulatory towards the relative safety of the New Sacristy. Baroncelli had meanwhile observed the failure of the two priests and now advanced menacingly towards Lorenzo and his companions. Lunging at the slightly wounded Lorenzo with his rapier, Lorenzo's bank manager Francesco Nori valiantly dove in front of Baroncelli's blade and was run through the stomach. Nori's act of self-sacrifice now gave Lorenzo's friends just enough time to drag him into the sacristy and bolt the heavy protective doors behind them.

Inside the cathedral there was general panic as the congregation, few of whom had any real apprehension of what was taking place, fought to find the quickest exit. Women screamed hysterically. Some people were foolishly shouting that Brunelleschi's dome was crumbling and about to cave in on their heads and in the confusion Giuliano's lifeless body was left abandoned in a widening pool of arterial blood. Inside the sanctuary of the New Sacristy, Lorenzo's friends quickly ascertained the extent of his injuries. Fortunately it was nothing too serious. The lacerated neck that he had received at the blundering hands of the priest was the only visible wound so far as they could make out. Nevertheless, the assailant's blade may have been coated in poison so one of Lorenzo's friends, Antonio Ridolfi, bravely sucked the blood from the wound and spat it out onto the stone floor. Lorenzo was frantic for news of his younger brother and kept calling out, asking if there was any word. Sigismondo della Stufa then climbed to the top of the choir loft and peered over. Giuliano's bloodied corpse lay lifeless and abandoned where it had fallen. Florence's beloved golden boy had been slain. For Lorenzo, however, it was not only his sibling but also his innocence which had been slain that day; innocence at having not suspected the motives of the assassins, innocence at having failed to detect the deadly perfidy of the Pazzi family; innocence at having ever placed trust in Pope Sixtus IV.

CHAPTER 11

Naples and into the Lion's Den

The letter written by the Florentines, full of contempt of Christ and of
His unworthy Vicar does not alarm us, but causes us to think that God
has destroyed their intellect and their judgment as a punishment for
their sins.

Pope Sixtus IV to the duke of Urbino

Baroncelli, the most capable of the assassins, had lost no time in making
his exit from the cathedral, quickly finding his horse and immediately
galloping off towards the city gates. The two incompetent priests Maffei
and Bagnone also took wing, this time into the narrow city streets. Francesco
de' Pazzi, bleeding profusely from his self-inflicted stab wound, stumbled home
and collapsed on his bed in a paroxysm of despair, depression and indecision.
The principle target of their plot had somehow, infuriatingly, managed to evade
them. How could this have happened? Everything had been planned so
carefully! With Lorenzo still alive and very much at liberty all bets were off.
Francesco de' Pazzi, the mainspring of the entire conspiracy, was now all too
painfully aware that the full force of the Medici *reggimento* would shortly be
mobilising against him and his family. Yet, dumbstruck and strangely passive,
he did nothing but lay in his bedchamber going over and over the events of the
past hour in his mind.

Back at the Duomo relief had soon come to the small group clustered
around the wounded and badly shaken Lorenzo de' Medici still sheltering inside
the New Sacristy. Some Medici supporters now signalled their presence by
banging on the bronze doors and Lorenzo was quickly ushered outside, passed
the lifeless body of Giuliano–which was mercifully screened from his view by
some thoughtful Medici militiamen–and out into the by now silent and deserted
streets of Florence. But a quarter of a mile across the city another crucial
drama was now playing out. Archbishop Salviati and Jacopo Bracciolini had
made their way to the Palazzo della Signoria with their armed band of *Perugini*
henchmen with the intention of seizing Florence's seat of government. Upon
arrival at the *palazzo*, Salviati spoke to the palace guards on the door,
demanding an immediate audience with the *gonfaloniere della giustizia*. The
guards replied that the *gonfaloniere* was otherwise engaged; he was at that
moment dining with the eight *priori*. Nevertheless, Salviati and his rough-
looking retainers were permitted to enter. The palace guards ushered Salviati
and Bracciolini into a waiting room upstairs whilst his armed guards were
shown into the Chancellery, a separate room which was equipped with heavy
doors and robust locks that could only be opened from the outside (a sensible

263

precautionary measure which was the result of centuries of factional conflict in Florence).

As luck would have it, the current *gonfaloniere* was none other than the capable Cesare Petrucci, the former *podestà* of Prato and the hero of the recent Prato rebellion. In gratitude to Messer Petrucci's decisiveness in putting down the Prato revolt Lorenzo had seen to it that his career had been advanced and he was now serving as Florence's highest government official. When *gonfaloniere* Petrucci entered the waiting room he encountered a visibly abstracted and seemingly incoherent Archbishop Salviati who now proceeded to make some vague speech of which Petrucci could neither make head nor tail. His instincts, however, told him immediately that something was badly amiss. Then, suddenly, Salviati lost his composure altogether and called loudly for his *Perugini* guards who were still at that moment locked inside in the Chancellery. None came running. There was only Jacopo Bracciolini, who now placed himself before Petrucci and made to unsheathe his sword. Before he could do so, the quick-witted *gonfaloniere* 'grabbed him by the hair, threw him to the ground, and called guards to watch him'. In the ensuing commotion, the palace guards were alerted and came running, but when the *Perugini* succeeded in breaking through the Chancellery door there were running battles and sword fights throughout the narrow corridors of the *palazzo*. Disconnected by the numerous doors of the *palazzo* however, 'the chiefs of the conspirators were separated. Thus divided, they lost much of the momentum of their attack.' Salviati's men were soon overpowered and pacified; the seat of government was secured. But as a precaution, Petrucci now ordered that the *palazzo* be barricaded and that an emergency bell, the *Sonare di Palagio*, be sounded to alert the city. Soon the warning peels intoned through the streets of the commune, drawing curious crowds to the Piazza della Signoria to find out what had happened.

The crowd which began to assemble was a mixed bag including both Medici supporters as well as their Pazzi enemies. Soon, the Pazzi family patriarch Jacopo himself arrived in the piazza with a small band of armed Pazzi militiamen. Cantering theatrically up and down on his stallion, Jacopo hoarsely bellowed that old Florentine rallying cry of '*Popolo e Liberta!*' This was supposed to be the cue for the crowd to storm the Palazzo della Signoria. But the *Perugini* had, as we have seen, failed miserably in their attempt to secure the seat of government for the rebels. As Jacopo's men tried to force their way inside they found the heavy doors and windows bolted and barricaded against them whilst, from the brick machicolations above, a steady and unwelcome stream of rocks, crossbow bolts and other projectiles began to pelt them. Watching this gathering fiasco from the *piazza*, the remainder of the uncommitted crowds now turned markedly hostile and some lone voices had begun chanting, hesitantly at first, and then with growing conviction, the old Medici rallying cry of '*Palle! Palle! Palle!*' Soon the entire mob in the *piazza* had taken up the Medici chant in unison and it was clear that the day was lost. In his account of the conspiracy, *della congiura dei Pazzi*, Angelo Poliziano describes Jacopo's despair in these moments: 'He had no success, and in fact, everyone called him an evil man; indeed, his voice was so broken by terror that he could scarcely be heard, and all men held him in contempt and cursed his crime'.

Cursing his nephew Francesco's incompetence, Jacopo rode back to the Palazzo Pazzi only to be informed by his brother-in-law Giovanni Serristori that Florence's people had adamantly refused to be roused in support of their cause. Hurling maledictions he fled on horseback for the city gate of Santa Croce, whose guards he had taken the precaution of bribing sometime beforehand. With the abandonment of the Pazzi patriarch the Pazzi rebellion effectively collapsed but this was as yet unknown to the Medici *reggimento*. At the Palazzo Medici, untold numbers of armed men rushed here and there, gathering weapons from the *palazzo's* private armoury and fortifying the building in expectation of an all-out attack. The expensive and elaborate repast which had been prepared for the two cardinals and other important guests lay untouched and spoiling in the banqueting hall. As Giusto Giusti recorded in his recollections of the event, armed men were stationed in the street to protect the *palazzo* from ill doers; the memoirist himself joined in the action, collecting a breastplate and a sword from the armoury and taking up position outside until five in the morning.

In his *camera*, attended by his closest *familiares*, Lorenzo de' Medici dashed off a diplomatic letter to Bona of Savoy beseeching the Duchess for 'as many men as you can with all speed'. Although Lorenzo could not have known about the proximity of Montefeltro and Tolentino's troops they had to assume the worst and prepare for the possibility that, as in 1466, outside military intervention was on its way. Word was sent to the Medici militia manning the various city gates and the commune now effectively went into a state of lockdown. Crowds began to gather outside the Medici *palazzo*, many Florentines noisily expressing their loyalty whilst other curious onlookers simply came to learn what all the commotion was about. Lorenzo decided it was a good idea to put in an appearance before his loyal supporters and so he appeared at an upstairs window, his neck wound still bandaged and his face visibly pale and drawn. Addressing the people, he called for calm and urged them to allow justice to now take its natural course. As emotional as he must have been by the knowledge of his brother Giuliano's death, Lorenzo would have had no desire to see the city erupt in a spasm of divisive violence and retribution. As Florence's past had shown, mob rule could so easily spiral out of hand and rebound upon the oligarchs themselves. But by now events had progressed past the point of containment and the mob was baying for Pazzi blood.

Giuliano de' Medici had been the golden son of Florence and his murder sparked off a wave of retributive killing by an irate citizenry. A priest who had nothing whatsoever to do with the conspiracy was captured by the angry crowd whereupon the unfortunate man was quartered and decapitated. Other armed mobs roamed the streets of the commune actively seeking out members of the Pazzi and Salviati families. Some of the *Perugini* foot soldiers and crossbowmen under the command of Montesecco had been quickly rounded up. In a macabre twist, random dismembered body parts of 'conspirators' began to accumulate in a grisly heap outside the Palazzo Medici. At the Palazzo della Signoria, meanwhile, the members of the commune's government had not paused for the slow gears of *giustizia* to grind. The *Perugini* who, just hours before, had been engaged in swordplay with the palace guards were lined up on an upper story and, one by one, unceremoniously defenestrated. After their crumpled bodies had piled up on the elevated dais of the *ringhiera* below, the waiting crowd merrily dragged and defiled their lifeless corpses from the Piazza della Signoria through the streets of Florence.

Francesco de' Pazzi, had by now been seized from his bedroom at the Palazzo Pazzi (where, at his wits end, he had been contemplating suicide) and was conveyed, stark naked, to the *signoria*. Here, the stern, scarlet-robed *priori* dispensed with the need for any form of trial and Francesco was hung from the *palazzo* balcony to the jubilation of the mob below. When it came to Archbishop Salviati's turn he was dragged out and offered the chance to make his final confession ('*Sacer, unctus, archiepiscopus sum*' he is said to have uttered: 'I am the holy, anointed archbishop'). Then, he too was hanged from the same balcony, still dressed in his ecclesiastical vestments. In a bizarre and gruesome twist to the day's proceedings the twitching, dying Salviati was seen by eyewitnesses in the *piazza* to sink his teeth into Francesco's corpse which hung lifelessly beside to his own. Other corpses, including that of the archbishop's brother Jacopo Salviati, soon joined them.

When it came to Lorenzo's brother-in-law, Guglielmo de' Pazzi, *il Magnifico* made a special case to the *signoria* to commute his sentence to exile. His elder sister Bianca had personally pleaded for her husband's life, denying (perhaps truthfully) that he had any foreknowledge of the conspiracy. For his part, Lorenzo had been loath to countenance the man's death in view of the happier times they had spent together hunting and on foreign state visits. Guglielmo would merely be confined to his country villa for the duration of the crisis and made to keep in touch with the *signoria* concerning his comings and goings. Guglielmo's relations were considerably less fortunate. Giovanni de' Pazzi, husband to the heiress of the Borromeo fortune, died in prison at Volterra, whilst the seven sons of Francesco's brother Piero de' Pazzi were either hung, condemned to perpetual exile, or else imprisoned for the term of their natural lives.

Less fortunate still was the family *capo* Jacopo de' Pazzi who was cornered several days later in the village of San Godenzo by a peasant farmer. Conveyed back to Florence by ox cart he too was hanged from the balcony of the Palazzo della Signoria. Laid to rest in the Pazzi family chapel at Santa Croce, Jacopo's cadaver was soon disinterred and re-buried next to the city wall. The diarist and apothecary Luca Landucci records what transpired next: 'Some boys disinterred it a second time, and dragged it through Florence by the piece of rope that was still round its neck; and when they came to the door of his house, they tied the rope to the door-bell, saying: "Knock at the door!" and they made great sport all through the town. And when they grew tired and did not know what more to do with it, they went to the Ponte al Rubiconte and threw it into the river. And they sang a song with certain rhymes, amongst others this line: "Messer Jacopo is floating down the Arno". And it was considered an extraordinary thing, first because children are usually afraid of dead bodies, and secondly because the stench was so bad that it was impossible to go near it.' Jacopo de' Pazzi's death and what came after remains one of the less edifying aspects of the conspiracy's aftermath. He had initially tried to talk Francesco out of going ahead but in the end had been railroaded into joining in; but, having made his decision, according to the law of vendetta blood called for blood.

The two incompetent priests were meanwhile tracked down to the monastery of the Badia where the mob subjected them to the Byzantine punishment of *rhinokopia* (their noses were sliced off) following which they were hanged on a gallows that had been hastily erected in the Piazza della Signoria. Giovanni Battista Montesecco was captured next on 4 May. Subjected to torture and interrogated by the *signoria*, the honourable Montesecco salved his uneasy conscience by offering a full confession and gave his Florentine inquisitors a comprehensive account of the history of the conspiracy before being executed by beheading at the Bargello. Montesecco was the only conspirator to be afforded the 'privilege' of being finished off at the customary Florentine place of execution. Presumably too, Montesecco would have been afforded the ministrations of the confraternities known as the *conforterie* or 'companies of justice'. These were comprised of lay people who devoted themselves to spending time with condemned individuals in their cells the night before their execution. Here, they would comfort the doomed and prepare them for their coming death as humanely as possible. Often the *conforterie* themselves were drawn from the highest social ranks and Lorenzo de' Medici was himself a member of the *conforteria* of S. Maria della Croce, who went by the name of 'the Blacks' on account of their solemn black robes. Michelangelo Buonarroti meanwhile belonged to the *conforteria* of S. Giovanni Decollato.

Cardinal Riario meanwhile had taken refuge among the canons of the Duomo during the initial tumult of the assassination. Officials of the government later found him still hunkering there and escorted him to the gaol in the Palazzo della Signoria where he was forced to compose a letter to Pope Sixtus IV detailing all that had taken place that day. The fact that Riario had apparently taken no active part in the assassination, and indeed had failed to join either Francesco or any of the other plotters after the dramatic events beneath the Duomo's cupola, seemed to indicate his essential innocence of any wrongdoing. But, on the other hand, he had spent the past few days lodged with the Pazzi as they had been forced to continually change and refine their plans. The closeted discussions and growing sense of paranoia at their plans becoming public must surely have been enough to alert the young man that a plot was afoot and it is inconceivable to imagine that he was completely in the dark. If he had in fact been wholly ignorant, the Florentines might have said of him 'You are rounder than the O of Giotto' which was a common phrase used to describe slowness or dim-wittedness. Cardinal Riario was probably only saved by his close family relationship with the Pope himself.

Bernardo Baroncelli, the adventurer who had joined the enterprise for personal gain and who had plunged the first dagger into Giuliano, was the last to evade capture. He fled to far distant Constantinople imagining that distance would be his salvation. Here, in the *Genovese* suburb of Galata across the channel known as the Golden Horn, he took refuge with some relatives. But the long arm of Florentine law knew no bounds. The authorities in Florence eventually learned of his location through their international intelligence network and, through the offices of Florence's consul in Galata, Lorenzo Carducci, they entered into negotiations with Sultan Mehmet, with whom the Florentines were on reasonable terms. The *signoria* was soon able to triumphantly announce: 'By letters of Bernardo Peruzzi [Carducci's associate] we have learned with great pleasure how that most glorious prince [Mehmet] has seized Bernardo Baroncelli, most heinous parricide and traitor to his country, and declares himself willing to do with him whatever we may want — a decision certainly in keeping with the love and great favour he has always shown toward our republic and our people as well as with the justice of his most serene Majesty'. A Florentine representative embarked for the Ottoman capital to make the necessary arrangements with Mehmet and returned with Baroncelli in his custody on 24 December 1479. Five days later, he too was hanged from the walls of the Bargello. One of the public spectators on that day, Leonardo da Vinci, made a pencil sketch in his notebook of the dangling corpse.

Lorenzo de' Medici thanked Sultan Mehmet by commissioning a medallion in his honour designed by his friend, the sculptor Bertoldo di Giovanni.

Giuliano de' Medici had meanwhile been laid to rest on 31 April 1478 in a service attended by most of Florence. Lorenzo lost no time in using this opportunity to send an unambiguous political signal to the Florentines. Giuliano's funeral was deliberately austere, as Piero and Cosimo de Medici's had been, and furthermore he was buried on the same day as Francesco Nori who had loyally sacrificed his own life to redeem that of his employer's. Lorenzo was re-affirming the Medici's ties with the republic and reminding the Florentines of their origins in good, solid, unpretentious mercantile stock. Indeed, the funeral of Giuliano's erstwhile love interest Simonetta Vespucci had proceeded with far more grandeur than his own. Angelo Poliziano lamented the misfortune which had befallen on his patrons: 'From this great upheaval of human affairs I am directly warned about the fickleness of fortune', he would later write. Echoing Virgil's *Georgica*, Poliziano then went on to compare Giuliano and Lorenzo with Julius Caesar and Augustus: 'We pray to God most high and most good "that at least that this young man [Lorenzo] be not hindered from helping this shipwrecked age"'.

Amidst the tragedy and gloom Giuliano had, however, succeeded in leaving behind him a more hopeful legacy. He had impregnated a woman of humble means named Fioretta Gorini seven months earlier and in June she gave birth to a healthy baby boy who was christened 'Giulio' in remembrance of his father. This child, fathered out of wedlock, was taken under the full protection and love of the House of Medici and was raised by Lorenzo alongside his own boys Piero, Giovanni and Giuliano. Like Lorenzo's second son Giovanni, Giulio was later destined to enter the Church, sponsored by his powerful adoptive family. Like his cousin Giovanni, he would eventually rise to the highest ecclesiastical rank imaginable. But even as Giuliano was still being entombed the vendetta against the Pazzi continued. Their banking and business assets were confiscated, their *palazzi* were appropriated and even the tombstones of their ancestors were systematically erased. Pazzi women were hereafter forbidden by order of the *signoria* to marry and the jewels, gemstones and personal possessions of Jacopo's pampered daughter were impounded by order of the *signoria*.

The public humiliation of the Pazzi did not end here, however. In the aftermath of the Pazzi Conspiracy, Lorenzo de' Medici would use art to pursue a propagandistic political agenda. Firstly, a decree was issued in 1478 that all Pazzi coats of arms around the city were to be destroyed. Next, to commemorate the infamy of the Pazzi and their confederates, Sandro Botticelli was commissioned to draw sketches of the corpses left dangling from the walls of the Palazzo della Signoria, which he later reproduced in life-size frescoes painted on either a wall of the Bargello or a wall of the Dogana, part of the government-complex. Those depicted were Francesco de' Pazzi, Bernardo di Bandino Baroncelli, Archbishop Salviati, Renato de' Pazzi, Messer Jacopo de' Pazzi, Antonio Maffei and Stefano de Bagnone. Nobody passing through the *piazza* on their daily business could miss this grim and macabre painting. Botticelli's frescoes especially angered Pope Sixtus IV who arguably had masterminded or at least acquiesced to the attack in the Duomo. Sensitive to Lorenzo's propaganda coup he called loudly for the portrait of Archbishop Salviati to be removed at once (the offensive cameos were only removed much later at the behest of Pope Alexander VI in 1494). This was not the only example of state propaganda indulged in by Lorenzo, for a commemorative medal cast in bronze by Bertoldo di Giovanni had depicted the assassination of Giuliano from two separate perspectives. Above both scenes loomed the dominating portraits of Lorenzo and Giuliano de' Medici themselves. Beneath their faces were inscribed the words 'Public Mourning' on one side and 'Public Safety' on the other. The medal was commissioned with a view to its being widely propagated within Florence, a reminder to the people that the Medici and the state were effectively one and the same entity.

The dramatic social and political downfall of the Pazzi in the aftermath of their failed conspiracy may have assuaged the Medici family's anger and their basic desire for retribution but, on a practical level, it hardly even dented the wider international problems that Florence now continued to face. The Pazzi had been the feckless instrument of Pope Sixtus IV's bitter vendetta against the Medici and the errant clan's removal from the picture did nothing to eradicate either the Pope's venom or his desire to see the total elimination of Florence's first family. Sixtus complained most vocally that Florence's hanging of the archbishop of Pisa in his full ecclesiastical vestments had been an outrageous challenge to the sanctity of the Church. His argument, flimsy as it was in view of Salviati's well-defined secular act of sedition against the Florentine state, was that priests could only be tried under Church jurisdiction. By making an example of Archbishop Salviati the Florentine *signoria* had flouted the very authority of the Church to try their own. Such an insult to the papacy, to Christendom, and to the established order itself could not go unpunished. It was a high-handed and sanctimonious posture in which the Pope could nevertheless feel confident of calling upon the support of other Christian countries and city-states to bring disobedient Florence to heel.

Moreover, the Pope's nephew and attack dog Girolamo Riario was also still very much at liberty, even if his fellow conspirators were by now either captured or dispersed, and he now demonstrated his ability to cause the Florentines continued harm from a prudently safe distance. Count Riario's first move was to have the Florentine ambassador in Rome, the eminent humanist Donato di Neri Acciaiuoli, hauled from his house by an armed guard of 300 soldiers and thrown into the Castel Sant'Angelo 'where', lamented the Florentine chronicler Vespasiano da Bisticci, 'he was imprisoned against all the customs of diplomacy'. Ambassador Acciaiuoli was soon the subject of numerous petitions and entreaties by his colleagues in the Italian and foreign diplomatic corps. Despite the Pope's attempts to persuade his nephew to allow the ambassador to go free he proved his base nature by sticking obdurately to his guns.

To neutralise the Pope's threat Lorenzo briefly considered using as leverage his hostage, the Pope's great-nephew Cardinal Raffaele Sansoni Riario. This gambit, however, had little merit in terms of public relations value and inevitably Lorenzo was soon inundated with petitions from most of the courts of Europe urging him to release the feckless young priest to the bosom of his great-uncle the Pope. This he finally agreed to do in June 1478 in exchange for his incarcerated ambassador Donato Acciaiuoli, but the whole process of setting up the prisoner exchange proceeded exceedingly slowly. By the time that the young cardinal reached Siena and freedom it was said that he had taken on the colour of paper and, until the end of his days, would never lose this deathly pallor. Donato Acciaiuoli, upon safely reaching Florence, was reassigned by the signoria as ambassador to Milan and Paris and the former ambassador to Imola, Guido Antonio Vespucci, was despatched in his place to Rome. However, instead of salving the Pope's fury all the gesture of releasing Cardinal Sansoni Riario succeeded in doing was to free the Holy Father's hand to now pursue an unrestrained policy of vengeance against Lorenzo and the Florentines. This came, on the day immediately after Cardinal Raffaele's release, in the form of a personal excommunication for Lorenzo direct from the papal court.

The damage of excommunication cannot be underestimated; through such means popes down through the centuries had destroyed the power of errant emperors, kings and princes by placing them beyond the succour of Holy Mother Church. Kings held their lands at the behest of the Pope who, according to the juristic metaphysics of the era, held the entire world as the proxy of Jesus Christ, the King of the Earth until he returned at the time of the earthly resurrection and Last Judgement. If a king was therefore excommunicated by the Pope, his liege lords and subjects were absolved from their duty to obey him; he consequently lost his place in the 'natural order' and was cast out into a kind of princely purgatory. If the pope of Rome was able to neutralize powerful kings and princes in this way, how much less could a lowly merchant-banker like Lorenzo de' Medici resist such a devastating denunciation from Christ's proxy on earth? In any staunchly Christian community it was usually the case that nobody would even associate with an excommunicant and indeed it was often dangerous for them to do so.

To make matters worse Sixtus had also couched his bull of excommunication in a lurid string of personal insults to Lorenzo himself, referring to him as 'that son of iniquity and foster-child of perdition' whose crime was 'kindled with madness, torn by diabolical suggestions'. In a fit of adjectival exuberance, Lorenzo was pronounced 'culpable, sacrilegious, excommunicate, anathematized, infamous, unworthy of trust and incapable of making a will'. Sixtus had, for the time being, taken care not to place Florence itself under a papal interdict. In so doing he hoped to drive a wedge between Lorenzo de' Medici and the people he governed. Provided the Florentines gave up their errant leading citizen, who had sinned against both heaven and the papacy, they would still receive the benefactorial succour of the Blessed Church, military action would not be forthcoming and life would go on for them as usual. There was a two-month deadline by which Florence was expected to respond to the papal ultimatum to bring the miscreant to punishment, after which the entire city could expect to be placed under a similar interdict. This meant that Florence would be stripped of its archiepiscopal and pontifical privileges and its lands and towns placed under papal control. Furthermore, Florence's neighbouring dependencies and dioceses such as Fiesole and Pistoia would share a similar fate. Writing to Tommaso Soderini, Lorenzo expressed his growing pessimism about the situation: 'Letters from Rome show that although the Pope knows that Cardinal Riario has been set at liberty, he shows no disposition to raise the excommunication or the interdict. This is a bad sign and makes one believe that he will do all in his power to injure us. We shall see what will happen and are determined to defend ourselves as well as we can.'

As Florence was currently threatened by the combined military forces of Rome and the Papal States, Naples, and the duchy of Urbino, Pope Sixtus's calculation was of course based on the practical-minded assumption that the people of Florence would prefer to put the emergency behind them and get back to their peaceful everyday lives as quickly as possible; the abandonment of Lorenzo de' Medici would, he surmised, be but a small price to pay for this. But His Holiness's reading of the national character of the Florentines could not have been more misinformed. What the citizens of the Florentine republic loathed above all else was outside interference in their domestic affairs by foreigners. In this regard the Pope was not considered the head of Christendom but just another secular ruler of a city-state which, jealous of Florence's economic success, now saw fit to meddle in Florence's business. Popes had always trodden with care the fine line between the spiritual and political realms and many a time a pontiff's position had become untenable through venturing too far into the secular world of power politics. Furthermore, in murdering Giuliano de' Medici the Pope's conspirators–led by local traitors the Pazzi–had slain the city's golden son, a young man who was almost universally adored by the *popolo*. This had caused deep offence, not least in the bloody and outrageous way in which the assault had taken place within the sacred confines of the city's cathedral. No, the people of Florence would stand solidly behind the surviving Medici son Lorenzo in this unseemly papal vendetta. As Pope Sixtus IV issued his bull of excommunication on 1 June, the young Medici ruler found himself overwhelmed outside his *palazzo* on the Via Larga by adoring mobs of Florentines of all social classes, eager to express their fervent support for their first citizen.

On 12 June, Lorenzo staged a piece of political theatre designed to gauge his actual level of tangible political support. In one of his most earnest and self-effacing performances to-date, he stood before the *signoria* and other assembled *principali* and assured them that, if it would serve the greater interests of Florence, then he was prepared to deliver himself up to Pope Sixtus in order to save the city from attack. One by one the assembled dignitaries and members of the government rose and reaffirmed their support for Lorenzo and their unbounded confidence in his continued leadership. Imprudently, the Pope had also issued direct threats against the *gonfaloniere* and members of the *signoria*, threatening 'to have all their property confiscated by the Church, their houses levelled to the ground, their every dwelling place rendered unfit for habitation of any kind'. Naturally this misstep had the effect of rallying the government firmly behind Lorenzo de' Medici. Through loyalty, common purpose and the Pope's own ineptitude Lorenzo had obtained the mandate he so badly needed. He immediately called a *dieci di balìa* on 13 June and placed himself at its head, a move which effectively bestowed upon Lorenzo emergency dictatorial powers.

Medici *reggimento* loyalists such as Tommaso Soderini and Luigi Guicciardini were also given prime places within the *dieci* and Lorenzo himself was granted the unprecedented privilege of an armed bodyguard of twelve soldiers to ensure his personal security at all times within the city's precincts. Assassins had attempted their brutal trade once before; Lorenzo would not be caught unprepared a second time. The Medici put the city firmly on a fighting basis to meet the coming threat from Rome and Naples. An embassy from Ferrante had by this time arrived in Florence to demand Lorenzo's expulsion from the city, thereby indicating that the King of Naples fully intended to honour his alliance with Pope Sixtus. To Tommaso Soderini, Lorenzo wrote: 'By yours and Orfeo's letters we understand that 1,000 men have been engaged and are ready for our service. If this is correct I think it will suffice if one half crosses our frontier, the rest being held in readiness for what I mentioned in my last, the assault of Imola. It must be remembered that in defending ourselves we are defending those Illustrious Lords [of Milan], and if we gain anything for ourselves it will be most unexpected, for these Venetian ambassadors declare that if peace is not made with the Turk we can hope for but small aid from them. In ten or twelve days we shall have 450 men under arms. If there is a chance of engaging any *condottieri* it would be an excellent thing.' Lorenzo singled out the *condottiere* Costanzo Sforza, *signore* of Pesaro, as one in whom he could probably trust.

By early July, the Pope had galvanised King Ferrante's son the duke of Calabria into action against Florentine territory backed up by the considerable forces of Federigo da Montefeltro. Eager to present a united front against the Pope, the *signoria* issued an open letter to Sixtus which was as notable for its acerbity as for its outright defiance. For the papal absolutists of that time, the Pazzi conspiracy had been a laudable and justifiable deed. The duke of Calabria, by now encamped at Montepulciano, had even gone so far as to defiantly despatch his own messenger to Florence carrying yet another missive repeating the Pope's grievances. The *signoria* of course saw things very differently and this latest affront, even more than the Pope's original Bull of excommunication of 1 June, seems to have motivated them to retaliate against Sixtus in similar fashion. 'Your Holiness writes to us that you are only waging war against our State to free it from a tyrant', the *signoria* wrote to Pope Sixtus. 'We are thankful for your paternal love, and for the consolation your letter affords to this people. It is a people which has ever been on the side of the Church, and has been the first in professions of obedience to your Holiness. It could not therefore without sorrow behold an army of the Shepherd entering its territories (even while the Turk was on the threshold of Italy), ravaging its crops, seizing its towns, and carrying off its maidens and its shrines as booty.'

In view of the looming invasion and conquest of the city of Otranto in August 1480 by the Ottoman Turks of Sultan Mehmet II, the *signoria's* defiant epistolary to Pope Sixtus was under the circumstances eerily prescient and poignant. In the event, however, the war of words only went into higher gear with Sixtus rephrasing his interdict in even more severe language on 21 July and the *signoria* countering that 'The Pope avers that Lorenzo is a tyrant, but we and our people, have proved him to be, and with one voice acclaim him, the *defender* of our liberties'. The architect of this fresh wave of rebelliousness was Lorenzo's old tutor Gentile Becchi, who had taken it upon himself to lead Florence's administrators, ecclesiastics, academics and humanists in their collective defiance of what they clearly regarded as papal tyranny over the spiritual life of the state. Issuing their own excommunication of Pope Sixtus, the affronted Catholic priesthood of Florence and its satellite towns and cities doggedly continued with their salvific Holy rites as normal in open disobedience towards the papal interdict. The *signoria* meanwhile spat its indifference to the pontiff's threats, insolently dismissing Pope Sixtus as 'Judas in the seat of Peter'.

Further welcome support came from the court of the French King Louis XI who wrote personally to Lorenzo condoling with him and vilifying the Pope. Consolingly, Louis stated that the murder 'of our said cousin Giuliano de' Medici' was tantamount to an attempt upon his own royal person 'and therefore consider the Pazzi guilty of *læsæ Majestatis*, we cannot permit this deed to go unpunished'. Louis had spent the better part of two decades since his accession in a state of antagonism towards the papacy. He had inherited from his father Charles VII the Pragmatic Sanction of Bourges (1438), a ruling which upheld the French conciliarist decree *Sacrosancta* which asserted the supremacy of a council over the Pope and made his jurisdiction subject to the will of the King.

Although Louis had revoked the Pragmatic Sanction in 1461 it was taken out, dusted off, and reasserted from time to time as relations between the French court and the papacy fluctuated. The French Crown was also displeased by the Pope's support of the royal claim of King Ferrante over and above the rival claim of the House of Anjou. King Louis's reprimand to the Most Holy Father was uncompromising in its tone: 'We are deeply grieved and still more astonished that such an outrage should have been committed against one of such a House as is that of the Medici; renowned in the whole world, and known as belonging to the Church and filling high offices, such as that of Cardinal and Archbishop, and in the precincts of a Church, a sacred place dedicated to God'. But as much as Lorenzo may have toyed with the idea of inviting Louis to Italy to renew his claim to the Angevin throne of Naples, thus providing a check to Ferrante, he wisely hesitated. Despite his own problems the introduction of France as a power player on the Italian peninsula would unquestionably have introduced a devastating new set of variables and complications. To his considerable credit, Lorenzo de' Medici was not prepared to destabilise the whole of Italy merely in order to save his own skin.

Venice also theoretically came down on the side of Florence although, as in the case of France, little practical support would be forthcoming due to the Venetians' preoccupation with on-going Ottoman encroachments on their traditional eastern trading routes. Writing to Giovanni Lanfredini, Florence's ambassador in Venice, Lorenzo urged that: 'We have need of more men than those who are on this side of the Po. If the *signoria* approve of our plan of attacking Imola in case war is declared against us, we should prefer that the above-mentioned men should be employed there. If they do not approve, then it is imperative that the men be sent with all haste to guard our territory, and we will give orders that they are to be allowed to cross our frontier.' Lorenzo's late friend Galeazzo Maria Sforza had cautioned him that the Venetians were fickle and not to be trusted and indeed the present predicament seemed to vindicate this assessment. The Venetian ambassador to Florence lamented the reluctance of his own government to get involved and replied to Lanfredini: 'I do not know what hope I can have, when, even such grave injuries as we have suffered, cannot persuade [the Venetians] to move. I see that at Rome they understand the humour of Venice and speak sweet words in order to send to sleep him who sleeps already.' Even a mission to Venice by the indefatigable Tommaso Soderini failed to sway the Venetians from their studied neutrality.

The aging Donato Acciaiuoli had been in charge of diplomacy with Milan but he had died suddenly whilst en route to France, his other diplomatic remit, and urgently needed to be replaced. Lorenzo recalled Guido Antonio Vespucci from Rome and named him Donato's replacement as ambassador to the duchy of Milan. Guido required a reliable assistant in his retinue and he chose a family member, the son of his cousin Ser Anastasio, whose name was Amerigo Vespucci. Upon arrival, the Vespuccis found that Milan was still deeply embroiled in its struggle for succession. The three remaining Sforza brothers would soon return to Milan in 1479 and, together with Roberto da Sanseverino, would force several outlying towns to submit to their rule. Besides which, the duchy was also busy fending off attacks by the Swiss as well as quelling a rebellion in Genoa around this time and could not be counted upon in the coming military conflict. As for Clarice's clan, the powerful warlords of the Orsini, although they went through the motions of publicly expressing their support for Lorenzo, the Orsini forces failed to mobilise. Florence now stood increasingly isolated in the looming showdown with Rome.

Florence turned instead to her less formidable ally Ferrara. Duke Ercole I d'Este of Ferrara had learned the military arts at the court of King Alfonso V of Aragon. Seizing his dukedom in 1471 following the death of his brother Borso, Ercole had in 1476 crushed a subsequent coup that had been staged by the rightful successor, Borso's son Niccolò. Although he was an acknowledged *condottiere* Ercole was not especially known for his military dynamism. Furthermore, he was married to King Ferrante's daughter Eleonora d'Aragona and would therefore be matched on the campaign field against his own brother-in-law Alfonso of Calabria. This was hardly a situation designed to inspire much confidence in Borso's Florentine employers but nevertheless beggars could not be choosers and Ferrara was one of the few friendly states which Lorenzo could call upon at this time.

True to form, once he received his commission, Ercole delayed joining his forces in the field while he continued to haggle over the terms of his *condotta*. When he did eventually take command of his army, the Ferrarese showed themselves to be slovenly and undisciplined and certainly no real match for the experienced and determined Spanish- *Napoletano* troops of Alfonso, or indeed the professional mercenaries of the terrifying monocular *condottiere* Montefeltro. On 13 July, the *Napoletani* formerly declared war upon the republic and the Florentine countryside was swollen with refugees fleeing from the advancing enemy. Less than one week later, Florence's old enemy Siena opportunistically entered the conflict on the side of the Pope and together with Alfonso and Montefeltro the combined papal forces made determined advances on Tuscan territory. In response, Ercole d'Este made a series of complicated feints and counter marches which amounted in reality to little more than a humiliating mass retreat on the part of Florence's hired mercenary army. By the end of 1478 the conflict had devolved into the usual series of inconclusive assaults and skirmishes which characterised the warfare of the Italian *condottieri*. Some atrocities had occurred, including most notably the destruction of the town of Rencine by the *Sienese*, but as winter set in both sides retired to their winter quarters affording some respite from the fighting. One particularly bitter pill for the Florentines was the loss to Genoa of the tiny yet strategically significant town of Sarzana, which lay on the border between Liguria and Tuscany. In 1468, Sarzana had been purchased by Piero de' Medici from Luigi di Campofregoso for 37,000 florins and its loss was keenly felt amongst Florence's military planners. Sarzana had been a key Florentine fortress which hitherto served to guard the Ligurian Apennines.

On the social and economic front, meanwhile, Lorenzo's troubles continued to multiply. Though he might confess to King Louis XI of France that his only transgression against the Pope was that he had 'remained alive' after the latter had attempted to assassinate him, the fact of the matter was that Lorenzo's subjects were now beginning to pay the price for their support of the House of Medici. Food supplies from the ravaged countryside were increasingly hard to come by inside Florence and raw materials for the wool and cloth trade had also dwindled to a trickle, thus bringing the economic life of the city to a virtual standstill. With little food or work many Florentines faced destitution and, to make matters worse, an outbreak of plague during the summer of 1478 in the city's Santa Croce district further added to the peoples' misery. The war commissioners moved the magistracy of the *dieci* to Fiesole as a temporary precaution. As Florence's pestilential streets swelled with dead bodies and the hospitals struggled to keep pace with the influx of patients the River Arno chose this inopportune time to break its banks and the city was flooded. In the *contado*, meanwhile, armed bands of outlaws masquerading as *Napoletano* or *Sienese* scouting parties ravaged the towns and villages of what meagre supplies they still had. In the face of these prodigious hardships a debilitating mood of lassitude and depression now descended upon the beleaguered commune. Opposition elements began to flourish. By 1479, Cardinal Francesco Gonzaga was reporting back to his master in Rome that anti-Medicean leaflets were being liberally scattered throughout Florence's streets.

To spare his family some of the worst hardships of the city, Lorenzo despatched Clarice and the children, together with his poet friend Poliziano, to various Medici residences in the surrounding countryside, being sure to switch their location every so often as a security precaution. Villas like Cafaggiolo were delightful as a summertime residence but, in the autumn and winter of 1478, there were merely damp and depressing. In the bleak and isolated countryside Clarice, the mother to several demanding children, began to show signs of early stage consumption. Her illness and the irritability it inevitably caused now led her and the opinionated humanist Poliziano to quarrel bitterly. Poliziano served as tutor to little Piero and Giovanni and Clarice was especially upset that he had the effrontery to teach the boys Latin from the pagan classics rather than the holy Psalms. Trapped together under the same roof, and seemingly oblivious to Florence's wider political problems, Lorenzo's beloved 'pagan' poet and his devout, Roman wife kept up a steady stream of correspondence with him in which each party took turns in airing their grievances. In a letter dated 18 December 1478, Poliziano complained that his access to his two young students was being impeded by one of Clarice's household allies, Ser Alberto di Malerba, who 'mumbles prayers with these children all day long'.

When Clarice returned from giving birth in Florence in early 1479, matters rapidly came to a head and Poliziano was unceremoniously expelled from the villa at Cafaggiolo. So sudden was his expulsion that he had been forced to leave his cherished books behind and his position as tutor was immediately filled by Martino della Comedia, who also taught the Tornabuoni progeny. Poor Poliziano was reduced to writing yet more letters to Lorenzo and Lorenzo's mother Lucrezia inquiring what was to be his fate (he was eventually made librarian to the household, a role which gave him considerably less access to Lorenzo and the family). Lorenzo's attention at this time, however, could not have been further removed from his wife's and his friend's silly domestic bickering. The situation was truly grim. In the wider scheme of things the suffering of the city had reached crisis point. Even worse however was the news that the Medici Bank itself, the very lynchpin of Medici political power, was facing imminent bankruptcy.

Pope Sixtus had used the outbreak of war to renege on all the Curia's outstanding debts to the Medici Bank. Not long afterwards the Neapolitan king had also followed suit. At a stroke, two of the most profitable branches of the family business, both of which had already been experiencing a contraction prior to the Pazzi Conspiracy, were effectively shut down. The bank's northern European branches fared little better. Years of mismanagement by the Medici agent Tommaso Portinari had produced catastrophic losses in both London and

Bruges. Lorenzo calculated that in the region of 70,000 florins had been lost but the actual losses were probably closer to 100,000. Tommaso had not repaid the debt of gratitude that he owed Cosimo de' Medici when the latter transferred his trust from the Bardi to the Portinari. Eschewing the Medici's tendency to arrange non-threatening middle class marriages for all their key bank employees, Portinari had struck out on his own and secretly married the upper class fifteen-year-old Maria di Francesco di Bandini Baroncelli. Not only was the girl a close relative of the head of the Pazzi Bank in Bruges but she was also related to Giuilano's assassin Bernardo Bandini Baroncelli. From the unnecessary and costly luxury of the Medici Bank's ostentatious headquarters at the Hotel Bladelin in Bruges, Tommaso Portinari's disastrous tendency towards social climbing had also brought him into the orbit of the duke of Burgundy, Charles the Bold.

Under the influence of Duke Charles he had made a series of monumentally poor deals such as purchasing a customs concession at Gravelines just before the Duke banned the import of English wool. He also helped Charles out of a bind by purchasing, with Medici Bank ducats, two expensive Burgundian galleys previously intended for the late Pope Pius II's abortive Crusade. These two vessels not only operated at a loss but were loaned out to the Duke to import tax and duty-free Burgundian goods into Pisa. Worse still, Portinari had repeated the fatal mistakes of the Bardi, the Peruzzi and the Acciaiuoli by loaning large sums to Duke Charles who channelled the money into making his court one of the most luxurious and admired in all Europe. The small, safe banking deals favoured by Portinari's elderly predecessor Agnolo Tani were ignored in favour of the quixotic search for one huge but elusive financial killing. The prima donna Portinari saw himself as an impresario of the banking world but all he had done was set his bank up for the oldest trap in the book. When Duke Charles was killed at the Battle of Nancy in January 1477 by the Lorrainers and the Swiss, his naked and badly mutilated body found some days afterward frozen into a nearby river, there was little chance of his massive outstanding debts being repaid by his successor Philip the Good.

Neither would the Medici be able to claw back massive loans which had been extended to the English king, Edward IV. Lorenzo de' Medici would later complain bitterly of his Bruges agent's mismanagement and borderline malfeasance, even going so far as to assert that Portinari had done him more harm than the Pope, but the fact of the matter was that Lorenzo himself had neglected the Medici Bank's business for years, preferring to appoint semi-autonomous managers who, like Portinari, were allowed a free rein to do as they pleased. The cumulative result of this absenteeism was that the London branch collapsed, the Bruges and Milan branches closed down, and the Lyons, Rome and Naples branches were plagued with insuperable difficulties. As a stopgap measure to stave off default and financial collapse Lorenzo begged Bona of Savoy for a loan of 12,000 ducats, seeking a further 40,000 ducats in the spring of 1479. He mortgaged some of his own Medici property too, including the villa at Cafaggiolo, which brought in 60,000 florins. Meanwhile, Even Lorenzo de' Medici's wife Clarice and his mother Lucrezia were forced to pledge personal jewellery and artworks valued at close to 20,000 florins to help stave off financial ruin.

In a move which would have disastrous repercussions much later on, Lorenzo also skimmed 50,000 florins from the large inheritance of his two younger cousins Lorenzo di Pierfrancesco and Giovanni di Pierfrancesco.

Lorenzo and Giovanni were descended from Cosimo de' Medici's brother Lorenzo, the former head of the Medici's cadet line, whose son was Pierfrancesco. It was Pierfrancesco who, aligned with his father-in-law Agnolo Acciaioli, had almost joined the ranks of the reformers in 1466. His wife Laudomia Acciaioli had died in 1469 and, when Pierfrancesco himself passed away in July 1476, his sons were left orphaned aged just thirteen and nine. Lorenzo assumed their guardianship, giving them the best possible education that Medici ducats could buy. Amongst their teachers had been Marsilio Ficino, Angelo Poliziano, as well as a learned friar of San Marco by the name of Giorgio Antonio Vespucci. The latter happened to be the uncle of Amerigo Vespucci, who had entered Medici service only the year before and was serving as assistant to Guido Antonio Vespucci, Florence's new ambassador to Milan and Bologna. By 1479, Lorenzo the Younger was already sixteen years old. Although he and his brother had benefited from having his namesake Lorenzo de' Medici as their guardian and benefactor, he was nonetheless old enough to know that they had been defrauded of their inheritance. The poisoned shoots of jealously at the cadet line's diminished status were already present and his guardian's overt embezzlement now only inflamed Lorenzo's resentment. It also soon became clear to Lorenzo di Pierfrancesco that his branch of the family would never be given access to quite the same financial opportunities enjoyed by the main line of the Medici through their political control of Florence. This fact was to become a recurring cause for dissatisfaction and jealousy as the decades wore on.

However, as the Medici *reggimento* continued to haemorrhage funds, mostly towards the ineffective army of Duke Ercole of Ferrara, even these emergency measures were insufficient to meet Lorenzo's public and private expenses. Facing bankruptcy and total political ruin at this point, Lorenzo de' Medici now opted to indulge in a little deft corruption and reluctantly dipped into Florence's public coffers. A discreet raid on the funds of the *monte dei doti*–a state fund intended to set aside money for dowries for the poor–netted Lorenzo the considerable sum of up to 80,000 florins. Established in 1425, the *monte dei doti* was an innovative state fund into which families could contribute regular fixed contributions in return for a dowry when their daughter married. The fund had bestowed dowries on around 20,000 women during the fifteenth and sixteenth-century. Should the underwritten girl remain unmarried then the contributions would default to the state. Lucrezia Tornabuoni was one of the directors of the fund and it may have been through her offices that Lorenzo gained access to its reserves.

Through these various means Lorenzo was able to remain financially afloat, albeit at the cost in later years of laying himself open to the charge of peculation. On the other hand, as Lorenzo himself might have argued, the fiscal relationship between the Medici and the Florentine state were nothing if not porous. Funds flowed in both directions, but more often than not from the Medici Bank into the needs of the state because ruling and political and administrative funding naturally went hand-in-hand. In 1479 and with the wolves at the door Lorenzo could have done little else but take a dip into the state coffers as Medici bankruptcy implied state bankruptcy.

The war meanwhile was not going well despite an auspicious start. The Florentine-*Ferrarese* army scored an initial military victory at Lake Trasimene against the troops of the Prefect of Rome, the Pope's nephew Leonardo della

Rovere. Florence's ambassador in Paris, Guidantonio Vespucci, described to the war council how 'When the king of France heard the news he gave signs of great joy, kneeling as is his wont three times and kissing the ground, thanking God. All that day he talked of nought else with his people, saying: "My friends the Florentines and my cousin Lorenzo de' Medici will have their revenge this year..."' However the good news was to be short-lived. Alfonso of Calabria had soon succeeded in scattering the Florentine forces at Poggio Imperiale (Poggibonsi) and proceeded to reduce the town of Colle Val d'Elsa just a few miles south of Florence itself. Alfonso might well have commenced to lay siege to Florence at this point were it not for the fact that winter had begun to set in. Both sides therefore gratefully retreated to camp after concluding a ceasefire agreement. Those within the city of Florence knew—without needing to be any great military strategist—that, come springtime, there would be nothing to stand between the papalists and Florence itself. Federigo da Montefeltro's smug formula, which stated that in time of war the Florentines were always defeated by the third year, looked depressingly prescient.

The long months of organising the war effort as head of the *dieci* had also taken its visible toll on Lorenzo. Most of his waking hours were spent scribbling urgent despatches to the frontline as well as organising the emergency life of a city which would most likely soon find itself invested by papal forces. There was little he could do in practice to alleviate the very real suffering now being experienced by the citizenry. The return, in the summer of 1479, of the pestilence only made conditions worse in the foetid, densely-packed tenements of the city. Wealthy and poor alike were struck down by the on-going miasmas and, in August of that year, Lorenzo himself succumbed to a fever. His poetry and his humanist studies, the things which gave him most joy, Lorenzo had been forced to forego during this time of crisis. Lorenzo knew that Pope Sixtus—gripped as he was by some dark, obsessive hatred for the Medici—would never relent while he still remained head of state. As for Federigo da Montefeltro, whereas once he had stood godfather to the infant Lorenzo, now he was no more than a subordinate in-law and creature of the Pope; a cold professional who would press on machine-like until Florence was vanquished. Lorenzo knew that Florence could not endure a third year of war without support from a powerful neighbouring state like Venice or Milan. But Florence's old ally Milan would this time fail the Medici.

Milan's internal political disarray had recently been settled on 7 September 1479 when Ludovico Sforza and Bona of Savoy finally came to an agreement concerning the regency of the duchy. Galeazzo Maria's son Gian Galeazzo Sforza was only ten years old and still too young to rule as duke in his own right. Ludovico, who had been kept at bay by his adversary, Milan's chief minister Cicco Simonetta, now made use of the intense animosity that existed between Cicco and Bona's lover Antonio Tassino. Cicco, an able administrator who ran a tight ship, deeply resented the fact that Bona often shared confidential matters of state with the low-born former footman Tassino. Ludovico gained the confidence of the naïve young Tassino, persuading him to facilitate an audience between himself and Bona. When the pair met, Ludovico won Bona's trust and she agreed to transfer Milan's regency to him. She required little persuading in fact; Bona had already been cowed by Roberto da Sanseverino's military successes and felt she had little choice at this point but to give way. Although one of the brothers, Sforza Maria, had died during the course of Sanseverino's campaigns, Ludovico and Roberto were now well entrenched in Milan and

Ascanio, who entered the episcopate with his appointment as Bishop of Pavia that same month, returned to Milan in October.

Bona's loyal and highly capable chief minister was disconsolate when he learned the news. He had earlier predicted that, should Ludovico ever gain power, he would be the first casualty of the new regime. His prediction proved chillingly accurate. Ludovico had not been in Milan three days when, falsely accused of treason, Cicco was arrested, imprisoned and tortured in Pavia's *castello* while Ludovico pillaged his house and seized his assets. One year later Cicco was finally beheaded in the fortress's tower and, to signify the end of his influence over *Milanese* affairs, his body was buried in the cloister of Sant'Apollinare outside Milan's city walls. It was a sad end for one who had served the House of Sforza so diligently for many years and furthermore it removed one of Lorenzo's more dependable allies from the picture. Despite Cicco Simonetta's long friendship to the House of Medici, Lorenzo was now forced to bite the bullet and make overtures to the new lord in Milan, Ludovico Sforza. He wrote effusively to the *Milanese* ambassador enthusing over Ludovico's appointment as regent but, despite Lorenzo's obeisance, little practical assistance would be forthcoming from *il Moro*. Ludovico would assert further control over Milan before the end of the year by detaching Bona from Gian Galeazzo and by having her lover Antonio Tassino exiled for a period of ten years. Left alone and isolated, Bona was finally forced by Ludovico to go to the fortress of Abbiategrasso and be confined there.

It was at this point, while his fortunes were at a low ebb, that Lorenzo de' Medici took his momentous decision to play a gambit which was so unexpected and so completely outrageous, that it was planned in secret and, once executed, stunned not only the citizenry of Florence but became the wonder of the entire Italian peninsula. On 6 December 1479, having secured his ally Tommaso Soderini in the crucial post of *gonfaloniere*, Lorenzo slipped quietly out of Florence accompanied only by his secretary Niccolò Michelozzi. His proximate destination was the Florentine city of Pisa. Halfway through his journey he paused at the town of San Miniato and penned a moving letter to the *signoria* which explained his actions and the reasoning that lay behind them. The letter began with an apologia. 'If I have not already informed Your Illustrious Excellencies of the reason for my departure it is not out of presumption but because it seems to me that the troubled state of our city demands deeds, not words'. The letter went on to explain how, perceiving the city's deep longing for peace, Lorenzo had decided to assume full personal responsibility for the quarrel with Pope Sixtus and accept the consequences himself rather than continue to allow the entire commune to be endangered. In the hope that his own fate would settle the fate of Florence, Lorenzo explained that he would place his person at the disposal of King Ferrante of Naples 'because', as he put it, 'I am the chief target of our enemies' hatred'. And if surrendering himself into Ferrante's custody did not bring a conclusion to the war, Lorenzo expressed the belief 'that our citizens will unite to protect their liberty, so that by the grace of God they will come to its defence as our fathers always did'. As his letter was being made public in Florence to the astonishment of the populace, Lorenzo himself was already boarding a galley which had been despatched secretly from King Ferrante. The ship would bring him south to the *Regno*, Italy's only kingdom, and his personal appointment with destiny.

How are we to account for Lorenzo's dramatic decision to place himself in the hands of the most untrustworthy prince in all Italy? Truly, the Florentines themselves were astounded at the inherent self-sacrifice in the gesture. By seemingly offering himself up as a sacrificial lamb to King Ferrante, Lorenzo had distracted them from two grinding years of suffering and privation. Whereas they had formerly begun to grumble about the trouble the Medici had caused them, the people of Florence now stood in collective awe at Lorenzo's apparent act of almost suicidal martyrdom on their behalf. But only when Lorenzo's stratagem is examined more closely is its true brilliance revealed. Firstly, he took care not to surrender himself into the hands of Pope Sixtus IV and his rapacious nephew Girolamo Riario. Had he done so, the darkest dungeon in the Castel Sant'Angelo, not to mention an intimate acquaintance with the castellan's full range of torture paraphernalia, would no doubt have awaited Lorenzo. Such a move would have been reckless to the point of perversity. No, by placing himself instead at the mercy of the volatile King Ferrante, Lorenzo was playing a far more subtle and astute geopolitical gambit. Ferrante may have been allied with the Pope for the time being however the centuries' long suspicion between Rome and the Papal States on the one hand and the kingdom of Naples on the other was well-documented. Naples's prestige as the sole kingdom on the Italian peninsula was predicated on the maintenance of a careful balance of power amongst the other city-states to the north. As the main competitors to Naples, neither Milan nor Venice could be permitted to grow too powerful and yet their relative strength or weakness also depended on the alignments of the smaller mercantile city-states of both Tuscany and Lombardy. By the same token, Rome–which already held substantial territory in the Papal States of the Romagna–could not be permitted to simply devour a key city-state such as Florence and its Tuscan dependencies. Even worse, should a considerably augmented Rome align with either Milan or Venice (or both) then their combined strength would prove more than a match for an isolated Naples in the south.

King Ferrante himself was most sensitive of all about the on-going Angevin claim to the Neapolitan throne currently being championed by King Louis XI of France. This tended on the whole to make Ferrante an insecure monarch and it was this fundamental insecurity and potential isolation of Naples's king that Lorenzo de' Medici, a maestro at international affairs, intended to tease and exploit. His strategy planned to sow doubt and paranoia as much as it sought to flatter and cajole the Neapolitan monarch. But in pursuing this subtle strategy, Lorenzo would still need to run the gauntlet of Ferrante's notoriously unpredictable temperament. We know from the *ricordi* of Lorenzo's agent Filippo Strozzi the Elder that Lorenzo had already been planning his Naples stratagem several months before he even set foot on the Neapolitan galley which had been sent to fetch him. Strozzi himself had been despatched to Naples in November to test the water with Ferrante and his assessment was that Ferrante was ripe for an individual diplomatic approach that excluded the Pope. The Medici prince was gambling on the assumption that Ferrante would prefer to deal with a humbled and belittled Lorenzo de' Medici, instead of a Florence that had lapsed into a protectorate of the papacy.

On the evening of 18 December, Lorenzo's galley and its single escort sailed into Naples harbour. One of the first people to greet Lorenzo upon his arrival was Duke Alfonso's brother Don Federigo. Lorenzo had grown close to Federigo in Milan during Ippolita Maria Sforza's proxy wedding to Alfonso, when Federigo had stood in for his older brother. Seeing Federigo beaming at him from the quayside, followed by a warm embrace was surely an encouraging sign of things to come. The trip down the coast had also been made in the convivial company of two other former *Napoletano* acquaintances: Gian Tommaso Caraffa and Prinzivalle di Gennaro, who were now both serving as advisers to King Ferrante. As for the King himself, Lorenzo was informed that he was away on a hunting trip but in his stead he was greeted by an array of *Napoletano* ministers, ambassadors and court dignitaries and, most encouragingly, was treated with all the pomp and fanfare of a visiting head of state. This must have come as a huge relief to Lorenzo, who could just as easily have been clapped in irons and thrown into a Neapolitan dungeon upon disembarkation.

His initial meeting with King Ferrante, when it came two days later, was also most reassuring. As Lorenzo himself later recorded, the mercurial king of Naples clasped him in his arms and 'greeted me most graciously and with many kind words, showing in many different ways the affection he had for our city'. It was clear to Lorenzo that Ferrante bore him no personal grudge, which certainly could not be said for the Pope. The King also showed much affinity for the people Florence and this positive reception was considered a good beginning. Lorenzo's initial euphoria at his friendly and diplomatic welcome soon gave way, however, to a growing sense of depression. In the days and weeks that followed, and as the negotiations dragged on, Ferrante showed that he could be frustratingly dilatory, inconclusive and vague. It became clear to Lorenzo that the King himself was caught on the horns of a dilemma. Although personally inclined towards peace at this point, Ferrante was at the same time still hesitant to incur the wrath of Pope Sixtus by making concord with Florence. Like Federigo da Montefeltro, Ferrante was in Sixtus's personal debt. The Pope had created one of Ferrante's sons a cardinal in 1477; Giovanni d'Aragona, cardinal-deacon of Sant'Adriano al Foro, was currently apostolic administrator of the see of Badajoz and would soon be named as papal legate to the court of Hungary. The fact that the Pope had named anyone outside of his immediate family as cardinal was in itself a remarkable event and the ambitious Ferrante was reluctant to jeopardise his son's blooming career in the Sacred College. His only recourse therefore was to do what any statesmen would do in this situation; King Ferrante stalled and played for time.

In his lodgings in the Medici Bank's Naples branch, Lorenzo ploughed the peaks and troughs of intense hope followed by the gloomiest of depressions as the unpredictable king advanced and then backtracked and then grew distant and fudged his former position. This was a dance which, to Lorenzo's despair, was repeated many times over. Niccolò Michelozzi recorded that his master 'seemed to be two men, not one. During the day he appeared perfectly easy, restful, cheerful and confident. But at night he grieved bitterly about his own ill fortune and that of Florence.' As an antidote to the emotional ups and downs caused by Ferrante's vacillation, Lorenzo sought relief in an activity which had always come natural to him, the dispensing of Medici philanthropic largesse. He had brought with him sizeable reserves of his state-embezzled funds and, in an unprecedented Florentine charm offensive, he now gave it freely to relieve many instances of poverty or need which he had witnessed in Naples. One of his first acts of benevolent theatrics was to free the one hundred Christian galley slaves who had conveyed him from Pisa to Naples at some considerable cost. The generous gesture proved to be a public relations coup in Naples. In addition, the state pension money which had been misappropriated from the poor brides of Florence was now freely dispensed to the poor brides of Naples. Fetes and festivals were staged for the amusement of the more well-to-do and local charities were bestowed with considerable Medici-funded endowments. During those rare and precious moments when Lorenzo was graced with Ferrante's time and attention he did his utmost to forget his own depression and concentrated instead on charming the King with his scholarly erudition and witty conversation. Ferrante, the murderous usurper who, so it was said, had the habit of embalming and exhibiting his dead rivals in a grisly private menagerie, yet who fancied himself a humanist and artistic dilettante, responded positively to Lorenzo's kindly, generous and nuanced overtures.

Lorenzo was accompanied in his benevolent pursuits by his friend Ippolita Maria Sforza, the duchess of Calabria. Lorenzo and Ippolita had had remained on close and friendly terms ever since all those many years ago in Milan when, aged barely sixteen, Lorenzo had represented the republic of Florence at Ippolita's wedding. In Naples, Ippolita was to become his staunchest local champion and confidante. The pair would take long walks together in the grounds of the Duchess's home, the Castel Capuano, built in the twelfth-century by William I, the second Norman king of Sicily. In their later correspondence, Ippolita would fondly remind Lorenzo of their idyllic strolls together, notifying him that 'our garden ... is now most beautiful and in full bloom'. Though a mere woman Ippolita was, like certain other high-born Renaissance ladies, savvy in the arts of statesmanship and knew how to broker a political deal. Increasingly she began acting as Lorenzo's go-between, proposing solutions and compromises to various diplomatic impasses and territorial disputations. Such was the level of her involvement in the on-going negotiations that Ferrante himself began humorously referring to the Duchess as 'Lorenzo's confederate'. In the meantime, Lorenzo continued to charm the *Napoletani* who, for the most part, were enchanted by this generous, cultured and chivalrous mercantile prince who moved amongst them like some beneficent saint.

The rest of Italy also continued to admire Lorenzo's act of placing himself at Naples' mercy. He had shown great personal courage and many, Lorenzo included, would have been mindful of the fate of the former *condottiere* Jacopo Piccinino, who had been summoned to Naples in 1465 under a flag of truce only to be seized and executed by Ferrante immediately upon arrival. The enormous risk Lorenzo had taken in coming to Naples was obvious to all observers of political events. But even so, January had by now turned into February and Lorenzo was being continually bombarded by entreaties from Florence's *signoria* and other *principali* to bring the tardy negotiations with Ferrante to a conclusion and return home. Florence's chancellor Bartolomeo Scala wrote to Lorenzo: 'We are all hoping against hope for the conclusion of this affair which has delayed so long' and assured him that 'if there is peace you will see how the city will flourish'. By this time Lorenzo was badly missing his family and had demanded regular updates on his children's progress. He was heartened when Antonio Pucci wrote to him with the news that his son Giovanni 'is fat and looks well'. Deciding that he could not remain in Naples one moment longer he now determined to force the matter. Boarding a galley at the port of Gaeta on 27 February 1480, Lorenzo made the fortnight-long voyage home. He arrived back in Florence around 13 March to much joyous celebration and the tolling of bells throughout the city.

Barely a few days later word arrived from Naples that King Ferrante had ratified Lorenzo's proposed peace treaty on the very day that he had returned home. Duchess Ippolita Maria had, in her capacity as Lorenzo's official representative, acted as witness and signatory to the treaty. The terms were that Florence should pay to Naples an indemnity, rectify certain outstanding territorial disputes between the two states, and release those members of the Pazzi that had not directly participated in the assassination who were still being imprisoned. Concrete considerations had after all trumped all other concerns. Recent naval incursions by the Ottoman Turks in the Mezzogiorno were already a growing cause for concern and at one point an audacious Turkish flotilla had even sailed right into the harbour of Naples itself. As works of literature like Luigi Pulci's romantic epic *Morgante* increasingly glorified medieval chivalry and the Crusades and implied that a fresh Crusade was needed to repel the looming Ottoman threat, Ferrante had responded to the more practical need to free up his *Napoletano* troops campaigning in Tuscany. Florence and Naples were, after two years, finally at peace once more. Their reconciliation also paved the way for closer ties between Naples and Milan; to cement this newfound peace that same year Ippolita Maria's daughter Isabella d'Aragona was betrothed to Milan's duke-in-waiting Gian Galeazzo Sforza. Nonetheless for all this it must still be remembered that the House of Sforza and the papacy continued to be linked through the marriage of Ippolita Maria's niece Caterina Sforza to Pope Sixtus's nephew Girolamo Riario.

With Naples neutralised Pope Sixtus IV had little alternative but to agree to join the peace. Although he still had the loyal support of the duke of Urbino this resource alone was insufficient with which to conquer Florence. In the chambers of the Apostolic Palace the Pope was gripped by apoplectic rage at Ferrante's betrayal, but what else could he do? Far more important problems had by now arisen in the Mediterranean and so the time had now come for him to put away his role as a petty secular ruler and don his more all-encompassing garb as the leader of Roman Catholic Christendom. Recent advances by the Ottomans had reduced the Eastern Mediterranean Sea to little more than a Turkish lake. Following Constantinople's fall in 1453, Mehmet the Conqueror had annexed the duchy of Athens in 1458, the despotate of Morea in 1460, and the duchy of Naxos (also known as the duchy of the Archipelago) in 1479. Crete, Cyprus, Corfu, Cephalonia and Rhodes still remained in Christian hands but the Turkish Sultan's intentions were as plain as day; to gain merit with his heathen god Allah by conquering as much of Christian Europe as he could for Islam and its prophet.

On 28 July 1480 a fleet of 128 Ottoman vessels made landfall at the southern Italian port of Otranto and lay siege to the fortified city. The Turkish troops were experienced veterans of Mehmet's earlier abortive siege of Rhodes against the Hospitaller Knights of St. John and they made short work of storming and capturing Otranto's weakly-defended citadel. In the ensuing carnage a total of 12,000 Italians were claimed by the Catholic Church to have been killed and a further 5,000, mostly women and children, were enslaved by the Turk. Bishop Stefano Pendinelli, together with the entire clergy of the town, was trussed up and executed. When 800 citizens of Otranto were rounded up and given the ultimatum to either convert to Islam or face execution, in fear and trembling for their immortal souls all of them chose death. The Turks gladly obliged them and they were despatched to their Christian Saviour in a mass ceremony of beheading and impaling; the Christian mayor of Otranto was meanwhile singled out for the special honour of being sawn in half whilst still alive. These 800 unfortunates became known as the famous 'Martyrs of Otranto' and were later canonised by the Church as saints. The entire Italian peninsula was by now in a state of uproar and alarm. From Rome a concerned Pope Sixtus IV renewed Paul II's 1471 call for a Crusade against the barbarous heathens and made contingency plans for the city's evacuation in the event that the scourge reached as far as Rome itself.

The ending of the Florentine war was therefore timely as Duke Alfonso of Calabria was able to withdraw his much needed troops from Tuscany and join forces with the armies of Hungary, France and several other Italian city-states. The Turks had moved slowly in consolidating themselves on the Italian peninsula and, despite further incursions against the cities of Lecce, Taranto and Brindisi, the Sultan's generalissimo Gedik Ahmed Pasha failed to establish a credible presence. Finding it difficult to provision his forces in Italy and aware of the close proximity of Alfonso's forces, Gedik Pasha now withdrew his fleet before the onset of winter, leaving the 1,300-strong Turkish garrison in Otranto to fend for itself. There was therefore little real sense of surprise when, in September 1481, the avenging Christian armies fell upon the city and eradicated every Muslim solider they could find. With the re-conquest of Otranto the Muslim threat now subsided. Already, Christendom had warmed to the welcome news in May that year of Sultan Mehmet's sudden death at the age of forty-nine. It was widely rumoured that he had been poisoned, perhaps even by his erstwhile trading partners the Venetians. Mehmet's successor, Bayezid II, now suspended hostilities with the Christians while he fought a bitter struggle for succession with his brother Prince Djem.

Following his dramatic and highly public journey to Naples, Lorenzo de' Medici–now safely ensconced once more in Florence–was being openly referred to by the soubriquet he will always be best remembered by, 'il Magnifico'. On 25 November 1480, a delegation of Florence's most prominent principali paid a visit of reconciliation to the Curia to bend the knee and kiss the slippered feet of Pope Sixtus IV. Amongst their ranks were the illustrious Florentine ambassador Guidantonio Vespucci, Gino Capponi, the son of Neri Capponi and father of Piero Capponi, who would shortly make his mark on Florentine politics, Lorenzo's uncle Giovanni Tornabuoni, and Luigi Guicciardini amongst several others. These envoys were forced to endure a savage dressing-down by Sixtus before a reconciliation Mass was celebrated. On 3 December 1480, peace was formally restored between Florence and the papacy. Two years later Sandro Botticelli would paint his *Pallas and the Centaur* which many saw as an allegory on the achievement of peace following the bitter years of the Pazzi wars. In the painting the personification of reason, the goddess Pallas-Minerva, her blonde tresses adorned with a wreath of entwined olive branches, tames the Centaur of instinct and passion who represents the 'primordially coarse' forces of Pope Sixtus IV, Girolamo Riario and the Pazzi.

In the immediate aftermath of his bold and risky diplomatic initiative in Naples, nobody was in any doubt that Lorenzo's authority within Florence had been vastly improved and consolidated. Nevertheless, the crisis had highlighted certain deficiencies within the Medici system, foremost amongst which was that system's dependence on the physical presence of Lorenzo himself as the lynchpin of the whole structure. When he was absent from the republic for any protracted period it was clear that Lorenzo's placemen, even his most loyal ones, were dangerously prone to waywardness and independence of action.

Lorenzo now therefore took the precaution of further tightening his grip on the machinery of political power.

The most significant innovation which Lorenzo devised to minimise this problem was the formation of a brand new executive council called the Council of Seventy. This body, which mainly comprised *uomini sicuri* or those key higher echelon members of the *reggimento* on whom the Medici could always count, no matter what, was tasked with the selection (from within its own ranks) of two further sub-councils known as the *otto di pratica* (the Eight) and the *dodici procuratori* (the Twelve). The former was given oversight on foreign policy whilst the latter was responsible for managing Florence's domestic and financial affairs. Lorenzo himself sat on both the Seventy and the Eight. Under this new system the *signoria* became more of a figurehead and a rubber stamp, whilst the Seventy became the new centre of power with Lorenzo inevitably perched at its apex. Furthermore, the Seventy now superseded the *accoppiatori* as the mechanism by which government officials were screened and selected for office; in effect this gave the Seventy the legerdemain to self-replicate itself indefinitely. The government reforms were henceforth merely another example of determined oligarchic rule basking in the hazy penumbra of conservative Florentine republicanism.

Knowing that this further contraction of power into fewer and fewer hands would prove unpopular with the old ruling élite who had seen their influence gradually eroded under Medici rule, Lorenzo took pains to ensure that representatives of these 'old money' families were included in the Seventy whilst 'new men' were studiously excluded. To a large extent this was a complete reversal of Medici political policy to-date. It had previously been the practise to show favour towards those middling families which had made their fortunes through astute business practise and who had shown unswerving loyalty towards the Medici *reggimento*. The measures were also bound to further alienate the other traditional allies of the Medici, the *popolo minuto*, who now found themselves more excluded from the political process than perhaps ever before. The change of emphasis would inevitably return to haunt Lorenzo's successors, as would his shameless raiding of the state funds at the height of the recent crisis.

Not all of Lorenzo's supporters were impressed by the political reforms he was undertaking. Benedetto Dei, that remarkable chronicler of Florentine and Mediterranean events, had remonstrated how the Medici had 'refashioned the government in such a way so that it was based on tyranny rather than on the public good ... so that it is a shame to see how this state is run.' Dei had travelled extensively throughout the Mediterranean and North Africa for many years, having also stayed for some time in Constantinople, before returning home to Florence. His vast network of personal contacts, acquired during these years of wandering, enabled him to compile a regular news broadsheet which he sent out to subscribers for a pre-agreed price. This practice, which was to later become even more coordinated under professional Roman and Venetian writers, helped by the growing reliability of the international postal service, was the origin of the modern news media as we understand it today. It would soon no longer be sufficient for rulers to impress their domestic subjects through galas and festivities, but if they were to retain a good reputation in any broader sense they would need to positively engage these self-appointed critics and commentators on current affairs. At the other end of the spectrum, of course, there would also soon arise those scurrilous writers whose output bordered on simple blackmail; writers such as Pietro Aretino for example, the self-proclaimed 'scourge of princes', who made an appreciable living out of threatening to reveal the deepest, darkest secrets of Italy's rulers to the general public.

Lorenzo also took strides to reach out once more to Ludovico Sforza, the regent of Milan. The *Milanese* alliance was still considered an important one and, although the Medici Bank branch in Milan was by now closed, Lorenzo was reluctant to see their families' relationship lapse for want of a goodwill gesture. That gesture was to send *il Moro* the services of his friend and treasured resource Leonardo da Vinci in September 1482. Leonardo, who had apprenticed with Verrocchio from 1466–76, had come within Lorenzo's circle around the year 1480. He had attended the Neo-Platonic Academy in the Garden of the Piazza San Marco and the Villa di Careggi although, unlike the other members of the Academy, he knew no Latin or Greek and always felt out of place amidst the educated banter of Lorenzo's young humanist friends. All the same, Lorenzo was as devoted to Leonardo's exquisite genius as he was irritated by the artist's tendency to flit from one project to another without finishing anything. As a case in point, in 1481 Leonardo had embarked upon a commission for the Augustinian monks of San Donato a Scopeto to paint *The Adoration of the Magi* but had been continually distracted from the process of completing it. Other artists amongst Lorenzo's coterie had proved rather more reliable. At the age of forty-seven, Andrea del Verrocchio was still a considerable artistic presence, whilst Domenico Ghirlandaio had recently completed the second of three frescos that he would paint depicting the Last Supper. Sandro Botticelli, meanwhile, would that same year complete one of his best known works – *La Primavera*, which would be followed three years later by the *Birth of Venus*. Leonardo could therefore be spared to serve a wider purpose.

Lorenzo decided that Leonardo's services would best be served as a kind of artistic ambassadorial gift to the new *Milanese* regent. According to a story later told by Giorgio Vasari, Leonardo–himself a talented musician–had created a silver lyre in the shape of a horse's head. Lorenzo now despatched Leonardo to Milan bearing the silver lyre as a gift to secure the trust and amity of Ludovico Sforza and it was said that only Leonardo himself knew how to play the instrument. As Vasari tells the story: 'And with this instrument he surpassed all the other performers, as no other musician were equal competitors to this sound. Moreover, Leonardo was also the best improvisational reciter of poetry of his time. The Duke, after listening to the marvellous rationale of Leonardo, fell in love with his virtues so much that it was incredible.' But, in addition to the present of music, Leonardo also bore other significant gifts such as his schemes for better fortifications, improved waterworks and inventive new weapons. These schemes he listed down in his famous 'Letter of Application' which was a kind of curriculum vitae of all the different artistic services he was able to offer Milan's duke. Amongst these was the proposal to create a massive equestrian statue of Francesco Sforza in bronze.

In Milan, the *maestro* found himself in good company since other luminaries such as Donato Bramante and the mathematician Luca Pacioli were already a part of the city's cultural life. However, it was only several months later, in April 1483, that Leonardo received his first commission from the court of *il Moro*. This was to paint the centre panel in an altarpiece triptych for the Chapel of the Immaculate Conception, attached to the church of S. Francesco Grande in Milan. Leonardo's panel, which now hangs in the Louvre, shows the Madonna and Child Jesus with the infant John the Baptist and an angel, in a rocky setting which gives the painting its name – the *Madonna of the Rocks*. Yet the commission was nevertheless a joint one which Leonardo shared with two local artists, the Predis brothers. Furthermore, this first commission of Leonardo's in Milan was to leave in its wake an interminable squabble over payment for the work. Years after it completion, the Confraternity of S. Francesco Grande persisted in lowballing the artists on the final balance of their fees, which had foolishly been left open-ended in the contract. As a result the painting was retrieved and re-sold, possibly to Ludovico Sforza, who probably thereafter gave it as a gift to either the Emperor Maximilian or the king of France. Leonardo was later commissioned to paint near identical a replacement for the Confraternity which today hangs in the National Gallery in London.

Beyond the *Madonna of the Rocks* commission, we have surprisingly little information about how Leonardo managed to eke out a living in Milan from 1483 to the late 1480s whilst trying to earn himself a place as court artist. Yet it is from this period that many of his most intriguing speculative drawings date. These included innovative ideas for military equipment such as multiple-barrelled cannons, armoured vehicles, flying machines and scythed chariots (the latter shamelessly plagiarised from Roberto Valtario's treatise *De re militari* of 1472 and offered with a word of caution that such devices were liable to do as much damage to one's own troops as to the enemy's). But these ideas were of less interest to Ludovico Sforza lately since, taking a leaf perhaps from the Medici playbook, his strategy had instead switched from reliance upon military strength to skilled diplomacy. It is also around this time that we find Leonardo experimenting with drawings and calculations relating to correlations of ideal human proportions with geometry, as described by the ancient Roman architect Vitruvius in Book III of his treatise *De architectura*. These would later become manifested in Leonardo's famous 'Vitruvian Man' or *Le proporzioni del corpo umano secondo Vitruvio* which was drawn around 1490.

Leonardo also made desultory attempts to commence work on his great bronze equestrian statue of the Sforza family *padrone* but true to form, and although he had already conducted dissections on horses cadavers in Florence in order to learn more about their anatomy, his efforts on this project were at best sporadic and intermittent. The memorialising of the Sforza name in bronze would, for the time being, have to wait. Other dynasties meanwhile did not feel they had the leisure to wait for their ennoblement and apotheosis. The most disruptive of these resided in Rome – the Riario-della Rovere family. Their hunger for legitimacy would soon propel northern Italy into yet another unwelcome and destructive conflict.

CHAPTER 12

The Settling of Scores

This man has lived long enough for his own immortal fame, but not for
Italy. God grant that now he is dead men may not attempt that which
they dared not do while he was alive.

King Ferrante of Naples upon learning
of the death of Lorenzo de' Medici

Whilst Lorenzo de' Medici concentrated on astute measures to shore up
his political control over the Florentine republic, his nemesis and the
sole surviving member of the Pazzi Conspiracy, Count Girolamo Riario,
blithely continued in his louche ways from a safe distance in Rome. Here, at the
Palazzo Riario, he continued to scheme and conspire with his uncle Pope Sixtus
IV to carve out a legacy for the formerly obscure Riario-della Rovere family. At
his side was the beautiful, vivacious and independent-minded Caterina Sforza,
a young woman who–though still in her first blush of youth–towered
uncomfortably over her husband in both natural intelligence and single-
mindedness of purpose. For himself, Riaro remained the low-born coward and
dilettante he had always been. His back-seat role in the failed Pazzi Conspiracy
and the abortive conquest of Florence which followed had cost him considerable
prestige in Rome and behind closed doors and in the many taverns of the city
he had become the butt of many ribald jokes. As *gonfaloniere* of the papal
armies he cut a particularly incongruous figure and had not even bothered to
learn the basic rudiments of the art of war. Pallid and obese, he could barely
ride his own horse let alone command troops in the thick of battle. Yet this
mattered little for family connections and not talent counted for everything
during these corrupt times. Seemingly immune to public criticism of his blatant
nepotism, Pope Sixtus continued to squander vast amounts of papal treasure
on promoting Girolamo's career and future prospects.

The hinge of Sixtus's policy of ennoblement for his nephew lay in the twin
towns of Forli and Imola; from these two fiefdoms a powerful new Riario-della
Rovere state would be created in the Romagna with Girolamo as its secular lord
and Cardinal Giuliano della Rovere as its spiritual enforcer within the Sacred
College. The late Cardinal Pietro Riario had already completed the purchase of
Imola for Pope Sixtus one year prior to the cardinal's own death in 1474.
Neighbouring Forli had meanwhile dropped like a ripe plumb into Sixtus's
hands thanks in large measure to the interminable family squabbling of the
ruling Ordelaffi clan. After the despised fratricide Pino III Ordelaffi of Forli died
in October 1480, he had left his infant son Sinibaldo under the regency of his
third wife Lucrezia Pico della Mirandola (the sister of the philosopher Giovanni

Pico della Mirandola who would soon enter Lorenzo de' Medici's humanist circle). The late Pino III's three nephews, sons of the brother Cecco whom he had murdered in order to obtain the lordship of Forlì, had returned and contested Lucrezia for ownership of the town and the widow had withdrawn to the fortress known as the Rocca di Ravaldino. Seizing their moment, Sixtus and Girolamo had despatched papal troops to Forlì to take possession of the town, declaring the Ordelaffi title to Forlì null and void. The ostensible reason given was that Forlì, like other towns in the Romagna, was a papal fief and the Ordelaffi had resisted previous attempts by the Church to reclaim its rightful property. Lucrezia Pico della Mirandola was bought off and re-housed in an alternative *castello* elsewhere whilst the three disgruntled Ordelaffi brothers had been banished. Predictably, Count Girolamo Riario was installed as lord of Forlì in their place.

The positioning of Riario in such a strategic economic and military crossroads as Forlì, controlling as it did the lines of communications from north to south and east to west, was both inflammatory and destabilising and yet the Pope seemed determined to transform his 'heir' into one of the most powerful dynastic lords on the peninsula. With these considerations in mind Riario had also lately been busy producing heirs. A daughter named Bianca, named for Caterina's grandmother Bianca Maria Visconti and born in March 1478, was the couple's first child. The daughter was soon followed in September 1479 by a son, Ottaviano, and then by another son, Cesare, in August 1480. Pope Sixtus IV looked on, intoxicated by the thought of Girolamo emulating the success of Francesco Sforza and siring a mighty and powerful clan destined to be greatly respected in Italy. The reality could not of course have been further removed from the dream. Girolamo Riario was no Francesco Sforza. Indeed, Girolamo's cowardice manifested itself at every turn. Even as the Count left the Palazzo Riario in Rome to take possession of his two new fiefdoms in the Romagna his paranoia took hold and he was gripped by the morbid fear of assassination. The defences of both towns, as well as measures for his and his family's personal security, were tightened up and the *rocca* at Forlì was substantially improved and upgraded to provide a secure refuge for the Count and his family in the event of invasion or domestic upheaval.

The Rocca di Ravaldino which still stands proud to this day in the town of Forlì boasted the latest state-of-the-art defensive innovations. At a pinch it could provide refuge for the entire 10,000 strong population of the town if necessary. Riario's growing obsession with safety from assassination was, with no small measure of irony, to prefigure later events. He held off visiting his new fief for the time being, instead assigning his trusted *condottiere* Giovanni Francesco da Tolentino to secure Forlì as the town's military governor. Putting in an intermediary to first test the waters turned out to be an uncharacteristically astute move; Tolentino, who had the instincts of a bloodhound, soon sniffed out a conspiracy by the banished Ordelaffi brothers and moved quickly to neutralise the threat. With the town's security now guaranteed, Count Girolamo Riario was formerly invested by Pope Sixtus IV in his new possessions in the Romagna and, in July 1481, the couple finally arrived in Forlì in person to much feasting and public festivity.

As Girolamo and Caterina progressed on to Imola the wheels of papal diplomacy were still turning, still scheming. Count Riario's two fiefs of Forlì and Imola were separated by a third town called Faenza and it was only natural that Girolamo should covet this independent town as well. Faenza, which was still harbouring the troublesome Ordelaffi brothers, was ruled by Galeotto Manfredi. Manfredi, who in his youth had fought for the Republic of Venice under the renowned *condottiere* Bartolomeo Colleoni, was however no pushover like the Ordelaffi. Furthermore, he was protected by the powerful Duke Ercole d'Este of Ferrara. In order to assimilate Faenza it therefore followed that Ercole d'Este, who had himself acquired a broad belt of former papal lands stretching from Reggio to Modena, would somehow need to be crushed. The duke of Ferrara had already earned the enmity of Pope Sixtus by choosing to fight on the side of his friend Lorenzo de' Medici in the Pazzi War. Claiming Ferrara for the papacy, Sixtus had in retaliation excommunicated Ercole and declared him deposed, gestures which were more symbolic than anything else and the duke of Ferrara had not been slow in demonstrating his contempt for papal fiat.

Ferrara had meanwhile also angered Venice by encroaching upon Venice's lucrative monopoly on the production of salt. To add insult to injury, Ferrara had used for this purpose certain lands in the Comacchio which had ironically been leased from *La Serenissima*. Furthermore, the Most Serene Republic's notional alliance with Florence in the Pazzi War had left her with little tangible gains to compensate her for the long and costly years of conflict. To make matters worse, Lorenzo's recent rapprochement with Ferrante of Naples sent warning signals that the Medici were once again planning to change the balance of power on the peninsula. The Venetians had never taken kindly to Ercole's 1473 marriage to the *Napoletano* Princess Eleonora d'Aragona and feared the intervention of her father Ferrante in Lombardy's affairs. Feeling increasingly isolated, Venice was actively seeking new strategic partners by this time.

Since Ferrante's change of heart concerning Lorenzo de' Medici meant that Rome could not act against Florence directly, Pope Sixtus IV now decided instead to focus his efforts on Lorenzo's ally Ercole d'Este. The shared purpose between the papacy and Venice over the question of Ferrara made them natural allies. By contrast, Milan could not be counted upon to support Riario's bid for Faenza, regardless of the fact that he was married to a daughter of the Sforza. Ludovico Sforza's rise to power had changed the nature of this particular alliance and Ludovico himself was notoriously jealous of anyone's advancement other than his own. In 1481, Ludovico had won his final victory over his sister-in-law Bona–with whom Caterina Sforza had always been especially close–forcing Bona from Milan and seizing the dukedom from Caterina's brother Gian Galeazzo. As such, Ludovico *il Moro* could hardly be counted upon to now assist his niece or her Riario husband. Pope Sixtus therefore orchestrated a state visit to Venice for Girolamo and Caterina with the intention of sealing a Papal-Venetian pact. This concordat would not only serve to weaken Ferrara (and thereby help secure Faenza) but, in a wider sense, it would contest the growing threat posed by the bloc of Naples, Florence and Ferrara.

In September 1481, Girolamo and his wife arrived in the Most Serene Republic to be met personally by the Doge himself, Giovanni Mocenigo, who descended the steps of the palace to greet them personally. Although she was eight months pregnant at the time, the young Caterina still exuded considerable beauty and glamour. As if being met personally by the Doge was not honour enough, the Venetians proceeded to confer upon the podgy former prune seller élite membership in the nobility of Venice. The countess of Forlì and Imola was meanwhile granted over one hundred Venetian ladies-in-waiting to attend upon her person. The Doge suspended matters of state to give the couple a personal guided tour of the city and, amidst the delightful amusements and endless socialising, the practical terms of the alliance were duly hammered out. Venice promised to assist Rome in her coming conflict with the duchy of Ferrara and would be awarded the *Ferrarese* possessions of Reggio and Modena in return for Venice helping to secure the town of Faenza for Count Riario.

However, although the pact seemed straightforward to Riario and the Pope, not everything was what it appeared. The Venetians were perhaps the most sophisticated and mercurial diplomatists in all of Italy and, although they treated their upstart guests with all due pomp and ceremony, behind closed doors they deliberated at length on the count's very obvious personal shortcomings. For one thing, they speculated whether Riario, who was still *gonfaloniere* of the Pope's army, could truly be depended upon as an effective and reliable ally in the coming war with Ferrara? The Medici agent inside Forlì, the archdeacon of the town, echoed these same sentiments back to Lorenzo, affirming that the Riario's state visit to Venice, though apparently a diplomatic success, had in reality produced little in tangible terms that Florence needed to be afraid of. Either oblivious of, or else complicit in, her husband's plotting against Ercole d'Este, Caterina meanwhile wrote amicable letters to Ercole's wife, her friend Eleonora d'Aragona, pleading with her to send her some of their renowned Ferrarese hunting dogs.

Emboldened by the news that the Venetians, plagued as they obviously were with reservations concerning Girolamo Riario's competence, were playing it coy, Lorenzo de' Medici decided to intervene in his enemy's affairs by backing a rebellion within Forlì. Both he and Ercole d'Este financed a blue collar plot by some discontented *Forlivese* tradesmen to assassinate Girolamo and Caterina whilst they were en route from Venice to Forlì. Because of the lowly occupations of those involved, this plot became known as 'the Artisan Conspiracy'. The plot, however, was quickly uncovered and neutralised by Riario's loyal *capitano* Giovanni Francesco da Tolentino. When the couple returned to Forlì it was to the reassuring sight of the artisan conspirators dangling by their broken necks from the walls of the Palazzo Riario. As a result of this, however, the Count lapsed back into his customary fits of paranoia, surrounding himself with hundreds of armed guards. It was not long before the family retreated once more to the relative safety of Rome as preparations continued for their war against Ferrara. The coming conflict was by now an open secret in Italy. Lorenzo de' Medici was galvanised into action and hasty Florentine diplomacy now drew the old allies of Florence, Milan and Naples back into each other's orbits in order to meet the joint threat presented by Venice and Rome.

Although Venice had doubted Girolamo's attributes as an effective ally in any conflict with Ferrara, circumstances had followed their own inevitable course and the on-going dispute between the two city-states over the lucrative salt monopoly had flared up once again. Ercole d'Este had refused point blank to cease using the leased lands of the Comacchio to produce salt however, as aggravating as this was, Venice could not go to war on this pretext alone. Instead, a minor jurisdictional dispute involving Venice's representative in Ferrara, the *visdominio*, was used as a casus belli and war was duly declared between the two states in the spring of 1482. Venice now called upon the papal *gonfaloniere* to put his troops into the field alongside the Venetians; these were then joined by additional forces supplied by Venice's sister maritime republic Genoa as well as by additional contingents from William VIII, Marquis of Montferrat. Lining up on Ferrara's side under the supreme command of

Federico da Montefeltro of Urbino was the army of Ercole's father-in-law Ferrante of Naples, commanded as usual by his son Alfonso of Calabria. Ludovico Sforza of Milan, Federico I Gonzaga of Mantua and Giovanni II Bentivoglio of Bologna, all of whom felt increasingly threatened by Venice's growing power on the mainland, contributed additional forces. Lorenzo de' Medici and the Florentine republic provided Ercole d'Este with supplemental mercenary troops as well as financial assistance. With the shrivelling of her maritime trade in the Eastern Mediterranean since 1453, Venice's compensatory tendency to flex her muscles on the Italian peninsula had brought her under considerable suspicion from the land-locked city-states; Florence's allies were therefore strongly committed to containing her influence.

The 'War of Ferrara' commenced with rapid Venetian advances in the north under the command of the *condottiere* Roberto da Sanseverino. The territories of Adria, Comacchio, Argenta, Ficarolo and Rovigo were quickly either overrun or besieged while other Venetian formations crossed the Po River and began laying siege to the city of Ferrara itself late in the year. Meanwhile, the duke of Calabria–on his way north to assist Ferrara–had entered papal territory from the south and begun laying waste to the land. Ordered by Pope Sixtus IV to confront Alfonso's *Napoletano* troops with his papal forces, the *gonfaloniere* Girolamo Riaro instead set up his headquarters at the basilica of St. John Lateran inside the Roman walls near the Appian Gate. Here, on the flimsy pretext that he was ensuring the domestic peace of the city, he idled his time away at dice and cards in the Sacristy as the rest of his troops lolled around the precincts of the papal cathedral or told bawdy jokes to one another much to the horror of the resident priests. Ferrante used the opportunity presented by Riario's rank incompetence to persuade the Colonna, Savelli and della Valle families to stir up trouble within the Roman patrimony and their rag tag bands of *bravi* and cutthroat thugs now joined forces with Alfonso's Spanish and *Napoletano* troops. Alfonso proved as active and vigorous as Girolamo had proven supine and ineffective. The food supply to the city of Rome was soon disrupted and, as municipal tensions grew, the Pope was compelled for the sake of his own safety to transform the Vatican into an armed military fortress.

In frustration at his nephew's inactivity, the Pope made a humiliating appeal to Venice for military help. Venice responded by sending the pontiff a relief expedition of fresh, well-drilled Venetian troops under the command of Roberto Malatesta, the lord of Rimini. Malatesta, who was married to Federico da Montefeltro's daughter Elizabeth, had been invested with the vicariate of papal Rimini by Sixtus IV in 1475, but during the Pazzi Wars he had fought on the side of Florence. Now reconciled once more with the See of Rome, he was a talented commander and certainly a match for the experienced soldier Alfonso. On 15 August he and Girolamo Riario marched their 9,000 troops in procession through the *piazza* of St. Peter as Pope Sixtus gave his solemn benediction from an upper storey window. The armies of Alfonso of Calabria and Roberto Malatesta met in pitched battle on 20 August 1482 in what was to become notorious as one of the bloodiest engagements of the entire Renaissance period, Campo Morto – the 'Field of Death'. The Battle of Campo Morto was fought near Frosinone in the Lazio, less than 100 miles south-east of Rome. The battle, according to Niccolò Machiavelli, 'was fought with more virtue than any other that had been made in fifty years of Italy'. The duke of Calabria had positioned his outnumbered troops in the inhospitable coastal marshes and lowland woodlands on a small hill which had just two entrances from the neighbouring marsh. He had in his army some contingents of the fearsome remnant Muslim Janissaries who had capitulated to him at Otranto in 1481. These Muslim troops bravely repulsed an initial attack by Malatesta's foot soldiers however, due to the marshy conditions and a sudden rain shower, the Venetian general's heavy cavalry was incapacitated and unable to follow up.

Fortunately for the Venetians, Malatesta had taken the precaution of drafting unusually large numbers of crossbowmen into his ranks as opposed to the preferred firearms of the era. As the *Napoletani* struggled to ignite their harquebuses, cannons and falconets, all of which were rendered ineffective by damp gunpowder, Malatesta's men were unencumbered by the wet conditions. Mounting flanking attacks with swarms of these lethal crossbowmen firing quarrels into the enemy's ranks, the Venetian and papal troops steadily gained the advantage. Seeing that his fellow *Napoletani* were on the verge of being routed by the crossbowmen, Alfonso finally abandoned his army and fled down the coast to Terracina. By the end of the horrendous engagement two thousand men lay dead from their wounds; it was one of the highest death tolls of any battle fought during this period. As several hundred *Napoletano* noblemen were led away in chains to Rome, Girolamo Riario counted himself fortunate that he had the strategic foresight to remain in the rear for much of the bloody battle, guarding the army's precious marquees.

Roberto Malatesta's death in Rome on 10 September from malaria probably contracted in the unhealthy marshes of the Campo Morto meant that Pope Sixtus IV–who had given the *condottiere* supreme unction at the very last–was largely unable to capitalise upon papal military successes in the Lazio. By sheer coincidence, the *Ferrarese* supreme commander Federigo da Montefeltro had also been struck down by a fever whilst campaigning in Ferrara and had died on exactly the same day as his son-in-law. Consequently, the duke of Urbino's daughter Elisabeth had to endure the twin misfortune of learning that both her father and her husband had died within twenty-four hours of each other. Disenchanted with the course of the war and particularly the appalling casualties of Campo Morto, and still prey to the domestic disturbances being caused by the ungovernable Colonna, Savelli and della Valle clans, Pope Sixtus meanwhile found himself in an unenviable position. For once the Pope had begun, not before time it must be said, to find fault with his incompetent nephew Girolamo Riario. Ludovico Sforza could not have summarised the situation better when he remarked caustically that the War of Ferrara was begun 'for Girolamo's ambitions, without regard for the men who are thrown to the wolves and the people who are ruined'. As Pope Sixtus's own position was being daily weakened, his arch enemy Lorenzo de' Medici seemed to ride out the conflict with ease. Indeed, Lorenzo had used the débâcle of Campo Morto to equip his *condottiere* Niccolò Vitelli with an army so that he could seize Città di Castello for Florence while the Pope was otherwise occupied.

Disgusted with the situation in which Girolamo's incompetence had placed him, Pope Sixtus now looked to Cardinal Giuliano della Rovere to resolve matters. Giuliano could not have been more different from his idle, porcine cousin. Shrewd, astute, ruthless and with an understanding of long term political and military strategy, the cardinal decamped to the city of Cremona where negotiations were opened with all the major combatants. As a result of these negotiations, in which Lorenzo de' Medici took an active and personal role, Pope Sixtus–who had already concluded a separate peace with Naples on 28

November–reached a general armistice with all the other belligerent powers except for Venice on 13 December 1482.

In the north, Sixtus had grown alarmed at the deadly efficiency of his Venetian ally's advance and the rapidity with which Venetian forces had laid siege to Ferrara itself. He now executed that most characteristic and ubiquitous of Italian diplomatic manoeuvres, a U-turn. When the Pope's entreaties to Venice to break off hostilities were ignored he excommunicated his former ally, which in turn retaliated by recalling its ambassador from Rome. Then, in early 1483, Pope Sixtus formed a new Holy League comprising Rome, Milan, Florence and Naples whose purpose was to oppose his erstwhile ally Venice for the 'crime' of having disobeyed his instructions and ignoring his interdict. At this point in Sixtus's deteriorating relations with Venice he now granted Alfonso of Calabria free passage through papal lands to counter the Venetians and assist their Ferrarese allies, the upshot of which was that the 2,000 odd casualties of Campo Morto had effectively suffered and died for nothing. As if this was not quite bad enough, Sixtus also despatched papal troops under the command of Virginio Orsini to assist in the relief of Ferrara. The Pope had already forgotten that suppressing Ferrara was still the key to obtaining Faenza; either forgotten or perhaps he genuinely no longer cared about Girolamo's interests. This notwithstanding, Sixtus appointed Caterina's uncle Ascanio Sforza as cardinal in March 1483, which nevertheless gave the couple, and Ludovico, another powerful Sforza ally, this time in the Sacred College.

Pope Sixtus IV had by now become a shadow of his fiery former self. At sixty-nine he was by now aged, weak and possibly suffering from remorse over the many inclement decisions that he had made during his pontificate. As his personal willpower waned so Girolamo Riario's influence in Rome increased and the nephew soon gained the ascendant in papal affairs, a development which would ultimately prove disastrous for the city of Rome. In the immediate aftermath of the peace terms gained at the Council of Cremona in 1483, Girolamo had joined forces with Cardinal Raffaele Sansoni Riario, the former stooge in the Pazzi Conspiracy, to extort and defraud the Curia of as much coin as was humanly possible. Merely in order for them to be allowed to keep their positions, priests and other papal employees were forced to pay the hefty fees and penalties extracted by Girolamo. He sold church benefices, imposed random taxes and openly stole moveable Church property. For his greed and rapacity Girolamo was denounced by his own relative Antonio Basso della Rovere who, on his death bed, declared that the count of Bosco, Forlì and Imola had 'committed crimes that had scandalised the universe'. Meanwhile, to his wife Caterina's disgust, he had gathered around him an entourage of thugs and flatterers who urged him on to ever more outrageous crimes and sacrilegious acts. He had placed one of his favoured henchmen, Innocenzo Codronchi, in charge of the Castel Sant'Angelo, the single most important fortification in Rome and the key to controlling the city as well as the Vatican and its Borgo. Another of his followers, the *condottiere* Giovanni Francesco da Tolentino, who governed Forlì with a rod of iron on his behalf, was now brought to Rome to help Girolamo sniff out dissent and conspiracies within the Curia itself. But most damaging of all was Girolamo's growing dalliance with Virginio Orsini, the lord of Bracciano. Egged on by his new Orsini ally, Girolamo now ruthlessly acted out his grudge against the Colonna for their treason in having backed Alfonso of Calabria's play at the Battle of Campo Morto.

In reality, the low-intensity conflict between the della Rovere papacy and the Colonna had persisted throughout the dreary War of Ferrara. Even before Campo Morto, in April 1482, Girolamo and Virginio Orsini's allies the Santa Croce family had assaulted the *palazzo* of the Colonna-allied della Valle and in the resulting scuffle a member of the Colonna had been killed. Although Pope Sixtus had stepped in to try to pacify the powerful Colonna by raising the houses of the Santa Croce as a quid pro quo it had not prevented Girolamo from taking his highly personal anti-Colonna crusade to the next level. In June he had Cardinal Giovanni Colonna and Cardinal Giovanni Battista Savelli arrested on charges of plotting his murder and the two unfortunate prelates were despatched to grim lodgings in the bowels of the Castel Sant'Angelo. Meanwhile, Girolamo had transformed the family's apartments in the Vatican into something resembling an armed military camp where soldiers and mercenaries came and went at all hours of the day and night.

In 1483, during the first weeks of Lent, Pope Sixtus suddenly fell ill and the Riario-della Rovere household slipped immediately into crisis mode. With uncharacteristic clarity, the count of Bosco and his wife Caterina could foresee that their own influence in Rome could not survive the death of the Pope. The Curia and the Roman populace at-large hated the Riario and della Rovere family; once removed from the protection of Pope Sixtus the mob was poised to consign them back to the dismal oblivion from whence they had sprung. As a precaution, the couple left Rome in June only to return again in November, by which time Caterina was already pregnant once more. Worryingly, however, the Pope's health showed no signs of improvement and their position in Rome continued to be precarious. But this still failed to dampen Girolamo's excesses. As the new year of 1484 got underway, Count Riario initiated all-out war on the Colonna, joyfully assisted by Virginio Orsini.

Coveting two of the most powerful Colonna fortresses at Palliano and Marino, the Count insisted that his uncle summon Lorenzo Colonna, lord of Marino and protonotary of the Church, to answer certain allegations against him. When Lorenzo prudently refused to answer the summons, Girolamo went with 200 heavily armed henchmen to the Colonna *palazzo* at the Piazza Venezia. Here, an argument at the front gate between Riario's intemperate *bravi* and the nervous Colonna guards led to a violent brawl which left several men on either side either dead or wounded. To prevent further bloodshed the protonotary Lorenzo surrendered his person into Virginio Orsini's hands and was brought back under guard to the Castel Sant'Angelo. Throughout the entire journey an enraged Girolamo Riario braced the protonotary and uttered murderous threats against his life, even attempting at one point to stab him with his dagger. Virginio Orsini had interpolated himself between Girolamo and the protonotary to prevent the latter from being killed on the spot. When an envoy from the Colonna subsequently begged for the protonotary's release, offering in return the Colonna strongholds of Marino and Ardea, a crazed Girolamo had the unfortunate messenger put to death. He did not need to be handed Colonna properties on a plate, he would *take* the Colonna fortresses by storm if he so decided. When his cousin Giuliano della Rovere attempted to intercede and inject a note of restraint into this escalating situation, Girolamo was enraged at his cousin's interference and threatened to burn the cardinal's *palazzo* down with the cardinal inside it.

On 29 June 1484, the unfortunate protonotary Lorenzo was executed at the courtyard of the Castel Sant'Angelo after a month-long imprisonment during which he was subjected to the cruellest torments imaginable. It was said that, when the Colonna opened the coffin in which the decapitated corpse had been returned to them, the body of the protonotary showed all the signs of having been suspended with heavy weights, an especially agonising and sadistic form of torture. Girolamo's motives in persecuting the powerful Colonna at this point when his own fortunes hung so precariously in the balance can only be guessed at. If he believed himself to be eradicating a future Colonna threat to his position once Sixtus was dead then he was sadly deluding himself. The only person who stood to gain from persecuting the Colonna was the Orsini lord of Bracciano. Colonna malice against Girolamo proliferated as a direct result and his actions had merely served to drive nails into his own coffin. Even his young wife Caterina saw the foolishness of his conduct and, in the aftermath of the protonotary Lorenzo's illegal and unjust execution, she now visibly distanced herself from her husband. This savage and unnecessary act had in fact outraged the whole of Roman society and Girolamo Riario was by now increasingly regarded by all except his closest henchmen as being completely beyond the pale.

Worse however was to come on 7 August 1484. On that day the Treaty of Bagnolo was concluded between all the belligerents in the on-going War of Ferrara, which had by now acquired the soubriquet 'the Diplomat's War'. Ludovico Sforza had already pulled out of the Holy League and Venice was indelicately lobbying for the international involvement of the French against Naples (in pursuit of her Angevin claim to the kingdom) and also against Milan (in pursuit of her Orléanist claim to the duchy). The involvement of France in Italy's affairs was the last thing anyone wanted and so it made sense to draw this most unproductive and pointless conflict to a close. By the terms of the treaty, Ercole d'Este ceded to Venice the territory of Rovigo in the Polesine, lost early on during the fighting whilst, for their part, the Venetian troops still occupying *Ferrarese* territory agreed to withdraw. Ferrara, furthermore, remained in the hands of the Este and was not to be absorbed back into the Papal States. The Peace of Bagnolo meanwhile arrested any further Venetian expansionism in northern Italy by ceding to the maritime state not only Rovigo but also a broad swath of the Po Delta. This acquisition agreed upon at Bagnolo marked the high-point of Venetian territorial gains on terra firma and never again would Venice control so large a swathe of land nor have so much influence in northern Italy as it did in the last half of the fifteenth-century.

Despite the peace, Pope Sixtus IV was greatly displeased with the terms which had been reached without seeking his personal consultation. On 11 August, emissaries arrived in Rome to deliver the specific terms of the treaty. According to several eye witness accounts, upon hearing these terms the Pope was suddenly seized by a palsy of impotent rage. He was heard to utter: 'Up to this time we have carried on a dangerous and difficult war, in order, by our victorious arms, to obtain an honourable peace for the security of the Apostolic See, our own honour, and that of the League ... This peace, my beloved sons in Christ, I can neither approve nor sanction.' In a long life of poor decisions and disappointments, a life which had mostly been devoted to elevating his humble but often maladroit relatives, the peace treaty was the final crushing humiliation. The pontiff withdrew to his private apartments and by the following morning Francesco della Rovere was dead.

The death of Pope Sixtus IV was received not so much with elation as with exhausted relief in Florence. Since the beginning of the Imola affair and extending through the bitter years of the Pazzi Conspiracy and the various wars which had followed in its wake, the Pope had proven to be the republic's most implacable enemy. Florence and the Medici had not only suffered both politically and economically as a direct result of the Pope's scheming but Lorenzo had been forced to endure the death of a cherished brother. By this time much of Italy also felt the same way. Years of pointless war had ravaged the peninsula all in the name of the Pope's misguided efforts to enrich and ennoble his undeserving family. The Curia and Sacred College also breathed a visible collective sigh of relief and Cardinal Rafaelle Sansoni Riario was duly appointed camerlengo of the Church in charge of guiding the appointment of his uncle's successor. It was an odd choice, to say the least, to select another Riario to be camerlengo but it was assumed that even a Riario cardinal would not be so foolish as to even attempt to engineer the election of another Riario or della Rovere pontiff.

Even as the cardinals were girding themselves to enter the papal conclave for the selection of the new bishop of Rome, the banished Colonna, Savelli and della Valle were pouring back into the city with their men. One of their first acts of retribution was to sack the Palazzo Riario–today known as the Palazzo Altemps–which had been constructed in 1479 for Count Girolamo by the mathematician Luca Pacioli with interiors designed by Pope Sixtus's own court painter Melozzo da Forlì. The *palazzo* was situated just north of the heavily-settled area around the Piazza Navona and across the street from the Church of St. Apollinare. A typical nouveau riche, Girolamo had insisted on the most ostentatious decorations and adornments that money could buy, including the most intricately carved marble pilasters and capitals. When the Colonna mob ransacked the *palazzo* these and innumerable other exquisite works of Roman Renaissance art were either removed or vandalised. As the Florentine ambassador Guidantonio Vespucci wrote to Lorenzo de' Medici, 'still they did not cease to destroy and take away until they came to the hinges and nails of the house'. The palace would later come into the possession of Cardinal Sansoni Riario.

The consequences of Girolamo's stupendous lack of foresight in persecuting the Colonna whilst he had the upper hand now came home to roost. All that his uncle had built for him in Rome and the Papal States of the Romagna were now in dire jeopardy. To evade the inevitable riotous Roman mobs which always attended the death of a pontiff, the Count and his wife stationed themselves east of Rome at the town of Paliano which, rather ironically, also happened to be a Colonna stronghold. Meanwhile, the College of Cardinals ordered Girolamo to cease hostilities with the Colonna forthwith whilst simultaneously denying his entry to Rome in order to safeguard his property. Not only were his *palazzi* and other property in the city in the process of being systematically looted and destroyed but it would have been negligent of him to not at least attempt to assert some measure of influence over the election of his late uncle's successor. However, as the civil disturbances spread through the city both he and Virginio Orsini were incapable of advancing further than the Ponte Molle, the Milvian Bridge, which spanned the northern section of the Tiber.

It was at this point, as the Riario's fortunes teetered on the brink of complete destruction, that Caterina Sforza abandoned the comfortable world of noble female domesticity and entered the realm of historical legend. Although already seven months pregnant and big with child, Caterina took to horse and with a small bodyguard rode from her husband's camp at Paliano to the Castel Sant'Angelo where, on 14 August, she took control of the fortress. The cannon of Sant'Angelo effectively controlled the city of Rome and so, dismissing her husband's castellan Innocenzo Codronchi, she ordered that the fortress's artillery be concentrated on the road leading from the city of Rome across the Ponte Sant'Angelo to the Vatican. This clever interdiction prevented the College of Cardinals from proceeding to St. Peter's to form the papal conclave and thus delayed the election process for the new pontiff. Her execution of this bold standoff was truly a move worthy of a Sforza; however it also had the added advantage of being more effective than her husband's dramatic yet ultimately impotent posturing at the Ponte Molle. The intelligent and perceptive Caterina knew that the only way the Riarios would be able to secure both their properties and their titles would be if the cardinals were forced to recognise them before they elected a new pope. As the uncertain period of *sede vacante* dragged on and the city of Rome descended into even greater chaos, Caterina's leverage over the cardinals only increased.

On 17 August, a funeral was held for Pope Sixtus IV which was attended by eleven members of the Sacred College, including Cardinal Giuliano della Rovere, the remainder of the Curia having been too afraid to run the gauntlet of Caterina's cannon in Sant'Angelo. Cardinal Raffaelle Sansoni Riario sent an emissary in an attempt to defuse the impasse but Caterina immediately saw through the ploy and the insincerity of motive which lay behind it. On 23 August, the College of Cardinals–led by the papal vice-chancellor Rodrigo Borgia–sought to cut a separate deal with Count Girolamo which would, they hoped, pull the rug from under his wilful and unruly wife. In return for a payment of 8,000 ducats, the assurance of his seignory over Forlì and Imola, and the promise that he would continue in the role of *gonfaloniere* of the papal armies, Girolamo agreed to withdraw from Rome. Caterina's contemptuous response to this independently-made deal with her incompetent spouse was to reinforce her garrison with an additional 150 soldiers and remain resolutely put. She now intended to parlay only with the newly elected pope. Caterina knew that Cardinal Borgia and the others could not be trusted to keep their word and she demanded more watertight assurances.

The matter was finally resolved when, on 25 August, she was visited at the Castel Sant'Angelo by her uncle Cardinal Ascanio Sforza and eight other cardinals. The delegation confirmed her demands in writing and assured her that she would be granted safe passage out of Rome and back to Forlì. The following morning she emerged from the fortress with her escort of heavily armed troops to the astonished gaze of the denizens of Rome who had gathered at the Ponte Sant'Angelo to watch the spectacle. Heavily pregnant, Caterina was exhausted and dirty from her ordeal yet her attire was nevertheless rich and impressive. From her belt hung a fresh accoutrement which she would continue to wear in the future: a man's sword. In the hypermasculine and sexually-exclusive world of Quattrocento politics, a world in which women were relegated to the discreet role of child bearers and housekeepers, Caterina had achieved a stunning settlement which quite possibly amazed her as much as anyone else.

Two minute's walk from the bustling Campo de' Fiori in Rome squats the city's first Renaissance palace, the Palazzo della Cancelleria, built in the Florentine style by Donato Bramante using fine, bone-hued travertine as well as original

299

Roman columns scavenged from the ruins of the nearby ancient Theatre of Pompey. The magnificent *palazzo*, which was originally commissioned in 1489 by Cardinal Raffaele Sansoni Riario, was said to have been financed by a single night's winnings at cards. The unfortunate loser that evening is rumoured to have been the *Genovese* aristocrat Franceschetto Cybò, son-in-law to Lorenzo the Magnificent of Florence and bastard son of Giambattista Cybò, the cardinal who had been elected to replace Pope Sixtus IV and who had taken the name Innocent VIII. For all his splendid family connections Franceschetto Cybò ranks perhaps as one of the most incompetent Renaissance gamblers of all time. He was, by all accounts, also something of a sore loser. After foregoing vast quantities of ducats at the gaming table to Cardinal Riario he is said to have run crying to his father the Pope and complained that this prince of the Church had cheated and bamboozled him.

Wastrel scions of the nobility are of course nothing new; the phenomenon was a widespread one in Renaissance Italy, as in other eras. However, it must be said that Franceschetto Cybò brought a whole new level of accomplishment to a lifelong vocation of gambling, drinking, whoring, gallivanting and depleting the papal coffers. You might be forgiven for imagining that to be as prodigiously and as studiously dissolute as young Cybò undoubtedly was required at least a certain level of functional intelligence. However, in this you would be wrong, for the young man's profligacy operated entirely independently from a mind which was, at bottom, utterly vacant. In this respect the apple had not fallen far from the tree.

Franceschetto's father, Pope Innocent VIII, had–upon his accession to the chair of St. Peter on 29 August 1484–proven himself to be weak-willed, unfocused, nepotistic and self-engrossed. All in the Curia acknowledged that Pope Innocent VIII's eight-year tenure was little more than a stopgap measure designed to solve the impasse between competing bids for the tiara by two of the papal court's bitterest rivals. These were Cardinal Giuliano della Rovere, nephew to the late and largely unlamented Pope Sixtus IV, and the Catalan Cardinal Rodrigo Borgia, the papal vice-chancellor. As one curtain had closed on the recent drama of Caterina Sforza in the Castel Sant'Angelo, so the stage was set for a new spectacle involving these two implacable ecclesiastical contenders. In the conclave, neither cardinal had possessed the requisite number of majority votes to ensure their own election. Coupled to this was the fact that, despite his huge ambition, or perhaps possibly because of it, Cardinal della Rovere had never been generally well-liked at the papal court. Far more popular than either of these men was the 'man of the moment', the Venetian cardinal and triumphant papal diplomat Marco Barbo. However, although Cardinal Barbo was held in high esteem, his native city's wider political ambitions were a cause for some concern in Rome and lingering Roman enmity towards *La Serenissima* had been the inevitable fallout from the fruitless War of Ferrara. In order to forestall the elevation of a Venetian pontiff it was therefore agreed by both antagonists that they would collaborate in the election of an inconsequential third party whom they could jointly manipulate. They settled without too much difficulty upon Cardinal Giambattista Cybò, the *Genovese* bishop of Molfetta. Such was the rancorous mood in Rome towards Venice that a candidate from Venice's rival maritime city-state of Genoa was embraced wholeheartedly by the Sacred College. As was customary, the usual bribes changed hands to speed the electoral process along.

Innocent VIII's reign, as may have been foreseen from its somewhat cynical genesis, was lacklustre and uninspiring. 'Cybò has not much experience in state affairs, nor much learning, though he is by no means illiterate', Guidantonio Vespucci had written to Lorenzo de' Medici. Vespucci then went on to affirm that under Pope Innocent it would be Cardinal della Rovere 'who may now be said to be pope, and will have more power than he had with Pope Sixtus if he knows how to hold his ground'. The most that can perhaps be said of Pope Innocent VIII is that, lacking as he did the unquenchable ambition of Sixtus IV, he was at least far less rapacious. Like Pope Paul II some years before, Innocent was at heart a sybarite who was far more interested in enjoying the immediate material comforts and perquisites of the papacy than in extending his family's actual power and influence. In the immediate aftermath of Pope Sixtus's exhausting papacy, however, this counted for much and the Curia as a whole now welcomed the hiatus presented by the installation of a pontifical underachiever.

Although they kept hold of their fiefs, Girolamo Riario and Caterina Sforza meanwhile received few benefits from Cybò's appointment. As a cardinal he had been no particular friend to the House of Riario and as pope he was well known to be on amicable terms with Girolamo's bête noir Lorenzo de' Medici. More troubling still, however, for Count Riario was the fact that his cousin Cardinal Giuliano della Rovere was now widely acknowledged as the éminence grise behind the papal throne. It had been through Cardinal della Rovere's good offices that Cybò had gained his elevation to the cardinalate, for it was he who had persuaded his uncle Pope Sixtus to advance the career of Molfetta's unprepossessing bishop. Pope Innocent naturally now owed his benefactor a debt of gratitude which tended to supersede any influence that della Rovere's rival Cardinal Borgia may have hoped to wield over His Holiness. Cardinal della Rovere had furthermore still not forgotten his cousin's threat, at the height of the Colonna crisis, to burn his *palazzo* down with him inside it.

When Pope Innocent VIII did genuinely attempt to do some good it usually came to nothing. An early promising rallying cry for a fresh Crusade against the Turk, whose sacking of the Apulian port of Otranto and martyrdom of 800 of its inhabitants was still keenly felt amongst the traumatised Italians, ultimately fell on deaf ears. The principle roadblock had been Naples's ever-irascible King Ferrante who had vigorously opposed the proposal in spite of the fact that Otranto and the Muslim incursions had occurred within his own dominions in the *Regno*. As had been noted at the Battle of Campo Morto, the *Napoletani* had made cynical use of the captured Ottoman Janissaries in their own armed forces. The king of Naples therefore harboured something of an equivocal attitude towards these godless (but useful) infidels in his midst. When Ferrante subsequently despatched Duke Alfonso of Calabria as Neapolitan envoy to the papal court, the son had proven every bit as coarse, intractable and ill-mannered as the father. Though an able soldier who had fought bravely in the Pazzi War and the War of Ferrara, Alfonso's rude and boorish manners at court succeeded in alienating not only His Holiness himself but also the powerful and influential Cardinal della Rovere. As a direct result, when in 1485 the hot-headed Alfonso persuaded his father King Ferrante to go to war with the eternally troublesome *Napoletano* barons, it was Cardinal della Rovere who counselled the Pope to come down on the side of the rebel lords. But this was to prove a considerable strategic mistake on the part of the papacy for, as Joseph Stalin would sardonically later remark to Pierre Laval in 1935, 'how many legions has the pope?' With little effective support from the militarily enfeebled papacy the insurgent *Napoletano* barons soon buckled and came to a compromise agreement with Ferrante. Naples had then marched one of its armies within sight of the city of Rome itself and it was only the military acumen of Cardinal della Rovere, deployed in an emergency hammer-blow, which managed to send the *Napoletani* recoiling back to the *Regno*.

Ferrante's concord with his barons proved short-lived. Having agreed to a marriage alliance between the son of the main conspirator, Count Francesco Coppola of Sarno, and the King's own grand-daughter Maria Piccolomini, Ferrante had the former rebels arrested during the course of the wedding feast and they were either publicly executed or else murdered secretly in prison. This put paid to Pope Innocent VIII's allies amongst the *Napoletano* barons and the papacy had been left ignominiously isolated against Naples. For his role in instigating the whole embarrassing affair, Cardinal della Rovere, whom the Florentine Ambassador had even described as the de facto pope, had lost much of his former influence at the papal court. He was now increasingly sidelined by his rival Rodrigo Borgia, whose reputation at the Vatican had remained intact throughout the entire Neapolitan crisis. Florence and Lorenzo de' Medici had meanwhile supported King Ferrante in this dispute. It was not a question of whether Lorenzo felt Ferrante's cause to be any more just than the Pope's; it was simply that the *Regno* was too powerful to have as an enemy while Florence's relations with Italy's other main power Milan were still strained. Besides, the papacy was at best an unreliable and inconstant ally. Lorenzo's opinion of Rome was uncompromisingly honest: 'This ecclesiastical state has always been the ruin of Italy because they are ignoramuses and they know nothing of governing states, and so they endanger the whole world'. Eventually a truce was signed between Naples and Rome in August 1486.

When Pope Innocent VIII was not failing dismally at his foreign policy, he was pandering to his two illegitimate offspring, his son Franceschetto ('Little Francesco') and a daughter, Teodorina Cybò. These two children had been sired during the Pope's intemperate and licentious youth. The latter was married off to the prominent *Genovese* merchant Gerardo Usodimare. The couple subsequently bore three children, including two daughters, Peretta and Battistina, and a son named Alarino. Peretta was to eventually marry the renowned *Genovese* admiral and hero Andrea Doria, whilst Battistina was married off to Luigi of Aragon, King Ferrante's grandson. As we have already seen, however, Franceschetto was something of a problem, embodying as he did all the worst hereditary traits of Pope Innocent VIII but with few of his father's saving graces. Franceschetto's gambling losses and dissolute, hard-drinking lifestyle were a continual strain on the Pope's strained finances, whose ledgers bore witness to years of largesse dispensed by his predecessor Pope Sixtus to his own nephews. The recent ill-conceived misadventure of the Neapolitan Barons War had left the papal coffers even more depleted. Pope Innocent kept pace with his son's expenses as best he could, underwriting them whenever necessary through the sale of papal offices, titles and indulgences, but even this was insufficient to keep the papal accounts in the black. The Pope needed viable ways of raising ready cash and he needed them quickly.

Fortunately for the Pope a lucrative opportunity had presented itself which promised to solve his financial worries. Innocent had lately come into the possession of one of the late Sultan Mehmet II's two sons, Prince Djem. The old

Sultan, the feared conqueror of Constantinople, had died in 1481 to be succeeded by his eldest son Bayezid II. As was the custom with the fiercely competitive sons of the Ottoman Sultan, who were often the offspring of different royal concubines, Bayezid's younger brother Djem had mounted a rebellion against his rule. When Bayezid prevailed, Djem had fled to the island of Rhodes where he took refuge with the Knights of St. John. The Christian Order's grand master, Pierre d'Aubusson, secretly came to an agreement with Bayezid to detain the troublesome Djem in return for an annual payment of 40,000 ducats. Knowing that possession of the Sultan's rival brother gave Christendom strong leverage in its war with the Turk, Pope Innocent VIII had subsequently persuaded d'Aubusson to hand Prince Djem into papal custody in return for a cardinal's hat and Djem was brought to Rome. At Rome, Djem was permitted to maintain what was, by anyone's standards, an exceedingly comfortable Turkish court-in-exile and Pope Innocent naturally inherited the annual 'pension' which Bayezid had previously paid out to the Hospitallers in order to keep his brother's nose out of his domestic affairs. Bayezid, who was keen to remain in the Pope's good graces lest he unleash the troublesome Djem in his domains, despatched an embassy to the papal court which dispensed an additional one-time payment of 120,000 ducats for Djem's guaranteed incarceration for a further three years. As a further sign of good faith, from one ruler to another, the Sultan also made the Pope a gift of the Holy Lance with which the Roman soldier Longinus was reputed to have pierced Christ's side during the Crucifixion.

In 1487, the Pope also contrived a way of palming the cost of his profligate son's maintenance onto the banker and Florentine ruler Lorenzo the Magnificent. Lorenzo, who had been so viciously persecuted by Pope Sixtus, had since Pope Innocent's elevation diligently moved to heal the breach between his family and the papacy. Innocent, who was already fairly well-disposed towards the Medici, had in fact had made the first move through one of Lorenzo's men, Pierfilippo Pandolfini. 'Lorenzo will know that there was never a pope who so loved his house as I do and having seen from experience his faith, integrity, and wisdom, I will govern myself according to his thoughts and wishes' were the Pope's words, as relayed by Pandolfini to *il Magnifico*. The restoration of good papal relations was certainly timely; the Medici Bank had gone into steep decline after Pope Sixtus had vindictively cancelled the bank's business with the Curia and closed down its Rome branch. Furthermore Lorenzo's heir apparent, his eldest son Piero, was not considered to have inherited the family intelligence and Lorenzo had sardonically begun to refer to his three sons as: 'the good' (meaning Giuliano), 'the wise' (meaning Giovanni) and 'the foolish' (which denoted Piero). It was something of an open secret that Lorenzo placed the lion's share of his future hopes for the Medici dynasty on the future governance of his plump and precociously intelligent ecclesiastical offspring Giovanni. In a shrewd piece of horse-trading, Lorenzo now finally managed to barter the long-awaited cardinal's red hat for the twelve-year-old Giovanni de' Medici. The price had been Lorenzo's consent to a dynastic marriage between the Pope's son Franceschetto and Lorenzo's daughter Maria Maddalena. At last the Medici and the current ruling papal family would be officially joined in a family and political union. The couple was given the confiscated Palazzo Pazzi in which to live and raise their future family.

No sooner had the wedding had taken place in January 1488 than the personal shortcomings of Lorenzo's new son-in-law became all too apparent.

Lorenzo doted on his daughters but not only did the inconsiderate, gallivanting Franceschetto prove to be the worst possible husband for the frail, shy, fifteen-year-old waif Maria Maddalena but, worse still, Pope Innocent showed no intention of bearing his end of his son's exorbitant upkeep. For his part, Lorenzo had already bestowed on the couple the confiscated Pazzi villa at Montughi for their residence, as well as another handsome villa at Spedaletto. Soon, however, *il Magnifico* was reduced to penning missives to His Holiness questioning whether Franceschetto could really be the son of a pope, receiving as he now did so little in the way of papal funding and maintenance. The Pope had, it was true, purchased the fief of Cerveteri from Bartolommeo della Rovere in 1487 and, after the death of Domenico d'Anguillara, Innocent VIII had also bestowed upon his son the fortress of Anguillara, the purchase of which was financed by the Medici Bank. By October 1489, however, Lorenzo was lobbying the Pope to intervene in the additional purchase of Santa Severa in order to secure Franceschetto's and his daughter's future. To Giovanni Lanfredini, who was by this time Florence's ambassador in Rome, Lorenzo wrote: 'It is urgent that His Holiness should for once and for all arrange the affairs of Signor Francesco so that I should not be daily worried about them, and that we can live in peace and harmony. To speak plainly, Signor Francesco has not the position the nephew of a Pope ought to have, and yet we are now approaching the seventh year of the pontificate. More regard should be shown to the increasing family, which is a valid reason for our Holy Father's aid.'

With his spendthrift son finally off his books and foisted on his new Medici father-in-law, Innocent VIII had meanwhile shifted his attention back to more pressing ecclesiastical affairs. The same year as his son's wedding, Pope Innocent had confirmed Tomás de Torquemada as Grand Inquisitor of the Holy Office for the Propagation of the Faith, which had been established in Spain at King Ferdinand and Queen Isabella's request in late 1478 by Pope Sixtus IV. The so-called Spanish Inquisition was not, however, properly within papal jurisdiction at all but was entirely answerable to the Spanish crown and Torquemada had in fact been Isabella's personal confessor prior to his infamous new role. Not content with placing his considerable weight behind the extirpation of heresy in Ferdinand and Isabella's Spanish domains, Pope Innocent also devoted himself wholeheartedly to the condemnation of the heretical Waldensian movement, issuing a bull for the extermination of the heretics which resulted in a brutal and horrifying 'Crusade' in the provinces of Dauphiné and Piedmont. The Waldensians were related to those other heretics the Lollards, as well as the Hussites of Bohemia, and the movement expressed a general dissatisfaction with the Roman Church amongst common grassroots peasants and townspeople which would later foreshadow that singular Church reformer Martin Luther and his Swiss counterpart Huldrych Zwingli. Opulence, nepotism, corruption, pluralism, absenteeism, worldliness and simony – far from exemplifying the transcendent values of the Kingdom of Jerusalem, the earthly Church was seen by many perceptive common people to embody these *all too human* failings.

Pope Innocent's avid activities against heresy also extended to book burnings. In 1486, he had judged thirteen of the 900 theses of the philosopher Giovanni Pico della Mirandola to be heretical and the book containing the theses was proscribed by the Church. Pico della Mirandola was by this time a good friend of Lorenzo and was a frequent guest at his philosophically-inclined dinner table. His terrifying inquisitorial cross-questioning by the Church had shaken him badly. In October 1489 we find Lorenzo de' Medici writing to Giovanni Lanfredini that 'The book has been examined by all the most learned priests here, well-known men of saintly life, and has been highly approved of by them as a Christian and a marvellous work. I am not so bad a Christian as to remain silent or to encourage him if I thought otherwise.' Sensibly, della Mirandola nevertheless kept a low profile after his brush with the Pope and as late as August 1490 we find Lorenzo once again writing to Lanfredini how 'Two days ago I met by chance the Count della Mirandola riding in the outskirts of Florence. He is living very quietly in a villa nearby, immersed in his studies. He desires at last to know what his future is to be, for having obeyed His Holiness hitherto and being decided to obey him implicitly in the future, he wishes to have some indication that His Holiness accepts his obedience in the form of a Brief, whereby the Pope acknowledges him as an obedient son and a good Christian, which I believe him to be.'

But whilst Lorenzo and his humanist friends such as Pico della Mirandola discussed Plato and Cicero at table, his new son-in-law could only find fault with the repasts being served. During a visit to Florence in June 1488, Lorenzo had not only received Franceschetto informally *en famille* but also with unassuming wholesome Tuscan dishes on the table as opposed to the lurid, candied confections which he was more used to in Rome. The Medici dinner table, complained Franceschetto petulantly, was decidedly rustic and uncouth. A more informed member of his entourage pointed out to him that Lorenzo was doing him great honour as an intimate member of the family by entertaining him in this simple Florentine manner, yet Franceschetto still pined for his complicated delicacies and lamented that he was doomed to live out his days ignominiously as a Tuscan *contadino*. His delicate wife meanwhile made the best of a bad situation, giving birth to their first offspring Lucrezia in 1489 and Clarice in 1490, and trying her hand at running a business. Acquiring the ancient Etruscan thermal bath resort in Stigliano, whose salt-iodine-sulphur waters were renowned for their healing of rheumatic and respiratory diseases, Maddalena turned the enterprise into a lucrative business. In this she was as enterprising as her grandmother Lucrezia Tornabuoni who, in 1478, had rented the thermal spa at Bagno a Morba near the Medici's Spedaletto estate near Volterra from the Knights of Monte.

The churlishness of his new son-in-law was of course a small price to pay in the more long term strategic Medici game of winning back the confidence and trust of the papacy. Fortunately for Lorenzo, Innocent VIII proved to be exactly the kind of venal personality which he, with his innate charm and knowledge of human psychology, was a past master at manipulating. Not only did the spendthrift pontiff have ready access to endless lines of Medici credit but Lorenzo was also adept at flattering and pleasing the uncomplicated and pleasure-loving man who wore the pontifical mitre. One of Pope Innocent's pleasures was to consume the ortolan, a small, olive green and yellow finch-like songbird about six inches long and weighing just four ounces. Considered a delicacy, the fat in which the ortolan was enveloped tasted like hazelnut and gourmands often consumed the flesh, fat and bones all in one, single exquisite bite. Lorenzo ensured that the Pope was kept well supplied with this epicurean treat for his dining table, sending him regular batches of the delicacy in the diplomatic bags from Tuscany. Such studied attentiveness to the Holy Father's taste buds, as well as his pockets, had paid off and in 1488 the lucrative papal alum concession was once more restored to the Medici Bank. Newly re-established as the bank's Rome branch manager, Giovanni Tornabuoni enthused that 'our affairs here, as I have told you, succeed better and better every day because of the love and affection Our Lord feels towards you'.

The Pope's beneficence also enabled Lorenzo greater freedom of action in military affairs as well. In 1487, *il Magnifico* laid siege to the *Genovese* fortress town of Sarzana with its impressive citadel, which had been lost to Genoa in the aftermath of the Pazzi Wars of 1478 and which guarded the important entrance to the valley of the Magra. It was chiefly thanks to heavy diplomatic pressure from the Pope in Rome that Florentine forces succeeded in coercing the fortress's *Genovese* defenders into capitulating. Not since the Albizzi and Capponi families had basked in the capture of Pisa had a Florentine ruler been so fêted following Sarzana's capture. When Lorenzo rode back to Florence after taking possession of the town and its fortress, the Ferrarese ambassador reported that 'The Magnificent Lorenzo arrived here on the vigil of San Giovanni and was received with more joy and caresses by the people than I care to describe, as they say they owe the taking of Sarzana to him more than to others'. Lorenzo's earlier act of attacking the *Genovese* fortress of Pietrasanta had not, however, gone down quite so well with the Ligurian pope.

For Lorenzo, the resurgence in his bank's profits and the acquisition of strategically important fortresses such as Sarzana were all very well, however his main sense of achievement during this time unquestionably lay in his having secured a cardinal's hat for the twelve-year-old Giovanni. Indeed, with regard to his second son's ecclesiastical career Lorenzo's accumulation of a multitude of rich benefices and preferment's would have caused even the late master of simony Pope Sixtus IV to blush. Having received the tonsure in 1482 at the tender age of six, just one year later Giovanni was made abbot of Font Douce in the French Diocese of Saintes thanks to the tireless efforts of the branch manager of the Medici Bank in Lyons, who also later lobbied King Louis XI to award the youth the Archbishopric of Aix-en-Provence. Additionally, Giovanni had been created apostolic protonotary by Pope Sixtus IV as part of his grudging process of reconciliation with Lorenzo. Upon his elevation in 1484, Pope Innocent VIII allowed Giovanni to possess riches accrued at the Abbey of Passignano and in 1486 he was created abbot of the historic and prestigious abbey of Montecassino, which Ferrante of Naples had conferred upon him in gratitude for Lorenzo's support during the Barons War. The reaction of the venerable Benedictine monks of Montecassino at having to take instructions from an absentee eleven-year-old boy can only be imagined. In addition to these rich pickings, by 1487 Lorenzo had also arranged for the precocious Giovanni to be awarded the important post within the Tuscan Church of bishop of Arezzo and abbot of the Cistercian monastery of Morimondo in Lombardy. These multiple benefices alone would have kept Giovanni de' Medici in exquisite luxury for the remainder of his life but Lorenzo's ambitions for his son knew no bounds. The House of Medici could not count itself as having truly arrived as Italian nobility without at least one cardinal in the family. On 8 March 1488, this long-awaited Medici ambition was finally realised. As a result of the marriage between Franceschetto and Maria Maddalena, Pope Innocent VIII confirmed the thirteen-year-old Giovanni as cardinal-deacon of Santa Maria in Domnica, a basilica church that was situated near the papal cathedral of St. John Lateran.

For years, Lorenzo had been forced to sit back and watch his old nemesis Sixtus IV nominate as cardinals Giovanni d'Aragona of Naples in 1477 and Ascanio Sforza of Milan in 1484. The long-awaited elevation of his son under the more pliable Innocent VIII was a victory of the highest order, yet there was one small problem. Giovanni's extreme youth (at thirteen years old he was the youngest cardinal ever appointed) meant that certain stipulations were imposed upon his cardinalate. To avoid scandal and accusations of partiality, Giovanni would not be allowed to wear the insignia or share in the deliberations of the Sacred College until three years had passed. Until then, the news of his elevation was to be kept strictly secret. During this interlude, Pope Innocent would provide the best humanists and scholars that money could buy to educate his young Medici protégé. Following the completion of his education by Lorenzo's humanist friends Angelo Poliziano, Marsilio Ficino, and Bernardo Dovizi, Cardinal Giovanni would be sent to Pisa to study theology and canon law under the celebrated jurists Filippo Decio and Bartolomeo Sozzini.

The stipulation that Giovanni's elevation remain, for the time being, *segreto* presented Lorenzo however with a quandary. If Pope Innocent VIII were to die within those three years, without having formally announced Giovanni's elevation to cardinal, his successor–if unfriendly to the Medici–might well refuse to ratify or perhaps even acknowledge the appointment. Keeping his peace for three whole years therefore presented far too great a risk. Lorenzo sidestepped the prohibition, and the problem, by simply ignoring it; within days of the appointment he had publicised the news abroad to Pope Innocent's considerable irritation. To placate His Holiness, Lorenzo had offered the following otiose excuse in a letter dated 14 March 1488: 'As to keeping this affair secret I should be much distressed if the knowledge of it had been made public by me. But Your Holiness may rest assured that it was immediately known in Rome, and then divulged by letters to people here, so that everyone came to congratulate me. I can affirm that the news was not published by me, nor did I cause any demonstration of joy to be made. In any case, whether by my fault or not, I am extremely distressed that Your Holiness should have experienced any annoyance.'

The news of Giovanni's red tasselled hat, though officially secret, therefore became common knowledge in the streets of Florence and thereafter throughout all of Italy. So identified by now were the ordinary people with the Medici *reggimento* that the mood was ecstatic; the Florentines regarded the joyous news of a Medici cardinal as their own civic good fortune. The apothecary Luca Landucci, for example, enthused: 'we have heard that the Pope had made six cardinals, who were as follows: two French, one *Milanese*, two of his nephews, and one Florentine, son of Lorenzo de' Medici. Thank god! It is a great honour to our city in general and in particular to his father and his house.' Lorenzo, elated at the fulfilment of this generations-old family ambition, declared that it was 'the greatest honour that has ever befallen our house'. Barely out of puberty, the young cardinal was destined to play a central role in rebuilding the fortunes of the house of Medici and in time would bring Florence and Rome even closer together. For the time being, however, he remained a corpulent, pleasure-loving youth who, born to Medici riches and privilege, seemed to take it all nonchalantly in his stride. Aware perhaps of Giovanni's shortcomings in this area, Lorenzo sent his son off from Florence with the following moralising sentiments: 'I remember the time when the Sacred College was full of learned and virtuous men. Theirs is the example for you to follow. The less your

307

conduct resembles that of those who now compose it the more beloved and respected you will be'.

In his eldest son Piero, Lorenzo was considerably less blessed. Interested in neither scholarship nor the art of statesmanship he grew into a haughty, ill-disciplined and impulsive young man whose sole preoccupation was cutting a dash in society. Preferring the thrill of the hunt to the boredom of his humanist classes with Angelo Poliziano and Marsilio Ficino, *il Magnifico* was acutely aware of his son's shortcomings as a potential heir to the complex political apparatus of the Medici *reggimento*. Piero's want of intelligence and lack of good judgement, not to mention his inflated ego, was only exacerbated by the almost universal adulation in which he was held by the common people of Florence. Regarding him as a new Lorenzo, they flocked to the Via Larga just to catch a glimpse of his comings and goings at the Palazzo Medici. Lorenzo's friend Matteo Franco had remarked humorously that 'the poor lad cannot go outside the door without all Florence running after him'. But not everyone was impressed with the Medici youth and many blamed Piero's 'foreign' Orsini blood as being the root cause of his insufferable arrogance.

With the more sensible and gifted Giovanni destined for a promising career in the upper echelons of the Church, Lorenzo de' Medici was forced to work with the shoddy heir material he had to hand. When Pope Innocent VIII ascended the papal throne Lorenzo himself had been prevented by ill health from offering his congratulations in person. The murder of his brother followed by the arduous years of conflict with Pope Sixtus IV, not to mention his personal military leadership during the Pazzi Wars, had taken their visible toll on *il Magnifico*. He had aged poorly and continued to suffer grievously from the family affliction of gout, added to which were the on-going problems with chronic eczema not to mention occasional bouts of asthma. Lorenzo had had little choice at that time but to assign the thirteen-year-old Piero to offer the Medici family's felicitations to Pope Innocent in Rome. Packing his son off, he followed up with a five-page missive on 26 November 1484 offering Piero helpful advice and urging him to 'be careful not to take precedence over those who are your elders for, although you are my son, you are but a citizen of Florence, as they are'. But corrupt and pleasure-loving Rome was hardly the sort of city to imbue Piero with either good sense or humility. Upon his return, he angered Lorenzo by infringing Florence's sumptuary laws with his expensive and extravagant new Roman costumes.

As unofficial first citizen of Florence, Lorenzo himself had for decades moved in the circle of kings, popes, emperors and princes. He also pursued a deliberate dynastic policy of marrying his firstborn offspring into the titled élite and, in 1486, Piero was betrothed to another Orsini girl, Alfonsina, who was the daughter of Count Roberto Orsini of Tagliacozzo and Alba and his wife Caterina di Sanseverino. Even before Giovanni's elevation to the College, Lorenzo had begun engraving the initials LAV.R.MED into his precious hardstone decorative vessels and vases which were displayed discreetly in showcases at the Palazzo Medici. Even if the initials are interpreted to represent the phrase *Lorenzo Rex Medicorum* ('Lorenzo, King of the Medici') this would still imply a clear ambition of hereditary nobility or kingship on Lorenzo's part. Indeed, Lorenzo's brother-in-law Bernardo Rucellai, a close member of the Medici family who had negotiated Piero's marriage to Alfonsina Orsini, unabashedly described the engraved initials as 'a future memorial for posterity of his royal splendour'.

It could be argued therefore that in pursuing the usual louche behaviour of a rich man's son, Piero di Lorenzo de' Medici was simply aping the princely pretensions of his own father and even that Lorenzo himself, surrounded as he now was by a sense of glamour and grandeur, had ceased to set a good 'republican' example. Just as during the Roman era the *triumvir* Octavian had gradually become Augustus so, it could be argued, had Lorenzo metamorphosed from first citizen into dictator. There was nothing inherently wrong with Lorenzo's princely effulgence, except of course for the fact that, in the eyes of the Florentines, their city was still a republic and not a hereditary duchy or principality. The affectations of élite ruling families had always been tolerated in the republic so long as those families brought wealth, prosperity and diplomatic success to Florence. Anyone who was found wanting in any of these attributes, yet who still believed he had any hereditary right to rulership, was nevertheless deluding himself. Though he was still not aware of it, Piero di Lorenzo was destined to become the shining example of this principle.

Ten years after Giuliano de' Medici's assassination in the Duomo the final chapter in the whole shameful Pazzi Conspiracy was about to be brought to a close. Following Caterina Sforza's gallant defence of her family's rights in Rome, the Riarios had retreated to their possessions in Forlì and Imola. Although Pope Innocent VIII had honoured the Sacred College's agreement to grant the Riario's descendants their hereditary rights, and even upheld Girolamo's status as papal *gonfaloniere*, the new pope had made it abundantly clear that the couple could expect no further support from the papacy and that Girolamo was expected to remain well away from both Rome as well as the Pope's armed forces. Cardinal Giovanni Battista Savelli, whom Girolamo had unwisely imprisoned in Rome at the height of the Colonna crisis, had meanwhile secured the position of papal legate to Bologna, from which city he could be relied upon to make diplomatic trouble for the Count. Meanwhile, the Manfredi family of neighbouring Faenza watched the Riarios both with fear and jealous suspicion.

With only the Bentivoglio of Bologna and Caterina's uncle Ludovico *il Moro* to count on as potential supporters, Girolamo for once held his usual boorish and alienating ways in abeyance, striving to win the hearts and minds of his subjects by reducing taxation and subsidising cheap public grain when the harvests failed from drought. There was little else he could do; he was no longer a great lord and he could not afford to alienate those few subjects he still had. But despite his efforts to reform his style of rule, bad luck and recurrent intrigues nevertheless continued to plague the Riarios. In October 1484, the Zampeschi brothers–whose family lands had earlier been ceded by Pope Sixtus IV to Count Riario in punishment for their support for Florence–had returned to the area and occupied three fiefs at San Mauro on the outskirts of Forlì. Then, in the spring of 1485, Taddeo Manfredi had staged an unsuccessful coup in Imola which had been suppressed by the Count's loyal *condottiere* Giovanni Francesco da Tolentino. In 1486, yet another plot was discovered, this time instigated by Antonio Maria Ordelaffi, one of the three ousted Ordelaffi claimants to Forlì. Neither did the subterfuge cease with the neutralisation of this latest plot. In September 1487, Antonio Maria was also behind a minor peasant's rebellion which had been led by his agents Nino Biagio and Domenico Roffi.

As the 1480s dragged on the Riarios' poor luck persisted. First Caterina and then her husband were beset with life threatening bouts of sickness and–when Girolamo's public subsidies threatened to bankrupt him–the Count was forced to reinstate taxation, a move which created immediate and widespread ill-feeling among the citizenry. In the spring of 1488, Count Girolamo fell out with two local *Forlivese* noblemen, Ludovico and Checco Orsi, over matters relating to taxation policy and tax farming. Ludovico Orsi had been one of Girolamo's closest friends and had even stood godfather to Girolamo's fourth child Giovanni Livio in 1484. The rift between the two men proved catastrophic and the Count's increasingly irrational and threatening behaviour towards Ludovico caused the Orsi brothers to fear that their lives might be in danger. Seeing little alternative they decided to strike the first blow. On 14 April 1488, during what was a busy market day in Forlì, Ludovico and Checco Orsi, together with two of the Count's disgruntled bodyguards, Ludovico Panseco and Giacomo del Ronche, stole into the Palazzo Riario where Girolamo was taking lunch in a room known as the Hall of the Nymphs. Here, they used their daggers to cut the unguarded Girolamo to ribbons, casting his bloody corpse from the window into the *piazza* below, where it was desecrated and spat upon by the *Forlivesi*. Lorenzo de' Medici's hated nemesis was finally dead at the age of forty-five, a victim of the same variety of extreme violence which he had so casually meted out throughout his own lifetime. As the shocking events of the day unfolded Caterina was taken prisoner together with her mother Lucrezia Landriani, her sister Stella, and all six of her children: Bianca (ten), Ottaviano (nine), Cesare (eight), Giovanni Livio (four), Galeazzo Maria (three) and the infant Sforzino. Also captured was Girolamo's illegitimate son Scipione, who was by now fourteen years old.

The Count's assassination now set in motion a complex chain of events in which the papacy reclaimed the town at the invitation of the *Forlivesi* but were countered by an army despatched by Ludovico *il Moro*. Cardinal Savelli, who had set out from nearby Bologna, attempted to mediate between the Orsi and the Sforza widow and in the ensuing standoff Caterina perpetrated the act for which she has become notorious down through history. The impregnable Rocca di Ravaldino, the key to Forlì, was in the hands of the late Girolamo's loyal castellan Tommaso Feo who refused to surrender it to the Orsi brothers, claiming that he was holding it for the Count's heir Ottaviano. Holding Caterina's family as hostages, the Orsi agreed to allow Caterina to confer with Feo to release the fortress into their charge. Feo agreed to this on the condition that Caterina be unaccompanied. In reality however, both Caterina and her castellan were playing a high-stakes game of deception. Once safely inside the *rocca* she refused to come out again. Growing increasingly desperate at their predicament, the Orsi dragged Caterina's mother, sister, son Ottaviano and four-year-old Livio beneath the ramparts and in full view threatened to slit all their throats unless Caterina surrendered the fortress to them. According to various reports of what happened next, Caterina–who was by now heavily pregnant with her seventh child–appeared at the edge of the battlements and called down: 'Go ahead and do it, idiots!' she yelled, 'in my belly is another child by the late count and I also have the means to produce many more heirs too!' More lurid accounts describe Caterina hitching up her skirts and pointing brazenly to her genitals to underscore her point.

As the time ticked by, and as Ludovico Sforza's troops drew closer to Forlì with each passing hour, the Orsi's bluff had been masterfully called. Desperately, they sent word to Lorenzo de' Medici, begging for him to intervene on their behalf. They had rid him after all of his most hated adversary. But Lorenzo saw no advantage in responding to their distress call; Girolamo was already gone, the blood feud was over and, without the support of the sitting

Pope, the Riario heirs were in a considerably weakened position and could no longer do Florence any real harm. In short, this was no longer Florence's fight. Bolstered by the timely arrival of *il Moro*'s troops, Caterina and her family retained control of Forlì, the Orsi brothers fled and the family's elderly patriarch Andrea Orsi was forced to watch his *palazzo* being demolished brick-by-brick before he was beheaded and then hacked into quarters for the crime of having squired traitors.

Barely two months after the assassination a rumour was put about that Caterina had agreed to marry Forlì's banished claimant Antonio Maria Ordelaffi, who had begun the process of courting her. Intensely irritated, Caterina lost no time in scotching these reports and imprisoned a number of the chief rumour mongers including her devoted chronicler Leone Cobelli. In reality, Caterina had fallen for Giacomo Feo, the poorly educated but handsome younger brother of her loyal castellan Tommaso Feo whose actions that shocking day had saved her family's possessions. Tommaso himself, however, was now considered a liability since his principal loyalties lay with his former master Girolamo and, consequently, with the Riario family of Savona. Caterina felt that she could no longer count on the Riarios to protect or promote her interests. Deciding therefore that she needed to control all the *rocca* in her territories, Caterina duped the unwitting Tommaso into vacating Ravaldino and installed his brother Giacomo in his place. When the two lovers eventually married it was in *segreto* so to avoid losing the regency of her dominions and custody of the late count's children.

1488, the year of Giovanni's elevation to cardinal and the year in which Lorenzo de' Medici's enemy was destroyed, was nevertheless tinged with a note of sadness for the House of Medici. On 30 July, Clarice Orsini died at the age of thirty-five from the tuberculosis which had afflicted her for some years now. On a purely romantic or emotional level, her relationship with Lorenzo could never be described as particularly close and even after their marriage Lorenzo had continued to fritter his affections away on other objects of affection. '*Nelle cose veneree maravigliosamente involto*' Machiavelli would later write of Lorenzo in his *Storie Fiorentine*, meaning basically that 'he was *fond* of women'. Most notable amongst these, especially towards the later period of his life, was Madonna Bartolomea who was the daughter of the banker Lorenzo Nasi, whose brother Piero Nasi was a close Medici *amici* of some considerable standing. According to the historian Francesco Guicciardini, Lorenzo persisted in his love affair with Bartolomea despite her being married to Donato Benci and notwithstanding the fact that she was 'neither young nor beautiful' (she was about twenty-nine at the time of Clarice Orsini's death and therefore considered very much middle-aged).

Though never romantically close, Lorenzo's marriage to Clarice had nevertheless served its purpose in producing no less than ten heirs including, most importantly of all, three healthy sons. The third son, Giuliano, had been born in 1479 and like his brother Piero was destined to marry into the nobility of Italy, in this case Filiberta the daughter of Duke Philip II of Savoy. Of Clarice's four surviving daughters, the long-suffering Maria Maddalena continued to produce children for Franceschetto Cybò; Lucrezia Maria married Jacopo Salviati in February 1488; whilst Contessina Antonia married Piero Ridolfi in 1494. Luisa Contessina was betrothed to Giovanni de' Medici, from the cadet side of the family, in 1486 when Giovanni was nineteen but sadly died

311

young two months before her mother at the age of ten. Between them, Lorenzo and Clarice's offspring were, in the successive generation, to produce no less than four cardinals and two dukes. Their firstborn, Lucrezia Maria, would give birth to a daughter, Maria Salviati, whose marriage in 1516 to Giovanni della Bande Nere (the son of Giovanni de' Medici, by then styled for republican reasons as Giovanni *il Popolano*) would eventually reunite the main branch and the estranged cadet branch of the Medici family. But all this was, as yet, far in the future.

When Clarice died on 30 July 1488, Lorenzo, who at the time was suffering from his own ailments, principally gout, was taking the mineral waters at Filetta. He was attended by his personal physician Pierleone of Spoleto who, drawing a sizeable salary of one thousand florins for his expertise, had confidently declared that 'he could not die of that malady'. Yet such was his own discomfort that Lorenzo was unable to return to Florence in time for his wife's funeral, which took place several days later at the basilica of San Lorenzo. For this absence, Lorenzo was subjected to considerable criticism but it was simply the final sad act in their relationship. The fact was that *il Magnifico's* civic responsibilities had, over the years, seldom left him much time to devote attention to his wife in her more prosaic domestic setting. Even so, there was still a genuine fondness there and Clarice's death nevertheless came as a bitter blow to Lorenzo. Just two days after his wife's death, Lorenzo would write to Pope Innocent VIII that 'The deprivation of such habitual and such sweet company has filled my cup and has made me so miserable that I can find no peace'.

As always, Lorenzo turned for solace to his art collections, his poetry and his humanist scholarship and patronage. In 1489 the master Ghirlandaio sent him, at Lorenzo's own request, the two brightest new pupils from his *bottega*. The candidates were to join the sculptor Bertoldo di Giovanni's informal arts and intellectual Academy in the Medici-sponsored Garden of the Sculptures near San Marco. One of these boys was the fourteen-year-old Michelangelo di Ludovico di Leonardo Buonarroti. Born on 6 March 1475, Michelangelo had arrived as one of Ghirlandaio's new apprentices from the small town of Caprese in the Casentino. His father Lodovico had previously earned his living as a minor bureaucrat, having served as *podestà* of Caprese, but upon relocating to Florence just after Michelangelo's birth the large family including five sons and a daughter fell into straightened circumstances and was forced to cohabit in the same house together with their Florentine relatives. Michelangelo himself was indentured to Ghirlandaio, who was then perhaps the most important painter in Florence, in the year 1488 when he was thirteen. The artist later tended to avoid mentioning his early apprenticeship under Ghirlandaio as he preferred to give the impression that his artistic talent was 'God-given'.

Michelangelo was nevertheless highly talented for his age and had made an immediate impression on those with whom he came into contact. According to his two contemporary biographers Vasari and Condivi it was at the suggestion of the classicist Poliziano that Michelangelo had been inspired to carve a marble relief of a centaur battle which showed evidence of true mastery of his craft. The piece, which depicted Ovid's tale of the drunken and inflamed centaurs attempting to carry off Perithous's bride Hippodameia and her handmaidens during her wedding feast, was the first iteration of a leitmotif with which Michelangelo would become obsessed for the remainder of his life – the male human figure in movement. Because of his immense promise Michelangelo was

312

subsequently taken under Lorenzo's own roof at the Palazzo Medici and here, in the intellectual hothouse environment, he positively thrived, participating in Ficino's and Poliziano's Platonic Academy at Careggi, soaking up the numerous references to classical mythology and avidly studying the works of the masters Masaccio and Donatello, the latter having been responsible for *David*, the first free-standing figurative statue cast since ancient times, and a subject which Michelangelo would also later tackle.

But not everyone in Lorenzo's household was as enamoured of the arrogant teenage prodigy whose name was Michelangelo Buonarroti. One afternoon in 1491, a fellow student named Pietro Torrigiano became so enraged at Buonarroti's incessant teasing, while the two students were quietly sketching together in the Chapel of Santa Maria del Carmine, that he landed a well-aimed punch which broke Michelangelo's nose. So enraged was *il Magnifico* by the senseless assault on his artistic protégé that Torrigiano was forced to flee Florence in fear of his life (and indeed the artist's notoriously bad temper would bedevil most of the rest of his career; many years later he was still complaining to the silversmith and autobiographer Cellini about how irritating he had found Michelangelo; but Torrigiano would still go on to carve out his own reputation regardless, being for instance responsible for the tombs of the English King Henry VII and his Queen, Elizabeth of York).

The year before, when the cartilage of Michelangelo's nose had still been shapely and undeformed, a thirty-eight-year-old Dominican friar named Girolamo Savonarola came to preach in Florence at the Convent of San Marco. He was exceedingly ugly with a huge hooked nose and his body was stick thin from his ascetic choice of lifestyle. At night he slept on a wooden pallet covered with straw and was a far cry from the peacocking and hypocritical friars singled out by Boccaccio for having cells that were secretly 'stocked with ointments and salves, huge boxes of sweets, phials and flasks of perfume and fragrant oils, and casks overflowing with Malmsey wine'. Savonarola had first visited Florence in 1482 as a guest lecturer at San Marco and, as he himself was the first to point out in his diary, his preaching had not gone down well initially. His speech was delivered in a strong *Ferrarese* accent, he gesticulated far too much, and his sermons were utterly devoid of the humanist rhetoric that the sophisticated Florentines had come to expect of their well-educated priests. Discouraged, he excused himself to lecture in Siena in 1485 and then again in 1486; but by 1490 he was back once more in Florence, having brushed up his style and polished his delivery to appeal to the Florentines. His refreshing brand of plain-speaking apocalyptic honesty caught on quickly. His first sermons were given informally at San Marco beside a damask rose bush but, by Lent of 1491, he had been invited to declaim from the pulpit of the Duomo itself, for this was by now the only holy space capable of holding the curious crowds which flocked to hear him.

Indeed, Florence had not seen anything quite like Savonarola before. Eschewing the clever and elaborate arguments and declamatory styles of the Florentine humanists (who had also, inevitably, influenced the preaching style of many well-to-do local ecclesiastics) Savonarola instead based his sermons on Biblical scripture and preached a simple Christian message of humility, poverty and morality. 'Why do we not become like little children, simple, trusting and pure?' he asked of the wealthy Florentine merchants who had assembled out of idle curiosity to hear him preach. To the *popolo minuto* and the *popolo magro*, however, the little friar's earnest and heartfelt entreaties to the people of

Florence to turn their backs on sophistication and material trappings and instead embrace the wealth and riches of the eternal, living Kingdom of Heaven struck a noticeable chord. In the opinion of many, Florence had begun to emulate a new Sodom and Gomorrah where any pleasure was available at any price and where any vice could be conveniently absolved with some jejune humanist piety quarried from pagan antiquity. His ire was reserved in particular for Florence's moneylenders, who–so he claimed–loaned out coin at exorbitant rates of interest to the poor. When, on 6 April 1491, he denounced Italy's many 'tyrants' the Florentines were left in no doubt that he was talking about none other than Lorenzo de' Medici who, as the leader of the city, was directly responsible for its failings and sins.

If Lorenzo de' Medici's golden age, encouraged by the example of Medici patronage, had opened men's minds to the innate possibilities of their own humanity and had entrained a glorious world of literary and artistic accomplishment, then the new Savonarolan fundamentalism garbed in sackcloth and ashes had arrived to cast doubt on this smugly confident worldview. 'Open, open, O Lord, the waters of the Red Sea and submerge the impious in the waves of Your Wrath!' This sort of preaching was not an encouragement to discover and extend and beautify but an exhortation to cringe and cower and repent of one's worldly sins. Two entirely contradictory and antagonistic philosophies had taken root in Florence's fertile intellectual soil and both were now poised to do battle in the hearts and minds of the Florentines. A twenty-two year old student named Niccolò Machiavelli was one of Savonarola's early onlookers and, although the pragmatic budding political theorist and future professional bureaucrat refused to be swept away by the friar's sermonising, he nevertheless tended to agree with Savonarola's supposition that a community's sins were rooted in the conduct of their lords and princes. An increasingly educated and articulate population had by now realised that the established order, both secular and religious, was rotten throughout with corruption, simony and ecclesiastical careerism; it was only natural that their longing for political reform should take root in Messianic visions of the Creator smiting those who had puffed themselves up whilst holding out the hand of salvation to those who had suffered under an unjust system.

To the chaste, puritanical Savonarola the evidence of Florence's political and spiritual corruption lay all around him and indeed was emblematic in the city's very obvious sexual and moral degradation. The streets and narrow *vicoli* (alleyways) of Florence were infested with prostitutes, many having come from other city-states or else from the relative poverty of the *contado*. Distinguishable by their little tinkling bells, their gloves and their high heels, they were virtually a population apart and even had their own city official, called the *onestà*, whose 'office of decency' was tasked with supervising their activities and making sure they adhered to the city ordinances regulating their trade. The ordinary Florentine citizen going about his daily business would have been quite literally surrounded by the temptation of companionable sex. Fatal diseases like syphilis, the notorious 'French disease', were consequently an ever-present risk for those who gave in to the perennial temptations of *bel viver italiano*. Yet all the same, there had been those Church Fathers who had taken a more tolerant and practical view of such things. St. Thomas Aquinas had considered brothels to be an unwholesome but necessary outlet for man's baser natural inclinations and their presence was as essential as 'a cesspit in a palace' to coin Aquinas's own colourful analogy. The pragmatic acceptance of sin was not however one of Savonarola's strong suits and to him the city's prostitutes were, as he himself put it, no more than 'pieces of meat with eyes'.

One of Savonarola's early sermons, even before arriving in Florence, had taken an allegorical approach to man's essential sinfulness but it could just as easily have been applied to the proclivities of the Florentines themselves: 'O flee these cruel lands, flee this shore of greed, flee the lands of Sodom and Gomorrah, flee Egypt and the Pharaohs, flee this most vile and proud people, these greedy youth, lascivious old men, fawning paupers!' Other sermons were less allegorical, more explicit: 'Pay! Pay! Murderers go free while the innocent are blamed. Young girls are exploited. Filthy sodomites—even some who have wives—have boys brought to them in their storerooms and shops. Women use the church as a brothel; the streets are full of whores. To the poor he can only say, be patient, bear up, wait for God. To the rich, however, the Lord said, "Woe to you patricians ... I will bring affliction upon you! No longer will the city be called *Florentia*, but [a place of] turpitude and blood and a robbers' cave [Jer. 7.11].'

That this kind of fundamentalist Christian rhetoric should arrive in Florence to plant its injurious seed of doubt at this particular moment in the twilight years of the great Lorenzo de' Medici was an unfortunate dice throw of history. Lorenzo's heirs badly needed to reinforce the 'magnificence' of Medici rule in order to retain their credibility as quasi-dynastic rulers. Savonarola, by contrast, advocated the cleansing of all earthly vanities. In his *Compendium Revelationum* the friar would soon write of the beatific vision he had experienced which had convinced him that 'if sinners had eyes, they would surely see how grievous and hard is this pestilence, and how sharp the sword'. Lorenzo meanwhile stood for an altogether more forgiving, satirical and jocose view of life as typified in his ribald collection of carnival songs, the *Canti Carnascialeschi*, whose *Canti della malmaritata, delle donne giovani e di mariti vecchi, delle vedove, dei giudei battezzati* sang of the sexual frustration of widows, unhappy wives, young wives with old husbands as well as, in the interests of poetic inclusivity, 'baptized Jews'. The two messages–playing to entirely dissimilar impulses in the human soul–were hopelessly opposed and contradictory and the whole dynamic became positively explosive. Savonarola's sermonising was of course distinctly demagogic. Like all successful popular leaders and rabble-rousers his preaching pandered to the prejudices of the *popolo minuto* and spoke directly to their eternally disenfranchised condition. What was more remarkable, however, was the friar's ability to reach and convert those amongst Florence's wealthier classes, those with a real vested interest in the continuation of the privileged Medici status quo.

In March 1492, the seventeen-year-old Giovanni de' Medici had been formally admitted into the Sacred College of Cardinals. Leaving Florence for the nearby town of Fiesole, he proceeded to the ancient cathedral-turned-Benedictine abbey known as the Badia Fiesolana. Here, after a night spent in solitary prayer and meditation, his insignia was blessed before the High Altar and he received the garments of his new rank: the *pallium* or cardinal's mantle, the *biretum* or scarlet cap, and the *galerus*, the broad-brimmed tasselled hat. Returning to Florence on a mule with his brother Piero and their cavalcade he was greeted at the city gates by the *signoria*, the assembled clergy and crowds of cheering Florentines. After High Mass at the Duomo he finally returned to the Palazzo

Medici where his gout-ridden father Lorenzo de' Medici was awaiting him. The moment is immortalised in a fresco by Giorgio Vasari in the Sala di Lorenzo il Magnifico at the Palazzo della Signoria. In his sumptuous scarlet robes of office, the young cardinal kneels before a proud Lorenzo offering him his cardinal's hat, attended by other humanist luminaries such as Angelo Poliziano and Marsilio Ficino; quirkily in the background can be seen the exotic giraffes which the Turkish Sultan had earlier presented to Lorenzo. That evening, the newly-minted cardinal was fêted at a sumptuous dinner held at the Palazzo Medici. Manfredo di Manfredi, the *Ferrarese* ambassador, reported to Ercole d'Este how 'a great number of chiselled silver vases were presented to the Cardinal on behalf of the *signoria*' which Manfredi estimated to be 'valued at 10,000 ducats or more, which may well be, as they weighed more than 1,000 pounds.' Manfredi then went on to describe how, modestly, 'His Lordship would not accept them and gave them back to the donors with fair words of thanks'.

This would prove to be one of Lorenzo's final happy moments together with Giovanni. As Manfredo di Manfredi had also reported to his master, *il Magnifico* was by this time suffering most grievously from gout and Manfredi opined that '*est res miranda* ('it is wonderful') how he can still live'. Eventually the time came for father and son to part ways and, in that same month of March, Giovanni was entrusted into the hands of Filippo Valori and Andrea Cambini for the journey to Rome. After Giovanni had arrived safely, Lorenzo wrote him a long letter rich in practical advice on how to comport himself as a newly-minted young cardinal. The message remains a remarkable document not only for the pithy words of accumulated wisdom but also because Lorenzo makes no allusion to the fact that, by this time, he almost certainly knew he was a dying man. Instead of dwelling on his own misfortune or allowing it to colour his final parting words to his beloved son, he concentrates on giving Giovanni the best possible send-off into adult life. Writing to the young Giovanni, Lorenzo offered simple, practical advice and guidance: 'One rule above all others I recommend that you follow with utmost diligence, and that is to rise early in the morning, for besides being good for your health, this will enable you to think about and arrange all the business of the day'. *Il Magnifico* then went on to exhort his second son to tend to 'both the goats and the cabbages' which was a homespun way of reminding Giovanni to look after both the interests of the Medici family as well as the Church. He then devoted some space to the perils of falling into bad ways as he took up his future life in the Sacred College: 'The rank of Cardinal is as secure as it is great', confided Lorenzo, 'men therefore often become negligent; they conceive they have done enough and that without exertion they can preserve their position. This is often prejudicial to character and to life, and a thing against which you must guard.'

His health had rapidly deteriorated in the days following Giovanni's elevation and, like his father before him, he had been carried to Careggi where the air was supposedly better in order to recuperate, accompanied by his sister Bianca. As his health now began to fail in these last remaining days of his life he received visits from those people who were closest to him. His son Piero and daughter Lucrezia soon came to be by his side. To his son Piero, he exhorted him to act honourably and not to distance those people who had helped place him in power (the son would not live up to his father's words and Piero di Lorenzo de' Medici would later be described by Francesco Guicciardini as being 'not only hated by his enemies, but also disliked by his friends, who found him almost intolerable: proud and bestial, preferring to be hated rather than loved, fierce and cruel'.) Lorenzo's final hours were passed tenderly with his dearest friends, the humanists Pico della Mirandola (now safely emerged from his recent brush with heresy) and Angelo Poliziano. Upon the arrival of the former at the villa, Lorenzo had politely asked his apology for disturbing him and assured Pico that 'he died more willingly after seeing so dear a friend'. As one bibliophile to another, he then joked 'that death had spared me until your library was complete'. During his final hours, so the story goes, Lorenzo was visited by Girolamo Savonarola, who supposedly denied Lorenzo the sacrament of last rites because the Medici ruler had refused to restore the Florentines to their political liberties. This story, however, is almost certainly apocryphal. According to Poliziano, another priest had already come and administered the last rites and therefore it made little sense for Savonarola to rush to Lorenzo's bedside in order to duplicate this simple ritual. Neither does it seem credible that a man of Savonarola's deep piety would have denied any man this final important sacrament on so capricious a pretext.

On 9 April 1492, aged just forty-three, Lorenzo the Magnificent died peacefully at his villa at Careggi. Lorenzo's personal physician Pierleone of Spoleto had, as reported by Bartolommeo Dei to his uncle Benedetto, been wrongly treating him, 'giving him cold things when he should have had hot' and when a more qualified doctor arrived from Milan his attempts to administer the correct remedies had been too late (Maestro Pierleone was so distraught at his failure that he committed suicide the following morning by drowning himself in a well belonging to the Martelli family). As Bartolommeo Dei recorded Lorenzo's passing to his uncle, 'he quitted this life in the flower of his age and most assuredly far too soon, to the great and bitter sorrow of the whole city; and with every reason, for no doubt we have lost the splendour not only of Tuscany but of all Italy. Every day we shall learn more what we have lost. As yet it cannot be calculated, but time will show.' It would indeed. Not long after Lorenzo's death his Byzantine agent Janus Lascaris returned from his second epic book-finding voyage overseas with a bumper crop of over two hundred rare manuscripts from Mount Athos, only to find that he was too late for his patron to ever be able to peruse them. 'How vain is every hope, each breath', Lorenzo had written in one of his sonnets, 'How false is every single plan. How full of ignorance is man against the monstrous mistress, Death'.

The body of Lorenzo the Magnificent was carried solemnly back to Florence where it lay in state at the monastery of San Marco. Bartolommeo Dei recorded that 'On Monday evening at one of the clock [an hour after sundown] the body of Lorenzo was borne by the Company of the Magi into the sacristy of S. Lorenzo in the coffin wherein it had been brought from Careggi the night before, with many torches and tapers. The next day, that is Tuesday, the 10th, the funeral took place without much pomp, as had always been the custom of their ancestors, without banners.' Lorenzo's coffin was lowered into the same tomb as his beloved younger brother Giuliano de' Medici, who had died under more violent circumstances some fourteen years earlier. The red porphyry sarcophagus which enclosed *il Magnifico's* body was that same one designed by Verrocchio for Cosimo de' Medici and his son Piero. Bartolommeo Dei went on to add that 'There were but three Orders of friars and one of priests; in truth, great pomp could not be shown, for the greatest splendour would have been small for such a man. But wonderful was the number of citizens and nobles, in long black robes touching the ground, who came to do him honour; it was a fine spectacle, and touching to see such manifest signs of sadness and of sorrow.'

The public encomium offered by the Florentine state for their former first citizen was both generous and sincere. Lorenzo, it stated, had neglected 'no opportunity of protecting, increasing, adorning and raising this city, but was always ready with counsel, authority, and painstaking in thought and deed'. The official epitaph went on to affirm that Lorenzo 'shrank from neither trouble nor danger for the good of the State and its freedom' and omitted nothing that could tend to raise our reputation and enlarge our borders'.

Pope Innocent VIII followed Lorenzo de' Medici to the grave that same year. A shameless glutton, Innocent had, towards the end of his pontificate, succumbed to morbid obesity and was in the unseemly habit of nourishing himself on milk from the brimming breasts of Roman midwives. On his deathbed, *père* Cybò is infamous for having received from his Jewish doctor an oral transfusion of blood–arguably the first recorded blood transfusion in history–from three young street urchins. Following the transfusion the urchins died from exsanguination; the single ducat which they had each been paid for the gift of their life essence was torn from their rigor mortised hands by the miserly papal officials. After his Holiness finally expired on 25 July 1492, Franceschetto Cybò opportunistically attempted to loot the papal treasury. As at the card table, he proved unlucky and was thwarted in his attempt by Cardinal Borgia, the vice-chancellor. But this was not all. Two months later to the day, Lorenzo's beloved Angelo Poliziano also died, his death perhaps accelerated by the loss of his beloved *padrone*. His sad Latin elegy for Lorenzo described his eyes as 'gushing a fountain of tears': '*quis dabit capiti meo aquam, quis oculis meis fontem lachrymarum dabit?*'

Curiously, one of Lorenzo's final acts had been to despatch his faithful thirty-eight-year-old clerk Amerigo Vespucci to Seville in Spain. Vespucci had been sent together with Donato Niccolini as confidential agents to investigate the affairs of the Medici branch office in Cádiz, whose principal agent Giannotto Berardi was under suspicion of defrauding the bank. Berardi was one of the financiers of Christopher Columbus, a *Genovese* navigator who wished to test his theory that the fabled Indies could be found just 2,500 nautical miles west of the Azores. Vespucci arrived in Seville in March 1492 and both Vespucci and Berardi helped Columbus to prepare and victual for his epic voyage of discovery. After Berardi died in 1495 Vespucci took over his business obligations to Ferdinand and Isabella for the provisioning of exploratory Spanish ships and also later began actively sailing on voyages of discovery himself, most notably together with the explorer Alonso de Ojeda. Lorenzo the Magnificent's act of sending his clerk to probe some shady business dealings in Spain would set in train the subsequent great controversy concerning the naming of the New World or, as it was simply known then, *Terra Firma*. In 1507, on his map *Universalis Cosmographia* the German cartographer Martin Waldseemüller would name the new continent 'Amerige' (or 'Americus' Land') in honour of the Florentine explorer and erstwhile Medici factotum Amerigo Vespucci (Americus Vesputius). 'Americus Vesputius' was, according to Waldseemüller and his cartographical collaborator Matthias Ringmann, 'a man of perceptive character; since both Europa and Asia have received their names from women'. Columbus would die just one year before Waldseemüller's epoch-making act of nomenclature, on 20 May 1506.

Niccolò Machiavelli in his *Istorie Florentine* leaves us perhaps the most poignant memorial to *il Magnifico*, as remarkable for its candour as for its understanding of common human failings and contradictions: 'His reputation grew every day because of his prudence; for he was eloquent and sharp in discussing things, wise in resolving them, quick and spirited in executing them. Nor can the vices of his be adduced to stain his great virtues, even though he was marvellously involved in things of Venus and he delighted in facetious and pungent men and in childish games, more than would appear fitting in such a man. Many times he was seen among his sons and daughters, mixing in their amusements. This, considering both his voluptuous life and his grave life, one might see in him two different persons joined in an almost impossible conjunction.'

PART FOUR

THE MEDICI
WILDERNESS YEARS

CHAPTER 13

Charles VIII's Invasion of Italy

In the year 1493 Count Lodowick began to solicit Charles VIII, now
reigning in France, to an expedition into Italy, to conquer the kingdom
of Naples, and to supplant and exterminate those who possessed it; for
whilst they were in authority, Lodowick durst not attempt what he did
afterwards; for at that time Ferrand and Alphonso his son were both
very rich, of great experience in the wars, and had the reputation of
being very valiant princes, though it appeared otherwise upon occasion.

Philippe de Commynes

When surveying the events of the 1490s it is all too easy to become
bewildered by the complex factors which led to the French King
Charles VIII's 1494 invasion of the Italian peninsula, an incursion
which would precipitate the disastrous so-called Italian Wars of 1494-1559.
These multifarious factors, both foreign and domestic, would come together to
create a perfect storm of geopolitical destabilisation which would draw France,
Spain, the Swiss cantons and the Holy Roman Empire into the affairs of Italy
and devastate the peninsula for decades to come. City-states would change
hands, dynasties would be toppled and even Rome itself would be sacked by a
mutinous imperial army in 1527. By the end of the conflict, Italy itself would be
drastically transformed and a completely new balance of power would come into
being, which would be largely dominated by the emerging superpower Spain.

The year 1492 in particular is one of those epic, monumental and epoch-
making years which produced a watershed in European affairs. The year
witnessed Western Christendom's horizons broadening out to encompass the
New World shortly to be discovered by the *Genovese* mariner known to his
Spanish sponsors as Cristóbal Colón but to the rest of the world as Christopher
Columbus. 1492 also saw the emergence of the unified kingdom of Spain, with
the capture on 2 January 1492 of the Emirate of Granada, thus bringing to an
end the last remnant of Islam's 781-year presence on the Iberian Peninsula.
With the consolidation of the Crowns of Castile and Aragon under King
Ferdinand and Queen Isabella, and with the vast wealth of the New World
which would soon be flowing like a golden stream into the Spanish treasury,
Spain was set to transform itself from embattled Catholic outpost to fully
fledged global empire.

France too, following its exhausting wars with a fiercely-independent
Brittany and the conclusion of a marriage between the twenty-one-year-old King
Charles VIII and Anne of Brittany, had also emerged stronger and more unified
than before, eager to project its diplomatic and military presence on the world

stage. To the East, meanwhile, Ivan III Vasilyevich, better known as Ivan the Great, the Grand Prince of Moscow and Grand Prince of all Rus, had finally managed to surmount the Mongol Golden Horde. By 1492, he had consolidated Muscovite dominance over all Rus territory and taken to wife Zoë Palaiologos, the niece of the last Byzantine *basileus*. The Orthodox Metropolitan bishop of Moscow had henceforth declared Moscow to be the 'Third Rome'. Casimir IV, King of Poland and Grand Duke of Lithuania, who had acknowledged Ivan III, had steered his two realms to the apogee of their power but by 1492 he was dead. To the south, in Hungary, Laszlo II fought increasingly desperate battles to stave off the encroaching Turks driving north-west from Constantinople.

Within Italy, the deaths in 1492 of both Lorenzo de' Medici and his ally and family member Pope Innocent VIII had removed two statesmen who were the most important stabilising influences on the peninsula. Lorenzo in particular had maintained the delicate balancing act between the natural adversaries Milan and Naples seemingly through the sheer force of his personal charisma alone. Lorenzo's role as both power broker and pacifier would not, however, be inherited in any meaningful sense by his shallow and ineffectual son Piero, whom Francesco Guicciardini later dismissed as 'not qualified by either age or understanding to carry so heavy a burden, nor capable of governing with that moderation with which his father had proceeded in both domestic and foreign affairs'. Instead, the new contender for kingmaker on the Italian peninsula was Innocent VIII's successor, Cardinal Rodrigo Borgia, who was elected as pope on 11 August 1492. Just eight days earlier Christopher Columbus had departed in his carrack the *Santa María* with two other smaller caravels, the *Niña* and the *Pinta*, from Palos de la Frontera on his epic voyage of discovery.

The Catalan Rodrigo Borgia, who was crowned as Pope Alexander VI on 26 August 1492, had prospered immeasurably since Pope Calixtus III had first elevated him to the Sacred College in 1456. As papal vice-chancellor he had seen his influence continue to grow under Innocent VIII. However, when the papal conclave went into session on 6 August 1492 with twenty-three cardinals (six of whom had been appointed by the former Pope Sixtus IV) it was widely acknowledged that the papacy now came down to a two-horse race involving Cardinal Giuliano della Rovere and Caterina Sforza's uncle Cardinal Ascanio Sforza of Milan. When neither candidate could summon the requisite votes to carry the election, Cardinal Sforza had agreed to divert his own votes to Rodrigo Borgia. The deal which Ascanio cut involved not only the vice-chancellorship of the Church but also several Borgia-owned *palazzi*, a number of lucrative new benefices and also, so the Roman chronicler Stefano Infessura claimed in his *Diarium urbis Romae*, an entire mule train laden with silver and gold. The transaction was nonetheless a poorly-kept secret and this overt purchasing of the papal tiara, even by so intelligent, capable and respected a man as Cardinal Borgia, somewhat scandalised the Church. But more shocking revelations were still to follow which would be fodder for endless salacious gossip amongst the Romans. Pope Alexander VI, whom Ascanio Sforza matter-of-factly described to his brother Ludovico *il Moro* as 'a carnal man', had not only sired two separate families during his years in Holy Orders, but as Supreme Pontiff he would also persist in openly indulging in carnal relations with his alluring married lover Giulia Farnese. The fact that Giulia was the wife of Orsino Orsini, who was the son of Rodrigo's own cousin Adriana da Mila, only served to add a zest of incest to the already adulterous and sacrilegious papal scandal.

Just as Pope Sixtus IV had used the papacy to favour his relations and Pope Innocent VIII had enriched his worthless son Franceschetto, so Pope Alexander VI would use the chair of St. Peter to transplant several generations of Catalan Borgias and establish them in noble positions in Rome and the Papal States. In 1480, Rodrigo had already secured for his sister Juana's son the position of corrector of apostolic briefs in the Curia. Upon his elevation, Rodrigo now created the forty-six-year-old Juan Borgia archbishop of Monreale and also cardinal. At the same time, the new pope passed his former archbishopric of Valencia to his seventeen-year-old son Cesare. The Sforzese had helped Rodrigo to secure the papacy and Cardinal Ascanio Sforza now proposed that the Sforza-Borgia alliance be formalised through a dynastic marriage between their respective families. A lesser member of the Sforza family, Giovanni Sforza, the lord of Pesaro, would be wed to the Borgia pope's youngest daughter Lucrezia. As a public signal of gratitude to Cardinal Sforza for facilitating his pontificate, Rodrigo consented to the match but was first compelled to break off an earlier marriage contract that had been signed with Don Gasparo, the count of Aversa. Although Giovanni Sforza–who was the cousin of both Ludovico and Ascanio– was descended from a collateral branch of the Sforza line, sharing ancestry with the counts of Cotignola, his lineage was in the eyes of the social climbing Borgias still deemed sufficiently eminent to make him a more attractive match than Don Gasparo and arrangements for the betrothal were duly initiated.

The Sforza-Borgia match was a welcome diplomatic fillip to Ludovico *il Moro* who continued to rule Milan as regent despite the fact that his nephew Gian Galeazzo had already come of age in 1490 and was therefore eligible for full instatement to the dukedom. That year, *il Moro* took the liberty of broadcasting, in a none too subtle way, who was the *real* power behind the ducal throne by minting coinage bearing his own image on one side and Gian Galeazzo's on the other. The *Milanesi* were by and large complacent about Ludovico's regency; for one thing he demonstrated none of the predatory sociopathic tendencies of his brother Galeazzo Maria Sforza (or indeed his maternal grandfather Filippo Maria Visconti). For another, their rightful duke, Gian Galeazzo, showed little inclination or indeed aptitude for ducal rule himself, preferring instead the pleasant diversions of hunting, game fishing and feasting to the affairs of state. He therefore remained at his estates in Pavia indulging his fondness for self-indulgence and recreation. There is every reason to suppose that Ludovico encouraged his nephew's indolence and deliberately aggravated his educational shortfall. But for Gian Galeazzo's wife Isabella d'Aragona, the daughter of Duke Alfonso of Calabria and Duchess Ippolita Maria Sforza of Milan, it was an entirely different matter. Following her marriage to her nineteen-year-old cousin Gian Galeazzo in 1488 she was, by 1492, now the lawful duchess consort of Naples. To her intense irritation, however, she was forced to play second fiddle to Ludovico's own wife, Beatrice d'Este, whom *il Moro* had only recently married in 1491.

Ludovico had requested Beatrice's hand from her father Ercole I d'Este in order to cement the friendly longstanding relations between Milan and Ferrara. Beatrice herself was one of the most beautiful and accomplished princesses of the Italian Renaissance; exquisitely educated, she had used her influence to gather around her such scholars, poets and artists, such as Niccolò da Correggio, Bernardo Castiglione, Donato Bramante and Leonardo da Vinci who flattered her with an endless round of pageants and masques in her honour. In

1492, Beatrice visited Venice as ducal ambassador and lobbied to have *La Serenissima* recognise her husband as the rightful duke of Milan. This naturally incensed the proud Aragonese Isabella d'Aragona, who was confined uselessly to Pavia while her witless and pleasure-loving husband frittered his time away in idle leisure pursuits. She wrote repeatedly to her equally proud Aragonese father Alfonso, remonstrating with him about her humiliating situation and describing herself as 'the most unhappily married woman in the world'.

Isabella's agitation and her canvassing of Naples had been brought to Ludovico's attention by her own clueless husband, who had let the intelligence slip in casual conversation with his uncle. Ludovico had every reason to fear the powerful Spanish-ruled kingdom to the south; despite his alliance with Ferrara, without a much broader coalition of allies in the north Milan alone was no match for the *Napoletano* army. However, his sense of isolation had already been planted some years earlier following Lorenzo de' Medici's historic visit to (and safe return in one piece from) Naples; ever since that time Florence had gravitated increasingly towards Naples and Rome and had neglected her traditional Medici-led alliance between with Milan. This was, as we have seen, due in large part to Ludovico's own insouciance towards this same alliance. *Il Moro*'s fear of Naples was not, in the scheme of things, entirely baseless. Responding positively to Isabella's requests for help, Alfonso of Calabria now sought to mount an invasion of Milan designed to oust Ludovico and Beatrice d'Este. In this enterprise, he was supported by a prominent *Milanese* exile named Giangiacomo Trivulzio, a captain who had served the Sforza faithfully for many years but who had defected to Naples after *il Moro* appointed the considerably less experienced Galeazzo Sanseverino as captain-general of the ducal armies in his stead.

Alfonso and Trivulzio were ready to mount an invasion of Lombardy to rescue the honour of Alfonso's daughter when, at the eleventh hour, his father King Ferrante had sagely stayed their hand. An attack on Milan was too rash, it was far better to attempt a diplomatic resolution first. The emissaries that Ferrante now despatched to Ludovico Sforza's court politely thanked *il Moro* for his wise regency up until this point but suggested that now might be the time for him to step down in favour of his nephew. *Il Moro* was cordial but evasive. Since his assumption of the regency, he had pursued a very deliberate policy of neglecting his nephew's education and pandering to his many human frailties. Furthermore, Ludovico's own son Massimiliano Sforza would be born in January 1493. It was therefore now inevitable that his mind would turn towards prospects of a dynasty of his own. Ferrante's envoys returned empty-handed to Naples.

The old king was acutely aware that far wider issues were at stake than merely his granddaughter's bruised pride. Ferrante's father King Alfonso V of Aragon had succeeded in wresting control of the kingdom of Naples from René of Anjou on 26 February 1443. Thereafter, he had obtained the agreement of Pope Eugenius IV that the kingdom of Naples would pass to his illegitimate son Ferrante upon his death. Several decades later, and despite the fact that Naples was technically a papal fief, the French still refused to concede defeat over the matter of their former Angevin possessions there and French jurists maintained that the true title to the kingdom of Naples had–upon René of Anjou's death in 1480–simply escheated back to the French Crown. This was because the present French King Charles VIII's grandfather, Charles VII, had married Marie of Anjou whose father had been Louis I of Anjou, King of Naples from 1389 until 1399. It was by now common knowledge that Ludovico Sforza and Charles VIII had reached an understanding to support one another in their respective objectives; if *il Moro* were to now encourage King Charles VIII of France to invade Italy and lay claim to his ancestral rights it would spell disaster for the ruling Spanish House of Trastámara in Naples. In an attempt to avert this, Ferrante attempted a fresh diplomatic gambit, despatching his second son Federigo of Aragon to Rome just before Christmas 1492 to congratulate Pope Alexander VI on his accession and to persuade him to abandon his *Milanese* alliance.

Federigo arrived in Rome 'with a huge retinue and he was received with great honour by Cardinal Giuliano della Rovere' who, after supporting the rebel *Napoletano* barons in 1485, had subsequently patched up his differences with Ferrante in the interests of uniting against their shared enemies the Sforza of Milan and in particular Ascanio Sforza who, through his manoeuvrings, had robbed della Rovere of the papacy, not to mention the consolation prize of the vice-chancellorship. Federigo's older brother Alfonso of Calabria had been confirmed in his succession as heir to the kingdom of Naples on 27 May 1492 by the late Pope Innocent VIII. Naples needed to test the water to determine whether the new Borgia pope would abide by his predecessor's ruling and continue to endorse the Aragonese primacy in the kingdom. Like Lorenzo de' Medici before him, Pope Alexander VI now rose to the challenge of playing one state off against another whilst maintaining a balance of power in Italy. It was a subtle game for which, both in terms of personality and training, he was peculiarly well suited.

Alexander VI was, unfortunately for Ferrante, already feeling ill-disposed towards the kingdom of Naples. As early as 3 September 1492, the new pope believed that Ferrante had conspired to undermine his authority in the Papal States. When Pope Innocent VIII had died his unprepossessing son Franceschetto had (sensibly for once) recognised that he had lost the authority with which to hold onto the many papal fiefs which his nepotistic father had bestowed upon him. Amongst these were a number of properties which held particular strategic value in the Campania such as Cerveteri, Anguillara, Canale Monterano and Rota. Wishing to trade properties which he had no chance of retaining for hard cash (Franceschetto *always* being in need of ready cash) he had approached Virginio Orsini, lord of Bracciano, who had enthusiastically agreed to purchase them for amalgamation into his own Orsini estates in the Campania. For the necessary financing, Orsini had turned to his in-law Piero di Lorenzo de' Medici. Piero–who was married to Alfonsina Orsini and whose mother had been Clarice Orsini–understandably felt strong bonds of commitment towards his Orsini relatives and in the spirit of good family relations had agreed to fund the purchases from the Medici Bank. In reality, however, the sale of the Cybò properties had in fact been mooted during the final months of Lorenzo de' Medici's life and it had been *il Magnifico* himself who had set in motion the transaction which was now dutifully carried out by his son Piero. When Pope Alexander got wind of these purchases coming hard on the heels of his election he was irate; behind the transaction he deciphered the hidden influence of King Ferrante of Naples who, so he concluded, was encouraging his *condottiere* Virginio Orsini to acquire the Campania estates as a stepping stone for some future Neapolitan invasion of Rome and the Papal States. In reality this was highly unlikely for, as we have already seen, Ferrante needed the friendship of the Pope to legitimise his own monarchical rule in the face of the claims of the French Crown. Aside from this, the Pope was also galled by the fact that Franceschetto Cybò was hawking papal fiefs which were not rightly his to sell, something which served to undermine Alexander VI's feudal overlordship in the Papal States.

Under these strained circumstances, Don Federigo's offer of a Borgia match with Duke Alfonso and Ippolita Maria's eldest son Ferrandino was snubbed by Pope Alexander and on, 10 January 1493, Federigo left Rome without any assurances from the Pope that he would entertain any future alliance with Naples. Disgusted that Pope Alexander persisted in siding with the Sforzese, Cardinal della Rovere and Virginio Orsini both left Rome and decamped to the cardinal's private *castello* at Ostia, which commanded the Vatican's strategic access to the sea. Alexander viewed this as the belligerent move which indeed it was. His response was to move papal troops to the nearby coastal town of Civitavecchia and, in reply to this, Orsini gave the cardinal his assurance that he would 'protect the cardinal's fortress as well as his life'. On 2 February came the signing of the marriage contract between Giovanni Sforza and Lucrezia Borgia and their wedding took place in a proxy ceremony from which Giovanni himself was notably absent. To confound the on-going efforts of the *Napoletani* to propose their own countervailing marriage alliance, the betrothal was conducted in intense secrecy in the presence of the Pope's nephew Cardinal Juan Borgia Lanzol de Romaní, Cesare Borgia, Cesare's elder brother Juan, Cardinal Ascanio Sforza, the *Milanese* ambassador Stefano Taberna and a small group of papal officials and notaries. Giovanni was in return given a papal *condotta* and Lucrezia brought with her an appreciable dowry of 31,000 ducats.

In March, Ferrante desperately attempted once again to heal the rift with the papacy. Sending envoys to attempt to settle the matter of Cerveteri, Anguillara and the other papal properties, Ferrante also offered Aragonese princesses for both Cesare and Jofrè Borgia, ignoring the fact that both were at this time in Holy Orders and therefore ineligible as candidates for marriage diplomacy. Rodrigo Borgia persisted in resisting Ferrante's offer. By this time he was more preoccupied with the process of forging an alliance between those two erstwhile adversaries Milan and Venice. Ascanio Sforza's diplomacy in this regard came to fruition on 25 April when Pope Alexander VI announced the formation of the League of Saint Mark between Venice, Milan, Rome and also encompassing the smaller states of Siena, Ferrara and Mantua. This broad front was arrayed against the kingdom of Naples and the detested Orsini. Ferrante, more isolated and distrustful than ever thanks to this latest development, complained bitterly to King Ferdinand of Spain on 7 June 1493 that 'the Pope has no respect for the chair he now occupies ... all he wants is war with me, and he has been victimising me ever since he was elected.' He then added for good measure: 'the Pope leads such a life that he is abhorred by everyone'. But King Ferdinand remained unmoved, and besides, this Catalan Borgia pope was proving inordinately helpful to Spain's wider international interests.

On 12 October 1492, Christopher Columbus had made landfall in San Salvador in the Bahamas and on 15 March 1493 he had returned from his transatlantic voyage with gold, colourful parrots, and specimens of the indigenous *Taino* Indians from the new lands he had discovered. These lands he still believed to be the fabled Indies where the immensely profitable 'Spice Islands' were located with their crops of pepper and nutmeg. Columbus's act of claiming these lands for the throne of Spain had meanwhile angered Portugal, who pointed to an earlier papal ruling granting Portugal rights to all newly-discovered lands, no matter how far west, extending along the African coast. To settle the dispute, Pope Alexander issued the papal bull *Inter Caetera* on 4 May 1493 which ruled that Spain would receive exclusive rights to everything west of a line drawn 100 Spanish leagues beyond the Azores. This perquisite was in open thanks to the Spanish monarchs for the *Reconquista*, which also led the Pope to bestow upon the two sovereigns the title of *Rex Catholicissimus* or Their Most Catholic Majesties. With such an obliging Spanish pope as Rodrigo Borgia in the Vatican, King Ferrante's anti-Borgia invective had largely fallen on deaf ears at the Aragonese court.

The official marriage celebrations of Giovanni Sforza and Lucrezia Borgia on 12 June 1493 only rubbed salt into Ferrante's already open wounds. The marriage ceremony and feast was celebrated with due pomp and Alexander spared no expense in putting on a lavish show. Lucrezia's trousseau and wedding dress was rumoured to be worth 15,000 ducats and Giovanni himself put in a good appearance with borrowed jewellery and a heavy gold chain which many recognised as being the property of the Gonzaga family. The king of Naples might, however, have taken cold comfort in the fact that the Pope had adamantly refused to allow his new son-in-law to consummate his marriage until November. This may have been done out of consideration for Lucrezia's age (she was still only thirteen, the groom twenty-six and already a widower) but, as more cynical tongues might have speculated, an unconsummated marriage would be considerably easier to annul than a consummated one, should the diplomatic alliance between Rome and Milan subsequently prove 'inconvenient'.

Despite Rodrigo Borgia's friendly favours towards the joint thrones of Spain, the Pope was on the receiving end of a tongue lashing from Their Most Catholic Majesties' ambassador one week later on 19 June. Not only had Ferdinand and Isabella begun to disapprove of the Pope's on-going provocation towards their Aragonese kinsman Ferrante, but the Spanish monarchs reprimanded Alexander for granting asylum to the many Jews who had been expelled from Spain in the wake of the Spanish Crown's Alhambra Decree (or 'Edict of Expulsion') on 31 March 1492. From their lofty pedestal as Crusaders against the infidel Moors, the Spanish monarchs, through their ambassador Diego López de Haro, also reproached the Pope for on-going corruption within the Curia and the continued lucrative but sinful sale of Church benefices. It was perhaps this royal rebuke from his own native monarchy which finally induced Pope Alexander to mend fences with the king of Naples. By late July, Alexander and Ferrante had hammered out an agreement whereby Virginio Orsini would be permitted to keep his purchases of papal property on condition that the purchase price was paid to the Pope, as feudal overlord, rather than to the former vassal leaseholder Franceschetto Cybò. Innocent VIII's son had, it seemed, accrued yet another substantial loss in a lifetime of miserable gambles and had little choice but to fall back on the charity of his wife and her Medici relatives, thereafter dividing his time equally between Florence and Genoa.

The resolution of the stalemate over the Cybò fortresses was celebrated in Rome with a feast on 24 July which was attended by Virginio Orsini and Cardinal della Rovere, who had come down under the banner of concord from his *castello* in Ostia especially for the occasion. To seal the agreement, Pope

Alexander finally consented in mid-August to the dynastic olive branch which had long been proffered by Ferrante; the Pope's youngest son Jofrè would be matched with the King's youngest daughter, Princess Sancia of Aragon. Jofrè and Sancha were twelve and sixteen years old respectively and, although Ferrante would have preferred for a son-in-law either the more vigorous and intelligent Cesare Borgia or the more senior Juan Borgia, Pope Alexander had already formulated other plans for his two older sons. For Cesare he had earmarked a career in the Church (and he would in due course receive his cardinal's hat on 20 September 1493). Juan, meanwhile, was named second duke of Gandia following the untimely death of the first duke, Juan's older half-brother Pedro Luis, and had already embarked for Spain on 2 August to be married to Pedro Luis's widow, Maria Enriquez de Luna, a niece of King Ferdinand of Aragon and Queen Isabella of Castile. This particular alliance had been mooted by Diego López de Haro and the proposal had been greedily accepted by Pope Alexander, who was already covetously eyeing numerous conquered Moorish estates in Grenada for Juan.

The Pope's friendly rapprochement with Ferrante, facilitated by Diego López de Haro, now gave the lie to the League of Saint Mark. Although–like the earlier Most Holy League–the alliance was supposed to remain in effect for twenty-five years, all the players in Italy knew full well that it was hamstrung from the start by Venice's on-going covetousness towards Milan's Lombard territories. With the Pope and the king of Naples now back on friendly dynastic terms it was the turn of Ludovico *il Moro* to feel isolated and insecure. In his insecurity, he now looked north to the court of the French king. On 9 August, Guillaume Briçonnet, the bishop of St.-Malo and Charles VIII's secretary of the treasury, arrived at the papal court with a mission to urge the Pope to recognise King Charles VIII's Angevin claim to Naples. As suzerain of Naples this was still the Pope's feudal prerogative and the French king still preferred his claim to go by the book, even if he planned to march south and seize the *Regno* by force of arms anyway.

The instinctual reaction of Pope Alexander was to prevaricate. After all, he had finally achieved reconciliation with all his Italian enemies, being now dynastically linked to both Milan to the north and Naples in the south, as well as reconciled with Virginio Orsini following the business over the Cybò properties. Councils would need to be called and lengthy discussions would need to be held as to the legalities and technicalities of the French request, Pope Alexander protested; this was not a decision that he could simply make at will. Although stymied by the Pope's diplomatic manoeuvres King Charles VIII was not deterred. As early as 1491 Charles had already given his commitment of support to Ludovico Sforza's bid for the ducal title. By August 1492, when he summoned his vassals and ministers to Tours to discuss the matter of Italy, the King had decided to combine his reclamation of Naples with a full-scale Crusade against the Turk. The conquest of Naples and consolidation of control over southern Italy would be but the prelude to the Crusade; the French would then embark from the Adriatic ports of the Mezzogiorno to the Holy Land. The *Napoletano* émigrés at his court, many of them dissidents from the Barons War of 1485, egged him on, assuring him that Naples was easy pickings for French arms. Charles now moved to secure his own international borders before making his move in Italy. In November 1492 he had already reached an accord with Henry VII of England at Etaples; next he sealed a truce with Ferdinand and Isabella in Barcelona in January 1493; finally he concluded a treaty with

Maximilian of Austria at Senlis in May 1493. The way was now theoretically clear for Italy.

Ludovico Sforza meanwhile was basking in his newfound self-appointed role as 'kingmaker of Italy' and diplomatic heir apparent to Cosimo and Lorenzo de' Medici, even going so far as to vainly boast to his retainers 'that the Pope was his chaplain, the *signoria* of Venice was his chamberlain, and the king of France his courier'. But this view was not shared, however, by Philippe de Commynes, who described *il Moro* thus: 'This Ludovico was a wise man but very timorous and humble when he was in awe – and false when it was to his advantage. And this I do not speak by hearsay but as one that knew him well, having had many transactions with him.' But the fact still remained that *il Moro's* invitation to Charles had been one of the decisive factors in the French king's decision to invade.

As for Rodrigo Borgia, if he would not lend papal support to the enterprise he would be declared illegitimate by a council of Charles's French cardinals and deposed, a more pliant pontiff being installed in his stead. Pope Alexander's efforts to manage the situation and walk the delicate tightrope between Milan, Naples and the court of the French king became increasingly fraught as the weeks and months ticked by. Many on the Italian peninsula were struck by portents of the coming doom and in Florence Friar Savonarola predicted an apocalyptic scourge which would soon fall upon both the republic as well as the whole of Italy. This judgement was a result of their collective wickedness and ungodliness, the blame for which he laid squarely at the feet of the Medici for their tyranny and mismanagement of the republic. Although he had, at last, secured the Pope's crucial support, King Ferrante of Naples nevertheless remained so fearful of the French threat that he became a shadow of his former self. With Charles's threats to march south growing daily, the peninsula teetered on the brink of a catastrophe.

In September, Pope Alexander made further enemies within the College of Cardinals when he gave out an unprecedented twelve new red hats, some of them to his friends and relatives. Not only was his son Cesare elevated to the Sacred College but also young Alessandro Farnese, the brother of his beautiful lover Giulia Farnese. For this reason, Cardinal Farnese would thereafter be referred to amongst the other cardinals as 'Cardinal Fregnese' or 'Cardinal Cunt'. Since no Neapolitan clerics received a red hat in this latest round both Ludovico and Ascanio Sforza were jubilant; Cardinal Giuliano della Rovere, meanwhile, was so upset by the news of the Pope's latest appointments, which did not in any way benefit his own cause, that he took to bed with a fever. Many factors had by now conjuncted to create the looming crisis and all that was needed to ignite the volatile situation was a suitable trigger.

That trigger came on 27 January 1494 when King Ferrante of Naples died 'without the cross and without God' as the priggish papal Protonotary Apostolic Johannes Burchard tartly put it. For nearly half a century, and in spite of his illegitimacy, Ferrante had wielded immense power and influence on the Italian peninsula. He was mercurial and cruel but he was also justifiably feared by the other magnates of Italy. His son Alfonso of Calabria embodied all the more vicious traits of the father without apparently having inherited any of the saving graces. He was boorish and cruel and had been unable to create for himself the same mystique enjoyed by his late father. Neither did his louche ways at the courts of other city-states especially endear him to his noble contemporaries.

Without the restraining influence of his father Alfonso was an even greater potential threat to Ludovico Sforza and consequently *il Moro* now moved to re-confirm the backing of both France and the Empire.

On 16 March 1494, *il Moro*'s niece Bianca Maria Sforza, the daughter of the late Duke Galeazzo Maria, was married to the king of the Romans Maximilian at Innsbruck. Maximilian had previously been married to Mary of Burgundy, to whom he had been devoted, but Mary had died tragically in a riding accident in 1482. A second, proxy marriage to Anne of Brittany had been dissolved by Pope Innocent VIII in early 1492 and Anne was instead induced to marry Charles VIII of France so as to consolidate the divided lands within the French realm. His third marriage to Bianca Maria was strictly a financial transaction for the impecunious Maximilian. She brought her husband a vast dowry of 400,000 ducats in return for which Maximilian would assert his imperial suzerain's rights to the duchy of Milan and so, in this capacity, proclaim Ludovico Sforza as its rightful duke. Even as Maximilian and Bianca Maria's marriage was being concluded, from his military camp at Lyons Charles VIII now threw his hat into the ring and made public his intention of invading Italy with a large standing army of French and Gascon veterans from the wars in Brittany, plus additional troops which were already mustering throughout the months of March and April. Driven by these developments to finally come down on one side or the other, Pope Alexander VI adhered to his Neapolitan alliance and issued a bull on 22 March confirming Alfonso II as king of Naples whilst simultaneously condemning Charles's plans for war. Following a tempestuous eight-hour long consistory the College of Cardinals relented to Pope Alexander's request to appoint a papal legate for the coronation of Alfonso in Naples.

Two days later, the Pope despatched his own nephew Cardinal Juan Borgia Lanzol de Romaní for this purpose. Cardinal Borgia's first task was to preside over the marriage of his cousin Jofrè to Sancia of Aragon. The following day, on 8 May, he officiated at the coronation of Alfonso II of Naples, who received the official title of *Rex Siciliae* at Naples Cathedral. Having been crowned, it was now Alfonso's turn to manifest his gratitude to Pope Alexander for the Borgia family's support. Firstly, Jofrè was invested as prince of the small and insignificant fief of Squillace, as well as made count of Cariati, and bestowed with a generous income. Alexander's eldest son, Duke Juan Borgia of Gandia, *gonfaloniere* and captain-general of the Church, was meanwhile invested as prince of Tricario and count of Chiaromonte, Lauria and Carinola. In return Pope Alexander gave a red hat to Alfonso's illegitimate brother Luigi of Aragon. Luigi had previously been married to the former Pope Innocent VIII's granddaughter Battistina Cybò Usodimare who, although mentioned as having attended the June 1493 wedding in Rome of Lucrezia Borgia and Giovanni Sforza, had died sometime soon afterwards; following his wife's death Luigi took holy orders, receiving the tonsure in May 1494 from Alessandro Carafa, archbishop of Naples. The new king of Naples had obtained the necessary approval of his feudal suzerain for his crown and the Borgia clan had also done rather well out of the arrangement as well, even if the transaction left the Pope open to the usual allegations of simony, to which he was anyway inured.

One might be forgiven for thinking that Pope Alexander's pact with Alfonso would have pleased Cardinal Giuliano della Rovere immensely as it created his long-awaited Papal-Neapolitan front against his sworn enemy the House of Sforza but, in the ever-shifting sands that were Italian politics, this turned out not to be the case. Ever the changeable intriguer, della Rovere now allowed himself to be suborned by the *Milanese* ambassador and was induced to switch his allegiance to the king of France instead. Mystifying upon initial scrutiny, della Rovere's change of heart can easily be explained by the fact that his dislike for Ascanio Sforza was surmounted only by his enmity towards the Borgia pope, whom he decried and abominated for his overt simony in having purchased the papal throne. It can also be explained in terms of the years of acrimonious rivalry between the two men as they vied for the favour of Pope Innocent VIII, a simmering low-intensity war which Rodrigo Borgia had ultimately won. Following Rodrigo's election, della Rovere had bitterly and imprudently denounced the new pope in consistory but his imprudent outburst had later caused him to fear for his life. Knowing Rodrigo Borgia's ruthlessness, Giuliano not unreasonably concluded that his interests would best be served if King Charles VIII, at the behest of the Sforza regent, were to march on Rome and depose the Borgia pope for having challenged his royal claim to Naples.

To this end della Rovere was soon calling for a general council to reform the Church and *'per tribulare il Papa'*. Furthermore, if he was already prominent in Charles's itinerant court, how much better he himself would be placed for election to the pontifical chair under the French king's close scrutiny. With these considerations in mind, Cardinal della Rovere garrisoned and provisioned his fortress at Ostia to hold out for two years and, leaving it in the hands of the *condottiere* Fabrizio Colonna (a somewhat puzzling move since Fabrizio was still also working for Naples at the time), he sailed for France by way of Genoa. Arriving in Lyons on 1 June, he was warmly greeted by a generally sympathetic King Charles VIII. Charles, who was at this time beginning to waver after the full enormity of his undertaking had begun to sink in, was coaxed from his irresolution by a militant della Rovere. 'What fears then, what confusions, what dreams have possessed your royal breast?' the fugitive cardinal asked. 'Where is the fierceness with which you boasted, only four days ago, that you would overcome all Italy united?'

While della Rovere was haranguing the king of France, Pope Alexander's *condottiere* Niccolò di Pitigliano, who had formerly been captain-general of the Church prior to his replacement by Juan Borgia, now moved against Ostia, invested it, and induced Fabrizio Colonna to surrender the port to the Pope. The absentee Cardinal Giuliano della Rovere was, to all intents and purposes, now at war with the Borgia pope. From the safety of France, Cardinal della Rovere struck back. The French ambassador to Rome delivered an ultimatum to the Pope to the effect that if he refused to place the crown of Naples upon Charles's head then a Church council would be called for the express purpose of investigating allegations of simony in the awarding of Pope Alexander's tiara. The fact that Rodrigo Borgia's simony was an open secret in Rome and all the other Italian city-states and that nobody (except perhaps della Rovere himself) had seriously objected to it until now, was neither here nor there – Cardinal della Rovere held the threat of an enforced Church council over Pope Alexander's head like the proverbial Damoclean Sword. As the brother of France's ally Ludovico Sforza, the vice-chancellor Cardinal Ascanio Sforza had little choice but to go along with della Rovere's portentous charade, which made Ascanio's position in Rome increasingly untenable. Ludovico himself was less impressed by Charles's threat to reform the Church, scathingly asserting that 'the king has more need to reform himself than setting about reforming other people'.

With the grim news from Lyons of Charles VIII's ever growing mobilisation, Pope Alexander met King Alfonso II of Naples at Vicovaro in mid-July to discuss their mutual plans for the defence of Italy. Alfonso proposed an assault on Genoa in order to deprive the French army of a sympathetic port from which to launch any seaborne invasion of Naples. This was to be achieved in concert with a landward attack on Milan itself, for which purpose Alfonso despatched an advance party of several hundred men-at-arms under the inexperienced command of his twenty-five-year-old son Ferrandino. Alfonso himself would remain on the kingdom's borders with the main force of thirty squadrons of horse and Virginio Orsini would position himself south of Rome with 200 men-at-arms. In reply to these meagre and heavily dispersed forces, the king of France was planning his invasion with a crushing army of 1,900 lances, 1,200 mounted archers and 19,000 infantrymen supported by a further 1,500 native Italian lances and between 2,000 to 3,000 Italian infantry. His army would also deploy a completely new weapon hitherto unseen on the Italian peninsula – mobile artillery which was capable of shredding entire formations of men with devastating and demoralizing chain-shot. Unlike Italian cannon, which were traditionally made from copper tubes encased in wood and animal hides, and which fired small carved stones, the French artillery was cast in solid bronze and shot wrought iron cannonballs which were the size of a human head. Unlike the slow-moving Italian weapons, which were dragged by slow-moving oxen, the French limbered their cannon to swift, powerful horses which meant they could rapidly place their artillery anywhere on the battlefield.

Even with such a formidable army Charles would nonetheless still need to pass through the territory of Milan, Florence and the Papal States in order to reach his ultimate objective of Naples; much therefore depended upon the reception he received from the various Italian city-states dotted along the route. Milan herself would guarantee free passage through Lombardy, although even now Ludovico Sforza began to regret his actions as reports of the sheer size of the French army trickled in to him at Milan. Ludovico *il Moro* had envisaged that Charles would fight the war in much the same way as the former dukes of Anjou had done, with minimal forces and amphibious assaults against Naples; he had not anticipated that Charles would deploy a vast land army which could simply bulldoze its way across Italy. When Charles's envoys approached Venice for a declaration of where they stood in the coming conflict their Doge, Agostino Barbarigo, professed studied neutrality. The republic was too busy, so the Doge argued, containing Ottoman threats to their Eastern interests to become embroiled in Charles's expedition. This was in spite of Charles' offer of certain ports in Apulia and the Balkans if the republic should agree to join forces with him. Aware of *il Moro's* dynastic marriage alliance with Maximilian, privately *La Serenissima* was more concerned about a possible joint invasion by France and the Empire which would leave her territory open to attack by the republic's traditional enemy the Germans.

Ferrara was in a rather more complicated position. Ercole I d'Este was devoted to his Aragonese wife Eleonora d'Aragona and had attempted on more than one occasion to mediate between his father-in-law King Ferrante and his son-in-law Ludovico Sforza. On the other hand, Venice persisted in her antagonism towards Ferrara. A cautious man, unlike his more flamboyant brother Borso, Ercole came to regard an alliance with France as being the lesser of two evils; accordingly he despatched his second son Ferrante d'Este to the French court by way of insurance. However, Ferrante's laziness and

334

inattentiveness when it came to the task of winning the French king's favour led Ercole to despair. 'We know that you have plenty of talent and that you know what your duty is, and that, if you wish, you can do yourself credit' was the anxious father's missive to the erring son. The fact that Ercole kept his son perpetually short of funds whilst milking him tirelessly for any useful intelligence from the French court was seemingly lost on Ferrara's elderly ruler. The chess pieces were now therefore in place for what was to follow, but where exactly did the Florence of Piero di Lorenzo de' Medici stand in all of this?

Florence too was caught in an impossible conflict of loyalties. The House of Medici was intermarried with the Orsini, whose fortunes were intertwined with those of the *Regno*, where many of their lands and estates lay. At the same time the Medici, like Florence's other banking houses, depended on the goodwill of the Curia and the Pope for continued business. Furthermore, there was Cardinal Giovanni de' Medici's career within the Sacred College to consider; any move construed as being contrary to papal interests might adversely affect his prospects (having waited so long for a Medici cardinal the family was loathe to endanger this achievement). Yet on the other hand, even Piero de' Medici (who was not exactly the sharpest strategist in Italy) recognised that if Florence stood by her alliance with Naples and Rome, and if these two allies subsequently either stood aside or refused to provide military support to the republic, then Florence would be the first of the three powers to have to confront the French army in Tuscany. Furthermore, in all likelihood, they would have to face it alone. It was still too early in Alexander VI's pontificate to be able to tell whether or not he was a reliable friend of Florence or whether the republic would be entertaining a *mésalliance* by standing with the Pope.

On the other side of the coin was the fact that, in international terms, Florence's economic life had always favoured cordial relations with France, the commune's major northern trading partner. Moreover, Cardinal Giovanni depended for a large part of his income from the French benefices (including Font Douce and Aix-en-Provence) that had been so generously bestowed by Charles's predecessor King Louis XI and in order to retain these the cardinal depended on the continued goodwill of the French Crown. In conclusion, caught between Scylla and Charybdis, even the great Lorenzo would have been hard pressed to make the right decision in his son's position. In early February 1494, Charles VIII had pointedly demanded that Piero de' Medici cease his dithering and procure 300 lances, 100 infantry and six galleys for amalgamation into the French army. This in itself was problematic. Even throughout the summer of 1494 certain on-going domestic problems within his own realm presented the possibility that Charles might not invade Italy after all; if Florence therefore declared openly for France, and King Charles subsequently failed to come, then Florence would be left isolated in the face of Naples, Rome and possibly even Venice as well. Subsequent developments also seem to bear out the assumption that Piero failed to consult either with his cardinal brother or indeed with the *signoria* of Florence as to which strategic direction to take. It was in these highly problematic circumstances, therefore, that Piero de' Medici rolled the dice and unilaterally declared Florence's official support for King Alfonso II of Naples.

King Charles VIII, as might have been predicted, took this news as a personal slight. It was made worse by the fact that he had, so he at least believed, a personal connection with the republic. During his minority, when the awkward and unattractive royal youth had been under the regency of his older sister Anne (who had been described by their father Louis XI as 'the least deranged woman in France'), Charles had developed a close friendship with Florence's ambassador Piero di Gino Capponi, who was the grandson of that towering Florentine statesman Neri Capponi. That Piero Capponi's Republic of Florence should now turn its back on Charles, when he needed their cooperation for his army to peacefully traverse Tuscany, both angered the King and placed the Capponi family in a difficult situation. Piero de' Medici's decision to abandon Florence's traditional trading ally to the north immediately set malicious tongues wagging. Just as his father had been known as '*il Magnifico*' and his grandfather as Piero '*il Gottoso*', so Piero de' Medici acquired a variety of less flattering sobriquets in the polite circles of Florence. Chief amongst these was the nickname 'Piero *il Sfortunato*' (Piero the Unfortunate), although others referred to him somewhat less politely as 'Piero *il Fatuo*' or Piero the Fatuous.

Charles despatched his counsellor, the diplomat and diarist Philippe de Commynes, to conduct a diplomatic reconnaissance of Italy and his agent hastened to Florence in May. Commynes was no stranger to Medicean Florence. He had conducted a similar embassy in 1478 in the immediate aftermath of the Pazzi Conspiracy and had witnessed for himself the unrestrained bloodletting which had accompanied the re-establishment of Medici authority. When he went to the Palazzo Medici to meet with Piero di Lorenzo–whom Commynes casually dismissed as 'a man of very little ability'–Florence's young ruler confirmed to the envoy that the French army would *not* be permitted safe passage through Florentine territory. It was at this point that the jealousy of the cadet branch of the Medici family, those descended from Cosimo's brother, Lorenzo the Elder, now finally manifested itself. *Il Magnifico's* defrauding of the inheritances of Lorenzo di Pierfrancesco and his younger brother Giovanni had created much bad blood. Lorenzo de' Medici had tried to make amends, assigning his extremely capable clerk Amerigo Vespucci in 1483 to serve as the brothers' *maestro di casa*; Vespucci managed their business interests competently and loyally when the brothers were aged only twenty and seventeen respectively. But when Lorenzo di Pierfrancesco came of age in 1485, *il Magnifico* had been forced by the courts to make full restitution, which he did partially through cash reimbursements and partly by the transfer of property, including the Medici Villa di Cafaggiolo. But even so, when Lorenzo di Pierfrancesco had claimed 105,880 florins were owed to him and his brother, *il Magnifico* managed to have the obligation whittled down to 61,400 florins. The mistrust and antipathy had run so deep that Lorenzo di Pierfrancesco had even created his own circle of humanist scholars and poets to rival his former benefactor's; in addition to Amerigo Vespucci this would also include Michele Marullo, a passionate devotee of Lucretius who would later reputedly drown in the River Cecina wearing full armour with a copy of *De rerum natura* tucked in his pocket.

The animus which Lorenzo and Giovanni di Pierfrancesco still felt for *il Magnifico* had unfortunately been passed down from father to son. In fact, on 30 March 1494, the bad feeling had reached a climax during the traditional Spring Ball, when Piero had publicly slapped Giovanni's face in an argument over the attentions of an attractive young woman. It was not uncommon for such balls and carnivals to be used as the occasion for settling quarrels, especially those concerning matters of the heart, beneath a façade of boisterous play. However, given his late father's plundering of the brothers' inheritance, Piero had gone too far. Humiliated by his display of arrogance and superiority

336

the two brothers reached out angrily to Ambassador Commynes. They assured the French agent that most of the city's population were in favour of maintaining the traditional French alliance and, in return for French support against Piero, they promised to provide Charles with financial aid once he and his army reached Tuscany.

Their indiscreet overtures to Commynes and King Charles were soon broadcast over the diplomatic grapevine; and when word of his cousins' secret negotiations reached Piero from Gentile Becchi, who was at this time assigned to Charles's court, the Medici state security apparatus swooped down and spirited Lorenzo and Giovanni away to the Bargello on 26 April. Luca Landucci recorded that many now called openly for the execution of the lesser Medici brothers on charges of subversion and treason against the state. Indeed, the Council of Seventy had also recommended the death penalty and the charges should at least have merited closer scrutiny. In the event, however, Piero, proved neither decisive nor ruthless enough to follow through and three days later, in a politically maladroit display of clemency, he had the brothers cautioned and then pardoned. Piero's actions in this matter, which were perhaps made under French diplomatic pressure, led merely to the brothers being confined to their respective country estates at Cafaggiolo and Castello. Here, his duplicitous cousins were left free to maintain a covert dialogue with Charles VIII which, in the eyes of the French monarch, further undermined Piero's domestic and diplomatic authority.

The tense summer months passed with an air of apprehension punctuated by one moment of excitement. In June there was attempt on the part of the *Genovese* exiles Obietto Fieschi and Cardinal Paolo Campofregoso to deprive the French of an embarkation port for Naples by instigating an uprising in the *Milanese*-held port. The two exiles sailed a Neapolitan fleet dangerously close to Genoa but were foiled by the timely arrival of King Charles VIII's cousin, Louis d'Orléans, who had with him a force of French, *Milanese* and 3,500 ferocious Swiss mercenary pikemen. With little chance of provoking any sort of local uprising with so many enemy troops in the vicinity, Fieschi and Campofregoso broke off their attack and made south for Portovenere but their attempt to take this other port was also similarly confounded by the French.

In the same month the Medici wound down their banking business at their Lyons branch, which was where Charles was presently mobilising his main force. The French king had finally lost patience with all diplomacy with Florence and had ordered the expulsion of the Medici from French territory. By April, both Commynes and King Charles were fully aware that Piero di Gino Capponi was discreetly working against Piero de' Medici's interests, actively encouraging the French to expel both the Medici Bank and the Florentines from France. In the event, the Florentines (who were known to be still sympathetic to Charles) were permitted to remain; only those associated with the Medici were ordered to leave Lyons. There is little indication at this point that the Medici were aware that Piero Capponi was sleeping with the enemy. Yet the breach had been some time in the making and Capponi had himself gradually come to enshrine the traditional political beliefs of his family. These beliefs, which were not altogether aligned with those of the Medici, tended more towards the reactionary and the oligarchical and, inimical to the 'new men' of the past hundred or so years, strove to salvage the primacy of the *signoria* (now little more than an ornament) from further Medici encroachment. To the south, meanwhile, Siena's former head of state Jacopo Petrucci had only recently been deposed. Piero de' Medici might, if his political sensibilities had not failed him at this critical time, have regarded developments in Siena as an omen touching upon the fortunes of his own family and the vagaries of fortune.

By this stage Alfonso of Naples was actively appealing to the Turkish Sultan for help in the coming conflict with the king of France. In August 1494, word reached the Venetian court that Alfonso had sent an emissary to the Sublime Porte to ask Bayezid II to attack Chios and so distract Genoa from its expected amphibious operations on behalf of the French. It was even rumoured that Alfonso had offered the Sultan the towns of Brindisi and Otranto in return, preferring to see these two Christian towns surrendered to the infidel Turk than yielded up to King Charles VIII of France. It was a truly remarkable proposal in light of the Islamic massacres which had occurred at Otranto just fourteen years earlier. Wary of the French and aware of Charles's expansive talk of a Crusade, Bayezid however had wisely declined. The Christian Pope Alexander VI still held his troublesome brother Prince Djem as a hostage. If the French king were to obtain Djem from the Pope and unleash him in the Balkans it could prove highly problematic for the Sultan. It was therefore better, so he reasoned, to stay well out of this parochial quarrel between fellow Christian powers.

The tedious, rumour-filled months of 'phoney war' came to an abrupt end on 3 September 1494 when the armies of King Charles VIII of France invaded Italy on three separate fronts. Charles himself crossed into Savoy by means of the Montgenèvre Pass with 30,000 men and, by 9 September, he had reached Asti where he was met and welcomed by Ercole d'Este of Ferrara and Ludovico Sforza of Milan. Reviewing the sheer size of the French army on display, *il Moro* was secretly horrified at the enormity of what he had done. Particularly terrifying were Charles's mobile artillery train, as well as his mounted lances, the paid professionals of the renowned *compagnies d'ordonnance*. But not all of the French who had poured into Italy were necessarily fighting soldiers, since any large army of the era attracted an equal or an even larger number of civilians; these were a mixture of soldiers' wives, people in various commissariat roles, and simple merchants, peddlers or hangers on who earned their living off the troops. Charles VIII himself had calculated that to field an army of 20,000 fighting soldiers he would need to feed at least 48,000 to 50,000 mouths a day. Having summoned such a host, what savage mischief would they now get up to in Lombardy? As Charles was reaching Asti, Louis d'Orléans had sailed south along the Ligurian coast from Genoa to Rapallo where he once more engaged the *Napoletano* forces under the joint command of Obietto Fieschi and Cardinal Paolo Campofregoso. Disembarking several thousand Swiss pikemen, the Swiss troops routed the amphibious forces of Naples and their exiled *Genovesi* allies, massacred the wounded where they lay, murdered any prisoners that were taken in cold blood, and concluded their victory by sacking the town of Rapallo itself. It was a truly shocking display of what French military might was capable of and most of the city-states of Italy looked on aghast at the brutality which had been unleashed. When word of the atrocities reached Genoa the people of the city were so enraged that they rose up and killed many of the Swiss billeted in their midst.

While these events were happening, the third prong of Charles's invasion was meanwhile advancing south through the Romagna under the command of the Scottish noble, Bérault Stuart, 4th Lord of Aubigny. D'Aubigny, who was accompanied by the *condottiere* Gianfrancesco da Sanseverino, Conte di

Caiazzo, with his own *Milanese* troops, advanced along the Via Emilia which ran from Piacenza though Bologna until it reached Caterina Sforza's two fiefs of Forlì and Imola. Here, they sought permission to march through Caterina's lands on their way to Rome. Caterina, who was in the awkward position of being not only Ludovico Sforza's niece but also a vassal subject of the Pope, had little choice but to attempt somehow to maintain her neutrality. By this time she was deeply under the sway of her former stable-boy-turned-lover, Giacomo Feo. Feo had appointed himself commander-in-chief of Caterina's armed forces and had control of both of her towns' key fortresses. With d'Aubigny and Sanseverino descending from the north and King Alfonso's son Ferrandino, supported by the exiled *Milanese condottieri* Giangiacomo Trivulzio and Niccolò di Pitigliano, advancing from the south, Giacomo Feo and Caterina Sforza resolutely closed their cities' gates to both antagonists.

But it was impossible for Caterina to remain neutral forever; she had to choose one way or the other. Eventually, in return for her support, Forlì's lady succumbed to Pope Alexander's offer of a 16,000 ducat *condotta* for her son Ottaviano. As an additional sweetener the Pope also undertook to restore to her the fief of San Mauro, which had been held by the Zampeschi since 1484. The 4th Lord of Aubigny, however, was not amused by this decision and resolved to teach Caterina–and Italy–an object lesson in the consequences of challenging French power. On 20 October the French and their *Milanese* allies assaulted the fortified town of Mordano which, together with its nearby twin fortress of Bubano, was situated just seven miles north-east of Imola. Mordano, which was defended by 200 of Caterina's loyal, handpicked *Imolesi* guardsmen, held out valiantly for most of the day. But when the French artillery tore a hole in the fortress wall, d'Aubigny's infantry poured through the breach and vicious hand-to-hand fighting ensued inside the town. In the aftermath, Caterina's surviving soldiers were drawn and quartered while the women of the town were carried off by the French troops and brutally raped. As a foretaste of the savagery of the professional French army, the twin massacres of Rapallo and Mordano sent shockwaves across the length and breadth of Italy.

As soon as the French had attacked, Caterina had sent urgent word to Alfonso to order Ferrandino to come to her aid. Although many of the defenders of Mordano were *Napoletano*, Ferrandino had remained aloof from their plight. After the massacre she angrily switched her allegiance to France, writing to Piero de' Medici in Florence: 'There was no reason to treat me this way ... I have kept [our treaty] and done more than I was obliged to.' Caterina's abandonment now left the door wide open for the French to come unmolested from the Romagna and occupy Florentine territory in Tuscany. Piero de' Medici's secretary, Bernardo Dovizi da Bibbiena, attempted in vain to bring Florence and Caterina back into harmony again; however Piero's intransigence defeated Bibbiena's desperate diplomacy and Forlì and Imola now spiralled away into France's orbit. Meanwhile, the ineffectual Ferrandino of Naples, having thus far accomplished little of any real military value, withdrew his troops to nearby Castrocaro and then pulled them back even further to Cesena by the end of October.

On 21 October, the rightful duke of Milan, Gian Galeazzo, died suspiciously at Pavia. His death came mere days after he had received a visit from King Charles VIII during which the erstwhile duchess Isabella had thrown herself at Charles's feet and begged him to restore her husband to the ducal throne and re-think his decision to invade her home state of Naples. The French monarch

339

had gamely promised to guarantee Gian Galeazzo's safety and protection, yet his promise was not sincere and Isabella's petition had probably led Ludovico to finally act. The precise timing of Gian Galeazzo's death led many to suspect foul play and indeed the gossip-loving historian Guicciardini reported: 'A rumour was circulated that Gian Galeazzo's death had in fact been caused by excessive copulation; nonetheless it was believed throughout Italy that he had died not from his carnal excesses but from poison. One of the royal doctors, who had been present when Charles visited him, indicated that he had observed evident signs of this. No one seriously doubted that, if he had been poisoned, that this was the work of his uncle.' On learning of his nephew's timely death, Ludovico Sforza quickly absented himself from Charles's entourage and hurried back to Milan. Here, the city's notables hastened to offer him the ducal crown, ignoring the preceding claim of the Dowager Duchess Isabella d'Aragona's three-year-old son Francesco, the infant count of Pavia. Inconvenient and surplus to dynastic requiresment, Isabella and her children were promptly imprisoned in Milan but she would die many years later in 1524. When her body was exhumed in 2012, anthropologists concluded from the traces of mercury in her system that she had contracted syphilis from her dead husband.

The acknowledged dukedom of Milan was what Ludovico Sforza and his brother Cardinal Ascanio Sforza had worked so assiduously towards. *Il Moro* was if truth be told also fairly glad to be leaving the company of the French king. It had not taken long for him to grow disillusioned with his erstwhile Gallic allies; King Charles had treated the new *Milanese* duke with scant respect. Not only had he demanded the keys to every Lombard town that he passed through, but he had also stipulated that French guards be stationed 'for added security' on their town walls. As if this was not bad enough, Louis d'Orléans had, since his arrival, made no great secret of his own ambition to revive the Visconti claim to Milan. Furthermore, this was not just idle talk; Louis possessed the troops and therefore the means at his disposal to accomplish his aims should he wish. Ludovico had little option but to put these doubts to the back of his mind and try to hasten the French army out of Lombardy. Ludovico received the somewhat qualified congratulations of King Charles, who was in truth unimpressed with his brazen murder of the rightful duke, who was also King Charles's cousin, but *il Moro* was able, for the time being at least, to weather the royal storm and enjoy his fleeting moment of triumph.

After a brief illness which itself had raised questions as to whether the offensive would be continued or abandoned, Charles VIII had by now left Asti and joined the main body of his army at Piacenza. From here the French king decided to take the westerly route to Naples, across the Ligurian Apennines into Tuscany and down the Tyrrhenian littoral. This would take him, in succession, through the *contado* of the city-states of Pisa, Florence, Siena and then through the Papal States and Patrimony of St. Peter to Rome. Sending his general Gilbert de Bourbon, Comte de Montpensier, on ahead through the Apennine passes with the French vanguard, the Florentines received their first taste of French arms at the walled town of Fivizzano in the historic region of the Lunigiana. Here, late in October, the defensive walls which Cosimo de' Medici had earlier ordered be restored and rebuilt, were battered into rubble by an artillery barrage, following which the French advanced and viciously put the town to the sword. In this they were aided by the troops of Gabriele Malaspina, Marchese di Fosdinovo, who upheld his own hereditary claim to Fivizzano. As

340

Fivizzano's inhabitants were either butchered or carted back to Lyons for ransoming off, all the other Florentine towns in the Lunigiana rushed to capitulate as the French continued their relentless advance towards Sarzana.

Ludovico Sforza, who was by now deeply regretting having called the French to Italy, had deviously encouraged Charles to attack the fortress town of Sarzana in the forlorn hope that it might cripple the momentum of the French juggernaut which his actions had conjured. The town was one of several key strongpoints (two others being Pietrasanta and Librafratta) which guarded the coastal road from Liguria as it merged with the Tuscan Riviera. In the aftermath of the Pazzi Wars of 1478, Florence had lost Sarzana to Genoa but had managed to recapture it again in 1487. Sarzana itself consisted of a walled settlement which incorporated a citadel called the Fortezza Firmafede. This was a pre-existing *Genovese* fortification which had been completely remodelled by Lorenzo de' Medici between 1487 and 1492. Sarzana's citadel was complemented by a neighbouring 'sister' *rocca* named the Sarzanello, a state-of-the-art diamond-shaped fortress designed by the renowned military architects Il Francione and Luca da Caprina. As Il Francione had only begun work on the Sarzanello in 1492 it is reasonable to assume that this second fortress would not have been fully completed by the time that Charles VIII's troops arrived in its vicinity. Nevertheless, the Sarzanello typified the newer design of fortress which had traded height for a system of bastions which overlooked each other. These bastions could cover one another and deliver devastating enfilade fire on any assaulting troops and their walls were built at a slight angle to deflect artillery fire.

Lorenzo di Pierfrancesco and his younger brother Giovanni had chosen this moment to slip away from their house-arrest in the Florentine *contado* and, to nobody's great surprise, they now fetched up at Charles VIII's mobile court. Upon arrival in the French monarch's presence they assured Charles that the people of Florence supported France in this affair but had been misled by their inexperienced, misguided leader Piero de' Medici. The news of his cousins' escape and subsequent defection came as an unwelcome blow to Piero *il Fatuo*. As each day passed and King Charles came ever closer to Florence it seemed that he was increasingly losing political ground in the republic. Horrified at Charles's virtually unopposed advance into the Florentine Lunigiana, the *otto di pratica* now urged Piero to effect some sort of belated reconciliation with the French king for the greater good of the state.

Angered by Piero's policy of alliance with Naples and Rome, the members of the Seventy had borne witness, throughout the summer and autumn of 1494, to Piero's frustrating indolence in the face of the advancing French threat. Now, Piero only added insult to injury by assigning his brother-in-law Paolo Orsini to lead a pitifully inadequate detachment of 100 mercenaries to ride against Charles's 30,000 seasoned troops. Not since the disastrous war against the *Lucchesi* had the *signoria* born witness to such ineptitude by one of its leaders. Piero was also by this time financially broke. So broke in fact that his relative Virginio Orsini was forced to mortgage some of his own estates to provide the funding for Florence's Lilliputian military gesture. As Piero's mother and wife were both Orsini it was the least that Virginio could do. But at the same time Virginio was a practical man of the world and must have been cognisant of the fact that, barring a miracle, things could only end in disaster for Florence if Piero persisted in his denialism.

Meanwhile, the friar Savonarola preached ever more apocalyptic sermons in the Duomo against Florence's (meaning the Medici's) wickedness. On 21 September, the day of Saint Matthew the Apostle, he had preached the Genesis story of the Flood and the chilling analogical similarities between the French tidal wave and the wrathful floodwaters of God were hardly lost on the Florentines. Pico della Mirandola, one of the latest Medici men to fall under the friar's spell, later admitted that the sermon made the hairs stand up on the back of his neck. Savonarola urged the Florentines to build their Ark out of penitence ('turn to him with your entire heart, because he is kind and merciful; but if you refuse he will turn his eyes from you forever'); he preached this apocalyptic message for days in a row until he was both physically and mentally exhausted. While the little friar was predicting fire, flood and torment for his parishioners, Piero de' Medici turned to increasingly desperate measures to avert the coming crisis. After news reached Florence of the horrific sack of Fivizzano, Piero appealed to Venice for help. The government of the Most Serene Republic did not even bother to send a reply. He next offered King Charles VIII a bribe, reported by some to be in the region of 300,000 francs, but once again this approach failed to bear fruit. The French had already assumed the form of the irresistible flood waters of Savonarola's vision and could not be stopped by a mere pay-off.

For Piero di Lorenzo de' Medici, a young man now almost universally despised by the city which had once acclaimed him during happier times of privileged and golden youth, the centre would not hold. Clearly, the growing emergency now called for one bold and climactic gesture on his part. Piero had been just eight years old when his father had left Florence and taken ship for Naples, placing himself at the mercy of the dreaded King Ferrante. It had been a desperate and romantic gamble, the stuff of legend, and despite the inherent danger Lorenzo had ultimately succeeded in charming the hostile king and bringing an end to the Pazzi War. The exploit had earned Piero's father the title of *il Magnifico* and the enduring love of his people. A vain and superficial youth, Piero di Lorenzo now hatched in his mind a plan which would attempt to replicate his father's legendary diplomatic coup. As head of his country it was down to him, and him alone, to ride out and meet the French king and barter a stay of execution for Florence. On his return, he would be lauded and eulogised and for his bravery given the laurel wreath of a triumphant returning hero. At least, this was the febrile mixture of fantasy and delusion which now took shape in Piero's mind, even as the Florentine government itself was increasingly distancing itself from their putative Medici leader.

On 26 October, Piero de' Medici rode out from the city gates of Florence with a tiny entourage and headed for the court of King Charles VIII. He had no official mandate to bargain or negotiate with the French king on Florence's behalf; according to the republic's constitution this was strictly the preserve of the *signoria*. This was the difference between Piero's and Lorenzo's respective journeys. The latter had ridden out on his own behalf to settle the personal differences which existed between himself, King Ferrante and Pope Sixtus IV. Piero, on the other hand, was placing himself at the head of the state in a quarrel between France and Florence and would negotiate on Florence's behalf. He had never been authorised to undertake such a mission by the *signoria*.

Just as his father had stopped at Pisa and written his famous explanatory letter to the *signoria*, so Piero now halted at the town of Empoli and with a flourish of his quill penned his own dispatch to the Florentine *signoria*. In this

342

communication he explained that he was offering up his person to King Charles of France in the hope that it would mollify the anger that the French monarch felt towards Florence. In a clumsy attempt to bathe in the reflected glory of Lorenzo de' Medici, he asked the Florentines to 'remain loyal to his father's memory'. However, when Piero reached Pisa he penned a second letter to Bibbiena in which he revealed the true extent of the depression and defeatism which lurked behind the outward show of bravado. Piero glumly confessed to his secretary that he would support his ally Alfonso 'with the desperation which leads me to place myself in the power of the king of France without condition or hope of any consideration'. Arriving at Pietrasanta on 29 October, Piero found the French army infesting the countryside around Sarzana like some biblical plague of locusts. He announced his identity to the French scouts and requested safe passage from King Charles for a parlay. In his own mind, he had probably already decided to give up some of Florence's most important possessions in Tuscany as diplomatic concessions to the French king. But with French forces quickly forcing the submission of nearby fortresses such as Ortonuovo and Nicola he was in danger of losing even those few bargaining chips that he planned to bring to the table. To this end Piero sent word to Bibbiena to reinforce Pietrasanta and Pisa with Florentine troops lest they be conquered before he could magnanimously give them away to Charles.

The next day his royal safe passage arrived and Piero set out to meet the King at Santo Stefano, several miles north-west of Sarzana. Here, amidst the martial din and clamour of the military encampment, the strange, inbred French monarch met the callow, Florentine boy wonder who had misguidedly appeared before him to plead the case of his city. Things did not go well from the start. A contemptuous King Charles VIII and his courtiers treated Piero brusquely rather than as befitted his status as Florence's first citizen. In the words of Philippe de Commynes: 'those who had dealings with Piero counted this as nothing, mocking him and paying little attention to him'. After allowing his Gallic disdain sufficient time to sink in, a ploy which threw the younger and more inexperienced Piero off balance, Charles asserted his peace conditions through intermediaries. Firstly, he commanded the immediate and unconditional surrender of the fortresses of Sarzana, Sarzanello, Pietrasanta and Ripafratta. Secondly, he demanded control over the Florentine protectorates of Pisa and Livorno for the entire duration of the campaign. Thirdly, Florence was to extend to him a loan of 200,000 ducats to help finance the French army's campaign.

As any military strategist worth his salt was able to see, such concessions were of enormous value to any invading army. The abandonment of Florence's hostile coastal fortresses relieved Charles of the immense difficulty of pushing his way along a thin strip of land that was bounded on one side by the sea and on the other by a high mountain range. Winter was coming and the coastal plains would be an unhealthy region for the French to become bogged down in. Furthermore, had Piero stuck to his guns and called Charles's bluff, the French king may well have decided to bypass Florence altogether rather than run the risk of a time-consuming siege followed by a confused fight in the narrow streets and *vicoli* of the city. After all, Charles needed to conserve his precious troops for the coming fight with Naples. Based on these considerations, King Charles perhaps expected the young Medici lord to offer a counter-proposal or at least raise detailed objections concerning this broad swathe of demands. But the King was perhaps as yet unaware of the true childishness of the intellect

343

which confronted him. To Charles's astonishment the youthful leader of the Florentine republic listened to the terms, blinked, and then merely nodded his assent, avidly agreeing to all the French demands without any further negotiation.

Before leaving Florence Piero had held no meeting with the *signoria* or any of the other important state councils, such as the *otto di pratica* which governed foreign policy; he had briefed no senior members of the Medici *reggimento*. As we have already noted, he had no mandate from Florence to surrender to France any of the republic's towns, cities or fortresses. None of this prevented Piero from doing what he believed to be necessary to preserve Florence's peace and independence. Not only did he relinquish to France what he had no legal or constitutional right to give, but Piero foolishly caused himself to look even weaker still by now offering *gratis* accommodation to King Charles at the Palazzo Medici.

While Piero de' Medici was busy at Santo Stefano genuflecting and capitulating to King Charles VIII of France, and giving away that which was not his to give, back in Florence Piero's harshest critic, Piero di Gino Capponi, had been elected as *gonfaloniere*. In the wake of Capponi's election there had been a successful coup d'etat against the Medici *reggimento* which had previously dominated the Council of Seventy. By 31 October word had reached Florence that Piero had exchanged Florence's possessions for his personal political survival. Around the same time Bernardo Dovizi da Bibbiena wrote to Alfonso of Calabria to regretfully inform him that, thanks to Piero's deal with Charles, diplomatically Florence was now firmly back in France's corner. On 4 November a meeting was called at which Capponi publicly denounced Piero, declaring that 'Piero de' Medici is no longer fit to rule the state. It is time to dispense with this government of children!' by which he was not only referring to the twenty-three-year-old Piero himself but also to his nineteen-year-old 'adviser' Cardinal Giovanni de' Medici. The Council then selected a committee of five, including Capponi himself, as well as Fra Girolamo Savonarola, to meet with Charles and renegotiate Florence's 'official' terms.

The delegation set out on 5 November with Savonarola perversely insisting on travelling on foot in the style of a penitent pilgrim; this simply meant that the party wasted much precious time in their search for the French king's elusive itinerant headquarters. According to the anonymous author of the text on Savonarola's life known as the *Pseudo-Burlamacchi*, the group tarried at the town of Ripafratta. Here, Savonarola was supposedly able to demonstrate his divinely-sponsored credentials by reproducing Christ's miracle of the bounteous fishing catch; with sufficient repast on hand for the local *podestà* to be able to feed his Florentine guests adequately, they ate and rested before moving on. But they had not left Florence long before advance contingents of French troops began arriving in the city to begin organising billeting for the French army. In an efficient, business-like fashion the foreign soldiers went from door to door in the city streets, marking with a chalk cross those houses which would be obliged to provide billeting for the troops. Niccolò Machiavelli, already a shrewd (though still obscure) observer of current affairs, witnessed these comings and goings and was later to remark indignantly that 'Charles the king of France was able to seize Italy with sticks of chalk'.

When Piero de' Medici learned of Capponi's coup d'état he wasted no time in leaving Charles's presence and hurried back to Florence, meeting Paolo Orsini and his small detachment of armed *bravi* along the way. At Lucca, Piero learned of Savonarola's and Capponi's separate embassy to Charles. He himself reached Florence on 8 November. Leaving Orsini and his men outside the Porta San Gallo, Piero rode into the seemingly deserted city alone. At the Palazzo Medici he found a small crowd of curious but strangely silent onlookers standing, gawking in the street. He ordered that sweet cakes and wine be sent out to them in celebration, as though he had just won a great triumph, and instructed his supporters to let off fireworks. Other streets of the usually bustling city were strangely empty; Piero subsequently learned that many of the wives and daughters of the city had been despatched for safety to Florence's abbeys and nunneries in anticipation of the French army's arrival. The following day, after attending a thanksgiving Mass at the church of Santissima Annunziata, Piero strolled with a small group of bodyguards to the Palazzo della Signoria to report on his meeting with King Charles of France. Upon arrival, however, a member of the *signoria* named Luca Corsini rudely slammed the front door in his face and instructed him instead to enter the building alone and by the small servant's door known as the *sportello*. As the Medici youth stood impotently in the street, allowing this direct insult to his authority to sink in, the deep mellow tones of the *vacca* began to boom out overhead. The *signoria* was calling the city to arms.

Curious crowds (which soon grew increasingly hostile) quickly gathered in the *piazza*. Piero, who was standing on the elevated dais of the *ringhiera*, made a perfect target. Somebody pelted him with a rotten vegetable. Many had probably wanted to do this to the Medici for years. More missiles followed, and then a volley of them, perhaps even a clump or two of effluent that had been scraped up from the street. The mood had turned ugly. Piero's bodyguard formed a protective screen around their youthful charge and, against the baying howls of the mob, which was punctuated by the inevitable cries of 'Popolo e Libertà!', they somehow shoved and heaved their way back to the safety of the Palazzo Medici. Here, they found an energetic Cardinal Giovanni de' Medici galloping up and down the Via Larga on horseback with a gang of armed *bravi* hollering the traditional Medici rallying cries of '*Palle! Palle! Palle!*' That Giovanni was in Florence at all was a fluke. When Charles VIII had advanced on Sarzana, Pope Alexander VI had summoned Giovanni to Rome where he no doubt planned to use him as a hostage against Piero's continued loyalty. Giovanni had reached his own abbey of Passignano when news had reached him of Piero's mission to Charles and he had wisely turned round and returned to Florence. Piero's Tornabuoni cousins were also meanwhile hard at work trying to drum up support from amongst those in their client network. Some curious pro-Medicean retainers from the traditional Medici quarter of San Giovanni had turned out in force outside the Medici *palazzo*, but when the young cardinal attempted to lead them to the Orsanmichele and the *palleschi* stronghold of San Gallo he was driven back by an even larger and more hostile republican mob. The scent of blood was by now in the air and the situation was rapidly spirally out of control.

Joining Piero di Gino Capponi in this popular revolt against Medici rule was an *ottimati* named Francesco Valori. Valori was no stranger to the Medici *reggimento*, having been one of its former insiders. He had been *gonfaloniere* four times under *il Magnifico* and, in March 1492, Valori had been appointed (alongside another Medici loyalist, Pierfilippo Pandolfini) to be the young Cardinal Giovanni's personal adviser. After Lorenzo de' Medici's death just one month later, Valori had openly sided with Fra Savonarola. Now, recently returned from Pisa with a detachment of Florentine soldiers, he commanded an assault against the Medici *bravi* who had by now fallen back to the Bargello, where they set about equipping themselves from the prison's armoury. Meanwhile, back at the Palazzo della Signoria, an emboldened *signoria* issued a decree forbidding any Florentine citizen to aid or assist Piero de' Medici 'upon pain of death'. This proclamation caused what few Medici loyalists and *bravi* who remained in the immediate vicinity of the Palazzo Medici to melt away back to their homes. The words of Savonarola, so recently bellowed like holy writ from his pulpit, rang in the ears of every Florentine. '*Tiranno è nome di uomo di mala vita*' – 'Tyrant is the name of a man who leads an evil life', Savonarola had thundered, adding: '*e pessimo tra gli aitri uomini, che per forza sopra tutti vuol regnare*' – 'and worst amongst all other men, the type who craves to reign over everyone else'.

With little choice available to them the Medici brothers now barricaded themselves and their terrified family inside their *palazzo*. Fortunately the architect Michelozzo had built the family residence to withstand rioting or even an armed assault. This was common practice amongst the wealthy in the city-states of Italy, and the only Italians who didn't fortify their palaces were the Venetians, who could never quite countenance the possibility that their political quarrels would ever spill over into their private residences, which were–by mutual agreement–considered sacrosanct. As stout as a castle, the Palazzo Medici had narrow barred windows, high walls and heavy doors. Yet at the same time, surrounded as they were by a sea of angry republican malcontents, Piero knew that they would not be able to hold out indefinitely if this kept up. Elsewhere, across other districts of the city, Valori's men were rooting out any prominent Medici supporters they could lay their hands on and forcing their way into their houses and *palazzi*.

One such supporter was Antonio di Bernardo di Miniato who was *provveditore* of the Monte, the Florentine treasury. Guicciardini described him as being an honest man who was nevertheless despised for his crude manners, his arrogance and his cruelty toward the underprivileged. Another was Giovanni Guidi da Pratovecchio who was *notaio della riformagioni* in charge of recording the meetings of Florence's legislative assemblies. Like di Miniato, he too was regarded as a detested Medici civil servant burrowed like a tick within the workings of the chancery. Despite their attempts to hide in San Marco and Santa Croce both men were captured, imprisoned in the Bargello and tortured. Scenting in the air the return of mob rule, many Medici officials had by now already fled the city. These included Ser Zanobi, notary of the hated police magistracy the *otto di guardia*, Piero's own private secretary Bernardo Dovizi da Bibbiena, and Francesco di ser Barone, secretary of the *otto di pratica*. It would be harsh perhaps to dismiss such individuals as rats leaving a sinking ship; officials like Bibbiena had after all done their utmost to provide Piero de' Medici with wise and balanced counsel. The unstable gyrations in Piero's diplomacy and his all-round ineptitude had, however, ultimately led to his downfall. Realistically there was now little left to do except *survive*.

It is sufficient praise at this point to affirm that Piero de' Medici had finally been brought to perceive the truth of his situation. The self-deluding romanticism, the self-dramatisation and tendency to cast himself in the heroic mould of his father now fell away completely, just as the scales also fell from his eyes. With

346

the streets outside the Palazzo Medici cleared of supporters and with the *signoria* sitting in emergency late night session, declaring him outlawed and the Medici deposed as first family of Florence, it was only a matter of time before the government came for him. There was little option now but to flee the city.

On 9 November 1494 Piero rode out from the Palazzo Medici together with his fifteen-year-old younger brother Giuliano de' Medici and their closest household retainers. The streets were still disconcertingly quiet. Nobody was especially keen to be found loitering and denounced by the black-coated men of the Night Watch as an acolyte of the Medici out to cause trouble. The citizens of Florence cowered behind locked doors and quietly watched and waited. This was the only opportunity Piero would have. Without tarrying, the small party clattered straight up the Via Larga on horseback towards the Porto San Gallo, still thankfully held for the time being by Paolo Orsini and his *bravi*. Once clear of the city, the group then took the road to Bologna. Piero's wife Alfonsina remained behind at the Palazzo Medici with their children, the two-year-old Lorenzo and one-year-old Clarice, as well as her widowed mother Caterina di Sanseverino. Exile did not customarily extend to wives or their young children and wives of the State's enemies were usually spared undue persecution, therefore she would remain behind in Florence attempting to safeguard the family's dwindling interests as best she could. It was an incredibly brave move on her part given the crescendo of anti-Medici feeling and she would not find the decision entirely unproblematic. The *signoria* would soon swoop down and seize the Medici family assets, especially those of the Medici Bank, and unfortunately Alfonsina's dowry–on which, in her husband's absence, she was legally permitted to subsist–was inextricably bound up with those same bank assets. She would face many taxing legal battles ahead to claim what was rightfully hers.

Cardinal Giovanni de' Medici meanwhile tarried for a while in Florence in an effort to gather what transportable Medici wealth he could, which included 200,000 ducats from the Medici Bank and the more portable items from Lorenzo's exquisite collections of *objects d'art* (including, one would hope, the hardstone vases on which *il Magnifico* had incriminatingly inscribed those inflammatory words *Lorenzo Rex Medicorum*). Disguised in the poor habit of a Franciscan monk, Cardinal Giovanni deposited some of this treasure with the monastery of San Marco before retracing his steps and making his egress from the city by means of the Porto San Gallo accompanied by the last of Orsini's mercenaries. After his departure, the convent of Sant'Antonio, the cardinal's official residence, was ransacked by the mob. Having sated their anger on the convent the mob turned next to the Garden of the Sculptures near San Marco, where Michelangelo had taken his first steps in the world of sculpture. Here, the priceless artistic masterpieces were indiscriminately either smashed or hacked to pieces. As Piero and Giuliano de' Medici made their way north to Bologna, and Cardinal Giovanni headed south to Rome via Passignano, Siena and then Viterbo, the *signoria* had issued a fresh decree placing a bounty of 1,000 ducats on Cardinal Giovanni's head and 2,000 ducats on Piero's.

Just as the members of the senior branch of the Medici were making their escape, the two principal members of the cadet branch of the family–Lorenzo di Pierfrancesco and his brother Giovanni–were returning to Florence from the peripatetic court of King Charles VIII. To evade the anger of the mob, and to distance themselves from Piero di Lorenzo, they now prudently changed their family name from Medici to *Popolano* (meaning 'Popular'). They also lost no time in immediately declaring themselves in favour of the restoration of Florence's ancient republic. Antiquity was also plundered for a conveniently fitting comparison; in his work *la rappresentazione dell'Invenzione della Croce*, Lorenzo di Pierfrancesco compares Piero di Lorenzo to the Roman tyrant Maxentius, whilst Charles VIII is incongruously likened to Constantine the Great. It had been just sixty years since Piero di Lorenzo's great-grandfather Cosimo de' Medici had returned from exile in triumph to rule Florence as unquestioned first citizen. In that time four generations had passed and the Medici had systematically eroded the political rights of the citizens of Florence, diverting power to an élite inner circle. For the Florentines, as they now steeled themselves to face the irresistible French army, the Medici years were now already a quickly receding memory. Piero de' Medici 'the Unfortunate' had in a matter of weeks thrown away that which had taken decades for his antecedents to build; thanks in large part to his own abject surrender to the king of France, his downfall was spectacular even by Florentine standards.

According to Michelangelo's biographer Ascanio Condivi, a musician in Piero de' Medici's household had experienced in a dream a premonition of Piero's downfall. Michelangelo had brought the man to Piero to tell of this portent but the latter had laughed them both out of the room. Michelangelo must also have felt undervalued when Piero commissioned him one winter to create a snow statue in the courtyard of the Palazzo Medici. The artist had listened to his inner *daemon* (as well as Savonarola's unsettling Flood sermon on 21 September) and had already taken leave of Florence by mid-October 1493. 'Fearing evil consequences from Piero's arrogance and bad government', as Vasari records, Michelangelo made his way first to Venice but then backtracked to Bologna after he failed to find work in the maritime republic. In Bologna he was taken under the wing of Giovanfrancesco Aldovrandi, one of the city's governors, who lodged Michelangelo in his own home for a year and commissioned him to create three pieces – depictions of the saints Petronius and Proclus, and an angel bearing a candlestick. He was soon joined in exile by other artists whom *il Magnifico* and the Medici had earlier patronised.

Michelangelo also got himself embroiled in an unnecessary quarrel with Leonardo da Vinci, who was by now established in Ludovico Sforza's service as the acknowledged artistic maestro of the city. The two old rivals quickly locked horns over the huge equestrian statue of Francesco Sforza which *il Moro* had commissioned from Leonardo, Michelangelo suggesting that such a behemoth would be quite impossible to cast. Da Vinci had struggled throughout the mid and late 1480s and early 1490s with this supremely difficult work and, as was his way, his industry had come in fits and starts. The twenty-six-foot clay model had only been completed in November 1493, when it was officially unveiled in the courtyard of the Castello Sforzesco as part of the festivities held to mark the departure of Bianca Maria Sforza to the court of her future husband-to-be, the Emperor-elect Maximilian I. Michelangelo had spoken true about the problems associated with casting such a gargantuan statue, but in the end this was not due to any deficiency in Leonardo's artistry; it was due instead to the simple absence of raw material. When, sometime earlier, Ludovico's exiled rival Giangiacomo Trivulzio had advanced towards Ferrara, the duke of Milan had diverted the seventy-five tons of bronze that had been prepared in readiness for the statue's casting down the River Po to his father-in-law Ercole d'Este. Here at Ferrara the precious bronze would go towards the casting of 'three small cannon, one in the French style and two in another style' under the supervision of Maestro Zanin di Albergeto, the *Ferrarese* master armourer.

The same day that Piero de' Medici fled the city of Florence in fear of his life, the Florentine delegation led by Fra Savonarola and the *gonfaloniere* Piero di Gino Capponi finally caught up with King Charles VIII as he was making his victorious entry into Pisa. Savonarola the mendicant was still stubbornly on foot; his refusal to ride his horse had wasted many precious days. Pisa had already been occupied one week before by the French advance guard under Gilbert de Montpensier and the *Pisani* had been quick to welcome the armour-clad Gallic northerners as glorious liberators. They had enthusiastically entreated the French king to free them from Florentine subjugation and give them back their liberty. King Charles had, however, misheard their request for 'liberty' as an appeal for 'greater liberties' and had only too gladly agreed to their demands, but a period of disambiguation necessarily followed when, to Charles's surprise, the *Pisani* promptly went ahead and expelled Florence's functionaries from the city entirely on their own initiative. Nonetheless, a friendly, appreciative and indebted 'free' city in his rear was certainly preferable, in a tactical sense, to a potentially hostile Florentine dependency. Charles therefore saw no reason to intervene on behalf of the Florentines in this matter.

It must have been with no small sense of bitterness therefore that the official delegation from Florence's *signoria* now wound their way through the crowded and jubilant streets of the city which Piero de' Medici had so fecklessly given away just several days earlier. They found King Charles taking his ease at the Citadella Nuova, a Florentine construction which squatted on the south bank of the River Arno between the Ponte della Vittoria and the Ponte della Fortezza. Citadella Nuova was one of the first fortresses in Italy to have been specifically designed to withstand bombardment by cannon and so it was doubly fortunate for Charles that he had not been forced to contest the city, which would certainly have squandered much valuable time and manpower. Here, within the fortress walls, the Florentines were confronted with the French king and his court in all its ambulatory royal majesty. Temporarily overawed, Capponi and the others hung back and allowed the less impressed and ever loquacious friar Savonarola to take centre stage in petitioning the French king.

Savonarola's attitude towards Charles VIII had always been favourable. In his own unique apocalyptic style Savonarola had long preached that Florence's ills had been a result of the wickedness of the city's corrupt élites. God, as he himself had predicted, could be counted on in the fullness of time to despatch a suitable scourge to root out this wickedness and chastise the Florentines for having fallen into bad ways. As soon as the King's decision to invade Italy had become common knowledge it was inevitable that Savonarola would extrapolate that Charles was the designated instrument of God's divine wrath. That the venerable friar had chosen to identify this gnomic and inbred French monarch as 'the hand of God' was an irony sadly lost on the devout and literal-minded prig Savonarola. He stood before Charles and, in a paroxysm or righteous prophetic ecstasy, declaimed: 'At last you are here, O' King! Just as I predicted all these years, you have come as the hand of divine justice. With joyful hearts and smiling faces we welcome you. God has sent you to chastise all the tyrants of Italy!'

As Capponi and the others stood in the shadows and quietly cringed, Savonarola then qualified his eulogy with a veiled warning to Charles that, although he was indeed the righteous hand of God, the Holy Father in heaven would not hesitate to 'wreak terrible vengeance upon even his own instrument' should the King bring any harm to the city of Florence. Listening to the friar's remarkable and often impertinent disquisition, Charles could spare himself the luxury of a certain measure of forbearance. As far as he was concerned the city's representative Piero de' Medici had already granted him everything– certainly in a strategic sense–that he had sought from Florence. Therefore, this second delegation had absolutely no teeth. The Florentines were not bargaining from a position of strength; no *condottiere* army was interposed between himself and his next objective, which was to bring his troops the short distance from Pisa up the Arno River Valley to Florence itself. Neither would it have mattered much if one had since he could have easily brushed it aside. The attempt by the *signoria's* delegation to exact some concessions from Charles prior to his arrival in Florence was therefore disregarded.

By this time the *signoria* had wisely decided to forego their alliance with Alfonso of Naples and were therefore ill-disposed to bear the brunt of any French attack just in order to protect the *Regno*. This was especially so when Alfonso's armies seemed reluctant to even enter the fray (Ferrandino's abandonment of Caterina Sforza at Mordano had gone neither unnoticed nor unremarked amongst tacticians). In Milan, Ludovico Sforza was however privately thwarted by Florence's capitulation. Unlike his late father, Galeazzo Maria Sforza, he seemed disinterested in Milan's old alliance with Medici Florence. Lorenzo de' Medici had been his father's friend, not his. Besides, the Medici were now blown to the four winds and Florence's only utility consisted in her ability to delay Charles's progress down the length of the peninsula. But with the Florentine fortresses given up without a fight this would no longer happen. Should Charles prove too successful in his own endeavours against Naples then Ludovico's rival Louis d'Orléans would be emboldened to press his own separate suit concerning Milan. Louis d'Orléans undoubtedly watched from the sidelines at nearby Asti with much the same thoughts.

The day after Savonarola's righteous harangue, King Charles set off with his army for Florence. Marching up the Val d'Arno he halted at the nearby town of Signa and allowed Savonarola to go on ahead to Florence and notify the population of his arrival. Savonarola arrived back in the city on 11 November. With an absent *gonfaloniere*, and many conflicting rumours abounding, he found a leaderless city on the brink of outright panic. Seeking to reassure the population he gave a sermon to a huge crowd in the Duomo, during which he reaffirmed that the scourge of God was indeed upon them in the form of King Charles VIII. Nevertheless, he assured his flock that all would be well provided they inflicted no harm on the conquerors or indeed on each other. Above all he called for calm and restraint. The temptation to conduct witch hunts for the last remnants of the by now despised Medici *reggimento* was strong but Savonarola remonstrated against the taking of human life; he reminded the Florentines that they had been fortunate to win back their city without major bloodshed or loss of life and he humanely discouraged them from further acts of vengeance.

It was this propensity for peace and godliness which had led Commynes to remark that, in spite of his lamentable fondness for Biblical fire and brimstone, Savonarola was at heart a fundamentally good and *decent* man. Despite the friar's strictures, however, there were still the inevitable reprisals against those few Medici confederates left skulking in the city. As Luca Landucci recorded, 'Girolamo Tornabuoni had his breastplate torn off by anti-Medici supporters in Orto San Michele, but when he pleaded for mercy they spared his life. Giovanni

350

Francesco Tornabuoni was badly wounded in the cheek, and returned home.'
Some of the French troops, who had already been billeted amongst the locals,
armed themselves and tried to join in this fracas on the side of the Medici. They
were volubly reminded by the Florentines that this was a purely local matter
and to keep their noses out, 'upon which', recorded Landucci, 'they returned to
their lodgings'.

CHAPTER 14

The Medici in Exile

Le temps revient ('our time will return').

Medici family motto.

On 17 November 1494, with his lance tip held pointing martially forward rather than peacefully reversed at rest over his shoulder, King Charles VIII entered Florence through the majestic early fourteenth-century gate known as the Porta San Frediano as a conqueror with over 9,000 men, the remainder of the French force having gone on ahead to Siena. At his request Florence's city gates had been unhinged and completely removed and a symbolic breach had also been knocked in the nearby defensive walls as an additional, humiliating sign of the city's compliance and submission. The King was greeted by a Florentine deputation comprising the city's dignitaries, the *primati* (leading citizens), and the *grassi* (fat cats) who had attired themselves lavishly 'in the French manner'. After the perfunctory speeches of welcome, the French king and his troops proceeded to the Duomo in a procession which took more than two hours to file past.

The Florentines made the best of things, turning out into the streets to cheer the spectacle of the French, Gascon and Swiss soldiers as they filed silently and grim-faced through the city streets accompanied by the steady, martial beating of their drums. The historian Marino Sanuto the Younger (who, as Venetian envoy to Florence, was an eyewitness to Charles's entry to the city) recorded in his work *La spedizione di Carlo VIII in Italia*, that at the head of all the French soldiers there marched 'a monster of a man (*'omaccione'*) with a polished sword like a spit for roast pork, and then four big drums played with both hands, and accompanied by two pipes, making an infernal noise, such as one hears at a fair'. He also noted with trepidation that the French weapons seemed 'better suited for splitting doors than for fighting'. 7,000 Swiss, perfectly arrayed in seven formations, trooped in first followed by 700 men-at-arms on finely caparisoned horses, then 500 mounted archers, then 1,000 archers marching on foot. Many of these were the companies of *francs-archers*, permanent full-time soldiers who were armed with a bow. Founded by Charles VII, they had been reorganised by Louis XI and now King Charles VIII had rehabilitated them as a fighting force. They were paid four francs a month and exempted from payment of the tax known as the *taille*. Conflicts between the *francs-archers* and their rivals, the Swiss mercenaries from the cantons, were however frequent and often bloody.

Finally, at the end of his army, came the French king himself on horseback and surrounded by the men of his personal Swiss guard, the *Compagnie des*

Cent Suisses, each of whom were a minimum of six feet tall. Attired from head to toe in white, King Charles VIII wore a crowned hat as opposed to either an iron crown or a crowned helmet. His guards were clad in yellow and red and were led by their French captain-colonel; their colours bore the Swiss cross and the motto *Es est fiducia gentis* ('such is the fidelity of this nation'). Despite his sumptuous garb and impressive bodyguards of giants, Charles did not however cut a particularly impressive figure to the Florentines. This was especially so when he dismounted from his horse upon reaching the Duomo and people could see how diminutive and bow legged he was. Observing the scene, Lucca Landucci remarked that 'he seemed to the people less imposing, for he was really a very small man'. Accompanying him rode two of his more manipulative advisers: Guillaume Briçonnet, the bishop of St.-Malo, and the Venetian Paul Zane, the bishop of Brescia. Forgetting their earlier misgivings, the delighted Florentines loudly cheered '*Viva Francia!*' *Il Magnifico* had always spoiled the citizens with enjoyable spectacles like his famous joust; the *popolo minuto* missed those exciting days. Lorenzo may (as Savonarola constantly reminded them) have deprived the ordinary people of their political rights, but at least he had diverted them with worthy entertainment.

As magnificent a display as it was, however, this was still a tense situation which might easily be ignited by a single spark of misbehaviour. Charles needed a friendly–or, at the very least, a neutral–Florence in his rear as he processed down the peninsula to Naples. Should his men provoke an uprising amongst a disgruntled Florentine population the French would be forced to fight a messy urban battle within the confines of these dark, narrow streets; his army would lose valuable men who would be better served fighting the armies of Naples. As for the Florentines, they now had an army of occupation in their midst and eggshells would need to be trodden, carefully, for as long as it remained. The memories of Rapallo and Mordano and the savage conduct of the Swiss pikemen were still uncomfortably fresh in most peoples' imaginations. Alarmingly aware of the precipice on which they now teetered, the city's magnates and officials of the *signoria* and its various governing councils had turned out in their finest ceremonial attire to greet the King and pay respectful homage. They may well have freed their city of the Medici but in fifteenth-century society there was always someone higher up the food chain to have to kow-tow to and Charles, for the moment, was that someone.

The King himself took up residence in the Palazzo Medici, which Piero had formerly offered him during their meeting and which had been festooned with France's royal coat of arms in preparation for his arrival. Some apartments at the *palazzo* had to be quickly tidied up for the King's habitation since, in the aftermath of Piero and Giovanni de' Medici's departure, the Florentine mob had ransacked and looted the building's ground floor of its remaining treasures. Only the upstairs rooms of the *palazzo*, the *piano nobile* and the landings above, had been spared thanks to the foresight of the *signoria*, who had assigned armed guards to forestall the worst of the looting and protect the Medici women and children who still remained in residence. But even so the damage was deeply dismaying. Donatello's *David* had been removed from the *cortille* and *il Magnifico*'s many valuable collections of *objects d'art* had disappeared into the hands of innumerable looters, only to reappear some years later. Only those selected items squirreled away by Giovanni de' Medici at San Marco still survived, in addition to those smaller transportable items, jewels and suchlike that could be pawned, items which he had hurriedly taken with him into exile.

As we have already noted, the garden of San Marco, which *il Magnifico* had established as an Academy for the advancement of sculpture, was tragically expunged by the rioting mob together with most of its exquisite marble treasures. As for the Medici Bank's Florence head office, the *signoria* had appropriated the last remaining stores of ducats which Giovanni, in his undoubted haste, had overlooked in the branch's strongbox. In spite of this the indefatigable French king still managed to find some loot for himself, having already discovered Medici jewels, vases and paintings that he had carefully crated for shipment back to France. He found, among other treasures, a whole 'unicorn's horn' (probably in reality the rare horn of a narwhal) and parts of two others. When ground, the horn made a powerful aphrodisiac and, if kept whole and intact, could be used to detect the presence of poison. This was surely a useful accoutrement for a king who was at that moment in the process of violating Italy, a country where vendetta held sway and the practise of poisoning one's enemies was rife.

While Charles was busy at the Medici palazzo the peace held for the time being, broken only by the occasional minor skirmish, none of which thankfully escalated any further. One of the King's more influential nobles, Philip de Bresse, had taken up residence with Piero de' Medici's kinsman, Lorenzo Tornabuoni. Tornabuoni lobbied his guest to take up the Medici cause with the King. As a monarch, Charles himself was instinctively uncomfortable with the idea of being allied to a republic and would unquestionably have preferred for the Medici dynasts to return to power. To this end he wrote to the exiled Piero de' Medici in Bologna, entreating him to return to Florence and assuring him that French military power would guarantee his family's personal safety.

In Bologna meanwhile, Giovanni II Bentivoglio had failed to provide the fugitive Piero de' Medici and his younger brother with quite the friendly reception that they had anticipated. On the surface Giovanni supposedly owed a debt of gratitude to the Medici siblings' father Lorenzo. In 1488, in a fit of jealousy, Giovanni's daughter Francesca had poisoned her husband, Galeotto Manfredi, the ruler of Faenza. Faenza's citizens subsequently rebelled against Francesca and installed Galeotto's young son Astorre III Manfredi as the town's ruler. Arriving at the city to suppress the revolt, Giovanni had been captured and was eventually released only through the personal intercession of Lorenzo de' Medici himself.

But if Piero de' Medici hoped for sympathy from a grateful Giovanni Bentivoglio he was sadly disabused. On the contrary, the crusty Bentivoglio ruler of Bologna reprimanded him for quitting Florence and all his many possessions without so much as even unsheathing his sword. This was not strictly fair since Cardinal Medici had undeniably attempted to lead his armed supporters against the rebels before force of numbers had thwarted his efforts. Be that as it may, Giovanni Bentivoglio's diffident attitude made it clear that Bologna could not be regarded as a safe place of refuge for the exiled Medici brothers. The members of the party now dispersed. Piero disguised himself as a valet and fled to Venice (where his cardinal brother would eventually join him) whilst his younger brother Giuliano de' Medici took shelter in Urbino with Duke Guidobaldo da Montefeltro and his duchess Elisabetta Gonzaga.

In Venice the climate was appreciably kinder to the Medici fugitive. The Doge, Agostino Barbarigo, sent an official delegation to formally receive Piero and he was greeted with all due honour and granted the privilege of wearing his arms within the city. Soon after Piero's arrival in Venice the letter from King Charles VIII (which had initially been sent to Bologna) finally caught up with him. At this juncture Piero once more demonstrated his political ineptitude. Instead of seizing the day and returning to Florence under Charles's armed protection Piero de' Medici hesitated. Rather than acting decisively, like an unschooled child he instead presented Charles's letter to the Venetian senate and asked them what he should do. The Venetians, having no desire to see a tranquil, stable or indeed French-backed Medici Florence, advised Piero to disregard Charles's request since, as they reminded him, kings were notoriously untrustworthy and the whole enterprise was far too risky. Instead, they assured Piero that, when the time came, Venice would assist in his family's restoration to power. Credulously, Piero swallowed their deceitful advice and remained immobile in the vain hope of better days to come. But although Charles's efforts to reinstate the Medici were politely rebuffed by the main beneficiary himself, the damaging rumours of the King's interference in Florence's domestic affairs soon leaked out. Not only had Lorenzo Tornabuoni been vocal in lobbying Charles on Piero's behalf, but Piero's wife Alfonsina Orsini still remained at large and she was known to have Charles's ear. This, taken together with Charles's indiscreet talk about bringing Florence within his civil and judicial jurisdiction as France's vassal, now stirred up a torrent of civic outrage. The day after his arrival in Florence, the King was visited by a 300-strong deputation of citizens led by Luca Corsini and members of the *signoria*. The meeting began cordially enough with a proposal that the Florentine militia would stand guard side-by-side with their French counterparts for the duration of their stay, and that candles should be placed in every window to illuminate the dark streets and discourage wrongdoing. Things rapidly degenerated, however, when some in the deputation began murmuring that the discredited Medici brothers were trying to persuade the French monarch to allow them to return.

Later, back at the Palazzo della Signoria, Volterra's Bishop Francesco Soderini spoke openly of Florentine resistance should King Charles attempt to restore Medici rule but he was shouted down by two Frenchmen who had suddenly barged their way into the council chamber. Many suspected that Lorenzo Tornabuoni was behind this intrusion and the decision was taken to send another official deputation to meet with the King to vehemently put the *signoria's* case against any Medici restoration. Having the most credibility with Charles, Savonarola was selected to lead this deputation but when he met with the King on 21 November the latter assured him that overthrowing Florence's prevailing government was the very last thing on his mind. But, at the same time, Charles also opined that permitting Piero de' Medici to return home peacefully was surely not such an unreasonable request. The situation was temporarily defused and the citizens went back to the uneasy round of carnivals and banquets, all of which were designed to make a polite show of celebrating the French king's 'visit'. Charles's diplomats, however, continued to negotiate with Genoa, Venice and Milan, all of whom were eager to see how they could benefit from Florence's recent subjection to France. Mundanely Charles himself went through the motions of sightseeing, attending Masses in the various historic churches and being given a private showing of the city's famous mascots, its mangy and malodorous pair of lions. But despite his reassurances and the innocuous way in which he spent his time in Florence, trouble was nevertheless brewing.

Towards the end of the French stay a detachment of either French or Swiss troops had been waylaid in Borgo Ognissanti by a Florentine mob and pelted with broken paving stones; some of the soldiers had even been drenched with boiling water. The French response was to secure the Arno bridges and the Porta San Frediano in case they needed to beat a hasty retreat from the city. Meanwhile, another mob had made its way to the Piazza della Signoria to once more advertise their disapproval of any Medici *reintegrazione*. Here they confronted a detachment of Charles's Swiss guardsmen and tumult quickly erupted. These too were pelted with missiles and just as matters were spiralling out of control the members of the *signoria* interceded to quieten things down. With calm temporarily restored, a noticeably shaken King Charles VIII now concentrated on parlaying the best deal possible for his army when it came time for their departure. He demanded from the *signoria* the continued friendly neutrality of Florence in return for which he would reinstate her favoured trading status with France. On top of this he demanded a lump sum payment of a 150,000 florins towards his campaign costs. The treaty was duly signed on the altar of Santa Reparata and was perhaps observed by the young Niccolò Machiavelli who—as a fledgling Florentine patriot—was no doubt intensely cynical of the French king's professions of long-lasting friendship towards the republic.

The French departed Florence on 28 November after a stay of just eleven days; but even the final day was not without its tense moments. When the time came for Charles to broadcast the final terms of his departure in the Piazza della Signoria he reiterated French possession of the Florentine fortresses, claimed feudal overlord ship of the city and demanded payment of the sum of 200,000 ducats—which Piero de' Medici had originally promised him at Santo Stefano—rather than the lesser amount of 150,000 ducats which had been negotiated with the *signoria* just a few days before. For Piero di Gino Capponi, who had formerly known Charles at the French court when he was but a callow youth untutored in the ways of the wide world, this final overweening outrage was too much to bear. Leaping upon the *ringhiera* he snatched the offensive treaty from the French herald's hands and, holding it aloft, defiantly tore it to pieces before the crowd. King Charles VIII shuddered with anger. Furiously, he quavered through his translator that the treaty must be signed otherwise he would order his trumpeters to sound the call-to-arms, which would have been the signal for his troops to sack the city. Undeterred, Capponi responded with the legendary words: 'Sire, if you sound your trumpets, we will ring our bells!' Instantly a roar of approval arose from the Florentine mob.

Charles's bluff had been called. Most of the French king's troops were still billeted amongst the general population. Many of them would be crapulous from eleven days of hard drinking and womanising in the city's many taverns and whorehouses. Some of them would even be missing their arms or armour, having pawned the instruments of their trade to cover the gambling debts they had accrued. If the Florentines were summoned into the streets in their droves it could well result in the wholesale massacre of his dispersed and unprepared army. Sensibly, and to his lasting credit, Charles backed down. With a face-saving quip on his former tutor's name he brushed Florence's defiance aside: 'Capponi! Oh Capponi! What a capon you are!' The explosive moment had been defused. An amount of 120,000 florins was eventually haggled by the Florentines, which of course they had absolutely no intention of paying, and

Charles and his bibulous army marched somewhat unsteadily out of Florence and turned south to join their comrades at Siena.

The French king continued on his historic appointment with destiny. After a brief sojourn in Siena he continued south to the Papal States, entering Rome at the end of December 1494. As usual, the vanguard under Montpensier entered Rome first, and Charles followed two days later while the Catalan Borgia pope cowered inside the Castel Sant'Angelo. At Charles's side rode the two Italian cardinals who had thrown their lot in with the French king, Cardinal Giuliano della Rovere and *il Moro's* brother Cardinal Ascanio Sforza. Also accompanying Charles VIII was Jean Bilhères de Lagraulas, earlier named governor of Rome by Innocent VIII and cardinal priest by Alexander VI the year previous. Since he was already familiar with the pontiff, King Charles despatched Cardinal Bilhères to entreat with Pope Alexander but the negotiations proved fruitless. When the two powerful men finally did meet it was through an artifice which saved face on both sides – the King accidentally 'bumped into' the Pope whilst strolling in the papal gardens; both initially pretended not to notice the other. But Charles's conniving cardinal allies still hoped that the King would dethrone Alexander VI and call for a new conclave (or, even better, simply appoint one of them as his successor) they were to be sadly disappointed. When they finally sat down for formal discussions, the sixty-five-year-old Borgia pope, schooled for decades in the complex, Byzantine politics of the Curia and razor sharp of mind, ran rings around the guileless King Charles. Alexander persuaded Charles that any papal dethronement which was done either through a Church council or by any secular authority would be manifestly unlawful in God's eyes. At the same time he demonstrated to Charles that he was a practical-minded pontiff with whom the French king could work by offering him the last minute concession of agreeing to recognise France's rightful claim to Naples.

These negotiations were greatly assisted by the wily Guillaume Briçonnet who was rewarded in turn by Pope Alexander with a cardinal's hat during a special consistory held in the King's presence on 16 January 1495. Briçonnet took the title of Cardinal of St.-Malo, from his episcopal see in France. As an additional concession, Pope Alexander grudgingly agreed to hand over his son Cesare Borgia as a hostage of the French king. He also consented to surrender Prince Djem to Charles, who planned to use the Sultan's brother to sew discord in the Ottoman ranks once he mounted his much-publicised Crusade against the Turk. Moreover, Pope Alexander was forced to agree to the additional bribe of a mule train full of gold and silver to help finance Charles's Italian campaign. These were all that the King required before taking his leave from Rome, which he did, quitting the city on 28 January 1495, much to the relief of the Romans who (historically used to sackings) knew that they had dodged a projectile.

Despite the protestations of Cardinal della Rovere, Pope Alexander VI retained the throne of St. Peter and the concessions which he had earlier agreed to now promptly dematerialised. Cesare Borgia engineered his escape from French captivity soon afterwards. Prince Djem was mysteriously poisoned and could be of no further use against his brother the Sultan. The mule train laden with treasure was discovered to be carrying only worthless iron bars and logs of wood. But as angry as Charles was at Pope Alexander's perfidy, he was by now nearing his ultimate objective and this had to take precedence. That same month, seeing the writing on the wall, King Alfonso abdicated in favour of his son Ferrandino and sought sanctuary in a Sicilian monastery, only to die in Messina later that same year. The new king put up scant resistance to the

French army before himself fleeing his realm. On 20 February 1495, Charles VIII entered Naples as its conqueror and its monarch. The *Napoletani*, who refused to fight and die in defence of Ferrandino's title, had frankly seen it all before and were philosophical about the transition. A long succession of foreigners had conquered the kingdom over the centuries from fierce Normans and brutal Germans, to French speakers from Anjou, and unpleasant and foul-smelling Spaniards from Aragon. Now it was the turn of the French; this was how it had always been in the *Regno*.

While these events were shaking the very foundations of Italy, Cardinal Giovanni de' Medici had meanwhile made his way from Pitigliano to Città di Castello which had for years been ruled by the *tiranno* Niccolò Vitelli. Like Giovanni Bentivoglio, Niccolò Vitelli owed the Medici a considerable debt of gratitude. Vitelli had served as *podestà* in Florence and also as a *condottiere* for the republic. When he had been besieged at Città di Castello in 1474 by the forces of Pope Sixtus IV, it had been Lorenzo de' Medici who had funded his subsequent return in 1482 and again in 1484. His four sons Giovanni, Camillo, Paolo and Vitellozzo, were all *condottiere* like their father and, upon Niccolò's death in 1486, rule of the town had passed to his eldest, Vitellozzo Vitelli. At Città di Castello, the cardinal was given a far warmer welcome by the tough roustabout mercenary Vitellozzo than Piero de' Medici had been afforded at chilly Bologna.

Lorenzo de' Medici's three surviving daughters Lucrezia Maria, Maria Maddalena and Contessina Antonia shared differing fates that fatal year of 1494. Lucrezia Maria de' Medici–who had been married in February 1488 to the Florentine nobleman Jacopo Salviati–was placed in the uncomfortable position of being the wife of one of the new republic's staunchest supporters. Nevertheless, like Alfonsina Orsini, she too rose to the occasion and would continue from this point forward to work discreetly behind the scenes to lobby for the return of her three banished brothers. The youngest daughter, Contessina Antonia de' Medici was married in that turbulent year of 1494 to Piero Ridolfi, the scion of an old, noble Tuscan family. The collapse of the young woman's family fortunes during that year must have proved the worst possible wedding present imaginable.

Maria Maddalena de' Medici was still at this time married to the gambler and wastrel Franceschetto Cybò. His parentage still made it impossible to reside in Rome therefore he and his wife continued to divide their time between Tuscany and Liguria. Matteo Franco, the Florentine cleric and humanist who had originally accompanied the young Maria Maddalena to Rome as her chaplain, had in January 1492 painted a vivid picture of Maria Maddalena's unhappy matrimonial life. Writing to Bernardo Dovizi da Bibbiena's brother Piero, Matteo expostulated at length on 'The bad health of Madonna Maddalena and the thoughtless behaviour of my Lord in keeping her up, for all this winter he has gambled every night, supping at six or seven and coming to bed at daylight, and she will not, and cannot, eat or sleep without him. Thus she has lost sleep and appetite and has become as thin as a lizard.' Matteo Franco had gone on to complain how 'Madonna's illness is caused by sitting up too late at night, eating at hours she is not used to, and remaining shut up in the house all day without taking any exercise ... She thinks and dreams of nought else, so great is her love of him. She is slowly pining away and this seems to me the most alarming symptom, for nothing she eats or drinks does her any good or gives her any pleasure.'

Charles VIII's passage through Tuscany had left the Florentine state in disarray. Not only was the republic left bereft of Pisa, Livorno and a number of important strategic fortresses guarding its borders, but the presence of the French had also presented an opportunity for both Arezzo and Montepulciano to throw off the Florentine yoke as well. Florence's *imperium* and its economic life had been drastically reduced all within the space of a single month. Its former alliance with Milan also lay in tatters thanks to the short-sighted and selfish policies of Ludovico Sforza. Lorenzo de' Medici and his father Cosimo may have used the threat of French arms to beat the other city-states into line, but they had never gone so far as to actually open Pandora's Box. Ludovico Sforza had been 'born for the ruin of Italy'. This was the mournful judgement of *il Moro's* contemporary, the Italian physician, historian, biographer and prelate, Paolo Giovio. But Ludovico's incautious act would not only serve to destroy the peace of Italy but would also return to plague both him and his new dynasty. For the time being, of course, this was still cold comfort for Florence.

In the aftermath of King Charles's occupation of the city, the Florentines returned to their favourite pastime *du jour*, the staging of witch hunts for any former Medici officials who had not already fled. Those unfortunate enough to be named and caught were not only dismissed from office but also suffered having their homes ransacked. This was the fate of Francesco di ser Barone, secretary of the *Otto di Pratica*, who had in any case already had the prudence to take flight from Florence. Not so fortunate, however, was Antonio di Bernardo di Miniato who, having endured the agonies of torture since his capture by the *signoria*, was executed by hanging on 12 December 1494. His death was recorded by Lucca Landucci who noted ruefully that di Miniato's corpse was left dangling from an upper storey window of the Bargello from early morning until eight in the evening. Others such as Bernardo da Ricci and Ser Antonio da Colle met with similar fates. The latter had been one of *il Magnifico's* 'new men' who had been sent as secretary to the Florentine ambassador to Rome. Most recently, da Colle had been tasked by Piero de' Medici with the delicate process of coaxing a cardinal's hat from Pope Alexander VI for his onetime tutor Gentile Becchi. The last official assignment which Becchi himself had undertaken had been to France, accompanied by Piero Soderini, to try to negotiate peace between Florence and Charles VIII, but upon learning of his former student's flight and subsequent exile a disenchanted Becchi did not even bother returning to the city but instead retired to his *villa alle Botte*. Other former Medici faction members to be scooped up included Bernardo del Nero, now well into his seventies and one of Lorenzo's old stalwarts, who had ridden alongside Cardinal Giovanni de' Medici through the streets of Florence trying to drum up support. Del Nero's life was only saved through the personal intercession of Savonarola himself, who gave a fire and brimstone sermon forbidding any further retribution against former Medici loyalists.

Savonarola's readiness to provide sanctuary and amnesty for distressed former Medicean loyalists, who were known at this time as the *bigi*, caused them to flock for safety to the *frate's* banner. Savonarola's own followers had quickly become known, somewhat pejoratively, as the *piagnoni* ('the wailers') and their more politically active members were called the *frateschi* (the 'frate's men') yet despite Savonarola's personal popularity they still remained largely disorganised as a political force and in the minority when it came to Florence's government. The *piagnoni* were therefore not entirely averse to having their numbers boosted by the influx of *bigi*. This marriage of convenience led many anti-Medici conservatives, however, to suspect the friar of secretly conspiring with the *bigi* for the return of Piero de' Medici. Their fears, which were in reality patently absurd for the frate disliked the Medici on principle, were a misconstrual of Savonarola's genuine intentions for the commune. Savonarola, who unquestionably envisaged a more theocratic system of government, had begun to define the new Florence as a prototypical 'City of God'. What Savonarola was attempting to bring about therefore was a universal peace and reconciliation in which Florence might be redefined as the *bene comune* of the Christian theologian and philosopher Saint Thomas Aquinas. Savonarola knew better than most that Florentine politics had always been vicious, little more than a license to persecute one's business rivals, and this had only served to create a self-perpetuating wheel of political hatred. He knew too that men like Cosimo and Lorenzo de' Medici had become especially adept at wielding these methods of political, legal and tax harassment. Savonarola did not hate the Medici per se; his verdict upon them was basically that they had, like the corrupt emperors of ancient Rome, merely lulled the simple-minded masses to sleep with bread and circuses: 'Many times the tyrant ... occupies the people in spectacles and festivals', had been Savonarola's judgement on Lorenzo de' Medici shortly after his death. Furthermore, Savonarola argued against the use of banishment for former Medici supporters, asserting with some justification that deportees only grew stronger in exile.

If Florence were to build a truly free and righteous New Jerusalem with a fresh slate it was imperative that the factional animosities of the past be forgiven and forgotten. With this political expediency of reconciliation in mind, Savonarola proposed firstly that discordant political speech and the use of divisive labels such as 'blacks', 'whites' or 'greys' be punishable by fines, torture and imprisonment. Secondly, the frate moved to blunt the stern penalties such as imprisonment, physical mutilation and even execution, which the *signoria* was able to mete out to those accused of treasonable offences against the state, by proposing a new law of appeal. The usual practice was for any guilty verdict to be confirmed by a majority vote of six to three amongst the eight *priori* and single *gonfaloniere*, what became known as the 'Law of Six Beans' because beans were used to cast their votes. Savonarola suggested instead that everyone be given the right of appeal before a committee of one hundred members of the Great Council and that a two thirds majority should be sufficient to acquit the accused. This proposal was an altogether fairer system which served to check the indiscriminate use by the *signoria* of their harsh punitive powers. While the mendicant preacher's all-too public rebukes poured out of the pulpit, the call for wider, more representative government steadily grew. This also threw the spotlight on other social injustices which were widely prevalent in fourteenth and fifteenth-century Italy; issues such as government corruption, unfair taxation, selective application of the laws, not to mention draconian punishment of workers who staged protests, were all called sharply into focus. Those amongst the wealthier sections of the community derided Savonarola's criticisms of the rich and powerful and his championing of the poor and their many social grievances.

As a result of Savonarola's attempts to improve the political hygiene of the state, opinion in Florence now bifurcated into two broad camps. On the one hand, Savonarola found support from such *ottimati* as Paolantonio Soderini, Giovambattista Ridolfi, and Piero Guicciardini, all of whom earnestly wished to

361

see the friar's idealistic political innovation of *governo largo* (rule by the majority) come into effect. On the other hand there were the more conservative *ottimati*, such as Piero di Gino Capponi, who preferred to see the more restricted old-fashioned *governo stretto* or 'strict government'. Both camps of course desired to see the Old Medicean Order swept away and so on 30 November 1494 the presiding *signoria* called to order a *pratica* ('consultation') which was an extraordinary council comprising all the past *gonfalonieri* who had been declared *veduti* ('eligible'). The *pratica's* task was to give advice on how the city should now be governed in the absence of the Medici. They recommended firstly that a *parlamento* be called which would be empowered to dismantle the two Medici councils known as the Hundred and the Seventy. They also advised that a new scrutiny be held since all the names in the current *borse* were from the last scrutiny of 1484, which had been held under Lorenzo de' Medici's auspices. Twenty *accoppiatori* would be appointed tasked with selecting *a mano* the new pool of available officials for the regime. A new constitution would also be drawn up and an interim magistracy of ten of Florence's 'noblest and ablest' citizens would, as their first order of business, ensure that Florence did not descend into political factionalism and chaos.

On 2 December 1494, just four days after the exodus of the crapulous French forces from Florence, Piero Capponi, Bernardo Rucellai and Lorenzo di Pierfrancesco (who was by now already styling himself, not as 'Medici', but as '*il Popolano*') ordered the tolling of the *vacca*. For decades, the Medici had used the presence of armed soldiers in the Piazza della Signoria to coerce the *parlamento* into rubber stamping a *balià* which was, in turn, pre-packed with Medici men through manipulative use of the *accoppiatori* and their *scrutinies*. This had been the inner secret of Medici authority. The new political élite now took a leaf from the Medici playbook. The Piazza della Signoria was, as before, ring-fenced with armed troops. Antonio Bartolomei, the new *notaio della riformagioni* since the arrest of the former incumbent Giovanni Guidi da Pratovecchio, solemnly read out the new Florentine constitution to the assembled past *gonfalonieri* and citizens waiting in the *piazza* under their various banners. The *parlamento* was then informed of the *signoria's* plans: to dismantle the 'fraudulent' councils which had been introduced by the Medici *reggimento* and to recall all those citizens who had been banished by the Medici since 1434. The new constitution was then affirmed and the people, in the understated words of one contemporary chronicler, were 'permitted to leave'.

At the instigation of Girolamo Savonarola, who was called in to consult with the *pratica* on the new system of government, a 'Great Council' was established on 22 December 1494. This council would comprise any male over twenty-nine years old who paid taxes, or whose family had in the past produced a senior member of the administration. As this came to around 3,600 people and there was no venue in Florence large enough to accommodate such a throng, the Great Council was for the time being divided into three smaller constituent councils, each of which would serve for six months at a time. In effect, this new political innovation involved a far greater number of ordinary citizens in Florence's political life than at any other time in the republic's history; it must therefore be seen as Savonarola's crowning political achievement. This was the little friar's way of giving those who lacked political representation a true voice in government. Antonio Sangallo was meanwhile engaged to combine several of the existing halls in the Palazzo della Signoria into a single massive council chamber so that the entire body could eventually meet in one sitting.

But, while the Great Council was still forming, business still needed to be taken care of. After the Medici councils had been abolished the twenty *accoppiatori* had set to work deciding whose names went into the *borse* and thereby determining the occupants of every important post in the new government. Amongst the presiding *accoppiatori* was Francesco Valori, who had led the rebel mob against the Medici, as well as Piero Capponi, Bernardo Rucellai, Giuliano Salviati, Domenico Bonsi and Lorenzo di Pierfrancesco *il Popolano*. Although the qualifying age for entry to the *accoppiatori* was forty an exception was made in the case of the thirty-one-year-old Lorenzo di Pierfrancesco on account of his steadfast opposition to his Medici cousins. These twenty men started out by replacing all those ambassadors whom Lorenzo *il Magnifico* and Piero de' Medici had hitherto appointed. Their next task was to appoint an interim *signoria*, an *otto di guardia*, Councils of the People and Commune and also a *dieci di balìa* (which was subsequently renamed the *dieci di libertà e pace*). If, in the wake of the Medici departure and the creation of the Great Council, the common people of Florence had hoped for a more populist style of executive it was sadly not to be. For the most part, the men who were now determining Florence's interim government were *ottimati*–grandees from the republic's old moneyed families and Medici men not so long ago–and the new *reggimento* which they now sought to create was, in a significant sense, every bit as exclusive as the one that had been ousted.

It soon dawned on the more populist members of the commune that little had changed in reality. Lorenzo di Pierfrancesco for example, whose change of name did little to hoodwink those more cynical Florentines, was of the Medici (cadet) bloodline. Piero Capponi had been taken under *il Magnifico's* wing as a young man and been sent as ambassador to various foreign courts, only coming out in open opposition to the Medici after Lorenzo died. A similar story attended the rise of Guidantonio Vespucci, one of the Medici's most tireless ambassadors, who had been despatched by *il Magnifico* to petition the king of France for support in the aftermath of the Pazzi Conspiracy. Another *accoppiatori* was Bernardo Rucellai who had been married to Lorenzo's elder sister Nannina de' Medici up until her recent death in May 1493. Thus, Bernardo Rucellai was by marriage the uncle-in-law to Piero, Giovanni and Giuliano de' Medici. The bitterest experience of all was reserved for those dissidents who had been repatriated after long years of exile only to find that old Medici men still held sway.

The new signoria which they had selected was sworn in on 1 January 1495. The gonfaloniere was a man named Filippo Corbizzi, who was a known conservative of the *governo stretto* persuasion. Corbizzi was also sympathetic to the extreme conservative faction whom Savonarola and his *frateschi* had come to label the *arrabiati* or 'enraged ones' (sometimes referred to less politely as the 'mad dogs'). The *arrabiati* were a group of around several hundred radicals from the lesser guilds who longed for the root and branch destruction of the Medici and their supporters, but who at the same time believed that ecclesiastics like Savonarola had no business leading the reform movement or indeed meddling in secular politics. Strategically they were allied with Pope Alexander VI and the duke of Milan and called loudly for Florence's membership of the Pope's newly-minted Holy League against France. Their spiritual leader, the elderly firebrand Baldassare Carducci, used Savonarola's clemency towards the Medici *bigi* to accuse the frate of fostering a fifth column which was ready to betray Florence once Piero de' Medici approached the city in any force.

363

Another opposition faction worth mentioning around this time was the *tiepidi* or 'tepid ones' who comprised a loose alliance of clerics and priests (many of whom were drawn from the better-off families) who saw no earthly reason why their clerical vows should disbar them from a life of permissive, sensual enjoyment. These wealthy, non-puritanically minded priests, many of whom had evidently retained close links with avowedly non-puritanical Rome, resented the friar's priggish strictures on morality and were ill-disposed to an existence based on penitential starvation, celibacy, hair shirts and self-mortification. Frightened at the popular democratic mood which had been stirred up by Savonarola's sermons, the *arrabiati* and the *tiepidi* joined forces in their agenda of excluding the cleric Savonarola from meddling in the affairs of secular government. They sponsored a Franciscan friar by the name of Domenico da Ponzo to come to Florence and challenge Savonarola's claims to have prophetic abilities and to question his involvement in politics. By rights, since he was both a cleric as well as a non-citizen, Savonarola was doubly ineligible to participate in the political life of Florence and da Ponzo should have been able to demolish the legitimacy of the frate's activities on these grounds alone. Savonarola, however, utterly trounced da Ponzo in a masterful sermon delivered on 13 January 1495 which became widely known as 'The Sermon on the Renewal of the Church'.

On 14 January, the next day, the Great Council, or at least one third of it, sat for the first time. In response, four days later the *arrabiati* gonfaloniere Filippo Corbizzi once again moved to challenge Savonarola's legitimacy by inviting two distinguished local theologians—Fra Tommaso da Rieti and Fra Giovanni Caroli—to debate Savonarola before an audience of clerics and laity. The debate was to refrain from touching on politics since Corbizzi refused to acknowledge that clerics had any business involving themselves in secular areas. As he had done before with da Ponzo, Savonarola held his own in the debate; however these repeated attacks on his sincerity and purity of purpose were in truth beginning to demoralise him. On 1 March, a fresh *signoria* was selected which had as its *gonfaloniere* the ultra-conservative ottimati Tanai de'Nerli, who was an altogether more capable operator that his predecessor Corbizzi. On 19 March, however, Savonarola was delighted when the Great Council abolished the Law of Six Beans and approved his proposal for a right of appeal before the Great Council. 'See, you have not been able to resist ... this has been done by God', he exulted to his followers after the landslide victory of 543 to 163.

With this latest defeat, the more conservative *ottimati* faction was seemingly unable to gain significant traction in their war with the little friar. Part of the problem lay in the fatal fractures within the influential *ottimati* class itself. Particularly destructive was the on-going feud between Piero Capponi and Paolantonio Soderini who–together with his three brothers Piero, Giovanni and Francesco Soderini, the bishop of Volterra–had already been active in Florentine politics for many years. When Piero Capponi had earlier blocked Paolantonio's appointment to the twenty *accoppiatori* the latter took his grievances outside the governing élite to Savonarola to adjudicate. The friar soon began preaching stern sermons denouncing the power of the élite *accoppiatori* and calling once more for *governo largo*, proclaiming that God had intended that Florence be ruled by 'its people, not by tyranny'. Approaching two members of the *accoppiatori*–Giuliano Salviati and Domenico Bonsi–Savonarola cowed the two men into resigning their positions. The ever combustible Francesco Valori was also approached for his resignation but had angrily refused. Despite Valori's obstinacy, however, the spirit of the city was soon firmly against the twenty and, by May 1495, those remaining *accoppiatori* had petitioned the *signoria* to accept their resignations.

That same month, Alfonsina Orsini asked permission to travel to re-join her husband in Rome, from whence he had subsequently gone from Venice, but she was denied her request. This may have had something to do with the misguided on-going suspicion that Piero de' Medici was planning his return with Savonarola's assistance. Instead, Alfonsina was forced to remain in Florence with her other female relatives and make the best of things. Later in September, however, she left Florence covertly without the *signoria's* permission and joined her husband Piero and his brother Giuliano in Siena. Her mother was only permitted to join her two years later, when she herself was exiled from Florence in March 1497.

King Charles VIII's brief sojourn in Naples earned him few loyal adherents in that kingdom. Although the *Napoletani* had tolerated him, he himself had largely spent his time in idleness and dissipation, enjoying the favours of a succession of local beauties whose likenesses he had pruriently captured in a sketch book. The estates and *Napoletano* lordships which he parcelled out to his French nobles were rapidly re-sold behind his back for ready cash since no Frenchman earnestly expected to remain behind in this subdued yet sullenly hostile country. Ferrandino of Naples, who had earlier escaped to the island of Ischia in the Bay of Naples, the very epitome of someone who had lived to fight another day, was meanwhile poised to return to his stolen kingdom as soon as the main French army had departed.

By the spring of 1495, the divided and quarrelling city-states of the Italian peninsula had come to their senses and realised that King Charles VIII posed the greatest threat to their liberty. Even the lord who had foolishly invited Charles to Italy, Ludovico Sforza, had been deeply shaken by the chilly and disrespectful reception which he had endured both from Charles and his cousin Louis d'Orléans, who even now remained menacingly quartered at nearby Asti from where he continued to threaten Milan. Pope Alexander VI too was champing at the bit for retribution for Charles's having taken his son Cesare as a hostage. Venice was leery of France's ambivalence towards the Turk, which threatened her maritime empire. The Emperor Maximilian I was suffering from bruised pride that the French king had so blatantly intervened in Italian affairs, something which he regarded as his own imperial remit. King Ferdinand of Aragon, the ruler of Sicily, could hardly be expected to tolerate a French adversary on the other side of the narrow Straits of Messina. The representatives of these five powers gathered in Venice and opened negotiations, striving to keep their discussions secret from Philippe de Commynes who was keeping his king abreast of all developments.

Finally, on 31 March 1495, the Holy League (or League of Venice) was formed comprising Venice, Milan, Rome, Spain and Sicily under King Ferdinand of Aragon, and Germany under the Emperor Maximilian. The League was represented nebulously to the world as a purely defensive alliance against 'any state threatening the peace of Italy' but, although the French king was not directly named, its real opponent was plain for all to see – Charles VIII of France, whom the League intended to drive from Italy by force. The League began the process of gathering an army of 20,000 *Milanese* and Venetian troops under the *condottiere* Francesco II Gonzaga, Marquis of Mantua, a brave enough mercenary who was well-known in Italy for his short stature and bug-eyed appearance. News of the formation of the Holy League came as an unwelcome development for Savonarola in Florence. The friar was primarily responsible for orchestrating Florence's alliance with France and Savonarola himself had deeply offended by the Borgia Pope by openly proclaiming that King Charles VIII was God's instrument on Earth, sent here to reform a sinful papacy. Many Florentines also felt ashamed that, whilst Italy's other states were banding together to expel the foreign interloper, they were still caught on the wrong side in the coming conflict. Should Pope Alexander decide to make a diplomatic issue of this fact, Florence could well face the retribution of the League's army at some point.

In Naples, Charles VIII had decided not to tarry any longer. The Crusade was no longer practicable. The loss of Prince Djem, for one thing, had hindered Charles's plans to unleash a distracting guerrilla war on the Turkish Sultan. But in truth, once he had become acquainted with the myriad perfumed comforts of the *Regno*, Charles had soon lost his appetite for campaigning for God in Anatolia or in the parched deserts of the Holy Land. Inevitably too, affairs in France eventually claimed his attention and the time had come to return north of the Alps. On 20 May 1495, Charles departed the kingdom with a large part of his army, around 1,000 lances of his *compagnies d'ordonnance* and some 6,000 infantry. He left Montepensier behind in Naples with the remainder of his forces, comprising 1,300 mixed French and Italian lances supported by 2,700 infantry. These now, in effect, constituted a French army of occupation. Four days later, an army of 5,000 lightly armed Spaniards sent by Queen Isabella of Spain landed under the command of Gonzalo Fernández de Córdoba near Naples. Two days after that Savonarola wrote to King Charles reminding him of his messianic promise to march on Rome and reform the papacy, but this was certainly not one of Charles's priorities by this point.

Charles VIII reached Rome on 1 June and learned to his disappointment that the Borgia Pope Alexander VI had taken flight to Orvieto and could not therefore formally invest him as king of Naples as he had hitherto promised. The Pope had left Charles a polite note to the effect that he had vacated Rome 'in order to offer him and his entourage better accommodations'. The King therefore had little reason to tarry long in Rome and he vacated the city after just two days. On 13 June, Charles reached Siena where he was petitioned by an embassy of disgruntled Florentine envoys who called for the restoration of Pisa to Florence. Their newfound liberty had recently emboldened the *Pisani* to seize the strategically important town of Ripafratta, which commanded the road between Lucca and Pisa. The French garrison in Pisa had even helped them do it. Savonarola's thirst for political liberty and greater representation extended only to the Florentines themselves and did not encompass subject states like Pisa; this fact alone indicated just how 'Florentine' he had become in his own thinking. But feeling that it was wiser for the time being to hold onto Pisa and Livorno, both of which lay across his lines of communication from Genoa to Naples, Charles VIII informed Florence's envoys that those towns would continue to be garrisoned by French troops until he reached Asti and made his final judgement regarding the matter. Privately, though, he had been impressed by Pisa's fiercely independent spirit and was privately in favour of granting its inhabitants their freedom once he was safely out of Tuscany.

Savonarola had one final meeting with King Charles at the town of Poggibonsi on 17 June. Charles continued to extend the little friar every courtesy, but since his mission in Italy was drawing to a close he no longer needed Savonarola's encouragement or endorsement. When the frate returned to Florence he boasted to the crowds that had turned out to hear his report: 'I've been in the field, which is like being in hell' but the *signoria* remained generally unimpressed by this latest ineffectual diplomatic mission. Meanwhile, on the war front, things had started warming up. Ludovico Sforza's captain-general, Galeazzo Sanseverino, was married to the duke's illegitimate daughter Bianca. Ludovico now despatched his son-in-law Sanseverino to attack Louis d'Orléans at Asti and demand his surrender. Louis, who had angered both Ludovico and the Emperor Maximilian by having recently declared himself duke of Milan, had stymied *il Moro's* plans by sallying out and capturing the town of Novara just 31 miles from Milan. Louis hoped that his royal cousin Charles VIII would now come to Novara and join forces with him in a French attack on Milan, the prospect of which caused general consternation amongst the *Milanesi* and led a panic-stricken Ludovico to barricade himself inside the Castello Sforzesco. It was only the cool-headedness of Beatrice d'Este which saved the day and, when reinforcements arrived from Venice, Galeazzo Sanseverino was able to besiege the French holed up inside Novara. By 6 July, Pope Alexander VI was safely back in Rome and Charles's army of around 10,000 men had retraced its steps back across the Ligurian Apennines and reached the small hamlet of Fornovo in the Taro Valley near Parma.

Charles had been closely shadowed this entire time by the army of the Holy League. Ignoring instructions from Venice to avoid battle and simply harry the French out of Italy, the glory-hungry Francesco Gonzaga instead committed his 20,000 League troops to battle. The result was an uncoordinated attack across the River Taro by four separate elements of Gonzaga's large and unwieldy Italian army. The ensuing battle consisted largely of confused skirmishing by the heavy cavalry of both sides. Gonzaga's two centre elements, commanded by himself and Bernardino Fortebraccio, had been compelled to ford the swollen river at a single crossing point and in doing so they became compressed together, lost all cohesion, and were beaten off by the French without difficulty. The Venetian *stradioti*, which were irregular mercenary light horse recruited from the Balkans, did however succeed in reaching and plundering Charles's baggage train; to the French king's chagrin, amongst the treasures lost was the sketch book of his amorous conquests during his stay in Naples. Still, despite the League's efforts, the main French army nevertheless succeeded in crossing the River Taro and escaped by way of Borgo San Donnino, Fiorenzuola and Tortona through the Lombard plain to the safety of Asti.

All things considered, the *Milanesi* and the Venetians came off largely the worse for wear at Fornovo and more judicious chroniclers like Guicciardini 'awarded the palm to the French'. The plain fact was that the French had given the patriotic Italians a savage mauling on their way out of Italy and the 'victory' had been at best a deeply pyrrhic one. Yet, at the same time, the battle rapidly entered popular mythology as an Italian triumph of arms which had shattered once and for all the belief in French invincibility. Fornovo had also been the first real, set piece battle since the French invasion and contemporary observers had been shocked at its sheer brutality, a far cry indeed from the orchestrated, rule-bound, protracted and essentially bloodless military pirouettes of the *condottieri*.

Following the battle, the two armies continued to shadow each other like wary dogs but were reluctant to re-engage and incur further loss of life and so Charles reached the town of Asti safely on 15 July. Louis was still under siege inside Novara, however Charles's battered army was in no shape to mount a rescue mission, besides which the Swiss reinforcements that he had procured were still trickling across the Alps at a painfully slow rate. Without his King's backing Louis therefore quit Novara (less than half of his troops survived the three month siege) and, on 10 October, Charles concluded his own separate treaty with Ludovico Sforza, the Peace of Vercelli. In return for the cessation of hostilities between France and Milan, the former would be permitted the continued use of *Milanese* Genoa as part of her supply route to Naples. Somewhat disingenuously Ludovico Sforza took pains to assure Charles that he would have Milan's full support during his next foray against Naples. The separate *Milanese* deal naturally gave the lie to hopes for patriotic Italian unity and the supposed cohesion of the Holy League against France.

Charles had barely extracted himself from Italy when his grip on his new kingdom in the south had already begun slipping away. Despite an early victory on 28 June 1495 by Stuart d'Aubigny over Gonzalo Fernández de Córdoba's small force at the Battle of Seminara, by 7 July King Ferrandino had returned by sea to his capital with fresh Spanish and Sicilian troops and had instigated a popular uprising in Naples that had taken the French completely off guard. By 4 October, the French forces under Montpensier were confined within the Castelnuovo and under heavy siege. By 27 November, Castelnuovo had capitulated and on 17 February 1496 its twin fortress of Castel dell'Ovo had also surrendered. Although French troops still remained in control of large pockets of the Neapolitan *contado*, Charles VIII's rule in the city of Naples itself was already a quickly fading dream. When Francesco Gonzaga sent reinforcements south from the armies of the Holy League to assist Ferrandino and Córdoba the balance was tipped against Montpensier and he yielded France's formal surrender on 27 July 1496. Out of spite, Ferrandino then interned the captured French troops on malarial marshlands near Pozzuoli where many, including the valiant Montpensier himself, succumbed to the unhealthy miasmas and died in their droves. In August 1496, with the kingdom once more firmly back under his control, Naples was able to celebrate King Ferrandino's wedding to his eighteen-year-old half-aunt Joanna. Unfortunately, *Fortuna* determined that he was not able to bask in his victory for long and by early the following month he was dead. In the absence of any children of his own Ferrandino of Naples was succeeded by his uncle Federigo, brother to the late King Alfonso II and the good friend of the late Lorenzo de' Medici. Federigo was crowned on 26 June 1497.

France's intervention in Italian affairs had opened Pandora's Box. Whereas previously Italy's warring city-states had contented themselves with battling with their hired *condottieri* for this small parcel of farmland, that minor town, or some obscure stretch of coastline, from this point forward vast tracts of Italy would be ogled greedily by the foreign powers. The Italians' experiences facing the heavy artillery of Charles VIII would also lead to a revolution in military engineering. From now on the peninsula would see the increasing rise of the *trace italienne* or star fort. Whereas the old fashioned citadels had been built with high stone walls, the newer star forts or 'bastion forts' were constructed with lower walls which were both thicker and made from brick, which did not shatter on impact with iron projectiles as did stone. The main walls were also protected by an often complex array of outer walls, bastions, earthworks, ravelins, moats and ditches which impeded the formerly straightforward task of simply battering down an outer defence with concentrated artillery fire. Michelangelo would become an exponent of such techniques as would such architects as Baldassare Peruzzi and Vincenzo Scamozzi. The new defensive methodologies perfected in Italy would subsequently be exported to the rest of Europe by the 1530s.

Although Charles VIII was by now back in France, he continued to harbour ambitions to reconquer Naples. His cousin Louis d'Orléans had meanwhile whetted his appetite with regard to the acquisition of Milan. It was at this point, in the spring of 1496, that the king of the Romans and Emperor-elect Maximilian I also entered the ring. He was summoned to Italy by Ludovico Sforza ostensibly to provide a counterweight to Trivulzio, who was still threatening Milan from his base at Asti. But as Ludovico and Maximilian both knew, their true objective was independent Pisa. Before departing from Italy in January 1496, Charles VIII's military governor in Pisa, Robert de Balzac, baron d'Entragues, had conducted a fire sale of most of Florence's prized assets. He sold Sarzana and Sarzanello to Genoa for around 20,000 ducats whilst Pietrasanta was sold to Lucca for 15,000 ducats. Both Genoa and Lucca were merely re-acquiring cities which had earlier been taken from them by Florence and were well satisfied with the arrangement. As for Pisa, Balzac sold the city's main citadel back to the Pisani for 20,000 ducats (which was financed jointly by Milan and Venice) and Venetian troops moved in to provide security against Florence. Pisa, however, was a tempting and juicy target for the duke of Milan.

The plan was for the Emperor-elect to come south to Italy for his investiture by Pope Alexander VI. The visit would thus give him the opportunity of going to relieve the Venetians at Pisa. In order to prevent Florence from regaining control the *Pisani* themselves were equally happy for either Milan or the Venetians to assume control over their city as both states had already provided Pisa with much-needed maritime support against Florence. Maximilian's intervention, which was for various reasons opposed by his fellow German electors, was nevertheless half-baked and he brought to Italy only a small fraction of the troops that *il Moro* had hoped for, depending instead on his Italian allies to make up the shortfall in manpower. In October 1496, Maximilian entered Pisa to popular jubilation. The statue of Charles VIII which had been erected in 1494 was torn down and replaced by imperial eagles. When Florence sent envoys to parlay with the Emperor-elect over the issue of Pisa's return, Maximilian proved evasive, referring the petition to the duke of Milan instead. But the initial elation at Maximilian's involvement soon grew stale. Venice had by now correctly apprehended that Ludovico was angling to have himself invested as lord of Pisa by Maximilian (he had already been invested as duke of Milan by the Emperor-elect's ambassadors on 26 May 1495). Maximilian himself was clearly only present in Pisa for this express purpose although, to be candid, the maritime republic was uninterested in acquiring Pisa for itself and was hesitant to commit to an acquisition which lay so deep inside Tuscany. Venice therefore now simply withheld the troops and funds upon which Maximilian was so heavily dependent. Seeing the perfidious game the Venetians were playing, Ludovico lost interest in the defence of Pisa and switched his animosity towards Venice, which naturally only resulted in a further loss of manpower for Maximilian.

In order to make it south to Rome for his investiture Maximilian felt it necessary to capture Savonarolan Florence and secure his supply lines back to Germany. But Venice and Milan's abandonment had put paid to that idea. He was also deeply in hock to the Fugger Bank for his Italian expedition. Finding his military position in Pisa now largely untenable, he made a perfunctory attempt to lay siege to nearby Livorno which ended in abject failure. His son, Philip the Handsome, Archduke of Flanders, meanwhile refused to fulfil his end of the plan by distracting King Charles in France. Disgusted at the whole affair, Maximilian now washed his hands of Italy altogether and scurried back to Germany. There he consoled himself with his favourite pastime, which consisted in clambering over the freezing precipices and glaciers of the Tyrol in the hunt for the agile mountain goat known as the chamois. As with Charles VIII's expedition, however, Maximilian's foray had set a dangerous precedent and the future adventurism of his grandson Charles V south of the Swiss Alps would later prove calamitous for Italy.

The opening moves in Florence's new war to reconquer Pisa continued to go miserably for Florence. Her war commissioner Piero Capponi, the anti-Savonarolan *ottimati* who had so courageously defied King Charles VIII was killed by a harquebus shot to the head whilst leading an assault on the fortress of Soiana on Pisa's coastline. The dead politician was transported on a barge up the River Arno back to Florence where his public funeral took place on 27 September 1496. The funeral attracted large crowds of mourners yet, at the same time, the *piagnoni* openly rejoiced since Capponi had led the party which was so vehemently opposed to Savonarola. In 1497, there came a six-month truce brokered by Federigo, Naples and Spain but when it expired Venice became more involved again and sent reinforcements to assist Pisa. By this time, with Savonarola encountering political problems both at home and with Rome, Ludovico Sforza (who disliked the frate intensely) had re-aligned himself with Florence and loaned them his support against Pisa. The upshot was a low-intensity war that would continue on and off between the two cities for the next fifteen years. Fortunately for the *Pisani* themselves the Florentines were throughout this time far too engrossed with their own domestic infighting to prosecute the war with any real political unity or military effectiveness. Indeed, far more worrying to the Florentines was the rumour that Piero de' Medici and his cardinal brother were raising their own private mercenary army and planned to march on Florence.

Aggravating this threat were the deep political divisions within Florence. The foremost source of tension lay in the on-going struggle between the theocratic reformer Savonarola and his opponents. At the end of July 1495 the friar had supposedly delivered his self-professed 'last sermon' before grateful retirement into a life of prayer and contemplation. The pressures of overseeing the reorganisation of the commune's government had proven a tremendous strain on the frate and he wished nothing better now than to set Florence on a righteous direction and then leave the stage. From the pulpit he had fulminated one final time against all those whom he regarded as being the true enemies of Florence: the sinners, the gamblers, the harlots, the sodomites (whom he wished to see burned at the stake) and the blasphemers. In a gesture of spiritual cleansing, he called for taverns to be closed down and dancing to be banned. His more puritanical adherents listened enthralled, as they had always done, to his parting words. His enemies on the other hand–the *arrabiati* and the *tiepidi*–were only too glad to see the back of the meddlesome priest.

Feeling that his talents were being wasted in quiet Bologna, Michelangelo had already returned to Florence by the winter of 1495 but he found the city much changed under Savonarola's influence. Donatello's bronze statue of *Judith and Holofernes* had, in a somewhat mean-spirited move by the *signoria*, been moved from its former location in the courtyard of the Palazzo Medici to a brand new position outside the Palazzo della Signoria itself. Here, it's metaphor of the 'victory of justice over tyranny' took on an entirely new anti-Medicean slant. Some of *il Magnifico's* old friends like Giovanni Pico della Mirandola were meanwhile clearly mesmerised by the frate's teachings. One of della Mirandola's circle, the humanist Girolamo Benivieni, had also fallen under Savonarola's spell and was by now enthusiastically composing lauds and other devotional songs for Florence's carnival processions to replace the bawdy *Canti Carnascialeschi* of Lorenzo de' Medici, the bowdlerisation of which would be far too onerous an undertaking for any hack. The Savonarolans' prudish rejection of nudity and denunciation of paganism contributed to a rather dull climate in which Michelangelo's genius could hardly be expected to thrive.

Lorenzo di Pierfrancesco came to his aid, hiring him to sculpt an infant St. John the Baptist (a *Giovannino*), after which the artist worked on his own project – a sleeping *Cupid* in marble. Baldassare del Milanese brought the *Cupid* to Lorenzo di Pierfrancesco's attention; thrilled at this latest work, Lorenzo recognised that having the statue artificially aged would allow it to be sold for a far higher price in Rome as an 'antique'. Michelangelo treated the work with acidic earth to give it a suitably ancient appearance and it was then passed by del Milanese to the middleman in the deal, Cardinal Raffaele Sansoni Riario. But when Michelangelo admitted the deception to the cardinal the latter furiously rejected the work, for which he had already paid 200 ducats. Michelangelo offered to accept it back; del Milanese declared that he would rather see it smashed into pieces. The whole *Cupid* affair became a terrible mess but there was nonetheless a silver lining, for Cardinal Riario later calmed down and, realising that *Cupid* was–despite the subterfuge–a masterful work of obvious genius, he invited Michelangelo to Rome in June 1496. Michelangelo was still the tender age of twenty-one and, under the appreciative gaze of the Cardinal, he would live and work in the Palazzo Riaro for a year.

Savonarola had also sidestepped an invitation from Pope Alexander VI to come to Rome and candidly discuss his prophetic visions with the pontiff. Behind this invitation lay the machinations of Fra Mariano da Genazzano, who had never forgotten or forgiven the scathing humiliation that he had once suffered at Savonarola's hands and who was now working closely with the Pope to exact his revenge. For his part, although he called attention to the papacy's numberless sins, Savonarola had until now been careful to avoid any explicit criticism of Alexander VI personally, but all this would soon change. During the second week of September 1495 another papal brief had arrived in Florence, addressed to the rival Franciscan order (Savonarola himself was a Dominican). The Brief denounced Savonarola as being 'So deranged by recent upheavals in Italy that he has begun to proclaim that he has been sent by God and even speaks with God... claiming that anyone who does not accept his prophecies cannot hope for salvation... Despite our patience he refuses to repent and absolve his sins by submitting to our will.' This time, the communiqué–which had also banned the friar from any further public preaching–was found to be fraudulent. It had been forged in the Pope's name by Bartolomeo Floridi, the bishop of Cosenza, and almost certainly at the behest of Piero de' Medici who had established the hub of his political opposition to Savonarola's regime in Rome. Savonarola bit the bullet and responded to the Pope at length, rebutting the accusations made against him as delicately as he could without being seen to impinge upon papal infallibility. He also wrote to the head of the Dominican order, Cardinal Carafa, seeking his support in the matter and commenting, 'I am well aware of who is behind all these lies about me, and understand that they are the work of perverse citizens who wish to re-establish tyranny in Florence'.

Cardinal Carafa's reply was depressing, indicating as it did that the Pope had chosen to support the exiled Medici in this matter and was doubtless even open to backing a Medici coup d'état in Florence if it came down to that. As a result, Savonarola felt he had nothing to lose by returning to the pulpit, despite the prohibition laid upon him by the forged papal brief. In October a further chilling remonstrance was received from Alexander VI stating tartly: 'We command you, by virtue of your vow of obedience, to cease preaching forthwith, both in public and in private, until such time as you are able to present yourself before us'. The mounting pressure on Savonarola simply caused him to dig his heels in. He was re-invigorated to undertake the earthly ministry which he believed he had been given by Almighty God, namely the expurgation of all Florence's sins. A small army of street urchins with shorn hair known as the *fanciulli* had taken up Savonarola's call to collect alms for the poor but their remit now widened as they scoured Florence's streets for gamblers, prostitutes, homosexuals, blasphemers and other sinners. In their rag-tag groups, the *fanciulli* went from door to door demanding that the occupants surrender their luxury items and other 'vanities' – silver plate, priceless illuminated manuscripts, candelabra, gold and jewels. If the ladies of the house answered the front door wearing sumptuous or 'indecent' clothing or furs these were pulled off them by the 'Blessed Bands' of near-feral holy children.

All these exquisite luxury goods were collected and then piled high in the Piazza della Signoria and burned to the glee of the common people, the *popolo*. This was the famous so-called 'Bonfire of the Vanities' and Savonarola's call spared no item however precious and no matter how much sentimental value was attached to it. He was especially aghast at the unbiblical scenes and depictions from Ovid and other 'pagan' poets that were often depicted on Florentine girls' dowry *cassoni*. The *cassone* was the chest in which the bride's dowry was prominently carried in the nuptial procession and many of these exquisite works of art had come from the workshop of the acknowledged master of *cassoni* painting, Apollonio di Giovanni di Tommaso. But no matter, for the preservation of beauty now took second place in Florence to pious demonstrations of voluntary poverty and simplicity in Christ's name. When offered up by their owners, the most exquisite *cassoni* were hacked into pieces and placed on the immense bonfire for kindling. On 7 February 1497, Savonarola's supporters collected and publicly burned thousands of objects. These even included several paintings by the artist Botticelli who, enamoured of the friar's devoutness, had allowed himself to be swept up in the city's religious fervour to the extent of gleefully destroying his own masterpieces.

In the political life of the commune, meanwhile, Piero Capponi's death in 1496 had cleared the way for the rise of his main political rival, Francesco Valori. Aged fifty-eight at the time of the great Bonfire of the Vanities, Valori's small yet influential family had formerly been part of Cosimo de' Medici's inner circle and Francesco himself had been amongst Lorenzo de' Medici's élite clique, having even been selected at one time by *il Magnifico* to counsel his son Giovanni. He was a statesman of considerable knowledge and experience, having served three times as *gonfaloniere*; however, Piero de Medici's inept handling of Charles VIII's invasion of Tuscany had caused Valori, like Piero Capponi before him, to turn his back on his former *padrone* and become an ardent anti-Medicean. In 1495 he had been one of the twenty élite *accoppiatori* who had been ignominiously obliged by Savonarola to step down, but at this point he thrust himself forward as a candidate to lead the friar's militant political wing, the *frateschi*. In a political sense the *frateschi* were, as Savonarola himself complained, still hopelessly disorganised, inexperienced and naive. If they were to be the conduit for the promotion of reformist Savonarolan policies in the Great Council they needed a qualified leader to guide them. Bounteously informed and knowledgeable in these matters, political leadership was something that Valori could readily provide. The *arrabiati*, the *bigi* and the *tiepidi* had earlier quipped that Valori was a head without a tail and the *frateschi* were a tail without a head but now–through some perverse political alchemy– the two were conjoined and now made common cause on the Great Council and in the *signoria*. In January 1497, Francesco Valori was selected to be *gonfaloniere* of Florence.

Valori immediately set to work modifying the entry requirements for the Great Council, which Savonarola had commented needed further 'refining'. In 1425, when it had first been proposed, the basic qualifications for sitting on the Council had been considerably more relaxed, such that even those candidates who owed back taxes could still qualify for a seat. Valori reversed these and other regulations however the resultant dip in council members impeded the *governo largo* which Savonarola had originally envisaged. In response, Valori lowered the mandatory admission age from thirty years of age to just twenty-four. This, as it turned out, was a colossal political blunder for it opened up the Great Council to a whole generation of young adults in the first blush of their *giovinezza* or 'youthful indiscretion and hot-headedness'. These young men had come of age during the twilight years of Lorenzo de' Medici's golden age; finding themselves now in a puritanical theocratic society they yearned for the lost glamour of the Medici days – the jousting and the carousing and the composing of sonnets to Florence's incomparable *belle ragazze*. Finding themselves with a larger share in government than they would otherwise have enjoyed, these young, pro-Medicean *bigi* were able, in March 1497, to vote in a new pro-Medici successor to Valori. This was the elderly Bernardo del Nero. Savonarola's sermonising had effectively saved del Nero's life three years earlier and, although he recognised this debt to the friar, del Nero did not intend to let it get in the way of his *bigi*-influenced political agenda. The respective factions of del Nero and Valori now became embroiled in a protracted and highly divisive political debate over electoral reform.

While this was in train, Savonarola himself became entangled in a very public farce concerning a rival seer and prophetess named suor Maddalena, who was a poor and obscure nun from Santa Maria di Casignano. Claiming that she had inside knowledge that Friar Savonarola was a fraud and maintaining that she was blessed with her own divine revelations concerning Florence's fate, the nun was used by the enemies of the *frateschi* to attempt to draw Savonarola into a highly damaging public debate with his accuser. Brought to Florence by *gonfaloniere* Bernardo del Nero and his chancellor Niccolò Altoviti, suor Maddalena now held consultations with such luminaries as the anti-

Savonarolan *Milanese* chancellor and the ambassadors of Duke Ercole d'Este of Ferrara and King Charles VIII of France. The well-publicised affair was a huge embarrassment to the embattled Savonarola who doggedly refused to debate with suor Maddalena. To have done so would not only have diminished his own authority but would have conferred a wholly undeserved legitimacy upon the nun, so he refused to dignify her accusations by publicly engaging with her. Eventually, the friar managed to have the Eight of Security escort the errant nun back to her convent where she was secluded under armed guard to prevent her from causing any further mischief.

The *bigi* cat was however already amongst the pigeons. The appointment of Medici loyalist Bernardo del Nero had convinced the exiled Piero de' Medici that Florentine public sentiment had changed and he chose this moment to make his long-anticipated move. Funded by Venice and his wealthy brother Cardinal Giovanni, he marched into Tuscany with, according to the diarist Luca Landucci, a hastily-assembled mercenary force of lancers, light cavalry and foot soldiers numbering around 2,000 men. On 25 April, Landucci recorded that Piero had already arrived with his troops at Siena, just forty miles to the south. Landucci added that Piero intended to take advantage of the current food shortages within the city by marching to the northern gate and distributing flour and corn to–what he evidently presumed would be–a grateful populace. Sensibly the *signoria* ordered that the city gates be kept closed as a precaution and quickly hired the *condottiere* Paolo Vitelli (whose brother Vitellozzo had earlier given Piero de' Medici sanctuary at Città di Castello) to set up a defensive perimeter around Florence. Several hundred pro-Medici sympathisers were meanwhile rounded up and interned as an additional safeguard. Piero's initial attempt to march on Florence ended in outright farce when a torrential downpour forced him bedraggled back to Siena. When his mercenaries marched out again, this time in less inclement weather and with the sunshine on their faces, the Florentines were ready and waiting for them. Bernardo del Nero, not wishing to be accused of treason, went through the public motions of ordering the Porto di San Piero to be closed in the face of the approaching Medici forces and hoisted falconets and other light artillery pieces and swivel guns to the city ramparts. Meanwhile, somewhat more fanatical *bigi* fifth columnists that were still at large in Florence sent word to Piero that if he stationed himself outside the city gates a pro-Medici uprising would ensue and those gates would be thrown open to him. Piero now sent word to his supporters within the republic insisting that a *parlamento* be called and then he planted himself outside the walls for his sympathisers to do the rest.

But both he and the *bigi* militants had miscalculated for the mood inside Florence–though by no means universally in favour of Savonarola's theocratic rule–was nevertheless unwilling to take the retrograde step of allowing the Medici oligarchs to return to power. Those few lonely riders who galloped with a growing sense of futility and desperation through the city streets shouting themselves hoarse with the Medici rallying cry of '*Palle! Palle!*' met with a lukewarm response. Piero was no Lorenzo de' Medici and he was certainly no Cosimo de' Medici either. The good people of Florence–even the *popolo minuto*– went quietly inside their homes, bolted their doors and waited for the crisis to blow over. Besides, the situation inside the encircled city was hardly as fraught as Piero's associates had optimistically reported to him; grain supplies had by now reached them from Livorno and the Romagna and so any attempt to starve the city into submission had been narrowly averted. Realising that his attempt had failed and lacking the troops with which to invest the wide city perimeter set up by Vitelli, in the words of Landucci, Piero de' Medici 'turned back and went away, seeing that he had no supporters in Florence. It was considered a most foolish thing for him to have put himself in such danger, for if we had wished, we could have captured him; if the alarm bell had rung outside, he would have been surrounded. As it was, he returned to Siena, not without fear.'

The inevitable political backlash now followed. At the beginning of the *signoria's* May–June term the fiercely anti-Medicean *gonfaloniere* Piero degli Alberti was elected to office. His first act was to create a commission of eight to track Piero's subsequent movements as well as his diplomatic efforts, Florence's greater fear being a Medici alliance with either Milan or else Venice (which at this time was lending considerable military aid and assistance to a defiant Pisa – as many as 1,000 horse and 1,000 troops). Their other mandate was to keep tabs on those known Medici sympathisers within the city. Alberti himself was no great friend to Savonarola and even churlishly reopened the old allegation that the *frateschi* were secretly in league with the Medici. In a move which seemed to be aimed directly against Savonarola, Alberti then decreed a two-month ban on unlicensed preaching, albeit with the concession that preaching may continue through 4 May, which was Ascension Day. But, on the morning of the friar's scheduled sermon, the Duomo had been found to be desecrated with the corpse of an ass and the cathedral walls adjacent to the pulpit were smeared with faeces. The mood towards the little friar, already by now somewhat unfriendly, was turning distinctly ugly.

By this time Savonarola had been abandoned too by his supporter Charles VIII who, having proven his military prowess, showed little inclination to return to Italy. The French king was still at this time preoccupied in a desultory effort to capture both Genoa and Savona, attempts which were led by the ecclesiastical exiles Cardinal Giuliano della Rovere and Battistino Campofregoso, but the French monarch's passion for martial glory in Italy had run its course and, by April the following year, he would be dead. Returning from watching a game of *jeu de paume*, the French king would strike his head on a low door lintel at the Château d'Amboise and would not regain consciousness. As Charles had no sons of his own, his cousin the duke of Orléans, who was next in line to the throne, succeeded him as King Louis XII. With no friendly, sympathetic French monarch to condone his messianic undertaking, Savonarola was now left bereft of his most powerful earthly shield.

Events now moved rapidly to a climax. On 12 May 1497, Pope Alexander VI excommunicated the little friar on the pretext that the 'so-called vicar of San Marco of Florence' had disseminated 'pernicious dogma', ignored the papal ban on his preaching, and had refused to comply with the Holy Father's summons to Rome to 'discuss' his alleged prophetic abilities. In addition, Savonarola had stubbornly refused to comply with the Pope's order of 7 November creating a unified Tusco-Roman Congregation, which had been done with the purpose of bringing Savonarola and his brother friars directly under Roman authority. Pope Alexander VI's breve of excommunication was delivered, after some delay, to the *signoria* as well as to other assorted churches of Florence. The order of excommunication was publicly read aloud on 18 June 1497 in no less than five of them.

Savonarola's mood nevertheless remained defiant. He looked upon the excommunication as a necessary stage in God's ultimate providential plan for

375

him. 'The Lord has placed me here: "I have put you here as a watchman in the centre of Italy that you may hear my words and announce them to the people"'. That said, he still kept up his end of the propaganda war by publishing two public letters, one for mass consumption denying that the Florentines had any compunction to obey an excommunication which was based on false information, and a second letter, intended for the more educated humanist scholars and clergy of Florence, describing in more learned terms the legal, theological and juristic limits of papal power. When on 15 June the murdered corpse of Pope Alexander's favourite son Juan Borgia, the second duke of Gandia, was fished out of the River Tiber, its throat slit and bearing nine stab wounds, many amongst the *frateschi* and the *piagnoni* self-righteously saw it as divine retribution for the Pope's ungodly ways and his persecution of their beloved prophet. But to Savonarola's credit the persecuted friar refused to take solace in the Pope's personal misfortunes and instead despatched a letter of condolence to the bereaved pope which seemed, to all intents and purposes, both genuine and heartfelt in its sentiments.

On 4 August 1497, amidst an outbreak of plague, came the shocking though not entirely unexpected discovery of a Medici plot to take over the government and restore the commune's banished banker leaders to power. How this all came about was as follows. Piero de' Medici's close friend Lamberto dell'Antella had followed Piero into exile but the two men had recently had a falling out and the more volatile Piero had subsequently threatened dell'Antella's life. The frightened man's requests to return to Florence and have his banishment quashed in return for divulging information about the exiles' seditious activities had been ignored. Nevertheless, dell'Antella had returned to his estates near Florence anyway and it was there that he was apprehended and brought to the city for questioning. When he was put to the torture his apparently innocent motives in seeking sanctuary from his former associate Piero now gave way and he was discovered to be carrying certain incriminating messages intended for Medici loyalists secreted throughout the commune. Under torture he revealed a list of those who were actively working to subvert the government and return the Medici to power. The list was questionable in view of dell'Antella's many known enemies in Florence and his own desire for revenge on them; however, based on dell'Antella's list, the *signoria* nevertheless went ahead with the drawing up of its own roster of those suspects who were to be arrested.

The *bigi* plot was said to involve, amongst others, the former *gonfaloniere* Bernardo del Nero, Gianozzo Pucci, Lorenzo Tornabuoni, Niccolò Ridolfi and Giovanni Cambi (who is not to be confused with the Florentine historian of the same name, who was devoted to the popular government). Of these five suspects, Tornabuoni, Ridolfi and del Nero were so unsuspicious that they presented themselves voluntarily at the Palazzo della Signoria for what they believed would be a discussion on what should be done concerning Lamberto dell'Antella. Instead, the three horrified men were clapped in irons and bundled off to the Bargello. In the subsequent 'investigation' which followed (meaning, subjecting the suspects to the excruciating agonies of the *strappado*), Piero de' Medici's sister Lucrezia Maria was also found to be implicated. She was placed under house arrest and later questioned, whereupon it was learned that she had spent 3,000 ducats of her own money to fund the plot to return her brother Piero to power. This notwithstanding, the latest round of allegations was based, to say the least, on the flimsiest of evidence. Lorenzo Tornabuoni's earlier act of lobbying King Charles VIII for Piero's return under French protection was already an open secret but by now he was thought to have made his peace with the republican government. Niccolò Ridolfi meanwhile admitted under torture to having fraternised with Savonarola's old enemy Fra Mariano da Genazzano; he had recounted his meeting to Bernardo del Nero, who had subsequently failed to act on Ridolfi's report. Bernardo himself may have had *bigi* associations but he was never personally in favour of returning Piero de' Medici to power, preferring instead an alternative *reggimento* headed by Piero's estranged relatives Lorenzo and Giovanni *il Popolano*.

Nevertheless, Lamberto dell'Antella's emotive testimony had been simply far too damning to overlook. He claimed that Piero had drawn up long death lists of his political opponents, to be bloodily dealt with upon his return to power. Dell'Antella also insisted that the conspirators had openly boasted that the reprisals which had taken place in the aftermath of the Pazzi conspiracy of 1478 would pale in significance compared to what Piero had in store for his current enemies. Foremost amongst these 'enemies' was the House of Valori. Piero's rivals would not only be executed but their *palazzi* would be torn up from their very foundations and expunged as in the days of Farinata degli Uberti. Chief amongst his most hated adversaries, so dell'Antella claimed, were the Valori, the Strozzi, the Nerli and the Giugni families. After several protracted and unruly debates, during which the right of appeal (an innovation for which Savonarola had fought so hard) was scandalously denied them, the five accused men were duly executed by beheading. The house leader and main force behind the indictments, Francesco Valori, could not however countenance the execution of a woman, even a Medici woman, and so Lucrezia Maria was pardoned, although thereafter kept under close official scrutiny.

Bravely, Lucrezia Maria would continue to build covert support for her exiled Medici relations, some of which was dynastic in nature. In 1508 she negotiated the marriage of her niece, Clarice de' Medici to Filippo Strozzi the Younger against the wishes of the prevailing regime. Most of the Strozzi had only returned from their thirty-two-year-long exile in 1466; the former family *capo* Palla Strozzi had died in 1462 at the venerable age of ninety-two whilst still in exile at Padua; the man who had once been Florence's wealthiest citizen had died a penniless pauper. There was therefore a fair degree of consternation at the match amongst Filippo's own kinsmen, who were reluctant to be associated with a family which was not only their traditional rival, but whose members were by now politically disgraced exiles themselves. Filippo the Younger was by all accounts a rather carefree young man with an earthy sense of humour who according to correspondence that he kept up with his close business associate Francesco del Nero was able to make himself the sexual scourge of Florence's convents thanks to his handiness with ladders, keys and pick-locks. Some of his nocturnal activities seem to have blithely continued well into his marriage years and when Clarice later chanced upon some of his illicit love letters she had furiously put a stop to her Strozzi husband's night-time assignations. Filippo seemed an unlikely ally on the face of it, but the choice of the Strozzi was to nevertheless bear fruit in later years.

In September of that year, Lorenzo de' Medici's cousin Giovanni *il Popolano* married Caterina Sforza in a secret ceremony. Caterina was, by this time, an available widow on the marriage market once more. In a repetition of history, her second husband, the former groom Giacomo Feo, had–like her first husband Girolamo Riario–been brutally assassinated. It had happened in August 1495 following a pleasant family picnic in the countryside just outside Forlì. Grief stricken, Caterina had descended upon the perpetrators, the Ghetti family, like an avenging angel. The assassin, Giovanni Antonio Ghetti, met his end in a graveyard at the hands of Caterina's bounty hunters who, with business-like diligence, staved in his head. Ghetti's wife Rosa, meanwhile, who had been the Countess's favourite lady-in-waiting, had been flung down a well in the *rocca* of Ravaldino together with several of their young children. Caterina then ordered her soldiers to slit the throat of Rosa Ghetti's remaining five-year-old. But her orgy of bloody revenge weighed heavily on Caterina's conscience; she needed to be transported out of herself.

Around this time, Giovanni *il Popolano* had arrived in Forlì like a breath of fresh spring air to recruit some of her superbly trained *Forlivesi* troops for Florence's on-going war against Pisa. Caterina was immediately taken by the charms of this gallant, cultured and well-read Florentine and the two had soon become business partners, with Giovanni shipping large quantities of much-needed *Forlivese* grain to a hungry Florence. She had learned about Savonarola's inspirational preaching from Giovanni and soon entered into private correspondence with the little friar. Savonarola could see that Caterina's soul was tortured by her past murderous misdeeds and replied back to the Countess extolling her to do good works because 'charity extinguishes sins, as water puts out fire'. Gladly she followed his advice, focusing her attention on relieving the suffering of her own subjects through a program of charitable deeds. To thank the friar she also dedicated her time and her funds to a community of nuns residing at the Muratte convent in Florence.

The romance ran its course and Caterina and Giovanni *il Popolano* were a good match for each other. When she eventually married Giovanni she was already pregnant with his child. The ceremony, however, had to be kept secret so as to prevent her uncle Ludovico from learning of their union. During their courtship the duke of Milan had kept up a steady stream of correspondence demanding to know her diplomatic status vis-à-vis Florence. Ludovico Sforza and his brother Cardinal Ascanio were no friends to Savonarola and were reluctant to initiate any rapprochement with Florence until the frate's influence upon the republic had been loosened. Understanding the game of diplomacy and dissimulation only too well Caterina wrote back to *il Moro* that her loyalties lay, as always, with her beloved home city of Milan. She would wait until Milan's interests were realigned once more with those of Florence before she made any official marriage announcement. On 5 April 1498, Caterina bore Giovanni a son, whom she named Ludovico Sforza de' Medici. Sadly however, by September her beloved new Medici husband was dead of a fever. Like most Medici males Giovanni too had suffered from gout and to relieve the symptoms he was in the habit of frequenting the thermal baths at Bagno di Romagna where he could sweat the toxins from his body. Here he had expired on 12 September 1498 in Caterina's arms. In memory of his dead father little Ludovico Sforza de' Medici was rechristened simply as 'Giovanni'. Unbeknownst to Caterina at this time, the infant would have a brief but glorious future ahead of him. The Venetian poetess Moderata Fonte would later allude to this in her chivalric poem *tredici canti del Floridoro* ('The Thirteen Cantos of Floridoro'):

See Pietro Francesco; and see together with him
Giovanni his son, who will take

378

a wife come from the Sforza's seed,
from whom the other Giovanni will come to the light.

Earlier that year, on 23 May 1498, Savonarola had succumbed to the irresistible wrath of the Renaissance papacy. He had stubbornly continued preaching, even after the Pope's prohibition, and had foolishly agreed to undergo a trial by fire in April of that year to prove that he spoke with God's authority and that his prophetic visions were divinely inspired. Many had taken a dim view of this 'heretical' fire walking stunt and the papal authorities themselves had, in the final analysis, proven far too calculating for so straightforward and idealistic a monk as Savonarola, who was always a far better preacher than a politician. From Rome, Pope Alexander VI's public relations campaign against the friar had cast him in an increasingly poor light as Florence's fortunes continued to suffer various reversals. Failed harvests and outbreaks of plague had made the people surly. When the tide of public opinion had finally, irrevocably turned against Savonarola there had been running battles outside the Dominican monastery of San Marco and, when the Florentine mob broke down the monastery doors, an incriminating cache of weapons had been found inside. The discovery was enough to condemn the little friar and seal his fate. The Pope had no need to act further for the customary course of Florentine justice now took over.

The friar was delivered up into the hands of the *signoria* for judgement on charges of fomenting sedition and armed rebellion. Transferred to the Bargello, he was tortured for days on end by the agonising *strappado*. Raised several meters in the air by his wrists, which were bound behind his back, he was dropped and his fall was arrested just short of the floor, which tore his shoulder blades out of their sockets. The process was repeated several times in succession. Each time, when he could bear the agony no longer he would confess; but once he had recovered his strength and composure a little he would subsequently recant his confession and the *strappado* would be administered all over again. This routine went on and on, over and over again without mercy. On 19 April Savonarola signed a lengthy confession in which he admitted that his divine revelations were fraudulent and that he had deliberately deceived his followers. Ironically, it was read aloud in the *Sala* of the Great Council which Savonarola had himself commissioned and, although many of the *piagnoni* were sceptical of the statement, believing that malicious notarial interpolations by the inquisitors had made the 'confession' even more incriminatory, the little friar's fate was nevertheless sealed from this point forward.

After the sentence of guilt had been passed Savonarola was publicly hanged and then burned in the Piazza della Signoria along with his two closest adherents, frate Silvestro and frate Domenico da Pescia. Before their execution all three friars were forced to undergo the humiliating ritual of 'degradation' or defrocking, during which their ecclesiastical robes were stripped from their bodies and their hair shaved. Luca Landucci witnessed the spectacle, recording that 'In a few hours they were incinerated, their legs and arms falling off little by little, bits and pieces sticking to the chains. Rocks were thrown to knock these pieces loose because it was feared that the people would collect them.' Finally, their ashes were thrown into the River Arno to discourage any determined relic hunters from amongst the *piagnoni* and to prevent the creation of a 'Savonarola cult'.

Accompanying the friar in his downfall was Savonarola's political ally the politician Francesco Valori. In the earlier riots of 8 April, which had led to the initial arrest of Savonarola, the secular leader of the *frateschi* had attempted to seek refuge at his home, the Palazzo Valori, where a mob had sadly already found and murdered his wife some moments earlier. He had been spotted by a crowd of *arrabiati* and been set upon and lynched. His corpse was stripped naked and dragged to the church of San Procolo where Vincenzo Ridolfi, the nephew of the Medici conspirator Niccolò Ridolfi (whom Valori had earlier condemned to death), hacked off Valori's lifeless head with a pruning hook. But, from the ashes of the old order, fresh shoots were already sprouting. On 28 May 1498, five days after Savonarola's corpse had smouldered in the *piazza*, a relatively unknown factotum with a cynical glint in his eye named Niccolò Machiavelli was appointed to the position of secretary of the second chancery. For Niccolò Machiavelli, Francesco Valori had been a very different kettle of fish from Cosimo de' Medici, being arrogant, hot-tempered and ambitious – someone who would wilfully transgress the law in pursuit of his goals. That would be his later judgement of the man in the *Discourses*; however in the *Natures of Florentine Men*, Machiavelli would soften his tone somewhat, characterising Valori fundamentally as a sincere and passionate patriot who was perhaps somewhat misunderstood. Savonarola was meanwhile almost certainly admired by Machiavelli (who claimed the frate embodied the qualities of both fox and lion – cunning combined with force) yet his failure, like that of Rinaldo degli Albizzi long before, had lain in his inability to rise above the limitations of being purely a factional leader. Ultimately his *frateschi* had been unable to unify the republic and had instead divided Florentine political opinion so badly that the resultant structural weaknesses had led the city to self-detonate.

The failure meanwhile of Piero de' Medici's *coup de main* and his inability to garner popular support in April of 1497 had proven the final humiliation for the proud and foolish young Medici *capo*. Upon his return to Rome he forgot his troubles by losing himself in a life of purposelessness and dissipation. Piero now embraced the kind of aimlessly intemperate life which Michelangelo's newly completed statue of *Bacchus*, commissioned and then, like *Cupid* before it, rejected by Cardinal Riario, implicitly warned people against. 'Self-indulgence will ultimately be the death of you' had been Michelangelo's implicit message, which came mind you from the ultimate ascetic – someone who seldom bathed, neglected his appearance and failed to eat properly. Of Michelangelo's Bacchus, Percy Bysshe Shelley would write: 'It looks drunken, brutal, and narrow-minded, and has an expression of dissoluteness the most revolting'. But any higher moral lesson which might otherwise have been learned from the artist's first sculpture since taking up residence in Rome was entirely lost on Piero.

His former friend Lamberto dell'Antella, his tongue loosened by the *strappado*, had disclosed to his Florentine interrogators the damning extent of Piero's lifestyle in Rome. Piero, so dell'Antella reported, 'Here abandoned himself to a licentious and most scandalous life. He would rise from his bed late in the afternoon for dinner, sending down to the kitchen to see if they had prepared any particular dish which took his fancy. If not, he would leave for the San Severino, where every day a sumptuous banquet was served and here he spent most of his time. When he had finished his meal, it was his custom to retire to a private room with a courtesan until it was time for his evening meal. Or sometimes he would stay there even later, and then head straight out for the streets of Rome with a bunch of dim-witted, loose-living companions. After carousing the night away he would return to his wife around dawn. In this way, he dissipated his time and energy in gluttony, gambling, lewdness and all kinds of unnatural vices.' He quickly used up the last dwindling jewels and plate which his brother the cardinal had salvaged during those final climactic days in Florence and came begging to Giovanni de' Medici for additional funding from the cardinal's many profitable sinecures.

The failure of Piero's reconquest and the execution of Fra Savonarola had not, however, solved any of Florence's problems or transformed her into some post-Medicean land of milk and honey. Far from it; Florence had lost much prestige in the intervening few years and her brief flirtation with theocratic government had made her seem vaguely absurd in the eyes of other secular city-states. The years of conflict and Savonarolan austerity had taken their toll. In Florence, poverty was by now widespread and even Sandro Botticelli, who had once enjoyed the patronage and admiration of Lorenzo de' Medici was now unemployed. Reduced to wearing drab, threadbare rags, Botticelli had been an ardent supporter of Savonarola and a member of the *piagnoni* but his devoutness had led him to abandon his craft as 'a worldly vanity' and he had little employment or income by this time. Botticelli's fate was a depressing metaphor for how low Florence's fortunes had sunk in the post-Medici milieu.

CHAPTER 15

Italy Aflame

But the worst quality weak republics have is to be irresolute, so that all
the decisions they make, they make as the result of force, and if ever
they do anything good, they do it as something forced and not as a
result of their prudence.

Niccolò Machiavelli, *Discourses*, 1.38

In the years immediately following their flight from Florence, the three Medici
brothers had dispersed like the proverbial Jews of Exodus. Whilst Piero de'
Medici had remained in Venice pursuing his forlorn hope of regaining
Medicean rule over the republic, the youngest brother, fifteen-year-old Giuliano,
had been given safe haven by the duke of Urbino, Guidobaldo da Montefeltro,
and Francesco Gonzaga, Marquis of Mantua. Cardinal Giovanni's situation was
far from impecunious for he still possessed a rich cornucopia of Church
benefices which gave him a handsome annual income. Piero's seemingly
insatiable thirst for money had, even as early as 1494, grown intolerable and
the elder brother showed little fraternal gratitude for Giovanni's support and
advice, being 'liable to treat the cardinal with such extreme insolence, even
when they were in public together, that his brother all but refused to see him ...
as soon as the cardinal received any new income from his many benefices, Piero
immediately turned up to claim a share but within two or three days this would
all have been squandered or gambled away.' Leaving Piero therefore to his own
avaricious and self-destructive devices, Giovanni obtained a papal dispensation
from Pope Alexander VI to travel north across the Alps. Despite having the
friendship and support of Pope Alexander and his vice-chancellor Ascanio
Sforza, the political climate in Italy had grown too chilly for the Medici cardinal,
hence the prudent decision to allow a cooling off period which he would use to
extend his knowledge of Europe. Such a trip would also prove invaluable in
extending his international diplomatic connections beyond the narrow
parochialism of Italy.

Cardinal Giovanni would travel north with his cousin, Giulio. Giuliano de'
Medici's illegitimate son had earlier been created a Knight of Rhodes by the late
Lorenzo *il Magnifico* but Giulio had later indicated his preference for an
ecclesiastical career. Thereupon, Lorenzo had made him prior of Capua and had
sent him to finish his canon law education at the Academy at Pisa, which his
uncle had–as one of his last acts–reformed and strengthened. Now, the cardinal
quit the Eternal City, collected Giulio from Pisa, and the pair travelled north
together in the company of a small group of friends. For the two young
churchmen their five-year peregrinations assumed the form of a colourful

Rabelaisian adventure. They travelled incognito and in drab secular clothing, not wishing to draw undue attention to themselves or their status as wealthy Medici princes of the Church. Setting out initially from Venice to Bavaria, the company visited the cities of Nuremberg and Ratisbon before arriving at Ulm. Here, the Emperor Maximilian learned that the young Medici cardinal was traveling through his kingdom and summoned him to his Imperial Court at Innsbruck in the Tyrol. Maxmilian was no barbarous German. Married to Bianca Maria Sforza he had surrounded himself with a retinue of artists, poets and scholars and was steeped in humanist learning. Amongst the many famous artists who gravitated to his court were Albrecht Dürer, Albrecht Altdorfer, Lucas Cranach the Elder, Hans Burgkmair and Peter Vischer. The humanist Willibald Pirckheimer meanwhile advised Maxmilian on literary matters. The Emperor's preoccupation was to promote his image as a great humanist prince. However, since much of his reign was preoccupied with countering his own troublesome German barons, his efforts in the artistic and scholarly arena tended to serve as compensation for his absence of real power.

Much impressed with the precocious pair of young ecclesiastics the Emperor sent a letter of introduction to his son Philip the Handsome in the Low Countries which paved the way for the next leg of their journey. From Bavaria they travelled north to the Netherlands where they narrowly missed meeting Desiderius Erasmus, the promising young humanist of Rotterdam who had struck up a friendly correspondence with Giovanni shortly after the latter's elevation to cardinal. Erasmus, who had been secretary to the bishop of Cambrai, had already departed for England where he was destined to meet Thomas More, John Colet and the future King Henry VIII, who was only seven years old at the time. From Brussels the Medici cousins sailed up the Flemish coast to Terouenne with the intention of visiting Henry VII's realm of England but, the mood of the London English not always being especially well disposed towards Italians, the majority overruled Giovanni's plans and instead they headed south for Rouen. Here, the two cousins and their small entourage were arrested and briefly detained by the suspicious civic authorities. Released at the behest of the French King Louis XII, their perambulations took them next to Marseilles. By 1500, they had taken ship for Genoa where Giovanni's sister Maria Maddalena was currently residing with her husband Franceschetto Cybò, the son of the late Pope Innocent VIII, but inclement winds and treacherous seas blew them prematurely to Savona.

Here they made contact with the still exiled Cardinal Giuliano della Rovere, who was staying at his magnificent Palazzo della Rovere, the most imposing building right in the heart of the city which had been designed by Giuliano da Sangallo in the mid-1490s. Since accompanying King Charles VIII on his invasion of Italy in 1494, della Rovere had been in Naples but afterwards, fearing the poisoned cup, had returned to France with the King. 'Vincula' had always been an implacable adversary of Rodrigo Borgia and was still in danger of the Pope's retribution for having sought unsuccessfully to have Charles depose him. In exile at Avignon, he schemed for the conquest of the 'Riviera di Ponente', the coastline to the west of Genoa which was his ancestral home. As his two separate attempts to drive the *Milanese* from Genoa and Savona in 1495 and 1496-7 were frustrated he could only look on with bitterness as the Pope's son Cesare Borgia succeeded, where his own kinsman Girolamo Riaro had failed, in turning the Papal States into a personal fiefdom. In 1498, he had been compelled to swallow his pride and welcome Cesare Borgia to Avignon, whose resident archbishop he was. Cesare had come in some considerable pomp and splendour to petition Louis XII for a noble wife, preferably Carlotta of Aragon, the daughter of Federigo of Naples, who was at that time serving as a lady-in-waiting to Louis's queen. Carlotta, however, had spurned Cesare's suit and he had been forced to settle instead for the hand of Charlotte d'Albret. Throughout Cesare's romantic intrigues and machinations, and because Louis had taken a liking to the magnificent Borgia prince, della Rovere had been forced to maintain the pretence of cordiality with the son of his rival the Pope.

Rough, masculine, syphilitic and a known sodomite, Giuliano della Rovere flaunted his anti-intellectual pretensions and boasted openly of having previously been a simple Ligurian boatman in the years prior to his elevation to the Sacred College, whose Dean he officially still was. More comfortable with a sword in his hand than a psalter book and more disposed to wearing a suit of armour than his clerical vestments, he was the archetypal man of action. He had sired an illegitimate daughter, Felice della Rovere, who was raised in the Palazzo della Rovere prudently distant from Borgia retaliation, and who would later be married off to Gian Giordano Orsini and become one of the most influential Renaissance matrons of her era. Curiously, the spare, athletic, dynamic Cardinal della Rovere took a distinct liking to the obese, cultured, short-sighted Cardinal de' Medici and his bastard cousin. Both men shared a mutual passion for hunting and despite his corpulence Giovanni de' Medici could still sit a horse as well as the next man. Notwithstanding his unprepossessing appearance Giovanni was nevertheless an extremely intelligent man, as was della Rovere. Giovanni de' Medici would remain a close confederate of the older man and, as he steadily climbed the ladder of the Curia, his alliance with della Rovere would bear decisive fruit in the years to come. It is curious to imagine the scene of these three future popes sitting down together at dinner. After Savona, the visiting prelates made their way down the coast to Genoa. Here, at Donna Maddalena's residence, the two well-travelled clerics were finally able to catch up on all the eventful news from home.

While Cardinal de' Medici and his young cousin had been away in Europe, the new French King Louis XII had come to Italy with his army in 1499 and, in a lightning summer campaign, had captured Genoa, Piacenza and Cremona. These towns were followed, on 6 October, by the plumb objective of Milan itself. The Milanese rebel condottiere Giangiacomo Trivulzio was installed as governor as Ludovico Sforza's son-in-law Galeazzo Sanseverino despairingly declared: 'No defence avails against the might of the French. If they wished to storm the gloomy city of Hades in quest of Proserpine and Eurydice, neither Cerberus nor Pluto would venture to resist them.' Standing by and refusing to commit to either France or the duke of Milan, Florence had only succeeded in offending them both. The duke of Milan, now regretting to his bones the decision to involve Charles VIII in Italy's affairs, had fled to the Tyrol seeking the protection of his nephew-by-marriage, the Emperor Maximilian. He met with a frosty reception however from the Emperor's Bavarian subjects.

When the French troops had entered Milan in triumph they encountered Leonardo da Vinci's massive clay model for the huge unfinished equestrian statue of Francesco Sforza, which Ludovico had commissioned some years earlier. The monument would have been considerably larger than either Donatello's equestrian statue of Gattamelata in Padua or Verrocchio's equestrian rendering of Bartolomeo Colleoni in Venice. Leonardo had tinkered with the commission on and off for years, disquieted by the technical challenges of producing something four times larger than life, but in 1494 Ludovico Sforza had donated the bronze to the duke of Ferrara for his cannon. Coming across the exquisite clay moulding for the so-called 'Gran Cavallo', Louis XII's troops lived up to the French reputation for uncouthness by using it for target practice and it was subsequently pulverised by their cannon. It was a fitting metaphor for refined and cultivated Italy's coming years of suffering under a succession of irresistible foreign powers – France, Spain, the Holy Roman Empire and even the Swiss cantons.

But having achieved his objectives, King Louis now unwisely dismissed the 12,000 Swiss troops in his service without pay and the disgruntled Swiss now went over to Duke Sforza's side. Ludovico *il Moro* eventually returned to Italy with a formidable force of between 20,000 to 30,000 troops comprising Swiss pikemen, Balkan *stradioti* and German *landsknechts*. The latter had come to prominence around the turn of the century as mercenary pikemen from the lowlands of Swabia and fought in similar fashion to the Swiss pikemen, except for certain stylistic differences – the Swiss fought with their pikes held level whilst the *landsknechts* held their own pikes slanting slightly upwards. During the months of February and March 1500, and in conjunction with his brother Cardinal Ascanio Sforza, Ludovico quickly succeeded in recapturing Bellinzona, Como, Pavia and Milan in quick succession. On 5 February 1500, Ludovico Sforza entered Milan by the Porta Nuova, the same gate by which Francesco had triumphantly entered the city fifty years earlier. 'If the walls, the trees and the earth had possessed voices, they too would have cried "Moro! Moro!"' declared the Mantuan ambassador at the time.

The Milanese were generally glad to see his return for the French occupation had soon grown unpopular and taxation was far more burdensome than it had been previously under the House of Sforza. Leaving the *castello* of Milan still defended by French troops, Giangiacomo Trivulzio had retired on Novara and Mortara, but on 22 March, Novara had capitulated to *il Moro's* troops. But sadly this had been the apogee of *il Moro's* success. During the recent siege of Novara, Ludovico's unwieldy and undisciplined mercenary army had melted away due to lack of funds ('No money, no Swiss', as the popular saying went). Meanwhile, a fresh French army under the experienced command of Louis de La Trémoille (who had fought with Charles VIII at Fornovo) had entered Italy and joined forces with both Trivulzio and Yves d'Alègre at Mortara. Together, the French and rebel forces counter-attacked Novara and Ludovico unwisely met them in open battle outside the city walls on 8 April. The resulting clash of arms was a fiasco. *Il Moro's* Swiss mercenary pikemen were leery of engaging their own countrymen serving on the French side and retired in disorder to the safety of the city along with the German *landsknechts*.

That evening, the captains of the opposing Swiss regiments on either side fraternised with each other and La Trémoille's Swiss agreed to allow their brethren trapped inside Novara safe haven in return for surrendering Ludovico Sforza to them. Yet the Duke's loyal Swiss were still keen to smuggle their employer to safety and so, the following day, as the duke of Milan's Swiss units filed past their countrymen one-by-one so that each man could be individually identified, *il Moro* marched along in their ranks incongruously disguised as a Swiss pike man. A Swiss mercenary named Hans Turmann of Uri gave the Duke up in return for 200 livres, however, and he was promptly arrested and taken as a prisoner back to France. *Il Moro* was afforded honourable treatment by

King Louis but was shut away at Lys-Saint-Georges in Berry, where he remained for the next four years, before being transferred to the Château de Loches in the Loire, where the captive duke enjoyed somewhat greater liberty. After an ill-conceived escape attempt in the spring of 1508, however, when he attempted to smuggle himself out in a bale of straw, he was locked away in the grim underground dungeons of the Château where he later died on 17 May 1508 at the age of fifty-seven. Ludovico Sforza had been a hereditary prince, one who was probably at least more entitled to govern than the nephew whom he had had deposed.

> 'I say therefore that in states that are hereditary and accustomed to the lineage of their prince there are many fewer difficulties in maintaining them than in new ones, for it suffices only not to break with the orders of one's ancestors and then to govern according to circumstances. So that if such a prince is of ordinary industry he will always maintain himself in his state unless an extraordinary and excessive force deprives him of it.'

Clearly, *il Moro* contradicted Niccolò Machiavelli's dictum in *The Prince* to the effect that hereditary princedoms are usually easy for their rulers to keep. He had lost his princedom not once but twice. On the other hand, unlike Piero di Lorenzo de' Medici, he had at least attempted to put up a decent fight for it.

Cardinal Ascanio Sforza, who had also been captured by the French and taken as a hostage to Bourges, was confined there until 1503. Another unfortunate figure like his ducal brother, Ascanio had been obliged to go along with *il Moro's* policies to the detriment of his own ecclesiastical career and had inevitably incurred the wrath of Pope Alexander VI. The judgement of Ascanio's countryman and biographer, the *Milanese* chronicler Bernadino Corio, was however harsh. Cardinal Ascanio, so Corio maintained, should have fought Rodrigo Borgia harder for the papal tiara, but he was a myopic simpleton who valued short-term term profit over long-term power and thus his fate was well-deserved. Whilst Ludovico and Ascanio were prisoners of the French, Louis XII made a royal progress through his new Lombard possessions and gaily danced with the elegant and bejewelled ladies of Milan, whom the Benedictine chronicler, Jean d'Auton, described as 'more like nymphs and goddesses than human women'.

Ludovico and Ascanio Sforza were not the only Sforza family members to have experienced dramatic reversals of fortune during the interlude when Cardinal Giovanni de' Medici had been absent from Italy. Ludovico's young sons Massimiliano and Francesco were, in his absence, raised at the Imperial Court by the Emperor Maximilian and his wife Bianca Maria Sforza. Gian Galeazzo Sforza's son Francesco Sforza, who was known as *il Duchetto* was carried off to be raised as a monk in France by Louis XII. *Il Moro's* wife Beatrice d'Este meanwhile retired to the city of Bari where she spent the remainder of her life. Ludovico's niece Caterina Sforza (also now Cardinal Giovanni's kinswoman by virtue of her recent marriage to the late Giovanni *il Popolano*) had also latterly been deprived of her fiefs of Forlì and Imola.

Meanwhile the war to regain Pisa, a conflict which would–in the words of the former Savonarola supporter Giovambattista Ridolfi–'give Florence back her soul', was not going well. Florence's domestic troubles had only encouraged the

Venetians to step up their involvement and they now reinforced the *Pisani* with 2,000 infantry and horse together with a further 100 Balkan *stradioti*. Savonarola's removal had, on the other hand, prompted Ludovico Sforza (who had always intensely disliked the friar's hold over Florence) to re-enter the fray on Florence's side and the commune had also gone to the considerable expense of hiring two top-notch *condottieri*, Paolo and Vitellozzo Vitelli, to lead their army. But the Venetians' response had been to open another front in the war against Florence by attacking from the east, in the hills around Casentino. Caterina Sforza had sided with Florence against Venice in this business.

Although the Vitelli brothers successfully countered this new Venetian offensive, the business of maintaining upwards of 20,000 mercenaries to continue blocking Venice proved cripplingly expensive for the republic. When Venice herself withdrew under the combined pressure of the Ottomans and the new French King Louis XII, they accepted an agreement whereby Florence would indemnify them to the tune of 180,000 ducats to be paid over the next twelve years. With the Venetians out of the picture, Paolo Vitelli was once again able to refocus on the offensive against Pisa. By August 1499, gaping holes had been torn in Pisa's walls by the *condottiere's* cannon but, when urged to attack by the *signoria*, Vitelli mystifyingly hesitated, pleading that both he and his army were 'too sick to fight'. By September he had lifted the siege altogether and struck camp. The *signoria* was incensed. Vitelli was arrested on suspected charges of treason and collusion with the enemy, brought to Florence, and beheaded. When Lucca's representative protested at Florence's draconian treatment of their *condottiere*, the second chancery secretary, Niccolò Machiavelli, defended the decision by claiming that Vitelli's failure to attack decisively had earned him 'No end of punishment'. Florence's actions only reinforced her image, in the eyes of other professional *condottieri*, as a hard taskmaster, a poor paymaster and a potentially lethal employer. At the same time, the Vitelli affair only reinforced Machiavelli's own conviction that Florence could not continue to depend on freelance *condottieri* and must endeavour to build its own communal army.

But this aspiration towards a national army still lay, for the time being, in the future. To pursue the immediate on-going objective of Pisa, Florence was forced to turn to her allies France and King Louis XII for help. The French king granted the republic a motley force of Swiss and Gascon troops for this purpose led by an incompetent commander named Hugh of Beaumont. But the enlistment of France's support soon made Vitelli's campaign look like a sensible military manoeuvre. The Swiss and Gascons looted and plundered their way across the countryside from Bologna to Liguria before arriving outside the walls of Pisa. Here, they set up a few token cannon and took a few pot shots but otherwise they occupied themselves instead with prowling the surrounding *contado* in search of booty. When the unruly mercenaries accused the Florentines of failing to provide sufficient stores of drink and foodstuffs they took as their prisoner Florence's official commissary Luca degli Albizzi. The French general Blaise de Monluc would at a later date lament the occasional unreliability of hired Swiss units, writing: 'It is true that they are veritable soldiers and form the backbone of any army, but you must never be short of money if you want them, and they will never take promises in lieu of cash'.

Niccolò Machiavelli was despatched along with Francesco della Casa to King Louis XII's court at Lyons to remonstrate with the monarch over the behaviour of his soldiers. He and his companion had no official ambassadorial status and furthermore the *signoria* kept them penuriously short of funds. In Lyons, where international diplomacy was largely carried out through the expensive purchase of personal favours, these two impoverished and lowly functionaries were unable to cultivate any of the status-conscious courtiers who surrounded the King. When della Casa fell ill and left Lyons to seek medical treatment in Paris, Machiavelli was left to deal with this impossible situation alone. Back in Florence, the *signoria* had little inkling how diplomacy was achieved at this, the most powerful court in all of Europe, and had completely unrealistic expectations of what their envoy could achieve. Increasingly frustrated by the parochial outlook of his employers, and existing almost like a beggar, Machiavelli chanced everything on one final climactic meeting with the cardinal of Rouen and prime minister, Georges d'Amboise, one of the most powerful men in the realm at this time.

During his conference with Cardinal d'Amboise, Machiavelli offered the fruits of his accumulated political wisdom to-date. If King Louis were to achieve his objectives in Italy, he informed the cardinal, it was imperative that he support those states which were friendly towards him – namely Florence, Genoa, Ferrara, Bologna, Mantua and Forlì. At the same time he needed to crush those states, like Venice, Spain and the Kingdom of Naples, who were France's equal in military power. The result had perhaps been somewhat predictable; d'Amboise had listened sympathetically but at the end of this disquisition he had brushed Machiavelli's views aside by assuring the Florentine envoy that Louis XII would always follow the course of action that he considered best. With absolutely no diplomatic ground achieved, Machiavelli mounted his horse and rode back to Florence without further delay. What he had failed to achieve in terms of diplomacy, however, he had more than made up for in learning the inner workings of a major royal court. This knowledge would be fed back into his vast, encyclopaedic mental storehouse on political practices and human nature.

Meanwhile, while Machiavelli was on his mission to France, Pope Alexander VI was–like the nepotistic Pope Sixtus IV before him–attempting to carve out a principality in the Papal States of the Romagna for his rapacious son Cesare Borgia. Cesare had, as we have noted, found a friend and kindred spirit in the French King Louis XII, whose power in Lombardy now rested upon the joint hinges of Venice and the papacy. To draw the Pope closer to his orbit, King Louis had created Cesare duke of Valentinois in August 1498, a not inconsiderable heraldic honour whose lands brought a handsome income of over 20,000 gold ducats per annum. He subsequently became known in his own country by the Italianised version of his ducal title, 'Valentino'. Cesare's marriage to the French noblewoman Charlotte d'Albret, who adored him, was a surprisingly happy one during the brief time they were together but unfortunately for Charlotte she had been left behind in France when Cesare returned to exert his iron will over Italy. Louis had also granted the newly minted Valentinois the blunt weapon–to do with as he wished–of one hundred French lances, to be generously paid for at France's own expense.

One of Valentino's first targets would be Caterina Sforza's dominions of Forlì and Imola, for which a pretext for open war was sought. Initially, his father the Pope argued that Caterina's papal rents had fallen into arrears, a fairly common excuse for eviction, but this pretext was soon set aside in favour of a stronger casus belli – Caterina, so the Pope claimed, had plotted to assassinate him. The method of assassination purportedly took the rather novel form of a diplomatic letter from Caterina to the Pope which had been dipped in the infected pus from Romagnol plague victims. Pope Alexander wrote to Florence's *signoria*, informing them of Caterina's alleged plot, but this time the *signoria* stood squarely behind their Sforza protégé, although in reality they failed to send her any troops. Caterina's erstwhile kinsman, Cardinal Raffaele Sansoni Riario, meanwhile fled the city of Rome in fear for his life.

On 17 December 1499, the proud, stubborn *Imolesi* defenders yielded to Valentino, followed shortly afterwards by the capitulation of Forlì, but Caterina still remained determinedly in charge of Forlì's citadel the Ravaldino. On 12 January 1500, Valentino stormed the *rocca* with his 12,000 papal mercenaries, supported by his French lances, and captured the defiant Caterina who, in a final desperate bluff had threatened to ignite the fortress's gunpowder magazine and blow herself, Valentino, and much of his army to smithereens (Guicciardini would later eulogise Caterina as being that day: 'the only one of manly spirit, among so many defenders of womanly spirit'). Cesare was able to talk her out of it however and, after being taken captive, she was allegedly raped by Valentino, who ungraciously bragged that she had defended her citadel with a good deal more determination than she had defended her person. Thereafter she was brought to Rome where she was housed in the Belvedere Palace, although a subsequent escape attempt led her to be transferred to a dungeon in the somewhat less salubrious Castel Sant'Angelo. Locked up in a cell which reeked of faeces, urine and the despair of innumerable past inmates, she received letters from her sons Ottaviano and Cesare Riaro which complained of their own straightened circumstances and gave little consideration to their mother's suffering. Amongst other trivialities, they grumbled over the expense of raising little Giovanni, their infant Medici half-brother.

While in Rome, Pope Alexander meanwhile honoured Valentino with the title of *gonfaloniere* of the Church and raised twelve new cardinals, the income from which was sufficient for Cesare to replace his dwindling French forces with the services of the *condottieri* Vitellozzo Vitelli, Gian Paolo Baglioni, Giulio and Paolo Orsini, and Oliverotto da Fermo. Together with this fearsome entourage Cesare now resumed his campaign of territorial conquest. Valentino's voracious land-grab in the Romagna quickly led to his ousting of a whole clutch of lords from their fiefs. Count Giovanni Sforza of Pesaro had been married to Cesare's sister Lucrezia but when the Sforza union had grown 'inconvenient' his union was humiliatingly annulled by the Pope on the grounds of non-consummation. When Valentino marched on the city of Pesaro, Giovanni Sforza fled from his former brother-in-law in fear of his life. Pandolfo Malatesta meanwhile lost control of Rimini and the young lord of Faenza, Astorre III Manfredi, was deposed and later drowned in the Tiber by Cesare's ruthless Catalan henchman, the notorious assassin Don Miguel de Corella, who went by the sinister moniker of 'Michelotto'.

This was the tumultuous Italy to which the Medici cardinal was now returning. But some events had nevertheless turned in his favour. Savonarola was no longer around to cause the Medici further mischief and, although Alexander VI was by now firmly in bed with the French ('The Pope is quite French since the Most Christian King has offered a Duchy to his son' Ascanio Sforza commented) he was also antagonistic towards the Florentine republic since they had supported Caterina Sforza against Valentino. The conditions were therefore fairly favourable for Cardinal Giovanni's return to Rome. Former canon law students together in Pisa, Giovanni de' Medici and Cesare Borgia had moreover always been on favourable terms even as the latter's relations with Florence fluctuated back and forth. It was also common knowledge that both Cesare and his autocratic father the Pope were fiercely anti-republican in their sympathies. Florence meanwhile had succeeded in making some powerful enemies aside from the Pope. Cesare's *condottiere* Vitellozzo Vitelli had neither forgiven nor forgotten Florence's execution, in October 1499, of his brother-in-arms Paolo. The betrayal had effectively driven the enraged Vitellozzo into Cesare's arms and he now watched and waited for his chance to wreak vengeance on perfidious Florence. But Florence, like Valentino himself, was by this time sponsored and supported once more by France and so the Borgia bull calf could not move openly against the republic for fear of upsetting his benefactor Louis XII. For the time being, therefore, Cesare confined his depredations solely to the Romagna.

Piero de' Medici's attempt to recapture Florence had already come to grief by this time and he was now languishing in Rome anxiously awaiting the return of his cardinal brother and his flowing ecclesiastical ducats. From Genoa, Giovanni de' Medici and his cousin Giulio returned to Rome in May 1500. They would eventually settle down to live at the comfortable Palazzo Medici (today known as the Palazzo Madama) which, completed in 1505, was the Medici family's main residence in Rome and which was situated adjacent to the Piazza Navona and built atop the ruins of the ancient baths of Nero. Here, financed by the income from Giovanni's benefices, the cardinal cultivated the life of the *bon vivant*, throwing extravagant parties, for which he often went into debt, and delighting in witty and entertaining companionship. One of his boon companions at this time was his former tutor (and his brother Piero's former secretary) Bernardo Dovizi da Bibbiena, a priest whose gifts as a natural courtier endeared him to the young cardinal. Baldassarre Castiglione in his *Il Libro del Cortegiano* ('The Book of the Courtier') later presented Bibbiena as a facetious, though polished, courtier-in-residence at the court of Urbino; the waggish Bibbiena was to distinguish himself by writing the first comedy of any literary importance written in Italian prose, *La Calandria*. On one level a complex farce involving the usual theatrical canards–a wager over a seduction and an exchange of identities–on another level it was a sexually-subversive tract which carried cross dressing and gender interchangeability to absurd and fantastical proportions. Not only do all the main characters of *La Calandria* swap clothes at some point or another but they also swap their sexual parts too! Bibbiena himself was an avowed libertine who, despite his priestly vocation, continued to flout the Vatican's rules on celibacy by cohabiting with his favourite concubine. But it was hard for the Church authorities to impose their code of moral superiority over Bibbiena when Pope Alexander himself openly lusted after the body of his married mistress, Giulia Farnese. Lust and adultery – the Borgia pope had effortlessly managed to combine two deadly sins into a single act.

Indeed, the diverting and engaging Bibbiena seems to have set the general tone for Giovanni's circle of friends. He would eventually come within the orbit of another famous wit in whom (to coin Alan Watts's expression) 'the element of irreducible rascality' was equally strong. This was the irrepressible Pietro Bembo, the noted scholar, poet, literary theorist and lover who was able to boast, as one of his romantic achievements, of an affair with Lucrezia Borgia, who was at this time by now the wife of Duke Alfonso d'Este of Ferrara (his father Ercole d'Este having died in 1505). Jacopo Sadoleto was another noted poet-priest who would later benefit from his friendship with Cardinal Giovanni, although he was to begin his ecclesiastical career under the patronage of the powerful *Napoletano* prelate, Cardinal Oliviero Carafa. Another frequent visitor to Cardinal Giovanni's lively *palazzo* was Galeotto Franciotti della Rovere, the nephew of Giuliano della Rovere. Just four years older than Giovanni himself, the young priest was befriended it seems initially for his family's political connections but later earned Giovanni's lasting affections. He would be made a cardinal priest in 1503 and vice-chancellor of the Holy Roman Church in 1505 but, after his death in 1507, it was said that Cardinal Giovanni could not hear his name mentioned without tears welling up in his eyes.

Giovanni's young brother Giuliano de' Medici was also a frequent visitor to the Palazzo Medici. By nature affable and even-tempered, he had earned the respect of the lords of Urbino and Mantua with whom he had sought sanctuary. More a devotee of literature and the arts than a man who excelled in the cut and thrust of political action, Giuliano's mild temperament proved resilient and equanimous in exile, unlike his more combustible brother Piero. Michelangelo, the genius with whom Giulio de' Medici would cross swords on later occasions, had by this time established his reputation as the ipso facto preeminent artist-in-residence at Rome, just as Leonardo da Vinci had held similar laurels in Milan. He had only recently completed one of his most celebrated creations, the Pietà, a representation of the Virgin Mary weeping over the dead body of Christ whom she holds in her arms. The work was commissioned by Cardinal Jean Bilhères, one of the powerful ecclesiastics who–together with Giuliano della Rovere and Ascanio Sforza–had ridden into Rome with King Charles VIII and who now served as France's ambassador to the Court of Rome. According to Giorgio Vasari, having completed such a masterpiece, Michelangelo was mortified to hear that another sculptor, Cristoforo Solari, was being credited with the work. Michelangelo angrily took up his chisel and signed the sculpture: MICHAELA[N]GELUS BONAROTUS FLORENTIN[US] FACIEBA[T] ('Michelangelo Buonarroti Florentine made this'); it was the first and only work that Michelangelo would ever personally sign.

In May 1501, Cesare Borgia, Duke of Valentinois, was summoned back from his campaigning to Rome where he was created hereditary duke of the Romagna by his father Pope Alexander VI. On his way back from Faenza he made a detour to Florence and, in a wholly characteristic act of provocation, encamped his troops just ten miles from the city gates. Although Florence and Cesare Borgia shared the same benefactor in Louis XII of France, Florence was suitably and justifiably intimidated. Having extorted an agreement from the *signoria* to pay him 36,000 florins a year in protection money, Borgia then went to Piombino on the Ligurian coast, where he left his *condottiere* Vitellozzo Vitelli in charge of the siege of that city. Thereafter he himself went to Prato with his 8,000 or so horse and infantry where, in the words of one Florentine coppersmith who witnessed these events, he stayed 'for four to six days trampling the fields, thieving and doing all sorts of harm, and leaving a huge amount of damage'. After a brief stay in Rome, where the Pope invested Louis XII as king of Naples on 4 July 1501, Valentino joined the French king on his march south to reconquer the kingdom with which he had just been bestowed.

Louis of France had earlier concluded two treaties (those of Chambord and Grenada in October and November 1500) with his adversary King Ferdinand of

392

Aragon. By the terms of these agreements the two kings had agreed to jointly invade and subsequently share the kingdom of Naples between them. Louis would receive the city of Naples itself as well as the neighbouring province of the Tierra di Lavoro and the Abruzzi to the north-east and be declared king; Ferdinand meanwhile would be made duke of Apulia and Calabria. The present incumbent, King Federigo, was to be deposed but given a fair pension by Louis by way of compensation. It was a puzzling arrangement in which Ferdinand betrayed his relative Federigo and Louis agreed to give up territory which, given sufficient time and resources, he probably could have conquered on his own anyway. It had certainly been contrary to the advice given earlier by Machiavelli to Cardinal Georges d'Amboise for Louis to crush its major military rival Spain. Cesare's one hundred French lances had already departed from his service and were loaned out to Yves d'Alègre, the French commander in the south. The conquest was achieved by August 1501, when King Louis XII accepted the surrender of Federigo who subsequently went into exile in France. The conquest had been marred only by the bloody sacking in July of the city of Capua, which was defended by Spanish and Roman troops under Fabrizio Colonna. Predictably, many had blamed Italy's *bête noire*, Valentino, for the appalling massacre of the city's inhabitants. Gonzalo Fernández de Córdoba meanwhile landed in Calabria to begin the conquest of Ferdinand's share of the *Regno*. King Federigo himself, the last reigning king of the Neapolitan branch of the House of Trastámara, perished in comfortable enough exile in Tours in 1504. King Federigo's son Ferdinand was meanwhile captured by Gonzalo Fernández de Córdoba, and sent into captivity in Barcelona. Nevertheless, in subsequent years he succeeded in gaining Ferdinand of Aragon's respect as well as his friendship and his exile was a relatively happy and privileged one.

Their respective conquests done, France and Spain settled down into an uneasy truce. The reality, however, was that both sides aspired to win 'all-or-nothing' and relations between Spain's viceroy Córdoba and France's governor Louis d'Armagnac, Duc de Nemours, soon degenerated into a low-intensity war of nerves. Ownership of the regions of the Capitanata and the Basilicata were contested, as was the *dogana* – the tax which was levied on the vast herds of migratory cattle in these regions. Conscious of wielding a far smaller army than the French, Córdoba withdrew to the town of Barletta while Nemours laid siege to Canossa in August 1502. With both France and Spain preoccupied over dividing the spoils of Naples, it had quickly dawned on the *signoria* that neither France nor Spain, and neither Milan nor Venice threatened the security of the Florentine state as much as Valentino himself, a warlord who possessed the full power and backing of the Borgia papacy. Not only was Rodrigo Borgia's family now dynastically linked with the House of Aragon through Jofrè's marriage to Sancia of Aragon, but Lucrezia Borgia's more recent marriage to Alfonso d'Este of Ferrara brought into the papal camp a neighbouring city-state which had always been, to say the least, somewhat ambivalent towards Florence. Alfonso d'Este himself was a dangerous enough figure in his own right. His explosive and unpredictable disposition was even hinted at in his official emblem or *impresa* which famously consisted of a blazing cannonball accompanied by the inscrutable maxim *loco et tempore* ('at the right time and place'). He cut a grim and somewhat lugubrious figure amongst his fellow Renaissance lords, seemingly interested only in his armed forces and in maintaining the state-of-the-art cannon and munitions foundry established by his father Ercole.

Already by May 1502, it was an open secret that Cesare Borgia, Duke of Valentinois and Duke of the Romagna, was planning his next move against Tuscany and possibly even against Florence itself. That same month, Cesare withdrew 54,000 ducats from the papal treasury to pay for his troops, spending a further 3,000 ducats on gunpowder alone. Piombino had already fallen on 3 September 1501 and on 6 June 1502 news had arrived to the effect that Vitellozzo Vitelli, out of spite for Florence over the execution of his brother Paolo, had together with his associate Gian Paolo Baglioni–the tyrant of Perugia–countermanded Cesare's direct orders by providing military support to a rebellion in Florence's protectorate of Arezzo. The Pope instructed Guidobaldo da Montefeltro to provide Vitelli with all possible assistance and Cesare himself set out for Urbino en route to Arezzo. Vitelli's actions were, however, an embarrassing setback to Cesare since attacking such an important protectorate of France now placed him in a poor light with King Louis XII. It was all the more infuriating since Vitelli had acted from deeply personal motives of revenge whilst representing his actions as springing from Cesare Borgia's own policy. Rather than jeopardise his relations with France it now behoved Cesare to try to mend fences with the Florentine republic. Cesare sent word to Florence's *signoria* to despatch some suitably qualified *oratori* to come and clear the air with him at Urbino. The *signoria* duly assigned Francesco Soderini, bishop of Volterra, and the secretary of the second chancery Niccolò Machiavelli.

This was precisely the sort of assignment that Machiavelli relished, travel outside of Florence, new experiences, and the opportunity to meet one of Italy's most illustrious personalities and gain his measure face-to-face. As usual, Machiavelli left the day-to-day running of the second chancery to his subordinates – men like Agostino Vespucci, Andrea di Romolo and Biagio Buonaccorsi, with whom he went out of his way to cultivate a friendly and familiar rapport rather than the stiff relationship which usually existed between master and employee. The members of the second chancery became therefore a tight clique, almost a sort of gang, and Machiavelli himself preferred to operate on this level since he felt more could be achieved through working with his staff as equals and allowing them to practice their initiative. Machiavelli himself was no saint and neither were his staff; they relished in the exchanging of ribald anecdotes. When Agostino Vespucci had been in Rome in 1501, he had for example written back to Machiavelli about the scandalous practices of the Roman poets and how they were 'continuously in the garden with women, ... where they awaken the silent muse with their lyre ... But, good God, ... how much wine they guzzle after they have poeticized... They have players of various instruments and they dance and leap with these girls in the manner of the Salij or rather the Bacchantes.'

The two officials Machiavelli and Bishop Soderini had barely even departed Florence when word reached them that–instead of simply passing through Urbino–Cesare Borgia had actually captured the city from Guidobaldo da Montefeltro, who had fled into exile at the court of the d'Este of Mantua without putting up any resistance at all. Nevertheless, the Florentine envoys pressed on towards Urbino where, upon arrival, they may well have passed by Michelangelo's *Cupid*, which had somehow found its way from Cardinal Riario's ownership to the ducal collection in Urbino (Isabella d'Este, Marchesa of Mantua, was desperately trying to convince Cesare to sell her the piece despite having sheltered the deposed duke of Urbino at her court!) In a well-orchestrated and somewhat intimidating *coup de théâtre*, Valentino received them by torchlight in the splendid ducal palace which had been built by Federigo da Montefeltro. Machiavelli would afterwards describe Cesare's impressive bearing and appearance to the *signoria* in an illuminating despatch: 'This lord is most splendid and magnificent and is so vigorous in military matters that there is no undertaking so great that it does not seem a minor thing to him, and he never ceases from seeking glory or enlarging his state, and he fears no effort or danger: he arrives in a place before it has been noticed that he set out from another; his soldiers love him; he has recruited the best men in Italy: and all of this makes him victorious and formidable, to which we should add that he is perpetually lucky.'

Valentino told the emissaries that, had he wished, he could easily have restored the Medici to power in Florence; he could easily have humiliated the republic, but he chose not to do so. He insisted that he wished to be Florence's friend and ally, but demanded that the city pay him the 36,000 florins they had promised him one year ago and furthermore overhaul their republican system of government. The two Florentines, themselves both ardent republicans, were deeply affronted. They replied that republicanism had served their city well for hundreds of years and all of Florence was deeply proud of their existing system of government. On hearing this, Cesare removed the kid gloves. He stated that he was not sorry that Arezzo had been conquered by his lieutenant Vitelli; on the contrary he was gratified by it. He told the Florentines that their city deserved no favours from him, in fact quite the contrary. The emissaries countered him by raising the issue of Florence's three-year defensive alliance with France; the first such treaty had been concluded back in October 1499 and secured King Louis's help in reconquering Pisa in return for a pledge of 400 Florentine men-at-arms and 3,000 infantry to assist in defending the French king's northern Italian territories. In April 1502, the *signoria* had found it necessary to renew the treaty at the cost of a 120,000 scudi payment to the French Crown. But Valentino merely scoffed, saying 'I know better than you what the King has in mind; you will be deceived'. Indeed, the truth of the matter was that the Florentines had found the king of France's military aid less than satisfactory.

Upon Machiavelli and Soderini's return to Florence the *signoria* expressed little enthusiasm for any alliance with the duke of Valentinois, although Francesco Soderini felt that Cesare spoke from the heart and genuinely desired the alliance. Strangely, Valentino's bargaining pitch subsequently altered in tone. Rather than simply bullying, he now cajoled Florence, insisting that he was their best bet in seeking to restrain the likes of Vitelli or the Orsini, who were kinsmen to the Medici and their powerful supporters. Still unconvinced, the *signoria* did what politicians do best and simply prevaricated. Since Savonarola's execution, Florence's government had been limping along, retaining the same essential structure as before; the Savonarolan Great Council was maintained in the interests of preserving continuity of government but the two-month long term of the executive branch of the *gonfaloniere* was now deemed to be manifestly inadequate. In response to this shortcoming the Great Council ruled, on 10 September 1502, that the office of *gonfaloniere* should instead now be conferred for life. The man appointed to be Florence's first *gonfaloniere a vita* was Francesco Soderini's brother, Piero Soderini. Hailing from the same family as the brothers Niccolò and Tommaso Soderini, Piero was not an open Savonarolan himself, and belonged neither to the *piagnone* nor the *frateschi*; neither indeed would he have been their first choice had they remained in power. But as a reformer he nevertheless pursued many avowedly Savonarolan objectives such as the reform of the fiscal system, overhauling the sumptuary laws, and establishing limits on the size of dowries. He also improved the Monte di Pietà, or communal loan fund, which had been a *piagnone* initiative created to assist the less well-off. It wasn't inspired government, but it was nevertheless a methodical step in the right direction.

As for the surviving *il Popolano* brother, Lorenzo di Pierfrancesco, he never quite managed to consolidate his political influence in Florence. Although he had been shown favour by the republican government, and in spite of the fact that his Medici origins did not seem to be unduly held against him, his reputation had nevertheless been destroyed by Savonarola shortly before the friar's execution. When he was suffering the *strappado*, the friar had identified Lorenzo di Pierfrancesco to his interrogators as the man whom he had earlier accused of aspiring to become Florence's tyrant. Although Savonarola always had a high regard for Lorenzo he worried that he was rather too close to the duke of Milan for comfort and, shortly after the friar's denunciation, Lorenzo left Florence never to return again. Compared to his other Medici relatives not terribly much is documented about Lorenzo di Pierfrancesco's life. However, he does have a small but unique place in the history of navigation and exploration. Prior to his death in May 1503, Lorenzo would be the recipient of three important and historic letters from his sometime employee Amerigo Vespucci in which the explorer described at length his on-going voyages of discovery in 'the Brazils'.

Lorenzo's former loyal *maestro di casa* seemed particularly fascinated by the Indian cultures he was encountering in these strange new worlds; they were cultures which evidently placed little importance on material wealth, an alien concept to Italians and especially to Florentine bankers. 'All of their wealth consists in feathers, fish bones and the like', Vespucci claimed but his letters to Lorenzo touching on this topic had met with considerable scepticism back in his home city of Florence. 'They vilify me because I declared that the inhabitants of those lands care not for gold not other riches esteemed by us and held in high regard', Vespucci complained bitterly. The scholar and physician Antonio de Ferraris had, for one, gone out of his way to rubbish Vespucci's claims about the native inhabitants' indifference towards gold and silver. Vespucci, however, was adamant that the explorers had discovered a culture which was entirely 'other' in terms of what a sixteenth-century Italian believed and understood about the world. 'We found the whole land to be inhabited by people who went naked, men and women alike, without any shame', he reported, going on to add that 'They have neither law nor any faith, live according to nature, know not of the immortality of the soul. They hold no personal wealth amongst them, for everything is in common. They have no words for 'realm' or 'province'; they have no kings, nor do they obey anyone: each is lord of himself.'

By the time that Machiavelli met Valentino for the second time on 7 October 1502, he had already been busily overseeing Vitelli's and Borgia's return of Arezzo to Florence and had made three visits to that city between August and September. By the time he and Cesare met the circumstances were now considerably altered. Vitellozzo Vitelli, unhappy that his conquest of Arezzo had been overturned by his employer, had by now fomented sedition amongst the Duke's other *condottieri* – Paolo and Giambattista Orsini, Oliverotto Eufreducci da Fermo, Gian Paolo Baglioni, Ottaviano Fregoso and Antonio da Venafro.

Since Cesare's recent dispossession of the duke of Urbino, these lords had all come to the private realisation that in supporting Valentino they were making a rod for their own backs; having already made an *amuse bouche* of the duchy of Urbino, the rapacious Cesare Borgia–as was now manifestly apparent–would eventually swallow them all for the *plat principal*. The conspirators met and fomented their plans at the fortress of La Magione near Lake Trasimeno. Both Cesare and the Florentine government had got wind of this rebel coalition and Valentino tried again to persuade Machiavelli that he was more a friend towards Florence than an enemy. He insisted that, after the defeat of Faenza, Vitelli had thrown himself at Valentino's feet and begged him to lead the army to the very walls of Florence and avenge the memory of Paolo Vitelli. According to Cesare Borgia's version of the tale, only he had prevented this from occurring.

Frustratingly for Machiavelli the *signoria* still remained unconvinced, preferring instead to watch Valentino and his enemies battle it out from a safe position of neutrality and observe who came out on top. Ever the astute statesman and political strategist, Machiavelli had meanwhile grasped that Valentino's olive branch towards the republic was wholly in earnest. An alliance with the Duke made considerable sense since, as he wrote to the *signoria*, Borgia is 'highly reputed, very fortunate, and accustomed to winning'. Cesare, who lived a strange semi-nocturnal existence, could disappear and resurface at will with alarming speed anywhere on the map of northern Italy. His was a peculiarly focused and intense kind of intelligence, the likes of which had never really been seen before in Italy. There had, it was true, been clever *condottieri* before–men like Sir John Hawkwood or Alberico da Barbiano or Federigo da Montefeltro–but Valentino was different; he refused to abide by the polite rules of Italian warfare and was totally ruthless. Cesare was also highly charismatic and inspired his troops through personal examples of valour. In addition, he was a visionary leader who was quick to take advantage of the latest military innovations. On 18 August 1502, Cesare had appointed Leonardo da Vinci (unemployed since the downfall of Ludovico Sforza) as his architect and military engineer and gave the artist a roving commission to inspect and upgrade the static defences of his various cities. In order to win Valentino's patronage, da Vinci had impressed him by producing a detailed map of the city of Imola, a truly revolutionary concept in those days.

Machiavelli almost certainly came into contact with the fifty-year-old da Vinci during his embassy to Cesare and the secretary was ultimately able to entice the artist away from Borgia's service and back to Florence in October 1503 to paint a fresco in the *Sala del Gran Consiglio*, the Great Council chamber of the Palazzo della Signoria, commemorating the victory of the Florentines over the Visconti at The Battle of Anghiari. The fresco was intended to be a companion piece to Michelangelo's proposed future painting of the Battle of Cascina of 1364, an episode in the republic's fourteenth-century conflict with Pisa (this painting was never completed although several notable copies do exist, including one by Michelangelo's pupil *Aristotile* Sangallo). While Leonardo experimented with revolutionary new paint techniques for his great martial fresco he also began work on a portrait of Lisa Gherardini, the wife of a Florentine cloth and silk merchant. For the next several years he would endlessly caress her features with his brush. The sitter was, so the story goes, prone to melancholy and so Leonardo had jesters and musicians play for her while he was painting. Their antics would occasionally cause a wry smile to play upon her features. But the commission would never ultimately be delivered to the client who commissioned it. He would eventually bring the canvas with him to France in 1518, where the painting would later come to be known as the 'Mona Lisa' – the most famous painting in art history.

As Machiavelli was the first to admit, though a visionary military genius, Valentino was also an inherently spontaneous and unpredictable politician who rarely knew what he was going to do until he himself had done it. This was borne out on 26 December 1502 when Valentino had left the dismembered body of his right-hand man Ramiro de Lorqua on public display in the town square of Cesena. Lorqua had angered Cesare by his inhumane treatment of Cesena's inhabitants and so he had delivered a brutal yet necessary object lesson in what it meant to work against Valentino's political interests. Though cruel, it was cruelty with a purpose and Machiavelli could not help but begin to admire Cesare for his systematic, cold-blooded and–most importantly–*decisive* style of rule, an attribute which was lacking in Florence's own dithering government. Chastened by Valentino's ruthlessness, Vitelli and the others had finally come to terms with Cesare after their brief and desultory attempts at fomenting rebellion. Dissembling false forgiveness, Valentino had held out an olive branch to his former lieutenants only to snatch it away at the last moment.

Lulled into a false sense of security during a reconciliatory meeting with Valentino at the fortress of Senigallia, the rebels dismissed their security detail and were immediately seized by Cesare's troops. Here, on 31 December 1502, Vitelli and Oliverotto da Fermo were slowly garrotted to death. Machiavelli himself was present to bear witness to (and record for posterity) the grisly spectacle. In January of the following year Paolo and Francesco Orsini met the same fate as Vitelli and da Fermo at the Castel della Pieve. Machiavelli's advice to the *signoria* of Florence had proven remarkably prescient; Valentino had always been the stronger party. As early as his June meeting at Urbino in fact, Valentino had decided to rid himself of these petty tyrants in his pay, which was the reason why he so desperately wanted to win Florence over to his side, so as to safeguard his rear when he made his move against them. But, by refusing to choose one way or another, Florence had squandered her opportunity to partner, on an equal footing, with Italy's most powerful and cunning new warlord. Instead, she now had a dangerous potential enemy who by now was nearing the very height of his powers.

Valentino's friendship may have been a good play for Florence at this time. Their expensive but not terribly effective alliance with France was in many ways proving unsatisfactory. Louis XII's prime minister, Cardinal d'Amboise, had by now proposed a highly unhelpful solution to the whole Pisa issue. The Florentines would be permitted access to Pisa, with the payment of the requisite tolls, whilst at the same time being obliged to foot the bill for an on-going French presence in the city. King Louis clearly remained aloof and uncommitted to the Florentine reconquest of her former possession. Florence instead resorted to an attempt to starve the *Pisani* into submission by ravaging their crops, but Pisa received material aid from the anti-Florentine cities of Genoa, Lucca and Siena which sustained her. Throughout the débâcle King Louis's attitude remained infuriating. You may attack Pandolfo Petrucci of Siena, the French king informed Florence; Petrucci still owed the French Crown 20,000 ducats for having reinstated him in his fief. But do not under any circumstances attack Lucca (the Florentines naturally wanted to attack their old adversary Lucca and not Siena). Louis only put a stop to *Genovese* support for Pisa when the Florentines applied all the diplomatic pressure at their disposal.

398

Amidst the political chicanery, Niccolò Machiavelli lured Leonardo da Vinci from his laborious painting of The Battle of Anghiari and the two collaborated on a fanciful scheme to divert the River Arno away from Pisa and so cut off the city's water supply. On 29 August 1503, a workforce of 2,000 labourers, protected by 1,000 Florentine soldiers, began digging a new course for the Arno. Under modern conditions and with industrial excavation equipment the plan, which was little more than a routine exercise in applied engineering, might easily have worked. But in the early sixteenth century the technical capability to accomplish what they set out to do simply did not yet exist. In an early test of the scheme, it transpired that the excavations were too shallow and, when the river water was diverted into a basin, it backed up, broke the surrounding dams and flooded the surrounding farmland on which the Florentines depended for their agriculture. The *signoria* cancelled the project in disgust and Machiavelli was to later write elliptically in his masterpiece *The Prince* of the 'dikes and dams' that control 'the river of fortune'. The ephemeral nature of *fortuna* and her favours also followed Leonardo back to his own studio. The new experimental method of mixing his paint for the fresco of the Battle of Anghiari proved unstable and, although the mural was completed, in subsequent years it faded away to little more than a ghostly shadow on the wall of the *Sala*. By all contemporary accounts it was an extraordinary work for which Giorgio Vasari has left us the following description: 'this battle expresses the complete rage, the contempt and the revenge of both men and horses, two of which are interlocked with their forelegs. They fight with their teeth, no less fiercely than their riders who are struggling for the standard.'

Of more practical concern for Florence than either misconceived military engineering schemes or indeed vanishing frescos was the growing intervention of Spain in Pisa's affairs. Pisa had lately applied to King Ferdinand II for support in recovering her territories lost to Florence in return for a half-share in the port city's future profits. Although the Spanish monarch did not wish to become directly embroiled in the conflict himself he nevertheless instructed his capable general Gonzalo de Córdoba to encourage the continued proxy support of Genoa, Lucca and Siena, and he also established a worrying Spanish presence at Piombino. In October 1503, Córdoba's Italian *condottiere* Bartolomeo d'Alviano had also concluded a *condotta* with the Orsini for the restoration to power in Florence of their kinsmen the Medici. However, King Ferdinand had instructed Córdoba to keep a tight leash on d'Alviano and only permitted him the use of 200 Spanish men-at-arms for the entire enterprise. It was not yet the Medici's time.

In the *Regno*, the on-going contest between France and Spain meanwhile continued. Gonzalo de Córdoba had by now been reinforced with troops from Spain – Galicians and Asturians, as well as German *landsknechts* who were more than a match for the Swiss mercenaries fighting in the pay of the French. On 28 April 1503, the Spanish under Córdoba achieved a crushing victory over the French, commanded by Louis d'Armagnac, Duc de Nemours, at Cerignola near Bari. It was here that Córdoba deployed the formation which had revolutionised the Spanish army, the 'Coronelía'. Like the more famous 'Tercio' which came after, this was a versatile mixed formation comprising a combination of pikemen, harquebusiers, halberdiers and swordsmen. Pitted against these innovative Spanish units were the more traditional Swiss pikemen and French heavy armoured cavalry, the famous *compagnies d'ordonnance*.

Nemours and Yves d'Alègre arrived at Cerignola near sundown, their men hot for the attack. The Spanish, however, had positioned themselves in advance on the lower slopes of a hill behind a well-prepared ditch and, when Nemours led several hundred men-at-arms in a bold frontal assault, his men's mounts could not navigate the trench which was moreover being defended by pikemen and halberdiers. Nemours's vaunted Swiss pike squares found the ground equally heavy going and soon the French assault had been flanked by Spanish horse and cut to pieces. In the resulting carnage the duc de Nemours himself was cut down by harquebus fire and d'Alègre retired from the field in disorder with the remnants of the French rear-guard. The battlefield was left strewn with the corpses of 2,000 French dead. One of the Spanish commanders, Fabrizio Colonna, later attributed Córdoba's victory primarily to the ditch which had the Spanish had dug.

Following his victory at Cerignola, Córdoba entered Naples in triumph on 16 May 1503. Angered at this reversal, King Louis XII despatched a fresh French army under the command of his new viceroy Ludovico II, Marquis of Saluzzo, which assembled at Gaeta between the months of June and August. With the French army was Piero de' Medici, who had finally been roused from his directionless life of dissipation and taken up arms in Louis's forces. Further reinforcements under Trémoille departed from Milan, many of his soldiers grumbling about being sent south to Naples which, with some justification, they already perceived to be a lost cause. These reinforcements had all but reached Rome when news had arrived that Pope Alexander VI had died.

On 6 August, the Pope and his son Cesare had been guests at the villa of Cardinal Adriano Castellesi da Corneto, one of the nine new cardinals which Rodrigo Borgia had created in May, the sale of which (according to a report of the Venetian ambassador) had netted the impecunious Curia a handsome 130,000 ducats in simoniacal earnings. Cardinal Castellesi's villa was located just outside Rome and, although Rome was in the grip of a minor malarial epidemic that month, Castellesi's guests dined *al fresco* that evening. Things were going well for the Borgias in the Romagna and it was an occasion for celebrating their good fortune. As well as the income from the new cardinals, the Pope had also recently sent word to Duke Ercole d'Este of Ferrara that Cesare was to be named lord of Siena, Lucca and Pisa through the good offices of the French. Cesare's proud motto *Aut Caesar, aut nihil* ('Caesar or nothing!') seemed on the verge of coming true. On 11 August, which happened to be the eleventh anniversary of the Pope's accession, Venice's ambassador Antonio Giustinian recorded in his *Dispacci* that Alexander was not his usual ebullient self. The following day both father and son lay stricken with 'tertian fever' and the Pope was vomiting up copious amounts of bile. By 18 August, Cesare, the younger and physically stronger of the two, had recovered a little thanks to an impromptu ice bath which had lowered his fever. The chronicler Pietro Martire d'Anghiera, who had earlier described the voyages of Christopher Columbus to Cardinal Ascanio Sforza, recorded the subsequent 'cure' which was proscribed to Cesare by his doctors. A mule was eviscerated and Cesare was made to take a bath in its steaming entrails. By the evening of the same day, however, having received extreme unction from the Valencian bishop of Carinola, Pope Alexander VI was dead.

Malicious tongues would later wag that the Pope and his son had been struck down by their own poison (or else were poisoned by one of their enemies) but the reality was almost certainly far more mundane; that the pair had quite simply succumbed–unluckily both at the same time–to malaria or else some other common infection caused by the poor sanitation of the era. There was the question of the malarial epidemic around this time – indeed, just several days before on 1 August, the Pope's loyal nephew Juan Borgia Lanzol de Romaní, cardinal-archbishop of Monreale, had also succumbed to the disease, leading Alexander to comment to Antonio Giustinian that the month of August was 'a bad month for those who are fat', by which he of course meant himself. Cardinal Castellesi and some of his other dinner guests had also fallen sick following the gathering. However the rapid decomposition of the Pope's obese corpse and the way that his blackened tongue became swollen to twice its normal size would, in the centuries to come, continue to feed the historians' lurid rumours of cantarella poisoning.

Following Pope Alexander's death Rome descended into its customary lawless interlude of rioting and pillaging. Cesare's loyal lieutenant Don Miguel de Corella managed to secure several hundred thousand ducats worth of gold, silver and jewels from his dead father's chambers. However, by this time the Orsini and Colonna had also begun streaming back into the city where they presented a challenge to Cesare's 12,000-strong papal army. Cesare ordered that the Orsini palaces in the Monte Giordano district be fired as a warning, but the real damage was being done outside of Rome where Cesare had his fiefs. In Città di Castello, Perugia, Urbino, Camerino and Piombino and in the Romagna, Cesare's representatives were already being challenged and thrown out of power. Venice under the Doge Leonardo Loredan (so realistically painted by Giovanni Bellini for posterity) moved in and occupied both Rimini and Faenza. Still very sick, Cesare was forced to leave Rome for the duration of the papal conclave which would soon follow.

He cut a deal with King Louis XII to persuade the eleven Spanish cardinals to vote for France's main favourite for Pope, Cardinal Georges d'Amboise, and to serve Louis as his vassal. In return, the French king would support Cesare in regaining any cities and territories which he had recently lost. Cardinal Ascanio Sforza was also recently released from his French prison cell on the proviso that he too promised to vote for d'Amboise. Trémoille's French reinforcements were meanwhile ordered to remain outside the city of Rome while the members of the Sacred College secluded themselves in conclave. But when the doors closed and the Sacred College got down to its deliberations the Spanish cardinals refused to cooperate with the French king's scheme and instead voted for their own countryman Cardinal Bernardino de Carvajal. This split the vote three ways between the Spanish, the French and several Italian contenders. Realising that he now had no chance of being elected, and fearing the election of his rival Giuliano della Rovere (who commanded an impressive fifteen votes in the first round), Georges d'Amboise proposed instead a neutral third party candidate. On 22 September, the sixty-four-year-old Cardinal Francesco Todeschini Piccolomini was elected as pope. Piccolomini was the nephew of the late Æneas Silvius Piccolomini who had served as Pope Pius II, and in remembrance of his uncle he assumed the name of Pope Pius III.

Although the new pope, grateful for the support of Cesare Borgia's French and Spanish cardinals, undertook to maintain Cesare in the position of captain-general and *gonfaloniere* of the papal army, and agreed to endorse his fiefs in the Romagna, the welcome respite that his reign provided was ludicrously short and by 18 October he was dead. The cause of death was a suppurating ulcer on the Pope's left leg and his surgeons had unwisely cut into it thus unleashing an infection which engendered a raging fever. Cesare had only just returned to Rome from the safety of the Borgia family fief at Nepi on 3 October. He had with him only a small force of several hundred foot soldiers and 150 horse, having committed the remainder of his army to King Louis for the enterprise of Naples. In the Romagna, the Baglioni, the Appiano, the Vitelli, the Varano, the Malatesta and Giovanni Sforza of Pesaro were by now all inveigling their way back into their former possessions, often with the open connivance of Venice. Gonzalo de Córdoba, *El gran capitán*, had meanwhile issued an injunction against any Spaniards entering Cesare's service as the Borgia duke was openly supporting King Louis. Unfortunately this injunction resulted in the loss of some of Cesare's most talented Spanish commanders.

When Pope Pius III died, Cesare was at that moment blockaded inside the Castel Sant'Angelo, whence he had fled when rumours of a credible Spanish-Orsini kidnapping plot had reached his attention. Here he received a visit from Niccolò Machiavelli, who had been ordered by the *signoria* to observe and report on current events in Rome. Machiavelli, by now one of Valentino's most ardent admirers, was flabbergasted to witness his former hero broker a deal with his own nemesis, Cardinal Giuliano della Rovere. In return for the votes of the Spanish cardinals who had been elevated by Alexander VI, della Rovere promised to confirm both Cesare's Romagnol duchy as well as his powerful military position as captain-general of the Church. To Machiavelli, this was truly a deal with *il diavolo*, for Cardinal della Rovere had always proven himself to be the most relentless and implacable enemy of the House of Borgia. With precious little political leverage, however, the embattled Valentino now had no alternative but to make the unwelcome arrangement with his erstwhile adversary.

Matters gained their own momentum from this point. On 31 October, in a conclave that lasted barely ten hours, the shortest in history, Cardinal Giuliano della Rovere was elected pope. He had been virtually the universal choice amongst the cardinals. The only votes which he did *not* receive were from himself and Georges d'Amboise who, with dreams of the papal tiara, had hurriedly departed his station with the French army and rushed to Rome, only to be frustrated in his hopes for the second time in the course of a single year. Giuliano assumed the fighting name of Pope Julius II thereby implying that he sought to be Cesare Borgia's successor as 'Caesar'. He had waited many years for his chance and when it came he was ready.

The honeymoon period between Cesare Borgia and Pope Julius II proved, as Machiavelli had no doubt foreseen, to be pathetically short-lived. It began promisingly enough, with the two men discussing the possibility of a marriage alliance between their two families, and with Julius giving Valentino the fortress of Ostia as a naval base of operations from which to recapture his lost Romagnol towns. Not only were the former lords of the Romagna newly resurgent but, more worryingly for Rome, Venice had recently taken the opportunity of expanding its own influence into the vacuum created by Valentino's disarray. The Venetians under their Doge Leonardo Loredan felt blasé about their recent reconquests. They had nicknamed Pope Julius *il Veneziano* on account of his pro-Venetian sympathies and did not expect him to retaliate. How wrong they were. With the armies of France and Naples currently facing off across the Garigliano River in the south of Italy, Cesare and the Pope agreed that this was the most opportune moment to confront Venice and the lords of the Romagna. The Pope engineered a truce with both France and the

Holy Roman Empire and then promptly excommunicated Venice in preparation for Valentino's military offensive.

But although it looked on the surface as though the Pope was honouring his pledge to Cesare, Julius was privately considering using Cesare to first roll back the Venetians from the Romagna before disposing of his hated Borgia *gonfaloniere*. In fact, Julius had revealed as much to a mortified Niccolò Machiavelli, who had in turn passed the intelligence discreetly on to the Florentine *Signoria*, who as usual did nothing. Finally, after interminable delays in granting Valentino his necessary safe conduct pass through Tuscany, Cesare (who was by now growing increasingly disorientated by the Pope's habit of keeping him continually in the dark) assembled his forces at Ostia intending to take ship for Genoa. There he would take possession of a large banker's loan and raise troops in Lombardy before marching into the Romagna by way of Ferrara. But when he reached Ostia he was apprehended by two cardinal-emissaries of Pope Julius and ordered by the new pope to give up the passwords to his various fortresses across the Papal States. Refusing to comply, he was then seized by the admiral of the papal fleet, and brought back to Rome in chains. On 24 November, Pope Julius effectively declared the end of Cesare's duchy of the Romagna when he appointed Giovanni Sacchi as the territory's governor. Through guile and dissimulation, Pope Julius II had outwitted his old Borgia adversary who surpassed him in martial vigour.

By this time too, Valentino's former ally Louis XII of France was experiencing further bitter reversals in the conflict with Naples. By mid-November, King Louis's army had broken out from the port of Gaeta and advanced to the Garigliano River where it attempted to forge a bridgehead and engage the forces of Gonzalo de Córdoba who was patiently waiting for them on the far side. Amongst the French troops was Piero de' Medici 'the Unfortunate', wearing a suit of armour the cost for which had probably been begged from his brother the cardinal. The French, who were commanded by Francesco Gonzaga (who, unhelpfully for a general, did not even speak his troops' native tongue), threw a pontoon bridge across the Garigliano and gingerly began to cross over. The Spanish counter-attacked, however, and although the French managed to hold onto their bridgehead they were now hemmed in and could neither advance further nor bring across the rest of their troops.

A miserable month and a half of stalemate ensued in which incessant rains turned the camps of both armies into a quagmire and pestilential sickness ravaged the rank and file. On 28 December, Córdoba and Bartolomeo d'Alviano made their move with an army which had been augmented by the private militia of the Orsini, as well the many unpaid mercenaries who had deserted Cesare Borgia's army following Valentino's downfall. Building their own separate pontoon some distance upriver, the Spanish crossed in force and caught the unprepared main body of the French in the flank. Demoralised by the sneak attack, the French were unable to stand-to-arms and form up. On the far side of the French bridgehead those stranded soldiers, who were now engaged by the Spanish rear-guard under Diego de Mendoza, rushed back across the pontoon for dear life.

Piero de' Medici had been assigned to the artillery train. Most of the French artillery had been loaded onto boats to ferry them across the river but the surprise attack had left them vulnerable in the middle of the open water. The French tried as best they could to get their exposed cannon back across the river but a sudden storm and torrential downpour now capsized many of the small, unstable boats. One of these boats had been requisitioned by Piero de' Medici who, together with several other persons of rank, were attempting to evade a detachment of Spanish cavalry that had suddenly appeared on the riverbank. The boat, overloaded by both men and artillery, foundered and capsized in midstream and Piero, weighed down no doubt by his expensively heavy cuirass and the weapons which dangled from his belt, sank to the bottom of the Garigliano River and drowned.

Despite Piero's many failings both as a leader and as an individual his wife Alfonsina Orsini had continued to stand by him in exile together with her two children, the eleven-year-old Lorenzo and ten-year-old Clarice. Piero de' Medici's watery and premature death, which ended as imprudently and as calamitously as it had been lived, now left Cardinal Giovanni as patriarch of the exiled Medici. He now assumed the responsibility and cost of providing a suitable upbringing for his orphaned niece and nephew. The secular fortunes of the family would also now need to be promoted through his younger brother Giuliano, aged twenty-four. Happily, Piero's death had on the other hand served to disarm some of Florence's general hostility towards the Medici. Fortunately too for the cardinal he had fostered cordial relations with Cardinal della Rovere which now stood him in good stead not only to prosper under the latter's papacy, but also to pursue his family's political objectives under the official mantle of papal policy.

Cesare Borgia, who had escaped the clutches of Pope Julius only to fall into the hands of Gonzalo de Córdoba whilst attempting to take ship in Naples harbour, had by now been transported to Spain, to the remote Castillo de La Mota in Valladolid. Borgia would end his life as he had lived – with style and panache. Executing a dashing escape from La Mota he fled to the little kingdom of John III of Navarre, brother to his wife Charlotte d'Albret. John gladly hired this famous Italian warlord to lead a campaign against the Castilian encroachments of Ferdinand of Aragon and the count of Lerín. The Castilian-held town of Viana was besieged but the citadel refused to capitulate. In the early morning of 11 March 1507, a clutch of enemy men-at-arms rode out from the town's fortress and, enraged at their bare-faced audacity, Borgia rode off in pursuit. Finding in his enthusiasm for the chase that he had left his escort far behind, he suddenly found himself alone and surrounded by the enemy knights. Disfigured by syphilis, having lost his duchy of the Romagna, not to mention his paternal papal protector, and far from his wife and child, there was nothing else for Cesare to do but charge valiantly to his death and into the pages of legend. After the Castilian knights had killed Valentino, he was left on the ground naked but for a strip of cloth covering his genitals.

Pope Julius II was now facing the same essential difficulties as his two immediate predecessors, chief amongst which was the sustained unwonted interference of hostile outside powers in Italy's affairs. Cesare Borgia's former fiefs of Rimini and Faenza, along with Ravenna, were by now under the direct control of Venice. Technically these were still papal vicariates and Pope Julius was not about to acquiesce in their loss to the maritime republic. First, however, the Pope would turn his attention and his resources towards the capture of two other important papal cities, Perugia and Bologna where he would earn his well-deserved soubriquet *il pontefice terribile*.

When Queen Isabella of Spain died in November 1504, her consort Ferdinand of Aragon was supplanted as ruler of Castile by their daughter Joanna the Mad and their son-in-law Philip the Handsome, who was the son of the Emperor Maximilian. Bowing out gracefully from his governorship of Castile, Ferdinand left Spain and sailed for Naples with plans to transform the *Regno* from a re-conquered territory into an integrated component of his Aragonese realm. Upon his arrival in Italy the King took immediate measures to check the unrestrained power of his powerful viceroy Gonzalo de Córdoba who, as a native Castilian, represented the interests of his dead queen rather than his own. Ferdinand's mission was reconciliation and integration and he had even brought with him certain Angevin barons who were to be reincorporated within the realm in the interests of reunifying these different competing interests.

At the same time King Louis XII had also returned to Italy where he first set about deposing Giovanni Bentivoglio from Bologna. Bentivoglio was an especially cruel tyrant who was much feared in his city. In 1504, he had consulted his court astrologer, the *Napoletano* Luca Gaurico, about the destiny of his son Annibale but, disliking the astrologer's prediction, he had subjected Gaurico to the torture known as *Mancuerda*. This involved tying a thin cord around a victim's arm and tightening it until it cut right through to the bone (despite the dreadful injury, Gaurico went on to enjoy a renowned career, accurately predicting both the elevation of Pope Paul III and the death of Henry II of France in a joust). Becoming a prisoner of King Louis, Bentivoglio himself would end his days in the dungeons of the Castello Sforzesco. With the Bentivoglio now deposed, the French king moved next against Genoa which had lately rebelled against French overlordship.

In August 1505, the pro-Medici Orsini confederate Bartolomeo d'Alviano appeared in Tuscany with his 200 men-at-arms augmented by another 200 light cavalry. The expedition was made on his own initiative since King Ferdinand was still blocking his mission against Florence ostensibly in support of Pisa. Fortunately for Florence, however, their own *condottiere* Ercole Bentivoglio and the Florentine war commissioner Antonio Giacomini drew d'Alviano into an engagement at San Vincenti and routed the small Spanish force, thus bringing the threat to an abrupt end. In the aftermath of this victory, Antonio Giacomini regurgitated the bold promises made by Ercole Bentivoglio that he could follow it up with the conquest of Pisa itself. Giacomini's impassioned speech to the *signoria* in the Room of the Council, the Sala dei Dugento, was later graphically depicted by the painter Giorgio Vasari. The motion was approved and Ercole Bentivoglio laid siege to Pisa on 6 September 1505. The enterprise was a total fiasco. Florence's artillery knocked a hole in the city walls through which Bentivoglio's troops attempted to enter the city but they were beaten back by the *Pisani* with relative ease and, when news arrived from Piombino that more Spanish troops were on their way, Bentivoglio struck camp and the siege was ignominiously abandoned.

Niccolò Machiavelli's judgement on the whole affair was, as usual, scathing. 'Hence I suggest that there is no easier way to ruin a republic where the populace has power than to engage it in bold campaigns, because where the populace carries weight in the deliberations, bold campaigns will always be accepted', he railed. Antonio Giacomini and others who had advocated the latest siege attempt had been made to look like fools and their *condottiere's* poor performance can only have reinforced Florence's reservations about the effectiveness of mercenary services. The former chancellor Leonardo Bruni had also complained as much in his 1421 work *De Militia*. As classical humanists, many in Florence's government reminisced fondly on the patriotic commitment of the legionaries of the ancient Roman republic; these citizen-soldiers had fought doggedly and with ruthless professionalism on Rome's most inaccessible frontiers in order to bring Roman light and reason to the darkness of tribal barbarism. The advent of barbarian mercenary legions had, by contrast, ultimately spelled the end of the Western Roman Empire. The disappointment felt at Bentivoglio's poor performance can only have strengthened the government's determination to finalise the creation of an effective, professional standing army of their own. This had already been initiated even before the 1505 disaster at Pisa and the instigator was as usual Florence's chief asset, the far sighted secretary of the second chancery Niccolò Machiavelli.

By May 1504, Machiavelli had obtained the political support of Piero Soderini for the scheme for Florence to create its own independent standing militia. Skirting the approval of the Great Council and the Council of Eighty, Soderini told his protégé to simply go ahead and raise the necessary recruits on his own initiative. Relishing the prospect of this new adventure, Machiavelli leapt on his horse and did precisely that. Wisely, he opted to raise volunteers from the *contado* around the Mugello and Casentino. Infantrymen raised in the countryside, where there was a paucity of strongholds and fortifications, presented far less of a security risk than those recruited either in Florence itself or indeed its subject cities like Arezzo, Sansepolcro, Cortona, Volterra or Pistoia. Machiavelli's departure from Florence at this time was probably just as well. 1504 had been a plague year and, in an attempt to contain the contagion, the *signoria* had ordered that all prostitutes who had recently arrived from plague-ridden cities were to leave Florence. For Machiavelli, who enjoyed sampling the favours of new whores from the countryside, this had curtailed one of the political theorist's principal pastimes.

Less welcome news to the Florentines had been a rumour that Cesare Borgia's former henchman Don Miguel de Corella, widely known as 'the Strangler' due to his complicity in numerous Borgia assassinations, was being mooted as the possible commander of Machiavelli's new Florentine militia. Corella had been taken prisoner in November 1503 in the Romagna whilst fighting to shore up his Borgia master's crumbling dominions and had been brought to Florence and briefly imprisoned. In the event, however, nothing came of the proposal to put him in charge of Florence's army although later in 1505, after having been tortured in Rome by Pope Julius II for any inside information he could provide on the Borgia family, Machiavelli graciously mediated with the Holy Father for Corella's release and he was brought once more to Florence to occupy the position of *podestà*, or chief of police, which was always held by a suitably qualified foreigner.

By 15 February 1506, Machiavelli was able to parade 400 former peasants from the Mugello, now the core of a full-time Florentine militia, before the *signoria* of Florence. Dressed in their uniform of 'white doublet, stockings with a white-and-red pattern, white caps and slippers, and iron breastplates' they carried a lance as their main weapon. A few were also armed with the rudimentary matchlock firearm which the Dutch called the Hakkenbusse, the French called the harquebus, and the Italians called the *scopietti*. The crowds which had assembled to watch Machiavelli's military tattoo enthusiastically applauded the display as 'the finest thing that had ever been ordered for the city of Florence'. The professional *condottieri* of Italy would doubtless have been less impressed. The famous English mercenary Sir John Hawkwood, who had fought for Florence during the War of the Eight Saints in the 1370s, and also against Gian Galeazzo Visconti in the 1390s, had on one occasion rudely reprimanded the *signoria* for their amateurish interference in military matters: 'go and make cloth and let *me* manage the army', he had brusquely told them.

Florence's new martial spirit gained further propagandising through a new public statue which the *signoria* had earlier unveiled on 8 September 1504. This was of course the iconic statue of *David* which Michelangelo had been steadily working on since 1501. The work was carved from a single huge block of marble which the artists Agostino di Duccio and Antonio Rossellino had both previously owned and failed to do anything meaningful with. Yet, because of their earlier botched work, the marble block was already quite narrow by the time Michelangelo came to sculpt it and so it was decided to place it against the wall of the Palazzo della Signoria so as to conceal *David's* slender side profile. It was placed on a raised plinth outside the seat of government where Piero Soderini stopped by to view it. The symbolism it embodied, of a pensive David facing a mighty Goliath alone and unaided, could not have been more poignant to the Florentines in these isolated and troubled times. But towards one of the supreme artistic achievements of the Renaissance, Florence's *gonfaloniere* adopted the exasperating pose of the dilettante. 'Isn't his nose just a little too big?' Soderini had asked Michelangelo. The genius might well have been forgiven for flying into a fury over this unwonted criticism of his life's crowning masterpiece but for once he kept his composure. 'I agree', replied the sculptor. Kneeling down and scooping up a handful of dust from the *piazza*, he climbed the ladder and pretended to chip gently away at the nose, releasing small puffs of dust for added effect. 'Better?' he asked the *gonfaloniere a vita* when he had finished. 'It is now perfect!' replied the satisfied *padrone*.

In the summer of 1506, Cardinal Giovanni de' Medici together with twenty-four cardinals of the Holy Roman Church had accompanied Pope Julius II on his military expedition against Perugia and Bologna. The Umbrian tyrant of Perugia, Gian Paolo Baglioni, did not wait for the Holy Father to come to him but instead met the pontiff at Orvieto and abased himself before him. Permitting Gian Paolo to remain in Perugia, the Pope then occupied his city with his military entourage, which consisted of a mere 500 men-at-arms and a train containing the papal treasure, a singularly risky undertaking given Gian Paolo's unsavoury reputation for untrustworthiness and enterprising banditry. Proceeding next to Cesare Borgia's former stronghold of Cesena, the Pope had met with Cardinal d'Amboise who had colluded with his master the French king in the ousting of the Bentivoglio family whilst the Pope had simultaneously issued a bull of excommunication against the recalcitrant lord Giovanni Bentivoglio. The combined pressure allowed Pope Julius to move in and occupy the city of Bologna with his papal forces on 11 November 1506. Amongst the throng of *Bolognesi* jostling to watch the Pope enter the city in his magnificent suit of armour was, quite by chance, the Dutch humanist, theologian and correspondent of Cardinal de' Medici, Desiderius Erasmus. His personal impression of this forceful and worldly Pope led him to begin work on a satirical tract entitled *Julius Exclusus*–'Pope Julius excluded from Paradise'–which satirised a recently deceased Pope Julius II as trying to persuade Saint Peter to allow him to enter heaven using the same worldly and 'Machiavellian' tactics that he had applied whilst still alive. For diplomatic reasons, however, Erasmus consistently denied authorship of the tract for years afterwards.

King Louis of France and King Ferdinand of Aragon met at Savona in late June 1507. Here, discussions seem to have centred on the need to form an anti-Venetian coalition together with the Emperor Maximilian, Venice's traditional enemy. But the Emperor jumped the gun and unilaterally invaded Venetian Lombardy in February 1508 with–as was customary for Maximilian–grossly inadequate land forces. By this time the *condottiere* Bartolomeo d'Alviano had now left Spanish service and was serving as Venice's captain. D'Alviano was able to soundly defeat Maximilian's advance guard at Pieve di Cadore and Maximilian himself was prevented from advancing south to Verona by Niccolò Orsini da Pitigliano, whereupon the Emperor was forced to conclude a humiliating truce. The agreement entered into by Venice and the Empire was worded in such a way, however, that the French Crown was completely disregarded and Louis XII was now seriously motivated to settle all outstanding differences with Maximilian and create the tripartite pact which had been mooted earlier at Savona. The result was the League of Cambrai, which was concluded on 10 December 1508 between France, the Holy Roman Empire, Spain and the papacy in opposition to the Republic of Venice, which was placed under a papal interdict in April 1509.

Indeed, during this period, the forceful Pope Julius II was dominating all around him including the unfortunate artist Michelangelo. Their first meeting in Rome had been the model of a promising future relationship – Michelangelo devoutly deferential, the Pope benignly avuncular. Julius commissioned him to build him a splendid tomb and Michelangelo had vowed to build him one worthy of the ancient Roman Caesars; in March 1505 he disappeared into the quarries of Carrara to seek out the perfect marble for the massive task. While he was gone, Julius got caught up in the other project to rebuild St. Peter's basilica. Placed in charge of designing the imposing new structure was the architect Donato d'Angelo Lazzari, whose constant petitioning of the Pope for building projects earned him the name by which he is more popularly known, Bramante, from the Italian word *bramare* meaning 'to yearn or solicit'. Many commented that Julius had only commissioned the new basilica in order to accommodate the ostentatious thirty-six feet high tomb, incorporating forty life-size statues which Michelangelo had promised the Pope. When Buonarroti returned to Rome he found that the tomb project had been cancelled and his formerly free and open access to the Pope was now severely curtailed. Donato Bramante had persuaded the Pope that it was bad luck to have one's mausoleum crafted during one's own lifetime, thereby diverting the pontiff's attention to his own more important project – the rebuilding of the Vatican.

The first stone of this great new basilica had been laid by Pope Julius II on 18 April 1506, and Julius would also set up a special commission, the *constitution Liquet omnibus*, to supervise the reconstruction. But the day before the cornerstone ceremony Michelangelo had fled back to Tuscany in a huff. Angrily, Julius sent his official papal despatch riders to order the artist back to Rome but Buonarroti stood on his pride and continued to hide out in Florence. When Julius marched against Bologna in 1506, the Florentines grew scared that Michelangelo was a liability who was placing their city in danger. Piero Soderini made an approach to the artist, complaining that the Pope was applying pressure on the *signoria* to return to him Florence's most famous resident artist. Michelangelo irritably replied that he would as sooner accept a commission from the Sultan to construct a bridge between Pera and Constantinople than return to work for the Pope; however Soderini had eventually induced Michelangelo to at least meet with Julius at Bologna and he had gone there in November when the Pope made his victorious entry to the conquered city. With letters of presentation in the name of Piero's brother, Cardinal Soderini, Michelangelo was presented to the Pope, who complained that the artist had waited for His Holiness to come to *him* (since Bologna was closer to Florence than Rome) rather than having the initiative to go to Rome when summoned. But in the end all was forgiven. The Pope commissioned the artist to fabricate a large bronze statue of himself, which turned out to be greatly favoured by the Supreme Pontiff. When Michelangelo asked whether he should place a book in the figure's left hand Pope Julius had replied 'Give me a sword, for I am not a man of letters!' Like the bronze reserved for Leonardo's equestrian statue, the bronze Pope Julius would eventually fall prey to Alfonso d'Este's munitions foundry, melted down to create a cannon christened 'the Julius'. The duke of Ferrara kept the Pope's bronze head, however, placing it in his cabinet – indicative perhaps of some symbolic triumph of Ferrara over the papacy.

In March 1508, Michelangelo–who had by now returned to Rome–had experienced a huge argument with Julius over the latter's constant interruptions and alterations to his on-going work on the Pope's tomb. Julius had already convinced himself that instead of completing the tomb he wanted Buonarroti to commence work on the ceiling frescos of the Sistine Chapel, the building which had been built by his uncle Pope Sixtus IV. The Pope commanded a reluctant Michelangelo, who regarded himself primarily as a sculptor rather than a painter, to commence work on the vault of the Sistine Chapel. Poor Buonarroti did everything in his power to avoid and abscond from the enforced commission and yet in the end he had no choice but to comply. It would prove to be perhaps the most epic achievement of his career, but he would be plagued at every turn by his nemesis Bramante who not only questioned his ability to complete the work but drilled holes in the ceiling to anchor the scaffolding which he'd constructed for the artists to work. The most famous panel from the Sistine Ceiling was destined to be that of God reaching out from the angelic heavenly realms and touching the finger of a recumbent Adam to infuse him with the gift of life. But while Michelangelo was celebrating the ultimate iconic act of divine creation, God's children were perpetrating the ultimate act of destruction here on earth.

On 14 May 1509, the vanguard of a League army led by King Louis XII caught up with the rear-guard of a Venetian army under the command of d'Alviano and da Pitigliano near the town of Agnadello, just twenty-four miles from Milan. The Venetians were around 30,000 men with a core of Romagnol pike infantry trained in Swiss methods, whilst the French had around 25,000 troops comprising mostly Swiss pikemen. The French troops had hemmed in d'Alviano's men on three sides and proceeded to destroy them piecemeal. When d'Alviano led his men-at-arms against the French centre, where the King himself was stationed, they were thrown back and in the fog of battle d'Alviano himself was captured. Louis had ordered that no enemy prisoners be taken that day and when the smoke had finally settled over the battlefield the countryside was found to be littered with thousands of Venetian corpses.

Following the dramatic events at Agnadello the Emperor and Alfonso d'Este of Ferrara took up the offensive in the Veneto, taking back the Polesine and advancing upon Friuli where towns such as Cividale, Udine and Treviso stubbornly refused to capitulate. At this point the Venetians saw the writing on the wall and assessed that, in a tactical sense, it would be preferable to surrender their contested lands and cities on *terra ferma* to the Emperor (and seize them back later) than to risk King Louis's deeper involvement. This was basically due to the fact that, to Venetian eyes, the French were judged to be far more formidable enemies than the imperial forces. It was also more prudent to maintain the Venetian army intact for a hypothetical defence of Venice rather than split it up into penny packets for the separate defence of their individual cities and possessions. Venice's Great Council therefore instructed their cities of Verona, Vicenze and Padua to surrender to the imperial forces and a minor farce now ensued when the Venetian officials realised that there were no imperial troops in the vicinity to whom they could surrender!

The Battle of Agnadello and its aftermath signalled the loss of virtually the entirety of Venice's acquisitions over a hundred year period on the Italian mainland. As such it was an absolutely devastating blow to the maritime republic. For their own part, those cities which had reverted to the Holy Roman Empire were largely thankful that Venetian tyranny had been replaced by imperial rule. The élite of those cities envisioned a situation similar to the semi-autonomous imperial city-states of the Holy Roman Empire, where the Emperor himself exercised only a distant, 'hands-off' style of overlordship. Venice herself used the lull period to reorganise its city militia for the defence of the lagoons. Many of the Venetian oligarchs were unhappy that Venice's aggressive policy of territorial expansion in Lombardy since the time of Doge Francesco Foscari had ultimately amounted to nothing. They were not so much disappointed that lands had been lost; rather that Venice–whose main strength lay in the maritime arena–had succeeded in making so many powerful enemies on dry land. Nevertheless Venice's resilient and combative spirit remained undaunted. By December 1509, Niccolò Machiavelli–who was at this time on a diplomatic mission to Mantua and Verona–was reporting back to the *signoria* that whenever Venice captured a new city the Lion of St. Mark was depicted as holding a sword in its paw rather than a book.

While King Louis XII was basking in his victory over the Venetians at Agnadello the Pope was in action against the rebellious fiefs of the Romagna. These were soon recaptured and Venice, still greatly weakened and in the process of regrouping, wisely decided not to contest them. By June, the Apulian ports demanded by the kingdom of Naples were also surrendered and restored to King Ferdinand. Like Lorenzo de' Medici before him, Pope Julius II had a fine grasp of geopolitics and understood the importance of maintaining a balance of power in Italy. Just as Lorenzo and Cosimo de' Medici before him had been able to determine the best long-term strategy for Florence, so Julius could be counted upon to engage secular policies and alliances that benefited Rome and the Papal States above all else. He was also seemingly unencumbered by that species of rampant nepotism which had so bedevilled his uncle Pope Sixtus's reign or the reign of Pope Alexander VI. But, as Julius II himself saw it, he was also working towards a much wider objective, namely the liberation of the Italian peninsula from *all* foreign subjection. The League of Cambrai had been a first step in this process and was instrumental in checking Venice's growing power in Lombardy, the Romagna and the territory of the Marches. Despite a concerted resurgence of Venetian efforts between 1509 and 1510, that objective had now largely been achieved and Pope Julius magnanimously lifted Venice's excommunication in February 1510.

The Pope's chief concern now was to prevent northern Italy from being carved up between the two European superpowers ruled by his erstwhile allies King Louis XII and the Emperor Maximilian. It was therefore now deemed opportune for Julius to abandon his former alliance with France and the Empire and bolster an embattled Venice, whilst at the same time maintaining friendly relations with the House of Aragon as well as the Swiss cantons. To this end the Pope had already re-opened diplomatic channels with the Venetians and by the late summer of 1509 Rome had no less than six Venetian ambassadors in residence. This constant shifting of alliances as the situation and opportunity dictated was of course nothing new in this era; indeed it was something of a leitmotif of the times. Pope Julius had also placed Ferrara squarely in his gun sights. Strictly speaking the city was a papal fief, although still contested by Venice, and Alfonso d'Este was receiving disconcertingly strong backing from King Louis of France.

Watching these developments from Florence, Niccolò Machiavelli broadly disagreed with the Pope's strategy of disengaging from France and the Empire and seeking to liberate Italy entirely from foreign dominion. When his friend Francesco Vettori mooted the possibility of a unification of Italian states against foreign domination his response had been 'don't make me laugh!' On the contrary, he regarded it as a largely destabilising move which would result in the much fuller domination of Italy by either France or Spanish Naples. To Machiavelli, the better course of action was to leave France in control of Milan and Spain in control of the *Regno* and thereby preserve the status quo. Then, if one side or other gained the upper hand, the independent Italian city-states could intervene to redress the balance as necessary. Machiavelli had not at this point evolved into the ardent Italian patriot that he was later to become, a mind-set which would later be shared by his humanist compatriots Giovanni Pontano, Marino Sanuto the Younger, Bernardo Rucellai or Bernardino Corio; intellectuals who in the fullness of time all came to realise the sheer magnitude of the calamity facing Italy from the continued presence of these hostile foreign armies.

But Julius II's inconvenient policies were meanwhile already placing Florence in a difficult corner. Not only would the Pope's end-game surround Florence with papal possessions but the republic was also being forced to choose between two evils. Noting that the papacy was distancing itself from him, King Louis demanded that Florence openly declare its allegiance to France. Meanwhile, from Milan, a beleaguered Cardinal d'Amboise was calling loudly for the assistance of Florentine troops. For Florence to have publicly sided with King Louis at this point would have left her highly vulnerable to attack from the Pope's forces. Not only was Julius firmly supportive of Cardinal Giovanni de' Medici, but the latter had by this time embarked upon an adroit charm offensive in Rome designed to win over the former Florentine enemies of his brother Piero the Unfortunate. If the Pope and the Medici were to combine their resources and move against Florence together, then the French army lay disconcertingly far away. Machiavelli was assigned to negotiate personally with the French king on Florence's complicated situation and he arrived back in Lyons in July 1510.

This was not Machiavelli's first diplomatic mission to France of course. As the reader will recall, he had first met King Louis XII and Cardinal Georges

411

d'Amboise in France a decade ago. This latest mission, nevertheless, was his greatest diplomatic challenge to-date. At least this time he was designated as Florence's fully-fledged ambassador. The main problem was the widening rift between France and the papacy, which was forcing Florence to choose between them. Piero Soderini had instructed Machiavelli to implore Louis to preserve cordial relations with the Pope whilst simultaneously undermining Venice and keeping on the good side of the Emperor. But ultimately the *signoria's* strategy was based on the desire to delay making any decision one way or another and to play for time, even though time was not on Florence's side. Machiavelli, who firmly maintained that Florence's security lay not in neutrality but in a continued alliance with France, now recommended a diplomatic initiative which would serve to place Florence in the most positive diplomatic light for that future eventuality. He proposed a peace conference between the two sides mediated by Florence. If the mediation was successful then Florence could bask in her role as arbiter of concord. If, on the other hand, the Pope were to reject the outstretched laurel then both France and Florence could gain merit in the combined eyes of Europe by at least having attempted to secure a peace. Their subsequent war on the Pope would therefore be regarded as both morally and diplomatically justified.

Predictably perhaps, Pope Julius rejected the offer of mediation out of hand, dismissing the Florentine ambassadors with the accusation that the republic was doing all in its power to thwart his efforts to free Italy from foreign domination. With conflict now inevitable, Machiavelli tried desperately to convince the *signoria* in his correspondence that to remain on the fence could only result in one conceivable outcome – Florence would be crushed between the adversarial forces of France and the Pope. It was necessary to choose a side and manage events in such a way that Florence itself would not be left undefended. To this end he briefed his French counterparts that the Florentine army must not under any circumstances be sent outside of Tuscany to support Cardinal d'Amboise in Milan. He argued that Florence's troops were of more value if used to hamper the Pope's operations within Tuscany than they were if dispersed to Lombardy and, although the French were at first sceptical, thanks to Machiavelli's persuasiveness and his diplomatic finesse, they eventually came round to his line of reasoning. By October 1510, the talented Florentine diplomatist had safely returned to Florence.

Meanwhile, by this time open war had broken out and Pope Julius had unleashed his offensive against the European powers by means of some underhand plays. Firstly, Genoa was encouraged in its rebellion against French rule and 10,000 Swiss mercenaries were procured in the cantons to menace Louis's general positions in Lombardy. Then, the Pope moved against Ferrara and the d'Este. With around 10,000 foot soldiers and 1,000 men-at-arms under the joint command of the papal legate Cardinal Francesco Alidosi and the Pope's nephew Francesco Maria della Rovere, Duke of Urbino, Julius advanced first to d'Este's second city of Modena, which was captured, and thenceforth moved against Bologna on 22 September 1510. Reinforcements were despatched to the Pope from a Venetian army in the Polesine and King Ferdinand sent an additional 100 men-at-arms under Fabrizio Colonna. When the king of France's commander, Charles Chaumont d'Amboise, went to lay siege to Bologna the *Bolognesi* fortified their city against France's re-imposition of the detested Bentivoglio family and he withdrew, reluctant to besiege a city which was under the personal command of the pope of Rome. Pope Julius's next victory was over the town of Mirandola, which was under the lordship of the Pico family. The town capitulated on 20 January 1511 and the Pope patrolled the streets in person to prevent his troops from running amok and sacking it. Julius was a capable and decisive military commander but he was not so fortunate in those who commanded beneath him. His on-going operations were especially bedevilled by a damaging feud which had arisen between his nephew the duke of Urbino and his secretary and legate Cardinal Francesco Alidosi.

Francesco Maria della Rovere was the son of Duke Guidobaldo da Montefeltro's sister Giovanna and Pope Julius II's brother Giovanni della Rovere. At Pope Sixtus IV's behest the heirless Guidobaldo had reluctantly agreed to adopt his nephew as his son and heir; when Guidobaldo subsequently died in 1508, Francesco Maria duly acceded to the title of duke of Urbino and also recovered his own private patrimony of Senigallia following the downfall of Cesare Borgia. That same year, Francesco Maria married Eleonora Gonzaga, the daughter of Francesco II Gonzaga, Marquess of Mantua, and Isabella d'Este (who was the late Duke Ercole's daughter). The eighteen-year-old duke's nemesis, however, was Cardinal Alidosi, a prelate who was already notorious for his diplomatic short-sightedness and cruelty (Pietro Bembo later described him with the damning words that 'Faith meant nothing to him, nor religion, nor trustworthiness, nor shame, and there was nothing in him that was holy'.) Upon being appointed papal legate of Bologna on 27 June 1508, Cardinal Alidosi had ordered Alberto Castelli, Innocenzo Ringhieri, Sallustio Guidotti and Bartolomeo Magnani to be strangled. The four accused men had been charged with a plot to return the Bentivoglio to power and were executed along with over thirty other local suspects, an act which had greatly alienated the *Bolognesi* from their new papal rulers. When, in early May 1511, the Pope relocated from Bologna to Ravenna, the disaffected *Bolognesi* immediately revolted, Giovanni Bentivoglio returned as ruler and Cardinal Alidosi fled the city to re-join his master, Pope Julius II.

The duke of Urbino had already twice attempted to have Cardinal Alidosi arrested and arraigned on charges of treason. When, on a papal mission to the court of King Louis, the French monarch had elevated him without papal approval to the bishopric of Cremona, it had been widely rumoured that Alidosi was in Louis's pay. The duke of Urbino had him arrested on 7 October 1510 and then again on 28 October but, on both occasions, Alidosi had used his close relationship with Julius II to wangle his way free. Now that Bologna had fallen, instead of assigning the obvious blame to Alidosi for having estranged the citizenry, Pope Julius's rash response was to instead assign the blame to his nephew Francesco Maria. Matters came to a head on 24 May 1511, when the Duke and his entourage met with the cardinal and his own followers just as the latter was hastening to a supper engagement with the Pope. When the cardinal's salute to Francesco Maria was misconstrued as a gesture of rudeness, some *bravi* in the Duke's party struck the cardinal from his mule and killed him with a blow to the head. Amidst this unnecessary crisis in his court affairs, Pope Julius later appointed Cardinal de' Medici as Cardinal Alidosi's replacement as papal legate to Bologna and also the Romagna on 1 October 1511.

The Holy League between Pope Julius II, King Ferdinand II and Venice was declared in Rome in October 1511. It simply made official the ruptures which had already been tearing northern Italy apart since after the Battle of Agnadello. Louis XII's latest strategy, an attempt to call a Church council at Pisa to repudiate the Pope, had caused Julius considerable personal offence but, aside from the support of a handful of estranged cardinals who had flocked to Louis's side led by Cardinal Bernardino López de Carvajal, the schismatic council had been largely ignored by the Italian clergy. Even the Florentines, who had been pressured by France to hold the *conciliabulum* at Pisa (which was finally back under Florence's control once again), were less than enthusiastic towards the French king's move and refused to compel their own clergy to attend. The Pope's war against France and the Emperor would pit his papal and Venetian troops, augmented by the Spanish under the new viceroy of Naples, Raimondo de Cardona, against the king of France's talented twenty-two-year-old nephew, Gaston de Foix. The latter now opened the ball with considerable panache.

Moving with lightning speed, de Foix's first act was to quickly relieve a siege of Bologna by Cardona. Next, he moved with equal swiftness to reconquer the city of Brescia, which had fallen to the Venetians, and his three-day sacking of that city in February 1512 was sadly one of the worst atrocities of the entire Italian Wars. King Louis then commanded de Foix to bring the reluctant Spanish army to a decisive engagement and defeat it conclusively. This was necessary in light of the fact that England's King Henry VIII, encouraged by his own separate alliance with King Ferdinand, had by now joined the Holy League and was planning his own invasion of France. In November 1511, Ferdinand and his son-in-law Henry had concluded the Treaty of Westminster, pledging mutual assistance between the two against both France and Navarre. By the summer of 1512 Henry, who dreamed of regaining the English Crown's ancestral lands in France, would launch a joint expedition to the Aquitaine in conjunction with Ferdinand (who would cynically use the eager young English king to safeguard his own flank while he campaigned against France in Navarre). It was imperative therefore for de Foix to smash the Spanish forces in Italy so that Louis XII could turn against his enemies' incursions in the French homeland. Gaston de Foix elected to undertake this objective in the vicinity of Ravenna.

On 11 April 1512, Cardinal Giovanni de' Medici accompanied the 20,000 Spanish and papal troops of Raimondo de Cardona and Alonso Carvajal as they dug in along the River Ronco to the south of the city of Ravenna, which was left fortified by Marcantonio Colonna and 1,500 men. Meticulously, they prepared a strong defensive position behind a long curving trench with their backs to the river and inside this they drew up their infantry, artillery, men-at-arms and Balkan *stradioti*. The French under Gaston de Foix crossed the river by pontoon and took up positions immediately facing the Spanish entrenchments. The French fielded around 30,000 troops and twice the cannon of the Spaniards thanks to the participation of Alfonso d'Este and his famous Ferrarese artillery. The Spanish had also been left short-handed due to the conduct of the captain-general of the Papal States, Francesco Maria della Rovere. Churlishly refusing to be placed under the overall command of the Spanish viceroy Cardona, the duke of Urbino had failed to put in an appearance at Ravenna.

The young Cardinal de' Medici, however, did not fail to distinguish himself by riding up and down the rank and file on a white palfrey, all the while admonishing the Spanish soldiers to fight well for the Pope. Not long afterwards the cannonade began. For two terrifying hours the artillery on either side pummelled one another with iron and stone shot. Within their defensive

414

position the Spanish infantrymen lay down in the mud to evade the projectiles tearing through their ranks, but the vulnerable Spanish cavalry to their rear were unable to emulate this and the bombardment soon ripped gaping holes in their squadrons. Unable to withstand the horror of seeing their cavalry reduced to a mass of dead riders and mangled horses the Spanish men-at-arms emerged from their positions behind the trench and charged the more disciplined French horse. As Jacopo Guicciardini wrote vividly to his brother Francesco: 'The Spaniards, seeing themselves wasted and destroyed without breaking a lance, rushed forward and with arms in hand gave battle at close quarters. It lasted about four hours, during the first two of which it was terrible, savage, and almost all the men-at-arms of the first squadron were killed, and many of those of the second.' Meanwhile, the French *landsknechts* moved in to engage the Spanish infantrymen who were dug in behind both the ditch as well as a line of bladed, fortified carts together with their harquebusiers. Pierfilippo Pandolfini in *Desjardins and Canestrini II* recorded that the Spanish withered under de Foix's frontal onslaught and, when the victorious French horse and rear-guard joined in the attack, Cardona and Carvajal abandoned their defeated army and fled the battlefield, Cardona taking with him around 200 badly needed men-at-arms.

By mid-afternoon casualties were upwards of 16,000 men according to Pandolfini, around 4,000 on the French side and 12,000 on the Spanish. Ravenna was the first occasion in which field artillery had been use decisively and *en masse* in a military engagement and thanks to their superiority in this arm the French had prevailed. The cannon had taken a particularly heavy toll on the Spanish heavy cavalry, scattering a maelstrom of bloodied heads, arms, legs and breastplates as well as the sundry body parts of their horses across the Spanish side of the battlefield. The French commander Gaston de Foix was himself butchered as he led a cavalry charge against one of the final stubborn Spanish infantry units. By the same token, the cream of the Holy League's commanders had been either killed or else captured and those taken into captivity included such figures as Pedro Navarro, Marcantonio Colonna, Fernando Francesco d'Ávalos, and Cardinal Giovanni de' Medici himself. Cardinal de' Medici was taken prisoner whilst performing ministrations and supreme unction for the dying soldiery of the battlefield.

Giovanni was transferred by the French from Ravenna, which had been all but destroyed during the engagement, to Bologna where Annibale II Bentivoglio and his brother Ermes treated him well, considering he was an ecclesiastic, despite the Pope's persecution of their family *capo* Giovanni. After Bologna he was taken thereafter to Modena where Annibale's sister Bianca Rangone generously pawned her jewellery to raise funds for his upkeep. Eventually the cardinal reached Milan, where he was provided with comfortable accommodation in the home of Cardinal Federigo Sanseverino, the son of Roberto da Sanseverino d'Aragona, former captain-general of the papal army, and his second wife Elisabetta da Montefeltro. Obtaining permission from a distracted Sanseverino for his cousin Giulio de' Medici to pay him a visit, the cardinal carefully instructed his kinsman Giulio to go immediately to Rome and report to Pope Julius both the death of Gaston de Foix and the ragged state of the French army. Giulio's report proved timely as the Pope, believing that all had been lost, had been seriously contemplating fleeing Rome by taking ship from Ostia. The Pope had good reason to be afraid; had Gaston de Foix survived the battle his victorious troops would almost certainly have pressed forward to Rome – the epicentre of the Holy League. However, paralysed by the loss of their charismatic leader and short on supplies, the French squandered their victory by lingering in the Emilia-Romagna.

Although the Battle of Ravenna was adjudged to have been a great French victory (Cardona's entire Spanish army having been practically annihilated and the Florentines having rung their bells loudly, just as they had done after Venice's defeat at Agnadello), nobody was quite prepared for the sudden French collapse which came shortly thereafter. Watching from the sidelines and impressed by the extent of anti-French sentiment in northern Italy, the Swiss cantons now decided to throw in their lot with the Holy League, not as hired mercenaries mind you, but as fully fledged members of the alliance itself. The chief architect of the Swiss intervention was the fiercely anti-French bishop of Sion, Cardinal Matthäus Schinner. As always, the isolated Swiss cantons were primarily motivated by the need to keep open their access to their primary food and trading source, the fertile Plain of Lombardy. The key to maintaining Swiss access to Lombardy had traditionally been the towns of Bellinzona and Domodossola which controlled several crucial Alpine passes including the important Simplon Pass. The Swiss had also lately come to question their traditional role as a source of paid mercenaries for the French king. French domination of Lombardy did not necessarily work in their favour and an anti-French faction had arisen within the cantons which sought greater independence of action.

Pope Julius II's Holy League was a natural ally to this new Swiss faction which was opposed to French supremacy. To Pope Julius, Schinner had advised: 'We know the Swiss malady; it is promptly cured with money', meaning that the Swiss would gladly work for whoever paid them. Sir Thomas More had said much the same thing in *Utopia* (1506) when he wrote of the Swiss: 'They go forth of their country in great companies together, and whosoever lacketh soldiers, there they proffer their service for small wages. This is the only craft they have to get their living by. They maintain their life by seeking their death.' As a result, Julius II had kept sufficient funds flowing in the direction of the Swiss cantons to ensure that their newfound ideological support against their former French allies remained suitably fervent (Louis XII meanwhile turned to their bitter rivals the lowland Swabian *landsknechts* for an alternative pool of mercenary support). A 20,000-strong Swiss army under Baron von Hohensax and Jacob Stapfer descended into Lombardy by the Brenner Pass. Marching along the shores of Lake Garda, they linked up with a smaller Venetian army on 1 June, occupied Verona, and proceeded to outflank the French under their new supreme commander Jacques de La Palisse. The latter found that he could only muster around 10,000 foot and 700 lances in response to the Swiss threat and, when the Emperor ordered 4,000 German *landsknechts* to leave French service, the unfortunate French general lost his best troops. The Bentivoglio family quit Bologna for good on 10 June and the French army retired to Pavia where it subsequently came under siege. Realising that his position was now untenable, La Palisse capitulated and withdrew from the city.

Such was the sheer enthusiasm of the Swiss to chase the French from Italy that the skirmish lines of the Swiss *enfants perdus* had stripped off their clothes and swam the freezing streams, halberds in hand, in an effort to get at the enemy. But thanks to an opportune disagreement between the Swiss and Venetian troops as to who should take the honour of evicting the French army from Lombardy, La Palisse managed to extricate himself from the closing net and his troops reached the safety of France by early July. With the French expelled from Lombardy their influence rapidly crumbled. Genoa quickly wrested their independence from French domination with Venetian assistance and the former exile Giano Campofregoso became Doge of the city. The Swiss meanwhile set about restoring the Sforza. Cardinal Schinner entered Cremona and extracted an indemnity of 40,000 ducats from the city, with which he paid off his Swiss troops. When he went to Pavia, Schinner received a deputation of citizens from Milan, who petitioned for the restoration of *il Moro's* son, Massimiliano Sforza, as their duke. Agreeing to the petition, Schinner left about 600 Swiss behind to protect the newly installed duke and the rest of his army trudged back across the Alpine passes to their cantons laden with booty.

The French had meanwhile brought their valuable hostage Giovanni de' Medici, Cardinal-Legate of Bologna, with them on their final retreat from Italy but he was spared the indignity of ransoming or of ending his days as a hostage in France. Thanks to the intervention of a friendly priest named Bengallo and two local magnates named Rinaldo Zazzi and Ottaviano Isimbardi a diversion was created just as Giovanni was about to board a barge across the River Po at a small village named Cairo. In the confusion, the cardinal managed to evade his French captors and–improbably disguised as a soldier–he went into hiding as the French angrily scoured the surrounding Piedmontese *contado* for their prized prisoner. Isimbardi then brought the fugitive to the dwelling of his friend, Bernardo Malespina and sought his assistance in hiding him but, to the cardinal's horror, instead of being given a room, fresh clothes and food and water, he was instead locked up in Malespina's filthy pigeon-coop. Unbeknownst to Isimbardi, his friend Bernardo Malespina was in fact a clandestine French sympathiser. Although Isimbardi pleaded at length with his friend to release Giovanni he replied that the best he could do was notify France's *Milanese condottiere* Giangiacomo Trivulzio about his captive and ask his advice on what to do. But the Italian Trivulzio, although in service to the French, was so impressed to learn of the cardinal's courageous escape attempt that he wrote back to Malespina giving him a nod and a wink for the prisoner's release. Obligingly, Malespina left the pigeon-coop gate conveniently ajar one evening so that the cardinal could slip away to freedom.

The sudden collapse of the French in Italy left the members of the Holy League unprepared as to what should now be done with those territories formerly under French protection. Pope Julius, for instance, still coveted Ferrara and summoned Alfonso d'Este to Rome where he was absolved by the Pope whilst at the same time being pressured to relinquish control of his city. D'Este's response was to slip away from Rome under the protection of Fabrizio and Prospero Colonna and by October he was defiantly back in his duchy. King Ferdinand meanwhile wished to maintain the Spanish army on Italian soil so that he could have a say in the disposal of Lombard territory, yet all the same he was hard pressed for funding and neither the Pope nor the Venetians would agree to subsidise his troops. At a conference held at Mantua it was agreed with Maximilian's representative Cardinal Lang that Ferdinand would cooperate with the Emperor in settling the affairs of Lombardy, but before this it was decided, with some additional persuasion from Cardinal Giovanni de' Medici, that the Spanish army would march to Florence and reinstate the Medici regime there.

With a sanguine Cardinal Giovanni de' Medici in tow, Raimondo de Cardona trudged into Tuscany with 5,000 foot and two-hundred men-at-arms but no papal reinforcements. On 28 August 1512, his famished troops reached the town of Prato which the Florentine *signoria* had reinforced with several thousand of Machiavelli's full-time peasant militiamen. As early as 1502, when the government had extended the office of the *gonfaloniere* to a life term, Niccolò Machiavelli had (as we have seen) argued that no city could defend itself with prudence alone, when prudence was unsupported by force. The presence of an unreliable ally in Louis XII of France alongside adversaries like Cesare Borgia, Venice and even Spain, made it imperative that Florence should be able to defend herself without having to depend on the traditional system of hiring expensive and unreliable *condottieri*. He took to rhetoric to state his case, giving the example of the fall of Constantinople to the Turk in 1453. In peacetime the Byzantine *basileus* Constantine XI Palaiologos had appealed to the citizens for funds to upgrade the city's armed forces but the people had merely laughed at him. But when the Turk appeared outside the walls of the metropolis those same citizens now panicked and ran to the *basileus* imploring him for his help, whereat he sent them away telling them 'Go die with your money in your pockets, since you did not wish to live without it'. Machiavelli was implying that the anecdote was as valid in the case of Florence as it had been in the case of the (now fallen and defunct) Christian capital of the East. Florence's government was being told in no uncertain terms to prepare for future military challenges or else face the dire consequences.

Niccolò Machiavelli's creation of Florence's first standing army, whose initial test was to be at Prato, was a sensible and well-intentioned gesture but in reality the hastily raised and drilled peasant militia from the Tuscan *contado* were no match for the experienced, battle-hardened veterans of Raimondo de Cardona. When the Spaniard's few artillery pieces knocked a small breach in Prato's town wall near the Mercatale gate his troops tried to enter but were initially repelled by the Florentine troops supported by the *Pratesi*. However, the Spaniards were renowned throughout Italy for their dogged ferocity during siege assaults and they now scaled the walls and succeeded in gaining entry to the town. They quickly overpowered the ill-trained and badly-equipped defenders who fled like sheep before ravening wolves. As Cardinal Giovanni wrote matter-of-factly to Pope Julius the following day: 'This day (29 August), at sixteen of the clock, the town was sacked, not without some bloodshed, such as could not be avoided ... the capture of Prato, so speedily and cruelly, although it has given me pain, will at least have the good effect of serving as an *example* and a *deterrent* to the others [italics added].'

Giovanni's words are self-censuring and the reality of the town's fall was, unhappily, considerably less restrained and altogether more horrific. The Spaniards, whose ranks included large numbers of Muslim mercenaries, proceeded to subject Prato to two days of unrestrained, merciless violence and barbarism. 'It was not a struggle', commented the historian Nardi on the atrocity, 'it was sheer butchery'. Niccolò Machiavelli later cited the incident in a letter dated 16 September. He related anecdotes from the refugees themselves which revealed the full horror of what had transpired in Prato. Around 4,000 people had been slaughtered and innumerable rapes and sacrilegious acts had been committed against women and sacred places in the town. 'It would be a lamentable thing to narrate the great cruelty they did there', said Jacopo Guicciardini, adding: 'women raped and ransomed, boys sodomised, and all the monasteries turned into brothels'. As the nineteenth-century *Pratese* writer Cesare Guasti recorded the words of a contemporary eyewitness, one Pistofilo, a secretary to Cardinal Ippolito d'Este, *'O Dio! O Dio! O Dio! Che crudeltà!'* ('Oh God, oh God, oh God, what cruelty!')

The citizens of Florence learned of the sacking of Prato from the steady stream of refugees, who arrived at their walls complaining luridly of unrestrained rape, torture, killing, looting and burning. The commune's government quite literally collapsed overnight. Piero Soderini received the brunt of it. 'The city here was full of confusion and fear because the *gonfaloniere* governed matters as usual ... many *uomini da bene* were dissatisfied', declared Jacopo Guicciardini. A group of aristocratic young *bigi* Florentines went to the Palazzo della Signoria and demanded Piero Soderini's immediate resignation; they were led by Antonfrancesco degli Albizzi, Paolo di Piero Vettori, Bartolomeo di Filippo Valori and the sons of Bernardo Ruccellai. Soderini sought sanctuary from the riotous *giovani* in the house of Paolo Vettori's brother, Francesco. The deposed *gonfaloniere* was unjustly vilified as the cause of all Florence's sufferings and sent into exile to Siena.

Soderini's replacement was, surprisingly, a Savonarolan, Giambattista Ridolfi, whose term of office was reduced from life to just fourteen months. Niccolò Machiavelli, who had asked his friend and confidante Francesco Vettori to stand surety for Soderini's safety, watched in sadness as the former republican head of state rode into enforced retirement and exile. Machiavelli's judgement of Soderini was, however, ultimately to be a harsh one. In his writings he later blamed the former *gonfaloniere a vita* for refusing to accept a peace offering which had earlier been proposed by Raimondo de Cardona. The Spaniard, so Machiavelli believed, could easily have been bought off with a shrewd one-time bribe. Now, instead, Florence was forced to pay 80,000 ducats for the upkeep of Cardona's Spanish troops, as well as a further extortion of 20,000 ducats to Cardona personally. Worst of all, however, the *signoria* was also now compelled to exculpate the Medici, restore their property, and agree to their return to Florence as the city's rulers.

On 1 September 1512, eighteen years after their ignominious flight, Cardinal Giovanni de' Medici returned to Florence accompanied by his cousin Giulio, their safety guaranteed by the presence of 1,500 grizzled Spanish soldiers. Here, in the full splendour of his ecclesiastical rank as a prince of the Church, the cardinal ruled as proxy for a brief period before Giovanni's brother, Giuliano de' Medici, was able to return from exile and take up his post as head of the Medici *reggimento* which, with the help of its supporters from the so-called *palleschi* (or 'ballers'), now once more held Florence's government tightly within its grip. Forged by his colourful life experiences into a mature, worldly and shrewd statesman, from the beginning Cardinal Giovanni had the air of a man who intended to rule. On 16 September, he demanded a *parlamento* and, as in the days of Lorenzo the Magnificent, it was stage-managed with *palleschi* horsemen galloping up and down the streets yelling the inevitable rallying cry of 'Palle! Palle!' and loaned-out Spanish troops securing the Piazza della Signoria. The subsequent *balià* appointed a council of fifty citizens of unequivocally Medicean sympathies to oversee the reform of the city's institutions. The Savonarolan Great Council of Three Thousand was immediately and unceremoniously abolished. Under the cardinal's gaze the crimson cross of the Florentine republic was erased and the Medici *palle* restored to all the public buildings.

But if Cardinal Giovanni was the political impresario deftly reinstating the Medici levers of power, then the unambitious affability of his brother Giuliano initially threatened to undermine the cardinal's diligent work in restoring the Medici regime. Arriving back in Florence after all these years, the ingenuous Giuliano entered the city not with pomp and fanfare as he should have done for political effect, but with simplicity and humility. He was accompanied by his companions Prinzivalle della Stufa and Girolamo degli Albizzi and just thirty-three armed men for security. Not only was his tiny entourage unbefitting as Florence's new head-of-state, but he was also dressed not in any great finery but instead wearing the traditional Florentine *lucco*. This wide, sleeveless garment with its open side seams, usually of plain black wool, was traditionally favoured by the older men of the commune. Under any other circumstances this would have been a prudent demonstration of 'old style' Medici modesty and decorum but the sartorial oversight was also compounded by a more serious *faux pas*. No sooner had Giuliano entered Florence than he now called at the *palazzo* of Antonfrancesco degli Albizzi, to whom he expressed his desire to be accepted as no more than 'a private citizen of Florence' and disavowing any interest in its political governance. Clearly somewhere along the line there had been a serious miscommunication between the cardinal and his younger sibling. Giuliano's naive diffidence to the outward show of government exasperated Cardinal Giovanni who had worked so hard towards the Medici restoration. The older brother had not engineered the city's subjugation only to hand it back on a silver platter to those republican interests which had joyously exulted all these years in the family's exile. Giovanni now put his foot down and used the continued presence of Cardona's Spanish troops to force the *signoria* to reinstate full dictatorial Medici power at sword point.

Even as the Medici were settling comfortably back into power, the unfortunate Niccolò Machiavelli's own personal ordeal was only just beginning. Seeking to redeem himself in the eyes of the restored Medici rulers Machiavelli wrote two letters to Giovanni de' Medici beseeching the cardinal to be magnanimous in his victory and clement in his restoration of Medici lands and preferments. In the second letter, written in early November and titled *Il ricordo ai Palleschi* ('To the Mediceans'), he pleaded the case of Piero Soderini arguing that, despite his opposition to Medici rule, Soderini had been a wise statesman whose name ought not to be denigrated. Cardinal de' Medici initially gave the letter writer the silent treatment. His response, when it eventually came, was however roundly unsympathetic. And then, the hammer blow. On 7 November 1512, the Medici-controlled *signoria* informed the secretary of the second chancery that he was no longer a member of the government. He was to remain within the dominions of Florence, pay a surety of 1,000 florins for his good behaviour, and was hereafter barred from entering the Palazzo della Signoria.

Broken in spirit by his exclusion from government, a vocation around which he had built his entire adult life, Machiavelli despondently retired to his private smallholding located just south of Florence. But worse was yet to follow when an anti-Medicean plot to assassinate Cardinal de' Medici, Giuliano de' Medici and their cousin Giulio was uncovered involving the noted republicans Pietro Paolo Boscoli, Agostino Capponi, Niccolò Valori (Machiavelli's close friend and family member) and Giovanni Folchi. The ringleader, Boscoli, had been an ardent admirer of Savonarola and refused to accept the inevitability of the Medici restoration. He gathered some like-minded conspirators together at the home of Lorenzo Lenzi sometime in early February 1513 and the conspirators had listed down on a piece of paper all those other potential anti-Medici

420

supporters whom they believed they could call upon. Unfortunately, the piece of paper, on which Machiavelli's own name had been mentioned, had been foolishly mislaid and subsequently found its way into the hands of the authorities. Boscoli and Capponi were promptly arrested and tortured by the *otto di guardia* and a guilty sentence pronounced.

Although he had nothing to do with the plot, Machiavelli was amongst those who were later picked up and imprisoned in the Bargello. Tortured by the *strappado* he bravely refused to incriminate himself and throughout his ordeal was terrified that at any moment he might be taken out and summarily executed. Death was indeed the fate of the principal conspirators themselves on 23 February 1513. Luca della Robbia, a relative of the famous artist, was present in Boscoli's prison cell the entire night beforehand and recorded the traitor's execution the following morning in his *Recitazione*: 'And placing himself down, and the executioner, giving him the shortest time, cleanly removed his head, which, so cut, continued to move its mouth for a time'. Machiavelli was not executed but, from his foetid jail cell in the Bargello, he wrote once again to the Medici brothers, pleading for clemency not for the former *gonfaloniere* this time but for himself. His letters were couched in the form of sonnets although, after Machiavelli's inimitable style, they were written with tongue firmly in cheek; even in prison the political theorist could not quite find it within himself to grovel. But the gesture cut no ice with the cardinal and Machiavelli remained incarcerated nonetheless.

The return of Medici power in Florence was marked by the inevitable carnivals and festivities, all gloomily bittersweet in the light of the recent Prato massacre. But as his father Lorenzo the Magnificent had done before him, Cardinal Giovanni de' Medici went out of his way to order the obligatory bonfires and gay celebrations to woo a sullen populace more inured to the puritan dreariness of a Savonarola, or the austerity of an embattled republic, than to the public confections of *il Magnifico*. Giovanni's own personal motto *Jugem enim meum suave est* ('Truly my yoke is easy') seemed to indicate that, provided the Florentines did not resist his will, the cardinal, who himself was at heart a pleasure-loving sybarite, a homosexual who enjoyed indulging his gluttony at merry feasts, would not be an unduly hard task master.

Aside from the recent beheading of Boscoli and his confederates (who had indicted themselves more through their own stupidity than through any genuine threat to the new Medici government; Boscoli himself had paid the price for his foolhardiness by requiring two excruciating strokes of the axe), the Medici restoration had, enticingly, been achieved with remarkably little in the way of retribution, vendettas or score-settling. To their credit the Medici had still not descended to the level of depravity commonplace amongst many of the tyrants and despots of Italy. That Giovanni was a prince of the Church was also a heartening sign and, as we have already noted, the kindly Giuliano de' Medici was not a person whose motivations were rooted in negative emotions such as fear or paranoia. It also helped the Medici cause considerably that Piero the Unfortunate was no longer in the picture. The Florentines gradually awoke, therefore, to the comforting realisation that, although their liberties had been abrogated, the new Medici regime might at the very least prove a humane one.

PART FIVE

THE MEDICI RESURGENT

CHAPTER 16

The Lion Pope

I used to be an exile, but I'm back in Leo's reign.
So burn your midnight oil, boys, and follow in my train.
For no one leaves my Leo without a handsome gain.
Bards will sing for prizes, and they'll not sing in vain.

Pasquinade, 1513

Pope Julius II died of a fever on 21 February 1513, after a nine-year pontificate which had consisted largely of military campaigning, but which had at least achieved its proximate goal of finally expelling the French menace from Italy. His reign had not been without its personal controversy and Giuliano della Rovere's homosexual proclivities were widely suspected (the murdered Cardinal Alidosi was rumoured to have been his catamite). Furthermore, the late pope had also sired an illegitimate daughter, Felice della Rovere, whilst he had been a cardinal (his predecessor Rodrigo Borgia almost certainly sired a child whilst he was pope – the notorious *Infans Romanus*). Today, peoples' sexual orientation is considered largely a private matter but in Renaissance Italy sodomy was considered a mortal sin and was punishable by the so-called 'Pope's Pear', a metal pear or leaf-shaped torture device which was administered to the victim's rectum and then screwed into an open position to inflict massive (more often than not, fatal) internal damage. It is conceivable of course that the lurid rumours of Giuliano's sex life were merely malicious gossip and certainly the later northern European Protestants were especially quick to make propaganda capital out of it; the French writer Philippe de Mornay (1549-1623) for example reproached all Italians for their buggery, but added with a special hint of mischievousness: 'This horror is ascribed to good Julius'.

Julius's personal contribution to the ecclesiastical life of the Church meanwhile had been minimal and, with the exception of a purely reactive Fifth Lateran Council (which had been called into being to disavow the actions of the schismatic *conciliabulum* at Pisa and later Milan), there had been no other major Church councils or pronouncements during his reign. The Pope had confined himself to the routine duties of any senior cleric and contented himself that his spiritual and pastoral duties had been fulfilled. He did, however, lay the cornerstone (quite literally) for the later Roman Catholic Church by commissioning the new basilica of St. Peter at the Vatican Hill, which was intended to replace the existing leaky and crumbling relic which had originally been ordered by the Emperor Constantine the Great. On a pettier note, Julius had also commissioned a new set of apartments in the Apostolic Palace as he could not bear to reside in the rooms formerly occupied by his hated enemy Pope Alexander VI (and indeed the Borgia apartments were subsequently shut up from the general public and all but forgotten, only to be reopened again in 1889 by Pope Leo XIII). Julius II was laid to rest in St. Peter's in the Vatican alongside the remains of his uncle Pope Sixtus IV.

The papal conclave of 1513 ensued, much to the relief of the Italian cardinals, in the absence of the overbearing and schismatic French cardinals including Guillaume Briçonnet and René de Prie. Giovanni de' Medici (who, suffering badly from ulcers and an anal fistula, had to be ported to Rome in a litter) arrived late and missed the opening proceedings. Laid up sick in his cot, the obese, perspiring invalid was not initially considered to be *papabile* – that is to say, a potential candidate bearing the innate qualities to sit on the throne of St. Peter. However, as the conclave progressed, and as conditions (and food) inside the walled-up chapel grew progressively worse, the Medici cardinal increasingly appeared to represent a solution to the deadlock. The conclave now became largely a two-horse race between himself and Cardinal Raffaele Sansoni Riario, who was supported by the older, more conservative element. The former meanwhile was seen to have the support of the younger, more aristocratic members of the Sacred College; cardinals such as Alfonso Petrucci (the son of Pandolfo Petrucci, former lord of Siena), Ippolito d'Este (the brother of Duke Alfonso I d'Este of Ferrara) and Ghismondo Gonzaga of Mantua, for whom the military papacy of the Ligurian Pope Giuliano della Rovere had proven disagreeable and incommodious. Understandably opposed to Giovanni's election were men like Cardinal Francesco Soderini whose brother Piero, the deposed former *gonfaloniere* of Florence, had been sent into exile following the return of the Medici. However, ever the consummate courtier and salesman, Bernardo Dovizi da Bibbiena had finessed Francesco's bruised family pride by bruiting the possibility of a Medici-Soderini marriage in return for his vote; the gambit worked and Cardinal Giovanni emerged with the necessary majority for election as pope.

As deacon of the Sacred College, Giovanni was able to announce his own nomination to the conclave and was crowned pope on 19 March 1513 at the age of thirty-seven. Cardinal Alessandro Farnese, the brother of Pope Alexander VI's lover Giulia Farnese and seven years Giovanni's senior, placed the papal tiara on his head. Giovanni's election had been marked for once by a distinct lack of simony. A non-priest (the last non-priest to be elected pope in fact), Giovanni was hastily ordained on 15 March and consecrated as bishop two days later. The night before his birth Giovanni's mother, Clarice Orsini, had supposedly experienced a prophetic dream in which she found herself in the Duomo giving birth not to an infant but to a huge and docile lion; Giovanni de' Medici therefore now honoured his late mother's vision by assuming the name of Pope Leo X (a name which also echoed back to an eleventh century reformer of the Church, Pope Leo IX). The Sacred College heaved a collective sigh of relief. Giovanni's humanist correspondent Desiderius Erasmus gave his seal of approval from distant England, describing Leo X as the complete reverse of Julius II, a pacific and conciliatory pope who would usher in 'an age of gold' that would replace his predecessor's belligerent 'age of iron'. A confirmed homosexual like Julius II before him, it was nevertheless hoped that Leo X's papacy would not be marked either by the martial prowess of Giuliano della Rovere or by the profane whoremongering and drink-fuelled orgies of Rodrigo Borgia and his uncontrollable Catalan offspring. Pope Leo himself bore this out when, orienting himself more towards a papacy characterised by elegant, tasteful fun and recreation, he is said to have quipped to his good-natured brother Giuliano: 'God has given us the papacy, now let us enjoy it!'

Leo's papacy began in the spirit with which it was to continue for the next eight years, with an extravagant and festive papal procession from the Vatican to St. John Lateran. This was the important Roman festival known as the *possesso* which signified the Pope's taking possession of the spiritual and temporal aspects of the bishopric of Rome. Intended as a statement of future political intent by the Pope for how he intended to run Rome and the Papal States, it involved a pageant-filled procession from St. Peter's to St. John Lateran along the now-defunct Via Papale. Riding a snow white Turkish horse (but seated side-saddle due to the intense pain from his haemorrhoids) he rode out in his finest vestments wearing the papal tiara as his equerries and flunkies scattered gold coins to an appreciative and cheering crowd. Morbidly obese and sweating profusely from the Roman sunshine, he must have seemed an unprepossessing figure compared to the more athletic, armour-clad Pope Julius II. Nevertheless the general positivity of the occasion seemed to dispel all doubts.

Giovanni's allies had worked hard to create a spectacle that would awe the Roman mob. 'I experienced so violent a desire to become pope myself, that I was unable to obtain a wink of sleep or any repose all that night. No longer do I marvel at these prelates desiring so ardently to procure this dignity, and I verily believe every lacquey would sooner be made a pope than a prince!' was the comment of Giangiacomo Penni, one eyewitness to Pope Leo X's procession. Before arriving at the ancient basilica of St. John Lateran the new pope had passed beneath a fabulous triumphal arch that had been erected and paid for by his wealthy banker friend Agostino Chigi. 'The era of Venus and Mars have now ended', proclaimed the arch's inscription, 'Now comes the rule of Minerva'. Chigi–probably the wealthiest man in Rome at this time–was crediting Leo's new papacy with the blessings and advantages of wisdom, as embodied by the ancient pagan goddess Minerva. But, in a fiscal sense, was it 'wisdom' for the new pope to be spending upwards of 100,000 ducats on his own coronation ceremony?

In Florence too the atmosphere was celebratory. Upon learning of the news of a Medici pope astride (indeed, overflowing) the throne of St. Peter, the *palleschi* and the *bigi* were ecstatic. Complimentary sweet wine flowed from fountains in the Piazza della Signoria and at night the rites of Bacchus were illuminated by huge bonfires in every street. These were not, for once, incinerators for peoples' worldly 'vanities', but instead beacons for a new and hopeful (if somewhat tipsy) Florence, the pleasure-loving and hedonistic Florence of old. So ubiquitous were these celebratory bonfires in fact that the roofs of the merchants' houses in the Mercato Nuovo district were almost entirely stripped for firewood, causing the city authorities to step in with an emergency ordinance banning the igniting of any more bonfires. To Raffaello Petrucci, one of his favourites, the Pope had declared: 'We begin gloriously, we live gloriously, we die gloriously', and it seemed during those early halcyon days that the Florentines had taken Giovanni de' Medici's philosophy to heart as the usually sedate and sensible citizens of the commune threw caution to the wind and lived like there was no tomorrow.

Newly released from the Bargello on 12 March, Niccolò Machiavelli was himself soon caught up in Florence's celebratory atmosphere. Reunited with his

427

old gang of friends from the second chancery, he would daily visit 'some girl to recover our vigour'. He was thankful to still be alive. His horrendous first-hand experience of political imprisonment and torture had been positively nightmarish but it had not, however, dampened his interest in politics. To his confidante Francesco Vettori he confessed: 'If you find that commenting on events bores you because you realise that they frequently turn out differently from the opinions and ideas we have, you are right – for the same thing has happened to me. All the same, if I could talk to you, I could only fill your head with castles in the air, because Fortune has seen to it that since I do not know how to talk about either the silk or wool trade, or profits or losses, I have to talk about politics.' Vettori, by now an important Florentine envoy to the papal court in Rome, kept Machiavelli appraised of political developments at the new Medici court of Pope Leo X. In spite of this, or possibly because of it, Machiavelli remained depressed at his on-going exclusion from the political life of the commune just as things were starting to become interesting again.

At a stroke, Cardinal Giovanni's elevation had altered the geopolitical standing of Florence in Italian affairs. From being an enemy of the Papal States under the reigns of Pope Sixtus IV, Pope Alexander VI and Pope Julius II, Florence was now, for the first time ever, politically joined at the hip with Rome and the papacy. It seemed that overnight everyone in Florence had suddenly become an ardent Medici supporter. What is more, the bankers and merchants of the city salivated at the thought of how much business they would soon be doing with the Court of Rome. That was all as it may be, but the new Medici pope was not merely content with the return of Florence to Medici control and the republic's subsequent prosperity. Like popes Sixtus IV and Alexander VI who had attempted to carve out realms for their family members, he also now aspired to the creation of a new Medici principality in central Italy and also like his predecessors he had few qualms about using the institution of the papacy to achieve this distinctly secular and personal end.

The first step was for Pope Leo X to consolidate his family members and foremost supporters in key positions of power. Firstly, in addition to his status as Medici representative (ruler basically) in Florence, Giuliano de' Medici was made a captain of the Church sometime before August 1513 (he would be further promoted to captain-general of the Church on 10 January 1515). The following month both Giuliano and his nephew Lorenzo would also be bestowed the honour of Roman citizenship by the Pope. By replacing Francesco Maria della Rovere, the duke of Urbino, in this important and prestigious military role Pope Leo would initiate a history of animosity between Francesco Maria and the Medici which would lead ultimately to catastrophic events, but for now all this lay in the future.

Leo X was to prove no less nepotistic than his three predecessors and would elevate many of his own cousins and nephews to the Sacred College, which was by this time anyway both a common and accepted practice. Giulio de' Medici, who had been the Pope's constant companion during those long and uncertain years of exile, was named archbishop of Florence on 9 May 1513 and raised to the Sacred College in the very first consistory of 23 September 1513. He was given the appointment of cardinal-deacon of Santa Maria in Domnica, a position which had been vacated by Pope Leo himself. Also elevated during the same consistory was the son of the Pope's sister Maria Maddalena, Innocenzo Cybò, who was not only created cardinal-deacon but also Protonotary Apostolic

428

(Innocenzo's father Franceschetto Cybò was meanwhile appointed governor of Spoleto in 1519, whilst his brother-in-law Giovanni Maria da Varano was made duke of Camerino). Neither had Leo's old and trusted friend, confidant and ally Bernardo Dovizi da Bibbiena been forgotten; he too received his cardinal's hat and would continue to serve as a loyal papal legate and nuncio over the next seven years. Several years later, in the consistory of 1 July 1517, Leo would also create three more Medici cardinals: his cousin Luigi de' Rossi, the son of Leonetto de' Rossi and Maria de' Medici (Piero the Gouty's daughter), was one. Another was Giovanni Salviati, the son of his older sister Lucrezia and her husband Jacopo Salviati. A third was Niccolò Ridolfi, the sixteen-year-old son of his youngest sister Contessina and her husband Piero Ridolfi. Piero Ridolfi himself would also be later rewarded for his loyal relationship with the Medici family with his election as *gonfaloniere*.

The exiled *gonfaloniere* Piero Soderini had meanwhile been recalled from Ragusa and, granted a pardon by Pope Leo, was reunited with his brother Cardinal Francesco Soderini in Rome. The latter, however, was not granted the Medici marriage alliance that he had been promised in return for casting his vote in favour of Giovanni (Bibbiena had averred that the Pope's twenty-one-year-old nephew, Lorenzo di Piero de' Medici, would make a suitable match but this proposal was almost certainly not made in earnest but merely dangled as bait for the gullible Soderini to swallow). For Lorenzo di Piero de' Medici, Pope Leo had altogether different plans. As the only son of Lorenzo the Magnificent's eldest son Piero, Lorenzo was the direct male linear heir to the main line of the Medici. Together with his sister Clarice, he had been raised in exile by his father Piero until his death at the Garigliano River in 1503, whereupon Cardinal Giovanni and his sister-in-law Alfonsina Orsini had taken on the shared responsibility for his upbringing and education. The boy showed the same early promise as *il Magnifico* and his murdered brother Giuliano and it was Lorenzo whom the Pope envisaged would eventually rule over a powerful new Medici principality which Giovanni de' Medici would create using papal funds and resources.

After the French departure from Italy, Pope Julius II had secured both Parma and Piacenza for the papacy, whilst Modena was still garrisoned by the Spanish. If the new pope could defeat Duke Alfonso d'Este in Ferrara and supplant Duke Francesco Maria della Rovere of Urbino then their two states could be united with Parma, Piacenza, Modena and Reggio into a single new domain straddling much of central Italy. This state could be further amalgamated with the papal vicariates of Rimini, Faenza and Ravenna provided that they could be coaxed from the control of Venice, which clearly entailed going to war with Venice at some point. La Serenissima herself had recently been rocked by a series of peasant revolts in the north-eastern region of Friuli which had been deliberately sparked off in February 1511 by the Savorgnan family in their feud against the aristocratic della Torre family and their supporters. Although the instigator was assassinated by March 1512, the peasants' discontent still continued to simmer in the Friulian contado. As regards Ferrara, Leo X played a game of dissimulation. Alfonso d'Este had journeyed to Rome on 30 March to offer the new pope his formal felicitations and Leo for his part had lifted the papal interdict on Ferrara for a period of three months. Alfonso then remained in Rome for the Pope's official coronation ceremony which followed on 12 April. By 29 April, Alfonso was back in Ferrara and reporting to his wife Lucrezia Borgia that he was satisfied that the new Pope was a man of good faith.

The other obstacle to Leo's plan lay in the proposed acquisition of Urbino, whose duke had shown much kindness to Giuliano de' Medici while he was in exile. Not only was the kind-hearted Giuliano reluctant to see Francesco Maria deposed but he quite literally considered such an undertaking to be a criminal enterprise. This notwithstanding, Pope Leo's objectives do not seem altogether dissimilar from those of Alexander VI, who had used the pretext of non-payment of the *denarii sancti petri* to allow Cesare Borgia to conduct punitive campaigns against all the semi-independent states of the Romagna as a possible precursor to establishing a unified Italy.

Lorenzo de' Medici had meanwhile been created captain-general of the Florentine republic on 12 August 1515, formerly replacing his affable but unreliable uncle Giuliano in the prime leadership role in the commune. In his duties he was supported both by his mother Alfonsina and by selected, trusted Medici kinsmen by marriage such as his aunt Lucrezia's husband Jacopo Salviati and Contessina's husband Piero Ridolfi, both of whom had been temporarily left in charge of Florence whilst Lorenzo was away in Rome being vested with his new powers by Pope Leo. In essence, Lorenzo had already been conducting himself as Florence's de facto supreme ruler many months prior to his official appointment. Lorenzo's increasingly haughty and imperious ways were, in truth, earning him few friends amongst the ordinary Florentines and half of the time he was not even present in the republic anyway, preferring to spend his days in Rome frittering away his days with his agreeable uncle Giuliano.

The proud Florentines quietly chafed at being treated by the young Medici princeling like some subject state of an absentee lord. On those occasions when he did condescend to come to Florence, he commanded that government meetings be held at the Palazzo Medici instead of the Palazzo della Signoria; meanwhile, the counsel of older, more experienced statesmen went unheeded while Lorenzo instead insisted on surrounding himself with obsequious young courtiers who carried out his every bidding without question. A far more capable servant of the state, Niccolò Machiavelli, languished for the time being in his farmhouse, putting the finishing touches to his masterwork of realpolitik, *The Prince*. In an effort to ingratiate himself with the Medici he would dedicate the book initially to Giuliano. When Giuliano was displaced as Florence's ruler by Lorenzo, the pragmatic student of the political arts quickly changed his dedication to Lorenzo instead. *The Prince* was the distillation of Machiavelli's experiences of statesmanship and especially his observation of the activities of Cesare Borgia, Italy's preeminent maestro in the art of both war and politics. But in his thinking and his writings Machiavelli was still centuries ahead of his time and great lords would continue to govern themselves not by pragmatic rational principles but as they had always done, according to the dictates of their pride. Cesare Borgia had been the first who had transcended this limited 'emotional thinking' and managed to turn reasoned strategy and fluidity of action to his advantage. He had truly earned his name for he was the first modern Italian to act with the cool calculation of Julius Caesar. His downfall had only been brought about by the vagaries of fate – he had never in his wildest imaginings foreseen that both he and his father the Pope would fall mortally ill at the same time.

The political landscape of Italy in the year 1513 had been left with some major changes compared to the lie of the land some years earlier. In Milan the Sforza now ruled once more, although as little more than puppets of far greater forces which had supplanted the French. As a compromise between the competing claims of Maximilian and the Swiss cantons, each of whom had their own ideas on how Milan's former possessions should be carved up, the nineteen-year-old Massimiliano Sforza, the eldest son of Ludovico Sforza and Beatrice d'Este, was brought back from Flanders (where he had been cared for by the Emperor Maximilian's only daughter Margaret of Austria) and installed as duke of Milan on 29 December 1512. In the event, it was the Swiss who won the battle for mastery of the young duke. In return for an annual payment of 40,000 ducats and the ceding of Lugano, Locarno and Domodossola to the Swiss, the cantons undertook to maintain the young duke in power. The Spanish and *Napoletani* also bolstered the new duke and even set about re-occupying various towns, including Parma and Piacenza, which they held in trust for Milan, thus foiling for the moment Pope Leo's own private plans for these two possessions. Preoccupied with their own parochial affairs and the aftermath of the Friuli peasants' rebellion, the Venetians largely kept aloof from this struggle between the Swiss and the Germans for control of the duke of Milan.

Massimiliano's brief dukedom would, however, be sadly undistinguished. He was a far cry from his strong forebears Francesco Sforza and Galeazzo Maria Sforza, and even his own father Ludovico who had made his fatal last stand at Novara. An upbringing in exile had led to his being undermined by a persistent weakness in character, as well as a nervous restlessness. Mario Equicola, a courtier of Isabella d'Este, had reported of Massimiliano: 'The Duke is never still, he does not sleep at night, he is always in motion even when he is doing nothing'. With little real aptitude for rule he dissipated his days in pleasant diversions and the citizens of Milan could only shake their heads at how low the once mighty House of Sforza had fallen. In the Po Valley and the Veneto, meanwhile, the armies of Venice had fallen back and consolidated their hold over former territories there which had been vacated in the wake of the French withdrawal. Venice was still hampered by unresolved differences with the Emperor and when the latter's representative Cardinal Lang had come to Rome to confer with the late Pope Julius II, His Holiness had, in return for Maximilian's undertaking to repudiate the schismatic Council of Pisa, agreed to use spiritual sanctions against Venice and to exclude the republic from the new Holy League between the Empire and the papacy. An increasingly isolated Venice had also been antagonised by the League's recapture of Brescia; it was the promise to return Brescia to Venetian rule–together with the towns of Bergamo and Cremona–that induced Venice to conclude a new pact with King Louis XII of France in March 1513, just prior to Pope Julius's death. That same month the Emperor Maximilian entered the Holy League.

Louis XII of France, who was by this time fifty-one, was still not finished with his lifelong intervention in the affairs of Italy. Even after everything that had happened, he still stubbornly refused to relinquish the Orléanist claim over the duchy of Milan, a claim which had occupied all of his reign and indeed much of his adult life. He now despatched a French army under the joint command of Louis de La Trémoille and the anti Sforzese *condottiere* Giangiacomo Trivulzio, which arrived in Piedmont in May 1513 and began its inexorable advance towards Milan. Desperately, Massimiliano Sforza traded the towns of Parma and Piacenza to Pope Leo in return for the promise of papal

431

troops, although none were subsequently forthcoming. The Pope also purchased Reggio and Modena from the Emperor for 40,000 ducats, a move which alerted Alfonso d'Este to Leo X's underlying bad faith. Guicciardini would write that the Pope 'having purchased Modena, he bent his mind exclusively to acquire Ferrara, more with intrigues than with open threats of force'. Openly, Leo refused to adhere to any public alliance with either Milan or Spain against the French. Secretly, however, the Pope had opened negotiations with the Swiss cantons and had funded an 8,000-strong army of Swiss pikemen at a reputed cost of 34,000 gold florins. These Swiss crossed the Alps and headed straight for La Trémoille whilst he was in the midst of laying siege to Novara, where Massimiliano Sforza had shut himself up. Here, at the Battle of Ariotta on 6 June 1513, the mainly Swiss pike infantrymen, unsupported by either artillery or horse, first put to flight the French men-at-arms and then decimated the German mercenary *landsknechts* fighting in the French army. Massimiliano himself later wrote that Ariotta 'was with such loss and discomfiture to the enemy that nearly 12,000 were killed. The rest were put to flight, the Swiss captains pursuing them together with us, leaving behind them all the artillery and provisions with infinite spoils.' It was an incredible feat of Swiss arms from which the French could not recover. Soon afterwards the remaining French units in northern Italy were driven out by the combined arms of the Swiss, *Milanese*, imperial and Spanish troops.

For his own part Pope Leo X had committed no papal soldiers of his own, at least not openly and so, diplomatically speaking, he remained in good standing with the French Crown. However the reign of Louis XII was by now limping to its inevitable closure. Its death knell corresponded with a sudden uptick in the King's marital life. Louis's second wife Anne of Brittany passed away in January 1514 having borne him four stillborn sons and two daughters who under the *Lex Salica* were disbarred from inheriting the kingdom. Desperate to squire a male successor to his royal throne he had rashly consented to marry the sprightly and vivacious Mary Tudor, the eighteen-year-old sister of King Henry VIII of England. With a thirty-three year age difference between them the more senior Louis struggled–despite the disabilities brought on by his recurring gout– to keep up with his wife's fondness for courtly dancing, not to mention his nightly toils in the bedchamber to produce an heir. After less than three months of these exertions Louis XII's constitution proved unequal to the challenge and he died in the royal hotel of Tournelles in Paris on 1 January 1515. Florence's ambassador to Rome, Machiavelli's old friend Francesco Vettori, snickered that the French king's English 'filly [had been] so young, so beautiful and so swift that she had ridden him right out of the world'.

When King Louis XII had acceded to the throne in 1498 the son of his distant cousin Charles, Count of Angoulême, a great-great-grandson of King Charles V of France, had become his heir apparent and *Dauphin* of France. This boy was the four-year-old François who, subsequent to the count of Angoulême's death in 1496, was raised in a lonely and unwelcoming French court by his newly-widowed, nineteen-year-old mother Louise of Savoy. It was not, however, expected that François would ever rule; Charles VIII had been a young man upon gaining the throne and his own successor Louis was also a young and virile man. After a highly public law suit in which Louis had obtained a papal divorce from Jeanne of France, his barren wife of twenty-two years, a law suit in which the King unchivalrously cited both congenital deformity and witchcraft on Jeanne's part, Louis was left free in 1498 to remarry the Queen Dowager, Anne of Brittany, who was still only twenty-one years old and assumed to be fertile. But, with each successive stillbirth, Anne's loathing for Louise of Savoy and her healthy young male heir grew exponentially and the two women became firm rivals. Louise happily returned the queen's animus, gloating in her journal after Anne had lost her latest son, 'He could not retard the exaltation of my own Caesar for he did not live'. King Louis, however, adored his future successor the infant François and lavished every attention upon him. Thus, François grew to manhood as a somewhat spoiled and indulged mother's boy; handsome and athletic, he gave up his privileged youth to the joys of hunting and the thrill of the chase.

The year during which the French king had been married to Mary Tudor had given Louise a scare however. Not only was it conceivable that Mary might give birth to a male heir but, in his youthful impulsiveness, François had begun a flirtation with the attractive young Queen. Happily, the dalliance had not yet come to the jealous attentions of the King, but Louise nevertheless had to take her son sternly in hand and remind him that, aside from the obvious dangers of the King finding out, if the liaison were consummated and a male child were the fruit of it, he may well have unwittingly supplanted himself as heir to the throne. Chastened by this sudden realisation, François withdrew from his pursuit of Mary and instead redirected his passions to the study of war and military strategy. Now, he only needed a suitable theatre in which to exercise these martial pretensions.

After Louis XII died, François was crowned as king of France in the Cathedral of Reims on 25 January 1515. A relieved Queen Dowager Mary, who had not been best pleased with her marriage of state to the elderly Louis, was left free to wed her paramour the English lord Charles Brandon, 1st Duke of Suffolk, whom she secretly wed at the Hotel de Clugny before departing for England in March. Upon learning of the new king's accession, Pope Leo X had sent his brother Giuliano north as emissary to France to congratulate King François I on his coronation. François was evidently charmed by the easy-going Medici princeling for in gratitude he raised him to the nobility, bestowing upon Giuliano the title of duke of Nemours and the hand in marriage of his aunt, Philiberta of Savoy. The dukedom of Nemours was an old and distinguished title, dating back to the twelfth-century. After Louis d'Armagnac had been killed at the battle of Cerignola in April 1503, King Louis XII had bestowed the title upon his nephew, Gaston de Foix, however *his own* untimely death at the Battle of Ravenna meant that the title escheated back to the French Crown. It was a singular honour for the Medici to now be granted membership of the French nobility; now Giuliano could get to work creating noble heirs to bolster the ranks of the increasingly aristocratic Medici. To-date, he had produced only one illegitimate heir, a four-year-old son named Ippolito who had been born at Urbino during his years in exile there. Baptised on 19 April 1511, the mother was a gentlewoman of Urbino named Pacifica Brandani.

In return for ennobling Giuliano, François asked for the Pope's blessing in his forthcoming recovery of the duchy of Milan as well as the towns of Parma and Piacenza. This would inevitably set the Pope on a collision course with the Empire, the Swiss cantons as well as Naples, all of whom were Milan's protectors. Although his late king and benefactor Louis had neglected to involve him in his on-going wars, François had nevertheless taken a keen interest in the affairs of Italy; upon King Louis's death the twenty-one-year-old François now took upon himself the glamorous royal role for which he was ideally suited, that of romantic warrior-king. In this he had a natural rival across the channel in the dynamic King Henry VIII of England, a young man equally in love with his youth and his own agreeable reflection, and both monarchs were determined to test the limits of their royal prerogative.

But the young French king's love of chivalry was no longer in tune with the times; the advent of the firearm and of artillery pieces had seen to that. In Italy it had been Ercole d'Este who had been the most visionary in exploring the capabilities of such weapons and this talent had since been taken up by his son. The current Duke Alfonso I of Ferrara, husband to the fabled Lucrezia Borgia, amused himself playing the combined roles of Vulcan and Tubal Cain. In the Stygian foundries of Ferrara, smaller and more mobile new ordnances were being developed such as the falconet, whimsically named for the aristocratic pastime of falconry. This was a small-bore light artillery piece whose high-velocity iron or (if necessary) carved stone projectiles were easily capable of penetrating steel breastplates, whereupon they would liquefy flesh and shatter bone. These were fearsome weapons which could rake an army's rank and file and cause devastating battlefield casualties, as indeed they had recently demonstrated to such deadly effect at the Battle of Ravenna. Soldiers unlucky enough to be struck in the extremities by such weapons might well have survived the initial injury; however the poor medical knowledge of the time almost invariably resulted in the victim's ultimate demise from either shock or septicaemia. Battles were no longer decided by the aristocratic cavalry charge either, in which expensively-armoured gentlemen knights delivered the *coup de grâce* with the inevitable moral conclusion that 'the better men had won' (recent savage clashes like the Battle of Ariotta had seen to that). Rather, wars were now being won by common, workaday soldiers like the drab Swiss who, due to their poverty, often went into battle shoeless and in rags. Gripped firmly in their grubby hands was their non-nonsense workaday weapon, the Swiss pike: ten to twenty-five feet long and tipped with a steel spike, the pike was wielded by a dense formation of men who were capable in an instant of creating an invincible Macedonian phalanx which neither horse nor swordsmen could penetrate.

If François I of France was not yet cognisant of the grim realities of war, he was apprised of one salient fact. He was aware that the wars in Italy had still not been conclusively played out and that honour and glory was still to be had on the peninsula. This was due in large measure to the Italians themselves. The simple fact was that the temperament of the Italians was such that they hated each other even more than they hated the foreigners who habitually intervened in their affairs. They would even ally themselves with the heathen Turk if this gave them some advantage over their neighbours. Indeed, on the eve of Charles VIII's invasion, Alfonso of Naples had boasted that if necessary he could put 20,000 of Sultan Bayezid II's Muslim troops into the field against France; later, when confronted by the army of King Louis XII, an embattled Ludovico Sforza had also sent word to Bayezid that he was prepared to pay the Sultan to create a diversion by attacking the maritime colonies of France's ally, Venice. Similar fraternisation had also taken place soon after the Muslims had occupied Otranto in 1480 when King Ferrante had approached the Turks for their assistance against his adversaries (sensibly, the Turks had elected to remain neutral).

François rapidly assembled a formidable new French army in the summer of 1515. It comprised some 20,000 ferocious German mercenary *landsknechts* along with around 10,000 French infantry under the command of Pedro Navarro, a turncoat Spanish commander who had been captured at Ravenna by the troops of Gaston de Foix and whose ransom had failed to be met by a niggardly King Ferdinand of Spain. In addition, François also dragooned into his service the noble horse known as the gentlemen pensioners, as well as 3,000 mounted French men-at-arms, the so-called Black Band (a fearsome mercenary *landsknecht* unit created by Duke George of Saxony). Completing this fearsome force, there was also a sizeable artillery train. This intimidating army, which was personally commanded by King François himself, was estimated at the time to have been as large as 100,000 men. The King's senior captains included the Constable of France, Charles III, Duke of Bourbon, as well as other famous and experienced commanders who had served in Italy under his predecessors, nobles such as Louis de la Trémoille, Giangiacomo Trivulzio, Jacques de La Palisse and Stuart d'Aubigny. The French would be joined upon their arrival in Italy by a sizeable Venetian force under the command of the veteran *condottiere* Bartolomeo d'Alviano, who (as usual) was instructed by the republic to maintain a conservative strategy and remain ready to fall back and defend Venice herself if the situation demanded it.

Opposing the French was the usual confederation of *Milanese*, Swiss, imperial and papal forces. Notwithstanding the king of France's recent preferments in favour of his brother Giuliano, Duke of Nemours, Pope Leo X refused to be enticed by this into an overt alliance with France. The French alliance was nonetheless a strategy that was strongly advocated by the retired but ever-astute Niccolò Machiavelli, whose discreet opinion the Pope had lately sought on the matter. But this consultation remained no more than the briefest of flirtations and ultimately Leo cautiously reverted to his old alliance with Ferdinand of Spain, in whose army he had fought at Ravenna. Papal troops were not, however, to be lavished on Duke Massimiliano Sforza for the protection of Milan itself but instead were despatched, under the command of Lorenzo de' Medici and with Cardinal Giulio de' Medici as papal legate, to protect the papal vicariates of Parma and Piacenza, situated less than 100 miles to the south-east of Milan. Clearly, the Pope had decided against simply handing these lands–which lay at the very centre of his Italian strategy–over to France. Still smarting from his replacement earlier that year as captain-general of the Church, the duke of Urbino refused to contribute his own forces to the armies of the Papal States. No matter; the Pope would deal with this most unreliable of lords in due course. The Spanish and *Napoletano* troops under the command of Raimondo de Cardona, meanwhile, tarried on their way north to take up position at Verona where they hoped to prevent any junction between the Venetians and the French. It was left largely to the Swiss pikemen, under Cardinal Schinner, and a detachment of several hundred Italian *bravi* under Prospero Colonna to defend Milan against France's huge juggernaut of an army.

The opening moves of the campaign soon got underway. The Swiss advanced to the town of Susa to block two key Alpine passes by which they expected the French to descend into Piedmont – the Mont Cenis and the Mont Genèvre. Trivulzio, however, used his local knowledge of the terrain to bring the French in by the less frequented Col d'Argentière and, descending unhindered onto the Lombard plain, a vanguard of several French companies surprised and captured Prospero Colonna and his men while they were billeted at Villafranca. This now left the Swiss standing virtually alone on the front lines, with the Spanish, *Napoletano* and Papal contingents holding back in reserve. When Pope

Leo showed no intention of committing his men to battle, and when Raimondo de Cardona vacated Verona thereby allowing the possibility of a junction between the French and Venetian forces, Cardinal Schinner pulled his Swiss back to the safety of Milan. Advancing down into northern Italy, the first objective of King François was to re-occupy the city of Novara, which had been deserted by the Swiss sometime earlier. Subsequently he moved south to Marignano (today known as Melegnano), which lay just several miles south-east of Milan, where he encamped with the intention of linking up with d'Alviano and his Venetians at Lodi before advancing on the Spanish and papal troops at Piacenza.

Most of the Swiss troops now shut up inside Milan were tired of years of fruitless campaigning in Italy and were by now keen to return home with their booty. The Swiss had, in fact, already entered into armistice negotiations with King François at Marignano preparatory to their withdrawal. These peace talks had been stymied, however, by the arrival of fresh Swiss mercenaries who had marched down from the cantons hungry for plunder. Cardinal Schinner—that implacable enemy of the French—had used the opportunity presented by their arrival to preach a fiery sermon urging that they now hit the French army hard and without delay. On 13 September 1515, before François could link up with d'Alviano's Venetians, the Swiss filed out of Milan and advanced on the French king's position at Marignano. Arriving just two hours before sunset, the Swiss were deployed by the pugnacious Cardinal Schinner (who later fought in the ranks along with Huldrych Zwingli) into three large battle squares in staggered echelon. At the blast of the Swiss war horns, the three solitary pike squares advanced slowly and steadily against the French lines.

The resulting Battle of Marignano lasted for two whole days. The ground was utterly unsuitable for the sort of close-quarter infantry tactics favoured by the Swiss, covered as it was by streams, ditches and orchards. They were also hampered by the fact that they had brought with them only six cannon and 200 cavalrymen. Initially, the French hammered the Swiss squares mercilessly with their own cannon, archers, harquebusiers and cavalry but still the Swiss held firm and with unbridled confidence persisted in manfully bringing the fight to the French, pushing François back nearly one kilometre. François brought up his 'Black Bands of Guelders' to reinforce his frontage as well as his *gendarmerie* on the flanks. As darkness fell, a series of confusing, inconclusive hand-to-hand mêlées occupied the gloomy battlefield. Sometime after midnight, both sides lay down where they had stood, utterly exhausted, and slept. King François himself took his rest that night on a gun carriage wearing full armour, having first slaked his thirst with bloody water from a ditch filled with dead bodies.

The following day, despite being outnumbered and lacking both artillery and horse, the Swiss once more valiantly brought the fight to the French. The latter, hard pressed and drawn up on the defensive with badly wavering morale, came within a hair's breadth of being routed by the shoeless pikemen of the Swiss cantons. But weakened by the cold, their numbers sapped by the relentless artillery and archery, the Swiss wavered. They mustered into a wedge formation in one final attempt to break through and, as the Alpine war horns sounded, one massive Swiss pike man managed to reach the French cannon before he was butchered where he stood. Then, suddenly, the timely arrival of d'Alviano's Venetian reinforcements in the Swiss army's rear tipped the battle in favour of the beleaguered French and saved the day. Knowing that all was lost, the Swiss reformed into one large hollow square with the wounded placed in the middle and, harried by d'Alviano's cavalry, quit the field and retreated in good order back in the direction of Milan. The exhausted Frenchmen could only stand and watch them go with a mixture of awe and admiration.

The two-day battle had produced a truly modern carnage. The cast bronze artillery of the French had torn through the Swiss squares and the latter, in their turn, had with their bristling forest of pikes taken their own equally heavy toll on the thin lines of *gendarme* cavalry. Adding to the confusion, Trivulzio had also somehow managed to inundate the field of battle with water and this had fatally hindered the deployment of the Swiss squares. But if Marignano had proven one new military reality of the age, it was that an army composed of heavy pike infantry alone could not hope to prevail against one in which mixed arms closely coordinated their efforts. Some estimates listed the total casualties for both sides as being as high as 16,000, a comparable number to those suffered at the Battle of Ravenna. In fact, Marignano was a slaughterhouse that need not have happened and, were it not for Schinner's bellicose rhetoric, the Swiss might well have negotiated terms for a peaceful withdrawal from Milan. The humble workaday Milanese narrator Giovanni Marco Burigozzo tells in his *Cronica* how the Swiss returned to Milan covered from head to toe in dust and looking like they had spent the past ten years in battle; greatly moved, the citizens of Milan emerged from their houses to offer 'the poor Swiss' food and wine 'to lighten their hearts'. Although the slaughter had been great, it could have been far worse had François pressed his suit against the single retreating Swiss square and in this he showed his tendency towards old school chivalry. When the matter was discussed in a later council of war, the French king concurred with his most trusted councillors that rather than harry a foe who was near-death anyway, it was more gallant and magnanimous of the victor to offer them 'a golden bridge' by which to escape (*'J'ai ouï dire à tous bons capitaines et gens savants en guerre que à son ennemi on doit faire un pont d'or pour fuir'*).

Leaving their prodigious numbers of wounded in the hospitals of Milan and around 1,500 troops to guard the city walls, Schinner and the Swiss now departed for home, bringing Massimiliano's younger brother Francesco with them to safety. King François laid siege to Milan, gaining access to the city itself whilst Massimiliano Sforza, his chief minister Girolamo Morone, and a small group of defenders retreated for refuge to the Castello Sforzesco. When French sappers dug beneath the citadel's foundations and began to lay mines, the young duke of Milan realised that his situation was hopeless and agreed to come to terms. On 11 October 1515, having quenched–for the time being at least–his youthful thirst for military glory, King François I of France entered Milan in triumph by the Porta Ticinese, attired in an outfit of sky-blue velvet embroidered with golden lilies. François continued to behave with great chivalry towards his former adversary Massimiliano: 'The King, having returned from hunting, was sitting in the room where his supper was spread, when the Duke was brought to him by the Grand Constable. As they entered the room His Majesty lifted his cap from his head, and, rising to his feet, embraced the Duke.' François promised the former Sforza duke that he would be well looked after, even promising him a suitable wife. With this, he departed for exile in France with a generous annual pension of 36,000 crowns.

The Battle of Marignano had much longer-lasting diplomatic effects for, in effect, it ended the independence of the Swiss Confederation as a political force in Italy. The so-called 'Eternal Peace' of Fribourg, signed on 29 November 1516, committed both parties to refrain in perpetuity from allying themselves with the enemies of the other. Switzerland renounced all claims to Milan and France paid the Swiss handsome compensation for her failed Milanese campaigns. The Alpine town of Domodossola reverted back to Italian ownership, although the Swiss retained her other key town of Bellinzona, as well as parts of Lake Lugano and Lake Maggiore. From now on, France could call upon the services of Swiss mercenaries at any time in the future. This 'Eternal Peace' between France and the Swiss Confederation would be kept for the next 282 years and would only be broken in the years following the French Revolution, with the French invasion of Switzerland in 1798.

Having played no part in the defence of Milan, Raimondo de Cardona marched his Spanish troops south back to the border of Naples where they took up position to defend the kingdom against any possible French invasion, though none would be forthcoming. Having, likewise, failed to contribute to the resistance against François, Pope Leo X now parleyed afresh with the French king, seeking urgent assurances that Parma and Piacenza would be left in peace by France. The defeat at Marignano had convinced the Pope that the Spanish alliance (which had conveniently restored the Medici to power in Florence) was now a thing of the past; for their part, the Florentines too were relieved to be back under their old, familiar French alliance. Magnanimously forgiving all past transgressions, King François now promised to place Florence, the Papal States and also the Medici family themselves under the protection of French arms. There was only one condition – that the Pope and the King hold a face-to-face meeting.

Pope Leo agreed to go and meet the French king at Bologna, a mission which would enable him to pay a visit to Florence on his way north (it had been deemed inadvisable for François to march south to meet the Pope at Rome, which would have led his troops dangerously close to Florentine territory). Leo left Cardinal Soderini in charge at Rome, another shrewd move on his part designed to prevent Soderini from showing his face in Florence and reminding the citizens of their lost republican liberties (despite Piero's recent pardon the Soderini were still being kept judiciously at arm's length). The Pope's journey took him through both Cortona, where he was lavishly entertained for three days at the house of Giulio Passerini, as well as Arezzo. Lorenzo de Medici's moment to shine came during this, Pope Leo X's first state visit as Supreme Pontiff and Vicar of Christ and the occasion would be one of the most extravagant affairs Florence had yet witnessed. With a huge budget of 70,000 florins at his disposal, the young captain-general busied himself hiring a small army of 2,000 guildsmen and renowned artists to erect a cavalcade of artificial triumphal arches, palaces, castles, obelisks and statues, all elaborate but temporary structures dedicated to courtly ritual. Upon arrival in the vicinity of Florence the Pope was met by riders from Lorenzo informing him that the preparation of the city's decorations had not yet been completed, therefore he took up temporary residence at the villa of Jacopo Gionfiliazzi in Marignolle while the workmen completed their task. In truth, it had been Lorenzo's mother Alfonsina Orsini who had been tasked with the actual responsibility of decorating Florence for Pope Leo's visit and she had accomplished the task efficiently to the credit and glory of her son, on whom she so clearly doted.

Pope Leo X's *ingresso* to Florence, on 30 November 1515, was every bit equal to the artisanship which had gone into the transformation and transfiguration of Florence into a courtly, fantasy city. Despite his extreme corpulence the Pope–preceded by a colourful procession of heralds, valets and horsemen all dressed in immaculate papal livery–would nevertheless have looked magnificent in his bejewelled silk pontifical robes and papal tiara. Foremost in his official entourage was the brightly coloured Pontifical Swiss Guard. The regiment had been founded by Pope Julius II on 22 January 1506, with a core of 150 men brought to Rome by Peter von Hertenstein and commanded by Kaspar von Silenen of Uri. The artist Raphael had designed their original uniforms in bright blue, yellow and red but, by this time, the Pontifical Swiss Guard may have worn either a doublet bearing the white cross of Switzerland, or else a motif featuring the papal crossed keys. Their chests may have been protected by an armoured cuirass or breastplate and their heads by a helmet, perhaps the popular Spanish-style *morion*, as with the modern day Vatican Swiss Guard. Their weapons were the traditional halberd and broadsword. Behind the neatly dressed detachments of Pontifical Swiss Guard and their commander on horseback would have followed the representatives of the Sacred College, an array of cardinals all dressed in their sumptuous scarlet or purple *soutane* (cassock) with the *mozzetta* or red hooded cloak. The more mundane priests and other members of the Curia, no less resplendent in their ceremonial dress, would have brought up the rear.

Wearing his papal tiara and cope, 'Papa Leone' and his entourage first arrived at the city's Porta Romana and passed on horseback through a magnificent triumphal arch created by Jacopo di Sandro and Baccio da Montelupo. From here, Pope Leo proceeded in state down the Via Maggio, nearby to which, in the Piazza di Santa Felice, had been constructed a second arch in which had been placed a statue of his late father Lorenzo the Magnificent. When Giovanni laid eyes on the bust's inscription, '*hic est filius meus dilectus*' ('this is my beloved Son'), he was said to have been deeply and visibly affected. Across the bridge of Santa Trinità the Pope now arrived at the Piazza Santa Trinità where a massive castle had been constructed which was designed to resemble the Castel Sant'Angelo in Rome; in its frieze was an inscription declaring that Florence was blessed to be under the protection of 'both the earthly and the heavenly Giovanni' – a clear reference to both Pope Leo X himself as well as Florence's patron saint John the Baptist or *Giovanni Battista*. When Leo arrived at the Mercato Nuovo he found it dominated by a fifty-foot high obelisk resembling Trajan's Column at Rome. Next, in the Piazza della Signoria he encountered an octagonal temple, whilst in the Loggia had been placed a colossal statue of Hercules.

To the ecstatic cheers of the crowds, he now turned north towards the Duomo. Remembering his father's penchant for display and carnival as an essential tool of political propaganda, Pope Leo would have been anxious to create as much of a spectacle as possible. As the procession passed, the Pope giving solemn benedictions as he went, his attendants scattering glittering scoops of *soldi* and *denari* at the gleeful *popolo*, Giovanni de' Medici was shrewdly calling down centuries of papal tradition and Christian belief in service to his own resurgent dynasty. Upon arrival at the Cathedral of Santa Maria del Fiore he found the western façade decorated by an exquisite trompe-l'œil devised by the Florentine sculptor and architect Jacopo Sansovino and painted in chiaroscuro with bas-reliefs and sculpted figures by the painter Andrea del Sarto.

Here, as the culmination of the whole glorious *mise en scène*, Pope Leo X gave his benediction and plenary indulgence whilst his cousin Cardinal Giulio de' Medici, the archbishop of Florence, recited the oration at Mass. After His Holiness had retired to the monastery of Santa Maria Novella to rest and remove his vestments, the people gave themselves over to wild celebration – festive fireworks were lit and cannon were ignited in salute; there was feasting and joyful dancing. The merriment continued for three whole days. On the third day, the Pope performed the Advent service in the private family chapel at the Palazzo Medici. Upon completing the service the Pope was visibly moved by emotion and, according to contemporary reports, shed copious tears.

At Bologna, from 11 to 15 December, the mood was somewhat more subdued in contrast to the celebratory fervour of Florence. Bologna had borne the brunt of some of the worst fighting in recent years. Although the city's despot Giovanni Bentivoglio had not been well-liked by his own people he was still preferable to either the French or indeed a papal vicar (the cruelty of the papal legate Cardinal Alidosi had by no means been forgotten by the *Bolognesi*). Consequently there were no cheering crowds to welcome Pope Leo as he made his entry into the city and duly convoked his consistory. Arriving at the Palazzo Pubblico sometime later, François I made his obeisance, kneeling and kissing the Pope's red velvet slipper and then his papal ring, after which he was permitted a more familiar kiss on the flabby jowl of the Supreme Pontiff and Vicar of Christ. Both the King and the Pope were then treated to the spectacle of a life-size clockwork lion which was able to walk forward, twirl its tail and bear its fearsome teeth; when its chest opened, out burst a clutch of French lilies – the automaton thereby embodying within itself both the symbols of the French Crown and also the Lion Pope. The mechanism had been created by that impresario Leonardo da Vinci and King François was so impressed by its novelty that the following year he brought Leonardo back to France as his court painter, philosopher, architect and court *mécanicien* or engineer. The ageing Italian master was given a pension of seven-hundred gold crowns a year, the beautiful Château du Clos Lucé, beside the River Loire in Amboise, and the official mandate to 'think, work and dream'. It was here that Leonardo da Vinci passed the remaining three years of what had been a truly remarkable life.

Entertaining diversions aside, once the formalities had been concluded Pope Leo found the French king in business-like humour. As discussions got underway it soon became evident that François was seeking to bolster his recent military victory at Marignano with diplomatic hegemony too. He implored the Pope to abandon his treaty with Ferdinand of Aragon and join France in banishing Spanish arms from Italy once and for all. As Pope Leo knew that such a move would, if successful, grant François unrestrained power over the entire peninsula he refused to discuss the crowning of François as king of Naples whilst King Ferdinand himself was still alive. Besides, replied Leo, playing for time, Rome's agreement with Naples still had another six months to run. François next demanded that Leo give up the papal vicariates of Parma and Piacenza through which the king of France had travelled on his way to Bologna. These, he claimed, were traditional satellites of Milan and ought therefore to be turned over to him since he was in effect Milan's new ruler. Even more galling was his demand that the Pope surrender the towns of Reggio and Modena to his ally the duke of Ferrara.

These two requests struck right at the heart of Leo's plans for a Medici principality and so the Pope prevaricated. Concerning Parma and Piacenza he gave his assent but cautiously added the caveat that he may change his mind at a later date. Regarding Reggio and Modena, which he had received from the Emperor Maximilian, the Pope refused to assent to the king of France's terms unless Alfonso d'Este reimbursed him the 40,000 ducats which he had advanced to the Emperor in return for his imperial investment with both cities. Leo also refused to climb down from his avowed intention of conquering Urbino from Francesco Maria della Rovere. The latter, so Leo argued, had abrogated his right to hold Urbino as a vassal of the Church when, as captain-general of the Papal States, he had neglected to provide his military support to the Spanish and papal army at the Battle of Ravenna.

The King and the Pope then went on to discuss their respective powers over the Gallic Church. Satisfied with the outcome, King François then asked the Pope to make his former tutor, Adrian Gouffier de Boissy, a cardinal. Boissy was related by marriage to Cardinal Georges d'Amboise and, during the consistory of 14 December, he received the red hat and the titular church of Santi Marcellino e Pietro al Laterano. As the discussions at Bologna finally drew to a close, François rather astonishingly, demanded to be given the classical sculpture known as *Laocoön and His Sons* as a parting goodwill gift. This was the magnificent statue of the mythical Trojan high priest which had been unearthed in February 1506 by a peasant digging in a Roman vineyard. Recognised for what it was by Giuliano da Sangallo and Michelangelo, the *Laocoön* had been placed in the personal collection of Pope Julius II. It was an unusual request but Leo mumbled some vague words of assent just so as to bring the proceedings to a close (the *Laocoön* would remain in Italy until another French invasion in 1798 finally carried it off to France). François left Bologna well pleased, the Pope considerably less so, having achieved very little of tangible value for himself, Rome or indeed Florence. The French king returned briefly to Milan where–before finally leaving the city on 8 January 1516–he oversaw the reconstitution of the duchy's administration and transferred its governorship to the highly capable but dour and humourless Constable of France Charles, Duke of Bourbon.

Pope Leo X returned once more to Florence where he found the River Arno had burst its banks and the city in the grip of an attack of famine. Worse still, he found his brother Giuliano sick with consumption at the Palazzo Medici. Moving the invalid to a more conducive Medici country property at Fiesole, the Pope watched as Giuliano faded away before his eyes. Giuliano was still lamenting the Pope's plans to move against the duke of Urbino and his talented, cultured wife Eleonora Gonzaga. In spite of all the times that Francesco Maria della Rovere had let his family down Giuliano de' Medici still stood by him, even as he himself teetered at death's door. Despite the best care that Medici money could provide, Giuliano's condition continued to deteriorate and he died on 17 March 1516 at the age of thirty-seven. The duke of Nemours had been married to Filiberta of Savoy on 22 February 1515 at the court of France and, by the time of his death, Filiberta had still failed to conceive. He was survived therefore only by his illegitimate five-year-old son, Ippolito (by Pacifica Brandano). The boy's upbringing would subsequently be sponsored by his uncle Pope Leo X and his cousin Cardinal Giulio, himself a dubiously legitimatised bastard. But despite being orphaned the future nevertheless looked bright for the privileged young Ippolito de' Medici. The following year, despite his age, the Pope made the boy archbishop of Avignon. Lorenzo, meanwhile, continued to rule Florence, presiding there with help from his mother Alfonsina.

On 23 January 1516, His Most Catholic Majesty King Ferdinand II of Aragon died at the age of sixty-three in Madrigalejo, Spain. On 14 March, his fifteen-year-old grandson the young Archduke Charles Habsburg, Duke of Burgundy and Prince of Asturias, was duly proclaimed King of Castile and of Aragon, a position which he was to hold jointly with his mother Queen Joanna *la Loca* ('the Mad'). On the epochal nature of this event we need not dwell, suffice to say that in one fell swoop it drew many diverse realms into a single coalition which comprised a unified Spain, the Low Countries, Burgundy, and the kingdoms of Naples, Sicily and Sardinia. If Charles's inheritance horrified King François I, then for Pope Leo X it offered tantalizing new possibilities. At Bologna, François had stymied the Pope's plans for a principality based around Parma, Piacenza, Modena, Reggio and Ferrara. As an alternative therefore, Pope Leo had clung to an earlier, vague hope that François might be willing to divest himself of his claim to Naples and confer the kingdom instead upon Giuliano de' Medici, who had been married to his aunt. For his part, François intended no such thing; in fact he still aspired to the throne of Naples himself and had hoped that Charles of Burgundy would make a gift of it to him, while he himself focused on consolidating his rule over Castilian Spain. Both king and pope were, however, to be disabused in their respective hopes and Charles remained committed to preserving the kingdom of Naples for his own Spanish descendants.

With Naples obviously off the table, Pope Leo looked closer to home in Tuscany. Florence's old enemies Siena and Lucca could, he surmised, both be amalgamated into a new Florentine state under Giuliano's lordship. With regard to Lucca, the Pope persuaded François not to renew his protection over that city. Siena meanwhile had, until Ferdinand's death, been under the protection of Spain and so the Pope now used the opportunity of the Aragonese king's demise to replace the ruling *signore*, Borghese Petrucci, with his cousin Raffaele Petrucci. Borghese was the son of Pandolfo Petrucci, the brutal authoritarian absolutist who had ruled Siena with a rod of iron since 1500. Chased from Siena by Cesare Borgia in 1503, he had subsequently returned and, following Valentino's removal from Italy, had continued to rule as one of the most influential lords in Tuscany. It was Pandolfo who had supported the *Pisani* during their fifteen-year long struggle with Florence. Pandolfo and Borghese had calculated, however, without the son of Pandolfo's brother Giacoppo, a young man who had chosen an ecclesiastical career. Raffaello Petrucci, bishop of Grosseto, was a notable pro-Medici cleric who had followed Giovanni de' Medici into his long years of exile from Florence during the pontificates of Alexander VI and Julius II. He had long been a personal advocate for the return and restoration of Piero de' Medici and, in March 1516, with the support of both the Pope and Florence, he instigated the coup that subsequently brought him to power in Siena. Pope Leo's unwonted interference in Siena's affairs had, however, earned him the enmity of Cardinal Alfonso Petrucci, who was Borghese Petrucci's brother.

When Giuliano died just three days after Charles was declared king of the joint Spanish kingdoms the plan to create him a great feudal prince of Tuscany had to be quickly revised. The person on whom the future prospects of the Medici dynasty now devolved was Piero the Unfortunate's proud and dissolute son Lorenzo di Piero de' Medici. In 1516 he was just twenty-four years old, an acceptable age considering that, in as many years, the remarkable Cesare Borgia was already duke of Valentinois and on the brink of embarking upon his epic conquest of the Romagna. The Pope had never abandoned his plans to subdue Urbino and, now that his younger brother was dead, there remained no further impediment to this undertaking. Furthermore, as Urbino was a papal vicariate, he could safely act this time without the unwelcome interference of either France or Spain.

Leo X first laid the necessary groundwork, taking Duke Francesco Maria della Rovere to task for a number of heinous acts that he had committed in the past; the cold blooded murder of Cardinal Alidosi for one thing, and the failure to answer Julius II's call to restore the Medici to Florence for another, not to mention his treacherous refusal to come to his and Cardona's assistance at the Battle of Ravenna. The notorious street killing of Cardinal Alidosi was cited, by itself alone, as grounds for disqualifying the Duke from holding his fief in the name of the papacy; it was an infamous act for which the Duke was even held up for comparison with Cesare Borgia, by now legendary as one of the most hated figures in Italy. He was ordered to appear in person in Rome to formally respond to the charges. A papal summons under such circumstances usually foreshadowed a rapid arraignment, a brief show trial, and a hasty conviction followed by a lengthy spell in the Torre dell'Annona, the dilapidated medieval tower in the rione of Ponte which served as Rome's notorious and much-feared pontifical prison. When unsurprisingly the duke of Urbino failed to present himself, Pope Leo duly excommunicated him and he fled his duchy for the safety of Mantua and the Gonzaga family. Lorenzo de' Medici advanced with his papal troops and quickly occupied the duchy in June. By August, his uncle the Pope had created him duke of Urbino.

But Francesco Maria della Rovere was not done. Like the *condottieri* dukes of Urbino of old, he would challenge the Pope's high-handed actions and he took himself off to Verona to recruit a fresh army. By February 1517, he had reached the border of the Papal States with a formidable force consisting of 7,000 Spaniards, German mercenary *landsknechts*, Gascons and Italians plus around 600 horse. Although the Pope had hired about 10,000 of his own *landsknechts* and Gascon mercenaries to counter the deposed duke, the native people of Urbino clearly favoured Francesco Maria and the struggle for the duchy was bitterly contested in the hills and mountains around the town of Urbino itself. The vicious tyrant of Perugia, Gian Paolo Baglioni, who had been created count of Bettona by Pope Leo X only one year before, had meanwhile entered the fray on the side of his new papal benefactor. In retaliation, Francesco Maria invested Perugia. The conflict now degenerated into what can only be described as an unruly and protracted mess. Lorenzo de' Medici and the Pope's *condottieri* Renzo da Ceri, Giulio Vitelli and Guido Rangoni dealt with the situation as best they could.

In March 1517, Lorenzo himself suffered a harquebus shot to the head which, although not fatal, refused to heal properly and was sufficiently serious to leave him a visibly changed man in the months which followed. Meanwhile, he was replaced as commander of the papal army by Cardinal Bibbiena. But no sooner had the handover been completed than many of Leo's *landsknechts* deserted to Francesco Maria's army for want of payment by the Pope. To make matters worse, Bibbiena next suffered a bad defeat at Monte Imperiale and, reeling under heavy losses, was forced to retreat to Pesaro. The Pope was only able to restore the deteriorating situation by mid-September when Francesco

Maria's own unpaid Gascons and Spanish mercenaries defected, in their own turn, to the Pope's army, having negotiated better terms for themselves with their former adversary. Once again, Francesco Maria bolted for Mantua where he was received at the Palazzo Ducale by his father-in-law Francesco Gonzaga, the by now heavily syphilitic former-*condottiere*, and his cultured wife Isabella d'Este. The dowager duchess of Urbino, Elisabetta Gonzaga and her niece Eleonora Gonzaga meanwhile fled to Ferrara without a ducat to their name and were taken in by Alfonso d'Este and Lucrezia Borgia (for his part, Alfonso was still irate that Reggio and Modena had still not been restored to him, despite his having already repaid Leo the 40,000 ducats that the Pope had paid Maximilian for the two towns). The Medici conquest of Urbino had ultimately been achieved at a staggering cost to the papal treasury of over 800,000 ducats.

In the summer of 1517, the Court of Rome was thrown into an uproar by the uncovering of a plot to murder the Medici pope. Pope Leo's aggressive efforts to carve out a Medici principality had quickly begun to win him powerful enemies in the Sacred College. The ousting of Francesco Maria della Rovere had upset Cardinal Raffaele Sansoni Riario, the former duke's kinsman and the last prominent remaining *nipote* of Pope Sixtus IV. Pope Leo's meddling in his family's affairs in Siena had, meanwhile, enraged Cardinal Alfonso Petrucci to the point of action, probably egged on by Duke Francesco Maria, whilst Cardinal Francesco Soderini (who had so far done well out of his career and now owned Girolamo Riario's former Roman residence, the Palazzo Altemps) still smouldered over the ousting of his brother Piero from the fulcrum of power in Florence. These malcontents were joined by other grumblers like Cardinals Bandinello Sauli, who had been denied the wealthy archbishopric of Marseilles by Pope Leo, and Adriano Castellesi, who had been influenced by a soothsayer's prediction that 'Adrian, a learned man of humble birth' would soon sit upon the throne of St. Peter (displeased with Pope Leo's profligate reign, Castellesi had decided to help the prophetic process along).

The plot which coalesced around these clerical malcontents would involve the Pope's physician, Battista Vercelli, a specialist in ulcers. Poisoned bandages would be applied by the doctor to the Pope's anal fistula and Cardinal Sansoni Riario would then be elected to replace him in the subsequent papal conclave. When Cardinal Petrucci left for Mantua to update Francesco Maria della Rovere on the plan, the plot came to light through the indiscretion of a household servant and Pope Leo swiftly took matters into his own hands. Cardinals Petrucci and Sauli were promptly recalled to Rome under a promise of safe conduct but were instantly arrested and cast into the *Sammorocco*, the deepest and worst dungeon of the Castel Sant'Angelo, where on a daily basis they were subjected to the horrific tortures of the rack. 'No faith need be kept with a poisoner', Leo would gruffly retort to the Spanish Ambassador who had stood surety for Petrucci. In their agonising suffering, the two cardinals implicated Cardinal Sansoni Riario and the others, most of whom were subsequently imprisoned. Castellesi escaped from retribution upon paying a fine of 25,000 ducats and was deposed from the Sacred College after he fled from Rome. Bandinello Sauli was initially deposed as cardinal, but was later restored and permitted to retire to his villa in Monterotondo where he died one year later under suspicious circumstances. Cardinal Soderini meanwhile was briefly detained by the Pope but was eventually allowed to leave Rome and go into voluntary exile upon payment of a 25,000 ducat fine.

Cardinal Riario had in fact refused to participate in the plot but the fact that he was aware of Petrucci's intentions, did not disclose the plot, and indeed stood to benefit from its successful outcome, ultimately sealed his downfall after forty years as a high-flying prince of the Church. Forced to bribe his way out of trouble by coughing up 150,000 ducats and surrendering his *palazzo* to the Holy See, Riario left Rome and would eventually die in Naples in 1521. His magnificent *palazzo*, built from a single night's gaming winnings, was handed over to Cardinal Giulio de' Medici, vice-chancellor of the Church, who subsequently made the building the seat of the Apostolic Chancery (accordingly, it would be known thereafter as the Palazzo della Cancelleria). Pope Leo had neither forgotten nor forgiven Sansoni Riario's role in the Pazzi conspiracy of 1478 and this outcome at least assuaged the Pope's desire for belated poetic justice and final closure over the murder of his late uncle Giuliano.

Neither Battista Vercelli nor Cardinal Petrucci was quite as fortunate as their co-conspirators. The former was tortured and then dragged through the streets of Rome before being drawn and quartered. When Cardinal Bembo read aloud his own sentence of execution Petrucci had replied with such a vociferous stream of invective and blasphemies that he could be heard all the way down the corridor. When one unfortunate priest approached to offer Petrucci the last confession, the condemned man had kicked him violently in the testicles. Lorenzo de' Medici had by this time arrived in Siena to confer with the condemned cardinal's relative Raffaele Petrucci, who had pledged to do anything within his power to bring his treacherous kinsman to justice. It was all the green light that Leo X needed. Cardinal Petrucci was garrotted in his prison cell by the Pope's Muslim executioner Roland the Moor, for no prince of Holy Mother Church could legally be killed by another Christian.

In a city inured to all forms of scandal in high places, the executions and rash of banishments had nevertheless shocked all of Rome. In the immediate aftermath, Pope Leo's sense of paranoia only increased. He ordered the papal guard to track down and execute those members of Cardinal Petrucci's family whom they could lay their hands on, as well as anyone formerly associated with him. In consistory he kept two deaf bowmen behind his throne to react swiftly to any sudden assassination attempts (Petrucci had confessed on the rack to having worn a dagger in consistory, waiting for an opportune moment to stab the Holy Father). In spite of the fact that all those implicated had confessed to the plot, the popular scuttlebutt in Rome was that there had been no such plot, but that the spendthrift pope had concocted the story purely for the vast fines that he could impose upon those wealthy cardinals that had been implicated.

The Pope's actions in the wake of the Petrucci Plot certainly do not seem to have been designed to disabuse people that his actions had been financially motivated. Immediately after the crisis had blown over, on 3 July 1517, Leo published the names of thirty-one new cardinals, a number of appointees almost unprecedented in the history of the Church, the appointment of which brought a windfall of ducats for the papal treasury. But generating income had not been the only motivation. Diluting the far too powerful Sacred College with an influx of new cardinals also served to create a more compliant cardinalate which would not object to his promotion of Medici interests throughout Italy. He also had some debts to settle in favour of those who had helped him in the past. In gratitude to Bianca Rangone of Modena, who had sold her jewellery to help pay for his expenses when he had been a prisoner of the French army, Leo created her son Ercole Rangone a cardinal. His two nephews Giovanni Salviati and Niccolò Ridolfi were also raised to the Sacred College at this time. Bishop Raffaello Petrucci (the executed Cardinal Alfonso Petrucci's cousin) also received a cardinal's hat in recognition of his long and loyal service to the Medici pope.

To the East, Bayezid II's sultanate had ended when he was forced to abdicate the throne on 25 April 1512 by his younger son Selim, who had staged a successful uprising against both his father and elder brother Ahmet. Sultan Selim had then sealed his power by dual acts of parricide and fratricide, earning himself the epithet 'the Grim'. Unlike Bayezid he was militarily ambitious. By early 1517 he had conquered the Mamluks at the battles of Marj Dabiq and Ridanieh and annexed the Mamluk Sultanate which, in addition to Egypt, also encompassed Syria, Palestine and much of the Arabian Peninsula. The by now massive Ottoman Empire stretched from Egypt to the Balkans and the Christian kingdoms were justified in being somewhat worried about Selim's intentions. In his Papal bull *Apostolici Regiminis* of 19 December 1513, condemning every proposition contrary to the truth of the enlightened Christian faith, Pope Leo X had declared: 'If the Almighty in his mercy allows us to settle peace among the Christian leaders, we shall press on not only to destroy completely the bad seeds, but also to expand the territories of Christ, and, supported by these achievements, we shall go forward, with God favouring his own purposes, to the most holy expedition against the infidels, the desire for which is deeply fixed in our heart.'

Pope Leo X persuaded the Fifth Lateran Council to now appoint a special committee of inquiry comprising eight cardinals to investigate future Ottoman plans and gather intelligence whilst he himself made overtures to the crowned heads of Europe for a proposed Crusade designed to hold the heathen in check. François of France was approached in addition to Henry VIII of England; Charles of Aragon, Castile, León, Sicily and the Netherlands was also approached, as was the Holy Roman Emperor Maximilian. The proposal found a favourable reception and the papal committee recommended that a general peace be declared across Christendom whilst the Crusade was launched. Both François and Maximilian came up with different strategies however. The former favoured a single campaign in which a 60,000-strong army would take ship from Ancona and land at Durazzo from whence they would march on the Ottoman capital Constantinople. Maximilian on the other hand preferred a three-year campaign, during which he, Charles of Spain, and Manuel of Portugal would first advance along the North African coast and seize Egypt; meanwhile, François would capture the Balkans together with the Poles and Hungarians, and in the third year the two converging Christian armies would jointly lay siege to Constantinople. It was a bold, spectacular plan which proposed to roll back most of the Muslim advances which had been achieved since the seventh-century.

To fund the campaign, François was given the dispensation to collect ecclesiastical tithes within France, a surprising concession which was looked upon askance by the other kings of Europe and which caused some suspicion. Many mumbled that the French king was only interested in harvesting the income and was not sincere about the Pope's Crusade at all. Nonetheless, by March 1518, the terms of a five-year Europe-wide truce had been hammered out in preparation for the venture. Its chief architect was Cardinal Thomas Wolsey the lord chancellor of England who, together with King Henry VIII, was wildly enthusiastic about the Crusade. On 3 October 1518, the French and

English were the first to sign Wolsey's Treaty of London which, somewhat optimistically, proclaimed an eternal peace throughout Christendom. This was a precursor to the rest of Europe joining the truce and the other signatories comprised Burgundy, the Netherlands, the Holy Roman Empire, Spain, and the Papal States. In gratitude for his proactivity in organising the truce, Pope Leo placed Cardinal Wolsey in charge of logistical preparations for the Crusade itself. An almost palpable *frisson* of expectation now settled over Europe.

The Crusade raised the inevitable question of funding. The Fifth Lateran Council had approved a suggestion that the Pope increase the sale of indulgences across Europe to help meet the costs. Leo X unreservedly approved this approach, stating to his cardinals: 'There are many, and there will be many, who will gladly purchase eternal life for a small price, if they see that others are fighting for God in earnest, rather than pretending to do so'. His choice of words were ironic for as the months dragged on and no Crusade materialised some critics questioned the Pope's mettle, others even going so far as to suggest that the Crusade had been nothing but a money-making ploy by a profligate bishop of Rome who could not live within his budget. This was certainly the observation of the Venetian ambassador, who noted that Leo's treasury was empty 'because of his generosity' and that he dispensed so much largesse that his native Florentines were loath to leave him so much as a *soldo*.

Since Lorenzo de' Medici was ennobled and established in his new duchy of Urbino, the time had now come for him to marry. When François and Pope Leo X had met in Bologna, the former had sealed their agreement with the promise of a suitable French dynastic match. To Lorenzo himself, the French king had written personally in 1516 to congratulate him on becoming ruler of Florence and had vowed: 'I intend to help you with all my power. I also wish to marry you off to some beautiful and good lady of noble birth and of my kin, so that the love which I bear you may grow and be strengthened.' The lady which François had selected for his young Medici protégé was one of his distant relatives and a member of the royal house of France, Madeleine de la Tour, the daughter of the count of Auvergne. The House of La Tour d'Auvergne was an old and illustrious one and Madeleine's father, Jean III de la Tour, was the last medieval count of Auvergne, Boulogne, and Lauraguais. Madeleine's mother, Jeanne de Bourbon-Vendôme, was a descendant of the French King Louis IX ('Saint Louis') through the House of Bourbon, which had been created by the union of Robert de Clermont and Beatrice de Bourbon. Should the House of Valois ever become barren of sons, the House of Bourbon was ever-poised to take up the French Crown.

The proposed wedding would be a dual celebration for, two months earlier on 28 February 1518, the French king's wife Claude of Brittany had given birth to his firstborn son, who had also been named François. The King had asked Pope Leo to stand as godfather for the child and it was decided that Lorenzo de' Medici would travel to France to act as his uncle's proxy. The royal couple had been most pleased with their healthy new child; upon giving birth, Claude is reputed to have gaily remarked 'tell the King that he is even more beautiful than himself'. For the *Dauphin's* christening, at which Duke Lorenzo was present and granted the honour of holding the infant heir to the French throne, the artist Leonardo da Vinci had continued to prove his versatility and value-for-money by designing the baptistery decorations. Three days after the baptism, on 28 April 1518, Madeleine and Lorenzo were themselves married at the gorgeous

Italianate palace of Château d'Amboise. This magnificent property was owned by the Queen Mother Louise of Savoy although, less happily, it had been where King Charles VIII had died after watching that fateful game of *jeu de paume*. Here, Leonardo da Vinci was already in residence, domiciled at the nearby (and conveniently accessible) Château du Clos Lucé. François had meanwhile brought from Italy other gifted artists such as the landscape designer Pacello da Mercogliano, who considerably improved the château grounds and gardens through a clever system of hydraulics that siphoned water from the nearby River Loire to irrigate the estate. All-in-all it was a magical setting for an aristocratic wedding and, as if the surroundings were not opulent enough, the royal decorators had also adorned the château's inner courtyard with brightly covered silk awnings and tapestries upon which the Duke's Florentine entourage feasted their eyes upon their arrival.

The wedding itself was a sumptuous affair which lasted a full ten days. There were feasts and balls, more feasts and masques and banquets and chivalrous tournaments and yet more feasting. To help digest the rich foods there was of course also plenty of dancing. King François, himself a great dance enthusiast, ensured that dance figured prominently in all the festivities. In honour of the Tuscan groom the King ordered that dancing be conducted in the Italian style, which would have involved for example the *basse danse*, or 'low dance', which was a dignified, stately, processional dance – the precursor to later dance styles like the *pavane* or the *galliard*. There was also the *balletti*, from which the French subsequently derived the modern word 'ballet'. For the wedding, seventy-two ladies were attired in Italian, German, and other fashionable costumes, providing a flourish of bright colour. François's wedding gift to Madeleine was 10,000 gold coins and a nuptial bed of tortoiseshell inlaid with mother-of-pearl and richly decorated with precious gems. Lorenzo received from the King thirty-six fine French horses. Not to be outdone, the wealthy Medici groom reciprocated by giving away rich gifts to the assembled French nobility.

Despite the grandeur of the occasion, however, the French aristocrats were less than taken with the Medici duke. For such a relative parvenu whose family had until very recently been not only 'merchants' but also political exiles, he was deemed to be brash and arrogant. Furthermore, his physique–which was never quite the same after his wounding during the wars of Urbino–seemed to them sickly and unimpressive. This was most probably due to the syphilis which was by now rampant in his body, a legacy of his aimless and dissolute days prowling the brothels of Rome. Be that as it may, however, François himself was in a celebratory mood due to the birth of his new heir and it was the King who set the tone as to how his magnates should respond to their 'low-born' Florentine guest. Consequently, when the King bestowed upon Lorenzo France's highest chivalrous honour, the Order of Saint-Michel, no one was especially surprised or taken aback. And when François granted the Duke a company of his mounted *gendarmes* (just as Louis XII had made a gift of 100 lances to Cesare Borgia some years before), no one murmured a syllable of dissent and all was light hearted celebration.

Lorenzo and Madeleine's triumphant return to Florence was closely observed by the Florentines, not least by the *fashionistas* amongst the more *grassi* families. Madeleine herself did not disappoint her eager audience, making her entry to the city in an embroidered dress of Lyons silk and the finest brocade from Paris, and peering from beneath a coif of Rheims linen.

Lorenzo meanwhile embarked upon a whole new chapter in good living and fine dining which was epitomised by his presidency of the *Compagnia del Broncone*. This was an exclusive gentleman's society which took its name from the Italian word *broncone*, which connotes a large tree trunk that is reborn and sprouts new leaves. The analogy was obvious; Florence had surmounted the recent years of difficulty and strife and was now poised to be newly reborn, surpassing even her earlier golden age under the tutelage of Lorenzo's grandfather *il Magnifico*. Before his death, Giuliano the duke of Nemours had enjoyed his own similar exclusive society, the *Compagnia del Diamante*. However the remit of these élite societies or brotherhoods was not always purely festive in nature; often it was deeply political as well. The fiercely anti-republican historian Bartolomeo Cerretani recorded in his *Sommario e estratto della sua storia* that nobody who was not either a member of the *Broncone* or the *Diamante* could expect to be elected as a magistrate in Florence and that the *compagnia* therefore governed the city virtually by default.

With Lorenzo's marriage affairs now resolved, Pope Leo once more settled down to his customary life of feasting, entertainments, hunting and general self-indulgence. Magnificent hunts were organised in the countryside around the papal villa at Magliana to the south-west of Rome in which His Holiness would ride out with several hundred retainers (and when his haemorrhoids were flaring up he would watch the *coup de grâce* being delivered to some unfortunate buck from a safe distance on horseback through a telescope). Masked balls were held. There was dancing and lute playing and poetry readings. A devotee of menageries, the Pope delighted in his beloved pet elephant Hanno, a gift from King Manuel I of Portugal. On the day of his extraordinary arrival in Rome, the beast had worn two scarlet slippers identical to the Pope's and had genuflected to the Supreme Pontiff three times, showing itself to be the most devout elephant in all of Christendom. Leo also had his boy-singer Solimando, the son of the late Turkish Prince Djem, who was widely rumoured to be the Pope's teenage catamite. There were also cavorting dwarves and jesters, leading the ever-irreverent Pietro Aretino to snark: 'It is difficult to judge whether the merits of the learned or the tricks of fools afford the most delight to his Holiness', whilst Sigismondo Tizio complained that 'It is injurious to the Church that her Head should delight in plays, music, the chase and nonsense, instead of paying serious attention to the needs of his flock and mourning over their misfortunes'.

But in Pope Leo's endlessly gay life there was precious little room for mourning. Instead, there were interminable performances of the Pope's favourite sex comedy *La Calandria* which had been written by his scabrous friend Cardinal Bibbiena. Machiavelli's play *Mandragola* was also performed, much to Leo's delight, even though the work was a thinly veiled satirical critique of Medici power in Florence. The Pope's friend the urbane *Sienese* banker Agostino Chigi threw the most extravagant banquets in all of Rome at his suburban Villa Chigi, later better known as the Villa Farnesina, which–built by the Sienese architect Baldassarre Peruzzi–was adorned with frescos by the likes of Raphael, Sebastiano del Piombo and Giulio Romano. Another notable contributor to the villa's wealth of frescos was the homosexual Piedmontese artist Giovanni Bazzi who revelled in the provocative name of *Il Sodoma* and who's *Nuptials of the Conqueror with Roxanne* (an episode in the life of Alexander the Great) was regarded as his life's masterpiece. In 1513, *Il Sodoma* presented the Pope with a picture of *the Death of Lucretia* in return for which

Pope Leo gave him a large sum of money and elevated the artist to the rank of *cavaliere*.

When the decadent feasting at Chigi's villa had been concluded the host made it a ritual to affect to demonstrate his vast wealth; his guests would be invited to make their way out into the garden where they would toss the gold and silver plate from which they had dined, like exotic discuses, into the adjacent River Tiber (the expensive dining services were retrieved later on from nets which had been carefully laid beforehand by the villa's footmen.) Chigi's fortune had brought many fringe benefits: his lovely Venetian mistress, Francesca Ordeaschi, was the toast of Rome and his name had also been formerly associated with the great Roman beauty Imperia Cognati, Europe's first high-profile celebrity courtesan, who also occasionally lent her favours to the painter Raphael. For others with less illustrious mistresses to go home to, the delights of Rome's many brothels always beckoned as an after-dinner option. In a Roman population of 50,000 souls, 7,000 of them were licensed prostitutes, leading Benvenuto Cellini to matter-of-factly remark that 'The kind of illness [syphilis] was rife - very common among priests'.

When he wasn't otherwise occupied enjoying himself with his friends (and their lovers), the Supreme Pontiff was overseeing the improvement of Rome and this encompassed both its intellectual, as well as its actual, architecture. Leo's greatest contribution to learning was to revitalise Rome's pontifical university, the *Sapienza*. Established by Pope Boniface VIII as a *Studium* under the papacy's direct control, Pope Eugenius IV had (with notable irony) used a tax on wine to raise funds for its reorganisation. Leo X brought in scores of new academics in a range of fresh disciplines from botany and mathematics to astronomy and medicine and established new chairs of Greek and Hebrew. Erasmus's first Latin/Greek Bible the *Novum Instrumentum* had been completed in 1516 and dedicated to Pope Leo X. It required numerous rewrites throughout the remainder of Erasmus's life. In 1519, the Pope wrote to Erasmus in anticipation of the latest revised edition: 'Go forward then in this same spirit: work for the public good, and do all you can to bring so religious an undertaking into the light of day'.

In his Physical building program Pope Leo continued a tradition which dated back to the public works first initiated by Pope Nicholas V. He constructed a new road, the Via di Ripetta, which provided a spacious new boulevard going north to the Piazza del Popolo and which took the name 'Via Leonina' after its builder. Together with the sculptor Andrea Sansovino, he added the façade portico of the Church of Santa Maria in Domnica with Tuscan columns and a fountain. Above all he continued, at astronomical expense, to fund the on-going work of Bramante in rebuilding the new St. Peter's basilica, conceived by Pope Julius II to be the showcase centre of worship for Roman Catholic Christendom. After Bramante died in 1514, Raphael was given the contract to take over as supervisor of works whilst still continuing his other painting commissions: in 1517 he painted the famous portrait of a plump and pensive Pope Leo flanked by a swarthy Cardinal Giulio de' Medici and Cardinal Luigi de' Rossi, the grandson of Piero the Gouty through his daughter Maria.

Other ecclesiastical building projects tended to fall by the wayside depending on the vagaries of the Medici papacy's ever-fluctuating finances. Leo had earlier commissioned Michelangelo to reconstruct the façade of the 'Medici' Basilica of San Lorenzo in Florence and to adorn it with sculptures.

450

Unenthusiastically, Michelangelo had agreed and spent the next three years drawing and planning the new façade. However, the Pope had by this time spent a small fortune on his military excursions; the conquest of the duchy of Urbino for instance and Leo's sponsoring of the imperial forces against the French had left him in an impecunious state; as time went by, so the funding for civic improvements like the façade of San Lorenzo had quite simply dried up. In spite of this, Michelangelo gamely carried on until 1520. Although Leo's patronage of art and architecture in no way matched that of his predecessor Pope Julius II, Leo X did nevertheless continue most of the structures begun under Julius, notable amongst which are the Vatican staterooms, the Stanze, which Raphael started work on in 1508 and whose decorations Leo paid to have completed. The frescoes in the Stanza della Segnatura had already been finished by the time Leo gained the papal throne, but those in the two adjoining rooms were painted during his papacy. In the Stanza di Eliodoro, Leo was depicted by Raphael mounted on the white horse which he had gallantly rode at the Battle of Ravenna; in the fresco he is depicted in the guise of Pope Leo the Great riding out to dissuade the Huns from attacking Rome. The frescoes in the Stanza dell'Incendio, meanwhile, were intended to establish and reinforce Leo's pontifical power. It was a continuation of the old story: the projection of Medici power and legitimacy through the finest art that money could buy.

But this kind of patronage never had come cheap. The construction of St. Peter's and the extravagance of Pope Leo's lifestyle left a gaping hole in the papal treasury and the Curia was reduced to increasingly inventive measures in the constant struggle to generate fresh sources of income. The sale of indulgences to both the living and the dead had already been approved by the Fifth Lateran Council as a revenue-raising solution for the proposed Crusade against Selim 'the Grim' and by now indulgences had become endemic across the whole of Western Latin Christendom as bishops in their dioceses were bombarded with instructions to keep raising their incomes and send ever larger Church tithes back to Rome. Commissioners for the collection of indulgences attracted some of the Church's most unscrupulous talent, some of whom were outright shysters. The *Milanese* papal protonotary Arcimboldi enjoyed spectacular success in raising revenues in Germany, Denmark and Sweden; so much so that a chronicle published in Lübeck in 1516 had criticised Arcimboldi for flaunting silver kettles and frying pans paid for by his revenues. Another commissioner, Albert of Brandenburg the archbishop of Mainz and Magdeburg and Primate of Germany, had taken out a 30,000 florin loan from the Fuggers of Augsburg to settle his *pallium* and was unable to repay the principal and interest solely from the income of his archdiocese. He therefore turned to one of Christendom's slickest ecclesiastical salesmen, the Saxon-born Johann Tetzel, Grand Commissioner for indulgences in Germany.

Johann Tetzel went from town to town, church to church, with his travelling roadshow. Whenever he entered a new town his carriage (the Papal Bull of Indulgences placed neatly next to him on a silk cushion) and his intimidating entourage of guards, clerics and Fugger bankers always made an impression. His presentation to the crowds included the most graphic depictions of Hell and all its nameless torments and he carried paintings specially designed to leave nothing to the simple, gullible, peasant imagination. It was Tetzel who became known for the notoriously jejune couplet:

'As soon as a coin in the coffer rings

The soul from purgatory springs'.

When asked whether an indulgence could also be purchased in remission of some future sin, Tetzel is reputed to have contradicted official Church dogma and avidly assented that it could. He also claimed that an indulgence could indemnify its purchaser for an act of sexual assault against the Blessed Virgin Mary herself. There was a set price list depending on one's social station: for lay rulers the price per indulgence was twenty-five gold guilders, the same as for bishops. For abbots, counts and barons the charge was ten and for lesser nobles and clerics six. For ordinary members of the laity the price was a half to one guilder depending on the person's income. Roman Catholic theology supported the concept of indulgences for it asserted that man cannot be justified by faith alone; only charity and good works could contribute to the salvation of one's soul. One such officially mandated 'good work' (indeed the most highly encouraged one) lay in the donation of coin to Holy Mother Church.

Within the remote lands of the Empire, however, this cynical hawking of papal indulgences stirred up considerable resentment amongst those who saw in the practice the inevitable cheapening of their faith. From the University of Wittenberg an audacious monk named Martin Luther had already denounced Cardinal Petrucci's trial and execution as a cynical 'financial operation' of the Pope and a tract which he wrote called the *Ninety-Five Theses* (officially known as the *Disputation of Martin Luther on the Power and Efficacy of Indulgences*) had been nailed for public scrutiny to the door of Wittenberg Cathedral on 31 October 1517. The technology of the printing press had spread Luther's cogent arguments throughout the length and breadth of the Empire and eventually Luther's own bishop, Prince Albert of Mainz, had relayed the subversive document to the Pope. Upon learning of the dissident monk, Pope Leo had reacted by punningly referring to Luther as 'Luder', which was the German word for 'carrion', and which also connoted that the bearer of the name was a beast, wretch, debauchee, whore, or scoundrel. At this point, however, Leo X had merely dismissed the brouhaha in Germany as a minor disagreement amongst contentious monks. Like the rest of the Roman hierarchy he had fatally overlooked the fact that if Luther could call into question the divine order of things, then the common low-born man could, by the same token, question the earthly hierarchy. The whole of Europe was a powder keg and Luther, in his sincere quest for simple spiritual truth free of accepted ritual and institutionalised superstition, was the spark that would set it off.

Lorenzo de' Medici's wife Madeleine de la Tour gave birth on 13 April 1519 to a daughter, whom she named Catherine Maria Romula. Neither parent was especially ecstatic that their first-born child was of the female sex. Lorenzo by this time was already chronically sick with both consumption and syphilis and there was now considerable doubt as to whether he would even survive long enough to procreate a legitimate male heir with his new duchess. He languished bedridden at the Medici villa at Careggi, where his new-born daughter was presented to him. Madeleine too was ill from complications arising from the birth and, indeed, it is highly likely that her husband had also infected her with syphilis. Like most wealthy, young Renaissance males he had philandered and it is probable that Lorenzo, taking after his dissolute father Piero, had picked up the disease in the brothels of Rome.

Already Lorenzo was father to an illegitimate eight-year-old son named Alessandro who had supposedly been born to a servant girl of North African descent, identified in documents as Simonetta da Collevecchio, who skivvied in the Medici household. Many gossiped that the boy was in fact Cardinal Giulio's bastard and that his nephew the Duke had only acknowledged him in order to spare the high-ranking cleric any undue social or professional embarrassment; the resemblance between the swarthy cardinal and the half-caste boy was especially remarked upon. Meanwhile, the seriousness of Madeleine's post-partum condition was not relayed to the Duke for fear that it might adversely affect his own delicate health. Her ailment worsened however and, despite the best doctors that Medici money could buy, nothing could be done to improve her condition. By 28 April, Madeleine was dead, having barely emerged from her teenage years. Lorenzo's own condition also rapidly deteriorated and, aged just twenty-six, he followed his young wife to the grave several days later on 4 May 1519. The poet Ludovico Ariosto, better known as the author of the best-selling romance epic *Orlando Furioso*, had been sent by Alfonso d'Este to convey his ducal master's condolences for Madeleine recent death; Ariosto arrived in Careggi shortly after Lorenzo's own demise and was unable to accomplish his mission. Devastated, Pope Leo X hid his grief behind a pall of Christian stoicism. 'God has given, God has taken away' he is reputed to have commented upon hearing of his nephew's passing. In Florence, Goro Gheri called out the guard and sent riders to speed word to the republic's favoured *condottiere* Vitello Vitelli to come with all haste but, in the event, the city remained calm and the professional soldiers were not needed.

Both Lorenzo and his late uncle Giuliano were interred at the Medici New Sacristy behind Brunelleschi's unfinished facade of the Church of San Lorenzo. Earlier attempts by Michelangelo to induce Pope Leo X to consent to his designs for the facade had foundered over the sculptor's choice of expensive marble from Carrara and Pietrasanta rather than cheaper marble from the quarries at Seravezza near Florence. When, in 1520, a workman was killed by a falling block of marble, the superstitious Michelangelo abandoned the project altogether after having devoted several wasted years to creating the necessary drawings and models; '*L'arte non è mai finita, ma solo abbandonata*' as Michelangelo's rival Leonardo da Vinci had epigrammatised. This is why, to this very day, the basilica of San Lorenzo strangely still lacks what should by rights have been a magnificent Michelangelo façade. Although they had grown up together beneath the same roof practically as brothers, the Pope and Michelangelo never could see eye-to-eye. The uncomplicated, pleasure-loving Pope could never understand Michelangelo's morose, pious personality. The same year that the facade was finally shelved, the pontiff had confessed to Sebastiano del Piombo that 'Michelangelo is a terrible man; one cannot get along with him'.

Nevertheless, in 1526, Buonarroti would begin work on the iconic tombs of Lorenzo di Piero and Giuliano di Lorenzo. The conception was for both tombs to incorporate an allegory of the four parts of day: Night and Day, and Dusk and Dawn. Four life-size marble statues would commemorate these four elements, Night and Day being placed on Giuliano's tomb, and Dusk and Dawn being placed on Lorenzo's. The two tombs were also originally intended to be paired with brand new tombs for Lorenzo the Magnificent and his brother Giuliano de' Medici, however Michelangelo never began the final pair and so these two relatively minor and short-lived Medici sons were immortalised by the great

Buonarroti instead. By working on the Medici tombs Michelangelo continued to neglect his outstanding commission on Pope Julius II's own tomb – a far grander affair which was by now contractually long overdue. The late Julius's relative Francesco Maria della Rovere complained to Michelangelo, accusing him of idling his time away in Florence whilst enjoying the 16,000 crowns that he had already been paid for the commission. To his chagrin, this onerous commitment would continue to plague Buonarroti for years to come, as would Francesco Maria della Rovere's periodic threats of violence, from which the artist prayed for deliverance.

As for Catherine Maria Romula de' Medici, the infant, who had been rapidly baptised on 16 April, would grow up to eventually marry the brother of the French *Dauphin*, Prince Henry and, through one of those strange quirks of fate, would eventually become the Medici queen of France. In truth, the Florentines were not sad to see the back of the imperious Duke Lorenzo. Both he and his mother Alfonsina Orsini had quickly squandered what little goodwill the Medici regime had carried forward from their lengthy period of exile. Like his illustrious grandfather he had begun to use the (in his case, undeserved) soubriquet *'il Magnifico'* and one unfortunate Florentine who instead described him as 'Lorenzo the Shit' was sent into exile for eight years. Alfonsina in particular had done much to alienate the Florentines during the many interludes when she governed in Lorenzo's absence. Unlike the Pope's elder sister Lucrezia, who called for a more dispersed and equitable form of Medici control, his sister-in-law Alfonsina had repeatedly called for sole power to be concentrated in her son's hands and continually interfered in the appointment of elected state officials. She herself pulled Lorenzo's strings from Rome and, when she moved back to Florence in 1515, she took up residence at the Palazzo Medici, which now became the de facto centre of Florence's government. Constantly preoccupied with financing Lorenzo's rule, not to mention the expensive conquest of Urbino from 1516-7, she pressured the Pope to appoint her son-in-law Filippo Strozzi the Younger to the position of depositor-general of the Vatican, giving her family direct access to the Vatican treasury. Filippo and his associate Francesco del Nero (whom Filippo got appointed as *vicedepositario* of Florence) happily made use of the sinecure to enrich themselves by earning commission on transfers of large sums of money between Florence and Rome as required by the Pope.

When she was not physically in Florence, Alfonsina acted through her chancellor, Bernardo Fiamminghi, or through her agent Goro Gheri, who had also acted as Lorenzo's secretary. Indeed, prior to her active involvement in Florence's government before the year 1515, Lorenzo had nominated a twenty-year-old cousin named Galeotto de' Medici to deputise for him whenever he himself was away in Rome. These deputies were able on many occasions to ignore the will of the *gonfaloniere* and the various governing councils and, in effect, became small, self-contained centres of government in and of themselves. More than anything, therefore, Alfonsina and Lorenzo's style of ruling prefigured a change to a more centralised and almost 'ducal or monarchical' form of government, unquestionably one of the factors which most offended many casual spectators of Florentine political affairs. Even as early as 1515, during Pope Leo's state visit to Florence, posters had been seen around the back streets protesting Alfonsina's avarice and denouncing her as an 'enemy of republican liberties'. When she finally died, one year after her son, malicious tongues spread rumours that she had left behind a vast fortune of over 70,000 ducats. In reality her legacy was probably closer to around 10,000 ducats, although she did also possess a splendid *palazzo* in Rome (the Palazzo Medici, which she acquired from Pope Leo X in 1509) as well as various dairy farms in Tuscany. She urged the Pope to use her legacy wisely to care for her surviving twenty-seven-year-old daughter Clarice as well as her infant granddaughter Catherine de' Medici (even though Clarice's husband Filippo was by now using his position as the Vatican's depositor-general to create one of Rome's great fortunes).

Without a candidate for rule, the duchy of Urbino itself was taken under the direct rule of the papacy, although the late Lorenzo's infant daughter Catherine was first created duchess of Urbino by Pope Leo. Florence, meanwhile, came under the rule and supervision of Cardinal Giulio de' Medici, who proved himself to be a considerably more tolerant and enlightened governor and who managed to reclaim some of the goodwill squandered by Lorenzo and his overbearing Orsini mother. As for the remaining male heirs of the main line of the Medici family, there were now only two bastard children remaining: the eight-year-old Ippolito de' Medici, only son of Giuliano di Lorenzo (who was now hastily legitimised); and Lorenzo's swarthy ten-year-old bastard Alessandro de' Medici, now referred to as 'il Moro', who had been raised comfortably but as yet obscurely under the privileged roof of the Palazzo Medici in Rome. Therefore, with the pope of Rome himself as the most adroit member of the main, male line of the Medici family, the future of the Medici now rested somewhat dubiously upon the shoulders of two illegitimate sons, a legitimised cardinal-cousin and an infant duchess (who, even as a grown adult, could not be able to govern anyway due to her status as a woman). The education of the two boys was prudently accelerated. Pierio Valeriano, one of the rising intellectual stars at Pope Leo's court, was entrusted with inculcating them with the humanist knowledge essential to their grooming as future leaders of Florence. Ippolito seems to have distinguished himself in this area from a young age; Alessandro considerably less so.

The cadet line of the family, which had so shrewdly re-invented itself as 'il Popolano', was by contrast flourishing. Lorenzo di Pierfrancesco together with his wife Semiramide d'Appiano had squired several children before his death in 1503, including Pierfrancesco the Younger who was already thirty-three by the year 1520. In 1511 Pierfrancesco had married Maria Soderini who was related to the disgraced Cardinal Francesco Soderini and his brother Piero Soderini, the former republican *gonfaloniere* during Florence's Savonarolan interlude. The couple had four offspring of their own: Lorenzino ('Little Lorenzo'), Giuliano, Laudomia and Maddalena. Meanwhile, Lorenzo di Pierfrancesco's younger brother Giovanni *il Popolano's* son Ludovico (but better known to all as 'Giovanni'), whom he had squired by Caterina Sforza just prior to his death, was by this time twenty-two years old.

When Caterina Sforza had died in 1509, after a long and exhausting custody battle with Lorenzo di Pierfrancesco over little Giovanni, the boy had inherited all his late father's considerable property holdings within Florence itself and had been sent to be raised as a ward of his distant relations Lucrezia de' Medici and Jacopo Salviati. As he grew to manhood under the Salviati's roof this violent and quarrelsome young man soon began to embody all the warlike qualities of his late mother, who had earned the nickname of *La Tigra* ('the Tigress'). In Florence, however, she had subsequently settled down to lead a quieter and more sedate existence than her former life, but her son had inherited her fire in full measure. Giovanni de' Medici's notorious rapier duel with Boccaccino Alamanni, reputed to be the best swordsman in the city, earned him a temporary banishment from Florence in 1515 and, at the age of seventeen, the youth had been summoned to Rome by Pope Leo X.

No sooner had he arrived in Rome than Giovanni again disgraced himself by his constant brawling, duelling and whoring in the brothels of the city. On one occasion, however, when Giovanni and a small group of friends were ambushed on the Ponte Sant'Angelo by a gang of Orsini *bravi*, who had tried to take the youth captive in order to ransom him back to his wealthy Medici relations, Giovanni had fought his way free with such violent and reckless élan that when the Pope heard of the escapade he knew immediately what to do with his uncontrollable young kinsman. Giving the young lion a squadron of 100 lances, he sent him to fight in Lorenzo de' Medici's war for the conquest of Urbino, and here–in the hills around the duchy, forged in the white hot maelstrom of battle– Giovanni had proved himself every inch his mother's son. Having found his calling in battle, Giovanni now embarked upon a military career which would ultimately lead to his reputation as 'the last great *condottieri* of Italy'.

Having been raised by Caterina, Giovanni de' Medici was trained by the best swordsmen money could buy; but not only was he a capable man of action, he also possessed an outstanding tactical and strategic mind as well. Quickly grasping all the factors which decided the outcome of modern battles he was able to adapt his military practices accordingly. He understood, for instance, how gunpowder had completely revolutionised the battlefield and foresaw the need to change the use and purpose of cavalry in battle. Equipping his men-at-arms with smaller, lighter and more mobile Turkish or Berber horses, he capitalised on the two major strengths of the cavalry arm–'speed and mobility'– and specialised in fast but devastating skirmishing tactics and ambushes. Also, in an era when professional soldiers were epitomised by the mercenary *landsknecht*, that is to say individualists with their tendency towards outlandish multi-coloured peacocking, Giovanni instead emphasised the importance of consistency and uniformity of dress. Consequently, where other battlefield units strove to outdo one another in the extravagance and outlandishness of their attire, his mounted units wore simple, drab tunics which were purposefully all alike.

In 1516, Giovanni had married Lucrezia and Jacopo's seventeen-year-old daughter Maria Salviati, Lorenzo the Magnificent's granddaughter, with whom he had been raised as an orphan. Unlike other dynastic marriages of the day this seemed to be a genuine love match. Maria had watched the energetic Giovanni grow up on a day-to-day basis and had sincerely fallen in love with the strong, capable, young man. Giovanni no doubt reciprocated the emotion and around him, at least in his later married life, there is not the same tell-tale gossip of dissipation and idleness of purpose as there had been in the case of Piero the Unfortunate or his dissolute son Lorenzo. The wedding was in a way a small reminder of the heyday of Florence under the reign of *il Magnifico*. For her own wedding, Maria's mother Lucrezia had been provided with a lavish and wide-ranging trousseau by her father Lorenzo. This trousseau had included the very latest ladies fashions such as the *gammura* (sometimes also called the *camora*), a style of dress which was to preserve its popularity well into the sixteenth-century, not to mention pretty chemises of linen from Rheims and fine silk from Lucca as well as hair-bands, handkerchiefs and other accessories which Lucrezia had never had occasion to use herself. These were now handed down to Maria as part of her own sumptuous wedding trousseau.

When in 1519 Maria gave birth to a son, Cosimo, the child succeeded in uniting once more the main and cadet lines of the Medici family. In a sense, Giovanni's genuine ability in war posed a danger to the Medici pope and his vice-chancellor Cardinal Giulio, who seems to have borne an especial animus towards the serious-minded young *condottiere*. The fact that such a successful and dynamic individual, a man of real power, hailed from the cadet branch of the Medici family must have been particularly galling. Giovanni quickly gained a loyal following amongst those who could divine his true qualities. The 'scourge of princes', that serial poetic blackmailer Pietro Aretino (who was notorious for such racy literary works as *Dialogue in which Nanna teaches her daughter Pippa to be a whore*), would later become Giovanni's close personal friend, constant traveling companion, confidante and chronicler. The painter Titian would much later capture for posterity the features of this self-proclaimed 'Secretary to the World' – a truly massive presence, fifty-three years old, bearded, dissolute, satyr-like; Aretino would remain with Giovanni de' Medici quite literally until the very end.

CHAPTER 17

The Battle of Pavia

Madame, that you may know the state of the rest of my misfortune,
there is nothing left to me but honour, and my life, which is saved.

King Francis I of France to Louise of Savoy

In the first half of 1519, Europe was rocked by further massive tectonic
changes in the political landscape. In January of that year the Emperor
Maximilian died and, on 28 June 1519 at Frankfurt am Main, the electors of
the Holy Roman Empire offered King Charles the Imperial Crown. Barely out of
his teens, as the Emperor Charles V, he now ruled a vast dominion extending to
all four points of the compass: from the Baltic to the Mediterranean, from Spain
to Germany and Austria. He was also soon to lay claim to the vast untapped
wealth of the New World as his conquistadors Hernán Cortés and Francisco
Pizarro would, within a few years, begin their epic drive inland to conquer both
Mexico and Peru. This evolution of the Holy Roman Empire into a truly *global*
empire was the worst conceivable scenario for King François as Charles's
dominions now effectively hemmed a more parochial France in from every side.
In a bid to forestall this outcome, the French king had himself lobbied
unsuccessfully for imperial election. He had despatched Robert III de La Marck,
Seigneur of Fleuranges and Marshal of France, on the well-nigh impossible
errand of inducing the electors to award him their votes. But it had all been for
nothing for Charles was bankrolled by the inexhaustible wealth of the House of
Fugger and some 850,000 ducats had been lavished on the electoral lobbying
campaign.

Meanwhile, from Charles's perspective, France was seen as a barrier which
lay inconveniently between his new German lands and the territories which he
held in both Spain and the Netherlands. Furthermore, through her occupation
of Milan, Genoa, Parma and Piacenza, France was also interfering in what
Charles saw as the *Regnum Italiae*, which is to say, those lands in northern and
central Italy which were traditionally considered to be part of the Holy Roman
Empire. As King Ferdinand of Spain had battled King Louis of France for
mastery of the Kingdom of Naples, so the Emperor Charles would now continue
that same conflict by battling François of France for mastery of the duchy of
Milan. But whereas the late Emperor Maximilian had always been hampered in
his military endeavours by lack of funding, the Emperor Charles faced no such
constraints. Not only did he now hold massive tracts of Europe, but the
treasure galleons plying the seas from the New World promised to make Spain
and the Empire the single wealthiest political bloc in all Christendom. It was

therefore time for Charles to intervene in the affairs of Italy and reclaim what was rightfully his by birth.

Upon Maximilian's death, Pope Leo X's Crusade had the wind taken out of its sails. The former Emperor had been the main driving force behind the venture and his successor Charles was seemingly eager to wash his hands of the whole affair. Peace in Europe was not what he desired; there was still unfinished business with the Crown of France and therefore the chastisement of Selim 'the Grim' would have to wait. Meanwhile, in Germany, the heretic Augustinian monk Martin Luther would soon write in 1521: 'How shamefully the Pope has this long time baited us with the war against the Turks, gotten our money, destroyed so many Christians and made so much mischief!' The Emperor would soon be preoccupied with the political and religious unrest which Martin Luther would stir up. It therefore made sense for him to make overtures to Pope Leo X; not only did he require the Pope's blessing for his own imperial investiture, but only the Pope could excommunicate the recalcitrant Luther, which he finally did on 15 June 1520 with the papal bull *Exsurge Domine* ('Arise O Lord'). In the midst of the furore of the Lutheran heresy, Charles was eager to prove his status as a devout Catholic king, even as his rivals were doing the same. In the summer of 1521, Henry VIII of England had published his treatise *Assertio Septem Sacramentorum* ('The Defence of the Seven Sacraments') in gratitude for which Pope Leo had, in October 1521, granted him the title *Fidei Defensor* ('Defender of the Faith'). It was also time for Pope Leo to reverse the concordat arrived at with François in Bologna in 1515 and to move closer to the Empire. The French Crown, it was now clear to Leo X, would never agree to relinquish Parma or Piacenza or indeed abandon their military support for the estranged papal vicariate of Ferrara. Furthermore, the French king's petulant insistence that the Pope accompany him in a joint conquest of Aragonese Naples was growing increasingly insistent and ever more tiresome for Pope Leo.

For the initial few years of his rule, Charles had been under the sway of his advisers and in foreign policy matters they had counselled caution. The price that he paid for détente with France had been demeaning. In return for the king of France's recognition of his throne of Naples, Charles was forced to pay the French Crown 100,000 ducats per year. As he grew into the role which destiny had forced upon him, however, his courtiers watched as the young man with the oversized Habsburg jaw (a result of inbreeding) and drooling speech developed a shrewd mind for statesmanship and strategy which belied his slightly absurd and inbred physical appearance. Terrified that the new Emperor would seek to be crowned in Rome and use the opportunity to acquire yet more territories on the Italian peninsula, François decided to distract Charles with a series of conflicts on his own borders. In the south, Henri d'Albret, the son of Queen Catherine of Navarre (who had been ousted from her kingdom by the Spanish in 1512), attempted a reconquest with French assistance. To the north, François encouraged Robert de la Marck, Seigneur de la Flourance, to invade Luxembourg. A more gifted soldier than a diplomat, de la Marck was perfect for such an assignment; at the Battle of Marignano he had his horse shot out from under him and had been knighted by the King with his own royal hand. On 22 April 1521, France formerly declared war on the Empire.

With the effortless, mercurial changeability of a Medici statesman, Pope Leo X now forged a new agreement with the Emperor. France would be expunged from Italy altogether; its fiefs in Milan and other neighbouring cities would be reconquered by a joint imperial-papal army. The second son of Ludovico Sforza, Francesco Sforza, known as *il Duchetto*, would be instated as duke of Milan. French Genoa was to be overturned and Antoniotto Adorno would be installed there instead. Charles would also assist the Pope against his rebellious papal subject Alfonso d'Este of Ferrara, who had long supported the objectives of the French Crown. Rome and the Papal States would furthermore agree to help Charles defend the borders of Naples and repel any attack by Venice. Florence and the Medici would trade French for imperial support and Charles, in return, pledged the Pope to do all in his power to extirpate the Lutheran heresy which was still spreading unchecked across his German lands. To finance the new campaign, both Emperor and pope would each contribute 100,000 ducats, much of which would go towards the hiring of 16,000 freelance Swiss mercenaries. The treaty was signed on 29 May 1521.

Charles initially began his offensive against France through proxies of his own. Antoniotto and Girolamo Adorno led a mixed fleet of papal and imperial galleys against Genoa's Ottaviano Campofregoso in June 1521, but the attempt proved unsuccessful. Rome and the Empire then refocused their attentions on consolidating their armies and selecting the best commanders to lead them. Joint overall command of the army was given to Prospero Colonna and the Neapolitan *condottiere* Fernando Francesco d'Ávalos, the marchese di Pescara. Antonio de Leyva, Duke of Terranova, was given command of the Spanish cavalry. The papal troops were meanwhile placed under the leadership of Federico II Gonzaga, Marquis of Mantua, who was already proving to be more assertive and more reliable than his late father, Francesco Gonzaga. Their total forces numbered around 20,000 infantry supported by 1,500 lances. It had been mooted at some point that the viceroy of Naples, the militarily uninspiring Raimondo de Cardona, would be sent north to act as supreme commander but this was universally unpopular amongst the existing commanders and, in the event, Cardona's own ill health put paid to the idea (indeed he was to die the following year). Opposed to the imperial force were around 8,000 foot and 1,200 horse under the command of Odet de Foix, Viscount of Lautrec.

In 1516, in order to gain the favour of his new mistress Françoise de Foix, Comtesse de Châteaubriant, the French king had summarily dismissed his capable Constable of France, Charles of Bourbon, from the position of Regent and Governor of Milan and appointed as his replacement the Comtesse's brother the viscount of Lautrec, effectively making him viceroy for all French affairs in Italy. The Comtesse herself held a special place in the King's affections and was known as '*La mye du roi*' ('the Sweetheart of the King') and, as for Lautrec, he was a gallant enough soldier who had also seen combat at the Battle of Marignano. Be that as it may, this was no way to conduct important military affairs, with key appointments being farmed out based on who was occupying the monarch's bedchamber at any given moment. Charles of Bourbon had kept his counsel and retired to private life for the time being; however the open wound inflicted by the King's dismissive and unjust conduct in this affair would eventually ripen to become an infected sore called 'treason'. Lautrec meanwhile plotted against his rival in Milan, the aged *Milanese* rebel Giangiacomo Trivulzio. By now in his mid-seventies, Trivulzio was accused of plotting with the Swiss for their return and control of Lombardy and summoned to France to answer the allegations and there he had died on 5 December 1518. Scheming with Lautrec had been Trivulzio's old adversary, Galeazzo Sanseverino, the son-in-law of Ludovico Sforza *il Moro*.

461

The imperial-papal campaign got underway in August with an attempt to lay siege to the French inside Parma, but when Lautrec approached with his army the siege was abandoned after a fortnight. The marchese di Pescara soon demonstrated his flair for leadership. Once, when Lautrec's brother, Lescun, was shadowing Pescara's column through the countryside, Pescara had flaunted his fearlessness by riding in the rear-guard on a slow and obstinate mule. When, in their determination to capture him, the pursuing French advance guard turned a predetermined point in the road, a company of Pescara's Spanish harquebusiers (whom he had surreptitiously placed in the hedgerows) suddenly opened fire on the pursuers, decimating the French troops. For flamboyant, morale-boosting exploits such as these the Neapolitan commander came to be much-loved by his men. Also serving in the imperial-papal forces was another *condottiere* who had already earned considerable respect during the course of his, as yet, short career. This was Caterina Sforza's son, Giovanni de' Medici, who led a small private company of soldiers who were ruthlessly dedicated to him. Giovanni earned distinction early on in the campaign by forging a passage across the River Adda, thereby opening the way for the imperial advance towards Milan, Parma and Piacenza. As both Lautrec and Lescun pulled back behind the line of the Adda River their Swiss mercenaries began deserting the French army for want of pay. The few troops that the Venetians had sent under the command of Teodoro Trivulzio were also next to useless. Lautrec and Lescun withdrew inside Milan and, in their wake, the Imperialists now advanced to lay siege to the city.

In seeking to bolster Milan's defences, Lautrec had unwisely levelled the suburbs outside of the city walls, a measure which had created deep resentment amongst the *Milanesi*. When Pescara and Prospero Colonna arrived outside Milan on 20 November, their intelligence network informed them of the local population's antipathy towards the occupying French and they decided to turn this situation to their advantage by mounting an immediate attack. The Spanish and Germans were unleashed against the city walls, whilst inside Milan the local population rose up in unison against the detested French. The few Venetians allied to the French fled in panic, leaving Teodoro Trivulzio behind to be captured as he lay wounded amidst the rubble. Lautrec himself withdrew with his best troops and, when the dust had settled, Milan had fallen within a matter of just two hours. The only drawback was that Milan's citadel had not fallen and was still occupied by the French, but this was of little consequence for the *castello* could easily be isolated from the rest of the city.

The fall of Milan, which had happened so rapidly and unexpectedly, sent shock waves rippling across Lombardy. In the immediate aftermath the demoralised cities of Pavia, Lodi, Como, Alessandria and the two episcopal cities sees of Parma and Piacenza, quickly capitulated to the imperial forces. Only Cremona and the fortresses of Milan and Novara still remained in French hands. Lautrec withdrew to Venetian territory, where he was unable to mount a counter-offensive for fear of upsetting the Venetians. An absentee Francesco Sforza was declared duke of Milan, with his adviser Girolamo Morone temporarily acting as regent in his stead. The new duke would ultimately reach Milan in early April 1522 with 5,000 German reinforcements which he had brought with him from Trent, where he had been living safely in exile. Upon arrival he was given a warm welcome by Federico the marquis of Mantua and the Spanish captain Don Antonio de Leyva who had been governing the city jointly together with Girolamo Morone. According to one eye-witness, there was 'such ringing of bells and firing of artillery as might have brought the world down in ruins'. For their part, the *Milanese* were overjoyed to see the return of a Sforza duke and looked forward once again to the days of Francesco and Ludovico Sforza. It therefore behove the Imperialists to play up to this Sforza patriotism in order to win the goodwill of the population. But even as the people of Milan celebrated their good fortune, all was not well within the Imperialist camp itself. When, garbed in the impressive robes of a Knight of Rhodes, the papal legate Cardinal Giulio de' Medici visited Milan and called upon the joint imperial commanders Prospero Colonna and Fernando Francesco d'Ávalos, the latter insulted his counterpart by claiming all the credit for Milan's conquest. Flying into a rage, Colonna challenged Pescara's presumptuous claims and he in turn indignantly drew his sword. It was left to the cardinal to enforce calm between the two incensed commanders but from that moment on all amity and cooperation between the two generals was at an unfortunate end.

Pope Leo X was taking his ease at the Villa Magliana outside Rome when news reached him of the fall of Milan and the recovery of Parma and Piacenza. His policy of aligning with the Emperor had been vindicated. He immediately returned to Rome, arriving back on Sunday, 24 November, with the intention of conferring with his war council and participating in the public festivities being planned to commemorate the great victory of the papal alliance. However, soon afterwards, he succumbed to a chill and took to his bed. By 1 December 1521, mere days after achieving all that he had hoped and planned for, Christendom's first Medici pope was dead at the age of forty-six.

In contrast to the minutiae set down about the lives and deaths of popes Sixtus IV, Innocent VIII and Alexander VI by the papal master of ceremonies, Johann Burchard, Pope Leo X's own major-domo, Paris de Grassis (who had succeeded Burchard in 1506), has left us with scant information in his chronicle, the *Diarium*, concerning Leo's illness, treatment and eventual demise. All that we know for sure is that, having been called upon to make the necessary funeral arrangements for the dead pope, Paris de Grassis entered the papal bedchamber and found that the Supreme Pontiff's body was 'already cold and livid'. The Pope had died so unexpectedly that the final sacrament of supreme unction could not even be administered. Pope Leo's funeral panegyric was delivered by Antonio da Spella, his chamberlain, who–either intentionally or unintentionally, we do not know–botched the oration completely and declaimed the words in so rude and unbecoming a way that no record of it was taken down for the official papal chronicle. The judgement of Alexandre Dumas was that under Pope Leo X's reign Christianity 'had assumed a pagan character' and even the Catholic Encyclopaedia blandly posits that Leo 'was possessed by an insatiable love of pleasure'. After his death, all the positive aspects of Leo X's rule were rapidly forgotten – his building works in the city and his bringing of a certain festive gaiety to Rome. All that was now remembered was how his addiction to lavish and self-indulgent pleasures and pursuits had virtually bankrupted the papacy.

The sudden and unforeseen nature of his passing led inevitably to the usual rumours of poisoning and, in the aftermath of his death, there was the unavoidable rash of public witch hunts for the likely 'culprits'. Suspicion fell firstly upon one Bernardo Malespina, the Pope's cup-bearer who was known to be a lifelong French sympathiser. In fact, it had been Malespina who had been responsible for holding the Pope captive in his pigeon-coop following his daring escape from the French army after the Battle of Ravenna, a role which Malespina himself no doubt bore with everlasting embarrassment and regret. Apparently Malespina had served the Pope a cup of wine several days before his death and Leo had complained that the drink tasted unusually bitter. In the absence of any firm evidence, however, Malespina was released and suspicions now came to bear on both King François of France and Francesco Maria della Rovere, the deposed duke of Urbino.

François, it was generally agreed, did not have the base nature required for such subterfuge as the assassination of a Pope and he was soon acquitted in the court of public opinion. Della Rovere, however, was an entirely different matter; he had both the brutal nature for assassination and indeed the motive for it. Not only had the Pope systematically deprived him of his duchy but he had proven before, in his cold blooded murder of Cardinal Alidosi, that he had a killer's sensibilities. The portrait which Titian painted of the duke of Urbino in 1538 depicts a bearded man of aristocratic bearing dressed in burnished black armour and grasping the baton of a Venetian general. His ferocious face is turned away at a slight angle but his piercing eyes glance towards the viewer, as if challenging. It is the portrait of both an uncompromising individual and a killer.

Another possible suspect was Alfonso d'Este, the duke of Ferrara, whose duchy had doggedly resisted all papal attempts at conquest for many years. Since the death of his wife Lucrezia Borgia in 1519, a much-maligned woman who had been an alleviating and steadying influence on the Duke, his dour soul had become even sourer than before. All he seemed interested in these days was experimenting with new manufacturing techniques in his *Ferrarese* cannon foundry. Still, the Romans could not place d'Este beyond the bounds of suspicion and Pope Leo's death did indeed serve to remove an unwelcome adversary who challenged his rule over the duchy.

The military consequences of Pope Leo's death were wide-ranging. The Florentine contingents promptly left the imperial-papal army whilst the spigots to papal funding, which had previously been crucial for the financing of the army, were effectively turned off overnight. Colonna and Pescara could no longer pay their troops and the majority of the Swiss who had come from Zurich to fight with the imperial army now promptly returned home. Cardinal Giulio de' Medici, who had travelled with the army as papal legate, now hurried back to Rome for the conclave; as vice-chancellor of the Church and the leading figure in the proceedings he nurtured hopes that he would be elected as Leo's replacement. As a candidate his qualifications were persuasive. Not only was he a Knight of Rhodes, a proven figure who had played a crucial role in the aftermath of the Battle of Ravenna, but overall he was seen as being an experienced, intelligent and dependable member of the Sacred College who had advised the former pope to the very best of his abilities.

When the papal conclave went into session Giulio was quickly able to command the support of fourteen out of a total of thirty-nine cardinals. However, Cardinal Francesco Soderini had already formed an alliance with Cardinal Pompeo Colonna and both stood firmly opposed to his election, dissuading the remaining cardinals from casting their votes in favour of the Medici candidate. Meanwhile, the mutually suspicious Spanish and French cardinals remained in a deadlock, whilst the king of France let it be widely known that if another Medici were elected as pope 'neither he nor any man in his kingdom would obey the Church of Rome'. This impasse left as *papabile* several other frontrunners that were nevertheless considered equally objectionable as candidates for Supreme Pontiff. One of these was Cardinal Alessandro Farnese, who could never quite shake off his uncomfortable affiliations with the hated Borgia family. Yet another, with seven votes in his favour, was Cardinal Thomas Wolsey the lord chancellor of England and a man who was by now at the very height of his powers.

But if the idea of a non-Italian pope was unpopular with the Latin cardinals then the prospect of an English pope was an abomination. The last (and only) English pope had been a certain Nicholas Breakspear, who ascended to St. Peter's throne in 1154 as Pope Adrian IV. In his struggle for power with Arnold of Brescia, the leader of the anti-papal faction in Rome, Adrian had taken the unheard-of step of placing Rome itself under a papal interdict. This extreme act had ruined the pilgrim trade and collapsed the local economy and consequently the Italian cardinals had come to an unspoken agreement to never again elect another Englishman as pope of Rome. Added to this was the Italians' natural xenophobia towards the English in general. In 1496-7, a popular Italian saying was doing the rounds to the effect that 'the English are great lovers of themselves, and of everything belonging to them; they think that there are no other men than themselves, and no other world but England; and whenever they see a handsome foreigner, they say that "he looks like an Englishman!"'. In the fourteenth-century, that other notorious Englishman, Sir John Hawkwood, had likewise given rise to the expression: *'Inglese italianato é un diavolo incarnato'* ('an Englishman Italianised is a devil incarnate').

To block the election of either of these two cardinals, Giulio de' Medici induced his colleagues to throw their support behind a complete outsider in the hopes that he would garner more votes in succeeding rounds. This nonentity was the Emperor Charles V's own former schoolmaster, the sixty-three-year-old Adrian Florensz, the cardinal of Tortosa in Spain. Florensz, at this time, was not even physically present at the conclave in Rome, but serving as Charles V's regent in Spain. Unfortunately the other voting blocs who were opposed to Cardinal Medici had exactly the same idea and, on 9 January 1522, they too threw their votes behind this largely compromise candidate. The gambit backfired on all the various factions as they now saw to their horror that the cardinal of Tortosa had garnered sufficient votes (almost a unanimous result in fact) for election. The new Dutch pope, who had been elected almost by mistake, would subsequently take the name of Pope Adrian VI.

The only other foreign pope to be elected in recent times had been the Catalan Rodrigo Borgia who, as Pope Alexander VI, had been widely despised by the Italians. The thought of another non-Italian, this time one from the far north, cast the Sacred College into a palsy of depressed soul-searching. As one cardinal cynically put the matter, 'the Emperor is now Pope and the Pope, Emperor'. The reaction of the Roman mob was far worse however. The Romans scoffed at the choice of this practically unknown barbarian from Utrecht. In the outdoor atrium of the Vatican palace they angrily pushed and jostled and jeered the red-robed cardinals as, mortified at what they had just done, they emerged ashen-faced from the conclave.

The Emperor Charles V was naturally delighted to learn that his old tutor had been named pope and wrote enthusiastically to the English ambassador to Spain that he was certain he 'could rely on the new pope as thoroughly as on anyone who had risen to greatness of his service'. The new pope, by contrast, was horrified by his nomination. Advanced in years, in failing health, and having more the temperament of the quiet scholar than of a potential leader of Christendom, he accepted the nomination only with great reluctance. Nevertheless to his credit, having accepted the nomination, Pope Adrian VI now determined to be the change that he so desperately wished to see in Holy Mother Church. He refused to be unduly partial to his former student Charles V and hastened by sea from Tortosa to the papal seaport of Civitavecchia and thereafter onward to Rome, where he was crowned pope on 31 August 1522. In his first consistory of cardinals he lost no time in accusing the clergy and the papacy of being 'so steeped in sin they could no longer perceive the stench of their own iniquities'. It was hardly what you might call an encouraging beginning.

Upon settling into the Vatican he promptly sacked most of the service staff of the Apostolic Palace, stressing the need to economise following the fiscal excesses of Pope Leo X. Instead, he moved into a small house in the Vatican gardens where he was attended by a modest staff of just four servants, including an old Flemish cook whom he had brought with him from the Low Countries. She was instructed to budget just one ducat per day for his meals. For his miserly and reclusive habits Pope Adrian was widely lampooned by the Roman people. On the base of the battered ancient Roman statue known as the Pasquino, to which the Romans attached their anonymous political critiques and tirades, leaflets known as *pasquinades* were pasted ridiculing the parsimonious new pope as a 'barbarian' from the cold north. To a people used to being courted and entertained by Pope Leo X with ever more expensive and extravagant festivals and spectacles, they simply did not understand the mentality of this earnest Dutchman who was living the sort of contemplative and Spartan lifestyle that the heretic Martin Luther himself would have approved of. The Pope's behaviour was not only inexplicable it was positively harrowing for the fun-loving Roman mob. One morning a *pasquinade* appeared which violently castigated the Romans for 'having lost the papacy to a bastard renegade tyrant'. As was by now fairly common, the tract offered little in the way of self-censorship: 'O vile rabble, O asses [good only] for beating beasts without learning, without intellect, born only to stuff your faces and go to bed with whores, boys, and buggerers!' This more or less summed up the mood of the Romans concerning Pope Adrian VI's election, by which time the Piazza de Pasquino had become a vibrant centre of opposition to papal rule and the scandalous excesses of the cardinals. Pope Leo had tolerated the ever more vitriolic *pasquinades* (and as a devotee of bawdy *poesie* perhaps even enjoyed some of them) but Pope Adrian lost no time in threatening to throw the revered statue into the River Tiber. A Spanish ambassador managed to dissuade him by comically suggesting that to do so might well yield an army of frogs who croaked *pasquinades*.

Adrian's parsimony was equally embarrassing for the members of Rome's Sacred College who, resplendent in their magnificent Roman *palazzi*, were not known as 'princes of the Church' for nothing. The office of cardinal was one of the most exalted positions within Renaissance society and entailed a considerable outlay in the form of living expenses, patronage and entertainment. Cardinals were also expected to foot most of their expenses during their often costly overseas missions as papal legates or nuncios for the Holy See. The average Roman cardinal subsisted on a salary of between 4,000 to 6,000 ducats per year. This was at a time when an ordinary priest might be expected to survive on only twenty-five ducats per year. The average size of a cardinal's household was between 150 to 200 individuals, from the major-domo at the head of the household down to the stewards, chamberlains, gentlemen of the wardrobe, stable hands, cooks and various other menials. Cardinals might also employ sizeable numbers of *bravi et capitani* to serve as their personal bodyguards as they negotiated the often violent and dangerous streets of Rome. When they themselves were at the centre of such a complex web of patronage it was demeaning and unbecoming of the Supreme Pontiff of the Holy Roman Church to subsist frugally in the manner of some scholar-hermit and naturally it reflected poorly on their own ingrained extravagance.

But even worse was to follow. Adrian himself spoke no Italian and insisted instead on conducting all consistory business in Latin. He also abased himself before the poor of Rome ('I love poverty', he reassured them) whilst upbraiding the princes of the Church for their self-indulgent ways, pestering them to shave off their beards and ordering the removal of many of the 'pagan' classical paintings and sculptures which he chanced across in his perambulations around the Vatican Palace. He gave few audiences, complained the Venetian ambassador, who also added that 'when he does consent to see anyone he says little except the same answer, we shall see'. All who came into contact with him derided his lack of social graces and his stultifying aura of austerity. Coming hard on the heels of Pope Leo's gracious and fun-loving papacy with its interest in art and fine living this new pope had delivered Rome and its citizens up into a kind of joyless purgatory which seemed wholly alien to them. The Italians mocked him behind his back, quipping that Pope Adrian had become '*divino*', by which they meant that upon arrival in Rome he had become 'drunk' (*di vino*) on the strong Italian wine.

Although Cardinal Giulio had been instrumental in securing his papal election, Pope Adrian VI proved a largely retrograde step for Medici interests in Italy. During the interval between Adrian's election in January and his coronation at the end of August, the ousted duke of Urbino, Francesco Maria della Rovere, had reconquered his duchy along with both Pesaro and Senigallia. Urbino had then lent his military assistance to Malatesta and Orazio Baglioni to recover their own ancestral lands in Perugia (in 1520, their father Gian Paolo, who had already survived a demeaning dressing down from Pope Julius II, followed by imprisonment at the hands of the Spanish, had been lured to Rome by his former *padrone* Pope Leo X only to be imprisoned and then beheaded as an accessory to Cardinal Petrucci's putative conspiracy. the Pope had then reabsorbed Perugia back into the papal territories.) This was not the only Medici reversal, however, for Borghese Petrucci had also meanwhile regained the lordship of Siena and Alfonso d'Este had recovered lands in the duchy of Ferrara which had hitherto been lost to the imperial and papal armies. Since Pope Adrian and the Sacred College had approved della Rovere's return to power, Cardinal Giulio de' Medici now had little option but to come to terms with the duke of Urbino, who–in return for being permitted to resume his duchy–agreed to relinquish to him those tracts which Leo X had hitherto granted to Florence. Cardinal Giulio himself was meanwhile made captain-general of Florence for a period of one year.

For the new pope, consolidating recent Medici territorial gains took a distant second place to attempting to become peacemaker to the quarrelling princes of Europe. To the Emperor Charles V's consternation, Pope Adrian stubbornly refused to renew Rome's anti-French alliance with the Empire and sought instead to make the papacy entirely neutral and independent. This break would initiate years of distrust and bad feeling between the Emperor and the papacy and would eventually run its course in the scandalous events of 1527. But even so, Pope Adrian the peacemaker was determined to try to reconcile the belligerents. The most obvious way for a pope to draw quarrelsome European kings together was to involve them in a papal Crusade against the Turk, and this is what Pope Adrian VI now attempted, in his own well-meaning way, to do.

The Ottomans had made worrying recent advances in Hungary and also in Rhodes, where a fleet of 400 Turkish galleys had landed in June 1522 to do battle with the Knights of St. John. After six exhausting months of fighting, the Turkish commander offered the knights generous terms by which to vacate Rhodes in peace and the Order subsequently decamped from the island forever. The Ottoman audacity had to be answered by Christendom. However, the Pope's well-meaning remonstrations fell on deaf ears. Both France and the Empire were oblivious to the wider Turkish threat, locked as they increasing were in a death match which would be played out in Italy. As King François replied to Adrian, 'We are ready to make peace and to come with great power against the Turk provided Milan, which is our patrimony, is restored to us'. The Emperor Charles was no less forthright in his rejection of the Pope's overtures for European peace and a Crusade. He placed the blame squarely on the Pope's own disobedience towards his former pupil, one whom he had raised up so high. Meanwhile, the refugee fleet of the Knights of Rhodes landed at Civitavecchia and the order's grand master Philippe de Villiers de L'Isle-Adam requested an audience with Pope Adrian to discuss where the knights might make their new headquarters. Despite his having fought bravely for Christendom against the heathen Turk Villiers was kept waiting by the Pope, probably for no other reason than that he was a Frenchman.

In addition to rebutting the Pope's entreaties for a truce in Italy and a Crusade to check the Turk, King François was also at this time preoccupied with the fallout from his attempts to put the Constable of France in his place. Charles III, 8th Duke of Bourbon, was the son of Gilbert, Count of Montpensier, and his Mantuan wife Clara Gonzaga (the sister of Francesco II Gonzaga and sister-in-law of Isabella d'Este). The duke of Bourbon-Montpensier, Auvergne and Châtellraut, Count of Clermont, Montpensier, Forez, La Marche and Gien and countless other titles was the last of the great medieval French nobles. Not only did his income dwarf that of King François but he also had the unnerving ability to raise his own private army of loyal subjects. Duke Charles, who was also a prince of Burgundy, ruled his vast domains from his seat at the town of Moulins, the historical capital of the Bourbonnais. Upon François's accession he had been appointed to the highest military honour in the land, Constable of France; Bourbon had exercised his role as supreme commander of France's armies with panache and proven martial ability, having been instrumental in the French king's much celebrated victory at Marignano.

Although Bourbon was himself a loyal subject of the King and a straightforward man of honour, a proud monarch like François could not be expected to co-exist with such a powerful magnate at the heart of his realm. François had already humiliated Bourbon by dismissing him as governor of Milan (effectively French viceroy in Italy) in favour of the brother of his latest aristocratic lover. When war had broken out again between France and the Empire in 1521, François appointed not the loyal and capable Charles of

Bourbon but instead his own incompetent brother-in-law the duke of Alençon to command his Flemish campaign. Insultingly, Bourbon was given the status of second-in-command, despite being by far and away the more experienced commander.

When Bourbon's beloved wife Suzanne died in April 1521 she bequeathed her Bourbon lands and title to him (for, whereas she had been a legitimate natural daughter of Peter II, Duke of Bourbon, Charles himself was a Bourbon of the lesser cadet line of Bourbon-Montpensier and held the title of duke only as consort to the Duchess Suzanne). Into Bourbon's grief-stricken life now stepped the king of France's mother, Louise of Savoy. As a Bourbon of the more senior line Louise now claimed ascendancy to the title over Duke Charles. She was also rumoured to be madly in love with the honourable but somewhat dour duke and it was now heavily intimated that the only way that Bourbon could regain his King's favour *and* retain his ducal possessions was to marry the forty-five year old Queen Mother Louise. If Bourbon had quietly done so, subsequent history might well have been very different. Instead, the proud duke of Bourbon spurned Louise's advances in such a humiliating and public way that the Queen Mother privately determined to crush him utterly. In the summer of 1521, Louise initiated a lawsuit against Bourbon which would, if successful, deprive him of his late wife's domains altogether.

As the French lawyers in Paris and Lyons greedily smacked their chops at the prospect of such a labyrinthine and high-profile case, the Emperor Charles V began to circle the increasingly embattled and disaffected duke of Bourbon, offering to unite Bourbon with the powerful House of Habsburg. The Emperor's sister Eleanor of Austria had just become widowed by the death of her husband, the king of Portugal. She was still only twenty-three and was quite a delightful young woman. Bourbon, always the straight-talking man of honour, refused the offer however, not because he did not desire the prestigious match but because he still hoped to heal the breach between himself and his sovereign. In the scheme of things, it was just too risky to upset the Queen Mother with such a union. But the damage had been done; François had already learned of the marriage offer on the diplomatic grapevine and was determined to have it out with Bourbon. The Duke was at court one day paying his respects to Queen Claude when an infuriated François entered the audience chamber and subjected Bourbon to a long and bitter harangue before the entire French court. The King's very public accusation that Bourbon had plotted against him with his bitter rival the Emperor could not have been further from the truth, and yet the woe-begotten duke was sadly forced to retire in disgrace.

In July 1522, Bourbon had consented to meet the Emperor's Spanish chamberlain, Adrian de Croy, at the château of Montbrison deep in the Bourbonnais. Here, the Duke now committed the treason of which François had earlier accused him. He would take Eleanor to wife and receive in return a staggering dowry of 200,000 ducats. In return, Bourbon agreed to attack François in Italy with an army of mercenary *landsknechts*, while the Emperor and Henry VIII of England each mounted their own separate coordinated invasions of France from the north and south with a combined army of 45,000 men. Charles of Bourbon had finally arrived at the grim realisation that the only way he could survive the struggle with his anointed king and the Queen Mother was if he were to depose François and seize the Crown of France for himself. For this reason he doggedly refused to agree to acknowledge Henry VIII's renewed claims to the throne of France.

Such a covert plan required massive organisation and, inevitably, word leaked out from one of the many supernumeraries and found its way back to the court of François. The King retaliated by arresting Bourbon's closest followers, the bishop of Autun and Jean de Poitiers, Seigneur de Saint Vallier (the father of the future King Henry II's famous royal mistress Diane de Poitiers). Bourbon had no choice but to flee his lands in the middle of the night with one hundred of his closest retainers and 40,000 ducats in gold secreted in his saddlebags. It was to his ancestral home of Mantua that Bourbon now fled. Bourbon's mother had been Clara Gonzaga and his uncle had been the late Francesco II Gonzaga, Marquis of Mantua. Francesco himself had by now already died from syphilis in 1519, to be replaced by his son Federico II Gonzaga. Bourbon's aunt-in-law, Isabella d'Este, was still very much in residence at Mantua and she welcomed the by now gaunt and careworn fugitive duke of Bourbon into her Mantuan *palazzo*. But Bourbon's sojourn in the idyllic ancestral Italian lands of his mother, Clara, was to be short-lived. The Emperor was planning for his big push to eject all remaining French troops from Italy and the exiled duke would figure prominently in those plans.

France was undaunted by her loss of Milan and launched an expedition in March and April of 1522 under Lautrec to recover the duchy; he was given 16,000 Swiss mercenaries with which to carry out the task and was joined as well by France's Venetian allies. Also by now fighting in the French forces under Lautrec's command was Caterina Sforza's son, the young *condottiere* Giovanni de' Medici. Since Pope Leo X's recent death his successor Adrian VI, buffeted by both of these countervailing forces and seeking to maintain his neutrality, had consistently refused to unleash, or indeed even hire, Giovanni and so the frustrated *condottiere* had simply picked his own side, going over into the pay of the French. Such easy-going loyalties were of course quite common for the *condottieri* and besides, the wages of his small private army still needed to be paid and French gold was just as good as imperial gold. In mournful commemoration of the late Pope Leo X, who had started him on his military career, Giovanni ordered that his men-at-arms burnish their armour to a black finish and decreed that fluttering black ribbons adorn both their uniforms and their lances. This unique uniform and decoration led to his being renamed Giovanni *della Bande Nere* or 'Giovanni of the Black Bands'. His small, professional regiment of mounted troops worshipped him and were an asset to any army that was fortunate enough to hire them at the right price. More than this, however, Giovanni della Bande Nere now increasingly took up the mantle which, hated as he had undoubtedly been, Cesare Borgia had formerly worn, namely the potential unifier of Italy.

Valentino's campaigns to carve out a duchy of the Romagna had unquestionably been a precursor to his wider ambition of mounting the throne of Naples and then combining both of these realms with Rome and the Papal States. But Valentino had already been dead now for fifteen years and his project, so energetically backed by Pope Alexander VI, had ultimately met with failure and death. A nascent Italian patriot movement, still only a vague but hopeful feeling amongst certain writers and intellectuals, now coalesced around the equally impressive figure of Giovanni and his Black Bands. It was hoped that they would be the beginning of a popular effort to expel all unwelcome foreigners from the Italian peninsula. This not only applied to the French, who had so scared the Italians in 1494 with their new-fangled artillery, or the rough

Imperialist Germans, many of whom by now comprised disrespectful and mocking Lutheran heretics, or even the Swiss, who seemed intent on proving to the world that in the military sphere they could be far more than mere Alpine sheep herders. It also applied to those *Napoletani* and Spaniards from down south who were seen by the more cultured Italians as rough, simple fellows who seldom bathed and who habitually enjoyed the pungent delights of chopped garlic and onions soused in vinegar. Italy needed a champion, a tip of the spear, a man of steel who would expunge these foreign interlopers once and for all. Political observers as wise and as prescient as Machiavelli, Aretino and Castiglione all came to believe that such a man had been sent to them in the rough-and-tumble form of Giovanni della Bande.

For the time being, however, even the presence of Giovanni of the Black Bands could not help the French regain Milan. Prospero Colonna had done a sterling job of fortifying the city ahead of the French offensive and Francesco Sforza's chancellor Girolamo Morone had meanwhile organised the *Milanesi* into an effective militia. The able-bodied men of the duchy had, according to Giovanni Marco Burigozzo, gathered together under their respective gonfalons 'to offer their lives and their possessions for the defence of the homeland and against the French'. Just as Savonarola had come to the fore to provide leadership to the Florentines at the height of their own crisis so an Augustinian friar named Andrea Barbato had also lately arisen amongst the Milanese to offer the population both succour and encouragement. Girolamo Morone made the best possible use of Barbato's inspirational eloquence to rally the *Milanese* however, like Savonarola before, him his prophetic pretensions were not entirely without critics. Even the humble observer Burigozzo derided the bearded Augustinian's followers as '*homenazzi, donazole e poltronaglia*' ('no-account men, idle women, and riffraff'). Nevertheless, by concentrating their efforts in a shared spirit of patriotism, the *Milanese* militia were able both to contain the French fortress garrison in their midst whilst fending off the French siege outside their stout walls with little difficulty.

Marching off instead to attack Pavia, which he deemed to be an easier target, Lautrec had been shadowed by Colonna and his 18,000 *landsknechts*, Spaniards and Italians who subsequently created a well-fortified encampment at the little farm called La Bicocca, which was situated several miles from Milan. Under pressure from his overconfident Swiss mercenaries, Lautrec was persuaded to attack Colonna on 29 April and, in the carnage which followed, the Swiss learned to their chagrin that a determined square of pikemen was no match for a well-coordinated defence by the combined arms of pike, harquebusiers and artillerymen (it was a lesson which they ought by rights to have learned at the Battle of Marignano some years earlier). Pescara had even prefigured later styles of fighting by ordering his harquebusiers to fire by ranks and kneel down to reload while their comrades continued firing over their heads. Impeded by the Spanish ditches and ramparts and trapped in an open killing field under withering handgun fire, the Swiss were butchered by the platoon, by the company, and by the regiment. The remnants of the mauled French army then broke up, the Swiss returning home and the Venetians departing for Venice. Lautrec himself left for France where the underachieving general received a distinctly icy reception from his king. Despite Lautrec's withdrawal the citadels of Cremona, Novara and Milan remained doggedly held by their French garrisons. Colonna and Pescara therefore diverted their operations to Genoa, which they now approached from two different directions.

Seizing the French-held city from Ottaviano Campofregoso and Pedro Navarro, the Imperialists installed Antoniotto Adorno as Doge of an independent *Genovese* republic which was now afforded imperial protection.

It was at this point, when the Emperor's power in Italy had reached its apogee that the tide was set to change once again. As always in Italy, when one or other foreign power held too much sway over the peninsula, the Italians themselves began to grow wary of losing their sovereignty. As previously noted, Italy was increasingly subject to a vague and as yet ill-defined yearning for independence from outside interference. This yearning came at a time when the ascendant Charles V began to make his presence felt where it hurt most keenly, in the pockets and purses of the Italians. The Emperor now ordered those reclaimed imperial cities to contribute to the cost of maintaining the imperial army in Lombardy. He attempted to extort subsidies from Florence, Siena and Lucca but those states argued on principle against having to contribute funding. The Emperor reacted by asserting that these cities, especially Florence, had been 'disobedient' for having had contact with the French in the past and he threatened to send imperial troops to chastise them if they did not pay the recompenses now demanded of them.

Increasingly Charles also tried to browbeat the Pope who in turn stubbornly refused to be pressured by his former pupil. Charles had quartered his imperial troops in the papal cities of Parma and Piacenza and, like Pope Leo X before him, Adrian had objected to this infringement of papal sovereignty. Stubbornly, Charles refused to move them. The Pope was further affronted by the Emperor's claims to hold suzerainty over both Modena and Reggio, both of which he was offering to sell to Alfonso d'Este in order to raise much-needed funds. There was little, however, that the papacy could do in reality in the face of such imperial hegemony. In retaliation for having sided with the Emperor, King François had, amidst a blizzard of recriminatory insults, withheld from the Pope all French Church tithes and this had reduced the Curia's income to perilous levels. The mounting pressure from the Emperor was too much for the elderly Pope Adrian VI to withstand and, in August 1523, Charles prevailed and the weary pontiff was forced to concede to a formal treaty with the Empire. The pact, which was ostensibly defensive in nature, would encompass Charles V, the Pope, Henry VIII, Charles's brother Ferdinand, Archduke of Austria, Francesco Sforza of Milan and the cities of Florence, Siena, Lucca and Genoa. All the signatories agreed to make regular contributions towards the League's funding, the ultimate objective of which was to drive out the French from their few remaining strongholds in Italy and keep them out permanently.

Relenting against his will to this imperial treaty would not yet be the final act of Pope Adrian VI's papacy. After all this time he had still not deigned to meet with the grand master of the Knights of Rhodes, Philippe de Villiers de L'Isle-Adam. Aware that he was becoming increasingly distanced from France, the Pope had postponed meeting the French aristocrat for months, but to his credit the latter–a loyal Roman Catholic–held no grudge towards his pontiff. Upon being ushered into the Pope's presence, the strikingly tall, white-haired warrior dropped to his knees and bent to kiss the Pope's velvet slipper. He then proceeded to give a blood-curdling account of the siege and fall of Rhodes which held all those present in dumbstruck awe. In gratitude for his services to Christendom, Villiers was given the town of Viterbo as a temporary headquarters for his military Order. It was to be one of the Pope's final acts. Exhausted and depressed by the impossible demands of papal diplomacy and the warp and weft of terrestrial power politics, this quiet scholar-pope died just two weeks later on 14 September 1523. As a final mocking irony, the very same day that he left this mortal coil, another French army crossed the border into Italy. Few mourned the unfortunate Dutch prelate who had been called only with great reluctance to occupy the shoes of the fisherman. His had been a well-intentioned papacy but the Italians had by now had enough of foreign pontiffs. The next inhabitant of St. Peter's throne would be drawn from their own ranks.

Rather unfairly, Pope Adrian VI was destined to be immortalised by the fiercely Protestant playwright Christopher Marlowe in *Doctor Faustus*. In the play, Pope Adrian is found disputing with a schismatic antipope named Bruno and invokes the principle of papal infallibility to prove that his arguments are correct versus those of a former (one presumes, equally 'infallible') pope. In short he was made to embody all those illogical and sophistical tendencies which the, by then well-entrenched, breakaway Protestant Church believed contaminated the entire Roman Catholic communion. And it was unfair too because, of all the recent popes, certainly from Sixtus IV onwards, Pope Adrian VI was the most amenable to the proposition that Catholicism was perhaps most at fault for its own ills. At the Diet of Nuremberg in 1522, for instance, Adrian had thwarted the efforts of his own papal nuncio, Francesco Chieregati, when he instructed him to convey the ambiguous edict that although action needed to be taken against Martin Luther, the very existence of this heretic monk was almost certainly due to the general moral decline of the Church. His meaning was clear: the Vatican itself was largely to blame for the heresies which had sprouted within the Church's own ranks. These were not the words of a divinely infallible papal autocrat but the heartfelt judgement of an austere Dutch outsider who could see with his own eyes the cesspool that was the Court of Rome.

Thirty-five cardinals went into seclusion in the Sistine Chapel on 1 October 1523 to elect Adrian's successor and once more the food and living conditions within the papal conclave progressively deteriorated as the days, weeks and then months rolled by. Yet again, Cardinals Soderini and Colonna conspired to keep Cardinal Giulio de' Medici from St. Peter's throne, engineering a stay of balloting until mid-November when three anti-Medici, pro-French cardinals could arrive in Rome. Giulio, however, had the full backing of the Emperor Charles V which, in addition to his own party within the Sacred College, also earned him the crucial votes of the Spanish cardinals. The English cardinals meanwhile still pursued the pipedream of another English pope and cast their votes in favour of Cardinal Thomas Wolsey. Cardinal Pompeo Colonna soon began to emerge as a frontrunner but, when divisions in the French bloc began to appear, some of the latter proposed to cast their votes in favour of Cardinal Franciotto Orsini, who had been educated in Florence under the auspices of Lorenzo the Magnificent. The prospect of an Orsini pope was too much for Pompeo Colonna to contend with; miserably he brokered a deal, agreeing to throw his backing behind the nomination of Cardinal Giulio de' Medici in return for the important and lucrative position of vice-chancellor of the Church. On 19 November 1523, Giulio de' Medici, the illegitimate son of the assassinated Giuliano de' Medici and his mistress Fioretta Gorini, was crowned as Pope Clement VII.

There had, so it seemed to some of the cardinals, been a supernatural foreshadowing of Giulio's election as pope. At the beginning of the conclave when the cardinals were drawing their lots for accommodation, Cardinal de' Medici had drawn the partitioned cell which lay directly beneath Perugino's painting of Christ Giving the Keys of heaven to Saint Peter and many had regarded this as a prophetic omen. But Giulio was no Peter. The new bishop of Rome was to begin his pontificate in the spirit in which it was to continue, with two poor decisions on his part. Initially, he had wanted to take his own name as pope, but it was quickly pointed out to him by the superstitious cardinals that every pope who had done so in the past had died before the year was out. He therefore opted to take a different name. Many were puzzled however when he had selected for his pontificate the name of the antipope Clement VII. The new pope was also certainly no Pope Julius, as Francesco Guicciardini–himself an ardent Medici *amici*–rushed to point out: 'No two men could have been more unlike in character than the Popes Julius and Clement. For while the former was of great and even excessive courage, ardent, impulsive, frank and open, the latter was of a temper inclining rather to timidity, most patient, moderate, and withal dissembling.'

Since he was an Italian and also perceived to be intelligent and accomplished there was nevertheless widespread relief and rejoicing amongst the Curia and the international diplomatic corps, not to mention the native Romans themselves. The Emperor's ambassador to Rome confidently, if somewhat prematurely, wrote back to Madrid assuring Charles that Pope Clement would prove to be 'your creature'. The English ambassador meanwhile reported back to the English king that 'There is as much craft and policy in him as any man of earth'. But although he was a Medici like the late Pope Leo X, the forty-five-year-old Pope Clement VII was an entirely different animal from his oafishly rotund yet shrewd and canny cousin. Whereas Leo X had surrounded himself with diversions and pleasant entertainments, Clement was staid and austere. Where Leo was carelessly spendthrift, Clement was parsimonious in the extreme, though it must be said not as frugal as Pope Adrian. If Leo was decisive when he needed to be, Clement vacillated endlessly (in fact he made Shakespeare's Hamlet look positively decisive) and, even when he eventually made a decision one way or the other, he would inevitably–infuriatingly to those around him–change his mind again later. The root of the problem lay not so much in Clement's intellect, which was still firmly analytical; it lay in his innate character and temperament. As vice-chancellor and adviser to both Leo X and Adrian VI, Giulio de' Medici could resolve any political or diplomatic issue down to its constituent elements, laying out all the necessary information on which the Vicar of Christ could make his final decision; this was really his forte and, as such, he had made an excellent papal legate. But put Clement VII in the midst of a problem and ask him to make a decision himself one way or the other and he was strangely paralysed by the infinite possibilities and courses of action that lay open before him.

Withal, Pope Clement's papacy began promisingly enough. He appointed an international committee of bishops to look into Martin Luther's grievances and also established the *Collegium LX Virorum* to survey the financing of the on-going construction of St. Peter's basilica. On 12 December 1523, Clement issued the papal bull *Admonet nos suscepti* which formally established the *Reverenda Fabbrica di San Pietro* in the Vatican, an administrative entity providing for the basilica's reconstruction and subsequent maintenance. It replaced Pope Julius II's constitution *Liquet omnibus* with a permanent college of 60 experts of international standing, directly dependent on the Holy See, and charged with providing for the building and administration of the basilica. This at least was an encouraging beginning. As a patron of the arts he also fared slightly better than as a papal statesman. Cardinal Giulio had gone through the motions of being every inch the Medici *padrone*. At the Palazzo della Cancelleria, where he had lived since its former owner Cardinal Raffaele Sansoni Riario had relinquished the property in the aftermath of the Petrucci Conspiracy, Giulio had entertained numerous prominent artists including the painters Parmigiano and Gianbattista Rosso, the architect Baldassare Peruzzi and the sculptor Raffaello da Montelupo, who had studied under and collaborated with the great Michelangelo himself. The old Medici protégé and family friend Michelangelo, who was by now forty-eight years old, was commissioned by Clement in the year of his papal election to design the *Biblioteca Medicea Laurenziana* (the Laurentian Library) which would showcase the immense private library of the Medici family and position them as learned humanist scholars rather than merely bankers and wool merchants made-good. Giorgio Vasari would later praise the 'handsome disposition of the windows and ceiling and the marvellous vestibule. Nothing so graceful and vigorous in every part was ever seen, comprising the bases, tabernacles, corners, convenient staircase with its curious divisions so different from the common treatment as to excite general wonder'. Florence's Laurentian Library remains one of Michelangelo's most important architectural achievements and Pope Clement VII, pensive and saturnine as he undoubtedly was, can at least claim some of the credit for this outstanding building.

Another frequent visitor at the Palazzo della Cancelleria was the Florentine gold and silversmith Benvenuto Cellini, who had earned Cardinal Giulio's respect based on a silver casket, some silver candlesticks, and a vase which he had fashioned for the bishop of Salamanca. Cellini was to become not only Clement's artist-client but also in many respects the Pope's friend, perhaps even his only true friend. But their friendship was nevertheless a stormy one often punctuated with fierce altercations. On one occasion the Pope grew so impatient at the length of time Cellini was taking over the commission of a chalice that he threatened to arrest the goldsmith if the work was not handed over immediately. Cellini had refused point blank, countering: 'having taken so much trouble to bring it near to completion I don't intend it to fall into the hands of some ignorant beast who would find it only too easy to ruin it'. The outburst possibly betrays Cellini's true feelings towards the Supreme Pontiff, a saturnine individual whose unreasonable whims Cellini had to pander to in order to earn a living. Clement's own feelings towards the artisan (who was also a chronicler and who would later meticulously record his great year of crisis in 1527) was revealed by a later somewhat controversial edict which absolved Cellini from all past and future crimes, effectively placing the goldsmith 'above the law'.

Like Leo X before him, Clement looked to his young Medici relatives in whom the family's future now lay. By the spring of 1524, Ippolito (thirteen), Alessandro (twelve) and little Catherine de' Medici (five) were all paraded at the papal court for their future dynastic promise to be evaluated. Ippolito de' Medici, archbishop of Avignon, was soon afterwards despatched to Florence under the joint supervision of Cardinal Niccolò Ridolfi (newly appointed by Pope Clement as archbishop of Florence in January 1524) and Silvio Passerini, the cardinal-bishop of Cortona. The fifty-five-year-old Passerini was a long time Medici confederate, having been raised and educated at the home of Lorenzo the

Magnificent; he had been especially close to the late Giovanni de' Medici and fought with him on campaign, being taken prisoner alongside him at the Battle of Ravenna. He was now effectively made Florence's regent until such time as Ippolito was old enough to rule. He arrived in Florence on 30 August attended by a small entourage of around ten pages and took up residence at the Palazzo Medici. The late Lorenzo di Piero's former secretary and agent, Goro Gheri, had advised that a period spent living as a private citizen of Florence would enable the boy to acquire a useful understanding of Florence's ways, something which Lorenzo himself had sadly lacked; evidently it was a forlorn hope since not long after arriving in Florence Ippolito also immodestly assumed the soubriquet 'il Magnifico', as the detested Lorenzo had done before him.

Ippolito was soon joined on 19 June 1425 by Alessandro and Catherine. Alessandro did not dwell in the city itself however, but was instead removed discreetly to the serene and luxurious Medici villa at Poggio a Caiano which Giuliano da Sangallo had designed for il Magnifico. Here, Alessandro was placed under the guardianship of Ottaviano de' Medici who managed the family's household affairs. Hailing from the cadet line of the family, the son of Lorenzo di Bernardetto, Ottaviano was married to Maria Salviati's sister Francesca and would become one of Alessandro's principal ministers and advisers in later years. So far, like Ippolito, Alessandro had done relatively well for himself despite his extreme youth and his illegitimacy. The year after Pope Leo's death Alessandro had been granted the ducal city of Penne along with the terra of Campli in the Abruzzo by the Emperor Charles 'in consideration', as the imperial diplomats quaintly put it, 'of the merits of the illustrious family of the Medici'. This small fief, situated not far from Pescara on the Adriatic coast, brought him an income of 3,000 ducats a year and the ability to refer to himself as 'duke'. But at this point it is noteworthy that Alessandro was ranked as distinctly inferior to Ippolito, due perhaps to the far lower conditions of his birth, his mother having been a coloured servant whereas Ippolito's had been an Italian gentlewoman. One of the late duke of Nemours' friends, Giovanni di Bardo Corsi assumed co-responsibility for Alessandro's guardianship and Pierio Valeriano continued his education. In the same schoolroom as the young Alessandro was the future painter, architect, writer, and historian Giorgio Vasari from Arezzo. The two lads were roughly the same age and Ottaviano de' Medici had taken the promising young artist under his avuncular wing. It would be Vasari who, as an adult, would eventually coin the term rinascita or 'rebirth' ('Renaissance') to describe the great flowering of art which had taken place in Florence during the previous century and a half.

Unfortunately for Clement VII he became pope at a time when Europe was approaching a veritable maelstrom in the relations between France and the Empire. This was a period when a firm, decisive pontiff was needed on the throne of St. Peter and unfortunately Clement simply failed to fit the bill. The Italian Wars were resuming once more. The final few months of the late Adrian VI's pontificate had witnessed a French relief expedition to Italy under the command of Guillaume Gouffier, seigneur de Bonnivet and Admiral of France. An enigmatic figure, Bonnivet was a reputed libertine who had competed (successfully one might add) with King François for the affections of the Comtesse de Châteaubriant. He also nurtured an implacable hatred towards the duke of Bourbon. Bonnivet crossed the River Ticino into Italy with 36,000 infantry and over 2,000 mounted men-at-arms on the same day in September

1523 that Pope Adrian VI had died. The League had held together however and Pope Clement had renewed his vow to uphold his predecessor's imperial alliance. In Milan, chancellor Morone encouraged the *Milanesi* to strengthen their fortifications in anticipation of the French onslaught. Meanwhile, Federigo II Gonzaga, Marquis of Mantua, and newly appointed captain-general of the Church, brought his troops up into a position of readiness together with those of the duke of Urbino. Since his Medici kinsman was now pope, Giovanni della Bande Nere (who was by now being dubbed 'the Grand Devil' by the French) had by this time left France's service and thrown his lot in with the Imperialists. When a Neapolitan army arrived under the command of the marchese di Pescara and the new Spanish viceroy Charles de Lannoy, the French were pushed back across the Ticino once again.

When the French retreated back to the line of the River Sesia near Romagnano, and attempted to make their crossing on 30 April 1524, the Imperialist forces under Pescara swooped down and raked their rear-guard with deadly harquebus fire. Admiral Bonnivet, who was personally supervising the rear-guard, was struck by a harquebus shot, although miraculously he was not killed. Another famous French knight who *was* however killed that day was the Chevalier de Bayard. Since 1495, the fifty-one-year-old Pierre Terrail, seigneur de Bayard, had participated in most of the major engagements of the Italian Wars. He had survived the Battles of Fornovo, Garigliano, Agnadello and Ravenna. He had also been present at the Sieges of Padua and Brescia. At Brescia he had been wounded just as his troops were entering the town, and had been carried to a local nobleman's mansion, whose wife had been forced to pay a ransom of 2,000 ducats to ensure the safety of her family. While his wound healed he had the two charming daughters of the house sing to him each night and, upon leaving to join the French troops for the Battle of Ravenna, he endowed the surprised girls with a gift of one thousand ducats each This had been the exact amount which their mother had been forced to offer up as ransom. It was due to appealing stories like this that the Chevalier de Bayard was habitually referred to as *'le bon chevalier'*, or 'the good knight'. But at the Sesia River the Chevalier's long career of gallantry was terminated by the new master of the battlefield; this was not the heavily armoured courtly knight-at-arms, but the lowly harquebusier, blackened by gunpowder soot and taking unchivalrous pot shots at the enemy's ranks. As he lay mortally wounded surrounded by his respectful enemies the Chevalier was hailed by his old comrade-in-arms Charles of Bourbon. The latter is said to have remarked: 'Ah! Monsieur de Bayard; I am very sad to see you in this state; you who were such a virtuous knight' to which the Chevalier de Bayard is reputed to have retorted: 'Monsieur, do not pity me for I die as a man of honour ought, doing my duty. But I pity you, because you fight against your king, your country, and your oath.' If true, these words must have bitterly stung Bourbon who, despite his incontrovertible treason, still regarded himself essentially as a man of honour. This, at least, was the report spun by the French chronicler Martin du Bellay, who knew the kind of anti-Bourbon slant that would edify the ear of the French king.

With the French army chased back across the Alps, the Emperor now ordered Charles of Bourbon to invade France while the opportunity presented itself. While Bourbon was attacking the French homeland, Charles himself would sweep into Toulouse with 28,000 Spanish and German troops, while Henry VIII would meanwhile take ship for Calais with his own army and invade

477

Picardy. The 'Great Plan', as it was called, was to crown Henry VIII as king of France in Reims and depose François once and for all. Burdened as he was by reservations about handing Henry the crown of France (which naturally he coveted for himself) Bourbon dutifully consented to attack his nemesis François. With the warlike motto *'Victoire ou mort'* ringing in the ears of his German, Spanish and Italian troops, Bourbon and Pescara crossed the River Var on 1 July 1524 and advanced deep into Provence along the coastal littoral, sweeping through Monaco, Vence, Antibes and Cannes until they reached the city of Marseilles on 14 August. Here, the French king's siege engineer Mirandel, his Admiral of France, Philippe de Chabot, and the Italian *condottiere* Renzo da Ceri, had diligently set about strengthening the city's defences to meet the approaching threat.

Despite a daily cannon bombardment from the Imperialists, the *Massiliots* bravely resisted for weeks all imperial attempts at taking their city. And when the news reached Bourbon that King François and the seigneur de Bonnivet were coming in person from Lyons with a massive army to relieve Marseille he was left with the difficult decision of whether to maintain the siege or withdraw back into Italy. Always the proactive leader, he decided on expediting the former option. But when his artillery had torn breaches in the city walls and the time came to mount an assault, Bourbon was betrayed by Pescara. As Bourbon's own German mercenary *landsknechts* vaulted through the opening, only to be checked by a few guns which the defenders had quickly moved into position, Pescara now turned to his Spanish troops who were following close behind the Germans and declared: 'If you want to sup in paradise today, then go forward. But if, like me, you have no such desire, then follow me back to Italy.' With these treacherous and demoralising words the attack had floundered and the siege had been lifted. The Imperialist army limped back to Lombardy in penny packets of undisciplined and near-mutinous companies. Meanwhile, Bourbon's allies Charles V and Henry VIII had deserted him, both having failed for an assortment of personal reasons to embark upon their own respective invasions of France.

Bourbon had intended to fall back on Milan but even this relatively straightforward objective was now unattainable. As the Imperialists threaded their way painstakingly back along the coastal littoral, François and Bonnivet had dragged their cannon and an entire army across one of the more inaccessible passes of the French Alps to intercept them. Instead of going to Milan, which was in the grip of plague, Bourbon instead distributed his army in a wide arc centred on the fortresses of Pavia, Piacenza, Cremona and Alessandria. By late October 1524, the king of France entered Milan practically unopposed and the benighted city changed hands once again. The *Milanesi*, worn down by the outbreak of plague in their midst, were in no fit state to resist a large, fresh French army equipped with heavy artillery. Bourbon and Pescara meanwhile made their headquarters at Lodi. Their army, once the formidable invaders of France, was by now little more than a rag-tag band of unpaid, footsore vagabonds.

In Rome, Pope Clement VII now shuddered at the idea of an alliance with such a pitiful, vestigial army as Bourbon's. As usual, he vacillated and he wavered, he calculated and he prevaricated. He could see possible reasons both for and against supporting this or that side. The vicious Tuscan satirist, Francesco Berni, lampooned Clement's by now famous tergiversations in four lines of *poesie bernesche*:

> A papacy made up of respects,
> Of considerations and of talk,
> Of yets, and then, of buts and ifs and maybe's,
> Of words without end that have no effect at all.

Eventually, Clement sent for the polished Mantuan diplomat Baldassarre Castiglione and prevailed upon him to go as the Vatican's nuncio to the court of the Emperor Charles V at Madrid. This Castiglione agreed to do; assured as he was that continued détente with Charles V against France was the key to an enduring peace in Italy. Castiglione's master, Federigo Gonzaga, was decidedly pro-Imperialist and had after all harboured the French traitor and Gonzaga family member, Charles of Bourbon.

What the cultured Mantuan diplomatist could not have known, at the time that he accepted his commission, was that his employer Pope Clement was however now playing both ends against the middle. The rapid decline in imperial fortunes had scared him once more into the French camp and he had meanwhile privately despatched his confidante and apostolic *datario* Gian Matteo Giberti to Lombardy for the express purpose of entering into fresh negotiations with King François. The French alliance was Clement's real intent; Castiglione's mission was merely a blind, a fool's errand to cover himself in the eventuality that the Emperor experienced a sudden revival of fortune. Pope Clement VII was playing a very delicate and dangerous game of diplomatic subterfuge for which he was probably the least qualified.

Due to the on-going plague epidemic in Milan, François had installed a sizeable French garrison in the city and then left with his army to go lay siege to Pavia, just twenty miles away to the south. Pavia was situated on the lower Ticino River, near its confluence with the Po, a waterway which served to protect the city's southern side. To the north of the city lay a large triangular-shaped area of enclosed parkland which was bounded by a great stone wall. Within its carefully landscaped confines, the park had been created as a hunter's paradise for a whole succession of Visconti and Sforzese dukes. In summer the setting was delightful, even magical. There were rivulets criss-crossing the whole expanse, as well as well-manicured lawns, copses, glades and forests. There were small farms and pavilions, follies, rotundas and pagan temples. Within this idyllic setting roamed pheasants, boar and other wild game; everything in fact to keep an active duke and his courtiers energetically entertained for days on end. The French army made its encampment in this sprawling leisure park and the French king himself took up residence at the ducal hunting lodge known as the Castello di Mirabello.

As October turned to November, however, the terrain became progressively less sublime. As the winter rains and frosts set in not only did the park become shrouded in heavy fogs but the ground beneath grew marshy and waterlogged. The French encountered considerable difficulty in dragging their artillery into position to bombard the town walls. Pavia's defences were reasonably stout and the city's principal fortress, the Castello Visconteo, was incorporated into the city walls and faced northwards out towards the park. Duke Galeazzo Maria Sforza had lavished considerable expenditure on this impressive bastion. The Brescian artist Bonifacio Bembo had been brought in during the 1460s to decorate the walls and ceilings of the *castello* with scenes of hunting and games and other activities from the Duke's daily life. Other rooms would contain portraits of the ducal family, including 'the duchess playing ball, and her maids playing *triumphi* in the garden'. Still other rooms would be adorned with landscapes filled with deer and assorted game. The sum of 7,880 ducats had been allocated for these beautification works although sadly, however, many of these pieces were to be destroyed in the subsequent military actions of the coming years. The French set about digging their entrenchments from the park side of the city and in the soggy mud they placed their cannon as best they could. Meanwhile, the duke of Montmorency crossed the River Ticino and invested Pavia from the south, completing the city's encirclement.

Commanding Pavia's garrison was the forty-four-year-old Don Antonio de Leyva. Leyva, who hailed originally from Spanish Navarre, had fought under Pescara in the recent failed Provence campaign; earlier still he had been wounded at the Battle of Ravenna. Although confined to both chair and portable litter by his debilitating gout he was widely known for his valour and was a level-headed and resourceful commander for Charles V to have in a siege situation like this. Under his command he had a mixture of 9,000 Swiss and German mercenary *landsknechts*. Moreover, as part of his preparations he had provisioned the city for a lengthy siege and, if necessary, he felt confident of being able to hold out for weeks and months to come. His only concern, though it was hardly a small one, was finding the means to pay his mercenaries as the months ticked by ('No money, no Swiss!')

For nearly four months, from late October 1524 to February 1525, the city of Pavia stubbornly held out. The initial weeks of the siege had witnessed a desultory artillery bombardment but the cannon had soon been silenced by the ever-present problem of damp gunpowder. There had also taken place sundry bloody clashes and skirmishes. But Leyva's determined and level-headed resistance to a French attack against a breach in the town walls on 21 November lessened the French interest on making any direct frontal assault on the city and, demoralised, they melted back into their trenches, hoping instead to starve the city into submission. Accordingly, as the weeks went by and the dwindling rations were consumed by the besieged population, Pavia's inhabitants began to consume their pets and beasts of burden. When it grew intolerably cold they ripped up their floors and the beams in their houses for firewood. As François himself wrote to the Queen Mother Louise, 'For more than a month now those inside have not drunk wine or eaten meat or cheese'. Still, the motivation of both the mercenaries and the citizens remained high. Pavia, for one thing, was traditionally a Ghibelline city which honoured and fought for the Emperor; now assailed by what were in effect French and papal Guelphs the city indignantly held out.

One of their number, Marchesa Ippolita Fioramonda, valiantly did all she could to keep the brave *Pavese* in good spirits. Wearing her heavenly blue satin dress sprinkled with moths stitched in gold (an allegory of *fatal attraction* that was intended to dissuade potential suitors!), she did the rounds of the city wall, hurling scorn at the French and encouraging the defenders with solicitous words. Castiglione was one of her greatest admirers and the author of the *Cortegiano* wrote to her encouragingly from across the Alps: 'your ladyship has shown to the entire world, in addition to her other qualities, to be a valiant lady in arms, and not only beautiful, but still bellicose'. The Marchesa Ippolita was, like Caterina Sforza, a virago in the true Renaissance tradition. Boccaccio, in his *De mulieribus claris* ('On Famous Women') had argued that remarkable women should be celebrated when and wherever they were encountered since the limitations of their sex made their achievements all the more admirable. Out of courtly respect, the French soldiers were forbidden to fire upon the Marchesa Ippolita when she made her regular appearances on the walls of Pavia.

Inside Pavia, meanwhile, the efforts of the Marchesa Ippolita Fioramonda to raise peoples' spirits only served to gloss over what was now fast becoming a desperate situation. Wages were as great a problem as dwindling food supplies. To pay his Spanish mercenaries the imperial governor of Pavia, Don Antonio de Leyva, had been forced to melt down all the church plate that he could lay his hands on. He had also been forced to raid the Carthusian monastery known as the Certosa for their treasure. If he could not pay his troops they would not fight and would simply abandon their posts. Worse still they might even decide to go over to the enemy. The French, on the other hand, were of good cheer. Retiring to their comfortable encampment deep within the game park, they had set up market stalls and brothels and there was lively music and dancing as the Christmas season approached. François himself enjoyed himself hawking and hunting during the day and at night he caroused merrily with his childhood friends the duke of Montmorency and Admiral Guillaume Gouffier, seigneur de Bonnivet. There was plenty of fine food from the Lombard countryside as well as the company of attractive young ladies eager to gain the attention of a king.

As Cardinal de' Medici, Pope Clement VII had formerly been the leader of the Imperialist faction within the Sacred College. As pope he had attempted, like Adrian VI, to walk the fine line of neutrality between France and the Empire. However, when John Stewart, Duke of Albany, was sent by François with one third of the French army to invade Naples by marching directly through Tuscany, Clement was naturally swayed by an overriding concern for the safety of Florence. Albany, a descendant of James II of Scotland who had until recently been second in line to the Scots throne, had up till 1524 been the all-powerful regent of that kingdom before being ousted by the Dowager Queen Margaret Tudor and the Scottish noble Archibald Douglas, 6th Earl of Angus. As his mother was from the illustrious de la Tour d'Auvergne family, he was now reduced to living in exile in France and selling his sword as a mercenary. He was given 5,000 foot and 500 lances and told by the French monarch to cross the Apennines and march through Tuscany recruiting local men into his army as he went. This he did, passing through Lucca and Siena and extorting manpower, funds and even some artillery pieces from both of those cities. A querulous Pope Clement was forced to acquiesce to the duke of Albany's presence, having been assured by François that Florence itself would not be disturbed by the intruding French forces. 'What would you have me do?' he remonstrated with his officials, 'The French are strong, and I cannot resist them. The imperial army needs money, and I have none to give. The Emperor is far off and cannot help me now.'

Pushed into a corner, he reluctantly signed a secret treaty with the French king on 12 December. Privately, Clement was satisfied however to see the restoration of a balance of international power to northern Italy; so long as France fought the Empire then the papacy could pick and choose its side depending on whoever happened to be in the ascendant. That at least was the theory. At the same time as the Pope was coming into alliance with France, the pro-French Orsini faction were being given *carte blanch* to raise additional recruits from within Rome and the Papal States, while Renzo da Ceri was instructed to come from France with his Italian mercenary troops and link up with Albany. Aside from Albany, another famous exile who had rallied to the French banner was Richard de la Pole, Earl of Suffolk, the last of the Yorkist claimants to the English throne whose nickname was, appropriately enough, 'White Rose'. As these events were in motion, the Venetians had meanwhile concluded a non-aggression pact with France and had entered into negotiations to renew their former offensive alliance whilst Alfonso d'Este of Ferrara also pledged his support and munitions to his old allies the French.

By the time that the hapless papal envoy Baldassarre Castiglione had journeyed across the freezing Alps and reached Lyons, he found France's Queen Mother Louise of Savoy in joyful mood for word had already reached the city of the new French-Papal-Venetian tripartite agreement. Poor Castiglione was beside himself at the Pope's duplicity but, ever the cool professional diplomat, he still insisted on completing his mission to the Emperor's distant Spanish court. Had he known Charles V's own response to the new papal orientation he might not have troubled himself. Upon learning of the papal alliance the Emperor's inscrutable demeanour, so it had been remarked by court onlookers, for once cracked and gave way to naked, raw emotion. He thundered to his shocked courtiers that he would march into Italy at the head of an army himself and take his revenge upon 'that villain of a pope'. He even openly entertained the possibility that perhaps Martin Luther had not been far wrong in his judgement of these treacherous Medici popes.

Into the park at Pavia one day rode the grim faced men-at-arms of the *Bande Nere*, all fluttering black ribbons and black burnished steel armour plate. Giovanni della Bande Nere had come to once more offer his arms to the king of France. Pope Clement's new French pact had been the main factor in this latest switch in his loyalties, but another incentive had been his frustration with the plodding and uninspiring Imperialist leadership. On one occasion, so the story went, Giovanni was in a military conference with several imperial generals, none of whom could decide on how to take a particular objective. Giovanni grew so tired of the endless debate back and forth that he stormed out of the room and, with the *Bande Nere*, quickly conquered the objective single-handedly. When he returned to camp and strolled back into the conference tent he found to his disgust that the 'strategy meeting' was still going on! Before arriving at Pavia, Giovanni had most recently been in action against Charles de Lannoy who had attempted to halt the duke of Albany's advance at the town of Fiorenzuola and had been defeated and retired to Lodi. The Black Bands had intervened on the French side and had returned with much-needed fresh supplies of gunpowder and shot provided by the duke of Ferrara. Despite Giovanni's earlier defection, François was for his part delighted to have the renowned *condottiere's* services once more. He rushed to offer him the highest honour that France could bestow, the Order of St. Michel. Giovanni della Bande Nere politely refused the chivalrous investiture, however, explaining as delicately as he could that he was free to offer his sword in battle but *not* his undying fealty. It was for this reason that the poet and satirist Pietro Aretino (who was travelling with the *Bande Nere* at this time), as well as other admirers like Machiavelli, began to refer to the fledgling patriot Giovanni as 'Giovanni d'Italia'.

The association, later to become a close and abiding friendship, between Pietro Aretino and Giovanni della Bande Nere was unusual not least because of the vast difference in temperament between the two men. Giovanni was the fearless warrior who would stand up for himself in any fight, whereas Aretino was that thing which Giovanni professed to hate most of all, a 'scribbler'. Following a recent assassination attempt in Rome by Pope Clement's apostolic *datario*, Gian Matteo Giberti, Aretino's first instinct had been to flee. The incident which prompted his attempted murder was the notorious affair surrounding the 1524 publication of *I Modi: The Sixteen Pleasures*. The engraver Marcantonio Raimondi had published sixteen erotic images which were based on a series of erotic paintings that Giulio Romano had conceived to decorate Federigo Gonzaga's new Palazzo Te in Mantua. Because Romano's paintings were not for public consumption he was left unscathed, but Raimondi–who had disseminated the smut through the printing presses–was imprisoned by Pope Clement, who also ordered the destruction of all copies of the engravings as well as the original plates. Aretino had managed to secure the unfortunate Raimondi's release from prison but then, to compound the injury, he had composed the notorious *sonetti lussuriosi* – sixteen explicit sonnets to accompany the erotic engravings as a gesture in favour of freedom of speech. Aretino had later tried to smooth over this disagreement with his patron Pope Clement, however the priggish Giberti had carried his grudge to extremes and had used strong-arm tactics to impress upon Aretino the advantages of a speedy departure from the Holy City. Aretino's ground breaking conjoining of erotic images and amatory verse marked the first time that this had ever been attempted and consequently the poet can be said to be the creator modern pornography. During this time Aretino also made liberal use of the Pasquino statue in Rome to spread his irreverent satire; so much so in fact that the aging effigy of Menelaus holding the dead body of Patroclus was acknowledged to be practically Aretino's mouthpiece during the 1520s and 1530s.

Their liking for the fairer sex was at least one area of common ground for the writer and the warrior. In this, the two men were–to coin that useful Italian expression–*simpatico*. But ultimately, Aretino–with his pseudo-poetic, commercialised porn and his ready adoption of technologies such as the printing press–was that unique Renaissance phenomenon, the man of the future, always once-removed from real life, the precursor of the literary pundit or the glib, televised talking head. Giovanni della Bande Nere, on the other hand, was firmly rooted in the past, a man of the sword who believed in destroying his opponents not from a remote distance with a quill pen, but up close and personal, where you could gaze into a person's eyes and, with grim satisfaction, watch as the lights went out. Moreover, Giovanni eschewed modern technological innovations such as the harquebus and consistently refused to incorporate large companies of harquebusiers into the *Bande Nere*. Both men were killers, but of an entirely different species. One was from the Old World, the other from the New, one wielded the sword, the other a quill.

While the French (who whose numbers were now thinned by the departure from the army of some 5,000 Grison Swiss mercenaries) were slowly and methodically reducing Pavia by starvation, the duke of Bourbon had travelled to Innsbruck and Nuremberg in December 1524 to meet Georg von Frundsburg of Mindelheim. The scion of an old line of Tyrolean knights from Swabia, the fifty-two-year-old Frundsburg was a fiercely loyal Imperialist who had dutifully answered his Kaiser's call-to-arms at this critical phase in the war. The proudly Lutheran German commander warily welcomed the Roman Catholic French exile to his military camp and eventually agreed to march south with his force

483

of 12,000 crack German *landsknechts*. In order to raise the necessary funding to pay for Frundsburg's troops Bourbon was forced to pawn the last of his family jewels while he was at Innsbruck. By mid-January, the two commanders were already back in Lombardy and at the city of Lodi they joined forces with the balance of the imperial army under Charles V's viceroy Charles de Lannoy.

At Lodi, Pope Clement VII made his irritating and ambivalent presence keenly felt by despatching a papal legate who implored the imperial generals not to attack the French. Meanwhile, Clement's Francophile papal nuncio Girolamo Aleandro, the archbishop of Brindisi, was at Pavia offering encouragement and succour to François. The irascible Frundsburg had lost patience with the papal representative, drawing his great sword and chasing the intimidated legate from the pavilion. Were they here in order to confront the French or not? Lannoy demurred. His own personal remit was Naples. He would much prefer to march back to the *Regno* and protect its borders. 'Nein!' replied Frundsburg firmly, the battle for Italy must be won right here in Lombardy. Besides, in feudal terms all territory north of the Papal States and west of Venice belonged to the Emperor as rightful feudal suzerain. Frundsburg's argument, forcefully stated, carried the day and the imperial strategy was finally agreed upon: to first fortify Lodi and Cremona and then march out and trap the French army against both of these cities as well as Pavia itself, which would serve as the anvil to the imperial army's hammer. Bourbon had meanwhile written to King Henry VIII to invade France from the north while the French king was distracted with military affairs outside of his realm.

The Imperialist army, numbering in the region of 23,000 to 25,000 troops, departed Lodi on 24 January 1525. Alfonso d'Ávalos, the cousin of Fernando Francesco d'Ávalos, the marchese di Pescara, quickly succeeded in capturing the French outpost at Sant'Angelo, thereby cutting the French lines of communication between Pavia and Milan, while meanwhile a separate column of imperial *landsknechts* advanced on the town of Belgiojoso. Despite an audacious raid led by Giovanni de' Medici and the seigneur de Bonnivet, the Imperialist troops occupied the town and by 2 February were only a few miles from Pavia itself. As they approached Pavia from the east, the imperial army attempted to draw the French army (which was of roughly equal size) away from the beleaguered city and into a pitched battle. François however knew the impecunious circumstances of the imperial generals and refused to accept the bait. Remaining firmly entrenched in the ducal game park outside Pavia he knew that if he dragged the campaign out long enough then Bourbon's German mercenaries would eventually just melt away for lack of pay. In almost everyone's experience, imperial armies usually did given enough time. The French king understood the situation perfectly; even the Spanish hero Pescara, always so beloved of his troops, was forced to use all his considerable powers of persuasion to keep his unpaid men from deserting.

In Rome, having made his choice and declaring finally for France, Pope Clement VII agonised over whether his decision had been the right one. 'I cannot tell you how great has been the Pope's anxiety and suspense, now that the armies are near one another', wrote Gian Matteo Giberti of Clement's mood. Meanwhile Cardinal Salviati, Clement's papal nuncio to François, unctuously informed the French king that 'As no sailor ever risks the storm of the open sea with only one anchor, so the Pope, confident though he is in your strength, will not stake all upon the single throw'. Having been dragooned into an alliance with France, the Pope still clung to his illusion that he was still operating as a neutral party who was free to align with the eventual winner. The reality was that he risked alienating both powerful monarchs through his unreliability and changeableness.

By early February, the imperial army had finally arrived in the vicinity of Pavia and bivouacked to the north, the other side of a stream which lay outside the park wall, just a stone's throw from the French forces. Their position effectively held the French in a vice between themselves and the 6,000 Spaniards besieged inside Pavia under the command of Don Antonio de Leyva. By the time they had arrived, however, they were lacking essential provisions, had not been paid for weeks and were suffering from generally low morale; Lannoy, who was in overall command, ordered that the army dig in and issued instructions that for the time being no units should go out of their way to engage the French army. Neither Pescara, nor his deputy Alarcon, nor the duke of Bourbon took much rest during this time; by night and by day they were seen to be everywhere, exposing themselves to all sorts of hardships and dangers. Other commanders such as the marquis of Civita Sant'Angelo, and the marquis del Gasto emulated their example. For four weeks the stalemate dragged on in the freezing mid-winter conditions. The tedium was occasionally punctuated by stirring morsels of encouraging news; word reached them on 6 February from Leyva informing that his troops had sallied out and killed several hundred of Renzo da Ceri's Grison soldiers in the suburb of San Salvador, capturing four guns and five barrels of gunpowder in the process.

In spite of Lannoy's command for general restraint on the part of the imperial army, a series of vicious skirmishes soon broke out between the two sides and during one of these Giovanni della Bande Nere was wounded by a stone ball from a harquebus and had to be sent down the River Po to recuperate at Piacenza. The French king would later miss his much-needed presence. Admiral Bonnivet sneered at Lannoy's caution and urged his king to action. The papal nuncio Girolamo Aleandro meanwhile tried to exert a moderating influence, cajoling François to simply let the Imperialists slowly freeze to death in their trenches. But the dire condition of Lannoy's army eventually decided the matter. The combustible *landsknechts* were on the verge of rebellion and the imperial governor of Milan, Don Antonio de Leyva, meanwhile sent word on 21 February that he could only hold out for several more days at the very most. If the army did not attack the French immediately not only would it fail in its mission to relieve Pavia, but its own safe withdrawal would be placed in jeopardy too. If the French refused to emerge from their safe haven of the walled park to engage with them, then the imperial army would up the ante, entering the park itself and bringing the battle directly to the French.

It was decided that engineers would create a breach in the northern side of the park wall near the Castello di Mirabello where François was believed to have made his headquarters. Through this breach the imperial forces would enter, engage the northernmost French forces, and then advance steadily southward against the enemy siege entrenchments so as to relieve the pressure on Pavia's garrison. The large number of conflicting contemporary accounts–often self-serving in tone–makes the battle of Pavia quite difficult to reconstruct in any coherent detail, but some broad brush strokes can nevertheless be made as follows. The two armies were roughly equally matched, in the region of 25,000 troops on either side give or take (the French perhaps less since some of their Grison troops had already abandoned the siege and returned to their cantons). These numbers do not include the 9,000 men of Pavia's Spanish garrison. The assault began on 24 February 1525, the Emperor's birthday and also the day of St. Matthias, who had replaced Judas as one of the twelve Apostles. In the early morning, just after midnight, the imperial sappers moved into position at the Porta Pescarina (named for the Spanish general Pescara) which was situated near the village of San Genesio. As quietly as possible so as not to alert the French inside, their sounds masked by an imperial bombardment of the French siege lines in the vicinity of the Torre del Gallo, the sappers painstakingly chipped and hacked a breach in the wall.

By 5 a.m. an advance force of 3,000 harquebusiers under the command of Alfonso d'Ávalos had gained entry to the park and advanced rapidly along the little stream known as the Vernavola towards the Castello di Mirabello. Arriving an hour and a half later, and finding that the *castello* was not in fact the French headquarters, they seized it with ease. Unbeknown to the Imperialists, François had shifted the royal camp from the Mirabello to the north-west sector of the park. The Spanish advance to the Mirabello therefore effectively cut him off from his main force which lay encamped to the north-east sector. Other smaller engagements were going on close to the Porta Pescarina but due to the morning fog it was difficult for the French captains to determine the exact magnitude of the attack and thereby see to the adequate disposition of their troops. The duke of Bourbon meanwhile was supervising the *ingresso* of his men and artillery, thousands of which now streamed into the park through two gates which his rangers had managed to open. The slow-moving, difficult to manoeuvre imperial artillery eventually had to be left behind. While this main attack was in progress, Don Antonio de Leyva's ragged Spanish troops emerged from the city of Pavia and now assaulted the 3,000 Swiss under the duke of Montmorency who had been manning the siege lines. Their attack was concentrated on the Torre del Gallo and Don Antonio himself led the attack, carried into battle on a chair for his gout prevented him from walking.

It was only by 7 a.m. that François, still isolated to the north-west with his 10,000 troops, was able to form up into battle formation and go on the offensive. He placed his aristocratic heavy cavalry and knights to the front, his Swiss pikemen and renegade Saxon *landsknechts* known as the 'Black Bands of Guelders' (not to be confused with the Italian *Bande Nere*) under the command of François de Lorraine and Richard de la Pole to the rear in their usual square formations, and the men-at-arms of the *Bande Nere* on the flanks. The French king's heavy cavalry had won the day at Marignano and so François sent them against a force of Spanish light cavalry which had emerged in front of them commanded by Lannoy himself. The French *gendarmes* under the command of Charles Tiercelin quickly dispersed Lannoy's cavalry who fled into woods to the east. But while the French knights were regrouping Pescara dispersed 3,000 harquebusiers into the many small copses and hedgerows from where they now took pot shots into the flanks of the vulnerable and preoccupied French horse. The French attempted to direct their artillery against the imperial foot soldiers, however their own horse lay to their immediate front and they were unable to fire without hitting their own men; Pescara had also instructed his men to lie down and take cover in the landscaped hollows or behind gentle slopes which were everywhere in the undulating park grounds. In fact, everything about the park's landscape was ill suited to the great sweeping cavalry charges favoured by the French. Bourbon brought up an additional 4,000 *landsknechts* who prodded the left flank of the French *gendarmes* with their pikes and halberds. When the imperial cavalry regrouped and counter-charged the French, the noble horse of France reeled back in shocked surprise. With the imperial harquebusiers and halberdiers also persisting in their deadly work, Paolo Giovio described the scene as 'a miserable killing of noble cavaliers and magnificent horses'.

The battles of the infantry meanwhile, resolved into countless small, random skirmishes amidst the copses and hedgerows. Robert de la Marck, Seigneur de la Flourance, advanced with a mass of Swiss pikemen to assist the wavering French horse, in the process overrunning a battery of Spanish artillery that had been dragged into the park. Overlooking the swarms of Pescara's harquebusiers in the vicinity of the Mirabello, he blundered instead however into 6,000 of Georg von Frundsburg's *landsknechts* and a fierce pike battle ensued. The French mercenaries were further disordered by squadrons of the fleeing French horse, who now rode amongst their ranks and threw them into a state of chaos as they tried to grapple with the *landsknechts*. It was now around 7:40 a.m. and while these events were unfolding, a fierce infantry battle was also being resolved elsewhere; the 'Black Bands' of the renegade Saxon mercenary pikemen under Francois de Lorraine, also advancing to support the French King's cavalry, had been virtually annihilated by the timely arrival of fresh regiments of Frundsburg's *landsknechts*. Amidst the mounting corpses lay the mangled and unrecognisable body of one of their commanders, Richard de la Pole the Earl of Suffolk, last Yorkist claimant to the English throne.

Right in the thick of the fighting, François himself made a magnificent cameo of the princely warrior. Surrounded by his steadfast courtiers, with his own sword he cut down the marquis of Civita Sant'Angelo. But on the flank his own brother-in-law, Charles IV, Duke of Alençon, had wavered and deserted the field with his mounted men-at-arms. Tiercelin and Flourance were unable to rally their troops either and as a result the French foot also now began to flee the field. These developments, along with the wholesale disintegration of the Saxon 'Black Bands', now effectively sealed the French king's fate. His calls for a rally were ignored by the fleeing troops who sought to put as much distance as possible between themselves and the harrying fire of the imperial harquebusiers. Eventually, the King's horse was shot from under him by an Italian mercenary named Caesare Herocolani and he stood alone, garbed in his surcoat of silver adorned with the French fleur-de-lis, an obvious target for the Imperialist mercenaries. The towering men of his Swiss Guard, the *Compagnie des Cent Suisses*, had each fought to the death defending their sovereign. The Spanish and Germans called for François to surrender but he disdained to capitulate to anyone but their most senior officer. When the duke of Bourbon drew near they called for the King to surrender to his former vassal but priggishly he refused to acknowledge any duke by the name of Bourbon on the field of battle. Eventually, Charles V's viceroy Lannoy came by in person and François finally surrendered to him.

François had very nearly been butchered by the impatient German *landsknechts* and France had lost the cream of its chivalrous commanders in Italy during this terrible engagement: La Pallise was dead, as was the Italian Galeazzo Sanseverino, the fourth son of the famous *condottiere* Roberto da Sanseverino; as too was Louis de La Trémoille, shot through the heart as he fought his way through the enemy to protect his king. De La Trémoille was the husband of Cesare Borgia's only daughter, Louise Borgia, the duchess of Valentinois. The King's friend Admiral Bonnivet also lay amongst the fallen whilst Lescun later succumbed to the fatal wounds that he had sustained. On the imperial side, Pescara had also sustained wounds which would eventually prove fatal. France's duke of Alençon survived, however, to his considerable shame and led what remained of the tattered French army off the field of battle and back to France. In their hurry to ford the River Ticino, however, the aristocratic French knights had destroyed the bridge behind them which condemned many of the retreating French infantry to drowning as they attempted to swim the river in their armour.

That night, King François I of France was entertained graciously at dinner by the viceroy Lannoy. The duke of Bourbon, swallowing his aversion to a master who had wronged him so extensively, stood by and served as his cup-bearer. Fascinated and a little in awe, Frundsburg's imperial *landsknechts* in their colourful, harlequin-like slashed jerkins and tunics crowded in for a stolen look at this 'Most Christian King'. François himself was, despite his defeat, in fine fettle. He had acquitted himself honourably on the field of battle and shown great personal courage. The traditional rules of chivalry would now run their course. The Emperor Charles would ransom him according to the usual chivalrous practise of aristocratic warfare; pending payment of a suitable ransom he would be set free and, after an appropriate interlude, the eternal game of kingly war would once more be afoot. That evening he wrote sadly yet reassuringly to his mother Louise: 'To inform you of how my ill-fortune is proceeding, all is lost to me save honour and life, which remain safe'.

But François had forgotten, or perhaps had never truly grasped, that the Emperor Charles was a man of the *future* and not of the chivalrous past. Winning valiantly at the head of his own army was not overly important to the Emperor, and indeed he would not be able to prove his own personal skill-at-arms and acquire the laurels of a victorious Caesar until ten years later when he would personally lead his men in the conquest of Tunis from the Muslims. What mattered to Charles was not the gallant spectacle of leading his armies onto the field of battle but the simple, pragmatic ability to *win* (through an array of talented generals) and then be in a position to dictate the victor's terms afterwards. And this is what he fully intended to do with the French king after Pavia – wring the best possible conditions from François in return for his release.

But Charles's largely hands-off approach was a disaster for Italian affairs. Allowing Bourbon, Frundsburg and Lannoy to run their own campaign with a fair degree of autonomy, as was Charles's style, the Emperor had been as surprised as anyone by the unexpected victory at Pavia. He had only learned of the news in Madrid as late as 14 March and had neglected to make the necessary arrangements to even pay his victorious army. His generals on the ground lost no time in demanding that Rome pay the army 100,000 florins for its upkeep and it was the unfortunate Florentines who inevitably ended up footing the Medici pope's bill. The Emperor's agents also fanned out across the peninsula finding inventive new ways to tax the other city-states for the cost of the imperial army's maintenance. Pope Clement VII's reaction to Pavia was muted and low key, marked principally by a withdrawal to prayer and contemplation at a time when the situation required a decisive mind and some quick diplomatic decision-making on the part of the papacy.

In the aftermath of Pavia, what remained of the French army quit Italy. The troops stationed on the Riviera went back to Provence; the duke of Albany was collected from the Papal States by the fleet of the *Genovese* admiral Andrea

Doria. Rome and Florence continued their alliance for the time being with a now kingless France; Charles found it inadvisable to wage a punitive war against these two states and so a compromise treaty was concluded in early April. Lombardy and the various city-states including Milan and Ferrara (the d'Este having prudently swapped sides) now fell in behind the Empire. Venice managed to maintain a modicum of independence. Alfonso d'Este had switched his allegiance to Charles on the principle that his greatest enemy was Pope Clement and so, logically speaking, the Pope's enemy was now his new friend. The case of Mantua was a little more complicated due to the fact that, on the one hand, Federigo Gonzaga was captain-general of the Church whilst, on the other, he was ardently pro-imperialist and indeed the Marquis's brother Ferrante was serving with Bourbon himself in the imperial army (the duke of Bourbon had also been given sanctuary by the House of Gonzaga).

Francesco II Sforza was reinstated as duke of Milan, albeit with the support of *Napoletano* troops furnished by Lannoy. He was acutely aware that he was little more than a puppet of the imperial powers and his depression at his predicament led to a general decline in his health. After the 100,000 florins extortion money had been divided up amongst the 20,000 Germans, Italians and Spanish there was in fact very little to go round, no more than several coins a apiece per man after months of near-starvation conditions. The bulk of the imperial army trudged moodily off home after receiving their wages and both Lannoy and Bourbon had sailed for Madrid, Lannoy with his prize catch the king of France as his prisoner to present to the Emperor Charles personally. Lannoy had not only succeeded in stealing Bourbon's thunder but he had also occluded the limelight of Pescara, who had in many respects been the mainstay of the whole Pavia campaign. What now remained behind of Charles's army looked in danger of disintegrating at any moment and meanwhile his imperial agents had alienated just about every city-state in Italy by ceaselessly badgering them for funds. The impecunious Spaniards left holding Milan now took matters into their own hands and began extorting money from the citizens of the city. Desperately the *Milanesi* appealed to His Holiness the Pope for some alleviation of the Spanish demands, but Clement was either powerless or unwilling to help.

Francesco Sforza's minister Girolamo Morone had by now devoted many years of his life to the expulsion of the French and the re-establishment of Milanese independence under the ducal rule of the Sforza dynasty. Seeing that Milan had merely traded one master for another, the Imperialists, he resolved to do something about it. Together with Pope Clement, he now intrigued for the restoration of the pre-1495 balance of power between Milan, Florence, Rome, Naples and Venice; and for the expulsion of Spain and the Empire. Clement, still allied as he was with the French, was sympathetic to the scheme and so this brought both Florence and Rome to the table. Venice too seemed prepared to cooperate. Naples was the only problem since Ferdinand, the last of the Neapolitan claimants of the House of Trastámara, was by this time living as a contented exile in Spain (having been married by Charles V to Germaine of Foix, both Germaine and Ferdinand were serving as joint viceroys of Valencia by 1537 and would go on to play a significant role in Mediterranean affairs). Morone therefore needed to identify a suitable candidate to assume the crown of Naples and he alighted on the notion of offering it to the capable Spanish general, Fernando Francesco d'Ávalos, the marchese di Pescara. A loyal subject of Ferdinand II of Aragon and a firm supporter of his Habsburg descendant

Charles V, Pescara had–as a 23-year-old cavalry troop commander–been taken prisoner by the French at the Battle of Ravenna but had been given permission to ransom himself off by the anti-Sforza rebel Giangiacomo Trivulzio. But his subsequent relationship with Charles V had been a chequered one. In his earlier rivalry with Prospero Colonna, the Emperor had sided with Colonna. Furthermore, although it was arguably Pescara who kept the imperial army together at Pavia it had ultimately been Lannoy who claimed most of the credit; hence Pescara had every reason to feel disaffected with his paymasters.

Seizing upon these antipathies, Morone now attempted to suborn Pescara to abandon Charles and seize the crown of Naples for himself, assuring the Neapolitan general that Pope Clement VII would readily crown him as king. The wily Pescara had played along with the plot, pretending to listen sympathetically, but in reality he had kept his imperial master in Madrid fully abreast of developments from as early as July. Charles gave him all the latitude he needed to lead the unsuspecting conspirator on by the nose. Morone was summoned to Novara to discuss his plans in more detail and Pescara secreted his deputy Don Antonio de Leyva behind an arras, where he became privy to the full details of the plot. Morone was arrested by imperial agents in mid-October 1525. Pescara had himself been suffering from ill health and was not long for this world and, when he died on 3 December 1525, he graciously left behind a petition to Charles V to spare Morone's life. The Emperor was only too glad to grant this last wish provided Morone agreed to implicate the duke of Milan. Francesco II Sforza had only just been invested with his duchy in July that year, at a total cost to himself of 700,000 ducats, but soon Morone was singing like a songbird in return for his life and liberty. Charles's emissary appeared in Milan and presented the ailing duke with an ultimatum – relinquish both Milan and Cremona forthwith. When he refused to comply he found himself deposed as a rebel and the Castello Sforzesco, where he had taken up residence, was promptly invested by an imperial army as was Cremona. The redoubtable Don Antonio de Leyva, Duke of Terranova, took over from Pescara as supreme commander of the imperial army in Lombardy and hence effectively governor of the duchy. Don Antonio now proceeded to mop up almost all the major fortresses in the duchy on behalf of Spain and the Empire, although lack of funding continued to plague him and it was all Leyva could do to keep the imperial army together.

Pope Clement's role in the whole Morone affair was just as Morone himself had indicated. By July, Clement had opened negotiations with both Venice and Sforza in Milan for a defensive league to expel the Imperialists. If Pavia had achieved anything it seemed to have finally made Clement more stubborn and less vacillating in his determination to honour his agreement with the recently vanquished French. It was still the Emperor, not the French, who was the real threat to the independence of Italy (the recent death of Pescara, who had spurned his offer to side with the papacy, had only served to bolster Clement's belligerence). Should the Pope willingly accede to the Emperor's demands, he ran the ever-present risk of being relegated to the 'Emperor's bishop'. On the other hand, any pope who asserted too much independence from the Emperor left himself seriously exposed to predatory powers such as France. This was the balancing act which the popes of Rome had always been forced to endure in their relations with the emerging great powers of Europe.

From Madrid, Baldassarre Castiglione kept the Papal Court well informed of all major diplomatic developments, offering his professional opinion on the political affairs of the day. He tirelessly maintained his position that peace could only prevail in Italy if both the Emperor and the Pope were in perfect agreement on all things. Charles, he insisted, was a godly man who had been undemonstrative upon learning the news of his victory at Pavia; he had neither gloated nor revelled in his victory but instead received the news with seemly dignity. Castiglione contended that 'Without union with Caesar, neither a general peace, nor union against the infidels, nor any other good result would ever be attained'. Though appreciative of the valuable intelligence being fed to him from Charles's court, Clement remained largely unmoved through the long year during which King François remained the Emperor's captive.

When, however, news reached the court of Rome that the French king had caved in to practically all of the Emperor's demands by signing the Treaty of Madrid on 14 January 1526, the Pope went into a tailspin of dejection. Not only had François agreed to the demand that the French Crown relinquish the duchy of Burgundy back to Charles, himself the former titular duke of Burgundy, but François had also agreed to renounce all former claims in Italy including those to both Naples and Milan. Furthermore he had consented to restore the duke of Bourbon's lost territories to the fugitive, to marry Charles V's sister Eleanor of Austria, and to hand over his two young sons François and Henri, who were just eight and seven years old respectively. The Pope could not care less about the holding hostage of the king of France's two vulnerable sons, the eldest of which his late nephew Lorenzo de' Medici had held at his christening. He was more concerned that the lack of a countervailing French presence in Lombardy would leave Italy open to the Emperor to assert his authority piecemeal over the various city-states.

Clement need not have worried for that *tramontane* prince François, as glib with his oath as the Italians themselves, had absolutely no intention of keeping his word to Charles. When he had crossed the frontier between Spain and France at the River Bidassoa he had passed by the barque carrying his two vulnerable young boys into captivity; this alone might have crushed the spirit of any normal loving father, nevertheless when the King reached the far side of the river he leapt onto dry land and with renewed vigour declared loudly: 'I am king once again!' Charles had been furious when he heard the news that François planned to keep none of the conditions he had formerly agreed to. He vented his anger on the French *Dauphin* and his brother, moving them to a dark and airless prison cell where their bed was a straw cot and their only companion a small dog. After three years in Charles's captivity the boys would even begin to speak Spanish as their natural first language. Neither boy would fully overcome the trauma which they experienced as hostages to their royal father's fortunes.

The statesman and historian Francesco Guicciardini was summoned to Rome in early 1526 to lend Pope Clement his advice and counsel on international affairs. Born in 1483 into a distinguished pro-Medicean *ottimati* family, the young lawyer Guicciardini–whose godfather was Marsilio Ficino and whose wife was a member of the Salviati family–had served the *signoria* with distinction as one of Florence's youngest ever ambassadors to King Ferdinand of Aragon. Following the elevation of Pope Leo X the ambassadorial prodigy was taken under the new Medici Pope's wing and had embarked upon a career in papal diplomacy. Leo created him governor of Reggio in 1516, Modena in 1517, and Parma in 1521. In 1523, Clement VII next appointed him vice-regent of the Romagna, where he ruled with a considerable degree of autonomy. But unbeknown to either Leo or

Clement, despite by now being fairly high up in the ecclesiastical bureaucracy, Guicciardini had a singular loathing for priests – he was simply very accomplished at dissembling his opinions, an ability which was helped by his naturally cold, austere and somewhat aloof disposition. A good friend of Niccolò Machiavelli's since making his acquaintance in Modena in 1521, it was an odd friendship since 'il Machia' was everything that he was not – a commoner and a social climber who was injudiciously free with his opinions on every matter under the sun. Guicciardini is often regarded as the father of modern history due to his scrupulous reference to archival government documentation and his most famous work, the *Storie Fiorentine*, spanned the period from the rebellion of the *Ciompi* in 1378 to the Battle of Agnadello in 1509.

On entering the papal apartments, Guicciardini found the Pope seized by a palsy of self-doubt, utterly incapable of making a decision and sticking with it. The triple tiara weighed heavily on his brow and the Holy Father was seemingly incapable of formulating any coherent policy. As Guicciardini himself observed, 'Everything is done haphazard, and often today's action is contrary to and ruins yesterday's'. Like Machiavelli, he agreed that war was unavoidable; his friend had written: 'For as long as I can remember, people have always been either making war or talking about going to war; it is now being talked about and in a short while it will be declared; when it is over, people will start talking about it again'. Perhaps due to Guicciardini's calming, steadying influence the Pope was eventually able to arrive at a plan and stick to it at last. To Guicciardini, a political realist and cynic, the pact which François had made with Charles at Madrid was basically meaningless and, as such, the king of France had no earthly reason to abide by it. And when word soon reached the Pope that François had indeed reneged on the treaty Clement found his motivation to act by following Guicciardini's advice and throwing his weight unequivocally behind the French monarch.

On 22 May 1526, Pope Clement VII concluded the Holy League of Cognac with Rome and the Papal States, Medici-controlled Florence, Venice and Francesco II Sforza of Milan as signatories. François had also signed for France and been duly released by Pope Clement from his holy oath to the Emperor. King Henry VIII of England was meanwhile named 'protector' of the Holy League. The Pope made it clear that the Emperor was permitted to join the League but only upon the condition that he release the French king's sons, vacate the duchy of Milan and restore the Sforza to power, and pay a huge indemnity to King Henry. As if to add insult to injury, Charles was also advised to refrain from entering Italy for his coronation as emperor *unless* the Pope and the republic of Venice had first approved his proposed retinue (they feared that Charles would bring another army). Clement made the ultimate objectives of the League known as regards the kingdom of Naples, which was regarded as a 'lapsed' papal fief. Spain and the Emperor were to be thrown out of the *Regno* which would be restored by the Pope to France; however the Pope would pay to François an annual sum of 75,000 ducats for the natural son of Henry VIII, Henry Fitzroy, Duke of Richmond and Somerset, to have his principality in Naples. All the signatories agreed in return to protect the Medici family and its interests.

Charles responded to Clement's waywardness by covertly escalating the diplomatic situation. He now placed one of his admirals, Don Ugo de Moncada, in charge of imperial negotiations with the court of Rome. Moncada had enjoyed a colourful career. He had marched on Naples under King Charles VIII and later served as one of Cesare Borgia's *condottiere* before *El gran capitán* Gonzalo de Córdoba's 1503 proclamation forbidding all Spaniards from serving with the Borgia duke. Later, under Ferdinand II of Aragon, he fought the Berber pirates who continued to infest the seas around Italy and Sicily and had also served as viceroy of Sicily. When war broke out in 1522 he conducted naval sorties for the Emperor Charles V but had been defeated and captured by Genoa's famous admiral Andrea Doria (following the Treaty of Madrid he had been liberated in a prisoner exchange with the French general Montmorency). Moncada was widely disliked in Italy, not least for being a native Spaniard, but also because he regarded the peninsula as a ripe fruit for the plucking. He belonged to that group of chauvinistic Spaniards known as the *exaltados* who dreamed of subjecting all of Italy to the Spanish Crown. Moncada was therefore the very distillation of everything the Italians disliked about the Spanish.

Initial negotiations on 16 June did not auger well. Moncada agreed to lift the siege of Milan provided the Pope agreed to arrange for the payment of the imperial troops. Clement rebutted that he would only countenance this on condition that the Imperialist armies leave Italy altogether and restore the king of France's two sons to him. On 23 June the Pope wrote to the Emperor Charles in the strongest of terms, detailing a long litany of grievances against the Empire and denouncing Charles's 'insatiable ambition'. He almost immediately regretted his intemperance and wrote a second brief a couple of days later, nevertheless there was no way of cancelling his diplomatic blunder and the two leaders continued their inexorable drift apart. Clement, for his part, was seeing promises from François but as yet no funding. Neither were any troops forthcoming as yet from the French.

The army of the League of Cognac which took shape that summer at Marignano was a complex and unwieldy beast. It comprised two main elements: the Venetian army whose commander-in-chief was the duke of Urbino (who was very much beholden to Pesaro, the Venetian *Proveditore*), and the 'ecclesiastical' army whose commander-in-chief was the *condottiere* Guido Rangone who had served under the late Pope Leo X. Rangone's army was further subdivided into the papal forces commanded by Giovanni della Bande Nere (by now recovered from the injuries sustained at Pavia) and the Florentine forces commanded by the republic's *condottiere* Vitello Vitelli. Commissioned by the Pope to keep an eye on things, Francesco Guicciardini served as lieutenant-general of the papal forces. In addition, Renzo da Ceri, who had repelled the duke of Bourbon at the gates of Marseilles, was also making his way to Italy with his own Italian mercenaries, whilst another force comprised of largely *Milanese* exiles under the command of Michele Antonio, Marquis of Saluzzo, set out from Provence and aimed to join up with the combined League army in Lombardy.

Even the aging armchair strategist Niccolò Machiavelli heard the call to arms and left the comfort of his hearth and home and marched to the sound of the drum. Asked by the *signoria* to report to the army of the League in order to see to the disposition of the Florentine militia contingent, Machiavelli gladly whipped them into shape. But, when he was afforded the privilege of drilling a detachment of Giovanni della Bande Nere's famous Black Bands, things did not go so well. To his shame and embarrassment, Machiavelli's confused orders left the regiment of 3,000 *Bande Nere* soldiers in a chaotic shambles and Giovanni himself was obliged to take over and restore order to the formation. Unfortunately for Machiavelli the parade ground fiasco had been witnessed by one of his more notable sceptics, the Dominican friar and novella writer Matteo

493

Bandello. 'Niccolò kept us under the hot sun for more than two hours that day while he tried to parade [us] in the way he had described in writing, and he was having a very difficult time in so doing', sniffed Bandello, who concluded from the experience: 'It became clear then how big the difference is between he who knows and never applied what he knows, and he who–besides the knowledge–gets his hands dirty, as it is customary to say' (*Novelle* I, 40).

Bandello was fortunate to get this opportunity to cock such an intimate snook at Machiavelli and his ambiguous attitude towards *The Prince* was common enough at the time. Whereas the Florentines might have been privately fascinated by Machiavelli's public revelation of the method as concerning the art of politics and statecraft, it was still not considered altogether seemly to admit one's admiration openly. That its author could not even drill a regiment of soldiers when push came to shove was simply too juicy a piece of scuttlebutt to pass up. Nevertheless, for all that, Machiavelli's strategic instincts were perhaps still far in advance of the Pope and his many generals. Niccolò had lately mooted to Guicciardini that, instead of depending on the alliance with the King of France, a far better play would be to place Giovanni della Bande Nere at the head of a great Italian army and allow him to send the Imperialists reeling from Italy – a task which few believed him incapable of carrying out, and in very short order too. But before the idea could be seriously discussed with Clement VII, Filippo Strozz nixed the proposal by reaffirming the papal alliance with François. Both Machiavelli and Guicciardini knew full well that a valuable opportunity had been missed.

When Guido Rangone and Francesco Guicciardini subsequently linked up with the duke of Urbino at the military camp at Marignano, the two papal commanders felt honour bound to recognise the Duke as overall supreme commander 'to avoid disputes – and because there was nothing to be done about it'. If only both Clement VII and Guicciardini could have seen it, Francesco Maria della Rovere was still no friend of the Medici papacy but Guicciardini had nevertheless felt the need to defer to the more experienced *condottiere* in matters of war. The duke of Urbino with his Venetians and 'ecclesiastics' had quickly occupied the imperial city of Lodi, but there still remained disgruntled pockets of unpaid imperial troops at Pavia, Alessandria, Cremona and also Genoa. As for the city of Milan, the French and Duke Francesco Sforza were still holding out in the citadel but would shortly be obliged to capitulate if they were not relived, and soon. In all, the Imperialist troops numbered in the region of 6,000 to 8,000 together with some lances and light cavalry. Having captured Lodi thanks to a disgruntled Italian officer having opened the gates to his army, the duke of Urbino next advanced against Milan. However, when on 7 July he came within sight of the enemy entrenchments he grew skittish and ordered the army's withdrawal under cover of darkness. '*Veni, vidi, fugit*' ('I came, I saw, I fled') had been Guicciardini's mocking comment on the whole embarrassing affair. Giovanni della Bande Nere had been the only commander to actually engage the Imperialists at Milan, having on his own initiative mounted a spirited attack on the Porta Romana. Outraged at their captain-general's display of spinelessness, he subsequently ordered that his Black Bands stand-to-arms until daybreak, at which they pointedly turned their backs on their Spanish adversaries inside the city and slowly marched away with their dignity intact.

Lacking relief from the army of the League, Milan's castello unavoidably fell on 24 July and Francesco II Sforza was finally taken by the imperial forces after

494

a brave eight-month-long resistance. Seemingly broken by the siege and little more than skin and bone, he was taken to Como where, given a pension of 30,000 ducats, he was to await the judgement of Charles for his alleged involvement in Girolamo Morone's plot. He did not wait for the outcome. Instead, Sforza proceeded to Lodi where the League of Cognac had its military headquarters. Here, the duke of Urbino's army was augmented by 14,000 Swiss which had been paid for by France. With these fresh troops Urbino proceeded to acquit himself somewhat by relieving the city of Cremona, whose fortress was still held by Sforza's troops. The duke of Milan would make Cremona his own base for the next few years.

Don Ugo de Moncada was under instructions from Charles to draw Ferrara into the coming conflict as allies against the Pope and to also use Siena against Florence and the Medici. Charles had been informed by his agents in Italy that Siena still remained loyal to the Empire and would agree to the stationing of imperial troops in their city. Pope Clement, however, was still engaged in his Medici quest to expand Florence's remit in Tuscany and in July he despatched papal troops together with some *Sienese* exiles to lay siege to Siena. Later that same month, however, the *Sienese* counter-attacked the Romans and scattered their forces just as they were breaking camp. This morale-boosting victory only served to harden the attitude of the *Sienese* towards Clement and Florence. As a powerful inducement to align Ferrara with the Empire, Alfonso d'Este was meanwhile given the incentive of being appointed imperial captain-general and was invested with the cities of Reggio and Modena. Ferrara had long been associated with the French but the House of d'Este were Italian enough to know which alliance suited their interests best at any given moment. François simply could not serve both the Pope and the duchy of Ferrara, and so the sensible decision was taken to embrace Charles V. The foundries of Ferrara now stepped up their production of artillery and falconets in readiness for the approaching tempest.

Ugo de Moncada was also busy opening a channel of communications with the Ghibelline Colonna through their spokesperson in the Sacred College, Cardinal Pompeo Colonna. Cardinal Colonna had still not forgotten, or indeed forgiven, Clement's victory in the last papal conclave. The Colonna resented the Pope's turning away from the Emperor to embrace the king of France and Pompeo Colonna himself was angry that Clement had declined to appoint him as papal ambassador to the Emperor's court at Madrid. He had been openly heard to boast that 'with 100,000 ducats I could take Rome!' and what's more the Colonna family had the military forces in their possession to do just that. In fact, this was the plan formulated by the Emperor and communicated to Moncada, to support and facilitate a Colonna attack on Rome from 'whence all the mischief springs' as Charles put it. As these back channel communications continued, the Pope grew increasingly disconsolate at his recent failure in both Milan and Siena. The French ambassador to Rome reported Clement's perplexity and noted discouragingly that 'His ministers are more dead than alive'.

Pope Clement's Holy League of Cognac was, in an ironic way, to have a directly positive effect on the rise of Lutheranism in Germany. On 27 August the Protestants of the Empire came together at the Diet of Speyer and agreed in unison that each German state should be permitted freedom of religious worship until such time as a general Church council could be convened to settle religious matters. The natural instinct of Charles V, himself a fiercely devout

Roman Catholic, was to fight the Edict of Speyer (and the Edict of Worms that had formerly been agreed by working in conjunction Pope Leo X). However, since Clement had insulted Charles by his releasing François from his oath to him, not to mention his masterminding of the clearly anti-imperial League of Cognac, he consequently needed the support of as many of his imperial city-states as possible; naturally this also encompassed the Protestant ones too. In other words, Clement had lost a valuable potential ally, perhaps his single most important supporter, in the war against the Protestant 'heresy'. In the nineteen years which intervened between the Edict of Speyer in 1526 and the formation of the Council of Trent in 1545, the Protestant faith had ample time in which to consolidate itself, not only in Germany but also later in England, Switzerland and the Low Countries as well.

The Colonna family had established themselves in Rome during the twelfth-century but during the era of Petrarch in the fourteenth-century the clan had begun spreading the fanciful story that they were descended from the Julio-Claudian dynasty. Their coat of arms was a representation of Trajan's Column, a suitable imperial landmark which was located close to their main family *palazzo* in Rome. Later, as fierce Ghibellines, they earned the right to place the imperial pointed crown on top of their coat of arms. The family's first cardinal was Giovanni Colonna di Carbognano in 1206. Six years later a second cardinal, Giovanni the Younger, was also appointed to the Sacred College. The family's first (and last) pope was elected in 1417; this was Oddone Colonna, Pope Martin V.

More often than not, however, the Colonna had suffered perceived wrongs from the papacy, and all incoming popes were forced to contend with Colonna power when seeking to establish themselves as rulers of Rome and the Papal States. In 1484 the protonotary Lorenzo Oddone Colonna had, as we have seen, been arrested and then executed on the orders of Pope Sixtus IV's nephew Girolamo Riaro. The Borgia Pope Alexander VI had then fallen into a bitter feud with Fabrizio I Colonna of Paliano, which caused the latter to offer his services to the king of Naples; he served at the Battle of Cerignola in which the Spanish were successful against the occupying army of the French and later offered his sword to King Ferdinand of Spain when he assumed direct rule over the kingdom of Naples in 1504. For the crime of going against Pope Alexander he had many of his lands and properties seized and appropriated by the Church, lands which were subsequently redistributed to the Catalan pontiff's own family members. Cardinal Pompeo Colonna was also from the Paliano side of the Colonna family and like Fabrizio had also fought with another pope, this time Julius II. As the Catholic Encyclopaedia sums him up, 'the sword was more congenial to him than the breviary', meaning that in other words he was just another Roman aristocrat wielding secularised power through the institution of the Church.

Pompeo Colonna, who had his finger on the pulse of the city at this time, had an intimate feel for the mood of the Roman mob. Pope Clement's chamberlain, Cardinal Francesco Armellino, camerlengo of the Holy Roman Church, was perhaps the most hated man in all of Rome. A confirmed simoniac, he enriched both the Church, as well as himself, by openly selling positions within the Curia, by inflating wheat prices, and by imposing taxes on wine consumption. He also demolished countless numbers of supposedly 'unsafe' structures in the city, most of which were the homes of the poor, so that he could benefit from the subsequent business deals on the redistribution of land parcels. It was the underprivileged sort who had suffered most but, in truth, the Pope's fiscal policies had won him few friends amongst all social classes in Rome ever since Armellino's appointment. The wine tax was especially resented by the party-loving Romans.

Cardinal Colonna was aware that if his forces were to make their move the Pope would be able to garner little support from either the Roman mob or the élite. With this consideration in mind, Moncada returned to Rome in mid-August and assumed the mantle of peace broker between the papacy and the Colonna. Playing upon the Pope's personal weakness, Colonna cajoled him and showered him volubly with blandishments, lulling him into a false sense of security by assuring him that the Emperor's intentions were strictly honourable. Meanwhile, the Colonna had secretly stepped up their recruitment from amongst the many Colonna estates in the Tusculan hills east of Frascati. By August, the private army of the Colonna was estimated to outnumber those papal forces which Clement was known to have stationed in Rome. At the Colonna's disposal was something approaching 3,000 men plus additional levies from the Colonna estates together with about 800 horse.

Moncada now managed to broker an agreement between the Pope and the Colonna which saw the Supreme Pontiff agreeing to pardon the Colonna family for their past transgressions and the lifting of an admonition on Cardinal Colonna himself for his personal disobedience. In return, the Colonna would supposedly agree to stand down their men, which would permit Clement himself to make economies against the upkeep of the papal guard. Against howls of protest from his advisers against this false economy, Clement VII dismissed the majority of the several thousand troops guarding the city of Rome and retained only a small force of 200 to 500 guardsmen supported by 100 horse. The stand down was precisely what Cardinal Pompeo Colonna had been waiting for. On 17 September, Charles V had published an open letter to Pope Clement cataloguing his many misdeeds towards the Emperor. The letter, which took on the form of a manifesto and which reminded the Pope that Christ himself had exhorted Peter to put away his sword, was published in Spain, Germany and the Netherlands. It censured Clement for furthering the Lutheran heresy because, in taking up arms against the Emperor, Charles would now be forced to depend on those same heretics for protection against the Pope!

On the early morning of 20 September 1526, about 3,000 infantry and 800 horse led by Cardinal Colonna, Ascanio Colonna and Ugo de Moncada entered Rome by the Lateran Gate and galloped past the Forum towards the Ponte Sisto. Once across the River Tiber and in Trastevere they advanced up the Lungara and entered the Vatican by the lightly-defended Porta San Spirito. The ordinary people of Rome, those who were already up at this early hour, cheered the Colonna troops. Not only did they bear intense hatred for the corrupt and rapacious Cardinal Armellino but they sincerely believed that the Colonna would not harm the Vicar of Christ. Besides, as the Romans saw it, this was purely a disagreement between the Pope and the Colonna and it hardly concerned them. In order to reduce expenditure on the papal guard Armellino had used the argument that the Colonna were ultimately harmless. The Supreme Pontiff had been left practically defenceless by this foolish policy.

There were desultory clashes in the Borgo and around the area of the Vatican where the Curia and the papal court had their dwellings. Pope Clement's handful of loyal guards was scarcely a match for Moncada's hardened

Spaniards and the savage Colonna *bravi*. Clement's first instinct was to declare that he would confront the aggressors in his full papal robes and, if he could not shame them into dispersing, he insisted that he would end his life in a flourish as a Catholic martyr. His officials quickly talked him out of this rash course of action and so the Pope prudently retired instead to the Castel Sant'Angelo which–thanks once more to Cardinal Armellino's thriftiness–had not been adequately provisioned in readiness for the flood of ecclesiastical asylum seekers which now descended upon it. From the battlements and embrasures of Sant'Angelo those who had sought sanctuary now watched helplessly as Colonna and Moncada's troops sacked the Vatican Palace, carrying off armfuls of vessels, altar chalices, croziers, candelabras and even the papal tiara itself, which in his haste the Pope and his officials had neglected to bring along with them.

By this time, Cardinal Colonna had clearly taken leave of his senses. Blinded by his loathing for the Medici pope, he harboured no other ambition than to lower the papal tiara upon his own head. Had he been more rational he would have realised that the members of the Sacred College would scarcely have permitted him to seize the papal throne by force, but at this point it is probable that–overcome as he was with his immediate success and bolstered by the military presence of the Emperor's agent Ugo de Moncada–he would be able to impose his will on the Sacred College by sheer force of arms. In all of this, however, Cardinal Colonna had failed to realise that he had been cleverly manipulated by Moncada. The latter was never intent on overthrowing Clement and installing a Colonna pope in place of a Medici one; he was merely interested in bringing Clement to the point where he could pressure him into signing a fresh treaty with the Emperor which would be dictated purely on the latter's terms. With meagre provisions laid in for a protracted siege of the Castel, and with the Spanish and Colonna running rampant in the streets of Rome, this was exactly what the Pope was forced to do the very next day when Moncada, very much against the wishes of Cardinal Colonna, went to the Castel to negotiate a truce.

Riding his horse up the gradual incline of the Castel's inner staircase which led upwards to the private papal apartments, Ugo de Moncada was ushered into the Holy Father's presence. With a flick of his quill the Medici pope now agreed to a four-month truce during which he would abandon the League of Cognac and remove all papal troops from Lombardy and Siena in return for the Colonna's withdrawal from the city of Rome. A papal fleet commanded by Andrea Doria, which had arrived off the coast of French-held Genoa that August, would also be withdrawn. Piero di Lorenzo's daughter Clarice de' Medici would furnish her husband, Filippo Strozzi the Younger, as a hostage against the Pope's good behaviour, along with several other selected cardinals. Strozzi, who considered himself Clement's friend and who had prospered under both Medici popes, went along with the scheme despite the obvious dangers to his person and his purse. He would not be in a position to see it at the time, but Strozzi would probably have done better to back Machiavelli's and Guicciardini's plan to arm and support Giovanni della Bande Nere against Charles V, because his obedient support for the Pope and his weak-minded policies would not work out well for him personally.

Moncada and Charles V had, meanwhile, played both Pope Clement and Pompeo Colonna like virtuosos. Much to Cardinal Colonna's disgust, the Spanish forces supporting his own departed Rome on 22 September, carrying

30,000 ducats worth of plunder with them. The Pope had been cleverly dislodged from the League of Cognac and the Emperor had been able to save face by disavowing the shameful attack and heaping all the blame on the unruly Colonna clan instead. The latter would pay the inevitable price for having served as Charles's dupes. In the weeks that followed some papal troops were pulled out of Lombardy and repositioned in Florence to enforce Medici hegemony there. Other troops were permitted to remain close to Milan under the pretext that they were in the French king's pay. Thousands of papal troops returned from the front and poured back into Rome, considerably bolstering the Pope's mood. In September the Lombard city of Cremona fell to the League's forces. The ink on Ugo de Moncada's treaty was barely dry before the slippery Pope Clement had thoughts of reneging on it.

More Papal troops were brought from Lombardy under the command of the *condottiere* Vitello Vitelli and, together with groups of *bravi* from the rival Orsini, were flung against the Colonna estates. Clement would smash the Colonna for their disobedience and their act of sacrilege in attacking St. Peter's. Cardinal Pompeo had managed to evade the Pope's troops and fled to his monastery at Grottaferrata where, in his absence, he was justly deprived of the vice-chancellorship. Vespasiano Colonna, the son of Prospero Colonna, was especially singled out for the Pope's opprobrium. The cardinal's cousin had never intended to attack the Pope and in the weeks prior to the sacking he had gone to Rome to reassure Clement that the Colonna would serve as the Pope's obedient vassals for the lands which they held in the Papal States. But as regards those lands which they held in Naples, they had no option but to serve the Emperor Charles V's interests.

Italians now fought Italians in the Papal States, seemingly oblivious to the myriad dangers which surrounded them on the broader world stage. In the Balkans, just three weeks before the Colonna had poured into Rome, King Louis II of Hungary and his small army of mostly heavy armoured knights had been pulverised at the Battle of Mohács by a vastly superior force commanded by Süleyman the Magnificent. Fleeing from the onslaught, King Louis had been thrown by his horse in the darkness and confusion and died alone, drowned in the ditch where he had fallen. In the aftermath of Mohács the Habsburgs now claimed the throne of Hungary but the Emperor's brother Ferdinand I of Austria feuded with another claimant, John Zápolya the incumbent Voyevod of Transylvania. Louis II's death effectively marked the breakup of the unified Hungarian empire with the Ottomans holding both central Hungary and wielding suzerainty over semi-independent Transylvania (in his bid for Hungary Zápolya was forced to recognise Süleyman's feudal overlordship). Furthermore, although Süleyman was ultimately unable to hold onto the conquered city of Buda, which he had recently added to his earlier conquest of Belgrade in 1521, the reality of the situation was that Christendom's Balkan bulwark against the Ottoman Muslims was now dramatically compromised. And since the Emperor Charles V and King François I of France continued their own feud through 1526 and into 1527 the major European powers were unable to come together to shore up the Christian breach in the East.

But, despite these setbacks, the savage Turks were in fact the very least of Pope Clement VII's worries. A much closer threat was looming which, though still 'Christian' in nature, was every bit as detrimental to papal interests. As Pope Clement's papal guardsmen clashed with the Colonna remnants, unbeknown to them an army of 16,000 fanatical Lutheran *landsknechts* under the able command of Georg von Frundsburg had stumbled over the freezing cold Alps and down onto the icy Plain of Lombardy. In their leader the prince of Mindelheim's saddle bags was a length of silk rope with which he professed that he intended to hang the pope of Rome and the entire membership of the Sacred College. For Rome and the papacy the day of reckoning which had once been prophesied by Savonarola, and which was now being promoted by Martin Luther and Huldrych Zwingli, would soon be at hand.

CHAPTER 18

The Sack of Rome

In Rome, the chief city of Christendom, no bells ring, no churches are open, no masses are said. Sundays and feast days have ceased. Many houses are burned to the ground; in others the doors and windows are broken and carried away; the streets are changed into dunghills. The stench of dead bodies is terrible; men and beasts have a common grave and in the churches I have seen corpses that dogs have gnawed. In the public places, tables are set close together at which thousands of ducats are gambled for. The air rings with blasphemies fit to make good men–if such there be–wish that they were deaf. I know nothing wherewith I can compare it, except it be the destruction of Jerusalem. I do not believe that if I live for two thousand years I should see the like again.

Anonymous Spanish eye-witness to the sack of Rome

Georg von Frundsburg and his army of *landsknechts* was just one half of a vice with which Charles V intended to punish the Pope and relieve the beleaguered imperial garrison of Milan (the other half of this vice would comprise a force of 10,000 Germans and Spaniards under the command of the viceroy of Naples, Charles de Lannoy, which would be transported by sea and land at the port of Gaeta just south of Rome). The fifty-three-year-old Frundsburg was an old school battlefield commander. His *landsknechts* were well-drilled, intensely loyal to him, delighted in their espirit de corps and took pride in their colourful and flamboyant dress. Modelled after the Swiss pike formations, the German *landsknechts* had shown themselves worthy inheritors of their craft and their pike squares, liberally peppered with halberdiers and harquebusiers, were a daunting formation on any field of battle. Frundsburg himself had fought with distinction at Pavia and was a Protestant convert who had spoken out in support of Martin Luther. The opportunity to serve his Emperor by marching down into Italy and chastising this errant and wilful Medici pope had been too good to pass up.

Although he was in straightened financial circumstances Frundsburg nevertheless mortgaged his ancestral estates in Mindelheim in order to raise the necessary funds to pay his army; this consisted principally of thirty-five companies of pikemen. Like their commander, these soldiers were also mostly followers of Luther and their expedition was in many respects to assume the nature of a righteous crusade against 'popery'. Many of them were also hoping to make better profits from plunder than they had done during their last undertaking south of the Alps during the Pavia campaign. Frundsburg's initial orders were to enter Italy and link up with Leyva's and Bourbon's imperialists, mostly Spaniards together with some Germans, who were still bottled up on the defensive inside Milan by the troops of the League of Cognac. Aside from this any other orders remained dismayingly vague although it was gleefully rumoured amongst the soldiers that Rome (with its immeasurably rich pickings) was to be their ultimate destination.

The *landsknechts* knew that many of the more accessible Alpine passes were well defended by the Italian and French troops of Clement VII's League of Cognac so they chose therefore to enter Italy through one of the more difficult and unexpected routes which led from the city of Trent. This would bring the army down beside Lake Garda in the vicinity of Mantua. The nine day crossing of the high Alpine precipices and gorges at the beginning of winter had been a nightmare for the 16,000 Germans. Cold, shivering, wet and exhausted, they had been unable to find any wood above the Alpine tree line with which to light their cooking fires and, by the time that they descended onto the Lombard plain, they were half starved and in a pitiful condition. But the sheer force of their general's personality fired their determination and, finding themselves at last on flat and level ground, their column now snaked its way down beside Lake Garda until they came to the difficult, marshy terrain around Mantua.

Waiting for the Germans, thinly strung out along a line corresponding with the length of the River Po, were the Venetians and papal troops of the League of Cognac under the command of the duke of Urbino. There were no Mantuan troops alongside them for Federigo Gonzaga, Marquis of Mantua, was still a supporter of the Emperor and turned a blind eye whilst Frundsburg trudged through his lands unharassed. However it so happened that the nearest League forces to the *landsknechts* were the Black Bands of Giovanni della Bande Nere, who were at that time encamped in the vicinity of Curtatone near Mantua. As the Imperialist army attempted to cross the River Po near Borgoforte they were repeatedly engaged in late November by the determined Black Bands. Time and again the Italian light armoured cavalry threw themselves against the *landsknechts* who, according to one eyewitness, 'stood with their pikes and halberds like a wall'. Eventually, however, the repeated onslaughts took their toll, forcing the Imperialists to withdraw downriver to Governolo, where the Po conjuncts its tributary the River Mincio. Here, on 25 November, Giovanni della Bande Nere engaged the German rear-guard on the freezing banks of the Mincio and was struck in the leg by a projectile from a German falconet, one of several which Alfonso d'Este had secretly supplied to the imperial army from his foundry at Ferrara.

Wounded in the same leg which had been injured just before the Battle of Pavia, Giovanni was carried from the field and sent back downriver to San Nicolò Po where no doctor could be found to treat him. Thereupon he was sent by stretcher to Mantua where he was housed in the Castel Goffredo, owned by a member of the Gonzaga family. Here he was treated by Abraham Arié, the same Jewish surgeon who had treated his earlier leg wound. Upon learning the news of his friend's injury, Pietro Aretino had rushed to Giovanni's bedside and found the surgeons at their grim work sawing off the *condottiere's* lower leg. Squeamishly, the writer of satire and *bon mots* fled the room in terror. In the sixteenth-century, amputation of the lower limbs technically consisted in the surgeon making guillotine-like incisions below the knee using a crescent-shaped knife and saw; but the surgical arts were primitive by today's standards and in reality little better than butchery. With no anaesthetic available, Giovanni required twelve strong men to hold him down during the procedure but, even so, he still insisted on holding aloft a candle so that Abraham could see better as he went about his grisly work. Upon returning some time later, Aretino found the patient both lucid and in surprisingly good humour, holding up his freshly amputated foot like a good sport and asking Aretino to make a cameo of it.

But the wound was neither closed nor adequately disinfected and so within a matter of days gangrene soon set in. The delirious *condottiere* presently asked to be moved from the bed to his military cot crying 'I am a soldier and will not die amidst these sheets and bandages'. Italy's last great hope for independence from foreign domination died in his ordinary military camp bed on 30 November 1526. Pietro Aretino would later describe his eyewitness account of Giovanni's final hours in a moving letter to his friend Francesco Albizzi. Giovanni de' Medici of the Black Bands left behind his devoted wife Maria Salviati and their infant son Cosimo. It was especially mortifying for the widow. Maria had frequently admonished her husband not to take the great risks that he habitually did in battle. She strongly suspected too, probably with good reason, that Giovanni's jealous kinsman Pope Clement VII was purposefully placing him on the front lines where he was always in the greatest danger of injury or even death. The irony in this was strong considering that Paolo Giovio would later opine in his work *Gli elogi: Vite brevemente scritte d'huomini illustri di guerra antichi et moderna* (1557) that 'Giovanni d'Italia' had been the living embodiment of Clement's father Giuliano. Maria never subsequently remarried and took to wearing the black garb of a novice until her death in 1543, and it is in these sombre mourning clothes that she is habitually depicted in her subsequent portraits by the likes of Pontormo and Agnolo Bronzino. The remains of Giovanni were transferred to Florence where they were buried in the crypt of the Medici Chapel.

Giovanni's constant companion during this final year, Pietro Aretino, having by now outstayed his welcome in Rome, remained for a while in Mantua where his friend had so recently died. Here, under the protection of Federigo Gonzaga, he was free to pour his scorn upon the ineffectual Medici pope from a prudently safe distance. He also fraternised with Gonzaga's much-treasured court painter and architect Giulio Romano, who had been recruited to the court of Mantua in 1524, and who like Aretino was a fellow *cognoscente* of the nude female form, as indeed was the duke of Mantua himself (Federigo's portrait by Titian shows us a handsome, whimsical man who–somewhat unfairly–would eventually die of congenital syphilis inherited from his parents).

However, when Aretino penned a bitter satire targeting the Pope and his court which was dedicated to his new benefactor Gonzaga, Clement VII got wind of it and there was the devil to pay. Gonzaga was forced to send Aretino packing. The poet-for-hire next found himself in Venice, a morally lax city which he found rather more congenial. He compensated for his recent *faux pas* by composing for an appreciative Gonzaga *La puttana errante* ('The Wandering Whore'), an erotic poem in which a wanton woman of Venice sets out on a vulgar odyssey of unabashed sexual indulgence. Her peregrinations lead her eventually, inevitably, to Rome where she enters the city in triumph proudly wearing a *corona di cazzi* ('crown of cocks') on her head. In Aretino's erotic satire it would be the courtesan who would enter Rome after an abundance of enjoyable violations; but, to the Lutherans now descending through the desolate plains of Lombardy, Rome herself was the prostitute and her own violation (no doubt to Aretino's intense satisfaction) would ultimately prove to be far less agreeable.

With the Black Bands effectively neutralised by the death of their leader, the duke of Urbino and his Venetians offered no further resistance to Frundsburg's army as it now crossed the River Po at Ostiglia on 28 November. Still bitterly cold and miserable, and badly mauled by the Black Bands, the Imperialists trudged south to threaten first Parma and then Piacenza where the feisty commander Frundsburg despatched a terse communiqué to the duke of Bourbon in Milan in which he stated: 'In the face of great dangers I have crossed the high mountains and deep waters, have spent two months in the country, enduring poverty, hunger and frost: that owing to the great patience of my soldiers and with the help of God I have divided and driven back the enemy. I now lay here in the enemy's country, attacked every day, and desire further instructions.'

Given the conditions he and his men had endured since arriving in Lombardy, Frundsburg can be forgiven his lack of patience and the slightly impertinent manner in which he communicated with his ostensible commanding officer. But what Frundsburg himself failed to grasp was that Bourbon too was facing insuperable problems of his own in Milan. Bourbon had only returned there from Madrid late in 1526. The idea which Charles V had floated earlier that year, of Bourbon himself taking over the duchy of Milan, had never materialised (indeed Francesco Sforza had still yet to be formerly indicted and found guilty of any treason) and so he had settled instead for the more modest rank of captain-general of the imperial army in Lombardy, taking over command from Don Antonio de Leyva. Once back in Milan, Bourbon could see first-hand the problems his subordinate faced in governing the unruly city. In April 1526, while Bourbon was still in Spain, Leyva had been faced with a popular rebellion which was caused when a salt-merchant was killed whilst trying to prevent some Spanish soldiers from looting his house. It was only through the peace-making efforts of the *Milanese* aristocrats Pietro Pusterla and Francesco Visconti that order was restored. However, plunder and extortion of the local population was the only way Leyva's troops had of getting paid, and in June the same year the grass roots disturbances had been re-ignited and several hundred Spaniards were killed by the *Milanese*.

The locals knew that the German troops were not as rapacious as the hated Spaniards and so they tended to flock to the districts where the Germans were billeted. These areas they described as *Cuccagna*, that mythical land of milk and honey which is derived from the Middle French expression *pays de cocaigne*, or 'land of plenty' (the fabled 'Land of Cockaygne' in Middle English). This constant friction between the occupying troops and the local population led inevitably to Milan becoming a grim and depressing city, a far cry from the glories of its heyday under the Sforza and the Visconti. When Leyva banished several of the leading *Sforzeschi* the ordinary people were left without any noble protectors and the depredations of the soldiers only grew worse. The Spanish troops were owed considerable arrears in back pay which could only be settled by extorting funds from the resentful *Milanesi*. The rough, unwashed Spaniards were experts at extortion and their cruelty in the pursuit of plunder knew no bounds. Even Bourbon, upon his arrival in November, was hard pressed to contain their rampant gangsterism and he now sent word to Frundsburg that if Milan could produce but one month's pay he would be able to entice the army from the city and fulfil the count of Mindelheim's urgent request of linking up with the *landsknechts*. However, unless they were paid they simply refused to move out and join up with their allies. Unlike the *landsknechts*, who fought–at least in part–for missionary zeal and love of their general, the Spaniards fought strictly for pay and were adamant than no further service would be forthcoming in the absence of coin. Eventually, by selling off the very last of his personal jewels, Bourbon managed to scrape together enough in the way of specie to settle his outstanding account with the troops under his command and the Spaniards finally agreed to march out of Milan. The two imperial armies linked up at Piacenza on 30 January 1527.

While the imperial forces were consolidating in the north of Italy, the viceroy of Naples, Charles de Lannoy, had landed with his troops at Gaeta and was marching inland to the papal fortress situated at Frosinone, which was defended by a detachment of the Black Bands. Cardinal Pompeo Colonna, who had met Lannoy at the coast, urged him however to abandon Frosinone's siege and instead mount a direct attack on Rome. He was ignored. At the prospect of Lannoy's close proximity, Pope Clement predictably went into a fresh tailspin of dejection. His papal nuncio in France wrote desperately to the French king that 'the coming of the *landsknechts* and the death of Giovanni della Bande Nere are mortal blows for the Pope'. François remained unmoved. He was still too preoccupied enjoying his freedom from Spanish captivity and was in no hurry to venture to Italy himself or indeed incur the expense of sending an army to rescue the Pope at this present moment. He preferred to wait things out and see if the army of his adversary Charles wore itself out in Italy first. When he finally did deign to send an emissary his demand to the Supreme Pontiff was that his son should be made king of Naples and be married off to the late Duke Lorenzo II de' Medici's daughter Catherine de Medici. Pope Clement rightly dismissed the proposal as ridiculous. How, when he was under direct threat from a *Napoletano* and Spanish army in the south, and still lacking any tangible French support, could he possibly promise an investiture which was not within his power to give?

When Lannoy left the siege of Frosinone and came to Rome for an audience with the Pope, his terms were equally unfeasible. Lannoy demanded that Clement surrender the papal cities of Parma, Piacenza, Pisa, Leghorn, Ostia and Civitavecchia, as well as the sum of 200,000 ducats, which was to be paid to the *landsknechts* in the north to persuade them to go home to Germany. Clement now turned to the Venetian ambassador. Would Venice provide the money to make the imperial army vanish from Italian soil? 'Highly unlikely' was the reply. The count of Frundsburg had mortgaged his ancestral estates in order to do his Kaiser's bidding; furthermore he was driven by an evangelical Lutheran zeal which was in equal measure both heretical and intense. It was unlikely that an infusion of Venetian or indeed papal gold would deter him from his mission at this late stage. Observers recorded that Pope Clement was so disconsolate by the impossible demands being placed upon him that he barely knew what day it was. Another member of the papal court dolefully recorded, 'We have already received a sentence of death and only await its execution'. It is at this point that Clement embarked upon his final, fatal downward spiral of vacillation and indecision.

On 31 January, at his wits end, Clement finally signed a treaty with the imperial envoy Lannoy, agreeing to abandon his allies in the League of Cognac and pay the Spaniards and *landsknechts* massing in Lombardy the sum of

200,000 ducats. The king of France expressed his shock and surprise at Clement's sudden abandonment. However, when the papal troops of the *Bande Nere* defending Frosinone inflicted an unexpected defeat on Lannoy's besieging Spanish forces, the Pope's mood swung wildly back again; exulting in his troops' victory and in a fit of defiant belligerence towards the Empire, he cancelled his recent agreement with Charles. He now sent fresh word to François through a papal nuncio of his eternal and undying loyalty to the crown of France. Upon hearing this, François had candidly remarked to an amused court that he wished the Holy Father would 'make his mind up'.

But as the Pope misguidedly rejoiced in some obscure skirmish on the border with Naples, a massive army of unpaid and disenchanted Germans and Spaniards continued to trudge south from Piacenza through the unrelenting mud and sleet of a northern Italian winter. Broken treaties between popes and Emperors neither interested nor concerned these men; the money which the Pope had formerly agreed to pay them would only amount to around several ducats apiece. Their objective was the infinitely richer pickings to be had in wealthy city-states like Florence and Rome. As Guicciardini had recorded, many of these men had set out from Germany with just a single ducat in their doublet pockets and yet, after everything they had endured, they were still remarkably buoyant and resilient. However this mood could not be expected to continue indefinitely and the army was by now assuming all the aspects of a titanic unstoppable and near-mutinous force.

Alfonso d'Este had been concerned to get the imperial army across his *Ferrarese* territory as quickly as possible. Persuading them to head south for Rome, d'Este had bribed the Germans and Spaniards with a small payment of money, some much-needed supplies, and four more of his superb little artillery pieces. By the time the army had crossed the River Panaro and reached the outskirts of Bologna they had already become adept at scouring the outlying countryside for plunder and most importantly of all, provisions. Inevitably this left in its wake a great many suffering and complaining peasants who were left without food and supplies for the rest of the winter. When the Germans and Spanish arrived at Bologna the duke of Bourbon threatened to sack the city if money and provisions were not forthcoming and if the city-state refused to permit him safe passage through *Bolognese* lands to Naples. Francesco Guicciardini himself was already at Bologna to assess the situation and had by now divined only too well that the Imperialist objective was not Naples but instead Rome, or else Florence. He therefore advised the lord of Bologna to ignore Bourbon's demand since the *landsknechts* had only light artillery and no heavy cannon with which to breach Bologna's stout defences. When an imperial trumpeter was sent to obtain the *Bolognese* reply he was pointedly ignored.

While Bourbon's troops were encamped at Bologna, Pope Clement had turned weathercock once more, summoning the viceroy Lannoy to Rome and hastily concluding the second treaty within the space of as many months. In Rome, a bemused Lannoy had been lavishly entertained at the Pope's Vatican apartments; Clement had ended the festivities by readily agreeing to an eight-month truce and had also caved in to the full range of imperial terms and conditions. More particularly, as it pertained to the troops of Bourbon and Frundsburg in the north, the Pope agreed to pay them the reduced amount of 60,000 ducats. He also consented, once again, to withdraw his papal forces from participation in the League of Cognac and disband most of the troops defending the city of Rome. This he subsequently did, leaving only 2,000

Pontifical Swiss Guard and 2,000 of the *Bande Nere* stationed in the city. But this latest treaty with the Emperor's representative in the south would cut little ice with the seemingly autonomous and independent army marching down from the north. Decisions made over their heads by the great lords of Italy were coming to hold very little water with men who meant to have their reward for the considerable hardships already endured.

Trouble broke out initially in the Spanish ranks. On the evening of 11 March an unruly group of Spaniards approached the duke of Bourbon's marquee and loudly demanded to be paid their long overdue arrears. '*Paga! Paga!*' ('Pay! Pay!') they are said to have shouted, as they approached the Duke menacingly through the ankle-deep mud of the camp. Bourbon, who knew the character of his Spanish mercenaries from long experience, grasped that they could neither be mollified nor reasoned with. While the angry soldiers ransacked his tent, Bourbon sought sanctuary amongst the German lines and could only look on helplessly as his personal belongings were carried off by the disgruntled Spaniards. These included the Duke's trademark silver surcoat which he always wore in battle and which, since no common soldier would be able to wear it, was later found discarded in a ditch.

The German *landsknechts* were, it was true, considerably more disciplined than the Spanish rabble but when the news from Bourbon's half of the camp reached them they also became agitated and rebellious. As the *landsknechts* began noisily debating and affirming that they too should have their rights, and be paid the arrears of pay owed to them, the venerable count of Mindelheim appeared amongst them, a towering figure who commanded their instant respect. For the briefest of moments it had seemed to Bourbon that his colleague would be able to quell the mutiny through the sheer force of his personality and physical presence alone. However, when an angry *landsknecht* threateningly lowered his halberd at Frundsburg, the German commander went to draw his blade; this caused several more German halberdiers to do likewise. As Frundsburg summoned the full force of his character and began to berate his unruly 'children' he suffered a sudden stroke on the spot and collapsed prostrate across a drum.

The sight of their aged commander rendered helpless, paralysed and dumbstruck served momentarily to humble the unruly *landsknechts* and even the Spanish mercenaries piped down when they learned of Frundsburg's misfortune. The Germans sincerely loved the leader who had recruited them, drilled them, and shaped them into the well-trained and highly experienced military force which they knew themselves to be. They liked how he fondly referred to his troops as 'my beloved children' and with sentimental tears in their eyes they now carried him by stretcher back to Ferrara for medical treatment. Here, the doctor prescribed that he be placed in a bath of warm oil in which a fox had carefully been boiled. But the exotic cure had little effect and so the prince of Mindelheim was ported back across the wintry Alps to his own estates in Germany. Here, broken hearted at the disobedience of his beloved 'children', he was to die the following year in August aged fifty-five.

Frundsburg's collapse, however unfortunate, had nevertheless bought the duke of Bourbon some precious time. But although the immediate crisis had passed the Germans, who preferred to debate matters democratically, promptly elected their own council of twelve soldiers to lead them and represent their wishes to their senior commanders. The less democratic, more mob-handed,

Spaniards remained the same unruly potential powder keg. Bourbon managed to wring a small subsidy of 6,000 ducats to propitiate the troops but it was a pittance compared to their expectations and they now demanded that Bourbon turn the army towards Florence, where rich plunder could be guaranteed, and wrung from him the concession that the traditional three day sacking of the city be granted to them. Meanwhile, an imperial envoy named Cesare Ferramosca had arrived in camp with word of the Pope's latest, second agreement with the Emperor. Understandably however, the fact that the Medici pope had reduced his proposed bribe from 200,000 ducats to less than a third of that earlier offer left the men stone cold. In vain Ferramosca tried to convince the army to accede to the instructions of the Emperor's viceroy in Naples and stand down but it was of no avail. Perversely, the Spaniards asserted that it was still necessary for them to go to Rome in order to obtain absolution for all the killing they had done so far on the campaign. As for the Germans, they sulkily walked out of the meeting.

When Ferramosca learned later that night that he was a potential target for the soldiers' wrath he fled the camp. He would later inform both Lannoy and the Emperor that the imperial army in the north was effectively out of Bourbon's control and 'as angry as lions'. After Ferramosca departed, Bourbon replied politely back to the Pope rejecting his 60,000 ducats but demanding instead 150,000 ducats in return for his leaving Rome in peace. With this, the army moved south on 30 March along the old Emilian Way. Their destination, so the imperial army believed, was Pope Clement VII's wealthy, mercantile, Medici city-state of Florence. From his comfortable hiding place in Bologna, Guicciardini wrote to Giberti in Rome to inform the Pope of his three remaining options: 'Yield everything in a fresh treaty; fly; or defend yourself to the death. The most honourable is to perish like a hero'. The marquis of Mantua, Federigo Gonzaga, himself a papal *condottiere*, was meanwhile astonished that Clement had dismantled his army in Rome, commenting that 'The imprudence and carelessness [of the Pope] is too great. Before the armistice has taken effect the Pope has entirely disarmed himself. All this has been done only to save a little money.' He wrote a warning letter to his mother Isabella d'Este who was at that time in Rome awaiting a cardinal's hat for her twenty-year-old son Ercole.

All this time the astute Florentines had been keeping a wary eye on the political situation. When the Imperialists had crossed the River Po they had delegated an aged, fifty-eight-year-old Niccoló Machiavelli to ride over the Apennines and discuss the matter with Francesco Guicciardini at Modena; bestirring himself once more in service to his beloved republic, Machiavelli reached the city on 2 December. An astute strategist, Guicciardini had informed Machiavelli of the fact that, regardless of the Imperialist objective, their army might be countered but only if the armies of the League consolidated into a single large force of around 20,000 men. He also relayed the cowardice of the duke of Urbino who, unlike Giovanni della Bande Nere, evidently had scant interest in delaying or interdicting the Germans and Spanish as they advanced south. This was despite the fact that he had recently been reinforced by the *Milanese* troops of the marquis of Saluzzo. By the way, you can forget about trying to negotiate with Bourbon, Guicciardini added tartly. If you are going to speak to anyone on the imperial side it is preferable to reach out instead to Lannoy or else make an approach to Ugo de Moncada.

On 7 February Machiavelli was in Parma to meet Guicciardini once more and obtain a fresh update. The latter informed him of the duke of Urbino's continued reluctance to place his and the marquis of Saluzzo's armies directly in the path of the imperial troops, preferring instead to follow at a safe distance behind them. Machiavelli reported back to Florence that although the imperial army was in a bad state, being half-starved and ill-equipped, that emergency precautions should nevertheless be taken. He recommended that the *signoria* at least augment the city's walls and defences. The virtue of the ancient Romans, Machiavelli knew, was that they 'never made peace with money; but always with the virtue of arms'. The Pope's appeasement policy was only aggravating the situation. If possible, Machiavelli added, Florence would also be well advised to return to Francesco Maria the fortress of San Leo which Medici Florence had been unwisely withholding from the Duke since his restoration, something that had fostered considerable resentment. It was small matters such as these, holdovers from the Duke's previous quarrel with Pope Leo X, which threatened to jeopardise the defence of Italy and placed Florence itself in peril. Machiavelli's advice, impeccable as always, was just as characteristically ignored by Pope Clement. Even when Guicciardini followed up with His Holiness the diplomat expressed much the same sentiments: 'without the assistance of the Venetians our forces are not sufficient to defend us; unless the Duke is satisfied, their health will be of little worth; I would like to know how much the weight of that fortress is holding him back, for by refusing to hand it over we are risking great ruin'.

The tragedy was that two of the greatest political minds of the era, Niccoló Machiavelli and Francesco Guicciardini, had understood and analysed the situation perfectly. While the Pope in Rome vacillated between wanting to make a determined stand on the one hand and capitulating by striking one of his latest (ever more humiliating) deals on the other, these two political geniuses perceived correctly that the only law which the bedraggled and near-starved imperial army would obey was that of brute force. Bourbon's men, who at this point in their odyssey had taken on the appearance of wild animals, had no need for treaties made over their heads by Emperors, popes, nuncios and viceroys clad in fine velvet robes. When Lannoy himself went to meet with Bourbon, on 20 April at San Stefano in the foothills of the Apennines, he reminded the Duke of the recent agreement that he had wrung from Pope Clement. In an astonishing display of disobedience to the Emperor's most senior representative in Italy one of the *landsknecht* officers had stormed into the marquee and angrily torn the treaty parchment up in front of Lannoy's face. Three days later Lannoy departed the camp for Siena, effectively washing his hands of the whole affair and leaving Bourbon to his own devices.

Before his departure, Bourbon had informed Lannoy that his previous counter-demand had now increased from 150,000 to 240,000 ducats. When this was relayed to Pope Clement one observer in the Curia protested that 'To produce two hundred and forty thousand ducats is as impossible as to join the heaven and earth together'. The Pope's plea to Venice, France and England to provide the necessary funds to save the seat of Christendom was stonewalled. Hearing of the Pope's problems, Bourbon's cold response was to now increase his demand unreasonably to the sum of 300,000 ducats. At this stage Bourbon had nothing to lose. As Lannoy was to all intents and purposes the eyes, ears and voice of the Emperor in Italy, his reluctance to press home his own argument that the army abide by his instructions may seem puzzling. Leaving

509

aside the simple fact that he probably feared for his life amidst these half-starved beasts he could at least have been expected to put up a stronger show. However, this leads us to consider that the Emperor himself may well have been behind Lannoy's dumb show. Charles V had been kept regularly updated on the progress of his northern army as it moved inexorably southward and he had it fully within his power to send Bourbon the necessary funds with which to maintain tighter control over the *landsknechts* and hence have a say in their final objective. Instead, the Emperor appears to have deliberately starved the imperial army of all funding and hope and therefore top-down command effectively now became impossible. It is reasonable to assume therefore that by this point the Emperor himself was determined to teach Rome and the Pope a well-deserved lesson, whilst at the same time striving himself to appear neutral and blameless.

As the army drew closer to Florence the city crackled with tension and fear. On Friday, 26 April, what began as a simple marketplace brawl turned ugly and a crowd of angry Florentine aristocrats took to the streets and occupied the Palazzo della Signoria in protest at Medici rule, barring the great doors to the city guards and flinging missiles from the upper storey of the building. A bench was thrown from an upper window which struck the arm of Michelangelo's *David*, breaking it off and shattering it into three pieces. The rioters had gotten wind of a rumour that Ippolito de' Medici had fled the city in fear of the Emperor's approaching army. In actual fact, Ippolito had gone with his relatives Cardinal Ridolfi and Cardinal Cybò to dine with the duke of Urbino at the old Medici Villa di Castello, which Giovanni *il Popolano* had bequeathed to his son Giovanni della Bande Nere. Fortunately, Machiavelli and Guicciardini's strictures to the duke of Urbino to be more proactive had finally had some effect and the Duke, together with the marquis of Saluzzo, had concentrated their papal and Venetian troops in Florence's vicinity to shield the city from any imperial attack.

The Venetian ambassador Marco Foscari reported that the whole of Florence 'seemed to have turned upside down'. The mob inside the Palazzo della Signoria bayed exuberantly for the dismissal of the Pope's proxy Cardinal Silvio Passerini, a man who was by now universally disliked by the Florentines, and they also demanded the banishment of the two Medici scions Ippolito and Alessandro. Cardinal Cybò's *condottiere* brother Lorenzo Cybò and another mercenary commander Federigo Gonzaga da Bozzolo had gone to investigate and had subsequently been taken prisoner inside the *palazzo*. When Medici troops tried to get close the rebels killed several of them with harquebus fire from the windows. It was only the smooth diplomacy of Francesco Guicciardini, backed by the duke of Urbino and the threat of his cannon, which persuaded the mob to relent. Putting down their arms, they emerged peacefully from the seat of government. According to one eyewitness, Giovanni Agnello, the sons of the Strozzi, Salviati and Martelli families had been foremost amongst the rioters. Such *ottimati* families may have intermarried with the Medici and been amongst their closest *amici* but what they would never acquiesce to was the Medici setting themselves up as Florence's *de jure* princely rulers. The Strozzi especially had grown highly critical in recent years of the autocratic nature of Medici rule. The Venetian Foscari was only too relieved that the imperial army had not been in the vicinity when the uprising had occurred because 'if they had been near, things would have gone badly'. To prevent a recurrence of such events the Palazzo Medici was now bolstered around the clock by armed guards.

On the same day that the rioters were taking over Florence's seat of government Bourbon had struck camp and was on the march. Fortunately for Florence, news of the duke of Urbino's military presence had soon reached Bourbon who, despite the opportunity presented by the anti-Medici uprising (which became known as the *Tumulto del venerdì* or 'Friday's turmoil'), now decided to pass the city by and instead make Rome the army's ultimate objective. Not only had Urbino bolstered the city's defences but most of the main passes through the upper Arno valley were snowed in and well-defended by troops of the League of Cognac. Florence's defences were also in excellent condition thanks, in large part, to the attentions of Niccoló Machiavelli and the Spanish turncoat and military engineer Pedro Navarro; both men had advised the Pope on the improvement of Florence's defences throughout the spring and summer of 1526. Commissioning an ever-grateful Machiavelli to undertake this important project had been one of Pope Clement's few moments of lucidity. One of Clement's favoured architects, Antonio da Sangallo the Younger (the nephew of Antonio da Sangallo the Elder, for many years Florence's chief military architect), had been duly charged with modernising and upgrading the town walls and he set to work. Between the Oltrarno hills of San Miniato and Giramonte a series of angled bastions were to be created and aligned with another new bastion at the Porta San Giorgio. Meanwhile, many of the higher towers built over the various city gates would be reduced as they represented far too great a target to modern artillery. These far-sighted precautions now paid dividends.

Bourbon informed his men of their change of destination, by which he again incurred their anger. The men's conditions had deteriorated by now to such an extent that they were reduced to plucking the unripe berries from bushes to assuage their groaning bellies. Florence was near, Rome lay far away. Why bypass Florence? Summoning all the powers of persuasion at his disposal Bourbon informed his officers and men that Florence was practically impregnable against an army which had no heavy siege artillery. If they attempted to lay siege to the city they would quite simply perish before Florence's walls, or else be trapped in a vice by the army of the League. Rome on the other hand was lightly defended and her walls were lengthier, were in a sorry state of disrepair, and moreover had fewer troops to guard them. Reluctantly the angry Germans and Spaniards saw reason and acquiesced. They would after all march on Rome and hang the Pope.

Bourbon's troops crossed the Arno near Arezzo and marched south. Covering eighteen miles a day, they laid waste to the surrounding countryside until they reached Siena where the city authorities placated them with some well-timed food and supplies. Pressing on, they arrived at Viterbo, where the grand master of the formerly refugee Knights of Rhodes also provided them with food on condition that they passed by the city in a spirit of Christian peace. As Hospitallers they were bound by their oath to feed the hungry and besides, the troops of the Emperor would probably have thought twice before engaging these fanatical papal warriors who had held off 100,000 Ottoman soldiers for half a year. By 4 May, the imperial troops had encamped at Isola Farnese, the old fortified farmhouse from which the by now distinguished Roman Farnese family had taken their name. The house was built on the old Etruscan ruins of Veii and lay just a few miles to the north of Rome.

The same day as Bourbon was arriving at Isola Farnese the Pope humiliated himself with the futile gesture of donning his ceremonial vestments and announcing a Holy Crusade against the Imperialists who were despoiling the *contado* around Rome (this notwithstanding the fact that the papal crusading order of Rhodes had ironically just given the invading *landsknechts* a hearty meal). The city's mystics and holy men were not convinced at the Pope's charade. During one public gathering of ecclesiastics one wild-eyed hermit known as Brandano (his real name was Bartolomeo Carosi from Siena) stood up in the midst of the unwashed masses and loudly denounced Pope Clement. He railed that Rome would be destroyed like Sodom and Gomorrah and unkindly labelled Clement VII 'the bastard of Sodom'. Brandano was hauled away by the Pontifical Swiss Guard only to be released shortly afterwards thanks to the kindly Pope's clemency. But the exhibition had done little to bolster the Roman public's confidence in their theocratic ruler's ability to withstand the coming cyclone.

Many of the city's more foresighted inhabitants evidently felt the same way. In the weeks leading up to 3 May, when Rome's various city gates were ordered closed, the exodus had already begun. Frightened people, many of them foreigners, carried as much of their transportable wealth as they could down to the city's old port on the Via di Ripetta, which had been renamed after Clement's papal cousin as the Via Leonina. From here, for a purse-full of ducats, a wealthy merchant could embark both himself and his valuables on one of the many barques down river to the sea port of Ostia, from where he could take ship to practically anywhere in the known world. This option had indeed been briefly considered by the papal court; as early as January Cardinal Farnese had urged the Pope to abandon the city but to Clement's credit he bravely elected to ride out the coming crisis together with his subjects. Nobody in any position of influence however was under any illusion as to the severity of the developing situation.

The Pope's mind now turned, if a little belatedly, to the preparations for the city's defence. The first thing required was money, both to raise fresh troops and also as a standby to try to buy off the attackers at the eleventh hour if all else failed. Clement asked the civil governor of Rome, Girolamo Rossi, to organise a meeting of Rome's wealthiest citizens for the purpose of soliciting what he expected would be generous donations towards the city's defence and protection. This was arranged at the church of Aara Coeli, the only space large enough to accommodate the vast crowd which duly assembled. But when Rossi stood up to address the meeting (and he was one of the most eloquent and persuasive speakers in Rome) the wealthiest citizen of the city, Domenico Massimi, who owned a vast *palazzo* reputedly staffed by five hundred retainers, stepped forward and offered a paltry one hundred ducats. This then set the tone for the whole donation drive and the financial targets fell far short of expectation. Unfortunately, thanks to the luxurious and spendthrift pontificate of Leo X, Rome had softened into a city of lotus eaters who had little appreciation of the horrors which awaited them if the *landsknechts* were to breach Rome's walls.

As a result, Clement was forced to fall back on an expediency–that of raising funds through the sale of cardinals' hats–which he had long avoided on ethical grounds. Indeed, the consistory which sat on 3 May 1527 was the first in which *any* new cardinals were created during the initial years of Clement's pontificate. There was no shortage of wealthy candidates who were willing to produce the

512

necessary 40,000 ducats for the privilege of purchasing the red tasselled hat of a prince of the Church. Isabella Gonzaga was naturally relieved to receive the bonnet on behalf of her young son Ercole, who waited in Mantua for hopeful news of his elevation. The four other beneficiaries were the Florentines Benedetto Accolti and Niccolò Gaddi, the Venetian Marino Grimani, and the *Genovese* Agostino Spinola. All were from wealthy and influential Italian families. As it would turn out, this act would break the dyke of Clement's reluctance to elevate new members to the Sacred College and, by the end of his pontificate, he would create no less than thirty-two new cardinals, only two less in fact than Pope Sixtus IV but eleven less than the Borgia Pope Alexander VI.

Optimistically, with fresh reserves of 200,000 ducats safely clinking in the papal strongbox, Clement now turned to the commander of the city garrison who was one of the heroes of the defence of Marseilles against the duke of Bourbon. This was the Italian *condottiere* Renzo da Ceri. Renzo had arrived in Rome in January 1526, having been despatched by the king of France. Coming hard on the heels of Pompeo Colonna's attack on Rome, Renzo's arrival had cheered Pope Clement considerably and he had entrusted him with some of the reprisals against the errant Colonna as well as the position of commander of the garrison of Rome. A competent enough mid-level field commander, Renzo was however a poor choice for the more significant responsibility of preparing and fortifying Rome. The city during this era was mainly a theocratic municipality of priests and pilgrims; her defences were long neglected and to fortify and defend Rome properly would require a drastic overhaul by the designated military commander. Unduly optimistic about the inadequate preparations which he now set about orchestrating, Renzo nevertheless infused the Pope with a newfound confidence which had little true basis in reality or the actual mechanics of withstanding a siege.

Renzo's first act was to beef up the city's existing 4,000-strong garrison of papal guard and *Bande Nere* by recruiting several thousand irregulars from the city's native population. There was no shortage of volunteers from amongst Rome's seedy underbelly – the liars, braggarts, cut-throats, cut purses, scroungers and unemployed mercenaries who haunted the city's innumerable taverns and brothels. At the very least these unwashed scum knew how to handle a weapon and understood the rudiments of fighting. Ordinary working men too came forward; shopkeepers, artisans, labourers and hot-headed youths who, less helpfully, were attracted only by the notion of cutting a swashbuckling *bella figura* in time of war. All personal weapons had been banned within the precincts of Rome for some years now and Rome's men had little opportunity to prove their manhood; these poorer quality recruits possessed little in the way of practical military knowledge or experience and were next to useless except as cannon fodder. What Rome really needed were professional reinforcements from outside the city.

Renzo's efforts to raise levies from the surrounding *campagna romana* were however ineffective. Few districts answered his call to arms and most country people regarded Rome's troubles as being of her own making, nothing more than a private matter between a foreign Emperor and a 'foreign' Medici pope and a matter in which they had no stake and still less interest. The duke of Urbino had meanwhile taken the precaution of insuring himself against allegations of treason by despatching an advance party towards Rome under the *condottiere* Guido Rangone which comprised 8,000 men and 500 horse. Rangone had caught up with the imperial forces at Viterbo the day after they had left but, when Renzo da Ceri learned of their approach from Rangone's own messenger, he ordered him to ride back and inform Rangone that he should turn back and re-join Urbino. Except for a small force of harquebusiers, which he requested be sent to assist him in Rome, Rangone's forces were not needed Ceri told him. Rome's defences, he boasted, were in good shape and Rangone and Urbino should consolidate their forces to deliver one final, climactic hammer blow to the Imperialists' rear should they attack the city walls. This instruction, which remained uncontradicted by the papal adviser Giberti, was the most ill-advised decision in Renzo's entire litany of errors. He had effectively turned away 8,000 desperately needed professional reinforcements.

But would Renzo fare any better in preparing Rome's physical defences? Rome's primary fortifications consisted of her old Roman walls built in the time of the Roman Emperor Aurelian. These encircled the city for roughly twelve miles, safely enclosing the main area to the east of the Tiber and also extending west across the river, running just beneath the Janiculum Hill, forming a smaller enclave which protected the mainly working class suburb of Trastevere. In Aurelian's day the Vatican Hill had not been enclosed, since it was of no particular importance being principally a necropolis. However in the ninth-century, following a devastating raid by Muslim pirates who audaciously sailed up the River Tiber and sacked the Vatican Palace, Pope Leo IV had built his so-called 'Leonine Wall' around both the Vatican and the adjacent residential district known as the Borgo. These newer forty-foot high walls of red brick peppered by well-fortified towers and gates terminated in the Mausoleum of Hadrian to which fifteenth-century popes such as Alexander VI had gradually added a moat and bastions thereby transforming it into the heavily-fortified Castel Sant'Angelo. During Pope Clement's day, however, both the Aurelian and the Leonine Walls were in a sad state of disrepair, having been denuded from the top and bottom over the preceding centuries. The well-planned subterranean tunnels which the ancient Romans had built beneath the foundations in order to move men quickly from one stretch of wall to another had, over the centuries, been blocked by an assortment of debris and refuse. The situation at the Vatican was even worse as one whole stretch of the Leonine Wall ran through the private property of Cardinal Armellino, who had used the area to plant a vineyard. In this vineyard there was a small dwelling which was built propped against the outside of the wall; this structure could provide both shelter and an access point for any attacking army. Indeed, at several places some holes had even been knocked in the wall so people could come and go more easily; these breaches had to be bricked up as hastily as possible.

Renzo da Ceri calculated that if Bourbon came from Viterbo by way of Isola Farnese he would have to traverse the western bank of the Tiber and attack Rome from the west (if, that is, Bourbon failed to cross at the Milvian Bridge further north. He was later to prove correct in his prediction). Renzo therefore placed his more seasoned troops on the north-western and western walls and assigned Lucantonio Tomassino, who was Giovanni della Bande Nere's successor, as the commander of the Black Bands assigned to defend the more vulnerable point where the Vatican's walls joined up with the Aurelian walls near the River Tiber. He meanwhile placed his own second-in-command, Orazio Baglione, across the Tiber in the eastern half of the city in case Bourbon attacked from the direction of the Milvian Bridge. Renzo's own son Giovanni Paolo was commanded to defend Trastevere's Porta Settimiana.

One essential defensive measure which Renzo had, however, neglected to undertake was the destruction of the bridges over the Tiber, most critically of all the Ponte Sisto which linked Trastevere to the eastern half of the city. He had lobbied the Pope to be allowed to demolish this important waypoint across the river but Clement, under pressure from the inhabitants of Trastevere, bowed to their demands not to be to be cut off from their sole means of escape should the Imperialists attack their western suburb. There were also those cultured art lovers who misguidedly protested that 'so pretty a bridge' should not be demolished. As events would turn out, this tactical oversight was to have grave consequences in the days and weeks that followed.

On Sunday, 5 May 1527, all these preparations were being observed by the duke of Bourbon, who had by now arrived outside Rome and established his headquarters at the Hieronymite hermitage of Sant'Onofrio al Gianicolo. The hermitage was situated on the Janiculum Hill, the ideal vantage point for any attacking general. Bourbon's personal tragedy was that he was not simply another military commander surveying an objective but a devout Roman Catholic who now stood before the seat of his faith as its potential despoiler. From the Janiculum he and the *landsknechts* could view the crumbling old Vatican basilica dwarfed by the soaring but still unfinished construction of Bramante's and Raphael's new St. Peter's immediately behind it. He could see the many church steeples and bell towers of the city and the gentle curve of the River Tiber.

Tactically the city had to be taken in one all-or-nothing attack. There were barely enough provisions for one more night let alone a protracted siege. Added to this was the danger that the forces of Urbino and Saluzzo may not be far behind; if they waited the army could easily be caught in the jaws of a deadly vice. In reality, on 5 May the duke of Urbino was still far away at Arezzo and on 6 May he would receive word by courier that Bourbon was still at Viterbo; by 8 May Guido Rangone would come within sight of the city but by that time he would be powerless to intervene. Bourbon would have known that he was about to go down in history alongside four other heinous characters who had conquered and sacked the city of Rome: Alaric and his Visigoths (410), Genseric and his Vandals (455), Totila and his Ostragoths (546), and Robert Guiscard (1084), whose Normans had casually fired huge tracts of the city in their efforts to rescue Pope Gregory VII from the forces of the Holy Roman Emperor.

To the German Lutherans now surrounding him, straining at the leash at their intended prize, everything was simple and uncomplicated: beneath them lay the Antichrist, *Der falsche Messias*, and they were here to do God's cleansing work and secure some plunder while they were at it. The Spaniards at least would devoutly ask for absolution from their army chaplains before they proceeded to lay waste to God's city. The Italians were arguably the worst of all three nationalities. This was an Italian city-state and the seat of Christendom but for those serving with the imperial army Rome was no more than a source of riches and the papacy an institution which needed to be taught a much-needed secular lesson in humility. Ironically, many of them would be facing their own blood kinsmen inside the city. Two such individuals were Cardinal Alessandro Farnese's illegitimate sons by his mistress Silvia Ruffini. His eldest, the combustible twenty-four-year-old Pier Luigi Farnese, who was in the service of Charles V, faced his eighteen-year-old brother Ranuccio Farnese who was just half a mile away guarding the Porta Settimiana together with Renzo da Ceri's son Giovanni Paolo.

At dawn on Monday, 6 May 1527, the ragged and starving army of the duke of Bourbon stormed the city walls of Rome in the vicinity of the Janiculum and Vatican Hill, concentrating their efforts on the vulnerable stretch of wall which lay between the Porta San Spirito and the Porta del Torrione. As they had left their heavy siege cannon far behind them in the marshes of Lombardy and the snowy fields of Tuscany they had no way of battering down the defences. Instead, they scaled the walls using flimsy ladders hastily assembled from whatever materials lay to hand including, somewhat unhelpfully, the vine trellises belonging to the hapless Cardinal Armellino. They advanced on the wall under cover of a heavy fog which concealed their movements to the defenders, who could hear them but could not see where they intended to strike. Renzo's men were ordered to stand-to-arms. In the distance the bells of Rome's innumerable churches were tolling the call-to-arms. The mist obscured the sight of the gunners at the Castel Sant'Angelo and hampered their ability to take good clean shots at the attackers. While Bourbon assailed the Vatican walls his cousin Philibert, Prince of Orange, had been ordered to launch a diversionary action further upstream at the Ponte Milvio (in the event, Renzo had done well to station his second-in-command Orazio Baglione across the Tiber in the eastern half of the city, just in case).

While the Spaniards applied pressure on the Porta San Spirito the *landsknechts* meanwhile threw themselves at the Porta del Torrione (also called the Porta Cavelleggeri). Despite the miasma which obscured much of the battlefield both imperial attacks were fiercely repelled by Renzo's troops. This was the area in which the Roman commander had placed some of his most valuable assets, the *Bande Nere* under Lucantonio Tomassino. Helping out in Tomassino's brigade was Michelangelo's former apprentice Raffaello da Montelupo and his friend Lorenzetto, also a sculptor and architect. Both artists had collaborated on the wealthy banker Agostino Chigi's tomb and Raffaello had contributed work on the tombs of Popes Julius II and Pope Leo X. But today they were destroyers rather than creators, gunners who now worked alongside other artists from Rome's arty district of Parione to pour as much shot into the enemy's ranks as they could. Raffaello would survive to later record his harrowing experiences in his *Autobiografia di Raffaello da Montelupo*. Against such a determined defence, albeit from artists and journeymen as well as the more well-trained men of the Black Bands, the imperial attack began to falter.

Seeing that the attack had wavered Bourbon now threw himself body and soul into the thick of the fighting. The self-doubt and impotence of the past few months were finally forgotten; he was back in his element as a soldier and military commander once more. He needed neither kings, nor lands, nor great wealth; all he required was the professional performance of the troops under his command. This professionalism in battle he never doubted for one moment as the Germans, Austrians and Spaniards applied themselves to their bloody trade. To his men he seemed to be everywhere at once, riding his great charger, sheathed in his finest armour overtopped by his distinctive and instantly-recognisable silver surcoat. Here he was encouraging, there he was urging, always he was on the front line inspiring his troops. To the Italians in his army he baited them – do you really want to be shown up by all these foreigners? Get to it! Most of the time he was well within the enemy's harquebus range and must have made a unique, tempting and identifiable target in his regalia, but for the moment he was as immune from enemy fire as great Achilles at the Siege of Troy. However, in his exuberance Bourbon got carried away and acted rashly. At the Porta del Torrione he dismounted his warhorse and brushed the German *landsknechts* to one side; going up to the nearest scaling ladder he could find he gripped it and began to climb the rungs.

Somewhere above him on the wall was another of Rome's artists-in-residence who had been dragooned into military service. This was Pope Clement VII's friend the goldsmith Benvenuto Cellini. Before the attack a harquebus had been thrust into his hands and he was now taking pot shots at the Germans milling beneath the walls. To Cellini it was like shooting fish in a barrel. What happened next is perhaps best described in Cellini's own words: 'Directing my harquebus where I saw the thickest and most serried troops of fighting men, I aimed exactly at one whom I remarked to be higher than the rest: the fog prevented me from being certain whether he was on horseback or foot. Then I turned to Alessandro and Cecchino and bade them discharge their harquebuses showing them how to avoid being hit by the besiegers. When we had fired two rounds apiece I crept cautiously up to the wall and observed among the enemy a most extraordinary confusion. I discovered afterwards that one of our shots had killed the Constable of Bourbon: and from what I subsequently learned, he was the man whom I had first noticed above the heads of the rest.' Cellini was of course a notoriously self-aggrandising writer of autobiographic confection. Be that as it may however, regardless of whether Cellini or either of his two friends was personally responsible for shooting the sometime Constable of France, the imperial army now lacked its most senior field commander. Bourbon lay at the foot of the ladder in an ever-widening pool of arterial blood which gushed from a gaping wound in his groin. He was carried to a nearby church where half an hour or so later he died with the words '*à Rome! à Rome!*' still on his delirious lips. Like the Chevalier de Bayard and Giovanni della Bande Nere, the chivalry of the duke of Bourbon had been trounced by the cold, indiscriminating methods of modern warfare – powder and ball.

Meanwhile, back at the city walls, the German *landsknechts* lost all restraint and now launched an all-out attack, redoubling their efforts to mount the walls. Depending on which national version one adhered to, either the Spaniard Don Giovanni de Avalos or else the German Nicolas Seidenstücker gained the top of the walls by the same ladder Bourbon had used. This imperial soldier was then shot dead, but not before he had created an opening for his comrades to establish a small foothold on the city ramparts. As this was happening, Sigismondo della Torre gained ingress through a small gap made in the wall near the Belvedere Palace and some other Spaniards had found a hole in the cellar of the abandoned lean-to which Renzo's captains, in their ineptitude, had neglected to demolish. Some Spaniards now crawled through the cellar hole. On the other side they encountered the commander of the garrison of Rome himself, Renzo da Ceri. According to one story, Renzo did not even stop to draw his sword but instead took to heel and fled back across the Tiber, not stopping until he had reached safety and declaring loudly to astonished onlookers that all was lost. By this time the infiltrators had succeeded in opening two gates and the imperial troops now poured through into the Borgo like a veritable floodtide.

Once the Vatican's main ramparts had been breached Rome's defence essentially collapsed. The *Bande Nere* and the gunpowder-blackened painters and sculptors of the Parione militia were either slaughtered where they stood by the overwhelming numbers of professional German mercenaries or else they tried to fall back on St. Peter's Square. Here, the thin ranks of the Pontifical Swiss Guard were already engaged in vicious hand-to-hand combat with the exotic, dandified *landsknechts* who surged like some irresistible force of nature into the *piazza*. As 147 of his loyal Swiss guards were being butchered to a man defending the Vatican, Pope Clement VII was still on his knees praying in his private apartments at the Apostolic Palace. His entourage, along with the 42 remaining members of the Swiss Guard defending the Vatican, pushed and prodded him along the *passetto*, the elevated walkway leading from the Vatican to the safety of the Castel Sant'Angelo. Amongst the small group which hastened along the causeway was Paolo Giovio. A man of many talents, Giovio was a prelate, a physician, a historical essayist and the biographer of the late Pope Leo X, who had been his benefactor and who had knighted him. Giovio would later be appointed bishop of Nocera in 1528. In 1517, Cardinal Giulio de' Medici had made him his personal physician and he was usually to be found at the Medici pope's side, often recording caustic observations for posterity. Seeing that the Supreme Pontiff was an obvious target in his white papal vestments and skullcap, Giovio removed his own purple cloak and placed it around the Pope's shoulders to obscure him from the watchful eyes of any imperial sharpshooters.

When they reached the safety of the Castel Sant'Angelo the Pope and his small entourage found it already teeming with 3,000 Romans who had fled thence before the castellan could let down the portcullis. Clement was quickly ushered through the terrified crowd and upstairs to his private pontifical apartments. The Pope's chamberlain Cardinal Armellino later arrived after the *castello* had already been sealed and, like a supply of common groceries, had to be ignominiously hauled up to the battlements in a *corbello* or wicker basket. He subsequently joined the thirteen other cardinals and two foreign ambassadors who had sought sanctuary inside. Another fugitive who had arrived from the Borgo around the same time as the Pope was Benvenuto Cellini, who had somehow survived the attack on the Vatican walls. Recognised by one of the Medici's long-time confederates, Marcello Pallone, as being the Pope's friend, he was admitted to the fortress but was in the process separated from his friend Alessandro. Since he was a man who knew how to handle himself, Cellini was delegated to assist the gunners under the overall command of Antonio Santa Croce. These, Cellini found to his disgust, were putting up a feeble performance. Some of the gunners, men like Giuliano Fiorentino, could clearly see the imperial troops ravaging their homes in the Borgo and, torn with anguish, they refused to fire on the enemy for fear of hitting their families who were still somewhere down there in the confusion. Cellini had no such qualms; taking charge of one of the falconet crews, he poured on the gunfire wherever he felt it would serve to impede the invaders.

By noon the Borgo and the Vatican were in the Imperialists' hands. Most of the looting and outrages against the civilian population which happened at this time were perpetrated, however, not by the imperial troops themselves but by the vengeful Colonna *bravi* and common peasants who had by now streamed in from the countryside in the wake of the imperial army. The imperial troops themselves remained disciplined and held formation for the time being. Philibert of Orange had immediately assumed command upon Bourbon's death and had ordered that no looting take place until the entire city east of the Tiber had been properly secured. The disposition of the duke of Urbino was still at this time unknown (Guido Rangone and his 8,000 troops were in fact still safely at Monterotondo). Trastevere as well as the main area of the city across the Tiber still remained in the hands of the defenders. In the brief interlude which ensued, Bourbon's corpse was laid out in the Sistine Chapel, which was declared off-limits to the imperial troops, although Philibert somewhat disrespectfully saw fit to stable his horses here.

Finding the Ponte Sant'Angelo interdicted by deadly fire from the gunners of Sant'Angelo the imperial army instead launched their next attack upon the mostly working class artisan suburb of Trastevere, which fell by early afternoon. Following a brief lull while the hungry and exhausted troops scoured the captured areas for food and drink, the attack resumed once again, this time across the Ponte Sisto into the main area of Rome which lay east of the Tiber. Like the historical Horatius Cocles on the Pons Sublicius, a small group of noble Romans formed up in a line to confront the Imperialists. These included Cardinal Farnese's son Ranuccio Farnese, Pier Luigi Tebaldi and his brother Simeono, Giulio Vallati, the three Orsini brothers Gianantonio, Camilo and Valerio and even the ineffectual Renzo da Ceri and his son Giovanni Paolo. But, when the Spaniards and *landsknechts* surged across the small bridge driving thousands of terrified denizens of Trastevere before them, the thin line of papal defenders was swept away in the human deluge like a spider's web in a sudden torrent. The Imperialists poured through into the eastern half of the city. By nightfall, however, the attackers were spent. Even if they had wanted to begin their sack of the city they had not the energy, besides which the darkened city streets and *vicoli* were now hazardous and regarded as *terra incognita*. So instead they hunkered down in their national contingents, the Spaniards in the Piazza Navona near their national church Santa Giacomo, the Germans in the Campo dei Fiore near their traditional church Santa Maria dell'Anima, and the Italians under Ferrante Gonzaga beneath the watchful, though now silent, falconets of the Castel Sant'Angelo. But, welcome as it was, this night-time lull was merely the calm before the storm.

As dawn broke the following day the first waking imperial soldiers were already up and about their business of murder, theft, rape and desecration. It did not take long for the screams of those being subjected to every kind of vile action to wake those remaining Spaniards, Italians and *landsknechts* who still slumbered. As Cardinal Salviati was later to write to Baldassare Castiglione, 'I shudder to contemplate this for Christians are doing what the Turk never did'. One of the participants in the sacking, the renowned German mercenary commander Sebastian Schertlin Burtenbach, would later write matter-of-factly in his autobiography: 'In the year 1527, on 6 May, we took Rome by storm, put over 6,000 men to the sword, seized all that we could find in the churches and elsewhere, burned down a great part of the city, tearing and destroying all copyists work, all registers, letters and state documents'. The acts of desecration seemed to come first, promulgated by the German Lutherans who had come to deal *Der römische Antichrist* a righteous death blow.

Throughout the city the Catholic churches were a principal target of the Lutheran soldiers. As roving bands of *landsknechts* wound their way through Rome's streets and *piazze* church doors were torn from their hinges and their contents tossed into the streets. Chalices, sacred vessels, candlesticks, monstrances, all were swept from their altars into the bags of the soldiers. This was loot which the Lutherans maintained had been unlawfully stolen by the

Church from the godly nations of the earth and it was destined to be either melted down or sold. 'Why does the Pope not build this basilica with his own funds instead of with the money of the poor faithful?' Martin Luther had asked during Leo X's reign. Any documents, manuscripts or parchments from the various church archives were meanwhile destroyed, thrown to the horses for stabling, used as bedding or else cast to the four winds. After they had looted what they could the soldiers then laid fires in an orgy of senseless destruction. In the vicinity of the Vatican, where some of the most precious possessions of the Church lay, the holy relics were turned out of their hiding places and paraded through the streets, whilst the skulls of saints were used as target practice for bored harquebusiers and blasted to fragments. The golden Cross of Constantine the Great was unearthed and carried triumphantly through the streets to the jeers of the men; later it was broken down into smaller pieces, shared out, and subsequently lost to history.

One of the mercenaries claimed that he had found the actual rope with which Judas Iscariot was purported to have hanged himself, it was a big thick rope which could easily have hanged a giant. The discoverer was Sebastian Schertlin Burtenbach who, despite many offers for the grubby piece of cord, insisted on bringing it home with him to Germany as a souvenir of the sacking. Another *landsknecht* had recovered the purported Holy Lance of Longinus which Sultan Bayezid II had presented to Pope Innocent VIII as a bribe to keep his troublesome brother Prince Djem a prisoner of the Vatican. The German soldier affixed the Holy Lance to the tip of his pike and jabbed it skyward laughing hysterically. The busts of the Apostles stolen from St. John Lateran were also carried through the streets on the end of poles to the collective jeers of the soldiers. The handkerchief of Veronica, once used to wipe the brow of Christ, was passed round by soldiers in a tavern to wipe their grimy necks as they drank (although reportedly in rags, it would later mysteriously reappear back in its shrine, as good as new, after the sack).

Nor did the outrages end here. In St. Peter's Basilica the soldiers lolled around the High Altar playing dice while drunken Roman prostitutes paraded in the Pope's ecclesiastical vestments. The soldiers raised the Vatican's best holy chalices to the strumpets' lips in lewd attempts to inebriate them even more. When they grew tired of dice and whores they went in search of Catholic priests and forced them to strip naked and perform the High Mass with braying donkeys serving as the communicants. When one such priest refused to perform the ritual he was butchered on the spot. In the four Raphael Rooms (Il Stanze di Raffaello), the soldiers went around etching random graffiti into the brightly-painted, ten-year-old frescoes with their weapons. On Raphael's work known as *the Disputation of the Holy Sacrament* the name of Martin Luther was rudely scratched. On another fresco Charles V was hailed as Emperor. Other Raphael tapestries were torn from their hangings and bartered in the city streets for coin. Michelangelo's ceiling, painted for Pope Julius II almost at the cost of the master's eyesight, was saved only by the fact that its sheer height (68 ft) prevented the soldiers from doing any serious damage.

Meanwhile, at the Castel Sant'Angelo, soldiers gathered in drunken crowds beneath the ramparts, jeering and cat-calling Pope Clement, shouting up at him 'Vivat Lutherus pontifex'. Four years earlier in 1522, Martin Luther and Philippe Melanchthon had produced a polemical pamphlet featuring an engraving of a monstrous 'papal ass' standing in front of the Castel Sant'Angelo; the outrageous imagery was clearly intended to portray the Pope as Antichrist, in this case visualised as a bestial chimera. Many Lutheran *landsknechts* were fired by such simple propagandistic metaphors and the anti-papal agenda which lay behind it. Clearly the Pope was a monster. If not, why then did he not 'liberate everyone from purgatory for the sake of love (a most holy thing) and because of the supreme necessity of their souls?' Luther had argued in his theses. However, although the Germans were intolerable, it was the ardent Roman Catholics who were singled out for displaying the worst conduct of all. The judgement of the Prior of the Canons of St. Augustine at the time was: '*Mali fuere Germani, pejores Itali, Hispani vero pessimi*' ('the Germans were bad, the Italians were worse, the Spaniards were the worst of all').

But greed for plunder remained, more than religious zeal, the prime motivation for most of these common soldiers. Anything remotely of value was lifted, extracted, prised or hefted. Precious statues and other *objects d'art* had their jewels picked out by the men's daggers and precious gems were roughly apportioned on the marble floor of St. Peter's by men with shovels. The heads of St. Andrew and St. John were kicked around the streets like footballs. The grave of St. Peter itself was profaned. The tombs of Julius II and Alexander VI were smashed open, their mouldering remains desecrated. The Sistine Chapel and the Vatican Library founded by Pope Nicholas V were only spared through the intercession of Prince Philibert of Orange, who had laid out the duke of Bourbon's corpse on his bier in the chapel and ordered that the area be rendered off limits to the common soldiers. But his authority as head of the army did not save him from being robbed at sword point by his own men; his secretary later recorded that whilst making his rounds Philibert had been 'robbed by *landsknechts* in the porch of Saint Mark'.

If the most senior commander of the imperial army was not impervious to extortion then the citizens of Rome were monumentally less so. Over the coming days and weeks the asset-stripping of both the city and its inhabitants assumed a grim and coldly systematic quality. Inhabitants of many of the wealthier *palazzi* were forced to pay huge ransoms so as to be left alone by the soldiers. After the Germans had called to collect their ransom money then the Spaniards in their turn would call and the hapless owners would be forced to cough up further large bribes. After that, the Italians too would call and the process would be repeated a third time, by which time there was frankly little left to give. Others were considerably less fortunate, despite their great wealth. Rome's richest citizen, the millionaire Domenico Massimi, who had been so niggardly in his contribution to Rome's defence fund, was forced to watch as his sons were put to the sword, his daughter raped and his *palazzo* burned to the ground before his eyes. Having suffered these unspeakable horrors he too was slain. Only those managing to gain sanctuary within some of the city's Ghibelline, Spanish, German or Dutch residences were spared and sometimes not even then.

To the imperial troops, every inhabitant of Rome was thought to have sequestered a small fortune in specie and no method was considered too harsh for prising its location out of them. Wrote Luigi Guicciardini: 'Many were suspended for hours by the arms; many were cruelly bound by the private parts; many were suspended by the feet high above the road, or over water, while their tormentors threatened to cut the cord. Some were half buried in the cellars; others were nailed up in casks while many were villainously beaten and wounded.' Neither were the young and innocent spared. Children were flung from windows or else had their heads dashed against walls; anything to induce the Romans to reveal their secret treasure troves. 'In the whole of Rome not a living soul above the age of three years old was exempt from having to pay a ransom', wrote one observer. Luigi Guicciardini took pains to emphasize that the cardinals especially were a favourite target for the soldiers. Some cardinals, so he recorded, 'were set upon by scrubby beasts, riding with their faces backwards, in the habits and ensigns of their dignity, and some were led about all Rome with the greatest derision and contempt. Some, unable to raise all the ransom demanded, were so tortured that they died there and then, or within a few days.' Other cardinals were subjected, whilst still alive, to their own mock funerals. Guicciardini writes: 'For the sake of ridicule and punishments, they carried Cardinal Aracoeli one day on a bier through every street of Rome as if he were dead continually chanting his eulogy. They finally carried his "body" to a church where ... about half of his unusual (out of reverence I will avoid saying "criminal") habits were detailed in a funeral oration ... They returned to his palace and drank his wine.'

As for the high class noblewomen of Rome, many of these were abducted and forced to work in impromptu brothels serving the unwashed common soldiery. The Sieur de Brantôme sneered that 'Marchionesses, countesses and baronesses served the unruly troops and for long afterwards the patrician women of the city were known as *the relics of the Sack of Rome*.' Very often convents were transformed into such brothels and the nuns repeatedly raped, being passed round amongst the men like sacks of wine. The inhabitants of the convent of Santa Rufina put up a remarkable resistance with any weapons that came to hand; knives, meat cleavers, kettles of scalding water. Nevertheless despite the fortitude of its defenders the convent was stormed, the inhabitants slaughtered and those who survived were tortured and raped in the most savage fashion imaginable.

Cardinal Pompeo Colonna arrived in Rome on 7 May with 1,000 followers and when he saw the destruction and the thousands of fresh corpses littering the streets he wept tears of remorse. Well he might for it had been his own treacherous actions which had arguably paved the way for Rome's prostration. Nevertheless, the cardinal opened up one of his undamaged Colonna *palazzi* to around 500 gentlewomen who sought refuge and did the best he could to alleviate the suffering he came across. But even so, many of his own *bravi* joined in the sacking in retribution for Pope Clement's recent police action against the Colonna lands and estates. According to eye witnesses they behaved even worse than the Germans and Spaniards. Little more than armed peasants, they now exulted in the evil and the suffering they could freely inflict on their social betters. They carried off those items which even the Imperialists had thought beneath them, including 'even the ironwork of the houses' and they gleefully joined in the sacking of the city's monasteries and convents. Pier Luigi Farnese, the illegitimate son of Cardinal Alessandro Farnese, amassed plunder worth in the region of 25,000 ducats. Leaving the city for the Romagna, in a satisfying episode of poetic justice if ever there was one, he was robbed of his ill-gotten loot along the way by a feral gang of peasants.

The same day that Cardinal Colonna entered Rome, the Mantuan ambassador Francesco Gonzaga was writing home to his master Federigo describing the '*exterminio et total ruina de Roma*' and lamenting the 'cruel spectacle that would move stones to pity', adding for good measure that 'one could very well say that Our Lord God wishes to apply the lash to Christendom, which will not forget this for many years'. He was speaking the truth for the carnage would not be so easily forgotten. By the first few days alone it was later estimated by a Franciscan friar that some 12,000 inhabitants of the city had perished. Rome's grave diggers, those who had not themselves been murdered, worked fitfully to bury the corpses; a great many were simply flung into the Tiber to wash downstream on the tide to Ostia, by far and away the easiest method of disposal, though hardly a pleasant prospect for Ostia's seaside residents. Most of the dead, however, simply lay at the spot where they had been slaughtered, quickly putrefying in the May heat, prey to swarms of flies and infested with maggots. From their sanctuary in the Castel Sant'Angelo, Pope Clement and the papal court caught nauseating whiffs of these untold acres of decomposing flesh carried across Rome on the breeze. Where in God's name, the Pope continually inquired of his entourage, was the duke of Urbino and the army of the League?

CHAPTER 19

The Humbling of a Medici Pope

I once told Pope Clement, who was wont to be disquieted by every
trifling danger, that a good cure for these empty panics was to recall the
number of like occasions on which his fears had proved idle. By this I
would not be understood as urging men never to feel fear, but as
dissuading them from living in perpetual alarm.

Francesco Guicciardini

On 8 May, when the city was being to subjected to its third agonising day
of sacking, the duke of Urbino and the marquis of Saluzzo were
encamped at Cortona a full 100 miles away from Rome. Francesco Maria
della Rovere was by this time fully informed of events in the city. Not only had
ample intelligence reached him from refugee papal soldiers but the bishop of
Motula had sent him a clear and unambiguous report which stated that the
Borgo had fallen and that the Pope was now a prisoner inside Sant'Angelo. If
anything this information seemed to deter Urbino rather than galvanise him
into action. If the Borgo had already fallen then surely all was lost? Francesco
Guicciardini strongly disagreed and made the counter-argument. If the League
were to march with all haste on Rome while the Imperialists within were still
running amok, and fragmented into small disorganised companies of looters,
they might be able to carry the day and bring the sack to an abrupt end. But
Francesco Maria della Rovere, who had already suffered so grievously at the
hands of one Medici pope, was evidently enjoying watching his successor twist
in the wind, besides which, the very idea of taking orders from a mere lawyer
such as Francesco Guicciardini deeply offended his noble sensibilities. Neither
did he seem very greatly concerned about the plight of his mother-in-law,
Isabella d'Este, who was also still trapped in Rome, holed up in the Palazzo
Colonna with sundry other gentlewomen whom she had graciously offered
sanctuary from the marauding and lustful soldiers. Frustrated at Urbino's
deliberate tardiness, Guicciardini was moved to write that 'the Pope remains in
the *castello*, begging for help so earnestly that his entreaties would melt the very
stones, and in so abject a state of misery that even the Turks are filled with
pity'.

The League's army moved ponderously south, eventually reaching Orvieto.
Here, the governor of the town refused to provide the troops with provisions
unless their commander gave his oath to march to the immediate relief of the
Pope. Urbino accused Guicciardini at conniving in this piece of theatrical
brinkmanship. On 11 May, one of Pope Clement's personal attendants, Pietro
Chiavaluce, reached the League's army with a bone-chilling eyewitness account

of Rome's sacking and the Pope's perilous captivity. Federigo Gonzaga and Ugo Pepoli were so stirred by the account that without even seeking Urbino's permission they led a small detachment of their men on a rescue mission to extract the Pope, not to mention Gonzaga's own mother Isabella d'Este, from the city. The expedition unfortunately ended in failure when Federigo carelessly fell from his horse in the darkness and sustained multiple fractures. It was only by 22 May that the League's troops reached Isola Farnese. By this time some 10,000 men had already deserted, either back to their homes or else, somewhat more cynically, to join in the sacking themselves. Urbino therefore only had at his disposal some 15,000 troops although, desertions aside, this was still sufficient to deliver a considerable hammer blow to the disorganised Imperialists. Guido Rangone had taken his light cavalry on a reconnaissance expedition close to the city walls some days earlier and had been startled to find that very few *landsknechts* had even bothered to rally to their *gonfalon* in opposition to their approach. If the League were to hit hard and hit fast then perhaps Rome and the Pope could be spared further weeks or even months of imperial subjection.

Ludovico Ariosto was to later write in *Orlando Furioso*: 'The League that should relieve sits still and gapes'. Francesco Maria della Rovere could have redeemed himself at this point had he risen to the occasion and ordered the attack. Instead, on 2 June, he concluded that the worst had already happened and, nothing more to be done, ordered his drummers to beat the retreat north, back to Viterbo. Guicciardini was beside himself with rage. This was surely high treason by the commander of the League's army. He openly accused the Duke of it, the strongest words he had used against his colleague to-date. It was an act of incredible bravery on Guicciardini's part considering that Urbino was not only his social superior but also a violent, potentially murderous, individual. But the latter had the backing of the Venetians, the single most powerful element in the League, and so the papal emissary and lieutenant-general of the papal army was powerless without Urbino's committed support. Meanwhile, inside the city, the situation had deteriorated to such an extent that a Roman noblewoman could be purchased for two coins, but an egg fetched six.

Prince Philibert of Orange was, despite his youth, still the most senior commander in charge and discussions to install either Lannoy or Moncada as the army's replacement general had met with a lukewarm response from both men. Indeed, Lannoy himself had fled Rome on 28 May for Naples, where he would sicken and die by September the same year; and when Madrid offered the *condotta* to Alfonso d'Este, he too had sensibly demurred. Nobody with any sense wished to assume responsibility for an already impossible situation. One day Philibert was knocked from his mule by a stray shot fired from the Castel Sant'Angelo and was carried to a nearby inn to recuperate. This was exceedingly bad timing, for Clement had recently entered into the tentative process of negotiation with Philibert and it left the imperial army without any superior commander or restraining force. Cellini himself hardly helped matters when he offered to aim his cannon at the inn where the entire imperial command was assembled round the bed of the injured Philibert. Clement wisely stopped his friend from blowing the enemy command structure to kingdom come with a single cannonball and in Philibert's absence the negotiations were continued instead by his emissary, Bartolomeo Gattinara. Gattinara, the regent of Naples, had served as the late duke of Bourbon's Spanish adviser. He had taken pains to dissociate himself (and therefore his Emperor) from the attack on Rome. But like all Spaniards Gattinara was a charmless man with little tact or diplomacy. As Clement professed his poverty and his inability to find the funds for the ransom which Gattinara demanded of him, Gattinara seized hold of the astonished Medici pope's hand and gestured to the fat golden rings which festooned his fingers.

With no sign of the duke of Urbino and with few other options before him, Pope Clement VII was forced to come to terms on 5 June. The demands were not only humiliating but they effectively terminated much of the temporal power which had been clawed back by his pontifical predecessors since the return from Avignon. In addition to a 400,000 ducat payment, to be paid in three instalments, Clement was obliged to relinquish ownership of the papal cities of Ostia, Civitavecchia, Modena, Parma and Piacenza. As a final stinging indignity the Pope was also forced to generously compensate the Colonna for his retaliatory attacks on their lands. Cardinal Pompeo Colonna had already met with Clement privately around this time and, despite all that had passed between them, supposedly the two men had embraced and kissed in a gesture of reconciliation. Two days later the 500 men of the papal garrison were permitted to march safely out of the Castel Sant'Angelo to their freedom whilst the Germans and Spaniards trooped in to relieve them. The irrepressible Sebastian Schertlin Burtenbach was amongst them. In his memoirs he recorded that he and a group of imperial soldiers found Pope Clement and his cardinals cowering in a small cell deep within the Castel. 'We took him prisoner. They wept bitterly. We were all moved,' he recorded concisely. But Burtenbach's ultimate judgement, which was hardly an uncommon one, not least amongst many of Clement's own advisers, was that the Vicar of Christ had largely brought all of his misfortunes upon himself.

Throughout the coming weeks and months the Pope was kept captive in the *castello* to ensure that he abided by his promise to pay the vast ransom. Beyond the mighty drum of the fortress, however, another misfortune had descended upon the city to add to the suffering already caused by pillage, murder, rape, desecration and starvation. The thousands of unburied corpses littering the city streets had by now given rise to an outbreak of plague, the proportions of which few of the Lutheran soldiers or the Spanish had ever witnessed before. The pestilence ravaged the Imperialist ranks even as the survivors continued doggedly to drink heavily of the strong Roman wine and wring what little plunder still remained in the city. Cardinal Armellino, so detested by the Romans, was one of those struck down by the pandemic. So too was Cardinal Ercole Rangone the bishop of Modena. Having earlier destroyed the aqueducts which brought fresh drinking water to the city, the imperial troops were also now denied this most basic of human amenities. Plague-ridden and thirsty, they died in their thousands. Those who failed to succumb sensibly fled Rome and set about pillaging the *contado* instead. The town of Narni refused to provide the roaming imperial soldiers with provisions and so the city was besieged, stormed and viciously sacked. During the days of the ancient Roman republic Narni had been referred to as Nequinam, from the Latin word *nequam*, meaning 'a rogue'. The town's inhabitants had always been regarded as rogues by the Romans and its greatest curse was its proximity to the city of Rome. At Narni, the Germans, Austrians and Spaniards put to the sword over 1,000 men, women and children.

Two thousand or so Imperialists still remained in Rome as the Pope's guards. Entombed deep within Hadrian's mausoleum, Clement VII listened to his captors in the apartments above him – drinking, merrymaking, whoring, arguing and occasionally fighting. He had managed with great difficulty to raise the first instalment of 100,000 ducats by plundering the assets of his own churches, and a further 195,000 was raised by appealing to sundry *Genovese* and Spanish bankers who deducted a hefty 25% commission from the Pope while he was *in extremis*. But the task of fulfilling the last instalment of 105,000 ducats was, to all intents and purposes, impossible.

Charles V received word of the sacking on 17 June, more than a month after the initial attack on Rome. In March the previous year, the Emperor had wed the twenty-six-year-old *Infanta* Isabella of Portugal, just three years his junior, and his mind was still preoccupied with sweet matters of the heart. When the news reached him he was at the tilt yard impressing his new bride with his prowess, but instead of cancelling the event as a mark of respect (or contrition) for the desecration of Christendom's holiest city he simply continued with the tournament. When a delegation of Spanish ecclesiastics held an audience with him the following day the Emperor had adjusted his demeanour to an appropriately sorrowful one, but even so he refused to accept any personal blame or responsibility for the tragedy. Instead he heaped blame upon his scapegoat, the deceased duke of Bourbon, and attributed the disaster to the ungovernability of Bourbon's troops. The fact that he had conveniently neglected to pay his own army for months on end was conveniently air brushed from Charles's internalised version of events. The Imperial Court nevertheless now went into crisis mode to determine the most fitting official response to the consequences of their own clandestine policies.

Charles's statement, when it came, was made in two parts. In a letter to Pope Clement on 25 July the Emperor censured His Holiness for forming an anti-imperial league with France following the French king's release from custody. It had, so Charles maintained, been his most earnest desire to join with France and the papacy in a Crusade against the Turk, but instead of this he had been compelled to defend himself against the Pope's secular aggression. On 2 August, the Emperor issued a second proclamation to all the courts of Europe asserting much the same self-serving argument: 'Since they wished to wage war on us, against all reason and justice, we were forced to take up arms in our own defence. But first we protested not only to the Pope but also to the College of Cardinals, so that no one might complain if, as a result of this war, which we did not seek, the Apostolic See should suffer some harm. Indeed we pointed out that they could only blame themselves for the consequences since they had been the cause of it all. Our protests availed nothing ... So we committed our cause to God and sent more troops from Germany into Italy in order that we might achieve through force what we had been unable to accomplish through love and virtue.' The Emperor's public relations initiative convinced many in Europe that he was largely blameless in this affair. Even the apostolic nuncio Baldassare Castiglione was persuaded of Charles's basic sincerity, but then Castiglione always had a soft spot for Spain and the Empire.

Castiglione at this time was working tirelessly at the Imperial Court for the Pope's release. Eventually his efforts paid off and Charles despatched an embassy to Rome tasked with bringing this about in practical terms. Cynical to the last, however, Charles had nevertheless considered all the different ways in which he could make capital from the Pope's predicament. Should he venture to Rome himself, for example, and release the Pope personally and be officially crowned Emperor in return? This could wait for now, it was decided. Clement showed no gratitude to his nuncio Castiglione; indeed he heaped much of the blame for his predicament on Castiglione's 'failed diplomacy'. He accused the latter of faithlessness and incompetence. On the contrary, however; it had been Castiglione and Castiglione alone who had stood by the Pope, and was still committed to the Holy Father's interests, even after Clement had knowingly sent him to Spain as a diplomatic patsy. Earlier, when Clement had assigned Cardinal Farnese and Cardinal Salviati to go to Madrid and plead with the Emperor for his release, both men had betrayed the Pope by failing to carry out their mission; for them it was enough to be free from Rome and captivity and they had both promptly gone straight home to their family estates. Clement's accusation of faithlessness was a bitter blow for the venerable poet-statesman. In a letter to Clement dated 10 December he rebutted the Pope's criticism that he had failed to keep the Curia adequately appraised of Charles's intentions. In a boldly admonitory move for a papal bureaucrat, Castiglione reproved the Pope's own inconsistent and provocative policies for the misfortunes that had befallen His Holiness. To his immense surprise Pope Clement sent a reply, apologising for having misjudged him. Nevertheless, the damage had already been done and Castiglione, broken hearted by the Supreme Pontiff's lack of faith in him, died of the plague in Toledo in the year 1529.

In 1528, the year before his death, Castiglione published the book for which he is most remembered, *Il Libro del Cortegiano* ('The Book of the Courtier'). The book hearkened back to Castiglione's own halcyon days at the Court of Urbino during the dukedom of Guidobaldo da Montefeltro, when Urbino was regarded as perhaps the most refined and elegant of court in all Italy. The work featured an elegant philosophical dialogue, taking place over a span of four days in the year 1507, between Guidobaldo's wife Elisabetta Gonzaga and her sister-in-law Emilia Pia on the question of what constitutes the ideal gentleman. Castiglione's ruminations, through the mouthpiece of his characters, concluded that the old medieval ideal of the chivalrous knight could no longer suffice in a Renaissance world in which humanist learning had shed new light on so many areas of intellectual darkness. Instead, the Renaissance courtier also needed a grounding in classical Greek and Latin and Castiglione advised a Ciceronian life of service to one's city-state, as advocated in Cicero's own treatises *De Officiis* ('The Duties of a Gentleman') and *De Oratore* ('On the Orator'). Castiglione himself was the very paragon of the ideal courtier whom he sought to describe. Despite Clement's own uncharitable opinions, history's judgement of him as an honest broker in relation to the tragic events of 1527 has largely been fair.

News of Rome's conquest had reached Florence on 11 May. The city's regent, Silvio Passerini the cardinal-bishop of Cortona, and his charges Ippolito and Alessandro de' Medici could only watch impotently as the Florentines once more took to the streets. On this occasion neither the duke of Urbino, nor the Marquis of Saluzzo, nor Guido Rangone were present to bolster the Medici regime. The angry mob openly thronged the streets brazenly insulting the Medicean Supreme Pontiff, describing him as *il Papa chi mente!* ('the Pope who lies!') On 16 May, Passerini and his two charges fled the city having agreed to a full restoration of the pre-Medicean republic in return for their safe passage out of the city. The cardinal-bishop of Cortona, Ippolito de' Medici and Alessandro de' Medici left Florence by the Porta San Gallo and made for the Medici villa at Poggia a Caiano, from whence they subsequently made their way to Lucca. This second fall of the Medici administration cannot, however, be laid entirely at Passerini's feet alone; the sack of Rome had precipitated severe and sudden economic problems all of which now combined with the general public's sense of dissatisfaction towards the Medici. In the weeks and months to come these problems would only worsen as Medici patronage dried up, trade and commerce with Rome and the Papal States came to a virtual standstill and Medici Florence's special financial status vis-à-vis the Medici Court of Rome was nullified by the Pope's imprisonment and consequent poverty, which in turn sounded the death knell for those Florentine banks that were heavily dependent on papal business. Filippo Strozzi the Younger, husband to Piero the Unfortunate's daughter Clarice de' Medici, had negotiated both Passerini's departure and the transfer of power. Since 1508, when he and Clarice had married, Filippo had enjoyed all the benefits of association with the House of Medici. Both Leo X and Clement VII had been his benefactors at the Court of Rome and, as the Medici papacy's foremost financial wheeler-dealer, he had prospered immensely under both their reigns; furthermore he had also enjoyed cordial relations with his late brother-in-law Lorenzo, the duke of Urbino.

Having said that, Filippo's wife Clarice de' Medici had always been a caustic critic of both Passerini and Ippolito de' Medici since their imposition on Florence in 1524. Strozzi had inevitably fallen in step with his wife's sentiments, having criticised Passerini's tendency towards self-rule without regard to Florence's traditional councils, and having furthermore claimed that Passerini 'ruled badly'. Clarice herself was no less critical either of her uncle, Pope Clement VII, despite his friendship and benefactorial support for her husband. Indeed, Filippo's own feelings towards the Pope had lately cooled to a large extent due to deeply personal reasons. When, in the aftermath of the Colonna raid on Rome, Filippo had volunteered to accompany the withdrawing Colonna as their hostage, he had subsequently languished in Naples's forbidding *fortezza* of Castelnuovo for many months whilst the Pope made no effort to settle his ransom or secure his freedom. Eventually, Filippo had been forced to cut a separate deal with the Colonna, agreeing to work behind the scenes with various dissident Florentine families to secure the expulsion of the Medici in order to secure his release. Another bone of contention between Pope Clement and the Strozzi was the fact that, having made numerous other Medici cousins and nephews cardinals, Clement consistently refused to do the same for Clarice and Filippo's own son Piero Strozzi who was compelled instead to take up the customary Italian nobleman's career of *condottiere*.

When Cardinal Passerini, Ippolito de' Medici and Alessandro de' Medici had sought sanctuary at the Palazzo Medici, the fiery Clarice–so Bernardo Segni informs us–had barred their way, declaring to the assembled crowd that she acknowledged no kinship with 'the three Medici bastards'. Clarice would die the following year on 3 May 1528 and be spared the sting of Medici retribution that was eventually to follow their acts of 'republican' disobedience. For the time being, however, Florence *was* for better or worse a republic once more and the arbitrary rule of the much-loathed Cardinal Passerini was now no more than a fading memory. Attendants busied themselves in the Palazzo della Signoria, cleaning and dusting Savonarola's majestic *Sala del Gran Consiglio* in readiness for Florence's Great Council to once more reconvene, pass laws and appoint magistrates following a fifteen year hiatus. On 31 May 1527, Niccolò Capponi (who was married to Filippo Strozzi's sister Alessandra) was elected as *gonfaloniere per un anno*, standard-bearer for one year with an option to further renew his appointment for two more years should he choose. Capponi, who was the son of Piero di Gino Capponi, was essentially a conservative moderate and a member of that clique of *ottimati* families who had long been Medici supporters but who now objected to their growing princely pretensions. He was a good choice and a largely stabilising influence on Florence, although he did face some opposition from the *popolani* and especially the popular party's sub-faction the *adirati*, who were decidedly adverse to his appointment.

Having obediently served Florence during the crisis of the past year, journeying outside of the city to meet with Guicciardini on a number of occasions and reporting faithfully back on the dispositions of the looming imperial army, Niccolò Machiavelli was hopeful that there would be a place for him in the new post-Medici regime. He was, after all a professed republican who–though he had served the Medici in recent years–had also suffered and been persecuted by them as well. Furthermore his work in strengthening Florence's defences had been instrumental in deterring Bourbon's rabble from attacking Florence when it really counted. Sadly, his career expectations were as usual to be disappointed. Instead of recovering his old post as secretary of the second chancery, the job went to a former Medici functionary named Francesco Tarugi. It was a final, bitter disappointment from which Machiavelli would not be able to recover. The Florentine republic which he professed to love more than his own soul could not have inflicted a more devastating blow to his spirit. Instead of earning him universal acclaim for their incisive and astute observations on statecraft, such works as *The Art of War* (1520), *Discourses on Livy* (1531), *The Prince* (1532), and *Florentine Histories* (1532) had–having been illicitly circulated for years in pamphlet form–afforded him instead the unwholesome reputation of a manipulative political cynic and 'an adviser to tyrants'.

In Book II, Chapter 22 of his *Discourses on Livy*, Machiavelli had written: 'Those who have found themselves witnesses of the deliberations of men have observed, and still observe, how often the opinions of men are erroneous; which many times, if they are not decided by very excellent men, are contrary to all truth. And because excellent men in corrupt republics (especially in quiet times) are frowned upon both from envy and from other reasons of ambition, it follows that a common deception (error) is judged good, or it is put forward by men who want favours more readily for themselves than for the general good.' The precept summed up the shortcomings of the Florentine state whenever it had tried to operate as an independent sovereign republic beyond Medici hegemony. Wise counsel, presumably such as his own, was habitually ignored whilst proud amateurs and fools were given free play in formulating state policy.

On 10 June, not long after learning of his disheartening rejection by the new governmental order, Machiavelli took sick and by 21 June 1527 he was dead at the age of fifty-eight. One of his final comments to the friends and family gathered around his death bed was that he much preferred to go to Hell and discuss politics and philosophy with the renowned ancients rather than join the blessed, but crushingly dull, saints in Heaven. Niccolò, perhaps more than most, had grasped the canker that conventional religion had become and he wanted none of it in the Afterlife: 'The evil example of the court of Rome has destroyed all piety and religion in Italy, resulting in infinite mischief and disorders, which keep our country divided and are the cause of our ruin ... This barbarous domination stinks in the nostrils of everyone.' His friend Francesco Guicciardini, whom he professed to love, and who was perhaps one of the few

531

men who truly understood him correctly, would outlive Machiavelli by a further thirteen years and continue to play an active role in Florentine affairs.

Clarice de' Medici's young ward Catherine had, upon the succession of the new republican government, been torn from Clarice's bosom and was moved from the Medici Villa di Poggio a Caiano to the Santa Lucia convent in the Via San Gallo. In December 1527 she would be relocated again to the convent of Santa-Caterina of Siena but at the insistence of the French ambassador (who described the place as a disease-infested slum) she was moved for a third and final time to the convent of the Santa-Maria Annunziata della Murate. Here, at this pro-Medicean convent, she was surrounded by largely sympathetic ladies of the nobility who had taken the veil. She was given the spacious cell once occupied by Caterina Sforza when she herself had sought sanctuary in Florence. The nuns predictably made a great fuss of the little Catherine de' Medici. Sister Niccolini described her as a 'dear little child ... with such gracious manners ... that she made herself loved by all'. Here, for now at least, she was safe.

Having ravaged the surrounding countryside, the imperial troops returned again to the pitiful remains of what remained of Rome in September. They extorted the few surviving inhabitants anew; then they threatened and ordered the Pope to cough up what he still owed and seized some well-bred hostages to make sure that he did. Losing patience, they eventually brought them out for execution and it was only through the actions of Cardinal Pompeo Colonna, trying perhaps to make amends for his earlier duplicity, that the hostages managed to escape their captors as they lay befuddled by the good cardinal's generous gift of several sacks of heady Roman wine. While the imperial army frittered away its time in Rome, an isolated Don Antonio de Leyva was left to hold Milan as best he could with no reinforcements. He was still confronted, indeed outnumbered four to one, by a hostile Venetian army which was allied with Francesco II Sforza. When the Venetians advanced to Marignano, south-west of Milan, Don Antonio brought his considerably smaller force to meet them in a forced night march and thrashed them with his Spanish and Italian contingents, the Germans having failed to muster to the field of battle on time. He then pursued them some distance and finished the Venetians off. For desserts, Leyva next defeated a Swiss army drawing French pay at the town of Monza. This time it was a more closely-contested affair but the elderly and gout-ridden commander nevertheless demonstrated that he had still lost none of his old fire.

Serious reversals followed, however, firstly when a French fleet commanded by Andrea Doria captured Genoa, thus cutting off Milan's communications with Madrid. Next, the city of Alessandria fell to the viscount of Lautrec who, by August 1527, was freshly returned to Italy and meant to do the Imperialists some harm. Massing with the Venetians and the Italians of Francesco Sforza, Lautrec now went to attack the city of Pavia. It was captured on 5 October and, in very personal retribution for the king of France's earlier defeat and capture here, the unfortunate city was subjected to a most brutal and incorrigible sacking. Now, instead of the logical next step of moving to attack an isolated Milan where Leyva could barely muster 6,500 unpaid Germans, Spanish and Italians, Lautrec turned south to march against Rome, free the Pope and then attack Spanish Naples. Although he now shed a sizeable portion of his forces (the 7,000 Venetians leaving for winter quarters and the Swiss likewise departing) he persuaded Alfonso d'Este to come over to the League with the promise of a match between Louis XII's daughter, Renée of France, and Alfonso's son Ercole. He also sweetened the deal by undertaking to recognise the duke's title to Ferrara along with the two papal fiefs of Modena and Reggio.

Upon Charles de Lannoy's death he had been replaced by Don Pedro de Veyre a Spanish chauvinist who, like Ugo de Moncada, had little liking for the Italians and even less sympathy for the Italian Medici pope. When he presented himself at the Castel Sant'Angelo in October it was with hardly more respect than Bartolomeo Gattinara had shown some weeks earlier. But under the circumstances Clement could not complain for the imperial hand was now outstretched, if somewhat insidiously, with the proverbial olive branch. The terms Clement had consented to earlier, both in terms of payment of the balance of the ransom and relinquishing of the papal fiefs, were ratified. The Pope was also forced to acquiesce to the gathering of a Church council thus reopening the whole Pandora's Box of conciliarism. By this time, Pope Clement VII had been locked away in the Castel Sant'Angelo for eight full months. Not only had the destruction of the Eternal City been an ever-present reality throughout this time, not to mention, starvation, plague and the very real threat of sudden death, but bitterest of all Clement had signed away a thousand years' worth of Church patrimony.

On 8 December, and with the assistance of Luigi Gonzaga (who resented the Spaniards' insolent treatment of the pontiff), Clement left his trusted Cardinal Lorenzo Campeggio 'in charge' of an utterly prostrate city of Rome and walked out of the *castello* dressed in the rude garb of a servant with a basket slung over his arm and a slouch hat obscuring his features. The guards, who were either astonishingly short-sighted or else under secret orders from Charles V to allow the Pope his liberty (for they had seen the Pope every day for months), permitted him to pass and he threaded his way nervously through the devastated, dung-besmirched, corpse-strewn streets of his capital. Once outside the walls he was met by Gonzaga's *bravi* who–shaking their heads sadly at the gauntness of the forty-nine-year-old pope with his long, grey, old man's beard–took him off on horseback to Viterbo and thence to sanctuary at Orvieto.

The remote hill town of Orvieto may have been remote and under-provisioned but it was almost halfway between Rome and Florence and hence put some much needed distance between the Pope and his former imperial jailors. Some would say that Clement was little better off at Orvieto than at the Castello Sant'Angelo–the countryside was still infested with roaming bands of *landsknechts* and the price of food and basic necessities was astronomical–but this is surely to misprize liberty after nearly a year of incarceration. He made his court as best he could in Orvieto's crumbling episcopal palace and was attended, according to the English ambassador who made his way there, by 'thirty persons – riffraff and others, standing in the chambers for a garnishment'. Feeling old beyond his years and suffering badly from that old Medici affliction of gout, Clement was physically free, though considerably constrained in his freedom of action, but remained melancholy over Rome's fate. The loss of Florence in particular was the bitterest pill but for the moment, as a papal cypher in an obscure Umbrian citadel, he had no power and little say in the matter. He grew and kept his beard long as a mark of mourning for the tragedy which had befallen Rome thanks in large measure to his own inept policies. The humanist Pierio Valeriano, tutor to the young Alessandro and Ippolito de' Medici (who had followed them into exile), obligingly penned the treatise *Pro sacerdotum barbis* which advocated the wearing of beards for priests. Outside of the priesthood beards were by now all the rage amongst gentlemen, having been in vogue since around the year 1500 when the European visitors to the New World found it increasingly desirable to distinguish themselves as genuine 'white men' from the equally fair-skinned but *unbearded* native Indians. Scorned since the days of Basilios Bessarion, Clement VII would usher in a new hirsute fashion in beards amongst ecclesiastics.

On 17 February 1528, those remaining Imperialist troops in Rome began their weary withdrawal. Of the 22,000 who had occupied the city just over half remained, the rest having succumbed to plague, infighting amongst themselves, heavy drinking, gluttony, or else they had simply dispersed to other parts in search of fresh plunder and adventure. They trooped out of a city which had been denuded of two thirds of its population and to all intents and purposes destroyed as a habitat. Many of those Romans left alive had taken to living a strange, feral, semi-subterranean existence amidst the ruins, tunnels and cisterns of the city. As the army withdrew they emerged from their hiding places, squinting unaccustomed to the sunlight, and viciously fell upon those German or Spanish soldiers foolhardy enough to have remained behind. Rome had been transformed into a city of ghosts and ghouls. 'This is not the ruin of one city but of the whole world', declared Erasmus sadly.

Any person of learning, scholarship or artistry, all those higher souls who struggled towards higher truths, had long since departed the city. The list of names read like a roll call of Rome's artistic and humanist Renaissance. Polidoro da Caravaggio, a pupil of Raphael who specialised in painting delightful frescos on the exteriors of Roman palaces, fled to Naples only to be tragically murdered later in Messina. His close friend and collaborator Maturino da Firenze is said to have perished during the sack. Giovanni da Udine, the discoverer of the art of Stucco, who had assisted Raphael in commissions such as the Vatican Loggie, returned to his hometown of Udine. The eccentric Florentine Mannerist painter Rosso Fiorentino fled Rome after suffering torture at the soldiers' hands. Rome's loss was France's gain and he wound up in service to the French king at the Château de Fontainebleau. Jacopo Sansovino fled to Venice where he became chief architect and superintendent of properties to the republic, one of the most senior artistic positions in the city. The Doge, Andrea Gritti, immediately gave him a commission to beautify the area around San Marco. Another Mannerist, Parmigianino, escaped to Bologna and later Parma. Here he was joined by the philosopher Lodovico Boccadifferro and the engraver Marcantonio Raimondi, the infamous creator of the pornographic *I Modi: The Sixteen Pleasures* so admired by Pietro Aretino. Pope Clement VII's friend Benvenuto Cellini, having marched out of the Castel Sant'Angelo with the rest of the papal troops that day, made his way to Florence and then eventually to Mantua. Death was nearly the fate of the *Sienese* architect Baldassare Peruzzi whom Clement had summoned to Rome to work on the new St. Peter's. On attempting to flee Rome during the initial days of the sack, Peruzzi had been captured by a group of German *landsknechts* and only escaped torture and death by sketching the corpse of the duke of Bourbon for the amusement of his captors, after which he was allowed to go free. However, Peruzzi was captured all over again and robbed of most of his possessions, arriving back in Siena resembling a half-naked scarecrow. Erasmus's correspondent Paolo Bombace died in the initial attack having been cut down in the Borgo whilst trying to reach the safety of the Castel Sant'Angelo.

Rome's intellectual fraternities and sodalities, which by their nature had been both religious and literary, were similarly devastated. Prior to the sack, Rome's main academic sodalities were concentrated around the figures of the papal protonotary Johann Göritz and his intellectual 'rival' Angelo Colocci. Göritz had to flee Rome during the initial attack, having been robbed blind by the *landsknechts*, and later died in Verona from injuries he had sustained. Colocci on the other hand survived but under heart-breaking circumstances. The scholar had amassed an impressive private library of old and rare books and manuscripts, as well as a wide-ranging collection of statues and antiquities at his villa near the Aqua Virgo. Prior to the attack he had the foresight to send some of his most precious items for safekeeping in Florence but during the sack not only had Colucci been forced to pay exorbitant bribes to remain alive, but much of the rest of his library had been sadly destroyed (though two hundred of his precious books still survived in the Vatican Archives).

In their grief over lost and irreplaceable treasures, Rome's humanists scrambled to position themselves to each other as the most hard done by. Bishop Jacopo Sadoleto, a client of the late Cardinal Oliviero Carafa, was especially guilty of this obscure sin of pride-in-victimisation, complaining to his correspondents that he was particularly wronged by the loss of his precious library at such an advanced and vulnerable age when little else remained left to him but scholarship. Nevertheless, Sadoleto still found the inspiration to write to Pope Clement in September 1527: 'if by our sufferings satisfaction is made to the wrath and strictness of God, and if this harshness of punishments is about to open up an approach to good morals and holier principles [then] perhaps the transaction will not have been made with us with the most unfavourable outcome'. Clement's response, if any, to this exhortation 'to keep his chin up' remains unrecorded. Fortunately, Sadoleto himself had had the prescience to flee Rome just before the sack took place, leading many in Rome to credit him with either divine foreknowledge or else some prophetic gift. The attack of the imperial troops on 6 May 1527 had come just ten days after the forty-ninth anniversary of Clement's father's assassination, which had fallen on 26 April 1478. Clement himself would have been deeply conscious of the proximity of those two dates for Giuliano de' Medici's murder had been commemorated annually in Florence for at least a full ten years after the event. One can only imagine the Pope's state of mind when this latest calamity had burst upon him.

At Orvieto, Pope Clement was being closely watched by imperial agents within his court. Not all the terms and conditions he had agreed to had been fulfilled and the final outstanding balance of the payment to the imperial army had never been settled but Charles still breathed easier allowing the Pope to enjoy some semblance of freedom. This was just as well since a new coalition was forming against Charles for a final challenge to Habsburg domination of Europe and Italy. On 22 January 1528, citing a litany of grievances against Charles V, the kings of England and France declared war on the Empire. It was all academic really. France and the Empire had continued their conflict with scarcely a breather throughout much of 1527 and at this point François (who had only recently awoken to the Pope's plight) still believed himself to have a fighting chance of quelling the Habsburgs in Italy. On paper the situation looked promising for the rump of the League. Leyva was still bottled up in

Milan, Como, Trezzo, Pizzighettone and Monza. The French, Swiss, Venetians and Italians of Francesco Sforza still held Alessandria, Vigevano and Pavia while Andrea Doria now held Genoa.

By 10 February, a French army had invaded the Abruzzi under Lautrec, with a truly massive host which had been further enlarged by the arrival of 3,000 *landsknechts*, 1,000 more Germans in Venetian pay, as well as the forces of Alfonso d'Este, Federigo Gonzaga, the Spanish turncoat Pedro Navarro, and the men-at-arms of Florence's Black Bands. All told Lautrec was believed to have had around 22,000 mercenaries under his command together with thousands more *aventuriers* tagging along. They quickly seized Aquila and then proceeded to invade Apulia, moving into position around the old Byzantine hill fortress of Troia. Facing this host was Philibert of Orange and the marchese del Vasto together with the 10,000-12,000 remnants of the imperial army. Although there was some desultory skirmishing and Orange was all for sounding the attack, del Vasto convinced him that they were too outnumbered and Orange allowed himself to be persuaded to fall back on Naples. After mopping up most of the rest of Apulia, Lautrec himself advanced on Naples where he dug in on the heights surrounding the city whilst the League's admiral Andrea Doria blockaded Naples harbour with his small fleet of eight galleys. When Ugo de Moncada sailed out of Naples harbour to challenge Doria with his own six ships Moncada himself was killed in the engagement and the marchese del Vasto, who was sailing with him, was taken prisoner. Doria meanwhile sat tight expecting a relief force of Venetian galleys to join him in re-enforcing the blockade.

With Orange and his dwindling forces pent up inside Naples all the pieces on the chessboard seemed to be moving rapidly towards checkmate for the imperial side. But now the fortunes of war shifted back once again, as they so often do, this time through the foolhardiness of the French king whose unfair treatment of Doria drove him back into the imperial fold. On 4 July 1528, Doria withdrew his fleet from Naples and by August he had concluded a progressive deal with the Emperor by which the latter promised to recognise (once freed from the French) a sovereign and independent Genoa released from the obligation to pay imperial protection dues. Doria's defection was the sea change that Naples's imperial garrison so badly needed and with raised spirits they sent their light horse to scour the countryside for supplies, some of which were being brought in from the nearby port of Gaeta, and went out of their way to harry their besiegers. Caught in the open on malarial marshlands, the League's army suffered attrition through the usual problems of sickness and desertion. Lautrec himself died on 16 August, as did his second-in-command, as did the Venetian war commissioner as well. Michele Antonio, Marquis of Saluzzo, led what remained of the once huge League army ('not so much an army as a walking pestilence') away from Naples on 29 August. They got as far as the old Norman hilltop town of Aversa in Apulia but were too weak to defend themselves against the imperial army which had shadowed them there. Saluzzo expired in the dungeons of Naples whilst the Spanish turncoat Pedro Navarro, who had given long years of loyal service to the French king (and who had helped Machiavelli rebuild the city walls of Florence), was sentenced to be executed on the orders of the Emperor. Before that could happen, however, Navarro was murdered in prison at the ripe old age of sixty-eight.

Yet there were still a few more movements before the final curtain. When Charles V and the Archduke Ferdinand sent Henry, Duke of Brunswick, into

Lombardy with 20,000 troops and 1,700 cavalry to reinforce Leyva in Milan, the French king responded by despatching the Comte de Saint-Pol with around 10,000 men and 400 lances. Linking up with the Venetian troops of the duke of Urbino, Saint-Pol conquered and sacked Pavia (earlier recaptured by Leyva) all over again on 19 September; the unfortunate German and Spanish garrison was offered no quarter. After this all sides retired to winter quarters and in the spring there was considerable confusion on both sides as to what their objectives should be. Saint-Pol, Urbino and Sforza would have liked to have moved against the key prize of Milan, by now only weakly defended by Leyva and some 2,800 German *landsknechts* and Spanish soldiers, however even they recognised that they possessed insufficient troops for the task of a siege. They therefore opted to mount an attack on the newly-independent Genoa of Andrea Doria instead. When Leyva learned of this he led his men out of Milan in a forced night march and attacked the League forces at the town on Landriano on 21 June 1529. The result was a crushing defeat for the League which ended with Saint-Pol's capture, Francesco Sforza's flight to Crema, and around 3,000 League soldiers being taken prisoner.

The 'Great Matter' of the English monarch Henry VIII had meanwhile pursued Pope Clement from Rome to Orvieto. Henry, who had fallen for the episodically-dispensed charms of the twenty-six-year-old Lady Anne Boleyn, was seeking in effect an annulment from his marriage with Charles V's aunt Catherine of Aragon. Catherine, who was the daughter of the late Queen Isabella I of Castile and King Ferdinand II of Aragon, was at that time forty-two years old and, as heir to the English throne, had only managed to produce one daughter, Mary. Although the English crown was not subject to the gender restrictions of the French Salic law and Mary could still mount the throne as the queen of England, Henry had already convinced himself by 1527 that in marrying Catherine, the former wife of his dead brother Prince Arthur, he had acted contrary to Leviticus 20:21. This verse stated: *Qui duxerit uxorem fratris sui, rem facit illicitam: turpitudinem fratris sui revelavit; absque liberis erunt* ('If a man takes his brother's wife, it is an unclean thing: he hath uncovered his brother's nakedness; they shall be without children'.) Henry had by now persuaded himself that the fruitlessness of his marriage and lack of male heirs was God's judgement upon an unholy union.

According to both Henry and Cardinal Wolsey (whose foreign policy by this time was almost entirely dominated by his attempts to secure his master's annulment) the Pope had never been empowered to dispense with this Biblical impediment and thus the marriage was unlawful in the eyes of God. Leaving aside the obvious question marks this created over issues of papal infallibility, it was a powerful if rather convenient argument for the English king to pursue. But arguing it was one thing; persuading Pope Clement VII to now dissolve the marriage was another matter entirely. Under different, more neutral, circumstances an annulment may well have been granted; indeed, not only was there precedent for such royal annulments but when Pope Clement had initially escaped to Orvieto he was, on a somewhat more personal level, feeling ill-disposed towards the Emperor for having left Rome, in his own words, 'a pitiable and mangled corpse'. In the spring of 1528, Clement VII may well have granted the annulment purely out of spite towards Charles (and Charles, far too preoccupied with the fallout from the defeat at Mohács to give overly much precedence to the marital woes of some distant Spanish aunt, would have had to stomach it). But as was usual with Clement, by the time he actually came round to making a decision one way or the other, he had usually made a 180 degree change of direction. This was certainly the case by August of 1530 when, as we shall see in due course, his interests and those of the Emperor all converged once again.

The English had started the ball rolling in the spring of 1527 when the bishop of Lincoln had questioned the underlying validity of Henry's marriage to Queen Catherine. This was followed in May 1527 by a secret papal inquiry (an *inquisitio ex officio*) into the legality of the marriage which was set up by Cardinal Wolsey in his capacity as permanent papal legate to the English court. In this, Wolsey had been assisted by Archbishop William Warham who, invoking his favourite phrase *ira principis mors est* ('the King's anger is death'), wearily co-signed the letter to Clement VII urging the Pope to assent to Henry's wishes. Unfortunately, their solicitation to Clement VII coincided almost exactly with the Sack of Rome. Locked up in the Castel Sant'Angelo and constantly menaced by imperial troops, Clement was in no position to rock the boat by openly defying Charles. Wolsey's argument, under these circumstances, was that since the bishop of Rome was incapacitated it was down to those cardinals who *were* still at liberty to convene a Church synod and take care of outstanding business. Since most of these happened to be French cardinals, then Wolsey would convene the council in France and naturally he would solemnly discharge his duty to the Church by advancing himself as Clement's temporary proxy. This was naturally very generous of him. The theory of course, more than a little cynical in conception, was that Wolsey would decamp to France, issue the annulment on Clement's behalf, and quickly return to London to bask in Henry's grace and favour. Wolsey for his part still hoped that Henry would see sense and recover from his absurd infatuation with the Boleyn girl; a dynastic alliance with a French princess would be of far more diplomatic value in view of England and France's on-going joint war with the Emperor and this idea was now mooted to the French cardinals as an incentive for them to convene Wolsey's synod.

It was around this time that Catherine herself got wind of Henry's plans and she entered into feverish correspondence with her nephew through his ambassador Don Inigo de Mendoza. Wolsey decamped in July to France in great style and pomp, where he proceeded to scandalise all present by arguing that, since the Medici pope was in effect a captive and no longer a free agent, that he should do the decent thing by immediately abdicating. By September, Henry had delegated a separate official to go to Rome and present Henry's case to His Holiness personally. This envoy was William Knight, Henry's fifty-two-year-old secretary of state and bishop of Bath and Wells. Receiving instructions from Wolsey at Compiègne, he obtained a safe conduct pass from Clement's protonotary Uberto Gambara and proceeded on to Rome. Narrowly avoiding being murdered at Monterotundo, Knight entered Rome by early December and, at considerable personal risk to himself, attempted to present his credentials to the Pope in the Castel Sant'Angelo. His efforts however were unsuccessful and by the month's end Clement had fled to Orvieto where he set up his exiled papal court. William Knight returned in failure to London in February 1528; that he had made it as far as Rome at all was a small miracle since, old and well past his prime, Knight was also known to be losing his eyesight at the time he was given his royal commission.

By March, two more English emissaries were at Orvieto petitioning Pope Clement on England's proposal to appoint a decretal commission empowered to investigate the King's 'Great Matter' in London. These emissaries were Cardinal Wolsey's two secretaries: Stephen Gardiner and Edward Fox. Pope Clement obliged them by consenting to such a commission and in May he further agreed to upgrade it with powers to issue an actual decree of annulment, although Clement shrewdly reserved the privilege to have the final say in the matter. Clement's trusted Cardinal Lorenzo Campeggio was then despatched from Rome to London, a ponderous journey made in slow, comfortable stages for he suffered badly from gout. Campeggio finally arrived in London on 7 October 1528. At Clement's suggestion, his representative met with Catherine on three different occasions; during one of these visits Campeggio proposed to Catherine that she graciously retire to a convent, thus leaving the King's marriage to resolve itself naturally without further conflict. He then reminded the Queen that Jeanne of France had taken this drastic step in order to graciously allow her former husband Louis XII to marry the former wife of his predecessor, Anne of Brittany, 'for the good of the realm'. Catherine however remained adamant. She claimed that she had come to her marriage with Henry as a virgin because at the time of her previous marriage to Prince Arthur she had remained, in her own words, both 'intacta e incorrupta'. Few who knew Catherine's upright and moral Catholic character could doubt the veracity of her words or indeed her resolve.

By July 1528, however, the military and diplomatic tide had already turned against England and France. France's efforts to regain its footing in Italy, and especially in Naples, had been sabotaged by Andrea Doria's defection to the Emperor and Henry VIII's secret negotiations with the Medici pope concerning his marriage had become inconveniently and embarrassingly public. In England there was almost universal sympathy for Queen Catherine who, as the daughter of two anointed monarchs and a devout Roman Catholic, had always been popular with her English subjects. With the recent defeat of the latest French offensive, Pope Clement had once more swung behind Charles V and the Empire. The day before Campeggio reached London, the Supreme Pontiff had returned once more to Rome by way of Viterbo. To the dwindling crowds of Romans who welcomed him back, the Pope was a visibly changed man. He was older and more haggard, with his flowing grey beard and his feebly benedictions to the sceptical and mildly hostile crowd. Clement entered the Porta del Popolo with a large detachment of imperial troops, clearly more a puppet of the Emperor than the secular sovereign lord of Rome and the Papal States. Rome itself was a total ruin; the Mantuan ambassador Francesco Gonzaga estimated that four-fifths of the city was by now uninhabited. Clement VII was no longer a free agent. He now wrote to Campeggio to delay the proceedings for as long as possible and the cardinal replied that, for his part, he was satisfied with the Queen's claim that the marriage was perfectly lawful. Wolsey meanwhile, nearing the end of his tether and with Henry's displeasure at his ineffectuality intensifying daily, retreated to the last weapon in his armoury and threatened the uncooperative pope with Schism if he failed to comply with the annulment.

On 10 January 1529, feeling tired, old and vulnerable, and seeking to create a future successor for himself in the papacy, Pope Clement elevated the eighteen-year-old Ippolito de' Medici (already archbishop of Avignon since the age of six) to the Sacred College. Like Cesare Borgia before him, a career in the Church was decidedly not to Ippolito's tastes. Like the 'Borgia bull calf' his interests lay more in the military sphere and as Giuliano de' Medici's heir he imagined himself carving out a great secular Italian principality instead. Clement on the other hand was thinking like any prudent Renaissance patriarch in reserving one son for the Church and one for more temporal responsibilities. The elevation certainly displeased Pope Clement's cousin Lucrezia de' Medici and her husband Jacopo Salviati, who now saw in Ippolito potential competition for their own son Cardinal Giovanni Salviati, an established cleric who had already been cardinal since Pope Leo X's consistory of 1 July 1517. The Salviati father and son's fears were not, if must be said, completely unfounded. Clement intended to enrich his young protégé as a prelude to aggrandising him within the Church hierarchy. When Cardinal Silvio Passerini died on 20 April 1529, Ippolito was given his former post as papal legate to Perugia. This was soon followed by the position of legate to Genoa and later that same year he was granted the benefice of Sant'Anastasio alle Tre Fontane and made administrator of the See of Casale Monferrato.

The English king's 'Great Matter' meanwhile rumbled to its inevitable climax on 17 June 1529 at Blackfriars, where an ecclesiastical tribunal chaired by cardinals Wolsey and Campeggio heard the case against the legitimacy of the Queen's marriage. By this time Campeggio was already heavily prejudiced against Lady Anne, having reported that she had 'certain Lutheran books, in English, of an evil sort' (perhaps referring to illicit copies of William Tyndale's English vernacular Bible). For Henry, what should have been a carefully stage-managed show trial, slipped from his grasp and degenerated into a farce as Queen Catherine, playing effortlessly to the gallery, proceeded to win the hearts and minds of the audience. The final crushing blow came when Cardinal Campeggio, who had deliberately delayed the proceedings for many weeks at Clement's secret behest, refused to issue any definitive ruling and averred instead that the tribunal would need to be shifted to a Vatican court in Rome. It was the final disappointment for Henry, who now came to the conclusion that he could never get his way whilst the Emperor stood guard, both literally and metaphorically, over the Pope of Rome.

Cardinal Thomas Wolsey's fate, as is well known was sealed by this last fiasco. He had assured Henry that he could obtain the papal dispensation and had thereby raised the King's expectations only for them to come crashing to earth. He had failed his monarch in just this one thing. The downfall of this obscure butcher's son from Ipswich, who had twice aspired to be Pope of Rome and Vicar of Christ, was spectacular indeed. Wolsey was stripped of both his public office and his personal property, including his magnificent residence of Hampton Court Palace, which Henry now appropriated as a replacement for the Palace of Westminster. Permitted to remain archbishop of York, he stoically travelled to bleak Yorkshire to take up his post but, before he could even arrive at his See, was arrested at Cawood in North Yorkshire on charges of treason. Ordered to be brought to London for trial and execution (at Anne Boleyn's personal instigation so many claimed) Wolsey fell ill on the return journey and died in Leicester on 29 November 1530 aged fifty-seven.

Following the final defeat and capture of the French commander Saint-Pol at the Battle of Landriano in June 1529, France and the Empire entered into peace negotiations. These were principally conducted behind the scenes although on 3 August France's Queen Mother Louise of Savoy and the Empire's Margaret of Austria came together in person at the border town of Cambrai to conclude the agreement with a woman's touch. 'Look', wrote the Dutch poet Johannes Secundus at the time, 'the treaty has been concluded through women's efforts' ('*En per femineas foedera pacta manus*'). The truce which came to be known as 'the Peace of the Ladies' (*the Paix des Dames*) largely preserved the terms of the Treaty of Madrid made some three years earlier. Importantly, France finally agreed to abandon her thirty-five-year-long quest for Milan and Naples. She also relinquished suzerainty to Flanders, Artois, Tournai, Genoa and Asti. In return for a ransom of two million gold pieces, France would however retain the prestigious duchy of Burgundy and François's two young sons would finally be returned to him (they were by now both fluent in Spanish and deeply traumatised by their incarceration). François was even moved by the conclusion of the peace to propose to the Emperor's ambassadors at the Louvre a joint Holy Crusade against the Sultan Süleyman, who had already reached the gates of Vienna and was by now threatening all of Central and Western Europe.

Officially, although the Empire's state of war with France was dissolved by the Treaty of Cambrai, a state of war still existed at least on paper between Charles V and Venice, Florence and the Pope. But the Battle of Landriano had precipitated a powerful epiphany in the mind of Pope Clement VII. Watching these developments from far off Orvieto, Clement now realised that the Empire had ultimately broken the back of French power and won the contest for Italy. But Clement cared little for Italy, only for his Medici patrimony Florence. Consequently, Clement saw that only Charles V had the power to restore Florence to the Medici and only he could make an effective future partner. Bowing to the inevitable, France was ditched and Clement finally admitted to his court: 'I have quite made up my mind to become an Imperialist, and to live and die as such'. Imperial relations with the papacy was settled by the Treaty of Barcelona of 29 June 1529. By the terms of the treaty, Pope Clement agreed to absolve the participants of the sack of Rome of any sins and promised to crown Charles V as Holy Roman Emperor in Italy. In return, the Emperor pledged to encourage certain towns in the Papal States to restore their allegiance to the Pope. Clement would also receive Ravenna and Cervia, two cities which the Republic of Venice had recently been forced to surrender. The duke of Ferrara would likewise be induced to relinquish Modena and Reggio to the Pope. Most importantly of all for Clement, Charles would provide the military assistance for an imperial reconquest of Medici Florence. Gallingly, however, for Clement, he would be forced to cooperate with the imperial commander Philibert of Orange who had so recently commanded the troops which had laid waste to Rome.

An earlier mooted plan to place Alessandro de' Medici on the ducal throne of Milan was however abandoned; neither the Emperor nor the Venetians were in favour of this, besides which, Clement came to realise that the Medici had no effective power base in Milan through which to rule. Instead, Francesco II Sforza would be permitted to return to Milan as duke in return for the sum of 900,000 scudi, provided he was found innocent of the charges of treason against him. Alessandro de' Medici would however by way of compensation be united in marriage with Charles V's illegitimate seven-year-old daughter Margaret of Austria, whom he had sired at the age of twenty-two by his Dutch lover Johanna Maria van der Gheynst. With this proposal in mind, the Florentine bishop of Sansepolcro, Leonardo Tornabuoni, had already journeyed to meet Margaret in Flanders and returned with a most favourable report, as well as her portrait, which pleased Clement greatly. With matters now settled between

Rome and the Empire, it was time for Charles to pay his long-awaited visit to Italy.

Charles had left Barcelona by late July and been conveyed by the fleet of his new nautical ally Andrea Doria to Genoa on 12 August where he paused for re-confirmation of the Treaty of Cambrai. He brought along an army of 9,000 Spanish troops and 1,000 horse just in case he needed it (and a further 8,000 *landsknechts* were also on their way from Germany). From here he proceeded over the Apennines to Piacenza on 6 September and by October he was at Modena with his personal entourage of 2,000 courtiers, retainers, servants and guards. The countryside of Lombardy was for once relatively peaceful and content although still far from at peace. The Empire and Venice were still officially at war and Charles's *landsknechts* set about pillaging the Venetian territories as soon as they arrived (the League's *condottiere* Renzo da Ceri, who had failed so signally in defending Rome, was meanwhile still at large in Apulia causing trouble for the Emperor's Neapolitan administration there). But the situation to the east was nonetheless looking more hopeful. By late October the Emperor had received joyous word that the Turk had been stopped in their tracks at Vienna by Graf von Salm and his determined defenders. Nevertheless, the Muslim threat had merely been checked not vanquished and Christendom would still need to unite to confront the threat. Charles's brother Ferdinand and his aunt Margaret of Austria had made it quite clear that his help was urgently needed on the Austrian front. A brief, formal period of healing with the Pope of Rome would hence be desirable before setting out on any eastern Crusade. Sensibly, Charles had been cautioned that it was inadvisable to visit Rome itself, which was still in a pitiful state, its bedraggled population ill disposed towards the Emperor whose army had caused so much suffering. It was therefore decided for prudence sake that Charles would meet the Pope on neutral ground at Bologna instead.

The Emperor Charles V arrived in Bologna *la Grassa* ('Fat Bologna' as it was widely known) on 15 November 1529. Dressed in a fine suit of armour covered by brocade and wearing a black velvet cap and wielding a golden baton, he was greeted at the Porta San Felice by Cardinal Campeggio who had only recently arrived home from his deliberations in London. In return for his loyalty to Charles's aunt Catherine of Aragon, Campeggio's family was adopted under the Emperor's patronage and Clement bestowed on him the Rocca di Dozza in the Emilia-Romagna, which the cardinal later converted into a pleasant residence by roofing over the courtyard and creating a number of congenial open loggias. The Emperor was then accompanied to the Palazzo Pubblico of Bologna by Duke Alessandro de' Medici of Penne and by his *Genovese* admiral Andrea Doria. The city had been transformed, for the occasion, into an imaginary 'Rome' through the addition of numerous *faux* triumphal arches featuring pagan Roman gods and statues of illustrious Roman generals such as Scipio Africanus, Quintus Caecilius Metellus Pius, Marcus Claudius Marcellus, and Marcus Furius Camillus. The enclosure in which Pope Clement awaited the Emperor was itself constructed to represent the Vatican consistory with a blue and white striped awning. The Emperor knelt and gently kissed the Pope's red velvet slipper, uttering the words 'I have come to where I long desired to be, to the feet of Your Holiness'. The reconciliation was enough to make a strong man weep. Alessandro's uncle Ippolito de' Medici was in Bologna too, watching the spectacle as a cardinal in the Pope's retinue; from the sidelines he jealously observed as the peacocking Alessandro gained the Emperor's eye and, as his

542

prospective son-in-law, increasingly came under his benevolent imperial patronage.

Since the date of the actual coronation had been set for 24 February 1530, the Emperor's thirtieth birthday, there would be several long weeks of negotiations in the interim between the imperial and papal delegations. Lodged in adjacent suites in the Palazzo Pubblico both Emperor and the Pope spent days on end closeted together. Most of what was privately discussed remains alas unrecorded for posterity. However, on 23 December, a peace treaty was finally concluded with the ambassadors from Venice. In return, Venice agreed to yield those cities that she had seized in Naples. Francesco II Sforza, belatedly absolved of all charges of treason and plotting, was meanwhile to be confirmed as duke of Milan, although it was agreed that imperial soldiers would maintain a presence in the Castello Sforzesco as surety for Sforza's 900,000 scudi fee, which had been negotiated earlier in the year. Charles would also consent, the following year, to Sforza's proposal that he should marry Charles's niece Christina of Denmark, still barely nine years old at the time, and that the wedding should take place in May 1534 once she had reached the age of thirteen. As with the suggestion that Alessandro de' Medici should marry his daughter Margaret, the proposal enshrined Charles's astute policy of binding the rulers of the key city-states of Italy to him through close family ties. The upshot of the various talks of 1529 was that a broad front was now created comprising the Empire, Ferdinand of Austria, Venice, Milan, France and the papacy.

Although the diplomatic ramifications of these months were epoch-making, for the younger members of the entourages of both sides it was a largely boring and frustrating time, with little else to do except carouse and hang around aimlessly. Cardinal Ippolito and his cousin Giovanni Battista Cybò did a little too much of the latter one evening and ended up embroiled in an armed brawl with some of Charles's Spanish followers. The fracas, which was an armed and violent one, resulted in several Spanish deaths. The matter, which might easily have escalated into a blood vendetta, was only smoothed over through the timely intervention of the thirty-eight-year-old Cardinal Innocenzo Cybò, who managed to calm the vengeful Spaniards down. In other respects the Imperialists were winners. Bartolomeo Gattinara, Charles V's regent of Naples, who–when Clement had pleaded poverty–had so rudely grasped the Pope's hands in the Castello Sant'Angelo and pointed out the amount of gold which adorned his fingers, was rewarded with a cardinal's hat; a sop to the Emperor who had always valued Gattinara's help and advice. When Charles was not engaged in diplomacy he passed the time with a favourite hound that he had brought with him to Bologna. Marino Sanuto the Younger described the animal as being a type of 'a large racing dog'. The painter Titian would make the Emperor's acquaintance in Bologna and three years later would paint Charles together with this most extraordinary canine.

The monotony of the endless negotiations was thankfully broken when on 24 February 1530 (the Emperor's birthday) Charles V was crowned in the Basilica of San Petronio. It was a dual crowning ceremony; first came the traditional Iron Crown of Lombardy, specially brought from Monza and hastily enlarged because it was too tight for Charles's head, and next came the crown of the Holy Roman Empire combined with the ritual anointing. During the ceremonies the marquis of Montferrat carried the imperial sceptre and the duke of Savoy the Iron Crown. The duke of Urbino, Francesco Maria della Rovere, who had kept his own sword sheathed during much of the Pope's recent tribulations, toted the imperial sword. Although nobody obviously knew it at the time, Charles V would be the last ever Emperor to receive a papal coronation in Italy. Given all that had transpired between both Pope and Emperor it must have been a moment of supreme triumph for Charles. The universal peace of Christendom was then, after so much Christian bloodshed, declared to the assembled crowd. The Dutch painter, engraver and etcher Nicholaus Hogenberg recorded the ceremonial procession to San Petronio in several rare engravings which were commissioned by the archduchess, Margaret of Austria.

Following the coronation the townspeople of Bologna were treated to an ox roast in the centre of the *piazza*, but it was not any old roast as one contemporary observer Guadalupi recorded: 'a whole ox was there for the taking, complete with head and very long horns, stuffed with a wether, itself stuffed with chickens, capons, partridges, pheasants, pigeons, hares, thrushes and pigs, also whole; and because no one could turn it, they had devised certain winches, turned by various *landsknechts* who were standing around'. By March 1530, Charles was already heading back in Innsbruck, his purpose accomplished, although it was a bittersweet homecoming since two of his most trusted advisers, Bartolomeo Gattinara and Margaret of Austria, were to both die by the end of the year. The timing of their deaths was especially inconvenient in view of the continuing spread of the Lutheran heresy, which plagued Germany and the Netherlands, and on top of everything else Charles was beginning to feel his age and was constantly plagued by headaches, asthma and gout.

Florence had been under siege since late October 1529 by Pope Clement's former jailor the twenty-seven-year-old Philibert of Orange. Lacking sufficient troops (Philibert only had around 10,500 infantry, 800 men-at-arms and disparate elements of light horse as well as about twenty-five good quality artillery pieces), a direct assault on the city had been ruled out. The imperial army therefore settled instead into the posture of a protracted siege, pitching their tents in an arc stretching from the imperial headquarters at the foot of San Miniato to the gate at Porta Romana. Thanks to the earlier efforts of both Antonio da Sangallo the Younger and the late Niccolò Machiavelli in improving the city walls, Florence was capable of repelling most direct frontal assaults on her defences and so the city would be a tough nut for the Imperialists to crack. The Florentines figured that all they needed to do was settle down and wait for the imperial forces to disintegrate through lack of pay, a factor which seemed to bedevil most of Charles V's armies throughout the long Italian Wars.

The artist Michelangelo, who during this time was back in his beloved Florence completing some work on the Medici chapel of San Lorenzo, answered the call of the republican government and dutifully assumed Machiavelli's old job as General Governor and Steward of Fortifications. As such Michelangelo became a member of the *Nove della Milizia*, the nine-man military leadership of the Florentine armed forces. Though raised under the roof of Lorenzo de' Medici, Michelangelo's love affair with the family had long since soured and he had no wish to see their political resurgence in the city which he adored; his relations with Pope Clement VII continued to be abrasive as the Pope himself observed in his remark: 'When Buonarroti comes to see me I always take a seat and bid him to be seated, feeling that he will do so without leave'. From 1528 to 1529, prior to Philibert's investment of the city, he helped to improve Florence's fortifications. One of Michelangelo's first recommendations was to strongly advise that the city walls be extended south to completely enclose the hill and convent of San Miniato al Monte which, being one of the highest points in the city and overlooking Florence's city centre, was a superb potential site for an enemy artillery battery. Peasants were put to work here both day and night to throw up a new protective wall consisting of unbaked earthen brick; they were paid with the usual daily rations of several loaves of bread and a flask of wine. Writes Vasari: 'He designed fortifications for the city and surrounded the hill of St. Miniato with bastions, not only earthworks with the usual fascines, but with framework below of oaks and chestnuts and other good materials, using rough bricks made of tow and dung, carefully laid'. Michelangelo also reinforced the various city gates with earthworks and ordered that ditches and trenches be dug right around the city walls. As a precaution, the Campanile of San Miniato al Monte was covered by mattresses to protect it from any stray cannon shot, although this did not stop a renowned bombardier named Lupo from Santa Croce from taking pot shots at the enemy from a gun emplacement situated high up within the bell tower.

Teaching himself military architecture *on the job* as he went along, the *signoria* sent Michelangelo briefly to Ferrara to inspect the famous city fortifications there, as well as Duke Alfonso's famous cannon foundry. Having masterminded these defensive innovations in the face of some resistance from Niccolò Capponi, Michelangelo then suddenly fled the city in fear of his life on 21 September 1529. He had got wind of some rumours that Pope Clement was concluding a secret treaty with the republican government and he had no intention of lingering in the city and being hung for treason. He quietly slipped out through the bastion at San Miniato al Monte, bringing with him his pupil Antonio Mini and his friend Piloto the goldsmith 'each of them carrying a number of crowns fastened in their doublets'. They headed for refuge at Ferrara, welcomed by Duke Alfonso, but made their way subsequently to Venice – that traditional city of sanctuary, where the Doge implored the maestro to design improvements to the Rialto Bridge. In Michelangelo's absence Antonio da Sangallo the Younger took over his duties and responsibilities.

Florence's city militia, another Machiavellian innovation, was this time considerably better trained and motivated than the green and untried units which had faced the Spanish army at Prato in 1512. Its numbers progressively swelled from an initial 4,000 men to 10,000 as the siege wore on and Florence's youths and *bravi* took up the call-to-arms. Taking an active role in the organisation of the militia was Donato Giannotti, Machiavelli's successor as secretary to Florence's war council and one the former political theorist's close friends. A historian like Machiavelli himself, Giannotti would produce his own political-historical work on Florence, the *Della repubblica fiorentina* of 1531. Giannotti's amateur militiamen were bolstered by the forces of professional mercenaries including Stefano Colonna and Mario Orsini (the Colonna and Orsini fighting on the same side for once) and by Malatesta Baglioni, widely regarded at the time as one of Italy's top *condottieri*, who received his commission as captain-general of the Florentine army in January 1530. The Florentine war commissioner Francesco Ferrucci meanwhile led Florence's military efforts in the wider region of Tuscany itself, maintaining firm control of valuable Florentine enclaves such as Pisa, Livorno, Empoli and Volterra, cities which remained crucial for Florence's resupply. As a commander Ferrucci was brutally effective but he was also cruel, perpetrating atrocities on many citizens of these occupied cities and stripping others of their wealth in order to fund his military campaigns.

Philibert of Orange made his headquarters to the south of Florence at the Villa Guicciardini and blocked the route north to nearby Prato with his German *landsknechts*. The siege officially began on 28 October when Malatesta Baglioni led a procession of Florence's musicians up the hill to the convent of San Miniato al Monte and, through a herald, issued a proclamation challenging the prince of Orange. The entire arsenal of Florence then opened up on the imperial positions for a full one hour. The following day, by way of response, the prince of Orange ordered his own cannon to barrage San Miniato al Monte, whose *campanile* sustained no fewer than fifty cannonball strikes in the fusillade. Meanwhile, Spanish troops were used to blockade the route leading to Bologna. From this city a steady stream of gunpowder and other essential supplies were sent by the Emperor and the Pope throughout the winter of 1529 and the spring of 1530. The civil authorities in Florence had meanwhile flattened the suburbs outside the walls for a mile in all directions thereby depriving the Imperialists of any cover. This heart-breaking task, which saw the demolition of some of Florence's finest villas *al di là delle mura della città* complete with their gardens, trees, olive groves and often even the precious works of art which they housed was nonetheless a necessary precaution. The Venetian envoy Carlo Capello witnessed first-hand the devastation ordered by the Council of Eighty and concluded philosophically that 'all riches lie in the preservation of public liberty, without which private possessions are not one's own'. Since he himself owned none of the fine properties which were being demolished he could afford to be philosophical.

One of the imperial commanders at the siege of Florence was Pier Maria III de' Rossi, the count of San Secondo. He was the son of Caterina Sforza's eldest daughter Bianca Riario and her second husband Troilo I de' Rossi, sixth Count of San Secondo. Just six years younger than his late uncle Giovanni della Bande Nere, with whom he had been educated during his childhood at the Medici court, he had spent some time fighting and learning his trade in France after which he returned to Italy and fought alongside his uncle in the *Bande Nere* defending their family estates. He was situated with a corps of infantry at the Torre del Gallo, a bastion which lay atop the hills of Arcetri which provided a magnificent panorama over the entire city. The scene, as perhaps it may have looked from the vantage point of Arcetri, was later to be painted by Giorgio Vasari as one of the frescos in the Sala di Clement VII at the Palazzo della Signoria. It gives a fair representation of the imperial siege encampments as they must have appeared at the time with their numerous tents, entrenchments and artillery batteries situated on the high ground. In the fresco one such cannon emplacement can be seen firing, amidst wispy puffs of white smoke, from the hill of Giramonte down onto the heavily fortified hill of San Miniato.

Morale within the city started out exceedingly high at the commencement of the siege. Ladies from the more radical republican families gladly auctioned off their best clothing and jewellery to help raise money for arms and weapons. Popular wisdom at the time maintained that Florence was protected by her fortunate natural situation. A large army could not, so it was imagined, fit within the plain that was bounded by Florence's narrow surrounding hills whilst, by the same token, a smaller army which *could* fit inside would be insufficient in number to storm the old fourteenth-century ring walls. It was a hopeful theory which had more in the way of wishful thinking than military science, however. The plain fact of the matter was that these walls had never been tested by modern artillery fire before and had not in fact been designed to withstand modern siege technology or heavy artillery barrages. Against Charles VIII and the duke of Bourbon they had fortunately never been tested, but this had only led to a peculiar sort of complacency on the Florentines' part, similar to the 'lotus eater' denialism which had been prevalent in Rome just prior to its sacking.

As for the political regime, despite the initial moderating influence of the *gonfaloniere* Niccolò Capponi, Florence's government had moved steadily to the more radical end of the spectrum. The remaining supporters of the Medici cause, still pejoratively referred to as the *palleschi*, had long been edged out in favour of those who were more fiercely opposed to the Medici. Most former Medici *amici* had by now sensibly fled the city, whereupon they served as advisers or informers or else took rank in the imperial army; those 'ballers' who were brave enough to remain behind had their property sequestered and more often than not found themselves incarcerated. The fact that Michelangelo was given a place on the military council shows just how far he had come in his own anti-Medicean odyssey. The zealous new regime, at the heart of which was the *Consiglio Maggiore*, was meanwhile fired by an almost Savonarolan spiritual and republican fervour; in 1528, Jesus Christ was declared to be Florence's 'sole and true lord and king' and to memorialise this piece of spiritual legislation a crown of thorns had been carefully placed over the front door of the Palazzo della Signoria. Certain elements in Florence still also insisted ungenerously that the Palazzo Medici be burned to the ground as an additional sop to the city's newly resurgent republican pride.

In opposition to these democratising *popolani* forces still stood the great *ottimati* names such as the Albizzi, the Strozzi and the Soderini. When Niccolò Capponi, who still believed in dialogue with the imperial side, was caught in the act of attempting to negotiate with Pope Clement VII, he was ousted and briefly imprisoned in April 1529. Gaining his liberty by means of a moving and impassioned speech to the *signoria*, Capponi was sent on a mission to meet the Emperor Charles at Genoa and soften his heart towards Florence. Returning from this assignment he ran into Michelangelo, who had recently left Florence in fear of his life, and the artist painted a doleful picture of the condition of the city. Physically ill and despairing of his beloved Florence, Capponi–so we are told–lay down and died in the little hamlet of Castelnuovo. His death came in October 1529, on the eve of the siege of Florence.

Capponi was replaced as *gonfaloniere* by his personal enemy the fiery *popolano* Francesco Carducci, who was the brother of the tempestuous *arrabiati* leader Baldassare Carducci. Baldassare had by this time served a brief prison sentence in Venice for the crime of calling Pope Clement VII a *bastardazzio* and both siblings certainly had a significant axe to grind with the Medici Pope. Under the Carducci brothers there were even calls from some quarters for Cosimo de' Medici's title of *Pater Patriae* to be rescinded, with one activist complaining that the Medici 'deserve to be burnt in their palace and given to the dogs', adding that, 'those who do not want this vote to succeed wish to have a foot in both camps: they want to protect themselves against the future, and they await the return of these tyrants'. Carducci may have been a good Savonarolan from modest *popolani* circumstance, but he was still reluctant to overly empower the armed plebeian militiamen on whom Florence's defence depended. It was the old story of the upper class's collective memory of the populist chaos of 1378. He therefore availed himself of every opportunity to exhort the militia on the virtues of 'obedience' towards the duly appointed government.

Just before Niccolò Capponi's fall from grace Donato Giannotti had penned the former *gonfaloniere* a *discorso* which sought to disentangle Florence's complex social and political structure and set down the preconditions in which her unique form of republicanism might be satisfied. Giannotti developed the formula that Florence was essentially composed of three distinct classes: the many, the fewer and the very few. The 'many' were all those plebeians who simply desired *libertà* ('liberty') and who could be mollified by the workings of the *Consiglio Maggiore*. The 'fewer' were all those *ottimati* and *popolani* who desired *onore* ('honour') and who could be accommodated by lifetime election to the senate. Finally, those 'very few' and rare individuals who seek the highest power of all were natural candidates for the exalted position of *gonfaloniere a vita*. Hence there was a place for everyone in this scheme of things. Giannotti's politico-philosophical navel-gazing, though certainly unoriginal when compared with the ideas of other aristocratic political theorists like Guicciardini, was emblematic of Florence's desperate endeavour to define those ideals for which the city was now supposedly fighting. The Florentines were being expected once more to unite behind the banner of 'republicanism' but, after some difficult soul-searching, many concluded that republicanism meant sacrificing one's life or livelihood so that the same old *ottimati* and *popolani* families could retain their usual privileges. In truth, four-fifths of the city's population desired neither *libertà* nor *onore* but far more basic, practical necessities like simple employment and a few loaves of bread a day to feed their family. In reality they would look to whosoever could provide the *pace* in which those elementary needs could be met, regardless of whether republican or Medicean.

The siege soon settled down into the usual monotonous round of desultory artillery exchanges salted by the occasional, infrequent but spirited sally by the defenders. In one artillery battle Mario Orsini was killed whilst in the routine process of inspecting the integrity of the fortifications. His relative Napoleone Orsini meanwhile accepted the Emperor's gold and quietly absconded from Florence with his *bravi et capitani*. There was only one major assault against the city, on 11 November, but it was beaten back by the determined defenders supported by cannon fire from Michelangelo and Sangallo's well-designed bastions. The main military actions took place well away from Florence in the depths of the Tuscan *contado*, principally around the regions of Empoli and Volterra. These towns were successively invested by the Imperialists under Alessandro Vitelli and the marchese del Vasto but were relieved by the vigorous and decisive actions of the Florentine war commissioner Francesco Ferrucci, who quickly acquired a reputation amongst the admiring Florentines for his dash and fire. But Ferrucci's accomplishments were offset by failures at Pistoia, Prato and also Pietrasanta on the coast. Food shortages began to tell by April and May of 1530 and plague was an ever-present danger as conditions in the city steadily deteriorated.

Bravely, Florence's youths kept their spirits up as best they could with lively games of Florentine-style football in the Piazza Santa Croce. Two opposing teams of twenty-seven brightly-liveried players would score *caccie* or 'points' by touching down the ball at their opponents' end of the pitch. It was generally a gentlemanly affair and a far cry from the more brutal English version of the game, which the diplomat Thomas Elyot would describe in 1531 as more a 'bloody and murthering practise, then a felowly sporte or pastime'. The youths who participated took pride in their beguiling appearance and their colourful clothing which showed off their physiques to the very best advantage. The painter Jacopo Carucci, better known as Pontormo, immortalised two such typical youths armed and wearing their militia clothing in two famous paintings completed in Florence during the time of the siege. In his *Portrait of a Man in a Red Cap*, which probably depicted the eighteen-year-old aristocrat Carlo Neroni, and in his more famous *Portrait of a Halberdier*, whose hotly disputed subject is possibly a youth named Francesco Guardi, Pontormo presents us with images of two self-assured, even cocky, *giovani* who are dressed and equipped ready to defend their republican liberties *fino alla morte*. This spirit of belligerence was briefly and terrifyingly manifested in June 1530, when there was a spirited sally from the city by the militia. Before launching their attack, the Florentine commanders had given instructions that, in the event of a rout, any militia still remaining within the city should slay the women and children, 'so that with the destruction of the city there shall not remain anything but the memory of the greatness of the soul of its people'. It might have fallen to young men like Pontormo's two subjects, Neroni or Guardi, to carry out this appalling patriotic atrocity. Fortunately, however, in the event no such order was ever given.

An eleven-year-old Catherine de' Medici was still trapped inside Florence. Although safely sequestered at the convent of the Santa-Maria Annunziata della Murate she rapidly became the focus for republican hatred and was terrorised and subjected to death threats. Some within the civil administration unkindly suggested that she be lowered naked in a basket before the city walls as a target for the Pope's own troops. Others advocated even more spitefully that she be despatched to a military brothel where, having been forced to service the common soldiers, her chances of a noble marriage would be sabotaged forever. It was under these conditions that Silvestro Aldobrandini was sent to fetch her on the evening of 20 July 1530 and move her to the Santa Lucia convent where she had begun her captivity several years earlier. Here, she would be at considerably less risk of being smuggled out of the city to safety with her Medici kinsmen while the authorities prevaricated as to her ultimate fate. Since Aldobrandini came for her in the middle of the night with armed soldiers Catherine had been deeply traumatised, believing that Aldobrandini had come to bring her to her execution. She had shaved her head and donned the habit of a novice nun, bravely challenging the authorities to commit sacrilege by executing a poor, devout novitiate. In the event, Silvestro Aldobrandini and his men kept Catherine safe as she travelled the short but perilous route by donkey, running the gauntlet of angry mobs of jeering Florentines. Aldobrandini himself whispered constantly to his young charge not to worry for he would protect her from the baying mob.

On 3 August 1530, the tide turned for the Florentines. Aware that the imperial army was by now emaciated and considerably weakened by disease and lethargy, their hero Francesco Ferrucci had planned to advance with all his forces to Florence's relief. Unfortunately, Philibert of Orange had learned of this plan from his agents within the city and marched out with several thousand men, joining forces with his Calabrian commander Fabrizio Maramaldo and Alessandro Vitelli in the vicinity of the mountain village of Gavinana. The imperial forces numbered around 8,000 foot and 1,500 cavalry. Ferrucci himself had only about half that number. Florence's military council ordered their captain-general Malatesta Baglioni to march out and support Ferrucci by attacking the enemy from the rear but, unbeknown to them, the treacherous *condottiere* had already concluded a secret agreement with Pope Clement. Baglioni had previously been the ruler of Perugia after wresting control of the city from the papacy, having eliminated both his brother and his uncle in 1527. However, prior to joining Florence's war, Baglioni had been forced to abandon Perugia and his other Umbrian lands to Philibert and the Imperialists. Clement now agreed to prevail upon the Emperor to reinstate him in Perugia and pay him blood money provided that he betrayed the republic. In this request Baglioni now serenely complied.

As Ferrucci advanced courageously with his smaller force, Baglioni remained resolutely immobile. As battle was joined Ferrucci is said to have learned of the condottiere's betrayal and uttered the now immortal words '*Ahi traditor Malatesta!*' Nevertheless, Ferrucci himself was no pushover despite being drastically outnumbered. He had learned his trade in the crack companies of the Black Bands fighting alongside Giovanni della Bande Nere and he made a ferocious assault on the Imperialists, managing to kill the prince of Orange himself in a withering hail of harquebus fire as the latter led his light horse against the Florentine lines. The arrival of Maramaldo's reinforcement *landsknechts*, however, sealed the desperate Florentines' fate and by the end of the day's fighting their forces had been virtually annihilated. Ferrucci himself was captured and lying mortally wounded in Gavinana's little *piazza*; when Fabrizio Maramaldo came across the wounded commander he brutally despatched him with a sword thrust. It was a vicious and gratuitous act which would earn Maramaldo the infamy of having his name become synonymous in the Italian language with 'villainy', whilst the verb *maramaldeggiare* would come to mean 'the bullying of a defenceless victim'. The tragic yet valiant Francesco Ferrucci is, by contrast, memorialised in the Uffizi colonnade as one of the Florence's great and enduring heroes.

Nonetheless, the setback at Gavinana had effectively broken the back of the Florentine resistance. Once word of the disaster reached the city the defenders knew that no further relief would not be forthcoming. As Benedetto Varchi chronicled, 'Everyone, men as well as women, adults as well as children, was beside himself with fright and bewilderment'. The *signoria* despatched a delegation to meet with the dead prince of Orange's replacement, Ferrante Gonzaga, and Pope Clement's representative Bartolomeo di Filippo Valori (the latter, formerly a staunch republican, having defected to Pope Clement VII and the Medici side), and both envoys now insisted unconditionally on the restoration of the Medici in return for the cessation of hostilities. The fanatical republican rallying cry of: 'Florence in ashes rather than the Medici!', which Michelangelo himself had once supported, had now begun to ring hollow. As concessions to this demand, the Imperialist side was willing to grant full amnesty to the rebels, restore all territories formerly under Florentine rule and 'guarantee liberty' but, when the envoys returned with these terms, the demand for Medici restoration was rejected out of hand and the *signoria* ordered Baglioni and Stefano Colonna to mount an attack on the imperial camp, urging the Florentines to emulate the sacrificial example of the citizens of Saguntum in 218 BC.

But by now it was effectively all over and Baglioni, who had already been bought off by Clement and Charles, simply declined to follow orders. Backed as he was by his professional troops the military council could do little. The city militia meanwhile, less fervent than the diehards in the anti-Medicean administration, refused to countenance the destruction of their city and agreed together with Baglioni to stand down and begin the process of disbanding. On 12 August 1530, Lorenzo Strozzi, Pierfrancesco Portinari, Bardo Altoviti and Jacopo Morelli signed Florence's terms of capitulation. The provisions were left accommodatingly vague and there was no explicit promise that the Medici would be permitted to return to Florence merely as private citizens rather than as rulers. The agreement simply stated that Florence would agree to swear fealty to the Emperor, who would decide within four months as to what form of government the former republic would be given. For his part, Charles demanded 200,000 ducats recompense from Florence to cover his military expenses and the imperial army lingered menacingly outside the city while this sum was hastily gathered. Fifty nervous Florentine citizens were surrendered as surety for the payment being met.

Pope Clement VII was meanwhile afraid that the city might be subjected to a sacking like Rome had recently experienced. He was not alone in this concern. Cardinal Ippolito de' Medici, still vainly harbouring hopes that he (and not Alessandro) would be assigned the job of ruling Florence, had written to Bartolomeo Valori urging him to do all in his power to prevent the imperial troops from despoiling the city or otherwise misbehaving themselves. Alessandro Vitelli's 600 Italians provided security for the interim regime during this time and Valori summoned a *parlamento* which called into being a *balia*. There would be no political reprisals, at least not for the time being, but this was the least of peoples' concerns. The city itself had been left in a parlous state by the siege. Francesco Guicciardini wrote that 'The misery and ruin of the city and the *contado* are unspeakable, greater than we can possibly imagine'. No harvest had been brought in for that entire year and there had been no sowing of crops either. Manpower for both industry and agriculture was in short supply and extraordinary taxes had drained peoples' wealth. Deaths from plague and malnourishment had skyrocketed and some 8,000 of Florence's defenders had been killed in open battle. In all, some 36,000 Florentines had ultimately perished during the ten month siege, a figure that represented one third of the city's entire population; only 54,000 people remained alive in the city.

When Charles V's prognostication came through in July 1531 it could not have been to the Florentines' liking although it must have seemed inevitable to the realists amongst them. The regime was to be restored to the status quo prior to 1527. Alessandro de' Medici would be known as the 'duke of the republic of Florence' and the Emperor's word as Florence's suzerain was to be considered final; if the former republicans dissented from the imperial ruling concerning the restoration of Medici power they would be treated as rebels and shown no quarter. But overall there was a valid concern by the *otto di guardia* not to entirely decimate Florence's ruling class, such as it was. In the event, only six of the more senior rebel leaders were beheaded. The presiding republican *gonfaloniere* Raffaello Girolami was sentenced to decapitation. He escaped death by loaning out the finger-ring of Saint Zanobi, which he had in his possession, to cure a malady then afflicting the son of his captor the imperial commander Don Ferrante Gonzaga. Girolami received instead the punishment of life imprisonment and was removed from Florence to the citadel of Volterra to prevent him from fomenting sedition against the new regime. Silvestro Aldobrandini was also spared death and, after a short detention in prison, was exiled thanks in large measure to the intercession of Bartolomeo Valori ('one of the least cruel although the most powerful of the *palleschi*') and Catherine de' Medici, to whom Silvestro had shown both care and kindness during her hazardous journey to the Santa Lucia convent.

A further 190 or so republican rebels were rounded up and sent into exile; however most of these were of the younger sort who had received military training in the militia, men such as those whom Pontormo had immortalised in his paintings. Such individuals, who were mostly little more than hot-headed youths, had no place in the mature political and office-holding process going forward and could be safely deported in the interests of public order. As Francesco Guicciardini had written to Bartolomeo Lanfredini on 6 November 1530, to penalise too many of the *huomini da bene* ('gentlemen of quality') 'would diminish too much the little *virtù* that remains in the city, which the weaker it is the weaker the government will be'. As always, Guicciardini's sentiments were coloured by class interest and to Lanfredini he further added: 'The city is very exhausted. Those men who used to be wealthy are now all afflicted. Shops are closed and if you should pass through San Martino, you would only be frightened to see that of 64 shops that used to be open before the war, only 12 remain, and even they are severely weakened. The same is true in all the other businesses where men used to turn a profit.' Guicciardini's message was clear – Florence's *ottimati*, those who traditionally *avere lo stato*, should be preserved as far as possible and not penalised since their wealth and commerce was the city's very lifeblood.

This invariably left the poorer sort, or else certain formerly vocal republican friars, to bear the brunt of the authoritarian crackdown as scapegoats. One particularly heinous episode involved the imprisonment of Benedict Tiezzi da Foiano, a Dominican friar from the Florentine convent of Santa Maria Novella. Upon the restoration of the Florentine republic Benedict had returned from exile in Venice to Florence, transforming the Convent of San Marco, Savonarola's old monastery, into a centre for political and spiritual reform. But when the republic subsequently fell he was arrested by Malatesta Baglioni and imprisoned on Clement VII's orders in the dungeons of the Castel Sant'Angelo, where he later died of neglect and starvation in September 1531. As a former member of the republican *Nove della Milizia*, Michelangelo himself was obliged to go into hiding. After his sojourn in Venice he had returned again to Florence to participate in the final weeks of the siege, making some much-needed repairs to the badly damaged Campanile of San Miniato al Monte and directing the restoration of the crumbling fortifications. Bartolomeo Valori despatched soldiers to Michelangelo's house to arrest him but, suspecting something was afoot, the artist had already fled and gone into hiding at the house of Giovanni Battista Figiovanni, the former Prior of San Lorenzo. Figiovanni appears at some point to have moved the fugitive to the crypt under the altar space of the Medici Chapel since these seem to bear the imprint of the bored Michelangelo's graffiti. Clement VII may have been many things but towards Michelangelo he could never be vindictive and when he learned that the genius had gone into hiding he sent word to Florence that he was not to be harmed. Michelangelo emerged from his place of refuge, not too much the worse for wear, although profoundly depressed by the recent turn of events; he went back to his studio, picked up his hammer and chisel, and stoically went back to work.

In order to spare his two nephews the backlash of the citizens' outrage Pope Clement held off from sending either of them to Florence for the time being.

Ippolito was kept at Rome whilst Alessandro was sent to accompany the Emperor on his progress through Germany. The Venetian ambassador to Rome, Antonio Soriano, noted that Clement was keen to keep Alessandro's interests front and centre with the Imperial Court and concerned that Charles's earlier promise of a union with his daughter Margaret may not be followed through if Alessandro were kept out of sight and out of mind. Knowing Alessandro's lazy and self-indulgent temperament, the Pope was also eager to entice the boy away from Rome's notorious fleshpots for a few months. The boy was already the most dreadful wastrel and Clement must have worried about placing so much responsibility for the future of the family on his undeserving shoulders.

CHAPTER 20

Florence's Black Prince

If the State's in peace and ever quiet,
Then never can its splendour wane
But ours, like one that's fared too well,
Whose wealth and beauty none could tell,
Has plunged us into dearth and pain.

Lamento di Fiorenza, 2, ii

In the aftermath of the Emperor's coronation visit Alessandro de' Medici's star was very much in the ascendant, with Ippolito increasingly playing, in effect, second fiddle to his younger cousin. Pope Clement's affections certainly seem to have been firmly in Alessandro's favour at this time, as reflected by the many honours and emoluments which he now showered upon the dark-skinned, frizzy haired 'prince'. On 13 November 1529, the Pope had made Alessandro governor of Spoleto in the Papal States. It was an effortless sinecure, one which he could delegate to one of his functionaries whilst he himself sat back and collected the fat governor's fee. Then, during the Christmas celebrations of 1529, Alessandro was further honoured by being given the role of water bearer for the papal ablutions, a role which was considered second only to the Emperor himself in order of ceremonial precedence.

On the reasons why Ippolito fell out of favour whilst Alessandro now rose in Clement's estimation we can only really speculate. The education, bearing and polish of the former, which received much praise from foreign diplomats, was certainly never in question. For this reason alone perhaps Clement had been resolute in his desire to see the more capable of his two nephews follow him into the high ranks of the Church. When the viceroy of Naples, Cardinal Pompeo Colonna, died on 28 June 1532, Ippolito replaced him as vice-chancellor of the Church, a move which–as was usual in the endless game of musical chairs that was papal vacancies–set tongues wagging with the customary allegations of 'poisoning'. But Cardinal Ippolito subsequently repaid the Pope for this prestigious, influential and highly profitable post by failing to attend Clement's consistories, using the time instead to go hunting with his *bravi* and other secular hangers-on. Born into privilege and at a young age advanced effortlessly through the upper echelons of society and the Curia, Ippolito had failed to grasp the essentials of how to please one's benefactor. It was a foolish mistake and one which to Ippolito's detriment his rival Alessandro would *not* make.

Meanwhile in Germany, Alessandro had his feet squarely under the imperial table. At Augsburg, Frankfurt, Cologne and Aachen the swarthy duke of Penne dined daily with the Emperor and his brother King Ferdinand of Hungary and in the evening they poured over maps discussing military strategy for the upcoming Crusade against the Turkish Sultan. There seemed little doubt in Charles's mind that his future son-in-law Alessandro de' Medici would rule as his personal representative in Florence, just as his prospective nephew-in-law Francesco II Sforza would rule in Milan as his imperial vassal there. Dynastic alliance with this now chastened and compliant Medici pope was very much a cornerstone of imperial policy in Italy and all Alessandro really needed to do was prove that, on a personal level, he was equal to the task of ruling in Charles's name. At Brussels, on 25 January 1531, he was rewarded for his successful charm offensive on his prospective father-in-law by being introduced to the young Margaret of Austria. It was the first time that the nine-year-old Margaret would meet her future husband-to-be and what's more it was also the first time she had met her natural father Charles V. Margaret had been raised under the tutelage of her namesake, Charles's aunt Margaret, but following the latter's death in December 1530 Margaret's guardianship had been assumed by Mary of Hungary, who had succeeded Margaret as regent of the Netherlands. In Ghent, Alessandro merrily hunted and jousted, earning the unending plaudits of his hosts and a small army of diplomatic observers who watched his every move with bemused interest. He must have cut a dashing figure for young Margaret, herself still only really a child, and her own immaturity led her to overlook Alessandro's numerous personal failings such as his impulsiveness and his volatility.

Back in Italy, Cardinal Ippolito continued to vex His Holiness. Despite his numerous rich benefices he lived extravagantly and well beyond his means. The Pope often took him to task over his spendthrift ways but it proved to no avail. On 18 April Ippolito suddenly quit Rome and showed up in Florence against the Pope's express orders, causing something of a diplomatic panic amongst Clement's administration. Was this the start of a coup d'état? If so, it would betray to the Emperor certain structural family weaknesses within the House of Medici; it might even jeopardise Alessandro's prospects of becoming an imperial vassal. The Pope's representative in Florence, Nicholas Schömberg, was notified to be on the alert, as indeed was Alessandro Vitelli the *condottiere* in charge of Florence's armed forces (this, incidentally, was the same Vitelli whose father Paolo had been executed by the Florentines in 1499 and many quietly questioned the wisdom of introducing Alessandro into a position of such power in Florence). Cardinal Innocenzo Cybò was meanwhile despatched from Rome to consult with Ippolito on his intentions. It seems, however, that the crisis had been a storm in a teacup, Ippolito's motivations had been driven more by the need to seek additional funding than by any real intention to seize power in Florence. On his return, a relieved but annoyed Pope Clement paid off his debts to the tune of around 12,000 ducats, and provided him with an income of 800 ducats a month to tide him over in his lavish lifestyle. But foreign observers remained sceptical. The move resembled, at least on the surface, a half-baked power grab. Ippolito's animus towards Alessandro was also well known and furthermore–despite his status as a cardinal–he had recently set his cap at marrying his young niece Catherine de' Medici, who was reportedly besotted with Ippolito. Through his erratic behaviour Cardinal Ippolito de' Medici had, in short, become the proverbial loose cannon on deck.

Alessandro de' Medici arrived back in Florence on 5 July 1531 by way of Prato, where he had stayed briefly since there was a plague scare in Florence. He was greeted outside the city gates by Roberto Acciaiuoli and Luigi Ridolfi who accompanied him into the city amidst much pomp and fanfare. The following day the provisional handover of power took place at the Palazzo della Signoria. Nicholas Schömberg the papal nuncio was in attendance, as was the Pope's secretary Jacopo Salviati, as was the imperial envoy Giovanni Antonio Muscettola and the new *gonfaloniere* Benedetto Buondelmonti. Muscettola treated the assembled ruling council to an uncomfortable harangue about the rebelliousness of the Florentines (unfairly, since Florence had never been an imperial fief to begin with) and vouchsafed that the Emperor would forgive them their past transgressions provided they settled down to loyally accepting the new *imperial* status quo. Duke Alessandro de' Medici was then named by the first secretary and chancellor, Francesco Campana, as ruler of Florence *in perpetuo* along with his male descendants, whereupon he was ceremonially handed the keys to the city's various fortresses.

For this young Renaissance prince life could hardly be any better. He held court at the Palazzo Medici (whose suites he had ordered to be considerably improved and upgraded with new expensive decorations and wall hangings) and spent most of his time honing his hunting and riding skills, activities which Baldassare Castiglione had greatly commended in any accomplished rising courtier. When not exercising and developing his physique by riding his many fine horses he was being fitted for the latest men's fashions in expensively imported silk, damask and velvet, Florence's once stringent sumptuary laws by now but a quaint memory of a more conservative mercantile past. The troublesome business of actually governing was left to his and Pope Clement's many functionaries and supernumeraries. Francesco Guicciardini, that tirelessly loyal servant of both Florence and the Pope, was one such reliable individual. The late Niccolò Machiavelli's good friend Francesco Vettori was another. Other family names who participated in day-to-day government read like a roll call of Florence's history: the Strozzi managed, despite their love-hate relationship with Pope Clement, to remain influential, not least in their capacity as papal bankers. The Capponi, Valori, Acciaiuoli, Ridolfi and Pucci families also took their share in government duties. Superficially at least it seemed like a return to the times of the old Medici oligarchy of Cosimo de' Medici and Lorenzo the Magnificent although with a twist – despite having been carefully positioned as 'first amongst equals' Alessandro de' Medici was in reality the undoubted hereditary duke of Florence in all but name. The observance of hallowed republican form was specious and its implementation a pretence. Backed by the twin power of the papacy on the one hand and the Emperor on the other, Alessandro exemplified this himself by wearing round his neck a heavy gold chain of office with which his future father-in-law had presented him in Germany along with many other fine and expensive presents. It was a symbol and a reminder, if ever one was needed, that behind Alessandro's personal rule lay the full backing of imperial power.

In early October, the Pope received the welcome news that Martin Luther's Swiss counterpart Huldrych Zwingli, who had once famously alluded to the 'silly little ceremonies' of the Roman Catholic Church, had been defeated and killed at the Battle of Kappel. It was one of the few victories that the Catholic powers seemed to be experiencing as the German and Swiss reformations continued apace north of the Alps. Basking in this success, Clement now turned his attention to Florence, canvassing the members of Alessandro's ruling council as to the exact form which the new government ought to take. Present at the session were Francesco and Luigi Guicciardini and Francesco Vettori as well as Roberto Acciaiuoli. All concurred that the government would need to be a narrowly-controlled one based around the core of the Medici family and its closest political *amici*. However, it was pointed out that, unlike in the past when Medici banking wealth had been able to construct a broad *reggimento* of clients and supporters, the present situation was somewhat different. The current Medici regime would have to be imposed on Florence by the minority and this depended upon the ruling acumen of Alessandro and the loyalty of the guards and pro-Medici forces which he had at his immediate disposal. None of the officials averred, however, that the political situation would in any way be improved by elevating Alessandro to the dukedom of the city. On 3 April 1532 a council of twelve men was established to put into effect the political reforms which had been discussed with the Pope. Florence's Great Council of Three Hundred was reduced to a two hundred strong body and was supplemented by a smaller council of forty-eight. Final political power was, however, to reside in a new body called the Supreme Magistracy. This would comprise Duke Alessandro, his lieutenant, and four councillors who were to be selected from amongst the council of forty-eight. The *otto di pratica* would continue to have oversight over foreign policy and the *otto di guardia* would monitor and regulate Florence's domestic security.

Despite the appearance of the same old *ottimati* family names in this new resurrected Medici *reggimento*, this was no longer the civic humanist republic of old; it was to all intents and purposes a Medici police state. The head of the *otto di guardia*, the dreaded police magistracy, was a *Milanese* named Ser Maurizio da Milano whose nickname was 'the Butcher'. He had a reputation around Florence for being a martinet. Benvenuto Cellini relates in his *Memoirs* how his friend Tribolo explained Ser Maurizio's strict enforcement of the rules against carrying personal weapons within the city limits. Maurizio, says Tribolo, was the sort of person 'who for the least offence used to plague and persecute everybody, so that travellers were obliged to keep their swords bound up till they had passed the gate'. Cellini, who had survived the Sack of Rome, found this practice vaguely amusing. The historian Benedetto Varchi writes of how Ser Maurizio's men habitually entered people's dwellings searching for weapons and other contraband. Varchi describes these men as '*la schiuma de ribaldi*', quite literally the 'froth, foam or dregs of humanity' ('scum' basically), what Giuseppe Baretti amusingly describes in his *Dizionario delle lingue Italiana* as 'hang-dogs' or 'Newgate-birds'. Meanwhile, Alessandro Vitelli obligingly served the role of military enforcer for the Duke.

Although personal weapons were made illegal within the city limits, Alessandro himself flouted these rules and made gifts of the very latest German-made harquebuses and matchlock handguns to his friends and hangers-on, who brazenly flourished them in the streets. Official permission was meantime required for anyone seeking to leave the city at night. A climate of fear and quiet paranoia settled upon the city. Anyone suspected of being a supporter of the *popolari* or radical republican element could be denounced in a trice. Paid spies and informers were rife throughout the city. Ironically, Alessandro's regime had, knowingly or unknowingly, adopted precisely those kinds of practical political measures that had been advocated in *The Prince*, techniques for which Niccolò Machiavelli had been so heavily censured by the Florentines (today we would probably think of Machiavelli in terms of having been a 'politically incorrect' outsider). Indeed, had they taken a leaf from Niccolò's many writings on political science, Florence's republicans may have been able to prevent the Medici restoration. Nevertheless, all this was now moot for on 1 May Alessandro formally assumed the reins of government. One of his first acts was to conduct an inventory of the contents of Florence's now defunct centre of government, the Palazzo della Signoria. The fire sale of the old republican government had begun.

Having secured and formalised control over the government, Alessandro's regime now felt sufficiently strengthened to magnanimously relax some of the restrictions which had been placed on the 150 or so exiled dissidents and their families. However they were still under orders not to live within thirty miles of Florence, Rome, Venice, Genoa or Ancona lest they associate together and foment sedition. Pope Clement's friend Benvenuto Cellini, who had taken up service in Alessandro's artistic entourage, came across a small group of such Florentine exiles while on a routine assignment to Ferrara. These were the brothers Niccolò and Piero Benintendi and an older man, the historian Jacopo Nardi, all from reasonably well-to-do *ottimati* families but by now far more radicalised than those dissidents like the Strozzi, the Ridolfi and the Salviati who had managed to remain in Florence. There had been an awkward confrontation followed by a slight altercation in an inn situated on Ferrara's great square. In no uncertain terms Niccolò Benintendi had loudly vented his feelings towards Florence's new ruler. Jacopo Nardi had tried to calm things down but Benintendi had persisted in his invective. When he went too far and called Cellini a jackass, Cellini (ever the hero of his own tales) had allegedly drawn his sword and sent the scoundrels tumbling down the inn's stairs in fright. Some dissidents meanwhile unwisely ventured too near to Florence thus infringing the terms of their exile. One such deportee, Giovanbattista da Castiglione, had been captured by 'the Butcher' and imprisoned at the Bargello. But luckily for him, instead of being executed he was subsequently granted clemency by Alessandro and set free.

Other more prominent dissidents were less fortunate. The deposed republican *gonfaloniere* Raffaello Girolami was still the cause of on-going agitation, despite having been removed from Volterra and thence to a more secure prison in Pisa. What is more, Girolami had a powerful advocate in Ferrante Gonzaga. Gonzaga had somehow persuaded Pope Clement to allow Girolami to come and go freely on a bond of 20,000 ducats but, as Luigi Guicciardini complained, this sort of leniency was no way for a new regime to imprint its authority upon the people. How would the Florentines take the regime seriously when Gonzaga and his ally Nicholas Schömberg, Clement's papal nuncio, were both understood to be lobbying the Emperor for a full pardon for Girolami? Neither was Girolami any dilettante when it came to diplomatic manoeuvring, he was potentially a very dangerous political adversary. In 1522, Niccolò Machiavelli had favoured him with an exhortative letter entitled *Advice to Raffaello Girolami when he went as Ambassador to the Emperor*. In this piece of helpful diplomatic prepping, Florence's maestro at simulation and dissimulation had famously advised Girolami that 'if, to be sure, sometimes you need to conceal a fact with words, do it in such a way that it does not become known, or, if it does become known, that you have a quick and ready defence'. Girolami's mastery of Machiavellian techniques would ultimately avail him nothing, however, and Alessandro's advisers had their way – at some point Girolami was found poisoned in his prison cell in Pisa and thus ended the threat which he posed to the new regime. The Duke's iron hand had finally emerged from the velvet glove and was on full display. Machiavelli might have offered sage advice to Raffaello Girolami but he had also counselled princes that 'Men should be either treated generously or destroyed, because they take revenge for slight injuries – for heavy ones they cannot'. Alessandro had acted within the full scope of Machiavellian principles.

Another casualty in the dungeons of Pisa was the hapless Giovanni Battista della Palla. In 1528, della Palla had been commissioned to collect for the French king 'large numbers of antiquities of every sort, that is, marbles and bronzes, and paintings by masters of his Majesty'. This was to be done with the cynical intention of luring François and his army to Florence's assistance with the bribe of the city's finest artworks. Della Palla went about his scheme with preternatural verve, syphoning up many of Florence's most exquisite private and public treasures. One of his principle appropriations was the great 8 feet high statue of *Hercules* which Michelangelo had carved in 1493 following the death of his *padrone* Lorenzo de' Medici, which was purchased by Filippo Strozzi and which had stood proudly for many years in the courtyard of the Palazzo Strozzi. Della Palla sent the piece to François who put it in his palace at Fontainebleau (after it was moved to the Jardin de l'Etang the piece subsequently vanished from history around the year 1714). When Margherita Acciaiuoli, the wife of Pierfrancesco Borgherini, learned that della Palla planned to ship her marriage bed to France because it contained some exquisite panels painted by Pontormo she had dug her heels in, excoriating della Palla as 'a vile salesman, a little tradesman who sells for pennies'. Della Palla received his comeuppance when he was tortured most cruelly by Alessandro's men before being murdered in his prison cell.

Many of these political exiles and dissidents now gravitated towards Alfonso d'Este. Although d'Este had joined the last French League to supposedly 'save the papacy' from Charles, the French king had nevertheless needed to bribe the duke of Ferrara with the papal cities of Modena and Reggio. Charles's own visit to Modena in September 1529 had only served to further legitimise d'Este's title and naturally this rankled with Clement who would have preferred to have seen both of these fiefs ceded to the papacy. But he swallowed his displeasure and instead wrung from d'Este the concession that the Duke would refuse safe haven to the Medici's enemies. Some exiles had even found their way to the court of King François I. One such was the poet and statesman Luigi Alamanni. Alamanni, a contemporary and associate of Machiavelli, was a native Florentine whose father had been a Medici *amici*. Alamanni himself had unwisely taken part in a conspiracy against Cardinal Giulio de' Medici, a plot for which his friends Luigi di Tommaso Alamanni and Jacopo del Diacceto had been executed, and he personally had been forced to seek refuge in Venice. After the expulsion of the Medici in 1527, he had returned to Florence and taken an active role in the republic's affairs, but in 1530 he had been forced to flee once again, this time to France. François warmed to him, recognising his obvious wit and intelligence and would later make him his official ambassador to Charles V (who was similarly charmed by Alamanni's obvious diplomatic gifts). He was a particularly fine poet (Alamanni's *Opere Toscane* ('Tuscan Works') were first printed at Lyons in 1532-3) and François took as much pride in his artistry with words as Pope Clement VII took in Benvenuto Cellini's artistry in metals. To Alessandro, however, he was merely just another rebel fugitive.

As the exile predicament still lingered with Alessandro's government vacillating uncertainly between draconian measures on the one hand and leniency on the other, Cardinal Ippolito persisted in getting himself into all sorts of trouble. In July 1532, he had been despatched as papal legate *a latere* to Charles's armies in Hungary as the Emperor confronted the Sultan Süleyman. Here, affecting Hungarian fashion in his personal dress, he demonstrated more interest in soldiering than in the life of a cardinal. He disembarked in the Balkans at the head of 10,000 papal and Italian troops. As G.P. Carpani notes in Thomas Roscoe's 1822 edition of Benvenuto Cellini's *Memoirs*: 'He possessed all the qualities fitted for a prince but by no means for an ecclesiastic. With a fine person, and accomplished in every manly and elegant art, he soon became weary of the churchman's gown, and delighted to wear the sword and mantle of the chevalier.' By September and October 1532, however, Ippolito was safely well behind the lines at Linz in Austria. In October a mutiny had erupted amongst the Emperor's troops over the usual thorny question of pay. Cardinal Ippolito had been in command of a flying column of harquebusiers who had been despatched to link up with the mutineers in northern Italy. At San Vito al Tagliamento, fifty miles east of Florence, he was however arrested by imperial officials upon suspicion of having himself participated in the mutiny. It was only through Pope Clement's desperate intercession that he was ultimately released and exonerated.

By November 1532, Charles V himself was back in Italy for further discussions with the Pope. Clement dragged himself reluctantly to Bologna to meet with his imperial overlord. The English Bishop of London, Dr. Edward Bonner, has left us with a vivid picture of a miserable and ailing Pope as he made his way to see his Emperor: 'you shall understand that the 18th of November the Pope, taking with him only in his journey and company six cardinals with no great number, entered his journey towards Bologna, not keeping the common way, which, as you know, is by Florence and foul enough, but by Perugia and the lands of the Church; six other cardinals to make up a brown dozen, and yet not all good saints, taking their journey by Florence with the rest of the company. The said journey to the Pope, by reason of the continual rain and foul way, with other unfortunate accidents, as the loss of certain of his mules and the breaking of the leg of one Turkish horse that he had, special good, and above all for the evil lodgings that he had with his company, was wondrous painful; the Pope divers times compelled, by reason of the foulness and danger of the way, to go on foot the space of a mile or two and his company; besides that pleasure and pastime, for lack of a featherbed, compelled to lie in the straw.'

Alessandro also went to see the Emperor Charles, but so too did a delegation from Florence's disgruntled exile community. While Alessandro spent time with Charles the government of Florence came under the control of a new face, that of Cardinal Innocenzo Cybò, who had arrived in Florence by the middle of November. The cardinal took up residence at the Palazzo Pazzi, which had formerly been owned by his parents Maria Maddalena de' Medici and Franceschetto Cybò, and which was now owned by his brother Lorenzo Cybò. Franceschetto himself had died in 1519 following a journey to Tunis, whilst Maria Maddalena had died in Rome in 1528 just after the Sack and had been interred in St. Peter's Basilica by order of her cousin, Pope Clement VII. Like

Cardinal Silvio Passerini before him, Cardinal Cybò was generally disliked by the Florentines not least because, being half *Genovese*, he was regarded as a foreigner. But his private life was at the same time held up to vigorous scrutiny by Florence's self-appointed prudes. It was whispered that the cardinal had made a cuckold of his own brother Lorenzo with his wife Ricciarda Malaspina, Marchesana of Massa (who was the sister of Alessandro's own lover Taddea Malaspina). Lorenzo himself had been appointed by Pope Clement as *capitano della guardia del palazzo apostolico* on 11 November 1527 whilst Clement had been secluded at Orvieto and had largely prospered under the rule of the Medici popes. Parmigianino's portrait of Lorenzo shows a rather fierce looking red-bearded *condottiere* whom one would not ordinarily wish to cross, so it is worth speculating whether he was aware that his brother was humiliating him behind his back or whether the illicit affair was by Lorenzo's own tacit consent. Ricciarda and her sister-in-law Caterina Cybò suffered no diminishment in their reputation for grandeur, by being courted by these lord cardinals, but for all that were nevertheless described in 1524 by one observer in Rome as being 'ugly as devils'.

On 13 December Alessandro and the Emperor Charles reached Bologna and met with Pope Clement. From Charles's perspective, the main purpose of the visit was to discuss ways in which to create an Italian league to defend imperial interests south of the Alps. To achieve his ends he held over the Pope's head the threat of convening a Church Council, something calculated to strike fear into the heart of any sitting pope. From Clement's side, he needed to somehow avert such a council on the one hand and, on the other, reach a resolution concerning the future of Lorenzo's daughter Catherine de' Medici, the titular duchess of Urbino. Charles had mooted that she might be married off to Francesco II Sforza in the place of his niece Christina of Denmark but Clement was distinctly unenthusiastic. He had already matched her with Prince Henry, the second son of King François I of France. This poor lad, now thirteen years old, had been locked up with his brother the *Dauphin* François in a Spanish gaol cell for almost four and a half miserable years. Like his brother, his temperament had, due to his suffering, grown distant and morbid. His father François was however characteristically unsympathetic, showing open favour towards his younger son Charles, Duke of Angoulême. As a coping mechanism young Henry had developed an overweening fondness for the man who had orchestrated his and his elder brother's release from the Spanish – Anne de Montmorency, the Grand Master of France.

Charles V was naturally opposed to any French match for Catherine. The Venetian ambassadors Bernardo Navagero and Nicholas Tiepolo wondered why Charles had pledged his own daughter to cement an alliance with a pope whom he fundamentally distrusted and who seemed intent on going his own divergent way in matters of foreign policy. Francesco Guicciardini deliberated that Charles might even cancel Alessandro's marriage with Margaret of Austria if the Pope persisted in his French plans. But in the event, Clement proved himself the shrewder diplomat. He knew that Charles could not take seriously the French King's intention of uniting his royal line with that of a mere Florentine burgher family. He therefore went ahead regardless and made his agreements with the Pope since he needed Clement's cooperation to consolidate his domination of Italy. He betrayed this weak hand by making a major concession to Clement; writing to Mary of Hungary in Brussels, he commanded that his daughter to made ready to travel to Italy for the completion of her remaining education. Clement, meanwhile, had obtained François's official confirmation for the betrothal from the French cardinals Tournon and Grammont in Bologna. By the end of February 1533, negotiations having reached their conclusion, the Emperor prepared to depart Bologna for Andrea Doria's independent imperial protectorate of Genoa.

Margaret of Austria, who had just turned eleven, arrived in Verona on 18 March 1533. The plan was for her to go to Naples and spend several years maturing there before her final betrothal to Alessandro de' Medici. Naturally, for the Medici there was some urgency in sealing the dynastic union with the Emperor's illegitimate daughter. Pope Clement VII was not getting any younger and his health was already failing (in truth he had never fully recovered from the experience of Rome's sacking); if he should die the next pope would almost certainly not be a Medici and so the scramble for papal and imperial benefices, titles and emoluments would begin all over again with a fresh pontifical dynasty in power. As may be imagined, Margaret's arrival in Florence was a lavish affair. No expense was spared to spruce the city up for her ceremonial entry. The streets had been decorated by hangings and tapestries and tables groaning with food and wine had been laid out for the common people. Margaret's chaperone was Madame de Lannoy, the wife of the late viceroy of Naples Charles de Lannoy.

On 6 May Margaret reached Rome where she held court and received the Venetian ambassador. Already she was learning the profession of imperial statesmanship at a tender age. Alessandro rode to Rome to be with his future bride, lodging with Ippolito de' Medici at the Medici palace. The two rivals made the best of things, appearing in public together and maintaining at least a semblance of cordiality, even though each of them seethed at the competing political designs of the other. After a stay of only one week in Rome, Margaret went on to Naples. As a farewell gift Alessandro gave her some fine gold work specially commissioned from Benvenuto Cellini. He then returned to Florence where he officiated at the celebrations of the feast of St. John the Baptist, the showpiece event of which was the horse race known as the *palio*. Whilst the Florentines enjoyed the spectacle of the *palio*, which at least hearkened back to the gay rule of Lorenzo the Magnificent and activities like his joust, they buckled under the weight of the new tax demands for the year. Alessandro had commissioned a new fortress for the city and a forced loan of 35,000 ducats had been levied to fund these new defensive works.

On 1 September 1533, Catherine de' Medici set off for Marseilles for her wedding with Prince Henry of France. She was attended part of the way by Alessandro de' Medici although her cousins Palla Ruccellai and Maria Salviati and her uncle-in-law Filippo Strozzi accompanied her the rest of the way to France. On 6 September she arrived at La Spezia where the duke of Albany awaited with eighteen galleys and six brigantines to bring her and her entourage the rest of the way to France. Catherine arrived off the port of Marseilles one week later and was welcomed with hovering boats filled with musicians who came out to greet her. Anne de Montmorency, the Grand Master of France, had arranged the passage of both Catherine and the Pope and no expense had been spared for their arrival. Clement himself had elected not to pass through Florence on his way to Marseilles. Some suggested that it was to avoid unnecessary expense to the city authorities; others ventured that he knew he would not be welcomed there (it was in fact the second time in recent years that he had avoided passing through Florentine territory, the other being when he had gone by way of Perugia to visit Charles in Bologna). The exiled dissidents were still causing trouble and some of them were now based in Lyons, not far from the wedding festivities at Marseilles. Clement, for his part, set sail from the mouth of the River Arno with thirteen of his cardinals in tow as well as a large entourage comprising lesser ecclesiastics and representative from Italy's secular nobility. He reached Marseilles on 11 October.

François, who had arrived several days earlier, watched the Pope's flotilla sail regally into port. When Clement stepped ashore he was greeted by a delegation of France's most senior ecclesiastics. The following day Pope Clement VII made his formal ceremonial entry into the town accompanied on either side by the dukes of Orléans and Angoulême. On 13 October, King François made his equally regal entry into the city and greeted his papal guest. Here too was Cardinal Ippolito and his entourage, newly returned from his recent stint as papal legate to Charles V's army in the Balkans. They were all flamboyantly dressed in the Turkish style, of which they had grown enamoured and they showed off to their French hosts by brandishing their exotic curved Turkish scimitars in place of their normal Italian dress rapiers. Ippolito was still thinking and behaving more like a secular prince than as a 'prince of the Church'. The obvious comparisons with Cesare Borgia could not have been plainer for all to see.

On 23 October Catherine finally made her own triumphant official entry to Marseilles attended by twelve maids-of-honour. The assembled dignitaries were exhausted from ten days of feasting and entertainments but, as bleary-eyed as they were, none could fail to be impressed by the magnificent show which the Medici had put on for Catherine's wedding. Catherine de Medici herself would never be acknowledged as any great beauty; her facial features bore the slightly heavy Medici characteristics about the cheeks and jowl and her eyes bulged slightly from their sockets. She compensated for her physical shortcomings, however, with her lively intelligence and winning courtly manners and also with her sumptuous dress sense, for which Florence had been taxed mercilessly in order to put on a suitably magnificent show to the French aristocracy.

Giorgio Vasari included the scene of Pope Clement presiding over the couple's marriage as one of his frescos in the Sala di Clement VII in Florence. Vasari had taken pains to seek out eyewitness testimony of the event before putting brush to canvas. The mural shows the Pope flanked by the bride and groom, the latter stooping slightly to take his bride's outstretched hand, his father King François standing just behind his son's left shoulder and Catherine's surrogate mother Maria Salviati–immediately recognisable by her black dress and coif–hovering just behind the Pope. From beneath Catherine's skirts peers her dwarfish female fool whilst Prince Henry's own dwarf swaggers proudly, hands on hips. Emerging from beneath the Prince's elegantly stockinged legs is a chimerical beast resembling a cross between a dog and a lion. No expense had been spared on the nuptials. Catherine had been granted a trousseau worth 100,000 scudi, which had been loaned by Filippo Strozzi's Bank against future papal earnings and which was to be repaid to Strozzi in two future instalments. François also granted the child bride an annuity of 10,000 livres a year and a fine château for her residence.

The bride and the groom were both fourteen years old. Prince Henry was tall, good looking and well-built but his years in Spanish captivity had made him reserved and taciturn. Still, egged on by his father, he made the best

564

impression that he could. In common with her new husband, Catherine too had experienced deep personal suffering during her time in captivity in republican Florence and the profound terror which she felt for civil war would remain with her for the rest of her days. The pair made for a melancholy match at best. No one was under any misapprehension that this was a love match. These two young people had been thrust together for the express purpose of joining the House of Valois, the House of Medici and the Court of Rome in a dynastic alliance designed to recoup France's power and prestige, lost since the Treaty of Cambrai. Nevertheless, when François witnessed their consummation that night he merrily reported that 'each had shown valour in the joust' and when the Pope visited them in their bedchamber the following morning they both appeared satisfied and serene in each other's company.

One might have imagined that the bitter experience of the Sack of Rome and his own subsequent humiliating flight to Orvieto would have chastened Clement into accepting the pre-eminence of the Emperor Charles V. However the marriage of Catherine and Henry betrayed the fact that Clement had not lost his taste for double-dealing, even though he had little talent for it. Secret negotiations between the Pope and François now ensued as in years past. Catherine's claim to her late father's duchy of Urbino was reinstated; François insisted that Prince Henry–in his capacity as consort to the Duchess–had claim to Urbino and plans were now laid to raise a French army to recapture the city-state from Francesco Maria della Rovere, by now a lord in his early forties. Before parting company the King and the Pope exchanged final gifts. The King gave Clement a gorgeous Flemish tapestry depicting the Last Supper, whilst the Pope reciprocated with a casket comprising of 24 panels of rock crystal which had been intricately engraved by Valerio Belli with scenes from the Life of Christ. Moreover, in the consistory of 7 November 1533, Clement created four new cardinals, all of them French: Jean Le Veneur, Claude de Longwy de Givry, Odet de Coligny and Philippe de la Chambre. Charles V was also in Marseilles for talks with the Pope and these went ahead separately from those being held with the king of France.

But François, in his eagerness to deal himself back into the game of Italy, had not demonstrated much foresight. The alliance was predicated solely on the continued good health of Pope Clement. Should Clement die it was almost certain that Cardinal Ippolito, notwithstanding his role as vice-chancellor of the Church, would not be able to garner sufficient support to be elected as his natural successor. He would therefore be unlikely to safeguard Medici dynastic interests using Rome's deep pockets. Nor, for that matter, did Ippolito have the slightest interest in becoming the next Pope, bent as he was on a more secular princely career. In Clement's absence, all that would be left would be the remnant of Duke Alessandro de' Medici in Florence, who was Charles's vassal, Cardinal Ippolito de' Medici at Rome and the four newly minted French cardinals together with their French colleagues. Cardinal Ippolito was all the more unreliable since he was known to be making his own independent approaches to the Emperor Charles. Ippolito had suggested, somewhat unsubtly, to the Emperor that if Charles replaced Alessandro with himself as duke of Florence it would be better received by the Florentines and hence less expensive for the treasury to maintain an imperial presence in the duchy.

But Charles was a very different person from Clement for, once he had made up his mind on a certain course of action, he stuck to it. Alessandro had been his chosen candidate for ruler of Florence and his regime was by now effectively synonymous with imperial authority there. It was highly unlikely that Alessandro would be unseated through any act of the Emperor. Indeed, having consolidated political control over Florence, by 1533 Alessandro was already happily expanding Florence's influence towards the *Pisano* plain. As part of his policy of establishing strongpoints in this formerly troublesome region he commissioned the construction of the Medici Villa di Camugliano. On the surface just another Medici country retreat, the villa was in fact a fine example of Renaissance fortified architecture, with its scarp walls and reinforced towers. The placement, on the huge square military parade ground of a lawn, of Giovanni Bandini's sculpture *Hercules Killing the Hydra* was moreover a none too subtle indication of Pisa's fate should it ever again challenge Florentine rule. Observing these chess moves, France's ambassadors concluded that Alessandro was a dutiful and obliging imperial proxy in Tuscany. Accordingly, they prayed for a long life for Pope Clement VII.

Ill feeling towards the Medici was still rampant. In December 1533 a servant of Gabriello de' Rossi had uttered 'very dishonest words about His Excellency the Duke and the state and the Pope' to his neighbour Orlando Bovarli. The former had suggested that Alessandro could be assassinated whilst he was out hunting, but their imprudent conversation had been overheard and the two men were swiftly detained and summarily executed. That same month, relations between Alessandro and the Strozzi were also marred by misbehaviour and acts of vandalism involving members of that family and their entourage; in May 1531 Roberto and Vincenzo Strozzi had abducted a young girl from the town of Prato and subjected her to rape. Then, on Christmas Eve in 1532, during a boisterous game of Florentine football in the Mercato Vecchio, Roberto and Vincenzo had repeatedly kicked their ball amongst the market stalls causing disruption to ongoing business and damaging merchandise. In May 1533, Leone Strozzi and his friends had further blotted their copybook by playing a gratuitously violent prank on a doctor from Pavia. Alessandro had by this time taken to wearing mail shirts beneath his clothing as a precautionary measure and had a small wardrobe of such garments which had been specially tailored for him. The House of Medici still had grim recollections of the murder of Giuliano de' Medici in 1478; a sore which was still an open one for Giuliano's own son Pope Clement VII. Having learned once that their enemies might stoop to assassination, the Medici would not be blindsided again. This fear of assassination caused the regime in Florence to drift inevitably towards ever greater authoritarianism.

Around this time, there now arrived in Florence the key figure of Lorenzino de' Medici. A problematic and somewhat quixotic character, Lorenzino ('Little Lorenzo') was, as we have already noted, the eldest son of Pierfrancesco the Younger and Maria Soderini. He had been born in Florence in 1514 and had been educated for a while at Camerino together with his cousin Cosimo di Giovanni della Bande Nere (born 1519) and his more distant relative from the main Medici line, Alessandro de' Medici. All three boys were from approximately the same generation. During the crisis of 1526, when the imperial *landsknechts* had nearly sacked Florence, the twelve-year-old Lorenzino and seven-year-old Cosimo di Giovanni had been spirited away to Venice for safety and they had not been present when Alessandro and Ippolito were ejected from Florence later the following year. As a youth Lorenzino led an itinerant life, moving from the Veneto to Bologna and thence to Rome. Here, however, he earned the opprobrium of Pope Clement VII for deliberately decapitating some ancient Roman statues in the forum with his sword and defacing some bas-reliefs on the Arch of Constantine. For this gratuitous act of vandalism, which scandalised Rome's cultural conservationists, Lorenzino earned himself the nickname *Lorenzaccio* or 'Bad Lorenzo'. Angrily ordered by the Medici pope to leave Rome, in 1534 he returned to the city of his birth to seek his fortune.

In Florence, Lorenzino was reunited with his younger brother Giuliano di Pierfrancesco as well as his two sisters Laudomia and Maddalena; both sisters would eventually marry Strozzi brothers – the two sons of Clarice de' Medici and Filippo Strozzi the Younger. Laudomia would marry Piero Strozzi in 1539, whilst at the same time Maddalena would marry his younger brother (the exonerated rapist) Roberto Strozzi in a double-wedding. As we have already seen, Filippo Strozzi's household had been quite outspoken in their censure of the reinstated Medici regime and this served to cast a pall on Filippo's relations with his former benefactor Pope Clement VII. The men's relationship was further tainted by the fact that the Pope had still not repaid Strozzi the debt he owed him for Catherine de' Medici's recent marriage trousseau. Soon, the hot-headed Lorenzino would find himself amongst future brothers-in-law who sympathised with their father's anti-Medicean sentiments. Furthermore, being half-Soderini as well, Lorenzino's maternal family had been fairly comprehensively victimised by the Medici during Pope Leo X's era. Not only had the republican Piero Soderini been deposed as *gonfaloniere* but Cardinal Francesco Soderini had also been disgraced by the Medici. Given his family background it was ironic therefore that, soon after arriving in Florence, Lorenzino should become a firm favourite of Duke Alessandro and one of his principle partners in crime. For a confused and tempestuous young man like Lorenzino the conflict of loyalties must have been akin to being pulled in opposite directions by wild horses. To further compound matters, being a writer–and a passably good one at that–Lorenzino was also afflicted by the classic 'artistic temperament' which contributed to his emotional turmoil. In fact, so gifted a writer was he that Alessandro would later commission Lorenzino to pen a play to celebrate his marriage to Margaret of Austria, no small honour; Lorenzino would oblige him with *Aridosia*, a comedy which incorporated stylistic elements of Plautus and Terence and which was much admired at the time by Florence's theatre-goers.

While Alessandro and Lorenzino were busy bonding, the architect Antonio da Sangallo the Younger was called in by Pope Clement to further upgrade Florence's defences. As an imperial city, the Pope now owed it to Charles V to provide adequate fortifications to protect his investment. This process had begun not long after the city's recapture when a committee of five Procurators for the Fortification of the City and the Countryside was appointed in October 1531. They maintained their predecessors' sensible policy of prohibiting any construction close to the city walls that would provide cover to a besieging enemy. Next they commissioned the upgrading of an existing bastion that was situated at the Porta alla Giustizia. This so-called 'Gate of Justice', which was situated at the end of the Via dei Malcontenti in the south-eastern portion of the city just north of the Arno, was so-named because during the fourteenth-century it had been the starting point for the long walk that all criminals took prior to their execution. This state-of-the-art new bastion was fitted with 160 emplacements for guns, cannon and falconets of varying calibre.

In March 1534, Sangallo was once more approached by Clement, in some secrecy it ought to be said, to consult on the design of a completely new *fortezza* to be constructed at the Porta a Faenza along the northern city walls. This would be the Fortezza di San Giovanni Battista, more popularly known as the Fortezza da Basso, and it would be completed by 1537. Assisted on the project by Pierfrancesco da Viterbo, da Sangallo created an impregnable, forbidding-looking, pentagonal monstrosity of a Renaissance fortress, the first of its size and technical sophistication in Italy. Distinguished by its five intimidating diamond bastions, the *fortezza* boasted a prison, an integral arms factory, covered walkways and underground tunnels for making rapid troop dispositions. Bearing the Medici coat of arms, the Fortezza da Basso was built just as much to threaten and coerce the poor Florentines than to repel any foreign invader. Ironically, the fort–as impressive as it undoubtedly was–would never fire a shot in anger.

At the same time that Alessandro's regime was entrenching its rule through the latest military technology the Medici continued to embellish their benign enlightened reputation and their dynastic legacy through the propagandising arts. That same year Giorgio Vasari painted Alessandro dressed in full armour wielding a great golden staff of office. If the authoritarian overtones were implicit (surprisingly this was the first armorial portrait of any member of the Medici) then the princely pretensions were also clear for all to see. Another Medici portrait, Vasari's strangely unsettling posthumous representation of Lorenzo *il Magnifico*, painted in 1533/34, depicts the former Medici *capo* seated amongst his treasured collections, one of which is a large vase which bears the inscription VAN OMNIUM VIRTUTEM ('the vessel of all virtues'). The inference was obvious – that both Lorenzo and the Medici family as a whole were to be considered 'repositories of virtue'. This was a far cry indeed from the injudicious rule by intimidation that was in fact taking shape in Florence around this time.

One particular individual who would undertake no further work on Florence's fortifications was Michelangelo. He had by now discharged his obligation to Clement VII (who had saved his hide) to complete the commissioned work on both the Laurentian Library as well as the Medici New Sacristy in the Church of San Lorenzo, delegating much of the final finishing work to his three assistants Niccolò Tribolo (who had been Cellini's good friend), Raffaello da Montelupo and Giovanni Angelo Montorsoli while he himself spent ever more frequent sojourns in Rome. By the time that he had left Florence for good towards the end of 1534 (he would never again return to the city) he had left behind him the completed so-called 'Medici Chapel'. The project had taken him, on and off, fourteen years to complete. It consisted of a square space, encircled by a cupola, the walls of which were festooned by various ornamental columns and fake windows; on opposing walls of the chapel stood the tombs of Giuliano and Lorenzo de' Medici, both of which were adorned by four fully completed sculptures of Night and Day, Dusk and Dawn. Between each set of allegorical sculptures sat funerary monuments of Giuliano the duke of Nemours and Lorenzo the duke of Urbino, both depicted as classical heroes of antiquity. Michelangelo had in this work succeeded in combining the Christian view of immortality with an entirely pagan and humanist meditation on the glorification of finite man himself. The project, which had its original genesis in the frustrated dynastic hopes of the Medici family, turned out instead to be an artistic triumph, a *tour de force* and one of Michelangelo's greatest artistic gifts to Florence. The ornamental embellishments, which were also a major feature too of the Laurentian Library, would inform the Mannerist movement in Baroque architecture which was to follow well into the late sixteenth-century.

568

Michelangelo himself had by now grown fearful of Alessandro and had no desire to linger further in what was fast becoming a somewhat sinister Florentine police state. He returned to Rome where, despite his earlier support for the Florentine republic, he was nevertheless warmly embraced by Pope Clement who, unlike his cousin Pope Leo X, recognised and admired the artist's genius. He took up residence near the church of Santa Maria di Loreto and the Pope commissioned him to paint a large fresco of The Last Judgement which would cover the entire altar wall of the Sistine Chapel. It was a suitably apocalyptic theme which reflected everything that Clement had recently endured. The fresco would depict the Second Coming of Christ and his Judgement of the souls of humanity. The dead would be portrayed as rising from their graves, anxiously twisting and writhing in torment, to be consigned to either Heaven or to Hell. Michelangelo had already drawn up some of the cartoons for the fresco and the Pope approved them. Clement intended the mural as a grim, propagandistic reminder to the Lutheran heretics that no conceivable salvation could possibly exist outside of the Roman Catholic Church. The artist's own troubled inner state at this time is made manifest in the work itself – the disturbing self-portrait that Michelangelo would eventually include depicts him as the flayed skin gripped in the left hand of Saint Bartholomew the Apostle. Michelangelo always did have something of a martyr complex it must be said.

It was well that Michelangelo had quit Florence for, in his absence, Alessandro was already establishing his reputation as a tyrant-in-the-making. In his *Storia Fiorentina del Secolo XVI, Volume 1*, the humanist and Church reformer Pietro Carnesecchi tells of how a certain Alessandro Schiattesi was playing *palla* one afternoon outside the Palazzo Medici with his eighteen-year-old son Ormanno, bouncing the ball off the wall of the *palazzo*. When a Medici servant emerged to remonstrate that they were making too much noise and telling them to buzz off, an altercation had followed in the course of which Ormanno had slapped the impertinent servant who then reported the assault to the Duke's major-domo. As a result of his intemperate act, the unfortunate Ormanno was hauled from his bed in the middle of the night by the gentlemen of the Watch and carted off to the Bargello where he was sentenced 'amidst infinite misery' to have his hand severed. This gory incident had transpired on 12 May 1534. The implication was clear: an assault upon the Duke's servants was to be construed as an assault upon the Duke himself.

Given his private republican opinions, Buonarroti therefore had every reason to fear for his safety. For the next seven years in Rome, while he laboured on *The Last Judgement*, he nevertheless found some semblance of peace. One of the more positive developments in his life around this time was the deep and enduring friendship that he struck up with Vittoria Colonna, the widow of Fernando Francesco d'Ávalos, Marchese di Pescara – the Neapolitan general who had been instrumental in the capture of King François at the Battle of Pavia. Vittoria had–during the sixteen years of their marriage–seen relatively little of her late husband, who had been continually in the wars, yet when he died she was grief-stricken and took solace in writing poems. Vittoria was a well-educated, accomplished poetess in her own right and maintained an avid correspondence with many of the luminaries of the age such as Pietro Bembo, Luigi Alamanni, Baldassare Castiglione, and the historian Paolo Giovio (she was also on friendly terms with Ambrogio Politi, the fanatical Dominican heresy hunter known as *Il Caterino*, who would later accuse *The Last Judgement* of being a sacrilegious work of art). Vittoria was forty-two and Michelangelo himself was by then approaching his sixtieth year when they first met. She became a generous benefactor and friend to the artist and Buonarroti would pen the following poem to his beloved muse, who would continue to excite and intrigue him until her death in 1547:

> Seeking at least to be not all unfit
> For thy sublime and boundless courtesy,
> My lowly thoughts at first were fain to try
> What they could yield for grace so infinite.
> But now I know my unassisted wit
> Is all too weak to make me soar so high;
> For pardon, lady, for this fault I cry,
> And wiser still I grow remembering it.
> Yea, well I see what folly 'twere to think
> That largess dropped from thee like dews from heaven
> Could e'er be paid by work so frail as mine!

Sebastiano del Piombo had painted Vittoria's likeness in 1520 when she was twenty-eight but the rather wooden portrait somehow does not seem to do her full justice. Giovio did better when he gave this description of her eyes: 'Resembling the eyes of Venus, Vittoria's eyes are black, as if edged by shining ivory. However, they are not coquettish. Their beauty is due to affectionate cheerfulness, protected and decorated by eyelids and eyelashes like tender wings. Her eyebrows are slightly curved in elegant lines.' Michelangelo's own drawings of Vittoria (he would never paint or sculpt her) are some of the most intimate and personal works that he would ever produce. This slightly melancholy, certainly depressed widow and the quiet, determined, inner strength of spirit with which she struggled against her diminished circumstances, fascinated him endlessly. One portrait shows a slightly androgynous profile with a Classic Grecian nose, a face not entirely dissimilar from his statue of *David*. Another sketch catches Vittoria as she turns her neck to glance wistfully across her shoulder. 'From near and far my eyes can see where your beautiful face appears' Buonarroti wrote achingly of his latest muse.

Tommaso Cavalieri, a strikingly handsome Roman nobleman then in his early twenties, was another of Michelangelo's close friends at this time. They had first met in 1532 and for the for the fifty-seven-year-old artist the infatuation, though most probably only Platonic, was instant and electric. 'If I yearn day and night without intermission to be in Rome, it is only in order to return again to life, which I cannot enjoy without [my] soul', the artist had written to the young courtier. Given his romantic tastes and proclivities Rome was certainly more conducive than Florence, especially under the fiercely anti-sodomite Savonarola who had detested Florence's reputation as Italy's capital of homosexuality. In fact, Michelangelo seems to have turned his back on his fellow countrymen by this time and, to all intents and purposes, was now living the life of a Florentine *fuoriusciti*. 'I never knew a people more ungrateful and arrogant than the Florentines', he would grumble to anyone who could be bothered to listen. Cavalieri himself would later be left many of the artist's works in his will but, louche Roman aristocrat that he was, he would fail to preserve many of these soon-to-be priceless heirlooms.

In Florence meanwhile, despite all the artistic propaganda, the brutal and licentious nature of Alessandro's rule were by now fast becoming apparent. Numerous historians have made particular reference to the Duke's promiscuity and not without good reason. Although betrothed to young Margaret of Austria, like most noblemen of the era he had an official mistress, Taddea Malaspina, to whom he seems to have been reasonably devoted. Taddea, the younger daughter of Alberico Malaspina, Marquis of Massa, and Lucrezia d'Este, would bear Alessandro two illegitimate children, Giulio and Giulia, sometime between 1533 and 1535. However, despite his status as a family man, Alessandro was also developing an unsavoury reputation for deflowering the daughters of Florence's aristocracy. When the Florentine exiles had earlier presented their case against the Duke to the Emperor Charles, their spokesman, Jacopo Nardi, had not pulled any punches. Florence, he informed Charles V, was now a city in which terror reigned alongside political repression and where men feared for their lives whilst women feared for their honour.

Nardi complained how Alessandro had overseen the construction of his 'great fortress, built with the blood of her unhappy people as a prison and slaughterhouse'. Nardi himself was an acknowledged admirer of Michele di Lando the low-born *gonfaloniere* during the *Ciompi* rebellion, which Nardi had likened to two heroes of ancient Rome, Curius and Fabricius. His sympathies therefore were perhaps somewhat left-of-centre for an avowedly Imperialist court like Charles's. Francesco Guicciardini was easily able to deflect Nardi's criticisms of his master the Duke, speaking eloquently (if perhaps somewhat tongue-in-cheek) in defence of Alessandro's 'prudence' and his 'virtuous habits'. Then again it must be borne in mind that it was Guicciardini, the master of double-edged rhetoric, who had once described Lorenzo the Magnificent as: '*sarebbe impossibile avesse avuto un tiranno migliore e più piacevole*' by which he gave *il Magnifico* the dubious back-handed compliment that 'it would be impossible for Florence to have had a better tyrant'. It therefore paid for Alessandro to have a man like Guicciardini on his payroll.

Objectively speaking, that Alessandro had other outlets for his animal passions aside from the aristocratic Taddea Malaspina is, given the habits of the time, probable; and whether all of his trysts were entirely consensual is perhaps questionable. The judgement of subsequent scholarship towards Alessandro's sexual peccadilloes has always erred on the harsh side. Some contemporary observers refused to beat around the bush. The Franciscan chronicler Fra Girolamo Ughi openly wrote of Alessandro's 'disordered lust' and alleged that 'He began to profane and dishonour convents and women both noble and plebeian, now with one and now with another', although adding somewhat more intriguingly, 'but never, however, with force', implying mischievously that the nuns themselves were already wanton. Ughi was merely reaffirming what the pious Jacopo Nardi had already vouchsafed to Charles V when he reported that Alessandro 'much inclined and turned towards love affairs and had little respect for the honour of women whatever their condition, so much that one believes that even the virgins consecrated to God in their convents were neither secure nor spared from his lust'.

It had taken several generations but, if their critics were to be believed, the Medici duke was now behaving towards his fellow Florentines in just as predatory a fashion as the debauched Visconti dukes or indeed the notable *roué* Galeazzo Maria Sforza had behaved towards the long-suffering *Milanesi*. By all accounts Alessandro's followers seem to have emulated his licentious ways, leading the eighteenth-century English historian James Pettit Andrews to conclude that 'This dissolute prince encouraged his courtiers to practice every odious violence with impunity'. Later, writing from the prudish perspective of the nineteenth-century, the historian Thomas Adolphus Trollope (elder brother to the novelist Anthony Trollope) was even more censorious of the Duke's lifestyle, commenting that 'His life was one continued orgy. The ministers to his lawless will were ruffians, chosen from among the vilest of mankind; ... and these men were made, not only the ministers to, but the companions of, his pleasures; and the companions also of the young, wealthy, and the beautiful among the aristocracy of Florence.' The sycophants and reprobates who surrounded Alessandro had seemingly become a law unto themselves.

One particular incident stands out and this was the sexual insult which had been offered (not once, but on several different occasions) by Giuliano Salviati to Luisa Strozzi, the daughter of Clarice de' Medici and Filippo Strozzi, a young woman who was the wife of one of the city's leading patricians, Senator Luigi Capponi (nephew to Florence's former *gonfaloniere* Niccolò Capponi). The remark offered had been: 'I'd really like to give you one!' or words to that general effect. Being one of Alessandro's boisterous *amici*, Salviati evidently felt that he was immune from the normal rules of gentlemanly conduct and had let the remark slip while intoxicated during a festive supper and ball held to celebrate the marriage of one of Duke Alessandro's favourites, Guglielmo Martelli. However, the matter had not simply rested there and Salviati had pushed his luck with Luisa on two further occasions. On the third occasion that he had uttered the suggestive remark it was overheard by Luisa's older brother Piero Strozzi who immediately took exception to Salviati's impudence. Piero Strozzi was not the sort of man anyone would have wanted to tangle with in sixteenth-century Florence; he had a foul temper, was a habitual duellist and in later years would become a well-known and fearless *condottiere*, fighting alongside Mary of Guise in Scotland. Several months elapsed before Giuliano Salviati was suddenly and mysteriously set upon by a gang of masked men as he was strolling alone through the streets of Florence. Stabbed a number of times in the torso and thigh, his wounds, though not fatal, left him crippled with a permanent limp. Not unsurprisingly suspicion fell immediately upon Piero Strozzi who, together with his brother Maso, spent a short spell in a cell in the Bargello before being released for lack of evidence and thanks also to his powerful family connections.

Understandably, the Luisa Strozzi affair did little to improve the Duke's relations with the already critical Strozzi clan, but it does call attention to the general tone of Alessandro's rule around this time. And this tone was further degraded with the arrival of 'Bad Lorenzino' who pandered to the Duke's tastes and proclivities as a way of gaining his master's trust. Indeed, Cellini mentions that he 'often found him [the Duke] taking a nap after dinner, with his kinsman Lorenzino de' Medici', so clearly the two men were already on friendly, intimate terms. Lorenzino's mother, Maria Soderini, disapproved of her son's conduct. She was still locked in the same bitter tussle over family assets and inheritances with Maria Salviati which had bedevilled relations between Caterina Sforza and Lorenzo di Pierfrancesco *il Popolano*. The fact that Lorenzino was spending far beyond his means in a fruitless attempt to keep pace with Alessandro's opulent lifestyle was a constant source of irritation to her.

In Rome, Pope Clement VII's health was by this time fading fast. He had already been suffering from stomach complaints upon returning to Italy from France in December the previous year. By July the situation was looking serious and, as July progressed into August, it looked downright grim. Cardinal Agostino Trivulzio, who had taken it upon himself to keep François meticulously informed of the Pope's condition, wrote to the king of France with the news that Clement's condition was by now grave and that his doctors believed essentially that the Pope was dying. One of Clement's final acts had been to rule in favour of Queen Catherine of England on 23 March 1534. Characteristically as usual, Clement's decision was, as the saying goes, a day late and a buck short. Anne Boleyn had already been crowned queen consort on 1 June 1533 and had given birth to Princess Elisabeth, the future queen of England, by September the same year. The very same day that Clement issued his pronouncement, Henry VIII was having his Act of Succession read aloud in Parliament for the third time (placing Princess Elizabeth first in line to the throne) and by November 1534 an Act of Supremacy was passed which effectively stated that the king of England was now the head of the Church of England and denying Rome's spiritual authority in the realm. By the time of Henry's illegal and bigamous marriage Clement had already excommunicated the English king, recalled the papal ambassador and severed all diplomatic relations with the kingdom. England would embrace the Protestant religion and its young and headstrong King Henry would assume the role formerly occupied by the Pope himself.

But Pope Clement VII was thankfully spared this final humiliation of learning of England's Act of Supremacy because by 25 September 1534 he was pronounced dead at the age of fifty-six. His death came just two days after he had welcomed Michelangelo back to Rome and discussed *The Last Judgement* with the maestro. The Pope had eaten a meal containing the highly poisonous 'death cap' mushroom known as *Amanita phalloides* and his already enfeebled constitution could not cope. Had he been poisoned? This may very well have been the case, for in truth nobody wanted him around any longer. In the ungenerous words of Francesco Guicciardini, Clement *'morì odioso alla corte'* ('died odious to the court'). Paolo Giovio was less circumspect, accusing Clement of '... divers abominations. He was a bastard, a poisoner, a sodomite, a geomancer, a church robber.' The late Pope's body would never again return to Florence but was instead interred at St. Peter's where person or persons unknown desecrated the tomb's inscription *Clemens Pontifex Maximus* by replacing it with the scrawled pun *Inclemens Pontifex Minimus*. His corpse had also at some point been transfixed by someone's sword, the final degradation in a pontificate which had been marked by failure, disillusionment, a devastating Sack of Rome, colossal doctrinal defeats for the Roman Catholic Church and the corresponding growth of heresy, and the final ascendancy of Spanish and German imperial power throughout Italy.

Clement himself had betrayed something of the cynicism and disenchantment which he felt at the lot which he had drawn when he remarked bitterly: 'I tell you that in this world the ideal does not correspond with the real, and he who acts from amiable motives is a fool'. Clement's corpse found its eventual resting place in the Dominican church of Santa Maria sopra Minerva in Rome where it lies to this day. As a pope, Giulio di Giuliano de' Medici had been a dismal failure. As a cardinal he had shone. As both a Medici and the illegitimate son of a low born Florentine woman, he had made the very best of his situation. But for better or worse the era of the Medici popes was now for the time being suspended and the political landscape would now change dramatically for the worse for the House of Medici. There would be just two further Medici popes, both largely undistinguished – Pope Pius IV (a descendent of a distant *Milanese* branch of the family) and Pope Leo XI (the great-nephew of Pope Leo X), whose reign was destined be one of the briefest in history, lasting just under a month.

Cardinal Alessandro Farnese, so often derided in the past by his peers as 'Cardinal Fregnese'–'Cardinal Petticoat' or rather, less kindly, 'Cardinal Cunt'– accepted the papal diadem after a single solitary day of deliberation in conclave and was elected on 12 October. The sixty-seven-year-old cardinal, who had rode his beautiful sister Giulia's petticoats all the way to the pontifical throne, would now be known throughout Christendom as Pope Paul III. Despite having been close to Cardinal Giovanni de' Medici in their younger years, this new pope would however be no friend to Florence; instead of Florentine bankers he would instead now look to *Genovese* financiers to provide new lines of credit for the Court of Rome. The great wheel of pontifical politics had revolved once more, as it always inevitably did.

Florence greeted the news of the Medici Pope's death with relative calm. From the as yet uncompleted Fortezza da Basso no armed troops were disgorged to settle an anti-Medici uprising which had been anticipated but which failed to materialise. No Florentines poured onto the streets this time around and, anticlimactically, the Spanish troops inside the Fortezza stood down. The peoples' republican spirit had finally been broken, but all the same, Alessandro's militia were nevertheless placed on a state of high alert throughout Tuscany in expectation of any trouble. Those few potential dissidents who unwisely raised their heads above the parapet during this time, or indeed anyone who casually uttered any incautious or inflammatory words in public, were dealt with harshly by the *otto di guardia*. As an additional precaution, the prohibition on the carrying of swords and daggers within Florence was further extended to a three mile limit around the city. This prohibition applied even to Alessandro's crony Lorenzino, who later resentfully recorded in his *Apologia* that the Duke 'never allowed me to carry arms and always kept me disarmed as he did with the other citizens, all of whom he suspected'.

In France, with Pope Clement VII's death, Catherine de' Medici's suitability as the consort of a prince of France was suddenly thrown into question. Overnight, those French naysayers who had disparaged the little *duchessina* as 'a grocer's daughter' and described the marriage as a *mésalliance* found themselves justified in their assessment of a Medici union which was now worth, in effect, zero. *'J'ai reçu la fille toute nue'* ('the girl has come to me stark naked') was, according to the Venetian ambassador's report, François's own exasperated comment on the situation. In today's parlance he had been sold a lemon. The territorial agreements between the King and the Pope still remained unfilled and only part of Catherine's dowry had ever been paid. Prince Henry himself quickly tired of his short, plain Medici wife, preferring instead the charms of his beautiful, much older, French mistress Diane de Poitiers (who was in fact Catherine's second cousin through her mother, Madeleine de La Tour d'Auvergne). Fortunately, Catherine had been able to find an ally in the King's mistress Anne d'Hailly, Duchess d'Etampes, who admired the Medici girl's feisty spirit and adopted her into her circle, which was known as '*La Petite Bande*'.

Alessandro's reaction to his unfortunate sister's predicament is not recorded. Soon after Clement's death he sat for a portrait by Pontormo, in fact one of the most famous portraits by which he is known. In the painting, Alessandro is seated dressed entirely in black robes, as though in mourning, his pale hands rest on a parchment on which he is sketching the likeness of a female head, his face is pensive and sorrowful. Behind him a casement window lies partially ajar, and through this open window there have been discerned traces of a *pentimento* – that is to say, an erased second figure whose identity remains unknown. Was the mystery figure the image of Pope Clement VII, reputedly Alessandro's true father? It is a mystery about which we can only speculate. The artist himself was by now in his fortieth year, descending into the melancholy and depression which would characterise his later years. An ardent admirer of Michelangelo, Pontormo strove to equal and even surpass the maestro's style but would always fall far short. He was a victim of that phenomenon which sometimes afflicts overly ambitious artists, that of epigonism, the slavish devotion to a master who came before, the word itself being derived from the ancient Greek ἐπίγονοι – 'progeny' or 'coming after'. Pontormo's artistic rival Giorgio Vasari, who operated a competing *bottega* to Pontormo's own school which was run in conjunction with Bronzino, would later use his famous chronicle '*Le Vite de' più eccellenti pittori, scultori, e architettori da Cimabue insino a' tempi nostri*' to demean Pontormo by making him appear silly and foolish in his old age. Competition for Medici patronage would always be a pretext for underhand dealings amongst Florence's artists.

The ramifications of the Medici pope's death would come in a slow burn, not in any immediate flurry of tumultuous disaster or any sudden uprising. It would for the most part be economic in nature. The Sack of Rome had, as we have already noted, dealt a body blow to Florence's local economy. The long months when the city had been under siege by the imperial army had removed one of the city's key markets. Placed, however, against the wider backdrop of decades of ceaseless war between France and the Empire played out on Italian soil, not to mention fresh competition from northern European city-states to Florence's traditional textile industries, many of the *ottimati* friends of the Medici had already by this time been financially ruined. Some of the greatest families of the city had lost merchandise, property, personal belongings and also–far worse–any possibility of obtaining future credit. It was just as bad for the professional bureaucrats and diplomats. Clement's demise and the abrupt end of the Medici papacy, that final spigot of largesse for the Medici *amici*, amongst them such loyal professional administrators as Guicciardini, Valori or Vettori, who had little independent means of their own, was merely the latest in a series of misfortunes.

But if Clement's demise had yet to make itself widely felt, one incident which does seem to have had more of an impact in Florence at this time was the sudden and unexpected death of Luisa Strozzi on 4 December 1534. Luisa had been dining the previous evening with her sister Maria and her brother-in-law Lorenzo Ridolfi but, shortly after returning home, had fallen sick with agonising stomach pains and 'died violently (*morì violentemente*) in ten hours'. Her death came barely nine months after she had been insulted by Giuliano Salviati at Guglielmo Martelli's wedding supper and speculation naturally now went into high gear amongst Florence's avid gossipmongers. In contemporary accounts there are two differing versions of what is alleged to have happened. Bernardo Segni (1504-1558) in his *Istorie fiorentine dall'anno MDXXVII al MDLV* suggested that, following Giuliano Salviati's infelicitous remarks to Luisa, Duke Alessandro himself had taken a shine to the vivacious young woman and had initiated his own sexual overtures towards her, which she had virtuously rejected. As a result of this rejection, claims Segni, Alessandro supposedly induced Salviati's wife to administer a poison to Luisa, which she gladly did (through a household servant) in revenge for the injuries inflicted on her husband by Piero and Maso Strozzi.

Benedetto Varchi (1502-1565) in his *Storia fiorentina* takes a very different tack, suggesting that Luisa's own family the Strozzi dispensed *un veleno corrosivo*, 'a corrosive poison', in order to pre-empt any stain on the family's reputation by this 'miserable and unhappy' (*misera ed infelice*) young man who was their duke. According to Varchi, Luisa was a lively and flirtatious girl who was in the habit of attending Duke Alessandro's debauched soirées and it was therefore concluded that her seduction was simply a matter of time. In other words it was an aristocratic 'honour killing'. However, as both of these historians were in service to Grand Duke Cosimo I, a healthy degree of scepticism is required when considering any account which automatically casts the shadow of blame on Alessandro. Whilst it was true that he was a notorious womaniser we must be careful not to give credence to the idea that he would have stooped to ordering the poisoning of a young woman simply because she rejected his romantic advances, as in Segni's account. Somehow this sort of heartlessness does not seem to be Alessandro's style at all. Varchi's account of an 'honour killing', on the other hand, sounds equally implausible and the death of Luisa Strozzi will doubtless remain, for now, one of those countless unsolved Renaissance mysteries that we must pass over in silence.

The Strozzi patriarch, Filippo the Younger, had meanwhile gone into self-imposed, voluntary exile together with his tempestuous son Piero. Following his participation in Catherine de' Medici's wedding celebrations in Marseilles, Filippo had declined even to return to Florence. Having made a favourable impression on King François, Filippo had determined instead to return with the newly minted French cardinals to Rome where he planned to assist them in the furtherance of French interests at the Curia. However, on his way back to Italy he was met on the border of the Romagna by his son Piero, who alerted him to the fact that both Alessandro and the crippled Giuliano Salviati were baying for Strozzi blood. Filippo weighed in his mind the malice which Alessandro harboured towards the Strozzi for having backed the republican rebellion that had cast him out of Florence all those years before. He decided that caution was the better part of valour and bypassed the republic. In the late autumn of 1534 he had also turned down the offer of an appointment as Florentine ambassador to the court of Pope Paul III and from now on Strozzi would be an outsider.

In exile, Filippo and Piero Strozzi were joined by Cardinal Giovanni Salviati, Cardinal Niccolò Ridolfi and Cardinal Niccolò Gaddi, all of whom were by now equally disgruntled with Alessandro's regime. Both Salviati and Ridolfi were grandsons of Lorenzo the Magnificent from two of his daughters – Lucrezia (Salviati) and Contessina (Ridolfi). As direct legitimate descendants of *il Magnifico* they chafed at the elevation of Alessandro, a youth who was little more than the illegitimate offspring of an exceedingly low-born woman, a mere household slave. Although himself not a member of the extended Medici family, Cardinal Gaddi had his own private reasons for disliking Alessandro. Like Filippo Strozzi the Younger he had been taken hostage by the imperial army and, like Strozzi, having been abandoned by the Pope, he too had been incarcerated in the *fortezza* of Castelnuovo for an inordinately long interval before gaining his freedom. Like Strozzi, Gaddi's own family was also a prominent Florentine mercantile and banking house which did extensive business in Rome alongside other *ottimati* houses like the Altoviti, the Capponi, the Salviati and the Ardinghelli. This included importing grain to Rome, a venture which required considerable capital outlay. Gaddi had been amongst the first batch of five cardinals whom Clement VII created in his consistory of 3 May 1527 just three days before Rome's sacking and his family had reputedly paid 40,000 ducats for the privilege. All these marginalised *ottimati* exiles naturally gravitated towards the court of Cardinal Ippolito de' Medici.

It would, on the surface, have made sense for these self-exiles to make common cause with the other dissidents already hunkering down in such places as Ferrara, Venice, Rome and Lyons, men such as the hotheads Niccolò and Piero Benintendi, for example, or the former republican enforcer Silvestro Aldobrandini whose life had been spared by Catherine de' Medici; or Luigi Alamanni in France, or Jacopo Nardi, the scholar-historian who would write his *Istorie della Città di Firenze* as a systematic justification for the exiles' arguments. There were others too, members of the Soderini, Giugni, Berardi and Carnesecchi families, who harboured their own individual grudges against the swarthy Medici ruler of Florence. However, be this as it may, there still existed a certain amount of mutual suspicion between these two factions – the *grandi* families who had until recently been heavily associated with the Clementine Medici regime on the one hand and, on the other, the more radicalised exiles who had been victimised by that same regime since the time of the proscriptions of 1531. The more moderate Jacopo Nardi tended to serve as an honest broker and go-between for the two factions.

They were soon secretly joined by one of the Medici regime's former insiders and key allies, Bartolomeo Valori. Valori had served as Pope Clement's papal commissioner to the imperial army which had laid siege to Florence from 1529-30. Most recently he had been Clement's governor of the Romagna but, with the recent nomination of Pope Paul III, he was now left unemployed and was forced to fall back on service within Alessandro's staff. But Valori had soon complained that the Duke 'did not account nor esteem him as he believed he deserved'. He also resented the fact that Alessandro had personally intervened to prevent his son's marriage to Filippo Strozzi's daughter. The Valori had always had a complicated relationship with the Medici. They had once been amongst Cosimo and *il Magnifico's* closest supporters, but in 1494 they had switched sides and joined that cluster of *grandi* families who had ousted the Medici from power. Bartolomeo's kinsman, Francesco Valori, had subsequently become *gonfaloniere* to the ardently anti-Medicean Fra Savonarola. However, Machiavelli's friend the writer Niccolò Valori had managed to claw back some family favour from Pope Leo X by writing a flattering and eulogistic biography of his father *il Magnifico* and thereafter the Valori were now Mediceans again. Bartolomeo's clandestine defection to Filippo Strozzi's side was merely the repeating of an earlier pattern of fluctuating allegiances that had been established well before. Aligning with both Strozzi and Cardinal Ippolito and the exiles would, so Bartolomeo believed, be a way back into political favour. But this final defection of the Valori would raise wider, more troubling, questions concerning the ultimate legitimacy of Alessandro's Medici ducal rule.

If the exiles believed that their fortunes would profit from being tied to those of Cardinal Ippolito the sad fact of the matter was that the latter was himself by now being increasingly marginalised at Rome. The sixty-six-year-old Pope Paul III had his own relatives to advance and the pope had been greedily eyeing Ippolito's ecclesiastical benefices for the greedy and expectant members of his family. Slyly the Pope encouraged Ippolito in his schemes, fully aware that if Ippolito ruined himself personally and politically his downfall could only serve to benefit his own Farnese relatives. In truth, Alessandro and Paul III were also closet adversaries and the Pope had little good to say about the Medici in general. Alessandro would, according to Varchi, also prevent the new pope from helping himself to any newly vacant Florentine benefices and this naturally raised tensions further.

In May 1535, the dissidents sent two discrete sets of delegations to Barcelona to lobby Charles V on Ippolito's behalf. The *grandi* emissaries comprised on the one hand Piero Strozzi, Lorenzo Ridolfi (acting for Cardinal Niccolò Ridolfi) and Giovanmaria Stratigopolo (acting for Cardinal Giovanni Salviati). The radicals meanwhile delegated Paolo Antonio Soderini, Galeotto Giugni and Antonio Berardi. The *grandi* and the radicals were mutually suspicious of each other's long-term motives; the radicals suspected with some justification, for example, that Ippolito merely intended to substitute Alessandro's ducal rule with his own. But this gesture to the Emperor could not have come at a more inopportune moment. Charles was busy that spring together with his admiral Andrea Doria assembling a fleet of 400 ships and an army of 30,000 men with which he planned to recapture the city of Tunis, which had fallen to the Sultan's Barbary admiral Kheir ed-Din Barbarossa. Barbarossa had been making a general nuissance of himself up and down the coast of Italy since July 1534. Appearing with his fleet off the coast of Campania he had sacked Capri and Procida before bombarding ports along the Gulf of Naples. Afterwards he bombarded and made amphibious sallies against Lazio, Gaeta, Villa Santa Lucia, Sant'Isidoro, Sperlonga, Fondi, Terracina and Ostia. The assault against Ostia caused the bells of Rome to be rung out *a stormo*. Attached to the imperial army were 700 Knights of Rhodes, newly re-christened as the Knights of Malta following the Emperor's donation of the island of Malta to the itinerant Order, who had most recently been based in Nice.

Charles, who had already indicated to Ippolito personally that he wished to see him prosper in the Church whilst Alessandro was to be the secular ruler of Florence, now turned to his trusted admiral and asked how he should handle this latest irritating petition. Andrea Doria was a highly intelligent man with a firm grasp of the intricacies of diplomacy. He advised Charles to support Alessandro, a prince who was already *in situ* and soon to be his son-in-law. To upset the arrangements which he had already made in Florence would prove troublesome and destabilising; and besides, Alessandro had proven loyal to the Emperor and deserved Charles's support. He advised Charles to proceed with the marriage to Margaret and indeed, in March of that same year, an imperial ambassador had already informed Alessandro that the union would go ahead as planned. When Doria spoke with the exiles, attempting in friendly terms to persuade them to abandon their plans, Lorenzo Ridolfi incautiously let slip that they planned to capture a certain town from which they proposed to harass Alessandro. Doria passed the intelligence on to the Emperor who relayed it to Cherubino Buonanni, who was Alessandro's agent in Barcelona. The Florentine exiles had not fully grasped, if they ever would, that they were not merely challenging Alessandro but the full might of imperial power in Italy, against which even the king of France had been unable to prevail.

From this point forward the low-intensity war between Alessandro and Ippolito erupted into more blatant plots and intrigues. In June 1535, Alessandro despatched a ten man team under the command of a Florentine captain named Petruccio who had allegedly been paid 100 ducats to assassinate Piero Strozzi in Lombardy. The plot however was uncovered by Piero's relative, Battista Strozzi, who was then serving as governor of Modena. In retaliation, Ippolito turned to his cousin and carousing partner Giovanni Battista Cybò who was by now bishop of Marseilles. Since Alessandro often visited and dined with his mistress Taddea and her sister Ricciarda Malaspina at the *palazzo* in Florence belonging to Ricciarda's husband Lorenzo Cybò, Giovanni Battista's status as a Cybò would gain him access and proximity to the Duke. The plan was for Giovanni Battista and his *bravi* to lay-in some casks of gunpowder and blow the Duke to smithereens during one of his regular social calls. But when he wrote to Ippolito begging for more men and money the letter was intercepted and came to the attention of both Alessandro and Cardinal Innocenzo Cybò. Giovanni Battista Cybò was immediately arrested under torture and confessed everything. Cardinal Cybò was reported to have been livid at the treacherous actions of his brother.

With the discovery of the Cybò Plot, Ippolito and the exiles' fortunes rapidly unravelled. Plans to gather arms and troops on Tuscany's borders were defused by imperial envoys; Cardinal Ippolito himself was expelled from the papal palace by the Pope after the plot was made public. The two factions of Florentine exiles nevertheless patched up their differences and now agreed to unify behind Ippolito, approving that–once in power–he should rule in the old style of Cosimo de' Medici as *primus inter pares*. Towards the end of July, Ippolito travelled south to Itri near Naples. Here he was joined by Francesco Corsini, Antonio Berardi, Dante da Castiglione, Berlinghere Berlingheri, Bartolomeo Nasi and several other notable exiles. His plan seems to have been to circumvent the ineffectual diplomacy of the exiles altogether and make his petition personally to Charles V. Ippolito would present the Emperor with a litany of *fuoriusciti* grievances offered in the form of a compilation of all the Duke's most reprehensible deeds and atrocities. The Emperor had recently succeeded in capturing Tunis on 21 July, at the age of thirty-five his first ever military victory at the head of his own army. From Tunis, he was expected to take ship for Italy and travel back through Naples and the *Regno*; Ippolito would be waiting for him in Naples and planned to make his petition there.

In the meantime, he was able to pass some pleasant days with his twenty-two-year-old mistress Giulia Gonzaga. Reputed to have been the most beautiful woman in all of Italy, Giulia had been the wife of the late Vespasiano Colonna who, until his death in 1528 had been count of Fondi and duke of Traetto. When Kheir ed-Din Barbarossa had menaced the Neapolitan coast the year before he had learned of Giulia's fabled beauty and resolved to capture the girl and ship her off to serve as a concubine in Sultan Süleyman's seraglio at the Sublime Porte. Landing at Fondi with 2,000 men, Barbarossa had already forced open the town gates and was hastening to Giulia's *palazzo* when, alerted by the commotion, the beauty had sprung onto a horse and made her escape to the nearby hills barefoot and half-naked. Ippolito, who had been commissioned by the Pope to lead a picked detachment of papal troops against the Muslims, had found Giulia hiding in the fields and had carried her triumphantly back to Fondi as her gallant rescuer. Soon afterwards she had become his lover.

After one such pleasurable visit, Ippolito had returned to Itri's impregnable hilltop *fortezza* on 6 August, where he had taken a light meal of chicken broth flavoured with pepper with some bread, but no sooner had he tasted it than he fell sick, crying 'poison!' and pointing the finger at his major-domo Giovanni Andrea who had prepared his meal. By 10 August he was dead, aged just twenty-four. Notwithstanding the fact that both Dante da Castiglione and Berlinghere Berlingheri also fell sick and died the following day of similar symptoms to Ippolito's, and the pronouncements of the doctors that all their deaths were due to the pestilential marsh air of the region, attention now fell on the unfortunate major-domo. Giovanni Andrea was seized and put to the torture. Eventually, as in the case of all men who are tortured (with the possible exception of Girolamo Savonarola), Andrea admitted to having poisoned his master.

He had been approached, so he claimed, by two associates of Duke Alessandro's: Matteo da Cortona and Otto da Monteaguto. Both had persuaded him to murder Ippolito since the Duke would take care of whosoever did him this favour. Accordingly, Andrea purchased a *grosso*-worth of poison from an apothecary in Città di Castello where he was from and then did the deed (his story later changed to Signor Otto having sent him a vial of 'greenish' poison from Rome). After securing Giovanni Andrea's signed confession the man was, rather surprisingly, released; perhaps to see where he would go and what he would do next. Unsurprising (to the exiles) the former major-domo headed straight for Florence where he was received by Alessandro at court. From there he went to Borgo san Sepulcro where he retracted his confession, professing that it had been made under torture; however the unfortunate fugitive was subsequently murdered by some townspeople there.

A story about a possible alternative culprit was also doing the rounds. The subject of this other rumour was the burlesque poet Francesco Berni who, thanks to his satirical sonnets (many of which were intensely critical of the papacy of Clement VII), was an equal familiar of both Alessandro and Ippolito. A bitter rival in letters of that other 'scourge of princes' Pietro Aretino, Francesco Berni had originally come to Rome around 1517 and found a willing patron in the fun-loving Cardinal Bibbiena but following his patron's death he had nearly been thrown out of Rome for his saucy 'Bernesque' verses on Pope Adrian VI. 'O, poor unhappy courtiers, who escaped from the clutches of the Florentines to be given in prey to Germans and Spanish renegades', he had written in his *Capitolo di papa Adriano*. After a brief spell working for Bibbiena's nephew Angelo, he next went to work for Pope Clement's faithful *datario* Gian Matteo Giberti but Berni's idleness and dissipation made him a poor candidate for the lower ranks of the papal bureaucracy. The poet's facetiousness and fondness for the fairer sex (he was habitually in love with some pretty face or other) did however make him an ideal boon companion for the competing Medici cousins, who had a tendency to surround themselves with an assortment of artists, poets, satirists, lechers, debauchees and buffoons. After Ippolito's death the story soon spread that Berni had been solicited by Alessandro to poison Ippolito and by Ippolito to poison Alessandro, but that he had refused them both. For his non-compliance, so the rumour went, Berni himself had been poisoned by Alessandro. The story was typical of the sensational scuttlebutt of the era and probably had little basis in fact; besides which the pleasure-loving and flippant Berni would hardly have made for a credible assassin.

When Charles V's previous viceroy of Naples Cardinal Pompeo Colonna (who had taken over from Philibert of Orange) had died back in June 1532, his replacement that September had been the forty-eight-year-old Don Pedro Álvarez de Toledo. A stern Spanish disciplinarian of the old school, he ruled the city of Naples and the *Regno* with an iron fist, but also took great strides to improve the seaward fortifications to protect against future Muslim landings such as had occurred throughout 1534. On 25 November 1535, Don Pedro welcomed his Emperor as he made his triumphant entry into Naples accompanied by his captains in the recent Tunis expedition, Alfonso d'Ávalos and Ascanio Colonna. A series of games and balls were organised to celebrate his visit and his recent military victory. Charles also took the opportunity of paying his respects to his daughter Margaret. This was Charles's first visit to the kingdom of Naples and he would remain in the *Regno* for the following six months holding court on a variety of pressing imperial matters from his headquarters at the twin strongholds of Castel Nuovo and Castel Capuano.

Indeed Charles had many things on his mind throughout the winter of 1535 and the spring of 1536. In Milan his son-in-law Francesco Sforza had died in early November at the age of forty after a long and painful illness. Charles's daughter Christina of Denmark had not been able to fall pregnant in the year or so since they had been married. The late duke's half-brother Giovanni Paolo Sforza, Marquis of Caravaggio, had immediately set out for Charles's court to present his own claim to the duchy but when he reached Florence he died under mysterious circumstances. Some speculated that he had been poisoned by the Emperor's loyal servant Don Antonio de Leyva, who had been appointed governor of Milan upon Francesco's death. There were in all likelihood some underhand dealings going on for Charles did not replace the Sforza duke with a Sforza kinsman but instead retained the duchy for himself. The assumption of personal Habsburg rule in Milan was peaceful and untroubled, although France was now given a pretext to resume her own intervention in Italy and as usual the conquest of Milan was the chief priority. As a bridgehead to conquering Milan, François had revived his mother Louise's old claim to the ducal lands of Savoy. By mid-February 1536 a French army under the Comte de Saint-Pol was back on Italian soil, having occupied Savoy and advanced across Piedmont towards the capital of Turin. The long-suffering Antonio de Leyva was once more told to hold Milan as best he could.

Even more troubling than François's renewed offensive in northern Italy however was the on-going détente between France and the Ottoman Empire which had been in effect since the two powers had opened diplomatic channels in 1533/34. Indeed, Barbarossa's coastal raids against southern Italy had been made with the specific intent of supporting France and, for his part, François had announced his intentions to the Venetian ambassador Giorgio Gritti as early as 1531, declaring: 'I cannot deny that I wish to see the Turk all-powerful and ready for war, not for himself – for he is an infidel and we are all Christians – but to weaken the power of the Emperor, to compel him to make major expenses, and to reassure all the other governments who are opposed to such a formidable enemy'. Süleyman, glad to have a powerful Christian ally right in the heart of Europe, had reciprocated by proclaiming that 'he could not possibly abandon the king of France, who was his brother'. Martin Luther, for once in agreement with his Emperor, was disgusted with French complicity in dealing on friendly terms with the Turk. 'Antichrist is at the same time the Pope and the Turk', he thundered. 'The spirit of Antichrist is the Pope, his flesh the Turk ... Both ... are of one lord, the devil, since the Pope is a liar and the Turk a murderer'.

Into Charles's world of diplomatic worry and care now came an exasperating renewal of the petition from the Florentine exiles, who had decided to press ahead despite having lost their putative leader Ippolito. Alessandro was summoned to Naples to reply to their allegations concerning his misrule. This business had to be solved once and for all. The stage was set for a showdown. The exiles had already despatched Silvestro Aldobrandini to Charles's court to judge the lay of the land and, following several inconclusive audiences with the Emperor, he sent word back to summon Filippo Strozzi and the three cardinals to add their weight to his own efforts. This put the other exiles' backs up as they suspected Charles and the *grandi* of double-dealing behind their backs. They delegated Antonfrancesco degli Albizzi to represent them at court, but Albizzi, having recently accepted Andrea Doria's assistance in reclaiming certain of his estates, was now ill-disposed to sully himself in the eyes of the Emperor by publicly siding with the exiles. Old Jacopo Nardi was therefore assigned in his place. This was perhaps for the best since Nardi, more than most, was prepared to bend the knee and show due deference to the Emperor, plus he was a good advocate. François's ambassador to Charles, the Florentine exile Luigi Alamanni, had noted as early as 1516 that his countrymen made poor courtiers and petitioners of royalty: 'accustomed as they are to pay respect to no one other than their own magistrates and citizens, they show themselves to be alien to court manners (*tanto alieni da' modi della corte*) in a way I think matched by few others'.

In contrast to the small delegation of Florentine exiles which presented themselves to Charles, Alessandro's entourage was in effect a travelling court comprising friends and followers, courtiers, bodyguards and troops. He left Florence with around 1,300 horsemen and made a great show when he stopped over in Rome, appearing suddenly with a flourish in the papal presence chamber, falling to his knees and kissing the new Pope's velvet slipper. But there were those who would cast a shadow over his visit if they could. '*Viva Alessandro da Collevecchio!*" read the graffiti which had been scrawled on the wall of his Roman *palazzo* to 'welcome' him, records Varchi. The unkind reference to Collevecchio indicated his natural mother whom he had never known – Simonetta, the freed Moorish slave who was now living as a poor peasant woman in the village of Collevecchio near Rome. The implication was clear: Alessandro was an imposter – the son of a former slave who aped the manners and lifestyle of a duke.

To his credit, Alessandro appeared unperturbed; brazenly he retorted 'I owe the writer a debt of gratitude for informing me where I was from, for I didn't know until now!' Onward to Naples, Alessandro brought with him not only Francesco Guicciardini, Roberto Acciaiuoli, Francesco Vettori, Matteo Strozzi, Luigi Ridolfi and Bartolomeo Valori (who was still covertly supporting Filippo Strozzi's cause) but also the seventeen-year-old son of Giovanni della Bande Nere, Cosimo de' Medici, who was accompanied by his uncle Alamanno Salviati. The composition of Alessandro's delegation illustrates just how divided some of the greatest Florentine families had become over the issue of the Duke's rule. We have already seen how Cardinal Innocenzo Cybò had broken with his brother Giovanni Battista Cybò over the latter's assassination plot. In addition, Matteo Strozzi was for example opposed in this matter to his cousin Filippo the Younger. Luigi Ridolfi meanwhile stood opposed to his brother Cardinal Niccolò Ridolfi.

The exiles found it difficult to gain an audience with the busy Emperor. He was probably avoiding them. On the morning of 3 January 1536, therefore, Nardi braced Charles on his way to Mass, his companions crowding round to physically obstruct the Emperor's path, though in as non-threatening a manner as possible. There and then Nardi made his case before the startled Emperor and his court. The main gist of Nardi's argument was that when Florence's republican government had surrendered to the imperial army no mention had been made in the truce about Florence's conversion from a republic to a duchy. Furthermore, they alleged that Alessandro was misruling in Florence, acting as a dictator in the assignment of government posts, raiding the treasury to fund his lavish courtly lifestyle, filling Florence's official positions with hostile foreigners, and enforcing harsh laws on the citizens. He had built, they complained, a mighty fortress adjacent to Florence's walls with the sole purpose of subjugating them. The fact that Charles had privately made the completion of the Fortezza da Basso a precondition of Alessandro's marriage to his daughter was probably unknown to the exiles at the time; by 5 December the *fortezza* had already been constructed and its new garrison of mostly Spaniards had moved in. Nevertheless, Charles seemed visibly moved by the pathos of Nardi's impassioned speech, whilst the rest of the exiles abased themselves on their knees before him. All the same, he ordered that the imperial response would be held in abeyance for a week while Alessandro's chief advocate Francesco Guicciardini made his official rebuttal on behalf of the Duke.

When Guicciardini addressed the Imperial Court some while later he demolished the exiles' case like the slick and expensive lawyer he was. Pointing to the *grandi* exiles clustered around the person of Filippo Strozzi the Younger, Guicciardini reminded the assembly that all these men had served Pope Clement's interests during the siege of Florence and therefore it was quite wrong of them to now suddenly feign surprise at its results – a Medici duchy. He then proceeded to explain that executions and confinements of certain dissidents had been prosecuted on the basis that they had violated the peace treaty. But Guicciardini then used some sophistry to clarify that in certain respects neither the Emperor nor the Pope had 'signed' the accord, and presumably were not therefore bound to it. He then went on to pick off the exiles' individual allegations one by one. The harsh sentences could not be laid at the Duke's feet since his magistrates had acted in these matters and not Alessandro personally. With regard to Nardi's insinuations about the Duke's disregard for the women of Florence, Guicciardini denounced these as being no more than libellous smears. 'The virtue of his excellency; the fame, the opinion which is spread through the city of his prudence and moral conduct, are a sufficient reply', Guicciardini asserted, adding for good measure that 'his proceedings being all so praiseworthy that the calumnies of the malignant are unable to obscure them'.

On 16 January, the exiles were allowed a rejoinder to Guicciardini's rebuttal, which was followed in turn by yet another rebuttal from Guicciardini. Ever the conservative, Guicciardini had painted alarming scenes of mob rule hearkening back to the anarchic days of the *ciompi* should the more radical republican exiles get their way. In February, Charles V finally issued his ruling

583

on the matter. The terms of the adjudication came as no great surprise to anyone at court. Duke Alessandro was personally vindicated and upheld unconditionally in his ducal privilege. There would be no reversion from an imperial duchy to a Florentine republic. But as for the exiles, Charles–who could never be accused of being an unreasonable man–held out an olive branch and guaranteed that they would be permitted to return in peace and safety to Florence, that they would be able to reclaim their property and promised them freedom from political reprisal. Under the circumstances, that the exiles had plotted Alessandro's murder and Alessandro in return had possibly been complicit too in Ippolito's death, the compromise was a gracious one on the Emperor's part.

The exiles however reached deep within themselves for their last reserves of republican pride. Indignantly Nardi replied to Charles that they had not come before him 'to recover our possessions, nor to return as slaves into a city whence but yesterday we issued freemen'. They had come before him in good faith to appeal for 'that entire and real liberty which his agents and ministers promised in his name to preserve for us'. He then concluded:

> 'But now seeing by the memorial just presented to us that more respect is paid to the desires of Alessandro than to the merits and justice of our cause, that the name of liberty is not even mentioned, and but little said of the public interests; and that the restoration of banished citizens is not free, as by justice and obligation it should be made, but limited and conditioned as if it had been sought as a favour; we have therefore nothing else to reply except that we are resolved to live and die as free as we were born, but again supplicating his majesty to deliver our unfortunate city from the yoke of so bitter a servitude'.

Coming as it did after so many decades of intermittent Medici rule the entire speech was a remarkable reaffirmation of the most heartfelt Florentine civic humanism. Renaissance Florence had been built on this republican ethos and had come to greatness and prosperity as a guild-based republic. Even if the machinery of government could be been manipulated from behind the scenes by clever families like the Medici, what was imperative, above all else, was the republic's continued preservation; Florence should not be permitted to slide into the casual absolutism of an imperial duchy.

Unfortunately they were advocating such ideas to entirely the wrong audience. Charles's Imperial Court had watched the proceedings as they unfolded; these privileged Spanish, German, Dutch and *Napoletano* courtiers were avowed dynasts and monarchists, they had little real sympathy for the snivelling republicans of Florence. Niccolò Machiavelli, an astute student of Cesare Borgia and of ancient Roman military power, could have told them: *fight fire with fire*. Francesco Ferrucci had been their best hope for maintaining Florence as a free and independent republic. If they had somehow rallied and beaten the imperial forces laying siege to their city, or else hung on for another four years, Clement would by now be dead and the Emperor would no longer have been under any obligation to sustain Medici interests in Florence. But their poor choice in making Malatesta Baglioni their supreme commander had resulted in Ferrucci's tragic betrayal.

As usual, the Florentines stood there whimpering about foreign officials in their midst but when the republic's very life had been jeopardised they had as usual consigned its military defence to a foreign *condottiere* who could not wait to betray them in order to further his own personal interests. This had been the lesson which poor Niccolò Machiavelli had so desperately tried to impress upon his beloved fellow Florentines, who repaid him with scorn and contempt. It was a lesson which the Florentines already *knew* back in the 1420s when Niccolò Piccinino had been made the subject of that notorious *pittura infamante* on the wall of the Palazzo della Signoria. It was a lesson which the Florentines ought to have heeded but never did and now they had lost their republic forever because of it.

Paolo Giovio, the scholar, physician and prelate who had famously shielded Pope Clement VII from the imperial army by throwing his cloak over his shoulders as he had hurried to the Castel Sant'Angelo in 1527 had, following his patron Clement's death, retired to his peaceful villa on the shores of Lake Como. Dubbed the *Museo*, Giovio's villa was home to numerous portraits of some of the most famous personalities of the day, as well as antiquities and other *objects d'art*. It was to the knowledgeable Giovio that Alessandro had sent word requesting a suitable personal emblem. Giovio had been in Rome when the king of Portugal had sent Pope Leo X the novel gift of a white elephant; as a great spectacle the elephant was intended to be displayed alongside–or perhaps even made to fight with–a rhinoceros, but the latter had unfortunately drowned during the sea voyage to Italy. Albrecht Dürer had made a woodcut of this strange creature in 1515 and, in his *Thesaurus*, the Elizabethan lexicographer Thomas Cooper would later describe the rhinoceros as 'a beaste enemie to the elephant, and hath an horne in his snout bending upward'. Although he had not seen one with his own eyes, from the accounts left by Pliny, Giovio ascertained that the rhinoceros was a deadly and intractable adversary. It was therefore selected as a fitting insignia for the Duke, along with the purposeful motto '*No buelvo sin vencer*' meaning 'I shall not return without victory'.

It was an appropriate *impresa* for the successful culmination of Alessandro's diplomacy at Naples. Having confirmed Alessandro as Florence's *capo assoluto* Charles now gave the official green light for the Duke and Margaret's wedding ceremony to go ahead. Antoine Perrenot, the teenage son of Charles's trusted Burgundian counsellor Nicolas Perrenot de Granvelle, concluded the marriage negotiations in just one day. One of the main stipulations was that, in view of Margaret's youth, Alessandro was to refrain from consummating the union for at least six months. On 29 February 1536, the ring ceremony took place in Naples amidst considerable pomp and ruinous expense (the celebrations had been so expensive in fact that later the same year Alessandro would seek the Emperor's permission to sell off some of his Neapolitan fiefs to recover the costs). Once again, the wedding would be the subject of a later Vasari fresco, the painter envisaging the Duke and his Duchess together with the Emperor Charles flanked by pagan marine gods of the Tyrrhenian Sea designed to connote that the ceremony is taking place on the Neapolitan coast; somewhere in amongst the crowd Vasari has also depicted Maria Salviati's son Cosimo de' Medici as well as Don Pedro Álvarez de Toledo's daughter Eleonora. This other, second couple would find matrimonial bliss together just three years later under considerably altered circumstances.

The celebrations showcased the best that Spanish, Neapolitan and Florentine culture had to offer. Conspicuously absent from the wedding crowd, however, were the Florentine *fuoriusciti*. In disgust at Charles's perceived betrayal, most had abstained from taking part even though, in the interests of concord, Charles had initially been willing to forgive and forget their opposition to his new son-in-law. However, when he discovered that Filippo Strozzi had been secretly funnelling large sums of money to François's army in Piedmont it was the final straw. Filippo was declared an outlaw and officially exiled from Florence together with two of his sons, Piero, the fiery character who delighted in fighting duels over every little slight to his honour, and his more temperate brother the banker Roberto Strozzi. These three sought temporary refuge in France alongside Filippo's two other sons the soldier Leone Strozzi and the priest Lorenzo Strozzi. Also declared exiled were Lorenzo Ridolfi and Maria Salviati's and Cardinal Giovanni Salviati's younger brother Bernardo, a knight of the Order of St. John of Jerusalem, now the Order of Malta, who had once famously described Alessandro as 'born of the basest slave, more likely the son of a coachman than of Lorenzo or Clement'.

Alessandro's new bride was scheduled make her official entry to Florence in June, where the third part of the marriage ceremony–the wedding Mass and consummation–would duly take place. However, Margaret of Austria's arrival was to be preceded by a state visit by Charles V himself. Before reaching Florence the Emperor made a triumphal first entry to Rome on 5 April 1536, where he was fêted as 'a new Scipio Africanus' or even a latter day Alexander for his victory in Tunis. Pope Paul III had had many of the city's ancient Roman monuments, palaces and triumphal arches repaired, even to the extent of replacing some of the existing friezes on the arches of Constantine, Titus and Septimius Severus with depictions of Charles's own military victories. The Pope greeted the Emperor in front of St. Peter's and brought him to the 'old' audience hall (a dazzling new papal audience chamber, the *Sala Regia*, had meanwhile been commissioned from Antonio da Sangallo the Younger, but was not yet ready for use). Here, the Emperor went to work trying to win his new pope over to his side.

One conference, which was attended by Pope Paul III as well as by the French and Venetian ambassadors, saw Charles complaining that François was endangering the general peace of Italy by occupying Savoy and Piedmont and once more moving against Milan. Charles challenged the Farnese pope to side with François if he truly believed that the French cause was just; Pope Paul III, however, was no ineptly politicking Clement VII who flipped this way and then that; resolutely he maintained his neutrality. But it was a biased impartiality. If there was to be peace it would necessarily need to be a *pax imperium*, an imperial harmony, since nothing further could be gained by baiting the imperial eagle. Charles V's motto was PLVS VLTRA, meaning 'further beyond', a fitting watchword in view of the fact that the Empire aspired to become the first truly global power. New Worlds had been discovered to the west and at Tunis Charles had proved that the Turks could be beaten. The Spanish and German Empire dominated all. François's own aspirations, by contrast, appeared be parochial and old fashioned. The French king was married to the old chivalric code of the past, when kings gaily led their armies into battle for glory. But times had changed.

Leaving Rome, Charles entered Florence on 28 April by the southernmost Porta a San Pier Gattolini accompanied by around 6,000 imperial troops and 1,000 horsemen. The Duke's small army of client artists led by the painter

Giorgio Vasari and Cellini's companion, the sculptor Niccolò Tribolo, had scurried amidst a sudden labour shortage to complete the city's festive *apparati* (decorations) and the various triumphal arches which comprised the scenographic procession through which Charles would ride. Many of the prominent artists of Florence had contributed to the creative preparations for the visit. Aside from the aforementioned there were also the painters Pontormo and Bronzino, as well as Ridolfi Ghirlandaio and Battista Franco and these were joined by sculptors such as Baccio Bandinelli, who had been knighted by Charles V into the Order of St. James in 1530 and who was inordinately proud of the thick gold chain and shell medallion of the order which he was entitled to wear in public. Unfortunately for these artistic luminaries, there was still insufficient time for them to finish all the planned pieces and one particular equestrian statue of Charles–an honour which, as in classical antiquity, was usually reserved for the emperor alone–could not be completed in time. The half-finished work sat embarrassingly as the Emperor Charles V regally rode past. Charles would remain in Florence until 4 May living in the Duke's own personal quarters at the Palazzo Medici, which Alessandro had donated to him while he himself moved into the nearby Palazzo Tornabuoni. The famous Medici *palazzo* on the Via Larga was lavishly bedecked with hangings in cloth-of-gold to receive its imperial guest. Even as Charles was moving into his temporary lodgings Giorgio Vasari was busy in the former ground floor loggia frescoing *Scenes from the Life of Caesar*. For this special occasion of the Emperor's visit, Vasari set up his preparatory cartoon in place of the final fresco that had yet to be finished and the Emperor admired his work-in-progress. Vasari had scored another point over his rival Pontormo.

When Alessandro's fourteen-year-old bride Margaret of Austria made her own entry into Florence on 8 June, the *apparati* and festivities were still grand but on a slightly lower key than those which had been arranged for her 1533 visit to the city. Also, many of the decorations which had been created for Charles V's entry were simply recycled to save money. The new duchess of Florence made her way through the streets by night in a flickering torchlight procession. Margaret was housed at the palazzo of Alessandro's former guardian and household manager Ottaviano de' Medici, who was now one of the Duke's most trusted counsellors and who devoted much of his time to overseeing the artistic affairs of the Medici (much to the intense irritation of Benvenuto Cellini who resented his constant interference). For the occasion of her stay, Ottaviano had Giorgio Vasari transform his home into a celebration of the pagan gods and emperors of Rome. Vasari proudly described his renovation works in a letter to Pietro Aretino, explaining how Ottaviano's own antiquities collection was made the centre-stage of the decorations. When Margaret entered the palazzo she was therefore confronted with an abundance of Roman busts and bas-reliefs. No expense had been spared and, when she retired for the night to sleep, she found that her bed had been fashioned from the finest red pernambuco wood, specially imported from Brazil and much favoured in the crafting of violin bows.

The consecration of the marriage took place on 13 June at the church of San Lorenzo and was officiated by Cardinal Antonio Pucci, who came from a long line of Medici *amici* going all the way back to Giovanni di Bicci's trusted associate Puccio Pucci. The wedding banquet took place at the Palazzo Medici but was overshadowed by a solar eclipse which many in the party privately took to be a bad omen. Alessandro's star, which had all day been so high in the ascendant, was briefly cast into shadow. After the banquet, the guests and general public enjoyed a lively mock battle staged in the Piazza San Lorenzo by Florence's companies of *potenze*. The *potenze* were *reami di beffa* (or ersatz 'realms of insult'), that is to say, brigades composed of mostly working class youths which had been established in the mid-fourteenth-century and which took an active role in Florence's many carnivals and other public festivities. In return for wearing costumes and carrying their weapons and gonfalons they were given 'money for their expenses and gifts of wine and food ... and they went around the city singing and dancing and playing'. Following this excitement a more sedate entertainment was arranged in the headquarters of the *arte della seta* (the silk weavers guild) in the Via San Gallo, which stood at the rear of the Palazzo Medici. This was a performance of the play *Aridosia*, a comedy in five acts which had been specially written by Alessandro's boon companion Lorenzino de' Medici and which contained numerous hilarious inside jokes and veiled references to personages associated with the Duke. The play, an engaging *jeu d'esprit* with its farsical catalogue of unwanted pregnancies, inadequate dowries, cunning servants, lost purses and exorcisms, was all accepted by the audience in a spirit of ribald fun.

Later that same year, on 10 August 1536, Duke François III of Brittany the heir to the throne of France had died unexpectedly at the age of eighteen. As the husband of the new *Dauphin* Henry, Alessandro's sister Catherine now moved up the food chain and was destined to become the future queen of France. However a high profile royal death always required an appropriate scapegoat and, since poisoning was suspected, a suitable candidate was found in the person of the late *Dauphin's* Page of the Sewer, the Italian nobleman Count Sebastiano de Montecuccoli. The most damning evidence against Montecuccoli was the book on toxicology that had been found in his possession. Furthermore, Montecuccoli had also previously served the Emperor Charles V, a fact which probably condemned him in the end. Seeking to avoid a painful interrogation by torture the unfortunate man blurted out that he had poisoned Duke François at the Emperor's behest and, although he later retracted his confession, which was almost certainly false, he was executed by the horrifyingly repulsive method reserved only for regicides, that of *l'écartèlement*. So, as Catherine de' Medici rose to the position of *Dauphine*, her fellow countryman Sebastiano de Montecuccoli–who had accompanied on her journey from Italy to France–paid for her price of admission by having all four of his limbs torn from his torso by wild horses.

More auspicious news arrived in September 1536 when Margaret of Austria had fallen pregnant. It was exactly the news that both Charles and Alessandro needed, Charles to secure an heir to the imperial duchy of Florence, Alessandro to cement his relationship with the powerful father-in-law who was the basis for his political power. Due to the withdrawal of support from the influential Florentine *fuoriusciti* families, Alessandro had increasingly distanced himself from these old houses beginning from around the time of his wedding celebration and, like his Medici forebears Giovanni di Bicci and Cosimo, sought instead to cultivate the support and approval of the masses. Patronising the largely working class companies of *potenze* was one strategy that he pursued, and dazzling the people with the magnificence of his reign through expensive trappings and extravagant ceremonial was another. The ordinary Florentines who, unlike the wealthy shared little in the way of real power, had always shown a proclivity towards enticement by spectacle and the on-going exhibition of the Duke and *Duchessina's* marriage was a convenient way to distract the people and focus their attention elsewhere. Much as many modern day working class people might invest inordinate amounts of emotional energy in the distant aristocratic figures of the British royal family, Alessandro shrewdly perceived that simple, ordinary Florentines longed to identify with splendour and majesty. Alessandro accompanied his father-in-law to Genoa where the latter intended to at last take ship for Spain. Charles had spent an unusually long time in Italy seeing to its future and now the remainder of his vast dominions urgently needed his attention. However, by October, the fourteen-year-old *Duchessina* had miscarried and both men's plans lay for now in ruins.

Despite the setback (Margaret was still young and healthy), life went on as usual for the Duke. Leisure, hunting and gallivanting after women occupied his time while his teenage wife recuperated. On the Saturday evening of 6 January 1537, the night of Epiphany, Duke Alessandro was looking forward to an assignation with the attractive Caterina Soderini Ginori. Caterina was the wife of Leonardo Ginori, an elderly and rather dull merchant who just so happened to be away from Florence around this time. She was well reputed for her virtue and temperance and yet Lorenzino de' Medici had approached Alessandro with the intriguing news that Caterina, who happened also to be his aunt, was willing to sleep with him. That Lorenzino had become well known around Florence not just as the Duke's cousin but also as his pimp seemed to bother neither man. Alessandro had a reputation as a ladies man to maintain and Lorenzino, glad to voyeuristically participate in Alessandro's hedonistic lifestyle, readily obliged him with a string of charming conquests. The engaging news concerning Caterina was merely the latest boost to the Duke's prowess and self-esteem. She would be his latest in a string of amorous conquests.

As Caterina lived in a house situated in the street behind the Palazzo Medici that was adjacent to Lorenzino's own dwelling, a house which was owned by Maria Salviati, the procurer suggested to the Duke that after dinner he should leave his friends and proceed to Lorenzino's house while he quietly fetched Caterina from the dwelling next door. Because the married lady was, however, understandably anxious to preserve her unsullied reputation Lorenzino urged Alessandro to come with just two of his bodyguards and have them remain discreetly outside in the street while the tryst was taking place. The Duke agreed readily and he left the Palazzo Medici with his two minders named Giomo and l'Unghero ('The Hungarian'). Lorenzino had also persuaded the Duke that his usual precautionary chainmail doublet was unnecessary and so he proceeded completely unprotected, except for the two bodyguards–who were by now well accustomed to such nocturnal duties–to Lorenzino's house. Once inside, Lorenzino showed the Duke to his own bedchamber in which a warm fire blazed invitingly. Alessandro, feeling sleepy after his heavy meal, unbuckled his rapier, lay down on Lorenzino's bed and took forty winks while waiting for his partner of the evening to arrive.

But a perfumed and lusty Caterina did not appear in the bedchamber *décolletage*. Instead, Lorenzino had returned with a cut-throat rascal named Scoronconcolo, 'a man ever ready to use his hands' who owed Lorenzino a number of favours. Creeping stealthily into the room where Alessandro lay snoozing he first removed the Duke's rapier from reach and then bent over him to ask if he was asleep. When the Duke stirred from his nap, Lorenzino suddenly plunged his sword into his torso. Alessandro screamed out in pain and surprise and rose, attempting to make an exit towards the door. As he did so, Lorenzino placed his hand over his mouth to muffle the sound and was bitten right down to the bone. Scoronconcolo, seemingly unperturbed to learn that his victim was none other than Florence's duke, now joined in and stabbed the convulsing victim several times with his dagger. It was all over within a matter of seconds. Alessandro was finally despatched by Scoronconcolo with a final fatal dagger thrust through the throat. The disturbance caused by the Duke's assassination failed to wake the household. Maria Salviati herself was by now quite habituated to Lorenzino's late night drunken comings and goings and, even if she did hear some untoward noises, she clearly paid them no heed. Placing the dead body back on the bed, Lorenzino and Scoronconcolo locked the door to the room and left the house discreetly by a side door. None the wiser, the two bodyguards Giomo and l'Unghero remained posted outside.

Lorenzino's escape plan had been just as carefully premeditated as the actual murder itself. He was fortunately armed with an official exit pass to get him through the city gates in the early hours of the morning. The pass had been obtained earlier from Bishop Angelo Marzi who was custodian of the city gates. Lorenzino had visited him sometime beforehand and spun him some fanciful story about needing to visit his brother Giuliano who was lying sick in Cafaggiolo. Lorenzino now mounted his horse and along with Scoronconcolo and a third accomplice named *Il Freccia* ('the Arrow') galloped like the wind from the city, putting as much distance as he could between himself and his murderous deed, his wounded and bleeding hand stuffed for the time being into a glove. He rode to the Mugello where he stopped briefly in the region's provincial capital Scarperia to receive some emergency medical attention on his injured thumb. Afterwards the small party headed for Bologna, arriving the following day in the early afternoon, and here Lorenzino sat down to write urgent despatches concerning the night's undertaking to the various exiles in Venice, Rome and France, urging them to unite and march on Florence. Following further treatment on his hand from Maestro Angelo da Parma he roused Silvestro Aldobrandini and informed him of his deed. Aldobrandini however was sceptical and decided to await confirmation from Florence before acting further. By 9 January the assassins were to be found in Venice where the Florentine diaspora there learned the news of Alessandro's butchering with palpable delight.

Back in Florence, the crime was not discovered until the next morning. Still posted outside Lorenzino's house almost twelve hours later, Giomo and l'Unghero approached Cardinal Innocenzo Cybò and asked when they could be relieved of duty, expressing concern that their master had still failed to emerge from the house after so long. Cybò in turn then learned from Bishop Marzi about the granting of the exit pass to Lorenzino and immediately grew suspicious. Fearing the worst, Cybò hastened to the first secretary and chancellor, Francesco Campana, who suggested that Lorenzino's house be sealed and guards posted outside. Cybò then issued a bulletin stating that the Duke was under the weather and would not be making an appearance at a joust which had been planned for later that same day. In the meantime he sent urgent letters to his brother Lorenzo in Pisa, to Jacopo de' Medici (Alessandro's cousin who served on the *otto di guardia*), as well as to the *condottiere* Alessandro Vitelli who was at this time in Città di Castello. Cybò ordered Vitelli to come to Florence post-haste with as many of his troops as could be mustered for there was no way of knowing if Alessandro's disappearance might be the prelude to a republican uprising. Cybò then gathered the members of Alessandro's governing council: Francesco Guicciardini, Roberto Acciaiuoli, Matteo Strozzi and Francesco Vettori. Together and in great secrecy they admitted themselves to Lorenzino's bedroom where, to nobody's great surprise, they discovered Alessandro de' Medici's bloody corpse. The cadaver was wrapped in a blanket and moved the short distance to the Church of St Giovannino of Scolopi, situated adjacent to the Palazzo de' Medici. Here it remained until the following evening when it was moved to the Church of San Lorenzo's New Sacristy and interred without ceremony or eulogy in the tomb created for Alessandro's father Lorenzo di Piero de' Medici.

By the time that the news broke in the city it was Monday morning and Alessandro Vitelli had arrived at the Porta San Niccolò with his reinforcements. Neither they, nor the garrison of the Fortezza da Basso, were needed and Florence remained tranquil. Lorenzino's act had, as it turned out, been planned and executed in isolation and he had failed to coordinate his efforts with the rest of the Florentine *fuoriusciti* families elsewhere hence the opportunity for the more hard core republicans was lost. However since Cardinal Cybò himself was now left isolated without imperial troops or other material support at this time it was in his interest to attempt a quick and favourable resolution of the looming constitutional and succession crisis. Florence's Council of Forty-Eight met that afternoon to discuss the problem. Cybò favoured the recognition of Alessandro's illegitimate son Giulio de' Medici, one of two children whom the late duke had fathered by his lover Taddea Malaspina. However as Giulio was no more than four years old and his recognition would have entailed that Cardinal Cybò would become de facto regent in Florence, the Council demurred on the proposal. At this point some of the Council members suggested that any decision be postponed until such time as some of the more influential exiles could return and be consulted. This was of course most unacceptable to such *palleschi* faction members as Francesco Guicciardini and Francesco Vettori. Other constitutional systems such as a *gonfaloniere*-for-life or *signore*, which had either been experimented with or been found wanting in other Italian city-states, were also ruled out. This left the door open only to some sort of Medici dynastic settlement, but whom?

Obviously, Lorenzaccio's murderous actions had disqualified both himself as well as his brother Giuliano, so their bloodline was not an option. The most obvious choice was the nineteen-year-old Cosimo de' Medici. His ancestry was conveniently ideal in fact for Cosimo united within himself both the main and cadet lines of the Medici family which had splintered off in different arcs during the time of Cosimo de' Medici *Pater Patriae* and his brother Lorenzo. On his mother Maria Salviati's side he was the great grandson of Lorenzo il *Magnifico*. On his father Giovanni della Bande Nere's side he was the grandson of Giovanni *Il Popolano*. His father, moreover, had been the greatly esteemed Italian *condottiere* of the Black Bands and through his paternal grandmother Caterina the noble blood of the Sforza also coursed through his veins.

Cosimo was at this time resident at the Villa del Trebbio in the Mugello, a property which had once belonged to Giovanni di Bicci but which had been owned by Cosimo's great grandfather Pierfrancesco since his coming of age in 1451. On the face of it Cosimo seemed like an underwhelming choice of successor, being interested in little else except hunting and hanging around with his cousins Duke Alessandro and Lorenzino. The year before he had also fathered an illegitimate daughter named Bia (short for *Bambina*) by an unidentified peasant girl from Trebbio. On the other hand, the fact that the boy was an inexperienced *tabula rasa* commended him to both Guicciardini and Vettori since they believed they would be able to control him easily. With the cooperation of Maria Salviati and Cosimo's uncle Alamanno Salviati, the two *palleschi* arranged for Cosimo's candidacy to be touted in the city's marketplaces and, once Cybò realised that he had no conceivable pretext for a Spanish coup d'état, he was forced to come to terms with Cosimo's *palleschi* backers, agreeing to support Cosimo's candidacy the following morning in the Senate. Cosimo duly hastened from the Mugello to Florence to offer his condolences.

On 9 January 1537, the Senate sat to deliberate Cosimo's candidacy but as the afternoon dragged on they could not come to any decision. At this point in their protracted deliberations Alessandro Vitelli, who had made a separate pact with the *palleschi*, now stepped in and encouraged his troops in the Piazza della Signoria to call loudly for Cosimo by name. He rushed into the Senate chamber warning the politicians that he would be unable to hold his troops in check any longer if they did not make up their minds and soon! In this way Florence's government was railroaded into agreeing to confirm Cosimo de' Medici as Alessandro's successor.

When on 9 January the Medici scion, who would eventually become grand duke of Tuscany, accepted the leadership of Florence it was not as 'duke' but simply as 'Signor Cosimo de' Medici', or at best 'Lord'. His *palleschi* handlers, who reserved for themselves the title of Cosimo's 'magnificent counsellors' thought that they had installed a compliant puppet but they had misjudged the extent of the youthful leader's power, which was in fact deeply limited. For the time being the real political power still resided in the Emperor's representative Cardinal Cybò and the military power rested with Alessandro Vitello who, backed by Spanish troops, was like Cybò similarly indebted to Charles V for his position and influence. Soon afterwards, acting together as Charles's imperial representatives, Vitelli and Cybò seized control of the Fortezza da Basso and moved themselves in along with the late duke's fifteen-year-old widow Margaret. Before commandeering the fortress, Vitelli ransacked Lorenzino's house, shared in common with Maria Salviati and her son, evidently making off with many valuable items and jewels including much of Cosimo's own personal correspondence.

Alessandro de' Medici's illegitimate son Giulio would be removed from the care of his natural mother Taddea Malaspina and raised in Cosimo's court and when he grew to adulthood he embraced a military career. Inducted into the nautical Order of Saint Stephen he fought the Muslim pirates and Turks in the Mediterranean and was present as admiral at the Great Siege of Malta in 1565. Here, his fleet assisted the Hospitaller knights of the Order of Saint John, by then commanded by their illustrious Grand Master Jean de Vallette, in their epic struggle against the Turk. Alessandro's daughter Giulia by Taddea Malaspina was likewise reared at Cosimo's court under the watchful eye of Maria Salviati. Both Maria and her young ward are depicted in a well-known painting by Pontormo, Maria dressed in her characteristic mourning black; the propaganda value of depicting Maria benevolently sheltering the orphaned child of Cosimo's predecessor is readily apparent. Following the death of her first husband, Francesco Cantelmo, Giulia was later painted by Alessandro Allori who depicted her this time not as a timid child but as a self-assured young woman in her early twenties. She later married a second time with Cosimo's first cousin Bernadetto de' Medici, who subsequently obtained the seigniory of Ottaiano in the Kingdom of Naples, which is where the couple resided for the remainder of their lives. The late Duke Alessandro had also left behind a younger third child named Porzia whose maternal parentage is unknown. Like Alessandro's other two offspring, Porzia was tended by Maria Salviati who placed her in the Augustinian convent of San Clemente in Via San Gallo where, as a Catholic nun, she later rose to become abbess before dying young at the age of twenty-seven.

And what of Lorenzino de' Medici himself, whose act of tyrannicide or patricide (Jacopo Nardi would debate in his *Istorie* how precisely Lorenzino's act should be defined) served as the catalyst for Florence's tumultuous new change of government? Upon his arrival in Venice several days after the assassination Lorenzino found himself fêted very much as the man of the moment. Republican writers as Varchi, Girolamo Borgia, Francesco Maria Molza and others tripped over themselves to memorialise and eulogise his deeds. Filippo Strozzi immediately compared Lorenzino with Caesar's killer Marcus Junius Brutus, conveniently forgetting the fact that Dante had placed Brutus in the bottommost pit (whilst Coluccio Salutati in *De tyranno* had vindicated this placement). Meanwhile, in Rome, the exiled former republican war secretary Donato Giannotti commissioned from his friend Michelangelo a bust of Brutus in commemoration of Lorenzino; the bust was presented to Giannotti's patron Cardinal Niccolò Ridolfi.

Back in Florence, Lorenzino was the subject of a rather less flattering *pittura infamante* painted above the gate of the Fortezza da Basso. In the usual mocking custom, the assassin was depicted dangling by one foot. In Florence, Lorenzino would be more commonly known by his nickname 'Lorenzaccio' from this point forward. Strangely, none of the exiles in either Venice or Rome appeared concerned to pause for one moment and examine Lorenzino's actual motives, intoxicated as they were with the 'news unexpected but most sweet' from Florence. Indeed, it served their cause little should it subsequently transpire that Lorenzino had acted out of purely personal motives or in retaliation for some trivial slight or insult suffered at the hands of the late Duke. Indeed, portraying Lorenzino as the Tuscan Brutus cast their endeavours in a specious patina of nobility and righteousness; taking the moral high ground served to justify any future rebellious actions against both Charles V and Cosimo. However, as Guicciardini had wrily observed, tyrannicide was practised by 'very few who were moved solely by patriotic emotions'.

Lorenzino himself conveniently shrouded his actions in the motives which had been attributed to him. He penned a public justification of his act, the *Apologia*, in which he (rather predictably) claimed to be acting as the modern heir of Brutus to rid Florence of a cruel tyrant. But the fact remains that, although he had always been a rather solemn, bookish and introverted youth, nothing in Lorenzino's adult behaviour prior to January 1537 displays the slightest iota of interest in either dissident republican politics or the lofty ideals of civic humanism. By contrast, his days had been filled with pleasurable and dissolute pastimes, many of which were sponsored and facilitated by his cousin 'the tyrant' Alessandro. Cosimo de' Medici would later condemn Lorenzino to death *in absentia*. After more than a decade of freedom and notoriety, not to mention the inconvenience of having to evade the various bounty hunters sent against him, justice finally caught up with Lorenzino de' Medici and he was killed on the steps of his home in the Campo San Polo at Venice. Recent scholarship strongly indicates that Lorenzino's killers were commissioned and paid for by Alessandro de' Medici's father-in-law, the Emperor Charles V.

When King François I learned of Alessandro's assassination his characteristic first instinct was to use the event to destabilise his rival the Emperor Charles. This threatened to occur in one of two ways. Firstly, Charles would not only reaffirm his overlordship of Florence as an imperial duchy but was also anxious to lay claim to the fortresses of Pisa and Livorno, which the late Duke had promised to bequeath to him upon his death. If Cosimo objected to their seizure he might reach out to France for assistance, which Charles obviously wished to avoid at all costs. Secondly, and more likely still, François might take the more obvious route and provide direct material support to the exiled *fuoriusciti*. The French king was already fairly enamoured of the Strozzi family members in his midst, especially the brash, fiery and unprincipled Piero Strozzi and his brother Leone, soon to become a knight of the Order of Malta in 1530; both men personified all those chivalrous qualities that he held dear and Piero was certainly just as prone to recklessness as François. Martial men such as these now become the foci for all the disaffected Florentine exiles whose egos had grown too large for the city of their birth. They milled around in military encampments in the Apennine foothills and posed an ever-present threat to Cosimo's new regime.

Charles V's ambassador Fernando de Silva, the count of Cifuentes, arrived in Florence in the spring of 1537 and confirmed Cosimo as head of state, an act which would be later ratified by Charles on 30 September. Charles had mooted that Florence should become an imperial fief. Cosimo, who would be declared his imperial vassal, would be invested with all of Alessandro's former powers and privileges but would not be proclaimed duke. Cosimo's own envoys to Charles, Averardo Serristori and Giovanni Bandini (whom Cosimo would later imprison for sodomy) objected to Florence's reduction to mere vassal status. Florence, they informed the Emperor, had always been a free state beholden to neither Emperor nor prince. Cosimo at the same time made a play for the hand of Alessandro's widow Margaret, who was well-loved by the Florentines. For her own part, it had not taken long for the unfortunate Margaret to realise her late husband's shortcomings. Although still only a teenager she had enough perspicacity to see that Alessandro's character was already fixed and, although she genuinely mourned his passing, her gaze now settled on his more temperate and sweet-natured successor Cosimo, to whom she found herself increasingly attracted.

Cosimo, not wishing to risk everything on a direct military confrontation, tried instead, in late January 1537, to undermine their support by offering full amnesty and restitution of property for any exiles who returned quietly to Florence. The strategy, a sensible one under the circumstances, failed largely due to the non-cooperation of Alessandro Vitelli and the pride of the exiled leaders like Filippo Strozzi and Cardinal Niccolò Ridolfi. Open conflict was the inevitable result. Rashly, Piero Strozzi led an expedition south in April, picking up support along the way from many foolish and idealistic Florentine students residing in Padua and Bologna. Strozzi's objective was Borgo San Sepulcro and its surrounding *contado* and his strategy was to slowly deprive Florence, the *Dominante*, of much of its outlying territory and support. The audacious plan foundered however over mundane matter of logistics and resupply and, unable to live off the land due to the non-compliance of the *contadini*, Piero Strozzi's followers soon became hungry and demoralised.

One of those followers was the Florentine historian Benedetto Varchi who had been exiled after fighting the Imperialists during the Siege of Florence in 1530. Varchi observed how Piero's impetuosity was tarnishing the image of the *fuoriusciti* wherever they went and lamented how 'The Florentine exiles, who were first held in admiration ... were brought to derision even among children'. Varchi, who would later be pardoned by Cosimo and commissioned to write Florence's official chronicle, the *Storia fiorentina*, found (much like Pietro Aretino before him) that scribbling about heroic deeds was infinitely preferable to emulating them. Besides which he missed his home comforts, chief amongst which was the embrace of young boys, a vice which led his critics to satirise him with the words 'O father Varchi, new Socrates ... his arms open and his trousers down, this is how your Bembo is waiting for you in the Elysium Fields.' Such pleasure-loving poets and youthful academics, led albeit by lions such as Piero Strozzi, were not the sort of men who could be depended upon to trump Vitelli's rough workaday Spaniards on the field of battle.

This was brutally attested on 1 August 1537 at the Battle of Montemurlo which was fought on the anniversary of Octavian's victory over Mark Anthony and Cleopatra at Actium, a coincidence which was not lost on Cosimo. Elements of the Florentine *fuoriusciti* under Filippo Strozzi, his son Piero, Bartolomeo Valori and the Hospitaller knight Bernardo Salviati had converged on the hamlet of Montemurlo which lay halfway between Prato and Pistoia and whose *rocca* stood on a hill overlooking the road running between the two towns. The strength of the exiles' forces remains unclear, ranging from Jacopo Nardi's estimate of fifty to sixty to Benedetto Varchi's assessment of about 200. The exiles were supported by at least a couple of thousand professional mercenaries, 1,200 of which were under the command of Piero who had marched down from Bologna. Bernardo Salviati's troops had yet to arrive when Filippo began fortifying Montemurlo's *rocca* and ordered Piero to send an advance party towards Prato. This vanguard was ambushed by Alessandro Vitelli's troops coming from the other direction and when Piero rode out to relieve them his forces were checked and fell back in confusion. Abandoned and now surrounded in the *rocca*, Filippo and the others were obliged to surrender. News of the engagement reached Florence that same day. Ambassador Girolamo Tantucci vividly reported back to the Balìa of Siena on the scenes of rejoicing: 'Throughout the city are heard cries of *Palle, Palle,* and victory, victory; many guns have been fired from the castle, so that these Signori are full merry ... There is great rejoicing, and from two windows on the ground floor of the Signor Cosimo's palace much bread hath been thrown and is still being thrown, and from two wooden pipes they are continually pouring out a quantity of wine.'

Although Piero Strozzi and Bernardo Salviati evaded capture that day, many other prominent exiles were captured alive including Filippo Strozzi himself as well as Lodovico Rucellai and the overbearing and haughty Antonfrancesco degli Albizzi. Also led back in chains was Pope Clement VII's former legate Bartolomeo Valori who, crying 'tyranny!', had openly declared for the rebel cause following Alessandro's murder. During Florence's annual Carnival of 1507, Filippo Strozzi and his brother had taken part in the *Carro di Morte* ('Cart of Death') in which the figure of Death perched on top of the float and brandished his scythe whilst Filippo and others posed as skeletons who popped in and out of their coffins to sing morbid songs to the delighted crowd. His return to Florence was no Carnival. Strozzi and the other opposition leaders were led humiliatingly through the streets of Florence by the triumphant Alessandro Vitelli to the jeers and abuse of the drunken multitude, following which many of them were despatched by beheading. As Francesco Guicciardini remarked: 'There can be no greater happiness as this world goes than to see your enemy prostrate before you; to this nought can be preferred'.

The Battle of Montemurlo would be allegorised that same year by the Mannerist painter Battista Franco Veneziano who painted Cosimo de' Medici as the beautiful boy Ganymede being carried off by a protective Emperor Charles V, symbolised by Jupiter in the guise of an eagle. Meanwhile, the engagement at Montemurlo rages beneath them whilst Florence and the Duomo may be seen far off in the distance. Giorgio Vasari's fresco *Il trionfo di Cosimo a Montemurlo* in the Palazzo Vecchio is equally propagandistic in tone. In Vasari's work, which is influenced by classical ancient Roman imagery, Cosimo–attired as a classical Roman general or emperor–gazes down at the naked, bound and vanquished figures of the republican rebels Bartolomeo Valori, Filippo Strozzi and Anton Francesco degli Albizzi. Here is a stern yet magnanimous victor whose bloody military accomplishment has been transmuted by art into a serene, aesthetic representation of the revivified Medici status quo.

But what was particularly galling for Cosimo, however, was the fact that certain of these political opponents had been ransomed back to him by Vitelli's Spanish troops. Some of these had their sentences commuted by Cosimo to a lengthy term of imprisonment. This was the fate of Bartolomeo Valori's own son Paolo Antonio Valori, as well as exiles (now termed 'rebels') such as Vieri da Castiglione or Battista Canigiani. As for Filippo Strozzi himself, he became Vitelli's own personal prisoner and was permitted to continue his life in captivity at the Fortezza da Basso with some degree of normalcy, being permitted to correspond with his fugitive sons and erstwhile republican allies. As such, Strozzi represented a constant hazard as he had the means to bribe his way free at any moment. There was no reason to imagine why Vitelli would not accept Strozzi's money; the *condottiere* was extremely limited in his ambitions, caring only for his family fief of Città di Castello.

In the event, thankfully Cosimo was saved by Filippo's own growing sense of despair and weariness with the whole republican struggle. Tired of his sixteen month incarceration, and the intermittent bouts of torture that he was made to endure, to induce him to admit to complicity in Lorenzino's assassination plot, Strozzi is said to have taken his own life on 18 December 1538 by falling on a sword left carelessly lying around by a guard. Since suicide was regarded as a sin, Cosimo took this as an indication of his 'most vile soul'. What really happened in that cell will perhaps never be known. Some speculated that Strozzi was killed on the orders of the marchese del Vasto at Charles V's instigation. As Charles's counsellor, Cardinal Antoine Perrenot de Granvelle (the son of Nicolas Perrenot de Granvelle) had remarked at the time: 'A dead man can make no war'. Others surmised that certain imperial officers wished to see certain debts which they owed to Strozzi wiped clean, whilst doing Strozzi 'the favour' of sparing him from the horrible torture which awaited him if Vitelli eventually surrendered him into the hands of Cosimo. Filippo supposedly left a suicide note, inspired by Cato, in which he requested 'Don Giovanni di Luna, the commandant of the citadel, to make a sausage with my blood, and to send it to the Cardinal Cybò, that he may be satiated after my death with what he always longed for during my life'.

The Grand Duke of Tuscany

Duke he will be of Florence as a young man
of eighteen, that generous son,
for his merits and his lineage elected
by the will of that whole council.
Thereafter called grand duke of Tuscany,
which he will guard from every peril;
nor certainly a worthier man will
the sun ever see, which spreads everywhere its rays.

Tredici canti del Floridoro, canto 58, Moderata Fonte

To be fair, the victory at Montemurlo was by no means the end of Cosimo de' Medici's problems. Enemies, both foreign and domestic, still remained aplenty. Of the *fuoriusciti* these included Filippo's hot-headed sons Leone Strozzi and the irascible Piero. The banker Roberto Strozzi was also still at-large, though by now in comfortable exile in Venice with his wife Maddalena de' Medici. In 1542, the artist Titian would paint their young daughter Clarice; the portrait, which depicts an angelic curly haired child playing with her pet dog, reeks of relaxed privilege and status, not desperation or dire financial straits (Roberto was by no means experiencing the poverty of his ancestor Palla Strozzi). But in truth the exiles were by now a spent force. Not only had all their more important leaders been either captured, imprisoned or executed but those who still remained at liberty either in Lyons, Venice, Rome or hovering on the periphery of Tuscany itself, now refused to place their confidence in the erratic leadership of Filippo the Younger's sons. Discreetly, many of these exiles now defected to Cosimo. Vincenzo Martelli, the less well known brother of Niccolò Martelli, the poet and co-founder of the *Accademia Fiorentina*, was one of these former exiles who saw no shame in making their peace with Cosimo. Martelli, who had sought refuge with his employer Ferrante Sanseverino, Prince of Salerno, was soon asking his friends in Florence 'to kiss humbly the hands of His Excellency the Duke of Signoria Maria' and before long we find him working in Cosimo's own household as major-domo.

Other remaining exiles who could not bring themselves to reconcile with Cosimo settled down into safe and largely humdrum lives. Luigi Alamanni continued to charm and to enjoy the confidence of the French king and, after François's death in March 1547 at the age of fifty-two, Catherine de' Medici's husband King Henry II would continue to sponsor his career. Alamanni would die in 1556 whilst serving as Henry's ambassador to Genoa. Michelangelo's acquaintance Donato Giannotti would meanwhile continue to live in Rome until the ripe old age of eighty-one, blessed with the patronage of Cardinal Niccolò Ridolfi, whom Giannotti would outlive by twenty-three years. The story was a similar one for other prominent *fuoriusciti* such as Bartolomeo Cavalcanti, Luigi del Riccio and Giovanni Battista Busini. Another longstanding Medici enemy was removed in October 1538 when Francesco Maria della Rovere, Duke of Urbino, was assassinated by his barber-surgeon who poured a poisoned unction into his ears. The Duke was forty-eight years old and his abrasive likeness had been painted earlier that same year by Titian. The murder, which had been instigated by the Duke's brother-in-law Luigi Gonzaga, became the basis for *The Murder of Gonzago*, the story-within-a-story which is recounted in William Shakespeare's play *Hamlet, Prince of Denmark*.

As for Michelangelo, who styled himself as one of the *fuoriusciti* but who had never taken up arms to challenge Florence's new ruler, his trials and tribulations still had many years to run. In Pope Paul III he found an even harder taskmaster than the late Sixtus IV and the Farnese pontiff ensured that Clement's final commission, *The Last Judgement*, was completed to his satisfaction (although the Council of Trent would later order that loincloths be painted over all the male genitals in the fresco). Some of his most famous work still lay ahead of him, such as the redesign of the Capitoline Hill and its *piazza*, and in 1546 Michelangelo was appointed architect of St. Peter's Basilica whereupon he returned the design to his old adversary Bramante's original concept. In his later years his mind turned increasingly to thoughts of mortality, as is evidenced from his preoccupation with drawing and sculpting a number of Pietàs. Upon his death in Rome in 1564, at the age of eighty-eight, Michelangelo's body was moved to Florence for burial at the Basilica of Santa Croce. Despite his many frustrations with the Florentines themselves, the artist had always had a deep devotion towards his beloved Florence and so this had been his final request.

Having pacified the *fuoriusciti*, Cosimo's next challenge was to wrest power from the 'magnificent *palleschi* counsellors' who had so smugly set themselves over him. This was accomplished relatively easily. As early as June 1537, the Emperor's ambassador Cifuentes was liaising directly with Cosimo on all matters of state, hardly bothering to go through *ottimati* intermediaries like Francesco Guicciardini or Francesco Vettori. Realising that he had been trumped by the young duke, who had effectively consolidated all political power in his own person, Guicciardini had the prudence to quietly remove himself to the Villa Ravà, a family-owned villa in the countryside round Arcetri, where he devoted the remaining months of his life to rewriting the *Storia d'Italia*. Angered by his dismissal, Guicciardini skewed his revised history to make it seem like he had never been one of the *palleschi* but was always a loyal servant of the republic. This formerly great Florentine statesman died quietly and without fanfare in May 1540 aged fifty-seven, having set the rigorous standard by which the modern discipline of history would later be judged.

Vettori also did likewise, retiring to his own villa and dying one year before Guicciardini. A minor historian of some note himself, having written the *Sommario della istoria d'Italia* ('Summary of the History of Italy'), Vettori is best remembered today however for his illuminating correspondence with his lifelong friend Machiavelli. The letter which Machiavelli wrote to him on 10 December 1513 has become one of the best known letters in all Italian history. It described the creative process from which his most famous book *The Prince* had arisen and lovingly recalled Machiavelli's habit of communing with the long dead statesmen and men of letters of ancient Rome:

'On the coming of evening, I return to my house and enter my study; and at the door I take off the day's clothing, covered with mud and dust, and put on garments regal and courtly; and reclothed appropriately, I enter the ancient courts of ancient men, where, received by them with affection, I feed on that food which only is mine and which I was born for, where I am not ashamed to speak with them and to ask them the reason for their actions; and they in their kindness answer me; and for four hours of time I do not feel boredom, I forget every trouble, I do not dread poverty, I am not frightened by death; entirely I give myself over to them.'

The third most important battle was reserved for last and it was the battle of wits with Charles V to prise Florence's liberty from the Empire just when it seemed doomed to be consigned to being little more than an imperial fiefdom. Cosimo's principal adversaries in this respect were Cardinal Innocenzo Cybò, the military commander Alessandro Vitelli and of course Charles V himself. Cosimo had tried to follow his former counsellor Guicciardini's advice in seeking to move closer to Charles's own family, a strategy which had worked especially well for Alessandro. However the match that Cosimo now demanded with the Dowager Duchess Margaret, who would have been glad to remain with him in Florence, was not to be. The Emperor was intent on making far greater political capital from his daughter's newly available status and, at this moment in time, he especially needed the cooperation of the Pope. In 1538, Margaret was henceforth married off–very much against her will–to Ottavio Farnese, the grandson of Pope Paul III.

As individuals, the Farnese family were hardly much of an improvement on the Borgia or the Riario/della Rovere. Not only had Ottavio's father Pier Luigi Farnese served in the imperial army which had sacked Rome in 1527 but ten years later he was also notoriously implicated in the brutal sodomising of the fifteen-year-old bishop of Fano, Cosimo Gheri. The scandal, which would become known up and down the length of Italy as 'The Rape of Fano', resulted in the young bishop's death a month later from shame and bowel trauma in equal measure. Recounted by Benedetto Varchi in his *Storia fiorentina*, the incident also gave the Lutherans ample excuse to further criticise popery ('the Catholics have found novel new ways to execute their Saints' they gleefully quipped). In protest at being absorbed into such an outrageously lawless family, Margaret initially refused to consummate her enforced marriage. Ottavio would, after Pier Luigi's assassination, succeed his father as the duke of Parma and Piacenza and Margaret became his duchess. As part of her generous dowry and inheritance settlement with the Medici family she obtained ownership of the late Pope Clement VII's beautiful Palazzo Medici in Rome which thereafter became known as the Palazzo Madama after its new mistress, who became known simply as 'Madama'. Margaret herself would be appointed as Governor of the Netherlands by her half-brother Philip II of Spain in 1559 and for twenty-seven years until her death enjoyed a career as a pliable political tool of the Habsburgs in the Low Countries. The couple's son Alexander Farnese would be the same duke of Parma who, in 1588, took such an active role in the Spanish

Armada's fruitless 'enterprise of England' and upon whom Queen Elizabeth I poured her 'foul scorn' during her famous speech at Tilbury.

With Margaret held out of reach, in June 1539 Cosimo arguably found an even more advantageous match in Eleonora de Toledo, the proud Spanish daughter of Charles V's powerful viceroy of Naples, Don Pedro Álvarez. Like many Spanish aristocrats of his ilk Don Pedro had become staggeringly wealthy thanks to shipments of gold bullion from the New World. For Cosimo he would be a powerful financier, backer and lobbyist with the Emperor. Whereas the immoral conduct of the former Duke Alessandro had provided discontented Florentines with ample grounds for challenging the whole idea of ducal rule, Cosimo's behaviour seemed by contrast beyond reproach. Indeed, Cosimo had wisely rescinded many of the more barbarous and unjust laws which, fired with Savonarolan piety, had been implemented during the 'good old days' of the republic.

For her part, Eleonora de Toledo was not such an asset in this respect; being perceived–as Spaniards usually were in Florence–as being both proud and haughty. When Cosimo, by now styling himself as duke, moved his official residence from the Palazzo Medici to the Palazzo della Signoria, his wife complained disdainfully about the draftiness and inconvenience of the building which had formerly stood for so many decades as Florence's proud republican seat of government. She would use her own money in 1549 to purchase the Palazzo Pitti, still the largest private *palazzo* in the city, as a suitably grandiose residence, whereupon the Palazzo della Signoria was renamed the Palazzo Vecchio, or the 'Old Palace'. Cosimo's mother Maria Salviati, wife to the beloved Giovanni della Bande Nere, continued on the other hand to be perceived by the citizens as pious, faithful and kind, and this helped to offset the dislike which Eleonora tended to provoke. Maria died on 29 December 1543, just one year after the death of Cosimo's illegitimate daughter Bia.

Of Cosimo's remaining adversaries within Florence itself, Charles's representative, Cardinal Innocenzo Cybò, had found like the *palleschi* that his power had eroded virtually to nothing. His last assignment of any importance was as Cosimo's envoy to a series of discussions being held at Nice and Aigues Mortes between June and July 1538 between Charles V, François I and Pope Paul III. During one of the smaller side conferences concerning Florence it was agreed that Alessandro Vitelli would be relieved from his duties as castellan of the Fortezza da Basso and the Spanish garrison would be reduced to a mere 200 soldiers, a great victory for Cosimo since the Florentine militia could now effectively assume control of the city. But in spite of winning this important concession, Cardinal Cybò fell into increasing disfavour with the Duke, not least for the exorbitant expenses bill that he had presented to Cosimo for his diplomatic services. Worse still, Cosimo soon learned that the good cardinal had been passing juicy snippets of court gossip to his former lover, his sister-in-law Ricciarda Malaspina in Rome. The promiscuous and mischievous Ricciarda would then pass the information on to her own circle of intriguers and troublemakers. Consequently every move and every decision made at Cosimo's court was known almost simultaneously in Rome and Cosimo complained bitterly to Bandini: 'no one could open his lips in my house ... but it was known there [in Rome] almost before the words were spoken'. Cybò's behaviour became increasingly unreliable and erratic. He had recently assumed custody of Alessandro's son Giulio, whom he kept a virtual captive in his *palazzo*. Not only was he now puffing the five-year-old up with high-sounding titles and treating him like royalty, but he was also mischievously putting it about that Cosimo had hired an apothecary named Biaggio to poison the child. But Cybò's propaganda campaign, poorly thought through as it was, could only backfire on him. When Cosimo, in a beautifully conceived *coup de théâtre*, sent the calumniated Biaggio to confront Cybò at his own dinner table, the latter realised that the game was up and promptly fled Florence.

In the years that followed Duke Cosimo I would maintain his policy of alliance with Spain and the Empire against France. As usual, the main bone of contention was the competing French and imperial claims to Milan, which François's successor Henry II of France continued to pursue after his father's death in 1547. But whereas Florence had suffered from the effects of the Italian Wars from 1494 to 1530, during the final 17 years of the devastating conflict Duke Cosimo I succeeded in turning the war to Florence's advantage. The borders of the duchy of Florence, created by Charles V and Alessandro de' Medici in 1530 from the ashes of the Republic of Florence, would be extended and expanded in ways which Cosimo *pater patriae* or Lorenzo *il Magnifico* could only have dreamt of. The island of Elba was purchased from Genoa in 1548 and it became the base for Florence's fledgling navy. Cosimo's next move was to establish the port city of Livorno, which would be dominated by the Medicean Fortezza Vecchia, designed by Antonio da Sangallo the Younger. In August 1554, Siena's army under the command of the exile Piero Strozzi was bloodily vanquished at the Battle of Marciano.

The Strozzi scion escaped yet again but despite his many military failures on behalf of the rebels his fortunes would continue to rise. In 1554 Strozzi would be appointed marshal of France under King Henry II and Queen Catherine de' Medici. Siena, which had misguidedly placed her trust in Piero Strozzi, was not so fortunate; after an eighteen month retaliatory siege, the city finally capitulated to the forces of Florence and Spain on 17 April 1555, marking the end of the *Sienese* Republic. Philip II of Spain, who was at the time massively in debt to the Medici, ceded Siena to Cosimo I and the illustrious city was absorbed into the duchy of Florence. On 3 April 1559, *La pace di Cateau-Cambrésis* was finally signed between France and the Empire, drawing the sixty-five-year-long Italian Wars to an end. But by now the monarchs flicking their quills across the parchment of the truce were no longer Charles V and François I for the baton had passed to a new generation, their sons Philip II of Spain and Henry II of France. Ten years after the peace was concluded, in 1569, Cosimo I de' Medici was elevated to the rank of grand duke of Tuscany by Pope Pius V. The Grand Duchy of Tuscany would be ruled by the Medici for the next 168 years until the main line of the family was extinguished in 1737.

Giovanni di Bicci's eldest son Cosimo de' Medici had arguably been forced to take power in Florence to protect his social position, his family and his thriving business. Thanks to their enormous reserves of capital and their sophisticated network of political patronage, the Medici had managed to forge a hereditary dynasty within the confines of an ostensibly republican system. That had culminated in the Medici dukedom of Alessandro in 1530 and the Grand Duchy of Cosimo I in 1569. But it is debatably Catherine de' Medici's marriage to Henry of France in October 1533 which launched the Medici upon the European royal stage. This first royal union of the Medici produced no less than three Valois kings of France and one Valois queen of France. These were Francis II, Charles IX, and Henry III. Furthermore, when Henry of Navarre assumed the throne in the aftermath of the French Wars of Religion, he married Catherine's spirited and beautiful daughter Margaret, making her queen of France. King Henry IV of France and Queen Margaret had no issue of their own and, when their union was annulled in 1599, Henry would subsequently remarry Marie de' Medici, the granddaughter of Grand Duke Cosimo I. Their union would produce a whole raft of Bourbon kings: Louis XIII would subsequently be followed by Louis XIV, Louis XV (through Louis the Grand *Dauphin*, the son of Louis XIV) and finally Louis XVI (through Louis the *Dauphin* of France, the son of Louis XV). We all know how the story of King Louis XVI of France ends. The French king who lost his head on 21 January 1793 at the Place de la Révolution was a distant blood relation of Grand Duke Cosimo I of Florence. The unfortunate king who perished under the guillotine that day had slickened the scaffold with blood which was tied to the Italian patriot Giovanni della Bande Nere; to Francesco Sforza (through the *condottiere's* mother Caterina Sforza); to Lorenzo *il Magnifico* (through his eldest daughter Lucrezia, the mother of Maria Salviati); and ultimately to Giovanni di Bicci, the founder of the dynasty.

Meanwhile, Henry IV and Marie de' Medici's daughter Élisabeth, Madame Royale, married Philip IV of Spain thereby becoming a Medici queen of Spain. Élisabeth's daughter Maria Theresa of Spain would marry Louis XIV the famous 'Sun King' of France. The Sun King's eldest son Louis, the Grand *Dauphin*, then produced a son, Philip, who fought the War of the Spanish Succession to become Philip V of Spain, a king of Spain who had Medici blood flowing through his veins.

Another of Henry and Marie de' Medici's daughters, Henrietta Maria, became the queen of England after marrying King Charles I, who subsequently lost his crown, as well as his head, to England's puritan parliamentarians. But Henrietta Maria's son Charles II later returned to his realm in triumph (in true Medici style in fact) and sired a small army of descendants with numerous mistresses, although not with his lawful wife Queen Catherine of Braganza. Charles II's illegitimate issue, just on the male side alone, reads like a chapter in Debretts. In addition to the duke of Monmouth, who was executed after contesting his uncle James II for the crown of England, Charles II sired Charles FitzCharles, the earl of Plymouth; Charles Fitzroy, the duke of Southampton and second duke of Cleveland; Henry Fitzroy, the earl of Euston and duke of Grafton (a distant relative of Diana, Princess of Wales); George Fitzroy, the duke of Northumberland; Charles Beauclerk, the duke of St Albans; and finally Charles Lennox, the duke of Richmond and duke of Lennox (and yet another distant ancestor of Princess Diana, as well as Camilla, duchess of Cornwall, and Sarah, duchess of York).

Through Grand Duke Cosimo I's eldest son Francesco I, Grand Duke of Tuscany, we find his daughter Eleanor de' Medici giving birth to Eleonora Gonzaga who eventually became the second wife of Ferdinand II, Holy Roman Emperor. By virtue of this union Eleanor became archduchess consort of Austria, queen of Germany, and queen consort of Hungary and Bohemia. A descendant of Eleanor de' Medici's other daughter, Margherita Gonzaga, duchess of Lorraine, would meanwhile become Francis I, Holy Roman Emperor, through the noble line of the dukes of Lorraine.

Through Grand Duke Cosimo I's second son Grand Duke Ferdinando I, the younger brother and successor to Grand Duke Francesco I, we find Ferdinando's daughter Claudia marrying Leopold V, archduke of Austria and thus becoming archduchess of Austria. Their son Ferdinand Charles, archduke of Austria, married Anna de' Medici (the daughter of Cosimo II de' Medici, Grand Duke of Tuscany) and with her he sired Claudia Felicitas of Austria, who in turn married Leopold I, Holy Roman Emperor, and sired the archduchess Anna Maria Sophia and the archduchess Maria Josepha. Therefore it is perhaps safe to say that the Medici had Austria sewn up at least until the late seventeenth-century.

It is with the above in mind that the full irony of this book's subtitle ('*Rise of a Parvenu Dynasty*') was intended. For when you trace their relatively humble origins in the Mugello *contado* and how the early Medici fought some of the most powerful *grandi* families in Florence to gain control of the state and then, having furnished two popes, how the family subsequently integrated–seemingly effortlessly, or at least by some quaint coincidence of fate–with the most powerful royal houses of Europe, it is a truly astonishing story of epic upward social mobility. Oxymoronically, the House of Medici was indeed both *parvenu* and a *dynasty* in the fullest possible senses of those two words. Yet, as Dante Alighieri had forewarned in Inferno, Canto XVI, the Republic of Florence ultimately had cause to regret the upward social mobility of the extremely wealthy. It was, after all was said and done, a phenomenon which began most laudably with the fulfilment of upstanding humanist civic obligations, but which finally ended in 'arrogance and intemperance' (*orgoglio e dismisura*). With regard to the final *dénouement* of Medici ducal rule, if the white Guelph Dante had had a crystal ball he could not have prophesied Florence's fate more accurately.

SELECT BIBLIOGRAPHY

Addington Symonds, J., Renaissance in Italy: *The Age of the Despots* (University Press of the Pacific, 2002).

Addington Symonds, J., *Renaissance in Italy: Italian literature* (Nabu Press, 2010).

Ady, C., *A History of Milan under the Sforza* (CreateSpace Independent Publishing, 2015).

Ady, C., *Bentivoglio of Bologna: A Study In Despotism* (Oxford University Press, 1969).

Ady, C., *Lorenzo De Medici and Renaissance Italy (Men & Their Times)*, (Hodder & Stoughton Ltd, 1970).

Ady, C., *Pius II: Æneas Silvius Piccolomini; The Humanist Pope* (Forgotten Books, 2015).

Ainsworth, W. H., *The Constable de Bourbon* (Library of Alexandria, 2015).

Ackroyd, P., *Venice: Pure City* (Anchor, 2011).

Albury, W. R., *Castiglione's Allegory: Veiled Policy in The Book of the Courtier (1528)*, (Routledge New edition, 2014).

Angeli, F., *Growing in the shadow of an empire. How Spanish colonialism affected economic development in Europe and in the world (XVI-XVIII cc.)*.

Armstrong, N. (editor), Tennenhouse, L. (editor), *The Violence of Representation (Routledge Revivals): Literature and the History of Violence* (Routledge, 2014).

Arnold, T., *The Renaissance at War (Smithsonian History of Warfare)* (Harper Perennial, 2006).

Babinger, F., *Mehmed the Conqueror and His Time* (Princeton University Press, 1992).

Baker, N. S., *The Fruit of Liberty: Political Culture in the Florentine Renaissance, 1480-1550* (Harvard University Press, 2013).

Bandi, G., *Pietro Carnesecchi: storia fiorentina del secolo XVI, Volume 1* (Nabu Press, 2010).

Beecher, D., *Renaissance Comedy: The Italian Masters - Volume 1 (Lorenzo Da Ponte Italian Library) (Vol 1)*, (University of Toronto Press, 2008).

Bicheno, H., *Vendetta: High Art and Low Cunning at the Birth of the Renaissance* (Phoenix, 2009).

Bietenholz, P.G. (editor), Deutscher, T.B. (editor), *Contemporaries of Erasmus: A Biographical Register of the Renaissance and Reformation* (University of Toronto Press, 2003).

Biow, D., *On the Importance of Being an Individual in Renaissance Italy: Men, Their Professions, and Their Beards* (University of Pennsylvania Press, 2015).

Bisaha, N. (editor), *Europe (c.1400-1458): Translated by Robert Brown Introduced and annotated by Nancy Bisaha* (The Catholic University of America Press, 2013).

Black, R., *Renaissance Thought: A Reader* (Routledge, 2001).

Black, R., *Machiavelli* (Routledge, 2013).

Bloom, H., *The Italian Renaissance* (Chelsea House Publishers, 2004).

Bondanella, J. C. (editor), Musa, M. (editor), *The Italian Renaissance Reader* (Plume, 1987).

Booth, C., *Cosimo I: Duke of Florence* (Forgotten Books, 2015).

Bornstein, D. E. (editor), Najemy, J. M. (editor), Peterson, D. S. (editor), *Florence and Beyond: Culture, Society and Politics in Renaissance Italy (Essays in Honour of John M. Najemy)*, (Centre for Reformation and Renaissance Studies, 2008).

Bradford, S., *Lucrezia Borgia: Life, Love, and Death in Renaissance Italy* (Penguin Books, 2005).

Brackett, J. K., *Criminal Justice and Crime in Late Renaissance Florence, 1537-1609* (Cambridge University Press, 2002).

Brewer, J. S., (editor), *Letters and Papers, Foreign and Domestic, of the Reign of Henry VIII, Volume 3* (Cambridge University Press, 2015).

Brion, M., *The Medici: A Great Florentine Family* (Bookthrift Co, 1981).

Brown, A., *Bartolomeo Scala, 1430-1497, Chancellor of Florence: The Humanist As Bureaucrat* (Princeton Univ Press, 1979).

Brown, A., *The Return of Lucretius to Renaissance Florence (I Tatti Studies in Italian Renaissance History)*, (Harvard University Press, 2010).

Brownworth, L., *Lost to the West: The Forgotten Byzantine Empire That Rescued Western Civilization* (Broadway Books, 2010).

Brucker, G. A., *Florence, the Golden Age, 1138-1737* (University of California Press, 1998).

Brucker, G. A., *Florence, Renaissance Florence, Updated edition* (University of California Press, 1983).

Brucker, G. A., *The Civic World of Early Renaissance Florence* (ACLS Humanities e-Book, 2008).

Bull, M., *The Mirror of the Gods: Classical Mythology in Renaissance Art* (Allen Lane, 2005).

Bullard, M. M., *Filippo Strozzi and the Medici: Favor and Finance in Sixteenth-Century Florence and Rome (Cambridge Studies in Early Modern History)* (Cambridge University Press, 2008).

Buonarroti, M. (author), Ramsden, E. H. (editor), Ramsden, E. H. (translator), *The Letters of Michelangelo Translated from the original Tuscan, edited and annotated in Two volumes* (Stanford University Press, 1963).

Burckhardt, J. (author), Murray, P. (editor), Middlemore S. G. C. (translator), Burke, P. (introduction), *The Civilization of the Renaissance in Italy* (Penguin Classics, 1990).

Burke, J., *Changing Patrons: Social Identity and the Visual Arts in Renaissance Florence* (Penn State University Press, 2004).

Burke, P., *The Fortunes of the Courtier: The European Reception of Castiglione's Cortegiano* (Polity, 2013).

Burke, P., *The Italian Renaissance* (Princeton University Press, 1999).

Burman, E., *Emperor to Emperor: Italy Before the Renaissance* (Constable, 1991).

Cahill, T., *Heretics and Heroes: How Renaissance Artists and Reformation Priests Created Our World* (Anchor, 2014).

Campbell, S. J., *The Cabinet of Eros: Renaissance Mythological Painting and the Studiolo of Isabella d'Este* (Yale University Press, 2006).

Capponi, N. (author), Naffis-Sahely, A. (author), *The Day the Renaissance Was Saved: The Battle of Anghiari and da Vinci's Lost Masterpiece* (Melville House, 2015).

Capponi, N., *An Unlikely Prince: The Life and Times of Machiavelli* (Da Capo Press, 2010).

Cavalcanti, G., *The Trattato politico-morale of Giovanni Cavalcanti (1381-c. 1451): A critical edition and interpretation (Travaux d'humanisme et renaissance, 135)*.

Cellini, B. (author), Bondanella, J. C. (translator), Bondanella, P. (translator), *My Life by Benvenuto Cellini* (Oxford University Press, 2009).

Cesati, F., *Medici: Story of a European Dynasty* (Mandragora Srl, 2006).

Chamberlin, E. R., *The Bad Popes* (Barnes & Noble, 2003).

Chamberlin, E. R., *The Fall of the House of Borgia* (The Dial Book Club, 1974).

Chamberlin, E. R., *The Sack of Rome* (Dorset Press, 1985).

Chamberlin, E. R., *The World of the Italian Renaissance* (Unwin Hyman, 1982).

Christiansen, K. (editor), Weppelmann, S. (editor), *The Renaissance Portrait: From Donatello to Bellini* (Metropolitan Museum of Art, 2011).

Ciappelli, G., *Memory, Family, and Self: Tuscan Family Books and Other European Egodocuments (14th-18th Century)*, (Brill Academic Publishers, 2014).

Cloulas, I. (author), Roberts, G. (translator), *The Borgias* (Franklin Watts, 1989).

Cochrane, E., *Florence in the Forgotten Centuries: 1527-1800* (University Of Chicago Press, 2013).

Cochrane, E. (author), Kirshner, J. (editor), *Italy, 1530-1630* (Longman, 1989).

Cohn, S. K., *The Laboring Classes in Renaissance Florence* (Academic Press, 1980).

Cole, B., *Titian And Venetian Painting, 1450-1590* (Westview Press, 2000).

Connell, W. J., *Society and Individual in Renaissance Florence* (University of California Press, 2002).

Connell, W. J. (editor), Zorzi, A. (editor), *Florentine Tuscany: Structures and Practices of Power* (Cambridge University Press, 2004).

Corfis, I. A. (editor), Wolfe, M. (editor), *The Medieval City Under Siege* (Boydell & Brewer Inc, 1995).

Corio, B., *Storia Di Milano, Volume 2* (Nabu Press, 2013).

Corkery, J. (editor), Worcester, T. (editor), *The Papacy Since 1500: From Italian Prince to Universal Pastor* (Cambridge University Press, 2010).

Cox-Rearick, J., *Bronzino's Chapel of Eleonora in the Palazzo Vecchio* (University of California Press, 1993).

Creighton, M., *A History of the Papacy During the Period of the Reformation* (Cambridge University Press, 2011).

Cropper, E., *Pontormo: Portrait of a Halberdier* (J. Paul Getty Museum, 1998).

Crowley, R., *1453: The Holy War for Constantinople and the Clash of Islam and the West* (Hachette Books, 2006).

Crowley, R., *City of Fortune: How Venice Ruled the Seas* (Random House Trade Paperbacks, 2013).

Crum, R. J. (editor), Paoletti, J. T. (editor), *Renaissance Florence: A Social History 1st Edition* (Cambridge University Press, 2008).

Cummings, A. M., *The Maecenas And The Madrigalist: Patrons, Patronage, And The Origins Of The Italian Madrigal (Memoirs of the American Philosophical Society)*, (American Philosophical Society, 2004).

Cunningham, L. S., Reich, J. J., *Culture and Values: A Survey of the Humanities* (Wadsworth Publishing, 2009).

Currie, E., *Fashion and Masculinity in Renaissance Florence* (Bloomsbury Academic, 2016).

Dall'Aglio, S. (author), Weinstein, D. (translator), *The Duke's Assassin: Exile and Death of Lorenzino de' Medici* (Yale University Press, 2015).

Dameron, G. W., *Florence and Its Church in the Age of Dante* (University of Pennsylvania Press, 2013).

Dandelet, T. J., *The Renaissance of Empire in Early Modern Europe* (Cambridge University Press, 2014).

Dandelet, T. J. (editor), Marino, J. (editor), *Spain in Italy: Politics, Society, and Religion 1500-1700 (Medieval and Early Modern Iberian World)*, (Brill, 2006).

Davies, J., *Florence and Its University During the Early Renaissance* (Brill Academic Pub, 1998).

Davies, J., *Aspects of Violence in Renaissance Europe* (Routledge, 2013).

Dean, T., *The Towns of Italy in the Later Middle Ages* (Manchester University Press, 2000).

De Grazia, S., *Machiavelli in Hell* (Vintage, 1994).

De Jong, J. L., *The Power and the Glorification: Papal Pretensions and the Art of Propaganda in the Fifteenth and Sixteenth Centuries* (Penn State University Press, 2013).

De Keyser, J., *Francesco Filelfo and Francesco Sforza: Critical Edition of Filelfo's Sphortias. De genuensium deditione. Oratio parentalis, and his Polemical Exchange with Galeotto Marzio* (Georg Olms Verlag, 2015).

Delbeke, M. (editor), Schraven, M. (editor), *Foundation, Dedication and Consecration in Early Modern Europe* (BRILL, 2011).

Delmarcel, G. (editor), Delmarcel, G. (contributor), *Flemish Tapestry Weavers Abroad: Emigration and the Founding of Manufactories in Europe Proceedings of the International Conference, Mechelen, October* (Leuven University Press, 2002).

Delph, R. K. (editor), Fontaine, M. M. (editor), Martin, J. J. (editor), *Heresy, Culture, and Religion in Early Modern Italy: Contexts and Contestations (Sixteenth Century Essays and Studies)*, (Truman State University Press, 2006).

Demchak, C. C., *Wars of Disruption and Resilience: Cybered Conflict, Power, and National Security (Studies in Security and International Affairs)*, (University of Georgia Press, 2011).

Dennistoun, J., *Memoirs of the Dukes of Urbino, illustrating the arms, arts, and literature of Italy, from 1440 to 1630 (Volume 2)*, (Filiquarian Legacy Publishing, 2012).

De Roover, R., *The Rise and Decline of the Medici Bank: 1397-1494* (Beard Books, 1999).

Dickie, J., *The Delizia!: The Epic History of the Italians and Their Food* (Atria Books, 2010).

Di Tuccio Manetti, A. (author), Enggass, C. (translator), *The Life of Brunelleschi (English and Italian Edition)*, (The Pennsylvania State University Press, 1970).

Dooley, B., *The Dissemination of News and the Emergence of Contemporaneity in Early Modern Europe* (Routledge, 2010).

Alexandre Dumas, A., *The Borgias* (CreateSpace Independent Publishing, 2012).

Earle, T. F. (editor), Lowe, K. J. P. (editor), *Black Africans in Renaissance Europe* (Cambridge University Press, 2010).

Edelheit, A., *Ficino, Pico and Savonarola: The Evolution of Humanist Theology 1461/2-1498* (Brill, 2008).

Eisenbichler, K. (editor), Grendler, P. F. (editor), Terpstra, N. (editor), *Renaissance in the Streets, Schools and Studies. Essays in Honour of Paul F. Grendler* (Centre for Reformation and Renaissance Studies, 2008).

Eisenbichler, K. (editor), *The Cultural Politics of Duke Cosimo I De' Medici* (Ashgate, 2001).

Ekserdjian, D., *Parmigianino* (Yale University Press, 2006).

Elliott, S., *Italian Renaissance Painting* (Phaidon Press, 2000).

Ewart, K. D., *Cosimo de Medici* (MacMillan, 1899).

Filarete, F. and Manfidi, A., *Libro Cerimoniale of the Florentine Republic, by Francesco*.

Finucane, R. C., *Contested Canonizations: The Last Medieval Saints, 1482-1523* (The Catholic University of America Press, 2011).

Fletcher, C., *The Black Prince of Florence: The Spectacular Life and Treacherous World of Alessandro de' Medici* (Oxford University Press, 2016).

Florescu, R. R. (author), McNally, R. T. (author), *Dracula, Prince of Many Faces: His Life and His Times* (Back Bay Books, 1990).

Forcellino, A., *Michelangelo: A Tormented Life* (Polity, 1625).

Fraser, A., *The Six Wives of Henry VIII*, Weidenfeld & Nicolson, 1992).

Freely, J., *The Grand Turk: Sultan Mehmet II-Conqueror of Constantinople and Master of an Empire* (The Overlook Press, 2009).

Frieda, L., *Catherine de Medici: A Biography* (Harper Perennial, 2006).

Frieda, L., *The Deadly Sisterhood: A Story of Women, Power, and Intrigue in the Italian Renaissance, 1427-1527* (Harper, 2013).

Gaetana Marrone G. (editor), Puppa, P. (editor), *Encyclopedia of Italian Literary Studies: A-J* (Routledge, 2006).

Gaisser, J. H., *Pierio Valeriano on the Ill Fortune of Learned Men: A Renaissance Humanist and His World (Recentiores: Later Latin Texts and Contexts)*, (University of Michigan Press, 1999).

Garin, E. (author), Cochrane, L. G. (translator), *Renaissance Characters* (University Of Chicago Press; 1 edition (May 9, 1997).

Garratt, E., *The Story of Florence* (J. M. Dent & Co.,1902).

Gaylard, S., *Hollow Men: Writing, Objects, and Public Image in Renaissance Italy* (Fordham University Press, 2013).

Geanakoplos, D. J., *Constantinople and the West: Essays on the Late Byzantine (Palaeologan) and Italian Renaissances and the Byzantine and Roman Churches* (University of Wisconsin Press, 1989).

Gill. A., *Il Gigante: Michelangelo, Florence, and the David 1492-1504* (St. Martin's Griffin, 2004).

Gill, J., *The Council of Florence* (Cambridge University Press, 1959).

Goldthwaite, R. A., *The Building of Renaissance Florence: An Economic and Social History* (Johns Hopkins University Press, 1982).

Goldthwaite, R. A., *Private Wealth in Renaissance Florence* (Princeton University Press, 1968).

Goodhart Gordan, P. W. (translator), *Two Renaissance Book Hunters: The Letters of Poggius Bracciolini to Nicolaus De Niccolis* (Columbia University Press, 1991).

Gosman, M. (contributor), MacDonald, A. A. (contributor), Vanderjagt, A. J. (contributor), *Princes and Princely Culture, 1450-1650 (Brill's Studies in Intellectual History)*, (Brill Academic Publishers, 2005).

Gouwens, K., *Remembering the Renaissance: Humanist Narratives of the Sack of Rome* (Brill, 1998).

Grafton, A. (editor), Glenn, M. (editor), Settis, S. (editor), *The Classical Tradition* (Belknap Press, 2010).

Greenblatt, S., The Swerve (New York, 2011).

Griffiths, A. G. F., *The History and Romance of Crime: Italian Prisons* (Library of Alexandria, 2016).

Guicciardini, F. (author), Alexander, S. (translator), *The History of Italy* (Princeton University Press, 1984).

Guicciardini, F. (author), Trevor-Roper, H. (author), *Guicciardini. History of Italy and of Florence* (New English Library, 1966).

Gutkind, C. S., *Cosimo De' Medici: Pater Patriae, 1389-1464* (Clarendon Press, 1938).

Hale, J., *The Civilization of Europe in the Renaissance* (Harper Perennial, 2005).

Hale, J. R., *Florence and the Medici* (Phoenix, 2001).

History of the City of Rome in the Middle Ages, Vol. 2, 568-800 A.D. (Italica Press, 2001).

Hankins, J., *Humanism and Platonism in the Italian Renaissance: Humanism* (2004).

Hankins, J., *Renaissance Civic Humanism: Reappraisals and Reflections* (Cambridge University Press, 2004).

Hay, D. (author), Law, J. (author), *Italy in the Age of the Renaissance, 1380-1530 (Longman History of Italy)*, (Longman Publishing Group, 1989).

Hay, D., *The Italian Renaissance in its Historical Background 2nd Edition* (Cambridge University Press, 1977).

Herlihy, D. (author), Cohn Jr., S. K. (editor), *The Black Death and the Transformation of the West* (Harvard University Press, 1997).

Hibbard, H., *Michelangelo* (Harper & Row, 1985).

Hibbert, C., Rome: *The Biography of a City* (Penguin UK, 1987).

Hibbert, C., *The Borgias and Their Enemies: 1431-1519* (Mariner Books, 2009).

Hibbert, C., *The House of Medici: Its Rise and Fall Paperback* (William Morrow Paperbacks, 1999).

Hollingsworth, M., *The Borgias: History's Most Notorious Dynasty* (Quercus Publishing, 2016).

Hook, J., *The Sack of Rome* (Macmillan, 1972).

Hourihane, C., *The Grove Encyclopedia of Medieval Art and Architecture, Volume 2* (Oxford University Press, 2002).

Janin, H. (editor), Carlson, U. (editor), *Mercenaries in Medieval and Renaissance Europe* (McFarland, 2013).

Jardine, L. (editor), Brotton, J. (editor), *Global Interests: Renaissance Art Between East and West* (Reaktion Books, 2005).

Johnson, M., *The Borgias* (Macdonald, 1981).

Jones, P. J., *The Malatesta of Rimini and the Papal States* (Cambridge University Press, 2005).

Jones, J., *The Lost Battles: Leonardo, Michelangelo, and the Artistic Duel That Defined the Renaissance* (Knopf, 2012).

Jurdjevic, M., *A Great and Wretched City* (Harvard University Press, 2014).

Jurdjevic, M., *Guardians of Republicanism: The Valori Family in the Florentine Renaissance* (Oxford University Press, 2008).

Kasaba, R., *A Moveable Empire: Ottoman Nomads, Migrants, and Refugees* (University of Washington Press, 2009).

Kaufmann, J.E. (author), Kaufmann, H.W. (author), *The Medieval Fortress: Castles, Forts, And Walled Cities Of The Middle Ages* (Da Capo Press, 2004).

Kent, D., *The Rise of the Medici: Faction in Florence, 1426-1434* (Oxford University Press, 1978).

Kent, F. W., *Household and Lineage in Renaissance Florence: The Family Life of the Capponi, Ginori and Rucellai* (Princeton University Press, 2015).

Kertzer, D., *The Popes Against the Jews: The Vatican's Role in the Rise of Modern Anti-Semitism* (Vintage, 2002).

Kidwell, C., *Pietro Bembo: Lover, Linguist, Cardinal* (McGill-Queen's University Press, 2004).

King, B. L., *Renaissance Humanism: An Anthology of Sources* (Hackett Publishing Company, Inc., 2014).

King, M, *The Renaissance in Europe 1st Edition* (McGraw-Hill Humanities/Social Sciences/Languages, 2003).

King, R., *Brunelleschi's Dome: How a Renaissance Genius Reinvented Architecture* (Bloomsbury USA, 2013).

King, R., *Leonardo and the Last Supper* (Bloomsbury USA, 2013).

Knecht, R. J., *Francis I* (Cambridge University Press, 1984).

Knecht, R. J., *The Valois: Kings of France 1328-1589* (Bloomsbury Academic, 2007).

Kohl, B. G. (editor), Witt, R. G., *The Earthly Republic: Italian Humanists on Government and Society* (University of Pennsylvania Press, 1978).

Kohn, G. C., *Dictionary of Wars* (Checkmark Books, 2006).

Konstam, A., *Pavia 1525: The Climax of the Italian Wars* (Osprey Publishing, 1996).

Langdon, G., *Medici Women: Portraits of Power, Love, and Betrayal in the Court of Duke Cosimo I* (University of Toronto Press, 2007).

Lantschner, P., *The Logic of Political Conflict in Medieval Cities: Italy and the Southern Low Countries, 1370-1440* (Oxford Historical Monographs), (Oxford University Press, 2015).

Larsen, A. R. (editor), Robin, D. (editor), Levin, C. (editor), *Encyclopedia of Women in the Renaissance: Italy, France, and England* (ABC-CLIO, 2007).

Lazzarini, I., *Communication and Conflict: Italian Diplomacy in the Early Renaissance, 1350-1520 (Oxford Studies in Medieval European History)*, (Oxford University Press, 2015).

Lee, A., *The Ugly Renaissance: Sex, Greed, Violence and Depravity in an Age of Beauty* (Anchor, 2015).

Lee, S. J., *Aspects of European History 1789-1980* (Routledge, 2001).

Leonard Simonde Sismondi, J. C., *Italian Republics: Or, the Origin, Progress, and Fall of Italian Freedom* (Nabu Press, 2010).

Lester, T., *Da Vinci's Ghost: Genius, Obsession, and How Leonardo Created the World in His Own Image* (Free Press, 2012).

Lev, E., *Tigress of Forli: The Life of Caterina Sforza* (Head of Zeus, 2012).

Levi, A., *Renaissance and Reformation: The Intellectual Genesis* (Yale University Press, 2004).

Levy, A. M., *Re-membering Masculinity in Early Modern Florence: Widowed Bodies, Mourning and Portraiture (Women and Gender in the Early Modern World)*, (Routledge, 2006).

Liss, P. K., *Isabel the Queen: Life and Times (University of Pennsylvania Press; 2 edition* (December, 2004).

Lockwood, L., *Music in Renaissance Ferrara 1400-1505: The Creation of a Musical Center in the Fifteenth Century* (Oxford University Press, 2009).

Lowe, K. J. P., *Church and Politics in Renaissance Italy: The Life and Career of Cardinal Francesco Soderini, 1453-1524* (Cambridge University Press, 2002).

Lubkin, G., *A Renaissance Court: Milan under Galleazzo Maria Sforza* (University of California Press, 1994).

Lunenfeld, M., *1492: Discovery, Invasion, Encounter : Sources and Interpretations* (Wadsworth Publishing, 1990).

Lynn, J. A., *Giant of the Grand Siècle: The French Army, 1610-1715* (Cambridge University Press, 2006).

Lynn, J. A., *Women, Armies, and Warfare in Early Modern Europe 1st Edition* (Cambridge University Press, 2008).

MacCarthy, D., *The Secretary of Macchiavelli (Volume 2); Or, the Siege of Florence. an Historical Romance* (General Books, 2012).

Machiavelli, N. (author), Constantine, P. (translator), Ascoli, A. R. (introduction), *The Essential Writings of Machiavelli* (Modern Library, 2007).

Machiavelli, N. (author), Banfield, L. F. (translator), Mansfield, H. C. (translator), *Florentine Histories* (Princeton University Press, 1988).

Machiavelli, N. (author), Bull, G. (translator), Grafton, A. (introduction), *The Prince* (Penguin Classics, 2003).

Mack, P. (Editor), Jacob, M. C. (Editor), *Politics and Culture in Early Modern Europe: Essays in Honour of H. G. Koenigsberger* (Cambridge University Press, 2002).

Madden, T. F., *The New Concise History of the Crusades (Critical Issues in World and International History)*, (Rowman & Littlefield Publishers, 2005).

Madden, T. F., *Venice: A New History* (Penguin Books, 2013).

Maguire, Y., *The Women of the Medici* (Dial Press, 1927).

Majanlahti, A., *The Families Who Made Rome: A History and a Guide* (Random House, 2006).

Mallett M. (editor), Mann, N. (editor), *Lorenzo the Magnificent: Culture and Politics* (Warburg Institute, 1996).

Mallett, M., *Mercenaries and their Masters: Warfare in Renaissance Italy* (Pen and Sword, 2009).

Mallett, M. (author), Hale, J. R. (author), *The Military Organisation of a Renaissance State: Venice C.1400 to 1617* (Cambridge University Press, 2006).

Maltby, W. S., *The Reign of Charles V (European History in Perspective)* (Palgrave Macmillan, 2004).

Malveaux, E., *The Color Line: A History* (Xlibris, 2015).

Manciolino, A., *The Complete Renaissance Swordsman: A Guide to the Use of All Manner of Weapons: Antonio Manciolino's Opera Nova (1531)*, (FreeLance Academy Press, 2010).

Margolis, O., *The Politics of Culture in Quattrocento Europe: René of Anjou in Italy* (Oxford University Press, 2016).

Martin, M., *The Decline and Fall of the Roman Church* (Putnam Pub Group, 1981).

Martines, L., *Fire in the City: Savonarola and the Struggle for the Soul of Renaissance Florence* (Oxford University Press, 2006).

Martines, L., *Furies: War in Europe, 1450–1700* (Bloomsbury Press, 2013).

Martines, L., *Power and Imagination: City-States in Renaissance Italy* (Johns Hopkins University Press, 1988).

Martines, L., *Strong Words: Writing and Social Strain in the Italian Renaissance* (The Johns Hopkins University Press, 2003).

Martines, L., *Violence and Civil Disorder in Italian Cities, 1200-1500* (Los Angeles, 1972).

Maxson, B. J., *The Humanist World of Renaissance Florence* (Cambridge University Press, 2013).

Meyer, G. J., *The Borgias: The Hidden History* (Random House, 2013).

Miller, K., *St Peter's (Wonders of the World)*, (Profile Books, 2010).

Minio-Paluello, M. L., *Jesters and Devils. A Venetian Ship of Fools, in Florence on a Midsummer Voyage in 1514. Is there method in this folly?* (lulu.com, 2008).

Mitterauer, M. (author), Sieder, R. (author), *The European Family: Patriarchy to Partnership from the Middle Ages to the Present* (University of Chicago Press, 1984).

Molho, A., *Marriage Alliance in Late Medieval Florence* (Harvard University Press, 1994).

Molho, A., *Women, Family and Society in Medieval Europe: Historical Essays, 1978-1991* (Berghahn Books, 1995).

Moudarres, A., (editor), Moudarres, C. A., (editor), *New Worlds and the Italian Renaissance: Contributions to the History of European Intellectual Culture (Brill's Studies in Itellectual History)*, (Brill Academic Publishing, 2012).

Mulryne, J. R., *Ceremonial Entries in Early Modern Europe: The Iconography of Power* (Routledge, 2016).

Murray, L., *Michelangelo (World of Art)*, (Thames & Hudson, 1985).

Murray, P., *The Architecture of the Italian Renaissance* (Schocken, 1997).

Murry, G., *The Medicean Succession (I Tatti studies in Italian Renaissance history)*, (Harvard University Press, 2014).

Musiol, M. Dr., *Vittoria Colonna: A Woman's Renaissance* (epubli GmbH).

Najemy, J. M., *A History of Florence 1200-1575* (Wiley-Blackwell, 2008).

Napier, H. E., *Florentine History, Vol. 1-6: From the Earliest Authentic Records to the Accession of Ferdinand the Third, Grand Duke of Tuscany* (Forgotten Books, 2016).

Nevile, J., *The Eloquent Body: Dance and Humanist Culture in Fifteenth-Century Italy* (Indiana University Press, 2004).

Niccoli, O. (author), Cochrane, L. G. (translator), *Prophecy and People in Renaissance Italy* (Princeton University Press, 1990).

Nicholl, C., *Leonardo da Vinci: Flights of the Mind: A Biography* (Viking Adult, 2004).

Norwich, J.J., *Absolute Monarchs: A History of the Papacy* (Random House, 2011).

Norwich, J. J., *Byzantium: The Decline and Fall* (Knopf, 1995).

Norwich, J. J., *History of Venice* (Penguin UK, 2003).

Norwich, J. J., *The Middle Sea: A History of the Mediterranean* (Vintage, 2007).

Ober, F. A., *Amerigo Vespucci* (Echo Library, 2007).

Owen, J. M., *The Clash of Ideas in World Politics: Transnational Networks, States, and Regime Change, 1510-2010 (Princeton Studies in International History and Politics)*, (Princeton University Press, 2010).

Oxford University Press, *Lorenzo de' Medici: Oxford Bibliographies Online Research Guide* (Oxford University Press, 2010).

Pagden, A., *The Languages of Political Theory in Early-Modern Europe* (Cambridge University Press; Revised ed. Edition, 1990).

Parks, T., *Medici Money: Banking, Metaphysics, and Art in Fifteenth-Century Florence* (W. W. Norton & Company, 2006).

Paoletti, C., *A Military History of Italy* (Praeger, 2007).

Paolucci, A., *Florence Art and Architecture* (H.F. Ullmann Publishing, 2012).

Parrott, D., *The Business of War: Military Enterprise and Military Revolution in Early Modern Europe* (Cambridge University Press, 2012).

Partner, P., *Renaissance Rome, 1500-59: Portrait of a Society* (University of California Press, 1977).

Pernis, M. G., (author) Adams, S. A. (author), *Federico da Montefeltro and Sigismondo Malatesta: The Eagle and the Elephant (Studies in Italian Culture)*, (Peter Lang International Academic Publishers, 2003).

Pernis, M. G., (author) Adams, S. A. (author), *Lucrezia Tornabuoni De' Medici and the Medici Family in the Fifteenth Century* (Peter Lang International Academic Publishers, 2006).

Pham, J. P., *Heirs of the Fisherman: Behind the Scenes of Papal Death and Succession* (Oxford University Press, 2004).

Phillips, J., *The Fourth Crusade and the Sack of Constantinople* (Penguin Books, 2005).

Phillips, M. S., *The Memoir of Marco Parenti: A Life in Medici Florence* (Princeton University Press, 1987).

Piccolomini, M., *The Brutus Revival: Parricide and Tyrannicide During the Renaissance* (Southern Illinois University Press, 2006).

Pius II, *Reject Æneas, Accept Pius: Selected Letters of Æneas Sylvius Piccolomini (Pope Pius II) annotated edition Edition* (The Catholic University of America Press, 2006).

Plaisance, M. (editor), Carew-Reid, N. (editor), *Florence in the Time of the Medici: Public Celebrations, Politics, and Literature in the Fifteenth and Sixteenth Centuries (Essays and Studies, Vol. 14)*, (Centre for Reformation and Renaissance Studies, 2008).

Plumb, J.H., *The Italian Renaissance Revised Edition* (Mariner Books, 2001).

Pohl, F. J., *Amerigo Vespucci Pilot Cb: Amerigo Vespucci Pilot Ma* (Routledge, 1755).

Polizzotto, L., *Children of the Promise: The Confraternity of the Purification and the Socialization of Youths in Florence, 1427-1785 (Oxford-Warburg Studies)*, (Oxford University Press, 2004).

Prager, F. D. (editor), Scaglia, G. (editor), *Brunelleschi: Studies of His Technology and Inventions* (Dover Publications, 2004).

Quaintance, C., *Textual Masculinity and the Exchange of Women in Renaissance Venice* (University of Toronto Press, 2015).

Randolph, A. W. B., *Engaging Symbols: Gender, Politics, and Public Art in Fifteenth-century Florence* (Yale University Press, 2002).

Reston Jr., J., *Defenders of the Faith: Christianity and Islam Battle for the Soul of Europe, 1520-1536* (Penguin Books, 2010).

Richardson, C.M., *Reclaiming Rome: Cardinals in the Fifteenth Century (Brill's Studies in Intellectual History* (Book 173).

Ridolfi, R., *The Life of Girolamo Savonarola* (Alfred A. Knopf, 1959).

Robin, D., *Filelfo in Milan: Writings 1451-1477* (Princeton University Press, 2014).

Rogers, C. J., *The Oxford Encyclopedia of Medieval Warfare and Military Technology, Volume 3* (Oxford University Press, 2010).

Roscoe, W. I., *The Life of Lorenzo de' Medici, Called the Magnificent* (Forgotten Books, 2016).

Roscoe, W. I., *The life and pontificate of Leo X, Volume 1* (Printed By J. M'Creery, for T. Cadell and W. Davies, 1806).

Rosenthal, M. F., *The Honest Courtesan: Veronica Franco, Citizen and Writer in Sixteenth-Century Venice (Women in Culture and Society)*, (University of Chicago Press, 1993).

Ross, J., *Lives of the Early Medici: As Told in Their Correspondence* (Laconia Publishers, 2016).

Rowlands, E., *Masaccio: Saint Andrew and The Pisa Altarpiece* (J. Paul Getty Museum, 2003).

Rubinstein, N., *The Government of Florence Under the Medici* (1434 to 1494) (Clarendon Press, 1998).

Sabatini, R., *The Life of Cesare Borgia* (CreateSpace Independent Publishing, 2013).

Satz, A. (editor), Wood, J. (editor), *Articulate Objects: Voice, Sculpture and Performance* (Peter Lang AG, Internationaler Verlag der Wissenschaften, 2009).

Saunders, F. S., *Hawkwood: Diabolical Englishman* (Faber & Faber, 2005).

Schmitt, C. B. (editor), Skinner, Q. (editor), Kessler, E. (editor), Kraye, J. (editor), *The Cambridge History of Renaissance Philosophy* (Cambridge University Press, 1988).

Scotti, R. A., *Basilica: The Splendor and the Scandal: Building St. Peter's* (Plume, 2007).

Setton, K. M., *The Papacy and the Levant, 1204-1571, Vol. 3: The Sixteenth Century to the Reign of Julius III* (American Philosophical Society, 1978).

Shaw, C., The Politics of Exile in Renaissance Italy (Cambridge University Press, 2007).

Shaw, C., *Barons and Castellans: The Military Nobility of Renaissance Italy* (Brill, 2014).

Shaw, C., *The Politics of Exile in Renaissance Italy* (Cambridge Studies in Italian History and Culture), (Cambridge University Press, 2007).

Shaw, C., *Julius II: The Warrior Pope* (Wiley-Blackwell, 1997).

Sider, S., *Handbook to Life in Renaissance Europe* (Oxford University Press, 2007).

Siena, K. P., *Sins of the flesh: responding to sexual disease in early modern Europe* (Centre for Reformation and Renaissance Studies, 2005).

Seward, D., *Prince of the Renaissance: The Golden Life of FranCois I.* (MacMillan Publishing Company, 1973).

Simonetta, M., *The Montefeltro Conspiracy: A Renaissance Mystery Decoded* (Doubleday, 2008).

Sismondi, J.-C.-L. Simonde de, *A history of the Italian republics: being a view of the rise, progress, and fall of Italian freedom* (University of Michigan, 1875).

Skinner, Q., *Machiavelli: A Very Short Introduction* (Oxford University Press, 2001).

Sohm, P., *The Artist Grows Old: The Aging of Art and Artists in Italy, 1500-1800* (Yale University Press, 2007).

Somervill, B. A., *Catherine de Medici: The Power Behind the French Throne* (Compass Point Books, 2006).

Spencer, J. R., *Andrea Del Castagno and His Patrons* (Duke University Press Books, 1991).

Stapleford, R., *Lorenzo de' Medici at Home: The Inventory of the Palazzo Medici in 1492* (Penn State University Press, 2014).

Starn, R., *Contrary Commonwealth: The Theme of Exile in Medieval and Renaissance Italy* (University of California Press, 1982).

Steen, C. R., *Margaret of Parma: A Life* (Brill, 2013).

Steinmetz, G., *The Richest Man Who Ever Lived: The Life and Times of Jacob Fugger* (Simon & Schuster, 2015).

Stinger, C.L., *The Renaissance in Rome* (Indiana University Press, 1998).

Strathern, P., *Death in Florence: The Medici, Savonarola, and the Battle for the Soul of a Renaissance City* (Pegasus Books, 2015).

Strathern, P., *Spirit of Venice: From Marco Polo to Casanova* (Jonathan Cape, 2012).

Strathern, P., *The Artist, the Philosopher, and the Warrior: Da Vinci, Machiavelli, and Borgia and the World They Shaped* (Bantam, 2011).

Strathern, P., *The Medici: Godfathers of the Renaissance* (Vintage Books, 2009).

Sturm, S., *Lorenzo de' Medici* (New York, 1974).

Sumption, J., *Hundred Years War Vol 3: Divided Houses* (Faber & Faber, 2000).

Tacconi, M., *Cathedral and Civic Ritual in Late Medieval and Renaissance Florence: The Service Books of Santa Maria del Fiore (Cambridge Studies in Palaeography and Codicology),* (Cambridge University Press, 2006).

Taylor, F. L., *The Art of War in Italy 1494-1529: Prince Consort Prize Essay 1920* (Cambridge University Press, 2010).

Terpstra, N., *The Art of Executing Well: Rituals of Execution in Renaissance Italy* (Truman State University Press, 2008).

Thiem, J., *Lorenzo de' Medici: Selected Poems and Prose* (Penn State University Press, 2008).

Thomas. H., *The Golden Empire: Spain, Charles V, and the Creation of America Hardcover – Deckle Edge* (Random House, 2011).

Thomas. H., *Rivers of Gold: The Rise of the Spanish Empire* (Weidenfeld & Nicolson History, 2003).

Thomas James Dandelet, T. J. (editor), Marino, J. A. (editor), *Spain in Italy: Politics, Society, and Religion 1500-1700* (Brill, 2006).

Thompson, B., *Humanists and Reformers: A History of the Renaissance and Reformation* (Eerdmans Pub Co, 1817).

Tilley, A. A., *Medieval France: A Companion to French Studies* (Forgotten Books, 2015).

Tomas, N. A., *The Medici Women: Gender and Power in Renaissance Florence (Women and Gender in the Early Modern World),* (Routledge, 2003).

Tracy, J. D., *Emperor Charles V, Impresario of War: Campaign Strategy, International Finance, and Domestic Politics* (Cambridge University Press, 2010).

Treherne, M. (author), Brundin, A. (editor), *Forms of Faith in Sixteenth-Century Italy (Catholic Christendom, 1300-1700),* (Routledge, 2009).

Trexler, R. C., *Church and Community, 1200-1600: Studies in the History of Florence and New Spain* (Storia e Letteratura, 1987).

Trexler, R. C., *Public Life in Renaissance Florence* (Cornell University Press, 1991).

Trexler, R. C., *Power and Dependence in Renaissance Florence: The women of Renaissance Florence* (Mrts, 1993).

Trinkhaus, C., *In Our Image And Likeness: 2 Vol.* (University Of Chicago Press, 1970).

Trollope, A. T., *Filippo Strozzi: A History Of The Last Days Of The Old Italian Liberty* (Nabu Press, 2011).

Tuohy, T., *Herculean Ferrara: Ercole d'Este (1471-1505) and the Invention of a Ducal Capital (Cambridge Studies in Italian History and Culture)*, (Cambridge University Press, 2002).

Tylus, J., *Writing and Vulnerability in the Late Renaissance* (Stanford Univ Press, 1993).

Unger, M. J., *Machiavelli: A Biography* (Simon & Schuster, 2012).

Unger, M. J., *Michelangelo: A Life in Six Masterpieces* (Simon & Schuster, 2014).

Unger, M., *Magnifico: The Brilliant Life and Violent Times of Lorenzo de' Medici* (Simon & Schuster, 2009).

Vasari, G. (author), Bondanella, J. C. (translator), Bondanella, P. (translator), *The Lives of the Artists* (Oxford University Press, 2008).

Vaughan, H., *The Medici Popes: Leo X and Clement VII* (Benson Press, 2015).

Verstegen, I. F., *Patronage and Dynasty: The Rise of the Della Rovere on Renaissance Italy (Sixteenth Century Essays & Studies, Vol. 77)*, (Truman State University Press, 2007).

Veseth, M., *Mountains of Debt: Crisis and Change in Renaissance Florence, Victorian Britain, and Postwar America* (Oxford University Press, 1990).

Viroli, M. and Shugaar, A., *Machiavelli's God* (Princeton University Press, 2010).

Viroli, M. (author), Shugaar, A. (translator), *Niccolo's Smile: A Biography of Machiavelli* (Hill and Wang, 2002).

Walker, L. J., *The Discourses of Niccolò Machiavelli* (Routledge, 2013).

Wallace, D., *Chaucerian Polity: Absolutist Lineages and Associational Forms in England and Italy (Figurae)*, (Stanford University Press, 1997).

Weinberger, M., *Michelangelo The Sculptor* (First edition, 1967).

Weinstein, D., *Savonarola: The Rise and Fall of a Renaissance Prophet* (Yale University Press, 2011).

Welch, E. S., *Art in Renaissance Italy, 1350-1500* (Oxford University Press, 2001).

White, A., *Plague and Pleasure: The Renaissance World of Pius II* (The Catholic University of America Press, 2014).

White. M., *Leonardo the First Scientist* (Little Brown, 2000).

Whitfield, J. H., and Woodhouse, J. H., *A Short History of Italian Literature* (Manchester University Press, 1981).

Wiesner-Hanks, M., *The Renaissance and Reformation: A History in Documents (Pages from History)*, (Oxford University Press, 2011).

Williams, G. L., *Papal Genealogy: The Families and Descendants of the Popes* (McFarland, 2004).

Witt, R. G., *The Two Latin Cultures and the Foundation of Renaissance Humanism in Medieval Italy* (Cambridge University Press, 2012).

Woolfson, J., *Palgrave Advances in Renaissance Historiography* (Palgrave Macmillan, 2004).

Young, G. F., *The Medici: Annotated and Illustrated in Two Complete Volumes* (BookRix , 2014).

Zöllner, F. and Nathan, J., *Leonardo da Vinci* (Taschen, 2011).

CPSIA information can be obtained
at www.ICGtesting.com
Printed in the USA
LVOW09s0211010217

522808LV00003B/25/P